COOKING
A TO Z

The Complete
Culinary Reference Tool

Jane Horn
Editor/Writer

Janet Fletcher
Contributing Writer

Gary Hespenheide
Interior Designer

Jane Horn, a Bay area cookbook writer and editor, is a graduate of Cornell University, with a master's degree in communication from Stanford University. In the California Culinary Academy series of cookbooks, she is the author/editor of *The Art of Eating In* and has contributed to *Chicken and Other Poultry, Microwave and More*, and other titles in the series. She also is the co-author of *The New Harvest* (published by The Cole Group/101 Productions), a guide to exotic and specialty produce. Her column on culinary equipment, "Cook's Tools," appears regularly in *Bay Food* magazine.

Janet Fletcher, a Bay area food and wine writer and editor, holds a degree in economics from Stanford University and attended the Culinary Institute of America in Hyde Park, New York. She has cooked in several west coast restaurants, including the highly acclaimed Chez Panisse, and writes a weekly restaurant column for the Oakland *Tribune*. She also writes for the food and wine industry. She co-authored *Appetizers & Hors d'Oeuvres* and *Italian Cooking* and was contributing writer for *Cookies*, all part of the California Culinary Academy cookbook series.

The California Culinary Academy In the forefront of American institutions leading the culinary renaissance in this country, the California Culinary Academy, founded in San Francisco in 1977, has gained a reputation as one of the world's outstanding professional chef-training schools. With a teaching staff recruited from among the best restaurants of Western Europe, the Academy educates students from around the world in the preparation of classical cuisine. The recipes in this book were created in consultation with the chefs of the Academy. For information about the Academy, write the Office of the Dean, California Culinary Academy, 625 Polk Street, San Francisco, CA 94102.

Copyright © 1992 The Cole Group

All rights reserved under international and Pan-American copyright conventions.

1 2 3 4 5 6 7 8 9
92 93 94 95 96 97

ISBN 1-56426-002-X

The Cole Group
4415 Sonoma Highway, PO Box 4089, Santa Rosa, CA 95402-4089

CONTRIBUTORS

Cakes, Pastries, and Breads
Tina Salter

Cooking Technique
Daniel Strongin

Equipment
Bill Hughes

Food Processor
Greg Patent

General Recipe Development
Susan Walter

Ice Cream and Frozen Desserts
Leonard D. Grotta

Jams, Jellies, Preserves, and Condiments
Katie Millhiser

Microwave Cooking
Lorinda Moholt

Additional Recipes and Text
Bruce Aidells
John Phillip Carroll
Ron Clark
Hallie Donnelly
Olivia Erschen
Lonnie Gandara
Michael Goodwin
Jay Harlow
Faye Levy
Susan E. Mitchell
Julie Renaud
Cynthia Scheer
Vicki Barrios Schley
Angelo Villa
Charlotte Walker
Naomi Wise

Consultants
Ron Clark
Joyce Jue
Julie Renaud

Illustrator
Edith Allgood

The Cole Group
Publisher
Brete C. Harrison

Associate Publisher
James Connolly

Director of Operations
Linda Hauck

Director of Production
Steve Lux

Senior Editor
Annette Gooch

Address all inquiries to
The Cole Group
4415 Sonoma Highway, PO Box 4089
Santa Rosa, CA 95402-4089

Distributed to the book trade by Publishers Group West.

Copy Chief
Melinda E. Levine

Copyeditors
Andrea Y. Connolly
Judith Dunham

Proofreader
Lorna Cunkle

Editorial Assistants
Karen K. Johnson
Kass Kapsiak
Tamara Mallory
Raymond F. Quinton

Layout Editor
Linda M. Bouchard

Typographer
Robert C. Miller

Indexer
Elinor Lindheimer

Production by
Studio 165

Special Thanks to
Joanne Bautista
John A. Brown Kitchenwares
Vivianne Coles
Cuisinarts
Peggy Fallon
Jane Frorath
Sylvia Hajak
Robert L. Iacopi
Rebecca Johnson
Sam Kellogg
Tricia Reuter O'Brien
Darryl Salter
Paula Schlosser
Mark Zielinski
    and
      Ted Evans
      Christine Robertson
      Sally W. Smith
      Ernie S. Tasaki

COVER DESIGN
Glenn Martinez & Associates

PHOTOGRAPHY

Cover
Deborah Jones, photographer
Sandra Cook, food stylist

Recipes
Kevin Sanchez, photographer
Susan Massey-Weil, food stylist
Liz Ross, photographic stylist
Chris Coughlin, photographer's assistant

Technique
Marshall Gordon, photographer
Kathleen Prisant, food stylist
Diana Torrey, stylist's assistant

Equipment, Chefs (at left)
Kit Morris, photographer
Carol Haagens, photographer's assistant

Additional Photographers
Patricia Brabant, pp. 7, 78, 81, 82, 86, 112, 125, 126, 127, 161, 162, 163, 164, 165, 186, 239, 260, 400, 421, 423, 431, 437, 454, 483, 484, 486, 495, 498; Victor Budnik, pp. 312, 313; Ed Carey, pp. 133, 206, 237, 270, 273, 328, 388, 582 (left); David Fischer and Patrick Lyons, pp. 25, 75, 111, 231, 563, 611; Joel Glenn, pp. 114, 122, 233, 358, 445, 447, 485, 595, 602; Dennis Gray, pp. 53, 134, 194, 199, 201, 202, 253, 450, 467, 527, 598; Michael Lamotte, pp. 6, 13, 14, 26, 27, 28, 39, 42, 56 (left), 61, 64, 92, 139, 141, 143, 144, 146, 147, 150, 159 (right), 169, 182, 185, 188, 234, 286, 293, 298, 300, 341, 395, 397, 424, 427, 458, 463, 496, 509, 514, 528, 541, 565, 631; Fred Lyon, pp. 46, 176, 219, 221, 265, 280, 335, 346, 357, 452, 453, 510, 519, 531, 581, 591, 597, 609, 610; Doug Manchee, page 131 (right); Bob Montesclaros, pp. 68, 174, 198, 296, 350, 417, 472, 474, 476, 513, 533, 557; Allan Rosenberg, pp. 91, 179, 181, 374, 491, 614, 618, 623, 624, 625, 629, 630; Tom Tracy, page 303; Jackson Vereen, pp. 224, 295, 392, 532, 536, 537, 538, 542, 544, 546.

Additional Stylists
Allison Anthony, Roz Baker, M. Susan Broussard, Sandra Cook, Joanne Dexter, Olivia Erschen, Amy Glenn, Sandra Griswold, Carol Hacker, Karen Hazarian, Robert Lambert, Sandra Learned, Bunny Martin, Cherie Miller, Amy Nathan, Janet Nusbaum, Jan Rhodes, Cynthia Scheer, Sara Slavin, Carla Tavaras, Kathleen Volkmann, Doug Warne, Maria Winston.

PREFACE

Cooking A to Z is a practical, comprehensive culinary reference book. It is also a collection of more than 600 specially selected recipes covering the basics and more. And it is a beautiful book that anyone who loves food will read with pleasure.

If you are a novice cook, through this book you can learn the fundamentals — the terms, techniques, and equipment you need to prepare any recipe with success. *Cooking A to Z* will also guide you through the constantly changing marketplace: it tells you how to shop for and cook with fresh ingredients and processed foods; how to stock pantry and cupboard; and how to identify, select, and care for kitchen equipment. More experienced cooks will appreciate the convenience of finding all the basic food and cooking information in one up-to-date volume, as well as a wealth of reliable and creative recipes. With so much to offer, *Cooking A to Z* will prove invaluable to cooks and (noncooking) food enthusiasts alike, both as a workbook and as a source of hours of fascinating reading.

The information presented on these pages reflects the expertise of consultants drawn from all aspects of cooking. Equipment entries offer the most current information on the range of basic culinary tools and appliances. You will learn how to use the equipment, how to decide whether or not it should be part of your personal *batterie de cuisine*, and which pieces are interchangeable. Each of the equipment entries is accompanied by a photograph that clearly shows the item. Cooking terminology, the culinary shorthand that is the foundation for every recipe, is fully explained; terms are often illustrated. More than 35 sets of step-by-step photographs, plus detailed text, demonstrate important techniques such as boning, beating egg whites, carving, filleting, and decorating cakes. For each ingredient, you are provided with specific information for use,

availability, selection, and storage. Throughout the book you will find over 75 special features that offer highlights and tips. The recipes are wide ranging, from sauces to cookies to roasts, and include exciting ways to use familiar ingredients and those that are new to you.

You will refer to this book when you come across something you don't know in a recipe, or when you hear of a recipe and want to know what it is or how to prepare it. For instance, perhaps you recently tasted the following dessert: an apple tart composed of a pastry base with a filling of sliced apples, finished with an apricot glaze and presented in a pool of custard sauce. Open *Cooking A to Z* and look up: *apple, tart, tart pan, tart pastry, glaze,* and *custard.* You will find information on selecting, storing, and using apples; on what a tart is and how to make one; on what a tart pan is and what different kinds there are; on the types of tart pastry and which one to use; on the definition of *glaze* and several representative types of glazes; and on custards and how to make a custard sauce. You will find a number of recipes for tarts, as well as one for apple pie (just in case, even after learning all about tarts, you still prefer pie).

Cooking A to Z is organized alphabetically; the encyclopedia format makes it easy to locate any subject. You can also use the thorough index. While each of the almost 500 entries tells a complete story, many will also direct you elsewhere in the book for further information or additional recipes. Hundreds of full-color photographs of both recipes and techniques complement the clear, straightforward text and also make browsing a pleasure.

Whether this is your first cookbook or the latest addition to an extensive culinary library, *Cooking A to Z* will prove indispensable, so give it a good spot on your shelf or kitchen counter.

A popular Chinese restaurant dessert, meltingly tender Chinese Almond Cookies, uses both almond extract and whole blanched almonds to impart nutty flavor. The recipe is on page 145.

ACHIOTE

The hard, brick red seed of the annatto tree is called achiote. The seeds are valued more for the golden yellow color they impart to other foods than for their flavor, which is somewhat dusty.

Use   The seeds, typically, are soaked in water or heated in oil or lard, then discarded, and the oil or water is used to color food. Latin American cooks often add ground achiote to the water when cooking rice; and they use it in spice pastes for stews and sprinkle it on meats before roasting. The seed is also used commercially in this country to color butter, margarine, and cheese.

Availability   Check Latin American, Caribbean, and Philippine markets for achiote. It is available as whole seeds, ground powder, paste, and liquid extract.

Selection   Achiote seeds should have a lively brick red color; a brownish color indicates age.

Storage   Both seeds and powder should be stored in a tightly covered jar in a cool, dark place. Seeds will keep indefinitely; powder will keep up to six months. The paste should be refrigerated after opening; it will keep indefinitely.

Preparation   To color cooking fat, heat 2 parts oil or lard with 1 part achiote seed over moderately low heat until fat turns a golden orange (5 to 10 minutes). Cool, strain into a jar, and refrigerate. To prepare seeds for grinding, cover with water, bring to a boil and simmer 5 minutes, then remove from heat and let soak until cool. Drain and grind with a mortar and pestle, clean coffee grinder, or electric minichopper.

ACIDULATED WATER

The flesh of certain fruits and vegetables, such as apples and pears, will darken when exposed to air unless used immediately after cutting or unless they are dropped into acidulated water, a dilute solution of 5 or 6 parts water to 1 part acid. Typically the acid is lemon juice or vinegar.

ADJUST, TO

In cooking, this term means to taste a dish after it has cooked for a while, or just before serving, and then add more seasoning if needed.

AL DENTE

The literal meaning of this Italian term is *to the tooth*. It describes the consistency of pasta and vegetables when cooked just to the point of doneness. At this stage food still offers some resistance when chewed (the technical term is *percussion*) and has developed a fuller and richer flavor than when raw.

ALLSPICE

The allspice berry resembles an oversized, reddish brown peppercorn. Its flavor and aroma suggest a pungent and spicy blend of cloves, cinnamon, and nutmeg.

Use   Allspice adds zest to both savory and sweet dishes, including stews, sauces (particularly tomato-based ones), marinades, relishes and preserves, cooked fruit, and baked goods of all kinds. It combines well with other spices. One of the pickling spices, it is sometimes part of the French blend *quatre épices* (four spices) used in pâtés. If necessary substitute a mixture of equal amounts of cloves, cinnamon, and nutmeg for allspice.

Availability   Buy it packaged or bulk, whole or ground.

Selection   Packaged seasonings lose quality after a while; try to buy from a store that restocks its spice section fairly often.

Storage   Keep in an airtight container away from light and heat. Ground spice stays pungent up to six months, whole berries even longer.

Preparation   Grind whole berries in a pepper mill, clean coffee grinder, electric minichopper, or with a mortar and pestle.

> ### *Recipes and Related Information*
> *Carrot Spice Cake, 86; Honeyed Chicken With Apricots, 557.*

ALMOND

Encased in a light-tan pitted shell, the almond is a white, oval, flat nut covered with a brown skin. Both bitter and sweet varieties exist. Raw bitter almonds contain toxic prussic acid, which is harmful except in small amounts, and so only sweet almonds are sold in the United States. Because the acid is destroyed by heat, commercial processors can use oil from the more intensely flavored bitter nut for extracts and liqueurs. For more flavor, European recipes may add a touch of bitter almond to the sweet almond.

Use   Extremely versatile, the almond is used as both ingredient and garnish. It adds texture and crunch to poultry, fish, rice, sauces, vegetables, salads, breads, desserts, cake and pastry fillings, and candy.

Availability   Almonds come packaged in cans or clear bags, or in bulk; in the shell or shelled; unblanched or blanched; whole, chopped, sliced, or slivered.

Selection   Buy nuts that are as fresh as possible.

Storage   Unshelled nuts can be stored in a cool place for up to six months. Shelled nuts will keep in an airtight container in the refrigerator for several months or in the freezer for up to six months (thaw before using).

Preparation   See NUT.

ALMOND PASTE AND MARZIPAN

Made from finely ground blanched almonds, sugar, and egg whites, marzipan and almond paste can be molded to form flowers, stems, leaves, and other fanciful shapes, or rolled out into sheets to decorate cakes and pastries. They have been used for making confections for centuries. They were originally two distinct products, but now have become essentially interchangeable, both in use and in name. If a difference must be stated: Marzipan is cooked and firmer and more pliable than almond paste, which is not cooked. They can be found in better supermarkets or gourmet shops, or you can make your own (see right).

To roll out either almond paste or marzipan, dust work surface lightly with confectioners' sugar and roll out with a rolling pin. Tint almond paste or marzipan by kneading in a few drops of food coloring. Pale tints are usually the most appetizing on pastry.

◼ HOMEMADE ALMOND PASTE
  2 cups very finely ground blanched almonds
  2¼ cups sifted confectioners' sugar
  1 to 2 egg whites, beaten until foamy
  Fondant (optional)

1. Combine almonds and sugar in a bowl. Stir well to blend. Gradually stir in enough egg whites to moisten almond mixture. Gather mixture into a ball; knead until smooth. Wrap well and refrigerate. Keeps for 1 week.

2. To make almond paste more pliable and easier to roll out, work a little fondant into it. Fondant is a sticky white icing available at bakeries or stores that sell cake-decorating supplies (see page 96). To roll out almond paste, dust work surface with confectioners' sugar.

Makes about 1 pound.

Food Processor Version   Use metal blade to process almonds and sugar until almonds are very finely ground. Add 1 unbeaten egg white and process 20 seconds. If paste does not form a ball, add more egg white.

◼ HOMEMADE MARZIPAN
  2 cups sugar
  ¾ cup water
  3½ cups very finely ground blanched almonds
  2 egg whites, beaten until foamy
  Confectioners' sugar, for dusting

1. Combine sugar and the water in saucepan. Cook to 240° F (soft-ball stage; see CANDY AND CONFECTION, Stages of Sugar Syrup). Remove from heat; stir until cloudy. Then stir in almonds.

2. Stir in egg whites and cook over low heat until mixture firms slightly. Dust work surface with confectioners' sugar. Knead marzipan until pliable. Wrap well and store in refrigerator for up to 1 month.

Makes 1¾ pounds.

Food Processor Version   Use metal blade to grind almonds in 2 batches. Add to recipe as directed. Process cooked mixture until pliable (30 to 45 seconds).

> ### *Recipes and Related Information*
> *Almond Meringue Cake, 361; Almond Torte 89; Apricot-Almond Squares, 143; Chinese Almond Cookies, 145; Panforte, 186; Raspberry-Almond Tart, 496; Ricotta Cheesecake, 119; Your Own Bridge Mix, 59.*

Green-tinted marzipan was rolled out and then applied to a leaf mold. The marzipan takes the shape of a leaf, even the detailing of the veins. After removal from the mold, it can be placed on a cake for decoration.

ANGELICA

A large perennial herb native to the northern hemisphere and New Zealand, angelica is valued principally for its roots and stalks.

Use Fresh angelica is eaten as a vegetable in the world's northernmost regions, such as Iceland, Norway, and Siberia. Because of its pungent flavor and alleged digestive properties, angelica root is used in the production of cordials and liqueurs, such as Benedictine and Chartreuse. The leaves and stalks may be used to flavor custards. When processed commercially, the green celerylike stalks are generally candied in sugar syrup for decorative use in breads, cookies, cakes, and fruitcakes. Candied angelica is expensive, and occasionally counterfeits made of dyed substitutes appear in the market.

Availability Fresh angelica is not grown commercially in the United States. Some home gardeners cultivate it, and it may be found wild. Angelica stalks candied in sugar syrup are available packaged or in bulk from specialty food markets or a bakers' supply outlet.

Storage Keep fresh stalks in a plastic bag in refrigerator crisper and use within a couple of days. Store candied angelica in a cool, dark place for two to three months, or freeze indefinitely.

Preparation Wash and trim fresh angelica. Halve lengthwise to be sure hollow stalks are clean. Cut stalks in smaller lengths and steep in milk for custards, or dice and candy in sugar syrup. Candied angelica can be marinated in brandy or liqueur for several hours before using.

> ### Recipes and Related Information
> *Candied Fruit, 93; Candy, 93.*

ANISE

An annual herb in the parsley family, anise yields small, pungent leaves and greenish gray seeds; both have a licoricelike flavor.

Use Add anise leaves sparingly to salads and vegetable dishes. Anise seed (also spelled *aniseed*) is popular in German and Scandinavian cookies, cakes, and breads, and in Italian twice-baked cookies (*biscotti*). Add it to pickles, cabbage slaw, or ground-pork mixtures. Anise oil is used as a flavoring agent in cough medicines.

Availability Whole anise seed is packaged in glass jars. It is rarely available ground but may be ground at home. Anise leaves are not available commercially.

Selection Packaged seasonings lose quality after a while; try to buy from a store that restocks its spice section fairly often.

Storage Keep in an airtight container away from light and heat. Anise seed will stay pungent up to one year.

Preparation Leaves are used whole; rub them lightly between the fingers to release oils. Seed may be used whole, or ground in a pepper mill, clean coffee grinder, electric minichopper, or with a mortar and pestle.

▪ BISCOTTI

Almost every Italian bakery sells several varieties of dry *biscotti,* twice-baked (*bis cotto*) cookies that are meant to be dunked in coffee or wine. They keep for weeks in an airtight container; offer them with afternoon tea or coffee or with a late-night glass of sweet wine. Note that the dough must chill at least overnight.

> ¼ **cup dried currants**
> 2 **tablespoons Marsala**
> ½ **pound unsalted butter, softened**
> 2 **cups sugar**
> 4 **eggs**
> 1 **teaspoon vanilla extract**
> 1 **tablespoon anise-flavored liqueur**
> 4 **cups flour**
> 1 **teaspoon baking powder**
> 1 **teaspoon baking soda**
> ½ **teaspoon salt**
> 2 **teaspoons grated lemon rind**
> 1 **teaspoon anise seed**
> ½ **cup half-and-half**
> 1 **cup coarsely chopped, toasted walnuts**
> 1 **cup coarsely chopped, toasted hazelnuts**

1. Put currants in a bowl with Marsala; soak for 20 minutes.

2. Cream butter; add sugar gradually and beat until light. Add eggs one at a time, beating until light and fluffy. Add vanilla, liqueur, and currants with their soaking liquid.

3. Sift together flour, baking powder, baking soda, and salt. Stir in lemon rind and anise seed. Add to creamed mixture alternately with half-and-half. Stir in walnuts and hazelnuts by hand. Cover and chill dough for at least 2 hours or overnight.

4. Divide dough into quarters and place each quarter on a length of waxed paper. Form into a roll about 15 inches long and 1½ inches thick. Wrap in waxed paper, then in aluminum foil. Chill overnight (dough can be frozen at this point for up to 1 month; bring frozen dough to refrigerator temperature before proceeding).

5. Preheat oven to 350° F. Unwrap rolls and place them on ungreased baking sheets. Bake until very lightly browned (20 to 25 minutes). Carefully transfer rolls to a cutting board and cut on a 45-degree angle into slices about ½ inch thick. Place slices cut side up on baking sheets and return to oven. Bake until golden (8 to 12 minutes). Cool cookies thoroughly on racks. Store in airtight containers.

Makes about 4 dozen cookies.

Food Processor Version As a timesaver, use standard shredding disk to process nuts.

Recipes and Related Information
Florentine Grape Coffee Cake, 279; Spiced French Honey Bread, 304.

APPLE

The sweet, round, thin-skinned fruit of a tree that grows in temperate zones, the apple is presumed a native of southwest Asia. Of the thousands of classified varieties, fewer than 20 are commercially important in the United States. Skin color of most varieties is green, yellow, or red; the moist, crisp flesh is white to creamy white, sometimes with yellow, green, or red tints.

Use Raw apples are commonly eaten out of hand or in fruit salads. Apples may be stewed and puréed for applesauce, baked whole, or used as an ingredient in a wide variety of baked desserts. Cooked apples are a popular garnish for savory pork dishes; they also figure in some classic French chicken and veal preparations. Apples may be pressed for juice, which, in turn, may be fermented into cider or distilled into brandy (also known as applejack and Calvados).

Availability Early varieties such as the Gravenstein and Astrachan are harvested in July and August. Late varieties begin in September and continue through November. Controlled-storage apples are available the rest of the year. Fresh apples are sold in bulk, overwrapped trays, or plastic bags. Cooked apples are available as canned or bottled applesauce or as canned apple-pie filling. Sliced apples are also available dried.

Selection Choose firm apples without bruised spots. Scald (irregularly shaped tan or brown area) has tougher texture than unblemished skin but does not seriously affect eating quality.

The following are suggested pairings of apple varieties and uses; eating apples such as Golden Delicious, Granny Smith, or Newtown pippin are fine eaten out of hand but also are good, all-purpose cooking apples. These groupings are offered for optimum flavor; or use what your recipe suggests.

Homey Apple Crisp (see page 10) is an early American baked fruit dessert with a sweetened crumb topping. Whipped cream or vanilla ice cream is the perfect, cool complement to the warm, fragrant fruit.

For Eating Try Golden Delicious (gold), Granny Smith (green), Jonathan (brilliant red), McIntosh (red to green), Newtown pippin (green), Red Delicious (red), Stayman (red), or Winesap (red).

For Pies and Applesauce Use tart or slightly acidic varieties: Gravenstein (yellow-green with red stripes), Grimes Golden (gold), Jonathan (brilliant red), McIntosh (red to green), Newtown pippin (green), Northern Spy (red); Rhode Island Greening (green), Stayman (red), Winesap (red), and York Imperial (red).

For Baking Use firmer-fleshed varieties preferably over 3 inches in diameter: Northern Spy (red), Rome Beauty (red), Winesap (red), York Imperial (red).

Storage Refrigerate apples until use; hardy varieties will last a month or more. Dried apples will keep indefinitely when stored in a plastic bag in the refrigerator.

Preparation Peel apples or not, as desired. For cooked dishes, halve or quarter apples and remove core. To core whole apples, use an apple corer, or use a small, sharp knife to cut all the way around the core and lift it out.

Cut full triangles for the base of the charlotte shell and blunt-tipped triangles for the sides. If possible, set a side piece on each bottom piece.

■ APPLE CHARLOTTE

A combination of puréed apples and crisp fingers of buttered bread, Apple Charlotte is baked and served warm. Although a charlotte can be prepared in any appropriately sized mold or baking dish, a round, tinned-steel charlotte mold with its flat bottom, slightly flaring sides, and heart-shaped handles is traditional.

> **Good-quality, firm-textured bread (French, brioche, bakery white)**
> 1 **cup butter, melted**
> **Sugar, for dusting mold**

Basic Glaze (see page 250; use apricot preserves)

Apple Purée

> 5 **pounds tart apples (Granny Smith or pippin), peeled, cored, and sliced**
> ¼ **cup butter**
> ¼ **cup water**
> 1 **teaspoon vanilla extract**
> **Sugar, to taste**

1. Prepare Apple Purée. Preheat the oven to 400° F. Cut bread into ¼-inch-thick slices and remove crusts.

2. Lightly butter a 4-cup charlotte mold or soufflé dish; dust with sugar. Cut bread to fit mold (see photograph at left). Dip slices in melted butter and line bottom, then sides of pan.

3. Fill lined pan with cooled purée and cover with another layer of butter-dipped bread.

4. Bake until golden brown and firm to the touch (30 to 40 minutes). Remove from oven and cool 5 minutes before turning out onto a serving platter. Brush well with glaze. Slice into wedges and serve.

Serves 6.

Apple Purée In a large pan, cook apples with butter, the water, and vanilla over low heat, stirring occasionally. As apples begin to soften, mash them with a wooden spoon and stir until a *very* thick purée forms (about 1 hour). Stir continually or the mixture will scorch and stick to pan. Add sugar to taste (take into account that the mold is dusted with sugar and the bread shell is brushed with a sweet glaze, so you may want to leave apples somewhat tart for a contrast of flavors); let cool.

■ NUTTY BAKED APPLES

A delicious stuffing of chopped nuts, brown sugar, and butter transforms plain apples into a satisfying and homey cold-weather dessert.

> 6 **large baking apples**
> ⅓ **cup finely chopped walnuts, pecans, or blanched almonds**
> ⅓ **cup firmly packed brown sugar**
> 2 **teaspoons butter or margarine, softened**
> 1 **teaspoon grated lemon rind**

1. Preheat oven to 375° F. Core apples and remove about 1½ inches of peel around stem ends. Arrange in a buttered, shallow baking dish just large enough to hold all the apples.

2. In a small bowl mix nuts, brown sugar, butter, and lemon rind. Fill each cored apple with an equal amount of the nut mixture. Add water to the dish to a depth of about ¼ inch.

3. Bake apples, uncovered, basting occasionally with liquid from bottom of dish, until tender when pierced with a fork (40 to 45 minutes).

4. Serve hot or at room temperature.

Serves 6.

Microwave Version Core large cooking apples (or firm, just barely ripe pears) and prick skin in 3 or 4 places. Fill core with a mixture of butter, brown sugar, walnuts, and raisins. Fit snugly in a casserole, cover, and cook according to the following timetable:

Number of Apples	Cooking Time (100% Power)	Standing Time
1	2–4 minutes	3 minutes
2	4–6 minutes	3 minutes
3	6–8 minutes	3 minutes
4	9–10 minutes	3 minutes

■ APPLE CRISP

Humble and homey, a crisp is a baked dessert of fruit with a crumb topping of butter, flour, and sugar. Crisps are at their best served hot or warm; they can be prepared ahead and baked during the main part of the meal.

> 5 **large tart apples (2 to 3 lb), Granny Smith or pippin**
> ½ **to 1 teaspoon vanilla extract, ground cinnamon, grated lemon rind, or brandy, to taste**
> **Sugar, to taste (depending upon tartness of apples)**
> **Whipped cream or vanilla ice cream, for accompaniment**

Crisp Topping

> 2 **cups flour**
> 1 **cup granulated or firmly packed light brown sugar**
> 1 **cup unsalted butter**

1. Preheat oven to 350° F. Peel, core, and slice apples. Place apples in a shallow, 2-quart ovenproof dish. Sprinkle flavoring of choice over apples and then sugar (see Note).

2. Sprinkle Crisp Topping over apples, covering them completely with crumbs. Bake until crumbs are golden and apples are tender when pierced with the tip of a sharp knife (about 30 to 45 minutes). If top browns before apples are cooked throughout, cover with aluminum foil and lower temperature to 325° F.

3. Serve hot or at room temperature with whipped cream or vanilla ice cream.

Serves 6.

Note If a thicker syrup is preferred, toss apples in 1 to 1½ tablespoons flour before adding flavoring and sugar.

Crisp Topping Into a medium mixing bowl, sift flour; blend in sugar. Cut in butter with a pastry blender or fingertips until mixture resembles coarse crumbs.

Oat or Nut Topping For a dense crust add ½ to 1 cup quick-cooking rolled oats or ¼ cup chopped nuts (walnuts, hazelnuts, or almonds) to topping with the flour. For a lighter, crunchier crust, use only 1 cup flour mixed with 1 cup oats.

Rhubarb Crisp For apples and flavoring, substitute 2 pounds rhubarb (use stalks only, not leaves), cut into 1-inch pieces and sprinkled with 1 teaspoon cinnamon and 2 tablespoons flour.

■ APPLESAUCE

Ground cinnamon, nutmeg, or fresh lemon juice can be added to the apples for extra flavor.

> **6 medium-sized tart cooking apples (about 2 lb)**
> **¼ cup sugar**
> **¼ cup water**

1. Peel, core, and cut apples into chunks. Place apples in a 2-quart saucepan with sugar and the water.

2. Bring to a boil, cover, reduce heat, and cook, stirring occasionally, until apples are very tender (15 to 20 minutes).

3. Stir with a fork until mixture has a saucelike consistency. (Put through a food mill or process until smooth in a food processor, if desired.)

4. Serve warm, at room temperature, or chilled.

Serves 6.

Microwave Version Place 6 apples, pared, cored, and cut into 1-inch chunks, in a 2-quart casserole. Add ¼ cup water, ¼ to ½ cup sugar (depending upon tartness of apples), and a sprinkling of cinnamon, nutmeg, or allspice to taste, if desired. Stir and cover. Cook at 100 percent power (7 to 9 minutes) until tender, stirring after half the cooking time. Mash with a fork for chunky applesauce or purée in a blender or a food processor for a smooth-textured sauce.

Recipes and Related Information
Apple Butter, 320; Apple Dumplings With Nutmeg Sauce, 193; Apple Filling, 627; Apple Pie, 437; Apple Turnover, 626; Corer, 156; Pecan Applesauce Cake, 87; Red Cabbage With Apples, 75; Walnut-Apple Strudel, 222.

APRICOT

The apricot is the round, thin-skinned fruit of a tree native to China. Most varieties range from about 1 inch to 2 inches in diameter, with a deep gold skin and flesh. The moist, juicy flesh surrounds a dark, almond-shaped pit.

Use Fresh apricots are eaten out of hand. Apricots may be poached for fruit salads or compotes, baked in pies or tarts, stewed with meats, or cooked with sugar for jam or preserves. Dried apricots are often used to add sweetness and texture to stuffings, fruit breads and fruitcakes, or as part of a pastry filling.

Availability The fresh crop is harvested in May, June, and July. Canned and dried apricots are available all year.

Selection Choose fragrant apricots with a red blush; ripe apricots give slightly to pressure. Avoid any that are hard and greenish yellow, or dull, soft, or mushy.

Storage Use ripe apricots immediately or refrigerate for up to two days in a plastic bag. To ripen firm apricots, store in a closed paper bag in a warm room. Dried apricots will keep indefinitely stored in a plastic bag in the refrigerator crisper.

Preparation To peel fresh apricots, drop into boiling water for 10 seconds, then transfer with a slotted spoon to ice water. Skin will slip off easily. Halve and pit.

Recipes and Related Information
Apricot-Almond Squares, 143; Apricot and Curry Chutney, 323; Apricot Filling, 627; Apricot Preserves, 319; Basic Glaze, 250; Broiled Duck Breasts With Apricot-Mustard Glaze, 475; Honeyed Chicken With Apricots, 557; Winter Fruit Compote, 186; Your Own Bridge Mix, 59.

ARROWROOT

A fine, dry white powder, arrowroot is valued for its thickening ability and neutral flavor. It is processed from a tropical rhizome occasionally eaten as a starchy vegetable in China and the Caribbean.

Use Arrowroot powder is used as a thickening agent for soups, sauces, stews, and desserts. It imparts a sheen to fruit glazes and sauces. The powder is ideal for thickening egg-bound sauces and other sauces that shouldn't be allowed to boil, because it thickens at a lower temperature than flour and cornstarch and, unlike those two agents, doesn't need to be cooked to remove rawness.

Availability Packed in boxes; it is less widely available and more expensive than cornstarch.

Storage Will keep indefinitely in a closed container in a cool, dry place.

Use a sharp knife to slice off artichoke stem and kitchen scissors or a paring knife to trim away thorny leaf tips. Rub cut surfaces with lemon juice to prevent browning.

Preparation   To use arrowroot powder for thickening, dissolve 1 part powder in 3 parts cold water before adding to sauce or stew. One tablespoon of arrowroot has the thickening power of approximately 3 tablespoons flour or 4½ tablespoons cornstarch. Avoid arrowroot in dishes that must stand more than 10 minutes or be reheated; it will not hold.

ARTICHOKE

A Mediterranean native, the artichoke was introduced to the New World by French settlers in Louisiana and, later, by Spanish settlers in California. The edible parts of this tall plant are the green, globelike buds, which give the most commonly available variety its name—Green Globe. Small young buds about the size of a large walnut are tender enough when cooked to eat whole. Large mature buds develop a fuzzy interior choke that must be removed. The Jerusalem artichoke resembles the regular artichoke in flavor but is a member of the sunflower family.

Use   Whole cooked artichokes are eaten hot, lukewarm, or chilled, most often with a dipping sauce. Hot artichokes are often accompanied by melted butter; lukewarm or chilled artichokes by a mayonnaise or vinaigrette. Large artichokes can be filled with seafood or bread-crumb stuffings. Whole bottoms can be stuffed and baked or garnished with poached eggs. When sliced and sautéed, the bottoms can be used as a garnish for pasta, pizza, or omelets. Small artichokes can be fried whole, pickled, or steamed and marinated for a salad garnish. Steamed and halved, small artichokes can be added to braised chicken, veal, lamb, or seafood dishes.

Availability   They are sold fresh, canned, marinated, or frozen. Fresh artichokes are generally available year around, but late fall and early spring are peak harvest times. Bottoms and hearts are available in cans or marinated in jars; artichoke hearts are available frozen.

Selection   Look for compact, heavy, plump globes that yield slightly to pressure and have large, tightly clinging, fleshy green leaf scales. Avoid browning (indicates old age, injury, or frost) and light weight.

Storage   Refrigerate fresh artichokes in a plastic bag for up to four days.

Preparation   See Preparing Whole Artichokes.

■ PREPARING WHOLE ARTICHOKES

Trim off thorny tips of outer leaves with scissors or paring knife. Snap or cut off smallest, toughest leaves close to stem. Rub freshly cut parts with lemon to prevent discoloration. Slice stem off to form a flat bottom. Set artichoke, stem side down, on a steamer above at least 1 inch of boiling water. Cover and steam until bases are tender (30 to 60 minutes, depending on size). Artichokes are now ready to eat or to be used in one of the following preparations.

Microwave Version   Outside leaves of microwaved artichokes will be tougher than if cooked conventionally. Wash artichokes. Trim stems and thorny tips of outer leaves. Slice away about 1 inch off of top. Rub cut edges with lemon juice to prevent discoloration. Securely wrap each artichoke in waxed paper or parchment paper. Cook according to the following timetable:

Number of Artichokes	Cooking Time (100% Power)	Standing Time
1	5–8 minutes	5 minutes
2	8–10 minutes	5 minutes
4	12–14 minutes	3 minutes

Artichoke Bottoms   Use large artichokes only. After steaming remove all leaves and scrape away choke, leaving a shallow cup that can be used to hold hot savory ingredients such as poached eggs or oysters. Leave artichokes slightly underdone if filled bottoms will be reheated with other ingredients.

Artichoke Cups   Use large artichokes only. Carefully spread outer leaves to expose heart. Remove small heart leaves and scrape out fuzzy choke with a spoon. Fill hollow with a sauce for dipping outer leaves or a salad such as shrimp with herbed mayonnaise.

Cream of Artichoke Soup   If you have a lot of leftover leaves from preparing artichoke cups or bottoms, make them into a cream soup. Simmer in chicken stock until quite tender, purée in a food processor or food mill, strain out fibers, add milk or cream, and thicken with a flour and butter roux.

Marinated Artichokes   Cut cooked artichokes into quarters or smaller wedges. Remove chokes and heart leaves. Trim tops of outer leaves down to entirely edible parts (pull off a leaf and test it). Marinate in a mixture of 3 parts olive oil, 2 parts water, 1 part vinegar or lemon juice, and salt and pepper to taste. Fresh or dried herbs, blanched whole garlic cloves, or red pepper flakes may be added to marinade. Store in refrigerator; artichokes will keep for weeks in the marinade.

■ ARTICHOKES WITH DIPPING SAUCES

Eating artichokes is an informal affair; there is no substitute for fingers. Pull off leaves one at a time, dip into sauce, and use your teeth to scrape off meat inside the base of each leaf. Discard small, fibrous heart leaves and cut out fuzzy choke. Eat base with knife and fork, dipping chunks into sauce. Have available plenty of napkins and a large bowl for discarding leaves.

1 medium to large artichoke per person
2 tablespoons dipping sauce per person

Curried Mayonnaise

    1 tablespoon vegetable oil
    ¼ teaspoon curry powder
    ¼ cup mayonnaise
      Fresh lemon juice, to taste

Herbed Vinaigrette

      Pinch *each* salt and freshly ground pepper
    1 tablespoon tarragon-flavored wine vinegar
    4 tablespoons olive oil
    1 tablespoon minced fresh herbs (tarragon,
      basil, dill, or chervil)

Lemon Butter

    ¼ cup butter
    ½ lemon, juiced
      Pinch freshly ground pepper or dash
      Louisiana-style hot sauce (optional)

Trim and steam artichokes (see Preparing Whole Artichokes on opposite page). Serve warm, tepid, or cold with dipping sauce of choice.

Serves 2 to 3.

Curried Mayonnaise   In a small skillet heat oil over low heat. Add curry powder and cook 2 to 3 minutes. Allow to cool, then stir into mayonnaise. Add lemon juice to taste. Flavor will improve if sauce is made several hours ahead and allowed to stand until needed.

Herbed Vinaigrette   Blend salt and pepper with vinegar. Whisk in oil and blend in herbs. Taste for seasoning and adjust to taste. This sauce does not keep well (herbs can become bitter), so make it the same day it will be used.

Lemon Butter   Melt butter, and add lemon juice and pepper (if used). Pour into warm individual bowls.

■ STUFFED ARTICHOKES

The most dramatic Italian vegetable dish is probably stuffed artichokes, their leaves bulging with well-seasoned bread crumbs. In this recipe, anchovies add bite to the stuffing mixture. Tomato sauce keeps the artichokes moist during baking and makes an excellent dip in which to dunk the filled leaves.

    2 medium, cooked artichokes (see Preparing
      Whole Artichokes, opposite page, slice a
      ¾-inch piece off the top before cooking)
    1½ cups seasoned bread crumbs
    1 hard-cooked egg, chopped
    2 anchovy fillets, finely chopped
      Salt and freshly ground pepper, to taste
    2 teaspoons olive oil
    1 cup Basic Tomato Sauce (see page 516) or
      canned tomato sauce
    ¼ cup freshly grated Parmesan cheese

1. To make a cavity for stuffing, gently pull out tender center leaves of cooked, cooled artichokes with a teaspoon; scrape out fuzzy choke.

2. Preheat oven to 350° F. Combine bread crumbs, egg, anchovies, and salt and pepper to taste.

3. Stuff prepared filling into center cavity of artichokes; fill between leaves with a teaspoon. Drizzle 1 teaspoon olive oil over each artichoke.

4. In a greased, shallow, 9-inch baking dish, pour ½ cup tomato sauce. Stand artichokes in dish and pour rest of sauce over them. Sprinkle with cheese, and cover with aluminum foil.

5. Bake for 20 to 30 minutes. Remove foil for last few minutes of cooking and allow sauce to thicken. Artichokes are done when hearts can be pierced easily with a metal skewer or long-tined fork.

Serves 2.

Steaming is a particularly good method for cooking artichokes because it locks in both flavor and nutrients. For more information on steaming, see page 554.

Recipes and Related Information
Artichoke Frittata, 204; Fennel and Artichoke Salad, 218; Jerusalem Artichoke, 324; Pheasant Brochettes With Baby Vegetables, 296.

A smooth, buttery sauce is an easy way to transform asparagus into a festive dish. Hollandaise Sauce (see page 516) and asparagus are a classic pairing.

ARUGULA

Also known as rugola, rocket, Italian cress, and roquette, arugula is a delicate salad green popular in Mediterranean countries. When young its slender, dark green leaves are tender and nutty, with a subtle peppery flavor; mature arugula has an unpleasantly hot, mustardlike character. The four-petaled, white blossoms are edible.

Use Arugula is enjoyed as a salad green, alone, garnished with the delicate flowers, or in combination with other greens. As part of a sandwich filling, it lends an appealing nutty flavor; small whole leaves can be added to potato or lentil soup at the last minute.

Availability It is sold loose or in clear bags, and is at its best in spring and fall.

Selection Buy fresh greens that are not limp and do not show any signs of decay.

Storage Keep in a plastic bag in refrigerator crisper for several days; wash just before using.

Preparation Trim away roots; wash leaves well and dry thoroughly.

ASPARAGUS

The asparagus plant is a member of the lily family. Its edible part is the long, slender shoot, which can range from pencil thin to about one half inch thick. Mostly asparagus is harvested green. White asparagus is harvested when the tip just breaks the ground; lack of exposure to the sun keeps the spear pale.

Use Steamed or boiled asparagus is served at room temperature or chilled as a salad, often with mayonnaise, vinaigrette, or other salad dressing; served hot, it is generally dressed with butter or oil or Hollandaise sauce and offered as a first course or side dish. Asparagus tips are a popular garnish for salads, soup, rice, and pasta dishes; for omelet and quiche fillings; and for Asian stir-fries.

Availability Asparagus is available fresh, frozen, or canned; whole spears or tips. The fresh crop is harvested between March and June.

Selection Choose bright green or white spears that are brittle, not limp, have tightly closed tips, and stalks that are at least two-thirds green.

Storage Refrigerate spears, upright, with stem ends in water; or wrap cut ends in wet paper towels or cloth, cover with a plastic bag, and refrigerate. Refrigerated asparagus keeps up to one week.

Preparation Break asparagus spears by hand where they snap easily. Alternatively, use a small knife or vegetable peeler to remove tough outer peel at stem end; tips are tender and do not require peeling. Leave whole or cut diagonally into 1- to 2-inch pieces.

Cooking See BOIL, STEAM, STIR-FRY.

◾ ASPARAGUS WITH LEMON, TOMATO, AND ONIONS

When asparagus and new onions turn up in Italian markets at the same time, the chefs of Bologna prepare this dish and put it in their windows.

1½ **pounds medium asparagus**
  2 **small, sweet new onions** *or*
    4 green onions, minced
  2 **tablespoons fresh lemon juice**
  ½ **cup extravirgin olive oil**
    Grated rind of 1 lemon
  2 **tablespoons snipped fresh chives**
  2 **tomatoes, peeled, seeded, and diced**
    Salt and freshly ground pepper, to taste

1. Bring a large pot of salted water to a boil. Add asparagus and cook until barely tender (about 5 minutes). Transfer with tongs to a bowl of ice water. When cool, drain and dry well. Transfer to a serving platter with all tips facing the same direction.

2. Combine onion, lemon juice, olive oil, lemon rind, and half of the chives. Whisk well, then stir in tomatoes. Season to taste with salt and pepper. Spoon sauce over asparagus, then garnish with remaining chives. Serve at room temperature.

Serves 4.

Food Processor Version Use metal blade to process onion, cut in 1-inch pieces, 10 seconds. Add lemon juice, olive oil, lemon rind, and half the chives; process 5 seconds. If you have a French-fry disk, process tomatoes, halved and squeezed to remove excess juice, into dressing in work bowl.

Recipes and Related Information
Beef With Asparagus, 558; Cream of Any Vegetable Soup, 563; Pasta Primavera, 414.

AVOCADO

The avocado is the pear-shaped fruit of a tropical tree. Some varieties, such as the common Fuerte, have a thin, dark green skin; others, such as the Hass, have a thick, rough, pebbly skin that changes from green to black as they ripen. The yellow-green flesh surrounds a large dark seed; when ripe, the flesh is smooth and buttery with a nutty flavor.

Use Avocados are generally eaten raw as a salad or first course. Halved avocados can be stuffed with seafood or eaten plain with lemon or vinaigrette. Sliced avocados add a buttery texture to green salads, seafood salads, sandwiches, and omelet fillings. They are commonly used to garnish Mexican tostadas, tacos, and other Latin American dishes, and are the major ingredient in guacamole. Seasoned mashed avocado makes a rich, creamy smooth, and delicious sandwich spread.

Availability The supply of winter varieties peaks in January; summer varieties appear in the market from June through late August. Because the fruit can be held on the tree for months without becoming overripe, avocados are generally available the year around.

Selection Choose avocados with full necks and with flesh that gives slightly to pressure. Dark-skinned varieties should be very dark; light-skinned varieties should have a soft, dull-looking skin with a velvety feel.

Storage If using within a few days, ripe avocados will keep at cool room temperature; or store in refrigerator for up to one week. Ripen at warm room temperature, preferably in a dark spot; ripening takes from three to five days (refrigeration will slow process). To ripen quickly, place in a paper bag. To store partially used avocados, rub cut surfaces with lemon juice, cover tightly with plastic wrap, and refrigerate.

Preparation Cut avocado in half, lengthwise, around seed. Twist halves apart. To remove seed, either slide tip of a spoon gently underneath and lift it out or carefully strike seed with a sharp knife, embedding knife in seed. Rotate knife to lift out seed. To slice or cube avocado, hold one half, cut side up, in one hand and use a large spoon to scoop flesh out of skin in one piece. Put half, pit side down, on a cutting surface and slice or cube. Sprinkle cut surfaces with lemon or lime juice to keep them from browning.

■ GUACAMOLE

Avocado is used extensively in Mexico. Often just sliced and served as a garnish, it provides one of the important textural contrasts so typical of the cuisine. Certainly its best known and most popular use is in guacamole.

Guacamole is a versatile dish. In Mexico it is most often served on lettuce as a salad or side dish, but it is used also as a garnish for tacos, burritos, tostadas, or *flautas* and, of course, as a dip accompanied by fried tortilla wedges or assorted raw vegetables.

> 2 **large avocados**
> 2 **teaspoons fresh lime or lemon juice**
> ¼ **cup sour cream (optional)**
> 1 **small clove garlic, crushed**
> 1 **small tomato, diced**
> 1 **canned jalapeño chile, seeded and finely chopped (optional)**
> ¼ **cup finely minced onion**
> **Few sprigs cilantro, coarsely chopped**

1. Halve avocados; remove pit, scoop out pulp, and mash with a fork.

2. Add lime juice, sour cream (if used), garlic, tomato, jalapeño (if used), onion, and cilantro, mixing after each addition.

Makes approximately 2½ cups.

Food Processor Version Use metal blade to process garlic and 1 small onion until finely chopped (10 to 15 seconds). Add avocado and process to desired consistency. Add lime or lemon juice, sour cream, jalapeño, and cilantro sprigs; process 5 seconds. Stir in tomato.

Quick Guacamole Follow Guacamole recipe through step 1. Mix mashed pulp with ⅓ cup prepared salsa. *To make in a food processor:* Use metal blade to process avocados to desired consistency. Add salsa and process a few seconds to combine.

Makes approximately 2 cups.

Recipes and Related Information
Avocado Bacon Burger, 44; Avocado, Jicama, and Grapefruit Salad, 281; Guacamole Burger, 44.

BAIN-MARIE

A hot water bath or bain-marie provides a constant, even source of heat to delicate foods such as custards, cheesecakes, and sauces. Restaurant kitchens use a bain-marie to hold sauces at serving temperature for long periods of time. The home cook will also use a water bath for this purpose, but more typically will use it to insulate oven-cooked foods. The cooking dish is set in a larger pan filled partway with water that is almost, but not quite, boiling and then placed in the oven. Any pan can be used as the bottom container, as long as it is large enough to hold the cooking dish with a few inches of clearance on all sides. Roasting pans or cake pans, found in most home kitchens, are commonly used for this purpose. A large saucepan is suitable for stove-top service. A double boiler is a form of bain-marie.

Recipes and Related Information
Cheesecake, 117; Custard, 168; Sauce, 512.

BAKE, TO

The process of baking, as well as that of roasting, its twin, involves cooking raw food in an oven with currents of dry, hot air. For all practical purposes, to bake and to roast mean the same thing. See ROAST.

BAKE BLIND, TO

To bake a pastry crust for a pie or tart, partially or completely, before it is filled. To keep pastry from puffing up during baking, it is pricked evenly with a fork, lined with aluminum foil or parchment paper, filled with dried beans or metal or ceramic pie weights, then baked until set (10 to 15 minutes). Foil and beans are removed and pastry is returned to oven until it is partially or completely baked, as needed.

Partially baked crusts are used for some custard and cream fillings, which tend to be soggy or undercooked if filled raw. Fully prebaked shells are used to hold an uncooked filling (fresh fruit), a cold filling (mousse, Bavarian cream, pastry cream), or a filling that is cooked on top of the stove and added later (lemon curd, pudding).

Recipes and Related Information
Cake and Pastry Tools, 92; Pie and Tart, 434.

BAKER'S PEEL

Professional bakers use wooden shovels called peels to slide yeast breads and pizzas into the oven and to retrieve them when done. The amateur pizza maker can find scaled-down peels in cookware stores. Use the peel for the final rising of pizza and bread dough, after first sprinkling with cornmeal to prevent sticking. To transfer pizza or loaf to oven, give peel a few preliminary shakes to make sure the pizza glides freely, then set far edge of peel at far edge of baking surface (either baking stone or baking sheet); give peel a sharp jerk, and slowly pull back as pizza or loaf slides off.

Baker's peels are made of smooth, pale basswood and are commonly available in three sizes: 12 by 14 inches, 14 by 16 inches, and 16 by 18 inches. Buy the size that fits your oven and suits your needs. If you make single loaves, or pizzas for one or two, the smaller ones are sufficient. Giant breads need a giant board. If you have two ovens and bake several pizzas or breads at one time or in succession, and if you plan on cutting and serving on the peels, consider buying several. They also make wonderful bread and cheese boards.

After using, wipe peel clean with a damp cloth; scrape off any pieces of food. Don't wash under running water or wood will warp and eventually split.

Recipes and Related Information
Baking Stone and Tile, 24; Pizza, 445; Yeast Bread, 613.

BAKING PANS, FOR BATTER AND DOUGH

Selecting bake ware can be confusing. Often the same baking pan is sold under different names and in a variety of materials. As a primary guideline, consider the function of the pan, and then buy the one that will do the job best, regardless of what it is called. See MATERIALS FOR COOKWARE for more information.

Increasingly, professional-quality bake ware is available for home use. Although these pans usually cost more, in the long run they will prove their worth and justify their higher price. The superior materials and craftsmanship mean a better-looking, higher-quality final product. Professional pans have a longer life expectancy as well.

Should you purchase every pan described here? Hardly. Before buying, ask yourself the following questions. What do I bake most often? What is the yield of favorite recipes?

Bake ware is available for home use in a range of shapes, sizes, and materials. Shown top row, from left: ring mold, angel food cake pan, miniature savarin rings, panettone pan, charlotte mold, loaf pans, brioche molds, cake pans. Middle row, from left: savarin mold, ladyfinger pan, madeleine pan, muffin and popover pans, flan rings, tart pans, quiche pan. Bottom row, from left: pizza pans, Kugelhopf pan, baking cloche, bundt pan, cake pans, pie tins, baking sheet, and baking pan.

Do I need more than one of each pan? What are the dimensions of my oven? How much storage space do I have? Then purchase what best suits your needs.

ANGEL FOOD CAKE PAN

This pan with high sides has a center tube that promotes even distribution of heat and supports the delicate air-leavened batter as it rises. As angel food cakes must cool upside down, these pans usually have small metal feet spaced around the rim or a tube higher than the pan sides for added stability and to allow air circulation. Pans are typically 10 inches in diameter by 4 inches tall and are made of aluminum, often with a nonstick coating. They have a 9-cup capacity. Most have removable bottoms.

BABA MOLD

These small, thimble-shaped, aluminum molds are used for baking the sweet, yeast-leavened French cake known as baba. The molds are as tall as they are wide—2¼ inches. Miniature savarin rings are often substituted for baba cups (see Savarin Mold).

BAGUETTE PAN

Adapted from professional bake ware, these black steel or stainless steel troughs hold the long, slender loaves of crusty bread known as baguettes during their final rise and in the oven. Most bread recipes yield two loaves, so that is the configuration commonly found in cookware stores;

other sizes are available by special order. Pans are 17 inches long, with 2-inch-wide troughs. Some have a vented band between each pair of troughs for circulation of heat.

BAKING CLOCHE

Commercial bakery ovens produce breads with superior crusts by injecting a fine spray of water into the oven cavity. The bell-shaped stoneware baking cloche re-creates this environment for home-baked breads. To use, the porous dome is first soaked in water. The dough is set on the base, which has been sprinkled with cornmeal to prevent sticking, then covered with the dome, and put in the oven. Steam forms within the dome and blankets the dough. If you bake bread often and have a lot of storage space (dome is 10 inches high and base is 11 inches in diameter), you may want to buy one. A covered, unglazed clay casserole will work as well; only the shape is different.

BAKING PAN AND BAKING SHEET

Baking pans have straight sides, ¾ inch tall or higher, all the way around. Baking sheets have a low lip on one or more edges for easy handling. Baking pans are designed to contain runny batters. Baking sheets, also called cookie sheets, work for any freestanding baked product—stiff cookie doughs, rolls and free-form yeast breads, biscuits, cream puffs, and meringues, for example.

Both pans and sheets are kitchen workhorses. Sheets are used to support bottomless flan rings and delicate tartlet pans. Pans set under pies keep ovens clean by catching bubbling juices. They can help organize setup by serving as a catchall for ingredients and equipment.

Buy baking pans or baking sheets of the heaviest weight and best quality available. Aluminum and heavy-gauge black steel are good choices. A typical baking pan measures 11 by 16 by 1 or 2 inches. A standard jelly-roll pan measures approximately 11 by 15 by ¾ inches. Bak-

ing sheets vary in size, but a 14- by 17-inch sheet should fit most home ovens. Consider buying several sheets if you have two ovens, or if you bake in big batches.

A relative newcomer, the air-cushioned cookie sheet, sandwiches a layer of air between two sheets of aluminum. Inspired by the professional baker's trick of double sheeting—baking on two stacked sheets as a way of controlling heat distribution—this design keeps dough from browning too quickly on the bottom. Sheets measure 9½ by 14 inches and 14 by 16 inches. An air-cushioned jelly-roll pan is also available.

PAN SUBSTITUTION

Whenever possible, use the size and shape pan recommended in the recipe you are using. Measure pan depth on the outside of one side, bottom to top; measure length and/or width across top of pan between inside edges. If you do not have the right size pan or wish to vary the shape, you can consult the chart below to find a reasonable substitute. Choose a pan that has the same volume and similar depth as the pan in the recipe. The depth may vary up to ½ inch as long as the volume remains the same. The volume of a pan is measured by the amount of liquid it holds when filled to the rim. (This does not refer to the amount of batter the pan holds.) You may need to bake your cake, pie, or bread a little longer if you choose a deeper pan than the one recommended.

Pan Measurements Sides × Depth	Shape of Pan	Volume of Pan
2¾″ × 1⅜″	Muffin cups	Scant ½ cup
9″ × 1¼″	Pie plate	1 quart (4 cups)
8″ × 1½″	Round	1 quart (4 cups)
8″ × 8″ × 1½″	Square	1½ quarts (6 cups)
7″ × 11″ × 2″	Rectangular	1½ quarts (6 cups)
4½″ × 8½″ × 2½″	Loaf	1½ quarts (6 cups)
10″ × 2″	Deep-dish pie	1½ quarts (6 cups)
8″ × 2″	Round	1½ quarts (6 cups)
9″ × 1½″	Round	1½ quarts (6 cups)
8″ × 8″ × 2″	Square	2 quarts (8 cups)
9″ × 9″ × 1½″	Square	2 quarts (8 cups)
5″ × 9″ × 3″	Loaf	2 quarts (8 cups)
9″ × 2″	Round	2 quarts (8 cups)
9″ × 3″	Bundt	2¼ quarts (9 cups)
9″ × 4″	Kugelhopf (tube)	2¼ quarts (9 cups)
8″ × 3¼″	Tube	2¼ quarts (9 cups)
9″ × 9″ × 2″	Square	2½ quarts (10 cups)
9½″ × 2½″	Springform	2½ quarts (10 cups)
9″ × 13″ × 2″	Rectangular	3 quarts (12 cups)
10″ × 2½″	Springform	3 quarts (12 cups)
10″ × 3½″	Bundt	3 quarts (12 cups)

BRIOCHE PAN

An egg-rich French yeast bread with a characteristic topknot of dough, a brioche is traditionally made in a flared, fluted tinned steel mold.

Molds range from individual ones, 3½ inches in diameter by 1½ inches high, to those sized to serve a whole dinner party, 8 inches by 2½ inches. Brioche pans also make charming soup bowls or containers for condiments and preserves.

BUNDT PAN

These deep tube pans are used to bake the popular, densely textured bundt cakes. Pan sides have curves and indentations that produce a cake with an attractive, sculptured exterior. The center tube allows heat to reach more of the batter and also shapes the cake into a ring, which is easier to slice. Typically, these pans are made of cast aluminum with a nonstick interior coating and measure 10 inches in diameter by 3½ inches high, with a 12-cup capacity. Also available is a tray of six miniature bundt cake molds. Each mold holds 1 cup of batter.

CAKE PAN

Every kitchen probably has at least one of these baking pans. They are basic equipment and very versatile. Round pans are used for layer and other types of cakes and for breads; square and rectangular ones for sheet cakes, bar cookies, and breads. Most recipes call for round or square pans 8 or 9 inches by 1½ inches high. The standard rectangular pan is 9 by 13 by 1½ to 2 inches. Deep cake pans with 3-inch sides, formerly only available from restaurant suppliers, are now sold at well-stocked cookware stores. Also called cheesecake pans, these produce a cake with more volume than one baked in a shallower pan, because the batter has more surface to grab on to as it rises. Often the cake is sliced horizontally to produce additional layers.

The best-quality cake pans are made of heavy-gauge aluminum. If square or rectangular, they have sharply angled corners that make a more professional-looking product. Other materials are tinned steel, black steel, stainless steel, and ovenproof glass. Round pans often have removable bottoms.

CHARLOTTE MOLD

Like jelly-roll and bundt pans, this round mold with slightly flared sides gets its name from what is traditionally baked in it. A charlotte is a type of sweet dessert with an outside shell of bread or cake fingers and a center of cooked fruit or chilled cream. The pan is well-suited for making any molded dish: baked entrées, soufflés, and bombes (molded ice cream), for example. The mold is of tinned steel, with heart-shaped handles and a lid. The better ones still come from France. Sizes range from ¾- to 8-cup capacity.

CORN-STICK PAN

Making cornbread in corn-shaped, cast-iron molds adds a homey, country touch. These pans make seven corn sticks and need seasoning so they won't rust. In addition to the traditional ears of corn, molds now come in many designs.

CRUMPET AND ENGLISH MUFFIN RINGS

Crumpets are flat, round, griddle-cooked English yeast breads made in molds because the batter is too liquid to hold its shape. English muffins are similar to crumpets but are made with a stiffer batter, so using rings is optional. The stainless steel, 4-inch by 1-inch rings are packaged in sets of four. If you don't make these breads often enough to warrant the purchase of special equipment, use well-scrubbed tuna fish cans, with tops and bottoms removed.

FLAN FORM

See Tart Pan.

KUGELHOPF PAN

This turban-shaped tube pan is used for *Kugelhopf*, a sweet yeast bread studded with raisins and almonds. It most closely resembles a bundt pan, with swirls and ridges molded into the sides. A 9-inch pan with a 9-cup capacity is standard. Materials used are tinned steel, black steel, aluminum, and ovenproof glass. Some have nonstick interiors. This attractive pan can do alternative service as a mold for layered salads.

LADYFINGER AND LANGUES-DE-CHAT PAN

Strictly speaking, ladyfinger molds have straight sides, and those for making the crisp French cookie known as *langue-de-chat* (cat's tongue) have slightly pinched middles, but they look enough alike to be used interchangeably. The tinned steel trays have 10 molds, each about 3¾ inches tall and about 1 inch wide. Both ladyfingers and langues-de-chat can also be formed without a mold, using a pastry bag and plain tip; directions are usually given in the recipe.

LOAF PAN

Another kitchen essential, loaf pans are multipurpose—for breads, pound and fruit cakes, meat loaves, and pâtés. The standard loaf pan for bread is 5 by 9 by 3 inches. Smaller pans measure 4½ by 8½ by 2½ inches. Miniatures are about 2 inches wide by 4 to 5 inches long. Other pans are longer, or shallower, or narrower, or taller, but whatever their proportions, all are rectangular. They are made of tinned or black steel, aluminum, ovenproof glass, or ceramic. Some have a nonstick interior finish.

Crinkle-Edged Loaf Pan   This rectangular pan with accordion-pleated ends resembles a stretched brioche mold. Several sizes are available.

Pullman Pan   Because it bakes with a lid, this specialty bread pan produces a loaf with a dense texture and thin crust. Used for sandwiches or canapés, it is known as a pullman loaf or *pain de mie*. Long and narrow, this pan usually measures 4½ by 12½ by 4 inches.

MADELEINE PAN

This tinned-steel tray has slightly elongated, shell-shaped molds used to prepare madeleines, the buttery, French sponge cookie-cakes. Full-sized madeleines are 3 inches long; miniature madeleinettes measure 1⅝ inches.

MUFFIN PAN

The standard muffin pan has 6 or 12 cups, each 2¾ inches wide at the top and 1½ inches deep. Large cups produce a product 4 inches in diameter by 2 inches deep. These come in 2-, 4-, and 6-cup trays. Miniatures (also called gems) are bite-sized, a mere 1⅞ inches across by ¾ inch deep. Gem trays have 12 or 24 cups. Buy a muffin pan made of a heavyweight metal of good quality, whether aluminum (coated or uncoated), tinned steel, or cast iron. Muffins and cupcakes will rise higher and bake more evenly if you do.

PANETTONE PAN

Tall and cylindrical with straight sides, this mold is used for an Italian holiday fruited yeast bread. Although not authentic, the bread will taste just as good if baked in a coffee can, charlotte or soufflé mold, or even a tall tube pan. The panettone pan is 7½ inches in diameter, with 4-inch sides.

PIE PAN

American pie pans have sloping sides, in contrast to European tart pans, which have straight sides. As with any bake ware, heavyweight metal pie pans produce a more evenly browned product, but ovenproof glass and ceramic make good, versatile pans as well. Standard sizes are 8, 9, and 10 inches in diameter by 1 inch deep; consider buying one in each size. Deep-dish pans are 1½ to 2 inches tall.

A note on recipe style: Some directions call for pie pans or tins, others for pie plates. Generally, the former are metal, the latter glass or ceramic. Regardless, use what you have as long as it's the correct size.

PIZZA PAN

Pizza is more popular than ever. In addition to the familiar round metal pans, several other choices are available to the home pizza maker.

Deep-Dish Pizza Pan Aficionados of thick Chicago-style pizza can try their hand at home with the same high-sided pan that restaurants use. Made of aluminum or black steel, the round pan measures 15 by 2 inches. Some even come with a metal gripper, for purists the only way to rush the pizza from oven to table. Aluminum pans will darken and season with use, which will improve their heat conductivity and produce an even better crust. Wash black steel and darkened aluminum with warm sudsy water and wipe dry. Don't scrub to remove baked-on food or the seasoning will wear away.

Perforated Pizza Pan As dough bakes, it produces steam. Unless this moisture is drawn away, the crust will be soggy instead of desirably crisp. One solution is to use this aluminum pan pierced with hundreds of holes that allow steam to escape and heat to penetrate crust. The pan does wonders for frozen pizza as well and is dishwasher-safe. It is available in 13-, 14-, and 15-inch rounds; buy the size that fits your oven.

POPOVER PAN

The pan for the American cousin to Yorkshire pudding must absorb heat well. Popover batter needs a quick shot of heat to convert its moisture to steam, which then forces batter to expand into a light, airy bread. Cast iron is the traditional material, but tinned and black steel are good alternatives. Most pans have 6 cups. Popovers can also be made in individual porcelain custard cups (see MOLD).

QUICHE PAN

Although many baking dishes can be used to prepare the savory custard pie known as quiche, the one most associated with it is a fluted, straight-sided ceramic or metal pan with a removable bottom. Quiche pans are usually 10 to 12 inches in diameter by 1½ inches tall. Quiches are often baked in shallower tart pans if they are to be used as a first course. A porcelain dish is an attractive choice if you are serving the quiche in its pan.

RING MOLD

The center hole of this pan is larger than that of a tube pan. It is typically made of aluminum, comes in a range of sizes, and is suitable for breads, cakes, molded rice, and gelatin desserts.

SAVARIN MOLD

A savarin is a sweet, yeast-leavened French cake similar to a baba, but is larger and baked in a shallow ring mold, as opposed to the tumbler-shaped cup used for the baba. After baking, the cake is drenched with liqueur, painted with an apricot glaze, and served with a mound of whipped cream, custard, or fresh fruit placed in the center. The mold, 7 to 10 inches in diameter, is made of tinned steel. As a variation, miniature savarin rings for single servings are also available (see Baba Mold).

SPRINGFORM PAN

Most cheesecake recipes call for this round baking pan with high sides, but it is also used for other dense cakes that need special handling to be unmolded. A clamp releases the sides from the base, ensuring that the cake can be removed intact from the pan. Sizes range from 6 to 12 inches, in half-inch increments. Standard height is 2½ inches, and most are made of tinned steel.

TART PAN

Tarts are baked in shallow, fluted, straight-sided pans that usually have removable bottoms or in bottomless metal bands called flan forms or rings, which are set on baking sheets for support. Tinned or black steel are the most common materials. Round tart pans range from 8 to 12 inches in diameter and are 1 to 2 inches deep. Other sizes include a 14-inch square and an 8- by 12-inch rectangle. Flan forms, which are round, rectangular, or scalloped, come in sizes corresponding to tart pans. Tartlet pans are miniature tart pans; some are shaped like diamonds, ovals, circles, or rectangles, with fluted, rounded bottoms. Boat-shaped tartlet pans are called barquette tins.

TUBE PANS

These cake pans have a center tube that supports delicate batters as they rise in the oven. This design also gives a boost of heat to the core of the cake, which promotes more even baking. Angel food cakes, bundt cakes, and yeast breads such as *Kugelhopf* are baked in tube pans. Most of these pans can hold a large amount of batter, anywhere from 9 to 12 cups. Some have a nonstick interior, although these should also be greased and floured if that step is called for in the recipe.

Recipes and Related Information

Angel Food Cake, 82; Apple Charlotte, 10; Babas au Rhum, 623; Baking Stone and Tile, 24; Cake, 77; Cheesecake, 117; Christmas Panettone, 628; Classic Brioche, 622; Cookie, 139; French Baguettes, 617; Kugelhopf, 628; Ladyfingers, 84; Madeleines, 147; Muffin, 374; Old-Fashioned Buttermilk Corn Sticks, 270; Pie, 431; Pizza, 445; Plump Popovers, 29; Quiche Lorraine, 443; Savarin, 623; Tart, 431; Yeast Bread, 613.

Currant-studded Irish Soda Bread (see page 24) is distinctively marked with a cross-shaped surface. Like all quick breads, it is quickly assembled. Serve it sliced and spread with fresh butter and homemade marmalade.

BAKING POWDER

A chemical leavening agent used for making baked goods, baking powder is a carefully balanced mixture of an acid or acid-reacting salt, or a combination of acid-reacting salts, and sodium bicarbonate. Most baking powders also contain a small amount of dry starch, such as cornstarch, to prevent absorption of moisture. In the presence of moisture or heat, the acid acts upon the alkaline component—sodium bicarbonate—to produce carbon dioxide gas. Single-acting baking powders release gas quickly upon contact with moisture. Double-acting baking powder, the most widely used today, releases a small amount of gas upon contact with moisture but requires heat for full reaction.

Use Baking powder leavens a variety of commercial and home-baked goods. It gives volume and an appetizing texture to cakes, quick breads, muffins, biscuits, pancakes, waffles, crackers, and cookies.

Availability Baking powder is packaged in tins.

Storage Keep in an airtight container in a cool, dry place. Routinely replace old baking powder every three to four months.

Preparation Baking powder is usually sifted with the other dry ingredients of a recipe to disperse it evenly before adding it to a batter. Because baking powder is activated in part by liquid, baking powder batters should be baked immediately after liquid is added.

Recipes and Related Information
Baking Powder Biscuits, 49; Baking Soda, 23; Leaven, 338.

BAKING SODA

Also known as sodium bicarbonate or bicarbonate of soda, baking soda is a chemical leavening agent used for a variety of baked goods. In combination with an acid ingredient, such as buttermilk or molasses, it releases carbon dioxide gas and causes expansion of a batter.

Use Because it is an alkaline substance, baking soda is used to neutralize and leaven batters with acid ingredients. It also absorbs odors; an open box in the refrigerator will keep air fresh. A tablespoon of baking soda dissolved in 2 cups warm water is an effective cleanser.

Availability Baking soda is packaged in boxes.

Storage Keep in a cool, dry place.

Preparation If used in excess, baking soda can impart a soapy taste to a finished product. To avoid unpleasant flavors, the rule of thumb is to use no more than 1 teaspoon of soda per cup of acidic liquid. If additional leavening power is needed, it should come from baking powder. This explains why many recipes call for baking powder in addition to baking soda. Baking soda is usually sifted with the other dry ingredients of a recipe to disperse it evenly before adding it to a batter. Because baking soda is activated immediately by liquid, batters leavened only by baking soda should be baked immediately after liquid is added.

■ IRISH SODA BREAD

This currant-studded bread is really a giant biscuit. It is immediately recognizable because of its distinctive cross-shaped surface. This design is formed by marking an *x* on the top of the dough before baking. It makes an inviting breakfast when slathered with butter and marmalade—and also goes well with a main-dish soup. It's as easy to make your own spread as it is to make a quick bread; see page 320 for a recipe for Classic Orange Marmalade.

    2¾ **cups unbleached flour**
    ¼ **cup wheat germ**
    3 **tablespoons sugar**
    1 **teaspoon *each* baking soda and baking powder**
    ½ **teaspoon salt**
    3 **tablespoons cold butter or margarine**
    ½ **cup dried currants or raisins**
  1¼ **cups buttermilk**
    2 **teaspoons milk**

1. Preheat oven to 375° F. In a large bowl stir together flour, wheat germ, sugar, baking soda, baking powder, and salt. Cut in butter until mixture is the consistency of coarse crumbs. Stir in currants.

2. Add buttermilk and stir only enough to moisten dry ingredients.

3. Turn dough out onto a floured surface and knead lightly until it is smooth enough to shape into a flattened ball about 1½ inches high. Place on a greased baking sheet and brush with milk. With a floured knife cut an *x* into top of loaf (cutting from center to within about 1 inch of edge) about ¼ inch deep.

4. Bake until loaf is golden brown (40 to 45 minutes). Test by inserting a wooden skewer in thickest part.

5. Slide loaf onto a wire rack to cool slightly. Cut into thick slices and serve warm or at room temperature.

Makes 1 loaf.

Food Processor Version   Use metal blade to process flour, wheat germ, sugar, baking soda, baking powder, salt, butter, and currants (10 seconds). Transfer to bowl and mix in buttermilk as directed.

> ***Recipes and Related Information***
> *Baking Powder, 23; Biscuit, 49; Leaven, 338.*

BAKING STONE AND TILE

A commercial brick baker's oven produces light, wonderfully crispy breads, cookies, and pizzas because its porous stone floor and side walls absorb moisture from the dough and distribute heat efficiently. To achieve similar results with a home oven, use round or rectangular baking stones made of smooth, unglazed, high-fire stoneware or unglazed, square quarry tiles. The former, also sold as pizza stones, are sold at cookware stores; the latter can be purchased from suppliers of floor tile. Buy enough individual tiles to cover oven rack or floor.

Stones are available in 13- and 15-inch rounds or 12- by 15-inch rectangles. Some are packaged with a stainless steel rack for carrying and serving. Which size should you buy? First of all, the one that fits your oven. Then, the size and shape that accommodate what you bake most often. Round stones are best suited for single pizzas or breads. Up to four small pizzas or several loaves can fit on a rectangular stone at one time, and they needn't be round.

To be effective, stone must preheat with oven, usually at 400° F or higher, on lowest rack. Pizza or loaf is transferred to stone with a wooden paddle (baker's peel). After baking, stone stays in oven to cool. If stone is used frequently, store it on oven rack.

Baking stones are fragile and apt to crack if exposed to sudden changes of temperature. Clean by wiping with a damp cloth, not in the dishwasher, as the porous material will absorb soap or detergent. With use, pale color will darken and stain, a superficial change that in no way affects performance.

> ***Recipes and Related Information***
> *Baker's Peel, 18; Pizza, 445; Yeast Bread, 613.*

BAMBOO SHOOT

The young, spring shoots of the tropical bamboo plant are a popular Asian vegetable. The ivory-colored shoots are conical, usually about 3 inches wide and 4 inches long, and covered with a multilayered brown husk. When harvested they may be sweet, but they quickly become bitter when out of the ground. Lengthy boiling in the husk removes the bitterness. Flavor of the cooked, husked shoot is mild and refreshing; texture is fibrous and crisp.

Use   Bamboo shoots add texture and sweetness to Asian soups, stews, and stir-fried dishes. Japanese diners prize fresh bamboo shoots as a first sign of spring.

Availability   Water-packed, canned bamboo shoots are available whole or sliced. Occasionally "fresh-cooked" bamboo packed in water in plastic bags is exported to the United States. Sun-dried bamboo shoots are sometimes available in Asian markets.

Storage   Once opened, canned bamboo shoots will stay fresh for 1 week to 10 days if stored properly; place in fresh water in a covered container, refrigerate, and change water daily. Store fresh bamboo shoots in water, cover the container, refrigerate, and change water daily. Bamboo shoots may be covered with water and frozen for several months, but they will lose some crispness.

Preparation   Rinse canned bamboo shoots well, washing off any grainy white calcium (a residue from commercial processing) caught in the ridges. If a canned flavor persists, blanch briefly in fresh water before using. Fresh-cooked bamboo packed in water should be parboiled 15 minutes.

Recipes and Related Information
Mu Shu Pork, 378; Pork and Cabbage Wontons, 192; Shanghai Spring Rolls, 389.

BANANA

The common yellow banana is generally about 7 to 9 inches long and about 1½ inches in diameter. The red banana is shorter and slightly fatter. When ripe, the flesh is moist, slightly sticky, soft, and sweet. Unripe bananas are hard, rather dry, and starchy.

Use   Ripe raw bananas are eaten out of hand, or sliced and used in fruit salads or as a topping for breakfast cereals. Bananas are baked as a dessert or blended with other ingredients to flavor cakes, quick breads, puddings, pies, or ice cream. Use slightly underripe bananas for baking with butter and brown sugar; save overripe bananas for cakes and breads.

Availability   Fresh bananas are sold all year.

Selection   Choose plump, well-filled fruit with unblemished skin and no signs of decay.

Storage   Bananas continue to ripen after harvest. Ripe yellow bananas have a solid yellow skin with brown speckles. Ripe red bananas have dark red skin with black speckles and feel slightly soft. With both varieties, the skin will continue to darken as the banana ages. To ripen bananas further after purchase, store at room temperature. A bright yellow fruit with a green tip will reach ideal ripeness in two to three days. After ripening, bananas may be refrigerated for several days.

Preparation   Peel. For use in fruit salads, sprinkle bananas with lemon or lime juice to prevent browning.

■ BANANAS FOSTER

This impressive flaming dessert from New Orleans is simple but must be prepared at the last minute in small batches; do not attempt it for a large dinner party. Flaming desserts are easier to prepare over a gas burner (see the directions in step 2). If you are cooking on an electric burner, heat the rum in a small saucepan until it just begins to boil. Then pour it over the bananas and use a match to ignite it. The liqueur and rum can also be warmed in a microwave oven. Use 100 percent power and heat 30 to 45 seconds.

>   2 **tablespoons unsalted butter**
>   2 **tablespoons light or dark brown sugar**
>   **Pinch ground cinnamon**
>   **Pinch freshly grated nutmeg**
>   2 **small, firm bananas, cut in half lengthwise**
>   ¼ **cup Drambuie liqueur**
>   ¼ **cup dark rum**
>   2 **scoops vanilla ice cream**

1. In a 10-inch omelet or saute pan over medium heat, melt butter. Add sugar, cinnamon, and nutmeg; mix well. Add bananas and sauté until they begin to soften (about 1 minute on each side).

2. Pour in liqueur and rum. Turn up heat and tilt pan to ignite liquor. Shake pan slightly to prolong flames. When flames burn out, place 2 banana halves on each serving plate. Place a scoop of ice cream between the banana halves and spoon the sauce over all.

Serves 2.

Recipes and Related Information
Banana Cream Pie, 440; Banana Split, 311; Toasted Coconut-Banana Bread, 491.

BARD, TO

To cover meats, poultry, or fish with thin slices of fat—usually bacon or pork fat—before cooking (see photograph, page 593). This technique developed as a way of keeping faster-cooking, lean parts moist and juicy until fattier areas are done, or to keep roasts with little internal fat moist. For example, the breast meat of chicken or turkey is lower in fat than the dark meat of the legs or thighs and thus is finished sooner. Barding the breast will keep it from drying out before the bird is fully cooked. Veal is another meat that also benefits from barding or the application of another type of baste.

Barding and larding are similar techniques in that they both use applied fat to maintain or add moisture; they differ in where the basting fat is placed. Barding adds surface fat. Larding bastes by inserting strips of fat into the meat's interior mass (see LARD).

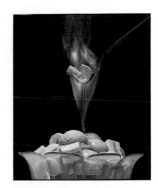

Bananas Foster makes an impressive grand finale to any meal. The bananas may be cut in chunks, as shown here, or halved, as in the recipe at left. Other fruits, such as fresh peaches, pears, or papayas, can be substituted for the bananas; you can also pour the delicious sauce over angel food cake.

Beef Soup au Pistou gets its name from the pungent paste of puréed basil and garlic that is stirred into the soup just before the tureen is brought to the table.

BASIL

A native of India, basil is cultivated as an annual culinary herb in temperate climates. Its soft green leaves are intensely aromatic, with a pungent, licoricelike flavor.

Use   Fresh basil flatters tomato salads and sauces. It is the principal ingredient in Italian pesto and French *pistou,* which are used as a pasta sauce and soup garnish respectively. Fresh basil leaves enhance mixed green salads, pasta and pizza, Mediterranean squash and eggplant salads and cooked dishes, vegetable soups, egg dishes, veal, lamb, fish, and chicken. To substitute dried basil for fresh, see HERB.

Availability   Fresh commercial garden basil is most plentiful in summer. Fresh hothouse basil is available all year. Dried basil is packed in airtight jars or tins.

Selection   Choose fresh, aromatic bunches that aren't limp and don't show signs of decay. Packaged seasonings lose quality after a while; try to buy from a store that restocks its spice section fairly often.

Storage   Fresh basil will last three or four days if wrapped first in damp paper towels, then in plastic wrap, and refrigerated. To freeze fresh basil, snip leaves finely and freeze in plastic bags. To dry fresh basil, hang bunches upside down in a warm, dry place. Store dried basil in a cool, dark place in an airtight container. Replace every six months.

Preparation   Wash leaves and dry thoroughly. Use whole or mince. Leaves cut with a knife discolor quickly; use only in cooked dishes. For uncooked dishes, tear leaves by hand.

■ BEEF SOUP AU PISTOU

This traditional French soup is usually made without meat, but ground beef makes it even better. The word *pistou* refers to the pestolike paste of basil and garlic that flavors the soup.

>   2   tablespoons olive oil
>   1½   pounds lean ground beef, crumbled
>   1   large onion, thinly slivered
>   1   clove garlic, minced
>   1   large can (28 oz) tomatoes, coarsely chopped; reserve liquid
>   3½   cups Beef Stock (see page 560) *or* 2 cans (14½ oz each) regular-strength beef broth
>   2   cups water
>   2   teaspoons salt
>   ¼   teaspoon freshly ground pepper
>   2   medium potatoes (about 1 lb), cut in ½-inch cubes
>   1   pound green beans, cut in 1-inch pieces
>   ¼   pound vermicelli, broken in half
>   ½   cup finely grated Gruyère or Swiss cheese
>   Grated Gruyère or Swiss cheese, for garnish

Pistou

>   ¼   cup olive oil
>   3   cloves garlic, minced
>   ½   cup loosely packed, fresh basil leaves *or* 2 tablespoons dried basil and ½ cup loosely packed, chopped parsley
>   ¼   teaspoon *each* salt and sugar
>   1   tablespoon red wine vinegar

1. In a 5- to 6-quart kettle, heat oil. Add ground beef and cook over medium heat, stirring often. As meat begins to brown, stir in onion and continue cooking until onion is soft. Stir in garlic. Add tomatoes and their liquid, broth, the water, salt, pepper, and potatoes.

2. Bring to a boil, cover, reduce heat, and simmer for 1 hour. Meanwhile cook green beans uncovered in a large quantity of boiling, salted water until they are tender-crisp (6 to 8 minutes). Drain and rinse immediately with cold water to stop cooking; drain and set aside.

3. After soup has cooked for 1 hour, add vermicelli and boil gently, uncovered, stirring occasionally, until pasta is just tender (10 to 12 minutes). Add green beans and cook just until beans are heated through.

4. Add the ½ cup Gruyère cheese, about 2 tablespoons at a time, stirring after each addition until cheese melts.

5. Place Pistou in a warm tureen, add soup, and stir until soup and Pistou are well blended. Serve at once, garnishing each serving with additional grated cheese to taste.

Makes about 16 cups, 6 to 8 servings.

Pistou In blender or food processor, combine olive oil, garlic, basil, salt, sugar, and vinegar. Whirl until smooth.

Makes about ⅓ cup.

■ PESTO

A summer sauce, pesto is made when basil is abundant and inexpensive. Its pungent aroma is unforgettable, whether it's tossed with hot linguine or stirred into steaming minestrone. For Genoese sailors long at sea, a fragrant *pasta al pesto* is the traditional welcome home.

> 2 **cups loosely packed, fresh basil leaves,**
> ½ **cup light olive oil**
> 2 **tablespoons pine nuts, toasted**
> 4 **large cloves garlic, minced**
> 1 **teaspoon coarse salt**
> ½ **cup freshly grated Parmesan cheese**
> 2 **tablespoons freshly grated Pecorino Romano cheese**
> 3 **tablespoons unsalted butter, softened**

Put basil, olive oil, pine nuts, garlic, and salt in a blender or food processor. Blend or process until smooth. Transfer to a bowl and stir in Parmesan, Pecorino Romano, and butter.

Makes 1 cup.

Make-Ahead Tip Pesto may be made up to 1 week ahead, covered with a thin film of olive oil, and refrigerated in an airtight container. Pesto may be frozen for up to 1 month, covered with a thin film of olive oil; if you plan to freeze it, make pesto without garlic and stir in minced garlic just before using. It is also possible to freeze pesto in ice-cube trays; each cube will provide sauce for 1 portion of pasta. In this case, wait to incorporate Parmesan, butter, and garlic until you are ready to serve it.

> ***Recipes and Related Information***
> *Northern-Style Tomato Sauce, 412; Osso Buco, 58; Pizza Margherita, 446; Tomatoes With Mozzarella and Basil, 507.*

BASTE, TO

This term, usually associated with meats and poultry, means to brush on or pour liquid over foods while they are cooking to keep them moist and flavorful and to develop an attractive finish. Usually the basting liquid is a combination of pan drippings and fat. Seasonings or other ingredients may be added to enhance taste.

> ***Recipes and Related Information***
> *Bulb Baster, 67; Cake and Pastry Tools, 89.*

BATTER

A batter is a mixture of flour and a liquid, such as milk, beer, or wine, plus eggs and other leavening or flavoring ingredients. The proportion of flour to liquid determines the thickness and end use of the batter, although by definition all batters must be thin enough to pour or drop from a spoon. Pourable batters, which have an equal amount of flour and liquid, are used for pancakes, popovers, and cakes. Thicker drop batters contain twice as much flour as liquid and are the basis for muffins, drop biscuits, fritters, and coatings for fried foods.

Batter coatings act as a puffy, protective barrier between oil and food. Coatings also improve the taste, appearance, and texture of fried foods. Quick-cooking foods that can hold their shape, such as fish, boned poultry, vegetables, and fruits, give the best results when dipped in batter and fried. *Frittered, French-fried,* and *batter-fried* are all terms used for batter-coated foods.

Batters have a wonderful flavor, but are not as convenient a coating for fried foods as a simple dip in flour or crumbs. It is a messy process, and one that allows little time between setup and cooking—once a food has been dipped in the batter, it must be fried at once, or batter will slide off. Although batter-coated foods cook quickly, preparation takes time. Most batters should rest at least 30 minutes to 1 hour before use to allow flour to blend completely with liquid, to give leavening a chance to activate, and to allow gluten to relax. But, this isn't always necessary, and usually a recipe will guide you. Remember to dry food thoroughly before coating or batter won't adhere. Dusting with flour (or confectioners' sugar in the case of fruit) is often recommended as a first step. Flour dries the surface of the food and gives the batter something to cling to.

For all batters, be sure the oven or frying fat is heated to the proper temperature. Deep-fried batter-coated foods cook at approximately 365° F. Test temperature with a deep-fat thermometer (see THERMOMETER); another test is to drop a cube of bread in the hot fat and slowly count to 60. The fat is ready to use if the bread is golden brown. For more information about cooking oils and frying, see DEEP-FRY and FRY.

Basting adds moisture and flavor to food. The best basting brushes are made of natural boar bristles. Make sure the bristles are securely attached to the handle.

Light, crispy tempura is probably the dish that most readily comes to mind when Westerners think about Japanese food. Always serve tempura immediately after frying. If left to stand, it becomes soggy.

■ BASIC FRITTER BATTER

Fritters are best served immediately after frying. To hold until the entire batch has been cooked, lay fritters on a wire rack and set in a 350° F oven. To keep warm for up to 20 minutes, hold in a 200° F oven. Use this batter for all kinds of vegetables, meats, and fish, cut in slices or bite-sized pieces. Note that the batter must chill for two hours before using.

  1 **cup flour**
  1 **tablespoon sugar**
    Pinch salt
  2 **eggs, separated**
  1 **cup white wine**
  2 **tablespoons butter, melted**
    Oil, for frying
    Diced vegetables, meat, or fish
    Kosher salt, to taste

1. Into a medium bowl sift flour, sugar, and salt. In a blender or food processor combine egg yolks, wine, and melted butter until smooth. Cover and refrigerate for 2 hours.

2. When ready to cook fritters, heat oil to 360° F to 375° F in a Dutch oven, heavy deep skillet, or other frying kettle. Meanwhile, beat egg whites to soft peaks; fold into chilled batter.

3. Dip food into batter and fry until golden (about 2 minutes per side). Serve immediately sprinkled with kosher salt.

Makes 2 cups batter.

■ BASIC FRITTER BATTER FOR FRUIT

This batter is similar to the basic version, but uses milk instead of wine and is sweetened to complement fruit.

  1 **cup flour**
    Pinch salt
  2 **tablespoons sugar**
  2 **eggs, separated**
  ½ **cup milk**
  2 **tablespoons butter, melted**
    Oil, for frying
    Slices or pieces of fruit such as banana, pineapple, apple, papaya
    Confectioners' sugar, granulated sugar, cinnamon sugar, fruit sauce, or melted preserves, for topping

1. Follow directions for Basic Fritter Batter (at left), substituting milk for wine.

2. Serve immediately sprinkled with confectioners' sugar, granulated sugar, or cinnamon sugar, or drizzled with fruit sauce or melted preserves.

Makes 2 cups batter.

■ TEMPURA BATTER

Use light, crispy tempura batter to coat firm-textured seafood such as prawns, sea bass, and sole, and pieces of carrot, broccoli, zucchini, eggplant, and sweet potato.

  1 **cup flour**
  2 **teaspoons baking powder**
  1 **teaspoon salt**
  1 **cup ice water**
  1 **egg, beaten**
    Oil, for frying (preferably peanut oil)

Dipping Sauce

  ¾ **cup Chicken Stock (see page 560)**
  4 **tablespoons Japanese soy sauce**
  3 **tablespoons mirin (sweet sake) or dry sherry**

1. In a small bowl sift together flour, baking powder, and salt. Place the ice water in a medium bowl; whisk in beaten egg. Add sifted dry ingredients and whisk together lightly just to combine (do not overmix—even if small lumps of flour are left in batter).

2. Use batter immediately. Make sure food to be dipped is dry. To fry at an even rate, cut food into pieces of the same size. Serve with Dipping Sauce.

Makes about 1½ cups batter.

Dipping Sauce   In a small saucepan combine Chicken Stock, soy sauce, and mirin; bring to a boil. Remove from heat and cool.

Makes about 1 cup.

■ PLUMP POPOVERS

Steam forming in this egg-rich batter billows each popover into a hollow puff that is virtually all crust—the better to lavish with butter and jam. You can make the batter ahead. Complete step 1, cover batter, and refrigerate for up to a day. When ready to bake, stir batter well and proceed with step 2.

    1 cup milk
    3 eggs
    1 tablespoon sugar
    2 tablespoons butter or margarine, melted
       and cooled, or vegetable oil
    1 cup flour
    ¼ teaspoon salt

1. In blender or food processor combine milk, eggs, sugar, butter, flour, and salt. Whirl until smooth and well combined, stopping motor once or twice and using a rubber spatula to mix in flour from sides of container.

2. Preheat oven to 400° F. Generously grease standard muffin or popover pans or custard cups. Pour batter into pans, filling about half full.

3. Bake until popovers are well browned and firm to the touch (35 to 40 minutes). Avoid opening oven until end of baking time. Serve hot.

Makes 10 to 12 popovers.

Recipes and Related Information
Biscuit, 49; Cake, 77; Deep-fried Zucchini
Blossoms, 238; Muffin, 374; Waffle and Pancake, 598.

BATTERIE DE CUISINE

Loosely translated, this French phrase means the *artillery of the kitchen*—all the pots and pans, utensils, and basic equipment used for cooking.

Although it is always fun to buy culinary paraphernalia, most cooks function extremely well with a collection of well-chosen, high-quality equipment that suits their particular needs. The following is a checklist of basic equipment (for specific information, consult the entries listed in Recipes and Related Information, at right).

Bake Ware   Baking pans and sheets, brushes, cake pans, cooling rack, loaf pan, muffin pan, pastry blender, pie pan, rolling pin, sifter, springform pan, tube pan.

Cookware   Double boiler, saucepans, sauce pot, sauté pan, skillets, steamer, stockpot.

Knives   Boning knife, chef's knife, paring knife, serrated bread knife, plus chef's fork, kitchen scissors, and knife sharpener or sharpening steel.

Machines   Coffee grinder or electric minichopper, food processor, electric mixer.

Measuring Tools   Dry and liquid measuring cups, measuring spoons, scale, thermometers (deep-frying, instant read, freezer, oven), timer.

Ovenware   Baking dishes, casseroles, broiler pan and rack, roasting pan and rack.

Small Equipment   Bulb baster, cheesecloth, citrus reamer, citrus stripper and zester, colanders and sieves, cutting board, food mill, funnel, garlic press, graters, kitchen twine, lacers and skewers, ladle, mixing bowls, molds, mortar and pestle, parchment paper, peeler, pepper mill, skimmer, spatulas, spoons (slotted and wooden), tongs, turners, whisk.

Recipes and Related Information
Baking Pans, 18; Cake and Pastry Tools, 89; Casseroles
and Baking Dishes, 103; Cheesecloth, 119; Chopping
and Cutting Board, 129; Citrus Reamer, 131;
Colander, Strainer, and Sieve, 137; Cookware, 151;
Food Processor, 240; Gadgets, 258; Grater, 281;
Knife, 328; Measure, 353; Mixers, 369; Mixing
Bowl, 369; Mold, 369; Needle and Fastener, 384;
Spatula, Scraper, and Turner, 548; Spoon, Ladle, and
Scoop, 551; Thermometer, 575; Timer, 579; Tongs, 582;
Whisk, 608

BAY

The evergreen bay shrub—also known as laurel—is a native of southern Europe. Its thick, glossy, dark green leaves are an important culinary herb. They contribute a pungent aroma to stocks, soups, and stews.

Use   Add bay leaves with restraint to flavor meat stocks, marinades, vegetable or dried bean soups, pot roast, roast chicken, and tomato or béchamel sauces. Remove leaves before serving. Whole bay leaf is a common component of bouquet garni. Add a pinch of ground bay leaf to stuffings, soups, or stews.

Availability   Dried bay leaves are packed in jars, tins, or plastic bags. Ground bay leaf is packed in jars or tins. Fresh bay is rarely available commercially.

Selection   Packaged seasoning loses quality after a while; try to buy from a store that restocks its spice section fairly often.

Storage   Keep dried and ground bay leaves in airtight containers in a cool, dark place for up to one year.

BEAN

All beans are members of the legume family, one of the world's most important food groups. Their genus is *Phaseolus*. Most beans consist of a pod with a single section that holds one row of seeds. Some varieties are cultivated more for their edible pod than for their seeds; others have tough, stringy pods and are cultivated primarily for their seeds, which may be used either fresh or dried. There are hundreds of varieties of fresh and dried beans. Those described here are among the most common.

Use   Beans with edible pods are enjoyed as a salad and as a side dish. French cooks serve tiny *haricots verts* both cold and hot—cold, with vinaigrette or mayonnaise; hot, with melted butter or olive oil. Chinese cooks often stir-fry beans with bits of seasoned minced pork or with oyster sauce. Italians add edible-podded beans to vegetable soups or sauté them with *pancetta* (unsmoked bacon). Indian cooks braise green beans with coconut and spices.

Shell beans may also be eaten as a cold salad or a hot side dish. They add body and flavor to soups and stews.

Availability   Fresh beans are available in bulk at produce markets and supermarkets. See specific beans for season. Dried beans come packed in plastic bags and are sold in bulk. Some beans are canned as well.

Selection   See specific beans.

Storage   Refrigerate fresh beans with edible pods in a perforated plastic bag for up to three or four days. Store fresh shell beans with inedible pods similarly and use within two or three days; shell just before using. Store dried beans in an airtight container in a cool place; they will keep up to one year.

Preparation   Varies depending upon bean; check specific entries for preparation information. Most dried beans (except lentils) require soaking before cooking. Cover with plenty of cold water and soak eight hours or overnight. Or use a quick-soak method: Boil beans and water 2 minutes; cover and let stand 1 hour. Discard water before proceeding with recipe.

Cooking   See Timetable for Cooking Beans on opposite page, and BOIL, SAUTE, STEAM, STIR-FRY.

AZUKI BEAN

Also spelled *adzuki,* this small, red bean is available dried, packed in plastic bags, from Asian markets. Chinese and Japanese cooks use these soft, slightly sweet beans in steamed rice dishes. Azuki beans are also boiled, mashed with shortening, and sweetened with sugar to make red bean paste, used by Asian cooks in a variety of sweet dishes, from jellies and puddings to stuffed pastry. The paste is available canned in Asian markets. Leftover bean paste will keep for months if refrigerated in a covered jar or plastic container.

BLACK BEAN

Also known as turtle beans, black beans are highly important to the various cuisines of Latin America and the Caribbean. These small, jet-black beans come to market dried, packaged in plastic bags or sold in bulk. Use within one year of purchase. Cooked black beans are also available canned in some parts of the country. They have an earthy, meaty flavor and a mealy texture. Black beans are used in soups, stews, salads, and bean dips. They go well with pork, rice, and greens.

BROAD BEAN

See Fava Bean.

CANNELLINI BEAN

See Kidney Bean.

CHINESE LONG BEAN

Also known as yard-long beans or asparagus beans, these thin, pliable green beans do grow to exceptional lengths, usually about 18 inches. Asian cooks use young, tender long beans in stir-fries. Mature long beans yield edible seeds similar to black-eyed peas. Long beans are available fresh in Asian markets in late summer and fall. Select thin, firm beans without wrinkles or spongy parts.

Long beans may be steamed or stir-fried; substitute them for green snap beans in any recipe, although their flavor is slightly milder and they have a crunchier texture. To prepare, trim ends and cut beans into small pieces.

CRANBERRY BEAN

Fresh cranberry beans have inedible whitish green pods with red striations and measure about 3 inches long and ½ inch wide. The shelled beans also have mottled reddish markings. The beans are occasionally available fresh in the summer; select firm, full pods with no signs of drying. To prepare fresh beans, open pods and remove beans. Dried cranberry beans are packaged in plastic bags or sold in bulk; use within a year of purchase. Canned cranberry beans are available in some parts of the country.

Add cranberry beans to stews and soups, especially Italian minestrone, or boil and serve as a side dish.

Recipes: Cranberry Bean Minestrone, 564.

FAVA BEAN

Also known as broad beans or horse beans, fava beans have pods that range from 4 to 18 inches long. When young and small, the whole pod may be eaten raw with oil and salt. More mature pods should be shelled; the moist green beans inside have a tough skin that should be peeled. Fresh fava beans are available in late spring and early summer. Select heavy, full pods that have good color and are without blemishes. To prepare, open pod and remove beans; use thumbnail to split and remove skin on each bean. Dried fava beans are packaged in plastic bags or sold in bulk. Cooked beans have an assertive, almost bitter flavor and a mealy texture.

Add fava beans to soups and stews or enjoy as a side dish dressed with butter or oil. Boiled favas may also be eaten cold or at room temperature as a salad dressed with vinaigrette.

■ BRAISED FAVA BEANS

A Sicilian specialty, these well-seasoned beans make a delightful hors d'oeuvre when wrapped up in cool lettuce cups, or serve them as a side dish to accompany a roast. Note that the beans need to soak overnight.

    1 pound dried fava beans
    1 cup chopped yellow onion
    3 tomatoes, coarsely chopped
    ½ cup tomato purée
    ½ cup coarsely chopped Italian parsley
    ½ cup coarsely chopped celery
      Salt and freshly ground pepper, to taste
      Red pepper flakes (optional)
      Lettuce leaves
      Olive oil, for garnish
      Parsley sprigs, for garnish
    4 ounces Parmesan cheese, sliced
      paper-thin, for garnish

1. Put beans in a large pot; add water to cover and soak overnight. The next day, add onion, tomatoes, and tomato puree. Bring to a boil, reduce heat to maintain a simmer, and cook until beans are just tender. There should be almost no water left.

2. Cool beans to room temperature, then add parsley, celery, salt, pepper, and hot pepper flakes (if used) to taste. Form cups with lettuce leaves and fill with beans; garnish with a drizzle of olive oil, a parsley sprig, and a slice of Parmesan cheese.

Serves 12.

Food Processor Version Use metal blade to chop parsley; set aside. Cut 1 stalk celery into 1-inch chunks and turn motor on and off to chop; set aside. Cut 1 large onion into eighths and process with metal blade, turning motor on and off 3 or 4 times; set aside. Process tomatoes with metal blade as for onion.

FLAGEOLET

A popular French shell bean, the *flageolet* has an inedible green pod about 3 inches long and small, light-green, kidney-shaped seeds. Fresh flageolets are occasionally available in the summer; look for well-filled, pliable pods that contain even-sized beans and do not show evidence

---

TIMETABLE FOR COOKING BEANS

To cook green beans (Chinese long bean, haricot vert, runner bean, snap bean): Steam in a small amount of boiling, salted water in a covered saucepan until tender (2 to 10 minutes, depending upon size and age); or cut in pieces and stir-fry in a skillet in 1 to 2 tablespoons vegetable oil until tender-crisp (2 to 5 minutes, depending upon size and age). Add salt or other seasoning just before serving and toss to blend. *To cook dried beans:* For all types except split golden gram (mung), cook as directed in a proportion of 3 parts water to 1 part beans; use a 4-to-1 ratio of water to beans for split golden gram (mung).

Type of Bean	Soak	Time
Azuki	Overnight or quick-soak	Boil 10 minutes; cover and simmer 1½ to 2 hours
Black	Same	Boil 10 minutes; cover and simmer 1 to 1½ hours
Cranberry	Same	Boil 10 minutes; cover and simmer 1½ to 2 hours
Fava	Same	Boil 10 minutes; cover and simmer 2 to 2½ hours
Flageolet	Same	Boil 10 minutes; cover and simmer 1½ to 2 hours
Great Northern	Same	Boil 10 minutes; cover and simmer 1½ to 2 hours
Kidney	Same	Boil 10 minutes; cover and simmer 1½ to 2 hours
Lentil	No soaking	Bring to boil; cover and simmer 20 to 25 minutes
Lima	Overnight or quick-soak	Boil 10 minutes; cover and simmer 1 to 1½ hours
Mung	Soak 1 to 4 hours	Bring to boil; cover and simmer 30 minutes
Navy	Overnight or quick-soak	Boil 10 minutes; cover and simmer 1½ to 2 hours
Pinto	Same	Boil 10 minutes; cover and simmer 1½ to 2 hours
Red	Same	Boil 10 minutes; cover and simmer 1½ to 2 hours
Soybean	Same	Boil 10 minutes; cover and simmer 1½ to 2 hours
Split golden gram (mung)	No soaking	Bring to boil; cover and simmer 20 to 30 minutes

---

of drying. To prepare, pull on tip of pod to split it open; remove beans. Dried flageolets are packaged in plastic bags or boxes or sold in bulk. Canned French flageolets are available in specialty food markets.

Braised flageolets are the traditional French accompaniment to leg of lamb. They may also be added to soups and stews or eaten cold as a salad with lemon and oil.

■ FLAGEOLETS WITH HERBS

Small, pale green flageolets are used frequently in French cuisine, particularly as a flavorful accompaniment to roast leg of lamb. Note that the beans must soak overnight, or quick-soak 1 hour (see Preparation).

      2 cups (about 1 lb) dried flageolets or
         small navy beans
     10 cups water
      1 bay leaf
      4 carrots, sliced
      1 onion, sliced
      2 cloves garlic, quartered
    1½ teaspoons dried rosemary
      1 teaspoon dried thyme
      2 tablespoons olive oil
      2 cups Beef Stock (see page 560)
      2 teaspoons salt
      1 teaspoon freshly ground pepper

1. Soak beans as directed on page 30, using 6 cups water. Add the remaining water, bay leaf, carrots, onion, garlic, rosemary, thyme, and oil.

2. Increase heat, and boil 10 minutes; reduce heat, and simmer 1½ hours; drain. Add stock, salt, and pepper, and continue cooking 30 minutes.

Serves 8 to 10.

GREAT NORTHERN BEAN

The Great Northern is a large white shell bean with a mild flavor. Dried Great Northern beans are packaged in plastic bags or sold in bulk. Use within a year of purchase. Cooked Great Northern beans are also available in cans and jars. Use in soups, stews, baked bean dishes, and salads.

GREEN BEAN

See Snap Bean.

HARICOT VERT

The haricot vert is an exceptionally slender, stringless green bean. Although long popular in France, this sweet, tender bean has only recently been commercialized in America. Now specialty markets generally have fresh haricots verts from July through September. Choose firm pods, ⅛ inch or less in diameter, with solid green color. To prepare, remove stem ends. Store beans in a perforated plastic bag in the refrigerator crisper; use within one or two days of purchase. Steam briefly, then sauté in butter or oil, and serve hot, or dress steamed beans with vinaigrette and serve at room temperature or chilled.

ITALIAN ROMANO (GREEN) BEAN

See Snap Bean.

KIDNEY BEAN

The kidney bean is the kidney-shaped seed of a common shell bean. Both red and white varieties exist, although the white kidney bean is more commonly called a *cannellini* bean. Dried red and white kidney beans are packaged in plastic bags or sold in bulk; use within a year of purchase. Canned kidney beans are widely available. The meaty flavor and mealy texture are appealing in soups, stews, chili, and salads.

■ RED BEANS AND RICE

This is the traditional Monday-night dinner of New Orleans. The custom probably began because folks had spent all their money on the weekend and needed a cheap but substantial way to feed themselves. Although it is an inexpensive meal, it does not lack in flavor and appetite appeal, and it makes an ideal dish for informally entertaining a large group. Note that the beans first have to soak overnight, and then when cooked should be refrigerated at least overnight.

      1 pound dried red beans
      4 quarts water
      2 meaty ham hocks
      8 cups Beef Stock (see page 560) or
         Chicken Stock (see page 560)
      4 bay leaves
    ½ teaspoon thyme
      1 teaspoon cayenne pepper
      1 teaspoon freshly ground pepper
      1 pound andouille (sausage)
    ¼ pound tasso (sausage), chopped (optional)
      2 cups chopped onion
    ½ cup chopped celery
      1 green bell pepper, chopped
      1 bunch green onions, chopped
      1 tablespoon minced garlic
      8 chaurice sausages (approximately 2 lb) or
         other fresh, hot sausages
         Salt and freshly ground pepper, to taste
         Red wine vinegar, to taste (optional)
      4 cups cooked rice
         Hot-pepper sauce, to taste

1. Wash beans and soak overnight in the water. The next day drain beans and wash well under cold running water. Place beans, ham hocks, and stock in a heavy, 6- to 8-quart stockpot or Dutch oven. Beans should be covered by about 2 to 3 inches of liquid; add more if necessary. Bring to a boil and skim any scum that collects on the surface. Reduce heat to simmer and add bay leaves, thyme, cayenne, and pepper. Simmer for 30 minutes while you prepare vegetables.

2. Chop ¼ pound of the *andouille* into ¼-inch pieces. Place in a 12-inch cast-iron frying pan (or other heavy frying pan) with *tasso* (if used). Fry for 5 minutes to render fat and brown meat. Add chopped onion and celery and cook until vegetables are soft (about 10 minutes). Add bell pepper, green onions, and garlic. Cook an additional 5 minutes, then add to simmering pot of red beans. Continue to cook beans until they are soft and some begin to break apart (about 1 hour). Allow beans to cool; refrigerate, covered, overnight or for up to 4 days.

3. When ready to serve, bring beans to a simmer. Place *chaurice* whole in a heavy frying pan, cover, and fry over medium heat for about 15 minutes, checking sausages frequently and turning them as they brown. Meanwhile, slice remaining andouille into ¼-inch slices and add to beans. Cook in beans for about 10 minutes. Taste beans for salt and pepper and correct if necessary; add a little vinegar (if desired). To serve, place about ½ cup hot rice in center of each plate, spoon beans over rice, and accompany with 1 chaurice. Serve with hot-pepper sauce.

Serves 8.

Food Processor Version Use metal blade to process vegetables, one after the other. Cut 2 large onions into eighths, put in work bowl, and turn motor on and off 3 to 4 times. Cut 1 stalk celery into 1-inch chunks and process same way. Cut bell pepper into 1-inch pieces and process same way. Cut green onions into 1-inch pieces and process 5 to 10 seconds.

LENTIL

The flat, disklike seeds of a leguminous plant, lentils are native to Asia Minor. Today lentils are marketed only dried, either packed in plastic bags or boxes or sold in bulk. Lentils are available in several different colors, including yellow, pink, and greenish brown. Store all varieties in a cool, dry place and use within a year.

Add lentils to soups and stews; boil until tender, drain, and dress with vinaigrette for a cool salad; or boil until tender, drain, and reheat with oil, butter, or bacon fat for a side dish.

LIMA BEAN

Also known as butter bean, the lima bean is a relatively large, kidney-shaped, light-green bean in an inedible green pod. Limas are occasionally available fresh in summer; choose solid-green, pliable pods without evidence of drying. To prepare, pull on string to open pod and remove beans. Limas are also available canned, frozen, and dried; dried limas are packed in plastic bags or sold in bulk. Store fresh limas in a plastic bag in refrigerator crisper; use quickly. Use dried limas within a year of purchase.

Add limas to soups and stews; boil until tender, drain and dress with butter or oil, and serve hot; or boil until tender, drain and dress with vinaigrette, and serve at room temperature or chilled as a salad.

■ SUCCOTASH

The name succotash derives from an Indian word, *m'sickquatash*, meaning corn not crushed or ground. Colonists learned from Native Americans the land-saving practice of planting corn and beans together, then training the bean vines up the corn stalks. At the harvest they simply combined the two in cooking. Today we usually make succotash with corn and lima beans, but many New England cooks prefer cranberry beans, and the Pennsylvania Dutch often add green bell peppers, tomatoes, and other vegetables. Some early recipes also called for fowl or meat plus potatoes or turnips, thus making more of a stew. This modern recipe is simple, colorful, and delicious, and it is very good made with frozen vegetables.

The classic Monday-night dinner of New Orleans, Red Beans and Rice, is embellished with Louisiana sausages and smoked meats. The hot sausage here, called chaurice, is flavored with fresh onions, parsley, and chiles and lightly smoked. Also pictured is tasso, a Cajun seasoning meat, which is more spicy and smoky than ham. If tasso is unavailable, you can use a smoked ham.

> ¼ cup butter
> 2 cups fresh corn kernels or frozen corn kernels, thawed
> 2 cups cooked lima beans
> ¼ teaspoon salt
> ¼ teaspoon freshly ground pepper
> ½ cup whipping cream
> 2 tablespoons chopped parsley

1. In a medium saucepan over medium heat, melt butter. Add corn, beans, salt, and pepper; stir to combine.

2. Add cream and simmer gently, uncovered, for about 5 minutes.

3. Stir in parsley and serve.

Serves 6.

"Never saw a man so tired he couldn't eat some beans," said the old prospector in Treasure of Sierra Madre. *Probably he was thinking of that southwestern indispensable, Frijoles, shown here, and its variation, Refried Beans.*

MUNG BEAN

The small cylindrical seed of a leguminous plant, the mung bean is most commonly green, but brown and black varieties exist. When shelled and split in half, the green mung bean yields a rectangular yellow bean called the split golden gram or *moong dal.* Both mung beans and split golden gram are highly valued by Indian cooks as a source of protein. Sprouted mung beans, an even finer source of protein, are used frequently in Asian cooking.

Fresh mung bean sprouts are widely available all year. Select firm white sprouts without brown areas. Refrigerate in a plastic bag and use immediately. If not using right away, blanch bean sprouts in boiling water for 30 seconds, then transfer to ice water. Refrigerate, covered with water, and change water daily. Blanched bean sprouts will stay fresh for five or six days. Mung bean sprouts are also available canned; rinse under cold water before using. Dried mung beans are packaged in plastic bags or sold in bulk. Use within a year of purchase.

Use whole mung beans in soups, stews, and pilafs. Mung bean sprouts add texture to salads, stir-fries, and omelets. Mung bean starch is the basis for the transparent "cellophane" noodles used by Chinese cooks. Indian cooks use mung bean flour for breads and sweets.

NAVY BEAN

The navy bean is a small, oval, white bean so named because it has long been a staple of the diet of the U.S. Navy. Dried navy beans are packaged in plastic bags or sold in bulk. Use within a year of purchase. Navy beans are also widely available canned; they are the variety used for most canned and home-cooked versions of pork and beans or baked beans. Use navy beans in soups, stews, and salads.

■ BOSTON BAKED BEANS

In colonial times, it was customary to begin cooking baked beans early Saturday, so they would simmer quietly all day and evening and be ready for an effortless Saturday supper, Sunday breakfast, or noontime dinner. Today, beans are no longer considered strictly Sabbath food (although they still take all day to cook). If you wish, add a little catsup to the recipe; it's not traditional, but it adds color and tang. Otherwise, pass catsup at the table.

> 2 cups (1 lb) dried navy beans
> 1½ teaspoons salt
> 3 tablespoons *each* molasses and brown sugar
> 1 tablespoon dry mustard
> ¼ cup catsup (optional)
> 1 onion, peeled and left whole
> ¼ pound salt pork

1. Pick over beans to remove pebbles or bits of dirt, then rinse well in a colander. Place in a large pan, add 1 teaspoon salt and enough water to cover beans by about 3 inches. Bring to a rolling boil over high heat, and boil for 2 minutes. Remove from heat, cover pan, and let stand 1 hour.

2. Uncover pan, bring back to a boil, reduce heat, and simmer until beans are tender (1 to 1½ hours). Add more water if necessary to keep beans well covered.

3. Drain well, reserving liquid. In a bean pot or casserole of about 2½-quart capacity, combine molasses, brown sugar, mustard, catsup (if desired), and ½ teaspoon salt. Add drained beans, and stir in enough reserved cooking liquid to cover beans; mix well. Push whole onion down one side of beans. Cut several gashes in salt pork and bury it on the other side.

4. Cover pot, place in oven, and turn heat to 350° F. Bake until beans are bubbling (about 1 hour). Reduce heat to 250° F and bake for 6 to 8 hours more, stirring every hour or so. As beans cook, they will absorb liquid; continue adding reserved cooking liquid (or water), a little at a time, to keep them moist but not soupy. Baked beans are done when thick, fragrant, and a deep brownish red. They can remain in a 200° F oven for 1 or 2 hours longer if you wish; just remember to add liquid occasionally so they do not dry out. Beans also reheat well the next day. Remove and discard onion before serving. Serve with sliced salt pork if you wish.

Serves 4 to 6.

PINTO BEAN

The pinto bean is the mottled oval seed of a common shell bean. Dried pinto beans are sold in plastic bags or in bulk; use within a year of purchase. Canned pinto beans are also widely available. Pinto beans appear in many southwestern and Mexican soups, stews, and chilis.

■ FRIJOLES

Homemade beans do taste better than beans from a can. Note that the beans have to soak overnight, or quick-soak 1 hour (see Preparation).

  1 **pound dry pinto beans**
16 **cups cold water**
  1 **large onion, coarsely chopped (about 1½ cups)**
  1 **tablespoon (about 2 cloves) minced garlic**
  ¼ **teaspoon red pepper flakes**
  1 **medium onion, finely chopped (about 1 cup)**
  3 **tablespoons bacon fat or lard**
  1 **large tomato, peeled, seeded, and coarsely chopped (about 1 cup)**
    Salt and freshly ground pepper, to taste

1. Soak beans overnight in 8 cups of the cold water.

2. Drain and add 8 cups fresh water, the coarsely chopped onion, garlic, and red pepper. Bring to a boil, lower heat, cover, and simmer until beans are tender (about 90 minutes).

3. In a medium skillet over moderate heat, sauté finely chopped onion in bacon fat until wilted; add tomato and sauté until soft. Place ½ cup drained beans in small bowl and mash well with a fork. Add mashed beans to skillet along with a little of their liquid (about ¼ cup); stir over low heat until a thick paste.

4. Spoon contents of skillet into bean pot. Simmer, stirring frequently, until liquid thickens (about 30 minutes). Season to taste with salt and pepper.

Serves 6 to 8.

Texas Jalapeño Pinto Beans Complete steps 1 through 3. Spoon contents of skillet into bean pot and add canned or pickled jalapeño chiles to taste—up to an entire 4-ounce can for a very, very spicy dish. Continue with step 4.

Refried Beans Complete steps 1 and 2. Drain cooked beans, reserving liquid. Mash well with a fork or a potato masher (not a food processor). In a large, heavy skillet, heat 3 tablespoons of rendered bacon fat with 4 tablespoons of lard until aromatic and almost smoking. Very carefully add mashed beans (they will spatter) and lower heat. Cook over medium-low heat, stirring frequently, until fat is absorbed. Thin to desired consistency with some of the reserved cooking liquid, stirring it in by tablespoons. Add ¼ pound Monterey jack cheese, coarsely grated, and cook about 15 minutes longer, until cheese is completely absorbed. Season with salt and pepper.

RUNNER BEAN

Also known as the scarlet runner bean, the runner bean has a flat, broad, green pod and small scarlet seeds. The edible blossom may be red or white. The runner bean is available fresh in summer and fall. Choose firm pods that have solid color, do not show signs of drying, and have beans that are not too pronounced. Steam and serve hot, with butter or oil, or cold with vinaigrette. Add to vegetable soups or mixed vegetable salads. To prepare, cut along each side of bean to remove strings and ridges. Slice across pod on the diagonal between each seed.

SNAP BEAN

Immature *Phaseolus vulgaris*, at the stage when entire pod is edible, is called snap bean. Snap beans include the common green or string bean, the Italian Romano bean, the yellow wax bean, and the purple-podded bean. Snap beans are available fresh, frozen, and canned. Some fresh varieties are available the year around, but the supply peaks in summer. Choose fresh snap beans that are firm, with smooth pods, and do not show signs of browning or drying. To prepare for cooking, remove strings and brown tips (see GADGETS, Bean Slicer). Snap beans may be steamed, braised, sautéed, stir-fried, or pickled. Serve hot, with butter or oil, or cold as a salad. They may be added to soups or hot, mixed vegetable combinations.

SOYBEAN

Fresh soybean pods are dark green with a soft outer fuzz; inside are two or four small oval beans. Soybeans can be yellow, green, brown, black, or mottled. When cooked their texture is firm, their flavor mild.

Because of their high protein content, soybeans are a valuable food source. They are made into a wide variety of products, from bean curd (tofu) to soy milk to soy sauce to soy flour.

Shell and boil fresh soybeans as you would English peas, or substitute soybeans for lima beans or fava beans in recipes that have a comparable flavor and texture. Dried soybeans can be sprouted for use in salads, stir-fries, and sandwiches, or boiled and served hot as a side dish. The salted black beans widely used in Chinese cooking are soft black soybeans that have been cooked, inoculated with a mold, and brined for about six months. Salted black beans are used to flavor steamed fish, pork ribs, clams, and many other dishes.

Fresh soybeans are available occasionally in Japanese markets and specialty markets in summer and fall; dried soybeans can be bought in bulk at Asian markets and health-food stores. Salted black beans are sold in Chinese markets in cans or small bags usually labeled "salted black beans." Do not confuse them with the uncooked variety, which is sold in similar packages.

Choose firm, well-filled soybean pods, without brown edges or spots.

Keep in a plastic bag in refrigerator for one to two days. Dried soybeans and salted black beans that are kept in an airtight container keep indefinitely in a cool, dry place.

Recipes: Bean Curd, 36; Flour, 234; Sauce and Condiment (Commercial), 523.

SPLIT GOLDEN GRAM (MOONG DAL)

See Mung Bean.

STRING BEAN

See Snap Bean.

TURTLE BEAN

See Black Bean.

WAX BEAN

See Snap Bean.

BEAN CURD

Also marketed under its Japanese name, *tofu,* bean curd is a highly nutritious soybean product that has been made in east Asia for over 2,000 years. Tofu is made from soybeans that are soaked, then puréed, and cooked to create soy milk. Soy milk is then mixed with a coagulant similar to the rennet used in making cheese. As curds form, they are shaped and pressed in rectangular molds to form tofu. Its texture is smooth, moist, and silky; its basic flavor is bland, but it readily absorbs other flavors.

Use   Tofu is an important source of protein for billions of people. It is eaten cold with a variety of seasonings and dipping sauces; it is also deep-fried, stir-fried, braised, stuffed, steamed, grilled, and poached in soups. Delicate Japanese-style tofu is suitable for soups and simmered dishes; Chinese-style tofu contains less whey and therefore is firmer and better for stir-frying, deep-frying, braising, and grilling.

Bean curd is used increasingly in non-Asian processed foods, from salad dressings to nondairy ice creams. The latter may be suitable for low-cholesterol and lactose-free diets; however, these products are generally not low-calorie as they are high in sugar and vegetable oil. Check package label for ingredients.

Availability   Both types of fresh tofu are sold packed in water in sealed plastic tubs or in sealed foil packages. The foil packages do not require refrigeration, until opening. Deep-fried bean curd is available in bulk or in sealed plastic bags. Japanese markets may also carry freeze-dried and charcoal-grilled tofu in cakes. The skin that forms on the surface of hot soybean milk is dried and sold as sheets, rolls, or sticks and is used as a meat substitute in some vegetarian dishes.

Storage   Fresh bean curd is highly perishable and should be used within two or three days of purchase. Refrigerate unused portion, covered with ample water, in a covered plastic container; change water daily.

Preparation   Rinse tofu briefly under cold running water. Cube, dice, or slice as recipe directs.

■ FRIED TOFU

Serve deep-fried tofu as a hot appetizer with a dipping sauce or use it as a meat substitute in such dishes as Mu Shu Pork (see page 378). The first step, pressing the tofu, may not be necessary if the tofu is firm enough; remember to drain it thoroughly. Softer, Japanese-style tofu will have to be pressed.

      7 ounces firm Chinese-style tofu
         Oil, for deep-frying

1. Drain tofu well. Wrap in a clean kitchen towel or several thicknesses of paper towel, place on a plate set in a sheet pan, and invert another plate on top. Place a 1-pound weight on top plate. Let stand 30 minutes, then unwrap and drain. Tofu will exude a lot of liquid. (This may be done ahead of time and the tofu refrigerated.)

2. Slice pressed tofu into squares, triangles, or other shapes about ⅜ inch thick. In a wok or other deep pan, heat oil to 350° F. Fry tofu pieces a few at a time, until puffy and golden brown (6 to 8 minutes).

Serves 4 to 6 as an appetizer.

BEARD, TO

Also called debeard; to pull out the byssus of a mussel, the bristly, beardlike hairs that are connected just inside the hinge of the shell (see photograph, page 536). Mussels attach themselves to rocks and each other with these threads. The byssus must be scrubbed from the outer shell and pulled from the inner shell before cooking. Mussels die soon after bearding, so preparation should follow immediately.

BEAT, TO

To mix ingredients by stirring rapidly in a circular motion by hand or with an electric mixer in order to make smooth (batters) or to lighten with air (egg whites and whipping cream).

BEEF

Technically, beef is any meat from a full-grown ox, bull, cow, or steer. In practice, however, almost all commercial beef comes from steers (castrated males). Ox meat is too tough, bulls are too unruly, and cows fatten too slowly to be suitable for commercial beef production.

The American beef industry is continually trying to improve the breed of cattle used for beef. Through selective breeding and cross-breeding for flavor, yield, disease-resistance, efficient feed-to-muscle conversion, and other characteristics, today's beef cattle are very different from the cattle brought to the colonies by seventeenth-century English settlers.

Most beef cattle today are black Angus or Hereford, although the French Charolais is gaining popularity. Crosses with Brahman bulls and Texas longhorns are also commercial successes.

WHAT DETERMINES QUALITY OF BEEF CATTLE

Diet is a major factor in determining the quality of meat on beef cattle. Grain-fed or grain-finished cattle develop more intramuscular fat (marbling), and therefore more flavorful and more tender meat, than do grass-fed cattle. Some experts claim that corn-fed cattle are superior in flavor to those fed a grain diet that also includes oats, barley, or sorghum. However, even grain-fed cattle have some hay or straw in their feed for roughage.

Age at time of slaughter is another determinant of quality. Young animals have tender meat but lack flavor. Older animals have more flavor but tougher meat. Most beef cattle today are slaughtered when they reach about 1,000 to 1,200 pounds, which generally takes 11 to 16 months.

How beef is treated after slaughter also affects its quality. Beef that has been allowed to hang, or age, on the carcass for two to six weeks at a cold temperature in a humidity-controlled room will be more tender than fresh beef. Under these controlled conditions, excess moisture in the meat evaporates and enzymes begin to break down the muscle fibers, thus tenderizing the meat. Few retail meat markets offer aged beef to consumers. Most aged beef is destined for restaurants.

WHAT MAKES BEEF CHOICE

The quality (how tender, juicy, and flavorful the meat is) of any piece of meat depends on its location on the animal and on the "grade" assigned to each meat carcass.

The choicest cuts of all meats come from the parts of the animal that do the least work. Just as in humans, the hard-working lower leg of an animal develops a strong, tough muscle, full of sinewy fibers and connective tissues, while the well-protected and rarely exercised little muscle right in the middle of the back (the filet mignon, on a steer)

remains tender. The tougher cuts can be just as tasty and nutritious as the tender ones if they're cooked by a method that tenderizes them.

GRADES OF BEEF

All meat sold in the United States is checked by government inspectors for wholesomeness. The United States Department of Agriculture also inspects most meat to determine its grade. The "quality" of beef that determines its grading by the USDA is based on its tenderness, juiciness, and flavor. The top grades for beef are USDA Prime, Choice, and Good. However, in most of the country, grading is voluntary, and only about 50 percent of American beef is graded. The major difference between grades is the degree of marbling.

Marbling is the small, paper-thin veins of fat that crisscross a piece of meat. Hard-working muscles, such as the flank and shin, have very little marbling; tender cuts, such as the rib and the loin, are finely marbled all over.

Prime, the highest grade of meat, containing the greatest degree of marbling, is produced in very limited quantities, and is generally sold at premium prices to finer restaurants and specialty meat markets. Prime cuts, because they are already expensive, also tend to receive the longest aging.

Choice is the grade generally sold at retail stores. It is preferred by consumers because it contains sufficient marbling for taste and tenderness and is less costly and less fattening than Prime.

Good, a lower-priced grade of meat, has less marbling than USDA Choice. It is as nutritious as the other grades, but less juicy and flavorful. Some supermarket chains sell it under their own quality designation rather than a USDA grade name. It is also used commercially for many canned meat items.

Use Beef is a major protein source in many of the world's cuisines. Some best-loved beef dishes include: Italian carpaccio, raw beef sliced paper-thin and served with a mustard sauce; French *boeuf bourguignonne,* beef stewed in Burgundy wine; Russian beef stroganoff with mushrooms and sour cream; English roast prime ribs of beef with Yorkshire pudding; and, of course, American hamburgers.

Availability Many retail stores have adopted the National Livestock and Meat Board's recommendations for standardizing meat labels (see Cuts of Beef). The names of the retail cuts vary sharply from region to region and store to store: London broil, for instance, may be flank steak in one market, a thick-cut top round steak in another. With the new form of labeling, the primal cut (chuck or rib, for example) is listed on the label along with the kind of meat (beef, pork, or other), and the retail cut, so that a well-informed consumer can best determine how to cook a particular piece of meat (see Cooking). The following are beef products also available in markets.

CUTS OF BEEF

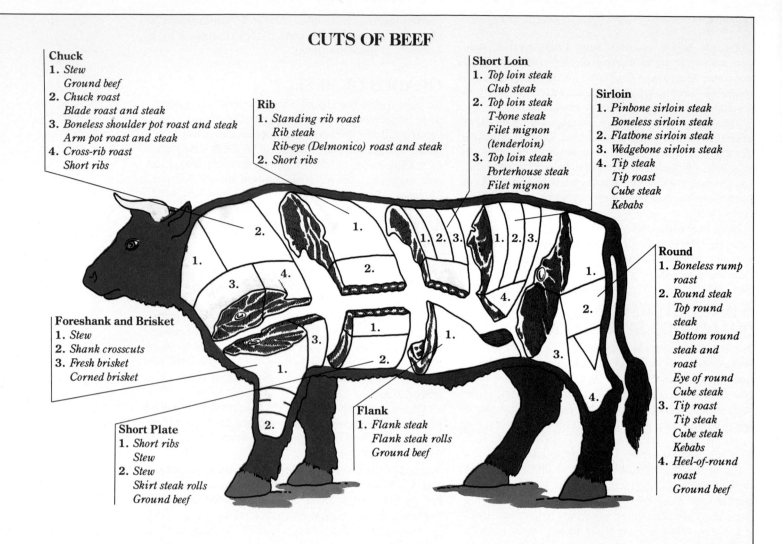

Chuck
1. *Stew*
   Ground beef
2. *Chuck roast*
   Blade roast and steak
3. *Boneless shoulder pot roast and steak*
   Arm pot roast and steak
4. *Cross-rib roast*
   Short ribs

Rib
1. *Standing rib roast*
   Rib steak
   Rib-eye (Delmonico) roast and steak
2. *Short ribs*

Short Loin
1. *Top loin steak*
   Club steak
2. *Top loin steak*
   T-bone steak
   Filet mignon
   (tenderloin)
3. *Top loin steak*
   Porterhouse steak
   Filet mignon

Sirloin
1. *Pinbone sirloin steak*
   Boneless sirloin steak
2. *Flatbone sirloin steak*
3. *Wedgebone sirloin steak*
4. *Tip steak*
   Tip roast
   Cube steak
   Kebabs

Round
1. *Boneless rump*
   roast
2. *Round steak*
   Top round
   steak
   Bottom round
   steak and
   roast
   Eye of round
   Cube steak
3. *Tip roast*
   Tip steak
   Cube steak
   Kebabs
4. *Heel-of-round*
   roast
   Ground beef

Foreshank and Brisket
1. *Stew*
2. *Shank crosscuts*
3. *Fresh brisket*
   Corned brisket

Short Plate
1. *Short ribs*
   Stew
2. *Stew*
   Skirt steak rolls
   Ground beef

Flank
1. *Flank steak*
   Flank steak rolls
   Ground beef

The tenderness of a cut depends upon what part of the animal it came from. Therefore, the cut should determine the cooking method. Tender cuts are usually cooked by dry-heat methods such as roasting, broiling, and grilling. These cooking methods enhance flavor but tend to toughen meat fibers. Less tender cuts require moist-heat cooking methods (stewing and braising); the cooking liquid tenderizes the meat and breaks down tough connective tissue. The gelatin that dissolves out of the connective fibers helps to thicken and enrich the cooking liquid. Marinating, pounding, cubing, and grinding can also be used to tenderize tough cuts. Commercial tenderizers such as papain, which partially predigest raw meat, are also used by many cooks; however, these tenderizers may affect both the flavor and the chewy, dense texture of beef. Some of the tougher cuts used for stir-frying and grilling are tenderized by slicing thinly and marinating.

There are eight primal (wholesale) cuts on a side of beef.
Chuck, Foreshank and Brisket, Short Plate, Flank, and Round The chuck and all the primal cuts on the lower half of the steer provide the lower-priced, less tender meats. Except for steaks cut from the flank, which are often grilled or used for kebabs and stir-fry dishes, these cuts are best suited to cooking in some sort of liquid. Cuts for pot roast include the chuck, the blade roast, the shoulder, the arm, the cross-rib roast, the brisket, the flank, and nearly all parts of the round, from the relatively tender top round to the medium-tough bottom round to the very tough eye of round. Stewing cuts include the entire chuck, the top of the foreshank, the short plate, and most of the round. The most popular cut for well-marinated *fajitas* (Tex-Mex marinated barbecued steak) is the skirt steak, but the flank and brisket are other good choices.

Ready-to-cook beef kebabs are usually cut from the round, but the long, thin kebabs favored in Thai cooking are sliced from the flank. In areas where Asian cooking is popular, flank steak—which at least has little waste—has become as expensive as porterhouse.
Rib, Short Loin, and Sirloin These primal cuts contain the tenderest meat, and are usually the most costly. From this area come the expensive steaks and roasts which are cooked by dry heat: rib roast, filet mignon, and rib, club, T-bone, porterhouse, and sirloin steaks. There is also a portion of the blade chuck roast that is actually an extension of the tender rib-eye muscle, and it, too, can be cooked as a steak. The top round is also sold as a roast or a steak for dry-heat cooking, but is not tender enough for all tastes, and many people prefer to braise this cut. Short ribs are suitable for moist-heat cooking methods.

Beef Jerky Thinly sliced lean dried beef, beef jerky doesn't require refrigeration. It is a good source of protein and has excellent keeping qualities. The original beef jerky was sun-dried or smoked over campfires. Most commercial beef jerky today is highly seasoned first, then oven-dried. It is available in supermarkets and sporting-goods stores. Latin American markets carry a version of beef jerky called *carne seca*. Armenian *bastourma*, available in Middle Eastern markets, is a similar, highly spiced sun-dried beef.

Chewy beef jerky can be eaten as is, diced and simmered in soups or stews, or soaked to soften, then added to eggs or hash. Store jerky in an airtight container at room temperature for up to three months, or refrigerate or freeze indefinitely.

Beef Marrow Beef bones yield a buttery edible marrow that adds richness and juiciness to dishes as it melts. The leg bones contain the most marrow. Have the butcher saw bones into chunks to make it easier to remove the marrow. To cut out raw marrow, use a small, sharp knife: Cut around the marrow and then pry it out. To store, wrap marrow and refrigerate for up to three days or freeze for up to two months. To use, chop and add to hamburgers, meat loaves, stuffings, and dumplings; chopped marrow is an ingredient in Bercy Butter, a classic garnish for grilled steak.

Corned Beef This preparation gets its name from the Old English word *corn,* for a small kernel or a grain of salt. Corned beef is brined beef, generally made with brisket or plate. Pickling spices, garlic, and sugar are usually added to the pickling medium. Most commercial varieties also contain saltpeter (sodium nitrate or potassium nitrate) for preservation and color retention. Some specialty markets offer their own fresh corned beef; it must be simmered in water until tender. Most supermarkets offer ready-to-eat corned beef, either canned or in a plastic package, in a large piece, or sliced for sandwiches.

Use corned beef in thick rye-bread sandwiches, in potato salad, in hash, as part of a dinner with potatoes and cabbage. Fresh corned beef in brine will keep for weeks in the refrigerator but gets saltier with time. Cooked corned beef may be refrigerated, well wrapped, for one or two weeks.

Pastrami A corned beef, pastrami is usually made with beef plate that is rubbed with black pepper and other spices, then smoked. It is a popular Jewish delicatessen item, usually steamed and sliced thin for thick rye-bread sandwiches. Some supermarkets also carry large chunks of pastrami packaged in plastic or sliced pastrami for sandwiches, also packed in plastic.

Because of its high fat content, pastrami is best served warm. Steam and slice thin. Leftover pastrami will keep, well wrapped, in the refrigerator for several days.

Selection The most tender cuts of beef come from the muscles that were rarely used, such as those in the loin and the rib. More active muscles—such as the shank, shoulder, tongue, and leg (or "round")—are tougher.

To select flavorful beef, look for marbling (intramuscular fat), which is a natural baster. Consumer concern about dietary fat has led to a demand for lean beef, but the most flavorful beef is well marbled. The beef's external fat should be creamy white, not yellow; the muscle should be red and firm. Avoid meat that is mushy or reddish brown. See also Grades of Beef.

Storage Large cuts of beef deteriorate less quickly than small cuts, such as stew meat or ground beef. However, all beef should be refrigerated or frozen immediately after purchase.

To refrigerate beef, remove store wrapping and rewrap loosely in waxed paper to allow for some air circulation. Set beef on a plate in the coldest part of the refrigerator. Use ground beef within one or two days, steaks within three or four days, roasts within one week.

To freeze beef, remove store wrapping and rewrap in moistureproof freezer paper; freeze immediately. To stack steaks or chops, put a double thickness of waxed paper between layers. Label and date packages with indelible ink. Thaw the oldest packages first. Transfer meat to refrigerator for slow thawing. Use thawed meat immediately; do not refreeze. Large roasts and steaks may be frozen for up to nine months, beef cubes for up to four months, ground beef for up to three months.

Preparation Most beef comes ready to cook from the butcher. Sometimes you may want to trim away some external fat, or slash the layer of fat on a steak to prevent it from curling as it broils or grills. Tough cuts can be made more tender if they are marinated, pounded, cubed, or ground. Commercial tenderizers, which partially "predigest" raw meat, are employed by many cooks, although these tenderizers may affect both the flavor and the characteristic chewy, dense texture of beef (see MARINATE, POUND).

Cooking Selecting the right cut of beef for a dish and applying the right cooking method to a given cut are essential to a successful result. Tender cuts of meat take well to quick, dry-heat cooking—roasting, broiling, panfrying, and grilling. Tougher cuts require slow, moist-heat cooking—stewing and braising.

Certain relatively tough cuts of beef are also used for stir-frying (usually following a brief marination period) and, after more marination, for barbecuing. In both cases, the meat seems tender because it is sliced very thinly across the grain (before cooking for stir-frying, and after cooking for barbecuing).

See BRAISE, BROIL, GRILL, PAN-BROIL, PANFRY, ROAST, STEW, STIR-FRY.

Tender, juicy strips of porterhouse steak need only the simple finish of an herb-seasoned butter, here flavored with fresh chives and parsley.

DRY-HEAT COOKING

These cooking methods—roasting, broiling, grilling, and pan-frying—do not include any added moisture. Sometimes fat is brushed or set on lean cuts to keep them from drying out during cooking. Sheets of beef fat can provide effective basting (see BARD) for lean beef roasts. Ask your butcher for thin sheets of exterior beef fat (not crumbly kidney fat). Arrange a single thickness of fat over top of roast and tie in place with string. As the roast cooks, the melting fat keeps the meat moist and juicy. The following recipes are for the more tender cuts of beef.

■ LONDON BROIL

Flank steak, a cut of meat from along the flank or underside of the beef, is traditionally used for this dish. A lean cut, it benefits from scoring and a flavorful marinade. The steak must marinate at least six hours, or overnight.

> 1 flank steak (about 1½ lb)
> 1 clove garlic, minced
> 1½ tablespoons vegetable oil
> ½ tablespoon red wine vinegar
>   Salt and freshly ground pepper, to taste

1. Score steak lightly and place in a shallow 9- by 12-inch nonaluminum pan. Sprinkle with garlic, oil, and vinegar. Turn to coat both sides and marinate in the refrigerator, loosely covered, 6 to 24 hours.

2. Preheat broiler. Drain marinade. Place steak on a rack in a shallow pan on top shelf of oven and broil 5 minutes on first side. Turn and broil 5 minutes on second side.

3. Place on a cutting board and slice across grain into diagonal strips about ¼ inch thick. Season with salt and pepper and serve immediately.

Serves 6 to 8.

■ ROAST PRIME RIB OF BEEF WITH YORKSHIRE PUDDING

Many family celebrations wouldn't be complete without this traditional dish that suggests everything bountiful and delicious. The Yorkshire Pudding is flavored with drippings from the roast. It cooks during the last half hour or so of the roast's cooking time.

> 1 prime rib of beef (4 rib, about 11 lb)
> 1 tablespoon salt
> ½ teaspoon freshly ground pepper
>   Horseradish Cream Sauce (see page 305), for accompaniment

Yorkshire Pudding

> 1 cup flour
> 1 teaspoon salt
> 2 eggs
> ½ cup milk
> ½ cup water
> 2 tablespoons hot beef fat

Gravy

> 2 tablespoons hot pan juices
> 1½ tablespoons flour
> 1½ cups Beef Stock (see page 560)

1. Preheat oven to 400° F. Rub beef with salt and pepper. Place beef in a roasting pan, fat side up, and roast 15 minutes per pound, approximately 2½ hours (or until internal temperature 125° F for rare, 135° F for medium-rare, or 140° F for medium).

2. Remove from oven. Reserve 2 tablespoons of pan juices; discard the rest.

3. Let meat rest 15 minutes. Remove roast to a carving board and carve.

4. Serve with Horseradish Cream Sauce, Yorkshire Pudding, and Gravy.

Serves 8.

Yorkshire Pudding

1. While meat is roasting, whisk together flour, salt, eggs, milk, and the water. Let rest 30 minutes.

2. Twenty minutes before roast is done, remove 2 tablespoons hot beef fat from roasting pan to a 10-inch cast-iron skillet and heat in oven 10 minutes.

3. Pour prepared Yorkshire Pudding batter into hot skillet and bake in 400° F oven until puffy and golden brown, about 25 minutes. (Pudding can be baked on same rack as roast if there is room, or on another rack, in another oven, or in oven used for meat while roast is resting.)

4. Remove, cut in 8 pieces, and set aside on platter to serve with meat.

Gravy Pour the reserved 2 tablespoons pan juices into a 1-quart saucepan over low heat. Stir in flour and cook 2 to 3 minutes. Whisk in stock and cook until slightly thickened (about 5 minutes). Serve over Yorkshire Pudding and prime rib.

■ BEEF TENDERLOIN

This method of roasting is useful for many tender cuts of beef that have little exterior fat and minimal marbling. Chateaubriand, which may be prepared in the same manner, is traditionally served surrounded with vegetables such as broiled tomatoes, small potatoes, and parsley sprigs, and accompanied with a sauce such as Béarnaise (see page 518).

    3 tablespoons vegetable oil
    2 tablespoons Dijon mustard
    2 tablespoons brandy
    1 teaspoon salt
    ¼ teaspoon freshly ground pepper
    2 pounds beef tenderloin, trimmed of
       exterior fat and any silvery membrane

1. In a small bowl mix together 1 tablespoon oil, mustard, brandy, salt, and pepper. Rub tenderloin with mustard mixture and rest 30 minutes.

2. Preheat oven to 400° F. Pour remaining oil in a Dutch oven or heavy cast-iron skillet and heat over medium-high heat. Brown tenderloin on one side (about 5 minutes). Turn meat and brown other side (about 5 minutes more).

3. Roast tenderloin in pan 25 to 30 minutes (or until internal temperature is 125° F for rare, 135° F for medium rare, and 140° F for medium). When done, let meat rest 15 minutes before carving.

4. To serve, cut the meat into ½-inch-thick slices.

Serves 6 to 8.

■ BROILED PORTERHOUSE STEAK
WITH SAVORY BUTTER

Place steaks on a lightly greased rack over a broiling pan; do not salt before starting to cook. To add flavor, if desired, rub steak with a cut clove of garlic or herbs of choice. In this recipe, delicious fresh chives and parsley flavor the butter that melts into a classic, thick steak.

    ⅓ cup butter or margarine, softened
    1 teaspoon fresh lemon juice
    ¼ teaspoon dry mustard
    1 tablespoon snipped fresh chives
    ¼ cup finely chopped parsley
    1 porterhouse steak (1½ to 2 lb), 1½ inches thick

1. Beat butter in a medium bowl until fluffy; gradually beat in lemon juice until well combined; then blend in dry mustard. Mix in chives and parsley, distributing evenly.

Shape butter into a roll about 1 inch in diameter; enclose in plastic wrap and refrigerate until firm (about 1 hour).

2. Preheat broiler. Trim excess fat from edges of steak; slash remaining fat at about 1-inch intervals. Place steak on greased rack of broiler pan about 4 inches from heat.

3. Broil, turning once, for 6 to 8 minutes on each side for rare (increase time for medium or well-done). When turning steak to broil second side, dot with about 1 tablespoon of butter mixture.

4. Place broiled steak on a carving board. With a short pointed knife, cut around the T-shaped bone; remove bone. Cut the smaller loin portion of the steak across the grain into several slices. Then slice the remaining meat across the grain about ¼ inch thick. Serve slices from each portion on warm dinner plates. Accompany with slices of herb butter.

Serves 2 to 3.

■ STEAK AU POIVRE

Club steaks are traditionally boneless, cut from the loin, and often called New York strip steaks. A variation of this recipe may be made with green peppercorns.

    6 club steaks (about ¾ lb each)
    6 tablespoons black peppercorns, crushed
    3 tablespoons vegetable oil
    3 tablespoons unsalted butter
       Juice of 1 lemon
    1 teaspoon Worcestershire sauce
    4 to 5 sprigs parsley, minced
    1 tablespoon snipped fresh chives
    4 tablespoons Cognac (optional)
    1 to 2 teaspoons salt

1. Coat both sides of steak with pepper, pressing firmly into meat. Let stand 30 minutes.

2. In a large, heavy-bottomed skillet, sauté first side of steaks in oil over medium-high heat until well browned (about 5 minutes); turn and sauté 3 minutes on second side. Remove steaks to a serving platter and keep warm.

3. To make sauce, add butter, lemon juice, Worcestershire sauce, parsley, and chives to skillet; whisk to combine. If using Cognac, pour into a small saucepan, heat slowly to warm, then ignite. Let Cognac cook until flame dissipates (about 3 minutes). Carefully pour Cognac over butter-lemon mixture in skillet and whisk together. Season with salt and pour over reserved steaks.

Serves 6.

Steak Diane Prepare steaks as for Steak au Poivre through step 2 but without peppercorn marinade. For sauce, use 3 tablespoons butter, juice of 1 lemon, 2 tablespoons snipped fresh chives, and 4 tablespoons Cognac (if desired). Prepare as in step 3 and season to taste with salt and freshly ground pepper before serving.

Making New England Boiled Dinner is slow, relaxed cooking, which can take care of itself while you attend to other matters. Once done, the meat can be kept warm for a couple of hours, or it can be reheated. The vegetables can be trimmed ahead of time, but should be cooked just before serving, so they retain their fresh color and shape.

MOIST-HEAT COOKING

Cooking with liquid will tenderize even the toughest cut of meat and draw out its flavor during the long, slow process. Braising and stewing are the methods used to tenderize lean, flavorful, but relatively tough cuts such as round, chuck, or brisket.

■ NEW ENGLAND BOILED DINNER

Just about every culture has its boiled dinner, dating back to the days when most cooking was done in a single pot slung over the fire. Since it's worth having leftovers for sandwiches or corned-beef hash, this recipe calls for a generous amount of corned beef.

    5 **to 6 pounds corned-beef brisket**
    8 **to 12 small beets, tops removed**
    8 **to 12 small boiling potatoes, peeled**
    8 **to 12 small boiling onions, peeled**
    8 **to 12 carrots, scraped**
    6 **small turnips, peeled**
    1 **head green cabbage, cored and quartered**
        Mustard, for accompaniment

Horseradish Sauce

    1 **cup chilled whipping cream**
    4 **to 5 tablespoons prepared horseradish**
    3 **tablespoons cider vinegar**
        Salt and freshly ground pepper, to taste

1. Rinse corned beef under running water and place in a large, deep pot. Cover with cold water and bring just

to a boil over high heat; skim off any scum that rises to the surface. Reduce heat to low, partially cover pot, and let simmer gently for 3 hours. (At this point meat may sit in the hot cooking liquid for another hour or two if you wish to delay serving. Bring back to a simmer before continuing with the vegetables.)

2. About an hour or so before you wish to serve, place beets in a medium saucepan, cover with water, and boil until tender when pierced (30 to 40 minutes). Drain; peel when cool enough to handle. Return peeled beets to saucepan, add a few ladlefuls of the corned-beef broth, and keep warm over low heat.

3. While beets are boiling, drop potatoes into simmering corned-beef pot and cook for 10 minutes. Drop in onions, carrots, and turnips, and simmer until vegetables are quite tender when pierced (about 30 minutes more). Add cabbage wedges and simmer exactly 3 minutes.

4. Remove meat from pot, slice thinly, and arrange on a large warm platter. Surround meat with vegetables from pot. Drain beets, and place in another serving bowl.

5. Serve with mustard and Horseradish Sauce.

Serves 6 to 8.

Horseradish Sauce   Whip cream until it stands in stiff peaks. Fold in horseradish and vinegar, and season with salt and pepper.

■ BASIC BOEUF EN DAUBE

France's ubiquitous wine-based beef stews are justly popular nearly everywhere that beef is eaten. Try the variation or make up your own: blanch seasonal vegetables until tender and add just before serving, vary the cooking liquid, or sprinkle with fresh herbs from your garden.

    ¼ **pound sliced bacon**
    3 **pounds beef round or chuck, in stewing pieces**
    2 **large onions, minced**
        Cooking oil, if necessary
    2 **tablespoons Cognac, Armagnac, or brandy**
    2 **pounds carrots, peeled, trimmed, and sliced thickly diagonally**
    4 **cloves garlic, crushed and peeled**
    3 **veal bones *or* 1 calf's foot (optional)**
    1 **bouquet garni**
    3 **cups dry red wine**
    1 **cup Beef Stock (see page 560) or canned beef bouillon (preferably low-salt)**
        Salt and freshly ground pepper, to taste
    6 **to 8 small boiling potatoes, scrubbed or peeled (optional)**
    6 **slices French bread and 1 clove garlic, halved (optional)**

1. Cut bacon slices horizontally into 1- by ¼-inch strips. In a very large, heavy skillet, sauté bacon until lightly browned but not crisp. Remove bacon with a slotted spoon; drain on paper towels and reserve.

2. Reheat bacon fat, and, over high heat, brown about one third of the beef. (If beef is crowded, juices will be released and meat will boil rather than brown.) Remove with a slotted spoon to a large, heavy casserole or Dutch oven, and brown remaining beef in two more shifts, transferring it to the casserole when brown. Over moderate heat, sauté minced onion in skillet until wilted (add vegetable oil to skillet if necessary), and transfer to casserole.

3. In a small saucepan over low heat, warm Cognac. (Have a long match ready.) Warm casserole over low heat. Pour Cognac into casserole, warm for a minute, and, very carefully (making sure nothing flammable is near the stove), set Cognac aflame. When flame dies down, add reserved bacon, carrots, garlic, veal bones (if used), bouquet garni, wine, and stock. Stir, carefully season to taste, cover, and simmer very slowly until beef is very tender (2 to 2½ hours) or slowly bake in oven at 250° F.

4. Meanwhile, boil potatoes, if used, in salted water to cover until tender (25 to 30 minutes). When stew is done, remove and discard veal bones and bouquet garni. Degrease stew (see DEGREASE). If desired, liquid may be poured off into a saucepan and boiled over a high flame until reduced by half, and/or it may be thickened and enriched with beurre manié made of 3 tablespoons butter and 3 tablespoons flour (see page 517). Return liquid to the stew along with potatoes, if used. Correct seasonings and reheat gently for a few minutes.

5. Toast French bread, if used, and rub while hot with cut sides of garlic. Float toasts on top of stewing liquid. Serve stew hot in widemouthed soup bowls; top each bowl with a piece of garlic toast from the main serving dish.

Serves 6.

Boeuf Bourguignonne (Burgundy Beef Stew) Decrease carrots to about ½ pound (2 or 3 large carrots), and add 1 pound of small white boiling onions, peeled and trimmed. Trim 1 pound of fresh mushrooms, wipe clean with a mushroom brush or slightly damp paper towel, and cut in quarters. In a heavy skillet, rapidly sauté mushrooms in 2 tablespoons of butter and 2 tablespoons oil until lightly brown. Add mushrooms to the stew 10 minutes before serving, and garnish stew with 2 tablespoons minced parsley. Omit potatoes and toast; serve stew over a bed of cooked, lightly buttered noodles.

Serves 4 to 6.

OTHER WAYS WITH BEEF

Whether sliced paper-thin, cut into strips, chopped, or ground, and whether served raw or cooked, beef stars in scores of international favorites, from the all-American burger to sophisticated carpaccio and the pastry-wrapped beef piroshki and baked empanada.

■ **STEAK TARTARE**

Beef of the best quality tastes delicious cooked or raw, as this well-known dish attests.

    1 pound raw, freshly ground, top-quality beef
      fillet, sirloin, or round steak
    2 egg yolks
    2 anchovies, chopped
    2 tablespoons capers
    1 shallot, minced
    4 sprigs chopped parsley
    ½ teaspoon dry mustard
    ½ teaspoon salt
    ¼ teaspoon freshly ground pepper
      Juice of 1 lemon
    2 teaspoons Cognac (optional)
      Buttered toast, for accompaniment

In a medium bowl mix beef, egg yolks, anchovies, capers, shallot, parsley, mustard, salt, pepper, lemon juice, and Cognac, if used. Serve on buttered toast.

Serves 4 to 6 as an entrée, 8 to 10 as an appetizer.

■ **NORTH BEACH GARLICKY MEAT LOAF**

This richly seasoned meat mixture captures the flavors of San Francisco's North Beach area, home to many wonderful Italian restaurants and cafés. Leftover meat loaf makes delicious sandwiches on a flavorful, homestyle bread. Do not slice the loaf until needed; it slices best when cold.

    1¼ cup dry bread crumbs
    5 tablespoons grated dried cheese
      (Parmesan cheese or a mixture of Parmesan,
      Romano, and dried Jack cheeses)
    5 tablespoons minced parsley
    1½ to 2 tablespoons finely minced garlic
    1½ pounds ground beef
    ½ teaspoon *each* salt and freshly ground pepper
    2 eggs
    ¼ cup (approximately) water
      Catsup, for coating

1. Preheat oven to 350° F. Mix bread crumbs, cheese, parsley, and garlic. Add meat, and salt and pepper, and mix together. Pour in eggs and a little of the water; knead mixture to an even consistency, adding more water if mixture seems dry.

2. Mold into a greased loaf pan, top with a very thin coat of catsup, and bake for 70 minutes.

Serves 6.

North Beach Meatballs Preheat oven to 450° F. Make meat mixture. Wet hands and roll mixture into 1½-inch meatballs. Place meatballs on a large, lightly greased baking sheet and bake for 20 minutes. Serve while still sizzling hot. (Meatballs may also be reheated in meatless tomato sauce of your choice and used to dress pasta.)

Serves 12 as an appetizer.

TIPS

ABOUT GROUND BEEF

As any supermarket shopper knows, ground beef, unlike other ground meats, comes in several grades and prices, determined by the amount of fat ground with the meat. The cheapest grade—usually just called ground beef—contains fully 30 percent fat (as much as sausage!). It's often identified as chuck, but other parts may be included in the grind. This grade can be used in dishes (such as spaghetti sauce) where the meat is browned first, and the fat poured off; however, considering the loss of nearly a third of the meat's volume, its economy is moot. It can also be used in meat loaf recipes that contain a high proportion of bread crumbs (which will absorb the fat) if calories and cholesterol aren't a problem. The middle grade—often called lean ground beef, lean ground chuck, or ground round—contains about 20 percent fat, and is the normal grade used for hamburgers, meat loaf, meatballs, and more elaborate ground-beef dishes. The leanest grade—usually identified as ground sirloin or extra-lean ground beef—contains approximately 15 percent fat. Although somewhat dry when cooked, it's the dieter's favorite for hamburgers.

■ ALL-AMERICAN HAMBURGER
WITH INTERNATIONAL TOPPINGS

The debate still rages over whether hamburgers should be panfried or broiled, rounded or flattened—these issues remain emphatically a matter of personal taste, and of experimentation. Rather than being served on the traditional hamburger buns, hamburgers may be accompanied by toasted English muffins, sourdough French rolls, or whole wheat pita bread. Burgers may also be topped with any Compound Butter (see page 68); anchovy butter and butter made with Roquefort or blue cheese are especially apt.

1¼ **pounds lean ground beef**
   Salt and freshly ground pepper, to taste
2 **to 4 tablespoons seasoning of choice, or a combination of the following: Worcestershire sauce, steak sauce, barbecue sauce, liquid smoke flavoring, salsa**
4 **hamburger buns, split (or other bread of choice)**
   Catsup, mayonnaise, mustard, sweet pickle relish (as desired)
1 **sweet red onion, thinly sliced**
1 **ripe tomato, sliced**
   Pickles, thinly sliced (optional)
   Shredded lettuce (optional)

1. Preheat broiler according to manufacturer's directions. As broiler heats, season meat with salt and pepper, and mix in any of the other suggested seasonings, if desired. Shape into 4 patties. (For thin hamburgers, place patties between 2 sheets of waxed paper and flatten with a rolling pin.)

2. Place patties on a lightly greased rack of broiler pan and broil 4 inches from heat until desired doneness is reached. The timing will vary with the thickness of the hamburgers. See BROIL, Timetable for Broiling Meat, for approximate broiling times.

3. During the last 3 minutes of cooking, place buns, cut side up, on rack with burgers to brown.

4. Spread hamburger buns with condiments of choice. Place burger on lower half of bun, and top with onion, then tomato, then pickle slices and lettuce, if desired.

Serves 4.

Avocado Bacon Burger   Gently fry 4 slices bacon until crisp, pouring off fat as it accumulates. Set cooked pieces aside to drain on paper towels. While burgers cook, peel, pit, and slice 1 small avocado and dribble a little fresh lime or lemon juice on slices. Top each burger with one slice of onion (if desired), one of bacon, one of tomato, and several slices of avocado.

Cheeseburger   Proceed as above, but during the last 1½ minutes of cooking, place a ¼-inch-thick slice of cheese (Cheddar, Monterey jack, or Swiss) on top half of each bun as it toasts under broiler; broil until cheese bubbles and melts. Do not let cheese burn.

Fast-Food Burger Dressing   Vigorously stir together 3 tablespoons catsup with 3 tablespoons mayonnaise. Stir in 1 tablespoon, or to taste, sweet pickle relish. Dress buns with catsup mixture. Top burger or cheeseburger with slices of sweet onion and tomato, and shredded lettuce.

Guacamole Burger   Peel, pit, and mash 1 small avocado (about 1 cup mashed flesh). Combine avocado with 1 small tomato, chopped, or ¼ cup Mexican salsa; 1 tablespoon fresh lime (or lemon) juice; 1 tablespoon grated onion; and salt, pepper, and cayenne pepper or bottled salsa jalapeño, to taste. Top each burger with onion and tomato, if desired, and a dollop of guacamole.

Little Italy Burger   In a medium frying pan, heat 1 tablespoon olive oil. Add one-half red and one-half green bell pepper, sliced; 1 medium red onion, sliced; and 2 cloves of garlic, minced. Sauté until limp. Stir in ½ teaspoon dried oregano leaves, crumbled, and 1 tablespoon minced parsley. Divide the mixture over 4 burgers.

Mushroom Cheeseburger   In a medium frying pan, melt 1 tablespoon butter. Add ¼ pound mushrooms, sliced; 2 cloves of garlic, minced; and 1 shallot, minced. Sauté until mushrooms have yielded liquid and are turning brown at the edges. Prepare broiled cheeseburgers and top each burger with the mushrooms.

Pan-fried Hamburger   Barely grease a large, heavy skillet (such as cast-iron) with a little vegetable oil. Heat empty skillet over a high flame until it begins to smoke. Add patties and sear on one side; whether thick or thin, use timing guidelines for 1-inch patties (see page 63). Turn and sear the other side. For medium or well-done hamburgers, lower heat to moderate after 2 minutes, and continue cooking until hamburger is cooked as desired. While hamburger cooks, lightly toast buns in toaster.

Philly Cheeseburger   Substitute split French rolls for buns. Make the Little Italy Burger dressing (see above). Follow directions for Cheeseburger (see above), topping the upper half of each roll with 2 slices of provolone cheese. Dress the lower half of the roll with sweet pickle relish, add hamburger, and top burger with Little Italy Burger dressing, and cover with the half of the roll with the melted cheese.

Ranchero Burger   Top each of 4 slices French bread with 2 slices Monterey jack cheese; broil 1 minute. Top cheese with a slice of tomato, a cooked burger, a fried or poached egg, and sliced ripe olives or chopped chives. Cover each sandwich with a second slice of bread. For more zest, add chopped chiles or salsa.

Russian Burger   On each broiled hamburger place 1 tablespoon sour cream or yogurt. Top each with 2 teaspoons red, black, or golden caviar. Sprinkle chopped green onions or chives over caviar. May be served open-faced on slices of dark rye bread.

CARPACCIO

To make the Italian dish carpaccio, lean raw beef is sliced and pounded tissue-thin, then dressed with Parmesan and a piquant vinaigrette. To make slicing easier, put meat in freezer until it is very cold but not frozen.

1½ pounds beef tenderloin, trimmed of all fat
1½ cups peeled, seeded, and chopped fresh tomato
½ cup minced Italian parsley
¼ cup minced fresh oregano
¼ cup minced fresh basil
⅓ cup fresh lemon juice
3 to 4 tablespoons olive oil
3 tablespoons freshly grated Parmesan cheese
   Salt and freshly ground pepper
2 tablespoons snipped fresh chives (optional)

1. Cut beef into 10 thin slices, approximately 2½ ounces each. Put each slice between two sheets of plastic wrap or waxed paper and pound with a mallet or the bottom of a skillet until beef is paper-thin.

2. In a bowl combine tomatoes, parsley, oregano, basil, and 1 tablespoon each of lemon juice and olive oil. Marinate at room temperature for at least 10 minutes or up to 1 hour.

3. To serve, arrange tenderloin slices on individual plates or large platters. Scatter tomatoes around them. Drizzle with remaining olive oil and lemon juice. Dust with Parmesan. Sprinkle salt and pepper over all and garnish with chives, if used.

Serves 10.

CORNED-BEEF HASH

Hash means a hodgepodge or jumble; in cooking it describes chopped food, usually meat with potatoes, which is browned in a skillet until crusty. It's a delicious way to use leftover cooked meat—here you use corned beef, but roast beef works well also. Allow a good 30 to 40 minutes to cook hash, since it must crust on the bottom twice before a final crust forms and the hash is turned out onto a platter. Chop meat and potatoes coarsely; if you use a food processor, don't chop too fine.

2 to 3 cups chopped cooked corned beef
2 to 3 cups chopped boiled potatoes
1 onion, finely chopped
¼ teaspoon freshly ground pepper
4 tablespoons butter or shortening
⅓ cup whipping cream

1. In a large bowl, mix beef, potatoes, onion, and pepper. In a 10-inch skillet (preferably well-seasoned cast-iron) over medium-low heat, melt butter. Spread meat mixture evenly over the bottom, forming a thick cake. Press down firmly all over with the back of a spatula. Cook about 10 minutes, giving pan a sharp jerk now and then to prevent sticking.

2. Scrape all over bottom of pan with a spatula to loosen the crust, and stir it into the hash. Again press firmly all over to make a flat cake, and cook 10 minutes more, giving pan a sharp jerk now and then to prevent sticking.

3. Pour cream over hash, then scrape up crust again and stir to incorporate cream. Flatten hash with a spatula and cook another 10 minutes, giving pan a few sharp jerks now and then to keep hash from sticking.

4. To serve, you may cut into wedges, flipping each piece over on a plate, crusted side up. Or, you may unmold the whole hash by flipping it from the skillet onto a platter. While this looks impressive, remember the skillet is hot and heavy, and you must work fast, so unmolding is a little tricky. It is easier if you get a friend to help you.

Serves 4 to 6.

Red-Flannel Hash   Add 2 cups diced cooked beets to the hash mixture and fry as directed.

Created at Harry's Bar in Venice, Carpaccio is an easy and elegant first course of thin-sliced beef. Here, it is ringed with herbed tomatoes and garnished with coarsely grated Parmesan cheese.

Fondue is not just party food. It makes a novel supper when served with a salad or vegetable casserole and warm French bread. Complement the meat with one or more dipping sauces.

■ BEEF FONDUE

Fondue pots for cooking meat are traditionally made of thin metal. The pot is placed over an alcohol burner or candle to maintain the temperature of the oil. The Mongolian hot pot is similar, although there the cooking liquid is stock. Meat for fondue is seared in hot oil; therefore it requires a tender cut that is best cooked rare. Generally, serve approximately ½ pound meat per person.

    2¼ cups vegetable oil
    1½ tablespoons red wine vinegar
     ½ teaspoon salt
     ¼ teaspoon freshly ground pepper
      2 pounds top round of beef, cut in 1-inch cubes

1. In a large bowl mix ¼ cup of the oil, the vinegar, salt, and pepper; toss with beef. Place remaining oil in a 2-quart fondue pot or saucepan. Heat oil on stove to approximately 360° F. If using range top, transfer to fondue pot over alcohol or canned heat burner; place at the table. Arrange meat and dipping sauces (see below) around fondue pot.

2. To eat, skewer meat with a fondue fork or bamboo skewer, dip into hot oil for 1 to 3 minutes (depending on the degree of doneness desired), and then dip into selected sauce.

Serves 4.

Dijon Mayonnaise Dipping Sauce Whisk 2 tablespoons Dijon mustard into ¼ cup homemade mayonnaise (see page 519).

Horseradish–Sour Cream Dipping Sauce Stir ¼ cup prepared horseradish into 1 cup sour cream.

Piquant Parsley Dipping Sauce Combine ½ cup olive oil, 2 tablespoons red wine vinegar, 1 tablespoon capers, 1 teaspoon anchovy paste, 1 bunch parsley, finely chopped, and 1 clove of garlic, finely chopped.

■ BEEF AND MUSHROOM PIROSHKI

The unusual, luscious filling of these savory Russian turnovers is especially designed to restore moisture to cooked beef. They can also be made with raw lean ground beef, if desired. The dough, too, is unusual, but not difficult to work with. As with nearly all pastries and turnovers, filled, unbaked piroshkis may be frozen until ready to use, but they shouldn't stand for too long at room temperature lest the dough grow soggy.

      4 tablespoons butter
      3 medium onions, minced (about 3 cups)
     ¼ pound mushrooms, wiped clean and
         chopped in fine dice
    1½ cups finely diced rare roast beef *or*
         ¾ pound lean ground beef
      1 teaspoon salt
     ½ teaspoon freshly ground pepper
     ¼ cup sour cream, at room temperature
      2 hard-cooked eggs, chopped fine
     ¼ cup finely minced fresh dill *or*
         2 tablespoons dried dill, crumbled
      1 egg, lightly beaten with 3 tablespoons water

Sour Cream Pastry

    1¾ cups flour
     ½ teaspoon salt
     ½ teaspoon baking powder
      4 tablespoons butter, chilled and cut
         into small pieces
      1 egg
     ½ cup sour cream

1. Prepare and chill pastry dough.

2. In a large skillet, melt butter. Add onions and sauté, stirring over moderate heat, until wilted. Add mushrooms, and continue stirring until lightly browned. If using raw ground beef, add it to skillet and sauté, stirring and breaking up with a fork, until it loses its redness.

3. Remove from heat, stir in roast beef, if used, salt, pepper, sour cream, chopped eggs, and dill; cool.

4. Preheat oven to 400°F. On a floured surface, roll out pastry to a large, very thin sheet. Using a 4-inch cookie cutter, cut pastry into rounds. (For larger piroshki, called pirogi, mark dough with an 8-inch pie plate and cut with a knife. Double quantity of filling for each pirogi.) Gather trims into a ball, wrap, and chill.

5. Dough shrinks after cutting; reroll each round. Place 1½ to 2 tablespoons of filling (for small piroshki) on half the circle of dough. Brush rim of circle with egg-water mixture, fold dough over to enclose filling, and seal by squeezing edges with fingers or by pressing with tines of a fork. Brush top with egg mixture. Repeat until all pastry circles have been filled. Roll out chilled dough trims, cut another set of rounds, and fill.

6. Bake on a lightly greased baking sheet 25 minutes (35 minutes for large piroshki). Serve immediately.

Makes about 18 small or 8 large piroshkis.

Sour Cream Pastry

1. *To make in food processor:* Mix all ingredients until blended thoroughly. *To make by hand:* Mix together flour, salt, and baking powder. Cut in butter until mixture forms a coarse meal. Blend in eggs and sour cream.

2. Set mixture on a lightly floured board or a sheet of waxed paper. Gather together and knead just until smooth and elastic. Flatten into a pancake, wrap in plastic wrap, and chill at least 2 hours, or overnight.

BEET

The beet is a root vegetable that thrives in cool climates. The common table beet is bulb-shaped with paper-thin, dark skin, dense, wine-red flesh, and edible green leaves with red veins and stems. Other, less common table varieties have golden or white flesh. A special horticultural variety is grown for its leafy tops rather than the swollen root. Yet another variety, the sugar beet, is rarely eaten, but is processed for sugar.

Use Cooked, peeled beets are eaten hot or cold, whole, or cut in pieces. They are served cold as a salad or salad garnish, or hot as a side dish with butter or a sweet-and-sour sauce. Beets may be pickled or made into relish. They are the principal ingredient in borscht, served hot or cold. Beet greens, when young and tender, may be added raw to a salad. Older greens must be cooked and may then be eaten cold, with lemon and oil, or hot, with butter or oil. Besides being delicious, the greens are an excellent source of vitamin A, calcium, and iron. They should not be discarded unless they are ragged or wilted.

Availability Beets are sold fresh, canned and pickled. Fresh beets are available all year, but peak months are June through October.

Selection Choose smooth, firm beet roots; small ones are generally sweeter. If green tops are still attached, they should look fresh, not wilted.

Storage Beets may be stored up to six months in a cool root cellar or storage shed; cut green tops off one inch above the root. Refrigerate for up to one month. Store greens in plastic bags in the refrigerator for three to five days; wash just before using.

Preparation *Roots:* Cut off beet greens 1 inch above crown. Scrub roots gently; do not break skin.
Greens: Wash greens well and dry. Young, tender leaves may be eaten raw as a salad. For older greens, separate stems from leaves.

Cooking See BAKE, BOIL, SAUTE (GREENS), STEAM.

▉ HARVARD BEETS
The natural sweetness of the beets may require adjusting the amount of vinegar in the recipe to suit individual taste.

    2 bunches beets (about 1 lb each)
    3 tablespoons sugar
    ¼ cup cold water
    2 teaspoons cornstarch
    5 tablespoons apple cider vinegar
      Juice and grated rind of 1 medium orange
    1 tablespoon unsalted butter
      Salt and freshly ground pepper, to taste

1. Remove stems from beets, leaving about ½ inch. In a 3-quart saucepan place beets and cover with water. Bring to a boil, reduce heat, and simmer until beets are easily pierced with a knife (approximately 30 minutes, depending on size of beets). Drain in a colander and cool for about 20 minutes. Trim stems and root tip from each beet and slip off skins. Slice beets ¼ inch thick.

2. In the same saucepan combine sugar, the cold water, cornstarch, vinegar, orange juice, and rind. Cook over low heat, stirring constantly until mixture is clear and thickened (4 to 5 minutes). Add sliced beets and butter. Stir to coat beets. Cook until hot (6 to 8 minutes). Season to taste with salt and pepper.

Serves 4 to 6.

Beets with their greens and young turnips make a distinctive winter salad. Serve as a first course before a hearty roast.

■ **WINTER SALAD OF BEETS AND TURNIPS**

Beet greens are mixed with beets and turnips for a hearty first course. Note that beets must bake for 1½ hours.

>   3 or 4 medium beets with greens attached
>   7 or 8 small turnips
>   2 tablespoons *each* fresh lemon juice and
>   red wine vinegar
>   1 tablespoon Dijon mustard
>   ½ tablespoon anchovy paste
>   ½ cup plus 2 tablespoons olive oil
>   3 tablespoons freshly grated Parmesan cheese
>   Salt and freshly ground pepper, to taste
>   ½ head *each* green-leaf and romaine lettuce,
>   washed and dried
>   2 tablespoons minced parsley

1. Preheat oven to 375° F. Remove beet greens and stems and set aside. Wash beets and put them in an oven-proof bowl or baking dish. Add water to come halfway up sides of beets, then cover tightly with a lid or aluminum foil and bake until beets can be easily pierced with a knife (about 1½ hours). Remove from oven and let cool. While beets are still warm, peel them and slice into rounds, then into thin matchsticks.

2. Wash beet stems and greens, then separate stems from greens. Bring a large pot of salted water to a boil and blanch greens for 30 seconds. Transfer greens

with a slotted spoon to a bowl of ice water. Drain and pat thoroughly dry. Boil stems 1 minute in same water; transfer to ice water and, when cool, drain and dry them. Coarsely chop both beet greens and stems.

3. In a large bowl, combine lemon juice, vinegar, mustard, and anchovy paste. Whisk in the ½ cup olive oil. Stir in 1 tablespoon of the Parmesan. Add beet greens and stems and marinate 15 minutes.

4. Bring another large pot of salted water to a boil. Wash turnips, then boil until tender. Very small turnips may take only 10 minutes, larger turnips up to 45 minutes. Drain and dry. While still warm, peel turnips, slice into rounds, then into thin matchsticks. Very small turnips may be left whole or halved.

5. Add beets, turnips, and remaining 2 tablespoons oil to marinating beet greens; let marinate 20 minutes. Add salt and pepper to taste. Line a serving platter with green-leaf and romaine leaves. Top with salad. Combine remaining Parmesan and parsley and sprinkle over salad.

Serves 4.

> ***Recipes and Related Information***
> *Budapest Borscht, 76; Red-Flannel Hash, 45.*

BELGIAN ENDIVE

Also known as French endive, or Belgian or witloof chicory, Belgian endive is the blanched shoots of a chicory root. To produce blanched (white) shoots, the roots are dug up and removed to a cool, darkened location or to forcing beds where they are covered with sand. The resulting shoots, harvested when 4 to 6 inches long and about 1½ inches wide, are made of compact, tightly furled, white leaves shading to yellow or light green tips.

Use   Belgian endive is eaten raw as a salad green or is braised in butter or cream sauce as a vegetable side dish. Braised with ham slices and cream sauce, it is a main course. Belgian endive leaves are perfect edible containers for cheese spreads or all kinds of hors d'oeuvres.

Availability   Fresh Belgian endive is sold in late fall and winter.

Selection   Choose bright white Belgian endive heads that are firm and unblemished.

Storage   Keep endive in a plastic bag in the refrigerator. Use within three or four days.

Preparation   Cut away bitter core with a knife. Rinse with cold running water. To braise, cook heads whole in butter in a covered pot, adding lemon juice to prevent discoloration. For salads, use raw leaves whole or cut into rings or strips.

Cooking   See BOIL, BRAISE.

■ **BRAISED BELGIAN ENDIVE**

Small heads of lettuce can also be braised.

    8 small Belgian endives
    3 tablespoons unsalted butter
    ½ cup Chicken Stock (see page 560)
       Juice of 1 lemon
    2 tablespoons parsley, minced
       Pinch sugar

1. Trim dry ends from endive. Remove any brown or shriveled leaves. In a heavy-bottomed, 10-inch skillet, place endives, butter, stock, lemon juice, parsley, and sugar.

2. Simmer over medium heat 8 minutes; turn and simmer 7 minutes more. Endive will be tender when pierced with a knife.

Serves 4.

BIND, TO

To cause ingredients to thicken and form a cohesive mass by adding another ingredient, called the binding agent. For example, Hollandaise sauce and mayonnaise are bound by egg yolks, puddings by tapioca, Bavarian cream by gelatin, some cream soups by potato, and many sauces, soups, and stews by flour, cornstarch, crackers, or bread crumbs.

BISCUIT

A biscuit is a quick bread made with a soft dough (3 parts flour to 1 part liquid), rather than the fairly moist batter used for quick loaf breads and muffins.

The ideal biscuit is uniform in shape, with straight sides and a level top, and has doubled its height during baking. The crust is crisp, tender, and golden brown, with lighter sides. The crumb is generally creamy white and fine grained, and pulls off in flaky sheets.

When shaping biscuits, use a floured, sharp-edged cutter or knife and cut by pressing downward. A dull edge will pinch top and bottom together, and the biscuits won't rise properly. Twisting the cutter produces lopsided biscuits.

Drop biscuit dough, too sticky to roll, is spooned directly onto an ungreased baking sheet. For dumplings, dough is dropped into boiling water or stock, or on a simmering stew, and gently steamed. Deep-dish fruit cobblers use either rolled or dropped biscuit dough for a top crust.

Biscuits are at their best served hot from the oven. If they must be reheated, wrap them in aluminum foil and heat in a 350° F oven for 10 minutes. To freeze, let cool and protect with freezer wrap, or tray-freeze: Set biscuits on a baking sheet, freeze just until firm, then package in plastic freezer bags labeled with the date. Frozen biscuits will keep for two to three months. Thaw in wrapping at room temperature; if wrapped in aluminum foil, place in a low oven.

■ **BAKING POWDER BISCUITS**

Although biscuits are traditionally shaped with a round biscuit cutter, the dough can also be cut with a knife into squares, rectangles, or diamonds. Whichever tool you use, flour the cutting edge so the dough will release easier.

    2 cups flour
    4 teaspoons baking powder
    ½ to 1 teaspoon salt, to taste
    6 tablespoons solid vegetable shortening
    ¾ cup milk
       Flour or beaten egg, for topping (optional)

1. Preheat oven to 425° F. Butter and flour a baking sheet or line with baking parchment.

2. Mix flour, baking powder, and salt; then sift into a medium bowl. With a pastry blender or with fingertips, cut vegetable shortening into dry ingredients until mixture is the consistency of fine crumbs. Pour in milk all at once and stir to mix. As soon as mixture holds together, turn out onto a floured work surface and knead lightly.

3. Roll or pat dough to a thickness of ½ to ¾ inch (depending on use); cut into 2½-inch rounds with a floured cutter.

4. For crustier biscuits place rounds about 1 inch apart on prepared baking sheet. For softer sides set touching or ¼ inch apart. Finish with a dusting of flour (for a soft surface) or brush with a beaten egg for a shiny surface. Bake until golden brown (12 to 15 minutes). Biscuits are best served hot from the oven.

Makes about 16 biscuits.

Drop Biscuits   Prepare as for Baking Powder Biscuits with these changes: Increase shortening to ½ cup and milk to 1 cup. For pebbly biscuits, scoop out a tablespoon (or more) of dough with a floured spoon, drop batter onto a baking sheet, leaving a few inches between each biscuit, and dust each with flour. For a smoother surface, scoop out batter with floured hands, roll lightly between hands to the size and shape of an egg, dip all sides in flour, and place on baking sheet; do not crowd. Bake until puffed and golden brown (10 to 12 minutes).

Cheese Biscuits   Add 1 teaspoon dry mustard to dry ingredients. After fat has been cut in, add ½ cup grated Cheddar or Swiss cheese and ¼ cup freshly grated Parmesan cheese and combine.

Herb Biscuits   Add 1½ teaspoons crushed dried dill or other herb and 1 teaspoon freshly ground pepper to dry ingredients.

TIPS

MIXING BISCUIT DOUGH

When mixing the dough be gentle and work quickly, or the biscuits will be tough. On the other hand, don't undermix the dough. Kneading further distributes the leaven and develops the gluten in the flour just enough to support the biscuit as it rises. Undermanipulated biscuits are squatty and will have yellow spots in the crumb and brown spots on the crust—the result of undissolved or poorly distributed leaven. With experience you will sense when the dough is ready.

■ CREAM BISCUITS

Using cream instead of milk will produce a richer biscuit. A topping of flour makes a soft crust, cream a browner one.

    2 cups flour
    1 tablespoon baking powder
    ½ teaspoon baking soda
    1 tablespoon sugar
    1 teaspoon salt
    2 tablespoons butter
    1¼ cups whipping cream
       Flour or whipping cream, for topping

1. Follow instructions for Baking Powder Biscuits (see page 49).

2. Brush lightly with flour or whipping cream and bake until golden brown (12 to 15 minutes).

Makes about 16 biscuits.

■ BUTTERMILK BISCUITS

These biscuits have a slightly tangy flavor and tender crumb because of the buttermilk. To create carbon dioxide, the gas that makes biscuits rise, the acid in the buttermilk must be balanced with an alkali, usually baking soda.

    2 cups flour
    2 teaspoons baking powder
    ½ teaspoon baking soda
    ½ teaspoon salt
    1 tablespoon sugar
    6 tablespoons unsalted butter
    ⅔ cup buttermilk
       Flour or buttermilk, for topping

1. Follow instructions for Baking Powder Biscuits (see page 49).

2. Brush lightly with flour or buttermilk and bake until golden brown (10 to 12 minutes).

Makes about 16 biscuits.

Orange Buttermilk Biscuits Increase baking powder to 1 teaspoon and sugar to ¼ cup. Reduce buttermilk to ½ cup; combine with ¼ cup fresh orange juice and grated rind of 2 oranges; add to fat-flour mixture as directed.

■ BERRY SHORTCAKE

Strawberries are traditional, but a mixture of fresh berries is also wonderful for this classic American dessert.

Shortcake

    2 cups flour
    1 tablespoon baking powder
    ½ teaspoon salt
    3 tablespoons sugar
    6 tablespoons butter
    ¾ cup whipping cream
       Cream, for brushed topping

Filling

    2 pints strawberries, hulled and sliced
    2 cups whipped cream, flavored with sugar,
       to taste, and 1 teaspoon vanilla extract

1. *For the shortcake:* Follow instructions for Baking Powder Biscuits (see page 49). Brush with cream and bake until golden brown (about 12 minutes).

2. To serve, split a biscuit in half horizontally. Place the bottom on an individual serving plate. Spoon on whipped cream and prepared fruit. Cover with biscuit top. Repeat with remaining biscuits and filling. For a marbled effect, purée half the fruit; just before serving fold purée into whipped cream.

Serves 12.

■ SCONES

The English upper classes pronounce this word as if it rhymes with "on" rather than "own." Webster's dictionary, a product of the colonies, says either way is acceptable. Traditionally, scones are split in two and eaten with butter, preserves, and, if available, Devonshire clotted cream (or substitute whipped cream). If etiquette is followed, the butter and preserves should be spooned on the plate, the scone sliced in half, and then only enough butter and preserves spread on for a mouthful. If cream is served, it is spooned on top of the preserves.

    3½ cups flour
    1 tablespoon baking powder
    1 teaspoon baking soda
    ½ teaspoon salt
    ¾ cup sugar
    ½ cup butter
    ½ cup buttermilk
    2 eggs, lightly beaten
       Butter, preserves, and clotted cream or
       whipped cream, for accompaniment (optional)

1. Follow instructions for Baking Powder Biscuits (see page 49). Before adding buttermilk, whisk with eggs.

2. Or, halve dough and knead gently to form 2 balls. Flatten each ball to a thickness of ½ to 1 inch. With a sharp knife, cut each round into 8 triangles. Arrange on prepared baking sheet and bake at 400° F until golden brown (20 to 30 minutes). Serve hot with butter, preserves, and cream (if desired).

Makes about 16 rounds or triangles.

Orange or Lemon Scones With buttermilk-egg mixture, add 1 tablespoon grated orange or lemon rind.

Raisin Scones With buttermilk-egg mixture, add 1 cup dark or golden raisins, dried currants, or a combination.

Spice Scones To dry ingredients, add 1 teaspoon mixed spices (equal amounts of ground cinnamon, nutmeg, cloves, and allspice).

Whole Wheat Scones For the 3½ cups all-purpose flour, substitute a blend of 2 cups all-purpose flour and 1½ cups whole wheat flour. Increase butter to ¾ cup.

■ FRUIT COBBLER

Grunt, slump, buckle, roly-poly, flummery, pandowdy, and cobbler—all are old-fashioned regional desserts of cooked fruit with a biscuit, dough, or bread topping of some type. In New England the fruit might be blueberries, in the South, peaches. Any juicy fruit or a combination of fruits would be equally delicious. Use the Cream Biscuit variation of Baking Powder Biscuits for the topping.

> 2 to 3 pints fresh blueberries or other
>   juicy fruit or berry
> ½ cup sugar, or more, to taste
>   Grated rind and juice of 1 lemon
> 2 tablespoons water
>   Cream Biscuits (see page 50)
>   Cream and sugar, for topping
>   Ice cream or whipped cream, for accompaniment

1. Preheat oven to 400° F. Wash blueberries and drain; pick over to remove any soft or bruised ones. Place blueberries in a shallow, 1½-quart, ovenproof baking dish. Sprinkle with sugar, lemon juice and rind, and the water; toss to combine.

2. After preparing Cream Biscuits, shape dough in one of the following ways: drop by tablespoons onto fruit; *or* roll out ½ inch thick, cut into 2-inch rounds, and set on fruit; *or* roll out ½ inch thick and just slightly smaller than baking dish, crimp edges, and set on fruit. Brush dough with cream and dust with sugar. Bake until biscuit dough is golden brown (30 to 40 minutes).

3. Serve hot straight from the oven, or at room temperature, with ice cream or whipped cream.

Serves 4 to 6.

Recipes and Related Information
Baking Powder, 23; Baking Soda, 23; Cut In, 171; Drop, 187; Dumpling, 189; Quick Bread, 490.

BLACKBERRY

A member of the rose family, the blackberry has black or deep purple, seedy fruit similar to raspberries, boysenberries, dewberries, olallieberries, loganberries, and youngberries in structure. The berries are composed of numerous small sacs on a fleshy stem. Ripe berries are sweet and very juicy.

Use Fresh uncooked berries are enjoyed as is, or with milk or cream and sugar, as a breakfast dish, snack, or dessert. Blackberries are used in tarts, pies, ice cream, fruit salads and compotes, shortcakes, crisps and cobblers, puddings, and preserves.

Availability Fresh, frozen, and canned. Fresh blackberries are in season from May through August, with peak supply in June and August. They are packed loosely in cardboard or plastic baskets with cellophane covers.

Selection Look for relatively bright berries with uniform dark color and plump, tender sacs. Stem caps should not be attached. Avoid stained containers, which may indicate spoilage and either unripe or oversoft berries.

Storage Pick berries over, discarding overripe or moldy ones. Spread remaining berries on a paper-towel–lined tray and refrigerate; use within two or three days.

Preparation Wash berries gently just before use.

Recipes and Related Information
Basic Berry Pie, 437; Fruit Cobbler, 51.

Biscuits and berries are a classic summer dessert. Strawberries are the usual choice, but try a combination of strawberries, raspberries, and blueberries for an appealing mix of color, flavor, and texture.

BLANCH, TO

To cook foods—most often vegetables—briefly in boiling water and set briefly in cold water until completely cool. Food is blanched for one or more of the following reasons: to loosen and remove skin (almonds, peaches, tomatoes); to enhance color and reduce bitterness (raw vegetables for hors d'oeuvres); to extend storage life (raw vegetables to be frozen); to draw out excess salt from meats such as bacon and salt pork.

Parboiling and blanching are identical processes, but although blanched foods boil only a short time, parboiled foods are cooked almost halfway. Parboiling is a great timesaving technique for stir-fries and sautés. It tenderizes longer-cooking ingredients so that all foods cook in the same amount of time, and it can be done in advance of final preparation, another convenience.

HOW TO BLANCH

Almost any vegetable can be blanched successfully in boiling water, and most can be blanched over steam. Steaming better maintains the shape of the vegetables and conserves more nutrients than water-blanching, but it takes a bit longer. Blanching in a microwave oven is quick and easy, and protects both nutrients and color. Time varies with specific vegetables and end use. In general, boil just until vegetable is tender-crisp. For peeling, usually 1 or 2 minutes is all the boiling time needed.

Microwave-Blanching You'll need appropriate oven-proof dishes. Prepare 1 pound of vegetables as for conventional cooking. Place in a glass casserole, add ⅓ cup water, and cover. Cook at 100 percent power until evenly cooked (4 to 6 minutes). When done, cool and drain as directed for water-blanching.

Steam-Blanching Use a large pot with a tight-fitting lid and a steaming rack that fits the pot. Fill pot with about 2 inches water and place rack in pot. Water should not touch rack. Bring water to a boil, loosely pack vegetables on rack in a single layer no more than 2 inches deep, and cover pot. When done, cool and drain as directed for water-blanching.

Water-Blanching Use a large pot with a tight-fitting lid, ideally one equipped with a strainer for lifting the vegetables in and out of boiling water. If your pot doesn't have its own strainer, use a basket, colander, or wire-mesh strainer that is large enough to allow the food to move around in boiling water. Bring lightly salted water to a hard boil; lower vegetable-filled strainer or basket into pot; return water to boiling point as quickly as possible; stir vegetables again once boiling resumes. Stir vegetables into ice water or hold under running water until completely cooled; drain immediately.

BLEND, TO

To mix two or more ingredients together by hand or with a machine until smooth or until they combine to produce uniform texture, color, or flavor.

BLENDER, IMMERSION BLENDER

The blender is often compared with the food processor, and often suffers in the comparison. Although it has slipped in popularity, its virtues should be kept in mind. The blender purées, makes mayonnaise and silky sauces, and mixes the best drinks. Its tall, narrow container is better designed for some jobs than the work bowl of the food processor. The shape also allows the machine to process small batches, sometimes a problem with the wider processor bowl. Processor bowls may have a problem with liquid seeping from the base. This can't happen with a blender. However, it cannot whip egg whites, which a processor can do if it has a whisk attachment, and the processor is better for chopping, shredding, and grating.

Blenders may have as many as 16 speeds, including an on-off pulse function designed to give more control over food consistency. Most cooks will use only a few settings and ignore the rest. Some models come with small jars that substitute for the standard container. These jars are a good size for small portions (including homemade baby food and salad dressings), and they come with covers so they can be stored in the refrigerator.

Do you need a blender? If you make a lot of purées for soups, sauces, ice creams, and sorbets, and have space for the blender, you'll find it useful. If you have room for only one appliance of this type—in your budget or on your kitchen counter—the food processor, although more expensive, is more versatile and therefore a better buy. An alternative is a relatively new (for the home cook) machine called the immersion blender.

IMMERSION BLENDER

Just making its debut in home kitchens, the immersion blender (also called a hand blender) has been a valued chef's tool for years. Essentially it is a blender without a container. It is a tall, narrow, handheld machine with rotary blades. Like a conventional blender, it excels at making sauces and purées. Unlike a conventional blender, this machine is portable. This means it can be used right in the cooking pot and can handle more food at a time because it ıs not limited by the size of the container. As another benefit, there are fewer dirty bowls to clean.

Why has a home version of this machine appeared only recently if it's been in restaurant kitchens for so long? The time is right. This appliance very much complements contemporary cuisine with the emphasis away from caloric, starch-thickened sauces, toward fresh purées and vegetable reductions—the types of preparations the immersion blender makes best.

Choose a model with variable speeds for optimum control. Soft foods blend at low speeds, but thick ingredients such as whole tomatoes or cooked potatoes need more mixing to work into a smooth purée. High speed also does a better job at creating emulsion sauces. If you have a blender with a whisk attachment, you can whip and beat as well as blend and purée. Other accessories include beakers for mixing drinks and blending small quantities, a strainer, and a wall mount.

The food processor will still perform more culinary chores than either type of blender, and if you only want one small appliance in this general category the processor should be it. If the portability and easy storage of the immersion blender appeal to you, you might consider acquiring one as a companion to the processor.

Recipes and Related Information

Food Processor, 240; Hollandaise Sauce, 516; Ice Cream and Frozen Dessert, 308; Mayonnaise, 519; Purée, 487; Sauce, 512; Stock and Soup, 558.

BLUEBERRY

The blueberry is a round, dark blue berry that grows wild in Scandinavia, the British Isles, Russia, and North and South America. Cultivated varieties date only from the early twentieth century and are larger than the wild berries. Ripe blueberries are sweet and juicy.

Use Fresh uncooked blueberries are enjoyed as is, or with milk or cream and sugar, as a breakfast dish, a snack, or dessert. When blueberries are blended with other berries, such as raspberries and strawberries, they make a simply prepared, visually appealing, and delicious fruit cup. Blueberries also add color and flavor to fruit salads, fools, yogurt, ice creams, muffins, and pancakes. They add sweetness to pies, tarts, cobblers, puddings, coffee cakes, tea breads, and other baked desserts. Blueberries make excellent preserves.

Availability Blueberries are marketed fresh, frozen, and canned. Blueberries are harvested from May to September, with peak supplies in July and August. They come to market in cardboard containers with cellophane covers. Frozen blueberries are packed in plastic bags or cardboard freezer packages. Canned blueberries, both cultivated and wild, are packed in water or sugar syrup.

Selection Choose firm, plump berries with a silvery bloom; they should not have stems attached. Avoid juice-stained containers and soft berries.

Storage Refrigerate fresh blueberries for up to two weeks; wash just before using. To freeze fresh blueberries, do not wash. Dry them thoroughly, repack in cardboard container, and overwrap tightly with plastic wrap, covering air holes at bottom of container. Alternatively, tray freeze: Spread blueberries out in a single layer on shallow metal pans and put directly in freezer. When berries are frozen solid, pack airtight in plastic bags or containers and refreeze. Frozen berries will keep at least a year. They do not have to be defrosted before using in baking recipes.

Preparation Wash berries just before using; discard any berries that appear moldy.

Served warm or at room temperature, Blueberry Coffee Cake is inviting for breakfast or as a midday treat with coffee or tea. The recipe is on page 54.

■ BLUEBERRY COFFEE CAKE

Dust confectioners' sugar over this almond-crusted fresh blueberry cake to dramatize its luscious appearance.

¼ cup *each* sliced almonds and
    firmly packed brown sugar
1½ cups flour
¾ cup granulated sugar
1 tablespoon baking powder
½ teaspoon salt
¼ teaspoon freshly grated nutmeg
⅓ cup butter
1 cup fresh blueberries
1 egg
½ cup milk
1 teaspoon vanilla extract
    Confectioners' sugar, for dusting

1. Preheat oven to 350° F. Generously grease a 9-inch tube pan with a capacity of 6 to 7 cups. Combine almonds and brown sugar; sprinkle mixture in pan; set aside.

2. In a large bowl mix flour, granulated sugar, baking powder, salt, and nutmeg; cut in butter until mixture resembles coarse crumbs. Lightly stir in blueberries.

3. In a small bowl beat egg lightly with milk and vanilla. Stir milk mixture into blueberry mixture just until combined. Spread batter gently in prepared pan.

4. Bake until coffee cake is well browned and a long skewer inserted in thickest part comes out clean (45 minutes to 1 hour).

5. Let stand in pan for about 5 minutes, loosen edges, and invert onto a serving plate. Serve warm or at room temperature, dusted with confectioners' sugar.

Serves 6 to 8.

Recipes and Related Information
Blueberry Buttermilk Pancakes, 600; Blueberry Muffins, 375; Fruit Cobbler, 51.

BOIL, TO

The process of heating a liquid to the boiling point (212° F at sea level). When it reaches the boiling point, all of the liquid will be in motion, with bubbles constantly rising and breaking on the surface.

Once water reaches 212° F, its temperature won't increase, but it will be more agitated and will evaporate faster. The following terms should help you create a type of boil by identifying the appearance of the surface of the water.

Shake Surface begins to shake, but bubbles have not yet appeared (for stocks).

Smile Small bubbles begin to pop up on the surface (for delicate sauces, poaching, stocks).

Simmer A continuous stream of small bubbles slowly rises to the surface (for slow cooking; soups, stews).

Moderate Boil Water surface is agitated but not rolling on top of itself (for most cooking).

Rolling Boil A great deal of turbulence is produced as bubbles form rapidly and rise to the surface, but break before reaching the surface (for green vegetables, pasta, reducing liquids).

BOILING VEGETABLES

An American cookbook from the turn of the century directed that string beans (cut in pieces) needed to boil one to three hours to tenderize. Few of us have probably been subjected to three-hour beans, but vegetables boiled to a dull, mushy, nutrient-depleted mass most likely were typical fare as we grew up. Today's emphasis on fresh, quality ingredients has resulted in a greater understanding of how to cook these foods to preserve their appearance, flavor, and nutrition.

Boiling is one of the principal cooking techniques for fresh vegetables. There are two approaches: using a large amount of water or using very little (usually ½ to 1 inch or enough water to cover). Green vegetables cooked uncovered in a pot full of water will keep their color better than if boiled in a small amount of liquid, but can lose important nutrients. When cooked in 1 or 2 inches of water in a covered pan, these vegetables retain nutrients but can turn dull and unappealing.

The challenge is to prepare vegetables so that nutrients are conserved and visual appeal maintained; most recipes will provide specific cooking instructions. In general, to avoid loss of nutrients, cook as briefly as possible in a small amount of water. To hold color, add a little salt to the water and begin cooking uncovered to allow gases that have a negative effect on color to escape, then finish in a covered pan; or lift cover several times during cooking to release gases. Bring water to a boil first, then add vegetables; quickly return to a boil and cover. Remember that vegetables cut in pieces of similar size will cook more evenly. To preserve the color of green vegetables, it's best to cook them uncovered in a large amount of boiling, salted water. Bring salted water to a boil and add vegetables. Stir vegetables until water returns to a boil, then let boil until done. Drain immediately and serve.

Cooking time depends upon freshness and maturity of vegetables and whether they are whole or cut up, and is usually measured from the point at which water returns to a boil after vegetables have been added. As a measure of comparison, broccoli spears will boil tender-crisp in about 7 to 10 minutes; florets need only 3 to 5 minutes to be ready. A head of cauliflower should cook 15 to 20 minutes; florets 5 to 10 minutes; slices only 3 to 5 minutes.

BONE, TO

A basic preparation technique used to separate the flesh of meat, poultry, and fish from the bones, and to trim away sinews, gristle, and fat in order to make eating easier and more enjoyable. All cooks, even those who prefer to have the butcher perform this service for them, should learn how to bone certain cuts, such as chicken breasts. Whole and bone-in poultry and other meats are less expensive per pound and will allow the cook last-minute flexibility when deciding what to prepare. Boned breasts are well suited to poaching, sautéing, and frying. Boneless legs and thighs are elegant when served with a savory stuffing. See FISH, for a discussion of filleting. See DISJOINT for a description of cutting up a whole chicken.

You will bone with less damage to the piece of meat if you use your hands to learn, by feel, the anatomy of the animal. That way you will get to know where the bones and joints are and then be able to cut in order to expose them. These preliminary cuts are exploratory ones that show you where subsequent cuts should be made. Use a sharp knife and a cutting board. Remember to wash the preparation surface thoroughly before and after it comes in contact with raw poultry.

BONING A CHICKEN BREAST

For a whole breast, remove skin and place breast skin side down. With tip of knife cut through membrane covering breastbone. Pick up breast with both hands and press back on ribs to break them away from breastbone, which will pop out. Pull out breastbone, including cartilage.

Cut away ribs by using tip of knife to make shallow cuts as close to rib bones as possible. Or, slip fingers between ribs and meat and work meat free from bones. Work wishbone free with fingers. Split breast in half, removing tough membranes lying along breastbone.

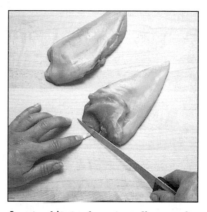

Locate white tendon on smaller muscle of each breast half. Place tendon side down on work surface and hold end with fingernail. With knife held vertically, scrape from end of tendon inward, removing meat from tendon. Trim into neat fillet shape.

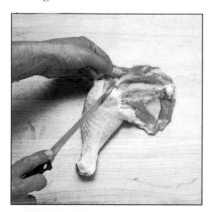

BONING A CHICKEN LEG AND THIGH

Do not separate leg and thigh. With boning knife, cut along thigh bone, to expose it, and then down drumstick.

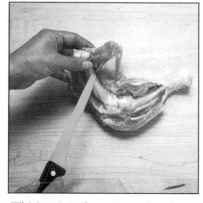

With hand, push meat away from bone. Then hold by exposed end of thigh bone so that leg and thigh hang down. Cut meat away from bone by making little cuts around the bone. Continue around knee joint to free leg bone.

If a larger piece of meat is desired, pound to flatten before stuffing. To separate into boneless leg and thigh, cut through at point where thigh and leg bone are joined.

Bouquet garni is a classic seasoning mixture made of fresh herbs that are tied in a bundle or wrapped in cheesecloth. The herbs will vary depending on usage and the cook's preference.

BORAGE

A hardy, highly ornamental, annual herb native to southern Europe and North Africa, borage has a stout stem, bristly gray-green leaves, and delicate, star-shaped, blue-violet flowers. The leaves have a cucumberlike flavor.

Use   Young borage leaves may be eaten raw as a salad or added to salads. Older leaves may be cooked and served like spinach. Fresh borage flowers make a colorful garnish for salads or iced drinks; dried borage flowers may be added to potpourri; candied flowers are used to decorate cakes and desserts.

Availability   Found in specialty markets from May through October.

Selection   Choose fresh leaves that are not limp and do not show any signs of decay.

Storage   Keep leaves and flowers loosely in plastic bags in the refrigerator. Use within a couple of days.

BOUQUET GARNI

A bundle of aromatic herbs and vegetables, bouquet garni is used to flavor soups, stocks, poaching liquids, stews, and braised dishes. It is always removed after cooking. The herbs are tied together with a string or gathered together in a cheesecloth bag to facilitate their retrieval from the finished dish. Traditional bouquet garni herbs include bay leaf, thyme, and parsley, although other herbs and vegetables such as tarragon, chervil, peppercorns, celery, and leeks may be included to enhance the flavor of a particular dish.

For a small bouquet garni, tie together with string three sprigs fresh parsley, two sprigs fresh thyme, and one bay leaf. If using dried or loose herbs, wrap all ingredients in a square of cheesecloth and tie with a string.

Recipes and Related Information
Bay, 29; Cheesecloth, 119; Herb, 299; Parsley, 406; Stock and Soup, 558; Thyme, 578.

BOWL CHOPPER

The bowl chopper is easy to recognize. It has a single stainless steel blade which is curved along the bottom at the cutting edge, and an easy-to-grip wooden knob as the handle. It chops and minces like a chef's knife, food processor, or electric minichopper, and is efficient for small tasks—a few tablespoons of garlic, herbs, or onion. Although it can be bought separately, most often it is paired with a small hardwood bowl whose curve matches the curve of the chopping blade.

A bowl chopper has homey appeal and is also practical. The bowl keeps the food contained so that it doesn't hop around when hit by the blade. Consider buying a chopper and matching bowl if you cook for one or two persons most of the time.

Select a blade that fits its bowl, or it won't be as effective. After each use, rinse the chopper in warm, sudsy water and wipe dry. Don't wash bowl; wipe away remaining food. Periodically treat wood with mineral oil. To protect blade, store chopper in bowl.

A *mezzaluna* is a large, double-handled, curved chopper, used on a flat chopping surface. A more serious piece of kitchen equipment than the bowl chopper, it has been referred to as the Italian chef's knife.

Recipes and Related Information
Food Processor, 240; Knife, 328.

BRAISE, TO

Braising is a combination of cooking methods designed to render tough cuts of meat and fibrous vegetables succulent and tender. Usually, food is first sautéed or browned for color and flavor, then cooked slowly in a small amount of liquid in an airtight pot. This creates a moist, steamy cooking environment that gently breaks down hard-to-chew connective tissue and muscle and releases the food's own juices. The browned meat is often set on a bed of chopped aromatic vegetables (*mirepoix*), which later may be puréed, mixed with pan juices, and used as a sauce. About ¼ to ½ inch of liquid—water, stock, wine, hard cider, tomato purée—is added to the bottom of the pot, which is tightly covered to prevent evaporation. Cooking is completed either on top of the stove or in the oven. Stewing is almost identical to braising, but uses smaller pieces of meat and requires more liquid.

Any casserole with a tight-fitting lid is suitable for braising. It is important that the vessel be of a material that conducts heat evenly and efficiently to prevent scorching and hot spots. The pot should not be much larger than the meat plus its liquid, so that the heat will be directed to the meat rather than the empty spaces.

The best foods for braising are shoulder cuts of beef (often called chuck), lamb, veal, and pork. Other good cuts are beef brisket, beef round, beef rump, veal shanks, and lamb shanks. Boneless cuts that are rolled and tied in a neat cylinder are ideal for braising because they are easy to carve. Whole chickens and Rock Cornish game hens are also delicious when braised.

BRAISING VEGETABLES

Although vegetables are commonly part of a meat or poultry braise for their wonderful flavor, they are also braised alone and served as a side dish. Root vegetables and leafy greens are superb when braised. Butter, or butter with some water, stock, or wine, plus seasonings, is a typical mixture for braising vegetables. Sugar is frequently added for flavor and to help develop a shiny syrup. Browning vegetables adds to their taste, but isn't always called for in many braised vegetable recipes. Often the first step is to toss vegetable pieces briefly in hot oil or melted butter; more liquid is then added and the vegetables cooked until tender. Alternatively, after slowly cooking in a small amount of liquid just until tender, vegetables can be finished in butter and seasonings for a short period of time until coated. Sometimes all ingredients are added at once.

Cooking times depend upon the size and shape of vegetables, their freshness, and maturity. As a rough guideline and comparison for other vegetables, celery hearts should braise for 10 to 15 minutes; Belgian endive needs about 15 to 20 minutes; blanch whole leeks to tenderize, then braise anywhere from 15 to 25 minutes, depending upon thickness; braise halved leeks 10 to 15 minutes without blanching (they will separate if precooked); braise carrots until tender and glazed with the reduced cooking liquid, anywhere from 8 to 15 minutes depending upon size of the pieces; braise greens just until wilted along with some sautéed onions and a small amount of liquid.

◼ ROLLED BEEF WITH PROSCIUTTO

Braciole is the Italian word for boneless meat cutlets, which are almost invariably stuffed, rolled, and tied. Here, in a Roman version, the cutlets are wrapped around a filling of prosciutto and celery, then gently braised with tomatoes and aromatic Italian mushrooms.

> 1 **pound bottom round of beef**
> 1½ **ounces dried porcini mushrooms**
> ⅓ **pound prosciutto, sliced paper-thin**
> 1 **cup coarsely chopped celery leaves**
> 3 **to 4 tablespoons olive oil**
> 1 **tablespoon minced garlic**
> 1 **cup minced onion**
> 2 **cups peeled, seeded, and diced tomatoes, fresh or canned**
> **Salt and freshly ground pepper, to taste**

1. Have butcher slice meat into eight 2-ounce slices, or freeze it briefly and slice it yourself with a sharp knife. Place slices between 2 sheets of lightly oiled waxed paper and pound with a mallet or bottom of a skillet until they are paper-thin. Soak *porcini* mushrooms in hot water to cover for 1 hour.

2. Place beef slices on a flat surface. Divide prosciutto slices evenly among them and sprinkle chopped celery leaves over prosciutto. Roll each beef slice into a neat bundle and tie securely with kitchen string.

3. Heat 3 tablespoons oil in a heavy skillet over medium-high heat until a light haze forms. Brown beef rolls on all sides, in batches if necessary, then set aside. If necessary, add a little more oil to coat surface of pan, then add garlic and onion and sauté over moderate heat until softened but not browned.

4. With a slotted spoon, remove mushrooms from soaking liquid and squeeze dry. Strain liquid through cheesecloth to remove any grit or sand. Add mushrooms, tomatoes, and reserved soaking liquid to skillet. Season with salt and pepper to taste. Return meat to skillet and bring sauce to a simmer. Cover, reduce heat to maintain a slow simmer, and cook 2 hours. Check meat after 1 hour, adding a little water if sauce has reduced too much. When meat is quite tender, transfer rolls to a warm serving plate, cut strings carefully with a small knife, and cover with sauce.

Serves 4.

Food Processor Version   Use metal blade to process 3 to 4 cloves of garlic for 10 seconds. Cut 1 large onion into eighths and add to work bowl. Turn motor on and off 3 or 4 times. Scrape bowl and pulse 2 to 3 more times until onion is minced.

Serve Osso Buco with buttered fettuccine and a tiny spoon for scooping the soft marrow out of the veal shank bones. The hollow bone gives the dish its name.

■ OSSO BUCO

Meaty veal shanks turn fork-tender when braised slowly with wine and vegetables, and they yield a delectable dividend: a nugget of marrow in each hollow bone (*osso buco*).

    3 veal shanks, each sawed into 6 to 8 pieces
       about 2½ inches long
       Salt and freshly ground pepper
    2 cups flour, for dredging
    ½ to ¾ cup safflower oil
 1¼   cups dry white wine
    2 cups Brown Veal Stock or Beef Stock
       (see page 560) or canned stock
    4 sprigs fresh thyme
    ½ cup parsley sprigs and stems
    3 bay leaves
    1 cup whole fresh basil leaves
    5 tablespoons butter
 1½   cups chopped onion
    1 cup diced celery
    1 cup diced carrots
    1 tablespoon minced garlic
    2 cups peeled, seeded, and chopped tomatoes

Gremolata

    2 tablespoons finely minced Italian parsley
    1 tablespoon grated lemon rind
    1 teaspoon finely minced garlic

1. Salt and pepper shanks well, then dredge lightly in flour and shake off excess. In a large Dutch oven over medium-high heat, heat oil. Add shanks and brown well on all sides, in batches if necessary. Transfer shanks to a plate as they are browned.

2. When all shanks have been browned, pour off excess fat, add wine to Dutch oven, and bring to a boil. With a wooden spoon, scrape up any browned bits clinging to bottom of pot. Add stock and simmer 2 minutes. If using canned beef stock, dilute with water to taste, to reduce strength and saltiness.

3. Place thyme, parsley, and bay leaves in a cheesecloth bag. Add to pot along with basil. Return shanks to pot and set aside.

4. In a large skillet over moderate heat, melt butter. Add onion, celery, carrots, and garlic, and cook until vegetables are slightly softened (about 5 minutes). Add tomatoes and simmer 5 minutes. Transfer mixture to Dutch oven, cover tightly, and bring to a simmer over moderately high heat. Reduce heat to maintain simmer and cook gently for at least 2 hours. (Dish may also be baked in a 325° F oven for 2½ to 3 hours; bring it to a simmer on top of stove first.) Check occasionally to make sure liquid has not reduced too much; add a little wine, stock, or water if necessary.

5. When meat is fork-tender, transfer shanks to a warm serving platter. Place pot briefly over high heat to reduce sauce slightly. Add Gremolata during final 30 seconds, then spoon sauce over meat.

Serves 8.

Gremolata   In a small bowl combine parsley, lemon rind, and garlic; mix to blend well.

Food Processor Version   Use metal blade to process 3 or 4 cloves garlic for 10 seconds. Cut 2 large onions, 2 celery stalks, and 2 medium carrots into 1-inch pieces. Add half to work bowl. Turn motor on and off 3 to 4 times to chop coarsely. Add to skillet in step 4. Repeat with remaining onion, celery, and carrot and add to skillet.

■ GAME HENS COQ AU VIN

Classic coq au vin uses an old rooster. The tender game hens are a tasty alternative and speed the cooking time considerably.

    2 Rock Cornish game hens (1 to 1½ lb each),
       cut into serving pieces
       Salt and freshly ground pepper
    ½ cup butter
    ¼ cup brandy
    4 cups (approximately) dry red wine
       Bouquet garni (3 sprigs parsley, 1 bay leaf,
       1 teaspoon dried thyme, 1 teaspoon dried
       marjoram, wrapped in 4-in. square of
       cheesecloth)
    3 slices (each ½ in. thick) salt pork
   12 small boiling onions, peeled
   12 mushroom caps
       Beurre manié (3 tablespoons each flour and
       butter kneaded together)

1. Wash game hens and pat dry; season with salt and pepper. In a large, heavy-bottomed sauté pan over medium-high heat, melt butter. Add game hens and sauté until golden brown (about 5 minutes per side). Drain fat from pan.

2. Pour brandy over game hens and flame it. When flame dies down, add enough red wine to cover hens. Add bouquet garni and cook, covered, over medium heat until game hens are tender when pierced with a fork (about 30 minutes).

3. After 15 minutes, brown salt pork in a medium, heavy-bottomed sauté pan over medium-high heat. Add onions and sauté until a rich brown color (about 10 minutes). Add mushrooms and continue cooking until just tender (about 1 minute). Set aside.

4. When chicken is tender, remove bouquet garni. Add vegetables. Drop beurre manié into sauce and whisk to blend; cook over medium heat until sauce has thickened.

Serves 4.

■ LEEKS BRAISED WITH TASSO

This dish demonstrates a typical and flavorful use of the Cajun seasoning meat called *tasso,* which imparts a smoky tang to the leeks and adds a contrast of color. Tasso is usually made from lean pork shoulder cut into chunks. It is richly seasoned with cayenne. Smoked ham can be substituted for tasso, but it is less smoky.

    3   medium-sized leeks
    1   carrot, diced
    2   shallots, finely chopped
    2   cloves garlic, minced
    ¼   pound tasso, finely chopped
    2   cups Beef Stock (see page 560)
    2   tablespoons butter

Split leeks and wash thoroughly. Place in a heavy pan over medium heat with carrot, shallots, garlic, tasso, stock, and butter. Cover, reduce to simmer, and cook until leeks are tender when pierced (30 to 40 minutes). Remove to a warm serving dish and reduce liquid until it turns syrupy. Pour over leeks and serve.

Serves 4 to 6.

BRAZIL NUT

The Brazil nut is the fruit of the tall bertholettia tree, which grows wild in Paraguay and Brazil. The tree yields 3- to 4-pound pods with thick shells that must be broken open with a machete. Inside are 12 to 20 three-sided Brazil nuts, with a dark brown shell that is rough and hard and has sharp edges. The large kernel inside has a thin brown skin and ivory meat; it is oily, with a flavor reminiscent of hazelnut and coconut.

Use   Shelled Brazil nuts are used in candies, cakes, and salted nut mixes. They add texture and nutty flavor to stuffings, chicken salad, and grain dishes.

Availability   Whole shelled nuts are packed in cans or plastic bags, or are sold in bulk. Unshelled nuts are available in bulk.

Selection   Buy as fresh as possible.

Storage   Keep unshelled nuts in a cool place for up to six months. Shelled nuts go stale quickly; store them in an airtight container in the refrigerator and use within three months. Shelled nuts may be frozen for up to six months, although they will lose some crispness.

Preparation   See NUT.

■ YOUR OWN BRIDGE MIX

Trail mixes, party mixes, bridge mixes, cocktail mixes—whatever the name, they are an addicting munchie, and best when you make your own. Fill small bowls with this nutty mix, which is naturally sweetened with raisins and dried apricots and spiked with wine. Place the bowls strategically around the room: on the bar, on the mantel, on the piano, or wherever guests are likely to gather. This recipe yields a large batch, enough for a crowd; store any extra in an airtight container.

    1   pound Brazil nuts, unskinned
    1   pound almonds, unskinned
    1   pound blanched cashews
    ½   pound shelled pine nuts
    ¼   pound muscat raisins or
        seedless dark raisins
    ⅓   pound golden raisins
    ⅓   cup Marsala or sweet vermouth
    ½   pound shelled pistachio nuts
    ¼   cup shredded unsweetened coconut
    ¼   cup lightly salted sunflower seeds
    ¼   cup finely minced dried apricots
        Kosher salt
        Worcestershire sauce (optional)

1. Preheat oven to 350° F. In separate batches, toast Brazil nuts, almonds, cashews, and pine nuts on cookie sheets until lightly browned and fragrant. Set nuts aside to cool.

2. In a medium saucepan combine muscat and golden raisins with Marsala. Bring to a boil, reduce heat, and simmer gently until liquid has evaporated (20 to 30 minutes). Set aside to cool.

3. Combine cooled toasted nuts with raisins, pistachios, coconut, sunflower seeds, and apricots. Add salt and Worcestershire sauce (if used) to taste.

Makes about 10 cups.

HOW TO BREAD FOOD

Holding food with fingers, dip food in flour and turn to coat on all sides; shake off excess flour.

Dip food in egg mixture, coating evenly with liquid. Do not get liquid on fingers. Remove food with a slotted spoon or wire skimmer, allowing excess liquid to drip off.

Set food in crumbs. Shake dish to coat food with some crumbs. Turn food and pat with fingers to firmly set top crumbs. Turn again and pat to set crumbs on other side; shake off excess.

BREAD, TO

To coat with bread or other crumbs, mostly to foods that will be fried. During cooking, the crumbs form a pleasantly crunchy crust that acts as a protective barrier between food and cooking oil. Often a layer of flour and then egg precedes the crumbs. The flour dries the outside of the food and gives the egg something to adhere to. The egg acts as glue for the crumbs. To develop an attractive, crisp crust, it is important to shake off excess coating before applying the next. The above directions will ensure that the crumbs coat the food and not your hands by keeping your hands free of egg wash, a very effective binder.

> ***Recipes and Related Information***
> *Deep-fry, 174; Fry, 254.*

BROCCOLI

A vegetable in the cabbage family, broccoli has a thick, rigid, green stalk, grayish green leaves, and a flowering dark green or purplish green head. All parts are edible.

Use The flowering heads of young broccoli may be eaten raw, dressed with vinaigrette, or accompanied by a dipping sauce. More mature broccoli is generally boiled or steamed and eaten cold as a salad or hot as a side dish. It is flattered by cheese sauce and cream sauce. Chopped broccoli may be made into soup, soufflé, or baked pudding. A variety of Chinese broccoli with more leaf than flower is used in Chinese stir-fried dishes.

Availability Fresh and frozen. Fresh broccoli is sold all year, with peak supplies in fall through winter. Frozen broccoli is available whole or chopped.

Selection Choose broccoli with tightly closed florets that do not show signs of yellowing. Avoid spears with tough, woody stems and wilted leaves.

Storage Keep broccoli in a plastic bag in the refrigerator for three or four days. It also freezes well.

Preparation Wash carefully. Trim butt end. If desired, peel tough green outer skin of stalks down to moist, pale green part. Flower heads cook more quickly than stalks; to cook heads and stalks evenly, split stalks lengthwise in halves or quarters, slicing all the way up to but not through flower heads.

Cooking See BOIL, STEAM, STIR-FRY.

■ **BROCCOLI SAUTEED WITH GARLIC**
Italian vegetables are often parboiled—partially cooked in water until almost tender—then sautéed in olive oil or butter, sometimes both.

>   1 bunch of fresh broccoli or
>   1 package (10 oz) frozen sliced broccoli
>   2 cloves garlic, minced
>   ¼ cup olive oil
>   Salt, to taste

1. Slice off and discard ends of fresh broccoli stalks; peel stalks if broccoli is tough. Split stalks in half or into quarters with florets left attached, or slice whole stalks horizontally into bite-sized pieces. Steam or drop into boiling salted water and cook until just fork-tender. Drain well. (Cook frozen broccoli according to package directions until barely tender.)

2. Over medium heat, sauté garlic in olive oil until golden. Add broccoli and salt and sauté about 3 to 4 minutes.

Makes 4 servings.

A quick, easy-to-make white sauce combined with grated Parmesan cheese transforms blanched broccoli into a golden gratin.

■ BROCCOLI GRATIN

A gratin is a popular way of preparing any vegetable that tastes good with cheese. The vegetable is cooked until tender, then baked with cheese sauce—try one flavored with grated Parmesan. Gratins can be made with one vegetable or with a mixture of cooked vegetables or vegetable purées.

   ¾ **pound broccoli**
      Pinch salt
   1 **cup Cheese Sauce (see page 513), finished with 1 egg yolk**
   2 **tablespoons grated Parmesan cheese**

1. Preheat oven to 425° F. Divide broccoli into medium florets. (Reserve stalks for soup.)

2. In a large saucepan boil enough water to cover broccoli generously and add a pinch of salt. Add broccoli and boil, uncovered, until just tender when pierced with a sharp knife (about 5 minutes). Drain broccoli, rinse with cold water, and drain thoroughly.

3. Butter a 4- or 5-cup shallow baking dish.

4. Arrange broccoli in one layer in baking dish. Spoon sauce over broccoli, covering it completely. Sprinkle with cheese. Broccoli can be kept, covered, up to 1 day in refrigerator.

5. Bake until hot (about 5 minutes if broccoli and sauce were hot, or about 15 minutes if they were cold).

6. If surface is not brown by the time mixture is hot, broil for about 1 minute. Serve hot.

Serves 4.

Recipes and Related Information

Beef With Asparagus, 558; Cream of Any Vegetable Soup, 563; Vegetable Purées, 487.

BROCCOLI RAAB

This leafy green member of the cabbage family figures prominently in Italian cooking. It has slender but firm stalks about 12 inches long, bright green leaves with jagged edges, and small green florets with yellow flowers. Its flavor is pleasantly bitter. It is marketed under a variety of similar names, including *cima di rapa, cima di rabe, broccolirab, broccoli di rape, rape, raab,* and *rapini.*

Use Broccoli raab may be steamed and served cool or chilled, as a salad with lemon and oil. Italian cooks briefly boil broccoli raab, then sauté it with oil and garlic for use as an accompaniment to pork roast. Alternatively, it may be very slowly sautéed in oil without preblanching.

Availability Fresh broccoli raab is most widely available fall through spring.

Selection Choose stalks with dark green, fresh-looking leaves and sturdy stems.

Storage Keep in a plastic bag in refrigerator crisper for three to four days.

Preparation Trim away any large wilted or bruised leaves; peel tough outer layer of stalk or cut away tough stem ends entirely.

Cooking See PARBOIL, SAUTE, STEAM.

■ ROMAN-STYLE BROCCOLI RAAB

The full flavor of broccoli raab stands up to garlic and cheese and is an excellent foil for pork or tomato-sauce dishes. Substitute Swiss chard if broccoli raab is not available.

> **2 pounds broccoli raab**
> **¼ cup olive oil**
> **½ tablespoon minced garlic**
> **Coarse salt and freshly ground pepper**
> **3 tablespoons fresh lemon juice**
> **2 tablespoons grated Romano cheese**

1. Wash broccoli raab and trim away any woody stems. Bring a large pot of salted water to a boil. Blanch broccoli raab 2 minutes. Drain and refresh in a bowl of ice water. Drain again and gently towel-dry.

2. Heat olive oil in a large skillet over moderate heat. Add garlic and sauté, stirring constantly, for 1 minute. Add broccoli and cook, turning often with tongs, until greens are coated with oil, hot throughout, and tender (about 2 minutes). Season to taste with salt and pepper; add lemon juice. Transfer to a warm serving platter. Sprinkle with cheese and serve at once.

Serves 4.

BROIL, TO

A cooking method which uses dry, radiant heat. It is appreciated for its convenience, speed, and simplicity. The goal for all broiled foods is to have the surface perfectly browned when the interior is cooked to taste. For a moist and tender final product, a delicate balance must be maintained between rapid surface cooking and slower internal heat transfer. The farther food is from the heat source, the more time it can stay under the broiler before overcooking. Thus larger pieces of meat, requiring a longer broiling time than thin fillets or skewered foods, may need to be set on a low oven rack to ensure a nicely browned surface and properly cooked interior.

Experiment with your broiler's temperature controls and rack settings. With experience you will develop an understanding of how to control the variables of this technique. As a general rule of thumb, however, place food about 4 to 6 inches from the broiler element. Broiled items should be uniform in size and at room temperature, so all will cook evenly and quickly.

SOME HINTS TO KEEP IN MIND

- Always preheat your broiler. If it's electric, have the door ajar when the unit is in operation.
- Line the inside of the broiler pan with aluminum foil to ease cleanup.
- Trim excess fat from meats and poultry before broiling since fat can ignite from high heat. For the same reason, drain off oil-based marinades and pat meat dry.
- Use tongs, not a fork, to turn meat; pricked meat loses its juices and becomes dry.
- Broiling *Fish:* Broiled fish is done when the meat is opaque and no longer clings to the bone. Cook 8 to 10 minutes per inch of thickness.
- Broiling *Meat:* See Timetable for Broiling Meat, opposite page. Any timetable should be considered merely a guideline, because so many variables should be taken into account when computing broiling time— shape of meat, amount of fat and bone, whether it was at room temperature, accuracy of your oven. Other ways than time for judging doneness include color of meat and touch. A few minutes before the estimated end of cooking time, make a small cut in the meat (near the bone if it has one; near center if boneless) to view the inside. Another way, used by professional chefs, takes into account how meat changes consistency as it cooks (see GRILL, When Is It Done?). When broiling steak, trim away most fat, leaving about ¼ inch; slash fat to keep from curling. For very thick steaks, use an instant-read thermometer to judge internal temperature. Very lean meats such as veal benefit from a baste or marinade to keep them moist.
- Broiling *Poultry:* See Timetable for Broiling Meat, opposite page. Broiled poultry is done when a meat thermometer inserted in the thickest part of the flesh reads 170° F to 175° F, or when the juices run slightly pink, or when the flesh springs back slightly when touched.
- Broiling *Vegetables:* Because they lack fat to keep them from drying out, baste vegetables with fat (oil or butter) or marinate them before broiling. Also ahead of time, blanch fibrous vegetables, such as leeks or celery, to soften slightly. Don't use the most intense heat, as vegetables may char before they cook completely. Broil until tender when pierced and slightly streaked with brown. Suggested for broiling: Japanese eggplant, leek, mushroom, onion, peppers, squash, tomato.

BROWN, TO

To expose food to high temperature in order to deepen surface color and intensify flavor. This is done under a broiler, in the oven, or by cooking in fat on top of the stove. Browned foods, properly cooked, have a crisp and pleasing texture without being brittle and burnt.

BROWNIE

How to define a brownie? Most often it's described as a square of rich, thin chocolate cake. Technically, however, it's a bar cookie, and it isn't always chocolate. Even the dictionary hedges in its definition of this extraordinarily popular sweet; Webster's describes it as "usually" chocolate and "often" made with nuts. What about texture? Brownie lovers argue whether the best is fudgy and chewy, or light and cakelike.

Actually there isn't a single, standard brownie recipe. There are numerous approaches, which have all evolved from the many techniques of making cakes. What is important is the final product, not what you had to do to make it or whether you've chosen to use solid chocolate, chocolate syrup, or cocoa powder to infuse the batter with its characteristic flavor.

Traditionally brownies are flat and square, although few of us would refuse one cut in a wedge or something even more unorthodox. The texture is either moist, chewy, and dense, or moist and cakey. Most often they are brown, but butterscotch brownies (blondies) are golden, those made with white chocolate quite pale, and marbled ones two-tone. The addition of chopped nuts is common, but controversial. Even more contentious is the inclusion of fruit, which some recipes may suggest.

In sum, a brownie is square or rectangular, made of chocolate, with nuts or other additions, and has a moist texture. But not always.

Note   These delicate formulations are created to produce a particular result. Varying proportions of ingredients, size of pan, and, most important, oven temperature and baking time even slightly will alter the final product. So, if you find *the* brownie recipe, follow it to the letter each time and you will be rewarded batch after batch.

CUTTING BROWNIES WITH PRECISION

Although even brownie crumbs taste wonderful, these bars look best when cut cleanly. For best results, refrigerate brownies in the pan to firm the chocolate before cutting. Turn out onto a dry, clean work surface and cut upside down to keep the top from crumbling. Use a sharp, serrated knife; for very fudgy brownies, dip knife in hot water before cutting. Wipe after each cut to prevent dragging. For brownies made in a square pan, cut in half each way, then halve each half. For larger rectangular pans, mark cuts lightly on the surface of the brownie using a ruler and sharp knife, and then cut along these lines. To make straight cuts, lay the ruler along the marked line and use the ruler's edge to guide the knife. If the brownie is especially moist, wipe the knife blade between cuts.

TIMETABLE FOR BROILING MEAT

A timetable such as this one can help you estimate how long a particular cut will take to broil to a particular degree of doneness. Keep in mind that the times are approximate and are based on a preheated broiler and meat at room temperature. Depending upon thickness and tenderness, cuts cook from 2 to 6 inches from the heat. Thicker cuts (1 inch thick or more) need to broil farther from the heating element and will need the longer cooking time. See also TEMPERATURE, Guide to Internal Temperatures.

Type of Meat	Thickness	Total Cooking Time (in minutes)		
		Rare	Medium	Well Done
Beef				
Flank steak	1 inch	4–5	6–8	
Hamburger	1 inch	3–5	9–11	13–15
	2 inches	4–6	11–13	15–17
Rib eye	1 inch	3–5	6–7	10–12
	2 inches	5–7	6–7	12–14
T-bone, porterhouse,	1 inch	5–6	9–11	13–16
club steak	2 inches	7–8	11–13	15–18
Tenderloin	1 inch	3–5	6–7	
	2 inches	5–7	9–11	
Top sirloin steak	1 inch	5–6	9–11	13–16
	2 inches	7–8	11–13	15–18
Lamb				
Loin chop	1 inch	5–7	8–10	12–14
	2 inches	7–8	10–12	14–16
Rack chop	1 inch	5–7	8–10	12–14
	2 inches	7–8	10–12	14–16
Shoulder chop	1 inch	5–7	8–10	12–14
Pork				
Loin chop	1 inch	8–10	12–14	
	2 inches	10–12	14–16	
Shoulder chop	1 inch	8–10	12–14	
	2 inches	10–12	14–16	
Tenderloin		10–12	14–16	
Poultry				
Boned breast				5–10
Chicken, turkey (bone-in pieces)				50–70
Halved game hen				12–15
Small whole bird				25
Veal				
Loin chop	1 inch	8–10	12–14	
Rack chop	1 inch	8–10	12–14	

Children of all ages love brownies, those ultimate bar cookies. Chewy or cakelike, nutty or plain, solid or layered, there's a brownie recipe to please every taste.

STORING AND FREEZING BROWNIES

Because brownies are so moist, they keep extremely well. When cool, remove bars from pan and wrap individually or leave in pan, tightly covered. Store in a cool, dry place. Moist, dense brownies will keep up to one week, drier, cakelike brownies one to two days. In warm weather you may want to store brownies in the refrigerator, where they will keep for three to four days. For longer storage wrap well and freeze for up to two months. Thaw slowly at room temperature.

■ CLASSIC FUDGE BROWNIES

These brownies have a moist texture and an intense, chocolate flavor. For a taste of mocha, try the Espresso Brownies variation.

  4 ounces unsweetened chocolate, chopped
  ½ cup butter
  3 large eggs
1⅓ cups sugar
  2 teaspoons vanilla extract
  ¾ cup flour
     Pinch salt
  1 cup chopped pecans or walnuts

1. Preheat oven to 350° F. Line bottom of an 8-inch-square cake pan with parchment paper; butter pan and dust with flour.

2. In a small, heavy-bottomed saucepan, melt chocolate and butter over low heat. Let chocolate mixture cool and continue with step 3.

3. In a large bowl beat eggs and sugar until thickened and lemon-colored; blend in vanilla. Sift flour and salt together and fold in; blend in chocolate mixture, then nuts.

4. Spread into prepared pan; bake until toothpick inserted near edge comes out clean (30 to 35 minutes).

5. Cool in pan. Refrigerate at least 2 hours before cutting. Serve chilled or at room temperature.

Makes 16 brownies.

Espresso Brownies Add 1 teaspoon instant coffee powder to chocolate-butter mixture as it melts.

■ WHITE-CHOCOLATE AND CHIP BROWNIES

The cocoa butter in white chocolate makes this brownie even richer; the color—dotted with dark bits of chocolate chips—makes it elegant.

  3 ounces white chocolate
  ½ cup butter or margarine
1½ cups flour
  ½ teaspoon baking powder
  ¼ teaspoon salt
  3 eggs, at room temperature
1½ cups sugar
  1 teaspoon vanilla extract
  1 package (6 oz) semisweet or milk chocolate chips
  ½ cup sliced almonds

1. Preheat oven to 350° F. Line bottom of a 9- by 13-inch pan with parchment paper; butter pan and dust with flour. In a small, heavy saucepan, melt white chocolate and butter over low heat; stir well to blend. Remove chocolate mixture from heat and let cool while continuing with step 2.

2. In a medium bowl combine flour, baking powder, and salt; set aside.

3. With an electric mixer beat eggs and sugar at high speed until thick and lemon-colored. Blend in vanilla. Gradually add white chocolate mixture, then flour mixture; beat well until combined. Stir in chocolate chips and ¼ cup almonds.

4. Spread batter in prepared pan, and sprinkle with remaining ¼ cup almonds. Bake until edges begin to pull away from sides of pan and center is nearly set when tested with a toothpick (30 to 35 minutes).

5. Let cool in pan on a wire rack for 10 minutes, then cut into bars. Remove from pan when cool.

Makes 3 dozen bars.

CAKE-LOVER'S BROWNIES

Not as dense and gooey as fudgy brownies, these bars have more in common with a rich chocolate cake.

    4 ounces unsweetened chocolate, chopped
    ½ cup butter, softened
    ¾ cup sugar
    3 eggs
    1 tablespoon vanilla extract
    ½ cup flour
      Pinch salt
    1 cup chopped pecans or walnuts
    ¼ cup chocolate chips or ½ cup raisins (optional)

1. Preheat oven to 350° F. Line bottom of an 8-inch-square cake pan with parchment paper; grease and flour.

2. In a double boiler over hot, but not boiling, water, melt chocolate; remove from heat and cool.

3. In a medium bowl cream butter and sugar until the consistency of whipped cream. Add eggs, one at a time, beating well after each addition. Stir in vanilla.

4. Sift flour and salt, and fold into egg mixture; gently blend in chocolate, then nuts and chocolate chips (if used). Spread into prepared pan; bake until toothpick inserted 2 inches from edge comes out clean (25 minutes; center may still look a little soft). Cool in pan.

5. Refrigerate at least 2 hours before cutting. Serve chilled or at room temperature. Best eaten within 2 days.

Makes 16 brownies.

BUTTERSCOTCH SAUCEPAN BROWNIES

The pecan-studded batter for these buttery blond brownies can be mixed in one saucepan to simplify preparation.

    1 cup flour
    ¾ teaspoon baking powder
      Pinch salt
    ⅓ cup butter or margarine
    1 cup firmly packed brown sugar
    1 egg
    1 teaspoon vanilla extract
    ½ cup chopped pecans

1. Preheat oven to 350° F. Line bottom of an 8-inch-square cake pan with parchment paper; butter pan and dust with flour. In a medium bowl thoroughly combine flour, baking powder, and salt; set aside.

2. In a 2-quart saucepan melt butter over medium heat. Add brown sugar, stirring until sugar dissolves and mixture bubbles. Remove from heat and let stand 5 minutes to cool slightly.

3. Beat in egg and vanilla, then gradually stir in flour mixture. Stir in pecans. Spread batter in prepared pan.

4. Bake until edges begin to pull away from sides of pan and center is nearly set when tested with a toothpick (25 to 30 minutes).

5. Let cool in pan on a wire rack 10 minutes, then cut into bars. Remove from pan when cool.

Makes 18 bars.

MARBLED CREAM CHEESE BROWNIES

Two batters—one made with cream cheese, the other with melted semisweet chocolate and chopped nuts—are swirled together to make these unusual brownies.

Cream Cheese Mixture

    2 tablespoons butter or margarine, softened
    1 small package (3 oz) cream cheese, softened
    ¼ cup sugar
    1 egg
    1 tablespoon flour
    ½ teaspoon vanilla extract

Chocolate Mixture

    4 ounces semisweet chocolate
    3 tablespoons butter or margarine
    ½ cup flour
    ½ teaspoon baking powder
    ¼ teaspoon salt
    3 eggs
    ¾ cup sugar
    1 teaspoon vanilla extract
    ½ cup chopped walnuts

1. Preheat oven to 350° F. Line bottom of an 8-inch-square cake pan with parchment paper; butter pan and dust with flour.

2. *For Cream Cheese Mixture:* In a medium bowl beat butter and cream cheese until well mixed. Add sugar and beat well. Add egg and beat until fluffy. Blend in flour and vanilla; set aside.

3. *For Chocolate Mixture:* In a small, heavy saucepan melt chocolate and butter over low heat; stir well to blend and set aside to cool. In a small bowl combine flour, baking powder, and salt; set aside. In a medium bowl beat eggs at high speed with an electric mixer until light-colored. Gradually beat in sugar, then vanilla. Gradually add flour mixture, mixing until well combined. Blend in chocolate mixture. Stir in walnuts.

4. Spread half of Chocolate Mixture in prepared pan. Pour Cream Cheese Mixture over it, lightly spreading to pan edges. Cover with remaining chocolate mixture. Swirl a thin spatula through all 3 layers to create a marbled effect.

5. Bake until edges begin to pull away from sides of pan and center is nearly set when tested with a toothpick (40 to 45 minutes).

6. Let cool in pan on a wire rack 5 minutes, then cut into bars. Remove from pan when cool.

Makes 18 bars.

Brussels Sprouts With Fresh Chestnuts is at its appealing best during the winter months, when chestnuts are in season.

BRUISE, TO

To partially crush a food—such as a clove of garlic—with the heel of a knife or with a mortar and pestle to release flavor. Bruising also facilitates removal of garlic's papery peel. When used for a sauce, berries are often bruised so they will absorb sugar more easily.

BRUNOISE

A mixture of aromatic vegetables cut in an even, fine dice, *brunoise* is used to flavor soups, stews, and sautés. Commonly included are onions, celery, carrots, and leeks, and less often turnips and parsnips; the choice is up to the cook. *Mirepoix* is a similar vegetable mixture used in the same way, but cut in coarser pieces.

BRUSH, TO

To apply a coating with a brush. Most often what is spread on is a flavoring agent, such as a glaze or a basting liquid; a fat, such as butter or oil; or a protective layer, such as an egg wash or aspic. A natural-bristle brush is recommended, as plastic bristles will melt and distort upon contact with heat.

> ***Recipes and Related Information***
> *Baste, 27; Cake and Pastry Tools, 89; Glaze, 268.*

BRUSSELS SPROUT

The Brussels sprout is a member of the cabbage family, native to northern Europe. Instead of one large head, the plant produces numerous small heads arranged in neat rows around a thick stalk.

Use Cooked Brussels sprouts may be eaten cold as a salad but are generally eaten hot as a side dish, dressed with butter, oil, or meat-roasting juices. Their nutty flavor is flattered by sliced almonds, braised chestnuts, and cream sauces.

Availability Fresh and frozen. The domestic fresh crop is harvested from mid-August through the first week of May. Imported Brussels sprouts from Mexico are available in late spring and summer. Brussels sprouts are generally removed from their stalk and sold in bulk (by the pound) or in cardboard buckets overwrapped with cellophane. However, they are increasingly coming to market still attached to their stalks. These sprouts have superior flavor; remove the heads from their stalk just before cooking.

Selection Choose Brussels sprouts that are small and odorless, tightly closed, and bright green, without yellowing or loose leaves around base.

Storage Refrigerate fresh Brussels sprouts in a plastic bag for three to five days.

Preparation Wash; trim stem ends and remove wilted or discolored leaves. Cut an *x* in stem ends for faster and more even cooking.

Cooking See BOIL, SAUTE, STEAM.

■ **BRUSSELS SPROUTS
WITH FRESH CHESTNUTS**
The European custom of roasting chestnuts and selling them on street corners is a romantic tradition that dates from antiquity. Brussels sprouts and chestnuts make a classic pairing for a holiday side dish.

    2 pounds fresh chestnuts *or*
       1 can (16 oz) chestnuts, drained
    2 pounds fresh Brussels sprouts
    2 cups Beef Stock (see page 560)
    ¼ teaspoon salt
       Freshly ground pepper

1. On the rounded side of each chestnut, make a deep *x* through outer shell and inner shell underneath. Place chestnuts in a 2-quart saucepan, cover with water, and boil for about 15 minutes; drain. Peel shell and inner skin. (If chestnuts are too hot to handle, cool briefly, but not for more than 1 or 2 minutes or they will be hard to peel.)

2. Trim the Brussels sprouts of dried stems and leaves. Cut an *x* into stem end of each so that they will cook more evenly and be less apt to separate.

3. In a large skillet combine stock and Brussels sprouts, and bring to a boil. Reduce heat and simmer 15 minutes. Add cooked chestnuts, salt, and pepper to taste, and cook 10 minutes more.

Makes 8 servings.

BULB BASTER

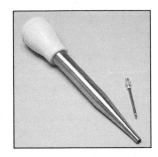

Bulb basters look like oversized eyedroppers and work in the same way. They are used to keep meats moist and flavorful by drenching them with pan juices or other liquid.

Their shafts are made of either nylon or stainless steel, both with a removable rubber bulb. Metal basters come with a long-handled cleaning brush to push out any food trapped in the narrow tip. Some are also packaged with a hollow metal injecting needle for internal basting and flavoring, which screws onto the shaft. Most basters measure about 10 inches from tip to top of bulb.

Nylon basters are considerably cheaper than metal ones; they also let you see how much liquid is drawn up into the shaft. Metal, however, is more durable and should last a lifetime. Both materials are safe to be put in a dishwasher. Remove bulb to clean. To reassemble, wet edge of shaft and bulb will slide on easily.

BURNET

A perennial herb native to Europe, burnet has rounded, toothed leaves that grow close to the ground, a tall flower stem, and rose-colored flowers. The leaves have a mild, cucumberlike flavor.

Use   Add whole burnet leaves to salads or float in iced drinks. Mince and add to mayonnaise or when using fines herbes. The leaves are a refreshing addition to salads, iced drinks, and herb vinegars.

Availability   Fresh burnet can be found in specialty markets from May through October.

Selection   Buy burnet that looks fresh and sprightly, without signs of wilting or decay.

Storage   Keep in a plastic bag in refrigerator crisper for one or two days.

Preparation   Wash just before using.

BUTTER

A solid fat, butter is made by agitating or churning cream (the fatty portion of cow's milk). It takes about 10 quarts of milk to yield 1 pound of butter. Most of the butter available commercially is sweet cream butter made from fresh (not sour) cream; it may be salted or unsalted. Sour cream butter, churned from cream that has been allowed to mature and sour slightly, is now hard to find commercially due to changing tastes; however, many who have grown up on sour cream butter prefer its pronounced flavor. It is probably still made for home use by many of those who keep dairy cows.

Although some consumers and cookbook writers use the term sweet butter to refer to unsalted butter, that term is misleading. A supermarket package labeled sweet cream butter may or may not be salted. If the butter does contain salt, it will be listed as an ingredient on the label. Unsalted butter is usually identified as such on the label. Salt adds flavor to butter and prolongs its refrigerated shelf life. However, many cooks prefer the delicate, fresh taste of unsalted butter. Vegetables sautéed in unsalted butter with a pinch of salt have a different flavor than those sautéed in salted butter. Because it is more perishable, unsalted butter is more expensive. Except in certain delicate cookies and pastries, it is rarely essential to the success of a dish.

Whipped butter is sweet cream butter, salted or unsalted, which is whipped with air or inert gas to make spreading easy.

Use   Butter adds flavor and richness to a variety of cooked foods and prepared dishes. Pouring melted butter on cooked vegetables; spreading softened butter on breads, muffins, biscuits, or other baked goods; swirling butter into a soup; and dotting butter on the top of a casserole before baking are all ways to use the nutty flavor of butter to enrich a dish.

It is the base of several important sauces, garnishes, and frostings. Both the classic Hollandaise sauce and its variations and the classic beurre blanc (white butter sauce) and its variations are butter-based sauces for savory foods. Compound Butters are classic garnishes for grilled meats, poultry, and fish. Butter provides the basis for buttercream frosting and hard sauce, the traditional accompaniment for steamed puddings.

Butter is also valued as a cooking medium. Cooking fish, meat, poultry, eggs, bread, vegetables, and batters in butter adds flavor and an appetizing brown surface.

As an ingredient in baked goods, butter adds tenderness and flavor and prolongs shelf life. Butter can also help leaven a baked product. Thoroughly creaming butter for a cake batter traps air and moisture; when cake is baked, hot air and steam expand and so does the cake. Similarly, layers of butter folded into a puff pastry dough will release steam in the oven, causing the pastry to rise.

Clarified butter has a clearer taste than whole butter and is preferred for light sauces. As it doesn't burn easily, it is often used for sautéing.

Availability   In retail markets butter is packaged in ¼-pound sticks or 1-pound blocks, wrapped in pure vegetable parchment or parchment-laminated metal foil to prevent absorption of other flavors or odors during storage. For added protection, it's usually packaged in waxed-paper cartons. Whipped butter is most commonly sold in 8-ounce tubs.

Selection   High-quality butter should have a sweet, not stale, aroma. It should have a semisoft consistency at room temperature and should not sweat, which would indicate excessive water content. It should melt smoothly on the tongue without leaving a deposit. Salted butter should not taste oversalted.

Storage   Salted butter will keep for several weeks in its original package in the coldest part of the refrigerator. Unsalted butter loses its delicate flavor after a week or two of refrigeration. Keep partially used butter in a covered dish in the refrigerator to prevent absorption of other odors. Store only what will be used within three days in the butter-storage compartment of the refrigerator. Butter freezes well—up to one month in its original package and up to nine months in freezer paper.

■ BROWN BUTTER (BEURRE NOISETTE) AND BLACK BUTTER (BEURRE NOIR)

The nutty flavor of both of these butter sauces complements poached fish, fried eggs, brains and other variety meats, green beans, cauliflower, and asparagus. To make Brown Butter, cook clarified butter over low heat until amber and fragrant. For Black Butter, cook clarified butter until very dark brown, almost black.

■ CLARIFIED BUTTER

Also known as drawn butter, clarified butter is butter with the milk solids removed. The clear yellow fat that remains can withstand high heat without burning. It will keep several weeks in the refrigerator or longer in the freezer.

To clarify butter: In a heavy pan, melt 1 pound of butter over low heat. Skim off froth and carefully pour clear yellow liquid from pan, leaving milky residue behind. Discard residue.

Makes about 1½ cups.

■ COMPOUND BUTTERS

Compound butters (also known as composed butters or flavored butters) are a mix of softened butter plus flavoring used as a sauce on grilled meats, fish, and poultry. They are also wonderful for basting. Compound butters freeze well, up to two months wrapped in waxed paper. Shape butter into a block or roll before chilling or freezing. To use, cut desired amount off block and store remainder.

Prepare butters as follows: In a medium bowl combine ingredients either by hand or with an electric mixer until well blended. Use immediately, or wrap in waxed paper.

Ancho Chile Butter

Adds heat to grilled meat, fish, or poultry. *Makes ½ cup.*

> 2 **large dried ancho chiles (or use New Mexico, pasilla, or California variety)**
> ½ **cup butter**

Cover chiles with boiling water. When they are rehydrated, drain and finely chop in a food processor or blender. Mix with butter.

Bercy Butter

Classically used for grilled beef and fish. *Makes ½ cup.*

> ½ **cup dry white wine**
> 1 **tablespoon minced shallots**
> 1 **tablespoon minced parsley**
> 1 **tablespoon fresh lemon juice**
> ¼ **cup cubed poached marrowbone**
>   **Salt and freshly ground pepper, to taste**

Boil wine and shallots until reduced to about 3 tablespoons; cool, then mix with parsley, lemon juice, marrowbone, salt and pepper.

Garlic Butter

Spread on bread or melt on meat, fish, or vegetables. *Makes ½ cup.*

> 5 **cloves garlic, peeled**
> 2 **cups water**
> ½ **cup butter, softened**

Boil garlic in the water about 5 minutes. Drain, cool, then crush garlic and mix with butter.

Herb Butter

Pair with fish, poultry, or vegetables. *Makes ½ cup.*

> 4 **tablespoons herbs of choice (chives, oregano, parsley, thyme, tarragon)**
> ½ **cup butter, softened**

Maître d'Hôtel Butter

Classically served with grilled meats, fish, or vegetables. *Makes ½ cup.*

> 2 **tablespoons chopped parsley**
> 1 **teaspoon fresh lemon juice**
> ½ **cup butter, softened**

Nut Butter

Use as a garnish for soups or toast, or as a sauce for fish or poultry. *Makes ¾ cup.*

> ½ **cup finely chopped, toasted hazelnuts, almonds, or pistachios**
> ½ **cup butter, softened**

Orange Butter

Use with fish, poultry, vegetables, breads, pancakes, or waffles. *Makes ½ cup.*

2   **teaspoons freshly squeezed orange juice**
     Grated rind of 1 orange
½   **cup butter, softened**

Red Pepper Butter

Use with fish and poultry. *Makes 1 cup.*

2   **shallots, finely chopped**
2   **large red bell peppers, peeled, seeded, and finely chopped**
1   **tablespoon balsamic vinegar**
1   **tablespoon butter**
½   **cup unsalted butter, softened**

Cook shallots, red pepper, and vinegar in 1 tablespoon butter until peppers soften; cool, then mix with butter.

Recipes and Related Information

Beurre Blanc, 518; Broiled Porterhouse Steak With Savory Butter, 41; Buttercream Frosting, 248; Butter Curler, 69; Hollandaise Sauce, 516.

BUTTER CURLER, MOLD, PADDLES, PRINT

Butter doesn't taste any better when it's curled, rolled, or pressed out of a mold, but it's certainly prettier and more fun to use. For all the butter shapes, store and serve over ice. Some of these shapes are tricky to produce. You may want to practice with each of these tools before attempting anything elaborate for a special dinner party. If you have time, prepare the shapes in quantity and freeze, well-wrapped. Then use the amount you need and leave the rest for another occasion.

BUTTER CURLER

The curved stainless steel blade has one notched edge that produces shell-like, ribbed curls of butter. To use, dip blade in warm water and draw across a block of butter that is soft enough to peel without falling apart, yet cold enough to hold its shape, but not shatter, when pressed.

BUTTER MOLD

Use this wooden cup to shape rounds of butter charmingly imprinted with a bird, flower, or other motif. Immerse mold in ice water for about 10 minutes. Fill cavity of mold with softened butter and refrigerate until butter firms. Press out butter by pushing down on plunger.

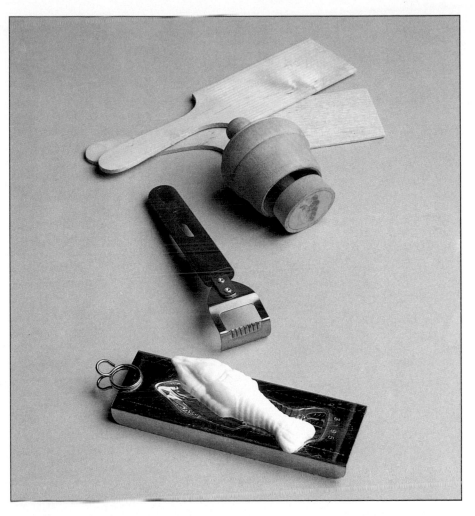

BUTTER PADDLES

To make butter balls, soak wooden paddles in water for about 10 minutes. Set a lump of cold butter about the size of a large marble on the ribbed surface of one paddle. Lay the other paddle, ribbed side down, on butter at a 90-degree angle and rotate until a ridged ball is formed.

BUTTER PRINT

This wooden or ceramic disk embosses a design on single servings of butter. Dip print in ice water, then press on a slightly softened pat or round of butter.

Whether rolled into balls, curled, or molded, shaped butter adds a decorative note to the table. Shown from top to bottom are: butter paddles, wooden mold with grape design, butter curler, metal mold with fish pattern.

BUTTERFLY, TO

This butcher's technique involves halving food horizontally, without cutting all the way through it, so that the two halves can be opened like the wings of a butterfly or the pages of a book. Often this is the first step when preparing a roast that is to be stuffed and rolled.

Braised Chinese Cabbage and Garlic, a richly seasoned vegetable side dish, is shown in a special earthenware casserole known as a clay pot or sand pot. This type of pot has been used in China for centuries for slow, gentle cooking over very low heat.

CABBAGE

One of the oldest vegetables cultivated by man, cabbage grows well in almost any climate and is appreciated in almost all of the world's cuisines. The cabbage or brassica family is quite large and includes such common vegetables as cauliflower, broccoli, mustard, kale, horseradish, radish, rutabaga, and turnip.

The members of the brassica family that go by the name cabbage are many and varied. Most are characterized by large round heads of tightly packed leaves, although some varieties are elongated, flattened, or loosely packed. Most varieties are white to light green, although red varieties exist.

Use   Raw and cooked cabbages are employed in many countries throughout the world. Raw cabbage can be shredded, dressed, and eaten as a salad, as in American cole slaw. It can be steamed, sautéed, braised, or baked, added to soups and stews, stuffed whole, or creamed. Steamed cabbage leaves can be filled with a stuffing, rolled, and braised. Thai diners often use whole cabbage leaves as a wrapper for spicy salads. Cabbage also makes a popular pickle: German sauerkraut, Japanese cabbage pickle, and the spicy Korean kimchee are all variations on the same theme.

Availability   Fresh cabbage is in the produce section all year, except for savoy cabbage, which is plentiful from fall until spring. Chinese cabbage is available at Asian markets, specialty produce markets, and well-stocked supermarkets. This entry details specific varieties of commercial importance.

Selection   See specific cabbages.

Storage   Western varieties may be stored in a plastic bag in the refrigerator crisper for at least two weeks. Chinese cabbage keeps, under similar conditions, for up to one week. Do not wash cabbages before storing.

Preparation   This varies depending upon variety; check specific types for preparation information.

Cooking   See BOIL, BRAISE, SAUTE, STEAM, STIR-FRY.

CHINESE CABBAGE

Several varieties of Chinese cabbage are available on the commercial market. Some form relatively compact, elongated heads. Others are open, leafy, flowering cabbages.

Bok Choy   This elongated, non-head-forming cabbage has long white ribs with dark green leaves; it resembles chard. Choose bok choy (also known as *pak choy* or *pak choi*) that has good color and firm white ribs; avoid wilting leaves. To prepare, trim stem and discard any discolored or ragged leaves. Bok choy is usually sliced across the ribs and stir-fried, but it may be eaten raw as a salad. A miniature version called baby bok choy or *bok choy sum* is occasionally available in specialty markets; it is particularly attractive when braised whole.

Napa Cabbage   Also called Chinese cabbage or celery cabbage, Napa cabbage has elongated, tightly furled leaves with wide white ribs and soft, pale green tips. Mild in flavor, it may be eaten raw or cooked. Choose heads that are heavy for their size, without bruised or ragged leaves; avoid very large heads, which may be bitter. To prepare, trim away any brown or bruised leaves. Slice and add raw to salads, or use in soups and stir-fries.

BRAISED CHINESE CABBAGE AND GARLIC

Braised and simmered dishes allow you to put together a Chinese dinner at a leisurely pace. The cabbage simmers unattended for the last 15 or 20 minutes, allowing plenty of time to prepare the rest of the meal. Lily buds are the dried, unopened buds of a tiger lily. Soaked in water and drained, they add a pleasant texture and slightly tart and tealike flavor to certain Chinese dishes. They are available at Asian markets, as are Chinese clay pots (see CASSEROLES AND BAKING DISHES, Chinese Clay Pot).

½ cup dried lily buds
  Oil, for stir-frying
1 large head garlic, separated into cloves and peeled
1 medium carrot, peeled and sliced on the diagonal
1 tablespoon minced fresh ginger
1 pound bok choy or other large-ribbed Chinese cabbage, cut crosswise into 1½-inch slices
2 or 3 green onions, trimmed and cut into 2-inch lengths
1 cup Rich Chicken Stock (see page 560) or duck stock, salted to taste
1 tablespoon black soy sauce

1. In a small bowl soak lily buds in lukewarm water until soft. Drain, squeezing out excess liquid. Cut or pinch off hard ends, and set lily buds aside.

2. Have ready a 1½-quart or larger Chinese clay pot (see CASSEROLES) or other flameproof, covered casserole. If using a clay pot, preheat it with hot water and dry it. Heat a wok or skillet over medium heat. Add a tablespoon or so of oil, and stir-fry garlic cloves and carrot until lightly browned. Add ginger and stir-fry until fragrant. Transfer contents of wok to casserole. Add a little more oil to wok, and stir-fry cabbage and green onions until just heated through. Transfer to pot. Add stock, soy sauce, and lily buds to wok and bring just to a boil. Pour over vegetables in pot.

3. Place casserole over medium-low heat, bring to a simmer, and cover. Simmer 15 to 20 minutes. Serve directly from pot.

Serves 6 to 8 with other dishes.

GREEN CABBAGE

The most common cabbage in American markets is the large round-headed variety with pale green or green leaves overlapping tightly around a central core. Select head cabbage that is heavy for its size, without drying around the core. To prepare, discard any wilted or damaged outer leaves and remove core with a sharp paring knife. Cabbage may be shredded and eaten raw as a salad or coleslaw; it may be steamed, braised, added to soups, or preserved as sauerkraut. The whole head may be blanched, then stuffed between the leaves and braised, or hollowed, stuffed, and baked. Individual leaves may be blanched to soften, then stuffed and braised. See Cabbage Preparation, page 76.

QUICK BUTTERED CABBAGE

This simple, basic technique is useful for cooking all green vegetables. They should be cooked until tender with just a touch of crispness; the easiest way to check is by tasting. When cooked in this way, cabbage remains bright green and has a delicate flavor. Serve it with any meat or poultry, or even with seafood.

1 medium (about 2 lb) green cabbage
¼ cup butter
  Salt and freshly ground pepper, to taste

1. Cut hard core from cabbage and discard. Rinse cabbage and cut in thin strips.

2. In a large saucepan boil enough lightly salted water to cover cabbage generously. Add cabbage and boil, uncovered, until just tender (about 5 minutes); check by tasting.

3. Drain cabbage, rinse with cold water, and drain thoroughly. Gently squeeze dry in a colander. Cabbage can be kept, covered, for 1 day in refrigerator.

4. Melt butter in a large skillet over medium heat. Add cabbage, salt, and pepper. Cook, stirring, until butter is absorbed (about 3 minutes). Taste and add more salt and pepper, if needed.

Serves 4 to 6.

STEAMED CABBAGE WEDGES

A very simple but delicious and attractive preparation for cabbage, the wedges can be dressed with a flavored butter, such as lemon butter, and served with a poultry or meat stew. See BUTTER, Compound Butters, for a selection of recipes for flavored butters. See STEAM for more information about steaming vegetables.

1 medium (about 2 lb) green cabbage

1. Trim any battered outside leaves from cabbage. Cut head in half lengthwise; cut each half into wedges, each including part of core. Steam until just tender (5 to 8 minutes).

2. Transfer wedges to a cutting board, cut away core, and transfer intact to plates (slide knife blade under wedge to lift it in one piece).

Serves 4 to 8.

Microwave Version For 1 pound of cabbage, prepare for cooking as directed in step 1. Place in a glass container and add 2 tablespoons water. Cook at 100 percent power 5 to 7 minutes. Let stand 2 minutes before dressing with lemon butter; serve.

■ BOHEMIAN CABBAGE ROLLS

Plump cabbage-wrapped packets of ground ham and pork are steamy and delicious. Serve with fluffy white rice.

  1 egg
  ⅓ cup whipping cream
  ¼ cup soft bread crumbs
  ¼ teaspoon salt
  ⅛ teaspoon *each* ground allspice, dill, and white pepper
  2 cups ground smoked pork picnic shoulder or leftover ham
  ½ pound ground pork
  1 large (2½ to 3 lb) green cabbage
    Paprika
    Flour
  2 tablespoons butter or margarine
  1 medium carrot, thinly sliced
  1 medium tomato, peeled and chopped
  1 medium onion, finely chopped
  ½ cup *each* dry white wine and tomato juice
    Sour cream and chopped parsley, for garnish

1. Preheat oven to 375° F. To prepare filling, beat egg with cream; mix in bread crumbs, salt, allspice, dill, and pepper. Lightly combine with ground meats; set aside.

2. To prepare cabbage, cut out core and carefully separate outer 6 leaves (reserve remainder for salad or other uses). Cut out thickest part at base of each leaf. Place leaves loosely in a large, deep frying pan; add just enough water to cover bottom. Cover and steam just until leaves are wilted and bright green (2 to 3 minutes). Remove cabbage from pan and drain.

3. Divide filling among the 6 prepared cabbage leaves. For each cabbage bundle, fold in sides, roll up loosely, and fasten with a toothpick (see Cabbage Preparation, page 76). Sprinkle cabbage rolls lightly with paprika, then coat with flour.

4. Pour out water from pan in which cabbage was steamed; in same pan brown cabbage rolls lightly on all sides in butter. Transfer rolls to a 2- to 3-quart casserole as they brown. Surround with carrot and tomato.

5. In same pan cook onion until it begins to brown. Mix in wine and tomato juice. Bring to a boil and cook, stirring, 3 minutes. Pour over cabbage rolls. (At this point casserole may be covered and refrigerated overnight.)

6. Bake, uncovered, for 1 hour. Uncover and continue cooking for 15 minutes longer. To serve, spoon vegetables and sauce over cabbage rolls, and top with a dollop of sour cream and a sprinkling of parsley.

Serves 6.

Food Processor Version   With slicing disk slice carrot and set aside until needed. Cut onion into quarters, put in work bowl, and with metal blade, turn motor on and off 3 or 4 times; remove from work bowl and set aside.

To grind meat: Cut lean pork and smoked pork into 1-inch pieces. Pulse motor about 10 times to chop. Add egg, cream, bread crumbs, salt, and spices. Process 5 seconds to combine.

Microwave Version   *To wilt leaves:* Place 6 cabbage leaves in a dish in the microwave oven; cover and cook at 100 percent power for about 2 minutes. Let stand, covered, if additional time is needed to soften the leaves; drain any liquid.

■ STUFFED WHOLE CABBAGE

Instead of stuffing individual cabbage leaves, try stuffing the whole head and cutting it into wedges to serve. When cabbage is sliced, the filling contrasts attractively with the subtle green of the leaves.

  1 large (2½ to 3 lb) green cabbage
  1 small onion, diced
  1 clove garlic, minced
  2 tablespoons vegetable oil
  4 tablespoons unsalted butter
  ½ pound ground veal
  ½ pound ham, minced
  3 sprigs parsley, minced
  ½ teaspoon salt
  ⅛ teaspoon freshly ground pepper
  1 egg
  ¼ cup Beef Stock (see page 560)
  ½ cup soft bread crumbs
  ½ cup whipping cream

1. Remove tough outer leaves from cabbage, reserve 2 or 3 to cover top, and discard remainder. Slice off top of cabbage and scoop out interior, leaving a shell about ¾ inch thick and a cavity approximately 4 inches in diameter (see Cabbage Preparation, page 76). Place cabbage in a 4-quart saucepan; cover with boiling water, reduce heat, and simmer until just tender (about 20 minutes). Drain upside down in a colander; let cool.

2. Preheat oven to 350° F. In a large skillet sauté onion and garlic in oil and 2 tablespoons butter over medium heat until soft but not browned (about 5 minutes). Add veal and ham, and sauté, stirring constantly and breaking up clumps as they form, until thoroughly cooked (about 10 minutes).

3. Mix in parsley, salt, pepper, egg, Beef Stock, bread crumbs, and cream. Cook briefly (2 to 3 minutes), stirring to combine. Stuff filling into hollowed cabbage. Cover stuffed cabbage with reserved cabbage leaves.

4. Grease a 3-quart casserole with remaining 2 tablespoons butter and set stuffed cabbage in dish. Cover casserole tightly with lid or aluminum foil and bake 90 minutes. Remove from oven, let rest 10 minutes, discard loose top leaves, and cut into 6 to 8 wedges to serve.

Serves 6 to 8.

CHOUCROUTE GARNI

Alsace is a region of France near Germany. Alsatian food often reflects both French and German cuisines. *Choucroute* is French for sauerkraut: the word gives this dish its name—sauerkraut with accompaniments. This recipe is easily made ahead for a gathering. Bring the piping hot casserole to the table and serve guests some meat, potatoes, and sauerkraut. Accompany with a glass of Riesling or dry white wine. Many cooks reserve duck, goose, or chicken fat to use here in place of vegetable oil.

    1   tart apple, diced
    2   medium onions, diced
    4   tablespoons vegetable oil
    ½   cup parsley, minced
    4   slices bacon, diced
   10   juniper berries, crushed
    1   teaspoon thyme
    1   bay leaf
   1⅔ cups Chicken Stock (see page 560)
   1⅓ cups Riesling or dry white wine
    3   to 4 skinless ham hocks
    2   pounds sauerkraut, rinsed
   12   small potatoes
    6   veal sausages
    3   smoked pork chops or pork steaks

1. In a 6-quart Dutch oven, sauté apple and onions in oil over medium heat until soft (10 minutes). Stir in parsley, bacon, juniper berries, thyme, bay leaf, stock, wine, and ham hocks. Cover and simmer 45 minutes.

2. Rinse sauerkraut in colander under cool water; pat dry. Scrub potatoes and cut each in half. Add sauerkraut, potatoes, and veal sausages to Dutch oven. Stir to combine, cover, and simmer another 15 minutes.

3. Remove pork chop meat from bone and cut into 2-inch cubes. Stir in pork cubes, cover, and cook another 40 minutes. Make sure each portion has a serving of meat, potatoes, and sauerkraut.

Serves 8 to 10.

Recipes: Crispy Coleslaw, 506; New England Boiled Dinner, 42.

RED CABBAGE

Ranging from reddish purple to dark purple, the firm, round red cabbage has tightly packed, overlapping leaves around a white central core. It is available the year around. Select compact cabbages that feel heavy for their size and do not have wilted outer leaves. To prepare, discard any damaged outer leaves and remove core with a sharp paring knife. Red cabbage may be pickled or eaten raw as a salad, braised, steamed, or sautéed. Adding vinegar or lemon juice to the cooking water (about 1 tablespoon per cup of water) will help preserve the bright color.

RED CABBAGE WITH APPLES

Apples and cabbage are a traditional pairing of flavors, sparked by a sweet-and-sour mixture of cider vinegar and brown sugar. Serve this alongside bratwurst or with any pork or beef dish.

    2   tablespoons vegetable oil
    1   onion, coarsely chopped
    ¼   cup cider vinegar
    2   tablespoons brown sugar or honey
        Salt and freshly ground pepper, to taste
    1   green apple, cored and thinly sliced
    1   small red cabbage, coarsely shredded

1. In a large frying pan, heat oil. Add onion and sauté until softened (5 minutes). Add vinegar, sugar, and salt and pepper to taste; stir to mix.

2. Add apple and cabbage. Bring liquid to a boil, reduce heat to medium, cover, and cook until cabbage wilts (about 10 minutes). Stir occasionally to coat cabbage with vinegar-sugar mixture.

Serves 4.

Microwave Version Prepare cabbage for cooking. Place shredded cabbage in a glass container and add 2 tablespoons water. Cover and cook at 100 percent power for 6 to 8 minutes. Add to recipe in step 2, after apple has cooked. Toss to coat with vinegar-sugar mixture.

Red Cabbage With Apples is part of a traditional German wurst supper. Shown with the cabbage dish are pan-fried bratwurst, sautéed onion, Spätzle (see page 190), and dark pumpernickel bread.

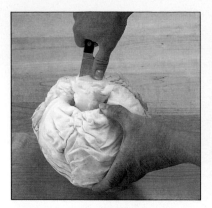  

CABBAGE PREPARATION

Coring cabbage   *Insert a sharp knife at edge of core, angled so knife tip points to center of cabbage head. Cut completely around core.*

Cabbage shell   *Remove any damaged outer leaves. Slice off about one fourth of top of cabbage. With a spoon scoop out center of head, leaving enough cabbage leaves to form a shell with walls about ¾ inch thick.*

Cabbage rolls   *Cut away a V-shaped piece from thickened base of each cabbage leaf. Lay leaves on work surface, with edges curling up. Set filling in center of leaf, fold in sides, then roll up from bottom to close package.*

◼ BUDAPEST BORSCHT

Developed in Eastern Europe, Budapest Borscht is a combination soup and stew and makes a substantial winter food. Serve with homemade whole-grain bread as a colorful first course or light supper.

  1½ **pounds red cabbage**
    5 **beets**
    5 **small boiling potatoes**
    6 **plum tomatoes**
  1½ **tablespoons vegetable oil**
    1 **onion, diced**
    2 **cloves garlic, finely chopped**
    6 **cups water**
   ½ **cup red wine vinegar**
    1 **tablespoon honey**
    3 **tablespoons parsley**
    1 **teaspoon thyme**
    1 **bay leaf**
  1½ **teaspoons dried dill**
    1 **tablespoon Hungarian paprika**
    2 **teaspoons kosher salt**
   ¼ **teaspoon freshly ground pepper**
   ½ **cup sour cream, for garnish**
    4 **tablespoons fresh dill, for garnish**

1. Slice cabbage into ¼-inch strips. Peel beets with a sharp knife and cut into julienne strips. Peel potatoes and cut in half. Peel and seed tomatoes; cut into quarters.

2. In a 4-quart saucepan, heat oil. Add onion and garlic. Sauté for 5 minutes. Add cabbage, beets, potatoes, tomatoes, the water, vinegar, honey, parsley, thyme, bay leaf, dill, paprika, salt, and pepper. Bring to boil and reduce heat. Simmer for 25 minutes. Serve with a dollop of sour cream and a garnish of chopped dill.

Makes 8 cups, 6 to 8 servings.

SAVOY CABBAGE

A large head-forming variety with crinkly, pale green leaves, savoy cabbage is especially popular among European cooks. It is milder and more tender than regular green cabbage, making it particularly suitable for salads. It may also be steamed, braised, stuffed, or added to soups. Savoy cabbage is available from fall until spring; select solid heads without signs of yellowing. To prepare, discard any ragged or discolored leaves and remove core with a sharp paring knife.

Recipes: Boiled Dinner Bolognese, 530.

◼ RED-AND-GREEN CABBAGE SLAW

Bright with slivers of red and green peppers, this cabbage salad has a zippy oil and vinegar dressing.

  1 **small savoy cabbage (about 1½ lb), thinly shredded**
 ½ **cup *each* seeded and slivered red and green bell pepper**
 ½ **cup *each* finely chopped parsley and thinly sliced green onions**
  2 **tablespoons vinegar**
1½ **teaspoons salt**
 ½ **teaspoon celery seed**
 ½ **cup white vinegar**
 ⅓ **cup vegetable oil**

1. In a large bowl mix cabbage, pepper, parsley, and onion. For dressing, shake (in covered jar) or stir together sugar, salt, celery seed, vinegar, and oil until sugar dissolves.

2. Pour dressing over cabbage mixture; mix lightly. Cover and refrigerate 30 minutes to 3 hours.

Serves 6 to 8.

CAKE

Both in our culture and throughout the world, cakes have a wonderful, long-standing tradition. In all sorts of celebrations, cakes play a central role—whether it's a cupcake with a single shining candle or a multitiered, elaborately trimmed bridal confection.

Although storebought cakes and those made from a mix have a place in lives that are increasingly busy and hectic, there is no substitute for the pleasure derived from baking in your own kitchen with the freshest, best-quality ingredients. Baking is one of the most satisfying and enjoyable ways to put your creative powers to work—and a light, richly flavored homemade cake is always appreciated and admired.

TYPES OF CAKES

Cakes are made from a thin batter, which is a mixture of flour and a liquid in approximately equal amounts, plus eggs or other leavening or flavoring ingredients, and often fat. In this country cakes are classified either by how they are leavened or by whether or not the batter contains fat.

Cakes rise because steam and gases force the batter to expand in the presence of heat. The liquid in the batter converts to steam in the oven, and bubbles of gas develop during the mixing process and during baking. The bubbles are created in two ways. A leavening agent such as baking powder, baking soda, or yeast produces carbon dioxide in the presence of moisture. Other bubbles are created by beating air into the ingredients, as when sugar and butter are creamed, when sugar and eggs are beaten together, or when egg whites are beaten separately and folded into the batter.

Angel food cake, sponge cake, and meringues are lightened by an airy foam of beaten eggs. Cakes that depend chiefly on carbon dioxide are the familiar American layer cakes, cupcakes, and dense tube cakes, and the yeast-leavened European specialties—French baba and savarin, and the Alsatian *Kugelhopf*.

Recipes that use carbon dioxide (except for yeast cakes) almost always begin by vigorously beating together butter and sugar (creaming). These are known as butter, shortened, or creamed cakes—cakes made with fat. They include layer cakes, pound cakes, and fruitcakes.

As in all cooking, the lines between these categories often blur. Chiffon cake and génoise are hybrids. Like an angel food cake, a chiffon cake incorporates beaten egg whites, but it also uses baking powder and is made with vegetable oil, a fat. Génoise batter is lightened with a whole-egg foam and enriched with melted butter. Pound cakes, perhaps the classic shortened cake, traditionally used 1 pound each of butter, sugar, eggs, and flour, and were leavened only by creaming air into the butter-sugar mixture. Today we are less lavish with the rich ingredients and prefer a lighter textured pound cake, so baking powder appears in many of these recipes.

Tortes, or flourless cakes, are like a classic sponge cake, but part or all of the flour has been replaced by ground nuts, cookie or bread crumbs, or a combination.

INGREDIENTS FOR CAKES: WHAT EACH DOES

Cakes are balanced formulas and each ingredient plays a role in the cake-making process. Sugar and fat tenderize the toughening action of flour and eggs. Liquid ingredients balance dry. For each type of cake, certain ingredients must be included, but the proportions can vary somewhat without affecting the quality of the final product. New recipes are created just that way—by starting with a basic recipe and changing amounts slightly or by substituting one ingredient for another.

Flour, sugar, milk, butter, eggs, nuts, raisins, fruits, and spices are just some of the ingredients that are transformed into cakes and pastries of all sorts. Using the freshest, best-quality ingredients will make a noticeable difference in the final product.

Flour Along with eggs, flour gives a cake its structure by forming an elastic network that traps expanding gas and steam. Use cake flour when indicated for a lighter, more tender cake. Sifting is recommended for most cakes, especially for more delicate ones such as angel food, sponge, and chiffon. Sifting results in a finer end product; it aerates the flour, removes specks of foreign material, and breaks up lumps. Cake flour should always be sifted; follow recipe directions about sifting before or after measuring. If you wish to substitute all-purpose flour for cake flour in a recipe, substitute 2 tablespoons cornstarch for the same amount of flour per 1 cup cake flour specified. It's unnecessary to sift all-purpose flour before measuring, although some older recipes may call for it. It's a good idea to sift after measuring to blend the flour with the other dry ingredients. For more information about sifting, see FLOUR.

Fat From fat, a cake gets tenderness, richness, and fluidity. Select a fat that is plastic (pliable) and easily beaten. Butter is preferred for its flavor, but is limited in the range of temperatures at which it can be beaten. Hydrogenated vegetable shortening is plastic at a wider range of temperatures than butter, but is tasteless. Some recipes compromise by calling for half shortening (for its superior creaming ability) and half butter (for excellent flavor). Butter creams best at room temperature. Let chilled butter warm on the counter until it is cool to the touch, but soft enough that a finger pressed into the surface leaves an impression. When oil is specified, use a light one such as safflower oil. Lard should be avoided because it doesn't cream well.

Sugar To balance the toughness contributed by flour and eggs, sugar is added to the batter to tenderize and, of course, to sweeten. When sugar is creamed with fat, its crystalline structure carries air into the mixture and contributes to the volume of a cake. Use granulated sugar unless otherwise indicated. Angel food cake recipes often specify superfine sugar which, like cake flour, is finely granulated and makes a finer crumb.

Eggs For foam cakes, eggs are the primary or only source of leavening and, along with flour, provide structure for all baked goods. They are a source of liquid and function as emulsifiers, which make the batter more uniform and stable. Unless otherwise directed, always use eggs graded large. Separate eggs when cold. Use whole eggs, egg yolks, and egg whites at room temperature. If desired, eggs may be measured by volume and weight. An egg is two-thirds white and one-third yolk. See EGG, Beating Eggs, for information about beating whole eggs, egg yolks, and egg whites.

Liquid In a cake batter, liquid adds moisture, which converts to steam with heat. Common liquids for cakes include milk, cream, sour cream, buttermilk, yogurt, fruit juices, and water. Recipes for foam cakes don't require liquids, other than what is provided by eggs or, in the case of chiffon cakes, by oil.

Acid Cream of tartar and lemon juice, both acids, help to stabilize an egg foam until it sets in the oven. Cream of tartar is commonly beaten into egg whites for this reason, especially if they are not whipped in a copper bowl. Acids help develop a finer texture and more tender crumb; for an angel food cake, they enhance its characteristic white color.

ABOUT CAKE PANS AND OTHER EQUIPMENT

By custom, an angel food cake has a hole in its center and a layer cake is round. We expect to see them that way and so most are, but angel food cakes in loaf form taste just as wonderful, as do square layers. The point is that any one of a number of baking pans will do a particular job well. Don't be compelled to buy every specialty pan you come across unless you have a lot of storage space, you bake a particular cake often, or different shapes appeal to you. Whichever you choose is up to you as long as the pan meets these criteria: it is of the proper volume and height for the recipe (regardless of shape); it is of good quality; it is made of a material that will conduct heat evenly and well. For information on specific pans and materials, see BAKING PANS, FOR BATTER AND DOUGH and MATERIALS FOR COOKWARE.

Other equipment useful for cake making includes such kitchen staples as wooden spoons, spatulas, measuring spoons and cups, mixing bowls, cooling racks, and a quality portable or stand electric mixer with a strong motor. Additional specialized tools, particularly those used for cake decorating—pastry bags, combs, turntables—are optional. See CAKE AND PASTRY TOOLS.

PREPARING PANS

Greasing and flouring baking pans aren't always necessary, but most recipes suggest that you do because it is less likely that the cake will stick. Some recipes call for greasing the bottom and sides, some only the bottom. Some recipes recommend adding a lining of parchment or waxed paper, others don't. Most call for dusting a pan with flour, but a few might suggest using sugar or crumbs. This powdery coat develops a thin, crisp crust and also keeps a cake from absorbing fat from the pan. Follow the directions in the recipe. If you are using a nonstick pan, grease and flour anyway if you are instructed to do so.

A few cakes need special treatment. Dense butter cakes such as pound cakes and heavy fruitcakes, which must bake slowly and for a long time, are baked in greased and paper-lined pans to protect the sides of the cake from overbrowning. Many bakers prefer parchment paper because it can withstand high oven temperatures and is very easy to peel off. Rich batters (those with a lot of sugar or eggs) and those with a large quantity of fruit should bake in greased and floured pans, even pans with nonstick interiors. Angel food cakes and chiffon cakes bake in ungreased pans so the delicate batter can cling to the sides as it rises.

When greasing pans, only a thin layer of fat is necessary, but it should be evenly applied. Use butter, solid shortening, oil, or vegetable cooking spray, and apply with a paper towel, pastry brush, or fingers. To make a paper liner, use bottom of cake pan as a guide, and trace around pan onto a piece of parchment or waxed paper. Cut paper to fit, and place it on the greased bottom of the pan. Grease the paper. If using paper, don't flour pan until after paper is in place. For dusting, place a few tablespoons flour, sugar, or other powder in greased pan, and tilt pan in each direction until entire surface is covered with a thin layer of flour. Invert pan and tap it on a counter or with your fist to remove excess flour (see PREPARING PAN FOR BAKING).

FILLING PANS

Cake batter should fill the pan from one-half to three-quarters full depending upon cake. The pan should never be so full that when the batter rises it overflows. For batters that rise high, such as angel food and sponge cakes, use deeper pans and less batter per pan. For heavier batters such as layer and pound cakes, pans are filled two-thirds to three-quarters full. When dividing a batter among several pans, as for layer cakes, use a ladle or spoon, rather than pouring from the mixing bowl, in order to maintain control and divide batter equally.

ABOUT BAKING CAKES

Place a cake in the oven as soon as possible. Leavening agents begin their action even before a cake is baked and need oven heat to finish the job or they will lose some of their power. Always bake in a preheated oven. Turn oven

SUCCESSFUL CAKE BAKING

If you are well organized and have thoroughly read the recipe before you begin, you will find baking a pleasure and will produce more successful baked products. Look up any unfamiliar terms or techniques. Assemble all of the equipment and ingredients in advance (a baking pan is a good catchall; the French call this process *mis en place*—all in place). Measure all ingredients precisely and carefully; have them at the specified temperature and in the condition indicated in the recipe. Finally, get into the habit of checking oven temperature and turning on the oven before you do anything else. Even the best bakers fail to achieve perfect results every time. Consult the following if you experience difficulties.

IF BUTTER CAKE BATTER CURDLES
- Each egg was not sufficiently mixed in before the next one was added.
- Batter was beaten at too high a speed. If it starts to curdle, ignore it or reduce the mixer speed to medium or medium-low and add 1 tablespoon flour per egg.

IF CAKE FALLS IN THE MIDDLE
- Batter was overbeaten, creating excess aeration which cake was unable to contain.
- Too much sugar was added to the batter.
- Too much baking powder was added.
- Too much liquid was added.
- Cake was undercooked.
- Oven door was opened before cake was set or cake was disturbed because oven door was closed with too much force.

IF CAKE PEAKS IN THE CENTER
- A hard (high-gluten) flour was used instead of soft flour (cake flour).
- Batter was overbeaten after flour was added. (This overactivates the gluten in the flour, creating a tough cake.)
- Oven was too hot. Cake rose too quickly.

IF CAKE IS TOUGH, FLAT, AND HEAVY
- Batter was underbeaten, causing insufficient aeration.
- Not enough sugar was added.
- Not enough baking powder was added.

on at least 10 to 15 minutes before you need to use it. Baking at the proper temperature and maintaining that temperature throughout the process are critical to the success of the final product. Cakes need to bake relatively fast to give their structure some rigidity. Without this framework, they would rise and then collapse because the leavening gases could not be maintained. Avoid opening the oven door during the first half of baking, which is the rising period. If the door is opened, the temperature will drop and the cake will fall; if you must open the door, do so quickly and close it gently without banging it shut.

Know your oven and how it bakes. Test it at several different temperatures with an oven thermometer to see if it is accurately calibrated. If it is off by 25° F or less, you can compensate by raising or lowering the oven temperature. If it is off by as much as 50° F, have it recalibrated. If you have two ovens and you often use both at one time for baking, you may find it convenient and helpful to leave an oven thermometer in each oven. See THERMOMETER.

In a standard oven, bake cakes on the center rack unless otherwise directed. Leave 1 to 2 inches between pans, and between pans and walls of oven. Try not to bake on more than one rack at a time; if you do, the goods baked on the bottom rack will tend to burn because they are close to the heating element and the heat will reflect from the pan on the upper shelf. If you are baking in quantity and need to employ more than one rack, use the middle rack and stagger the pans; once the cake is set rotate pans so they will bake evenly.

You can bake any of the recipes in this book in a convection oven, but you may need to adjust the oven temperature or baking time; see manufacturer's instructions.

USING A MICROWAVE OVEN
Baking cakes in a microwave oven produces mixed results. They won't brown and can bake unevenly; however, they can be moist, airy, and light, and they can have greater volume than those baked in a conventional oven because they don't develop a crust and therefore can rise more. The best cakes for baking in a microwave are rich cakes made with whole eggs, pudding cakes, and cakes made with oil. Boxed cake mixes also can be baked in a microwave with good results—just omit one egg when making the mix to improve texture and volume.

Round and ring shapes bake most evenly. Cakes often bake more evenly on the bottom when elevated on a plastic trivet or inverted glass dish. Rotating the cake dish once or twice, a quarter to a half turn, also facilitates even baking, especially in older ovens.

Experiment with several recipes to see if cakes from a microwave are to your liking; that's the best way to determine which ones are suited for this type of cooking.

WHEN IS THE CAKE DONE?
Experienced cooks rely not only on baking time to know when a cake is ready to come out of the oven, but also on how it looks, smells, sounds, and feels. A cake is done when it springs back lightly when touched in the center with a fingertip and when it begins to pull away from the sides of the pan. It will have developed an aroma, and the popping and sizzling of the batter will have slowed down (if these sounds have stopped completely, cake may be overdone). Start checking about 10 minutes before the end of the recommended baking time. A cake tester, toothpick, or wooden skewer should come out clean when inserted into the center of the cake.

COOLING AND TURNING OUT OF THE PAN
Cool the cake as directed in the recipe. Sponge cakes and butter cakes are often left to sit in their pans on wire cooling racks for 5 or 10 minutes before turning out. During this brief period they will continue to shrink from the sides of the pan. In addition, steam builds between cake and pan, which will help release the cake. Before unmolding, run a knife around the cake to loosen it from the sides of the pan, then sandwich it between two cooling racks and invert. Remove pan, sandwich cake gently between two racks, and flip again. Cool completely at room temperature before icing or storing.

Angel food cakes and chiffon cakes cool by hanging upside down in their pans. Set the angel food cake pan on its legs, or invert and place on the neck of a bottle or a funnel. Chiffon cakes in their pans can be inverted and set directly on a cooling rack because they don't rise as high as angel food cakes and won't be crushed by the rack.

STORING AND FREEZING CAKES

Cakes with fat, such as butter cakes and chiffon cakes, have the best keeping qualities; sponge cakes taste freshest when eaten the day they are baked or within a day or two. Ideally, cakes should be frozen unfrosted and unfilled, then frosted or filled after thawing. Butter-based icings can be frozen successfully for up to two months in rigid containers; thaw in the refrigerator, then bring to room temperature to make spreadable. If icing curdles during thawing, add a little hot, clarified butter and whip at high speed until it comes together. Icings based on egg whites or whipped cream do not freeze well. If you must frost a cake before freezing, select a butter-based icing. Always allow cake to cool completely before freezing. Certain spices, such as nutmeg and cloves, intensify in flavor when they are frozen, so use slightly less than the amount called for in the recipe.

Wrap cakes well with plastic wrap and aluminum foil, date, and freeze for time indicated. Cakes stored longer than the recommended period will suffer a loss of quality but will still be safe to eat. The freezing times are for goods stored at 0° F. Storing foods at temperatures higher than 0° F shortens the storage period considerably.

Angel, Chiffon, and Sponge Cakes Wrap first in plastic wrap and then airtight in a plastic storage bag: angel food cake—four to five days; chiffon cake—up to two weeks; sponge cake—two to three days. To freeze, follow directions for butter cakes. For added protection, store in a box or rigid container, sealing edges with freezer tape; label. Freeze unfrosted cakes up to six months, frosted cakes up to two months.

Butter and Pound Cakes Wrap well and store airtight, five to seven days. To freeze unfrosted, wrap, label, and date. Freeze for up to four months. To thaw, loosen wrapping and thaw at room temperature. To freeze a frosted cake, chill on a tray in freezer (uncovered) until firm. Wrap, label, and date. Freeze for up to two months. To thaw, remove wrapping and thaw at room temperature or in refrigerator.

Cheesecakes Refrigerate, loosely covered with aluminum foil, up to three days. To freeze, chill on a tray in freezer (uncovered) until firm. Wrap, label, and date. For added protection, store in a box or rigid container, sealing edges with freezer tape; label. Freeze for up to four months. Thaw in wrapping in refrigerator.

Fruitcakes Store in an airtight container; will keep up to three weeks when cut; freeze after that. To freeze, wrap, label, and date. Freeze for up to 12 months. Thaw in wrapping at room temperature.

FREEZING CAKE BATTER

As a timesaver, batter for butter cakes can be frozen, unbaked, for up to four weeks, and baked just as it comes from the freezer.

Prepare batter and spoon into pan in which it will be baked, first lining pan with heavy-duty foil. Freeze, uncovered, until solid (this usually takes 6 to 12 hours). Remove batter from pan, wrap it completely, label and date package, and return it to freezer. To bake, grease baking pan in which batter was frozen, peel away foil around batter, and place batter back in pan. Add at least 5 to 10 minutes to normal baking time; cake is done when a wooden pick inserted in center comes out clean.

Proper packaging is important for protecting batters during storage. Package materials must be resistant to both moisture and air. Aluminum foil is excellent; use either heavy-duty foil or a double thickness of regular foil. Heavy plastic bags designed for freezer storage are suitable for packaging cupcakes. Be sure to check the label on the package—if it does not say the bags are suitable for freezing, choose another bag.

Air pockets between food and package material collect moisture, resulting in frost and freezer burn. When wrapping frozen batters, press out as much air as you can and mold wrappings as close to food as possible. To extract air from plastic bags, insert a drinking straw in the opening, squeeze the opening shut around the straw, inhale to draw out air, and fasten tightly. Label and date all packages.

Most batters will keep up to four weeks at 0° F. If your freezer doesn't maintain a temperature of 0° F (and many combination refrigerator-freezers don't), do not keep the batter frozen more than two weeks.

CAKE DECORATION

Some cakes look and taste fine when unadorned. Others require a finish, whether simple or elaborate. The process of cake decoration ranges from the texturing of icing spread on a cake to the application of intricate patterns. When cakes are baked to celebrate an occasion or event, you can tailor their shape and decorations accordingly. Rectangular cakes are good picnic fare because they can be simply iced and easily carried. The same cake base can be baked in layers and elegantly adorned with buttercream rosettes or piped scrolls to serve at a dinner party. See FROSTING, ICING, AND FILLING for specific techniques.

FINISHING THE CAKE

The outside of a cake can be covered with one of the following treatments.

Almond Paste Almond paste or marzipan can be rolled out and used to form the top layer or outside covering of a cake. Almond paste can also be molded or shaped to form cake decorations (roses, flowers, leaves, stems, animals, fruits).

Confectioners' Sugar For a simple, quick finish, sift a light layer of confectioners' sugar over the cake. Create a design by laying a stencil, a fancy paper doily, a cutout snowflake, or strips of paper on the surface of the cake. Sift confectioners' sugar over the pattern, and carefully

With an easy-to-make paper piping cone (see page 246), you can decorate any cake, cookie, or pastry with all types of designs or messages. Lines 1 through 4 are typical borders. Line 5 shows a sample of script. Line 6 is a classic repeating design.

This slice of Devil's Food Cake with Chocolate Buttercream Frosting is an irresistible temptation. The recipe is on page 86.

remove pattern to reveal design. Powdered cocoa may also be used alone or in combination with confectioners' sugar to create contrasting designs.

Glazes A glaze is thinner than an icing. It is often poured over a cake rather than spread on. Cakes can be covered with a jelly glaze, a chocolate glaze, a confectioners' sugar glaze, or a fondant icing glaze.

Icing Applying icing in a smooth, flat layer is a common decorating technique. A textured surface (swirls, peaks, lines) can be created with a flat metal spatula or knife. Icing can also be applied in a smooth layer and textured with a comb scraper (serrated metal triangle) to create grooves. Of the many kinds of icings, some must be spread on with a spatula or knife, and others can be piped on with a pastry bag and tip.

TYPICAL CAKE DECORATIONS

These decorations are applied to the icing, glaze, or other surface covering on the cake to create patterns and add complementary flavor.

Chocolate Melted and tempered chocolate can be used in many ways. Make chocolate curls, rolls, and ruffles out of melted chocolate, wrap the cake in a paper-thin chocolate ribbon, or pipe chocolate through a pastry bag onto an iced or plain cake. See CHOCOLATE for directions; see FROSTING, ICING, AND FILLING for information on using a pastry bag.

Cookie Crumbs Finely crushed cookies can be patted around the sides of the cake to add flavor, color, and texture to the icing.

Fresh Fruit Either whole or sliced fresh fruit can be arranged decoratively on top of a cake. Fresh fruit is usually brushed with a thin jelly glaze to make it shine.

Miscellaneous Decorations Candied (glacé) orange, lemon, or citrus peel (chop candied peel, or cut in julienne strips, or dip pieces in melted chocolate); dried fruits (raisins, currants); crystallized violets, roses, or mimosas (available from well-stocked cookware shops or stores specializing in equipment for cake decorating); candied coffee beans; silver balls, gold leaf, and crystal sugar; preserved ginger; a cloth or paper ribbon tied around the cake after icing is firm; fresh flowers or leaves (free from harmful sprays).

Nuts Finely chopped, coarsely chopped, slivered, or sliced nuts, nut halves, or whole nuts can be used. Whole or halved nuts can be dipped in caramel or chocolate. Nuts taste and look best when lightly toasted in the oven before they are used to decorate a cake.

Sauces Serve a sauce on the side or set cake slices in a pool of sauce. Chocolate sauce, fruit sauce, purée (raspberry or strawberry), and vanilla custard sauce (*crème anglaise*) are good choices.

SLICING AND SERVING

Let the cake cool before attempting to slice it. Use a sharp knife with a thin blade. For iced cakes, clean the knife after each cut to remove accumulated frosting. Angel food cakes and sponge cakes are pliable and hard to slice. For these cakes, a serrated knife works best. Cut with a sawing motion; don't press down as you slice or you will compress the cake.

A cake slice can be presented lying down on its side or standing up (when possible or when more attractive). Try to include part of the top decoration, if any, in each serving.

◼ ANGEL FOOD CAKE

This foam cake is pure white because only egg whites—no yolks, no fat—are used. Food for angels, indeed! If the idea of 14 egg whites overwhelms you, remember that they freeze well. Stockpile them in your freezer when preparing recipes that call for egg yolks only. See EGG, Storage for freezing information. Work quickly and gently when making an angel food cake. If the batter is overmixed, it will lose volume and the final product will be tough. Remember that the cake must cool upside down. For a light summer dessert, accompany cake slices with fruit sauce or sliced fresh fruit. Slices of angel food cake make delicious French toast.

  1½ **cups sifted cake flour**
  1¾ **cups sugar**
  14 **egg whites**
      Pinch salt
   1 **teaspoon cream of tartar (optional)**
   2 **teaspoons vanilla extract**
  ½ **teaspoon almond extract**
   1 **teaspoon fresh lemon juice**

1. Preheat oven to 300° F. Sift flour again into a dry mixing bowl. Sift sugar into a separate bowl and set both bowls aside.

2. In a copper or stainless steel bowl, beat egg whites to soft peaks; add salt when whites are just foamy (if bowl is stainless steel, add cream of tartar at this point as well). Gently fold in sugar with a rubber spatula; fold in flour in 2 batches, then add vanilla and almond extracts and lemon juice. When all is completely incorporated, pour batter into a 10-inch tube pan and smooth top.

3. Bake until cake is a pale, creamy brown color, top springs back when gently touched with finger, and a wooden skewer inserted in center comes out clean (about 1 hour). Cool upside down in pan. (If pan doesn't have its own feet, invert pan over the neck of a bottle or balance on 4 small ramekins.)

4. To serve, gently remove from pan, releasing sides with a knife. Decorate and serve as desired.

Serves 10 to 12.

ROLLING A SPONGE CAKE

Turn cake out onto kitchen towel lined with a piece of sugar-dusted parchment paper; carefully roll.

When cool, gently unroll and spread with filling, leaving a narrow margin of bare cake all around. If cake is covered completely, the filling will be forced out of the cake as it is rerolled.

Carefully roll again and decorate. For a special effect, shown here, roll partway; pipe whipped cream rosettes along edge and top with raspberries. Dust with confectioners' sugar, if desired.

◼ BASIC SPONGE CAKE

This extremely versatile cake has a light, soft, and fine crumb. Sponge cakes depend on egg yolks and egg whites for leavening, each beaten and incorporated separately. Simple garnishes are best—such as fresh fruit, whipped cream, ice cream, or light frostings. To layer, halve cake with a serrated knife.

    6 eggs, separated
    1 cup sugar
    2 teaspoons vanilla extract
       Pinch salt
    ½ teaspoon cream of tartar (optional)
    1 cup cake flour, sifted

1. Preheat oven to 350° F. Lightly grease and flour an 8- or 9-inch-diameter cake pan. Line bottom with parchment paper.

2. In a large bowl beat egg yolks to break them up; add ¾ cup sugar and continue to beat until mixture falls from beater in a ribbon and leaves a slowly dissolving trail on surface (ribbon stage). Beat in vanilla.

3. In a separate large copper or stainless steel bowl, beat egg whites until just foamy; add salt (if bowl is stainless steel, add cream of tartar at this point as well). Beat whites to soft peaks; add remaining ¼ cup sugar and beat until stiff, glossy peaks form.

4. Fold flour into yolk mixture in three stages. Then fold in one third of whites to lighten. Very gently fold in remaining whites; fill prepared pan with batter.

5. Bake until pale gold color, top springs back when pressed gently with finger, and a wooden skewer inserted in center comes out clean (20 to 30 minutes). Cool in pan 10 minutes, then turn out onto rack and cool completely. Decorate as desired.

Serves 8.

Chocolate Sponge Cake   Substitute ¼ cup cocoa powder for ¼ cup of the flour.

◼ BASIC SPONGE CAKE ROLL

Cake rolls are not difficult to prepare and decorate, and are always very pretty when served. Typical of sponge cakes, they are appealing when simply filled and dusted with confectioners' sugar or cocoa powder. For a more substantial filling, use any flavor of buttercream frosting.

    4 eggs, separated
    ⅔ cup sugar
    1½ teaspoons vanilla extract
       Pinch salt
    ¼ teaspoon cream of tartar (optional)
    ⅔ cup cake flour, sifted

1. Preheat oven to 350° F. Lightly grease and flour an 11- by 15-inch jelly-roll pan. Line bottom with parchment paper.

2. Prepare according to directions for Basic Sponge Cake through step 4. Fill prepared jelly-roll pan and bake until top springs back when gently pressed with finger (about 15 minutes). Cool in pan 5 minutes.

3. Turn cake out onto a kitchen towel covered with a sheet of parchment paper that has been dusted with confectioners' sugar, superfine sugar, or cocoa powder (depending on recipe). Remove paper from cake bottom and trim crusts all around. Carefully roll up in parchment, wrap with kitchen towel to secure, and cool completely on a wire rack.

4. Gently unroll, then spread with filling of choice to within 1 inch of edges. Reroll carefully; finish as desired.

Serves 6 to 8.

Chocolate Sponge Cake Roll   Substitute 3 tablespoons cocoa powder for 3 tablespoons of the flour.

Elegant, sugar-dusted Ladyfingers are a classic example of the pastry maker's art. To shape them into even lengths, the cake batter is piped onto a baking sheet with a pastry bag.

■ LADYFINGERS

These soft, spongy fingers of cake are probably best known as the shell for Charlotte Russe (see page 170). They are also delicious eaten alone. Quick to make, they store well in an airtight container for one week. For longer storage and in damp, wet weather, they should be frozen.

> 1   cup cake flour
>   Pinch salt
> 4   eggs, separated
> ½   cup sugar
> ¼   teaspoon cream of tartar (optional)
> 1   teaspoon vanilla extract
>   Confectioners' sugar, for dusting

1. Preheat oven to 350° F. Line a baking sheet with parchment paper; butter paper and lightly dust with flour. Sift flour and salt together and set aside.

2. In bowl of heavy-duty mixer or other medium bowl, beat yolks and ¼ cup sugar together until mixture falls from beater in a ribbon and leaves a slowly dissolving trail on surface (ribbon stage). In a copper or stainless steel bowl, beat egg whites to soft peaks (if bowl is stainless steel, add cream of tartar when whites are just foamy); add remaining sugar and beat until stiff peaks form.

3. Stir one-fourth beaten egg whites into yolk mixture to lighten; sift in half the flour and fold into batter. Add remaining flour, then most of remaining beaten egg whites. Fold in rest of whites and vanilla.

4. Fill a pastry bag fitted with a ½-inch plain tip half full with batter. Pipe 4-inch-long fingers onto paper-lined baking sheet, about 1 inch apart (see Note). Sprinkle with confectioners' sugar and bake until edges are just beginning to brown (15 to 18 minutes). Cool on wire racks.

Makes 3 dozen ladyfingers.

Note If ladyfingers are to be used to line a charlotte mold, you can pipe fingers ½ inch apart so that as they bake they will expand and touch. To line mold, don't separate ladyfingers. Trim them to proper height, then lift in a sheet and set around inside of mold. For a variation, pipe rows of ladyfingers on the diagonal.

■ GENOISE

A sponge cake is leavened with a foam made of separately beaten egg yolks and egg whites, and without fat; a génoise uses whole eggs and is enriched with butter. It is the classic French cake, and the foundation for almost all of the French *gâteaux*. Eggs will beat to greatest volume if utensils and ingredients are at room temperature.

> 4   eggs
> ⅔   cup sugar
> 1   cup cake flour, sifted twice
>   Pinch salt
> 3   tablespoons unsalted butter, melted and cooled

1. Preheat oven to 350° F. Lightly grease and flour an 8-inch-diameter cake pan; line bottom with a circle of parchment paper.

2. *To prepare in a heavy-duty mixer:* In warmed bowl of mixer (fill bowl with hot water and drain), beat eggs at medium speed to break up; add sugar and beat until mixture falls from beater in a ribbon and leaves a slowly dissolving trail on surface (ribbon stage). *To prepare with a portable electric mixer or balloon whisk:* Beat eggs and sugar to ribbon stage in a large mixing bowl set over a pan of hot, but not boiling, water (make sure that pan does not touch water).

3. Gently fold in one third of flour, then another third. Mix some batter with melted butter; continue mixing until butter is incorporated, then fold into batter with last third of flour.

4. Pour batter into prepared pan and smooth surface, making a slight hollow in center. Bake until a pale gold color, the center springs back when gently pressed with finger, and a wooden skewer inserted in the center comes out clean (25 to 30 minutes). Cool in pan 10 minutes; turn out onto a wire rack to cool completely.

5. Slice horizontally into 2 layers with a long, serrated knife (see photograph at right). To moisten and flavor cake layers, brush with a soaking syrup (see SUGAR AND SYRUP), then fill with fruit, buttercream, or any of the frostings or icings in FROSTING, ICING, AND FILLING.

Serves 8.

LEMON CHIFFON CAKE

An American creation of the 1920s, the chiffon cake is a cross between a foam cake and a shortened cake. Because it uses oil instead of butter, it is extremely moist and stores well. Chiffon cake has a pleasing light texture and keeps its shape well, so it can travel to a potluck or picnic without damage. The cake tastes equally delicious if made with fresh orange juice and orange instead of lemon (see Orange Chiffon Cake variation). Glacé icing is extremely simple to prepare and apply.

        2 **cups cake flour**
    1½ **cups sugar**
        1 **tablespoon baking powder**
      ½ **teaspoon salt**
      ½ **cup vegetable oil**
      ¼ **cup fresh lemon juice**
      ½ **cup milk**
        1 **teaspoon finely grated lemon rind**
        6 **eggs, separated**
      ½ **teaspoon cream of tartar (optional)**
          Citrus Glacé Icing (see page 250)

1. Preheat oven to 325° F. In a large bowl sift flour, sugar, baking powder, and salt. Add oil, lemon juice, milk, and grated rind.

2. In a copper or stainless steel bowl, beat egg whites to soft peaks (if bowl is stainless steel, add cream of tartar to whites when just foamy). Gently fold one third of whites into flour mixture to lighten, then gently fold in remaining whites.

3. Pour batter into 10-inch bundt or tube pan. Bake until wooden skewer comes out clean and top springs back when gently pressed with finger (about 1 hour). Cool upside down on wire rack.

4. When cool, remove from pan and decorate with Citrus Glace Icing.

Serves 8 to 10.

Orange Chiffon Cake Substitute grated orange rind and fresh orange juice for the lemon rind and juice. Prepare icing with orange flavoring.

BASIC YELLOW LAYER CAKE

The American counterpart to the French genoise, the versatile layer cake appears at all celebrations. It can be dressed up or down, and is rich and moist. This is a butter or creamed cake, which means that fat and sugar are beaten together to incorporate air. The creaming step gives the cake its characteristic velvety texture. Remember that fats cream to best volume at room temperature. A chocolate variation follows. The batter can also be used for cupcakes. Fill and frost with any of the frostings in FROSTING, ICING, AND FILLING.

    2½ **cups cake flour**
    2½ **teaspoons baking powder**
        1 **teaspoon salt**
    1⅓ **cups sugar**
      ¾ **cup solid vegetable shortening or butter**
        3 **eggs**
        1 **teaspoon vanilla extract**
      ½ **cup milk**

1. Preheat oven to 350° F. Lightly grease bottoms of two 9-inch-diameter cake pans; line bottoms with circles of parchment paper; lightly grease and flour pans and paper.

2. Sift together flour, baking powder, and salt; set aside. In a large bowl cream sugar and shortening until combined. Add 1 egg; beat until light, fluffy, and a pale, ivory color. Add remaining eggs, beating well after each addition. If using a heavy-duty mixer, stop beating as soon as eggs are incorporated and mixture is light and fluffy. Blend in vanilla.

3. Remove beater from mixture. By hand, gently fold in sifted flour mixture in 3 stages, alternating with milk, and beginning and ending with flour.

4. Divide batter evenly between 2 prepared pans. Bake until golden brown, top springs back when gently pressed with finger, and a wooden skewer inserted in center comes out clean (20 to 25 minutes). Cool in pan 10 minutes, then turn out onto wire rack and cool completely. Decorate as desired.

Serves 8.

For an 8-Inch Layer Cake Use two 8-inch cake pans. Bake 25 to 30 minutes. Each layer can be split in half to make a 4-layer cake.

Basic Chocolate Layer Cake Substitute ½ cup unsweetened cocoa powder for ½ cup flour; sift cocoa powder and flour together to blend.

Basic Cupcakes Spoon batter into lightly greased and floured muffin pans or line pans with paper cupcake liners. Bake 15 to 20 minutes.

Makes 18 to 24 cupcakes.

Unlike American layer cakes, which are formed from two separately baked rounds, a layered génoise is created from a single layer sliced in half horizontally. Use a sharp, serrated bread knife, longer than the diameter of the cake, to make a clean slice.

This scrumptious Carrot Spice Cake is topped with Cream Cheese Frosting, partly piped on with a pastry bag, and walnut halves. The sides are covered with chopped, toasted walnuts.

3. Stir baking soda into buttermilk. Add ½ cup flour to egg mixture; then add ⅓ cup buttermilk mixture. Continue to add flour and buttermilk alternately, beating well after each addition. Stir in cocoa mixture.

4. Divide batter evenly between the 2 prepared pans. Bake until top springs back when gently pressed with finger and a wooden skewer inserted into center comes out clean (30 to 35 minutes). Cool in pans 5 minutes, then turn out onto wire racks and cool completely. Frost with Chocolate Buttercream.

Serves 8.

■ CARROT SPICE CAKE

For a simple finish to this delicious cake, follow the directions given in the recipe. For a more elaborate presentation, see photograph at left.

- 1⅓ cups unsalted butter
- 1¾ cups sugar
- 4 eggs
- 2 cups flour
- 2 teaspoons baking soda
- 1 teaspoon ground cinnamon
- ½ teaspoon ground allspice
- ¼ teaspoon freshly grated nutmeg
- ¼ teaspoon ground cloves
- 3 cups (about 1 lb) grated carrots
- 1¼ cups chopped walnuts
- ¼ cup golden raisins
- ¼ cup coarsely chopped walnuts, for decoration

Cream Cheese Frosting

- ¼ cup unsalted butter, softened
- 6 ounces cream cheese, softened
- 2 cups sifted confectioners' sugar
- 2 teaspoons fresh lemon juice

1. Preheat oven to 325° F. Lightly grease and flour a 9- by 13-inch baking pan.

2. In a large bowl cream butter to lighten; gradually add sugar and cream until light, fluffy, and a pale, ivory color. Add eggs, one at a time, beating well after each addition.

3. Sift together flour, baking soda, cinnamon, allspice, nutmeg, and cloves. Add to butter mixture and blend well. Stir in carrots, the 1¼ cups walnuts, and raisins.

4. Spread batter evenly in pan. Bake until top springs back when gently pressed with finger and a wooden skewer inserted into center comes out clean (45 to 55 minutes). Cool in pan on wire rack. Spread Cream Cheese Frosting on cool cake. Sprinkle the ¼ cup walnuts on top.

Serves 10 to 12.

Cream Cheese Frosting Cream butter and cream cheese. Add confectioners' sugar and lemon juice; beat until smooth.

■ DEVIL'S FOOD CAKE

Perhaps this rich, dark chocolate layer cake got its name because it contrasts dramatically with the snowy whiteness of angel food cake. Split the layers, if desired, to create a four-layer extravaganza.

- ¾ cup unsweetened cocoa powder
- ¾ cup boiling water
- ½ cup solid vegetable shortening or butter
- 2 cups sugar
- 2 eggs
- 1 teaspoon vanilla extract
- ¼ teaspoon salt
- 1½ teaspoons baking soda
- 1 cup buttermilk
- 2 cups sifted cake flour
- 2 cups Chocolate Buttercream Frosting (see page 248)

1. Preheat oven to 350° F. Lightly grease bottoms of two 8-inch-diameter by 2-inch-deep cake pans; line bottoms with circles of parchment paper; lightly grease and flour pans and paper. Stir cocoa into the boiling water until dissolved; set aside.

2. In a large bowl cream shortening and sugar together until light and fluffy. Add eggs, one at a time, beating after each addition. Beat in vanilla and salt.

PECAN APPLESAUCE CAKE

Chunks of homemade applesauce keep this cake moist for days. If you are looking for a healthier snack, replace the flour and sugar with whole wheat flour and honey.

    ½ cup unsalted butter or corn oil
    ½ cup firmly packed brown sugar
    2 eggs
    ½ cup honey
    ½ cup apple juice
    2½ cups sifted unbleached flour
    1½ teaspoons baking soda
    1 teaspoon salt
    ¼ teaspoon baking powder
    1 teaspoon ground cinnamon
    ½ teaspoon ground cloves (optional)
    ¼ teaspoon ground allspice (optional)
    ½ cup dried currants
    1 cup chopped pecans
      Pecan halves, for decoration

Chunky Applesauce

    4 apples
    ¼ cup sugar
    2 tablespoons water

Whipped Cream Icing

    6 ounces cream cheese, softened
    ⅓ cup firmly packed light brown sugar
    1 teaspoon vanilla extract
    1 cup whipping cream

1. Preheat oven to 350° F. Lightly grease and flour a 9- by 13-inch baking pan. Make Chunky Applesauce; cool to room temperature.

2. In a large bowl cream butter with brown sugar until light and fluffy. Add eggs and beat. Combine honey with apple juice; set aside.

3. Sift together flour, soda, salt, baking powder, cinnamon, and cloves and allspice (if used). Add to egg mixture alternately with honey–apple juice mixture, beating after each addition. Stir in currants, pecans, and Chunky Applesauce.

4. Bake until cake tester comes out clean (40 to 50 minutes). Cool in pan on wire rack.

5. Spread Whipped Cream Icing over top of cake. Decorate each serving with a pecan half.

Serves 10 to 12.

Chunky Applesauce Peel, core, and slice apples. In a medium saucepan combine apples with sugar and the water; cover and cook until apples are just tender but not mushy (do not overcook).

Makes 1½ cups.

Whipped Cream Icing Beat cream cheese with brown sugar until smooth. Add vanilla. Whip cream until it holds peaks, and gently fold into cream cheese mixture.

GINGER-PEACH UPSIDE-DOWN CAKE

Spicy gingerbread makes a delicious partner to peaches or nectarines in this unusual version of the classic American dessert—upside-down cake. The cake batter is spooned on a layer of sliced fruit. When turned upside down after baking, the fruit slices glow under a buttery brown-sugar glaze that drips delicately down the sides of the cake.

    1 cup firmly packed light brown sugar
    6 tablespoons unsalted butter, melted
    3 peaches or nectarines
    2½ cups flour
    2 teaspoons baking soda
    ½ teaspoon ground cinnamon
    2 teaspoons ground ginger
    ⅛ teaspoon freshly grated nutmeg
    ⅛ teaspoon ground cardamom (optional)
    ½ teaspoon salt
    ½ cup dark molasses
    1 cup boiling water
    1 scant cup unsalted butter, melted,
      or safflower oil
    1 cup granulated sugar
    2 eggs, lightly beaten
    2 teaspoons finely grated orange rind (optional)

1. Preheat oven to 350° F. Butter sides of a 10- by 3-inch springform pan. Stir brown sugar into the 6 tablespoons melted butter; spread evenly in bottom of pan. Peel and pit peaches; cut into ½-inch-wide slices. (If using nectarines, do not peel.) Arrange slices (packed closely together) in concentric circles on sugar in bottom of pan.

2. Sift together flour, baking soda, cinnamon, ginger, nutmeg, cardamom (if used), and salt; set aside. Combine molasses and the water in a bowl; set aside.

3. In a large bowl beat the 1 cup melted butter and granulated sugar until light. Beat in eggs and orange rind (if used). Add the molasses mixture. Stir in dry ingredients; beat until well blended. Pour batter into the peach-lined pan. Bake until cake tester comes out clean or cake springs back when lightly touched in center (about 1 hour). Cover top of cake with aluminum foil if it begins to burn at the edges.

4. Allow cake to cool in pan for 30 minutes. Invert cake on serving platter, remove cake pan, and allow glaze to drip down sides of cake. Serve while still warm or at room temperature with whipped cream.

Serves 10 to 12.

CHOCOLATE MARBLE CREAM CAKE

Here's a chocolate marble cake designed to be eaten with your fingers. It's perfect fare for picnics or box lunches.

> 4 ounces semisweet chocolate, coarsely chopped
> 2¼ cups sifted cake flour
> 1½ teaspoons baking powder
> ¾ cup granulated sugar
> 1 cup whipping cream
> 2 tablespoons fresh lemon juice
> 2 extralarge eggs
> Confectioners' sugar, for decoration

1. Preheat oven to 375° F. Lightly grease bottom of a 5- by 9- by 3-inch loaf pan. Line bottom of pan with parchment paper; lightly grease and flour pan and paper.

2. Melt chocolate in a bowl over hot, not boiling, water. When chocolate is just melted, remove from heat; cool 10 minutes.

3. Sift flour with baking powder twice; set aside. Combine granulated sugar, cream, and lemon juice in a medium bowl. Add eggs, one at a time, beating well after each addition.

4. Divide batter evenly between 2 medium bowls. Stir melted chocolate into half of batter. Stir half of flour into each half of batter. Fill loaf pan, alternating layers of chocolate and vanilla batter. To create a marbled effect, run a knife through batter in a figure-eight pattern.

5. Bake 20 minutes. Reduce oven to 350° F and bake until golden brown, top springs back when gently pressed with finger, and a wooden skewer inserted in center comes out clean (20 to 30 minutes). Turn out onto wire rack to cool. When cool, sift a light layer of confectioners' sugar on top.

Serves 8 to 10.

POUND CAKE

A very rich creamed cake, pound cake was originally made with 1 pound *each* butter, sugar, eggs, and flour. The eggs were the sole leavening. Today, a little baking powder is often added for additional lightness. If you prefer a less sweet version, omit the 3 tablespoons sugar.

> 1½ cups flour
> ½ teaspoon baking powder
> 1 cup butter
> 1 cup plus 3 tablespoons sugar
> 4 eggs

1. Preheat oven to 350° F. Lightly grease and flour a 4½- by 8½- by 3-inch loaf pan. Sift flour and baking powder together; set aside.

2. In a medium bowl cream butter and sugar together until light, fluffy, and a pale, ivory color. Add eggs, one at a time, beating well after each addition (if mixture begins to curdle, add 1 tablespoon flour).

3. Fold in flour and pour immediately into prepared pan. Bake until golden brown and a wooden skewer inserted into center comes out clean (25 to 30 minutes). Cool in pan 10 minutes, then turn out onto wire rack and cool completely. Serve sliced with fresh fruit or ice cream.

Serves 8.

RICH FRUITCAKE

Although the English may not have invented fruitcake, it is certainly associated with that country. There, fruitcakes are made for all sorts of celebrations, from Christmas to weddings to birthdays. Compared with an American version, this is more cakelike. It is dark, rich, and very traditionally English. The fruits mixed into the spiced batter are a combination of dried and candied—raisins and currants, glacé cherries, and candied citrus peel. For more flavor, let fruits macerate in either sherry or brandy several hours or overnight.

> 2½ cups flour
> 1 teaspoon baking powder
> ½ teaspoon *each* ground cinnamon and nutmeg
> ¼ teaspoon *each* ground allspice and cloves
> 1½ cups dark raisins
> 1½ cups golden raisins
> 1½ cups dried currants
> 1 cup glacé cherries
> ½ cup candied citrus peel
> ½ cup slivered or sliced almonds
> ½ cup sherry or brandy
> 1 cup butter, softened
> 1⅓ cups firmly packed brown sugar
> 4 eggs
> ½ cup milk
> Grated rind and juice of 1 lemon

1. Preheat oven to 350° F. Lightly grease a deep, 8-inch-diameter cake pan; line with a double layer of parchment paper. Lightly grease and flour paper. Into a medium bowl sift flour, baking powder, cinnamon, nutmeg, allspice, and cloves; set aside.

2. In a large bowl combine dark raisins, golden raisins, currants, cherries, citrus peel, and almonds. Sprinkle with sherry and set aside (preferably several hours or overnight).

3. In a large bowl cream together butter and sugar until light, fluffy, and a pale, ivory color. Add eggs, one at a time, beating well after each addition. Fold in flour mixture alternately with milk. Drain fruit if any liquid is left and fold into batter.

4. Spoon batter into prepared pan. Bake 1 hour. Reduce heat to 300° F and bake until golden brown and a wooden skewer inserted into center comes out clean (1½ hours). Should cake begin to overbrown before it is done, cover with aluminum foil.

Serves 10 to 12.

■ ALMOND TORTE

In the winter this very moist cake is delicious with cooked fruit compotes. In the summer accompany it with fresh fruits and fruit sauces.

1¼ cups flour
1 teaspoon baking powder
¾ cup sugar
¾ cup butter
1 package (7 oz) soft almond paste
4 eggs
½ teaspoon almond extract
Raspberry Sauce, for accompaniment
(see page 522)

1. Preheat oven to 350° F. Lightly grease bottom of a 9-inch-diameter cake pan; line with a circle of parchment paper; lightly grease and flour pan and paper. Sift flour and baking powder together and set aside.

2. In a large bowl cream together sugar, butter, and almond paste until light and fluffy. Add eggs, one at a time, beating well after each addition; stir in almond extract. Fold in flour mixture.

3. Pour batter into prepared cake pan. Bake until golden and a wooden skewer inserted into center comes out clean (40 to 50 minutes). Cool 10 minutes in pan, then remove from pan and cool on rack to room temperature. Serve accompanied with Raspberry Sauce.

Serves 8.

Recipes and Related Information
Cheesecake, 117; Chocolate Ruffle Torte, 127; Gingerbread, 267; Greek Walnut Torte, 605; Lemon Roulade Charlotte, 171; Poppy Seed Cake With Cream Cheese Frosting, 454.

CAKE AND PASTRY TOOLS

Having every tool and utensil described here does not guarantee that your pie crust will be flaky or that your angel food cake will rise light and airy, but the better equipped you are, the easier baking will be. On the other hand, buy only what you need and have room to store.

BOWL SCRAPER

This thin, flat, flexible piece of nylon has one edge that is curved to fit the curve of a mixing bowl. Many cooks prefer it to a rubber spatula for getting at the last bit of batter left in a bowl or for scooping up frosting, cream puff paste, or other light mixtures. Usually either kidney-shaped or rectangular, it has a general overall measurement of 5¾ inches by 3¾ inches. It is dishwasher-safe.

BRUSHES: PASTRY AND BASTING

Use a pastry brush if you need to apply a delicate jelly glaze to a fruit tart or cake; coat breads, rolls, and pastries with an egg wash, milk, or butter; or wipe away excess flour or other crumbs on a pie or a serving plate. These brushes tend to have short handles (1½ to 4 inches long), and the best are made of long-lasting boar bristles rather than nylon. They are either flat (½ inch to 4 inches wide) or round (usually about 1 inch in diameter). Round brushes and wide flat ones make fast work of buttering pans and wide sheets of filo dough. For laying on the thinnest glaze or liqueur bastes, some pastry makers use a brush made of goose feathers, which are braided at the ends to form a handle.

Brushes with longer handles are used for basting meats and poultry or for buttering pans. Handles average about 12 inches long and bristles are often offset, at an angle. This design lets the cook stand back at a safe distance from a hot oven or grill, yet still be able to reach the food.

Select a brush with bristles that fit deep into the handle and are connected securely to it so they stay on the brush and do not end up in the food. Some nylon and plastic brushes can go in the dishwasher. Natural-bristle brushes should be washed by hand with warm, soapy water right after using and air-dried.

CAKE COMB

The swirls and grooves that texture the frosting of many cakes are easily made with this tool, which is also known as a decorating comb or comb scraper. It is a rigid metal triangle with serrated teeth on all three sides; each row of teeth is of a different size. Made of stainless steel, the comb measures approximately 5 by 5 by 4 inches.

Fresh fruit best complements the rich, buttery flavor of Almond Torte. Try a summery sauce of puréed and whole raspberries.

Many specialty tools are available to assist the home baker. Clockwise from bottom left are: pie weights, pastry bag and tips, dough scraper, cooling racks, pastry blender, pastry brushes, flour dredger, cardboard cake trays, cake tester, cookie press, pastry crimper and wheels, rolling pin, cookie cutters, and a marble board.

CAKE-DECORATING TURNTABLE

By elevating a cake above the counter, this device allows more room for your hand to maneuver. Because the platter rotates, you can apply frosting, chopped nuts, or other surface decoration more evenly and with a more professional-looking result. Plates come in 12-, 14-, and 16-inch rounds or 12- by 16-inch rectangles; all sizes sit on a 4-inch-high base. The better ones are metal, with a cast-iron base and an aluminum alloy disk. For the occasional user, a less expensive plastic version with a shorter base will serve the same purpose.

CAKE TESTER

A cake is considered done if crumbs or batter does not adhere to a tester inserted into the center. For this task you can use a special tool made of a rigid stainless steel wire with a plastic-coated loop handle, or, perhaps more handily, a toothpick, bamboo skewer, broom straw, or sharp knife.

CARDBOARD CAKE TRAYS

These are invaluable aids for cake-decorating. Set under cakes to give them support so they can be easily maneuvered, these trays are especially helpful when applying frosting or other finishing touches. The trays are coated and are available in standard cake sizes, in rounds, rectangles, and squares. Look for them at better cookware stores and at cake-decorating supply stores. You can make your own tray by cutting cardboard slightly smaller than the cake and wrapping it smoothly and tightly with aluminum foil.

COOKIE PRESS

With this hand-operated machine you can transform butter-rich spritz cookie dough into dozens of fanciful shapes. The body is an aluminum and chrome cylinder that you fill with chilled dough. A removable aluminum collar at one end holds one of over a dozen accompanying pattern disks; a mechanism at the other end—either a lever, screw, or plunger—forces the dough through the disk. A press can also function like a pastry bag if you use one of the decorating tips. Look for a cookie press that allows you to regulate the amount of dough ejected through the disk. Even with the best presses, it takes some practice to produce uniform results, but you can always recycle the rejects and try again. After use, wash each part thoroughly in warm, sudsy water, and dry immediately before storing.

COOLING RACK

Wire cooling racks allow air to circulate around baked goods as they cool so steam won't build up underneath and cause them to get soggy. Round racks are good for a single layer of cake; rectangular ones hold two layers, a sheet cake, several loaves of bread, or a big batch of cookies. A good assortment would be two or three round racks and two rectangular ones. Select rectangular racks as large as you can store; these allow you to cool several baking sheets' worth of cookies at a time. Buy racks made of sturdy, heavy-gauge wire strong enough to support cakes and breads without sagging. Larger racks should have feet in the center as well as the corners. Round ones measure 11½ inches in diameter; well-sized rectangular ones are 10½ by 17 inches and 13 by 19 inches.

DREDGER

A cup-shaped dredger is a handy way to coat a cake or pastry with confectioners' sugar, cinnamon sugar, or cocoa, or to flour a work surface. Flour dredgers have about a 2-cup capacity, with a perforated metal screw-on cover and a handle. Sugar dredgers are smaller, holding no more than ½ cup, have a mesh cover, and do not have a handle.

FLOUR SIFTER

See COLANDER, STRAINER, AND SIEVE.

ICING SPATULA

See SPATULA, SCRAPER, AND TURNER.

PASTRY BAG AND TIPS

With a pastry bag you can inscribe a cake with a special message or adorn it with chains of stars, shape delicate ladyfingers and elegant éclairs, or border a roast with a ribbon of mashed potatoes. To use, the cone-shaped bag is filled with batter or icing; when pressure is applied to the bag, the filling is pushed out through a decorative tinned or chromed steel tip held at the pointed end of the bag.

Pastry bags are made of lightweight nylon, canvas, or plastic-lined cloth. Nylon is preferred because it doesn't retain odors, is flexible, and is easy to care for. Most useful sizes are 12, 14, and 16 inches long. Smaller bags are better suited for small designs and for decorating cakes and cookies. Larger bags hold more and can pipe a larger

surface without needing a refill. They can be purchased alone or in a set with an assortment of the most common tips: *plain* for writing and for making lines, stems, dots, or line drawings; *open-star* for small or large rosettes, stars, and border designs; *closed-star* for rosettes and flowers; *leaf* for piping leaves; *slit* for ribbons. Hundreds of specialty tips can be bought singly or in sets. A plastic coupling unit allows you to change tips without switching to a new bag or to use tips that would otherwise not fit the bag. If you don't want to bother with the coupler, consider buying several sizes of bags and a selection of tips for each.

After use, wash pastry bag, tips, and coupling unit in hot, sudsy water; rinse well and air-dry completely or bag will mildew and tips rust.

For information on how to use a pastry bag, see FROSTING, ICING, AND FILLING.

PASTRY BLENDER

To cut fat into flour when making pastry or biscuit dough, most people use a pastry blender. This hand tool has six U-shaped, thin stainless steel wires that are held in place by a wooden or plastic handle. The wires evenly distribute the cold fat, which is worked until the flour-fat mixture is the desired consistency, usually described as coarse crumbs. The more rigid the wires, the better the tool will work. Make sure wires are fastened securely to handle.

PASTRY BOARD

For rolling out pastry and for making candies, you want a surface that stays cool. Marble is considered best because it naturally maintains a surface temperature 20° F cooler than air. It is nonporous and therefore won't absorb moisture from the dough and cause it to stick. Marble, however, is heavy and expensive. A less costly, less weighty, but quite effective alternative is a board made of a dense, white, synthetic polycarbonate. Like marble, this material stays cool; it has the additional attribute of being dishwasher-safe.

Portable marble boards weighing about 20 pounds are ½ inch thick and measure 18 inches square. Boards of synthetic materials come in many sizes; 16 by 18 inches and 16 by 20 inches are practical dimensions. Choose the largest board that will easily fit your work space and allows you to roll out dough comfortably.

PASTRY CLOTH

Made of canvas, pastry cloths are used as a surface for rolling out pastry. Some are printed with guides representing standard diameters of pie crusts; others are set in a frame that keeps the cloth taut and wrinkle-free. Before use, flour is rubbed into the weave, which creates a somewhat nonstick finish. Before storing, the cloth should be shaken out; occasional washing will keep it sanitary. Cloths measure 17 by 18 inches or 21 inches square.

Many European cookies are shaped by pressing soft dough into whimsical, charming carved wooden molds, like these Dutch ones.

PASTRY AND COOKIE CUTTERS

Anyone can be an artist with the help of these cutters. Buy ones with a thin cutting edge that will slice through dough without dragging. Sides should be strong enough so they do not bend under pressure or deform when squeezed. Make sure cutters are deep enough for the thickness of the dough they will cut; cookie dough is usually ⅛ to ¼ inch, biscuit dough usually ½ inch. Most cutters are tinned steel and should be dried thoroughly after washing so they won't rust.

Pastry Cutters   Also used for biscuits, they come in a graduated set and have plain or fluted edges. Special puff pastry cutters are available to stamp out pastry cases (vol-au-vents) for savory or sweet fillings or to roll out triangles for croissants.

Cookie Cutters   Hundreds of different cookie cutters are available, some with handles, some with a rolled edge, singly or in sets. Specialty cookie cutters include the following:

Cookie Boards   Springerle, the traditional German anise cookies, are formed by rolling the stiff dough over a wooden board incised with cutout figures of birds, flowers, animals, houses, and people, each separated by double lines. The lines are cutting guides for separating the cookies before baking them. Boards come in two-, four-, and six-cookie sizes and as individual boards that make a single, giant figure. Also available for springerle are rolling cookie cutters and incised wooden rolling pins. Multiple and single-cookie boards for the rich Dutch spice cookies called *speculaas* (see photograph at left) are similar to those for springerle. The large board makes 12 cookies.

Cookie Stamps   Some of these round or square forms are large and attractive enough to hang on the wall. Made of wood, glass, or ceramic, they have a pattern cut into the surface. After dusting with flour to prevent sticking, the stamp is pressed into a small ball of dough. The dough is flattened and impressed with the reverse of the incised design.

Rolling Cookie Cutters   These are like jigsaw puzzles. The shapes are mounted on a drum attached to a wooden handle. The drum is rolled across the dough with pressure; the raised design cuts an interlocking pattern so dough is not wasted.

Shortbread Molds   Ceramic shortbread molds are concave, with the traditional Scottish thistle carved in the center and fluting, said to represent the rays of the sun, trimming the rim. The rich shortbread dough fills the hollow space and bakes right in the mold. Another version, a shallow, concave wooden mold, shapes the cookie by having the dough rolled over it. The dough is trimmed of any excess, turned out of the mold, and baked. Shortbread can also be baked in a baking pan.

PASTRY CRIMPER

This tool looks like tiny, flat-headed tweezers and fits over the upper and lower edges of a double-crust pie. When pinched together, a crimper seals the edges and impresses a design into the dough. Made of stainless steel, it measures about ¼ inch wide and 1½ inches long.

PASTRY/DOUGH SCRAPER

Extend the life of a wooden work surface by scraping it clean with this rigid metal scraper rather than by soaking it in water. Use it also to turn dough, to cut dough into small pieces, or to manipulate dough that is too wet and sticky to handle easily. The dough scraper is a rigid, stainless steel rectangle, measuring 3 by 6 inches, with a plastic or metal handle. It can go in the dishwasher.

PASTRY AND PIZZA WHEELS

When selecting one of these rolling-bladed tools, make sure the wheel turns freely and that, if it is large, there is a guard to protect your fingers. Use wheels to cut anything flat—pastry, pizza, cookies, pasta dough, and ravioli. Wheels with a crinkled edge are known as pastry jaggers; they cut a pinked line and are usually used to fashion strips of dough for weaving into a lattice pie crust. The wheels are stainless steel, aluminum alloy, or wood (one version of a jagger), with a wood, plastic, or molded metal handle; diameters range from ½ inch to 3 inches.

PIE WEIGHT

To blind bake a pie or tart crust means to bake it without a filling. Pie weights, which are ceramic or aluminum pellets or beans, keep a crust flat as it bakes so that it doesn't puff up, deform, and shrink. Crust is first lined with aluminum foil or parchment paper and then filled almost full with weights. When crust is done, foil and weights are removed. One package of weights fills two pie crusts. Before there were weights, bakers used dried beans or rice, still good choices.

ROLLING PIN

A well-designed rolling pin is heavy, so it, rather than you, does the work of shaping pastry and bread dough into a smooth, flat, even sheet. A heavier pin requires fewer runs across the dough to do the job. There are several types. The *American* is the familiar wooden cylinder with a handle on each end. The *French straight* is a slender wooden dowel without handles; the *French curved* is also a wooden dowel without handles, but it tapers from center to each end. The *tutove*, which has a grooved, rigid nylon cylinder and handles, is a special tool used for rolling puff pastry. *Marble* rolling pins are specifically for pastry work because they keep dough cool, although they are very cumbersome and expensive.

Which rolling pin should you use? Choose one that you are comfortable with and that produces the desired results. The American type is probably easier to manipulate than the others, although some pastry chefs feel that a rolling pin without handles gives you a better sense of the thickness of the dough. Regardless of the design, select one of smooth hardwood that is heavy, well balanced, and of a length that is wider than the pastry so it won't leave ridges in the dough as you roll. A rolling pin with a handle rotates more smoothly if handles move on ball or nylon bearings. A 15-inch length is very versatile—long enough and heavy enough to do a good job.

During use, keep rolling pin and work surface well-dusted with flour to prevent sticking. Flouring the surface works better than covering the pin with a cloth stocking, which usually wrinkles and makes an unwelcome pattern on the dough. Always wipe wood clean with a soft cloth before storing.

Recipes and Related Information
Biscuit, 49; Cake, 77; Cookie, 139; Frosting, Icing, and Filling, 244; Pie and Tart, 431; Pizza, 445.

CANDIED FRUIT

Many types of fresh fruit are candied for use in cakes, pastries, and confections. Cherries, pineapple, citron, angelica, orange rind, and lemon rind are among those most readily available in candied form. The candying process involves cooking or steeping the fruit in a highly concentrated sugar syrup, then drying it. The sugar penetrates and preserves the fruit.

Use   Candied fruits add festive color and a sweet note to breads, cookies, and cakes. Holiday fruitcakes are usually well endowed with liquor-soaked candied fruits. Because good candied fruits can be expensive, they are looked upon by many as an indulgence to reserve for holiday specialties.

Availability   Specialty shops, candy stores, and some health-food stores offer a selection of candied fruits. Many supermarkets carry packages of mixed candied fruit the year around and offer a wider selection at Christmas time.

Selection   Many packaged supermarket mixes depend heavily on artificial colors and preservatives; read the label for ingredients.

Storage   Keep candied fruits in a cool, dark place for up to three months. They may be frozen indefinitely.

Recipes and Related Information
Candy, 93; Christmas Panettone, 628; Divinity, 96; Rich Fruitcake, 88.

CANDY, TO

To glaze or preserve by cooking in sugar syrup, or to coat with sugar. A favorite presentation for cooked yams, sweet potatoes, and carrots is to coat them with a mixture of butter and sugar. Citrus peels are candied and used to flavor or decorate baked desserts.

CANDIED CITRUS PEEL

When strips of peel are cooked in a sugar syrup, the peel becomes infused with sugar, which acts as a preservative. This is a two-day process; the peel must sit in its syrup at room temperature overnight and then be cooked again. However, you can candy up to six fruits' worth at a time. Increase the recipe accordingly. The candied peel will keep up to one month. Use a sharp knife to cut the candied peel into strips or sharp-edged aspic or truffle cutters to form decorative shapes.

  1 **grapefruit, 2 oranges, *or* 2 lemons**
  ½ **cup sugar**
  ¼ **cup water**
  1 **tablespoon corn syrup**
     Sugar, for dusting candied peel

1. With a paring knife or vegetable peeler, remove peel from fruit in strips, leaving some white pith, but no more than ⅛ to ¼ inch, attached. Reserve fruit, wrapped airtight, for another use.

2. Place strips in a medium, heavy-bottomed saucepan and cover with cold water; boil 5 minutes. Drain, rinse with fresh water, and repeat process; set drained strips aside in saucepan.

3. Meanwhile, in a small, heavy-bottomed saucepan combine sugar, the water, and corn syrup, stirring over low heat until sugar has dissolved; raise heat and boil 2 minutes.

4. Pour sugar syrup over drained peel and cook over very low heat 1 hour. Cool, cover, and let sit at room temperature overnight.

5. The next day, bring to a boil, reduce heat to very low, and cook 1 hour. Remove peel from syrup and drain on wire rack set over parchment paper or baking sheet. Let dry completely (on a damp or cool day, let dry in a gas oven or in a still-warm oven that has been recently heated and turned off).

6. Roll in sugar and serve as is, or cut up for use as a flavoring, or cut into decorative shapes for garnishes. Store in an airtight container between layers of parchment paper. Will keep 1 month.

Recipes and Related Information
Candied Fruit, 93; Crystallized Flowers, 238; Glazed Carrots, 100; Lucia Buns, 99; Maple-Glazed Sweet Potatoes, 569; Sugar and Syrup, 567.

CANDY AND CONFECTION

That sweets delight us is evident. Our terms of endearment—"sweetheart" or "honey"—are sugarcoated. We express affection and goodwill with gilt-wrapped and be-ribboned boxes of all manner of confections. Although we tend to buy our candy rather than make it, homemade sweets are a tradition with many cooks during the holidays or are prepared occasionally as a special treat at other times of the year. Candy making is an enjoyable group activity and, along with baking cookies, is often our first experience with cooking.

SUGAR SYRUPS AND CANDY MAKING

The word candy comes from the Arabic *qandi*—made from sugarcane. Generally speaking, candies are made by boiling a solution of sugar and water to a particular concentration—that is, cooking the solution until a desired amount of water has evaporated. We have learned that certain syrup concentrations produce certain types of candies. For example, the more moisture a sugar syrup contains, the softer the candy is, like a caramel. Conversely, a very concentrated sugar syrup, containing just a little water, produces a hard candy, such as a brittle.

There are two measures commonly used to gauge the concentration of a sugar syrup: temperature and a cold water test. Temperature has proven to be an accurate guide to the stages that sugar syrup passes through as it cooks (see Stages of Sugar Syrup). Cooks who often make candy might want to buy a special candy thermometer (see THERMOMETER). The thermometer is clipped to the side of the pan, with its tip immersed at least one inch in the boiling syrup but not touching the pan bottom. When the syrup reaches the specified temperature, it is removed from the heat. Lacking a thermometer, concentration can be measured by dropping a small amount of hot syrup into cold water and noting its reaction. This is a well-known and long-used method, but one that is more subjective than temperature and is therefore considered less reliable. Syrups with a great deal of moisture form wispy threads. As the water content decreases, the syrup becomes a soft, pliable mass; at higher concentrations the ball loses elasticity and becomes brittle and increasingly hard. Candy recipes usually specify both temperature and physical stage—238° F, soft-ball stage, for example.

ABOUT CRYSTALLIZATION

Molecules in a sugar syrup have a natural attraction. When they join together, they form crystals. For some candies, like fondant and fudge, this crystallization is desirable, although in a controlled way. The object is to develop many minute crystals, rather than a few large ones that create a grainy, coarse texture in the candy. For noncrystalline candies, such as caramels, toffee, and brittle, the aim is to prevent crystal formation altogether. Substances called interfering agents, commonly corn syrup or an acid such as cream of tartar, are added to interrupt, partly or completely, the linking of these molecules.

TO CONTROL CRYSTAL FORMATION

Crystals need very little encouragement to develop; sometimes a speck of dust, a grain of sugar, or the slightest agitation of the sugar syrup is all that is required. The following are points to remember when working with sugar syrups to avoid undesirable crystal formation.

- Follow recipe directions exactly; don't make substitutions and don't hurry the cooking time or cook syrup too long, or the texture will be adversely affected.
- Keep sides of pan free of crystals, if they develop. As the sugar dissolves, brush away any crystals with a brush dipped in hot water. When making fondant and similar candies, after sugar dissolves and before raising heat, cover saucepan and cook for a few minutes. The steam that develops will wash down the pan sides.
- Don't stir syrup once sugar dissolves and syrup begins to boil. If you have to stir (to prevent scorching of caramels or toffee, for instance, or for testing syrup), use a clean and dry spoon.
- Pour syrup out of pan onto cooling surface; do not spoon or scrape. Marble is the preferred surface, but a heavy metal tray works well also.
- If the candy must be beaten or kneaded (to reduce the size of its crystals), allow it to cool to the suggested temperature before beating, and then work it continually until the desired consistency and color have been reached.

ENVIRONMENT AND EQUIPMENT

Like meringues, candies can be affected by the weather. The cooled syrup can actually absorb moisture from the air on a humid day and set softer than it should. Save candy making for dry, cool days or, if the weather is damp, cook the syrup a few degrees higher than the temperature specified in the recipe.

Use a deep, heavyweight pan for cooking the syrup, made of a material that conducts heat well so that the candy will not burn (see MATERIALS FOR COOKWARE). As it cooks, the liquid mixture can bubble up to almost four times its original volume, so be sure that the saucepan is large enough to contain it. The classic sugar pan is made of unlined copper (see COOKWARE, Caramelizing Pot), but a heavy-bottomed one made of aluminum lined with stainless steel is fine and less expensive. Other useful equipment includes a long-handled wooden spoon (wood can sit in the extremely hot sugar syrup without itself getting hot, a safety feature for the cook), candy thermometer, parchment paper, and a smooth surface for cooling, such as a marble slab, heavy metal tray, or flat ceramic platter.

CARAMELS

When heated, sugar slowly melts into a thick syrup and then begins to color, at first a pale yellow then gradually progressing to deeper tones of warm, dark brown. Accompanying this visual change is an intensifying of flavor. These soft, chewy tan candies are named for this process called caramelization, which gives them their distinctive color and flavor (see SUGAR AND SYRUP, Sugar Syrups). The candies keep up to two weeks wrapped in plastic and stored in a cool, dark spot.

- 3 cups sugar
- 1 cup light corn syrup
- 2 cups whipping cream
- ¾ cup butter
- 1 tablespoon vanilla extract

1. Butter a 9-inch pan. In a large, heavy-bottomed saucepan combine sugar, corn syrup, and cream; stir over low heat until sugar has completely dissolved. Increase heat to medium and cook until mixture turns a pale tan color (238° F on a candy thermometer, soft-ball stage).

2. Remove from heat, stir in butter and vanilla, and pour immediately into prepared pan. Cool to lukewarm and mark in 1-inch squares. When completely cool, cut into squares and serve. Or, wrap individually in plastic wrap and store in a cool, dark spot for several weeks.

Makes about 7 dozen candies.

TOFFEE

Although toffee and caramels are made similarly, the toffee mixture is cooked to a greater sugar concentration (soft-crack rather than soft-ball stage), resulting in a candy with a deeper color and a slightly brittle, although still chewy, texture.

- 1½ cups sugar
- 1½ cups whipping cream
- 1 tablespoon vanilla extract

1. Butter an 8-inch pan. In a large, heavy-bottomed saucepan dissolve sugar in cream over low heat. Increase heat to medium, bring mixture to a boil, and cook until mixture begins to thicken (about 5 minutes), turning the mixture over once or twice to keep bottom from overcooking.

2. Cook until mixture pulls away from sides of pan and turns golden brown (280° F on a candy thermometer, soft-crack stage; see Note). Immediately remove from heat, add vanilla, and pour into prepared pan. Cool to lukewarm and mark in 1-inch squares. When completely cool, cut or break into squares and serve. Or, store airtight wrapped individually in plastic wrap or layered between sheets of parchment paper. Toffee keeps for about 2 weeks.

Makes about 5 dozen candies.

STAGES OF SUGAR SYRUP

The concentration of sugar in a sugar syrup can be measured by its temperature reading on a candy thermometer or by its appearance when dropped into ice water. For the inexperienced, a candy-thermometer reading is the most reliable measure of sugar concentration. Other ingredients added to a basic sugar syrup affect concentration, causing these syrups to be ready at a lower or higher temperature than one without such additions. For this reason, a range of temperatures is given for each stage.

Check the accuracy of your candy thermometer by placing it in water and bringing the water to a boil. The thermometer should register 212° F at boiling point. If it doesn't, note the difference and adjust recipe temperatures accordingly. Before using, warm the thermometer by placing it in a glass of hot tap water. Then insert the thermometer into boiling syrup so that its tip is immersed in the liquid at least 1 inch and continue to boil gently until the required temperature is reached. Use the syrup at once.

To test the syrup without a candy thermometer, remove a few drops of syrup from the pan with a clean, dry wooden spoon. Then dip spoon in ice water, gather syrup in fingertips, and try to roll it into a ball. The sugar will exhibit characteristics of one of the stages described below.

Thermometer Reading	Stage	Cold Water Test
230°–236° F	Thread	Forms 2-inch threads when spoon is dipped in syrup and then some of the syrup on spoon is dropped into ice water; threads cannot be gathered into a ball
234°–240° F	Soft-ball	Forms a soft pliable ball when rolled between fingers in ice water
244°–248° F	Firm-ball	Forms a ball firm enough to hold its shape when rolled between fingers in ice water
250°–265° F	Hard-ball	Forms a hard ball that holds its shape when rolled between fingers in ice water, offers some resistance when pressed
270°–290° F	Soft-crack	Syrup stretches into firm but still-elastic strands in ice water
300°–310° F	Hard-crack	Syrup solidifies when dropped in ice water and can be easily snapped in half
320°–338° F	Light-caramel	Syrup turns an amber color when poured onto a white plate
350° F	Dark-caramel	Caramel turns a dark red-brown color; if caramel is cooked beyond this stage, it burns and becomes very bitter

Note It is difficult to determine the color of the mixture since the surface remains pale even when the bottom is cooking to caramel. To check color, slip a wooden spoon down side of pan to note if mixture is pulling away from sides and if lower portion is turning golden brown. If bottom seems to be darkening too quickly, turn mixture over, and continue cooking until desired color is reached.

PEANUT BRITTLE

Peanuts are synonymous with this hard, richly flavored candy, but other nuts, such as almonds, pecans, or hazelnuts—or a mixture—will be equally delicious.

> 2 cups sugar
> 1 cup light corn syrup
> ¾ cup water
> 2 cups raw peanuts (whole or halved),
>   skins removed
> 2 tablespoons butter

1. Oil or butter a baking sheet. In a large, heavy-bottomed saucepan, combine sugar, corn syrup, and the water; stir over low heat until sugar has completely dissolved. Increase heat to medium and cook without stirring until a rich golden brown (300° F on a candy thermometer, hard-crack stage).

2. Immediately remove from heat, add nuts and butter, and stir until nuts are coated. Pour onto prepared sheet, spreading quickly with a buttered spatula to about ½-inch thickness. Cool, break into pieces, and serve. Or store airtight; brittle keeps for about 2 weeks.

Makes about 1½ pounds brittle.

FONDANT

Crystalline, creamy fondant is a foundation or base for other confections, including some frostings. When making fondant the goal is to develop sugar crystals that are fine enough that the candy won't have a gritty texture (see To Control Crystal Formation). After kneading, fondant should be stored for several days before using. Making fondant is hard work and many cooks prefer to purchase it ready-made from cake-decorating supply stores.

> 2 cups sugar
> 2 tablespoons liquid glucose (available at
>   cake-decorating supply stores)
> ⅛ teaspoon cream of tartar
> ½ cup water
> ¼ to ½ teaspoon vanilla or almond extract (optional)

1. In a large, heavy-bottomed saucepan combine sugar, liquid glucose, cream of tartar, and the water and dissolve over low heat, washing down any crystals that may form on the sides of the pan with a brush dipped in hot water.

2. Bring to a boil and cook without stirring to 238° F on a candy thermometer (soft-ball stage). Immediately remove from heat and pour onto a marble slab or other smooth work surface. Cool undisturbed to 110° F. With a dough scraper or 2 metal spatulas that have been dipped in hot water, lift fondant from edges and push back to center.

3. Work fondant continuously, lifting and folding from edges to center, until it becomes white in color and smooth, pliable, and satiny. If desired, the final kneading can be done with buttered hands. If the fondant

becomes too stiff to work, cover with an inverted metal bowl and let sit briefly to soften; work again when ready.

4. Before using, let fondant ripen in an airtight container for several days to become more pliable. *To flavor:* Knead in vanilla or almond extract. *To tint:* Pierce mass and sprinkle a few drops of food coloring (pastel colors are most appropriate, so don't add too much coloring) into holes; let color seep into fondant, then knead to distribute evenly. Fondant keeps for up to 3 months if well wrapped and stored airtight in a cool place.

Makes ¾ to 1 pound.

DIVINITY

Divinity is creamy, like fondant, but is fluffier because the sugar syrup is beaten into whipped egg whites. If made with brown sugar, the candy is called seafoam. Wrapped airtight, Divinity will keep one to two weeks.

> 3 cups sugar
> ¾ cup light corn syrup
> ¼ cup water
> 2 egg whites
> 1 tablespoon vanilla extract
> 1½ cups chopped toasted nuts, chopped
>   candied citrus peel, or chopped glacé cherries

1. Oil or butter an 8-inch baking pan or set out sheets of parchment paper. In a medium, heavy-bottomed saucepan combine sugar, corn syrup, and the water; stir over low heat until sugar has dissolved completely. Increase heat to medium and cook without stirring until 250° F on a candy thermometer (hard-ball stage).

2. While syrup is cooking, beat egg whites until soft peaks form. When sugar syrup reaches temperature, slowly pour in a thin stream onto egg whites, beating continuously at high speed. Fold in vanilla and nuts.

3. Continue to beat until mixture cools slightly; pour immediately into prepared pan or drop by tablespoonfuls onto parchment paper. Let stand until firm. If made in pan, cut into squares to serve.

Makes about 5 dozen candies.

CHOCOLATE FUDGE

In older cookbooks, fudge recipes are often named for one of the New England women's colleges, because making this candy was such a popular pastime with students at these schools—Smith, Vassar, and Wellesley all have their own versions.

> 1½ cups sugar
> 1 cup whipping cream
> 1 jar (7 oz) marshmallow cream
> ¼ cup butter, cut in pieces
> 1 pound semisweet chocolate, chopped
> 1 teaspoon vanilla extract
> 1 cup chopped nuts (optional)

1. Oil or butter an 8-inch baking pan. In a large, heavy-bottomed saucepan, combine sugar, whipping cream, and marshmallow cream; stir over low heat until sugar has dissolved completely. Increase heat to medium and cook without stirring until 238° F on a candy thermometer (soft-ball stage).

2. Remove from heat and add butter and chopped chocolate; stir until completely melted and smooth. Stir in vanilla and nuts (if used).

3. Pour into prepared pan and cool until firm. Cut in 1-inch squares and serve. Stored airtight between layers of parchment paper, fudge keeps for 2 to 3 weeks.

Makes about 5 dozen candies.

■ CHOCOLATE TRUFFLES

Truffles are extremely easy to make because they have few ingredients and aren't dependent upon a temperamental sugar syrup for their base. Note that the truffle mixture must chill overnight before shaping.

> 1¼ **cups whipping cream**
> 1 **pound semisweet chocolate, chopped**
> ½ **cup unsalted butter, cut in small pieces**
> **Unsweetened cocoa powder or chopped nuts, for coating**

1. In a large, heavy-bottomed saucepan, bring cream to a boil. Add chocolate in small bits. Then add butter a little at a time. Stir until all is smooth. Cover and chill 8 hours or overnight.

2. If using cocoa, sift onto a plate. If using nuts, place in a layer on a plate. Scoop up chocolate mixture in teaspoonfuls. With hands, shape into ¾-inch balls (chocolate will melt a bit when handled). Roll in cocoa or nuts and set on another plate. Store, covered, in refrigerator until ready to serve. Truffles keep up to 1 month.

Makes about 6 dozen truffles.

Grand Marnier Truffles Before chilling and shaping chocolate mixture, add ¼ cup Grand Marnier and 1 teaspoon grated orange rind.

> **Recipes and Related Information**
> *Icing Fondant, 251; Pralines, 424; Sugar and Syrup, 567.*

CAPE GOOSEBERRY

Despite its name, the cape gooseberry is not a gooseberry at all, but a relative of the husk tomato (or tomatillo) and the ground cherry. It is also known as Chinese lantern, golden gooseberry, or strawberry tomato. Of Peruvian origin, it was later cultivated and highly regarded in South Africa, especially around the Cape of Good Hope. Today it is a commercial crop in New Zealand.

The small, golden, oval fruit is concealed by a brown, papery, outer husk, which must be removed. Its texture is firm and moist, its flavor mild.

Use Cape gooseberries are eaten raw as part of a fruit salad and cooked as an ingredient in a fruit compote. They may be added to stuffings of bread and fruit, made into jams or dessert sauces, used for pie and tart fillings, or added to gingerbread.

Availability Fresh cape gooseberries are available in specialty markets from March through June.

Selection Choose fruit with undamaged husks.

Storage Refrigerate in a plastic bag in crisper for up to two days.

Preparation Remove husk and rinse fruit. Slice, halve, or leave whole.

Perhaps not since the introduction of fudge has a confection appealed to the American sweet tooth as much as the French candy, truffles. Set in individual foil cups, they make a glamorous dessert.

CAPER

The small, unopened flower buds of a Mediterranean bush are called capers. They have a firm, almost crunchy texture and, depending on how they're packed, a piquant, salty or pickled flavor.

Use Capers provide a piquant note to sauces, dressings, and salads. Their pungent bite is appreciated with smooth-textured foods such as smoked salmon, brains, and eggs; in creamy dishes such as Vitello Tonnato; and as a garnish for fried fish or veal.

Availability Capers are generally pickled in vinegar and packed in jars. Some Italian markets carry salt-packed capers in bulk.

Capers vary considerably in size, depending on the variety and the stage of development at harvest. Many connoisseurs consider the smallest capers—the nonpareil variety from southern France—to be the finest, although larger capers are not necessarily stronger in flavor. The brining or salting process has a more important effect on flavor than does size. Try several brands to find one that you like.

Storage Capers in vinegar keep for months in the original jar in the refrigerator. Salt-packed capers may be stored for several months at room temperature in an airtight container.

Preparation Before using capers packed in vinegar, drain off liquid. Salt-packed capers should be rinsed and dried. Large capers may be coarsely chopped.

■ EGG AND CAPER SALAD

If you will be using Egg and Caper Salad as picnic fare, it's better to assemble the open-faced sandwiches at the picnic site. Pack the salad in a plastic container and bread and oregano sprigs garnish in plastic bags to keep them fresh. Remember to also bring a serrated knife to cut the bread into quarters.

- 4 **eggs, hard-cooked**
- 2 **stalks celery**
- 2 **tablespoons mayonnaise**
- 2 **tablespoons plain yogurt**
- 1 **tablespoon Dijon mustard**
- ¼ **teaspoon kosher salt**
- 1 **tablespoon capers**
- 4 **slices whole grain bread**
- 16 **small sprigs fresh oregano**

With a sharp knife, dice hard-cooked eggs and place into a 1-quart mixing bowl. Mince celery and add to eggs. Add mayonnaise, yogurt, mustard, salt, and capers. Stir to mix well. Place ½ cup on each slice of bread, garnish with sprigs of oregano, cut into quarters, and serve as open-faced sandwiches.

Serves 2 for lunch, 8 as part of a picnic.

Food Processor Version Trim away leaves from celery, cut celery stalks into 3-inch lengths, and wedge tightly in feed tube with slicing disk in place; process. Remove disk, leaving celery in work bowl, and insert metal blade. Add eggs, mayonnaise, yogurt, mustard, salt, and capers. Pulse rapidly a few times to chop egg and combine mixture.

Recipes and Related Information
Eggplant Relish, 208; Steak Tartare, 43;
Tapénade, 399; Vitello Tonnato, 594.

CARAMBOLA

Also known as star fruit or star apple, carambola is the waxy, yellow-green fruit of a tropical evergreen tree native to India and Malaya. It has five pronounced exterior ribs. Crosswise slices display a striking star pattern with five dark seeds in the center. Carambolas range from 2 to 5 inches long, depending on place of origin, and are usually about 2 inches wide. The flesh is watery and, depending on variety, can be sour or sweet.

Use Carambolas are eaten raw in fruit salads or out of hand (discard seeds) with a sprinkling of lime juice. Carambola slices can be used to garnish salads or desserts or as an ingredient in fresh fruit tarts or sorbets. Indian cooks make pickles and chutney with carambola and add it to stews; they also make a refreshing drink with crushed fruit, sugar, and ice.

Availability Peak season for fresh carambola is August to February.

Selection Ripe carambolas have a golden color with some browning on the edge of the ribs. Green-tinged carambolas are better for cooking.

Storage Refrigerate in a plastic bag in the crisper and use within three or four days.

Preparation Peel is edible.

CARAMELIZE, TO

To cook sugar slowly until it melts and turns a deep, golden brown. Caramel syrup is used to coat molds for custards and ice cream, as a glaze for cakes and pastries, and to add flavor and color to soups, sauces, and stews. Caramelizing also refers to a type of browning that occurs during cooking.

Recipes and Related Information
Caramels, 95; Crème Brûlée 170; Crème Caramel, 169;
Sugar and Syrup, 567.

CARAWAY SEED

A biennial plant of the parsley family, caraway is native to Asia Minor. It yields a hard brown seed, about ¼ inch long, that is curved and tapered at the ends. Caraway seed has a pungent, slightly sweet flavor akin to anise.

Use Caraway seed is frequently used in the cuisines of middle Europe (Germany, Poland, Austria, Hungary) and Scandinavia. It is kneaded into bread doughs, especially rye bread, and added to cheeses, to pork and sauerkraut dishes, to noodles and cabbage, to short ribs, goose, and other rich meats. It is also the principal flavoring ingredient in kümmel, a cordial.

Availability Caraway seed is sold whole, packed in jars or tins.

Selection Packaged seasonings lose quality after a while; try to buy from a store that restocks its spice section fairly often.

Storage Keep caraway seed in a cool, dark, dry place for up to one year.

CARDAMOM

Also spelled cardamon, cardamom is one of the most aromatic and pungent spices on the spice shelf. It is the dried fruit of a plant in the ginger family, native to India. The plant is low-yielding, and as the fruit must be snipped by hand with scissors, cardamom is necessarily expensive. The fragrant, hard black seeds are encased in a small round seedpod.

Use Indian cooks add cardamom to curries, rice pilafs, and stews for its special aroma and stimulating flavor. It is a common ingredient in an Indian *garam masala*. Scandinavian cooks use cardamom in sweet breads and buns, mulled wine, cakes, and braised meat dishes. In the Middle East, cardamom is used to flavor coffee. It adds an exotic fragrance and sweetness to applesauce and baked apples, poached fruits, and fruit pies.

Availability Whole cardamom pods are packed in jars or plastic bags or are sold in bulk. Whole cardamom seed and ground cardamom seed are packed in jars and tins.

Selection Packaged seasonings lose quality after a while; try to buy from a store that restocks its spice section fairly often.

Storage Keep in a cool, dark, dry place. Ground cardamom will stay pungent for three or four months, whole cardamom pods for about one year.

Preparation Crush whole cardamom pods gently and remove seeds. Add seeds whole to dishes, or grind in a pepper mill, clean coffee grinder, or electric mini-chopper, or with a mortar and pestle. Use sparingly.

LUCIA BUNS

Swedish bakers fashion these inventively shaped, cardamom-spiced rolls for December 13, Saint Lucia Day.

    2 packages active dry yeast
    ½ cup warm (105° to 115° F) water
 1¼ cups warm (105° to 115° F) milk
    ½ cup butter or margarine, softened
    ¾ cup sugar
    1 teaspoon *each* salt and ground cardamom
    2 tablespoons grated orange rind
    6 to 6½ cups flour
    2 eggs
    ½ cup dried currants
      Raisins
      Candied cherries, halved
    1 egg white, beaten with 1 teaspoon water
      Coarse sugar (pearl or decorating sugar, or crushed sugar cubes)

1. Sprinkle yeast over the warm water in large bowl of electric mixer. Let stand until soft (about 5 minutes).

2. Stir in milk, butter, sugar, salt, cardamom, and orange rind, stirring until sugar dissolves. Add 3½ cups of the flour. Mix to blend, then beat at medium speed until smooth and elastic (about 5 minutes).

3. Beat in eggs, one at a time, beating until smooth after each addition. Mix in currants. Gradually stir in about 2 cups more flour to make a soft dough.

4. Turn dough out onto a board or pastry cloth coated with some of the remaining ½ to 1 cup flour. Knead until dough is smooth and satiny and small bubbles form just under surface (12 to 15 minutes). Add enough flour to keep dough from being sticky.

5. Turn dough in a greased bowl. Cover with plastic wrap and a towel; let rise in a warm place until doubled in bulk (1 to 1½ hours).

6. Punch dough down; turn out on a floured surface, cover with inverted bowl, and let rest for 10 minutes. Divide dough into 2 equal portions. Roll each into a 12-inch square. Cut each square in half to make two 6- by 12-inch rectangles. Cut each rectangle crosswise into 12 strips. Roll each strip into a pencil-thin strand 8 inches long.

7. On greased baking sheets cross 2 strands to make an *x*. Curl each end into a small coil. Place a raisin in center of half the coils; place a cherry half in remaining coils. Repeat until all dough is shaped into rolls. Brush rolls lightly with egg white mixture. Sprinkle with coarse sugar. Let rise until almost doubled (30 to 40 minutes). Preheat oven to 400° F.

8. Bake rolls until golden brown (12 to 15 minutes). Serve warm or at room temperature.

Makes 2 dozen rolls.

CARDOON

Although the cardoon resembles celery, it's actually a thistle, like the artichoke. It has foot-long, pale green stalks, a tender white heart, and a flavor reminiscent of both artichoke and celery. Cardoon is much appreciated by both French and Italian cooks.

Use   Cardoon heart (inner stalks) may be steamed or boiled, then drained and buttered or dressed with anchovy sauce, or baked with cheese sauce. Italian cooks steam it, then coat it with egg and bread crumbs, and deep-fry it. It is also a traditional component in an Italian *bagna cauda.*

Availability   Fresh cardoon is a winter vegetable. Peak season is October through December.

Selection   Choose bunches with sturdy, pale green stalks and fresh-looking leaves, and without signs of wilting or decay.

Storage   Refrigerate in a plastic bag in crisper for one to two days.

Preparation   Remove and discard tough outer stalks. Trim spurs and leaves from inner stalks. String outside surfaces of stalks as you would celery by scraping with a paring knife. Cut stalks into ½-inch or larger lengths and keep in water acidulated with vinegar or lemon juice to prevent discoloration before cooking.

Cooking   See BOIL, BRAISE, DEEP-FRY, STEAM.

CAROB

Also called St. John's bread, carob is the pod of a tree native to Syria. According to legend, carob sustained St. John in the wilderness. Although carob is unrelated to chocolate, it has a vaguely similar sweet flavor.

Use   Mediterranean children eat dried carob pods as a sort of candy. In the United States, the seeds are sold in health-food stores and enjoyed as an out of hand snack. The seeds are also ground to produce carob powder or flour, for use in beverages, cakes, cookies, and breads. Carob chips are used as a substitute for chocolate chips in cookies and health-food snacks. Because carob does not contain caffeine and has a naturally sweet taste, some consider it a nutritious alternative to chocolate.

Availability   Carob is sold in most health-food stores as whole seeds, unsweetened chips, toasted powder, or chunks sweetened with dates.

Storage   Refrigerate carob seeds. Store carob chips, chunks, and powder in an airtight container in a cool place; they will keep indefinitely.

CARROT

A root vegetable, carrots have feathery green tops; commonly cultivated varieties are a deep orange color and average about 7 to 8 inches long and ¾ inch in diameter; they get larger and less sweet with age. Baby carrots are increasingly available commercially and are especially attractive on raw vegetable platters.

Use   Carrots have the highest sugar content of any vegetable after beets. They are delicious raw—whole, in sticks, or grated in salads. Carrot sticks are a nutritious addition to a child's lunchbox or an appetizer assortment of raw vegetables. Steamed and buttered or sugar-glazed carrots are a common side dish. Carrots may be creamed or pickled, added to stews, baked in a pudding, made into soup, or added to soups; because of their natural sweetness, they are an essential ingredient in a good basic stock. One of the most popular American desserts— spiced carrot cake with cream cheese frosting—depends on grated raw carrots for its moist, appealing texture and distinctive flavor.

Availability   Fresh carrots are sold all year, in bulk or in plastic bags. Frozen and canned carrots are also available.

Selection   Choose small, slender carrots that are rigid, not rubbery. If tops are attached, they should be fresh looking and bright green. Avoid carrots that are split, pale, or deeply discolored around the stem, which indicates age.

Storage   Remove carrot tops, if attached. Store fresh carrots in a plastic bag in the refrigerator crisper. They will keep for several weeks but will gradually lose sweetness and rigidity.

Preparation   Peel if desired; trim ends.

Cooking   See BOIL, BRAISE, GRILL, STEAM.

■ GLAZED CARROTS

Baby vegetables are charming, especially when dressed up with a buttery glaze. This very simple preparation is one to remember for an impromptu dinner.

   16 baby carrots, scrubbed and trimmed
   ¼ cup butter
   2 tablespoons brandy or fresh lemon juice
   1 tablespoon brown sugar or honey

1. In a large skillet bring salted water to a boil. Add carrots, cover, and simmer until tender-crisp (10 to 15 minutes). Do not overcook. Drain.

2. Push carrots to one side and add butter, brandy, and sugar, stirring to combine. Sauté carrots over medium-high heat, shaking skillet, until carrots are well coated and lightly browned. Serve immediately.

Serves 4.

When combined with white wine and dark raisins, simple root vegetables such as carrots and baby onions become a sophisticated vegetable side dish.

■ CARROT AND BABY ONION STEW WITH RAISINS

Raisins and white wine give this vegetable stew a delicate, sweet-and-sour flavor. When the vegetables are tender, their cooking liquid becomes a buttery glaze. Serve this stew as an accompaniment to any roast, broiled meat, or poultry, especially beef, pork, chicken, and duck. Note that the stew can be prepared as much as two days ahead of serving and stored in the refrigerator until needed.

¼ cup butter
1 pound carrots, quartered and cut in 2-inch pieces
½ pound baby onions, peeled (see Note)
½ cup dark raisins
⅓ cup dry white wine
⅓ cup water
Salt and freshly ground pepper, to taste
1 bay leaf

1. Melt butter in a large frying pan over medium heat. Add carrots and onions and sauté until lightly browned.

2. Add raisins, wine, the water, salt and pepper to taste, and bay leaf. Bring to a boil. Reduce heat to low, cover, and simmer, stirring occasionally, until vegetables are tender (about 35 minutes).

3. Raise heat to medium, uncover, and cook until liquid forms a syrupy glaze (about 10 minutes). If mixture is too watery and vegetables are beginning to fall apart, remove them carefully with a slotted spoon and boil liquid until it thickens; return vegetables to liquid and heat gently. Stew can be kept, covered, up to 2 days in refrigerator; reheat in a covered frying pan over low heat.

4. Taste and add more salt and pepper, if needed; best if served hot.

Serves 4.

Note To peel the baby onions, drop them into a saucepan of boiling water and boil 1 minute. Drain, rinse with cold water until cool, then peel with a paring knife.

Recipes and Related Information
Carrot-Raisin Salad, 507; Carrot Spice Cake, 86; Cream of Any Vegetable Soup, 563; Vegetable Purées, 487.

CARVE, TO

The process of cutting up a whole piece of meat into attractive, serving-sized pieces. The ritual of carving need not be an intimidating process. The proper equipment and a relaxed attitude will make all go much easier. Have on hand a carving knife with a long narrow blade about 8 to 10 inches long and 1 inch wide, made of a material that can be sharpened and that will hold an edge, such as high-carbon stainless steel. Also useful are a two-pronged chef's fork and a carving board with a well.

It's best to let roasts sit anywhere from 15 to 30 minutes, depending upon size, before carving. This resting period allows the juices to recirculate and the internal temperature to equalize. As a rule, carve only what is needed. The rest of the meat will stay moist if stored whole or on the frame. Save juices from meats for a sauce.

Arrange carved meat in an attractive manner on a serving platter, rather than randomly laying slices one on top of another. A garnish, whether the standard sprigs of parsley or a more imaginative choice, always enhances the visual appeal of the food when it is presented at the table. See GARNISH for examples of some basic plate decorations that are easy to master.

Recipes and Related Information
Beef, 37; Lamb, 335; Pork, 455; Poultry, 468; Veal, 591.

CARVING A TURKEY

Cut away trussing string and discard. Insert point of knife into bird where meaty part of leg meets breast; slice through skin down to the hip joint to expose joint. Stick knife directly into the joint and sever leg from body. Leg should fall away easily. Repeat on other side.

Turn leg skin side up; locate joint with knife and cut through to separate drumstick and thigh. Slice meat off drumstick and thigh. Remove wing by slicing through at corner of breast to expose shoulder joint; slice through joint. Remove other wing.

If carving at the table, remove breast meat by slicing at angle in slices about ¼ inch thick. If slicing in the kitchen, remove breast meat in one piece by inserting blade of knife flat along breastbone. Follow contour of bone with knife, and breast half will come away from frame. Repeat on other side. Slice breast meat.

CARVING A STANDING RIB ROAST

Place rib roast on cutting board fat side up. Remove feather bones by cutting down between bones and roast until bones fall away.

Separate meat from rib bones by making a clean vertical cut. Angle knife slightly toward rib bones, beginning at the small end, and continue cutting directly against the bones until you reach and are stopped by the backbone.

Using the rib bones as a guide, slice meat into serving pieces by making even, horizontal slices. Loosen the slices from the backbone and lift away by resting slice on knife and steadying with chef's fork.

CARVING OTHER MEATS

Carving a leg of lamb   This technique can also be used for veal or pork. Have butcher remove the hip bone. Slice away a small piece of meat from underside of leg to stabilize. Starting at narrow (shank) end, make vertical slices into the leg at regular intervals. Free slices by cutting horizontally along bone from shank end to hip joint (big end).

Carving a flank steak   To produce the most tender slices, carve across the grain of the meat and slice very thin. Lay the knife perpendicular to the grain and cut into the steak. Larger slices are produced by cutting diagonally. The more parallel the knife is to the meat— the more it is angled—the bigger the surface area of the slice.

Carving a boneless roast   Don't remove strings until you come to them; they help hold roast together. For a large roast, have it stand on end, then carve horizontally. Hold roast firmly in place with chef's fork below where you will cut. Slice into the meat with a steady sawing motion, keeping the knife as level as possible. For smaller roasts, carve vertically or on a slight diagonal.

CASHEW

The cashew nut is the seed of a tropical fruit called the cashew apple or pear cashew. The fruit itself is pear-shaped and soft like a peach, and may be white, red, or yellow. The kidney-shaped nut, encased in a shell, hangs outside the fruit. The shell is toxic and must be removed and the nuts cleaned before marketing. Cashews have a rich, buttery flavor and a crunchy texture.

Use   Roasted or fried cashews are enjoyed as a snack or predinner nibble. Chopped cashews may be added to cakes, cookies, pies, vegetable sautés, fruit chutneys, and relishes. Indian cooks add fried cashews to rice pilafs, breakfast cereals, and dumplings; they also use cashew nut butter, made from ground roasted cashews, as a thickener for curries.

Availability   Most cashews are roasted before being packed in jars or cans. They are available salted and un-salted. Health-food stores and specialty stores some-times carry raw (unroasted) cashews in bulk; they have a milder, less buttery character than roasted cashews.

Selection   Buy cashews that are as fresh as possible.

Storage   Keep roasted cashews in airtight jars or cans at room temperature for up to one month. They will keep longer if refrigerated or frozen. Raw cashews should be refrigerated or frozen if not used within a few days.

Preparation   See NUT.

CASSEROLES AND BAKING DISHES

Many of these pans are multipurpose. Primarily intended for slow cooking such as making stews and braises, which require extended cooking to tenderize tough cuts of meat, they are also suitable for roasting and for baking such combination dishes as layered entrées, vegetable accom-paniments, and fruit desserts. The more attractive ones can be presented at the table. Capacity ranges from as little as 2 cups to sizes for a crowd. Dishes are made in earthenware, porcelain, copper and other metals, and heat-resistant glass. Most casseroles are safe to use in the microwave oven. Some, however, have ingredients in the materials or glazes that make them unsuitable. To check, follow directions on page 364. See MATERIALS FOR COOKWARE for more information.

Casseroles are lidded pots, designed for slow, moist cooking in the oven; they are often suitable for use on top of the stove as well if they can withstand direct exposure to heat. The best are made of materials that absorb and hold oven heat evenly and efficiently, without scorching or producing hot spots. They have tight-fitting lids that trap steam, thus creating a moist interior that keeps food from drying out during the long cooking period. Because casseroles need little manipulation by the cook and must fit into the oven cavity, they have short handles or none at all. These versatile cookers are optimally effective when food fills most of their interior; the heat is then directed to the food and not to empty space. Buy several in sizes that match what you cook most often.

Casseroles and baking dishes are used for slow-cooked foods such as stews and braises, for roasting, and for baking. Some are multipurpose; they can go in the oven and can also withstand the direct heat of a burner. Clockwise from left to right are small and large covered roasters, electric slow cooker, marmite, bean pot, covered casserole, clay baker, gratin dish.

Baking dishes are low and fairly shallow in comparison with casseroles, don't have covers, and usually don't have handles either. They are suited for foods that need prolonged exposure to steady, even oven heat to evaporate liquid or to provide firmness in the case of fish, custards, egg dishes, rice and grains, vegetable side dishes, and baked entrées. Usually made of porcelain or earthenware, baking dishes can be utilitarian or dressed up enough to take to a dinner party.

CLAY BAKERS

Based on an ancient cooking method used by the Romans and Chinese, these earthenware casseroles are used for baking poultry, slow-cooking meats, and meat dishes. They allow food to bake in its own juices without added fat or basting. Because fragile pottery should not be subject to extreme temperature changes, they are put in a cold, not preheated, oven. Before filling with food, clay bakers without a glazed interior are first soaked in cold water. In the oven the water held in the porous clay converts to steam, which adds moisture to the cooking environment. Interior glazing makes the dish easier to clean, but eliminates its porosity. Never clean unglazed clay cookware with soap or detergent; it will be absorbed into the pores. After using, fill with hot water and let sit for a few hours, then scrub with coarse salt and a plastic sponge. Rinse and thoroughly air-dry. Don't be overly concerned with stains and dark spots, which naturally develop on this type of cookware.

Chinese Clay Pot   With its sand-colored, unglazed exterior and dark brown interior glaze, this pot is ideal for slow cooking over very low heat. The most common design, available in various sizes, is about two thirds as tall as it is wide, with rounded or sloping sides. It may have one long handle or two short loop handles, and may or may not be reinforced with wire on the outside. A 3-quart pot, big enough to hold a whole chicken, is the most useful size. To safely use these fragile pots: Always heat the pot partially filled with liquid, never empty; heat gradually, first over low heat and then increase to medium heat if needed. If cooking on an electric burner, use a heat diffuser to raise the pot up off the heating coils. When a braising calls for an initial stir-frying or browning, do this step in a wok or skillet, not in the heat-sensitive clay pot. To avoid breakage, cool pot before putting on a wet or cold surface. Any heatproof casserole with a tight-fitting lid will work as well as a clay pot for Chinese-style braising. Do not use unglazed earthenware clay bakers for braising; they cannot stand direct heat.

DUTCH OVEN

The cast-iron forerunner of today's Dutch oven hung from a special hook in the large, open fireplaces of colonial American kitchens or was set on a stand over the fire. Cast-iron pots are still popular, but today the Dutch oven has come to mean any large, heavy, lidded pot intended for slow cooking. Other materials used are enameled cast iron, aluminum alloys, and stainless steel. Buy one with a heavy bottom and a tight-fitting cover. Standard size is 5 quarts.

ELECTRIC SLOW COOKER

Essentially an automatic casserole, the electric slow cooker provides slow, moist cooking through a steady, even transfer of heat from heating elements to food through a stoneware insert bowl (stoneware is an excellent absorber of heat). Because the food is cooked so gently and is tightly covered, there is little evaporation; thus meats and poultry are kept from becoming dry. The electric slow cooker is designed to cook throughout the day—8 to 10 hours. It is energy efficient, a boon to those cooks who work out of the home, and it functions at such a low temperature that it doesn't heat up the kitchen. Guidelines for converting. conventional recipes to the slow cooker are provided by the manufacturer. Typically, a stew that requires an hour on top of the stove needs at least six hours in the slow cooker. Capacities range from a compact 1-quart size, for one or two people, to a 6-quart model suitable for large families and for entertaining.

ROASTING PANS AND RACKS

Whether you roast turkey or other meats frequently or only for holiday meals, a heavyweight roasting pan and rack should be considered basic equipment. Roasters are either rectangular or oval and one of two types: high-sided with a domed cover or shallow and open. Covered pans are most commonly used for roasting turkey or chicken. To keep the bird from cooking in its own fat, it is elevated on a rack or on ridges that are part of the bottom surface of the pan. The enclosed interior provides a moist, rather than dry, environment, so the bird actually steams rather than cooks in dry heat. These pans are made of many different materials, usually enameled steel or cast iron, and are sized to match common weights and sizes of poultry. The low and open roasting pan is the choice of most cooks because it is so versatile—for roasting and for casseroles, and for use as a bain-marie (hot water bath). It is sold under several names, sometimes called a roasting pan, lasagne pan, or cake pan. The best materials for the low roaster are aluminum, enameled steel, or copper.

Regardless of type, select a roasting pan that offers the most versatility. Don't buy an oversized pan unless you really need it. If you prepare large birds or roasts, select a pan as large as your oven will hold, but allow several inches of space all around for air circulation. It should be sturdy enough to support a large roast or turkey, but not so heavy that lifting is a struggle. The handles should be well attached and easy to hold; if they are extensions of the sides of the pan, they should be large enough to grip comfortably. For making gravy, be sure the pan can safely cook on the top of the stove as well. Some roasting pans can do double duty for broiling; however, the best broiler pans are still those that come with your oven.

A rack both provides open space beneath a roast so that heat can reach its underside and allows drippings to fall into the pan. Without a rack, the bottom of the roast will stew in the pan juices instead of staying dry and crisp. The most practical racks are collapsible for easy storage; they are made of chromed steel, sometimes coated with a nonstick finish, and are adjustable. Rigid racks are sturdy, but require more storage space when not in use.

SPECIALTY POTS

The shape of each of these three pots evolved to best prepare a particular dish, but all are considered slow cookers.

Bean Pot This pot has a narrow neck, a tubby, rounded bottom, a snug lid, and curved, lug handles. This ungainly but somehow appealing vessel is thought best for developing the characteristic flavor and consistency of that New England favorite—baked beans. Made of ceramic, bean pots come in 2-, 3½-, and 5-quart capacities.

Gratin Dish A gratin has a characteristic crisp, golden brown crust achieved by browning it in the oven or under the broiler. It cooks in a special shallow dish designed to expose a maximum amount of surface so that as much crust as possible is produced; it is the crust that makes a gratin, not what's underneath it. These oval pans often have little ear-shaped handles for transporting dish from oven to table. Sizes range from 4-inch, single-serving dishes to 14-inch dishes designed for multiple servings. They are available in porcelain, tin-lined copper, enameled cast iron, stainless steel, and ovenproof glass.

Marmite In French, *marmite* means casserole. Like the bean pot, this earthenware vessel is wider at the bottom than at the top. Certain soups and stews cooked in a marmite take their name from it; *petite marmite,* a hearty baked soup flavored with meat, poultry, root vegetables, and beef marrow, is one of the best known of these dishes. This pot has rustic charm and you will enjoy serving from it. Capacity ranges from 1½ to 6 quarts.

CAULIFLOWER

A member of the cabbage family, cauliflower is produced by blanching—wrapping the large green leaves around the developing head to block out sunlight. The result is a solid white head made up of small, tightly compacted white flowers on thick stems. Although most people eat only the florets, the entire plant is edible, including the leaves.

Use Cauliflower may be eaten raw, with oil and salt or a dipping sauce. It is a common addition to *crudités* assortments. Steamed or boiled cauliflower may be simply buttered, or dressed with cheese sauce, browned sliced almonds, or buttered bread crumbs. It may be cooked, cooled, and dressed with vinaigrette or mayonnaise. Cauliflower may be pickled, added to soups or stews, or fried tempura style.

Availability Fresh cauliflower is sold all year but is most abundant late fall until spring. Cauliflower is also available frozen.

Selection Choose cauliflower with fresh-looking green leaves, if they are still attached, and without brown spots on the head.

Storage Refrigerate fresh cauliflower in a plastic bag in the crisper for up to four or five days.

Preparation Wash thoroughly, trim stem end, and remove leaves (cook separately, if desired). Cook whole or use a small sharp knife to separate into smaller florets.

Cooking See BOIL, STEAM.

■ PAKORAS

Indian vegetable fritters or *pakoras* can be fried before guests arrive and reheated at the last minute in a 375° F oven for 10 minutes. Instead of wheat flour, Indian cooks traditionally use chick-pea flour. Because this flour is very difficult to find in this country, the recipe has been developed with all-purpose flour. You may substitute cooked potato cubes or shredded carrots for the cauliflower.

> 1 **head cauliflower (about 1 lb), cut into florets**
> 1 **onion, minced**
> 1 **clove garlic, minced**
> 2 **tablespoons vegetable oil**
> 2 **teaspoons jalapeño chile, minced**
> 4 **sprigs parsley, minced**
> 2 **sprigs fresh mint, minced**
> 1½ **cups flour**
> 1 **tablespoon baking powder**
> 1 **teaspoon salt**
> 1 **teaspoon cumin seed**
> ¼ **teaspoon turmeric**
> ¼ **teaspoon freshly ground black pepper**
> ⅛ **teaspoon cayenne pepper**
> ¾ **cup water**
> ½ **cup milk**
> **Oil, for frying**
> **Cilantro Raita, for accompaniment**
> **(see page 522)**

1. Cook florets in 3 quarts boiling water for 3 minutes. Remove with a slotted spoon, drain, and pat dry.

2. In a medium skillet sauté onion and garlic in oil over medium heat until softened (about 8 minutes). Stir in jalapeño, parsley, and mint; cook 2 to 3 minutes more. Reserve.

3. In a medium bowl combine flour, baking powder, salt, cumin seed, turmeric, black pepper, and cayenne pepper. Slowly stir in the water and milk to make a thick batter. Let rest 30 minutes.

4. Stir in reserved cauliflower and onion mixture. To deep-fry, heat 4 to 5 inches of oil in a 3-quart saucepan or wok to 375° F. Add batter, 1 teaspoon at a time, taking care not to crowd pan. Fry 3 minutes, carefully turn over with wire skimmer or slotted spoon, and fry second side 2 minutes. Remove from hot oil with skimmer and drain on paper towels. Cool briefly. Serve with Cilantro Raita.

Makes 36 to 40 pakoras.

CAVIAR

Although caviar refers traditionally to the roe of sturgeon, the word is being used increasingly to designate the roe of other fish such as salmon and whitefish.

Most sturgeon caviar comes from one of three varieties of sturgeon, whose principal home is the Caspian Sea bordering Russia and Iran. Beluga caviar from the beluga sturgeon is the most desirable; the eggs are gray to almost black, are the largest of sturgeon caviars, and have the most delicate taste. The eggs of the osetra sturgeon are golden yellow to brown and have a stronger flavor. The sevruga sturgeon yields the eggs with the strongest flavor; they are light to dark gray. Domestic caviar comes from Washington and Oregon sturgeon.

Although beluga caviar is generally the finest, quality depends to a large extent on the individual fish and on how carefully roe is processed. To prepare caviar, eggs are removed from the roe sac, inspected and cleaned, then pushed by hand through a screen or cotton sieve to separate them from membrane. The roe is then brined to flavor and preserve it before it is packed with salt in tins. The best caviar is *malossol,* Russian for *lightly salted.*

Pressed caviar is made from mature eggs, usually from sturgeon caught late in the season. The eggs are pressed together to make a strongly flavored concentrate. It is less expensive than other sturgeon caviars, and some prefer its full flavor.

Salmon caviar ranges from light orange to dark red depending on the salmon variety. The eggs are larger than sturgeon roe but are processed in a similar fashion.

Whitefish caviar, also called golden caviar, is from Great Lakes whitefish. The eggs are a bright yellow-gold and quite small.

Use Caviar is enjoyed as an appetizer, with buttered toast or blini to support it. The best caviar does not require another garnish; roe of lesser quality may be served with lemon, sour cream, minced hard-cooked egg, or onion. Caviar may also be used as a garnish for pasta or raw oysters. It should never be cooked.

Availability Sturgeon caviar is usually available fresh or pasteurized; it cannot be successfully frozen. Salmon caviar is available fresh, pasteurized, or frozen. Whitefish caviar is sold fresh or frozen. Caviar is always packed in tins or jars.

Selection All fish eggs (except for pressed caviar) should be firm, crisp, and separate, not mushy or soupy. They should have a clean, fresh briny smell and flavor.

Storage Pasteurized, vacuum-packed caviar does not require refrigeration until opening. After opening, refrigerate and use as soon as possible. Fresh caviar should be stored at 28° F, which is warmer than a freezer but cooler than a home refrigerator. For best storage, pack tin or jar in ice and store in coldest part of the refrigerator. If unopened, it will keep for up to one month. After opening, use within a couple of days. Pressed caviar should be stored and used similarly. Frozen caviar should be slowly thawed in refrigerator and eaten immediately.

Preparation To serve, rest caviar tin or jar in a bowl of ice and open at the last moment. Pressed caviar should be removed from refrigerator half an hour before serving to facilitate spreading.

■ NEW POTATOES WITH CAVIAR
Caviar need not be expensive imported sturgeon roe (although it can be). Let your budget be your guide in selecting from among the variety of colorful caviars on the market (see left). The contrast of warm potato and ice-cold caviar makes a memorable mouthful. This recipe would be sophisticated picnic fare: To carry to picnic site, wrap potatoes in aluminum foil to keep them warm and pack caviar in ice. If desired, substitute sour cream for Lemon Crème Fraîche.

    3 dozen tiny red-skinned new potatoes
    Olive oil
    Kosher salt
    Juice of 1 lemon
    12 ounces assorted caviar (golden, red, and black)
    Lemon wedges

Lemon Crème Fraîche

    1 cup whipping cream, buttermilk, or sour cream
    2 tablespoons fresh lemon juice

1. Steam potatoes over boiling salted water until they are just tender when pierced. Dry them well; drizzle them while hot with olive oil, then sprinkle with salt and lemon juice. Cut off top of each potato about ¼ inch down; scoop out and discard some of the inside pulp, leaving a firm, thick-sided shell. Wrap potatoes in foil and place in a tightly sealed container.

2. At serving time, set out potato shells, caviars, crème fraîche or sour cream, lemon wedges, some tiny serving spoons, and plenty of napkins. Guests can fill their potato shells with crème fraîche or sour cream and the caviar of their choice, with a little lemon juice squeezed over the top.

Serves 12.

Lemon Crème Fraîche In a small bowl or a jar, mix whipping cream and lemon juice and let sit at room temperature until mixture thickens to the consistency of sour cream. This will take 12 to 24 hours depending on the temperature of the room. Refrigerate after thickening; it will keep for several weeks.

Makes 1 cup.

Recipes and Related Information
Basic Crêpes, 602; Blini, 602.

CAVIAR FOR THE BUDGET CONSCIOUS

Serving good sturgeon caviar at a cocktail party is out of the question for most hosts and hostesses. Some people compromise by buying inexpensive lumpfish, but although it may look like the real thing, it is salty and indelicate and only serves to remind its eaters of what they're missing. Others may splurge on a little of the good stuff but have to spread it so thin that no one gets to enjoy it. Such economy combined with extravagance brings to mind the legendary Colette, who flatly stated (speaking of truffles), "If I can't have too many, I'll do without."

Now there's a better way. The golden caviar of Great Lakes whitefish is being sold across the country and at very reasonable prices relative to its quality. These tiny golden eggs not only look good but taste good if they've been well cared for.

Most golden caviar is flash-frozen after processing; otherwise, the eggs get soggy and collapse almost immediately. When you buy it, it should still be frozen, or you should ask how long it has been out of the freezer.

(Some markets take a tin or so out of the freezer each day to display on ice.) Don't buy a tin that has been out of the freezer more than one day.

Ideally, caviar should be stored at 28° F, which is colder than a refrigerator, but not as cold as most home freezers. When you bring caviar home, fill a bowl with ice, nestle the tin in the ice, and set the bowl in the coldest part of the refrigerator. (Make sure water cannot seep into the tin.) Then serve it within one or two days.

You can serve golden caviar just as you would black caviar. The only difference is that you don't have to scrimp! Spread it on warm buttered toast and serve with lemon. Spoon liberally onto blini (see page 602) with sour cream. Serve slices of small boiled potatoes topped with sour cream and caviar. Spoon a dollop of sour cream and some caviar atop crêpes (see page 602) and sprinkle all with dill. Spoon a little onto raw oysters on the half shell. Fill tiny Cream Puffs (see page 163) with sour cream, caviar, and chopped chives.

CAYENNE PEPPER
Finely ground red pepper from a variety of dried red capsicum peppers (chiles) is the source of cayenne pepper. Orange red to red, depending on the chiles used to prepare it, it varies in intensity but is always hot.

Use Cayenne pepper adds a spark of heat to foods. It is used in numerous cuisines to flavor just about everything, including dessert. Cooks add it to eggs, fish, vegetables, sauces, soups, stews, curries, chutneys, and chili. Just a pinch will heighten the flavor of almost any dish; before adding cayenne pepper to a recipe, see Preparation for a caution about variation in pungency.

Availability Cayenne pepper is sold packed in jars or airtight bags.

Selection Packaged dried seasonings lose quality after a while; try to buy from a store that restocks its spice section fairly often.

Storage Keep in an airtight container in a cool, dry, dark place. Replace every six months.

Preparation Because cayenne blends vary in pungency, use with restraint at first, then taste and adjust seasoning as desired.

Recipes and Related Information
Corn Maquechoux, 158; Stuffed Mirliton, 110.

CELERIAC

Grown primarily for its swollen root, celeriac is a type of celery. About the size of a baseball, the knobby, brown-skinned root has long, celerylike stalks that are usually removed in processing for the retail market. The appearance of this vegetable gave rise to its other common names: celery root, celery knob, and turnip-rooted celery. It has firm, crisp white flesh with a flavor that very much resembles that of celery.

Use   Celeriac may be eaten raw in salads or cooked in soups, stews, and casseroles. Boiled celeriac may be whipped with butter and cream, or mixed with whipped potatoes. Sliced celeriac may be baked in a cream or cheese sauce. French cooks cut raw celeriac into fine matchsticks and dress it with a mustard mayonnaise to make *céleri-rave rémoulade,* a salad popular with both home cooks and chefs.

Availability   Fresh celeriac is most readily found fall through winter.

Selection   Choose small to medium celery root that is firm, not spongy.

Storage   Celeriac will stay fresh in a plastic bag in the refrigerator crisper for up to one week.

Preparation   Peel with a small, stainless steel paring knife (carbon knives discolor celeriac). Plunge immediately into acidulated water to prevent discoloration. Slice, grate, or cube as recipe directs. Celeriac may also be washed and boiled in its skin, then peeled.

Cooking   See BOIL.

■ CELERY ROOT SALAD
Céleri-rave rémoulade

The unglamorous celery root, when peeled and shredded, can be transformed into an elegant salad, often served as a first course in French restaurants. A creamy dressing made of mustard and shallot coats the crunchy pieces. Use a food processor, if you have one, fitted with a shredding disk, for the tedious shredding job. A food processor also makes quick work out of emulsifying the ingredients for the piquant dressing.

       1   **large (1 to 1½ lb) celery root**
       2   **tablespoons fresh lemon juice**
       1   **egg yolk**
       2   **tablespoons tarragon wine vinegar**
       1   **tablespoon Dijon mustard**
       ½   **teaspoon salt**
           Pinch cayenne pepper
       1   **shallot, finely chopped**
       ¼   **cup** *each* **olive oil and vegetable oil**
           Butter or Boston lettuce leaves
           Chopped parsley, for garnish

1. Peel celery root thoroughly, cutting out any deep bits of peel. Shred quickly, using a food processor or grater (you should have 5 to 6 cups). Immediately mix well with lemon juice to prevent discoloration. Cover and refrigerate for about 1 hour.

2. In a medium bowl beat egg yolk with vinegar, mustard, salt, cayenne, and shallot. Using a whisk or fork, gradually beat in oils, a small amount at a time, until dressing is thick and creamy.

3. Shortly before serving, mix celery root lightly with dressing to coat.

4. Serve celery root mixture on lettuce leaves, sprinkled with parsley.

Serves 6.

Food Processor Version   Use a metal blade to process egg yolk, vinegar, mustard, salt, cayenne, and 1 tablespoon oil for 1 minute. Slowly add remaining oil. Add shallot and process 10 seconds more.

Recipes and Related Information
Sherried Oxtail Soup, 501; Vegetable Purées, 487.

CELERY

A member of the same vegetable family as carrots and parsley, celery has long, crisp stalks that may reach a foot in length. Some varieties are forcibly blanched and are white or very pale green throughout. Most commercial celery, however, has green outer stalks and pale green inner stalks furled around a central heart. Celery has pungent green leaves that are often removed in processing for the retail market.

Use   The crisp texture of raw celery is appealing in salads or as an hors d'oeuvre, often stuffed with a creamy cheese. It adds texture and flavor to soups, stuffings, and stews. Its flavor is important, if not essential, to stock-making. It is also a required ingredient in a classic French *mirepoix,* the mixture of diced aromatic root vegetables used to flavor sauces, soups, and stews. Braised celery hearts (the tender, innermost stalks) are a good companion to game, duck, or pork.

Availability   Fresh celery is sold the year around, either loose or packed in cellophane bags.

Selection   Choose celery that looks moist and crisp, and does not show signs of limpness or drying. Generally speaking, the darker the color, the stronger the flavor.

Storage   Refrigerate celery in a plastic bag in crisper for up to 10 days.

Preparation   Trim ends, remove leaves, and peel away any tough outer strings. Save leaves for use in stock.

Cooking   See BOIL, BRAISE, STIR-FRY.

■ BRAISED CELERY WITH WALNUTS

Although usually thought of as a salad vegetable in this country, celery is delicious cooked and served as a side dish. As celery is fibrous and won't cook tender with a brief sauté, it must first be parboiled to cook partway.

        1 head celery, separated into stalks and washed
        2 tablespoons butter
        1 small onion, finely chopped
        ⅓ cup walnuts, coarsely chopped
            Grated rind of 1 lemon

1. Cut celery diagonally into 1½-inch pieces. In a medium saucepan bring to a boil enough salted water to cover celery; add celery and parboil 5 minutes. Drain.

2. Meanwhile, in a large frying pan melt butter. Add onion and walnuts and sauté briefly. Add lemon rind and celery. Toss to coat celery.

Serves 4.

CELERY SEED

This tiny, pungent seed is the fruit of wild celery, which is also known as smallage.

Use Celery seed adds a celerylike flavor to soups, salad dressings, pickling mixtures, tomato juice, potato salad, cole slaw, stuffings, meat loaf, and shellfish stews. It is ground and mixed with salt to make celery salt.

Availability Celery seed is packaged in airtight jars or plastic bags.

Selection Packaged seasonings lose quality after a while; try to buy from a store that restocks its spice section fairly often.

Storage Keep in a cool, dry, dark place; replace celery seed once a year.

CHAYOTE

Also known as mirliton, vegetable pear, *chocho,* and christophine, the chayote is a pear-shaped, tropical squash native to Central America. It has been grown in North Africa and exported to Europe for years as a gourmet vegetable. Chayote is becoming increasingly available in markets throughout the United States. Its skin is smooth, thin, pale green to green with slight ridges; its flesh is moist and creamy white, with a delicate, slightly sweet flavor often compared to that of a cucumber. The single flat seed is edible with a nutty taste. On the average chayotes measure 4 to 6 inches in length and weigh about 1 pound.

Use Chayote may be used like any other squash: baked, steamed, boiled, stuffed, or fried. Its mild flavor is a good

counterpoint to spicy stuffings and other spicy treatments, although it is often simply steamed and buttered or cooled and dressed in vinaigrette.

Availability Peak availability for fresh chayote is October through April. If you cannot find chayote, try a large pattypan squash.

Selection Choose small unblemished chayotes with dark green skins.

Storage Refrigerate in a plastic bag in crisper for up to two weeks.

Preparation Young chayotes with tender skins do not need to be peeled; peel mature squash. Halve or quarter and remove seed.

Cooking See BOIL, SAUTE, STEAM.

Céleri-rave rémoulade is the French name for this very popular salad made of shredded celeriac (celery root) tossed in a tangy mustard-shallot dressing.

■ STUFFED MIRLITON

The mild flavor of chayote takes well to the spicy stuffing given in this recipe from Louisiana, where the vegetable is known as mirliton.

    2   chayotes, cut in half lengthwise
    4   cups water
    ¼   cup unsalted butter
    ½   pound andouille (sausage), chopped
    1   cup chopped onion
    ½   cup chopped celery
    ½   cup chopped green bell pepper
    1   tablespoon minced garlic
    ½   pound raw shrimp, shelled, deveined,
        and chopped
    ½   cup chopped green onions
    ½   teaspoon basil
    ¼   teaspoon thyme
    ½   teaspoon cayenne pepper
    1   teaspoon Worcestershire sauce
    ¾   to 1 cup dry bread crumbs
        Salt and freshly ground pepper, to taste

1. Place halved chayotes in a pan large enough to hold them in a single layer, cover with the water, and bring to a boil. Boil over medium heat until flesh of squash is tender (about 30 minutes). Remove from pan and cool under cold water. Remove seeds and scoop out pulp, being careful not to break through skin of chayotes. Chop pulp; reserve pulp and shells.

2. Preheat oven to 350° F. In a 12-inch frying pan over medium heat, melt butter. Add *andouille* and cook until slightly browned (about 5 minutes). Add onion and celery and cook until vegetables are soft (about 10 minutes). Add green pepper and garlic and cook for another 2 minutes. Add chopped shrimp and cook until shrimp turns pink (1 to 2 minutes). Add green onion, basil, thyme, cayenne, Worcestershire, and chopped chayote pulp. Add enough bread crumbs to bind the stuffing. Taste for salt and pepper; correct if necessary. Fill chayote shells with stuffing and bake for 30 minutes.

Serves 4.

Food Processor Version   Use metal blade to chop 1 medium onion and 1 stalk celery. Add to andouille. With metal blade process 1 small green pepper, cut in 1-inch pieces, and 3 cloves garlic; add to pan.

CHEESE

Despite their remarkable variety, almost all cheeses start cut as coagulated milk. The milk is coagulated by adding bacteria that cause it to curdle—to separate into solid curds and liquid whey. The vast differences in taste and texture depend on three factors: the source of the milk, the treatment after coagulation, and the aging process.

Most of the world's cheeses are made from cow's, goat's, or sheep's milk. Italian buffalo-milk mozzarella is one notable exception. Not only do the different types of animals yield milk of very different character, but the flavor of the milk is affected by the season and the region. Summer milk from cows that have grazed on pastureland tastes different from—many say better than—winter milk from grain-fed cows. Microorganisms in a given region also contribute to the flavor of a cheese, which partly explains why cheeses made by the same methods in different regions will not taste the same.

PROCESSING

Cheeses may be made from whole milk, skimmed milk, or milk with added cream (such as the French double and triple creams). The higher the fat portion of the milk or milk and cream mixture, the creamier and smoother the final cheese.

Cheese may also be made from either pasteurized or unpasteurized (raw) milk. Pasteurizing kills bacteria that impart flavor to cheese, which is why many consumers claim that a raw-milk cheese has better flavor than the same cheese made from pasteurized milk. Raw-milk cheeses are strictly regulated because raw milk is a potential carrier of disease-causing bacteria. Raw-milk cheeses, both imported and domestic, must be aged at least 60 days. Many cheeses—such as Maytag Blue from Iowa and Parmesan and Fontina Val d'Aosta from Italy—are made from raw milk and meet this aging requirement. Others, such as French Camembert and Brie, are aged less than 60 days and must be made from pasteurized milk if intended for sale in this country.

Raw-milk cheeses depend on natural bacteria to produce lactic acid, which curdles the milk by coagulating its protein (casein). Pasteurized milk does not contain these acid-producing bacteria; they must be introduced with a culture or starter. Sometimes rennet, an enzyme extracted from the stomachs of young calves, is added to speed coagulation. For some cheeses, coloring is added at this point; to make blue-veined cheeses such as Gorgonzola, the milk is inoculated with mold spores.

After coagulation the curd is cut into smaller pieces to encourage draining of the whey—the liquid, noncoagulating portion. The size of the cut and the length of the draining period determine the texture and moisture content of the finished cheese. Curds cut into large pieces and left to drain briefly produce a moist, soft cheese. Smaller cuts and a longer draining period yield a firmer cheese. Sometimes the curd is cooked or briefly heated with the whey before draining; this process produces a firm hard cheese such as Gruyère.

Some curds are ladled into molds and allowed to drain naturally. Others are molded and pressed, either lightly or heavily, to establish a shape and expel even more whey. Pressed cheeses have a firmer, more solid texture than unpressed cheeses.

After molding, cheeses may be soaked in brine or repeatedly washed with water, brine, or alcohol. They may be sprayed with spores to produce an exterior mold; they may also be waxed, smoked, wrapped with herbs or leaves, coated with ashes, or soaked in oil.

Lastly, some cheeses are aged or ripened under controlled temperature and humidity. Aging develops flavor and causes moisture loss. Generally, the longer a cheese has been aged, the stronger in flavor and drier it will be. Young Parmesan can be sliced and has a smooth, nutty flavor; aged Parmesan, best for grating, has a sharp flavor.

TYPES OF CHEESE

To make sense of the enormous variety of cheeses, it helps to classify or categorize them in some way. One helpful system is to classify them by texture: Are they hard or soft? Sliceable? Spreadable? Another system is to classify them by the source of the milk: cow, sheep, goat. Some cheeses are traditionally grouped together because they're made by a common process, such as the blue-veined and *pasta filata* cheeses.

Some of the more traditional classifications are outlined below. Categories inevitably overlap, and placement of a cheese in a particular category is somewhat arbitrary. A cheese may be semihard when young but hard when aged. Blue cheeses may be classified by texture—Gorgonzola is semisoft, Stilton is semihard—but they are generally grouped together because of their color.

CLASSIFICATION BY TEXTURE: SOFT CHEESE

Soft-textured cheeses, also known as fresh cheeses, include such popular varieties as cottage cheese, cream cheese, and French *fromage blanc*. They are uncooked and unripened or barely ripened; they are often not molded, but simply spooned into tubs. Soft cheeses are usually very mild and creamy.

Use Fresh cheeses such as cream cheese may be spread on crackers or bread. Cottage and pot cheeses may be salted and eaten with crisp vegetables as a salad, or sugared and eaten with fruit for breakfast or dessert. Serve slightly chilled. *Mascarpone* or whipped, sweetened cream cheese may be used to fill crêpes or fruit tarts. Fresh cheeses may also be made into cheesecakes and cheese pies.

Selection Buy soft cheeses from a market that has a rapid turnover.

Storage Because of their high moisture content, soft cheeses are highly perishable; all should be refrigerated in a covered container and most should be eaten within one week.

Cheeses in This Category Cottage cheese, pot cheese, farmer cheese, cream cheese, Neufchâtel, Gervais, *fromage blanc,* ricotta, *stracchino, mascarpone.*

■ COEUR A LA CREME

This charming molded cheese dessert is traditionally made in a heart-shaped basket or porcelain dish that is pierced on the bottom so the mixture can drain as it sets. The molds are available at better cookware stores.

1 pound cottage cheese
1 pound cream cheese, softened
1 teaspoon vanilla extract
  Pinch of salt
1 cup confectioners' sugar, sifted
2 cups whipping cream
1 pint whole strawberries *or* 1 cup Raspberry Sauce (see page 522), for garnish

1. Have ready a heart-shaped, 8-cup *coeur à la crème* mold. Dampen a towel and press into mold, leaving towel ends free.

2. Press cottage cheese through a sieve or whirl briefly in food processor; place in a 2-quart mixing bowl. Stir in cream cheese, vanilla, and salt. Add confectioners' sugar.

3. Whip cream to soft peaks; fold into cheese mixture. Pour mixture into prepared mold and cover with towel ends. Place mold in a shallow dish and chill 8 to 12 hours.

4. To unmold, fold back towel. Set serving plate over cheese and invert. Remove mold and towel from cheese. Garnish with whole strawberries or Raspberry Sauce.

Serves 8 to 10.

Recipes: Buttermilk Blintzes, 600; Cheese Roulade, 206; Figs With Flavored Ricotta, 220; Gnocchi Verde, 190; Marbled Cream Cheese Brownies, 65; New York–Style Cheesecake, 117; Ricotta Cheesecake, 119; Unbaked Cheesecake, 118.

A simple, but appealing dinner finale in the European tradition features a variety of cheeses in wedges, slices, or balls, served with fruits, nuts, and crackers. Offer a selection of fruit liqueurs or serve a dessert wine such as a late-harvest Zinfandel, a port, or a Muscat Canelli.

BRIE IN PUFF PASTRY

Center wheel of Brie on top of smaller puff pastry circle. Brush water on pastry from cheese to pastry edge. Cover with larger circle of pastry and press gently on top piece of dough at edges to seal the two circles together. Freeze until dough is firm but not frozen (about 10 minutes).

Cut a scallop pattern around edge of dough. Cut a ¼-inch hole in center of pastry (do not puncture cheese). Roll a 1-inch by 1½-inch piece of foil into a tube; set in hole in pastry (will serve as a steam vent).

Brush pastry decorations with water and apply to top. Freeze 20 minutes. Remove from freezer. Brush top of pastry with egg wash. Bake 20 to 25 minutes at 425° F.

CLASSIFICATION BY TEXTURE: SOFT-RIPENED CHEESES

Soft-ripened cheeses have not been cooked or pressed. Instead they are cut in large curds and allowed to drain naturally. They are then sprayed with spores or washed with brine, water, or alcohol to promote development of a rind. Sprayed cheeses develop a powdery white rind; washed cheeses develop an orange-hued rind.

These cheeses ripen from the rind inward. When fully ripe, they have a smooth, almost spreadable texture and range in flavor from mild to quite strong.

Use   Soft-ripened cheeses are delicious dinner cheeses, served after the main course but before dessert. They are traditionally offered with bread or crackers and wine. The rind is edible, although some prefer to cut it away. Serve soft-ripened cheeses at room temperature.

Selection   These cheeses should give slightly to pressure. They should feel supple but not liquid. Avoid any that have a chalky white center (they are underripe) or a strong ammonia odor (they are overripe). The rind should be evenly colored and slightly moist.

Storage   Keep them in the refrigerator, wrapped airtight in plastic; change wrapping every few days. Use within a couple of weeks.

Cheeses in This Category   Boursault, Brie, Brillat-Savarin, Camembert, *Caprice des Dieux, Carré de l'Est, Chaource,* Coulommiers, Liederkranz, Limburger, Muenster, Pont l'Eveque.

■ BRIE OR CAMEMBERT IN PUFF PASTRY

Soft-ripened cheeses, such as a round of Brie or Camembert, are a special treat when baked in puff pastry (see photographs at left). Wedges of the pastry served with a glass of wine and fresh fruit are delicious after dinner. You can enclose any size wheel of Brie or Camembert in puff pastry. Allow 2 ounces of cheese per person for a small serving. One recipe of puff pastry can easily enclose a 1-pound wheel of cheese. You can make circles of puff pastry from 1½ pounds virgin puff pastry and use trimmings to decorate the outside of the pastry.

    1½ recipes (2 lb) Classic Puff Pastry
        with 6 turns (see page 482)
    2   wheels (8 oz and 4 in. diameter each)
        Brie or Camembert, well-chilled, *or*
    1   wheel (16 oz and 8 in. diameter)
    1   egg, lightly beaten with 1 teaspoon water

1. Roll out Classic Puff Pastry a little less than ¼ inch thick. Chill sheet of dough until firm. If using two 4-inch wheels of cheese, cut out two 6-inch circles and two 7-inch circles of puff pastry. If using one 8-inch wheel, cut out one 10-inch circle and one 11-inch circle. Cover and refrigerate 30 minutes. Gather scraps of dough into a ball; refrigerate 30 minutes.

2. Roll out trimmings of dough as thin as possible (less than ⅛ inch thick) ; freeze until very cold but not frozen. Use pastry cutters or a sharp knife to make cutouts for decorating top of puff pastry (stems, leaves, flowers, grapes, etc.). Freeze decorations until firm. Freeze wheels of cheese no longer than 20 minutes.

3. Place two 6-inch circles (or one 10-inch circle) of puff pastry on a parchment-lined baking sheet. Place a wheel of cheese in center of each. Brush water around the border from cheese to edge of pastry. Cover each wheel with a 7-inch circle of puff pastry dough (or an 11-inch circle if using larger wheel). Press down on dough around base of cheese with fingertips to seal edges of dough together. Firm dough in freezer 10 minutes.

4. When dough is well chilled but not frozen, cut a scallop pattern at edge of pastry with a sharp knife. Create a hollow aluminum foil tube (a chimney) by wrapping a 1-inch by 1½-inch strip of foil 2 or 3 times around a pencil; butter exterior of foil tube and remove pencil. Cut a ¼-inch hole in center of top layer of pastry and fit buttered tube into it. This will allow steam from inside pastry to escape. Brush cutout decorations with water and apply in an attractive pattern on top. Return to freezer for 20 minutes. Preheat oven to 425° F.

5. Remove pastry rounds from freezer, and brush top of each with egg wash (take care not to drip any down sides of pastry). Bake until golden brown (20 to 25 minutes). Cool for 30 to 45 minutes before cutting. If served immediately, cheese will run out after pastry is cut. Cut each pastry into 4 (or 8 if using a large wheel) wedges.

Serves 8.

CLASSIFICATION BY TEXTURE: SEMISOFT CHEESES

The cheeses in this category have generally been pressed but not cooked. Ranging in flavor from very mild to strong, they have a soft texture but can be sliced. Many of these cheeses were originally made by European monks and are known as monastery cheeses.

Use   Serve semisoft cheeses as part of a cheese board, with bread or crackers and wine. Bring to room temperature before serving. Because they can be sliced, they may be used for sandwiches. Because they melt well, they may be used in grilled sandwiches or as a topping for many types of casseroles.

Selection   Choose semisoft cheeses that give slightly to pressure. They may smell strong, but they should not smell rank or ammoniated.

Storage   Keep semisoft cheese in the refrigerator, wrapped airtight in plastic; change wrapping every few days. Semisoft cheeses keep for up to one month.

Cheeses in This Category   Bel Paese, brick, Esrom, Gouda, Havarti, Livarot, Monterey jack, *morbier*, Oka, Port Salut, *reblochon*, Saint Paulin, Samsoe, Sonoma jack, *taleggio*, Tilsit.

Recipes: Cheese Roulade, 206; Chiles Rellenos, 428; Refried Beans, 35; Tiropita, 223.

CLASSIFICATION BY TEXTURE: SEMIFIRM CHEESES

These cheeses have been cooked and pressed to eliminate excess moisture. They may or may not have a rind. Texture is firm but smooth and allows cheeses to be sliced; flavor ranges from mild to sharp.

Use   Serve semifirm cheeses as part of a cheese board, with bread or crackers and wine. Bring to room temperature before serving. Because they can be sliced, they may be used for sandwiches. Most semifirm cheeses also melt well and may be grated for use in a range of cooked dishes, such as omelets, soufflés, sauces, breads, puddings, pies, and casseroles.

Selection   Avoid semifirm cheese with a cracked rind or a dry, crumbly texture.

Storage   Keep in refrigerator, wrapped airtight in plastic; change wrapping every few days. For long storage, overwrap plastic with aluminum foil and store in bottom of refrigerator. Coating cut side of cheese with butter or hot paraffin before wrapping prevents drying and the development of surface mold. Semifirm cheeses keep for several months under these conditions. They may also be frozen for up to two months. Wrap tightly in plastic, then in foil, and freeze quickly. Thaw slowly in refrigerator.

Cheeses in This Category   Appenzeller, Asiago, Caerphilly, Cantal, Cheddar, Cheshire, Danbo, Derby and Sage Derby, Double Gloucester, Edam, Emmentaler, fontina, Gjetost, Gruyère, Jarlsberg, *raclette*.

◼ FONTINA FRITTERS

Golden brown outside and molten within, these fritters are a heavenly mouthful. The batter may be made ahead, but the cheese must be fried at the last minute. Serve with a crisp, white Italian wine, such as an Orvieto or a Soave.

 ¾ **pound chilled fontina, not too ripe**
 ¼ **cup dry white wine**
 2 **eggs, separated**
 1 **teaspoon minced garlic**
 1 **teaspoon baking powder**
1½ **cups flour**
 1 **teaspoon salt**
2½ **tablespoons olive oil**
 ½ **to ⅔ cup ice water**
   Vegetable oil, for deep-frying
 ½ **cup minced fresh basil**
   Salt, to taste

1. Cut cheese into 1-inch cubes. In a bowl whisk together wine, egg yolks, and garlic. Whisk in baking powder, flour, and 1 teaspoon salt. Whisk in oil, then add enough of the ice water to make a thick but pourable batter, about the consistency of pancake batter. Let rest at room temperature for 2 hours.

2. When ready to serve, heat 2 inches of vegetable oil in a frying pan to 360° F. Beat egg whites with a pinch of salt until stiff but not dry. Fold into batter along with minced basil.

3. Dip cheese chunks into batter. Allow excess batter to drip off; fry chunks in oil until uniformly golden. Drain fritters on paper towels and salt lightly. Serve fritters immediately.

Serves 8 with other hors d'oeuvres.

Dip cubes of fontina cheese in batter, then fry until crisp and brown. The piping-hot Fontina Fritters makes a fine appetizer, served with chilled white wine and herbed olives.

CLASSIFICATION BY TEXTURE: FIRM CHEESES

These pressed, cooked cheeses have been aged until dry and hard. When young, they can be sliced; when aged, they must be grated.

Use   Hard cheeses are rarely used as table cheeses, except when young. Young Parmesan, dry jack, and Asiago can be sliced and may be served after dinner with fruit or nuts. Dry, aged cheeses are designed for grating. Use

A crock of English Stilton cheese mixed with mellow port makes a royal spread for small toasts or crackers.

CLASSIFICATION BY PROCESS: BLUE-VEINED CHEESES

Inoculating cheese with mold spores will, with time, produce a blue-veined interior. Blue-veined cheeses are generally pungent; they range in texture from the moist creaminess of Gorgonzola to the firm, slightly crumbly Stilton.

Use   Blue-veined cheeses are a pleasing addition to an after-dinner cheese board. Complemented by apples, pears, and walnuts, they should be served with crackers or bread and a rich red wine or port. Bring to room temperature before serving. Crumbled blue cheese makes a piquant addition to salads and salad dressings. Blue cheese may be whipped half and half with butter to make a cracker spread or a topping for grilled meats.

Selection   Blue cheeses may smell strong but should not smell rank or ammoniated. If possible, sample before buying; avoid cheeses that are overly salty or chalky.

Storage   Small pieces may be stored in the refrigerator, wrapped in plastic, for up to one month; change plastic wrap every few days. Large pieces or whole wheels keep longer if covered with a damp towel; cut cheese as needed and rewrap carefully.

Cheeses in This Category   Bleu de Bresse, Danablu, Fourme d'Ambert, Gorgonzola, Maytag Blue, Oregon Blue, *Pipo Crem'*, Roquefort, Stilton.

◾ STILTON CROCK WITH PORT WINE

A wedge of blue-veined Stilton cheese and a decanter of port are a venerable British tradition, usually served in the drawing room at the end of a formal meal. This pair can also be packed into a handsome crock for a predinner spread, the flavors melding during the course of a week-long aging. If you are hosting a large party, you can order a whole wheel of Stilton (usually in 10- or 16-pound pieces). Slice off the top and scoop out the cheese, leaving a sturdy wall all around. Then mash the cheese with about one bottle of port, refill the wheel, and replace the cover for aging. It makes an impressive buffet centerpiece, especially at holiday time.

> 2 **pounds Stilton cheese**
> ⅓ **to ½ cup imported port**
>   **Crackers, for accompaniment**

1. Trim any rind from cheese; place cheese in a bowl. Add port. With back of a wooden spoon, blend port and cheese. Pack into a 4-cup crock, cover with plastic wrap, refrigerate, and let age 1 week.

2. Bring cheese to room temperature and serve with crackers.

Makes 4 cups, or enough for 20 to 30 cocktail servings.

Recipes: Blue Cheese Soufflé, 205; Stilton Snow Peas, 419.

them in pasta, on soups, in casseroles, on pizzas, and in rice or egg dishes. Because hard cheeses go stale quickly after grating, it is preferable to buy them in blocks and grate them at home just before using.

Selection   Firm cheeses should be hard but not dried out. If possible, sample before buying and reject any that taste overly salty or bitter.

Storage   Because of their exceptionally low moisture content, hard cheeses store well. Follow storage and freezing advice for semifirm cheeses.

Cheeses in This Category   Aged Asiago, *Grana Padano*, Parmesan, Pecorino Romano, Sapsago, Sbrinz.

Recipes: Gnocchi di Patate, 189; Pesto, 27.

CLASSIFICATION BY PROCESS:
PASTA FILATA CHEESES

A specialty of Italy, *pasta filata* (spun paste) cheeses are made by washing the curd in hot water or whey, then kneading and stretching it to the desired consistency and shape. The process produces a pliable cheese that can be molded by hand; occasionally these cheeses are formed into animal or pear shapes. The finished cheese should be smooth and elastic but not rubbery. Pasta filata cheeses are usually mild in flavor and are occasionally smoked.

Use   In Italy fresh mozzarella is drizzled with olive oil and served as a first course, often with sliced tomatoes or roasted peppers. Fresh or factory-made mozzarella may be used in baked pasta dishes, such as lasagne, or layered in vegetable casseroles.

Selection   Fresh mozzarella should be purchased and used within two or three days of its manufacture. Other pasta filata cheeses have a longer shelf life. Avoid any that have a rubbery texture.

Storage   Refrigerate, wrapped airtight in plastic. These cheeses keep for several weeks. Serve at room temperature.

Cheeses in This Category   *Cacciocavallo,* mozzarella, Provolone, Scamorza.

Recipes: Deep-fried Zucchini Blossoms, 238; Pizza, 445; Tomatoes With Mozzarella and Basil, 507.

CLASSIFICATION BY PROCESS:
WHEY CHEESES

Most cheeses are made from coagulated milk curds, but a very few are made from the liquid whey. To make a whey cheese, the whey is heated until its solid matter coagulates. The best-known examples are Italian ricotta, made from the whey drained from provolone and mozzarella, and Norwegian Gjetost.

Use   Ricotta may be sugared and eaten with fresh berries or sliced fruit. It may be salted and eaten as a salad with crisp vegetables, olives, and olive oil. Seasoned ricotta is used as a filling for baked pasta dishes, as a stuffing for breast of veal, and in cheesecakes.

Norwegian Gjetost is usually sliced thin and eaten with toast for breakfast or with spiced fruit cake.

Selection   Fresh ricotta is very perishable; it should be purchased and used within a few days of its manufacture.

Storage   Keep in a covered container in the refrigerator. It is moist and creamy, with a very mild, almost sweet flavor. Domestic factory-made ricotta has a slightly longer shelf life but lacks the creamy texture and pure flavor of the fresh version.

Gjetost, an unusual cheese, is made from whey heated slowly until the water evaporates and the natural sugars caramelize. Lactose and brown sugar may be added. The result is a golden brown cheese with a smooth, creamy texture and a pronounced caramel flavor. It stores well, wrapped in plastic and chilled; change wrap often.

OTHER CLASSIFICATIONS:
PROCESSED CHEESES

Most processed cheeses derive from a natural cheese that has been ground and mixed with emulsifiers to make it uniformly smooth, then is pasteurized and packed. Some processed cheeses contain preservatives and colorings. Products labeled cheese spread or cheese food may contain flavorings as well as liquid or powdered milk for added moisture and spreadability.

These cheeses generally have a mild flavor and a uniformly smooth texture. Although they keep well and are often conveniently packaged, they lack the distinctive character and complexity of natural cheeses.

OTHER CLASSIFICATIONS:
CHEESES FOR SPECIAL DIETS

Today's market is full of cheeses made to comply with special diets. Low-fat and low-salt or low-sodium cheeses are widely available and are identified as such on their labels. Because fat adds richness and texture to cheese, low-fat cheeses may lack the full flavor and good melting qualities of the comparable full-fat cheeses. Part-skim mozzarella, for example, does not melt as well as whole-milk mozzarella but may be preferred by those counting calories.

CLASSIFICATION BY MILK SOURCE:
GOAT CHEESES

Also known as *chèvre* (French for goat), goat's milk cheese has a distinctive chalky color and tangy flavor. Young, fresh goat cheese is mild and creamy. As it ages, it gets stronger and drier. Goat cheeses are made in a variety of shapes and sizes. They may be coated with ash or dried herbs or sprayed with mold spores to produce a rind.

Use   Goat cheeses are a pleasing addition to a cheese board; offer them with crackers or bread and wine. Small, round goat cheeses may be coated with soft bread crumbs and sautéed or baked until warm throughout. Goat cheese adds a creamy tang to stuffings, salads, pizza toppings, souffles, and omelets.

Selection   Young, highly moist goat cheeses have a short shelf life. Buy them from a shop that has a rapid turnover and try to sample before purchase. Reject any that have a sour or ammoniated flavor.

Storage   Keep moist goat cheese in refrigerator, covered with plastic wrap; it will keep for one or two weeks. Change plastic wrap every few days. Aged goat cheese keeps slightly longer.

Cheeses in This Category   Banon, *bucheron,* California chévre, *caprino,* Chabichou (or *Cabécou*), feta (some feta is made from sheep's milk or part sheep's milk), Montrachet, Sainte-Maure.

ENTERTAINING WITH WINE AND CHEESE

Cheese and wine are ancient foods that go back to the earliest days of agriculture. It is not surprising, then, that they pair very well. There is probably not a wine that cannot be matched to one cheese or another, nor a single cheese that cannot be served with some wine. But some combinations of wine and cheese go together better than others.

A wine and cheese buffet can make excellent party fare, as long as you avoid the familiar "Cheddar, Swiss, and Brie, burgundy and chablis." A good cheese board can consist of as few as three or four cheeses, or a dozen or more, depending on the number of guests. The key is to provide a variety of flavors and textures. Wines should also be chosen for variety, so that at least one wine will suit every guest's personal taste.

Here are some pointers on assembling a selection of wines and cheeses:

- For a party at which dinner will not be served, allow about ¼ pound of cheese per person and one bottle of wine for every three or four guests. Allow half as much for a before-dinner cocktail hour. Remember, cheese is filling; don't overwhelm appetites before dinner.
- Try for a balanced selection of cheeses by choosing one example from each category. To get you going, you might want to plan around one soft-ripening cheese (such as Brie, Camembert), one semisoft cheese (consider Port-Salut, Monterey jack), one firm cheese, either of the Swiss or Cheddar type, and one blue-veined cheese. With more guests, for variety add a stronger soft or semisoft cheese (two are Pont l'Evêque, Esrom), a hard cheese (such as quality Parmesan, aged Gouda), a goat's-milk cheese, a double- or triple-cream cheese (such as Boursault, Saint-André), an herbed or spiced cheese (including Havarti with dill or Cumminost), or whatever other types you like.
- Follow the same approach with the wines. Start with one dry red, say a Zinfandel or a lighter-style Cabernet, and one white wine that is slightly sweet, such as Chenin Blanc or Riesling. Next, add both a dry white (Chardonnay or Sauvignon Blanc) and a different style of red (such as Gamay Beaujolais). Unless the purpose of the party is to provide an opportunity for tasting as many wines as possible with a variety of cheeses, keep the wine selection simple.
- Serve an assortment of breads or crackers. Avoid highly seasoned crackers if you want the flavor of the cheese and wine to come through. With really fine cheeses, thin, unsalted crackers or matzos are best.
- Other nice accompaniments to a cheese board are crunchy raw vegetables, nuts, olives, and fresh fruits, especially apples and grapes. Some guests might also enjoy a few condiments like fancy mustards, chutney, and gherkins.
- To show cheeses at their best, serve them at room temperature. Provide plenty of knives or cheese slicers, at least one for each cheese, to facilitate serving.

■ BAKED GOAT CHEESE SALAD

The richness of the goat cheese complements the pungent winter greens and a tangy wine vinegar. When baked, the cheese becomes creamy. This is a good company dish as the cheese must marinate one hour before baking, so preparation is completed before guests arrive.

```
 1   small goat cheese log (about 5 oz)
9½   tablespoons olive oil
 ⅓   cup dry bread crumbs
1½   tablespoons red wine vinegar
 ¼   teaspoon salt
 ⅛   teaspoon pepper
 ¼   cup snipped fresh chives
10 to 12 cups washed, dried, and torn salad
     greens (endive, chicory, watercress, arugula)
 ½   red bell pepper, cored, seeded, and
     cut into thin strips
     Freshly ground black pepper
     French bread, for accompaniment
```

1. Slice goat cheese into ½-inch-thick rounds. Pour 4 tablespoons olive oil into a shallow bowl; place bread crumbs on a sheet of waxed paper. Dip goat cheese rounds into olive oil to coat completely, then into bread crumbs; shake off excess crumbs. Set breaded rounds on a tray and chill for 1 hour. Toward the end of chilling period (or about 30 minutes before serving), preheat oven to 375° F.

2. In a small bowl whisk together 3 tablespoons oil, vinegar, salt, pepper, and chives; reserve. Thirty minutes before serving, let salad greens come to room temperature, if chilled.

3. Pour remaining olive oil into an 8-inch square baking dish. Set chilled goat cheese rounds in dish and bake until a light golden crust forms (about 8 minutes). Turn with a spatula (handle rounds gently so that they don't break) and bake on second side for 2 minutes.

4. To serve, toss salad greens with two thirds of the dressing; divide among 6 individual salad plates. Remove cheese from baking pan and place one breaded round in the center of each nest of greens. Arrange red peppers around goat cheese, drizzle with remaining dressing, and grind black pepper over top. Serve immediately with French bread.

Serves 6.

Recipes: Deep-fried Zucchini Blossoms (goat cheese and sun-dried tomato variation), 238.

CLASSIFICATION BY MILK SOURCE: SHEEP'S MILK CHEESES

Sheep's milk cheeses have a sharp tang that immediately distinguishes them from cow's milk cheeses. Most sheep's milk cheeses are made in countries and regions that have too little pasturage to support cattle—such as Greece, Spain, the Pyrenees, and the Middle East.

Use   Depending on their moisture content, sheep's milk cheeses may be sliced for use in sandwiches, snacks, and salads, or grated for use as a flavor accent on salads and cooked dishes.

Selection   If possible, ask for a sample before buying. Sheep's milk cheeses may be sharp but should not be excessively salty or bitter.

Storage   Keep them in plastic wrap in the refrigerator, changing the wrapping every few days. Highly moist cheeses deteriorate more quickly than varieties with low moisture.

Cheeses in This Category   Feta (some feta is made from goat's milk), *kasseri*, Liptauer, *manchego, pecorino*, Romano, Ricotta Pecorino (also known as *ricotta salata*), Roquefort.

Recipes: Greek Salad, 507; Tiropita, 223.

CHEESECAKE

This rich, creamy confection has achieved an enduring popularity that seems to transcend food fads and concern for calories. A cheesecake is a cake or pie with a custard-like filling whose main ingredient is cream cheese, cottage cheese, ricotta cheese, or some combination, contained in a cookie or crumb crust, or baked without a crust.

In New York, "real" cheesecake is a tall, dense, lemony, cream cheese–based cake. Elsewhere, preference might be for something lighter, perhaps flavored with liqueur or finished with a coat of sour cream or a layer of fresh fruit. Then there's marble, mocha, pumpkin, savory, chocolate chip, Italian, no-bake, and many, many others.

PREPARING CHEESECAKE

Regardless of the version you prefer, there are a few points to remember that apply to all. Packaged cream cheese usually contains gum, which makes a cake denser. Natural cream cheese, available at cheese and specialty food stores and well-stocked supermarkets, is free of gum and will produce a lighter-textured cake. Whichever type you favor, have the cream cheese at room temperature before using; it will mix easier and blend more quickly with the other ingredients.

Most recipes specify using a springform pan, whose sides release for easier removal of the cake. If the cheesecake is to bake in a hot water bath (bain-marie), wrap the outside of the pan with foil. The foil acts as a barrier to keep the water from seeping through the seams of the pan and into the cake, making it soggy. An alternative is to use a cheesecake pan, which is a deep layer-cake pan preferred by commercial bakers. Because it is made in one piece, it stays watertight, but for that reason the cake is more difficult to unmold.

■ NEW YORK–STYLE CHEESECAKE

This is always a dense, rich cake, served in thin slices because it is so filling. To suit today's taste for lighter desserts, cottage cheese has been added, but the texture is classic. Serve it as it comes from the oven or top with a lemon or raspberry glaze. The thick batter may strain the motor of some portable electric mixers. Use a heavy-duty mixer if possible; first beat by hand completely or partway to soften and blend the ingredients, then finish mixing with the machine.

    1 pound whole-milk cottage cheese
    1½ pounds natural cream cheese,
        at room temperature
    1½ cups sugar
        Grated rind and juice of 1 lemon
    5 eggs
    ¼ cup cornstarch
    1 pint sour cream
    2 tablespoons vanilla extract

Lemon Custard Glaze (optional)

    1 egg
    2 egg yolks
    6 tablespoons sugar
    ¼ cup fresh lemon juice
    1 teaspoon finely grated lemon rind
    4 tablespoons unsalted butter, softened
        Cookie crumbs (optional)

Raspberry Glaze (optional)

    1 package (10 oz) frozen raspberries
    2 tablespoons sugar
    1 tablespoon cornstarch
    2 teaspoons raspberry liqueur or kirsch

1. Preheat oven to 300° F. Butter bottom and sides of a 10-inch springform pan.

2. To refine texture of cottage cheese, force cheese through a wire-mesh sieve or purée in a blender or food processor. In a large bowl blend softened cream cheese and cottage cheese purée with a heavy-duty mixer and paddle attachment, or by hand with a wooden spoon. Add sugar and lemon rind; mix well to incorporate.

3. Add eggs, one at a time, beating well after each addition. Sift in cornstarch; beat to combine. Stir in sour cream, vanilla, and lemon juice. Pour into prepared pan and bake 50 minutes (it will be pale yellow—not at all brown—set around the edges, and still wobbly under the surface in the center). Turn off oven, leave door slightly ajar, and allow cheesecake to cool completely. When cool, spread with either glaze (if desired) or leave plain; refrigerate at least 6 hours, or overnight. Before serving, bring cake to room temperature. To slice cleanly and evenly, use a sharp, thin- and narrow-bladed knife. It may be necessary to dip blade in hot water and wipe clean after each slice, so knife draws easily through cake without drag.

Serves 12 to 16.

Lemon Custard Glaze In a medium stainless steel bowl, combine egg, egg yolks, sugar, lemon juice, and lemon rind. Immediately place over a pot of boiling water (double-boiler fashion) and whisk egg mixture until it thickens to the consistency of mayonnaise (do not boil or mixture will curdle). Remove from heat and immediately whisk in butter. Spread on cake while custard is still warm. If desired, sprinkle cookie crumbs around border of cake to decorate top.

Raspberry Glaze Thaw raspberries; drain, reserving juice. In a small saucepan combine juice with sugar, cornstarch, and about half of the berries. Bring to a boil, stirring, and cook until thickened and clear. Strain to remove seeds. To strained sauce add liqueur and reserved berries. Cool to room temperature, then spoon on cake, letting some glaze spill over top onto sides, if desired.

A specialty of southern Italy, Ricotta Cheesecake has a ricotta filling encased in pastry. Raisins, pine nuts, almonds, and a hint of chocolate enrich the filling.

■ UNBAKED CHEESECAKE

This mildly flavored cheesecake benefits from the addition of one of the fruit variations. Because the filling sets with gelatin, only the crumb crust needs to be baked.

    1 **pound natural cream cheese, at room temperature**
    ½ **cup superfine sugar**
    2 **tablespoons vanilla extract**
      Grated rind and juice of 2 lemons
    3 **egg yolks**
    1 **envelope unflavored gelatin**
    1 **cup whipping cream**
    3 **egg whites**
    ¼ **cup granulated sugar**

Graham Cracker Crumb Crust

    2 **cups fine graham cracker crumbs**
    2 **tablespoons granulated sugar**
    ¼ **cup melted butter**

1. Preheat oven to 350° F. Butter bottom and sides of a 10-inch springform pan. Prepare Graham Cracker Crumb Crust.

2. In a large bowl beat cream cheese until smooth; add sugar, vanilla, and lemon rind, and beat well. Add egg yolks, one at a time, beating well after each addition. In a small saucepan dissolve gelatin in lemon juice over low heat. Pour into cream cheese mixture.

3. Whip cream to soft peaks and fold into cheese mixture. Whip egg whites to soft peaks; add ¼ cup granulated sugar and beat briefly just to incorporate sugar. Stir one third of beaten egg whites into cream cheese mixture; gently fold in remaining whites.

4. Pour filling over cooled crust. Smooth surface with a spatula. Refrigerate until set (2 to 3 hours, or overnight). To serve, decorate top and sides with whipped cream or one of the fruits suggested in the variation.

Serves 8 to 12.

Graham Cracker Crumb Crust   In a medium bowl combine graham cracker crumbs and sugar; add melted butter and mix thoroughly. Press into prepared pan. Bake 10 minutes. Cool on a wire rack.

Food Processor Version   Use metal blade to process cream cheese, lemon rind, vanilla, and superfine sugar until smooth, scraping work bowl as necessary. Add all egg yolks at once and process 15 seconds. With motor running, pour dissolved gelatin through feed tube and process 10 seconds. Transfer to large mixing bowl and complete recipe as directed.

Fruit Cheesecake Mix in any of the following fruits with whipped cream in step 3: 1 pound fresh ripe, pitted cherries poached in ½ cup water and puréed in food processor or blender; *or* 1 cup dried apricot purée (soak in water for several hours or overnight, then poach in soaking water until tender, about 15 minutes; sweeten to taste and purée); *or* 1 package (10 oz) frozen raspberries, thawed, drained, puréed, and strained through a fine sieve to remove seeds.

▮ RICOTTA CHEESECAKE

Cheesecakes in southern Italy are made with ricotta, raisins, and pine nuts, and are commonly flecked with chocolate and flavored with rum. This version incorporates crunchy pine-nut brittle, a delicious candy to savor on its own. Offer this rich *torta* in the afternoon with a glass of Marsala, or serve it as the luscious finish to a light meal. Note that the raisins must macerate in the rum for 1 hour.

   1 **cup superfine sugar**
   3 **tablespoons water**
   5 **tablespoons pine nuts**
   4 **tablespoons golden raisins**
   2 **tablespoons rum**
3¼ **cups flour**
   1 **tablespoon baking powder**
  ½ **cup firmly packed dark brown sugar**
1¼ **cups ground almonds**
   4 **tablespoons chilled unsalted butter,**
     cut in small pieces
   1 **egg**
   1 **teaspoon vanilla extract**
1½ **pounds whole-milk ricotta cheese**
   1 **teaspoon grated lemon rind**
   2 **ounces milk chocolate, coarsely chopped**

1. In a 1-quart saucepan heat ¼ cup superfine sugar and the water over high heat. When mixture boils and sugar dissolves, add pine nuts. Continue cooking, swirling pan often, until sugar turns light brown. Turn mixture out onto an oiled baking sheet and let cool. Break up into small chunks. Combine raisins and rum in a small bowl and set aside for 1 hour.

2. *To make dough in a food processor:* Combine flour, baking powder, brown sugar, and almonds; process 5 seconds. Add butter and process until mixture resembles coarse meal, about 10 seconds. Whisk egg and vanilla together, then add to food processor with motor running. Process just until dough nearly holds together. Turn dough out onto a board, gather into a ball, and wrap in plastic. Do not knead or work dough, even if it doesn't hold together well. Refrigerate at least 1 hour. *To make*

dough by hand: Stir together flour, baking powder, brown sugar, and almonds. Cut in butter with a pastry blender until mixture resembles coarse crumbs. Whisk egg and vanilla together, then add to flour mixture. Toss lightly with a fork, just until dough holds together. Gather into a ball and wrap in plastic; refrigerate 1 hour.

3. In a large bowl combine ricotta, remaining sugar, lemon rind, raisins, and rum. Add chocolate bits and pine-nut brittle; mix well.

4. Preheat oven to 350° F. Line bottom and sides of a 10-inch springform pan with aluminum foil. Place a little more than half the pastry dough on bottom of pan, patting it into place and pushing it up sides. Spoon in ricotta filling. Roll out remaining pastry into a 10-inch round and lay over top of filling. Bake until top colors slightly (50 to 55 minutes).

5. Transfer cheesecake to a rack and cool in pan. Release sides of springform pan and gently peel back foil from sides. Lift bottom of cake gently with a spatula and pull out foil. Serve barely warm or at room temperature.

Serves 12.

Make-Ahead Tip Pastry dough may be made 1 day ahead and refrigerated. If stored airtight, brittle can be made up to 2 weeks ahead.

CHEESECLOTH

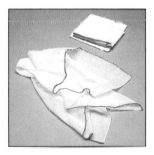

Soft, lightweight, and porous, cheesecloth is woven of natural cotton, which won't fall apart in hot liquids or add flavor to food. It is used as a neutral, porous wrap. Flavoring infusions such as bouquet garni and mulling spices are bundled in cheesecloth so they can be easily dropped into and retrieved from soups, stews, and beverages. Delicate poached foods such as whole fish and pasta rolls are wrapped in this material to preserve their shape while they cook. Some baked goods, such as fruitcakes, which benefit from slow soaking in liquor, are swaddled in alcohol-soaked cheesecloth to season. It also serves as a flexible strainer for stocks and other liquids.

Cheesecloth is sold in both coarse and fine weave. Each has its place in the kitchen. Coarse cheesecloth resembles bandage gauze. Inexpensive and widely available in supermarkets and cookware stores, it can be cut, used, and thrown away without too much concern for cost. Better quality, fine-mesh cheesecloth is harder to find and seems expensive in comparison with the coarse type, but because it can be washed and reused, it lasts longer.

CHERIMOYA

A heart-shaped fruit native to Ecuador and Peru, the cherimoya is now cultivated in southern California. Its dull green skin has thumbprintlike indentations edged in brown. The fruit inside is creamy white with large black seeds; it has a creamy, custardlike texture and a flavor reminiscent of banana, pineapple, and pear. Its other common names—custard apple and sherbet fruit—attest to its flavor and texture. Cherimoyas range in weight from ¼ pound to 2½ pounds.

Use   Cherimoya is refreshing when eaten chilled "on the half shell." The flesh is scooped out with a spoon and the seeds discarded. The peeled, diced fruit may be added to fruit salads or puréed for sherbet, ice cream, or daiquiris.

Availability   Fresh cherimoyas are in season from November through May. Because they must be hand-pollinated and handpicked and because the trees are low-yielding, cherimoyas are always expensive.

Selection   Choose green cherimoyas that give slightly to pressure; brownness indicates overripeness.

Storage   Hard cherimoyas may be ripened at room temperature. Ripe cherimoyas should be refrigerated and used within one or two days.

Preparation   Scoop from skin and remove seeds.

CHERRY

Although wild cherries are a prehistoric fruit, cherry cultivation probably originated in Asia Minor. Today cherries are cultivated throughout the world's temperate zone. Most of the many cherry varieties can be classified as either sweet (for eating raw) or sour (for cooking). The most commercially important sweet varieties in America are the yellow-orange Royal Ann and the dark red Bing; other varieties include Black Republican, Black Tartarian, Chapman, Lambert, early Burlat, and Schmidt. The most important sour varieties in America are red Montmorency and English Morello.

Use   Sweet cherries may be eaten out of hand or added to fruit salads, fruit compotes, tarts, or ice cream. They may be preserved in brandy for use as a garnish for ice cream or cake. Sour cherries are best for pies, cobblers, preserves, jams, dessert sauces, and pickles. Vinegared sour cherries are a piquant garnish for pâtés and other cold meats. Sour cherries are also used for commercial maraschino liqueur and syrup and for distilling.

Availability   Depending on the variety and the area, fresh sweet cherries are available late spring through August. June is the peak month for most varieties. Sour cherries are harvested from mid-June to mid-August but are rarely available fresh outside the immediate area of cultivation. Most domestic sour cherries are canned whole, in light or heavy syrup, often identified as cherry-pie filling. Wild cherries called *amarena* are imported from Italy packed in syrup or brandy. Dried sour cherries and wild cherry preserves are occasionally available in Greek markets.

Selection   With the exception of Royal Anns, dark color is the best indication of good flavor. Cherries should have a bright, glossy, plump appearance and fresh-looking stems. Avoid soft cherries or any with brown discoloration.

Storage   Handle fresh cherries carefully; refrigerate and use within a few days of purchase. Transfer leftover canned cherries to a covered plastic container; refrigerate for up to two weeks.

Preparation   For compotes and fruit salads, remove fresh cherry stems; remove pits with a cherry pitter, if desired. Fresh sour cherries should be pitted before cooking.

■ **SOUR-CHERRY PIE**

A lattice-top cherry pie shows off the ripe, red fruit to perfection. A cherry pitter (see opposite page) will make quick work of ridding the cherries of hard-to-remove pits.

    1 **9-inch double-crust Flaky Pastry or**
       Egg Pastry (see pages 434, 435)
 1¼ **cups sugar**
    5 **tablespoons flour**
  ⅔ **cup cherry juice or other red fruit juice**
  ½ **teaspoon ground cinnamon**
  ⅛ **teaspoon almond extract**
    1 **tablespoon fresh lemon juice**
    5 **cups pitted tart red cherries**
    1 **egg white, lightly beaten**
 1½ **tablespoons unsalted butter**

1. Preheat oven to 425° F. Roll out pastry for bottom crust and line a 9-inch pie plate. Roll out remaining pastry to form top crust or lattice top (see page 433).

2. In a saucepan combine sugar, flour, cherry juice, cinnamon, almond extract, lemon juice, and cherries. Cook over low heat, stirring frequently, until mixture thickens; set aside to cool.

3. Brush inside of bottom crust with egg white to moistureproof the crust. Pour in cooled filling. Dot with butter.

4. Moisten edges of bottom crust and cover with top crust or lattice top; finish edges. Bake for 20 minutes. Lower heat to 400° F and continue baking until crust is golden brown (40 minutes). Cover edges of crust with strips of aluminum foil, if necessary, to prevent excessive browning.

Serves 8.

■ **CHERRY CLAFOUTI**

Buttery pastry, sweet red cherries, and custard are baked together to create a French *clafouti*, a type of custard tart. A clafouti can be made from a batter, something like a fruit-dotted puffy pancake or popover, or with a pastry dough that is covered with fruit. If made with a batter, the dish is served from its baking pan. When baked in pastry, it is served in wedges. This version is a combination of a soft filling contained in a tart pastry crust. Although cherries are traditional, when the fresh fruit is unavailable, you can substitute sliced fresh kiwis, poached pears or peaches, or fresh berries. Boysenberries, loganberries, or olallie-berries make delicious clafouti.

    1 (9½-in.) Sweet Tart Pastry (see page 441)
    ½ cup milk
    ½ cup whipping cream
    2 whole eggs
    2 egg yolks
    ½ cup sugar
       Pinch freshly grated nutmeg
    1 tablespoon kirsch
    1 egg white, lightly beaten
    2¼ cups pitted sweet red cherries
    ¼ cup confectioners' sugar

1. Place pastry dough on a lightly floured surface and roll out to form a circle ⅛ inch thick and large enough to line a 9½-inch tart tin with removable bottom. Blind bake until partially baked (see page 18); cool in tart tin on a wire rack.

2. Preheat oven to 400° F. In a heavy-bottomed saucepan bring milk to a simmer over medium-low heat; add cream. In a mixing bowl whisk together eggs, egg yolks, sugar, and nutmeg. Add a little of the milk-cream mixture to gently raise the temperature of the eggs and keep them from curdling; stir well to blend. Blend in remaining milk-cream mixture; cool. Stir in kirsch. Set custard aside.

3. To prevent crust from getting soggy, gently brush tart shell with a thin layer of lightly beaten egg white. Arrange cherries (whole or cut in half; if halved, arrange cut side down) in an even layer over bottom of tart shell. Carefully pour custard over cherries (do not fill tart shell more than three fourths full).

4. Bake for 10 minutes at 400° F. Reduce heat to 325° F and bake until custard is set (about 35 minutes).

5. Sift confectioners' sugar over tart. Place under preheated broiler to caramelize sugar. Watch carefully—sugar burns easily. Serve slightly warm.

Serves 6 to 8.

Recipes and Related Information
Cherries Jubilee, 315; Fruit Cheesecake, 119.

CHERRY PITTER

Like a hole puncher, which this hand tool resembles, a cherry pitter makes quick work out of a most tedious chore—removing pits from cherries and olives. All the models are variations of a basic press system: the device holds the round or oval fruit in place while pressure is applied to a plunger that pushes out the pit. The simplest model handles one or two cherries at a squeeze and must be continually reloaded. If this procedure seems too time-consuming, look for an automatic pitter with a built-in container that can hold up to 3 cups of cherries. A funnel feeds the stored fruit to the pitter each time you press the plunger. It *is* child's play. If you have a junior chef who wants to help with meal preparation, this is exactly the type of repetitious work that young hands love to do.

Recipes and Related Information
Cherry, 120; Olive, 398.

CHERVIL

An annual herb native to Asia and Eastern Europe, chervil resembles a very delicate form of parsley. It has soft, feathery, green leaves atop slender stems and umbrella-shaped clusters of tiny white flowers. The leaves have a faint anise flavor.

Use   The aniselike flavor of chervil complements egg, tomato, and fish dishes. Add it to green salads and potato salads, cream soups, mayonnaise, and herb butters and sauces. Chervil is an ingredient in the classic French fines herbes mixture.

Availability   Fresh chervil, tied in bunches or packed in plastic bags, is occasionally available in specialty markets. Dried chervil is sold in airtight jars.

Selection   Buy chervil that is fresh-looking without signs of wilting or decay. Packaged seasonings lose quality after a while; try to buy from a store that restocks its spice section fairly often.

Storage   Keep fresh chervil in refrigerator, wrapped in damp paper towels then in plastic, for up to three days. Store dried chervil in an airtight container in a cool, dry, dark place.

Preparation   Mince fresh chervil leaves just before using. For cooked dishes, add chervil at the last moment; its delicate flavor dissipates with cooking.

Sidewalk chestnut vendors are a familiar winter sight in New York and the cities of Europe. They tuck the steaming nuggets into paper cones for shoppers and strollers, who probably appreciate the warmth as much as the rich, nutty taste. Chestnuts become harder to peel as they cool, so serve them hot from the cooking container or in a napkin-lined basket.

CHESTNUT

The chestnut is the fruit of a tree native to several continents. Chestnut trees flourished in America until the early twentieth century, when they were destroyed by a fungus blight. They still have not been reestablished, although efforts are being made.

The golden chestnut is encased in both a fine, reddish brown membrane and an inedible hard, brown shell. The shelled, cooked chestnut is simultaneously sweet and starchy, with a moist, crumbly texture.

Use   Fresh chestnuts may be roasted in their shells, then peeled and eaten whole as a snack. Peeled chestnuts may be simmered in stock or milk and served as an accompaniment to game or rich meats or made into soup. Whole chestnuts are often braised with red cabbage or Brussels sprouts. Cooked and puréed chestnuts may be seasoned with butter, salt, and pepper for a savory side dish, or sweetened with sugar and cream and used for dessert. French and Italian cooks use sweetened chestnut purée as a filling, garnish, or ingredient for a variety of desserts. Whole candied chestnuts are a popular Christmas confection in Western Europe and an autumn treat in Japan. Chopped candied chestnuts may be added to ice cream, dessert sauces, or confections. Americans add chopped cooked chestnuts to holiday poultry stuffings. Japanese steam autumn chestnuts with rice. In northern China, dried chestnuts are added to stews.

Chestnut flour, made from dried, ground chestnuts, is used in Europe for breads, soups, and desserts.

Availability   Fresh chestnuts are available in winter. Whole peeled chestnuts packed in water are imported from France. Unsweetened chestnut purée, packaged in cans and identified as *purée de marrons,* is imported from France and Switzerland. Sweetened chestnut purée, labeled as *crème de marrons,* is imported from France in cans and tubes. Also from France come whole candied chestnuts (*marrons glacées*) and chestnut pieces (*marrons débris*) in vanilla-flavored syrup, packed in cans and jars. Dried chestnuts are available in Italian and Chinese markets. Chestnut flour is sold in health-food stores and some Italian markets.

Selection   Choose glossy chestnuts that fill their shells and feel heavy for their size. Those with air pockets are likely to be older and dried out. Chestnuts can appear fresh and still be spoiled inside, so it's a good idea to buy a few more than you need.

Storage   Fresh chestnuts will keep up to one week in a cool place or up to two weeks in a plastic bag in the refrigerator. Unused chestnut purée or tinned candied chestnuts will keep in a covered plastic container in the refrigerator for several months. Dried chestnuts will keep in an airtight container in a cool place for two months or in the refrigerator or freezer indefinitely. Chestnut flour keeps one month in the refrigerator.

Preparation   To shell fresh chestnuts, cut an *x* in the flat side. Roast in a preheated 350° F oven for 10 minutes, then peel. Alternatively, blanch them in boiling water for 3 to 4 minutes. Remove from water one at a time and peel (easiest when chestnuts are hot).

■ ROASTED CHESTNUTS

Cook chestnuts at home in the oven as described below, or wrap them in heavy-duty aluminum foil and roast them outdoors over coals. You can also roast them on a grate in the fireplace or over an open fire, using a heavy, lidded skillet with a long handle or a popcorn popper; shake the pan repeatedly until the shells pop open.

> **2 dozen chestnuts**
> **Olive oil**
> **2 tablespoons water**

1. Preheat oven to 425° F. With a small, sharp knife, cut a cross in the flat side of each chestnut. Place chestnuts in a casserole with a tight-fitting lid; add a few drops of oil, toss nuts to coat lightly, add the water, and cover.

2. Bake until chestnuts feel tender when squeezed and peel easily (25 to 30 minutes). Remove to a napkin-lined basket or serve from the casserole.

Makes 2 dozen.

CHICORY

A variety of mostly perennial plants go by the family name *chicory*. Some chicory is grown for its leaves, some for its roots. Chicory grown for its roots is rarely seen in retail markets; the roots are dried, ground, and used as a coffee substitute or additive, popular in New Orleans.

The chicory family includes Belgian endive, escarole, and radicchio, as well as the salad green often labeled chicory in retail markets. The latter chicory is also sometimes labeled *frisé* or curly endive.

Because several of the major members of the chicory family are described in separate entries, this entry deals primarily with the salad green commonly called chicory. A head of chicory contains loosely grouped leaves that are frizzy and have spiky edges. Outer leaves are dark green; inner leaves are pale green, becoming yellow at the heart.

Use Chicory adds texture and a slightly bitter flavor to green salads. Because of its coarse texture, it is often mixed with other greens.

Availability Fresh chicory is sold all year but may be more abundant in early spring or late fall.

Selection Select chicory without evidence of wilting or browning on leaf tips.

Storage Keep chicory in a plastic bag in refrigerator crisper; use within two or three days.

Preparation Wash well just before using. Trim root end and discard any dark or ragged leaves.

CHIFFONNADE

A French term, *chiffonnade* refers to leafy greens and herbs cut into thin ribbons. A chiffonnade of basil, for example, can serve as a flavoring mixture or as a bed for other foods. Shredded lettuce or sorrel is a classic garnish for soups. To prepare a chiffonnade, trim leaves of their stems and any woody parts. Then roll leaves together into narrow tubes and slice into fine strips.

Chiffonnade is also a salad dressing that is based on a French dressing with the addition of chopped hard-cooked egg and strips of green bell pepper, chives, and other vegetables.

CHILL, TO

To make something cold by placing it in the refrigerator or by stirring it over ice water. Salads, gelatin-based dishes, pâtés, soups, mayonnaise-based sauces, custards, pastry dough, and fruit desserts are examples of foods that may require chilling.

CHIVE

A member of the onion family, chives grow in long, thin, hollow green shoots.

Use Snipped chives add a delicate onion flavor to soups, salads, vegetable dishes, eggs, fish, and cheese spreads. They are frequently used as a topping for baked potatoes, along with sour cream. Because of their delicate flavor, they are best as a raw garnish; if possible, add them to cooked dishes at the last minute. Chives are one ingredient in the classic French fines herbes mixture.

Availability Whole fresh chives are sold the year around, tied in bunches or packaged in plastic bags. Snipped freeze-dried chives are packed in airtight jars or tins. Snipped frozen chives are also available in supermarket freezer cases.

Selection Buy fresh shoots without evidence of wilting or decay. Dried seasonings lose quality after a while; try to buy from a store that restocks its spice section often.

Storage Wrap fresh chives in damp paper towels, then in a plastic bag, and refrigerate; use within three or four days. Store freeze-dried chives in an airtight container in a cool, dry, dark place and use within three months. Use frozen chives within six months.

Preparation Mince fresh chives with a knife or snip with kitchen scissors just before using. There is no need to reconstitute freeze-dried chives or thaw frozen chives before using.

■ **CHIVE POTATO SALAD**

In this version of a popular salad, tiny whole potatoes are tossed in a creamy dressing, punctuated by the oniony flavor and bright green color of fresh chives. Note that the potatoes cook a day in advance, and that, once tossed in dressing, they will keep another 24 hours.

> 2 **pounds small new potatoes**
> ¾ **cup Mayonnaise (see page 519)**
> ¾ **cup Crème Fraîche (see page 161) or sour cream**
> 1 **bunch fresh chives, snipped**

1. The day before the salad is prepared, peel off a strip of skin from around the middle of each potato. Bring a 4-quart pot of salted water to a boil. Add potatoes and cook, covered, until easily pierced with the tip of a sharp knife (20 to 30 minutes). Drain and cool completely. Refrigerate, covered.

2. The next day, combine Mayonnaise and Crème Fraîche in a medium bowl. Add potatoes and toss to cover with sauce. Sprinkle with snipped chives. Serve immediately or refrigerate, covered, up to 24 hours before serving.

Serves 6.

CHOCOLATE

The seeds of the tropical cocoa (or cacao) tree, called cocoa beans, are the source of chocolate. The seeds themselves are quite bitter; although the Aztecs enjoyed a beverage made from roasted ground cocoa beans mixed with hot water, today's taste demands further processing. Numerous advances in processing have led to a variety of chocolate products, from unsweetened cocoa to milk chocolate.

PROCESSING

The processing of chocolate begins with the harvest of the pods of the cocoa tree. Pods are broken open and seeds and pulp removed. Seeds are allowed to ferment for two to nine days to develop flavor; they are then dried, graded, packed, and shipped.

The chocolate manufacturer generally blends seeds from several sources to produce a consistent style and desirable flavor. After cleaning and blending seeds, the manufacturer roasts them to develop flavor and aroma. After roasting and cooling, seeds are shelled. The meat or nibs are saved; the shells are sold for animal feed or fertilizer. The nibs, which are slightly more than 50 percent cocoa butter, are then ground to produce chocolate liquor. The chocolate liquor is then used alone or blended with other ingredients to make specific types of chocolate or chocolate products (see Availability).

Use   Chocolate is little used in Asian cuisines, but it is undoubtedly one of the favorite flavors of the Western world. Indeed, in America chocolate ice cream is second only to vanilla. It is employed both as an ingredient and as a food in itself. Sweetened chocolate bars, either plain or flavored with milk, vanilla, nuts, or a variety of other flavorings, are a favorite snack food. Chocolate is used in countless candies and confections. It may be made into a syrup for use on ice cream and in sodas. Chocolate and chocolate products—in the form of either powdered cocoa or solidified bars—are an ingredient in frostings, cakes, cookies, pies, breads, puddings, mousses, ice creams, soufflés, and dessert sauces. It adds richness and mellow flavor to savory sauces and stews, such as Mexican mole and Sicilian caponata. Chocolate milk is a favorite of American schoolchildren, and hot chocolate or hot cocoa is a popular beverage in cold weather in many Western homes. Melted chocolate is used as a coating for dipped fruits, cookies, candies, and even pretzels.

Availability   Chocolate is sold in many forms. For the best flavor, choose a chocolate of high quality.

Chocolate-Flavored Syrup   This syrup is primarily corn syrup and cocoa with preservatives, emulsifiers, and flavorings. Chocolate syrup is packed in cans or plastic squeeze bottles.

Commercial Coating Chocolate (also known as *couverture*)   Professional confectioners use coating chocolate for dipping and for making chocolate curls, ruffles, and other garnishes. It has more cocoa butter than regular baking chocolate and thus melts and spreads well. In its original, unmelted form, coating chocolate contains cocoa butter made of stable fat crystals. If you melt and recool the chocolate without tempering it (carefully heating and cooling chocolate to a precise temperature), some of the fat crystals may recrystallize as unstable crystals. The unstable fat crystals rise to the surface of the chocolate and form dull gray streaks called fat bloom. Tempering melted chocolate promotes the formation of fat crystals and prevents the occurrence of fat bloom; this process also produces chocolate with a very shiny, unstreaked surface (see Working With Chocolate).

Couverture is not readily available to the home baker. It may be obtained from wholesale bakery supply houses and some mail-order suppliers, usually in 10-pound bars. If it is unavailable, use a good-quality semisweet or bittersweet chocolate with a high cocoa butter content. Many brands of European chocolate bars can be used in place of coating chocolate. See also Compound Chocolate Coating.

Compound Chocolate Coating   Although it has chocolate in its name, this is an imitation product. It may be simply melted and used directly for dipping or spreading.

Eating Chocolate   To make eating chocolate, cocoa butter and sugar are added to the chocolate liquor. Surprisingly, distinctions of bittersweet, semisweet, and sweet do not correspond to any fixed degree of sweetness; the amount of sugar in each depends on the formula of the individual manufacturer. According to U.S. Food and Drug Administration regulations, *sweet chocolate* may contain less than half the chocolate liquor required in bittersweet chocolate. Although different manufacturers use different formulations, *bittersweet chocolate* is usually the most intensely chocolate-flavored and the least sweet, with *semisweet chocolate* being sweeter, and *sweet chocolate* being sweeter still. The three are usually interchangeable in recipes.

Most bittersweet, semisweet, and sweet chocolate is sold in paper-wrapped bars. Semisweet chocolate is also made into chips and packed in bags; chips may be substituted for semisweet chocolate bars ounce for ounce. The chips, however, usually have a lower cocoa butter content than semisweet chocolate bars, thus their flavor is less intense and they melt less easily.

German's Sweet Chocolate   First made by a Mr. German, this type of chocolate has been popularized by the recipe for German's Sweet Chocolate Cake on the package. German's Sweet Chocolate is a proprietary name of the Baker Chocolate Company.

Milk Chocolate To make milk chocolate, dried milk solids are added to sweetened chocolate. It is widely used for candy bars and other confections but is rarely used in cooking. It should not be used in recipes unless specified.

Powdered Cocoa For powdered cocoa, enough cocoa butter is pressed out of the chocolate liquor to leave a press cake with a content of 10 to 24 percent cocoa butter. The cake is pulverized to make cocoa powder. *Dutch-process cocoa* is made by treating either whole nibs or chocolate liquor with an alkaline solution, yielding cocoa with a darker color and mellower flavor. *Instant cocoa* contains lecithin, an emulsifier that makes cocoa easier to dissolve in cold liquids. Many brands of instant cocoa also contain added sugar. Cocoa and instant cocoa are generally packed in airtight tins.

Solid Unsweetened Chocolate Chocolate liquor that has been poured into molds and solidified, solid unsweetened chocolate is usually sold in 8-ounce boxes, with the chocolate divided into tissue-wrapped 1-ounce squares for easy measuring.

White Chocolate Not technically chocolate at all because it lacks chocolate liquor, white chocolate is cocoa butter with added sugar, milk, and flavorings. It may contain lecithin and it usually contains vanilla or vanillin. It should not be substituted for chocolate in recipes.

Storage Keep solid chocolate, wrapped airtight, in a cool, dry place for up to four months. Chocolate kept in the refrigerator will sweat when brought to room temperature and may not melt properly. Chocolate stored in a warm place may develop bloom—a dusty white coating caused by melted cocoa butter rising to the surface. It is harmless and the chocolate may safely be used.

Cocoa will keep indefinitely in an airtight tin in a cool place. Store chocolate syrup in a covered container in the refrigerator; it will keep indefinitely.

WORKING WITH CHOCOLATE

Chocolate is an ingredient with many qualities and uses. Melted chocolate can be worked to create a variety of decorations (see photographs, page 126). The Chocolate Ruffle Torte on page 127 is an example of how chocolate ribbons and ruffles can be used.

All work with chocolate should be done at a cool time of the day in a cool room. Handle chocolate quickly and lightly to avoid melting. These techniques are not easy for people with hot hands.

To Melt Chocolate Chocolate is temperamental. It burns easily and should always be melted slowly. When melting chocolate by itself for any purpose, it is best to chop it into small pieces. Place chopped chocolate in the top of a double boiler or in a stainless steel bowl over a pan of hot (not boiling) water; adjust heat so water remains just below a simmer. Take care not to let water

To keep its surface shiny and free of streaks, chocolate must be heated until it melts and then cooled to a specific temperature. This process is called tempering.

boil or allow steam to rise and settle in pan of chocolate. If there is a speck of water in the container used to melt the chocolate, the chocolate will tighten (seize) into an unmeltable mass. To salvage tightened chocolate, stir in 1 teaspoon of vegetable shortening per ounce of chocolate.

Chocolate will melt well in liquid (such as milk or cream) as long as there is at least 1 tablespoon of liquid per ounce of chocolate.

Chocolate can also be melted in a microwave oven. Put chocolate in a glass container and set oven on medium or high heat; chocolate will melt in 1 to 3 minutes, depending on volume.

To Temper Chocolate Coarsely chop chocolate to be tempered. In addition, finely grate a few ounces of unmelted semisweet or bittersweet coating chocolate. You will need 1 tablespoon grated chocolate for every 4 ounces of coarsely chopped chocolate. Melt chopped chocolate in a dry bowl set over hot water; stir until smooth. Do not allow chocolate to exceed 115° F (test with an instant-read thermometer). Remove bowl from hot water and set on a towel to steady it. Gradually stir in grated chocolate, a spoonful at a time, stirring until melted before adding another spoonful.

If the dipping chocolate is semisweet or bittersweet, cool to 86° to 90° F; if milk chocolate, cool to 83° to 88° F. Return bowl to warm water to maintain desired temperature. If temperature drops too much, mixture will be too thick to coat properly. If it rises above 90° F, it will have to be retempered.

MAKING CHOCOLATE RUFFLES

To make a thin chocolate sheet for a ruffle   Refrigerate a piece of marble for several hours or place a rimmed baking sheet filled with ice on top of marble for 30 minutes to chill it. (Chocolate can be spread on the back of a baking sheet but ruffles will not look as shiny when finished.) Dry marble with paper towels. Pour a 1-inch-wide strip of melted and tempered chocolate on ice-cold marble. Use a flexible metal spatula and swift, smooth, even strokes to spread chocolate into a thin sheet about 3 inches wide and 10 inches long.

To form a fan-shaped ruffle   When chocolate begins to set but is still pliable, slide a wide-bladed putty knife under right edge of chocolate. To form a fan-shaped ruffle, push chocolate toward left side of marble by moving putty knife from right to left (flexing wrist back and forth as you push). Use index finger and thumb of left hand to gather chocolate into a ruffle as you go along. Transfer ruffle to a waxed paper–lined baking sheet and immediately place in refrigerator.

For the Chocolate Ruffle Torte   Make enough ruffles to cover the top of the cake in an overlapping design of rose petals. Rechill marble as necessary. Store ruffles between pieces of waxed paper in a pan in refrigerator until ready to place on cake, after cake has been wrapped with chocolate ribbon (see below). Cover top of pan with plastic wrap.

MAKING CHOCOLATE RIBBONS

Cut out a sheet of waxed paper that is slightly wider than cake is tall and as long as circumference of cake. With a flexible metal spatula, spread a thin layer of melted and tempered chocolate on waxed paper. When chocolate begins to set but is still pliable, place one end of strip against cake (with wet chocolate toward cake). Wrap rest of chocolate strip around cake so it rests smoothly against sides of cake. Press top edge of chocolate down onto top of cake. Chill in refrigerator until chocolate is firm and waxed paper peels away easily.

MAKING CHOCOLATE LEAVES

Choose thick, waxy plant leaves with visible veins. Paint melted and tempered chocolate evenly on undersides of leaves. Chill in refrigerator until chocolate is firm. Slide fingernail between leaf and chocolate near stem to loosen chocolate from leaf. Pull leaf away from chocolate. Use these delicate leaves to decorate all sorts of cakes.

MAKING CHOCOLATE CURLS

It is easiest to produce chocolate curls from a 4-ounce or larger bar of chocolate (at room temperature). Scrape long side of bar with a potato peeler. When chocolate is just the right temperature, this will produce chocolate curls. If chocolate is too cold, you will end up with short chocolate shavings or shredded chocolate.

■ CHOCOLATE RUFFLE TORTE

This stunning chocolate mousse torte requires some knowledge of the properties of chocolate and a little experience in working with melted chocolate. If you are a beginner to chocolate work, see Working With Chocolate.

- ¾ cup unsalted butter, softened
- ¾ cup sugar
- ¾ cup (3 oz) finely ground almonds
- 6 ounces bittersweet chocolate, melted and cooled
- 6 egg yolks
- 6 egg whites

Chocolate Mousse

- 1¼ cups whipping cream
- 6 ounces semisweet chocolate, melted and cooled
- ½ cup water
- 7 tablespoons sugar
- 4 egg yolks

Chocolate Ribbons and Ruffles

- 1 pound semisweet chocolate

1. Preheat oven to 350° F. Butter and lightly flour 2 round cake pans 2 inches tall and 8 inches in diameter (see Pan Substitution Chart, page 20, if you don't have pans this size). Line bottom of each with a circle of waxed paper.

2. In large electric mixer bowl, cream butter with half of the sugar until light. Add almonds and beat until light. Beat in melted chocolate.

3. Add egg yolks, one at a time, beating well after each addition; beat until light and fluffy.

4. Beat egg whites in a separate bowl until they begin to hold peaks. Gradually add remaining sugar and beat until stiff but still glossy.

5. Stir one fourth of egg whites into chocolate mixture to lighten batter. Gently fold in remaining whites. Whites should be completely incorporated but not deflated.

6. Divide batter equally between the 2 pans and gently smooth top of batter. Bake for 30 to 40 minutes, or until done. Cool in pans 10 minutes, then turn out onto wire racks to finish cooling. This cake tends to sink in the middle as it cools. Trim top with serrated knife to create even layers.

7. Place one layer on a cardboard cake circle that is ⅛ inch smaller than the cake. Spread half of the Chocolate Mousse over this layer. Set next layer on top of mousse. Spread remaining Chocolate Mousse on sides and top of cake. Refrigerate until mousse is firm (about 45 minutes).

8. Decorate cake with Chocolate Ribbons and Ruffles.

Serves 8.

Chocolate Mousse Whip cream until it holds soft peaks. Refrigerate. Melt chocolate; cool to tepid. Combine the water and sugar in saucepan. Bring to a boil to dissolve sugar. Boil 1 minute. Measure out ½ cup hot syrup. Place egg yolks in a deep, 4- to 5-quart stainless steel bowl. Whisk in hot syrup. Continue whisking in one direction (either clockwise or counterclockwise) over a double boiler until mixture holds soft peaks (5 to 7 minutes). Beat yolks off heat with electric mixer or by hand until they are cool. Stir in melted, tepid chocolate. Fold in one eighth of whipped cream. Gradually fold in remaining whipped cream. If you fold in cream too quickly, it will cause chocolate to harden and form chocolate chips.

Chocolate Ribbons and Ruffles Melt and temper (see page 125) 1 pound of semisweet chocolate. Follow step-by-step instructions on opposite page to form ruffles and ribbons.

Chocolate Ruffle Torte, adorned with pleats of rich chocolate, is a cake that borders on being a work of art. Inside the chocolate case are both chocolate cake and chocolate mousse—a chocoholic's fantasy.

■ CHOCOLATE-DIPPED FRUIT

When dipping fruits in chocolate, first dry the fruits completely. Any residual moisture will cause the chocolate to seize, or become stiff. Strawberries, glacé apricots, candied ginger, candied citrus peels, dried figs, and prunes look fabulous half-dipped. Fruits that tend to darken when exposed to the air, such as bananas, apples, and pears, are best totally coated. Moist fruits, such as orange sections, raspberries, and seedless grapes, should also be completely coated. The amount of chocolate required depends on the size of the pieces of fruit being coated. A dipping fork, with two or three thin prongs or a loop, is useful, although many professional candy makers use the tips of their fingers. Have ready a baking sheet covered with aluminum foil or parchment paper to set the fruit on after dipping. Fruits completely covered in chocolate can be refrigerated, loosely covered, up to 48 hours, or layered in a container between sheets of waxed paper or parchment paper. Partially covered moist fruits such as strawberries should be served within 12 hours.

    1 orange, sectioned
    1 apple
    1 box (8 oz) raspberries
   14 ounces semisweet chocolate, tempered
       (see page 125)

1. Section orange. Using a sharp knife, remove skin and white membrane of orange, exposing flesh beneath. Carefully cut out each section by cutting next to membrane from edge to core on each side of section. Place sections on paper towels to dry.

2. Wash apple and pat dry. Core apple and cut into 12 pieces. Pat sections dry. Wash and dry raspberries. Discard any that are moldy or bruised.

3. Using a dipping fork or 2 fingers, dip orange sections and apple slices into tempered chocolate. Coat fruit completely, lift from bowl of chocolate, shake gently to remove excess chocolate, and place on a baking sheet lined with aluminum foil or parchment paper. Dip raspberries in same manner, being extremely gentle. Store dipped fruit in the refrigerator if not serving immediately.

Makes about 4 dozen coated fruits.

■ STRAWBERRIES IN WHITE CHOCOLATE

White chocolate is very perishable due to the milk solids that are combined with sugar and cocoa butter to make this product. The best method for melting and tempering white chocolate requires a bain-marie (hot water bath). Water is boiled in a large pan while the chocolate is finely chopped and placed in a metal mixing bowl. The heat is then turned off under the water, and the bowl of white chocolate is placed in the hot water. The chocolate is stirred constantly as it melts, and the tempering process

continues as for semisweet chocolate (see page 125). Many American companies make a confectioners' coating, or summer coating, which is similar to white chocolate but uses vegetable fat instead of cocoa butter.

   30 large strawberries, with long stems
   10 ounces white chocolate

1. Wash strawberries and thoroughly pat dry. Temper chocolate according to instructions in the introduction and on page 125.

2. Hold strawberries by their stems. Dipping one at a time, lower tip of strawberry into chocolate to cover half of the fruit. Gently shake strawberry to remove excess chocolate and place on a baking sheet lined with aluminum foil or parchment paper. Repeat with remaining strawberries, setting berries about ½ inch apart on baking sheet. Place fruit in refrigerator if not serving immediately. Refrigerate for up to 12 hours. Because strawberries are perishable, they are best eaten within hours after dipping.

Makes 30 strawberries.

■ DIPPED AND STUFFED STRAWBERRIES

Strawberries in white chocolate are taken one delicious step further—they are filled with rich cream cheese.

   20 large strawberries, with long stems
    ½ cup natural cream cheese
   10 ounces semisweet or white chocolate,
       tempered (see preceding recipe)

1. Wash strawberries and thoroughly pat dry. Cut a slit in each strawberry from tip almost to stem. Gently pry slit apart until it is about ¼ inch wide at tip.

2. Taking about 1 teaspoon of cream cheese, fill opening. Smooth edges with a knife to conform to the contour of strawberry.

3. Dip as directed in step 2 of Strawberries in White Chocolate (preceding).

Makes 20 strawberries.

Recipes and Related Information

Baked Chocolate Custard, 169; Cake-Lover's Brownies, 65; Chocolate Doughnuts, 180; Chocolate Fudge, 96; Chocolate Fudge Frosting, 248; Chocolate Glaze, 250; Chocolate Ice Cream, 312; Chocolate Mousse Torte, 373; Chocolate-Pecan Waffles, 599; Chocolate Pretzels, 146; Chocolate Soufflé, 207; Chocolate Sponge Cake, 83; Chocolate-Swirled Babka, 630; Chocolate Truffles, 97; Classic Fudge Brownies, 64; Devil's Food Cake, 86; Hot Fudge Sauce, 522; Marbled Cream Cheese Brownies, 65; Old-fashioned Chocolate Sauce, 523; Pain au Chocolat, 626; Philadelphia-Style Chocolate Ice Cream, 313; Ricotta Cheesecake, 119; White-Chocolate and Chip Brownies, 64.

CHOP, TO

To cut food into small, but not necessarily even, pieces with a knife, a bowl chopper, in a food processor, or in an electric minichopper. Chopped pieces are larger than those that are minced or diced, and can be evenly or randomly shaped. See KNIFE, Cutting Techniques, for information on proper hand position when chopping with a knife and specifics on chopping particular foods. Also see specific entries on other chopping equipment.

CHOPPING AND CUTTING BOARD

A cutting surface must be soft enough to cushion the edge of a knife blade so that it will not dull the knife, but hard enough to resist splintering or otherwise disintegrating into the food. Wood is the favorite cutting surface of most cooks. Laminated hardwood cutting

boards and end-grain butcher blocks are both excellent choices. Wooden boards have some disadvantages, however. They require a lot of care, including periodic sanding and oiling. They also tend to absorb odors from food and are harder to sterilize and deodorize than nonporous materials. For this reason, some cooks prefer a synthetic surface for cutting meats, poultry, and especially seafood. The best synthetic boards are made of a dense, opaque white polycarbonate and have a slightly uneven surface that gives under the knife blade much as wood does. They are easy to clean with dishwashing detergent (which should never be used on a wooden board). Do not confuse these boards with decorative boards of shiny, clear plastic or any other hard surface, which will dull knives.

Whether you use a wooden or synthetic cutting board, choose the largest size that will easily fit your work space. Nothing is more frustrating than trying to cut a lot of foods on a tiny board. Although sizes may vary from one manufacturer to another, boards are typically available sized 15 by 20 by ⅜ inches, 18 by 24 by ⅜ inches, and 16 by 9 by ⅜ inches.

HOW TO CLEAN WOODEN CUTTING SURFACES

After each use, scrape wooden boards clean with a metal dough scraper. Never soak with water. If a film remains, sprinkle with coarse salt and scour with a plastic or wire scrub brush; wipe with a clean, damp sponge. For minor stains, rub with the cut side of a lemon half. Deep stains can only be removed by sanding. Occasionally, sanitize the wood by cleaning with a solution of equal parts of bleach and water; rinse away solution with a clean, damp sponge. To keep wood from drying out and splintering, oil occasionally with mineral oil, or special wood oil available at hardware stores, home improvement stores, and better cookware stores.

> *Recipes and Related Information*
> *Cake and Pastry Tools, 92; Knife, 328.*

CILANTRO

Also known as coriander or Chinese parsley, cilantro is a pungent herb often used in Latin American and Asian cooking. It has small, fragile green leaves and thin stems. Although cilantro resembles parsley, its slightly musty aroma and flavor are entirely different. The aromatic seeds, which have a sweet flavor far removed from the flavor of the leaves, are an important and ancient seasoning marketed as coriander seed.

Use Cilantro leaves and stems add pungent flavor to Latin American soups, salads, and stews; they are an aromatic, all-purpose garnish for countless Latin American dishes, used in much the same way minced parsley is in French or American cooking. Chinese steamed fish and shellfish, noodle dishes, soups, and stews are also commonly garnished with fresh cilantro leaves. Fresh cilantro is also used in Indian chutneys, Moroccan stews, and Thai salads.

Coriander seed is an ingredient in most commercial curry powders and pickling spice mixtures. Ground coriander is added to hot dogs and other sausages, to gingerbreads, coffee cakes, Danish pastry, and Swedish butter cookies, and to lamb, pork, chicken, and cheese dishes.

Availability Fresh cilantro, tied in small bundles, is available all year. Coriander seed is available whole or ground, in bulk or prepacked in airtight containers or plastic bags.

Selection Buy fresh-looking bunches without evidence of wilting or decay. Packaged seasonings lose quality after a while; try to buy from a store that restocks its spice shelves fairly often.

Storage Keep fresh cilantro, root ends down, in a jar of water. Cover with a plastic bag and refrigerate up to one week. Store coriander seed in an airtight container in a cool, dry, dark place. Replace ground coriander every six months. Whole coriander seed will last longer, anywhere from one to two years.

Preparation Trim root ends of fresh cilantro; mince or add whole to dishes. Toast whole coriander seed briefly in a dry skillet to bring out its flavor.

■ CILANTRO CHUTNEY

To prepare a fresh coconut, see page 132. Serve this refreshing sauce with all kinds of fish.

⅓ cup fresh lemon juice
2 cups cilantro leaves
½ cup peeled, chopped fresh coconut
⅓ cup finely chopped green onion
1½ tablespoons minced fresh ginger
1 tablespoon seeded, chopped red or green chiles
2 teaspoons sugar
1 teaspoon ground cumin
Kosher salt and freshly ground pepper, to taste

Place lemon juice and half the cilantro in a food processor fitted with a steel blade; purée. Add remaining cilantro, coconut, onion, ginger, chiles, sugar, and cumin; process until smooth. Taste and season with salt and pepper. Serve as soon as possible.

Makes 2 cups.

Recipes and Related Information
Cilantro Raita, 522; Cold Fillet of Sole With Cilantro, Lime, and Pomegranate, 232; Guacamole, 15.

CINNAMON

The most important baking spice in America, cinnamon is the dried bark of an evergreen tree. The cinnamon used by American bakers is *Cinnamomum cassia*, imported from Indonesia and China. It is a dark reddish brown and has a robust warm, sweet flavor. Another variety of cinnamon, *Cinnamomum zeylanicum*, comes from Sri Lanka and is considered by many to be superior. It is pale tan and has a delicate flavor that strikes most American palates as too subdued.

The cinnamon bark, left to dry in the sun, rolls up into tight curls, the form in which it is usually shipped.

Use   Cinnamon is used throughout the world to flavor both sweet and savory dishes. American bakers use it in cakes, apple pie, sticky buns, and other sweet rolls. It flavors eggnog, mulled wine, and Mexican hot chocolate. Cinnamon is an ingredient in Chinese five-spice and Indian *garam masala*. Greeks add it to beef stews, ground lamb dishes such as moussaka and *pastitsio,* rice pudding, and pastries such as baklava and nut cake. Moroccans use it in carrot salad, the flaky pigeon pie called *pastilla,* couscous, and sweet puddings. Cinnamon also flavors the Vietnamese beef noodle soup called *pho* and a variety of Spanish and Portuguese custards and baked cakes, pastries, and breads.

Availability   Cinnamon is available ground or in rolled sticks, in bulk or prepacked in airtight glass jars, tins, or plastic bags.

Selection   Packaged seasonings lose quality after a while; try to buy from a store that restocks its spice shelf fairly often.

Storage   Keep cinnamon in an airtight container in a cool, dry, dark place. Replace ground cinnamon every six months; stick cinnamon will stay pungent indefinitely.

Preparation   Stick cinnamon is added directly to stews, syrups, or liquids as a flavoring agent but should be removed before serving. The most fragrant ground cinnamon is ground at home from the stick; break cinnamon stick into smaller pieces by hand, then use a clean coffee grinder or electric minichopper to grind to a powder just before using. To clean grinder, whirl a piece of bread in it briefly; the bread will pick up any powdery remains.

■ CINNAMON TOAST

This nursery and camp food is a perennial (although perhaps secret) favorite with most of us all of our lives. For a dressy version, use a rich sweet bread, such as leftover brioche, panettone, or raisin bread. For a different flavor, add a little grated nutmeg or grated lemon rind to the cinnamon-sugar mixture.

6 slices bread
Butter
Cinnamon Sugar (3 parts granulated or
light brown sugar to 1 part ground cinnamon)

1. Lightly toast bread. Butter one side and sprinkle with Cinnamon Sugar.

2. Toast under broiler to melt sugar. Serve immediately.

Makes 6 pieces of toast.

Recipes and Related Information
Baklava, 222; Braised Pork With Prunes, 458;
Cinnamon Balls, 144; Cinnamon-Raisin Muffins, 375;
Cinnamon Rolled Danish, 626; Fruited Coffee
Ring, 493; Herb and Spice Blends, 301; Moroccan
Pastilla, 221; Snickerdoodles, 145; Spice
Doughnuts, 180; Winter Fruit Compote, 186.

CITRON

A citrus fruit, citron resembles a large, thick-skinned lemon. Among Western cooks, it is valued primarily for its thick peel, which is candied for use in fruitcakes and confections.

Use   Minced citron may be added to puddings, fruitcakes, and hot cross buns, and to any recipe calling for candied fruit.

Availability   Some health-food stores sell large pieces of candied citron in bulk. It is also available in specialty stores and through mail-order suppliers of candied fruit.

Minced candied citron packed in plastic tubs is sold in some supermarkets; it is also an ingredient in many diced candied fruit mixes. Most supermarket varieties contain preservatives.

Storage Citron obtained from health-food stores or mail-order services will probably be made without preservatives and should be stored in the freezer. Even supermarket citron containing preservatives should be refrigerated, covered, and used within six months.

Preparation Chop with a knife.

CITRUS REAMER

The intense, natural flavor of freshly squeezed citrus juice can't be matched by the bottled product. A citrus reamer is used to extract juice from the fruit. Many designs are available, but in fact all are essentially variations of a single idea— an upright, pointed, ribbed

cone, shaped like half a lemon, which, when forced into the flesh of a lemon, lime, or orange, breaks it down and releases the juice.

At its most basic is the reamer made of wood with a handle. Juice, pulp, and seeds drip into a bowl. Slightly more elaborate in design, a plastic, metal, or ceramic reamer is attached to a base that is perforated to allow juice to drip through into a separate bowl while trapping pulp and seeds. This type often comes with its own container, which has a lip for easy pouring.

Both manual and electric machines are available to ease the chore of squeezing a pitcher full of juice. Some food processors offer optional reamer attachments. A long-popular, hand-operated model made of chromed steel features a reamer fixed to an upright support that rests on a horseshoe-shaped base. A lever works a hinged cap that fits over the reamer and the fruit set on it; the juice passes through a strainer and into whatever type of container has been set beneath it.

A citrus spout looks like a metal or plastic hose nozzle. Inserted into unpeeled fruit, it extracts drops, rather than spoonfuls of juice, useful for sprinkling on vegetables, fish, and salads. Fruit can be refrigerated with spout still inserted. In addition to convenience, this device is appealing because fruit that has not been cut open keeps fresher longer. Avoid spouts made of aluminum as they blacken the skin of the fruit at the contact point.

CLARIFY, TO

To make clear by removing impurities. Two foods that are clarified are butter and stock. To clarify butter, it is first melted; then the surface foam is skimmed off and the milk solids, which have settled to the bottom, are discarded. Stock is clarified by adding egg whites to lukewarm liquid; the whites coagulate and, as they rise to the surface, trap materials floating in the stock. The liquid is then skimmed and strained.

> ***Recipes and Related Information***
> *Clarified Butter, 68; Stock and Soup, 558.*

CLOVE

In cooking, *clove* refers to both the dried bud of a tropical evergreen tree, which is the source for clove spice, and one section of a head of garlic or shallot. This entry discusses clove spice. Also see GARLIC and SHALLOT.

The dark, nail-shaped clove is picked by hand just before it opens and is then dried in the sun. Because of the labor involved, it is one of the world's most expensive spices but also one of the most aromatic, with a warm, sweet, almost peppery flavor. Eighty percent of the world's supply comes from Zanzibar, the remainder from Madagascar and Brazil.

Use Cloves add a sweet, pungent aroma to cakes, gingerbread, fruit pies, fruit compotes, and baked fruit. Whole cloves are used to stud hams before baking and to stud onions for flavoring stock. Mulled wine and hot chocolate are often scented with clove, as is Swedish Glogg. Around the world cloves are added to meat stews, such as German sauerbraten, and to such spice blends as Indian *garam masala*. Cloves are also commonly used in pickling and preserving mixtures.

Availability Cloves are available whole or ground, in bulk or packed in airtight jars, tins, or plastic bags.

Selection Packaged seasonings lose quality after a while; try to buy from a store that restocks its spice section fairly often.

Storage Keep cloves in an airtight container in a cool, dark, dry place. Whole cloves will keep indefinitely; replace ground cloves every six months.

Preparation Whole cloves may be added directly to a dish but should be removed before serving. To facilitate removal, whole cloves are sometimes wrapped in a cheesecloth bag or studded in an orange, onion, or other suitable flavoring ingredient.

Old-fashioned pomander balls are simply fruits studded with whole cloves, then dried. These natural air fresheners are as decorative as they are practical. They can be added to a Christmas punch, hung in the closet to repel moths, used as tree ornaments and place-card holders, stacked in a bowl as a centerpiece, or given as gifts.

COAGULATE, TO

To transform a liquid substance into a soft, semisolid mass. A prime example of coagulation in cooking is the thickening of eggs when heated. Custards, cream pie fillings, egg-based sauces, and coddled eggs use coagulated egg proteins as a way to thicken or set the mixture. The word has the same derivation as curdle—which means to form into solids and a liquid—but implies a stage where a mixture thickens but isn't lumpy. In one sense, coagulation is a controlled curdling, where proteins begin to solidify but are kept from separating by monitoring temperature and by gentle stirring.

> **Recipes and Related Information**
> Custard, 168; Egg, 194.

COARSE CRUMBS

This pastry term, specifically for making pie crusts and biscuits, describes the appearance of flour and fat—butter, lard, vegetable shortening, or a combination—when properly and sufficiently mixed. To achieve this texture, fat is cut in to the flour, or reduced to smaller and smaller flour-coated pieces, with a pastry blender, a fork, two knives, or skilled fingers, until the desired consistency is reached. Coarse meal and small peas are other common recipe descriptions for coarse crumbs.

> **Recipes and Related Information**
> Biscuit, 49; Cake and Pastry Tools, 91; Cut In, 171; Pie and Tart, 431.

COAT, TO

To cover with a dry ingredient such as flour, crumbs, sugar, or nuts, or a liquid such as sauce, glaze, aspic or gelatin, or a frosting. Typically, foods that are sautéed, fried, or broiled are given a dry coating, which adds texture and flavor, preserves natural juices, and serves as a protective barrier between food and cooking fat. Liquid coatings are decorative, keep foods moist, and add flavor.

COAT A SPOON, TO

To leave a velvety film on the back of a spoon dipped in soft custard; a test for the doneness of a soft custard (see CUSTARD). As an additional test, if a track made by running a finger down the coated spoon stays clear, the custard is ready and should be removed from the heat immediately or it will curdle.

COCONUT

Cultivated in Latin America, Africa, Indonesia, and other tropical areas, the coconut is the fruit of the towering coconut palm tree. The round nut has a hard, hairy brown shell, a thin brown skin, and firm, sweet, snow-white flesh.

Use   There are uses for almost every part of the coconut and the coconut palm. The hairy fibers on the shell are woven into mats and ropes or are made into brooms. The palm leaves are used to thatch roofs, the trunks for timber, and the sap of the tree is distilled for a beverage. Dried coconut meat is used in the manufacture of soaps and margarine. Coconut oil serves as a cooking oil and coconut shells as serving bowls.

The coconut palm is the main source of food in the Pacific Islands and is extremely important in Southeast Asia, India, and Latin America. Coconut milk and coconut cream are used in beverages, sauces, soups, and desserts. In Asia the grated fresh meat is an ingredient in vegetable, rice, and noodle dishes and in condiments such as Indonesian *sambals* and Indian chutneys. American cooks use sweetened coconut in pies, cakes, puddings, cookies, candies, and candy bars, and as a garnish for fruit salads and fruit compotes.

Availability   Whole fresh coconut is marketed all year, with peak supplies from September through January. Grated coconut is available in some supermarket freezer cases. It is also dried and packed, either sweetened or unsweetened, in plastic bags or tins. Grated coconut is also sold in bulk in many health-food stores.

Selection   The average coconut weighs about 1½ pounds and should sound full of liquid when shaken.

Storage   Unopened coconut will keep in the refrigerator crisper for up to one month. Once opened, the coconut meat should be used immediately. Any leftover meat, in pieces or grated, may be frozen with the liquid from inside the coconut for several months. Dried coconut will keep in an airtight container in a cool, dry place for several months.

Preparation   To open a whole coconut, puncture one or two of the round "eyes" near stem end with a screwdriver or ice pick. Let interior liquid drain out. (Leftover coconut may be frozen in this liquid.) Put whole coconut on a baking pan in a preheated 350° F oven for about 20 minutes; remove from oven and tap with a hammer in several places. It should crack open. Use a screwdriver to chip away shell from meat, or carefully pry them apart with a knife. Then use a small, sharp paring knife to peel away the thin brown skin. Grate a few chunks at a time in a hand grater, food processor, or blender.

Recipes: Cilantro Chutney, 130; Coconut Cream Pie, 440; Coconut Custard Pie, 440; Coconut Flake Crust, 436; Toasted Coconut-Banana Bread, 491; Your Own Bridge Mix, 59.

The meat, milk, and cream extracted from the tropical coconut are important ingredients in the cuisines of the Pacific Islands, Southeast Asia, India, and Latin America.

■ COCONUT MILK AND COCONUT CREAM

Coconut milk and cream are used to enrich and flavor beverages, puddings, stews, rice dishes, and sauces. Coconut cream is available packed in tins in Asian and Latin supermarkets. Store leftover commercial coconut cream in an airtight container in the refrigerator for up to one week; homemade coconut cream should be used within a few hours. Both homemade and purchased versions may be frozen indefinitely. However, frozen coconut milk and cream never have quite the smooth texture of the fresh or canned versions.

To make coconut milk and coconut cream, blend 1 cup of freshly grated coconut with 1 cup of hot water in a blender or food processor. (If using dried coconut, substitute milk for hot water.) Let steep 30 minutes, then strain through a sieve, pressing down on pulp to extract as much liquid as possible. Repeat with the same coconut but use fresh water or milk. Discard pulp. The resulting liquid is a rich coconut milk. The richer liquid that rises to the top as the milk cools is coconut cream, which may be spooned off and used separately, or stirred into the milk to enrich it.

CODDLE, TO

To cook in water just below the boiling point. The most common application is coddling eggs for Caesar salad. Coddling warms the yolk so it will hold more oil in suspension when incorporated into the dressing. The egg is left in the hot water only long enough to coagulate the surface of the white and to warm the egg slightly.

Recipes and Related Information
Caesar Salad, 506; Egg, 194.

Call it what you wish—java, café, brew—there is nothing in the world quite as satisfying as a hot cup of coffee for starting out the day.

COFFEE

Native to Africa, the coffee tree produces small red berries containing two flat-sided oval beans. These beans, when cleaned, skinned, dried, and roasted, are the basis for one of the world's most popular beverages.

The best coffee beans are the fruit of *Coffea arabica*, a tree that flourishes at high altitudes in the tropics and subtropics. *Coffea robusta*, a disease- and frost-resistant tree that thrives at lower altitudes, yields lesser-quality beans that are the basis of most commercial blends.

Today Brazil produces about half of the world's crop, with the rest of Latin America accounting for one quarter and Africa for one sixth.

Use　Coffee is enjoyed as a beverage and as an ingredient in other beverages. It adds richness and mellow flavor to stews, barbecue sauces, and the classic southern red-eye gravy. It may be added to pumpernickel bread for flavor and color, to spice cakes and fruitcakes, to mousses, custards, ice cream, puddings, dessert sauces, and frostings. Some recipes call for brewed coffee, others for instant coffee, instant espresso, or coffee extract.

Availability　Coffee is sold as whole roasted beans, in bulk or bags; ground, in bulk, bags, or vacuum-packed jars or cans; or as instant powder or granules, in vacuum-packed jars or cans.

Selection　The best coffee is made from freshly roasted beans. If possible, buy coffee beans in small batches directly from the roaster or from a retailer with a rapid turnover.

Storage　To slow oxidation and loss of flavor, store whole beans and ground coffee in airtight tins in freezer. Whole beans should be used within one month, ground beans within one week. Store instant coffee in an airtight jar in a cool place.

PROCESSING AND ROASTING

After harvesting, most coffee berries are sun-dried and allowed to ferment for two to three weeks to facilitate removal of the pulp and thin skin surrounding the beans. In some countries with abundant water, the berries are processed by a wet method: They are washed first, then mechanically stripped of pulp; next the beans are fermented in concrete tanks for up to 24 hours, washed repeatedly, then dried—either in the sun or mechanically. Finally, the papery outer skin is removed. The wet method is costlier, but yields higher-quality beans.

Whether processed by the wet or dry method, all beans are then sorted by size and picked over by hand to remove faulty specimens.

Coffee beans are shipped green (unroasted) and roasted by the packer, the wholesaler, or, in some instances, the coffee retailer. The temperature of the roast determines the flavor of the beverage. The longer the bean is roasted, the darker and more strongly flavored the coffee made from it (see Coffee Roasts).

DECAFFEINATED COFFEE

Caffeine is removed from coffee by one of two processes: a water method or a solvent method. In the water method, unroasted coffee beans are soaked for several hours in a mixture of water and coffee components until 97 percent of the caffeine has been leached out. The beans are then dried and roasted. The soaking liquid is treated with methylene chloride, which draws out the caffeine and allows liquid to be reused on subsequent batches.

In a variation of the water method called Swiss water process, the unroasted beans are soaked in a water solution until about 97 percent of the caffeine has been leached out. The solution also leaches out soluble flavor components. To retrieve them, the liquid solution is filtered through charcoal that has been treated to trap the caffeine but allow most of the flavor components through. The filtered liquid is condensed and added back to the beans, which are then dried and roasted.

There are four different solvents used to remove caffeine from coffee: methylene chloride, ethyl acetate, carbon dioxide, and triglycerides. Solvent methods are quicker and less expensive and they disturb fewer of the flavor components. Nevertheless, many people concerned about solvent residues continue to prefer a water-process decaffeinated coffee.

INSTANT COFFEE

Instant coffee is made from brewed coffee from which the water is removed either by evaporation in a vacuum or by freeze-drying. It is quickly reconstituted with hot water.

GRINDING

Coffee beans must be ground before they can be brewed. Because ground coffee oxidizes (and therefore turns rancid) faster than whole coffee beans, it is advisable to employ a home grinder and grind beans just before using.

TYPES OF GRINDS

The type of coffee maker determines the optimum grind. The finer the grind, the more quickly water extracts the flavor. Consequently, fine grinds are best suited to coffee makers that complete their brewing cycle quickly, such as espresso machines, Italian stove-top steam-pressure pots, and open-pot Turkish or Greek coffee makers. A medium or drip grind is designed for drip pots and plunger pots. Coarse or regular grind is suitable for machines with slow brewing cycles, such as percolators.

COFFEE GRINDERS AND MILLS

A few models of electric drip coffee makers have a built-in grinding system, but most are freestanding machines, either manual, functioning like a pepper mill, or one of the two types of electric units.

Electric Coffee Grinder   This is the more elementary of the two systems. Stainless steel blades pulverize the whole beans as they rotate; the fineness of the grind is controlled by how long the push button governing the motor is depressed. Drawbacks include unevenly ground beans, blades that may jam if the container is packed too tightly, and small capacity. These grinders can, however, do double duty for grinding spices and nuts. If you use one to prepare more than just coffee, the container should be cleaned before storing so flavors don't transfer from one food to another. Use the brush that comes with the machine, or whirl a slice of soft bread until reduced to fine crumbs; bread will pick up leftover powder or oils.

Electric Coffee Mill   Variable settings and grinding disks rather than blades ensure a more precise, uniform grind each time. Most have two receptacles—a hopper for whole beans and a container for the ground coffee. Mills can hold and process more beans than a grinder, which means more coffee per operation.

BREWING

Although there are many brewing methods, each does essentially the same thing: infuses ground coffee with water in order to extract the flavor essences. This process can be as basic as pouring hot water over coffee grounds and then straining out the liquid. For many coffee lovers, however, brewing the "perfect cup" is a much more complex affair. For them it is a careful, studied pairing of bean with brewing system, filter with coffee maker.

Regardless of how much time and effort you care to put into your morning cup of coffee, the most satisfying beverage is the offspring of good beans and a good coffee maker. Understanding the brewing process is also important.

Studies have determined that for optimum flavor and body, water temperature should be slightly less than boiling, or about 200° F. Higher temperatures extract too much of the coffee solids, producing a bitter brew lacking aroma, which boils away with the steam. Coffee made with water that is too cool is thin and insipid. The ideal extraction is 20 percent of the coffee solids, a point that occurs when grounds have been in contact with 200° F water for about two minutes. If extraction is too fast, the result is weak, flat, and off-tasting. If brewing is too slow or too long, the product is bitter and sour.

Whatever method you prefer, always start with cold water. Then make sure that the water is heated to the proper temperature (at least 185° F), and that extraction isn't rushed or dragged out. Finally, make sure that hot water reaches all the grounds.

COFFEE STRENGTH

How strongly to brew coffee is entirely a matter of taste. The higher the proportion of grounds to water, the stronger the coffee. To make a medium-strong cup of infused or drip coffee, use 2 tablespoons grounds (1 coffee measure) to 6 ounces water. Reduce proportions of grounds for weaker coffee. For espresso, use 2 tablespoons of ground coffee to 3 ounces water.

BREWING METHODS AND COFFEE MAKERS

The design of the coffee maker determines how the coffee is to be brewed. The following is a general guide to the variety of coffee makers available in America and the brewing method required by each.

Espresso Makers: Manual and Electric   The stovetop espresso maker, also known as *la moka*, is a three-part cast aluminum or stainless steel coffeepot with a spout and handle. The bottom is filled with water; a small coffee basket filled with very fine grounds is set atop it; then the upper chamber is screwed on and the machine placed over heat. As the water boils, steam is forced up through the grounds and then condenses as coffee in the upper chamber. To produce the intensely dark, rich espresso favored by the French and Italians requires a more complicated espresso machine. Several home models exist, all based on the same principle—that of rapidly forcing a combination of steam and water through tightly packed, very fine grounds. Some have a steam nozzle to froth milk for Italian cappuccino and *caffè latte* or the French version of the latter, café au lait.

Stove-top espresso makers are relatively inexpensive and are available in 1- to 12-cup sizes. Cost of home espresso machines ranges from less than $100 to more than $500, and you get what you pay for. Cheaper models tend to have inexpensive gaskets, seals, and pump systems, and as a result break down sooner. If you are one of the growing number of coffee enthusiasts who want to enjoy espresso at home, invest in the best machine you can afford.

Filter Drip System: Manual and Electric   The manual filter drip system consists of a pot fitted with a paper-lined cone. The cone and carafe are either a single unit or two separate pieces. The grounds are placed in the paper filter, then hot water is slowly poured over the grounds and allowed to drip into the pot below. For optimum extraction, begin by wetting the grounds, making sure you've moistened them completely, then let them steep for about 30 seconds. Pour more water to the top of the filter and let drip through; repeat until you've brewed the number of cups you want. To keep coffee hot, set pot on a heat diffuser over a low flame.

The electric filter drip system is merely an automatic version of the above method. The machine heats cold water poured into a special reservoir to the proper temperature. Within moments, hot water begins dripping down through the grounds held in a paper-filter–lined basket; brewed coffee is deposited in the pot below, which sits on a warming plate.

Whichever system you use, always remove grounds from cone after brewing because they absorb aroma from the coffee.

TIPS
COFFEE ROASTS

A pale roast (also called light city roast) produces delicate, fairly acidic coffee because the heat was not strong or long enough to decompose or evaporate most of the acids in the bean.

A light medium roast (also called American or full city roast) is the one used in most of the nationally distributed, commercial blends.

A dark roast (also known as French or Viennese roast) produces a rich-tasting, full-bodied coffee. Although the nomenclature is not regulated, generally a Viennese roast is lighter than a French roast.

A very dark roast (also known as Italian or espresso roast) produces dark, shiny beans used in making the richly flavored, bittersweet Italian espresso.

Coffee lovers can choose from a wide variety of coffee-making equipment. Shown from left to right are: manual filter drip pot, coffee mill, coffee grinder, French plunger pot, electric drip coffee maker, manual and electric espresso makers, open pot (ibrik), percolator, and Italian filter pot.

Manual systems are sized from 1 to 12 cups. Cones are plastic or porcelain. One-piece drip pots are made of heat-resistant glass with a wooden grip at the center of the pot. Electric machines offer many options: 4-, 8-, 10-, and 12-cup capacities; two brewing cycles (1 to 4 cups and 5 to 12 cups) so that smaller amounts aren't brewed too quickly; a stop-drip valve that interrupts brewing briefly if carafe is pulled off the base; built-in grinders; and an electronic start feature that can be programmed to begin brewing automatically at a preset time. Bells and whistles don't brew a better cup of coffee, however; most of these models are comparable. Choose a coffee maker that is easy to use. That means the filter can be installed without effort and the water cannister is easily accessible. After that, get what appeals to you.

Italian Filter Pot This pot, also known as the *napoletana* or *machinetta*, consists of two identical mug-shaped aluminum cylinders—one with a spout, the other without—and a coffee filter basket. The cylinder without a spout is filled with water and topped with a basket filled with grounds, then joined lip-to-lip with the spout, which faces downward. The machine is set over high heat, and when the water begins to boil, the entire apparatus is turned upside down by the handles. Hot water then drips down through the grounds and deposits brewed coffee in the lower cylinder (the one with the spout).

Open Pot The open pot, also known as an *ibrik* or Greek or Turkish coffeepot, is undoubtedly one of the oldest coffee makers. Today's models resemble a tall, narrow mug with a long handle. Water and sugar are placed in the mug and brought to a boil; pulverized coffee is added and the mug is returned to heat. When mixture boils up, mug is removed from heat until froth settles. The procedure is repeated twice, then the mixture is divided among small cups.

Percolator The pump percolator is the least desirable method for brewing coffee because the water gets too hot and only a little bit passes through the grounds at a time. The percolator consists of a pot with a basket that sits on a tube. The basket is filled with grounds and the pot with water. The pot is then set over heat or, if electric, is plugged in. The water is heated to boiling and is forced up the tube and into the basket, dripping back down into the pot repeatedly for up to 20 minutes. To compensate for the slow brewing process, the grind is usually coarse, which takes longer to extract.

Plunger The French plunger pot brews coffee by infusion. The pot is a glass cylinder with a fine mesh filter and plunger; the pot sits in a chromed metal frame that has a black, heat-resistant handle. Grounds and hot water are combined in the pot and allowed to steep for 3 to 5 minutes, with the plunger fully raised. Then the plunger is depressed, pushing grounds to bottom of pot and trapping them there. The clear coffee is poured into small cups. The result is the strong and flavorful *café filtre* often served in restaurants. This is a fast method that makes a good cup of coffee, but it isn't automatic because the water must be preheated and the coffee served immediately as it can't be held at serving temperature. The better models are expensive, but have a superior filter system and are extremely attractive. They are available in 4-, 8-, and 12-cup sizes.

Recipes and Related Information

Coffee Eclairs, 164; Coffee Fondant, 251; Coffee Ice Cream, 312; Country Ham Slices With Red-Eye Gravy, 462; Espresso Brownies, 64.

COLANDER, STRAINER, AND SIEVE

This family of equipment separates liquids from solids as in draining and rinsing a food, sifts flour and other dry ingredients, makes purées, and refines the texture of sauces and custards. Although thousands of seemingly different strainers and drainers are available, they are really all modifications of the same idea—a container with holes. They vary only in overall size, in the size of the openings, whether they are made of flexible mesh or more rigid material, and whether they can stand alone or need support of some kind. As a group they overlap one another in what they can do and are often interchangeable. A few, however, such as flour sifters or the cone-shaped chinois, are specialists. These designs have evolved to perform a particular separation better.

COLANDER

These freestanding metal or plastic bowls have relatively large holes that allow liquid to pass through quickly. They sit on a ring base or legs and have two handles. Some are made with a long handle and without bottom support and are used for draining over a pot or the sink. Colanders are best suited for rinsing food and draining cooked pasta and vegetables. Small handheld versions are useful for transferring cooked food from pot to plate. Buy a colander as large as will fit in your sink and on your shelf. They are made of stainless steel, enameled steel, nylon, tinned copper, and ceramic.

These straining, sifting, and refining tools are variations of a basic design—a container with holes. Shown clockwise from left to right are: small bowl strainers, rigid and wire mesh chinois, large bowl strainer, colander, drum sieve, flour sifter, flour and sugar dredgers.

STRAINER AND SIEVE

These are made of fine to coarse wire mesh supported by some sort of rigid frame. The basic bowl strainer is a kitchen staple because of its versatility: it drains, separates liquid from solid, solid from solid, and refines. Job for job, however, it doesn't perform as well as the specialty strainers—flour sifter, tamis, drum sieve, and chinois—each of which is designed to excel at a particular task. How many strainers do you need? A bowl strainer is a must; have several in different sizes and gauges of mesh. Buy the others if you would use them often and if you have a place to store them when you're not. Always choose a strainer with stainless steel mesh and a nonrusting frame.

Are strainers and sieves different? Not really. A strainer can be called a sieve when it is used to separate coarse particles from fine or to reduce soft solids to smooth purées—a very minor distinction.

Chinois (China Cap) Part of the classic French *batterie de cuisine*, the cone-shaped chinois gets its name from its resemblance to a peaked Chinese hat. Made of very fine mesh and equipped with a handle, it does an excellent job of separating stock from flavoring ingredients. A colander draped with several layers of dampened cheesecloth can be substituted for the chinois. Another version is rigid rather than mesh, with hundreds of tiny holes, and is used in conjunction with a pointed wooden pestle or pusher to make purées. A jelly-making chinois comes with a stand so it does not need other support; others have a handle and a lip and are set over a bowl or pan. Typically, a chinois is 8 inches in diameter and 10 inches tall. The mesh is tin and the frame tin-plated steel; to avoid rusting, wash promptly and dry thoroughly.

Drum Sieve/Tamis   Traditionally the frame for both of these European tools was wood; now it is more often metal. The round or teardrop-shaped tamis is a baking tool—for dusting cakes and pastries with confectioners' sugar or cocoa, or work surfaces with flour. Drum sieves are round and are used for puréeing, for refining custards, and to sieve egg yolks. European in origin, these strainers are not very common in American kitchens.

Flour Sifters   Most recipes no longer insist that flour be sifted, but many home bakers still do (see FLOUR, Is Sifting Necessary?). Sifting lightens the flour, breaks up clumps, and is a way to blend dry ingredients so that they are evenly dispersed. Wire bowl strainers work well for this job, but flour sifters do it just a little better. Their cylindrical shape directs the flour downward into cup or bowl; a bowl strainer lacks this control and flour tends to drift onto the work surface. Sifters have a mechanism to push the flour through, although many bakers move the flour along by banging the side of the sifter with the heel of their hand. Hand sifters that have a rotary handle to force the flour against the wire mesh are easiest to operate. Electric sifters can clog and aren't recommended, nor are triple-mesh hand sifters as they can trap food between layers and are hard to clean. Buy a sifter that holds at least 3 cups of flour, or more if you bake often or in large quantity.

COMBINE, TO

To mix two or more ingredients until blended. Sometimes in cooking this term also means to put ingredients that will be blended in one bowl or pan as a preparatory step.

CONDUCTION

To transfer heat by direct contact, molecule to molecule. For example, the interior mass of a steak or a turkey is heated by conduction; the heat touches the outer surface of the food and then is slowly passed along from one molecule to another through the interior to the center. Liquid in a saucepan is heated by conduction; the flame heats the pan, which in turn heats the liquid. A metal spoon sitting in a bowl of hot soup gets hot because of conduction as the heat travels from the soup to the bottom of the spoon and then up to its handle.

Microwave ovens, to a great degree, depend upon conduction for cooking. Microwaves penetrate the outer surface of food only an inch or two; the food is then finished by conduction. Times required for cooking with a microwave often include resting periods after cooking so that interior heat has time to work its way to the center.

Some materials are better conductors of heat than others. Metals in general are good conductors, as is hot fat. Water conducts less well than fat because it is unable to be heated to as high a temperature. Wood is a poor conductor of heat, which makes it an excellent material for cookware handles and cooking spoons.

Recipes and Related Information
Convection, 138; Materials for Cookware, 351;
Microwave Oven, 362.

CONVECTION, CONVECTION OVEN

The process of transferring heat by the circulating motion of air or liquid (including fat) is called convection. As heat is applied to a liquid (water or fat, for example) or a gas (air), whether from a flame or coil underneath a pan or from the heating unit of an oven, the molecules  closest to the heat source rise and those farther away sink. Moving currents are created when rising molecules cool and others heat up and so start to reverse their direction. (Once the hot gas or liquid touches the food, however, it is carried into the food by conduction.)

The convection oven creates extremely even oven heat because a fan in the oven cavity blows air over the heating element and keeps the hot air constantly moving. The circulating air results in even cooking, no matter how many pans are on a rack or how close they are to one another. Thus, these ovens are ideal for foods requiring hot, dry, circulating air—roasted and broiled meats and poultry, fish, and baked goods of all kinds.

A favorite with professional bakers since the early 1950s for its even browning and fast cooking, the convection oven cooks up to one third faster than conventional ovens and at lower temperatures for many foods. As a result, these ovens save energy as well as time. Unlike a microwave oven, this system does not need special utensils, and except for broiling, preheating is not required. Most home convection ovens are portable, designed to sit on a counter or recessed into cabinet space.

If you bake frequently or enjoy roasted or broiled meats, you will appreciate the unique capabilities of this type of oven. Options include dial or electronic touch controls, temperature probe, multistage programming, and dehydrator racks.

When determining time and temperature, follow the manufacturer's recommendations. As a general rule, to adapt a recipe written for roasting in a conventional oven, decrease roasting time by 30 percent and keep temperature the same. To bake a casserole, you should be able to keep heat and time about the same as a conventional oven. For leavened baked goods, you will need to decrease temperature by 50° F to 75° F; time may be slightly less.

Some cooks feel that although home convection ovens have their advantages, they do not perform as well as commercial models. Before buying a portable convection oven, you might want to talk to someone who already owns one and, if possible, try cooking with it.

Recipes and Related Information
Conduction, 138; Microwave Oven, 362.

COOKIE

Although American history has a decidedly English flavor, our word for cookies, the small, flat cakes that delight us from childhood on, derives from an earlier colonial influence: *koekje* is Dutch for "little cake." In England they are known as biscuits. Whatever they are called, these sweet baked treats are popular throughout the world in many forms and flavors.

Cookies fall into five basic categories, grouped primarily by the way they are shaped: drop, bar, molded and pressed, refrigerator, and rolled.

EQUIPMENT FOR BAKING COOKIES

One of the pleasures of making cookies is that they don't require lots of obscure or expensive ingredients or utensils. Nevertheless, baking will be easier and more fun if you are equipped with the basics.

Since making cookies is probably the most popular form of baking, have on hand several baking sheets. They should have a flat or barely turned-up edge so that the oven heat can reach every cookie evenly from all directions. Buy ones that are made of a heavyweight, heat-conductive material such as aluminum; they won't warp and will bake more evenly.

Insulated baking sheets have air sandwiched between two sheets of aluminum. The layer of air prevents cookies from burning on the bottom and promotes even baking. If you use an insulated baking sheet, you may find baking times increase slightly—generally requiring the maximum baking time given in the recipe.

Nonstick baking sheets are useful if they are made from heavy-gauge metal and coated with a top-quality nonstick material or silicone resin (see MATERIALS FOR COOKWARE, Nonstick Surfaces). When removing cookies from nonstick pans, use a spatula that won't scratch the surface.

Most bar cookies are baked in standard square or rectangular pans. The most frequently used sizes are an 8-inch square, a 9-inch square, and a 9- by 13-inch rectangle. The same baking characteristics can be found in these pans as in baking sheets of comparable materials. Bar cookies can also be baked in glass ovenware of the same dimensions as just specified.

Level wire racks enable cookies to cool quickly and evenly, with air circulating from all directions. Their shape doesn't matter, but having enough of them is a must if you bake often. Cookies are at their best if they can cool completely before you stack and store them.

Other equipment that is considered basic includes measuring spoons and dry and liquid measuring cups; a timer; a narrow metal spatula for leveling off dry ingredients and loosening edges of bar cookies from a pan; a wide, flexible metal spatula for transferring cookies from baking sheets; a rubber scraper for removing batter from a bowl or the blades of an electric mixer and for spreading batter in a baking pan; sifters and sieves for blending flour and other dry ingredients, for removing lumps from confectioners' sugar or cake flour, and also for sifting a decorative coating of confectioners' sugar or cocoa over the surface of baked cookies; rulers for measuring the dimensions of bar cookies to be cut uniformly, the thickness of a rolled-out dough, or the diameter of a roll of refrigerator-cookie dough; parchment paper; heavy-duty electric and portable mixers; food processor; blender; and specialty equipment such as cutters, molds, and a cookie press.

ABOUT MAKING AND BAKING COOKIES

Although making cookies is not a complicated procedure, any culinary undertaking goes more smoothly if you use the proper equipment and are organized. Read the recipe before you begin and have all equipment at hand and ingredients measured and in the form specified.

Grease pans only if the recipe calls for it. Use vegetable shortening or a nonstick vegetable spray (not butter). Another option is to line baking sheets with parchment paper. This method saves cleanup and permits easy transfer from baking sheet to cooling rack. Set unbaked cookies on cool baking sheets only. If you drop or set cookie dough onto a hot baking sheet, it will begin to spread or even bake before all the cookies are in place. If you are baking many cookies at one time, have several sheets available to use in rotation.

Good circulation of hot air in the oven is needed to bake cookies evenly. In general, use the middle oven rack, positioning a single baking sheet in the center of it. If you

Using whimsical, charming cookie cutters makes artists of us all. Who could resist these appealing sugar cookie rabbits?

have a wide oven, you may be able to place two narrow baking sheets side by side, but allow at least one inch of space between them, and between the baking sheets and sides of the oven. If time dictates baking two sheets of cookies at once, place one baking sheet on one side of the upper oven rack and the other baking sheet on the other side of the center rack. Halfway through the baking time, reverse the position of the two baking sheets.

Use a timer when baking cookies and know the idiosyncrasies of your oven. Many ovens have hot spots, or don't heat to the temperature they are set for. Test your oven frequently with an oven thermometer; if it is off, adjust the time or temperature accordingly. Check cookies for doneness toward the end of the low range of suggested cooking time, and then keep an eye on them until they are ready. They can quickly overbake.

COOLING AND STORING COOKIES

Some cookies are sturdy enough to be removed to cooling racks as soon as they come from the oven. Others are more delicate and must first cool slightly on the baking sheet. Each recipe should tell you how the cookies are to cool, but keep in mind that fragile cookies need very gentle treatment.

Cookies kept for short periods of time (up to one week) are best stored in a tightly covered tin at room temperature. Be sure the cookies have cooled completely before packing them in the container. If you are storing more than one kind of cookie, keep them separate. If placed together, crisp cookies will absorb moisture from soft cakelike cookies; before long all will be soggy. If cookies have icing or another topping, separate successive layers with sheets of waxed paper or kitchen parchment.

Cookies stored for longer periods of time (up to three or four months) can be kept in the freezer. Package each kind of cookie separately in an airtight enclosure of freezer wrap, freezer-weight plastic bags, heavy aluminum foil, or a foil-lined container. Rich, buttery, crisp cookies tend to freeze better than soft, moist, cakelike ones. Brownies are the exception; they can be frozen with great success. Thaw frozen cookies in their freezer wrapping or container at room temperature for 15 to 30 minutes. If cookies need frosting, glazing, or sprinkling with sugar, wait until they are thawed to add it.

DROP COOKIES

Made from a soft dough, drop cookies are extremely easy to prepare; they are often a child's first baking experience. They don't need to be molded, just pushed from a spoon onto a baking sheet.

To shape drop cookies, use two spoons. Scoop up the specified amount of dough with one, then use the other to help transfer the dough onto the baking sheet. Use both spoons to shape the spoonfuls of dough into a smoothly

rounded mound. Some bakers prefer to use a very small ice cream scoop to make a uniform round. Try to make all the cookies the same size and shape so they will finish baking at the same time.

■ OLD-FASHIONED SOFT SUGAR COOKIES

Nutmeg and lemon rind punctuate the familiar flavor of these tender, cakelike cookies.

> 2½ cups flour
> 1 teaspoon *each* baking soda and freshly grated nutmeg
> ¼ teaspoon salt
> ½ cup butter or margarine, softened
> 1½ cups sugar
> 2 eggs
> ½ teaspoon *each* vanilla extract and grated lemon rind
> 1 cup sour cream
>   Vanilla Granulated Sugar (see page 585), optional
> ¼ cup (approximately) raisins

1. In a bowl stir together flour, baking soda, nutmeg, and salt to combine thoroughly; set aside.

2. Preheat oven to 375° F. In mixer bowl combine butter and sugar, and beat until well blended. Beat in eggs, one at a time, mixing until fluffy after each addition. Add vanilla and lemon rind and mix to blend thoroughly.

3. Add flour mixture alternately with sour cream, mixing until smooth after each addition.

4. Drop by tablespoons, placed well apart, onto well-greased baking sheets. Sprinkle each cookie lightly with Vanilla Granulated Sugar (if used). Place one or more raisins in the center of each. Bake until cookies are golden brown (12 to 14 minutes). Remove at once to wire racks to cool.

Makes about 5 dozen 2¾-inch cookies.

■ TRADITIONAL RAISIN-OATMEAL COOKIES

Oatmeal, which replaces part of the flour, brings a chewy texture and nutlike flavor that are an unforgettable part of enjoying these cookies.

> 1½ cups flour
> 1 teaspoon baking soda
> ½ teaspoon ground cinnamon
> ¼ teaspoon *each* salt, freshly grated nutmeg, and ground cloves
> ¾ cup butter or margarine, softened
> 1½ cups firmly packed brown sugar
> 2 eggs
> 1 teaspoon vanilla extract
> 2 cups quick-cooking rolled oats
> 1 cup raisins

1. In a bowl stir together flour, baking soda, cinnamon, salt, nutmeg, and cloves to combine thoroughly; set aside.

A bar of delectable imported chocolate, coarsely chopped, transforms Favorite Chocolate Chip Cookies into luxurious Chocolate Chunk Cookies. You can bake these cookies to your taste—either crisp or chewy.

2. Preheat oven to 375° F. In mixer bowl combine butter and brown sugar, and beat until well blended. Add eggs, one at a time, beating well after each addition. Add vanilla and mix to blend.

3. Gradually add flour mixture until just blended. Stir in rolled oats and raisins.

4. Drop by tablespoons, placed about 2 inches apart, onto lightly greased baking sheets. Bake until cookies are lightly browned (about 10 minutes). Cool on wire racks.

Makes about 4 dozen 2½-inch cookies.

■ FAVORITE CHOCOLATE CHIP COOKIES

These cookies will be crisp if baked at the temperature specified in the main recipe, and soft and chewy if baked at the lower temperature suggested in the variation.

    1¼ cups flour
    ½ teaspoon baking soda
    ¼ teaspoon salt
    ½ cup butter or margarine, softened
    ½ cup firmly packed brown sugar
    ½ cup granulated sugar
    1 egg
    1 teaspoon vanilla extract
    1 package (6 oz) semisweet chocolate chips
    ½ cup chopped walnuts (optional)

1. In a bowl stir together flour, baking soda, and salt to combine thoroughly; set aside.

2. Preheat oven to 375° F. In mixer bowl combine butter and sugars; beat until fluffy and well blended. Beat in egg. Add vanilla and mix well.

3. Gradually add flour mixture until just blended. Stir in chocolate chips and walnuts (if used).

4. Drop by rounded tablespoons, placed well apart, onto lightly greased or nonstick baking sheets. Bake until cookies are well browned (12 to 14 minutes). Cool on wire racks.

Makes about thirty 2¾-inch cookies.

Chewy Chocolate Chip Cookies Bake cookies in a 325° F oven until they are a light golden brown (10 to 13 minutes). Cool on baking sheets for 3 minutes before removing to wire racks to cool completely.

Chocolate Chunk Cookies Omit semisweet chocolate chips. Coarsely chop a 3- to 4-ounce bar of semisweet chocolate, and fold it into cookie dough in step 3.

Peanut Butter–Chocolate Chip Cookies After beating butter and sugars, add ½ cup peanut butter (smooth or chunky). Beat well, then continue as for Favorite Chocolate Chip Cookies. Omit chopped walnuts.

TILE & LACE COOKIES

Making tiles Remove warm cookies, one at a time, from baking sheet and immediately drape over rolling pin (for small cookies, use small rolling pin) or curl in metal baguette pan. When cool, transfer to wire rack. If using sliced almonds in dough, drape or roll cookies so nutty sides are up.

Making cigarettes Roll each warm cookie around buttered handle of wooden spoon or cone. Remove when cool.

Making tulips Let each lace cookie cool on baking sheet until just firm enough to handle. Drape, bumpy side down, over inverted 2½- to 3-inch-diameter drinking glass, pressing draped portions of cookie softly into a cup shape. When set, transfer to wire rack or carefully place on baking sheet.

■ LEMON ROOF-TILE COOKIES

A drop-cookie batter, baked wafer thin, produces cookies of remarkable flexibility. While still warm from the oven, they can be rolled or curled into a variety of whimsical shapes. Curved into distinctive U shapes or twirled into "cigarettes" or cones, French *tuiles au citron* are a classic accompaniment to homemade ice cream or sorbet. They can also be baked as large cookies, then shaped into stylized tulips as edible containers for a frozen dessert, or left flat, stacked, and filled with any flavor mousse or a lemon curd. Although crisp when they are freshly baked, they may absorb moisture from the air and soften after standing. You can restore their crispness by arranging the cookies in a single layer on a baking sheet and placing them in a 200° F oven for 20 to 30 minutes.

   ¼ **cup blanched almonds**
   ⅓ **cup sifted cake flour**
   ¼ **cup butter or margarine, softened**
   ½ **cup sugar**
   2 **egg whites (about ¼ cup)**
   ¼ **teaspoon lemon extract**
   1 **tablespoon grated lemon rind**
   ½ **cup (approximately) sliced almonds (optional)**

1. In blender or food processor, whirl blanched almonds until powdery. In a small bowl combine almonds with cake flour, stirring to blend thoroughly; set aside.

2. Preheat oven to 400° F. Grease baking sheets and dust with flour (or line baking sheets with lightly buttered parchment paper).

3. In mixer bowl combine butter and sugar; beat until light and fluffy. Beat in egg whites until well blended. Stir in lemon extract and lemon rind. Gradually add flour mixture, beating until smooth.

4. Drop batter onto prepared baking sheets by rounded teaspoons, about 2 inches apart, to make tiles as shown in top photograph, or cones or cigarettes as shown in middle photograph. Batter can also be dropped by level tablespoons, about 3 inches apart, to make tulips as shown in bottom photograph. Sprinkle each with sliced almonds (if desired) to cover sparsely. With small spatula or back of a spoon, spread batter to a 3-inch-diameter circle for tiles or cones or to a 4-inch-diameter circle for tulips.

5. Bake until edges of cookies are brown (4 to 6 minutes). Let stand on baking sheets until cookies are barely firm enough to handle but still pliable (30 seconds to 1 minute). Carefully remove with a spatula and shape into tiles, cones, cigarettes, or tulips as shown in Tile and Lace Cookies (at left), or transfer to wire racks to make flat cookies.

6. If cookies become too cool to shape, return to oven for a few seconds until they are pliable again.

Makes about 30 small or 16 large cookies.

■ PECAN LACE COOKIES

These cookies can be shaped and served in all the ways suggested for Lemon Roof-Tile Cookies (at left). Shaped into tulips, they are delectable filled with apple or butter-pecan ice cream and topped with hot caramel sauce.

   ¼ **cup butter or margarine**
   ¼ **cup firmly packed brown sugar**
   ¼ **cup light corn syrup**
   ⅓ **cup flour**
   ½ **cup finely chopped pecans**
   1 **teaspoon vanilla extract**

1. Preheat oven to 350° F. Grease baking sheets and dust with flour.

2. Melt butter in a 1½- to 2-quart saucepan over medium heat. Stir in brown sugar and corn syrup. Increase heat to high and bring mixture to a boil, stirring constantly until brown sugar dissolves.

3. Remove pan from heat. Stir in flour and pecans until well combined. Blend in vanilla.

4. Drop batter onto prepared baking sheets by rounded teaspoons, placed about 2 inches apart, to make tiles as shown in top photograph or drop by rounded tablespoons, placed about 3 inches apart, to make tulips as shown in bottom photograph. With small spatula spread batter into an even circle.

5. Bake until cookies are browned (6 to 8 minutes for small cookies, 8 to 10 minutes for large ones). Let stand on baking sheets until cookies are barely firm enough to handle (30 seconds to 1 minute). Remove carefully with a spatula and shape as shown in Tile and Lace Cookies (at left), or transfer to wire racks to make flat cookies. If cookies become too cool to shape, return to oven briefly.

Makes about 30 small or 8 to 10 large cookies.

BAR COOKIES

Like drop cookies, bars have a soft-dough base. They are even more straightforward to put together because the batter isn't shaped at all before baking, just spread in a pan; the cookies are cut apart when they've cooled.

   Brownies are the ultimate bar cookie (see BROWNIE). They are addictive and in a class by themselves. But don't let their stellar reputation blind you to the appeal of other members of this cookie family, equally easy to make and wonderfully varied in flavor and appearance. In general, bar cookies need to cool in the pan on a wire rack until barely warm (usually 15 to 20 minutes) before cutting them into bars or squares. After you've cut the specified number of cookies, let them cool completely in the pan before removing them. Bar cookies look best if cut cleanly and uniformly. Use a ruler and mark where you will cut before doing so by scoring the surface with a knife.

   Most bar cookies freeze well. The richer and more buttery they are, the better they will store in the freezer.

■ APRICOT-ALMOND SQUARES

A crisply toasted almond pastry and a moist, tart apricot filling characterize these elegant bar cookies.

- 1 **cup dried apricots**
- ½ **cup unblanched almonds**
- ½ **cup butter or margarine, softened**
- ¼ **cup granulated sugar**
- 1 **cup flour**
- ½ **teaspoon baking powder**
- ¼ **teaspoon salt**
- 2 **eggs, at room temperature**
- 1 **cup firmly packed brown sugar**
- ½ **teaspoon vanilla extract**
- ¼ **teaspoon almond extract**
  Confectioners' sugar

1. Preheat oven to 350° F. Place apricots in a small saucepan; cover with water. Bring to a boil over medium-high heat. Cover and simmer until tender (6 to 8 minutes). Drain and pat dry with paper towels. Cut into thin slivers and set aside.

2. Spread almonds in a shallow pan. Bake until toasted (8 to 10 minutes). Let cool; whirl in blender or food processor to form coarse crumbs.

3. In mixer bowl beat butter and granulated sugar until fluffy. Blend in ½ cup of the flour and ground almonds. Spread evenly over bottom of an ungreased, 9-inch baking pan. Bake 20 minutes; remove pan from oven.

4. While pastry is baking, in a small bowl stir together remaining ½ cup flour, baking powder, and salt to combine thoroughly; set aside.

5. In mixer bowl beat eggs and brown sugar at high speed until thick. Gradually blend in flour mixture, then vanilla and almond extracts. Stir in apricots. Spread over baked layer.

6. Bake until well browned (about 30 minutes). Cool about 10 minutes, then cut into squares. Sift lightly with confectioners' sugar. Remove from pan when cool.

Makes 3 dozen squares.

■ FRESH LEMON BARS

A classic among cookies, these refreshing bars have a special appeal for lovers of lemon meringue pie.

- 1 **cup butter or margarine, softened**
- ½ **cup confectioners' sugar**
- 1 **teaspoon vanilla extract**
- 2 **cups flour**
- 4 **eggs**
- 2 **cups granulated sugar**
  Grated rind of 1 lemon
- 6 **tablespoons fresh lemon juice**
- ¼ **cup (approximately) confectioners' sugar, for topping**

1. Preheat oven to 350° F. Generously grease a 9- by 13-inch pan.

2. In mixer bowl combine butter, the ½ cup confectioners' sugar, and vanilla; beat until fluffy. Gradually add flour, mixing until well combined. Spread evenly in prepared pan. Bake for 20 minutes.

3. While pastry bakes, in a bowl combine eggs, granulated sugar, lemon rind, and lemon juice; stir to blend all ingredients (do not beat). Pour lemon mixture over baked cookie layer.

4. Return to oven and bake until topping is set and lightly browned (18 to 22 minutes).

5. Sift additional confectioners' sugar over warm cookies to generously cover top. Cut into bars. Remove from pan when cool.

Makes 3 dozen bars.

Tangy, layered Fresh Lemon Bars are simply prepared and simply delicious, which makes them an appealing dessert for entertaining.

Festively wrapped in white tissue paper, sugar-dusted Mexican Wedding Cakes are given to guests at Oaxacan nuptials as keepsakes of the special day.

■ CLASSIC SCOTCH SHORTBREAD

The word *short* has a number of meanings. When the subject is cookies, it means crisp and tender, due to an abundance of butter. These traditional cookies are not overly sweet. If you prefer a sweeter flavor, sift an additional tablespoon of Vanilla Confectioners' Sugar (see page 585) over the cookies after you cut them into wedges. The cookies have the characteristic sandy texture.

> 1 **cup flour**
> 6 **tablespoons Vanilla Confectioners' Sugar (see page 585)**
> ½ **cup firm butter or margarine, diced**

1. Preheat oven to 325° F. In a medium bowl stir together flour and Vanilla Confectioners' Sugar to combine thoroughly.

2. Using a pastry blender or your fingers, cut or crumble in butter until all the particles are uniformly small and well coated with flour mixture. Use your hands to firmly press crumbly dough into a flattened ball.

3. Place dough in an ungreased 8-inch-diameter pan, preferably with a removable bottom. Press dough evenly and firmly into pan. Use your index finger to impress a row of uniformly spaced dimples around outer edge. With tines of a fork, score dough into 12 wedges; then pierce randomly between scores to keep cookies flat.

4. Bake until color is pale golden brown (30 to 35 minutes). Cool on a rack for about 10 minutes. Cut cookies into wedges along previous scorings. When cool, remove pan sides and cookies.

Makes 1 dozen cookies.

MOLDED AND PRESSED COOKIES

There is some art to these rich, buttery cookies, because they are handshaped or formed with a cookie mold. The simplest of these cookies are shaped into balls before baking. The more complex are formed into other shapes by hand, by forcing through a template of a cookie press, or by using a mold. Although the typically sweet, butter-rich dough used for molded cookies can withstand a certain amount of handling and still stay tender, these cookies will be best if your touch is light.

■ MEXICAN WEDDING CAKES

Rich with butter and ground nuts, these tender cookies are coated generously, while still warm, with confectioners' sugar, which seems to melt into the cookies. In the Mexican state of Oaxaca, they are festively wrapped in fringed white tissue and given as favors to wedding guests.

> 2½ **cups flour**
> ¼ **teaspoon salt**
> 1 **cup finely chopped pecans**
> 1 **cup butter or margarine, softened**
> ½ **cup confectioners' sugar**
> 2 **teaspoons vanilla extract**
> 1½ **cups (approximately) confectioners' sugar**

1. In a bowl stir together flour, salt, and pecans to combine thoroughly; set aside. Preheat oven to 350° F.

2. In mixer bowl combine butter and the ½ cup confectioners' sugar; beat until fluffy. Blend in vanilla. Gradually add flour mixture, beating just until dough clings together.

3. Shape dough into 1½-inch balls. Place about 2 inches apart on ungreased baking sheets. Bake until firm and lightly browned (20 to 25 minutes).

4. Spread about ¾ cup of the remaining confectioners' sugar on a rimmed baking sheet. As cookies finish baking, remove them to sugar-lined baking sheet; generously sift some of the remaining confectioners' sugar over warm cookies, turning in sugar if necessary to coat all surfaces liberally. Transfer to wire racks to complete cooling.

Makes about thirty 1¾-inch cookies.

Cinnamon Balls   To flour mixture add 1 teaspoon ground cinnamon. Shape dough into 1-inch balls; place about 1 inch apart on baking sheets. Bake 20 minutes.

Makes about forty-two 1¼-inch cookies.

CHINESE ALMOND COOKIES

When selecting from the varied attractions of certain Chinese take-out restaurants, many people find rich almond cookies, packaged to go in a waxed-paper bag, virtually irresistible. They are just as compelling when baked at home. Making the cookies with a combination of butter and lard brings together the best quality of each ingredient—the flavor of butter and the tender crispness that lard imparts to pastry. See photograph, page 6.

    2 cups flour
    ½ teaspoon baking powder
    ½ cup *each* butter and lard, softened
    1 cup sugar
    1 teaspoon almond extract
    ½ teaspoon vanilla extract
    2 egg yolks
    ⅓ cup (approximately) blanched almonds
    2 teaspoons water

1. In a medium-sized bowl stir together flour and baking powder to combine thoroughly; set aside. Preheat oven to 350° F.

2. In mixer bowl combine butter and lard; beat until fluffy. Add sugar and beat until well combined. Blend in almond and vanilla extracts, then 1 egg yolk. Gradually add flour mixture, beating until well combined.

3. Shape dough into 1-inch balls. Place about 1½ inches apart on lightly greased baking sheets. Slightly flatten each cookie with fingertips; press almond into center.

4. In a small bowl beat remaining egg yolk with the 2 teaspoons water until blended. Lightly brush top of each cookie with egg-yolk mixture.

5. Bake until cookies are golden brown and feel firm when touched lightly (15 to 18 minutes). Let stand on baking sheets for 1 to 2 minutes, then transfer to wire racks to cool.

Makes about forty-two 2-inch cookies.

SNICKERDOODLES

Charmingly old-fashioned, these cookies, covered with cinnamon sugar, recall long afternoons on a porch swing, sipping homemade lemonade.

    1⅓ cups flour
    1 teaspoon cream of tartar
    ½ teaspoon baking soda
    ⅛ teaspoon salt
    ½ cup butter or margarine, softened
    ¾ cup sugar
    ½ teaspoon vanilla extract
    1 egg

Cinnamon Sugar

    ¼ cup sugar
    2 teaspoons ground cinnamon

1. In a bowl stir together flour, cream of tartar, baking soda, and salt to combine thoroughly; set aside. Preheat oven to 400° F.

2. In mixer bowl combine butter and sugar; beat until fluffy. Blend in vanilla. Beat in egg until well combined. Gradually add flour mixture, beating until just well combined.

3. Drop cookie dough by rounded teaspoons, 6 to 8 at a time, into Cinnamon Sugar spread in a shallow pan. Roll cookies to coat well, shaping them into balls as you roll. Arrange balls about 1½ inches apart on greased baking sheets.

4. Bake until edges are golden brown (8 to 10 minutes). Transfer to wire racks to cool.

Makes about 3 dozen 2½-inch cookies.

Cinnamon Sugar In a shallow pan mix sugar and cinnamon until thoroughly combined.

CHOCO–PEANUT BUTTER COOKIES

Speckled with grated semisweet chocolate, these peanut butter cookies give a classic recipe new flavor. You can also make these cookies with almond butter, with or without the chocolate.

    1½ cups flour
    2 teaspoons baking powder
    ⅛ teaspoon salt
    ½ cup butter or margarine, softened
    ½ cup peanut butter
    ½ cup *each* granulated sugar and
        firmly packed brown sugar
    1 teaspoon vanilla extract
    1 egg
    1 square (1 oz) semisweet baking chocolate, grated

1. In a bowl stir together flour, baking powder, and salt to combine thoroughly; set aside. Preheat oven to 375° F.

2. In mixer bowl combine butter and peanut butter; beat until fluffy. Add sugars and beat until well combined. Blend in vanilla, then egg, and beat until fluffy. Gradually add flour mixture, beating until well blended. Stir in chocolate.

3. Shape dough into 1-inch balls. Arrange balls about 1½ inches apart on ungreased baking sheets. Flatten each cookie with a fork, pressing tines once into dough and then crisscrossing the first pattern to make the characteristic crosshatch design.

4. Bake until cookies are lightly browned and feel firm when touched gently (10 to 12 minutes). Transfer to wire racks to cool.

Makes about forty-two 2-inch cookies.

Almond Butter Cookies Substitute almond butter for peanut butter; omit chocolate, if desired.

**MAKING
SPRITZ COOKIES**

*Ribbons   Use a ridged
plate. Form long strips, cut,
separate slightly, and
bake. When cool, dip into
chocolate glaze.*

*Rosettes   Use the snowflake
plate. Press candied cherry
half in center of each cookie
and bake.*

*Wreaths   Use the star plate.
Form long strands; cut into
5-inch lengths. Shape into
circles, decorate with silver
balls, and bake.*

■ SPRITZ

Buttery Spritz cookies are as much fun to make as they
are to eat. With one easy dough and different plates in a
cookie press, you can make wreaths, ribbons, rosettes,
and other shapes. Before baking, dress up the shapes with
decorating sugars or candied fruit, or flavor the dough itself with chocolate or ground almonds. Don't be disheart-
ened if your first efforts aren't as perfect as you would
wish. Just scoop up the failures, put the dough back in the
cookie press, and try again. Practice does make perfect
with these cookies. Be sure to wash both press and plates
before using them for the first time.

  1 **cup unsalted butter, softened**
  ½ **cup sugar**
  ¼ **teaspoon salt**
  1 **teaspoon vanilla extract**
  1 **egg**
 2½ **cups (approximately) sifted flour**

1. Preheat oven to 350° F. In large mixer bowl cream
butter; gradually add sugar, beating until light. Add salt,
vanilla, and egg; beat well.

2. Gradually add flour, beating until just blended. Dough
should be firm—neither sticky nor stiff.

3. Transfer dough to cookie press and press dough onto
ungreased baking sheets (see photographs at left).
Bake until lightly browned around edges (about 10 minutes). Transfer to wire racks to cool. Store in airtight
containers.

Makes about 8 dozen 1½-inch rosettes.

Chocolate Spritz   Add 3 ounces melted and cooled
semisweet chocolate to butter mixture; beat until blended.
Increase flour to approximately 2¾ cups.

Toasted-Almond Spritz   Use ½ teaspoon each vanilla
extract and almond extract. Add ¾ cup finely ground,
toasted almonds to butter mixture; beat until blended.

■ PINE NUT CRESCENTS

Croissants are not the only crescent-shaped French pastries. These crescent cookies, *croissants aux pignons,*
come from Provence.

  2 **cups flour**
  ¼ **teaspoon freshly grated nutmeg**
    Pinch salt
  ⅔ **cup butter or margarine, softened**
  ½ **cup firmly packed brown sugar**
  2 **egg yolks**
  1 **tablespoon grated orange rind**
  ½ **teaspoon vanilla extract**
  2 **tablespoons honey**
  ¾ **cup pine nuts or slivered almonds**

1. In a bowl stir together flour, nutmeg, and salt to blend
thoroughly; set aside. Preheat oven to 350° F.

2. In mixer bowl combine butter and brown sugar; beat
until fluffy. Add egg yolks, one at a time, beating well
after each addition. Blend in orange rind and vanilla.
Gradually add flour mixture, beating until thoroughly
combined.

3. Using about 1 tablespoon of dough for each cookie,
shape dough into a strand about 3 inches long, then curve
into a crescent. Place crescents about 2 inches apart on
greased baking sheets.

4. Heat honey in a small pan over low heat until fluid and
just warm to the touch. Lightly brush honey over tops
and sides of crescents, then liberally coat with pine nuts,
pressing them in gently.

5. Bake until cookies are golden (10 to 12 minutes). Let
cool on baking sheets for 1 to 2 minutes, then transfer to
wire racks to complete cooling.

Makes about 30 cookies.

■ CHOCOLATE PRETZELS

These trompe l'oeil pretzels, brushed with a wash of egg
white and speckled with coarse sugar, are as appropriate
with a demitasse of strong coffee as are their salty coun-
terparts with a stein of beer. Note that the dough must
chill for 45 minutes to firm before it can be rolled into
ropes and shaped.

 1⅔ **cups flour**
  ¼ **cup unsweetened cocoa**
  ¾ **cup butter or margarine, softened**
  ¾ **cup granulated sugar**
  1 **teaspoon vanilla extract**
  1 **egg white, slightly beaten**
  2 **tablespoons coarse sugar (pearl or
    decorating sugar, or crushed sugar cubes)**

1. In a bowl stir together flour and cocoa to combine
well; set aside.

2. In mixer bowl combine butter and granulated sugar;
beat until fluffy. Blend in vanilla. Gradually add flour
mixture, beating until smooth. Gather dough into a ball
and enclose in plastic wrap. Refrigerate until firm
enough to shape (about 45 minutes).

3. Preheat oven to 350° F. Work with one fourth of
the dough at a time, keeping remainder in refrigerator.
Divide each portion into 8 equal pieces. On a lightly
floured pastry cloth or board, roll each piece into an
8-inch-long strand using the palms of your hands. Twist
each strand into pretzel shape. Place cookies about
1 inch apart on lightly greased baking sheets.

4. Lightly brush each cookie with beaten egg white, then
scatter coarse sugar over surface.

5. Bake until cookies feel firm when touched lightly
(12 to 14 minutes). Let stand on baking sheets for about
2 minutes, then transfer to wire racks to cool completely.

Makes 32 cookies.

Madeleines, the delicate, shell-shaped cookies made famous by the French novelist, Marcel Proust, are especially delicious as an accompaniment to tea.

MADELEINES

The delicate cookie the French call a *madeleine* was the inspiration for Marcel Proust's evocative novel *Remembrance of Things Past*. These cookies have a gentle flavor derived from browned butter and a texture similar to that of a sponge cake. Traditionally, madeleines are baked in gleaming tin plaques. The special madeleine pan, with its distinctive shell-shaped molds, is available at better cookware stores.

- ½ **cup unsalted butter**
- 2 **eggs**
- ½ **cup sugar**
- 1 **teaspoon finely grated lemon rind**
- ¼ **teaspoon fresh lemon juice**
- ¼ **teaspoon vanilla extract**
- ⅛ **teaspoon baking powder**
- ¾ **cup sifted cake flour**

1. In a small, heavy-bottomed saucepan over medium heat, melt butter until milk solids turn a golden brown color. (This will occur just after the foam subsides.) Transfer to a small stainless steel bowl and allow to cool for 10 minutes.

2. In a medium stainless steel bowl over boiling water, whisk eggs and sugar until mixture is tepid (98° F). Remove from heat and whisk in lemon rind, lemon juice, and vanilla. Sift baking powder and flour together; stir into egg mixture. Stir in melted and cooled butter. Cover bowl with plastic wrap and allow to rest for 1 hour at room temperature.

3. Preheat oven to 450° F. Brush inside of shells of madeleine pans with a thin layer of melted butter. Dust with flour, then invert pan and rap briskly on counter to remove excess flour. Spoon batter into shells, filling each three-fourths full.

4. Bake until cookies rise in center and are very light brown on the bottom and edges (3 to 4 minutes for 1½-inch madeleines, 10 to 12 minutes for 3-inch madeleines). When done they spring back when lightly touched in the center. Remove madeleines from oven, invert pan over wire cooling rack, and tap lightly to release cookies from pan.

5. Cookies are best when served while still warm. Otherwise, cool completely and store in an airtight container or freeze until ready to use.

Makes 40 small or 15 large madeleines.

**MAKING
MULTICOLORED
COOKIES**

*Checkerboards   For each
log, arrange 3 strips of Light
and Chocolate Dough side by
side, alternating colors.
Stack three layers of strips as
shown in photograph (first
and third layer should be
identical, middle layer
should be opposite of top and
bottom); chill and slice.*

*Pinwheels   Roll chilled or
frozen Light and Chocolate
Dough to 1-inch-thick
rectangles. Stack doughs and
tightly roll up, jelly-roll
fashion. Chill well, then slice
and bake.*

*Mosaics   Cut logs of Light
and Chocolate Dough into
¼-inch-thick slices. With
same small decorative
cutter, remove center from
each slice. Place Light Dough
cutouts in chocolate slices
and Chocolate Dough
cutouts in light slices.*

REFRIGERATOR COOKIES

Long before there were cookie mixes or plastic-encased rolls of cookie dough in the supermarket refrigerator case, there were homemade icebox cookies. The rich dough can be prepared ahead and stored for up to three days in the refrigerator. The cold dough is sliced and baked; and it is sturdy enough to be worked into eye-pleasing, two-color checkerboards, pinwheels, and mosaics (see photographs at left).

If making refrigerator dough is unfamiliar to you, keep in mind the following: Because refrigerator cookies are sliced thinly from a roll of dough, solid ingredients must be either finely chopped or pliable enough so the dough can be sliced easily without tearing. Always shape dough before chilling it. After beating in dry ingredients and other added elements, dough will be quite soft and creamy. Divide it roughly in half, then turn out each half onto a square of plastic wrap or kitchen parchment. Using two spatulas—and the wrap as a guide—coax dough into a long, fat, sausagelike shape. While lifting and rolling, enclose dough in the wrapping. When dough is confined, you will be able to use your hands to mold it into an even more regular shape.

Keep wrapped dough in the coldest part of the refrigerator (or in the freezer—but keep track of the time, because it will begin to freeze after about 45 minutes). If dough is very soft and you want to keep the round shape, remove dough and smooth its contours once or twice during the chilling period.

To freeze dough for longer storage, enclose it in a moisture-proof wrapping such as freezer wrap or heavy aluminum foil. (Cookies enclosed in waxed paper or plastic wrap should be overwrapped in a sturdier material if you decide to freeze part of the unbaked dough.) Well-wrapped cookie dough can be kept frozen for up to a month. To thaw frozen dough, transfer it from freezer to refrigerator one to two hours before you plan to slice and bake it.

■ MULTICOLORED REFRIGERATOR COOKIES

With the photographs at left as your guide, you can combine tender, crisp chocolate and butterscotch doughs to make checkerboards, pinwheels, or mosaic refrigerator cookies. Note that the dough needs to be chilled or frozen several times during the process for easier handling.

Light Dough

1⅓ cups flour
   ½ teaspoon baking powder
   ¼ teaspoon salt
   ½ cup butter or margarine, softened
   ¼ cup solid vegetable shortening
   ½ cup each granulated sugar and firmly
       packed brown sugar
   ½ teaspoon vanilla extract
   1 egg yolk

Chocolate Dough

   1 cup flour
   ¼ cup unsweetened cocoa
   ½ teaspoon baking soda
   ¼ teaspoon salt
   ½ cup butter or margarine, softened
   ¼ cup solid vegetable shortening
   ½ cup each granulated sugar and firmly
       packed brown sugar
   1 egg

Light Dough

1. Combine flour, baking powder, and salt; set aside.

2. In mixer bowl blend butter and shortening. Add sugars and beat until fluffy. Beat in vanilla, then egg yolk.

3. Gradually add flour mixture, beating until just blended. Chill and shape dough as directed for the cookie style of your choice.

Chocolate Dough

1. In a bowl stir together flour, cocoa, baking soda, and salt to combine thoroughly; set aside.

2. In mixer bowl combine butter and shortening; beat to blend well. Add sugars and beat until fluffy. Add egg and beat until well blended.

3. Gradually add flour mixture, beating until just blended. Chill and shape dough as directed for the cookie style of your choice.

To Make Checkerboards

1. Transfer Light Dough to a large sheet of plastic wrap or waxed paper. Using a spatula and the plastic wrap, shape dough into a 2-inch-square log about 9 inches long. Wrap tightly and refrigerate until firm (at least 2 hours, or overnight; or place in freezer for 30 to 45 minutes).

2. Repeat shaping and chilling procedure described in step 1 using Chocolate Dough.

3. To make long strips, slice Light Dough lengthwise into halves or thirds. Separate layers and slice each lengthwise into halves or thirds. You will have 4 strips if you cut dough into halves or 9 strips if you cut dough into thirds.

4. Repeat cutting procedure described in step 3 using Chocolate Dough.

5. Following the photograph, place strips of Light Dough and Chocolate Dough side by side to form 2 logs, alternating colors to make each layer. Wrap each log tightly in plastic wrap, firmly pressing multicolored strips together. Return to refrigerator for at least 3 hours, or overnight.

6. Preheat oven to 350° F. Remove one roll of cookie dough at a time from refrigerator. Slice cookies to a thickness of ¼ inch, and arrange slices about 1 inch apart on ungreased baking sheets.

7. Bake until cookies feel firm when touched lightly (8 to 10 minutes). Transfer to wire racks to cool.

Makes about 6 dozen 2½-inch cookies.

To Make Pinwheels

1. Transfer Light Dough to a large sheet of plastic wrap or waxed paper. Using a spatula, flatten dough into a rectangle about 1 inch thick. Wrap tightly and refrigerate until firm (at least 2 hours, or overnight; or place in freezer for 30 to 45 minutes).

2. Repeat shaping and chilling procedure described in step 1 using Chocolate Dough.

3. Place Light Dough between 2 sheets of plastic wrap; roll into a 12-inch by 16-inch rectangle. Remove top sheet of plastic.

4. Repeat shaping procedure described in step 3 using Chocolate Dough.

5. Invert Light Dough over Chocolate Dough; peel off top sheet of plastic wrap. Starting with a 16-inch edge, and using bottom sheet of plastic and a spatula to guide dough, tightly roll 2 sheets of dough together, jelly-roll fashion. Cut roll in half to make two 8-inch-long rolls. Enclose each tightly in plastic wrap; refrigerate for at least 3 hours, or overnight.

6. Preheat oven to 350° F. Slice and bake until cookies are golden brown and feel firm when touched lightly (10 to 12 minutes). Transfer to wire racks to cool.

Makes about 5 dozen 3-inch cookies.

To Make Mosaics

1. Divide Light Dough in half. Transfer each half to a sheet of plastic wrap or waxed paper, and shape into a 2-inch-diameter log. Wrap each tightly and refrigerate until firm (at least 2 hours, or overnight; or place in freezer for 30 to 45 minutes).

2. Repeat shaping and chilling procedure described in step 1 using Chocolate Dough.

3. Preheat oven to 350° F. Cut 1 roll each of Light Dough and Chocolate Dough into ¼-inch-thick slices. Use a small decorative cutter to remove center from each cookie slice. Place light centers in chocolate slices; place chocolate centers in light slices. Repeat with remaining rolls of dough. Bake as for Checkerboards.

Makes about 6 dozen 2½-inch cookies.

ROLLED AND CUT COOKIES

These thin, crisp cookies are shaped by rolling out chilled dough and then cut with cookie cutters or around a hand-made pattern of your own design. Because they can be extremely decorative, they are popular for holidays. Plan to make these cookies when interruptions are few. Prepare the rich, buttery dough, and wrap and refrigerate it on one day; then roll out, cut, and bake the cookies on the next. There are cookie cutters in just about every shape you can imagine. To custom-design your own, find a simple shape that you like, trace it onto heavy cardboard, cut it out, and use it as a pattern.

The dough should be firm, but not too hard or it will crack when it is rolled out. On the other hand, if it is too soft it will stick to everything. Roll out only a small amount of dough at one time to avoid letting unused dough get too warm. Don't use too much flour when rolling out the dough or the cookies will be tough. Lightly flour the rolling pin and use a pastry cloth, or roll the dough between two sheets of waxed paper. If the dough sticks to the cutters, flour the cutters lightly by spooning flour into a shallow dish and dipping cutters into it when necessary. Use a wide spatula or turner for transferring cookies to baking sheets and for removing from sheets to cooling racks.

■ TRADITIONAL SUGAR-COOKIE CUTOUTS

This classic cookie is rich, crisp, and faintly spiced with either ground mace or nutmeg—a perfect dough to cut into valentine hearts, Easter chicks, Halloween pumpkins, George Washington hatchets, or Christmas trees. If desired, use a pastry bag or piping cone to decorate them with Royal Icing (see page 250). Note that the dough must chill several hours or overnight.

> 1¾ **cups flour**
> 2 **teaspoons baking powder**
> ¼ **teaspoon ground mace or nutmeg**
> ½ **cup butter or margarine, softened**
> 1 **cup sugar**
> 1 **teaspoon vanilla extract**
> 1 **egg**
>   **Vanilla Granulated Sugar**
>   **(see page 585), optional**

1. In a bowl stir together flour, baking powder, and mace to combine thoroughly; set aside.

2. In mixer bowl combine butter and sugar; beat until light and fluffy. Blend in vanilla. Add egg and beat again until fluffy. Gradually add flour mixture, beating until just well combined.

3. Enclose dough in plastic wrap and refrigerate until firm (1 to 2 hours or overnight).

4. Preheat oven to 325° F. Work with about half of the dough at a time, keeping remainder in refrigerator. On a lightly floured board or pastry cloth, roll out dough to a thickness of about ⅛ inch. Cut with cookie cutters into rounds or other fancy shapes. Carefully transfer to lightly greased baking sheets. Sprinkle with Vanilla Granulated Sugar (if desired).

5. Bake until cookies are golden brown (10 to 12 minutes). Let stand for about 1 minute, then transfer to wire racks to cool.

Makes about 3 dozen cookies.

Decorating gingerbread people, a holiday tradition, is one of the pleasures of childhood that even the youngest artists can do.

1. In a small bowl combine raisins and brandy; let stand 30 minutes. Add walnuts, sugar, and cinnamon; stir to blend; set aside.

2. Preheat oven to 425° F. Divide Cream Cheese Pastry in half. On a lightly floured surface, roll each half into a thin round. With a sharp knife cut 10-inch-diameter circles from each round of dough by placing bottom of a 10-inch tart tin (or a 10-inch-diameter pattern cut from paper) on dough and cutting around it. Roll scraps from both circles into another thin round, and make an 8-inch-diameter circle.

3. Sprinkle surface of each 10-inch circle with ⅔ cup raisin-nut filling; use ½ cup filling for 8-inch circle (a few tablespoons of filling will be left over). Press filling lightly with your hands to make it adhere to dough.

4. With a floured knife cut 10-inch circles into 12 wedges and cut 8-inch circles into 8 wedges. Starting with wide edge, roll each wedge toward tip, encasing filling.

5. Arrange rolls on ungreased baking sheets. Place sheets in oven and immediately reduce heat to 400° F. Bake until lightly browned (12 to 14 minutes). Transfer to wire racks; when cool sprinkle cookies with confectioners' sugar.

Makes 32 cookies.

Cream Cheese Pastry   In a bowl beat cream cheese, butter, salt, sugar, and vanilla until light and smooth. Add flour and beat until just blended. Gather dough into a ball and enclose in waxed paper or plastic wrap; refrigerate several hours or overnight.

■ GINGERBREAD PEOPLE

These little cookie people, cut from a thick slab of spicy molasses dough, are wonderful for a children's party. Make a batch and allow children to decorate their own. School-age children can maneuver an icing-filled paper piping cone. Provide younger children with a confectioners' sugar glaze, sprinkles, and decorating sugar.

> ½ cup unsalted butter, softened
> ½ cup firmly packed brown sugar
> ½ cup molasses
> 1 egg
> 2½ cups flour
> 1 teaspoon baking soda
> ½ teaspoon salt
> 2 teaspoons ground ginger
> 1 teaspoon ground cinnamon
> ½ teaspoon freshly grated nutmeg
> ½ teaspoon ground cloves
>   Dried currants, for decorating
>   Royal Icing (see page 250)

1. In large mixer bowl cream butter; gradually add sugar and beat until light. Add molasses and egg and beat to blend well; set aside.

■ RUGELACH

Although Jewish delicatessens sell Rugelach throughout the year, these cream cheese crescents are a Hanukkah tradition. They may be stuffed with nuts and raisins, as they are here, or with jam or poppy seed filling if preferred. They do not keep well and should be eaten within a few hours of baking.

> ½ cup raisins, coarsely chopped
> 1 tablespoon brandy
> 1 cup finely chopped, toasted walnuts
> ½ cup granulated sugar
> 1 teaspoon cinnamon
>   Confectioners' sugar, for dusting

Cream Cheese Pastry

> 1 package (8 oz) cream cheese, at room temperature
> ½ cup unsalted butter, at room temperature
> ¼ teaspoon salt
> 1 tablespoon sugar
> 1 teaspoon vanilla extract
> 1 cup flour

2. In a bowl stir together flour, baking soda, salt, ginger, cinnamon, nutmeg, and cloves. Gradually add flour mixture to butter mixture, beating until just blended. Gather dough into a ball and enclose in plastic wrap; refrigerate at least 1 hour.

3. Preheat oven to 325° F. On a lightly floured board, roll out gingerbread to a thickness of ¼ inch. Cut out cookies with a floured, 4½-inch-long cutter and transfer to greased baking sheets. Bake until cookies are lightly browned around edges and feel barely firm when touched gently (about 10 minutes). Transfer to wire racks. While each cookie is hot, press in currants to create eyes, mouth, and buttons. When cool, decorate with Royal Icing piped from a paper cone.

Makes about 1 dozen 4-inch-long cookies.

Recipes and Related Information
Baking Pans, 18; Biscotti, 8; Cake and Pastry Tools, 89; Linzer Hearts, 298; Macadamia Crisps, 346.

COOKWARE (POTS AND PANS)

In simplest terms, cookware permits controlled exposure of food to heat. The best pots and pans conduct heat evenly and efficiently and are most responsive to changes in temperature, usually due to their material and construction (see MATERIALS FOR COOKWARE). Size and shape are adaptations that have evolved over time for specific purposes; these features are subjective ones, having less to do with performance than with personal cooking styles or manufacturers' preferences.

Quality cookware is an investment that will return long-term dividends of reliability and durability. How do you judge quality? Price is a clue; better cookware costs more. But with proper care, each piece can be a one-time purchase. Resist the prepackaged appeal of a set. More than likely these collections include at least one pan that you wouldn't buy if you didn't have to. What appears to be a bargain, then, really isn't. If you don't need it, you don't want it. Resist, too, the seduction of surface flash—color and pattern don't keep a sauce from burning or make water boil faster. A material with good heat-conducting qualities offers those attributes. If it's pretty, consider its appearance a secondary bonus. Today's home cooks have come to appreciate and even prefer the clean, spare, utilitarian lines of commercial cookware, choosing a decorative pan only if it will go to the table.

BUTTER WARMER

This is a very versatile little pan, despite its single-purpose name. It is perfectly sized for melting jellies and preserves for glazes; warming syrups, single portions of soups,

and baby foods; softening honey and ice cream sauces; and heating alcohol for flambés. Most hold about 2 cups. Choose one with a wide, stable, flat bottom. A pan this small should also have a long handle, so the cook's hand is at a distance from the burner. Most cookware lines offer a version, in the usual materials. Some are enameled steel or cast iron—decorative enough to come to the table.

CARAMELIZING POT

If you make sugar syrups and candies more than occasionally, you might consider investing in this heavyweight, straight-sided pot traditionally used for sugar work. Copper is the metal of choice because it is extremely sensitive to heat; this affords important control of sugar syrup, which can quickly deepen from brown to burned in a matter of seconds. Unlike most copper cookware, caramelizing pots aren't lined with tin: copper and sugar are compatible (other foods and copper are sometimes adverse) and the high temperatures that sugar work requires can melt tin. They come in 1- and 2-quart sizes and have a hollow, rolled handle and a pouring spout.

CHICKEN FRYER

An American invention, the chicken fryer is a deep, covered frying pan well-suited for frying, browning, and braising. With its short handle and lip (to more easily pour off accumulated fat), it resembles a cast-iron skillet, and is usually made of cast iron or enameled cast iron. To help control spattering, its sides are higher than those of a skillet; and its domed lid is useful for slow, covered cooking. Both are about 12 inches in diameter. Although extremely versatile, the chicken fryer isn't as popular as it once was; those who saw their grandmothers using one to make great fried chicken do know its value.

DEEP-FAT FRYER

A deep-fat fryer should be tall enough to hold at least several inches of fat with sufficient additional room for the hot fat to bubble up without spilling over when food is dropped in; the fryer should be wide enough so that food can float freely to an evenly browned crisp. Depth is more critical than surface area, as safety is a key issue for this technique; width is a convenience that allows more food to fry at a time. French-style models are deep and wide, with a narrow base and wider surface, and ear handles. American deep-fat fryers resemble oversized saucepans, with a single long handle. Four quarts is a standard size and is appropriate for most recipes; steel, enameled steel, and aluminum are the usual materials.

Basket inserts, useful for lowering food into the fat, then lifting it out again when done, are often packaged with the pot. These baskets are also sold separately, to use with a pot you already have. The handles on some models are designed to hold the basket up out of the pan so that the fat can drain away. Other pans have a clip attached to one side for the same purpose. Helpful accessories include wire and mesh skimmers and deep-fat thermometers. Thermostatically controlled, electric deep-fat fryers are also available in large and small sizes.

DOUBLE BOILER

Foods that need some protection from direct heat—custards, chocolate, egg-based sauces—usually cook in a double boiler, which is, in effect, a pair of stacked saucepans. The lower pan holds a few inches of simmering or boiling water that gently heats food held in the upper section. The water diffuses the heat and softens its impact. Most manufacturers make double boiler inserts to fit their cookware. Double boilers are also available; 1½ and 2 quarts are basic sizes. Common materials are stainless steel, aluminum, enameled steel, clad metals, and copper with a porcelain upper pot.

Some cooks devise their own double boilers by setting a large bowl partway in a pan of smaller diameter. Or, they use a footed, cast-aluminum ring called a double boiler maker; this trivet sits on the bottom of a saucepan and keeps a bowl set within the pan about an inch above the pan bottom, away from the direct heat.

FISH POACHER

Typical dimensions for this long, narrow, covered pan are 18 inches long, 5 inches wide, and 3½ to 4 inches deep—sized to hold a medium-sized whole fish. It is used for poaching, whether fish, chicken breasts, or even pasta rolls. The rack lifts food off the pan bottom, providing gentle cooking in surrounding poaching liquid. The rack also permits the poached food to be safely removed from the pan. The most beautiful of these pans are of tin-lined copper; these are also the most costly. Stainless steel and tinned steel are acceptable alternatives. Although useful, fish poachers require a great deal of storage space.

GRIDDLE

These thick, flat pans are used for pancakes, French toast, scones, crumpets, bacon, sausage, hamburgers, thin steaks, fish, and eggs. Griddle-cooking is quick and requires little water or fat; heat is transferred by conduction directly from burner to pan to food. Unlike a skillet, which can also function as a griddle, these flat pans can have a trough or shallow rim, rather than true sides, to collect or contain excess fat or cooking oil. They are typically 12- or 14-inch squares or rounds, or 12- by 18- or 20-inch rectangles. They should be made of a material that heats evenly and quickly and holds heat well. After cooking, wipe away bits of food, rather than scrubbing the cooking surface, so a seasoning will develop; then lightly grease and store dry.

GRILL PAN (STOVE-TOP BROILER)

A hybrid, this pan functions as a combination griddle, skillet, and grill. The bottom surface is ridged, so, like a grill, food doesn't cook in its own fat—a boon to those restricting fat intake. It has raised sides, like a skillet, and is made of a heavy material such as cast iron or enameled cast iron since it is often used with high heat.

OMELET PAN

Strictly defined, an omelet pan is French, made of spun steel, and only used for this preparation. But with the development of nonstick finishes and the increasing demand for versatile cookware, there is less call for a single-purpose pan. Today, most so-called omelet pans are actually small—6-, 7-, or 8-inch—skillets. They have an open, slope-sided shape that allows eggs to slide around the pan as they cook and lets the finished omelet ease effortlessly from the pan onto a plate. Long, angled handles permit the cook to keep the pan in motion on the burner. Choose one made of heavy-gauge metal, for good heat control, and preferably with a nonstick interior.

PRESSURE COOKER

Although uncommon in American kitchens today, pressure cookers were much appreciated by our mothers and grandmothers for their ability to cut cooking time by one third to one half for foods requiring long, moist cooking, such as stews, soups, and stocks. A flavorful chicken stock is pressure-cooked in 30 minutes; artichokes are ready in 15 minutes. They are still used by a majority of European home cooks and seem to be on the verge of a comeback in the United States.

Pressure cookers work by steam action, which builds up in the tightly sealed pot. A valve system controls the amount of pressure, releasing excess steam through a series of openings in the cover. These pots scare away many cooks, who perhaps recall their mothers' dire warnings about standing near the stove when the pressure cooker was in action. Today's versions have improved safety controls, so there is little danger that the valves will blow off the pot from uncontrolled internal pressure, as they sometimes did in previous generations of these cookers. They are also much quieter than older models, emitting occasional quiet hisses instead of tooting like a steam engine. The busy cook who has embraced the microwave oven because it is quick and clean will find a pressure cooker appealing for similar reasons.

Most are manufactured in Europe; some American companies distribute these imports under their own labels. The most common size is 2 liters (about 2 quarts), perfect for small families; larger pots are 4, 6, and 8 quarts. They are made of heavy-gauge stainless steel and aluminum, and can also be used as a conventional pot.

SAUCEPAN

The versatile saucepan is best for making sauces, cooking vegetables and rice, reheating and warming, and melting solids such as chocolate, butter, and other fats, and viscous liquids such as honey and molasses. Ideally it should heat quickly and evenly, sit firmly on the burner, pour without dripping, have a snug-fitting lid, and be well balanced, easy to clean, not too heavy, and nonreactive to acid foods. Because it is moved around a great deal, the handle should be in proportion to the pan's size and weight for easy lifting.

Saucepans range in size from 2 cups to 6 quarts, and are made of copper, aluminum, stainless steel, enameled cast iron, ceramic, glass, and clad metals. They can be either tall and narrow or wide and shallow; each is useful, but a unique shape can also be the manufacturer's way of making a statement about a product as much as anything else. Saucepans with tall sides are well suited for warming and reheating; less surface area is exposed to the air, so less evaporation occurs. Low-sided saucepans, which give greater surface exposure to air, are perfect for quick cooking, mixing, and reductions. A shallow pan can also function as a water bath or double boiler; the pan is filled with several inches of gently simmering water and a bowl smaller in diameter is set in it. You will probably want to have at least two saucepans, probably more; 1-, 2-, and 3- to 4-quart capacities are basic sizes.

SAUCEPOT

These large, useful pans, with ear handles and covers, are also called Dutch ovens and casseroles. They are invaluable for cooking in large quantities: pasta, vegetables, soups, and stews. Because they are used for slow cooking, which requires holding a simmer for long periods of time, they should be made of a material that conducts and holds heat well. Sizes range from 4 to 14 quarts; 5 quarts will meet the needs of most households. Materials include aluminum, stainless steel, enameled steel, enameled cast iron, and clad metals.

Quality cookware is one of the most important purchases the home cook will make for the kitchen. Select those pots and pans that suit your cooking needs and personal cooking style. Shown clockwise from bottom left are: sauté pan, skillets, stove-top broiler, griddle, chicken fryer, deep-fat fryer, stockpot, saucepans, couscousière, steamer, pressure cooker, Chinese steamer, asparagus steamer, fish poacher, folding steamer, double boiler, wok, caramelizing pot, butter warmer.

SAUTE PAN

Wide, straight-sided, and shallow, with an extralong handle, sauté pans are designed for quick cooking in a small amount of oil or butter over high heat. *Sauter,* in French, means to jump. Traditionally, the pan is moved rapidly back and forth to prevent food from sticking to it, so the food jumps about from the constant motion. More typically today, sautéed food is turned rather than tossed, but the process is still fast moving. Like the slope-sided skillet, this pan is useful for browning and stir-frying meats, poultry, and vegetables; unlike a skillet, this one offers more protection against spattering fat and liquid, and it is better suited for combination cooking—stews, fricassees, and braises, for example. Any heavyweight skillet can substitute for a sauté pan.

Most sauté pans have 2½-inch sides; sizes range from 2 to 7 quarts (3 to 5 quarts are the most useful sizes) and most come with covers. Look for a sauté pan made of a heavy-gauge metal that picks up and transmits heat evenly without burning or hot spots and that has a handle made of a material that stays relatively cool; if very large, a long handle and a lug handle on the opposite side ease lifting. Materials are copper, aluminum, stainless steel, enameled steel, and clad metals.

SKILLET (FRYING PAN)

While the straight-sided sauté pan developed out of French culinary tradition, the flare-sided skillet (also called a frying pan) has American roots. The two evolved as slightly different approaches to the same process—rapid stove-top cooking in fat of some sort. The skillet is a shallower pan, with less bottom surface, but still tall enough to contain liquid for a sauce or stir-fry. Cast iron is the traditional material: it is heavy, an excellent heat conductor, works equally well on top of the stove and in the oven (perfect for Pommes Anna), and with use develops a seasoning that functions like a nonstick finish. Unless the seasoning is maintained and the pan kept dry, cast iron can rust, however (SEE MATERIALS FOR COOKWARE).

Other materials include aluminum, stainless steel, enameled steel, enameled cast iron, and clad metals. A skillet with an applied nonstick finish, which permits frying with little or no fat, is extremely useful. These are generally inexpensive and are worth buying in addition to your other skillets. The most popular sizes for skillets are 10 and 12 inches in diameter; if you can store them, buy both sizes. If you cook for a large family, you may even want the 14-inch-diameter pan. Smaller pans (6, 7, or 8 inches) are commonly used for omelets.

Electric frying pans with automatic controls permit precise regulation of temperature; if you have extra storage room, they are good backups for stove-top skillets, especially when frying in quantity. Many are now available with nonstick finishes. Those made of heavyweight metal will perform better and last longer.

STEAMERS

Steaming apparatus come in all sizes and shapes, but the idea is always the same: to support the food over a quantity of boiling water, with room for the steam to circulate around the food. The size and configuration depend upon what is being steamed.

All-Purpose Steamer   A traditional steamer is made of two (or more) stacked pots with bottoms that are perforated to allow the steam to rise from the lowest pot through the upper layers. Three quarts is a typical size. Steaming pots are larger—as much as 8 quarts—and have an insert that is perforated on the bottom. Like all steamers, they have tight-fitting lids that prevent steam from escaping. Blanching inserts have holes on the sides as well as the bottom. They are used to cook pasta as well as vegetables. Sometimes steaming pots are packaged with both inserts and sold as vegetable-spaghetti cookers. Many cookware manufacturers offer separate steaming and blanching inserts in a variety of sizes to fit their saucepans and stockpots.

Asparagus Steamer   A specialty steamer, this is a tall, narrow pot with an insert to hold asparagus stalks upright; the stalks partly boil and partly steam. The insert, with handles, makes it easier to remove stalks and then drain them. Although definitely not a necessity, the asparagus steamer is convenient to use if you have the space to store it.

Chinese Steamer   The Chinese steam with a rack of some sort: either a cross-shaped wooden or metal rack, a circular, stainless steel ring that looks a little like a cake cooling rack, or a perforated metal tray. These are usually set in a wok. Stacking steamer baskets of bamboo or metal are also used in Asian cooking; they allow you to steam several different items over one pot of water.

Couscousière   To prepare couscous, a stew considered the national dish of Morocco and other north African countries, grains of semolina steam in a perforated pan set over the pot containing meat and vegetables (couscous can refer to either the stew and grain in combination or just the grain). The moisture given off in the lower pan rises up and cooks the grains, which should be light and fluffy. A *couscousière* consists of two stacked pieces, both bulbous in shape; the stew pot on bottom has considerably larger capacity than the upper grain steamer. It is made of aluminum and stainless steel, and, if you are fond of ethnic stews, is a great presentation piece at a meal for guests.

Folding Steamer Insert   Almost any pot, narrow or wide, can be transformed into a steamer with this collapsible insert. Made of stainless steel, it is constructed of perforated, overlapping rectangles attached to a circular base, also perforated, which sits on three tiny legs. The device expands and contracts like the petals of a flower to fit most sizes of saucepan or saucepot. Inexpensive and compact, it has probably introduced more people to the pleasures of steamed food, particularly vegetables, than has any other piece of equipment. It has a 5½-inch base and when flat measures 9½ inches in diameter.

STOCKPOT

Tall, narrow stockpots are fixtures on restaurant ranges, sometimes kept simmering 24 hours a day to provide the liquid foundation for myriad sauces and soups. Their shape is well suited for slow, gentle cooking of liquids; less moisture is lost through evaporation in a deep pot than in one that is shallow and wide. The high sides also keep the flavoring elements—bones, meat, and root vegetables—immersed throughout cooking so that the gently bubbling water can slowly extract their essences into the broth. For the home cook, a stockpot is useful for making soup and stock and for cooking large amounts of food such as corn or lobster for a crowd. This pot uses less cooking surface than a saucepot of similar capacity, making room for other foods to cook at the same time. The pot isn't moved around on the stove, but may be carried when full, so it has two lug handles rather than one long handle.

Think big when choosing a stockpot—at least 8 quarts. Making stock is time-consuming; it's more efficient to produce it in quantity. Make sure the pot has a thick bottom; this extra weight prevents scorching of both ingredients and pot, and keeps the pot from warping. Stockpots are commonly made of aluminum, stainless steel, clad metals, and enameled steel.

WOK

The most famous symbol of Chinese cooking is the wok, and it is hard to imagine a more versatile or better-designed piece of cookware. Its round bottom allows food to be stir-fried or deep-fried with a minimum of oil. A steel or cast-iron wok is an excellent conductor of heat, making it possible to cook over a very small fire. With a cover and a steaming rack or basket, the wok becomes a steamer for everything from whole birds and fish to bite-sized pastries. You can simmer, braise, and even smoke foods in a wok.

Woks are available in many designs and materials. The traditional shape has a round bottom, for cooking over a gas flame (originally a charcoal brazier). Cooks with electric ranges should use a flat-bottomed wok for more efficient heating. A wok may have two metal loops as handles, two similar handles trimmed with wood, or one long wooden handle with or without a handle on the opposite side. A long handle is useful, especially for stir-frying, since it allows you to lift the wok with one hand to pour the contents out onto the serving platter without being spattered by oil.

Woks come in all sizes, from 9 to 30 inches in diameter. The 14-inch size is the most common for home use and is included in the standard wok sets sold in most cookware and department stores. The best material for woks is 14-gauge spun steel. Cast iron is also traditional, but many home cooks find it too heavy. Avoid those with nonstick surfaces that clean easily but do not allow foods to brown as well as steel or iron surfaces do. Stainless steel is pretty, but conducts heat poorly and food tends to stick to it. Anodized aluminum performs well but is very costly.

Among the essential wok accessories (included in most wok sets) are a wok ring, cover, Chinese-style wire strainer, ladle, and spatula. Optional accessories include steaming racks and bamboo steaming baskets (see Chinese Steamer), wire draining racks for fried foods, bamboo cleaning brushes, and extralong chopsticks for stirring while food cooks.

Like a cast-iron skillet, a steel wok must be carefully seasoned; see MATERIALS FOR COOKWARE.

COOL, TO

To bring hot food to room temperature (approximately 70° F). This is not the same as chilling food, which involves temperatures of 40° F or less.

COPPER EGG-WHITE BOWL

For centuries, cooks have recognized that egg whites beaten in an unlined copper bowl have appreciably more volume. Experiments suggest that copper binds with a protein in the whites to help create a more stable foam. This means that the beaten egg whites will keep  their volume longer. For home use, the most popular bowls are 10 and 12 inches in diameter. They are deep, with a rounded bottom and sloping sides. Ideal for developing airy foam, this shape best accommodates a balloon whisk, whose bulbous, open design incorporates more air into a mixture than a narrow, more tightly constructed whisk. To use, the bowl is set on the counter and rotated as eggs are whisked, or is held against the body with one arm and secured by looping the thumb through a ring attached to the rim. Copper inserts are available for some heavy-duty portable electric mixers.

Recipes and Related Information
Egg, 196; Whisk, 608.

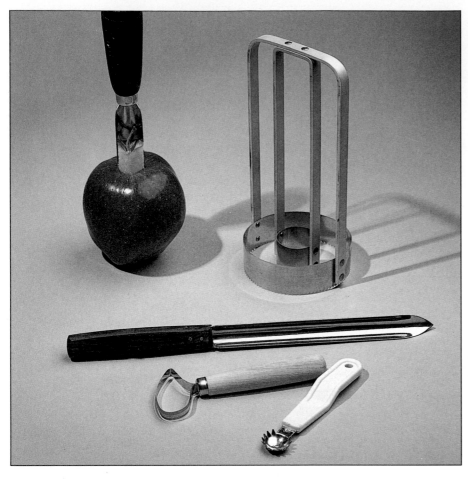

Coring tools make quick work of removing the core of a fruit or vegetable. Be sure to select a corer with a cutting edge that is sharp enough to do its job.

CORE, TO; CORER

The central seed-bearing structure of a fruit is the core; the tool with which to remove it is the corer. Apples, pears, pineapples, tomatoes, cucumbers, and zucchini have cores that may need to be removed for certain uses; special tools are available to perform this procedure on each of these foods. A knife or vegetable peeler will also do the job.

CORERS: APPLE, PEAR, PINEAPPLE, TOMATO, ZUCCHINI

These are straightforward, form-follows-function tools that do what their name suggests: remove the inedible or otherwise undesirable core from certain fruits and vegetables. When hollowed these foods are more attractive to serve, whether whole or sliced, and make versatile containers for stuffing.

Before you buy a cutting tool, check that its edge is sharp by running your finger lightly across the blade. Remember that although these machine-made corers are perfectly straight or round, chances are the fruits and vegetables aren't; even with the best technique, all the core or seeds will not come away on the first try.

APPLE CORER
Buy one that is long enough to cut all the way through an apple and has a wide enough shaft to remove all of the core and seeds in one operation. These corers usually have a hollow stainless steel shaft that traps the core. The handle is wood.

PEAR CORER
The blade is a ribbon of metal that looks like a baby pear. Cored pears are poached and served whole, or sliced or halved for use in a pastry.

PINEAPPLE CORER
This device removes peel and core at the same time. It consists of two round, serrated metal cutters, one inside the other, joined by a pair of tall, arched handles. The corer cuts down through the pineapple, whose top and bottom have been removed, with a clockwise rotating motion. The outer cutter separates peel from flesh as the inner cutter removes the core.

TOMATO CORER
Dubbed the tomato shark by manufacturers and retailers, this small stainless steel bowl has a toothy, zigzag edge. This tool also cleanly removes the ribs and seeds of cherry tomatoes to ready them for stuffing.

ZUCCHINI CORER
This tool resembles an apple corer, but the metal shaft is elongated to match the shape of a zucchini and comes to a point that better pierces the end of the squash. It works with cucumbers, apples, and pears as well.

Recipes and Related Information
Baked Pear Tart, 423; Nutty Baked Apples, 10.

CORK-PULLING DEVICES

All the devices available for pulling the cork from a bottle of wine can be divided into two categories: corkscrews and everything else. The simplest corkscrew is a coil of wire; one end is pointed and the other is attached to a handle. You screw the point of the coil into the cork and, lifting with the handle, pull out the cork.

Unfortunately, not every cork is willing to come out easily. As a result, corkscrews have been designed with every variety of leverage imaginable. In choosing a corkscrew, be sure to look for one with a helical (open-centered) screw, rather than the type that looks like an oversized wood screw. Because the latter bores a hole straight through the center of a cork, the screw will likely pull out of a stubborn cork. In general, whatever design you select, the simpler the better.

An air-pump cork puller—a long hollow needle attached to a compressed gas cylinder or hand pump—is not recommended. Once the needle is inserted through a cork, the gas pressure is activated to push out the cork. Table wine bottles, however, are not built to withstand internal pressure, as sparkling wine and soda bottles are. It may never happen, but the possibly explosive combination of a weak bottle and a stubborn cork is a frightening scene to contemplate.

DOUBLE SCREW

This corkscrew uses a second screw to pull the cork. Both the wooden model and the all-metal version rely on the same principle, but one screws a threaded tube out of the body, and the other screws a threaded handle down around a sliding tube, drawing the cork out with it. Both of these draw the cork smoothly and slowly without jostling the bottle, which is an important advantage in an older wine that has thrown a sediment.

DOUBLE-WING CORKSCREW

To operate this basic chrome and plastic device, the coiled wire is screwed into the cork until the wings are forced upward and the body rests on the rim of the bottle opening. Pressing both wings down draws the cork up and out. A reverse-thread version is available to ease the job for left-handed oenophiles.

PROFESSIONAL LEVER CORKSCREW

A commercial wine opener for serious wine tasters who think they have everything, this extravagant cork puller is more home accessory than basic kitchen equipment. Various models are made of solid copper, chrome-plated steel, or cast aluminum, often accented with wood. Extremely elaborate and in a class by itself, it is at the same time extremely simple to use: push the handle up and the cork pulls out; push down and the bottle is recorked.

SCREWPULL

One wine writer called this plastic device the first real advance in corkscrew technology in almost two centuries. Its ingeniously simple design uses a very long screw and a body to locate it on top of the bottle—nothing else. To pull the cork, the body is aligned on top of the bottle, and the tip of the teflon-coated screw is inserted, then rotated. The screw penetrates the cork until the handle stops against the body; with further turning (and very little effort), the cork climbs up the screw. A pocket version complete with a folding knife for cutting capsules allows devotees of this cork-pulling device to have it always close at hand.

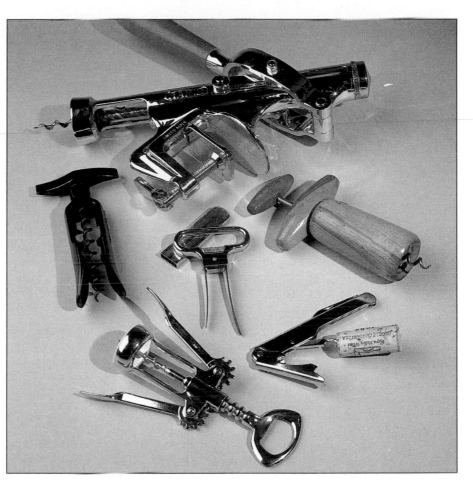

TWIN-BLADED CORK PULLER

This tool does not use a screw, but two flexible metal blades that slip down between the cork and the neck of the bottle. You pull the cork by simultaneously twisting and pulling up the handle. This device takes a little practice to master and a good deal of brute force, and if used incorrectly, it will neatly shove the cork back into the bottle. Once mastered, however, this tool makes pulling the cork a fairly quick operation. A minor advantage is that you can reverse the cork-pulling procedure to recork the bottle.

WAITER'S KNIFE

Although a bit harder to master than the double-wing corkscrew, the metal waiter's knife is a popular and reliable design. An arm attached to one end of the corkscrew hooks onto the top of the bottle, and the hinge forms the fulcrum. The waiter's knife also includes a small knife for cleanly cutting the capsule (lead or foil wrapping). The inexperienced user might find that the cork breaks or gets pushed into the bottle with this cork puller; novices should practice on *vin ordinaire* before attempting to open a vintage selection.

An assortment of cork-pulling devices, clockwise from top: professional lever corkscrew, simple corkscrew with wooden handle and case, waiter's knife, double-wing corkscrew, Screwpull, twin-bladed cork puller.

CORN

Also called maize, corn is not technically a vegetable, but a grass native to the New World. Of the hundreds of cultivated strains, most can be classified as either popcorn, field corn, or sweet corn. Popcorn is a type of corn whose kernels burst open when exposed to heat, revealing the familiar dry, white, puffy interior (see POPCORN). Field corn is used for animal feed or is dried for hominy; when ground, it yields hominy grits or *masa harina*. For a discussion of dried corn products (cornmeal, dried sweet corn, hominy, hominy grits, masa harina), see GRAIN. Corn marketed for the table, whether fresh, frozen, or canned, is sweet corn, which stores more sugar than starch; this entry will discuss sweet corn.

Sweet corn may be yellow or white, in full-sized ears or baby corn that may be eaten in its entirety. When sweet corn is picked, the sugar it contains begins rapidly converting to starch, so it is advisable to cook corn as soon as possible after purchase.

Use   Fresh sweet corn on the cob can be steamed, boiled, oven-roasted, or grilled and eaten out of hand. Fresh corn kernels may be made into soup or added to soup; used in salads, vegetable sautés, fritters, and relishes; creamed or made into puddings or soufflés. In Peru, chunks of steamed sweet corn are added to stews and served with seviche.

Availability   Fresh corn is sold almost the year around, with peak supplies in summer. Florida supplies most off-season corn in the United States. Frozen corn on the cob and corn kernels are also available. Corn kernels are canned, either water-packed or creamed.

Selection   Choose ears that feel full and heavy for their size; kernels should be relatively small and milky when pierced, and silk should be moist, without any signs of drying or decay.

Storage   Keep fresh corn in the refrigerator in a plastic bag and use as soon as possible. Do not remove husk and silk until ready to use. These natural wrappers will help keep the corn from drying out when exposed to the cold air of the refrigerator. Leftover frozen or canned corn may be stored in an airtight container in the refrigerator for up to three days.

Preparation   Remove husk and silk from fresh corn if steaming or boiling. To oven-roast or grill, peel back husk but leave attached. Remove silk and replace husk, tying it shut at the tip with string. Soak in cold water 30 minutes to moisten husk, then roast or grill. Alternatively, remove husk and silk, wrap ears in foil with butter, and roast or grill. To prepare fresh corn kernels, remove husk and silk, then run a sharp knife down cob from tip end to stem to cut kernels away, or use a corn kernel remover, which automatically shears kernels from cob.

Cooking   See BOIL, GRILL, STEAM.

■ ELOTES
Corn on the cob with lime-chile butter

In this dish, corn on the cob (with husk intact) is roasted on the grill and seasoned with a surprising combination of lime and chili powder. These sour and piquant flavors actually bring out the sweetness of the corn. Elotes can also be cooked indoors if the weather turns bad.

> Fresh ears of corn (about 2 per person), silk removed, husks left intact
> ¾ to 1 cup butter, at room temperature
> ¼ cup (generous) fresh lime juice
> 2 to 3 tablespoons Texas chili powder or powdered hot chiles (such as New Mexico chiles)
> Salt, to taste

1. *To cook corn outdoors:* Prepare fire in grill. Drench corn with water until husks can absorb no more; twist shut. If fire is very hot, wrap ears in aluminum foil. Place corn on grill and roast for about 20 minutes, turning frequently, until tender. Keep warm until ready to serve. *To cook corn indoors:* Preheat oven to 400° F. Remove husks and smear ears with a small amount of butter. Wrap each ear in aluminum foil and roast in oven until tender (20 to 25 minutes).

2. As corn roasts, use a fork to beat together butter, lime juice, chili powder, and salt, adjusting proportions to taste. When ready to serve, remove husks and coat corn with the mixture.

Serves 6 to 8.

■ CORN MAQUECHOUX

This Creole version of creamed corn is best served in summer when corn is sweetest, peppers are at their best, and fresh basil is abundant. With three colors of bell peppers—red, green, and yellow—plus the yellow corn, it makes a festive and flavorful accompaniment to fried or roast chicken.

> 3 tablespoons unsalted butter
> 1 cup finely chopped onions
> 2 shallots, finely chopped
> ½ cup chopped red bell pepper
> ½ cup chopped green bell pepper
> ½ cup chopped yellow bell pepper
> 3 to 4 cups fresh or frozen sweet corn kernels
> 2 tablespoons chopped parsley
> 4 tablespoons chopped green onion
> 1 cup whipping cream
> ¼ teaspoon dried thyme
> 1 tablespoon chopped fresh basil *or* ½ teaspoon dried basil
> ½ teaspoon cayenne pepper
> Salt and freshly ground black pepper, to taste
> Sugar, to taste

Melt butter in a heavy 3- to 4-quart saucepan over medium heat. Add onions and shallots and sauté until vegetables are soft but not browned. Add peppers and cook another 2 to 3 minutes. Add corn, parsley, green onions, cream, thyme, basil, and cayenne, and simmer for 10 to 15 minutes. Adjust taste with salt, pepper, and, if necessary, sugar.

Serves 4 to 6.

Food Processor Version Cut 1 medium onion into quarters and put in work bowl with metal blade in place; add shallots. Turn motor on and off 3 or 4 times to process. Cook as directed. Cut 1 *each* small green, red, and yellow bell peppers into 1-inch pieces. Process with metal blade, turning motor on and off 3 or 4 times. Cook as directed.

Recipes and Related Information
Basic Fritter Batter, 28; Corn Kernel Remover, 159; Corn Relish, 322; Succotash, 33.

CORN KERNEL REMOVER

If you love corn on the cob, corn salsas, chowders and soups, creamed corn, fritters, puddings, and all the many other wonderful ways there are to prepare corn when fresh and seasonally plentiful, this tool may prove handy even though it has limited uses. It does only what its name promises—cuts kernels off the cob— but it does it very well. The device consists of a plastic, metal, or wood trough with a fixed blade and movable teeth set across it; the corn slides along the trough and under the blade, which shears off the kernels. The teeth act like mashers if you want creamier corn; they can be moved away from the blade when not needed. This tool is not a year-round item in cookware stores; it's most available in summer months, when corn is at its most plentiful in the market.

Recipes and Related Information
Corn, 158; Corn Relish, 322; Succotash, 33.

CORNSTARCH

Derived from corn, cornstarch is a powdery white thickener. It gives a transparent sheen to sauces, syrups, and stews. Where appearance is important, as in a glaze for a fruit tart, it is preferred to flour, which produces a more opaque finish.

Use Cornstarch is used to thicken sauces, soups, stews, puddings, and syrups. It is a frequent ingredient in Chinese cooking to thicken sauces and to coat meats and fish before frying. Cornstarch also gives a light texture to baked goods. To substitute all-purpose flour for cake flour in baked goods, replace 2 tablespoons flour per cup with 2 tablespoons cornstarch.

Availability Cornstarch is widely available at supermarkets packed in boxes.

Storage Cornstarch will keep indefinitely in a cool, dry place.

Preparation To thicken a sauce, dissolve cornstarch in a small amount of cold water or stock before stirring into simmering liquid. Cook gently for a few minutes to remove the raw cornstarch flavor. Cornstarch-thickened sauces should not be boiled very long or they will separate. One tablespoon cornstarch has approximately the thickening power of 1½ to 2 tablespoons flour.

Recipes and Related Information
New York–Style Cheesecake, 117; Sauce, 512.

CRANBERRY

The small, tart red cranberry is the fruit of a low-lying vine native to North America and northern Europe. Wild cranberries were an important nutrient for Native Americans, who mashed them with dried meat and animal fat to make pemmican, a long-lasting food that nourished them through cold winters and extensive hunting expeditions. Today cranberries are cultivated commercially, with half the American crop grown in Massachusetts. Raw cranberries have a firm, crunchy texture and are very tart.

Use The naturally high acidity of the cranberry makes it excellent for relishes and jellies. It adds zest to salads, stuffings, cakes, muffins, quick breads, pies, and puddings. Cranberry juice is particularly refreshing and can be used in punches or cocktails. Cranberry relish, cranberry sauce, and other cranberry preparations are traditional dishes served on American Thanksgiving tables.

Availability Fresh cranberries are available from September to December, packed in plastic bags. Frozen cranberries, packed in plastic bags, are sold in most supermarkets all year. Canned cranberry relish and cranberry sauce are marketed the year around, as is bottled cranberry juice.

Storage Keep fresh cranberries in an unopened plastic bag in the refrigerator for up to four weeks. Store leftover fresh cranberries in an airtight container in the refrigerator. To freeze, wrap package in a plastic bag; freeze up to one year.

Cranberries were a staple in the diet of Native Americans during this country's early days. The berries were part of pemmican, a long-lasting dried food that nourished the Indians through the long, cold New England winters.

Preparation Wash berries and remove any stems; drain. It is unnecessary to thaw frozen berries before adding to batters or dishes that will be cooked.

■ WHOLE-BERRY CRANBERRY SAUCE

Although cranberries are synonymous with turkey, they are also delicious with roast pork, beef, and chicken. For a chunky sauce, cook 1 to 2 minutes more until the berries break down. For a smooth sauce, purée the berries in a blender or food processor for about 2 minutes.

> 1 package (12 oz) fresh or frozen cranberries (about 2½ cups)
> 1 cup sugar
> 1¼ cups water
> Juice and grated rind of 1 orange

1. Wash cranberries and pat dry. In a 2-quart saucepan combine sugar, the water, orange rind, and juice; cook, stirring, over medium heat, until sugar dissolves. Add cranberries to sugar syrup, bring to a boil, and cook until cranberry skins start to break or pop (about 1 minute).

2. Remove cranberries from the heat and pour into a 3-cup bowl or storage jars with lids to cool. Sauce can be stored, covered, in the refrigerator for up to 10 days, or placed in airtight jars in the freezer for up to 3 months (leave ½-inch headspace between sauce and jar lid).

Makes 2⅓ cups.

Variation Stir 1 cup coarsely chopped, toasted walnuts into cranberry sauce after removing from heat.

Makes 2¾ cups.

> ### *Recipes and Related Information*
> *Cranberry Conserve, 320; Cranberry-Orange-Nut Loaf, 492.*

CREAM

If freshly drawn milk is left to settle, the high-fat portion rises to the top to form a thick layer of cream. The modern dairy skims cream using a centrifugal cream separator and markets it in several different versions.

Use The high fat content of cream gives it a rich buttery flavor and a velvety texture. Cream is used to enrich sauces, soups, stews, and hot and cold beverages. Poured over berries, sliced bananas, poached fruit, and hot and cold cereals, it is a sauce in itself. Brushing cream on just-baked breads and rolls gives them a soft, shiny crust. Adding cream to baked goods such as biscuits and shortcake provides added richness and tenderness. Cream contributes body to a variety of sweet and savory puddings, custards, and mousses, and is, of course, the basis for all ice creams and many other frozen desserts. Cream also adds richness and texture to such confections as caramels, truffles, toffee, and pralines.

Due to its high fat content, cream holds a shape when whipped. A dollop of whipped, lightly salted cream is used to garnish and enrich soups. Sweetened whipped cream garnishes pies and tarts, cakes, puddings, mousses, sundaes, fresh berries, and cooked fruit desserts. Whipped cream gives body to mousses and parfaits; it may be flavored with chocolate or vanilla and used as a filling for cream puffs, or folded into pastry cream and used as a filling for crêpes and cakes. Whipped cream is also spooned on top of coffee, hot cocoa, Irish coffee, and many other coffee drinks.

Half-and-half or light cream may be substituted for heavy cream or whipping cream in many instances, although they yield a lighter, less rich dish. Half-and-half and light cream are unable to hold a foam and cannot be substituted in a recipe that calls for whipped cream.

Crème fraîche, a cultured cream often used by the French in sauces, is made by adding natural ferments to pasteurized heavy cream. It may be used whenever sour cream is called for: in soups, doughs and batters, salad dressings, and sauces, for example. It may also be lightly sweetened and spooned over berries or fruit desserts.

The smooth texture and rich, tangy flavor of sour cream are appreciated in dips, salad dressings, cold soups, and frostings. Sour cream gives a tender crumb to baked items such as cakes and biscuits.

Availability Although raw (unpasteurized) dairy products are sold in some health-food stores, most commercial dairy products, including cream, have been pasteurized (see MILK) to destroy disease-causing organisms and extend shelf life. If the product is not labeled as raw or unpasteurized, it has been pasteurized. Some cream is ultrapasteurized to extend shelf life.

Half-and-half is usually homogenized (see MILK) to prevent milk and cream from separating, and light cream may be homogenized. Whipping cream is not homogenized because that would interfere with its whipping ability. Cream is available in the following forms:

Half-and-Half A mixture of milk and cream, half-and-half contains between 10.5 percent and 18.0 percent milk fat.

Light Cream, Coffee Cream, or Table Cream The milk fat content is between 18 percent and 30 percent.

Light Whipping Cream or Whipping Cream The milk fat content is between 30 percent and 36 percent.

Heavy Whipping Cream or Heavy Cream The milk fat content is at least 36 percent.

Sour Cream This cream product is made in one of two ways: either by adding lactic acid–producing bacteria to pasteurized cream and letting it culture for about 24 hours until it reaches 0.5 percent acidity, or by adding vinegar or another acidifier to pasteurized cream and letting it stand until it curdles. The former procedure produces cultured sour cream; the latter method, acidified sour cream.

Any sour cream must contain at least 18 percent butterfat and may contain rennet, emulsifiers, and stabilizers. The requirement drops to 14.4 percent butterfat if nutritive sweeteners or bulky flavorings are added.

Crème Fraîche This cultured cream is thickened, or curdled, by the action of the acid-producing bacterial culture. Crème fraîche is thicker than whipping cream but less thick than American sour cream. It has a smooth, pourable texture and a tangy, nutlike flavor.

Heavy whipping cream, light whipping cream, coffee cream, and half-and-half are packed in cardboard containers. All are available in supermarkets, although light whipping cream and coffee cream may not be sold in smaller markets. Whipped cream is also marketed in pressurized aerosol cans, although it may contain sweeteners, flavoring, or stabilizers. Check the label. Sour cream is widely available at supermarkets packed in plastic tubs. Crème frâiche can be easily made at home (see right) or may be purchased in selected supermarkets, specialty gourmet shops, and cheese stores, in bulk or packed in plastic containers.

Storage Cream is highly perishable. Make it one of the last purchases at the supermarket and refrigerate it at home as soon as possible. Pasteurized cream stays fresh for at least one week. Ultrapasteurized cream keeps for six to eight weeks in an unopened container; after opening, use within one week. Sour cream should be refrigerated and used within one week. Crème fraîche should be refrigerated, covered, and used within one week.

Preparation To produce a more stable foam, chill cream, bowl, and beaters before whipping. Generally, 1 cup whipping cream yields 2 cups whipped cream. Choose a bowl large enough to handle the increased volume comfortably but small enough to allow beaters to maintain good contact with cream. It is best to whip cream shortly before using. It also may be whipped ahead, covered, and refrigerated for several hours. Some liquid will probably separate from the mass, but it will reincorporate readily; at serving time, rewhip lightly.

When folding whipped cream into another, heavier mixture, it's sometimes easier to add the whipped cream in stages, to lighten the other mixture. Fold in about one-third whipped cream to blend, then fold in remainder. For information about proper folding technique, see FOLD.

Sauces, soups, and stews containing sour cream should not be allowed to boil or they may curdle. Unlike sour cream, imported crème fraîche and crème fraîche made with buttermilk do not curdle when boiled and may be added to simmered dishes. Crème fraîche made with sour cream or yogurt curdles when boiled.

■ CREME FRAICHE

Some buttermilk or leftover crème fraîche is added to the whipping cream to start the curdling action. Heat 1 cup whipping cream in a small saucepan to 95° F. Transfer cream to a clean jar with a tight-fitting lid. Add 1 tablespoon buttermilk and shake well. Let stand at room temperature until thickened (12 to 24 hours). Refrigerate. Save 1 tablespoon from each batch and use in place of buttermilk in future batches. Do not try to make crème fraîche with ultrapasteurized cream, because it does not contain enough bacteria to curdle.

Cream will whip to greatest volume if liquid, bowl, and beaters are first chilled. It is best to whip cream just before using.

Recipes and Related Information

Banana Cream Pie, 440; Candy and Confection, 94; Chantilly Cream, 252; Chocolate Marble Cream Cake, 88; Coconut Cream Pie, 440; Cream-Basted Fried Eggs, 200; Cream Biscuits, 50; Cream Sauce, 513; Horseradish Cream Sauce, 305; Horseradish–Sour Cream Dipping Sauce, 46; Lemon Crème Fraîche, 107; Parmesan Cream Sauce, 412; Sour Cream Pastry, 47; Whipped Cream Icing, 87; Whipped Crème Fraîche, 264.

CREAM, TO

In baking, to beat fat—butter or solid vegetable shortening—with sugar until soft, smooth, and light. This process traps air that expands in the oven to help create a baked product with more volume. Creaming is especially important for butter (shortened) cakes, which depend on this step for some or all of their leavening. For cookies, creaming serves to combine ingredients rather than aerate and is done to produce a smooth texture.

To incorporate the most air, butter should be at warm room temperature (75° to 79° F). Let refrigerated butter sit out on the counter for about 30 minutes before using. An instant-read thermometer is the most accurate gauge of temperature, but you can also judge by touch. If butter yields slightly to pressure, yet still feels cool, it's ready. Solid vegetable shortening is plastic (pliable) at a wider range of temperatures than butter, and so it needn't soften before using.

Beat fat briefly to make it soft and pliable before adding sugar, then beat them together until light—a pale, ivory color—and the consistency of whipped cream. Scrape down sides of bowl occasionally to incorporate fully both ingredients.

How long should you cream a mixture? You want to continue long enough to accomplish your purpose; if you are creaming to leaven a cake, you may be directed to continue for as long as 6 to 8 minutes. For other mixtures follow this rule of thumb: cream until color lightens, consistency becomes fluffy, and batter is less grainy from sugar when you rub it between your fingers.

Chocolate Eclairs are made from fingers of cream puff pastry filled with vanilla pastry cream and iced with Bittersweet Chocolate Sauce. The flavor of the pastry cream can be easily varied. The éclair recipe appears on page 164.

CREAM OF TARTAR

A by-product of wine making, cream of tartar is the acid salt of tartaric acid. The crystallized sediment that falls to the bottom of a wine cask after fermentation and the crystalline substance that collects on its sides are crude tartar. To refine it for commercial use, it is decrystallized in a basic solution, then recrystallized, then bleached and allowed to crystallize again. The layer of white crystals that forms on the surface of the cooling liquid is powdered to make commercial cream of tartar.

Use Cream of tartar is a common ingredient in commercial baking powders, along with baking soda. In the presence of moisture, cream of tartar and baking soda react to produce carbon dioxide gas, thereby leavening the mixture or batter. Due to its acidity or low pH, a pinch of cream of tartar promotes coagulation in beaten egg whites if added partway through the beating process. Confectioners add cream of tartar to sugar syrup to impede crystallization, thereby yielding creamier, less grainy candies.

Availability Cream of tartar is widely sold packaged in airtight jars or tins.

Storage Keep in an airtight container in a cool, dry place; it will keep indefinitely.

Preparation Sift with other dry ingredients before adding to a batter. Because the leavening action of cream of tartar commences immediately upon contact with moisture, work quickly after adding moisture to batter.

Recipes and Related Information
Baking Powder, 23; Egg, 196.

CREAM PUFF PASTRY

The French call this pastry *pâte à choux*, cabbage pastry. It is the base for such delicacies as cream puffs, éclairs, and profiteroles. During baking, the little mounds of cream puff dough grow into knobby-surfaced pastries that do indeed resemble cabbages. These crisp, puffy shells can be filled with a variety of creams and glazed with numerous icings. The usual fillings are pastry cream, Chantilly cream, ice cream, or mousse. The toppings range from a dusting of confectioners' sugar to a rich chocolate sauce or crunchy caramel glaze. The fully baked puffs can also be filled with savory mixtures and served as finger foods that are perfect for cocktails.

INGREDIENTS FOR CREAM PUFFS

The dough is quickly and simply made from a paste, called panada, of water, butter, salt, sugar, and flour. Eggs are added one by one, causing the pastry to inflate like a balloon in the oven. Like the batter for popovers—those other steam-leavened crispy, hollow shells—cream puff paste\has an equal amount of flour and liquid. But cream puffs are much richer than popovers because the dough contains about eight times more fat. The fat also contributes tenderness, elasticity, and, with the water and egg, is a source for the steam-generating moisture that puffs the pastry as it bakes. Eggs add structure, richness, and liquid, and serve as an emulsifier to blend the liquid and fat into a smooth paste.

CREAM PUFF PASTRY BASICS

The technique for making cream puff paste is straightforward and simple (see Making Cream Puffs at right). The water, butter, salt, and sugar are combined in a heavy-bottomed saucepan and heated until the butter melts and the mixture just comes to a boil. At that moment the pan is removed from the heat and the flour is beaten in. With further beating the mixture thickens to a lumpy paste that later becomes smooth as each egg is incorporated. The paste has been beaten sufficiently when it pulls away from the sides of the pan in a ball. After the paste has cooled enough that it won't curdle the eggs (about 5 minutes), the eggs are added one at a time. The smooth, shiny finished mixture is a rich golden color and ready to be shaped as desired.

The most efficient way to create precise shapes is to pipe the cream puff paste onto parchment-lined baking sheets using a pastry bag with the tip specified in the recipe (see FROSTING, ICING, AND FILLING, page 244, for directions on using a pastry bag). If a pastry bag is not available, use two spoons and your fingers (dipped in egg wash or water) to roughly shape the paste.

Cream puff paste should be used while still warm. If you want to keep leftover paste, rub the surface with butter, cover, and refrigerate for up to 8 hours. To use, bring to room temperature and handle as you would fresh paste. Leftover paste does not puff as high as fresh paste and should be used only for small puffs, such as profiteroles or miniature éclairs.

■ CREAM PUFF PASTRY
Pâte à choux

This is the foundation for all types of classically shaped cream puff desserts—including éclairs, large and small cream puffs, profiteroles, and *gougères*. Unbleached white bread (hard) flour is best for making cream puffs. If hard flour is unavailable, substitute all-purpose flour.

For 1⅓ cups

  ½ **cup water** *or*
  ¼ **cup water and ¼ cup milk**
  4 **tablespoons unsalted butter, cut into pieces**
  ½ **teaspoon sugar**
  ¼ **teaspoon salt**
  ½ **cup unbleached white bread flour, sifted**
  2 **eggs**

For 2 cups

  ¾ **cup water** *or*
  ⅜ **cup water and ⅜ cup milk**
  6 **tablespoons unsalted butter, cut into pieces**
  ¾ **teaspoon sugar**
  ¼ **teaspoon salt**
  ¾ **cup unbleached white bread flour, sifted**
  3 **eggs**

For 2⅔ cups

  1 **cup water** *or*
  ½ **cup water and ½ cup milk**
  8 **tablespoons unsalted butter, cut into pieces**
  1 **teaspoon sugar**
  ½ **teaspoon salt**
  1 **cup unbleached white bread flour, sifted**
  4 **eggs**

1. Preheat oven to 425° F. Place the water, butter, sugar, and salt in a 2½-quart saucepan; bring to a boil over low heat. The mixture should be heated slowly so butter is just melted when water reaches a boil. When mixture boils, remove from heat immediately and add flour all at once. Stir vigorously with a wooden spoon. Return to medium heat and stir until mixture pulls away from sides of pan and forms a ball (about 30 seconds), leaving a white film on pan.

2. Remove from heat; cool 5 minutes. Add eggs, one at a time, beating thoroughly after each addition. The paste should look smooth and shiny but be stiff enough to hold its shape when piped or dropped onto a baking sheet.

If paste looks dull and is very stiff, lightly beat another egg and add a little of it to paste; beat until mixture is smooth. Add more egg if needed.

3. Fit pastry bag with a ¾-inch plain ornamenting tip. Fill bag half full with cream puff pastry. Pipe or spoon cream puff pastry onto parchment-lined baking sheets into shapes specified in individual recipes. Bake as directed.

1⅓ cups yields 8 éclairs, 10 cream puffs, or 40 profiteroles; 2 cups yields 12 éclairs, 15 cream puffs, or 60 profiteroles; 2⅔ cups yields 1 gougère.

■ CREAM PUFFS

For a dessert, fill Cream Puffs with whipped cream or pastry cream and dust lightly with confectioners' sugar. Once shells are filled with cream, they must be refrigerated to avoid spoilage unless served right away. However, shells quickly lose their crispness in the refrigerator. To use as an hors d'oeuvre or first course, fill with a savory mixture such as creamed crab, herbed cream cheese, or sour cream and caviar. Fill no more than 2 hours prior to serving. Cream puffs are good choices for stand-up cocktail parties when you plan to pass all or most of the food. The pastry makes a neat little package that can be eaten with ease. Unfilled shells can be frozen, wrapped airtight, and reheated in a 400° F oven 5 minutes to crisp.

  1⅓ **cups Cream Puff Pastry (at left)**
  1 **egg lightly beaten with 1 teaspoon water**
  2 **cups Chantilly Cream (see page 252)** *or*
    1½ cups Pastry Cream (see page 251) folded with 1 cup Chantilly Cream
  ¼ **cup confectioners' sugar, for dusting**

1. Preheat oven to 425° F. Line a baking sheet with parchment paper. Attach paper to baking sheet with a few dots of Cream Puff Pastry. Place Cream Puff Pastry in a pastry bag fitted with a ¾-inch tip. Pipe 2½-inch-diameter mounds of pastry about 2 inches apart on baking sheet (or drop mounds of pastry onto sheet using 2 spoons). Brush surface of each mound with egg-water mixture.

2. Bake at 425° F for 15 minutes; reduce heat to 400° F and continue baking 15 minutes longer. Make a few small slits in the side of each cream puff to allow steam to escape; turn off oven and return cream puffs to oven for 10 minutes. Prop oven door slightly ajar with a wooden spoon. Cool cream puffs on wire racks.

3. To fill cream puffs: Slice shells in half horizontally with a serrated knife. Remove any uncooked dough from inside. Place Chantilly Cream in a pastry bag fitted with a medium star tip. Pipe cream into bottom half of shell until cream extends 1 inch above the rim; cover with top half of shell. Sift confectioners' sugar over filled puffs. Serve immediately or refrigerate until ready to serve.

Makes 8 to 10 large puffs.

MAKING CREAM PUFFS

After adding flour to butter mixture in saucepan, cook, stirring vigorously, until mixture pulls away from sides of pan, forms a ball, and leaves a white film on saucepan.

This photograph shows how paste looks just after one egg has been added. Notice how paste separates into several lumps after the addition of an egg. When stirred vigorously the paste will return to a smooth consistency.

Cream puff pastry is ready to be piped or spooned onto a baking sheet when it reaches this smooth, shiny consistency. It should be stiff enough to hold its shape when piped.

To form éclairs, pipe 5-inch strips of paste 2 inches apart on a parchment-lined baking sheet (see Chocolate Eclairs, right). To form cream puffs, pipe 2½-inch mounds of paste 2 inches apart on baking sheet (see Cream Puffs, page 163).

■ CHOCOLATE ECLAIRS

Eclairs, fingers of cream puff pastry, are filled with flavored (chocolate, praline, or coffee) pastry cream and iced with a thin, shiny glaze. They are shaped by piping the pastry onto baking sheets with a pastry bag and plain tip (see photograph at left). Several delicious variations follow this recipe. Before using the Bittersweet Chocolate Sauce, cool to 90° F; then spread 1 to 2 tablespoons on top of each éclair or finish by dipping top of each pastry into the warm icing.

   1⅓ **cups Cream Puff Pastry (see page 163)**
    1 **egg lightly beaten with 1 teaspoon water**
   1½ **cups Pastry Cream (see page 251)**
    ½ **cup whipping cream**
    1 **cup Bittersweet Chocolate Sauce (at right)**

1. Preheat oven to 425° F. Place Cream Puff Pastry in a large pastry bag fitted with a ¾-inch tip. Cut a piece of parchment paper to fit a baking sheet; using a dark pen or pencil, draw along the long edges of the paper two parallel lines that are 5 inches apart; then turn paper over on baking sheet.

2. To form éclairs, pipe eight 5-inch strips of pastry, 2 inches apart, onto paper-covered baking sheet, using the lines on the paper as a guide. Brush éclairs with egg-water mixture. Run the back of a fork along top of each éclair to score top and keep it flat during baking.

3. Bake 15 minutes; reduce heat to 400° F and bake 15 minutes more. Remove éclairs from oven and make a few small slits along one side of each éclair to release steam. Turn off oven; return éclairs to oven for 10 minutes, keeping oven door slightly ajar with a wooden spoon. Cool éclairs on wire racks.

4. Prepare Pastry Cream and flavor as desired. Stir cold Pastry Cream until smooth. Beat whipping cream until it holds stiff peaks and fold into Pastry Cream.

5. Just before serving (no more than 2 hours before), place filling in a pastry bag fitted with a ¼-inch tip. Poke a hole in one end of éclair with the tip and fill with 3 to 4 tablespoons of the filling. If you don't have a pastry bag, use a serrated knife to slit each éclair along one side and then spoon filling inside.

6. To ice éclairs spread 1 to 2 tablespoons warm (90° F) Bittersweet Chocolate Sauce on top of each éclair, or dip top of each éclair in warm icing. To do as much as possible in advance (up to 4 or 5 hours before serving), ice éclairs before filling them. Store iced pastries in a cool, dry place; to keep them crisp, fill them carefully just before serving.

Makes 8 éclairs.

Caramel Eclairs   Dip éclairs in a sugar syrup that has been cooked to a medium caramel color (see SUGAR AND SYRUP); cool éclairs icing side down on a cold baking sheet. Fill with vanilla- or praline-flavored Pastry Cream.

Coffee Eclairs   Fill pastries with coffee-flavored Pastry Cream. Glaze with Glacé Icing flavored with coffee or chocolate (see page 250).

Double Chocolate Eclairs   Fill pastries with Pastry Cream flavored with chocolate. Glaze with Bittersweet Chocolate Sauce or chocolate-flavored Glacé Icing (see page 250).

Mocha Eclairs   Fill pastries with Pastry Cream flavored with chocolate and coffee (to make mocha). Glaze with Bittersweet Chocolate Sauce or Glacé Icing flavored with coffee or chocolate (see page 250).

■ ICE CREAM–FILLED PROFITEROLES

Tiny cream puffs filled with ice cream and topped with a deep, rich chocolate sauce are the classic dessert: profiteroles. The sauce is everything a chocolate sauce should be, it flows easily and coats well.

   1⅓ **cups Cream Puff Pastry (see page 163)**
    1 **egg lightly beaten with 1 teaspoon water**
    1 **pint vanilla or coffee ice cream**

Bittersweet Chocolate Sauce

    3 **tablespoons water**
    3 **tablespoons sugar**
    6 **ounces semisweet chocolate, broken into pieces**
    2 **ounces unsweetened chocolate, broken into pieces**
    1 **cup whipping cream**

1. Preheat oven to 425° F. Line baking sheets with parchment paper. Attach parchment to baking sheet at corners with dots of Cream Puff Pastry. Place Cream Puff Pastry in a pastry bag fitted with a ½-inch tip. Pipe forty-eight 1-inch-diameter mounds of pastry onto paper-lined baking sheets (at least ½ inch apart). Brush each puff with egg-water mixture, flattening the top slightly.

2. Bake 10 minutes; reduce heat to 400° F and bake until crisp and brown (about 10 minutes). Remove from oven and poke a ⅛-inch hole in bottom of each puff with tip of knife or tiny pastry tip. Turn off oven; return puffs to oven until dried out (5 to 10 minutes); prop oven door slightly ajar with a wooden spoon. Cool cream puffs on wire racks.

3. To fill pastries: Place a baking sheet in freezer. Slice each puff in half horizontally. Form 48 tiny mounds (1 rounded teaspoon each) of ice cream on cooled baking sheet. Flash-freeze. Cover ice cream mounds and store in freezer until ready to fill profiteroles. Before serving, fill bottom half of each shell with one of the ice cream mounds, then cover mound with top half of shell. Place 6 to 8 filled profiteroles in each dessert bowl. Pour about 3 tablespoons warm Bittersweet Chocolate Sauce over puffs. Serve immediately.

Makes 4 dozen profiteroles, serves 8.

Bittersweet Chocolate Sauce

1. Combine the water and sugar in a saucepan; bring to a boil over low heat, stirring constantly until sugar dissolves. Remove from heat and cool to 120° F (test with an instant-read thermometer).

2. Combine semisweet and unsweetened chocolates in top of double boiler; place over hot (not boiling) water until chocolate is just melted. Remove from heat. Pour in sugar syrup (at 120° F) all at once. Stir until smooth.

3. Heat cream in a small saucepan over low heat to 120° F. Pour into chocolate mixture and stir until smooth and shiny.

■ GOUGERE

In the Burgundy region of France, this cheese-flavored, seasoned cream puff pastry ring is a traditional specialty. Gruyère or Swiss cheese is mixed into the dough and sprinkled on top of each dough mound. Serve it as an appetizer or salad accompaniment.

> 2⅔ cups Cream Puff Pastry (see page 163)
> Pinch *each* cayenne pepper and
> freshly grated nutmeg
> 1 cup diced Gruyère or Swiss cheese

1. Preheat oven to 375° F. Prepare Cream Puff Pastry, stirring into mixture the cayenne and nutmeg just before adding flour. Mix in ¾ cup of the cheese after all the eggs have been added and mixture is smooth and shiny.

2. Spoon out dough to make 8 equal mounds in a circular shape on a parchment-lined or greased baking sheet. Sprinkle mounds with remaining ¼ cup cheese.

3. Bake until ring is well browned and crisp (40 to 45 minutes). Serve hot.

Makes 1 ring, serves 8.

cessor or blender; for dry bread crumbs, use day-old (or older) slices and dry slowly in a 325° F oven until completely dried out (at least 15 to 20 minutes). Tear into pieces and process as for fresh crumbs. To make cracker crumbs, crush crackers with a rolling pin until of the desired coarseness or fineness (it's less messy if what is to be crushed is contained in a plastic bag or between sheets of waxed paper).

Profiteroles are a variety of cream puff pastry petits fours. They make a stunning presentation and are sure to be the highlight of any party.

CRIMP, TO

To create a decorative pattern on the edge of a pie or pastry by using a fork or other tool such as a pastry crimper. This device resembles a pair of wide-armed tweezers, which grabs the dough between its "teeth." If a pie has two crusts or a lattice top, crimping will also join top and bottom crusts. The seal will be tighter if crusts are first bonded with water, milk, or beaten egg (egg yolk makes a stronger bond than a whole egg).

CRUMB, TO

To break up bread, crackers, or cookies into crumbs or to coat food with crumbs. Fresh, soft crumbs are made by processing pieces of bread (crusts removed) in a food pro-

CRUMBLE, TO

To break into small pieces with the fingers, as in crumbling blue cheese for use in a salad dressing.

CRUSH, TO

To reduce to crumbs (crackers or dried bread) or fine particles (peppercorns) by pounding with a mallet, rolling pin, or other device or machine (such as a food processor) or by grinding with a manual or electric mill. Garlic is crushed, typically with a garlic press or with a knife, to release as much of its flavor as possible.

CUBE, TO

A butchering term meaning to cut meats into measured cubes of even sizes (usually ½ or 1 inch) for use in stews. Vegetables cut this way are said to be diced; the pieces are usually smaller.

CUCUMBER

The cucumber is a gourd of the same family as pumpkin, zucchini, and other squashes. There are basically two types of cucumbers: pickling varieties and slicing varieties. Pickling varieties, such as the gherkin, the American dill, and the *cornichon* (small French pickle), are relatively small. The gherkin and the cornichon are rarely more than 2 inches long, the American dill rarely more than 4 inches. All of the varieties have dark green skin with knobby warts or spines.

Slicing cucumbers may be either outdoor varieties with seeds or greenhouse varieties, such as the long, thin-skinned English cucumber, which has few seeds. Outdoor varieties have a smooth, dark green skin and are usually about 8 inches long and 1½ inches wide, tapering at each end. The skin is often waxed to prolong shelf life. Greenhouse varieties, such as the English cucumber, are about 12 to 15 inches long.

Other commercially available slicing cucumbers include the round, pale yellow lemon cucumber, which has a very mild flavor, and the Japanese cucumber, a narrow, thin-skinned variety with few seeds.

Cucumbers have a crisp texture, a moist, cool flesh, and a mild flavor. Pickling cucumbers are appreciated for their crisp, firm texture, slicing varieties for their refreshing, juicy flavor.

Use Pickling cucumbers are packed in brine for use as a relish. Slicing cucumbers add crunchy texture and cool flavor to salads and sandwiches; they may also be steamed or sautéed and eaten as a vegetable. Cucumbers, hot or cold, have a particular affinity for fish and are often used to garnish salmon dishes. In Japan, cooks use cucumbers in sushi and cold salads, and in England, tea wouldn't be tea without cucumber sandwiches.

Availability Slicing cucumbers are available all year but peak season is the summer months. Most pickling cucumbers are sold only during the summer months. Many of the greenhouse varieties are wrapped in plastic to prevent dehydration.

Selection Choose firm cucumbers without soft spots. With the exception of lemon cucumbers, they should have a solid green color without signs of yellowing or puffiness.

Storage Keep cucumbers in refrigerator crisper for up to one week.

Preparation Pickling cucumbers should be scrubbed to remove loose spines. Greenhouse slicing cucumbers do not need to be peeled or seeded. Outdoor varieties may be peeled and seeded or not, as desired. Waxed cucumbers, however, should be peeled.

To seed a cucumber, slice it in half lengthwise and scrape out the seeds with a small spoon.

■ SWEET-AND-SOUR CUCUMBER SALAD

This dressing is also good with carrots, beets, cabbage, and zucchini. Also see the sour cream variation.

    ¼ cup cider vinegar
    1 teaspoon sugar
    ½ teaspoon salt
    ¼ teaspoon white pepper
    2 English cucumbers, sliced
    1 small red onion, diced

In a medium bowl whisk vinegar, sugar, salt, and pepper. Stir in cucumber slices and onion to coat with dressing. Cover and chill 2 hours.

Serves 6.

Sour Cream Cucumber Salad Stir ½ cup sour cream and 1 tablespoon dried dill into dressing.

> ### *Recipes and Related Information*
> *Bread and Butter Pickles, 321; Cucumber-Mint Sauce, 294; Dill Spears, 322; Jam, Jelly, Preserve, and Condiment, 316; Pickle, Commercial, 430.*

CUMIN

Native to the eastern Mediterranean, cumin is the tiny aromatic seed of a plant in the parsley family. The amber seed is about ⅛ to ¼ inch long and resembles caraway. Its aroma and flavor are very pungent, spicy, and sharp.

Use Cumin is widely used in Latin American cuisines and is the predominant flavor in many Latin sauces, soups, and stews. Cumin flavors Moroccan lentil soup and tomato salads, Texas chili (it is an ingredient in most chili powders), and Indian curries. The French serve cumin seed with Muenster cheese.

Availability Cumin can be purchased whole or ground, in bulk or packaged in airtight jars or tins.

Selection Packaged seasonings lose quality after a while; try to buy from a store that restocks its spice section fairly often.

Storage Keep in an airtight container in a cool, dry, dark place. Replace ground cumin every six months; cumin seed will keep indefinitely.

Preparation Freshly toasted and ground cumin seed is much more aromatic than purchased ground cumin.

Toast seeds in a skillet over low heat, shaking pan constantly, until they are aromatic and just begin to smoke; do not allow to burn. Grind in a clean coffee grinder or electric minichopper or with a mortar and pestle.

> **Recipes and Related Information**
> *Cilantro Chutney, 130; Hummus, 418; Pakoras, 106.*

CURDLING

This is the often undesirable state when a mixture containing egg, milk, or cream separates into solids and liquid. Curdling can be a sign of spoilage in milk, temporary or permanent failure of Hollandaise sauce, or complete failure of custards, but is the first step in making cheese and the process by which cultured crème fraîche is produced. The villain (when there is one) is usually heat or acid.

In the presence of heat, proteins in egg (and to a lesser degree in milk or cream) slowly form a gel (a semisolid network that traps liquid and serves as a thickening agent). When overheated, the gel clumps (shrinks into curds) and the liquid is squeezed out of the gel—resulting in a curdled custard or sauce. An acid acts on milk or cream in a similar manner, causing it to thicken or even produce clumps, for example, when cream and fruit are combined. Sometimes this process is intentional: crème fraîche, a French cultured cream, is purposely curdled by adding an acid-producing bacterial culture to pasteurized whipping cream. It can be made at home by adding buttermilk, an acid, to cream.

To avoid curdling, the key is control. Heat these mixtures slowly to set the protein and keep stirring to break up clumps of protein as they begin to form. You want the proteins to start to solidify—that is the thickening process—but not more than necessary. When adding eggs to a hot liquid, first mix some of the liquid slowly into the eggs to bring up their temperature; then add warmed egg mixture to hot liquid.

CURE, TO

To preserve foods, particularly meats and fish. Most curing involves a brine, which is a mixture of salt and other ingredients. By effecting chemical changes in the food, the brine protects it from harmful bacterial growth.

There are two basic types of brines, a dry and a wet. A sugar-cure is perhaps the best-known dry brine; a sugar-salt mixture is rubbed on a food, which is then packed tightly, weighted slightly, and turned every few days until the cure is completed. Prosciutto, bacon, and *gravlax,* the Scandinavian salmon dish, are sugar-cured.

A wet cure uses a brining stock made with water, salt, and flavorings; a food is covered in the brining liquid until

cured. Corned beef is wet-cured. Saltpeter (sodium nitrate or potassium nitrate) is usually added to preserve color. Most smoked foods are first brined to add flavor and to help preserve them. Pickling, curing, and brining are very similar processes.

> **Recipes and Related Information**
> *Beef, 39; Gravlax, 233.*

CURRANT

The currant is the small round berrylike fruit of a prickly shrub. It is probably native to Scandinavia, where it is still a popular fruit; it is also much appreciated in England and Germany. Although currants have been cultivated in America, cultivation is now discouraged—and in some areas forbidden—because the shrub is host to a parasite that kills neighboring white pines.

Currants may be red, white, or black. All are tart but the former two may be eaten raw with sugar; the black variety is too bitter to eat fresh. The small, raisinlike dried Zante currant is actually a grape but is discussed here.

Use Fresh red or white currants may be eaten with cream and sugar; along with the black variety, they may be cooked with sugar and made into pie fillings, puddings, dessert sauces, jams, and jellies. Red currant jelly is stirred into Cumberland sauce, an English sauce for game. It's also used to fill jelly rolls and Danish pastry, to fill and glaze baked apples or pears, and to sweeten braised red cabbage. Black currants are made into jams and jellies; in France they are made into a nonalcoholic syrup called *sirop de cassis* and an alcohol-based liqueur called *crème de cassis*, used in French apéritifs.

Dried Zante currants add sweetness to cakes, cookies, breads, and scones. They may be used whenever raisins are called for.

Availability Fresh currants are rarely available commercially. Specialty produce markets may occasionally carry them in July and August. Currant jelly is widely sold packed in jars; whole currants packed in light syrup are available in some specialty food stores.

Fresh Zante currants are not widely distributed commercially but may be found in some specialty markets in midsummer. Dried Zante currants are available in bulk or packed in boxes.

Storage Keep fresh currants in a plastic bag in the refrigerator and use within a couple of days. They may be frozen for up to two months. Store dried Zante currants in an airtight container; they will keep indefinitely.

Preparation When using fresh currants, discard any crushed or bruised fruit, wash, dry, and remove stems.

CUSTARD

Beloved by children of all ages, custard is a mixture of eggs, milk, sugar, salt, and flavoring, either gently cooked on top of the stove until thickened but still pourable (stirred custard), or slowly baked until firm (baked custard). Although a seemingly simple food, custard is temperamental and must be assembled and cooked with great care and attention. It is such a classic dish, with so many applications, that all cooks should develop a level of comfort with its preparation.

Stirred custard, also known as *crème anglaise*, is used as a sauce, as a pastry filling, and as the base for many chilled and frozen desserts, including ice cream and Bavarian cream. Baked custard is wonderful simply garnished with fresh fruit or whipped cream, or bathed in caramelized sugar syrup as in the famous French dessert *crème caramel* and its Latin counterpart, flan.

Made properly, custard is creamy and tender, not the curdled or weepy mess that has frustrated most cooks at one time or another. Custards thicken because egg proteins jell (form a semisolid network that enmeshes liquid) in the presence of heat. As a general rule, 1 whole egg or 2 egg yolks will thicken 1 cup milk. Problems occur when mixture is cooked too quickly and at too high a temperature. Always cook custards slowly and with gentle heat.

Stirred custards usually take about 10 to 12 minutes to thicken. Don't rush the process by raising the temperature. The line between a thickened custard and a curdled one is often only a few degrees of heat. Protect stirred custards by using a double boiler over hot, but never boiling, water. Keep stirring throughout cooking time to break up and evenly disperse the gel as it forms; this action will develop a thick mixture that is not rigid or lumpy. A custard has thickened sufficiently when it leaves a velvety coat on the back of a spoon and if a track made by running a finger down the coated spoon stays clear. It will have the consistency of cream whipped to soft peaks. Remove finished custard from heat immediately as it will continue to thicken as it cools. Strain into a bowl to achieve a smooth texture (for the same reason, strain baked custards before pouring into baking dish). Set pan in a bowl of ice or ice water to stop cooking. If you think custard has overheated, add a few slivers of ice to lower temperature. If the custard starts to curdle while cooking, remove from heat immediately and beat.

Although baked custards aren't stirred, they still must be prepared with care. They need to cook in a moderate oven and should be insulated from the heat by being set in a pan of hot water (a bain-marie or hot water bath). They are done when the center still jiggles slightly and a knife inserted halfway between center and edge comes out clean. Another test is to touch the surface with your finger; if it comes away clean, custard is ready. When properly cooked, texture is smooth and fine. An overheated baked custard is watery.

■ STIRRED CUSTARD
Crème anglaise

This is the basic vanilla custard sauce. It can be used right away or held in the refrigerator. For additional flavor, add 2 tablespoons orange-flavored liqueur (or liqueur of choice) to the finished sauce.

  2 cups milk
  ½ vanilla bean *or* 1 teaspoon vanilla extract
  4 egg yolks
  3 tablespoons sugar

1. If using vanilla bean, bring milk to a boil with bean in a heavy-bottomed saucepan, remove from heat, and let sit for 10 to 15 minutes to infuse milk with vanilla flavor. If using extract, it is added later; bring milk without flavoring to a boil.

2. In a medium bowl beat yolks and sugar together until thickened and lemon-colored. Add milk, stirring to combine well.

3. Turn mixture into a double boiler or return to same saucepan and cook over low heat, stirring, until it thickens and coats back of a spoon (about 10 minutes; a finger drawn across back of spoon should leave a trail). Remove custard from heat and strain through a fine sieve into a clean bowl set over ice to stop cooking; if using vanilla extract, stir in. Note that if using vanilla bean, which has now been strained out of custard, it can be put back into custard to enhance flavor further, or it can be washed, dried, and stored for later use.

4. Use custard immediately as a sauce, or refrigerate, with plastic wrap laid on surface to prevent a skin from forming, for up to 24 hours.

Makes about 2 cups.

■ BAKED CUSTARD

This is true comfort food, enriched with the addition of extra egg yolks. For a smooth consistency, remember to strain the custard before putting into the baking dish. Baked custard may be served immediately after cooking or set in the refrigerator to chill.

  2 eggs
  2 egg yolks
  2 cups milk
  3 tablespoons sugar
  Vanilla extract or freshly grated nutmeg, to taste

1. Preheat oven to 350° F. In a medium bowl beat eggs, egg yolks, milk, sugar, and vanilla together; strain through a sieve into a 1-quart baking dish or soufflé dish.

2. Set in a larger pan and fill pan with enough hot water to reach halfway up sides of baking dish. Bake until just set (30 to 35 minutes; center will be slightly wobbly). Serve warm, or refrigerate and serve chilled.

Serves 4 to 5.

A hot water bath (bain-marie) is used for Baked Chocolate Custard to ensure very gentle cooking and to guard against overheating.

■ BAKED CHOCOLATE CUSTARD
Petit pots de crème

Little porcelain custard pots with matching lids have given their name to the rich custard dish that is served in them. The most common flavor for this custard is chocolate, although coffee and vanilla are other popular choices. The custards must chill for several hours or overnight; they will keep up to one day, covered, in the refrigerator.

> **6 ounces semisweet chocolate, chopped**
> **3 cups half-and-half**
> **1 vanilla bean**
> **1 egg**
> **8 egg yolks**
> **⅓ cup sugar**
> **2 teaspoons instant coffee powder dissolved in 2 tablespoons hot water**

1. Preheat oven to 325° F. Melt chocolate in a double boiler over hot, but not boiling, water. In a medium, heavy-bottomed saucepan, bring half-and-half to a boil with vanilla bean, remove from heat, and let sit for 10 to 15 minutes to let milk infuse with vanilla flavor.

2. In a medium bowl beat egg, yolks, and sugar until thickened and lemon-colored. Add milk, stirring to combine well. Add dissolved coffee and warm, melted chocolate. Stir well to combine into a creamy mixture. Strain mixture through a sieve into a pitcher and skim off any bubbles or foam from surface. Fill 7 individual molds (5 ounces each) or 8 *pots de crème;* set custards in

a baking dish or pan and fill with enough hot water to reach halfway up sides of molds.

3. Bake until set (35 to 40 minutes). Remove from oven and cool to room temperature; cover and refrigerate at least 3 hours, or overnight. Serve lightly chilled.

Serves 8.

■ CREME CARAMEL

The Spanish counterpart for this satiny smooth, syrup-drenched, baked French custard is flan. Note that the dish must be prepared at least six hours in advance of serving, and preferably the day before.

> **½ cup sugar**
> **¼ cup water**
> **Baked Custard (opposite page)**

1. In a small, heavy-bottomed saucepan, dissolve sugar in the water over low heat (stir only until dissolved; do not stir while it colors). As soon as sugar is dissolved, raise heat to a boil and cook until it turns light brown (8 to 10 minutes). Remove caramel from heat and pour into a 1-quart ovenproof baking dish or soufflé dish. Set aside.

2. Prepare Baked Custard through step 1. Strain through a sieve onto reserved caramel. Bake as for Baked Custard. Cool and refrigerate for at least 6 hours, or preferably overnight (you will have more caramel syrup if you make the dish a day in advance).

Serves 4 to 5.

■ CREME BRULEE

This famous dessert, also known as burnt cream or Trinity cream, is a rich custard protected by a sugary crust broiled golden brown. England claims it as its own, although its lineage is often debated. It is a standard dish on the menu at celebratory dinners at Trinity College in Cambridge, where it is said to have originated.

> 3 cups whipping cream
> 1 vanilla bean, split
> 6 egg yolks
> 3 tablespoons granulated sugar
> 1½ cups superfine or brown sugar, for topping

1. *To make custard:* In a medium, heavy-bottomed saucepan, bring cream to a boil with vanilla bean, remove from heat, and let sit for 10 to 15 minutes to infuse milk with vanilla flavor.

2. In a medium bowl beat yolks and granulated sugar together until thickened and lemon-colored. Add warm cream, stirring to combine well.

3. Turn mixture into a double boiler or return to same saucepan and cook over low heat, stirring, until mixture thickens and coats back of a spoon (about 10 minutes; a finger drawn across back of spoon should leave a trail). Remove custard from heat and strain through a fine sieve into a clean bowl. (Vanilla bean can be washed, dried, and stored for later use.)

4. Pour into a 3-cup shallow baking dish or 4 individual 5-ounce molds. Chill 2 to 3 hours, or overnight.

5. *To make sugar crust:* Preheat broiler. Remove custard from refrigerator; sieve superfine sugar over custard. Brown sugar under broiler until caramelized; watch carefully so that sugar doesn't burn (to keep custards cold while they broil, set them in a tray of ice, if desired). Chill until ready to serve.

Serves 4.

Variation   For a firmer custard use 2 whole eggs and 4 egg yolks instead of all yolks.

■ BAVARIAN CREAM

When a stirred custard is lightened with whipped cream and set with gelatin, it becomes a delightful chilled dessert called Bavarian Cream. Shape in a lightly oiled mold or use as a filling for desserts such as Charlotte Russe (at right) or Lemon Roulade Charlotte (see page 171). The filling for the Charlotte Russe is a basic vanilla Bavarian; if desired, substitute 2 tablespoons rum, orange-flavored liqueur, or other liqueur for the vanilla extract. To use by itself, spoon into a 4- to 5-cup oiled mold and chill four hours or overnight. For a fruit-flavored Bavarian cream, use the Lemon Bavarian Cream filling recipe from Lemon Roulade Charlotte and substitute an equal amount of lightly sweetened, puréed fruit for the Lemon Curd. Spoon into an oiled 4- to 5-quart mold and chill four hours, or overnight.

For a particularly effective presentation, layer two colors of Bavarian cream in one mold or marble two of contrasting colors, such as vanilla and strawberry.

■ CHARLOTTE RUSSE

A special tinned steel charlotte mold with flaring sides is traditional for this dish, but any ovenproof dish of the proper size will work.

> 24 to 30 ladyfingers (see page 84 and Note, below)
> 2 cups whipping cream
> 4 egg yolks
> ⅓ cup sugar
> 1 envelope unflavored gelatin
> 2 tablespoons water
> 1 tablespoon vanilla extract
> 1 cup Chantilly Cream (see page 252), for decoration
>   Raspberry or Strawberry Sauce (see page 522), for accompaniment

1. Tightly line a 6-cup charlotte mold or soufflé dish with ladyfingers, standing them on end, sides touching. Cover with plastic wrap and set aside. Whip 1 cup whipping cream to soft peaks and set aside.

2. In a medium, heavy-bottomed saucepan, bring remaining cup of cream to a boil. In a medium bowl beat yolks and sugar together until thickened and lemon-colored. Add cream to yolk mixture and stir well.

3. Turn mixture into a double boiler or return to same saucepan, and cook over low heat, stirring, until mixture thickens and coats back of a spoon (about 10 minutes; a finger drawn across back of spoon should leave a trail). Remove custard from heat and strain through a fine sieve into a clean bowl set over ice to stop cooking.

4. In a small saucepan sprinkle gelatin over the water and let stand to soften; dissolve over low heat (3 to 4 minutes). Pour into warm custard and stir to blend thoroughly. Add vanilla and keep stirring until mixture is on point of setting (it will have the consistency of cream whipped to soft peaks); fold in whipped cream.

5. Pour mixture into lined mold, smooth top, cover, and refrigerate until set (2 to 4 hours). Any leftover ladyfingers can be crumbled and sprinkled over top of custard before refrigerating.

6. To serve, unmold charlotte by carefully running a knife between ladyfingers and mold. Invert onto a serving platter. Pipe rosettes of Chantilly Cream around top edge (if desired), and spoon a pool of Raspberry or Strawberry Sauce around bottom of charlotte.

Serves 6.

Note   If using packaged ladyfingers that are a little sticky, sprinkle them with sugar before lining mold.

■ LEMON ROULADE CHARLOTTE

This is a spectacular rolled charlotte. Although the preparation takes time, so much of it can be, or needs to be, done in advance that it's actually a good party dessert. Use lemon or any flavor Bavarian cream (see opposite page) and fill with a fruit preserve instead of the Lemon Curd.

> 1 **Basic Sponge Cake Roll (see page 83)**
> 1 **cup Lemon Curd (see page 252)**
> **Basic Glaze (use apricot preserves; see page 250), for topping**
> **Raspberry Sauce (see page 522), for accompaniment**

Lemon Bavarian Cream

> 1 **cup whipping cream**
> 1½ **cups milk**
> **Grated rind of 1 lemon**
> 4 **egg yolks**
> ⅓ **cup sugar**
> 1 **envelope unflavored gelatin**
> ½ **cup fresh lemon juice**
> 1½ **cups Lemon Curd (see page 252)**

1. As smoothly as possible, line a round-bottomed 1½- to 2-quart bowl or mold with aluminum foil. On flat Sponge Cake Roll, evenly spread Lemon Curd, stopping 1 inch from each edge. Gently roll up, jelly-roll fashion. Cut into ½-inch slices. Lay slices in lined mold, beginning in center and working out to make a complete, balanced shell (save any leftover slices and lay over filling). Cover and set aside.

2. Pour Lemon Bavarian Cream into cake-lined mold, cover, and refrigerate 4 hours, preferably overnight.

3. To serve, unmold by laying a serving platter on top and inverting; lift off foil-lined mold. Brush with Apricot Glaze. Serve as is or with Raspberry Sauce (if desired).

Serves 8.

Lemon Bavarian Cream

1. Whip cream to soft peaks and set aside. In a heavy-bottomed saucepan bring milk and lemon rind to a boil. In a medium bowl beat yolks and sugar together until thickened and lemon-colored; combine with milk.

2. Turn mixture into a double boiler or return to same saucepan and cook over low heat, stirring, until mixture thickens and coats back of a spoon (about 10 minutes). Remove custard from heat and strain through a fine sieve into a clean bowl set over ice to stop cooking.

3. In a small saucepan sprinkle gelatin over lemon juice and let stand to soften; dissolve over low heat (3 to 4 minutes). Pour into warm custard and stir to blend thoroughly. When custard is cool, add 1½ cups Lemon Curd, stirring continually until mixture is on point of setting (it will have the consistency of cream whipped to soft peaks); fold in whipped cream.

■ ZABAGLIONE

Zabaglione is an Italian wine custard; sabayon is the French counterpart. Serve the frothy whipped egg custard warm or cold with crunchy *biscotti* for textural contrast, or spoon it over sliced strawberries.

> 6 **egg yolks**
> ½ **cup sugar**
> ½ **to 1 cup Marsala, sherry, or Madeira**
> **Sliced strawberries, or Biscotti (see page 8), for accompaniment**

1. Whisk egg yolks, sugar, and wine in a double boiler over simmering water. Whisk by hand or with electric mixer until mixture doubles in volume and is very smooth and fluffy.

2. Serve immediately with strawberries or Biscotti. Mixture is unstable and will separate if left standing. To serve it cold, set over ice and continue whisking until chilled. It will then hold for about 3 hours; serve as is, or fold in whipped cream, or gelatin and whipped cream.

Serves 4 to 6.

CUT IN, TO

To mix solid fat (butter, solid vegetable shortening, or lard, or a combination) and dry ingredients (flour, mixed with any or all of the following: salt, baking powder, baking soda, sugar) with a cutting motion. The process, used when making pastry, whittles the fat into smaller and smaller flour-coated pieces by the action of a pastry blender, two knives, a fork, the fingers, or the metal blade of a food processor, until reduced to the desired texture. *Rub in* is another recipe term that has the same meaning, but this process is done with the fingertips.

To develop flakiness, fat is left in relatively large pieces, usually described as coarse crumbs or small peas, rather than being ground so fine that it merges with the flour. As pie crust or biscuits bake, particles of fat melt and create empty spaces that fill with steam and expand. This expansion causes pie crust or biscuit to rise, and creates layers of crust or crumb called the flake. Large particles of fat leave bigger air pockets and create a lighter, more flaky pastry or biscuit; fine particles hardly leave a trace and produce a dense, sandy pastry or a biscuit that lacks characteristic texture.

Work with chilled fat and utensils (even the fingers, especially on a hot day). If fat starts to melt, briefly chill mixture; try not to heat the room with other cooking. Work quickly but gently so as not to toughen dough.

Recipes and Related Information
Biscuit, 49; Cake and Pastry Tools, 91; Pie and Tart, 431.

D&E

When deep-frying, use a wire skimmer to scoop food out of the hot fat; the open mesh lets the fat drain off the food and back into the pot. A deep-fat thermometer helps the cook monitor the temperature of the oil.

DASH

There are many arguments about what constitutes a dash. For dry seasonings such as ground cayenne pepper and chili powder, a dash is best described as a small pinch— what can be held between one finger and the thumb. For liquid seasonings, it's a few drops shaken from the bottle.

DATE

The ancient date palm, cultivated in the Sahara from Neolithic times, produces a glossy oval fruit that is as sweet as candy. Fresh dates are generally about 1 inch to 1½ inches long and ½ to ¾ inch wide. They have a thin golden skin; moist, sweet golden flesh; and a small brown pit. Most dates are marketed in their dried state, however. Dried dates are a darker brown with chewier, drier flesh and an almost candylike sweetness.

The date palm ripens fruit only in warm arid climates. Today most of the world's crop comes from Iraq, although most dates eaten in America are grown in the Coachella Valley in California. The main variety is the Deglet Noor, although the Medjool—a large and exceptionally moist variety—is increasingly grown in California.

Use   Dates may be eaten out of hand as a snack or dessert. They may be pitted and stuffed with marzipan or whole nuts; wrapped with bacon or stuffed with sausage and broiled; chopped and used to sweeten cakes, cookies, stuffings, breads, muffins, cooked cereals, and fruit salads. Moroccan cooks add dates to salads and stews.

Availability   The fresh crop is available from September through May, with peak supplies in November. Dried dates are sold the year around, in bulk or packed in plastic bags or boxes. Packaged pitted dates are also readily available.

Selection   Look for plump, lustrous dates with a rich golden brown color.

Storage   Keep soft fresh dates in the refrigerator in a plastic bag and use within one week. Dried dates will keep indefinitely if wrapped airtight and refrigerated.

Preparation   Unpitted dates are usually pitted before use, although Moroccan cooks add them whole to stews.

> ***Recipes and Related Information***
> *Date Filling, 627; Dried Fruit, 184.*

DEEP-FRY, TO

To cook food in deep, hot fat. As down-home as crisply fried fritters, as formal as chicken Kiev, deep-fried foods have wide appeal and can assume a multitude of guises.

Most people love the crunchiness of these foods but often hesitate to prepare them at home. Yet deep-frying is neither complicated nor difficult. Fried foods have a bad name, but it is not all deserved. Improperly frying foods can cause a lot of oil absorption, making them both unappetizing and unhealthful; but good technique prevents this. The keys to good frying are the quality of the oil, its temperature, and the coating on the foods to be fried.

OIL AND TEMPERATURE CONTROL

The best oil for frying is a clear, relatively flavorless vegetable oil with a high smoke point (that is, an ability to withstand high temperatures without burning). Oil temperature is critical. For best results the oil should be between 360° and 390° F. At this temperature, the batter or other coating seals almost instantly, preventing any further oil absorption. Oil that is too hot can burn the outside of the food before the inside is fully cooked. The oil itself will begin to burn at over 400° F, giving a burnt flavor to the food. Oil that is too cool is equally bad; below 350° F, the food will absorb a lot of oil before it is cooked.

To control oil temperature, either fry in a thermostatically controlled deep-fryer or use a thermometer specially made for deep-frying and candy making (see THERMOMETER). To keep the temperature up during frying, do not try to fry too many pieces of food at a time. Watch the temperature: If it drops below 350° F and does not recover quickly, you are frying too much food for the quantity of oil. One obvious solution is to use as much oil as you can safely and conveniently. Be careful, however, to leave enough room for the oil to bubble up during frying. As a general rule, the frying container should be no more than two-thirds full of oil.

Oil can be used three or four times before it is no longer suitable for cooking. Oil will last longer if particles of food are skimmed off after each batch of food has been fried. To store, cool the oil in the pot, strain through cheesecloth, and keep in the refrigerator for up to three months. Check for rancidity before using (see RANCIDITY).

COATINGS FOR DEEP-FRIED FOODS

In general, a coating shields the food from the oil. Because deep-fried foods come into contact with more fat than foods that are sautéed or stir-fried, there is a greater chance of overabsorption of the fat. The cook can prevent overabsorption by maintaining the proper cooking temperature and by sealing the food with a protective coating. There are three basic types of coating: Flour is the simplest one and forms a thin, crisp crust; the second type, which adds extra insulation, is a dipping of food in flour, egg, and bread crumbs, which form a crunchy barrier that preserves the moistness of the food within; the third alternative, fritter batter, forms a fluffy coating.

DEEP-FRYING TECHNIQUE

Deep-frying is most suitable for pieces of chicken, seafood, and vegetables. Foods to be deep-fried must be similar in size and thickness so all will cook at the same rate. They must be dry and at room temperature. Lower food into the hot oil gently; to avoid splashing hot oil, do not drop the food from a height. A slotted spoon, wire skimmer, or basket insert is best for removing the cooked food from the pan. Hold the spoon or other utensil containing fried food over the oil for a few seconds to drain, and then transfer to a plate or tray lined with paper towels to drain further. If frying many items, transfer the cooked pieces to a low-heat oven to keep warm.

To proceed, follow the general frying guidelines outlined in FRY.

THE DEEP-FRY PANTRY

The basic requirements for deep-frying are mainly coatings and oils. If you're going to be doing a fair bit of deep-frying and have extra storage space, you may want to purchase a fry basket, a slotted spoon, a spoon rest, and a deep-fat thermometer. These tools are a help in mastering the process.

In the Refrigerator Eggs, beer, milk, yeast.

On the Shelf Flour; cornstarch; dry bread crumbs; baking powder; salt, pepper, and other seasonings; vegetable oil; solid vegetable shortening; wine.

Equipment Kettle with wire basket insert and lid (the pot should have a flat bottom for stability), or an electric fryer; a deep-fat thermometer; a slotted spoon or wire skimmer; a spoon rest; paper towels.

■ PAPER-WRAPPED CHICKEN

Bite-sized pieces of chicken fried inside a wrapper of paper or aluminum foil are a popular Chinese appetizer. Marinades for the chicken can be complicated mixtures of condiments, or a simple combination such as the following. Parchment paper suitable for cooking is available at well-stocked supermarkets and cookware stores. Note that the chicken pieces must marinate at least 30 minutes and up to several hours.

> 1 **chicken breast half, skinned, boned, and cut into ½-inch cubes**
> 1 **tablespoon** *each* **soy sauce and Shaoxing wine or dry sherry**
> 1 **tablespoon grated fresh ginger**
> 1 **teaspoon sesame oil**
>   **Oil, for deep-frying**

1. Combine chicken, soy sauce, wine, ginger, and sesame oil; marinate for 30 minutes to several hours. Cut eighteen 4-inch squares of parchment paper or aluminum foil.

2. Place a square of paper on work surface, one corner facing you ("south"). Place 2 or 3 chicken cubes across center of square. Fold south corner over chicken to ½ inch from north corner. Crease fold. Fold in east and west corners so that they overlap each other, and crease edges. Fold whole package toward north, forming an envelope shape. Tuck north corner into envelope and crease to seal. Repeat folding procedure with remaining packages.

3. In a wok or other deep pan, heat oil to 375° F. Fry chicken packages, a few at a time, until paper turns golden brown (about 1 minute). To facilitate unwrapping, slit open each package along folded edge before serving. To undo package and eat contents, use fingers or chopsticks.

Serves 4 to 8 as an appetizer (2 to 4 pieces per serving).

Deep-fried packets of Paper-Wrapped Chicken are easily unwrapped with the fingers. Inside are juicy, tender pieces of ginger-flavored chicken breast.

HOW TO DEGLAZE

The instructions given here for making a deglazing sauce are based on Chicken Breasts With Sherry, Cream, and Mushrooms (see page 611). Sauté the lightly floured chicken breasts in the butter.

Transfer browned breasts to warmed plates. In the same skillet, sauté aromatic ingredients—mushrooms, garlic, and green onions. As they cook, scrape up any bits of chicken or flour stuck to the pan.

Add wine and boil vigorously to reduce in volume and cook away alcohol; add cream and reduce sauce again. Season to taste.

■ COUNTRY FRIED CHICKEN

This version of a classic southern preparation comes from North Carolina. The cook insists that its special flavor is the result of salting the bird a day ahead of frying.

    2 whole frying chickens, cut up
       Salt
    1 cup milk
    1 egg
    2 cups flour
    2 tablespoons paprika
    2 teaspoons salt
    1 teaspoon ground white pepper
       Dash cayenne pepper
    5 cups (approximately) solid vegetable
       shortening, for frying

1. One day ahead of serving, wash chicken pieces and pat dry. Lightly salt, and refrigerate 12 to 24 hours.

2. Two hours before serving, mix together milk and egg in a small bowl. In a sturdy plastic bag sift together flour, paprika, salt, white pepper, and cayenne.

3. Dip chicken pieces in egg-milk mixture; then shake pieces in plastic bag to coat with flour; shake off excess flour. Place chicken on a rack and let stand 30 minutes to allow coating to set.

4. In a kettle or deep-fryer over medium-high heat, melt shortening and bring to 365° F (use a deep-fat thermometer).

5. Gently slip chicken into hot fat and fry until golden brown on both sides (about 15 minutes per side). With a slotted spoon remove chicken pieces from pan to a rack lined with paper towels to drain.

Serves 6 to 8.

■ FRITTO MISTO WITH CAPER MAYONNAISE

A traditional Italian Christmas Eve food, *fritto misto* means mixed fry. Use any combination of fish and shellfish and serve as part of a buffet with an assortment of salads.

    2 cups flour
    2 teaspoons fresh rosemary *or*
       1 teaspoon dried rosemary
 1¼ teaspoons salt
    2 tablespoons dry sherry
    2 tablespoons vegetable oil
 1½ cups water
    1 pound squid, cleaned
  12 small smelt
  ½ pound angler, cut in ¼-inch medallions
    1 pound shrimp, cleaned
       Salt and freshly ground pepper
    4 to 6 tablespoons fresh lemon juice
       Oil, for deep-frying
       Lemon wedges (optional)

Caper Mayonnaise

    1 cup Mayonnaise (see page 519)
    3 tablespoons fresh lemon juice
  ¼ cup capers, drained

1. In a large bowl combine flour, rosemary, and the 1¼ teaspoons salt. Add sherry and 2 tablespoons oil to the water. Beat water mixture into flour mixture until smooth. Cover and let batter rest 1 hour.

2. Cut bodies of squid into 1-inch circles. Leave tentacles whole. Lay squid pieces, smelt, angler, and shrimp on a platter. Sprinkle with salt, pepper, and lemon juice. Let stand for 5 minutes; then pat dry.

3. In a kettle or deep-fryer heat oil to 375° F. Dip fish and shellfish into batter, then gently slip a few pieces at a time into hot oil to deep-fry. Cook until golden. Remove with a slotted spoon and drain on paper towels. Keep pieces in a warm (200° F) oven until all are fried.

4. Serve with lemon wedges or Caper Mayonnaise.

Serves 8 to 10.

Caper Mayonnaise Prepare Mayonnaise; whisk together with fresh lemon juice and drained capers until well blended.

> ### *Recipes and Related Information*
> *Batter, 27; Cookware, 151; Fat, 216; Oil, 394.*

DEGLAZE, TO

To pour liquid—water, stock, wine, or liquor—into a pan in which food has been roasted or sautéed in order to absorb the glaze and the browned, crusty bits formed on the bottom of the pan. These concentrated, coagulated meat essences add wonderful flavor to a dish or sauce.

To deglaze, remove meat from pan. If more than a thin film of fat remains in the pan, discard excess. Pour one of the above liquids into the pan and cook over high heat, scraping bottom of pan to loosen drippings into the liquid. From this point, a sauce can be made. It can be simple—using a mix of fresh lemon juice and stock—or rich, with whipping cream and grated cheeses. A variety of flavorings, from tomatoes and fresh herbs to mustard and soy sauce, can add excitement to deglazed sauces. As you become comfortable with this method, you will be able to create your own sauces. See photographs at left.

> ### *Recipes and Related Information*
> *Chicken Breasts With Sherry, Cream, and Mushrooms, 611; Drippings, 186; Sauce, 512; Stock and Soup, 558; Wine in Cooking, 608.*

DEGREASE, TO

To remove grease from roasting pans (being careful to leave the drippings in the pan), and to remove congealed fat from chilled stock, stews, or essences. Skimming fat is essentially the same as degreasing.

There are several ways to degrease a pan. *With a ladle or serving spoon:* Use a ladle for stocks and large quantities of liquid; use a spoon for sauces and small quantities. Stir the surface of the liquid to force fat to the edges of the pan; don't stir below the surface or the fat will be mixed with the other liquid. Tilting the ladle slightly, dip edge into layer of fat just enough so that fat streams into bowl of ladle or spoon. Move ladle around perimeter until full; repeat until all fat is spooned off. With a spoon, tip the pan to make a pool of fat, slide spoon in, and fill. *With a skimmer:* The wire mesh or perforated-metal skimmer is a cleanup tool used to catch any fat that remains after degreasing with a ladle or spoon. Use as you would a spoon, tipping the pan to pool the little fat that may remain. Slide skimmer into pan and trap fat. *With filter paper:* A coffee filter (or paper towel) can be used to soak up small amounts of fat. Lay paper on surface and let it absorb fat; pull away and repeat as needed. *By chilling:* Bring stock, sauce, or soup to room temperature; cover and chill until fat hardens, then carefully spoon off solid fat. See photographs at right.

> **Recipes and Related Information**
> *Stew, 555; Stock and Soup, 558.*

DEVEIN, TO

To remove the black intestinal vein that runs along the outside curve of a shrimp (see photograph, page 537). This often cosmetic procedure is usually unnecessary on small- or medium-sized shrimp. On larger shrimp, the vein contains grit that would interfere with the taste and should be removed. To devein, slit shrimp along the back with a sharp knife or a deveining tool and pull away vein. Sometimes the vein snaps; to remove the pieces, hold shrimp under cold running water and vein will wash away.

DICE, TO

To cut into even, tiny cubes. Dicing results in smaller pieces than does chopping but larger than with mincing. This term refers primarily to vegetables, but can apply to any food that can hold this shape. To dice a vegetable, cut first into sticks, then cut sticks into cubes. The size of the sticks and how thick you slice them control the size of the dice. See KNIFE, Cutting Techniques.

DILL

A member of the parsley family, dill is both an herb and a spice. The soft feathery leaves are harvested for use as an herb called dill weed; the small, hard, dried seeds are used as a spice. The leaves have a refreshing, cool quality; the seeds have a warm, slightly bitter pungency. Dill seed is a component of most pickling spice mixtures.

Use   Dill weed is the main flavoring agent in dill pickles. It may be added to other vegetable pickles or used in salads, soups, cream sauces, vegetable sautés, and savory yeast breads. It has an affinity for cucumbers and fish. Scandinavian cooks use it to flavor salt- and sugar-cured salmon (*gravlax*); they add it to shrimp dishes, to cucumbers in sour cream, and to open-faced sandwiches. Use dill seed in breads, pickles, sauerkraut, and cole slaw.

Availability   Fresh dill is sold the year around in many supermarkets, with peak supplies in summer months. Dried dill weed and dill seed are sold in bulk or packed in jars, tins, or plastic bags.

Selection   Choose fresh-looking bunches without evidence of drying, wilting, or decay. Packaged seasonings lose quality after a while; try to buy from a store that restocks its spice section fairly often.

Storage   Wrap fresh dill in damp paper towels, then in a plastic bag and refrigerate in crisper; use within a few days. Keep dried dill weed in an airtight container in a cool, dark, dry place and use within six months. Store dill seed in an airtight container in a cool, dark, dry place; it will keep indefinitely.

> **Recipes and Related Information**
> *Bohemian Pork Goulash, 459; Dill Spears, 322; Gravlax, 233; Herb Biscuits, 49; Sour Cream Cucumber Salad, 166; Stuffed Grape Leaves, 281.*

DILUTE, TO

To weaken or tone down a liquid because its flavor is too strong for a particular purpose. For example, if an oil and vinegar dressing has too much bite, it can be tamed by increasing the amount of oil in the mixture.

DISJOINT, TO

A butchering technique that means to separate at the joints, it most often refers to poultry. A joint is the point where bones connect to one another; they are held together by tendons and cartilage, which have more give than bone and are therefore easier to cut through. With some experience, your hands will learn to recognize this elastic tissue by touch.

HOW TO DEGREASE

With a ladle or serving spoon   Dip edge of ladle or spoon into surface and let fat flow into bowl; repeat until all fat is spooned off. If needed, trap any remaining fat with a perforated metal or wire mesh skimmer.

With filter paper   Lay a paper coffee filter (or paper towel) on the surface of the liquid; it will absorb fat. Remove filter when saturated and repeat until all fat is absorbed. Change filter paper as needed.

By chilling   When chilled, fat will harden into a solid layer and can be easily removed. Let liquid come to room temperature before placing in refrigerator; remove hardened layer with a spoon.

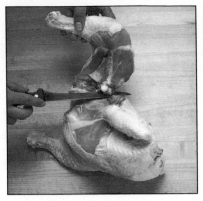

DISJOINTING POULTRY

With a sharp boning knife, cut with even strokes through skin between leg and breast to expose joint. Hold body with one hand and leg with other hand; lift leg up and pop the hip joint free.

Cut along remaining connective tissue with smooth, easy strokes until leg has been cut free. Hold leg up as you cut it away so weight of carcass is in counterbalance to leg; this tension will help to separate leg from body. Repeat for other leg.

To separate drumstick from thigh, if desired, rotate leg to locate joint. Lay piece right side up. At line where leg and thigh join, cut through to see joint, then cut through completely.

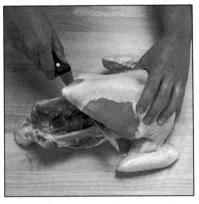

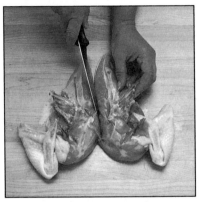

To remove breast, use rib cage as guide, cut through flap of skin just below rib cage until you hit resistance (point where rib cage begins). Pull back with hands to pop backbone; cut through tag of flesh that still holds backbone. At sides of rib cage, cut down just until you meet resistance (just below wing joint). Pull back slightly on rib cage between wing joints and cut to free wing joints on each side. Reserve back for stock.

To halve breast more easily, first remove breastbone: Turn whole breast underside up and make a slit through the white protective covering of the breastbone cartilage. Grab the breast with both hands, thumbs on either side of slit, and pull back to pop the breastbone free. With fingers, run along breastbone on both sides to loosen. Then gently but firmly pull bone to loosen further; cut away completely with a knife.

Cut through breast to wishbone. With a chef's knife or poultry shears, halve breast by cutting completely through wishbone. To remove wing, pull away from breast and cut at joint. You will now have two breast halves (with wings attached or separate), two drumsticks, two thighs, plus the back.

Disjointing is a simple, quick procedure if you know where the joints are or how to locate them, use a sharp knife and a cutting board, and have a relaxed approach to the whole process. By learning to cut up a whole bird yourself, you'll save money; poultry pieces cost more per pound because labor costs have been built in to the price. You'll also be a more confident and flexible cook, as you will have more control over food preparation even if you choose to have the butcher perform this service for you most of the time. See POULTRY, Preparation, for information on how to ready a bird for disjointing.

Recipes and Related Information
Bone, 55; Carve, 102; Chopping and Cutting Board, 129; Knife, 328.

DISSOLVE, TO

To add a solid to a liquid and cause it to become completely incorporated in the liquid or, in scientific terms, to pass into solution. Examples in cooking are dissolving gelatin or yeast in hot water, salt in a soup or stew, and sugar in hot cocoa. *Dissolve* also means to liquefy or melt, as when thinning honey or molasses by heating.

DOLLOP

A heap or pile of indeterminate size, *dollop* describes a generous spoonful of a semiliquid substance such as sour cream, whipped cream, or jelly added as a garnish or finish to a dish. The exact size of a dollop depends on the cook's taste.

DOT, TO

Usually part of the phrase "to dot with butter," meaning to place small bits of butter across the surface of food to be baked in the oven. The fat keeps the surface moist, adds richness, and can promote browning.

DOUGH

An uncooked mixture of flour, liquid, and often salt, eggs, sugar, fat, flavorings, and leavening, which is stiff enough to work with the hands. (Although a batter has the same basic composition, it is too wet to handle; batters are poured or dropped from a spoon.)

Doughs are classified by the ratio of dry to liquid ingredients. A soft dough, of the type used for biscuits and yeast breads, has approximately 3 parts flour to 1 part liquid. Stiff doughs, such as those for cookies and pie crusts, have more dry ingredients in proportion to liquid.

Recipes and Related Information
*Batter, 27; Biscuit, 49; Cookie, 139; Cream Puff
Pastry, 162; Doughnut and Fried Bread, 179; Pie and
Tart, 431; Puff Pastry, 480; Quick Bread, 490; Waffle
and Pancake, 598; Yeast Bread, 613.*

DOUGHNUT AND FRIED BREAD

A doughnut is a small fried cake, usually ring-shaped and leavened with yeast or baking powder. Fried cakes and breads are pieces of dough cooked in hot fat. Sometimes they are glazed, filled with jelly, or dusted with sugar.

If you've grown up eating only storebought doughnuts and fried breads, you'll find your own far more flavorful and delicate. Many of the recipes take no more time to prepare than a cake batter or a batch of cookies. You can also prepare dough the day before, so it takes only a few minutes to fry a batch of fresh doughnuts.

For frying you will need a deep kettle of hot fat. Peanut oil or corn oil is better than solid shortening for frying, since either oil can be heated to a higher temperature without smoking. The oil can be used again, but no more than four or five times. After that it becomes very dark and has an unpleasant odor when heated. After each use, cool oil completely, strain through cheesecloth into a bottle, cap tightly, and refrigerate.

The frying vessel can be either a thermostatically controlled electric skillet or deep-fryer, or a small roasting pan or Dutch oven heated on the stove top. Whichever you choose, have at least 2 to 3 inches of oil in the pan. A pan measuring 9 to 10 inches in diameter needs 2 to 3 quarts of oil, for example.

Choose your favorite from this doughnut array: iced Maple Bars (see page 183), Old-fashioned Cake Doughnuts dusted with confectioners' sugar (see page 180), sugar-sprinkled Yeast-Raised Doughnuts (see page 183), and plain cake doughnuts (see page 180). Fry the cutouts for bite-sized doughnut holes.

Keep frying temperature fairly constant—although it's bound to fluctuate a few degrees while you're cooking. A deep-fat or candy thermometer (see THERMOMETER) is the best gauge. Chopsticks or knitting needles are handy tools for turning breads as they fry.

You should wrap and freeze any fried breads you won't use in a day. To reheat, brush off any ice crystals and set on a baking sheet in a 350° F oven for about 7 minutes.

■ OLD-FASHIONED CAKE DOUGHNUTS

These favorites, with a slightly crunchy outside and a soft, cakelike inside, are easy and inexpensive to make. Serve while still warm.

    1 cup sugar
    4 teaspoons baking powder
    1½ teaspoons salt
    ½ teaspoon freshly grated nutmeg
    2 eggs
    ¼ cup butter, melted
    1 cup milk
    4 to 4½ cups cake flour
       Oil, for frying

Cinnamon Sugar (optional)

    ¾ cup sugar
    1 tablespoon ground cinnamon

1. In a large bowl stir together sugar, baking powder, salt, and nutmeg to combine.

2. Add eggs, butter, and milk; beat well.

3. Add 3 cups of the flour, beating until thoroughly blended. Add 1 more cup of flour and beat well. Dough should be rather soft, sticky, and just firm enough to handle. If necessary, gradually stir in enough of the remaining flour to make a shaggy-looking, barely manageable mass.

4. Cover with plastic wrap and chill for at least 1 hour or overnight.

5. In a Dutch oven, heavy deep skillet, or other frying kettle, begin heating at least 2 inches of oil to 360° F.

6. Scrape half the chilled dough onto a floured surface, then push, pat, and roll to make a mass about ½ inch thick. Cut doughnuts with a floured doughnut cutter. Set doughnuts and their holes aside on a lightly floured baking sheet. Push scraps together, reroll, and cut again. Repeat with other half of dough.

7. Fry about 4 doughnuts and holes at a time. Gently drop them into hot fat, and flip them over as they rise to the surface and puff. Turn a few more times as they cook. They are done when they turn golden brown all over (2 to 3 minutes). Remove with a slotted spoon and drain on paper towels. While doughnuts are still warm, toss in Cinnamon Sugar (if used).

Makes about 25 doughnuts and holes.

Cinnamon Sugar   In a small bowl mix sugar and cinnamon until well combined.

Chocolate Doughnuts   Omit nutmeg. Stir ½ cup unsweetened cocoa with dry ingredients in step 1, and add 1 teaspoon baking soda. Also add 1 teaspoon vanilla extract when milk is used in step 2.

Spice Doughnuts   Add 1½ teaspoons ground cinnamon, 1 teaspoon freshly grated nutmeg, ½ teaspoon ground cloves, and ½ teaspoon ground ginger to the dry ingredients in step 1.

Whole Wheat Doughnuts   Substitute 3½ to 4 cups whole wheat flour for cake flour. Doughnuts will not be quite as light and delicate.

■ CRULLERS

Some sources say that this twisted fried doughnut was once called an Aberdeen *crulla* (small cake), perhaps the origin for the name we know it by today. Whatever you call them, these spiced, lemon-accented Crullers are delicious for dunking in tea or coffee. They are tangy and tender because of the buttermilk in the batter.

    4 cups flour
    2 teaspoons baking soda
    1 teaspoon baking powder
    ½ teaspoon ground cinnamon
    ¼ teaspoon freshly grated nutmeg
    ¾ cup butter, cut in pieces
    ½ cup sugar
    ½ teaspoon grated lemon rind
    4 eggs
    ¼ cup buttermilk
    1 teaspoon vanilla extract
       Oil, for frying
       Sugar, for dusting

1. Into a large bowl sift flour, baking soda, baking powder, cinnamon, and nutmeg. Cut in butter until mixture resembles fine crumbs; stir in sugar and lemon rind. Make a well in center and add eggs, buttermilk, and vanilla. Stir to combine ingredients; turn out onto a lightly floured surface and knead 2 to 3 minutes.

2. In a Dutch oven, heavy deep skillet, or other frying kettle, begin heating at least 2 inches of oil to 365° F.

3. Shape dough into a square, then pat or roll into a rectangle approximately 10 by 24 inches and ½ inch thick. With a sharp knife cut dough into 5-inch-long by 1-inch-wide strips. Twist 2 strips together and fry, turning once, until golden on both sides (2 to 3 minutes total). Several can be fried at a time as long as they are not crowded.

4. Remove from oil, drain on paper towels, and sprinkle with sugar. Serve warm.

Makes 24 Crullers.

■ BUÑUELOS

Often available in Mexican bakeries, *buñuelos* are small, round, puffy pillows of sweet dough. The hollow centers make them perfect for Jelly Doughnuts (see page 183).

    ¼ cup butter, softened
    ⅓ cup sugar
    2 eggs
    1 teaspoon vanilla extract
    1¾ cups flour (more as needed)
    2 teaspoons baking powder
    1 teaspoon salt
    ¼ cup milk
        Oil, for frying
        Cinnamon Sugar (opposite page)

1. In medium bowl of electric mixer, cream butter and sugar together until blended. Add eggs and beat well. Stir in vanilla.

2. Stir and toss 1 cup of the flour with baking powder and salt. Add to first mixture and mix until blended. Beat in milk. Add remaining flour and mix to make a soft dough.

3. Turn onto a floured surface and knead 1 or 2 minutes until dough is smooth, kneading in more flour (you may need up to ½ cup more) if necessary to keep it from being too sticky.

4. Roll dough until it is about ¼ inch thick, flouring it lightly if it sticks. Cut into 3-inch rounds.

5. In a Dutch oven, heavy deep skillet, or other frying kettle, heat about 2 inches of oil to 360° F.

6. Fry about 6 Buñuelos at a time, turning them often, until they look like puffy, golden pillows (1½ to 2 minutes). Drain on paper towels and toss in Cinnamon Sugar while still warm.

Makes about 2 dozen Buñuelos.

■ CHURROS

Another Mexican fried bread, *churros* are made with long ropes of cream puff paste. In Mexico, the churro stand laden with these freshly cooked, golden sweet pastries is a common sight at all festivals. They should be eaten warm, when the outside is crisp and golden and the inside so puffy it's almost hollow.

    1 cup water
    ½ teaspoon salt
    1 tablespoon sugar
    ½ cup butter
    1 cup flour
    4 eggs
        Oil, for frying
        Cinnamon Sugar (opposite page)

1. Place the water, salt, sugar, and butter in a heavy saucepan. Heat slowly until butter melts, then bring to a full boil.

2. Add flour all at once, and beat vigorously until mixture is thick and smooth. Continue beating over medium heat for about 2 minutes, then remove.

3. Add eggs, one at a time, beating vigorously after each addition until mixture is smooth. (A handheld electric beater is useful.)

4. In a Dutch oven, heavy deep skillet, or other frying kettle, heat about 2 inches of oil to 390° F.

5. Scoop mixture into a large pastry bag fitted with a ½-inch star tip and fold down top of bag to seal. Squeeze bag over hot oil, pushing out a rope of paste 4 to 5 inches long. Cut with a knife, letting rope fall gently into oil. Rapidly form about 6 more Churros the same way. Turn them frequently until golden (about 2 minutes). Remove with a slotted spoon and drain on paper towels.

6. Fry remaining paste the same way, and while Churros are still warm, toss in Cinnamon Sugar.

Makes 3 to 4 dozen 4- to 5-inch Churros.

Churros and Buñuelos are both Mexican fried breads. Churros are ropes of cream puff paste, while Buñuelos are round, hollow, puffy pillows of dough.

Sopaipillas are light, airy puffs of deep-fried dough. Served piping hot, these weightless "pillows" are ready to receive a spoonful of honey in their hollow centers.

■ NAVAHO FRY BREAD

This specialty of the American Southwest proves to be both simple to make and addictive to eat. The bouncy, elastic dough is very forgiving and is even more easily handled when well chilled.

- 2 cups flour (more as needed)
- 1 tablespoon baking powder
- 1 teaspoon salt
- 1 tablespoon shortening or lard
- 1 cup boiling water
- 2 cups corn or peanut oil

1. Combine flour, baking powder, and salt. Add shortening and rub mixture between your fingers until shortening is well broken up. Pour the water into flour mixture and stir with a fork until mixture forms a ball. If flour remains dry, add very hot tap water, ¼ cup at a time, and knead in with fingers. If flour becomes too wet to form a ball, add flour by tablespoons. As soon as dough forms a firm ball, cover with plastic wrap and

allow to rest at room temperature for 45 minutes, or refrigerate overnight or longer. (Dough will keep, chilled, for about 1 week. It may also be frozen for up to 2 months and defrosted in refrigerator when needed.)

2. Lightly flour a pastry board or a sheet of waxed paper. Take a lump of dough about the size of a lime or a plum and lightly sprinkle it with flour. Place dough on floured work surface and push it down with the heel of your hand so that it forms a slightly flattened round. Sprinkle flour on both sides of the round and swiftly roll out to a rough circle about 5 inches in diameter (like a small corn tortilla). As each circle is rolled out, place it on an individual sheet of lightly floured waxed paper until ready to fry. (Dough will hold up to 1 hour.)

3. In a Dutch oven, heavy deep skillet, or other frying kettle, heat oil to 375° F. Just before frying poke a small hole in the center of each round of dough. Fry rounds, one at a time, until they are browned, puffed, and crisped on the outside (about 2 minutes per side), turning with tongs halfway through cooking. Regulate heat to maintain a temperature between 350° and 370° F. Remove from oil when done and drain on paper towels. Serve hot.

Makes 8 to 10 rounds.

■ SOPAIPILLAS

Another southwestern favorite, these airy fried puffs can be served for breakfast, at dinner (in place of bread), or even for dessert.

- 2 cups flour
- ½ teaspoon salt
- 2 teaspoons baking powder
- 2 teaspoons sugar
- 2 tablespoons lard or shortening
- ½ scant cup (approximately) hot tap water
  Oil, for frying
  Confectioners' sugar, for sprinkling
- 1 cup (approximately) honey, for accompaniment

1. In a medium bowl sift together flour, salt, baking powder, and sugar. With a pastry blender or fingers, cut in lard to make an even, lumpy meal. Add the water, stirring with a fork, until a dough forms. Flour your hands and rapidly knead dough about 12 times. If dough sticks to your hands, sprinkle on more flour by tablespoons and knead it in until dough is easily handled. If dough is too crumbly and dry to knead, add more hot water by tablespoons. After kneading, cover dough with plastic wrap and let stand at room temperature for about 30 minutes, or refrigerate overnight.

2. Preheat oven to 325° F. In a Dutch oven, heavy deep skillet, or other frying kettle, heat at least 2 inches of oil to 375° to 380° F. Meanwhile, flour a work surface and roll out dough in a rectangle about ¼ inch thick. Cut dough into 3-inch squares. Drop squares into hot oil, a few at a time, regulating heat to maintain a temperature between 360° and 385° F. The squares will fall, then rise, as they puff into little pillows. Push them down and turn often until they are golden. Remove with a slotted spoon, drain on paper towels, and keep warm in oven. Sprinkle with confectioners' sugar and serve hot with honey to spoon into the cavities.

Makes 16 puffs.

■ YEAST-RAISED DOUGHNUTS

These doughnuts are lighter and more tender than Old-fashioned Cake Doughnuts (see page 180) because they are leavened with yeast.

    1 cup warm (105° to 115° F) milk
    1 package active dry yeast
    ½ cup sugar
    1½ teaspoons salt
    ¼ teaspoon *each* ground cinnamon and nutmeg
    2 eggs
    ¼ cup butter, melted
    3½ to 4 cups flour
        Oil, for frying
        Cinnamon Sugar, optional (see page 180)

1. Pour milk in a large mixing bowl, sprinkle on yeast, stir, and let stand a few minutes to dissolve.

2. Add sugar, salt, cinnamon, nutmeg, eggs, and melted butter, and beat vigorously until blended. Add 2 cups of the flour and beat until batter is heavy but smooth. Add 1 more cup of flour, beating well, then add enough of the remaining flour to make a soft but manageable dough.

3. Turn out onto a lightly floured surface and knead a few minutes, until dough is smooth and elastic, sprinkling on a little additional flour if necessary to keep it from being too sticky.

4. Place in a greased bowl, cover with plastic wrap, and let rise until doubled in bulk (or refrigerate and let rise overnight if you wish to make fresh doughnuts the next morning).

5. Turn dough out onto a floured surface, punch down, then roll and pat until dough is about ½ inch thick. Cut with a floured doughnut cutter and set aside on baking sheets covered with waxed paper, leaving about 1½ inches between doughnuts. Reroll scraps and continue until all dough is cut. Cover with a towel and let rise until doubled in bulk.

6. When you are almost ready to fry doughnuts, heat 2 to 3 inches of oil to 360° F in a Dutch oven, heavy frying skillet, or other frying kettle.

7. Gently drop 3 or 4 doughnuts and their holes into hot fat. Turn frequently until golden brown on both sides (2 to 3 minutes). Remove with a slotted spoon and drain on paper towels. Fry remaining doughnuts the same way and toss while warm in Cinnamon Sugar (if used).

Makes about 18 to 20 doughnuts and holes.

■ MAPLE BARS

For authentic maple flavor, make the glaze with real maple syrup instead of an imitation product.

    1 recipe Yeast-Raised Doughnuts (at left)

Maple Glaze

    1 cup confectioners' sugar
    4 to 5 tablespoons maple syrup

1. Prepare Yeast-Raised Doughnuts through step 4. Turn dough out onto a floured surface, punch down, then press, pat, and roll to a fairly even rectangle about ½ inch thick. With a sharp knife, trim off any uneven edges. Cut into rectangles about 2 inches wide and 4 inches long. Set aside on baking sheets covered with waxed or parchment paper, cover with a towel, and let rise until doubled in bulk.

2. Fry as in Yeast-Raised Doughnuts. While still warm, brush top of each with Maple Glaze.

Makes about 15 bars.

Maple Glaze Beat confectioners' sugar and 4 tablespoons of the syrup together until smooth. If glaze is too stiff to spread, beat in a little more syrup.

Makes about ½ cup.

■ JELLY DOUGHNUTS

Another name for jelly doughnuts is Bismarks.

    1 recipe Old-fashioned Cake Doughnuts
        (see page 180) or Buñuelos (see page 181) or
        Yeast-Raised Doughnuts (at left)
    2 cups jelly or thick jam (do not use preserves;
        they will clog pastry bag)

1. Prepare one of these recipes, cutting cake doughnuts or raised doughnuts into rounds, not rings.

2. After pastries have cooled, use a knife point to make a small slit in the side of each pastry. Fill a pastry bag, fitted with a round tip, with about 2 cups jelly or jam. Pipe a generous tablespoon of jam or jelly into pastry.

Makes 18 to 24 doughnuts, depending upon recipe.

Recipes and Related Information
Deep-fry, 174; Fry, 254.

DRAIN, TO

To separate liquids and solids by setting both in a colander or strainer and letting the liquid pass through the holes (pasta from its cooking water), or by setting on absorbent paper (fat from fried food). This process also describes removing excess fat by pouring from the cooking pan into a receptacle, leaving only the pan juices.

DREDGE, TO

To coat food by sprinkling with a powder, for example, flour, cornstarch, or confectioners' sugar. For fried foods, a powdery coat ensures that the surface of the food will remain dry (moisture causes hot oil to sputter and drop in temperature; wet food steams instead of fries and won't brown properly). A coating of sugar sweetens fritters and other fried desserts.

DRESS, TO

The term *to dress* can refer to a number of processes. In classic French cuisine, it means the art of placing foods on a serving platter or plate in an attractive manner. It is sometimes used incorrectly to mean to eviscerate, but it can describe the preparation of meats by a butcher for retail sale.

DRIED FRUIT

Fruit may be dried by the sun or in commercial dehydrators. Valued not only for their packability and natural sweetness, dried fruits are also produced for their long shelf life and intense flavor.

Use   Dried fruits make a nutritious and convenient out-of-hand snack. Because they can be kept at room temperature for a few weeks without danger of spoilage, and because they are so light, they are an excellent energy source for backpackers and campers. Dried fruits are used in candies and confections, cookies, cakes, and breads. When used in baked goods, they are often presoaked to soften them; large ones may be cut up or minced. Dried fruits can be added to a stew or to a fruit compote. Raisins or minced dried fruits can be added to cooked or dried cereals. If plumped in beverage alcohol to keep from freezing, dried fruits can be added to ice cream or other frozen sweet desserts.

Availability   Most supermarkets carry a selection of packaged dried fruits, including raisins, prunes, apricots, and figs. Some supermarkets also carry dried fruits in bulk and mixed cut dried fruits. For a broad selection of dried fruits, both individual types and mixed, check health-food stores. The most commercially important dried fruits are discussed in this entry.

Storage   For long keeping, store all dried fruits in a plastic bag in refrigerator. Cut fruits (apples, pears, apricots, for example) may be kept for up to one year, and whole fruits (prunes and raisins) up to 18 months.

Preparation   If a recipe calls for chopped dried fruit, the fruit will be easier to chop if first tossed with oil or frozen. For 1 cup fruit, use 1 teaspoon vegetable oil. If the fruit is to be plumped, cover with very hot tap water and soak 2 to 5 minutes (longer results in flavor and nutrient loss).

CUT DRIED FRUITS

Some fruits—such as grapes, prunes, and figs—are dried whole. Others are cut and pitted or cored before drying. These include apples, apricots, pears, peaches, pineapple, papaya, mango, banana, and persimmon.

Among cut dried fruits, dried apricots are probably the most popular. Tree-ripened apricots are harvested at peak sweetness, cut in half and pitted, then placed, cut side up, on drying trays. Most apricots are then exposed to burning sulfur for several hours to prevent oxidation. They are then sun-dried and stored until shipment. When ready for shipment, they are cleaned, graded by size, and packed.

Most peaches intended for drying are freestone varieties. They are processed similarly to apricots.

Dried apples are made from mature apples that have been peeled, cored, sliced, and dried in modern dehydrators. When ready for shipment, they are graded and then packed.

Dried pears are processed similarly, although they are generally left in halves.

Cut dried fruits make a convenient and nutritious out-of-hand snack. They may be poached for a breakfast or dessert fruit compote or added to fruitcakes, quick breads, breakfast cereals, grain pilafs, steamed puddings, and stuffings. If desired, soak first in warm water to soften.

Recipes: Apricot-Almond Squares, 143; Apricot Filling, 627; Fruited Coffee Ring, 493; Your Own Bridge Mix, 59.

DRIED DATES

See DATE.

DRIED FIGS

Commercial dried figs may be sun-dried or dried in dehydrators. After drying, they are sorted and sent to processing plants, where they are inspected, graded by size, and stored until ready for shipment. Figs are packed just before shipment.

Although figs are one of the world's oldest fruits, the finest dried fig available today—the Calimyrna—is a fairly recent development. It is derived from the Turkish Smyrna fig, which was introduced to California in the late nineteenth century. It has a golden skin, a chewy moist flesh, and a particularly rich, nutlike flavor. The Black Mission fig is another fig variety that is frequently dried.

Dried figs are a delicious out-of-hand snack. They may also be poached whole for breakfast or dessert compotes. Minced figs add sweetness and chewy texture to cookies, cakes, breakfast cereals, grain dishes, steamed puddings, yeast breads, quick breads, and stuffings. Whole figs may be baked with butter and honey or steamed and dipped in chocolate for a rich dessert. See FIG.

PRUNES

Dried plums made from plum varieties that can be dried with the pit intact and without fermenting are called prunes. The fresh fruit is called a prune or a prune plum.

After harvesting, prunes are taken directly to a commercial dehydrator. After dehydrating, they are shipped to a processor or packager where they are inspected, graded by size, and stored until ready for shipment. Just before shipping, they are washed and cooked slightly to make them tender, drained, sorted again, and packed.

Prunes may be eaten out of hand as a snack or stewed and eaten cold or hot for breakfast or dessert. They make a delicious addition to fruit compotes or, when chopped, to fruit salads. Prunes add natural sweetness to savory stews and are an especially pleasing complement to rabbit, duck, chicken, and pork. Chopped prunes contribute sweetness and chewy texture to stuffings, fruit cakes, quick breads, breakfast cereals, grain dishes, cookies, and sweet fillings.

Recipes: Braised Pork With Prunes, 458; Prune Filling, 627.

RAISINS

California supplies about half the world's raisins, and about 95 percent of those are from the Thompson Seedless grape. Other grapes grown for raisins include Muscat, black Zante currant, and sultana.

To make raisins, grapes are harvested by hand at about 22 percent sugar content, laid out on paper trays between rows of vines, and sun-dried for three to five weeks. The trays are rolled and set under the vines for one to three weeks, then shipped to packing plants where they are washed, sorted, sized, packaged, and shipped.

To make golden raisins, Thompson Seedless grapes are not sun-dried, but instead are sent to the processing plant immediately after harvest. There, they are dipped in hot water and treated with sulfur dioxide to retain color, then dried in commercial dehydrators. Golden raisins are valued for their amber color and moist texture.

Muscat grapes have a distinctive perfume and flavor. The fresh grapes contain seeds, but the seeds are usually removed before the grapes are made into raisins. Raisins made from the round sultana grape have a small edible seed. Zante currants are very small, dark grapes (see CURRANT). Raisins made from them are correspondingly quite small and dark.

Raisins are a convenient and nutritious out-of-hand snack. They add natural sweetness and flavor to cakes, cookies, stuffings, stews, breads, muffins, breakfast cereals, grain dishes, salads, and fruit desserts. If desired, soak raisins in warm water to soften them or in brandy to flavor them before using in cakes and pastries. Sultanas and Zante currants are used in commercial baking to make a variety of cakes, steamed puddings, sweet rolls, and mincemeat.

Recipes: Biscotti, 8; Carrot and Baby Onion Stew With Raisins, 101; Carrot-Raisin Salad, 507; Cinnamon-Raisin Muffins, 375; Irish Soda Bread, 24; Lucia Buns, 99; Mincemeat Pie, 438; Nut-Currant Muffins, 375; Raisin Rice Pudding, 275; Rich Fruitcake, 88; Ricotta Cheesecake, 119; Roast Chicken With Rice, Fruit, and Almond Stuffing, 470; Rum Raisin Ice Cream, 312; Scones, 50; Sole With Almonds, Pine Nuts, and White Raisins, 533; Stuffed Grape Leaves, 281; Traditional Raisin-Oatmeal Cookies, 140; Your Own Bridge Mix, 59.

Dried fruit makes a delicious, chewy snack or a naturally sweet addition to baked goods, salads, entrées, and vegetable dishes. Pictured here are dried apples, pears, and persimmons.

Panforte is a specialty of the Tuscan city of Siena. Typical of Italian baked desserts, it is rich in nuts and dried fruit. A cup of espresso is a perfect accompaniment.

■ PANFORTE

Panforte is a nut-filled Italian confection that is a cross between a dessert and a candy. It can be served in tiny pieces accompanied by a cup of espresso after dinner. It also makes an excellent gift for those who love sweets.

>   ½ **pound whole almonds**
>   ½ **pound whole hazelnuts**
>   6 **ounces dried figs**
>   5 **ounces dark raisins**
>   5 **ounces golden raisins**
>   **Rind of whole orange**
>   **Rind of whole lemon**
>   ½ **cup flour**
>   ¼ **cup cocoa**
>   2 **teaspoons ground cinnamon**
>   ⅛ **teaspoon white pepper**
>   ⅛ **teaspoon mace**
>   ¾ **cup honey**
>   ½ **cup sugar**
>   **Juice of 1 orange**
>   ½ **cup confectioners' sugar**

1. Preheat oven to 350° F. Toast almonds and hazelnuts on baking sheet for 10 to 15 minutes. Remove from oven and cool. Reduce oven temperature to 300° F. Line an 8- by 8-inch baking pan with aluminum foil.

2. *If using a food processor:* Place figs, raisins, and orange and lemon rinds into food processor. Mix ingredients and process to purée. *If processing manually:* On a cutting board, finely chop figs, raisins, and orange and lemon rinds to a paste. Place mixture into a mixing bowl and stir to combine.

3. Sift together flour, cocoa, cinnamon, pepper, and mace. Add to dried fruit purée or mixture.

4. In a 1-quart saucepan heat honey, sugar, and orange juice until sugar dissolves. Carefully pour hot liquid into dried fruit and flour mixture. Add toasted nuts and stir to combine. Place fruit and nut mixture into prepared baking pan. Bake in preheated oven 50 to 55 minutes.

5. Cool in pan 10 minutes. While Panforte cools, dust a 12-inch square of foil with ¼ cup confectioners' sugar. Turn Panforte upside down onto coated foil and peel back foil used to line pan. Dust top with remaining ¼ cup confectioners' sugar. Cool completely.

6. Cut into 1-inch squares and serve immediately. To give as a gift, cut into quarters, cover in plastic wrap, and tie with ribbon.

Makes 32 bite-sized pieces or 4 squares for gifts.

■ WINTER FRUIT COMPOTE

This dish of dried fruits, plumped in spiced port, would be perfect for Sunday brunch.

>   ½ **pound (about 1¼ cups) dried prunes**
>   1 **package (6 oz) dried apricots**
>   1 **stick (2 to 3 in.) cinnamon**
>   ½ **lemon, thinly sliced**
>   **Juice of 1 orange**
>   3 **tablespoons brown sugar**
>   ¼ **cup port wine**

1. In a 2-quart saucepan combine prunes, apricots, cinnamon stick, lemon slices, and orange juice. Sprinkle with brown sugar. Add just enough water to cover fruits.

2. Bring to a boil, cover, reduce heat, and simmer until fruits are plump and tender (8 to 10 minutes).

3. Stir in port; transfer to a glass bowl. Serve fruits (with their liquid) warm, at room temperature, or chilled.

Serves 6.

DRIPPINGS

The juices that collect in the bottom of a roasting pan when meats or fowl are roasted are called drippings. After excess surface fat is removed, the drippings, full of the essences of the meat, are used as a flavoring agent, particularly for sauces and gravies.

Recipes and Related Information
Deglaze, 176; Perfect Gravy, 515.

DRIZZLE, TO

To pour a liquid such as butter or glaze in a thin stream over a surface to create a pattern of irregularly spaced, fine lines. For large amounts of food, drizzling is most effectively accomplished with a small ladle swirled in a tight circle so that the liquid just spills over the top. For smaller portions, dip a spoon in the liquid and shake lightly over food so that liquid falls in a stream.

Danish, cakes, and sweet breads are often drizzled with a confectioners' sugar icing as a final touch or with a thin crisscrossing of chocolate.

DROP, TO

To let a soft mixture fall from a spoon—such as dumpling batter into a simmering liquid or cookie dough onto a baking sheet.

DRY, TO

To remove moisture from raw foods before cooking, especially from those foods to be browned in some way, by patting with a towel. To dry also means to preserve food by drawing out its moisture. Drying can be accomplished at home in a dehydrator, in an oven, or in the sun. It is a relatively inexpensive way to preserve food. You pay only for the energy to heat the dehydrator or oven, and for the materials to make the trays.

METHODS FOR HOME DRYING: SUN, DEHYDRATOR, OVEN

There are several methods of home-drying: in the sun, in a dehydrator, or in an oven. The method you choose will depend upon the amount of time and money you wish to invest in drying and the types and quantities of food you intend to dry.

DRYING IN THE SUN

Sun-drying is by far the oldest method of preserving food. Although it takes longer than other methods—4 to 5 days of hot sun for most foods—it requires little investment. It's an ideal method in areas that have consecutive hot, dry days with temperatures in the nineties or higher, low humidity, and relatively clean air—for example, central California, the Southwest, and parts of the Midwest. Avoid sun-drying in areas where the air is dusty, animals are housed, or heavily traveled roads are nearby. People living in humid areas such as the South have had unsatisfactory results when sun-drying.

Certain fruits and vegetables are recommended for sun-drying because they won't spoil during the several-day drying period: apples, apricots, cherries, citrus peels,

TRAYS FOR DRYING

Drying trays can be simple cooling racks from your kitchen or elaborate home-constructed wooden models. Ultimately, your choice will depend on the drying method you select, the amount of time and money you want to invest, and the materials or equipment you have on hand.

Factory-made dehydrators usually come with trays, which are frequently made of plastic-coated or stainless steel screen embedded in a plastic or metal frame. Trays made entirely of plastic may warp and sag over time. Dehydrator trays are easy to maintain: Simply soak for a few minutes in warm water and wipe clean.

Trays for oven-drying and sun-drying are interchangeable. If you're planning to dry only a small quantity of food, rely on readily available tray materials. Cooling racks tightly covered with several layers of cheesecloth or nylon netting (available at fabric stores) work well. Secure the cheesecloth with straight pins; sew the nylon netting into a pillowcase shape and slip over each cooling rack.

If you plan to dry a large quantity of food in the oven or the sun, it's easy to make wooden trays. You'll need pieces of wood approximately the width and thickness of a stretcher for a painter's canvas, cut to appropriate lengths for the frame, kitchen string, and cheesecloth, nylon netting, or stainless steel mesh. Do not use aluminum, fiberglass, copper, or galvanized screen; all of these materials will negatively affect the quality of the dried food.

You can construct trays of any size, but keep these points in mind: For oven-drying, determine the dimensions of the trays by subtracting at least 1 inch from width and depth measurements of the interior of your oven to permit air circulation. Trays for sun-drying can be as large as you can handle comfortably; the larger the tray, the more drying space it offers.

When you have built the frame, run strings diagonally across the frame, tacking them at opposite corners, to support the cheesecloth, nylon netting, or stainless steel mesh. Stretch and tack the cheesecloth, netting, or mesh to the other side of the frame.

figs, grapes, nectarines, peaches, pears, plums, and pineapple among the fruits and chile peppers, lentils, peas, shell beans, sweet corn, and tomatoes among the vegetables. Meats and fish should not be sun-dried because there is a risk of spoilage. The only limit to the amount of food you can sun-dry at one time is the number of trays you have on hand. The recipe will give you specific directions for this method.

DRYING IN A DEHYDRATOR

Using a dehydrator is by far the simplest method of drying because it involves fewer variables than do sun- or oven-drying. You can dry virtually any food in a dehydrator, and, on the whole, dehydrator-dried food has a better appearance than food dried in the sun or an oven. Food also dries more evenly, and is almost impossible to scorch or overdry, in a dehydrator. The appliance can be left unattended and can be operated day and night. Finally, dehydrator-drying—unlike sun-drying—is not dependent on climatic conditions, although dehydrators perform best indoors, in a dry, well-ventilated room. Operating instructions vary from model to model, so consult the manufacturer's manual.

Dehydrators contain heating elements, which draw moisture from the food, and a fan, which blows warm air across the food to absorb the released moisture and carry it away. You can choose a ready-made dehydrator, available at department stores, hardware stores, or through mail-order catalogs, or you can construct your own.

Dried tomatoes in oil are a flavorful addition to salads or pasta, and they are not difficult to make in a dehydrator or in your oven.

DRYING IN AN OVEN

Oven-drying involves little or no investment in equipment. It is especially suited for drying a small quantity of food and for areas where sun-drying isn't possible.

Whether your oven is suitable for drying depends upon the *lowest* temperature it can achieve. Test your oven by heating it to its lowest setting, opening the door 4 to 6 inches, and measuring the temperature with an oven thermometer. The oven should maintain a temperature of 120° to 140° F. Too high a temperature will cook the food rather than dry it. Unfortunately, some older ovens offer a minimum temperature that is too high for oven-drying.

Heat should only come from the bottom of the oven. If your oven has a top heating element that gives off heat when the "bake" setting is on, remove the top element or place a large baking sheet on the top shelf as close to the heating unit as possible to deflect heat.

Options for trays to use in oven-drying are described in Trays for Drying (see page 187). Baking sheets are not recommended because they do not allow air to circulate all around the food. Tray size depends on the size of your oven. To allow air movement, trays should be at least 1 inch smaller than the inside of the oven. Use blocks or bricks to stack trays about 3 inches apart, allowing at least 3 inches of clearance at the bottom and top of the oven.

In general, to oven-dry, spread food on trays in a single layer; pieces should not touch each other. Preheat oven to 140° F; add loaded trays. Place a thermometer on the top tray toward the back of oven and monitor the temperature frequently, adjusting the oven thermostat to maintain a temperature between 120° and 140° F. To improve air circulation, prop the oven door open 4 to 6 inches and use an electric fan to keep moist air from accumulating. Place the fan on a chair or stool outside the oven. Position it to move air through the opening and across the oven, and set the fan on "low." Change the position of the fan from one side of the oven to the other every few hours.

Rotate the trays from top to bottom and from front to back every 2 to 3 hours. Turn pieces of food at least once. Food at the outer edges of the trays will dry faster, so needs removal before the inner pieces. Watch food carefully toward the end of the drying period because oven-dried foods can scorch easily when they are almost dry.

If you need the oven for cooking before food is dry, remove trays and keep in a dry spot. When you have finished cooking, allow the oven to cool to 120° to 140° F, replace the trays, and continue drying. The more frequently you remove the trays from the oven, the longer it will take the food to dry. Remember that food reabsorbs moisture at room temperature.

■ DRIED TOMATOES

The dried tomatoes will keep at room temperature for as long as the olive oil remains fresh. Refrigerate for longer storage. Add them to salads, serve as an appetizer, toss in pasta, or use to top pizza.

> 3 pounds Roma or other small
>   pear-shaped tomatoes
>   Salt, to taste
> 2 or 3 cloves garlic, peeled
> 2 or 3 small sprigs rosemary
>   Olive oil

1. Choose the smallest tomatoes you can find. Slice lengthwise almost in half and lay them open like a book (cut side up). Sprinkle cut surfaces lightly with salt.

2. Place tomatoes, cut side up, on drying trays. Dry in a dehydrator or the oven at 120° to 140° F: 4 hours or longer in a dehydrator or 24 hours or longer in the oven. When tomatoes are dry, they will be shriveled to small, flattish ovals and will feel dry but still pliable, not brittle.

3. Pack tomatoes, garlic, and rosemary loosely into 2 or 3 half-pint jars. Pour in enough oil to cover tomatoes completely—they may mold if exposed to air. Cap jars.

4. Let stand in a cool, dark place for 1 month for flavors to develop.

Makes 2 to 3 half pints.

DRY INGREDIENTS

This baking term refers to flour or other meal, salt, sugar, dry seasonings, and a chemical leavening such as baking powder or soda, as opposed to the liquids of a recipe—milk, water, butter, eggs, extracts, and the like.

DUMPLING

A small amount of dough cooked by boiling or steaming, a dumpling sometimes has a savory filling or is made into a sweet baked dessert of pastry-wrapped fruit. Dumplings are homey foods that are part of the culinary traditions of many cultures. Savory dumplings give substance to soup (Chinese wontons and Jewish matzo balls), can kick off a meal or be the main course (Italian *gnocchi*), and serve as a satisfying conclusion to a family supper or casual dinner party (American apple dumplings).

■ CHICKEN SOUP WITH DUMPLINGS

In one form or another, this straightforward, satisfying soup probably nourished all of us as children. Cake flour or a mixture of half cake flour and half all-purpose flour makes a lighter dumpling. An Herbed Dumplings variation is offered at the end of this recipe as is a recipe for Matzo Balls, which are dumplings made with matzo meal (ground from unleavened bread most often eaten at Passover).

> 2 cups cake flour
> 4 teaspoons baking powder
> 1 teaspoon salt
> 2 eggs, lightly beaten
> ¾ cup milk
> 16 cups Chicken Stock (see page 560)
> 6 small carrots, diced
> 6 stalks celery, diced
> 3 onions, finely chopped

1. In a large bowl sift together flour, baking powder, and salt. In a small bowl combine eggs and milk. Make a well in center of flour; pour egg-milk mixture into well and stir until well combined. Set aside.

2. In an 8-quart stockpot or Dutch oven, bring stock to a boil. Add carrots, celery, and onions; reduce heat to medium-low and simmer 10 minutes.

3. Drop dumpling batter into simmering broth, 1 tablespoon at a time. Cover and simmer for 10 minutes without lifting lid. Serve at once.

Makes 16 cups.

Herbed Dumplings Depending on herb used, blend 1 to 2 teaspoons of crushed dried herbs in with the dry ingredients. Continue as directed in step 1.

Matzo Balls In a medium bowl beat 4 eggs and combine with ⅓ cup melted shortening, ¼ cup water, 1 teaspoon salt, and a dash of pepper; mix in 1 cup matzo meal. Chill, covered, about 20 minutes. Shape mixture (with wet hands) into golf ball–sized balls and drop in simmering salted water or stock; cover and simmer about 30 minutes. If desired, recipe can be halved; cooking time will be the same.

■ GNOCCHI DI PATATE

Gnocchi are chewy Italian dumplings, most often made with potato as a base, although others are prepared with semolina flour or flavored with spinach. They may be served as a first course or main course, topped with butter or a sauce. Try Pesto (see page 27) or Ragù Bolognese (see page 412).

> 2 pounds Idaho baking potatoes (the older the better), unpeeled
> 1½ cups (approximately) flour
> 1 teaspoon salt
> 1 egg, slightly beaten (optional)
> ⅔ cup freshly grated Parmesan or Romano cheese, plus additional cheese for passing

1. Cook potatoes whole in boiling, salted water until tender. Drain and peel, then purée in a food processor or potato ricer, or put through a medium-mesh wire sieve. Place purée in a large bowl.

2. Add 1 cup of the flour, salt, and egg. Knead with fingers until smooth, adding more flour a little at a time until dough is no longer sticky.

3. Shape into long rolls about ¾ inch thick, then cut into lengths about 1¼ inches long. With your fingers, press each piece against the back of a fork so that one side will have impression of tines and the other will have a dent in the middle made by your finger. Each piece can also be rolled against the work surface with your finger to form a bow shape; set aside on lightly floured surface. Rest completed gnocchi on a lightly dusted board.

4. Cook immediately after shaping all the dough: Drop about ⅓ at a time into 4 quarts boiling, salted water. After they rise to the surface, continue to cook for 10 to 15 seconds, then remove with a slotted spoon to a heated bowl and toss in a little melted butter or some of the heated sauce in which you plan to serve them. Cover container with aluminum foil to keep warm while you cook rest of gnocchi.

5. To serve, pour selected sauce over gnocchi, add about ⅔ cup grated Parmesan cheese, and mix well. Pass additional grated cheese at the table.

Serves 6.

TIPS
PREPARING STEAMED DUMPLINGS

Light and fluffy dumplings are not difficult to make, but they are tricky enough that successful ones are applauded by appreciative guests, and failures deemed more suitable for bouncing than for eating. The secret is in what not to do. For those dumplings that are cooked covered, resist the urge to lift the lid while dumplings are steaming and you will be rewarded with an airy, tender product. When the lid is raised, steam escapes and cooking temperature lowers. In the time it takes to raise the temperature again, dumplings will overcook. Use a pan large enough to allow dumplings to expand as they steam, and keep cooking liquid at a simmer.

■ GNOCCHI VERDE

Green *gnocchi,* made with chopped spinach and green onion, can be prepared several hours ahead of time, then dropped into boiling water for cooking just before serving. (Gnocchi dough can also be frozen and used later.) Serve with the same sauces that accompany Gnocchi di Patate (see page 189) or use Tarragon Cheese Sauce, which appears at the end of this recipe. This dish can precede any roasted, grilled, or sautéed meat or fowl. Gnocchi are also delicious as garnishes for any clear soup, such as a plain consommé or a flavorful chicken stock.

> 1 **pound fresh spinach, chopped,** *or*
> 1 **package (10 oz) frozen chopped spinach, thawed completely**
> 1½ **cups ricotta cheese**
> 1 **cup fine dry bread crumbs**
> 2 **eggs, beaten**
> ¼ **cup freshly grated Parmesan cheese**
> ¼ **cup finely chopped green onion**
> ½ **teaspoon salt**
> 1 **teaspoon freshly grated nutmeg**
> **Flour, for coating**

Tarragon Cheese Sauce

> 2 **tablespoons butter**
> 3 **tablespoons flour**
> 2½ **cups milk**
> ½ **cup homemade Chicken Stock (see page 560) or regular-strength canned broth**
> ½ **teaspoon dried tarragon**
> **Pinch freshly grated nutmeg**
> **Salt and freshly ground pepper, to taste**
> ½ **to ¾ cup freshly grated Parmesan cheese**

Crumb Topping

> 3 **tablespoons fine white bread crumbs**
> 2 **tablespoons freshly grated Parmesan cheese**

1. If you are using fresh spinach, wilt leaves for about 30 seconds in a pot of boiling, salted water. Drain spinach well by putting it in a sieve or colander and pressing with a wooden spoon. When drained, chop finely.

2. In a mixing bowl combine spinach, ricotta, bread crumbs, eggs, Parmesan, green onion, salt, and nutmeg. Blend well, cover, and refrigerate for about 2 hours to firm.

3. When chilled, form gnocchi by rolling about 1 teaspoon of the mixture between palms of your hands into small, walnut-sized balls. Roll lightly in flour. Arrange on a tray lined with waxed paper. Refrigerate until cooking time.

4. To cook gnocchi, butter a shallow, baking dish; set aside. In a large pot bring several quarts of salted water to a simmer. Drop in gnocchi a few at a time, depending on size of pot, and regulate heat so water remains at a simmer. Gnocchi are done when they rise to the surface.

5. Remove cooked dumplings to buttered baking dish, using a slotted spoon for ease in handling. Continue until all the gnocchi have been cooked.

6. Fold sauce into gnocchi in baking dish. Sprinkle on topping and place under a hot broiler for 2 to 3 minutes to melt cheese and brown bread crumbs. Serve immediately.

Serves 4.

Tarragon Cheese Sauce   Melt butter in a saucepan. When it begins to froth, add flour and stir frequently over medium heat. Meanwhile, combine milk and stock and bring to a simmer. After flour and butter mixture has cooked for 4 or 5 minutes, remove pan from heat. When cooled slightly, add simmering liquid all at once and blend with a wire whisk until smooth. Return saucepan to medium heat and stir until sauce coats a spoon lightly and flour taste disappears. Add seasonings. Taste carefully and simmer 2 to 3 minutes. Add cheese and stir until fully incorporated.

Crumb Topping   Combine bread crumbs and Parmesan cheese; toss to blend.

■ SPATZLE

A traditional favorite German side dish, these nutmeg-scented morsels of batter are quickly boiled and then sautéed in butter until golden. A metal *spätzle* maker (see page 549), which looks like a strainer with ¼-inch-diameter holes, is handy to have. It's inexpensive and can be found in cookware shops. In a pinch, however, you can force the Spätzle batter through a flat cheese grater or a colander with large holes.

> 8 **cups water**
> 2 **cups flour**
> ¼ **teaspoon salt**
> ¼ **teaspoon freshly grated nutmeg**
> 3 **eggs, lightly beaten**
> ¾ **cup (approximately) milk**
> **Butter or margarine, to taste**

1. In a large saucepan bring the water to a boil.

2. Meanwhile, in a medium mixing bowl, combine flour, salt, and nutmeg.

3. Stir in eggs and gradually add enough milk to make a heavy batter.

4. Force some of the batter through holes of a spätzle maker or colander into the boiling water. Spätzle will cook quickly. As they rise to the surface, remove them with a slotted spoon to a colander. Rinse Spätzle with cold water and drain. Repeat until batter is used up.

5. Traditionally, Spätzle are sautéed in butter until golden brown. They're also good simply tossed with a little butter. Serve as a side dish with meat or poultry.

Serves 4 to 6.

Two different cooking techniques—panfrying and steaming—give Potstickers their unique combination of crisp, browned bottoms and tender tops. Try them with an assortment of fillings.

■ POTSTICKERS

These dumplings from northern China get their name from their method of cooking, a combination of panfrying and steaming that causes the bottoms to stick to the pan slightly. Getting just the right amount of "stick" without destroying the dumplings takes a little practice, so don't despair if the first few batches tear when you try to lift them from the pan. Practice this dish with family or not-too-fussy friends. The Pork and Shrimp Stuffing makes a delicious filling. Or, try the Pork and Cabbage Stuffing suggested for Wontons (see page 192). If you are in a hurry, use 1 pound of seasoned ground pork. Fresh potsticker wrappers are available at markets that specialize in Chinese foods. Well-stocked supermarkets should also carry them.

> ½ pound potsticker skins
> Oil, for frying
> ¾ cup water or thin chicken stock
> Soy sauce, chile oil, and black or rice vinegar for dipping, or one or more dipping sauces (see page 522)

Pork and Shrimp Stuffing

> ½ pound boneless pork
> ½ pound shrimp, peeled and roughly chopped
> ¼ cup *each* minced green onion and water chestnuts
> 4 teaspoons minced fresh ginger
> ¼ cup finely shredded carrot
> 2 tablespoons *each* soy sauce and Shaoxing wine or sherry
> 1 teaspoon sesame oil
> 1 egg

1. Prepare stuffing. Place 1 heaping teaspoon of stuffing across center of a skin and lightly moisten entire edge with a little water. Lift both sides of skin and pinch together in center of arc, above stuffing. Working on one side of center at a time, seal edges, making 3 or 4 pleats toward center as you work your way toward edge. Repeat on other side of center. Dumpling will naturally curl away from pleats to form a flat-bottomed crescent with a pleated ridge across top.

2. Heat a heavy, flat-bottomed skillet (nonstick or well-seasoned cast iron) with a tight-fitting lid over medium-high heat. Add enough oil to coat bottom generously. Arrange dumplings in pan in a closely packed circle, pleated sides up. Cook until edges begin to show browning on bottom. Add the water (careful—it will splatter a bit), and immediately cover pan. Reduce heat to medium and cook until dumplings are swollen and liquid is nearly evaporated (6 to 8 minutes).

3. Remove lid and increase heat to medium-high. Cook until liquid boils away and dumplings begin to sizzle in remaining oil. If oil is nearly all gone, add a little more for the final browning. Continue cooking until bottoms become crisp and golden brown. Loosen with a spatula and transfer to a serving plate. Serve one or more of the Chinese dipping sauces on page 522.

Makes 16 potstickers, 4 to 8 servings.

Pork and Shrimp Stuffing Grind pork finely in a food processor or mince by hand to a fine texture. Combine with shrimp, green onion, water chestnuts, ginger, carrot, soy sauce, wine, sesame oil, and egg.

Makes 2 cups.

Whether steamed or fried and paired with a dipping sauce, or simmered in soup, Wontons are among the most versatile and popular of Chinese dumplings. They can be cooked immediately after assembling, or frozen uncooked for later use.

▪ WONTONS

Probably the most familiar Chinese dumpling to Western-ers is the wonton, a relatively large noodle skin wrapped around a small amount of stuffing. Most often served in soup, they can also be fried or steamed. Fried, they go well with tangy sweet-and-sour sauces or mustard dips; steamed, they are best with soy sauce dips. To fill the wontons, use the Pork and Cabbage Stuffing given here, the Pork and Shrimp Stuffing from Potstickers (see page 191), or 1 pound seasoned ground pork.

> 1 pound wonton skins
> Oil, for deep-frying (optional)

Pork and Cabbage Stuffing

> ½ cup shredded cabbage (bok choy, Chinese, or any green variety)
> ½ teaspoon salt
> 1 pound boneless pork
> ¼ cup *each* minced green onion and bamboo shoots
> 1 tablespoon minced fresh ginger
> 2 tablespoons *each* soy sauce and Shaoxing wine or dry sherry
> 1 teaspoon sesame oil
> 1 egg
> 1 teaspoon cornstarch

1. Have at hand a small bowl of water with a brush for sealing edges. Peel off 2 or 3 wonton skins and place on the table, one corner "south" or toward you. Keep remaining skins covered with a towel to prevent drying.

2. Place a scant teaspoon of stuffing just south of center of skin. Brush near edges lightly with water and fold south corner over stuffing to within ½ inch of north corner. Press edges to seal. Pick up east and west corners and bring together at south end. Pinch or twist

slightly to seal corners together. Repeat with remaining skins and stuffing.

3. Keep finished Wontons covered with a towel to prevent them from drying, or freeze on a baking sheet and transfer to plastic bags when fully frozen. Boil in plain or lightly salted water before adding to soup, steam 6 to 8 minutes as a simple appetizer, or deep-fry in 375° F oil until golden brown and crisp.

Makes 60 to 70 Wontons.

Pork and Cabbage Stuffing Toss cabbage with salt and place in a colander to drain 30 minutes. Squeeze out excess moisture. Grind pork finely in a food processor or mince by hand to a fine texture. In a large bowl, combine pork, drained and squeezed cabbage, green onions, bamboo shoots, ginger, soy sauce, wine, oil, egg, and corn-starch; blend thoroughly.

Makes 2 cups.

Variation Substitute beef, lamb, or dark meat from chicken or turkey for pork.

Pork and Mushroom Stuffing Add ¼ cup soaked and minced black mushrooms (about 3 caps) to Pork and Cabbage Stuffing.

▪ GOLDEN CHICKEN STEW WITH CHEESE DUMPLINGS

Choose an attractive Dutch oven in which to stew this creamy chicken dish. After the fluffy, cheese-flecked dumplings have steamed atop the bubbling chicken, the stew is served directly from the pot.

> 4½ to 5 pounds meaty chicken pieces (thighs, drumsticks, and breasts)
> Salt, white pepper, grated nutmeg, and paprika
> 2 tablespoons butter or margarine
> 2 shallots, finely chopped (about ¼ cup)
> ½ pound large mushrooms, quartered
> 1 stalk celery, thinly sliced
> 3 medium carrots, sliced about ⅛ inch thick
> ½ teaspoon dried tarragon
> ¼ teaspoon dried thyme
> 2 cups water
> ½ cup *each* dry white wine and whipping cream
> 3 tablespoons cornstarch, blended with 3 tablespoons cold water
> ½ cup shelled fresh or frozen peas
> ¼ cup chopped parsley

Cheese Dumplings

> 2 cups flour
> 1 tablespoon baking powder
> ½ teaspoon salt
> Pinch freshly grated nutmeg
> ⅓ cup grated sharp Cheddar cheese
> ¼ cup butter or margarine
> 1 cup milk

1. Sprinkle chicken pieces lightly on all sides with salt, pepper, nutmeg, and paprika. Melt butter in a 4½- to 5-quart Dutch oven over medium heat. Add chicken pieces, about half at a time, and brown lightly on all sides, removing them as they brown.

2. To the same pan add shallots and mushrooms; cook, stirring occasionally, until mushrooms brown lightly. Spoon off and discard as much fat as possible. Mix in celery and carrots. Return chicken pieces to pot. Sprinkle with tarragon and thyme. Add the water and wine. Bring to a boil, cover, reduce heat, and simmer until chicken is tender (1 to 1¼ hours).

3. Remove pot from heat. Remove and reserve chicken pieces. Skim and discard fat from cooking liquid. Blend in cream. Place over medium heat; blend in cornstarch mixture. Cook, stirring, until mixture thickens and boils. Add peas and parsley, then return chicken pieces to sauce. Reduce heat to low.

4. Using two tablespoons to shape them, drop rounded dumplings about 1 inch apart over chicken pieces. To prevent dough from sticking, dip spoons into sauce before forming next dumpling. Cover and simmer until dumplings feel firm when touched lightly (15 to 20 minutes; do not uncover until dumplings have cooked for 15 minutes). Serve directly from Dutch oven.

Serves 6 to 8.

Cheese Dumplings   In a large bowl stir together flour, baking powder, salt, nutmeg, and cheese. Using two forks or a pastry blender, cut in butter until mixture resembles coarse crumbs. Add milk all at once, stirring just until ingredients are moistened and a soft dough forms.

■ **APPLE DUMPLINGS WITH NUTMEG SAUCE**
These dumplings from New England are made of whole apples wrapped in a rich biscuit dough, baked until tender and golden, and served with creamy Nutmeg Sauce. They are a perfect conclusion to a family dinner and a wonderfully homey dessert for guests. If you wish, omit the Nutmeg Sauce and serve with any remaining pan juices and a pitcher of cream or a scoop of vanilla ice cream. The amount of dough given here is generous, since it's far easier working with too much than too little.

    6 **Golden Delicious apples**
    2 **tablespoons** *each* **sugar and butter**
  1½ **cups apple juice**

Biscuit Dough

    3 **cups flour**
    2 **tablespoons sugar**
    4 **teaspoons baking powder**
    1 **teaspoon salt**
    1 **cup solid vegetable shortening**
    ¾ **cup milk**

Nutmeg Sauce

    1 **cup apple juice**
    1 **cup whipping cream**
    ½ **teaspoon freshly grated nutmeg**
    2 **tablespoons sugar**
    ¼ **cup butter**

1. Preheat oven to 375° F. Butter a 9- by 13-inch baking dish. Peel and core apples, leaving them whole; set aside.

2. On a smooth, lightly floured surface, push, pat, and roll Biscuit Dough to a rectangle 13 by 20 inches, keeping sides as even as possible and lifting and flouring often to prevent sticking. Cut in half lengthwise, then in thirds crosswise, thus making six 6½-inch squares.

3. Place an apple in the center of each dough square. One at a time, bring the 4 corners of each square together at the top to enclose apple. Twist and pinch attached corners together to seal. If dough tears, just patch it; don't worry if it looks a little ragged.

4. Place dumplings in prepared baking dish about 1 inch apart. Sprinkle with sugar and dot with butter; pour apple juice around dumplings. Bake until dough is golden brown and apples are tender when pierced with a toothpick or skewer (about 45 minutes). If they brown too much while baking, cover loosely with foil. While apples bake, prepare Nutmeg Sauce.

5. When apples are done, remove dumplings to a platter. Pour juices remaining in baking dish into Nutmeg Sauce, reheat if necessary, and pass sauce with dumplings.

Serves 6.

Biscuit Dough   In a medium bowl stir and toss together flour, sugar, baking powder, and salt. Cut in shortening until mixture resembles coarse crumbs. Pour in milk and stir with a fork just until dough holds together in a shaggy, cohesive mass. Turn onto a smooth, lightly floured surface and knead 10 times.

Nutmeg Sauce   In a medium saucepan combine apple juice, whipping cream, nutmeg, and sugar. Bring to a boil and boil until reduced to about 1¼ cups (about 10 minutes). Swirl in butter and set aside.

DUST, TO

To sprinkle very lightly with a powder. Dusting implies a fine coating, as opposed to dredging, which involves covering food with a heavier layer. Greased baking pans may be dusted with flour to keep batters and doughs from sticking; cakes and pastries are often given a light dusting of confectioners' sugar, cocoa, or ground nuts as a finishing touch.

Extremely versatile, eggs are a delicious food on their own. As a recipe ingredient, they add nutrients, flavor, richness, leavening, and thickening properties.

EGG

Among the most versatile and nutritious foods available, whole eggs contain vitamins, minerals, fats, and complete protein. The white is mostly water with some proteins; the yolk contains much of the protein and all of the fat, vitamins, minerals, and cholesterol. Although the eggs of ducks, geese, and other poultry are important to some cuisines, chicken eggs are by far the most commonly used. In general, this entry pertains to chicken eggs only; see Availability for information about eggs from other types of poultry.

Use   Eggs are enjoyed both as a dish in themselves and as ingredients in many other dishes.

Availability   Although the commercial baker has access to dried, frozen, and liquid eggs, these products are rarely available to the home cook. Fresh whole eggs are sold in all supermarkets, reaching most markets within four or five days.

Shortly after eggs are collected, they are graded for quality and size. Quality gradings are AA, A, and B, although B-grade eggs are rarely seen in stores. Gradings do not indicate freshness, but are based on thickness of white, firmness of yolk, and size of interior air pocket. To grade eggs, they are passed in front of a light source that reveals their interior. High-grade eggs have thick whites, compact, rounded yolks, and a small air pocket.

Size classifications are based on the minimum allowable weight per dozen (see below). Size does not reflect quality or freshness. Most recipes, however, are based on large eggs; using smaller or larger eggs may require adjustment of a recipe. Some markets carry both white and brown eggs. Shell color does not affect nutrition, quality, flavor, or appearance; it is determined by the breed of the hen.

Egg Size	*Minimum Weight per Dozen*
Jumbo	30 ounces
Extralarge	27 ounces
Large	24 ounces
Medium	21 ounces
Small	18 ounces
Peewee	15 ounces

Duck Eggs   Substitute duck eggs in any recipe calling for chicken eggs, although they are larger and impart a richer flavor and deeper yellow color. They may even be used in baking if the recipe is adjusted to account for the added volume. In China, duck eggs are used to prepare Thousand-Year Eggs (see page 195).

Quail Eggs   Black-and-white-speckled quail eggs are usually no more than 1 inch long. Their flavor is similar to that of chicken eggs, but their daintiness gives them a special appeal. In Japan, raw quail eggs are served with sushi as an accompaniment. Use hard-cooked peeled quail eggs to garnish salads, or pickle them and serve as an appetizer. Fresh quail eggs are available in some Japanese and specialty markets; cooked, peeled quail eggs are available in some specialty markets in cans or jars.

Salted Duck Eggs (Preserved Eggs)   To prepare salted eggs, duck eggs are soaked in brine for 30 to 40 days. The brine turns the yolk firm and bright orange and makes the white salty. Salted eggs are used in small quantities to add spark to a bland dish. Unlike Thousand-Year Eggs, they must be cooked. Hard-cooked salted eggs are eaten with steamed rice or are steamed with minced pork.

Store salted duck eggs in refrigerator for up to six months. To prepare, wash away salt covering. Cook in simmering water 1 hour, changing water several times (fresh water should be at a simmer, not cold). Cool, shell, and slice or quarter.

Thousand-Year Eggs (Preserved Eggs) These duck eggs are a Chinese delicacy available in many Chinese markets. To make them, raw duck eggs are coated with a mixture of lime, salt, ashes, and tea, then buried in earth for six to ten weeks. The claylike mixture colors, preserves, and flavors them. When peeled, the whites are amber, the yolks green; the texture is smooth and creamy, like a ripe avocado, and the flavor is strong and cheesy. Thousand-Year Eggs are quite rich and are eaten in small quantities, usually at breakfast or as one element of a cold appetizer platter. They do not require cooking and may also be made with chicken eggs.

Store eggs at room temperature for up to 10 days or wrapped in plastic and in the refrigerator for up to one month. To prepare, soak in cold water for 1 hour to soften outer black coating; scrape it away. Crack gently and shell. Slice or quarter. The eggs are sometimes served with a dipping sauce of soy, ginger, and vinegar.

Selection As a rule, buy eggs as fresh as possible. To test an egg for freshness, place it in a bowl of cold water. A fresh egg will remain on the bottom; an older egg will float to some degree. Discard any egg that rises to the surface of the water.

Storage Eggs deteriorate quickly under improper storage conditions. Refrigerate eggs immediately, small end down. Because they lose moisture and absorb odors through their thin shells, it is better to store them in their container than in an open refrigerator rack. Most commercial eggs have been coated with mineral oil to prevent loss of moisture and improve shelf life; they remain edible for up to five weeks, although the egg white gradually thins and the yolk flattens.

Keep leftover whites in a covered container in the refrigerator for one week to ten days. Cover leftover yolks with water and store in an airtight container in the refrigerator; use within two or three days. Store leftover whole eggs in an airtight container in the refrigerator and use within 24 hours.

Leftover yolks and whites freeze well. Ice-cube trays or muffin pans make ideal containers for tray-freezing separated eggs. Fill tray or pan with yolk or white and freeze; when firm, place individual cubes in plastic freezer bags. Calculate the capacity of a single ice-cube mold or muffin cup. How many whites or yolks will it hold? They can also be packaged in plastic containers, allowing ½-inch headspace for expansion. To prepare yolks for freezing, stir slightly, without producing foam (air bubbles beaten into egg will cause it to dry out during freezing). Add ½ teaspoon salt (if yolks will be used for savory dishes) or 1½ teaspoons sugar (if used for desserts) to each cup of egg yolks before freezing; this will prevent yolks from thickening and becoming gummy during freezing. Freeze egg whites without stirring or adding salt or sugar. Frozen egg whites whip just as well after thawing as when they are fresh.

EGGS AS AN INGREDIENT

As an ingredient in other dishes, eggs are used for a variety of purposes: to adhere, bind, clarify, emulsify, glaze, leaven, and thicken. In the process, they impart richness, color, and flavor to dishes.

Adhere Breaded fried foods often use eggs as glue to hold their crumb coat in place; the moisture in raw egg performs this function before cooking and the coagulated egg protein holds all together afterward.

Bind Egg acts as a binder in many cooked foods, giving structural support to ground meat mixtures, croquettes, pancakes, breads, and cakes. For baked products, the egg fulfills a variety of functions: the fat in the yolk contributes a shortening (tenderizing) effect; the moisture in the egg helps gelatinize the starch (flour); and, perhaps most importantly, the coagulation of egg proteins when heated gives the baked product much of its structure.

Clarify Egg whites are used to remove the impurities from cooked stock that cause it to become cloudy. To clarify, egg whites are added to simmering stock. As whites set with heat, they trap minute food particles; this "raft" of coagulated material floats to the top of the stockpot and, when strained off, reveals a clear stock.

Emulsify Eggs act as a stabilizing agent for emulsions—a dispersion of one liquid within another (such as oil and water)—which cannot freely mix except in the presence of an emulsifier that forces them together. In egg-based emulsions, oil, butter, wine, or stock is evenly dispersed in egg yolk to form a variety of sauces, from mayonnaise to Hollandaise to sabayon. Emulsions may be either cooked or uncooked. The principal uncooked egg emulsion is mayonnaise. Hollandaise sauce and its variations are examples of cooked egg emulsions. Whisking cooled clarified butter into warmed egg yolks produces a delicate emulsion with many uses. To make a sweet sabayon, another cooked egg emulsion, eggs and sugar are whisked over hot water until thick and warm. Then wine is whisked in and the mixture is beaten for several more minutes over heat. It doubles in volume and forms a thick, airy, fairly stable emulsion.

Emulsions, by their very nature, are unstable. Strict attention to timing and temperature is required to ensure success. Follow recipe instructions carefully.

Glaze Brushing bread or pastry before baking with an egg wash—beaten egg mixed with water, milk, or cream—imparts a shiny surface. An egg-yolk–water wash results in a golden surface; egg white with water creates a sticky surface that holds seeds in place; an egg wash containing milk or cream produces a soft crust.

Leaven The ability of egg whites to form a stable foam when beaten enables them to give volume to soufflés, angel food and sponge cakes, mousses, and meringues; air trapped in the beaten white expands in the presence of

---

WORKING WITH EGGS

TO CRACK AN EGG

Gently tap side of egg against an angled hard surface, such as the edge of a countertop or the side of a mixing bowl, and as close to the center of the egg as possible. If egg does not crack in half, crack it again once or twice, or use a knife to tap egg gently around its midsection. Break egg apart over a clean bowl.

TO SEPARATE YOLKS
FROM WHITES

It's easiest to separate eggs when they are cold because yolk is firmer, making it less likely to break. Egg whites beat most easily, however, when they are at room temperature. Therefore, when you need to beat whites, the best working procedure is to separate eggs as soon as you remove them from the refrigerator and then leave them at room temperature while preparing other ingredients for recipe.

Whites will not beat properly if there is a trace of egg yolk in them, so it is essential to separate eggs with care. When a recipe calls for several separated eggs, you can avoid the frustration of ruining a bowl full of whites with egg yolk by first breaking each egg over a small bowl. If white separates neatly, add it to a bowl set aside to hold all of the whites. If it picks up even a speck of yolk, try to scoop up yolk with a piece of egg shell; if this proves impossible, save white for another use.

To separate an egg, have ready two small bowls (use three bowls if separating more than one egg). Crack egg as described above. Holding half of shell in each hand, transfer yolk carefully from one half to the other, letting egg white drip into a bowl. When all of white has dripped into bowl, put yolk in second bowl. Another method is to crack egg into your clean palm; the less viscous white will drip through your fingers into a bowl set beneath your hand while the yolk stays on your palm.

---

heat. Whole-egg and egg-yolk foams are used as leavening agents in sponge cakes.

Thicken Eggs are used to thicken sauces, soups, and custards. With heat, the egg proteins gel, thereby thickening or setting a liquid. Making a classic custard sauce (*crème anglaise*) by heating milk, sugar, and eggs; thickening a soup with a mixture of cream and beaten eggs; and setting a baked rice pudding with eggs are examples of the thickening power of eggs.

BEATING EGGS:
WHOLE, YOLKS, AND WHITES

When eggs are beaten until they thicken and expand in volume, they form a network of air bubbles which is referred to as a foam. An egg-white foam is probably the most familiar of these, but whole-egg and egg-yolk foams also play important, although less common, culinary roles. Whole-egg foams lighten génoise, the delicate French cake; egg-yolk foams leaven the American sponge cake; a souffléed omelet uses both types.

Beaten whole eggs or egg yolks lighten in color and thicken as air bubbles are incorporated, but because of the physical properties of yolks, the resulting foam is unstable and will not set. In fact, an egg-yolk foam, unless used right away, will separate.

Often a recipe will direct you to beat eggs—whole or yolk, with or without sugar—until thick and lemon-colored, a readily discernible transformation. Another term used to describe this point is *to beat to a ribbon;* this is the stage at which the mixture falls slowly from the beater in a thin, ribbonlike band and leaves a trail in the bowl that remains for a few seconds, then disappears. When making génoise with anything but a heavy-duty stand mixer, the egg-sugar mixture is first beaten with a whisk over simmering water until mixture is lukewarm; the bowl is removed from heat and the mixture beaten to ribbon stage. This treatment both dissolves the sugar and gives the eggs greater elasticity so that further beating will develop a foam of great volume.

The process of beating causes egg whites to trap air bubbles. In the presence of heat, beaten whites expand and increase the volume of whatever mixture they are combined with—soufflés and cake batters are leavened completely or in part this way. Uncooked beaten egg whites, although they don't expand further because of the absence of heat, are used to lighten the texture of cold dishes such as mousses.

Fat, such as that found in egg yolks, hampers the ability of egg whites to develop a stable foam and results in less volume. For this reason, be sure that bowl and whisk or beaters are scrupulously clean and dry; even a speck of butter or egg yolk will inhibit the process and can decrease volume by as much as two thirds.

An unlined copper bowl and balloon whisk will develop a very stable foam with maximum volume; studies suggest that copper and the protein in egg whites form a very strong bond that results in a longer-lasting structure of air bubbles. A stainless steel bowl is next best; avoid plastic, glass, ceramic, and aluminum. Plastic, a petroleum product, can retain an oily film even with repeated washing; the slippery surface of glass, ceramic, and plastic make it harder for whites to billow up; aluminum will gray whites. Also keep in mind that properly beaten whites will increase to three times their original volume, so choose a bowl with sufficient capacity.

Recipes may suggest adding an acid, such as cream of tartar, to whites if you aren't using a copper bowl. As little as ⅛ teaspoon cream of tartar per egg white will make foam less prone to collapse; this addition will delay foam formation, however, so add it to whites after they have been beaten slightly and are just bubbly. Sugar acts as a stabilizer as well. A meringue, which contains sugar, is far more stable than sugarless whipped egg whites. Egg whites foam more slowly, however, in the presence of sugar and develop less volume. The best way to add sugar to egg whites is as follows: By hand or with an electric mixer at low speed, slowly beat whites without sugar just until frothy; then add 1 teaspoon sugar per white and whip egg whites until almost stiff (be carefully not to overbeat). Fold in remaining sugar by hand.

Remember that although eggs are easiest to separate when cold, both whites and yolks beat to greater volume when warm. Let cold yolks and whites sit at room temperature for at least 30 minutes before they are beaten.

BEATING EGG WHITES

Foamy   Egg whites are just slightly beaten; white suds begin to form in a matter of seconds. The mass is still transparent and liquid. Salt and cream of tartar (if used) are added at this stage once some foam develops. If these ingredients are added right away, the whites will need to be beaten longer before they will start to foam.

Soft peaks   The foam in soft peaks is thicker, whiter, and finer. When beater is lifted from bowl, whites form droopy, moist-looking, but definite, peaks. Use at this stage for soufflés.

Stiff, but not dry   Some sugar is added now. With continued beating, foam thickens and develops a glossy sheen; it should still look moist. Volume has increased. When beater is lifted from bowl, peaks stand in stiff points. When bowl is tipped, mass does not slide.

STAGES OF BEATEN EGG WHITES

Less experienced cooks tend to overbeat rather than underbeat. If you are unsure whether whites have reached the desired stage, it's best to stop. If you continue beating until they are stiff and dry, they lose elasticity. When whites attempt to expand further in the oven, they will collapse. Dry whites are overbeaten and cannot be rescued. The structure looks dry and curdled, and liquid will separate out. See Beating Egg Whites, above, for photographs of stages of beaten egg whites.

FOLDING EGG WHITES

When beaten egg whites are to be combined with other ingredients, the recommended procedure is folding. To fold means to incorporate one mixture into another gently without deflating the air in the lighter mixture. For a complete discussion, see FOLD.

EGG DISHES

As a dish in themselves, or as the main component of a dish, eggs may be hard-cooked, soft-cooked, poached, fried, baked, scrambled, or used for omelets, frittatas, and soufflés.

HARD-COOKED EGGS

Peeled, hard-cooked eggs make a nutritious snack or addition to a lunch box. They may be mashed for egg salad; quartered and simmered in a cream sauce; pickled; sliced as a garnish for a salad or sandwich; minced for a salad or vegetable garnish. Scotch Eggs, a popular dish served in English pubs, consists of peeled, hard-cooked eggs coated with ground sausage and bread crumbs, then deep-fried. Chopped hard-cooked eggs are often added to potato salads; tuna, chicken, or shellfish salads; or giblet gravy.

The best eggs for boiling and peeling are at least one week old. Very fresh eggs are difficult to peel. Both fresh and older eggs will peel more easily if dropped immediately into cold water after boiling.

However, hard-cooked eggs are easier to peel when they are warm, so if they are to be peeled soon after cooking, remove from cold water before they cool completely. Peel by tapping all around shell with a knife to form a network of cracks. Peel shell away under cold running water. Use shelled eggs immediately or store in a bowl of cold salted water in the refrigerator up to two weeks.

After boiling and cooling, unshelled hard-cooked eggs may be refrigerated for up to one week. Mark with an *x* to distinguish from raw eggs. If you forgot to mark an egg and can't remember if it's cooked or not, spin egg on counter. A raw egg will whirl evenly; a cooked egg will falter. Peel eggs just before using.

◼ NO-FAIL HARD-COOKED EGGS

Fill a pan with enough cold water to cover eggs by 1 inch. Add 2 teaspoons salt per quart of water; bring water to a boil. Using the oldest eggs in your refrigerator, lower them into boiling water with a slotted spoon. Reduce water to a simmer, with bubbles that barely break on the surface. Simmer, uncovered, 10 minutes. Immediately plunge eggs into cold water or set under cold running water (eggs will be easier to peel and won't develop a green ring around yolk). Cool 1 hour in cold water if not peeling right away.

Deviled eggs look particularly decorative when the egg-yolk filling is piped into the cooked white with a pastry bag.

DEVILED EGGS

Highly seasoned foods are sometimes referred to as "deviled." In this recipe, the spice is mustard.

> 6 hard-cooked eggs, peeled and halved lengthwise
> 3 tablespoons mayonnaise
> 1 tablespoon Dijon mustard
> ⅛ teaspoon salt
> Paprika, for sprinkling

1. With a small spoon lift egg yolks out of whites. Place yolks in small bowl.

2. Add mayonnaise, mustard, and salt to egg yolks; mix well with a fork to make a very smooth paste. Adjust seasonings, if necessary.

3. Arrange egg white halves on a serving platter. Mound some of yolk mixture into each and sprinkle with paprika. Serve immediately or store, covered, in refrigerator until ready to use.

Makes 1 dozen Deviled Eggs.

SCOTCH EGGS

An excellent picnic food, Scotch Eggs have an herbed sausage and bread crumb coat that protects the hard-cooked eggs secreted inside. When sliced in quarters or rings, they make a pretty addition to a buffet breakfast.

> 1 pound ground sausage
> 1½ teaspoons dried basil
> 1 teaspoon dried oregano
> ½ teaspoon salt
> ¼ teaspoon freshly ground pepper
> ¼ cup parsley, minced
> 1¼ cups soft bread crumbs
> 2 raw eggs
> 1 tablespoon water
> 6 hard-cooked eggs, peeled
> Oil, for frying

1. In a large bowl combine sausage, basil, oregano, salt, pepper, parsley, ½ cup bread crumbs, and 1 raw egg.

2. In a small bowl beat remaining raw egg and the water. Place remaining bread crumbs in a small dish. Wet hands with cold water to prevent sausage mixture from sticking. Place one sixth of sausage mixture in palm of your hand; flatten slightly. Place a hard-cooked egg in center of mixture and enclose in sausage. Roll in beaten egg, then bread crumbs, and place on a plate. Repeat with remaining hard-cooked eggs. Chill 1 hour.

3. Pour oil into a wok or 2-quart heavy-bottomed saucepan to about 3 inches deep; heat to about 365° F. Carefully add eggs and fry 5 minutes. Turn and fry 4 minutes. Remove with a slotted spoon to paper towels to drain and cool briefly.

Serves 6.

PICKLED EGGS

Walk into almost any English pub and you'll spot a jar of pickled eggs on the bar. Patrons down them with pints of ale for a quick, nourishing snack, or add cheese and a chunk of bread and call it lunch. As hors d'oeuvres, they can be served sliced atop buttered dark bread, or halved as a garnish for a platter of cold meats. Exceptionally easy to make, they also keep well; store them in a covered glass jar in the refrigerator for up to one month.

> 3 cups cider vinegar
> 3 cups water
> 2 tablespoons mixed pickling spice
> 1 medium onion, sliced
> 1 teaspoon salt
> 1 dozen hard-cooked eggs, peeled

In a saucepan combine vinegar, the water, pickling spices, onion, and salt. Bring just to a boil, then remove from heat and let cool 15 minutes. Pack eggs into a large, clean glass jar and pour in warm liquid; let cool, then cover and refrigerate at least 1 day before using.

Makes 1 dozen eggs.

SOFT-COOKED AND CODDLED EGGS

Prepared in the same manner as hard-cooked eggs but in less time—usually 4 to 5 minutes—soft-cooked eggs have a firm white and a soft yolk. Soft-cooked eggs are generally set in an eggcup; the top is cracked with a knife and removed, the egg then eaten directly from the shell with a spoon.

Coddled eggs are soft-cooked eggs that are gently finished away from heat. As with soft-cooked eggs, coddled eggs start in boiling water. They are then immediately covered, removed from heat, and left to stand until set to desired firmness. Consequently, they take slightly longer to cook—6 to 8 minutes—than soft-cooked eggs. Coddling produces an especially tender white. Eggs for Caesar salads are traditionally coddled. Special ceramic egg coddlers are available; to use, the egg is broken into the cup, topped with butter and seasonings, and covered with a metal lid. The cup is immersed in boiling water, then removed and set aside until egg is done to taste. The coddled egg is served in its cup.

To avoid rapid temperature changes that might crack the shell, bring refrigerated eggs to room temperature before soft-boiling or coddling. Steeping egg in tepid water will bring it quickly to room temperature.

NO-FAIL SOFT-COOKED EGGS

Follow directions for No-Fail Hard-Cooked Eggs (see page 197) and simmer, uncovered, until eggs are done to taste (3 to 5 minutes). Serve each egg, in the shell, in an eggcup, cracking top lightly with a spoon and peeling away about ½ inch of shell so egg can be eaten from remainder of shell. Alternatively, quickly cut egg in half, then use a spoon to scoop egg out into a small, warm dish.

■ SHRIMP-CROWNED EGGS

A simple soft-cooked egg becomes quite another story when you top it with buttery little shrimp to stir into each spoonful. Another topping you might present in the same way is a teaspoon of caviar and a dollop of sour cream seasoned with chives. Part of the charm of soft-cooked eggs is the eggcups they are served in. If this preparation is one you make often, you may want to collect a variety of eggcups to make your breakfast or brunch table even more decorative.

> 2 teaspoons butter or margarine
> 1 green onion, finely chopped
> ¼ cup tiny peeled, cooked shrimp
> 6 eggs
>   Hot, buttered toast strips, for accompaniment

1. Melt butter in a small frying pan over medium heat. Mix in green onion and stir just until limp. Add shrimp and mix lightly, just until shrimp are heated through. Remove from heat and keep warm.

2. Soft-cook eggs according to directions on page 198. Place eggs in eggcups and carefully slice off top fourth of each egg, using a serrated knife or egg scissors.

3. Scoop out and discard white from each egg top. Fill each eggshell with about 2 teaspoons of shrimp mixture. Quickly invert shrimp-filled top onto eggs and serve at once, accompanied by toast strips to dip into egg yolks.

Serves 6.

Recipes: Caesar Salad, 506.

POACHED EGGS

To poach is to cook gently in liquid. The best eggs for poaching are very fresh; a new-laid egg has a thick white and a firm yolk that tends to hold together when simmered. When poaching an egg, the goal is to produce a just-set egg with a neat, round shape. Sometimes the shape has to be helped along by trimming away trailing bits of cooked white before serving. Specially designed egg-poaching equipment makes the job easier but is not a must. Adding a little lemon juice or vinegar to the poaching liquid helps coagulate the white more quickly and preserve the shape of the egg, but also flavors the egg adversely. After cooking, poached eggs are drained and served alone or in a variety of savory preparations: nestled in artichoke bottoms and covered with Hollandaise or béarnaise sauce, dressed with brown butter, served atop toast with wine sauce, or simply accompanied with buttered toast.

■ BASIC POACHED EGGS

If not using poached eggs right away, have a bowl of ice water ready for cooling the cooked eggs. Eggs can be poached hours ahead, even as far as two days in advance of serving, and refrigerated in a bowl of ice water.

Bring water to a boil in a large, nonreactive saucepan (add 2 tablespoons vinegar per quart of water, if desired). Reduce heat to medium-low so that water just simmers. Break an egg into a small cup or ramekin and slide egg into bubbling water (or break directly into water). Repeat with remaining eggs. Reduce heat to low and poach eggs, uncovered, for 3 minutes. Lift each egg carefully with a slotted spoon and touch it; white should be firm and yolk still soft. Remove poached eggs from cooking water with a slotted spoon and serve at once, or transfer to a bowl of ice water. When eggs cool, remove from water and trim edges with a knife or kitchen scissors. Return to ice water.

To reheat eggs, transfer to a bowl of water that is just hot to the touch and let stand 5 to 10 minutes. Remove carefully to paper towels to drain.

Soft-cooked eggs have a firm white and a runny yolk. They are usually served in a decorative eggcup with the top part of the shell removed, an always appealing presentation.

■ EGGS BENEDICT

Most restaurant breakfast or brunch menus feature this well-known open-faced poached egg sandwich. The eggs can be poached ahead of time, even up to two days in advance, and held in the refrigerator. When needed, reheat in hot water. The Hollandaise is more delicate, but it can be held briefly in a double boiler or thermos.

    16 eggs
    16 slices Canadian bacon or ham, cut in
        ¼-inch-thick rounds
     4 to 6 tablespoons butter or margarine
     8 English muffins, split
     2 cups Hollandaise Sauce (see page 516)

1. Poach eggs according to directions on page 199, and refrigerate until ready to reheat.

2. Keep Hollandaise Sauce warm over hot (not boiling) water in a double boiler.

3. In a large frying pan over moderate heat, cook Canadian bacon in a little of the butter, adding more butter as needed (1 tablespoon at a time), until meat is lightly browned on both sides. Keep warm.

4. Reheat poached eggs as directed on page 199. Broil split English muffins until crisp and golden brown.

5. For each serving, place 2 muffin halves on a warm plate and cover each with (in order) Canadian bacon, poached egg, and Hollandaise Sauce. Serve at once.

Serves 8.

FRIED EGGS

Very fresh eggs are best for frying; the thick white of a fresh egg will not spread like the thin, runny white of an older egg. Eggs may be fried in butter, bacon fat, or oil, on one side (sunny-side up) or both (over easy). They may be served as is, on buttered toast, or in a sandwich. Mexican *huevos rancheros* are fried eggs served atop fried tortillas with a spicy tomato sauce.

■ BASIC FRIED EGGS

Using a frying pan just large enough to hold the number of eggs to be cooked, melt enough fat over medium heat to cover bottom generously; when fat foams, break eggs gently into pan.

Reduce heat to medium-low and cook, uncovered, occasionally spooning butter over eggs, until whites are set and yolks are covered with a pale, translucent film. As an alternative, after adding eggs to pan and reducing heat, cover and cook until eggs are done to your liking as in first method. For eggs sunny-side up, cook on one side only in a covered pan until whites set (about 1 minute) and transfer eggs to warm plates. For eggs over easy, cook in an uncovered frying pan on one side until underside sets (about 1 minute), turn carefully with a spatula, and cook on other side for a few seconds just to firm white.

■ HUEVOS RANCHEROS

This hearty breakfast or brunch dish is perhaps the best known of all Mexican egg dishes.

        Oil, for frying
        Salt, as needed
     6 corn tortillas
     6 eggs
        Sour cream and avocado slices,
        for garnish

Salsa Frita

    ½ small white onion, minced
     1 clove garlic, minced
     1 tablespoon oil
     2 fresh or canned jalapeño chiles, seeded
        and chopped, *or* 1 can (4 oz) diced green chiles
        for a milder salsa
     2 large tomatoes, peeled and chopped
        Salt, to taste
     1 tablespoon chopped cilantro or
        pinch dried oregano

1. Heat a thin (about ⅛ inch) layer of oil in a skillet. Lightly salt tortillas and fry them one at a time. Fry briefly until golden brown but not hard or crisp. Drain on paper towels.

2. Fry eggs to suit individual taste. Eggs sunny-side up are traditional for this recipe.

3. To serve, top each tortilla with a fried egg. Spoon warm Salsa Frita over egg. Garnish with a dab of sour cream and several avocado slices.

Serves 3 to 6.

Salsa Frita Chiles can burn the skin. When handling them, keep hands away from face, especially eyes. When finished, wash hands thoroughly with soap and water. In a skillet sauté onion and garlic in oil until soft. Add chiles and tomatoes, and simmer for 15 minutes. Check seasoning and add salt to taste. Stir in cilantro.

Makes 2 cups.

Variation Eggs can be poached in Salsa Frita. To serve, spoon eggs and salsa onto fried tortillas.

■ CREAM-BASTED FRIED EGGS

For a delicious Sunday breakfast, pair these eggs with a chunky applesauce, seasoned sausage, and sweet rolls. A recipe for applesauce appears on page 11, one for sausage is on page 530, and one for nut-filled, cinnamon-flavored pecan rolls is on page 629.

     2 tablespoons butter or margarine
     2 tablespoons whipping cream
     4 to 6 eggs
        Salt and white pepper, to taste

To flavor Parmesan Baked Eggs, you can add such toppings as thinly sliced green onions, snipped fresh chives, salsa, crumbled bacon, or grated cheese.

1. In a large, heavy frying pan over medium-low heat, melt butter. Swirl in cream. Break eggs into pan, being careful not to break yolks.

2. Cook, uncovered, occasionally spooning cream mixture over eggs, until whites are set and yolks are covered by a pale, translucent film (3 to 5 minutes). Serve at once, seasoned with salt and pepper.

Serves 4 to 6.

BAKED EGGS, SHIRRED EGGS, AND EGGS EN COCOTTE

Also known as shirred eggs, baked eggs are oven-cooked in buttered ramekins until just set. The eggs may be baked on a bed of creamed spinach or tomato sauce, or they may be broken over asparagus spears or buttered bread, then baked until set. To keep top of eggs moist and tender, they are lightly basted with cream or butter. Some recipes call for covering eggs during baking to keep tops soft.

After baking eggs, if desired sprinkle on a topping such as snipped fresh chives or thinly sliced green onions (including some of the green tops), red or green salsa, caviar, sour cream or crème fraîche, crumbled crisp bacon, or grated Swiss or sharp Cheddar cheese.

To make eggs *en cocotte* (eggs baked in ramekins), break eggs into buttered round porcelain cups and dot with butter and cream. Place cups in a pan of barely simmering water (bain-marie or hot water bath) and bake until eggs are set (about 7 minutes in a 400° F oven).

■ PARMESAN BAKED EGGS

In the basic recipe, eggs are baked in buttered shallow casseroles with Parmesan cheese. For variety try Prosciutto Baked Eggs or the topping variations suggested at right.

   2 tablespoons butter or margarine
   ¼ cup freshly grated Parmesan cheese
   4 eggs
     Salt, freshly grated nutmeg, and freshly ground pepper, to taste
     Chopped Italian parsley, for garnish

1. Preheat oven to 325° F. Using about half the butter, grease 4 shallow individual baking dishes about 5 inches in diameter. Coat each with 1 tablespoon cheese.

2. Break one egg into each dish. Sprinkle lightly with salt, nutmeg, and pepper. Dot with remaining butter.

3. Bake, uncovered, until eggs are set to your liking (12 to 15 minutes). Garnish with Italian parsley.

Serves 4.

Prosciutto Baked Eggs Do not coat baking dishes with Parmesan cheese. Instead, cook 4 thin slices prosciutto or other ham in butter or margarine until lightly browned, and line each baking dish with a prosciutto slice. Pour in any butter from frying pan. Continue as in basic recipe with eggs, salt, nutmeg, and pepper. Then sprinkle each egg with 1 tablespoon grated Parmesan cheese before baking, instead of dotting with butter.

In a medium frying pan over moderate to low heat, melt enough butter or margarine to coat bottom generously. When butter foams, add beaten eggs. Cook, stirring constantly with a wooden spoon, until eggs are set but still shiny and moist looking. For luxuriously creamy eggs, cook in top of a double boiler set over barely simmering water. Cooking time will be about 20 minutes, but eggs will be extraordinarily soft and moist.

Other ingredients might be added to the butter in the same pan in which the eggs are to be scrambled. For example, first cook onions, chopped green bell pepper, sliced mushrooms, or bits of ham, then reduce heat before adding eggs. Eggs can be sprinkled with grated cheese when they are nearly cooked. A scattering of snipped parsley or other fresh herbs at the finish also adds flavor. Other garnishes include cooked tomatoes, cream cheese, smoked fish, salami, asparagus tips, and bacon bits.

■ HANGTOWN FRY

Soon after the gold rush of 1849, the town of Placerville, California, in the Sierra foothills, became a major center for transacting business and administering justice. The latter activity prompted the miners to nickname it Hangtown. As the story goes, a miner who had struck it rich came to one of the hotels in Placerville and asked for the most expensive breakfast in the house. The most precious delicacy on hand was fresh oysters, which the cook fried and combined with scrambled eggs—Hangtown Fry.

>   1 pint small shucked oysters, drained
>   ½ to 1 teaspoon Worcestershire sauce
>   1 cup plain or seasoned bread crumbs
>   Oil, for deep-frying
>   2 tablespoons *each* butter and oil
>   12 eggs, beaten, at room temperature
>   Salt and freshly ground pepper, to taste
>   1 tablespoon snipped fresh chives or
>   chopped parsley, for garnish

1. Place oysters in a bowl and sprinkle with Worcestershire sauce. Roll oysters one at a time in bread crumbs; shake off excess crumbs and set aside.

2. In a saucepan or deep skillet, heat 2 inches of oil to 375° F. Fry oysters, a few at a time, until golden brown (3 to 5 minutes each). Drain on paper towels and keep warm.

3. Heat 1 tablespoon each butter and oil in a large skillet over medium heat. Add half of beaten eggs. Cook until eggs on bottom begin to set (about 1 minute), then gently stir whole mass once. Continue cooking, stirring only occasionally, until eggs are mostly set in large curds but still quite moist. Stir in half the oysters and season with salt and pepper. Transfer to a warm serving platter. Garnish with chives or parsley. Repeat with remaining eggs and oysters.

Serves 8.

Hangtown Fry is a dish with roots in the gold-rush era of California history when oysters were as precious as miners' nuggets.

SCRAMBLED EGGS

For scrambled eggs, raw eggs are first whipped with a fork to blend. Adding a little cream, milk, or water (1 tablespoon per egg) will produce a moister, softer texture; water gives a lighter flavor, milk or cream a richer one. Scrambled eggs are generally cooked in butter. Slow cooking yields soft, moist curds; cooking at high heat toughens eggs and produces dry curds.

To add interest, other ingredients such as herbs, cheese, or chopped vegetables can be blended into the eggs as they cook or can be used as garnish.

■ BASIC SCRAMBLED EGGS

Place eggs in a bowl large enough to allow for brisk beating. Season with salt—about ¼ teaspoon for every 3 eggs (unless you plan to add other salty ingredients)—and a pinch of pepper. Add about 1 tablespoon water, milk, or cream per egg (or less, if desired). Then beat with a fork, wire whisk, or egg beater until yolks and whites are completely blended.

JOE'S SPECIAL

San Francisco has had a number of restaurants named Joe's, all claiming to be the "original" Joe's and all featuring some variation of the following recipe. According to local legend, the dish was concocted when a hungry patron arrived at the end of a particularly busy night. About all the cook had left was eggs, spinach, and sausage (hamburger in some versions of the story)—and Joe's Special was born.

  ¼   pound mild Italian sausage or ground beef
  2   tablespoons olive oil
  1   small onion, sliced
  2   cloves garlic, minced
  1   bunch (about 1½ cups) spinach,
      washed, trimmed, and shredded
  4   eggs, lightly beaten, at room temperature
      Salt and freshly ground pepper, to taste

1. Remove casing from sausage and slice or crumble. In a large skillet over medium heat, sauté sausage in oil until meat loses raw color. Pour off all but 2 tablespoons of fat; gently cook onion and garlic until onion begins to brown.

2. Reduce heat to medium-low. Add spinach, eggs, salt, and pepper (season more heavily if using beef, less with sausage). Cook, stirring frequently, until eggs are nearly set. Serve on warm plates.

Serves 2.

Food Processor Version   Use metal blade to mince garlic; leave in work bowl. Use slicing disk for onion; remove and cook as directed. Use thick slicing disk to shred spinach. Pack leaves in feed tube loosely and process.

OMELETS AND FRITTATAS

The classic omelet is made with three whole eggs, is cooked quickly, and is often embellished with a filling. Total cooking time should be less than one minute. The inside of a properly cooked omelet is creamy; the outside is barely browned. The simplest fillings are minced herbs or grated cheese; more elaborate fillings include sautéed mushrooms or asparagus tips, smoked salmon with cream cheese, roasted chiles with Cheddar cheese, and sautéed chicken livers.

For a puffy or souffléed omelet, whites and yolks are separated; the whites are beaten to firm peaks, then are folded into yolk mixture. The omelet is cooked over medium heat on both sides. It may be filled or not, as desired.

Frittata (the Italian word for *omelet*) is a thick, open-faced egg pancake. Like an omelet, a frittata may incorporate a wide variety of foods, such as sweet peppers, artichoke hearts, herbs, cheese, sliced potatoes, onions, or leeks. Although omelets are usually served as soon as they are cooked, a frittata may be eaten hot, lukewarm, or even cold. It is usually turned out before it has completed cooking, then is inverted and returned to the frying pan to brown on both sides.

BASIC SINGLE-SERVING OMELET WITH HERBS

Try the fillings suggested here or create your own. Allow 3 to 4 tablespoons of filling for each single-serving omelet

  3   eggs
  1   tablespoon water
      Pinch salt and freshly ground pepper
  1   tablespoon butter
  1   teaspoon *each* minced fresh parsley,
      tarragon, and chives

1. In a small bowl mix eggs, the water, salt, and pepper with a fork until well blended but not foamy.

2. In a 7- or 8-inch omelet pan, heat about 1 tablespoon butter over medium-high heat until it begins to foam; add eggs.

3. At first, slide pan back and forth to keep omelet from sticking. As bottom begins to set, slip a thin spatula under eggs, tilting pan and lifting cooked portion to let uncooked egg mixture flow under it to the center. Repeat until most of omelet is set, but center and top are still moist and creamy.

4. Add herbs or filling of your choice (see below). For a filled omelet, spoon filling across center in a line with handle. Have a warm serving plate ready. Loosen one side of omelet with spatula and fold it over to cover about one third of the remainder. Then hold pan over serving plate so the other side begins to slide out. Flip omelet so that previously folded side flips over, producing an omelet folded into thirds with center third on top.

Serves 1.

Apple-Roquefort Omelet   Sauté half a tart green apple, cored and thinly sliced, in 1 tablespoon butter. In step 4, add apple, grated Parmesan or shredded Monterey jack cheese, and ½ to 1 ounce Roquefort cheese. Garnish with watercress leaves.

Mexican Omelet   Sauté 2 tablespoons chopped onions in a little butter. Add diced green (mild) or jalapeño (hot) chiles, black olives, and any shredded cheese, to make a total of ¼ cup. Add to omelet in step 4 and top with a dash of salsa or a dollop of sour cream or yogurt.

Princess Omelet   Cook ½ cup asparagus tips; mix half with a little whipping cream. Add to omelet in step 4. Garnish with sliced raw mushrooms and remaining cooked asparagus tips.

Provençale Omelet   Sauté ¼ cup diced tomatoes and a pinch minced garlic in olive oil. Add to omelet in step 4. Sprinkle omelet with minced parsley before serving.

Spinach Omelet   Sauté ¼ cup chopped fresh spinach and 1 anchovy fillet, diced, in a little butter. Add to omelet in step 4; top with 1 tablespoon shredded cheese and a sprinkling of freshly grated Parmesan cheese. Garnish omelet with a fresh spinach leaf.

**HOW TO MAKE
AN OMELET**

As egg mixture sets, tilt pan and gently lift cooked portions with a spatula, enabling the uncooked egg to flow underneath.

When most of the omelet is set but top is still slightly moist, spoon filling across center in a line with the handle of pan.

Loosen omelet with spatula and fold a third of it (from far side) toward the middle; tip pan over serving plate, then flip so that previously folded side turns over.

SOUFFLEED OMELET

Beaten egg whites folded into the separately beaten yolks cause the omelet to puff and lighten when cooked. Compared to a traditional omelet, a souffléed version is not a quick preparation; it needs almost 30 minutes of slow, gentle cooking to expand and set. When done it has developed a rich brown surface.

   6 eggs, separated
   ⅛ teaspoon salt
      Pinch freshly ground pepper
   1½ tablespoons unsalted butter
   2 tablespoons grated Gruyère cheese

1. Beat egg yolks in a small bowl with salt and pepper. Beat egg whites until soft peaks form. Fold one third of whites into yolks to lighten. Fold remaining whites into yolks.

2. Heat butter in a large skillet. Pour in omelet mixture and smooth with a spatula. Cook over low heat until puffy and set (25 to 28 minutes). Sprinkle center with cheese. Loosen edges with a spatula and fold in half. With a spatula slip omelet onto a serving plate.

Serves 2.

SWEET SOUFFLEED OMELET

For an after-theater bite, this omelet is an alternative to dessert. Chunky preserves, fresh fruit, whipped cream, or sweetened soft cheeses are some alternative toppings.

   ¼ cup milk
   4 eggs, separated
   1 tablespoon *each* Cognac or orange-
      flavored liqueur and granulated sugar
   1 tablespoon butter
      Confectioners' sugar, for dusting
   2 tablespoons orange juice
   2 to 3 tablespoons orange-flavored liqueur, warmed

1. Preheat oven to 350° F.

2. In a medium bowl combine thoroughly milk, egg yolks, Cognac, and granulated sugar with a fork.

3. In a separate bowl beat egg whites until stiff but not dry (do not overbeat).

4. Stir one third of the whites into yolk mixture. Fold in remaining whites.

5. Melt butter in an ovenproof skillet over medium-high heat. Add batter and cover skillet. Cook 5 minutes, slashing once to bottom crust with a knife to permit heat to penetrate.

6. Remove lid and transfer omelet to oven until top is set (about 2 minutes).

7. Remove omelet from skillet; sprinkle with confectioners' sugar and orange juice. Pour warm liqueur over and around it and ignite. Serve immediately.

Serves 4.

Variation Substitute any of the following for the topping of confectioners' sugar, orange juice, and orange-flavored liqueur: apricot-pineapple preserves; sliced fresh fruit topped with confectioners' sugar or honey; whole berries and sour or whipped cream mixed with a little grated lemon rind and lemon juice; almond liqueur, sliced almonds, and sweetened sour cream, whipped cream, or ricotta cheese; or orange-flavored liqueur and orange slices.

ARTICHOKE FRITTATA

Although a frittata is often described as an open-faced omelet, it's thicker than an omelet and it is often served barely warm. Like an omelet, it is the basis for a cook's own inspirations. Butter-steamed fresh asparagus tips, tiny shrimp, minced fresh herbs, spring onions—all are suitable for a frittata. The version below is a Roman classic: tiny artichoke hearts, dusted with Parmesan, baked into the eggs. Serve it as a first course or as a lunch or brunch dish. Easy to assemble from ingredients usually on hand, it's a perfect dish for unexpected company.

   8 large eggs
   1 tablespoon olive oil
   1 tablespoon butter
   1 jar (6 oz) artichoke hearts, quartered,
      marinated, and drained
   2 tablespoons freshly grated Parmesan cheese
      Salt and freshly ground pepper, to taste
      Thinly sliced sweet red onion, for garnish
      Baguette slices, for accompaniment

1. Preheat oven to 375° F. Beat eggs lightly. Heat oil and butter in a 9- or 10-inch nonstick skillet over moderately high heat. When fats are sizzling, add eggs and reduce heat to low. Arrange artichokes in a pretty pattern on top of eggs. Cook gently, lifting edges of frittata to let uncooked egg run underneath, until it is just set on top. Dust with Parmesan, salt, and pepper. Transfer skillet to oven and bake just until frittata is firm on top; do not overcook or it will be tough.

2. Cool in skillet, if desired, then slide onto serving platter and cut into wedges. Frittata can be eaten hot, warm, or at room temperature. Serve with raw onion and baguette slices.

Serves 4.

SOUFFLES

The base for a savory soufflé is generally a fairly thick white sauce, to which may be added puréed or cooked vegetables or fruit, cheese, or wine—or some of each. Egg yolks are blended into the sauce. Then it is leavened with beaten egg whites. As the soufflé bakes, the expansion of the whites makes it rise and billow. A sweet soufflé has a cream, custard, or fruit base. Although soufflés can be hot or cold, a cold soufflé is actually more of a mousse set with gelatin.

The key to a light, airy soufflé is proper handling of the egg whites; they must be beaten enough but not too much—just until small, slightly curved peaks form. Then they must be folded lightly and carefully into the sauce just until incorporated, using a rubber spatula and a circular, up-and-over motion (see FOLD). Stirring in or overfolding egg whites may release so much air that mixture will fail to rise. Because it is always easiest to fold together similar mixtures, remember to add some of the beaten egg whites to the sauce base to lighten it, then carefully fold in the remaining whites.

Bake on the middle rack of a preheated oven and allow plenty of room for the soufflé to rise. Follow the recipe for timing; the French prefer a soufflé with a soft, custardlike center, which becomes a sauce for the crisper outside. When removed from the oven, this type will not be firm; when moved it will shake slightly, indicating that its center is slighty underdone. Other versions will cook the mixture through. To serve, use two spoons to break the crust, and combine some of the soft center (if of that type) and firmer crust for each portion.

Although the straight-sided soufflé dish is traditional, any number of full-size or individual ovenproof containers will work. The baking dish is generally buttered and frequently coated with crumbs and grated cheese, or, for a dessert soufflé, granulated sugar. This coat will create an appealing crust. If you wish the soufflé to develop a "crown" as it bakes, draw a circle with the tip of a knife or spatula around the circumference of the mixture about 1 inch from the edge of the dish (see photographs at right). The portion of the soufflé within this circle will rise higher than the mixture that surrounds it.

Some soufflé recipes call for wrapping the dish with a paper or aluminum foil collar to support the mixture as it rises above the dish; other recipes are developed so that the collar is unnecessary. Cold soufflés frequently use a collar as an extension of the mold so that when the paper is removed the mixture has the appearance of having puffed. The collar can be made of parchment paper, aluminum foil, or waxed paper; it is cut so that it wraps around the mold and overlaps by several inches. The inside is always oiled or buttered (see photographs at right). If the collar is supporting a hot soufflé, it can be sprinkled with bread crumbs, cheese, or granulated sugar, depending on whether the mixture is savory or sweet.

Although soufflés have an intimidating reputation, timing the process is not as hard as you might think. If you are really pressed for time, the mixture can be completely assembled, covered, and left out at room temperature an hour or more before baking; or, preferably, the base can be made ahead and the whites beaten and folded in at the last minute. Haste is critical at serving time; when a baked soufflé is ready, serve it at once because it will deflate quickly. Sound advice for this delicate dish is to let your guests wait for the soufflé if need be, but never the other way around.

▦ BLUE CHEESE SOUFFLE

This makes an elegant first course. Served with a salad and with fruit and cheese for dessert, it can also be the main dish for a light supper. French Roquefort is the best cheese to use, but the excellent Maytag Blue from Iowa makes a very good second choice. This recipe is easily expandable to up to twice the proportions given, as long as you have a baking dish large enough to contain the soufflé. Allow a little more baking time for larger soufflés. Try the suggested variations as well.

> 2 tablespoons finely grated Parmesan cheese
> 2½ tablespoons butter
> 3 tablespoons flour
> 1 cup milk
> 3 ounces blue cheese, crumbled
>   Pinch freshly grated nutmeg
>   Salt and freshly ground pepper, to taste
> 4 egg yolks
> 6 egg whites, at room temperature

1. Preheat oven to 400° F. Choose a soufflé dish or other deep baking dish of about 6-cup capacity. Rub inside of dish with a little butter, add grated cheese, and roll cheese around to coat bottom and sides of dish evenly.

2. Melt butter in a heavy saucepan over moderate heat. Stir in flour and cook until flour turns a pale tan. Stir in milk and cook until sauce is thick, stirring frequently to break up any lumps. Add blue cheese to sauce and season to taste with nutmeg, salt, and pepper. Stir in egg yolks and set sauce aside to keep warm.

3. Beat egg whites just until they hold stiff peaks. Remove sauce from heat and stir a fourth of the egg whites into sauce. Fold remaining whites into sauce with a wide spatula. Immediately pour mixture into baking dish and place it in upper half of oven.

4. Reduce heat to 350° F and bake until soufflé is puffy and lightly browned, and a skewer or knife inserted into center comes out moist but clean (25 to 30 minutes). Serve immediately.

Serves 2 as a main course or 4 as a first course.

Parmesan-Gruyère or Parmesan-Cheddar Soufflé For the blue cheese, substitute 2 ounces freshly grated Parmesan and 2 ounces grated Gruyère or Cheddar.

Parmesan-Spinach Soufflé To Parmesan-Gruyère (or Cheddar) Soufflé, fold in ⅓ cup cooked, chopped, and well-drained spinach to sauce just before adding beaten egg whites in step 3.

Spinach-Ham Soufflé To Parmesan-Spinach Soufflé, fold in ½ cup ham, cut into ¼-inch dice, along with chopped spinach in step 3.

Spinach-Shrimp Soufflé To Parmesan-Spinach variation, fold in 1 cup coarsely chopped cooked shrimp along with chopped spinach in step 3.

HOW TO MAKE A SOUFFLE

After the soufflé base has been prepared—generally a thick sweet or savory white sauce—beaten egg whites are carefully folded in just until incorporated.

As an optional finish, the soufflé can be made to puff into a crown in the oven. To create this effect, run the tip of a knife or narrow-bladed spatula around the edge of the mixture about 1 inch from the sides of the dish.

Some soufflés need the support of a paper collar as they bake. The collar should be of double thickness and is set around the exterior of the dish, ends overlapping. Secure the paper with ovenproof kitchen twine.

1. Preheat oven to 350° F. Line a 10- by 15-inch jelly-roll pan with parchment paper, or grease with butter and dust with ¼ cup Parmesan cheese. Spread soufflé mixture into prepared pan and bake until puffed and golden brown (10 to 15 minutes); cool in pan 5 minutes.

2. While roulade is cooling, place a piece of parchment paper or a towel on work surface. Sprinkle with remaining ¼ cup Parmesan cheese. Loosen edges of soufflé and invert onto parchment. Roll parchment and roulade together, jelly-roll fashion, and cool completely (about 1 hour).

3. Slice mushrooms about ¼ inch thick. Heat butter and sauté mushrooms until lightly browned (12 to 15 minutes). Remove to a 3-quart mixing bowl to cool for 10 minutes.

4. Place jack cheese in bowl with mushrooms. Add garlic, chives, ricotta, and salt. Mix well to combine.

5. Carefully unroll roulade and spread with filling, leaving 1 inch uncovered around edge. Roll up again and refrigerate until serving time.

6. To serve, remove and discard parchment, and cut roulade into 2-inch-thick slices. Place on individual plates. Top pieces with Tomato-Shallot Sauce.

Serves 8.

Tomato-Shallot Sauce   In a small bowl mix together tomato, shallots, vinegar, oil, oregano, salt, and pepper. Marinate for 1 hour before serving.

Food Processor Version   Use metal blade to process Parmesan cheese (about 1 minute) and remove. Slice mushrooms with slicing disk and remove. Use shredding disk to process well-chilled Monterey jack cheese with light pressure and remove. Use metal blade for garlic and chives. Use ingredients as directed in recipe.

■ HOT LEMON SOUFFLE

Dessert soufflés are often sprinkled with confectioners' sugar as soon as they come out of the oven. The most efficient way to do this is to put the sugar in a shaker (also called a dredger) made for this purpose. With a slight change in ingredients, this versatile base becomes the classic Grand Marnier version or the popular chocolate soufflé. See the variations at the end of the recipe.

> 1   cup milk
> 3   egg yolks
> 6   tablespoons granulated sugar
> 4   tablespoons flour
> 2   tablespoons fresh, strained lemon juice
> 4   teaspoons grated lemon rind
> 5   egg whites
>   Confectioners' sugar, for dusting (optional)

1. Set aside 2 tablespoons milk. Bring remaining milk to a boil in a small, heavy-bottomed saucepan.

Although a baked soufflé must be served immediately, the soufflé base can be made ahead so that the only work at the last minute is beating egg whites and putting the soufflé in the oven. Soufflés make a wonderful main course for lunch or light supper, along with a salad and a fruit dessert such as the sorbet shown here.

■ CHEESE ROULADE

The word *roulade* indicates that this cheese soufflé is baked flat and rolled. Any of the variations suggested for the Blue Cheese Soufflé (see page 205) will work for the roulade. The filling is a tasty combination of sautéed mushrooms and ricotta cheese, complemented by a seasoned, uncooked tomato sauce. This roulade is delicious served warm from the oven or chilled for a festive picnic. Parchment paper makes assembly and cleanup easier.

> 1   recipe Parmesan-Spinach Soufflé
>   (see page 205)
> ½   cup freshly grated Parmesan cheese or
>   dry bread crumbs, for dusting
> ½   pound mushrooms
> 1   tablespoon butter
> ¼   pound Monterey jack cheese, grated
> 1   clove garlic, minced
> ¼   cup snipped fresh chives
> 2   cups ricotta cheese
> 1½ teaspoons kosher salt

Tomato-Shallot Sauce

> 1   large tomato, minced
> 4   shallots, minced
> 2   tablespoons red wine vinegar
> 6   tablespoons olive oil
> 1   teaspoon oregano
> ½   teaspoon kosher salt
> ¼   teaspoon freshly ground pepper

2. In a medium bowl whisk yolks lightly. Add 4 tablespoons granulated sugar and 2 tablespoons reserved milk and whisk until thick and smooth. Stir in flour with whisk.

3. Gradually whisk in half the hot milk. Return mixture to milk in pan and whisk. Cook over low heat, whisking, until mixture comes to a boil.

4. Remove from heat and whisk in lemon juice and rind. If not using immediately, dab mixture with a small piece of butter to prevent a skin from forming. Mixture can be kept, covered, up to 8 hours in refrigerator.

5. Preheat oven to 425° F. Generously butter a 5-cup soufflé dish.

6. Transfer lemon mixture to a heavy saucepan and whisk until smooth. Heat over low heat, whisking, until just hot. Remove from heat.

7. Beat egg whites until stiff. Add remaining granulated sugar, beating at high speed. Continue beating for about 30 seconds. Stir about one quarter of whites into lemon mixture. Spoon this mixture over remaining egg whites and fold together as gently but as quickly as possible, until just blended.

8. Transfer soufflé mixture to buttered soufflé dish and quickly smooth top with spatula. Bake until puffed and browned (about 15 minutes). When you carefully move dish, soufflé should shake very gently in center.

9. Set soufflé dish on serving platter, sprinkle soufflé with confectioners' sugar (if desired), and serve immediately. Dish up with 2 spoons so that each portion includes some soft center and some firmer crust.

Serves 4.

Chocolate Soufflé Substitute 2 teaspoons vanilla extract and 2 ounces semisweet chocolate, melted, for lemon juice and lemon rind.

Grand Marnier Soufflé Substitute grated orange rind for lemon rind and Grand Marnier or other orange-flavored liqueur for lemon juice.

■ CHILLED LEMON SOUFFLE

Cold soufflés are more like mousses. Set with gelatin, they give the appearance of rising because they expand upward from their dish. Of course, this is an illusion. The sides of the mold are made taller with the use of a paper collar. Orange juice and rind can be substituted for the lemon juice, if desired.

¾ **cup fresh lemon juice**
1 **envelope unflavored gelatin**
3 **eggs, separated**
¾ **cup superfine sugar**
2 **teaspoons finely grated lemon rind**
1 **cup whipping cream**
   Pinch cream of tartar (optional)
1 **cup Chantilly Cream (see page 252),**
   for decoration

1. Wrap a 4- to 5-cup soufflé dish with a collar made from parchment paper, aluminum foil, or waxed paper. To make collar, cut a 12- by 19-inch rectangle; fold in half so that it is 6 by 19 inches. Turn folded edge up about 2 inches and tape collar around mold, with double fold hugging rim of dish. Fasten with kitchen string. Lightly oil inside of collar.

2. Place half the lemon juice in a small saucepan; sprinkle gelatin over juice and let soften (3 to 4 minutes); dissolve over low heat. Set aside.

3. In a double boiler over simmering water, whip egg yolks and sugar until thick and lemon-colored (ribbon stage); add remaining lemon juice and half the grated lemon rind.

4. Add gelatin mixture to egg-yolk–lemon mixture and continue to whip until blended. Set bowl over ice and stir until mixture is on the point of setting (it will have the consistency of cream whipped to soft peaks). In a separate bowl whip cream to soft peaks; fold into egg mixture.

5. In a copper or stainless steel bowl (add cream of tartar if not using copper bowl), whip egg whites until stiff, but not dry, peaks. Fold one third of whites into soufflé base to lighten, then fold in remaining whites and finally remaining lemon rind.

6. Pour soufflé into prepared mold and chill until set (2 to 3 hours).

7. When ready to serve, remove soufflé from refrigerator, carefully unwrap paper collar, and decorate with Chantilly Cream.

Serves 6.

Recipes and Related Information
Angel Food Cake, 82; Basic Sponge Cake, 83; Bind, 49; Cake, 77; Clarify, 131; Copper Egg-White Bowl, 155; Custard, 168; Egg and Caper Salad, 98; Egg-Preparation Equipment, 210; Egg Wash, 211; Emulsion and Emulsifier, 212; Génoise, 84; Hollandaise Sauce, 516; Mayonnaise, 519; Meringue, 359.

EGGPLANT

An ancient fruit probably native to India, the eggplant belongs to the nightshade family along with the tomato. Eggplants are cultivated in a variety of shapes, sizes, and colors. All have a thin, glossy, edible skin, a pale whitish green flesh that becomes soft and watery when cooked, and a mild flavor that combines well with oil, cheese, herbs, and other seasonings. The flesh of the large, globular Western eggplant has more moisture and is more bitter than that of the Asian varieties. To draw off some of the bitter juices, Western eggplants are often salted before cooking; Asian eggplants do not require salting.

Use Eggplants can be steamed or boiled to soften the pulp, then baked in a casserole with eggs, cheese, and bread crumbs; sliced and fried, either in flour or in batter; skewered and grilled; halved, stuffed, and baked; stewed with tomatoes and peppers or with oil and garlic; or sliced, layered with cheese and tomato sauce, and baked parmigiana. Indian cooks include eggplant in curries.

Asian cooks pickle it, braise it with pork, or fry it in tempura batter. In southern Italy, eggplant is part of pasta sauces, baked dishes, and the popular relish caponata. Greek moussaka is a baked casserole of eggplant, lamb, and cream sauce. The mild flavor of eggplant makes it a good foil for spicy sauces or highly seasoned dishes. It readily soaks up oil and seasonings.

Availability In the United States the most common variety is the large, globular, purple type, weighing about 1 pound each. The Japanese eggplant is long, slender, and deep purple; a similar Chinese variety is slightly longer, with a lavender skin. Other cultivated varieties, usually grown on farms near Asian communities, are the small, round, white Thai eggplant and the tiny, round, white Chinese variety used for pickling. Peak availability is July and August, but eggplants are available all year.

Selection Choose eggplants that feel heavy for their size. Skin should be smooth and shiny; flesh should feel firm, without bruised areas.

Storage Place eggplant in a plastic bag and refrigerate in crisper for up to four days.

Preparation Eggplants do not need to be peeled. Wash and trim stem ends. Large globe varieties may be bitter; to remove some bitterness, slice and salt eggplant liberally, then drain for one hour between sheets of paper towels weighted with a heavy plate. Pat dry.

Cooking See BRAISE, BROIL, DEEP-FRY, GRILL.

■ MEDITERRANEAN EGGPLANT SPREAD

The warm flavors of the Mediterranean come through in this coarse eggplant spread, designed to be made in a food processor. Serve it with savory crackers or wedges of pita bread before a dinner of garlicky roast lamb or chicken. It can be stored in the refrigerator for up to two weeks.

- 1 **eggplant (about 1 lb)**
- ¼ **cup olive oil**
- 2 **red bell peppers, chopped**
- 2 **large tomatoes, peeled, seeded, and chopped**
- 1 **medium zucchini, chopped**
- 2 **cloves garlic, minced**
- 1 **teaspoon paprika (preferably Hungarian)**
- 1 **teaspoon ground cumin**
  Juice of 1 lemon
  Salt, to taste
  Crackers, pita bread wedges, or Belgian endive leaves, for accompaniment

1. Preheat oven to 450° F. Trim ends of eggplant; cut eggplant into lengthwise slices, about ¼ inch thick.

2. Brush a baking sheet with 2 tablespoons oil, then heat in oven 5 minutes. Place eggplant slices on heated baking sheet and bake 10 to 15 minutes. Remove from oven and let cool.

3. Place eggplant in food processor and purée coarsely, turning motor on and off rapidly. Set aside.

4. In remaining oil, sauté peppers over medium heat until soft (7 to 8 minutes). Add tomatoes, zucchini, garlic, paprika, cumin, lemon juice, and salt to taste and continue cooking 2 minutes. Remove from heat and cool slightly.

5. Combine pepper mixture and eggplant; process briefly. Spread should be very coarse. Pack into crocks and seal with a little olive oil.

6. At serving time, taste and adjust salt and lemon as necessary. Serve with crackers, warm pita bread, or leaves of Belgian endive.

Makes 2 cups.

■ EGGPLANT RELISH

Sicilians are renowned for their sweet-and-sour dishes, a particularly winning example of which is caponata. This eggplant relish of wonderfully complex flavors and textures is scooped up with hearts of lettuce or chunks of bread. Smooth and crunchy, hot and cool, sweet and tart—it's all there in this beguiling dish.

- 3 **large eggplants** *or* **6 small Japanese eggplants**
- 1½ **cups olive oil**
- 3 **cups minced onions**
- ⅓ **cup minced garlic**
- 1 **cup diced celery**
- 2 **cups peeled, seeded, and chopped tomatoes (½-in. chunks)**
- 3 **tablespoons capers**
- ⅔ **cup minced carrot**
- ½ **cup toasted pine nuts**
- 2 **cups oil-cured black olives**
- ⅓ **cup sugar**
- ⅔ **cup red wine vinegar**
- ½ **teaspoon cayenne pepper, or more to taste**
  Salt, to taste
- ⅔ **cup minced parsley**
  Olive oil, for garnish
  Minced parsley, for garnish

1. Preheat oven to 375° F. Peel eggplants and cut into ½-inch dice. Oil a large baking sheet or roasting pan with 3 tablespoons olive oil. Toss eggplant with ¾ cup olive oil to coat well, then transfer to baking sheet or pan. Bake, tossing eggplant frequently, until soft and lightly browned (about 20 minutes).

2. Heat remaining oil in a large skillet over moderate heat. Add onions and garlic and sauté until soft (7 to

10 minutes); do not allow garlic to brown. Add celery, tomatoes, capers, carrot, pine nuts, olives, sugar, vinegar, and cayenne. Simmer slowly 30 minutes. Add salt to taste. Add eggplant and cook an additional 10 minutes. Add the ⅔ cup parsley and let cool. Taste again and correct seasoning. To serve, transfer to a bowl, drizzle with olive oil, and garnish with minced parsley.

Serves 12.

Food Processor Version   Use metal blade to process parsley, onions, garlic, celery, tomatoes, and carrots to desired consistency. Process each vegetable individually. For best results, process parsley first.

▨ MOUSSAKA

Plan a Greek dinner with this layered lamb and eggplant casserole as the main course. Start with a lemon and rice soup. For dessert, serve Baklava (see page 222), a sweet pastry made with tissue-thin filo dough, ground almonds, and honey.

> 1 **large eggplant (about 1½ lb)**
> **Salt, as needed**
> ⅓ **cup (approximately) olive or vegetable oil**
> 1 **pound ground lamb, crumbled**
> 1 **large onion, finely chopped**
> 1 **clove garlic, minced**
> ¼ **teaspoon ground cinnamon**
> 1 **teaspoon salt**
> ⅛ **teaspoon *each* freshly grated nutmeg and white pepper**
> ¼ **teaspoon dried oregano**
> ¼ **cup chopped parsley**
> 2 **tablespoons tomato paste**
> ½ **cup dry red wine or Beef Stock (see page 560)**
> ½ **cup freshly grated Parmesan cheese**

Cream Sauce

> 2 **tablespoons butter or margarine**
> 2 **tablespoons flour**
> ½ **teaspoon salt**
> **Dash *each* freshly grated nutmeg and white pepper**
> 2 **cups milk**
> 2 **eggs**
> 1 **egg yolk**

1. Preheat oven to 350° F. Cut off stem end of eggplant; cut unpeeled eggplant in half lengthwise. Cut crosswise in ½-inch slices; liberally sprinkle both sides with salt. Set in a single layer between sheets of paper towel and weight with a heavy plate; set aside for 1 hour to drain.

2. In a large frying pan, heat 1 tablespoon oil and cook lamb, stirring, until browned. Spoon off excess fat. Mix in onion and cook, stirring occasionally, until onion is tender. Mix in garlic, cinnamon, salt, nutmeg, pepper, oregano, parsley, tomato paste, and wine. Bring to a boil,

reduce heat, and simmer, covered, for 15 minutes. Uncover and continue simmering until sauce is thick (about 5 minutes).

3. Pat eggplant dry with paper towels. Arrange slices in a single layer in a large shallow pan. Brush with some of the remaining oil. Broil, about 4 inches from heat, until lightly browned (about 5 minutes). Turn, brush second sides with oil, and broil until browned (5 minutes longer).

4. To assemble, place half the eggplant slices in a single layer in an ungreased square or oval casserole of about 2-quart capacity. Top with meat sauce; sprinkle with 2 tablespoons Parmesan cheese. Cover with remaining eggplant; sprinkle with 2 more tablespoons cheese. Pour on Cream Sauce; sprinkle with remaining cheese. At this point casserole can be covered and refrigerated overnight.

5. When ready to serve, bake until top is lightly browned (45 minutes to 1 hour).

Serves 6.

Cream Sauce   Melt butter in a medium saucepan; stir in flour, salt, nutmeg, and pepper. Remove from heat and gradually stir in milk. Return to heat and cook, stirring, until thickened. In a small bowl beat eggs and egg yolk. Mix in a little of the hot sauce. Over low heat, blend egg mixture gradually into sauce and mix well.

Food Processor Version   Use metal blade to process Parmesan cheese, then parsley, onion, and finally garlic.

Moussaka, a Greek lamb and eggplant casserole, should be on everyone's list of dinner party entrées. It can be prepared up to the point of baking and then refrigerated overnight, if desired. An hour before serving, put the casserole in the oven to cook while the rest of the meal is being assembled.

■ EGGPLANT PARMESAN

This popular recipe is similar to lasagne, but here slices of eggplant replace the flat lasagne noodles. Eggplant has a meaty, satisfying texture. Note that the eggplant slices must drain for 1 hour to remove bitter juices before they are browned.

2 medium eggplants, peeled
Salt, as needed
Flour, as needed
Olive oil, for frying
2 cups Basic Tomato Sauce (see page 516)
½ pound mozzarella cheese, coarsely grated
½ cup freshly grated Parmesan cheese
3 tablespoons butter

1. Cut eggplants horizontally in ½-inch slices; liberally sprinkle both sides with salt. Place in a single layer between sheets of paper towel and weight with a heavy plate; set aside for 1 hour to drain. Pat dry with paper towels. Dredge with flour and fry slices in a shallow amount of olive oil in a heavy pan over medium-high heat until lightly browned, adding more oil as necessary. Salt to taste and drain on paper towels.

2. Preheat oven to 400° F. Butter a 9- by 13-inch baking dish. Place a single layer of fried eggplant in dish; cover with ⅓ of the tomato sauce, ⅓ of the mozzarella cheese, and ⅓ of the Parmesan cheese. Continue layering eggplant, sauce, and cheese for 2 more layers, ending with Parmesan. Dot with butter and bake until bubbling hot throughout (about 30 minutes).

Serves 4.

■ RATATOUILLE

Complement this robust red pepper and eggplant stew with grilled garlic sausages and a green salad.

¼ cup olive oil
1 small unpeeled eggplant (about 1 lb), cut in ½-inch cubes
1 medium onion, slivered
½ pound mushrooms, thinly sliced
1 sweet red or green bell pepper, cut in strips
1 clove garlic, minced
¾ teaspoon *each* dried basil and dried oregano
½ teaspoon salt
⅛ teaspoon freshly ground black pepper
Pinch cayenne pepper
1 can (1 lb) tomatoes

1. In a large frying pan over medium heat, heat olive oil and cook eggplant and onion, stirring often, until vegetables are soft (about 10 minutes). Add mushrooms and pepper; cook, stirring occasionally, until the mushrooms brown lightly. Mix in minced garlic, basil, oregano, salt, pepper, cayenne, and tomatoes (coarsely chopped) and their liquid.

2. Bring mixture to a boil, reduce heat, and simmer, stirring occasionally, until mixture is thick and reduced to about 4 cups (20 to 25 minutes). Remove from heat and let cool for about 10 minutes.

3. Serve warm or at room temperature.

Serves 8.

> ***Recipes and Related Information***
> *Tempura Batter, 28; Vegetable Mixed Grill, 296.*

EGG-PREPARATION EQUIPMENT

These devices won't make your cooked egg more tender, but they aid preparation in some way and are quite popular according to retailers. See EGG for cooking information.

EGG CODDLER

These are servers and cooking pans in one. They are made of porcelain with a screw-on metal lid, or of heatproof glass with a plastic top. To use, one or two eggs are broken into a cup, covered with butter, cream, some chopped herbs, or other seasoning, and the lid is fastened. To cook the egg, the cup is immersed in simmering water. The finished dish is presented in the coddler. Some versions have an optional rack with handle that holds one or two cups and makes it easier to lower coddlers into hot water and draw them out when eggs are ready.

EGG POACHERS

Perfectly shaped poached eggs—cooked in the classic manner, in simmering water—can be difficult to achieve, especially if you are trying them for the first time. Help is available if you seek it out.

From England come deep, round rings; from France, egg-shaped perforated stands; from the United States, a multiple-egg poacher that fits into a skillet. All three give a poached egg a regular shape and prevent most of the white from drifting away from the yolk as egg cooks.

To use rings or individual stands, butter well or spray with a nonstick vegetable cooking spray. Place one in a pan with simmering water, break egg into it, then cook as directed in recipe. Rings can also be used for frying eggs—handy if you want to make them exactly round to match an English muffin.

The multiple-egg poacher is an aluminum plate coated with a nonstick finish. It has four separate wells—one egg goes in each—which maintain shape of the eggs as they poach. The plate has short feet that sit on the bottom of a shallow pan and holes between egg cups so that the cooking water can rise up through the plate, cover eggs, and cook them.

These tools are designed to simplify egg preparation or cookery. Shown clockwise from top right are egg poacher, egg slicer, egg wedger, egg separator, egg coddlers.

EGG SEPARATOR

This utensil is for those who lack confidence to separate yolk and white with the eggshell transfer technique or are too squeamish to crack the egg into their palm and let the white slip through their fingers. The separator is an aluminum, plastic, or ceramic saucer with slots cut around a cuplike center depression. To use, set over a receptacle of some sort. The design takes advantage of the differing viscosities of yolk and white; the thicker yolk gets trapped in the saucer while the more fluid white slides through the slots into the bowl set beneath.

EGG SLICER AND WEDGER

These devices create perfect slices or wedges of hard-cooked eggs. Both slicers and wedgers are two-part, hinged devices. The lower section holds the egg in place and is slatted or divided; the upper arm is made of stainless steel wires strung parallel for slicers, or intersecting for wedgers, across a metal frame. A shelled egg is set on the base and the wires are brought down and through white, yolk, and between the slats or sections. Slicers and wedgers also work for slicing mushrooms.

EGG WASH

This mixture of egg or egg yolk lightly beaten with water or milk has several uses. When brushed on pastry or bread, it promotes a shiny surface; it also works as a glue to join two pieces of raw pastry or to give seeds something to adhere to when sprinkled on raw dough. If milk or cream is used rather than water, a soft, rather than crusty, surface develops. The term can also refer to beaten egg combined with a splash of water or milk, a typical binding mixture for bread coatings.

Egg washes fall into three categories: whole egg, egg yolk, and egg white.

Whole-Egg Wash This mixture can be used for sweet or savory dishes. It creates a medium-brown finish and works well as a glue.

Egg-Yolk Wash This is the strongest. It promotes a rich, brown color when baked, is usually seasoned with a pinch of salt, and is used on savory dishes.

Egg-White Wash Often used on sweet dishes as a base for a dusting of sugar, this wash promotes a silvery, crispy surface and is suitable for sweet pies and pastries.

A warm, sweet-and-sour dressing softens the raw crispness of the greens in Hot Romaine and Escarole Salad. Like all wilted salads, this one should be served immediately after tossing.

EMULSION AND EMULSIFIER

When two liquids usually incapable of forming a stable mixture are in suspension, the combination is called an emulsion. What links them together is the addition of a third substance, called an emulsifier, which is compatible with both. For example, oil and water will mix when beaten, but will separate as soon as the beating stops unless stabilized with an emulsifying agent. Emulsions can be temporary (lasting a few minutes, such as an oil and vinegar salad dressing) or more permanent (lasting hours, days, or longer, such as mayonnaise).

Egg yolk is the most effective emulsifier for sauces. Other common ones are acids (lemon juice, vinegar, wine), dry and prepared (wet) mustard, and paprika, which is why these ingredients are basic to vinaigrette dressings.

Recipes and Related Information
Hollandaise Sauce, 516; Mayonnaise, 519; Vinaigrette Dressing, 520.

ENRICH, TO

To add an ingredient, known as an enrichment, to a dish to deepen its flavor and develop a luxurious finish, both visually and to the taste. Butter and cream, and sometimes egg yolks, are enrichments that are often swirled into sauces and cream soups just before serving.

ESCAROLE

A sturdy salad green of the chicory family, escarole has broad, wavy, jagged-edged green outer leaves that whiten near the core. The flavor is slightly bitter; the texture is firm and crisp.

Use   An escarole salad can stand up to hot bacon dressings or assertive vinaigrettes. Wilted escarole leaves can be added to bean or vegetable soups. Just a few hearty escarole leaves contribute pleasing texture to a mixed green salad.

Availability   Escarole is sporadically available throughout the year. However, it is at its best and most abundant in the winter.

Selection   Leaves should be crisp and creamy inside; avoid wilted heads with browning edges.

Storage   Keep escarole in a plastic bag in refrigerator crisper for up to three days.

Preparation   Discard ragged or dark green outer leaves. Wash well and dry, trim core end, and tear by hand into smaller pieces.

■ HOT ROMAINE AND ESCAROLE SALAD

This barely wilted salad combines two greens with substantial texture—romaine and escarole—in a piquant sweet-and-sour dressing with bacon and tomato.

> 2 **tablespoons fresh lemon juice**
> 1 **tablespoon catsup**
> 1 **teaspoon *each* sugar and Dijon mustard**
> ½ **teaspoon Worcestershire sauce**
> 1 **clove garlic, minced**
> 6 **slices bacon**
>   **Vegetable oil, as needed**
> 1 **medium onion, finely chopped**
> 6 **cups torn romaine lettuce**
> 4 **cups torn escarole**
> 1 **medium tomato, cut in thin wedges**
>   **Freshly ground pepper**

1. In a small bowl mix lemon juice, catsup, sugar, mustard, Worcestershire sauce, and garlic.

2. Cut bacon crosswise into ½-inch strips. In a large frying pan, cook bacon until crisp and brown, stirring often; remove with a slotted spoon and drain.

Measure ¼ cup bacon drippings; add oil (if needed) to make ¼ cup, or discard any drippings in excess of ¼ cup. In the same pan cook onion in drippings over medium heat, stirring, for about 1 minute. Add lemon juice mixture; bring to a boil.

3. Add romaine, escarole, and tomato; immediately remove from heat. Mix lightly to coat well with dressing. Transfer to a salad bowl and sprinkle with bacon and pepper. Serve at once.

Serves 4 to 6.

▓ ESCAROLE SOUP

Try this very simple soup that can be prepared and served within one hour. Fresh spinach or other greens may be substituted for escarole.

- **⅓ cup butter**
- **1 small onion, minced**
- **1 head escarole, well washed and coarsely chopped
  Salt and freshly ground pepper, to taste**
- **4 cups homemade Chicken Stock (see page 560)
  or regular-strength canned broth**
- **¼ cup crushed vermicelli**
- **¼ cup freshly grated Parmesan cheese, for topping**

1. In a large saucepan melt butter and sauté onion over medium heat until browned. Add escarole and salt and pepper to taste. Sauté briefly, then add stock. Cover and cook over low heat for 15 minutes. Add vermicelli and cook an additional 15 minutes.

2. Taste and season. Serve with Parmesan cheese.

Makes about 8 cups, 4 servings.

EVAPORATE, TO

To release steam from a liquid by boiling. Cooks use this principle when boiling liquids to decrease their volume and to intensify their flavor. Sauces are often thickened or reduced this way. A shallow, wide pan promotes faster evaporation than does a deep, narrow one, because the heat reaches more of the liquid at one time and the greater surface area allows water vapor to escape more quickly.

EVISCERATE, TO

To remove the internal organs from freshly killed birds, animals, and fish. Because the viscera spoil quickly and the enzymes in the digestive tract speed deterioration, evisceration is done for sanitary reasons. Also called draw and gut, it is typically done by slitting from the base of the gullet to the bottom of the belly and trimming the entrails from where they are attached to the chest cavity.

EXTRACT AND ESSENCE

The many extracts and essences used to flavor foods are derived from aromatic plant oils, from natural, nonplant ingredients, and from synthetics combined in a laboratory.

The characteristic taste and fragrance of many fruits, flowers, spices, and other plants are contained in the essential oils of the plant. Pure extracts are made by distilling these essential oils and dissolving them in alcohol or a diluted alcohol base, which keeps the oil in suspension. Pure vanilla and almond extracts, for example, are made in this fashion. Unlike extracts, flavorings—butterscotch and rum are two examples—are neither alcohol-based nor derived from plants.

Some flavors, such as maple or banana, cannot be extracted by distillation. In place of pure extracts, scientists have developed imitation and artificial flavorings. Imitation flavorings contain all or some nonnatural ingredients; artificial flavorings such as butterscotch may contain natural or synthetic flavors but do not have a natural counterpart that they are attempting to reproduce.

Use   Extracts and essences impart flavor to a given dish without adding solids or excess liquids. They are most commonly used in baking. Home cooks add vanilla, almond, lemon, and peppermint extracts and butter and rum flavorings to cakes, puddings, ice creams, custards, cookies, and candies. Rose water and orange flower water are used not only in baked goods and custards but also in savory rice dishes.

Extracts and essences are highly volatile; they dissipate rapidly in the atmosphere, even more rapidly in the presence of heat. As a result, they should be added to cool or cooling mixtures for maximum effect. When creaming butter and sugar for cakes or cookies, add extracts to the fat to slow vaporization and promote even distribution.

In general, 1 teaspoon of extract is enough to flavor 1 pint or 1 pound of food. Delicate flower waters—orange flower water and rose water—may be used more liberally.

Availability   Although many extracts and flavorings widely used in commercial food manufacturing are unavailable to the consumer, dozens of extracts and essences are packaged for consumers and are sold on spice shelves in supermarkets.

Selection   Pure extracts will give a truer, more concentrated flavor than imitation or artificial flavorings. For flavorings unavailable in pure form, such as banana or pistachio, an artificial extract will probably taste less harsh than the imitation product.

Storage   Extracts lose potency when exposed to light and heat. Stored in a cool, dark place, they will keep indefinitely.

F

Solid cooking fats such as butter, margarine, and lard, along with liquid oils, play important culinary roles: They add tenderness, flavor, and color, keep foods from sticking to cooking pans, and add richness to sauces and dressings.

FAT

Fats and oils have similar chemical compositions. Both are made up of triglycerides (glycerol molecules with three fatty acids attached). However, fats are solid at room temperature and oils liquid because fats contain more saturated fatty acids. As a result of this difference, fats and oils have different cooking qualities.

The following section looks at the role of solid fats in cooking. Also see BUTTER; MARGARINE; PORK, About Pork Lard; and POULTRY, About Chicken Livers, Giblets, and Fat. For information on liquid fats, see OIL.

Use   To the cook, solid fats are especially important in baking, deep-frying, and sautéing. In addition, they are useful as flavor enhancers, emulsifiers, and sealants. The best fat for a particular dish depends on the flavor and texture desired.

Storage   Although the decomposition process is not entirely understood, it is known that saturated fats oxidize and turn rancid more slowly than unsaturated fats. Beef, for example, has a longer freezer life than chicken or pork because its fat is more saturated. Pastries made with lard stay fresh longer than those made with poly-unsaturated oils. These facts probably have more implications for the commercial food processor than for the home cook who will choose a cooking or baking fat for its flavor and texture.

For specific storage instructions, see individual fats.

FAT IN BAKING

The primary role of fat in baking is as a shortening or tenderizing agent. When fat is combined with flour in a batter or dough, it limits development of gluten, an elastic protein network that gives a baked product its structure. If less strands of gluten are developed, the result is a more tender cake, cookie, pie dough, or loaf of bread; more gluten means baked goods will be tougher. Cookies without solid fat, such as meringues, are hard rather than tender.

Fat is also responsible for making pastry doughs flaky. In puff pastry and Danish pastry, for example, the fat content (usually butter) is extremely high. Butter is rolled between the layers of dough to make alternating layers of gluten and fat. When baked, the fat melts and generates steam, which leavens the dough and produces flaky sheets of pastry.

Fat imparts flavor and color to baked goods. An all-butter pie crust has a noticeably different flavor and color than an all-lard crust. The flavor of lard is important to Mexican and Chinese breads and pastries; the flavor of butter is important to French pastries. Although, technically, butter can be substituted for lard (or vice versa), the authentic, characteristic flavor of the product often depends on the fat used.

Some baked goods use fat as a leavening agent. When fat and sugar are creamed, the air trapped in the dough or batter adds volume to the baked product. For this reason, thorough creaming is essential to producing a cake with a light texture. Fats at room temperature cream more easily; they incorporate and hold air better (see CREAM).

Fat adds richness, smoothness, and sheen to the crumb of baked goods. High-fat breads such as brioche have a richer flavor and smoother, shinier crumb than fat-free breads such as a French-style baguette.

Fat improves the longevity of baked goods. By coating the starch granules, it slows moisture loss. Breads with fat last for several days, in contrast to the fat-free baguette, which goes stale in one day.

FAT IN DEEP-FRYING

Deep-frying requires a fat that does not burn or break down at high temperatures or in the presence of moisture. The temperature at which a fat or oil begins to deteriorate is called its smoke point. In general, saturated fats are more stable and have higher smoke points than unsaturated fats. The presence of free fatty acids in a fat, however, lowers its smoke point. Animal fats such as suet and butter have lower smoke points than vegetable oils because of their high proportion of free fatty acids. The best fat for deep-frying, then, would be a saturated (fully hydrogenated) vegetable shortening. These shortenings have a smoke point of about 460° F, compared to 320° to 330° F for butter and 340° to 350° F for lard.

Repeated use will lower the smoke point of a fat because of the moisture and the food particles left behind from previous use. To extend the life of a frying fat, carefully strain or filter it after each application, and store in a tightly capped container away from light and heat. Frying in a deep kettle, as opposed to a shallow, wide pan, exposes less of the fat to air and thus extends its life somewhat (and is safer). Fat that smokes or foams has broken down and should be discarded.

FAT IN SAUTEING

In panfrying and sautéing, the hot pan is coated with a thin layer of fat. The hot fat keeps the sautéed food from sticking to the pan and it aids in the formation of a crust, which helps to contain juices. It also imparts flavor and helps conduct heat from the pan to the item being cooked.

Although the mild flavor of butter may be desirable in sautéed items—especially in delicate foods such as fish and veal—butter burns easily. Clarified butter (see page 68) is preferred for high-heat sautéing because it has a higher smoke point than whole butter. Alternatively, adding oil to the butter in the sauté pan raises its smoke point.

OTHER USES FOR FAT

Apart from cooking, the most obvious use for fat is as a flavor enhancer. Adding butter to mashed potatoes or spreading goose fat on toast is the cook's way of taking advantage of the flavor of fat. Fat also adds what food scientists call mouthfeel to a dish, a palate sensation that largely determines whether we accept or reject a particular dish.

Fat also acts as an emulsifier in some sauces. To make a classic French beurre blanc, softened butter is whipped into a reduction of wine and shallots. The acid in the wine holds the butter in suspension and creates a filmy sauce. Whisking a few tablespoons of butter into a sauce enriches it, emulsifies it, and gives it sheen.

English potted meats and French *rillettes* (potted pork) and duck *confit* (preserved duck) are packed into jars or crocks and sealed with a layer of melted fat—usually fat rendered from the meat itself. The fat effectively keeps out moisture and air, and extends the storage life of the food. Potted meats sealed with fat will keep for several weeks under refrigeration.

> ### Recipes and Related Information
> Bard, 25; Beurre Blanc, 518; Cake, 77; Cream, 161; Cream Puff Pastry, 162; Deep-fry, 174; Emulsion and Emulsifier, 212; Fry, 254; Lard, 338; Panfry, 404; Puff Pastry, 480; Sauté, 531; Stir-fry, 557; Yeast Bread, 613.

FEIJOA

Also known as the pineapple guava, the feijoa is a small oval fruit with a smooth, gray-green skin, a creamy white flesh with a juicy, pearlike texture, and a sweet flavor reminiscent of pineapple, pear, and banana. It is native to South America but is now grown in California and throughout the South Pacific.

Use Enjoy feijoa "on the half shell," with lime or lemon. Peel, slice, and serve with prosciutto, or use it in fruit salads, preserves and jellies, sorbets, and mousses.

Availability The New Zealand crop is available from March through June, the California fruit from September through December.

Selection Ripe feijoas are fragrant and give slightly to gentle pressure.

Storage Place ripe fruit in a plastic bag in the refrigerator crisper. Underripe fruit will ripen if kept at room temperature. Use ripe fruit as soon as possible.

FENNEL

Also known as finocchio, fennel is a plant of Mediterranean origin, valued for its bulb, leaves, stems, flowers, and seeds. The greenish white bulb is made up of overlapping ribs like those of celery, broad at the bulbous base but narrowing to tubular stems. Feathery green leaves grow up from the middle of the bulb. Raw fennel has a licoricelike flavor and a crunchy, celerylike texture. Cooking mutes the flavor somewhat and softens the texture.

PREPARING FENNEL

Cut off and discard upper portion, including feathery leaves and ribs; remove bruised or discolored outer ribs; trim base.

Halve trimmed bulbs and remove a wedge of tough core from each.

Slice halves thinly lengthwise; bulbs can also be sliced crosswise, depending upon use.

Use   Fennel bulb is eaten raw or cooked. Slice thinly and add it to salads, or dress with lemon, olive oil, and freshly grated Parmesan cheese for a first course, or serve it raw with an assortment of vegetables and a dipping sauce. Bake it with butter and bread crumbs, add it to soups or stews, or steam it and dress with butter and lemon or cheese sauce. Fennel bulb is particularly compatible with white-fleshed fish and lobster.

French cooks stuff fish with feathery fennel leaves or add leaves to salads or fish soups. The edible flowers may also be added to salads. Young fennel branches may be eaten raw with oil and salt or with a dip. Adding dried fennel branches to a fire imparts a special fragrance to grilled fish.

The small, yellowish brown fennel seed adds a licorice-like flavor to fish soups, breads, sausages, pork roasts, stuffings, and apple pie. Indians often serve fennel seed after dinner as a digestive and breath freshener.

Availability   Fresh bulb fennel is sold in Italian markets and many supermarkets in fall and winter. Fennel seed is available on supermarket spice racks.

Selection   Fennel bulb should be smooth and whitish green without cracks and discoloration; leaves should look fresh and lively, not wilted. The bulb should be compact; spreading at the top indicates overmaturity. For fennel seed, remember that packaged seasonings lose quality after a while; try to buy from a store that restocks its spice section fairly often.

Storage   Keep fennel in a plastic bag in the refrigerator crisper; use within three to four days. Store fennel seed in an airtight container in a cool, dark place; it will keep indefinitely.

Preparation   Trim bulb base and cut away feathery stalks (save for other uses). Remove thick, tough outer ribs. Halve, core, and slice crosswise or lengthwise. See Preparing Fennel at left.

Cooking   See BOIL, BRAISE, GRILL, STEAM, STIR-FRY.

■ BRAISED FENNEL

This simple treatment brings out the subtle, sweet flavor of fennel. Although the fennel takes some time to tenderize, the preparation is easy and needs little attention other than occasional stirring. If desired, substitute chicken stock for the water or use a mixture of half stock and half water. If stock was used, taste the finished dish before adding salt; most stocks are already seasoned.

> 3 **large fennel bulbs**
> ½ **cup olive oil**
>   **Salt, to taste**

1. Remove and discard damaged or wilted outside parts of fennel, as well as tops, and cut a slice off bottom of bulbs. Cut bulbs into lengthwise slices and wash slices in cold water.

2. Place fennel slices, olive oil, and water to barely cover in a saucepan. Cook over medium heat, uncovered, until fork-tender (30 to 40 minutes), stirring occasionally. If fennel becomes dry, add a bit of hot water. Add salt to taste and serve on a preheated platter.

Serves 4.

■ FENNEL AND ARTICHOKE SALAD

The first spring artichokes are a delicious partner for the last of the fennel. Marinated in oil and lemon, then served with toast and Parmesan cheese, the two vegetables flatter each other and almost any main course. Grilled fish, roast lamb, or chicken are all fine choices.

> 1 **large *or* 2 small fennel bulbs**
> 3 **lemons**
> ¾ **cup olive oil**
>   **Coarse salt and freshly ground pepper, to taste**
> 4 **small artichokes (about 2 to 3 in. diameter)**
> 12 **slices toasted baguette (see Note)**
> ¼ **pound Parmesan cheese, sliced in long, thin slabs**
>   **Olive oil and freshly ground pepper, for garnish**

1. Wash fennel bulbs and remove any tough outer stalks. Halve and core them, and slice thinly lengthwise. Put fennel slices in a stainless steel, glass, or ceramic bowl. Add juice of 2 lemons, olive oil, and salt and pepper to taste. Toss to blend and set aside to marinate.

2. Remove dark green outer leaves of artichokes; cut off top third of artichokes with a serrated knife. Rub all cut surfaces with lemon. Cook in boiling, salted water until just tender (12 to 15 minutes). Drain and refresh under cold running water, then drain thoroughly and pat dry. Cut artichokes in half. Add to fennel in bowl and stir to coat with oil. Marinate an additional 30 to 45 minutes. Taste and add more salt or remaining lemon if necessary.

3. To serve, spoon a little of the marinade onto individual salad plates. Arrange fennel atop marinade. Surround with slices of baguette. Top bread with artichoke hearts. Alternate Parmesan slices with bread slices on plates and drizzle salad with a little additional olive oil. Serve immediately and pass the pepper mill.

Serves 4.

Note   If desired, brush toast with garlic oil while bread is still warm.

FENUGREEK

The small, yellowish brown seeds inside the pods of the fenugreek plant are actually legumes, like peas and beans, but they are so aromatic when dried and roasted that they're used as a spice. Fenugreek is especially important to the cuisines of India and North and East Africa.

Use Fenugreek is an important ingredient in most curry powder blends. It is also, surprisingly, used to flavor imitation maple syrup. Ethiopians eat the tiny fenugreek seeds as a vegetable, cooking them as they do peas or beans; they also use fenugreek as a spice in stews. In India, fenugreek is an ingredient in chutneys and mango pickles as well as curries; in Morocco, fenugreek is added to breads.

Availability Whole fenugreek seed can be found in Indian and Middle Eastern markets and some specialty and health-food stores, usually in bulk.

Selection Packaged seasonings lose quality after a while; try to buy from a store that restocks its spice section fairly often.

Storage Keep fenugreek in an airtight container in a cool, dark place. It will last indefinitely. Ground fenugreek quickly loses its aromatic qualities; for maximum flavor, grind whole fenugreek as needed.

Preparation The full flavor of fenugreek is brought out by roasting. Toast whole seeds in a skillet over low heat, shaking skillet often, until seeds are fragrant. Soak them in water to soften, then grind in a pepper mill, clean coffee grinder, or electric minichopper, or with a mortar and pestle.

FERMENTATION

For home cooks, the most relevant application of fermentation relates to the action of yeast in breadmaking. When yeast is mixed with sugar in a moist, warm environment (around 80° F), a chemical reaction occurs, which as a by-product gives off carbon dioxide gas—the primary leavening agent for yeast bread doughs. Sugar is introduced into these doughs directly in granulated form and indirectly as the yeast converts starch present in flour into glucose, a simple sugar. Alcohol is also released during fermentation, but evaporates during baking. The appealing, yeasty aroma of making bread is in part due to products of fermentation.

Fermentation begins when the dough is mixed. Under conditions of proper temperature and the availability of fermentable sugars, it continues until the dough heats to 138° F in the oven, a temperature that kills yeast. Many bakers believe that a more flavorful yeast dough develops from slow fermentation. Most recipes more commonly refer to this process as rising or proofing.

Fermentation is also the process by which wine is made. A yeast naturally present on the skin of grapes feeds on the sugars in the fresh, crushed fruit to produce ethyl alcohol (ethanol) and carbon dioxide gas. Vintners commonly kill most of the wild yeast at the time of crushing with sulfur dioxide, because it produces inconsistent fermentation, and then add a "pure" strain of cultured yeast with known properties.

Once yeast starter is added to grapes (or juice) in the fermenting vessel, the yeast quickly multiplies, and before long millions of yeast cells are alive in the must (unfermented juice). For several days, the must ferments rapidly, and the carbon dioxide quickly bubbles out of the fermenting tank. Gradually, as the sugar is consumed and the alcohol level rises, the yeast cells begin to die and settle to the bottom of the tank.

Left alone, the wine will ferment completely dry, that is, until all the sugar is consumed. The vintner will step in, however, to control the fermentation process by monitoring temperature and adding sulfur dioxide, and, by filtering, to achieve a desired result.

Some wines undergo a second type of fermentation, known as malolactic fermentation, after the sugar fermentation is complete. Malolactic bacteria transform one of the natural grape acids, malic acid, into the less-tart-tasting lactic acid.

Recipes and Related Information
Yeast, 613; Yeast Bread, 613.

Ripe grapes, such as those shown here entering a stemmer/crusher, can contain as much as 25 percent sugar by weight, making them among the sweetest fruits. Fermentation by microscopic yeast cells turns the sugar to alcohol, and the juice into wine.

FIDDLEHEAD FERN

The ostrich fern, which grows wild in New England and Canada, puts forth tightly curled green shoots every spring. These shoots, known as fiddlehead ferns, are gathered when they are 2 to 5 inches long and very tightly curled and are a prized wild delicacy. The texture of the shoots resembles that of string beans; the flavor is akin to asparagus and spinach. The unfurled, mature shoots are poisonous.

Use Fiddlehead ferns are eaten both raw in salads and cooked. Steamed, they are delicious hot with butter or cold with vinaigrette. Stir cooked fiddleheads into scrambled eggs or toss with pasta; try them deep-fried or stir-fried with other vegetables.

Availability Fiddlehead ferns are gathered wild in the late spring in New England and Canada. They are available fresh in some markets at that time. Some specialty shops carry frozen and canned fiddlehead ferns.

Selection Choose the smallest fiddlehead ferns with solid green color and without browning. They should look tightly curled and crisp, not wilted.

Storage Wrap in damp paper towels, then place in a plastic bag in the refrigerator for no longer than one or two days.

Preparation Rub off fuzzy scales or wash under running water to remove them. Cook whole.

Cooking See DEEP-FRY, SAUTE, STIR-FRY.

FIG

The plump, soft fig is the fruit of the ficus tree, of which there are hundreds of varieties. The ficus tree probably originated in Asia Minor and is certainly one of the most ancient edible plants. When ripe, figs are one of the sweetest fruits. Depending on variety, the most common cultivated figs are purple, green, yellow, or white skinned, with flesh that ranges from gold to deep red. The skin is edible, the ripe flesh moist and intensely sweet. See DRIED FRUIT, Dried Figs, for information on the dried fruit.

Use   Fresh, ripe figs are a nutritious out of hand snack. Sliced, sugared, and drizzled with milk or cream, they make a delicious breakfast or dessert. Serve halved figs as an appetizer with thinly sliced prosciutto. Slice or halve them and add to fruit salads, or poach them briefly for fruit compotes. Baked fresh figs flavored with butter, lemon, and honey are a delicious late-summer or early-fall dessert. Sliced figs make a beautiful, softly colored topping for a fruit tart.

Availability   Fresh figs are sold sporadically from June through October, with the best supply in August and September.

Selection   Choose figs that are as soft and ripe as possible. However, overripe fruit will have a sour odor due to fermentation of juice. Avoid bruised fruit, but fruit shriveled by the sun will be especially sweet.

Storage   Leave underripe figs at room temperature until ripe. Ripe figs are highly perishable; store on a paper-towel–lined tray in the refrigerator and use as soon as possible; hold no more than one or two days.

Preparation   Remove stem ends. Fresh figs do not require peeling, although some recipes may call for it.

Cooking   See POACH.

■ FIGS WITH FLAVORED RICOTTA

This elegant dessert only takes a few minutes to assemble. The citrus-infused ricotta-cheese filling can be prepared in advance and held in the refrigerator until needed. The nuts can be chopped ahead as well. All that is left to do is slice the figs and fill them.

> 12   medium-sized ripe fresh figs
> 1   cup ricotta cheese
> 1   teaspoon *each* grated lemon rind
>   and orange rind
> ¾   teaspoon vanilla extract
> ¼   cup honey
>   Chopped pistachios, hazelnuts,
>   or almonds, for garnish

1. Remove stem ends from figs. Cut each into a tulip shape by slicing in quarters from stem almost to blossom end. Press on stem end to open petals.

2. In a blender or food processor, whirl ricotta, citrus rinds, vanilla, and honey. Stuff each fig with 2 tablespoons flavored ricotta. Serve garnished with chopped nuts.

Serves 6.

FILET; FILLET, TO; FILLET

Filet refers to slices cut from the narrow end of a beef tenderloin, the most well-known being filet mignon steaks.

To fillet is to completely bone and trim a cut of meat or fish; *fillet* is the name of the long, boneless piece of meat or fish that results.

> ### *Recipes and Related Information*
> *Beef, 37; Bone, 55; Fish, 223.*

FILO PASTRY

Also spelled *phyllo,* filo pastry is made from a wheat-flour dough rolled into tissue-thin sheets. It is a common ingredient in Greek and Middle Eastern cooking. Although filo resembles strudel leaves, it is generally rolled thinner. In fact, filo dough is rolled and stretched so thin that it is difficult and time-consuming to make at home. When basted liberally with butter and baked, filo makes a crisp, flaky wrapper for turnovers and other baked dishes.

Use   Traditionally filo dough is used as a wrapper for the Greek feta cheese–stuffed turnovers called *tiropita* and for the spinach-stuffed *spanakopita.* Filo is layered with walnuts and honey to make a sweet dessert called baklava. Substitute filo dough for other pastry wrappers in turnover recipes or as a replacement for strudel leaves in cabbage or apple strudel. Filo can also be substituted for *warka,* the thin pastry used in Morocco for *pastilla* (a pigeon pie) and *brik* (a large fried turnover).

Availability   Filo pastry is found frozen in most supermarkets and fresh in some Middle Eastern markets. It is generally packaged in 1-pound boxes.

Storage   Filo dough may be frozen for up to one year. Refrigerated filo dough may be frozen immediately after purchase or refrigerated unopened for up to three weeks. After opening, use within a few days. Thaw frozen dough 8 hours or overnight in the refrigerator; do not refreeze.

Preparation   Filo is fragile and dries out quickly. It must be handled rapidly and kept moist. Open package only after remaining ingredients are ready. After removing filo from its plastic bag, lay flat and cover with waxed paper weighted with a damp towel. (Do not allow towel to touch filo.) For further guidance, follow package instructions or a particular recipe.

MOROCCAN PASTILLA

Moroccan restaurants serve small portions of this dish as a first course, but it also makes a substantial main dish. In this recipe chicken has been substituted for pigeon, the traditional bird. The pastry is filo, the same thin dough as used for Baklava on page 222.

> 1 frying chicken (3 to 3½ lb), cut up
> 2 small onions, 1 coarsely chopped and 1 finely chopped
> ¼ cup finely chopped parsley, plus 1 sprig
> 2½ teaspoons salt
> ⅛ teaspoon dried thyme
> 2 cups water
> 1 cup finely chopped blanched almonds
> ¼ cup granulated sugar
> 2 teaspoons ground cinnamon
> ½ teaspoon ground ginger
> ¼ teaspoon *each* freshly grated nutmeg and ground cardamom
> 1 cup butter or margarine
> 6 eggs
> 2 cloves garlic, minced
> ¼ teaspoon freshly ground pepper
> ½ pound (half package) filo dough, thawed 8 hours in refrigerator if frozen
> ¼ cup confectioners' sugar, for dusting
> ½ teaspoon (approximately) ground cinnamon, for dusting

1. In a large skillet or Dutch oven, combine chicken with coarsely chopped onion, parsley sprig, 1½ teaspoons salt, dried thyme, and the water. Bring to a boil, reduce heat, cover, and simmer until chicken is very tender (about 1½ hours). Strain and reserve broth for another use. Remove chicken from bones in large pieces, discarding bones and skin.

2. Preheat oven to 350° F. Place almonds in a shallow baking pan; bake, stirring occasionally, until golden brown (10 to 15 minutes). Cool. In a small bowl mix granulated sugar, 2 teaspoons cinnamon, ginger, nutmeg, and cardamom.

3. In a large frying pan, cook finely chopped onion in 3 tablespoons butter until limp but not browned. In a medium bowl beat eggs with garlic, 1 teaspoon salt, pepper, and chopped parsley. Add to onion mixture and cook over low heat, stirring occasionally, until eggs are softly set. Remove from heat.

4. Melt remaining butter. Use it to brush a 9-inch springform pan generously. Unfold sheets of filo dough so they lie flat. Cover with waxed paper, then a damp towel, to prevent them from drying out. Line pan with 1 sheet of dough, allowing dough to extend over edge of pan; brush generously with butter. Top with a second sheet of dough and brush with butter. Fold 6 more sheets of dough to fit pan and stack in pan one atop the other, brushing each with butter.

5. For filling, arrange a layer of prepared chicken, egg mixture, then toasted almonds. Sprinkle sugar and spice mixture over almonds.

6. Fold remaining sheets of filo dough to fit pan. Reserve 2 sheets for topping. Stack filo over almonds, brushing each layer with butter. Fold edges of filo that extend beyond the pan in toward center. Top with last 2 sheets, folded to fit pan; tuck any protruding edges down inside rim of pan. Brush with remaining butter. Using a razor blade or small sharp knife, cut through top layers of dough down to the almonds to mark pie in 8 wedge shapes. (At this point, you can cover and refrigerate pie for several hours or until you are ready to bake it.)

7. Bake until well browned and heated through (45 minutes to 1 hour). Remove pan sides. Sift confectioners' sugar over pie, then ½ teaspoon cinnamon. Serve immediately; cut in marked wedges.

Serves 8.

Food Processor Version Use the metal blade to process the following, setting each aside until needed: almonds, onion, parsley, and garlic. If you wish, leave parsley and garlic in work bowl. Add eggs, 1 teaspoon salt, pepper, and chopped parsley (if not already in bowl) and process 10 seconds.

Made with delicate filo dough, a common ingredient for many Middle Eastern cuisines, Moroccan Pastilla makes for an exotic Sunday brunch. This dish combines the light flavor of chicken with a nutty mixture of almonds, cinnamon, ginger, nutmeg, and cardamom in a crisp shell.

Honey-sweetened Baklava, made with layers of paper-thin filo dough and ground almonds, is a satisfying accompaniment to a cup of rich, strong coffee.

3. Carefully fold 2 sheets of filo to fit pan; place in pan one at a time, brushing each with butter. Sprinkle about 3 tablespoons of the almond mixture over top sheet. Fold 1 sheet of filo to fit pan; brush with butter. Sprinkle evenly with another 3 tablespoons almond mixture.

4. Continue to add layers, using 1 folded sheet of filo, a generous brushing of butter, and 3 to 4 tablespoons almond mixture for each, until nut mixture is used up (there should be about 10 nut-filled layers).

5. Fold remaining 2 to 3 sheets of filo to fit pan. Place on top, brushing each with butter before adding the next. With a very sharp knife, carefully cut diagonally across pan to make small diamond shapes—about 1½ inches on a side—cutting all the way to bottom of pan. Pour on any remaining butter.

6. Bake until golden brown (about 45 minutes). Pour warm Honey and Rose Water Syrup over top. Decorate each piece with an almond slice. Cool before serving.

Makes about 2 dozen pastries.

Honey and Rose Water Syrup   Combine sugar and the water in a 1½-quart saucepan; bring to a boil, stirring. Mix in honey and cook until syrup boils again. Remove from heat; mix in rose water.

◼ WALNUT-APPLE STRUDEL

Strudel is a typical Hungarian dessert, which traditionally uses homemade, paper-thin dough as the wrapper. The dough is extremely time-consuming and difficult to prepare. Using frozen filo dough streamlines the process.

> 6 sheets filo dough, thawed 8 hours
>   in refrigerator if frozen
> ½ cup unsalted butter
> 1 cup soft white bread crumbs
> ½ cup coarsely chopped walnuts
> 2 large baking apples, cored and coarsely chopped
> ¼ cup sugar
> ¼ cup raisins
> 1 teaspoon ground cinnamon

1. Unfold sheets of filo dough so they lie flat. Cover with waxed paper, then a damp towel, to prevent them from drying out. Preheat oven to 350° F. Butter a baking sheet.

2. In a small sauté pan over medium heat, melt ¼ cup butter. Add bread crumbs and sauté until golden brown (about 7 minutes); set aside.

3. In a medium bowl combine walnuts, apples, sugar, raisins, and cinnamon; toss to coat walnuts and apples thoroughly.

4. Melt remaining butter in a small saucepan; remove from heat. Spread a slightly damp cloth over work area. Stack 2 sheets filo dough on cloth. Brush top sheet with melted butter. Repeat twice, stacking 2 sheets of dough each time.

◼ BAKLAVA

These aromatic Greek pastries make a nice addition to a dessert buffet. They also freeze well.

> ½ pound (half package) filo dough,
>   thawed 8 hours in refrigerator if frozen
> 2 cups ground blanched almonds
> ¾ cup sugar
> 1 teaspoon grated lemon rind
> ¾ teaspoon ground cinnamon
> 1 cup unsalted butter, melted
>   Sliced almonds, for garnish

Honey and Rose Water Syrup

> ¼ cup *each* sugar and water
> 1 cup honey
> 1 tablespoon rose water

1. Unfold sheets of filo dough so they lie flat. Cover with waxed paper, then a damp towel, to prevent them from drying out.

2. Preheat oven to 325° F. In a medium bowl combine almonds, sugar, lemon rind, and cinnamon. Generously butter an 8- or 9-inch-square pan.

5. Spread sautéed bread crumbs on top sheet of dough, leaving a 3-inch border of dough uncovered. Cover bread crumbs with walnut-apple mixture.

6. With longer edge of dough facing you, fold nearest edge back over filling, then lift cloth and roll dough and filling like a jelly roll. Seal seam with water. Pinch edges to seal; tuck under.

7. Place on buttered baking sheet; brush top with melted butter. Set sheet on center rack of oven and bake until strudel is golden brown (25 to 35 minutes). Slice roll into individual servings about 1½ inches wide.

Serves 4 to 6.

Food Processor Version Tear slices of fresh bread into pieces and put in work bowl with metal blade. Process 15 seconds and set aside. Use shredding disk for walnuts and set aside. Put cored, quartered apples in work bowl; turn motor on and off a few times to chop.

■ TIROPITA

Because the cheeses vary in saltiness, taste the filling first and reduce the salt, if necessary. The little triangles can be frozen up to two months and baked direct from the freezer for quick party fare.

    2 bunches green onions, minced
    ½ cup parsley, minced
    1 clove garlic, minced
    ¼ pound Monterey jack cheese, shredded
    ¼ pound feta cheese, crumbled
    2 eggs
    ¼ teaspoon salt, or to taste
       Freshly ground pepper, to taste
   12 sheets filo dough, thawed 8 hours
       in refrigerator if frozen
    ¾ cup unsalted butter, melted

1. In a medium bowl stir together green onions, parsley, garlic, jack cheese, feta cheese, eggs, and salt and pepper to taste.

2. Place filo dough on work surface. Cut into strips about 3 inches wide; cover strips with waxed paper and a damp cloth to keep from drying out. Working with one strip at a time, brush with melted butter. Place a rounded tablespoon of cheese mixture at bottom of strip. Fold on diagonal to create a triangular shape; bottom edge of filo dough will touch left side of strip. Bring bottom of triangle up against straight edge. Fold again on diagonal so that left edge now touches right side. Repeat folding to top of strip, forming an enclosed triangular pastry. Brush folded triangle with melted butter. Repeat with remaining dough and filling.

3. Preheat oven to 400° F. Bake triangles on a baking sheet until lightly browned and hot (about 20 minutes). Cool about 2 minutes before serving.

Makes 3 dozen triangles.

Food Processor Version Cut green onions into 1-inch pieces. Use metal blade to chop green onion pieces, parsley, and garlic, turning motor on and off until desired consistency is obtained. Transfer to mixing bowl and add feta, eggs, salt, and pepper. Have jack cheese well chilled; process cheese with shredding disk and add to mixing bowl. Stir to blend with other ingredients. Continue with recipe.

FINISH, TO

Adding the final touches to a dish. This can include bringing food prepared ahead of time to serving temperature, arranging the food attractively on its plate, and adding garnishes to enhance visual appeal.

The term also specifically refers to the final attention paid by the cook to a sauce before serving it: to correct seasonings; to enrich with one or more of certain ingredients (butter, sour cream or crème fraîche, cream, or essences); and, when deemed appropriate, to add a splash of liquor to heighten the aroma.

FISH

How to purchase, prepare, and cook fish could be the subject of a multivolume cookbook. The world's lakes, rivers, and oceans are full of hundreds of species, many of which are unique to each region. Indeed, some cooks will argue that a bouillabaisse is authentic only when made in or near Marseilles, France, with local fish.

Modern transportation has improved that situation somewhat, bringing fresh Dover sole to Dallas and Maryland soft-shell crab to San Francisco. However, it is still true and worth acknowledging that fish is extremely perishable, that it ships successfully only under the most carefully controlled conditions, and that the most delicious fish is the one eaten within hours of capture. Anyone who has ever panfried and eaten a trout within moments of hooking it knows that even day-old fish has a markedly different flavor and texture. Freshness in fish is the first key to enjoyment. The second is selecting the proper cooking method.

This entry includes information to help the home cook select and prepare fish successfully; also see SHELLFISH.

CATEGORIZING FISH

Despite their great diversity, fish may be readily categorized in ways helpful to the cook. The three most important distinctions are: Is the fish round or flat? Is its flesh lean or oily? Is it from salt water or fresh water? The first question affects how the fish is cut for cooking. The second affects the choice of cooking method. The third has important health and safety implications.

There are two types of whole fish: flat and round, as illustrated by the top two fish in the photograph. Starting below the flatfish and moving clockwise, the most common cuts of fish include: whole pan-dressed fish (a small fish with head and tail, scaled, fins removed, and gutted); pan-dressed body (without head and tail); steak (a cross-section of a fish); butterflied fillet (both sides of fish still connected); fillets without skin; and fillets with skin.

basted generously during cooking to keep them moist, they may also be baked, broiled, or grilled.

Oily fish contain 5 to 50 percent fat. Their flesh is stronger tasting, richer, and less white than that of lean fish. Examples of oily fish are swordfish, trout, salmon, tuna, mackerel, catfish, sturgeon, smelt, sablefish, pompano, herring, anchovy, and eel. Because of their high oil content, they stay moist when cooked with little or no added liquid or fat (grilling, baking, and broiling). Only those oily fish lowest in fat, such as salmon, are appropriate choices for poaching.

SALT WATER OR FRESH WATER

As the popularity of sushi increases in the United States, it is important that cooks be aware of some dangers regarding raw fish. Freshwater fish from lakes and streams may carry parasites harmful to humans. Consequently, freshwater fish should never be eaten raw and are never used in sushi. Cooking to doneness—by any method—will kill any parasites present.

Parasites harmful to humans cannot survive in the flesh of saltwater fish. Consequently, such saltwater fish as tuna, halibut, salmon, and shellfish of all kinds are safe to eat raw if caught in nonpolluted waters.

Use   Depending on the character of the meat, fish may be poached, steamed, baked, panfried, grilled, broiled, braised, fried, smoked, or eaten raw. Fish bones can be used to make a stock for soups and sauces. Cooked cold fish can be used in salads, chowders, sandwich fillings, layered casseroles, fried cakes, or baked loaves. Whole fish can be stuffed and baked. Delicate fillets such as sole can be stuffed and rolled before baking. Firm-fleshed fish such as halibut and swordfish can be cubed and skewered for grilling.

Availability   Fish is available fresh or frozen, with the best selection usually found at specialty fish markets. Some markets keep fish in holding tanks for live purchase. For information on the most common retail market cuts, see Roundfish or Flatfish, Lean Flesh or Oily Flesh, and photograph at left.

Selection   Some people define fresh fish as fish that has never been frozen. However, a never-frozen fish can be considerably less than fresh. A truly fresh fish should not smell fishy—a sign of age or improper handling by the fishmonger. A fresh fish has a mild odor; firm, elastic flesh that springs back when pressed; clear, protruding eyes; reddish or pink gills; and scales that are shiny, bright, and tight to the skin.

As always, there are a few exceptions. Shark, skate, and ray, primitive fish with unique metabolisms, will have an ammoniated odor when freshly killed. Soaking them in milk or lightly acidulated water eliminates the smell. Without soaking, the odor will dissipate in a day or two, making shark, skate, and ray among the few fish that are better when not quite fresh.

ROUNDFISH OR FLATFISH

Based on their skeletal structure, all fish can be classified as either round or flat. Roundfish can be cooked whole or cut off the bone into two fillets. Large roundfish, salmon for example, can be cut crosswise into steaks. The fillets of some roundfish are thick enough to slice crosswise. Flatfish, such as flounder, cannot be satisfactorily cut into steaks or slices. They are either cooked whole or cut from the bone into four fillets, two top and two bottom.

LEAN FLESH OR OILY FLESH

Leaner fish have a mild flavor and firm white flesh. The oil or fat (5 percent or less of the total body substance) is concentrated in the liver, which is removed during cleaning. Sole, halibut, flounder, snapper, sea bass, burbot, turbot, and rockfish are examples of lean fish. Because their flesh dries out readily, they are well-suited to cooking with some sort of liquid or fat (poaching, steaming, sautéing); if

Some deep-water fish may have cloudy eyes from pressure changes when raised to the surface. Also, some flatfish may have dark, muddy gills, but they should be red or pink when washed.

If the fish has been frozen, ask how long it has been defrosted. Do not buy anything that has been defrosted for more than two days. It is better to purchase frozen fish and defrost it at home. For best quality, try to find fish that were individually quick-frozen on the fishing vessel.

Fillets offer fewer clues to freshness than whole fish. Look for flesh with a natural sheen; avoid fillets that are yellowing or browning around the edges. As with whole fish, the odor should be fresh and the flesh firm. If buying packaged frozen fillets, avoid packages that look as if they may have been thawed and refrozen. The telltale signs of fish that have been thawed at least once include a misshapen package and interior ice that is bloody.

When planning a meal, choose a recipe appropriate to the fish in season. When marketing, be prepared to change the recipe if the required fish is unavailable in good condition. It is wiser to buy the freshest fish available and plan the recipe around it.

Storage   The colder the storage temperature, the less rapidly fish deteriorates. To store fresh fish, pat dry, arrange in one layer in a baking dish lined with paper towels, cover with plastic wrap, and refrigerate. If possible, set the baking dish atop crushed ice in a larger pan, making sure the melting ice cannot enter the dish. Use as soon as possible.

Store frozen fish immediately in freezer, preferably at 0° F or below. Never refreeze thawed fish. One of the best ways to freeze a whole fresh fish is to ice glaze it. First set fish on a baking sheet and freeze just until firm. Dip frozen fish in ice water; a glaze will form immediately. Return fish to freezer to solidify glaze. Repeat glazing process until fish is coated with a layer of ice at least ⅛ inch thick. Wrap in heavy-duty foil, freezer paper, or a large plastic freezer bag and freeze. To freeze fillets and steaks, wrap individually or stack between sheets of freezer wrapping material. Wrap tightly, then overwrap. Always thaw frozen fish slowly in refrigerator.

Lean fish can be frozen longer than oily fish, large fish longer than small ones, whole fish longer than steaks or fillets. Freeze whole oily fish no longer than two months, whole lean fish no longer than six months. Freeze oily fillets no longer than one month, lean fillets no longer than three months.

Preparation   Both roundfish and flatfish need to be cleaned before use, but the cleaning procedures vary. Although a fishmonger can clean and cut up fish, there are advantages to buying fish whole: You will have a better idea of how fresh the fish is; you will have the bones and trimmings for stock; and on some fish, particularly salmon, you will get a better price per pound if you cut it up yourself.

Almost all fish require scaling. Some exceptions are trout, which have scales that are an integral part of the skin, and catfish, which have tough skin that must be removed altogether. If poaching the whole unboned fish, leave the dorsal and anal fins attached; they will help hold the fish together during poaching. See Scaling and Finning, page 227.

Gutting—removing the viscera or internal organs—can be done by the fishmonger or you can do it yourself. Because the entrails contain the bacteria that start decomposition, fish should be gutted as soon as possible—ideally, the moment it is caught, or immediately after being removed from the holding tank. If you plan to bone and fillet the fish, remove the entrails by gutting through the belly. If serving the fish whole, preserve the shape by gutting through the gills. The gutting techniques for roundfish are different from those used for flatfish. See Gutting, page 227.

Though many pan-sized fish have tasty skin that enhances flavor, some fish, such as largemouth bass and butterfish, have strong-tasting skin that interferes with the flavor of a dish. Leave skin on when poaching or grilling a whole fish. See Skinning, page 227.

Fillets are pieces of boneless fish. Steaks are cross sections cut from a whole fish. Roundfish and flatfish require slightly different filleting techniques. See Cutting Fillets and Steaks, page 228.

Cooking   The type of fish determines the most suitable cooking method. Select lean fish such as cod, sole, sea bass, or snapper for moist-heat or fat-based approaches. Use dry-heat methods on oily fish such as mackerel or tuna. Lean fish may be cooked by dry-heat methods if basted during cooking to prevent drying out. Frozen whole fish may be cooked from the frozen state. Fillets may have to be thawed to separate them; otherwise, cook from the frozen state.

See BRAISE, BROIL, DEEP-FRY, GRILL, PANFRY, POACH, SAUTE, STEAM, STEW, STIR-FRY.

The Common Fresh Fish chart on page 226 indicates preferred cooking methods for the major types of fish available in this country.

DRY-HEAT COOKING

Dry-heat cooking methods include baking, broiling, and grilling. Whatever the means, the goal is the same: cooking without robbing the food of moisture. Fish with a high internal fat or oil content are especially well suited for dry-heat cooking because they baste themselves. However, most fish have little internal fat to keep them moist during cooking, so to prevent them from drying out, a variety of precautions are available: wrapping with grape leaves, leafy greens, aluminum foil, or parchment paper; covering with vegetables, cream or bread crumb topping, or another coating; marinating and basting; stuffing; and leaving the head and tail attached.

COMMON FRESH FISH

Improved transportation, refrigeration, and freezing methods have broadened the choice of fish species available to cooks across the country. This chart offers cooking information for the most commonly available fish.

Type of Fish	Source	Flesh	Cooking Method
Anchovy	Salt water	Oily	Bake, Deep-fry, Grill, Pickle
Angler (monkfish, goosefish, lotte)	Salt water	Lean	Bake, Braise, Broil, Grill, Poach, Steam, Stew
Bonito (bonita)	Salt water	Moderately oily	Bake, Broil, Grill
Butterfish (Pacific pompano on West Coast)	Salt water	Oily	Bake, Broil, Grill
Carp	Fresh water	Moderately oily	Bake, Braise, Panfry, Poach, Steam, Stew
Catfish	Fresh water	Moderately oily	Bake, Braise, Broil, Grill, Panfry, Poach, Steam, Stew
Cod	Salt water	Lean	Bake, Braise, Broil, Grill, Panfry, Poach, Steam, Stew
Corbina (corvina)	Salt water	Moderately oily	Bake, Broil, Grill, Poach, Steam
Drum (redfish)	Salt water	Lean	Bake, Broil, Grill, Poach, Steam
Eel	Fresh water and salt water	Oily	Bake, Braise, Grill, Stew
Flounder	Salt water	Lean	Bake, Broil, Grill, Poach, Sauté, Steam
Grouper	Salt water	Lean	Bake, Braise, Broil, Fry, Grill, Poach, Steam, Stew
Haddock	Salt water	Lean	Bake, Braise, Broil, Fry, Grill, Poach, Steam, Stew
Hake	Salt water	Lean	Bake, Braise, Broil, Grill, Panfry, Poach, Steam, Stew
Halibut	Salt water	Lean	Bake, Broil, Grill, Poach, Sauté, Steam
Herring	Salt water	Oily	Bake, Broil, Grill, Pickle
Lake trout	Fresh water	Oily	Bake, Broil, Grill, Poach, Sauté, Steam
Mackerel	Salt water	Oily	Bake, Braise, Broil, Grill, Pickle, Stew
Monkfish (see Angler)			
Perch	Fresh water	Lean	Bake, Braise, Broil, Grill, Panfry, Poach, Sauté, Steam, Stew
Pike	Fresh water	Lean	Bake, Braise, Broil, Grill, Panfry, Poach, Sauté, Steam, Stew
Pollock	Salt water	Lean	Bake, Braise, Broil, Grill, Poach, Sauté, Steam, Stew
Pompano (Florida pompano)	Salt water	Moderately oily	Bake, Broil, Grill, Panfry, Sauté
Porgy	Salt water	Lean	Bake, Broil, Grill, Panfry
Ray	Salt water	Lean	Bake, Braise, Poach, Sauté, Steam, Stew
Red snapper (many fish labeled "snapper" are actually rockfish)	Salt water	Lean	Bake, Braise, Broil, Grill, Panfry, Poach, Sauté, Steam, Stew
Rockfish	Salt water	Lean	Bake, Braise, Broil, Grill, Panfry, Poach, Sauté, Steam, Stew
Sablefish (fillets known as butterfish on West Coast)	Salt water	Oily	Bake, Braise, Broil, Grill, Stew
Salmon	Salt water and fresh water	Moderately oily	Bake, Broil, Grill, Poach, Sauté, Smoke, Steam
Sea bass	Salt water	Lean	Bake, Braise, Broil, Grill, Panfry, Poach, Steam, Stew
Sea trout (weakfish)	Salt water	Moderately oily	Bake, Braise, Broil, Grill, Panfry, Poach, Steam, Stew
Shad	Fresh water	Moderately oily	Bake, Braise, Broil, Grill, Stew
Shark	Salt water	Lean	Bake, Braise, Broil, Grill, Panfry, Poach, Steam, Stew
Skate (see Ray)			
Smelt (whitebait)	Salt water	Oily	Bake, Broil, Grill, Panfry
Sole (petrale sole, rex sole, lemon sole, Dover sole)	Salt water	Lean	Bake, Broil, Grill, Poach, Sauté, Steam
Striped bass	Salt water and fresh water	Moderately oily	Bake, Braise, Broil, Grill, Poach, Sauté, Steam, Stew
Sturgeon	Salt water and fresh water	Oily	Bake, Broil, Grill, Sauté, Smoke
Swordfish	Salt water	Moderately oily	Bake, Braise, Broil, Grill, Stew
Tilefish	Salt water	Lean	Bake, Braise, Broil, Fry, Grill, Poach, Sauté, Steam, Stew
Trout	Fresh water	Moderately oily	Bake, Broil, Grill, Poach, Sauté, Smoke, Steam
Tuna	Salt water	Oily	Bake, Braise, Broil, Grill, Sauté, Stew
Turbot	Salt water	Lean	Bake, Poach, Sauté, Steam
White	Salt water	Lean	Bake, Broil, Grill, Panfry, Poach, Sauté, Steam
Whitebait (see Smelt)			
Whitefish	Fresh water	Oily	Bake, Broil, Grill, Smoke

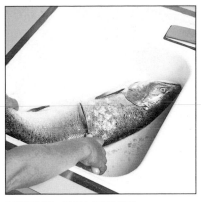

SCALING AND FINNING

Wet fish and salt hands for a better grip. With a knife or scaler, start at tail and scrape toward head. Rinse fish well.

The dorsal (back) fin can be clipped with kitchen scissors, although this leaves part of the fin connected to the fish. Cut against the grain, tail to head.

To remove the whole dorsal fin, cut along each side of fin with a filleting or boning knife and pull fin toward head to remove it. Use the same method to remove anal fin (closest to tail at bottom). Clip other fins with scissors.

GUTTING

Flatfish   To gut a flatfish, make a small cut behind gills and pull out viscera. Rinse.

Roundfish   To gut through belly, cut off head behind gill opening. Cut open belly from head end to just above anal (tail) fin area. Remove membranes, blood veins, and viscera. Rinse.

To gut through gills, open outer gill with thumb. Reach a finger into gill and snag inner gill. Pull gently to remove inner gill and viscera. Rinse.

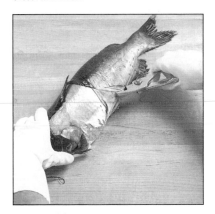

SKINNING

Catfish   Cut skin just behind head all around body. Wear gloves to protect hands from whiskerlike barbels and barbed fins. Hold head firmly and use pliers to peel skin toward tail.

Flatfish   Place dark side of fish up, and cut across skin where tail joins body. Beginning at the cut, with knife or hand, pry up a piece of skin. Grasp skin flap with one hand while anchoring fish with other hand. Pull skin away from cut and over head. Turn fish over. Holding head, pull skin down to tail.

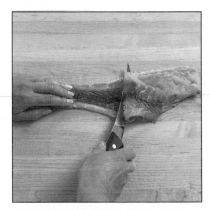

Roundfish   Make a slit across body just behind gills and another slit just above tail. Make another cut down back. Using a thin knife, separate skin from flesh, starting at tail. Pull (don't saw) knife toward head, holding skin firmly with other hand.

CUTTING FILLETS AND STEAKS

To fillet a skinned flatfish Place skinned fish on a board with eyes up. Cut through flesh to the backbone (which is in the middle of the fish) from head to tail. Insert knife blade at a shallow angle between ribs and end of the fillet close to the head. Cut down the length of a fillet on one side of the backbone and remove it. Cut remaining fillet using the same technique. Turn fish over and remove two bottom fillets; rinse fillets in cold water.

To fillet flatfish with skin left on Cut along line that runs along skin to expose backbone. Cut around backbone to expose ribs. Insert knife between ribs and the end of fillet close to the head. Continue as for skinned flatfish. Turn fish over, cut through line on skin, and cut back away from backbone for one fillet; repeat on other side for second fillet.

To skin a flatfish fillet Place fish skin side down on a board; at tail end cut down at a 45-degree angle to the skin, but not all the way through. Pick up flesh at slit to get at skin. Holding skin taut, slide knife along skin without cutting it, wiggling skin back and forth (this motion will help the knife scrape through between flesh and skin).

To fillet a roundfish Make a very shallow cut along either side of the backbone with the tip of a paring knife, just to release ribs from backbone; don't cut into flesh. Entering fish at dorsal fin hole, slice along backbone from hole to tail; cut across tail, reverse direction, and cut up to head, stopping at gill cut. Trim half fillet from head by cutting down through backbone.

To remove backbone Slip knife under backbone about half way down from head; cut back to tail; reverse and cut back to head. Pull bone up and off to head; cut away head. To remove ribs, slip knife just under rib; cut away from you to remove ribs. Use tweezers or strawberry huller to remove any fine bones that may remain.

Cutting a steak Using a large, sharp knife, cut off the head just behind gills. Slice the fish crosswise into steaks of the desired thickness, usually between 1 and 1½ inches.

CLASSIC BAKED FISH

This recipe lends itself to the use of any number of sauces, which can change the flavor of the fish in a variety of interesting ways.

 1 whole fish (3 to 4 lb), cleaned
 1½ teaspoons salt
 ½ teaspoon freshly ground pepper
 ½ lemon, sliced
  Unsalted butter, for greasing
 ½ cup water

1. Preheat oven to 425° F. Rub fish with salt, pepper, and lemon slices. Generously grease a large baking dish with butter. Place fish in dish and pour in the water.

2. Grease parchment paper or foil with unsalted butter and place over fish in baking dish.

3. Bake for 20 to 35 minutes; baking time depends on thickness of fish. Serve with sauce of your choice.

Serves 4 to 6.

BROILED SALMON
WITH SOUFFLE TOPPING

If you substitute dried herbs for fresh, use whole leaves. Serve this salmon dish with Fried Green Tomatoes (see page 581).

 ¾ cup unsalted butter
 1 large shallot, minced
 2 tablespoons minced fresh tarragon *or*
  1 tablespoon dried tarragon
 1 tablespoon minced fresh dill *or*
  ½ tablespoon dried dill
 2 tablespoons snipped fresh chives
 6 salmon fillets or steaks

Soufflé Topping

 1½ cups Mayonnaise (see page 519)
 2 tablespoons minced fresh *or*
  1 tablespoon dried tarragon
 1 tablespoon minced fresh *or*
  ½ tablespoon dried dill
 2 tablespoons snipped fresh chives
 2 egg whites

1. Preheat broiler. In a small saucepan melt butter. Add shallot, tarragon, dill, and chives. Place salmon in a large, heat-resistant gratin dish, and brush fish with the herb butter. Broil until fish is cooked (about 10 minutes); broiling time depends on thickness of fish.

2. Cover salmon with Soufflé Topping. Broil until puffy and brown (2 to 3 minutes).

Serves 6.

Soufflé Topping In a small bowl combine Mayonnaise, tarragon, dill, and chives. Mix well. Beat egg whites until stiff but not dry; fold into mayonnaise mixture.

STURGEON BROCHETTE
WITH HONEY MUSTARD SAUCE

A brochette is usually served on a bed of rice. Try delicious Onion and Rice Soubise instead.

 4 sturgeon steaks (6 oz each), cut in
  6 to 8 equal pieces
 1 cup whipping cream
 3 tablespoons dry white wine
 1 tablespoon honey
 1 tablespoon coarse-grain mustard

Onion and Rice Soubise

 2 pounds white onions
 3 tablespoons unsalted butter
 ¾ cup rice
 2 cups Fish Fumet (see page 451) or
  Chicken Stock (see page 560)
 1 teaspoon salt
 ⅓ teaspoon white pepper
 ⅓ cup whipping cream
 2 tablespoons unsalted butter

1. Preheat broiler. Place fish on metal skewers.

2. In a small saucepan over medium-high heat, reduce cream by half (watch carefully to prevent cream from boiling over). When reduced add wine, honey, and mustard. Mix well, simmer 1 minute, and remove from heat.

3. Brush sturgeon with sauce. Place fish on baking sheet and broil 2 to 3 minutes, turning once. Serve with remaining sauce on a bed of Onion and Rice Soubise.

Serves 4 to 6.

Onion and Rice Soubise Peel and coarsely slice onions. Melt the 3 tablespoons butter in a saucepan, add onions and cook for 5 to 7 minutes. Add rice, mix well, then add fumet, salt, and pepper. Cover and simmer 30 minutes. Purée the mixture in a food processor, adding cream and the 2 tablespoons butter. Reheat over low heat. Adjust seasonings and serve.

SWORDFISH PAILLARD WITH SALSA

In this recipe, *paillard* refers to a large, thin slice of fish. Serve with tortilla chips or warm corn tortillas.

 6 swordfish steaks (each ½-inch thick)
 3 tablespoons unsalted butter, melted
 1 teaspoon salt
 ½ teaspoon freshly ground pepper
  Salsa Cruda (see page 521)

1. Preheat broiler. Brush fish with butter and sprinkle with salt and pepper.

2. Broil fish 4 inches from heat for 1½ minutes. Turning the fish is unnecessary. Serve with Salsa Cruda.

Serves 6.

COOKING IN OIL

Sautéing, stir-frying, panfrying, and deep-frying are different cooking methods that have in common their reliance on the use of fats, a term that includes oils. Sautéing uses a very small amount of fat that often becomes part of the finished dish. Deep-fried food, on the other hand, is totally immersed in fat, which is not served with the final dish. Both of these cooking processes use extremely high temperatures; this seals in the flavor and succulence of the fish. To avoid greasy fried foods, it is important to monitor the temperature of the cooking fat; if too cool, the food could absorb the fat, and if too hot, the food will burn on its surface before being done inside.

■ PAN-FRIED CATFISH

As a bottom feeder, the "wild" catfish has an uncertain culinary reputation, but the rolling green hills of Tennessee are studded with limpid freshwater ponds where catfish are carefully bred and raised. Typically, a catfish farm includes a ramshackle roadside restaurant, from which an irresistible aroma of crisp, cornmeal-coated fried catfish wafts up and down the highway. One taste is enough to improve the catfish's reputation.

     4 to 6 small catfish (about 1 lb each) *or*
        2 to 3 pounds thick fillets from larger catfish
     ½ cup flour
     1 teaspoon salt
     ½ teaspoon coarsely ground pepper
     2 eggs
     1 tablespoon water
     1 cup white cornmeal
        Oil, for frying

1. Rinse catfish in cold water; dry with paper towels.

2. Mix flour, salt, and pepper. Dredge fish in the mixture and shake off excess. Place fish on waxed paper. Place eggs in a pie pan, add the water, and beat lightly to combine. Spread cornmeal on a large plate.

3. Heat ¼ inch oil in a large, heavy skillet (or two skillets, to cook all the fish at once). While oil is heating, dip fish in egg mixture, then roll in cornmeal to coat thoroughly, gently pressing the cornmeal onto fish. Place each coated fish on waxed paper.

4. When oil is rippling and fragrant (350° F), gently add fish to skillet(s), using long tongs to protect against spattering oil. Fry until coating is browned and fish is cooked through, turning carefully midway through cooking. Whole fish takes about 3 minutes per side, fillets 2 minutes per side. (For fillets, check doneness by inserting a knife; flesh should flake easily. For whole fish, inspect the flesh at the opening. Catfish retains a slightly pink color when cooked, but the flesh turns opaque.) Drain fish on paper towels and keep in the oven at low heat until ready to serve.

Serves 4 to 6.

■ HOT-AND-SOUR SHARK

Shark is a wonderfully full-flavored and versatile fish that lends itself to many types of cooking. Its lean flesh makes it well-suited for cooking techniques that use fat or other liquid—here a combination of deep-frying and stir-frying. The technique of coating with egg white and partially cooking the fish is called velveting and is common in Chinese cuisine. It produces a particularly attractive, crispy finish. Serve with steamed rice. For directions on how to prepare the sticky type of rice favored by the Chinese, see About Cooking Rice, page 274.

     2 cups water
        Zest of 1 orange, julienned
     2 egg whites
     2 tablespoons dry sherry
     3 tablespoons cornstarch
     4 tablespoons peanut oil
     1 teaspoon salt
     1 pound shark, cut in 1- by ½-inch cubes
        Oil, for deep-frying
     ½ cup fresh orange juice
     ½ cup Chicken Stock (see page 560)
     4 tablespoons rice vinegar
     2 tablespoons sugar
     2 tablespoons soy sauce
     ½ cup julienned ginger (2-in. strips)
     2 dried red chiles, seeded and minced
     ½ cup slivered green onion (3-in. strips)
     1 cup seeded, julienned red bell pepper
     2 tablespoons minced green onion

1. In a medium saucepan bring the water to a boil over medium-high heat. Add julienned orange zest and boil 1 minute. Remove zest from saucepan with slotted spoon, drain, and reserve.

2. In a medium bowl combine egg whites, sherry, 2 tablespoons of the cornstarch, 2 tablespoons of the peanut oil, and salt. Add shark pieces to mixture and toss to coat well.

3. In a Dutch oven, heavy deep skillet, or other frying kettle, heat at least 2 inches of oil for deep-frying to 350° F. Add shark pieces and fry until golden brown on all sides (2 to 3 minutes). Remove shark and drain on paper towels. Keep warm.

4. In small bowl combine orange juice, Chicken Stock, vinegar, remaining 1 tablespoon cornstarch, sugar, and soy sauce. In wok heat remaining 2 tablespoons peanut oil. Add ginger and chiles; stir-fry 1 minute. Add the ½ cup slivered green onion and bell pepper; stir-fry 1 minute. Add orange juice mixture; stir until it thickens.

5. Transfer shark to wok, add zest, toss, and reheat. Garnish with the 2 tablespoons minced green onion and serve immediately.

Serves 4 to 6.

Fresh trout is at its best when prepared simply. Here it is sautéed quickly, then served with a sauce of butter, lemon juice, and parsley, and garnished with toasted sliced almonds.

■ TROUT WITH ALMONDS

Golden sautéed almonds are a crisp, flavorful contrast to the delicate trout. You can use almost any small whole fish in this recipe.

    4   medium trout, cleaned
        Fresh lemon juice
        Freshly cracked black peppercorns
    6   tablespoons butter
    2   tablespoons oil
    ½   cup sliced almonds
    ¼   cup *each* fresh lemon juice or white wine
        and minced parsley
        Lemon slices and dill sprigs, for garnish

1. Rub trout with lemon juice and pepper.

2. Warm serving platter for fish in 200° F oven.

3. In a wide frying pan large enough to hold the 4 trout (use two pans if necessary), melt 2 tablespoons of the butter with the oil over medium-high heat. Add trout and sauté until lightly browned on one side. Turn when edges become opaque and curl slightly (3 to 5 minutes). The fish is done when it flakes at the touch of a fork at the thickest portion near the backbone. Remove fish to warm platter. Wipe out pan.

4. Melt the remaining ¼ cup butter in pan. Add almonds and sauté until golden.

5. Combine lemon juice and parsley and add to almonds. Swirl and pour sauce over trout. Garnish with lemon slices and sprigs of dill.

Serves 4.

■ BLACKENED FISH

The technique of charring fish in a hot cast-iron skillet was created by Paul Prudhomme especially for Louisiana red-fish. It is now prepared coast to coast in Cajun and Creole restaurants. A good exhaust fan is essential because a great deal of smoke is given off during cooking. The fish cooks rapidly, so to avoid fish that are finished on the outside but underdone within, use fillets that are not more than ½ inch thick.

    ½   cup unsalted butter, melted
    4   tablespoons vegetable oil
    1   teaspoon salt
    1   teaspoon cayenne pepper
    ½   teaspoon freshly ground black pepper
    ½   teaspoon dried thyme
    ½   teaspoon paprika
    4   fish fillets (about 2 lb total), each ½ inch thick

1. Place a cast-iron skillet over high heat until white hot (about 10 minutes).

2. Combine 4 tablespoons of the butter with oil in a shallow bowl. In another small bowl mix salt, cayenne, black pepper, thyme, and paprika. Dip each fish fillet in butter-oil mixture, then sprinkle with about 1 teaspoon seasoning mixture.

3. Place fillets in hot pan for exactly 2 minutes. Turn fillets over and cook second side for exactly 2 minutes. Remove from pan and serve immediately, drizzled with remaining butter.

Serves 4.

MOIST-HEAT COOKING

Fish requires delicate cooking. Moist heat provides a gentle means of cooking that is suitable for any type of fish. Moist-heat cooking methods—poaching, steaming, braising, and stewing—use liquid as a cooking medium. The differences among these methods lie in whether the food is cooked above the liquid (steaming) or in it (poaching, braising, and stewing), and in whether the cooking liquid is served as a part of the finished dish (braising and stewing) or not (poaching and steaming).

■ STEAMED WHOLE FISH, CHINESE-STYLE

This presentation of steamed fish is a Chinese classic. The use of more fresh onions and herbs at the finish enhances the dish. Serve with steamed or fried rice.

    1 whole carp or sea bass, cleaned
    2 tablespoons soy sauce
    2 tablespoons dry sherry
    ¼ cup julienned peeled fresh ginger
    2 green onions, slivered (4-in. strips;
       use part of the green)
    8 sprigs cilantro
       Cilantro, for garnish
       Green onion, slivered, for garnish

1. Place fish on plate in steaming rack. (If you do not have a steamer large enough, put the plate on a rack in a turkey roaster.)

2. Sprinkle soy sauce, sherry, ginger, and the 2 slivered green onions over fish. Arrange the 8 sprigs of cilantro on top of fish.

3. Pour boiling water into pan until it comes within 1 inch of fish. Cover and steam about 15 minutes (cooking time depends on the size of the fish).

4. Remove plate from steamer and serve fish directly from plate. Garnish with cilantro and green onion.

Serves 6 to 8.

■ COLD FILLET OF SOLE WITH CILANTRO, LIME, AND POMEGRANATE

This dish makes a wonderfully cool summer lunch or a fine first course to balance a heavy entrée such as lamb. To seed a pomegranate, see page 453.

    8 fillets sole
    1 teaspoon salt
    ½ teaspoon freshly ground pepper
   16 sprigs cilantro
    2 jalapeño or serrano chiles, seeded,
       deveined, and minced
    6 to 8 cups Wine Court Bouillon (page 450)
       Cilantro leaves
       Lime juice
    8 thin slices of lime, for garnish
    ½ cup pomegranate seeds, for garnish

1. Pat fillets dry. Place outer side of fillet down and sprinkle with salt and pepper. Place 2 sprigs of cilantro and some of the minced chiles in the center of each fillet. Fold the fillets in thirds and place folded side down in a wide, shallow saucepan.

2. Pour court bouillon over fish. The fish should be completely immersed. Cover and bring to a simmer. Poach 8 to 10 minutes. Remove from heat and cool in poaching liquid. When cool, remove from liquid.

3. To serve, sprinkle fish with the cilantro leaves and fresh lime juice. Top each fillet with a slice of lime and some pomegranate seeds.

Serves 8.

■ PORTUGUESE FISH STEW

The distinct flavors and the herbaceous quality of the kale provide a perfect foil for the fish. The original dish used salted cod instead of fresh fish; in this version the smoked ham supplies the extra flavor.

    3 tablespoons olive oil
    2 pounds cod
    ¼ cup fruity olive oil
    3 pounds new potatoes, cooked, peeled,
       and cut in ½-inch dice
    8 cloves garlic, peeled and quartered
    1 pound kale, shredded in ¼-inch strips
       Salt and freshly ground black pepper
    ¼ pound smoked ham cut in slivers
    1 cup dry white wine

1. In a large Dutch oven heat the 3 tablespoons olive oil. Add fish to pan, fry 1 minute on each side, and remove from pan.

2. Add the ¼ cup olive oil to pan. Add potatoes and toss over medium heat until coated. Add garlic and sauté 1 minute. Add kale to pan, turning to coat with oil. Cover and cook until the greens begin to wilt (2 to 3 minutes).

3. Sprinkle potatoes and greens with salt, pepper, and slivered ham. Arrange fish on top and pour in wine. Add enough water to barely reach top of greens.

4. Cover and simmer 25 to 35 minutes, shaking pan occasionally. When potatoes are done, correct seasonings and serve.

Serves 6 to 8.

OTHER WAYS WITH FISH

Not all fish is cooked in the conventional way, or even cooked at all. The recipes here are for Japanese sushi (see opposite page), which is vinegared rice garnished with raw fish and served with various condiments. Scandinavian gravlax (see opposite page) consists of raw fish in a dry, sugar-based marinade; and Latin American seviche (see page 234) uses citrus juice to firm up fish protein in much the same way that heat does.

◼ NIGIRI SUSHI

Although it takes many years to become a full-fledged sushi chef, any cook with a sharp knife can make a modest platter of *nigiri* sushi. Nigiri are thin slices of raw fish draped across "fingers" of molded sushi rice. Tuna and shrimp both lend themselves to this treatment. See the photographs at right for guidance in making sushi. Accompany sushi with warm sake (Japanese rice wine), a dry white wine, or cocktails.

    1 tablespoon wasabi (Japanese horseradish, available powdered in Japanese markets)
    2 tablespoons rice vinegar
    1 cup water
1½ pounds fresh tuna fillet, in one piece
    2 cups Sushi Rice (recipe follows)

Wasabi Dipping Sauce

    2 tablespoons wasabi (see note, above)
¼ cup soy sauce
    2 tablespoons minced green onion
    1 tablespoon rice wine

1. In a small bowl mix *wasabi* with just enough cold water to form a thick paste. Set aside. In another bowl combine rice vinegar and water. Slice fish into twenty-four 1-ounce portions.

2. Using the vinegar-water solution to keep your hands damp, pick up a small portion of rice and gently form it into a small oval. Dot the top of the oval with a little wasabi paste and place a slice of tuna on top. Repeat with remaining rice and tuna. Arrange sushi on a platter, preferably a Japanese style lacquer or porcelain tray. Serve with dipping sauce.

Makes 2 dozen sushi.

Wasabi Dipping Sauce Combine wasabi with just enough cold water to form a thick paste. Just before serving, combine wasabi paste, soy sauce, green onions, and rice wine.

◼ SUSHI RICE

A vinegar dressing adds flavor to this rice, which has a sticky, but not mushy, consistency.

3⅓ cups short-grain rice
    4 cups water
    1 three-inch square of konbu (dried kelp, available in Japanese markets); optional

Vinegar Dressing

    5 to 6 tablespoons rice vinegar
    5 tablespoons sugar
    4 teaspoons salt

1. Place rice in a large bowl; cover with cold water. Run hands through rice to remove starch, until water turns cloudy; drain. Repeat until water remains clear; drain.

2. Place rice in saucepan with the 4 cups cold water. Place *konbu* (if used) on top. Cover saucepan and bring to a boil over high heat; boil 2 minutes. Reduce heat to medium and boil, covered, for 5 minutes. Reduce heat to lowest possible setting and cook until all moisture is absorbed (about 15 minutes). Uncover; place a towel over top of pot, and cover again. Let rest 15 minutes.

3. With a thin tool like a wooden spatula held vertically, cut dressing into cooked rice, being careful not to mash rice. Mix until rice is glossy and holds together but is not mushy. Rice may be kept in a cool place, covered with a damp cloth, for up to 2 days; it should not be refrigerated.

Makes about 6 cups.

Vinegar Dressing In a small saucepan over low heat, combine all ingredients and cook until sugar and salt dissolve. Cool to room temperature. Keeps indefinitely.

◼ GRAVLAX

Salt and sugar draw out juices, while the flavors of herbs and spices are absorbed by the fish.

    1 salmon (4 lb), boned, head removed, skin intact
¼ cup kosher salt
¼ cup sugar
    1 tablespoon crushed white peppercorns
    1 cup chopped fresh dill

Mustard Sauce

    4 tablespoons Creole mustard
    1 teaspoon hot mustard
    3 tablespoons sugar
    2 tablespoons white vinegar
⅓ cup vegetable oil
    2 to 3 tablespoons chopped fresh dill

1. Cut salmon into 2 pieces along the backbone. Wipe dry. In a small bowl, combine salt, sugar, and peppercorns, and rub fish on both sides with mixture. In a large, deep dish, sprinkle part of salt mixture and one third of the dill. Lay one piece of fish in dish, sprinkle with one third of the dill, and some salt mixture. Lay other piece of fish on top of the first piece. Sprinkle with remaining salt mixture and dill.

2. Cover tightly with foil, place heavy book or two bricks on top of foil to press down on fish. Refrigerate. After 4 to 6 hours some liquid will leach out; discard it. Refrigerate for 3 days, turning periodically so that the salt and seasonings penetrate evenly.

3. Before serving, drain fish on towel and scrape off the marinade. Place each fillet skin side down on serving board and cut thin diagonal slices across the grain. Serve with Mustard Sauce.

Serves 10 to 12.

Mustard Sauce In a small bowl combine all ingredients. Mix well.

HOW TO MAKE NIGIRI SUSHI

Slice boned fish fillet across the grain, approximately ¼ inch thick, to fit the shape of the rice oval (see middle photograph). To butterfly shrimp, using a sharp knife, slit the shrimp down its back, being careful not to cut all the way through. Gently flatten out the shrimp, with the cut side down.

Moisten hands with mixture of rice vinegar and water (see Nigiri Sushi recipe at left). Form a small amount of Sushi Rice (see recipe at left) into an oval.

Finished Nigiri Sushi: Rice oval is topped with a dab of wasabi paste and a slice of fish or a butterflied shrimp.

Fresh cauliflower and broccoli florets can be tray-frozen (see page 242) and then packaged airtight for later use.

■ SEVICHE

Putting limes in boiling water for one minute will yield more juice, as will warming them in a microwave oven at 50 percent power for one minute.

- 1½ **pounds white-fleshed fish, skinned and boned**
- 1½ **cups fresh lime juice**
- 1 **cup vegetable oil**
- 1 **cup fresh orange juice**
- 1 **to 2 hot red chiles, seeded and slivered**
- 1 **small onion, sliced paper-thin**
- 1 **clove garlic, minced**
     Kosher salt and freshly ground pepper, to taste

1. Cut fish into ½-inch cubes; place in a small glass dish and cover with lime juice. It is extremely important that lime juice covers all of the fish. Add more if necessary.

2. Cover with plastic wrap and refrigerate for 4 to 5 hours. In the meantime, combine vegetable oil, orange juice, chiles, onion, and garlic. After fish has marinated for 3 hours, add orange juice mixture. Chill at least 2 more hours. Add salt and pepper to taste.

Serves 6 to 8.

Recipes and Related Information
Alder-Grilled Salmon, 296; Bombay Tuna, 509; Cioppino, 556; Coulibiac, 377; Dry Spice Rub for Fish, 350; Fritto Misto With Caper Mayonnaise, 176; Grilled Tuna, 295; Makizushi, 392; Poached Fish Steaks With Fresh Herbs and Cream, 452; Quenelles, 241; Steamed Salmon Steaks With Black Bean Sauce, 554.

FLAMBE, TO; FLAME, TO

To ignite foods that have liquor added, done for dramatic effect and to develop a rich flavor. Cherries Jubilee (see page 315)—vanilla ice cream with a sauce of cherries, brandy, and kirsch—is finished this way. Many savory sautés are flamed to enhance the perfume of the sauce.

If using a gas burner, tip pan slightly so wafting fumes ignite. For either gas or electric burners, ignite with a long kitchen or fireplace match. Let cook until flame disappears (at this point all alcohol has burned off). To retain some alcohol for its flavor, cover flaming dish to extinguish, or snuff out by adding wine or stock.

Liquor can also be heated in a microwave oven: Set in microwave-safe dish and heat 30 to 45 seconds at 100 percent power.

Caution Never pour liquor from a bottle into a pan that is near an open flame. The flame can follow the stream of alcohol into the bottle and cause it to explode. Remove food from heat, add liquor (from a small pan or dish; if from the bottle, remember to set bottle away from cooking area after use), and return pan to burner.

FLAVOR, TO; FLAVORING

To give or enhance taste by the addition of extra ingredients. Extracts, herbs and spices, and wines and liqueurs are commonly used for this purpose.

A flavoring is any substance that adds taste.

Recipes and Related Information
Extract and Essence, 213; Herb, 299; Spice, 549; Wine in Cooking, 608.

FLORET

These bud clusters that form the head of broccoli and cauliflower are often cut from their stalks and cooked separately. They are also called flowerets. Fresh broccoli has tightly closed flower buds, without yellowing; a head of fresh cauliflower should be creamy white and free of brown spots.

FLOUR, TO; FLOUR

To coat with flour; the finely ground meal itself. Flour is often used as a covering for foods that will be sautéed or panfried. It acts as a barrier to keep the surface of food dry (moisture causes hot oil to sputter and drop in temperature; wet foods steam instead of fry and don't brown properly). A light first layer of flour also helps batters and bread crumb coatings adhere better. Bakers often dust cake pans with flour to prevent sticking and, in some cases, to give batter something to grip as it rises. Always remove excess flour; otherwise the coat will be unpleasantly thick. To do this, lightly tap the food or pan with your hand so that the coating is even, but fine.

Flour as an ingredient is a difficult word to define precisely. Although it most commonly describes the powdery meal derived from a grain (wheat flour, rye flour), some flours (soy flour, chick-pea flour) are ground from legumes or are made from potatoes and other starchy vegetables, nuts, and carob. For clarity of presentation, the following remarks apply only to wheat flour. Other flours are discussed separately at the end of the section.

FROM GRAIN TO FLOUR: MILLING, BLEACHING, AND AGING

Milling is the process that turns whole hard grain into fine flour. Historically most grains were ground into flour between rotating stones. Although stone-ground flour is still available, especially in health-food stores, most flour today is milled between two grooved rollers.

The mechanical rollers crack the grain, allowing germ and bran to be sieved off the endosperm (the heart of the grain). The endosperm is then ground to desired size. For whole grain flours, bran and germ are then added back. The mechanical rollers generate considerable heat; if the high-fat germ and bran were left in during grinding, the heat would accelerate rancidity.

Wheat flour has a light yellow color after milling. For aesthetic reasons, some wheat flour is bleached, usually with chlorine dioxide, to turn it white quickly. If allowed to age for one or two months it would turn white naturally through oxidation. Aging improves baking qualities but takes time and space. To speed the process, both bleached and unbleached flours are chemically aged with potassium bromate or iodate.

Use Wheat flour serves as a thickener; as a coating for fried foods; as the basis for noodles; as the foundation of many batters such as those for pancakes, waffles, and fritters; and as the main ingredient in an enormous variety of baked goods, from breads, muffins, and biscuits to cakes, cookies, pies, and pastries.

Wheat flour is a protein food that is highly absorbent. When mixed with a liquid and manipulated, two of the water-soluble proteins—glutenin and gliadin—combine to form gluten. As a batter or dough is stirred, beaten, or mixed, strands of gluten develop into a cellular, elastic network that traps air and other gases released by leavening agents. In the oven, heat causes these gases to expand, which in turn stretches the gluten. This expansion creates volume and lightness in breads, cakes, pastries, and all leavened baked goods. Toward the end of the baking time, the proteins firm, giving the final product its structure. The amount of gluten that can be developed in any batter or dough is directly related to the protein content of the flour (see Availability for a discussion of the types of flour, including protein content; also see About Nonwheat Flours).

Baking Flour gives structure to an endless variety of baked goods. When a firm, sturdy texture is desired, as for breads, the dough is kneaded repeatedly to help develop gluten (see KNEAD). When a tender, crumbly texture is desired, as in cakes and pie crusts, the moistened flour is handled lightly to avoid development of gluten.

Batter Flour gives structure to batters for fritters, pancakes, waffles, and crêpes. To avoid development of gluten and to ensure a tender texture, flour should be mixed in lightly; overmixing produces a tough texture.

Coating Pan-fried foods, such as fish, veal and pork scallops, and sliced eggplant, are usually dusted with flour before cooking to prevent them from sticking. Deep-fried foods, such as chicken, fish, and onion rings, are frequently given an initial light dusting with flour to promote the formation of a protective coating that will keep moisture in.

Thickening When dissolved in a hot liquid, the starch granules in flour swell, absorbing water molecules and causing the mixture to thicken. Flour is added to sauces, stews, soups, puddings, and creams for this purpose. As a rule, using 1 tablespoon flour per cup of liquid produces a thin sauce; using 2 tablespoons per cup produces a medium-thick sauce; using 3 tablespoons per cup produces a thick sauce. In general, flour-thickened liquids should be cooked for at least several minutes after flour is added to remove any raw flour taste.

Availability The flours sold to consumers are of three basic kinds: hard-wheat, soft-wheat, and all-purpose.

All-Purpose Flour A blend of hard- and soft-wheat flours, this type is a hybrid. Its medium protein and starch content makes it acceptable for most culinary purposes. All-purpose flour can successfully be used in both bread and cake recipes, although it will not produce the superior product a specialized flour will. In most recipes that call simply for flour, use all-purpose flour.

Durum Flour Ground from durum wheat, the hardest wheat grown, durum flour makes an extremely sturdy dough and is thus the choice for commercially manufactured dried pasta. Durum flour is also known as semolina. It is coarsely ground and never bleached.

Enriched Flour When bran and germ are removed from wheat flour during milling, most of the A and B vitamins and iron are removed as well. To make enriched flour, the B vitamins and iron are added back. Some manufacturers also add calcium and vitamin D. Enrichment is not mandated at the federal level; however, 38 states require enrichment of white flour to specifications determined by each state.

Gluten Flour or High-Gluten Flour This flour is derived from hard wheat that has been treated to remove some of its starch and concentrate its protein. It contains at least 70 percent pure gluten. Gluten flour is used in special diets for people who cannot otherwise tolerate wheat flour. It can be used in combination with low-gluten flours to improve the gluten-forming abilities of a dough, or it can be combined with regular wheat flour in bread doughs in the ratio of two to one. If used this way, decrease kneading time by one fourth to avoid overdeveloping gluten. The first rising will be quicker, the second rising slower than for a regular wheat dough.

Hard-Wheat Flour (Bread Flour) This type is generally packaged as bread flour. It is ground from hard wheat—wheat with a high protein and low starch content. The relatively high quantities of glutenin and gliadin make hard-wheat flour preferable for baking bread.

Self-Rising Flour The miller has preblended chemical leavenings and salt into flour to make self-rising flour, most common in southern states. Unless self-rising flour is stored under ideal conditions and turns over quickly in the

---

TIPS

IS SIFTING NECESSARY?

Almost all commercial flours available to the home baker today have been sifted many times before packaging. "Presifted" commonly appears on package labels to indicate that the flour does not require sifting before use.

Technically it does not. Given modern milling practices, it is highly unlikely that home bakers will find foreign particles or coarse bits of grain in their flour; removing these undesirable additions was a primary reason for sifting. Sifting does, however, aerate flour, giving it greater volume. Because most recipes, especially older ones, are written under the assumption that cooks have sifted the flour before measuring, it is a good idea to do so whenever a recipe calls for sifted flour. Sift, then measure as directed in Preparation. The aeration provided by sifting is more important with delicate cakes that have little or no chemical leavening, such as angel food, sponge, and pound cakes. Wherever sifting is not specifically suggested, it may be omitted.

store, the leavenings may lose some of their potency. It is inadvisable to use self-rising flour in recipes that don't specify it.

Soft-Wheat Flour   This flour has a low protein and high starch content. When moistened, it develops weak gluten, so the products made from soft-wheat flours are tender and crumbly. Consequently, soft-wheat flour is preferred for cakes and some pastries. The product identified in supermarkets as cake flour is a soft-wheat flour. Pastry flour contains less protein than all-purpose flour and more protein than cake flour.

Whole Wheat or Graham Flour   This flour is milled from the whole kernel: endosperm (the central, starchy cells), bran (the skin of the kernel), and germ (the portion containing the seed). Used alone, whole wheat flour produces a heavy, compact, dark bread. The bran and germ tend to hamper gluten formation by shearing the developing gluten strands. The resulting dough rises slowly and forms a finished bread that is denser than a comparable bread made with white flour.

Storage   Refined flour should be kept in an airtight container in a cool, dry, dark place and used within six months. Whole grain flours turn rancid much faster because they contain the oil-rich germ and bran. They should be stored in an airtight container, refrigerated, and used within three months.

Preparation   Measure flour by spooning it lightly into a measuring cup, then leveling off the top with the straight edge of a metal spatula or knife. For greatest accuracy, professional bakers and some home bakers use a scale to measure flour (see MEASURE). Most yeast bread and certain quick bread recipes call for a varying amount of flour (3 to 3½ cups, for example). This range is indicated because different flours absorb different amounts of liquid. Softness or hardness of the wheat from which the flour was milled affects absorbency, as does humidity in the air. Add just enough flour to produce the type of batter or dough described in your recipe.

ABOUT NONWHEAT FLOURS

Nonwheat flours have very little or no glutenin and gliadin, the two proteins that combine with water to form gluten (see Use). Rye and triticale flours have more than other nonwheat flours, but neither has enough to make a light-textured bread on its own. To yield a loaf with a pleasing texture, nonwheat flours must be combined with wheat flour. The following individual entries give recommended proportions of nonwheat flour to wheat flour to produce a satisfactory final product. Exceeding the proportion results in a heavier loaf.

Barley Flour   This type is available in some health-food stores. On its own it makes a dense, heavy bread. To add its nutty, malty flavor to a loaf while retaining a light texture, use no more than 1 part barley flour to 5 parts wheat flour.

Brown Rice Flour   Available in some health-food stores, brown rice flour contains rice bran and germ. It has a nuttier, richer flavor than white rice flour and produces a darker loaf. Use no more than 1 part brown rice flour to 4 parts wheat flour in a bread dough. Store brown rice flour in refrigerator to slow rancidity.

Buckwheat Flour   Carried in some health-food stores, it adds a full-bodied, earthy flavor to wheat breads but on its own makes a dense, heavy bread. To make a light-textured loaf, use no more than 1 part buckwheat flour to 4 parts wheat flour. Buckwheat flour is also traditionally used in Russian blini and in French Brittany crêpes.

Corn Flour   Cream-colored and slightly sweet, corn flour is more finely ground than cornmeal; some health-food stores carry it. Because of its lack of gluten-forming proteins, use no more than 1 part corn flour to 4 parts wheat flour in a bread dough. Do not confuse with cornstarch, which is used as a thickener.

Millet Flour   It adds a nutlike, slightly sweet flavor to wheat breads, and is available in some health-food stores. To retain a light texture, use no more than 1 part millet flour to 4 parts wheat flour in bread doughs.

Oat Flour   This flour contains a natural antioxidant and will improve the longevity of a loaf of bread. It is, however, very low in gluten-forming proteins. To add its sweet, earthy flavor to a loaf while retaining a light texture, use no more than 1 part oat flour to 3 parts wheat flour. Buy oat flour at health-food stores.

Potato Flour   Also known as potato starch, potato flour is made from steamed potatoes that have been dried and ground. It is stark white and very fine. Potato flour is a useful thickening agent for some delicate sauces. Because it gelatinizes quickly and does not impart a flavor of its own, it is good for last-minute corrections. Sauces thickened with potato flour will not hold very long and should not be heated over 175° F. Potato flour is a tender starch and is desirable in some cakes and cookies; it is called for in many cakes for Jewish Passover to replace the wheat flour forbidden during the holiday. It is also a suitable flour for those on a gluten-free diet.

Rye Flour   Well-stocked supermarkets and most health-food stores sell rye flour in both medium and dark varieties. Dark rye contains the bran; medium rye sometimes does. Both produce a loaf with full-bodied, bitter, slightly sour flavor; in a dark rye loaf, the flavors are simply more pronounced. Rye flour contains some gluten-forming proteins but not enough to raise loaves well. For best results, use at least 1 part wheat flour to 2 parts medium rye, or 1 part wheat flour to 1 part dark rye in bread baking. Gluten formed by rye flour is fragile; knead a rye dough gently to avoid breaking gluten strands.

Soy Flour and Soya Flour   These are both derived from soybeans: Soy flour is ground from raw beans, soya flour from lightly toasted beans. In addition to a high protein content, both varieties have a high fat content; however, it is possible to find them with the fat partially or fully extracted. Soy and soya flours add a slightly sweet, pleasantly musty flavor to breads and improve shelf life. Because they do not have gluten-forming ability, use no more than 1 part soy or soya flour to 4 parts wheat flour in a bread dough. Breads containing soy flour brown quickly; reduce oven temperature about 25° F. Some health-food stores carry these types of flour.

Triticale Flour   This flour is ground from triticale, a cross between rye and wheat. Available in most health-food stores, it has the slightly bitter flavor of rye as well as the sweetness of wheat. On its own it produces a heavy, dense loaf. For best results, use no more than 1 part triticale flour to 1 part wheat flour in a bread dough. Like rye, triticale forms delicate gluten strands; doughs containing triticale should be kneaded and shaped gently.

White Rice Flour   Available in some health-food stores, white rice flour imparts a slightly sweet flavor to a loaf of bread. It is, however, very low in gluten-forming proteins. Use no more than 1 part rice flour to 4 parts wheat flour in a bread dough. Rice flour absorbs more liquid and absorbs it more slowly than wheat flour; adjust recipe and mixing times accordingly.

FLOWER, EDIBLE

Many plant blossoms are edible and tasty. Before experimenting with edible flowers, however, learn with certainty which ones are edible and make sure they have not been treated with pesticides or other harmful sprays often used on ornamental plants. Among the more familiar varieties of edible flowers are acacia and mimosa blossoms; almond blossoms; alyssum; apple, peach, and plum blossoms; borage; chrysanthemums; daisies; daylilies; dianthus; English primroses; geraniums; hollyhock; jasmine; lavender; lilacs; lily of the valley; nasturtiums; orange and lemon blossoms; pansies; pot marigolds; roses; squash blossoms; violas; and violets.

Use   Edible flowers make a beautiful garnish for all manner of dishes. Float them on drinks, sprinkle them on soups, or use them to brighten canapés. Some, such as nasturtium blossoms, have a peppery flavor that makes them a delicious addition to salads. Others, such as rose petals, are full of aromatic oils; they may be infused in creams and syrups to extract their perfume, then removed. The scent of fresh fruit blossoms or other aromatic blossoms flatters ice creams, puddings, and liquids for poaching fruit. Squash blossoms, especially zucchini, are often large enough to stuff; Italians serve them deep-

fried, filled with cheese, and coated with egg and bread crumbs. When crystallized with egg white and sugar, edible flowers are a striking adornment for ice cream and other desserts.

Availability   Large, fresh zucchini blossoms are occasionally available in Italian or specialty markets. Some supermarkets now carry zucchini blossoms, tiny purple borage flowers, and nasturtium flowers in season, packed in plastic bags. Few other edible flowers are available commercially; home gardens are the best source for most edible varieties.

Selection   You are most certain of obtaining unsprayed blossoms if you harvest them from your own garden. If buying commercially grown flowers, confirm that they are free of pesticides. In cooking, flowers are used for their appearance as much as anything else, so choose those that look fresh, not bruised or wilted.

Storage   All edible flowers are fragile, some extremely so. If possible, use shortly after picking. Store flowers loosely in an airtight plastic bag in refrigerator.

Experiment with a range of edible flowers for a salad that's interesting and beautiful as well as tasty. The salad shown above includes nasturtiums, violets, rose petals, and rosemary blossoms, plus a mixture of less common greens such as arugula, chicory, and mâche.

Preparation If possible gather flowers in the early morning when dew has just dried on them. If necessary, wash gently and pat dry. If they must be held for several hours, dip in ice water to refresh them just before using. When adding flowers to a salad, incorporate them after salad has been dressed and tossed, just before serving.

■ DEEP-FRIED ZUCCHINI BLOSSOMS

Fried squash blossoms are an Italian specialty that has stimulated many creative American chefs to develop their own versions. This recipe uses zucchini blossoms, available at specialty produce markets or from a home vegetable garden. The filling is a rich, seasoned blend of mozzarella cheese and hot peppers; a variation made with goat cheese and sun-dried tomato is offered as well. Serve this dish as an appetizer or first course.

Batter

> 2　eggs, separated
> ½　cup water
> ¼　cup white wine
> 2　tablespoons vegetable oil
> 1　teaspoon Worcestershire sauce
> 1　cup flour
> ½　teaspoon salt

Blossoms

> ½ to ¾　pound mozzarella cheese, cut into
> ½-inch cubes
> 2 to 4　jalapeño chiles, chopped, *or* 1 can (4 oz)
> diced green chiles for a milder taste
> 30　squash blossoms, flowers cleaned and
> stems removed
> Oil, for frying
> Salt and freshly ground pepper

Tomato Dipping Sauce

> 3　shallots, finely chopped, *or* ½ onion,
> finely chopped
> 2　tablespoons olive oil
> 3　cloves garlic, finely chopped
> ½　teaspoon *each* crushed dried oregano, thyme,
> and basil *or* 1 teaspoon *each* chopped fresh
> oregano and thyme, and 1 tablespoon chopped
> fresh basil
> 1　teaspoon sugar
> 1　can (28 oz) plum tomatoes (preferably
> peeled, crushed, and with added purée)
> ½　teaspoon *each* salt and freshly ground pepper
> Dash hot-pepper sauce, or to taste
> Dash Worcestershire sauce, or to taste

1. *For the batter:* In a blender combine egg yolks, the water, wine, oil, Worcestershire sauce, flour, and salt on high speed. Let batter stand at least 1 hour.

2. *For the blossoms:* In a medium bowl toss together mozzarella and chopped chiles (do not handle chiles with bare hands; use a wooden spoon or wear gloves). Gently fill blossoms with cheese mixture. Twist ends of petals to enclose stuffing. (Blossoms may be prepared ahead to this point, chilled on paper towels, and brought to room temperature about 30 minutes before frying.)

3. *To cook:* In a Dutch oven, deep, heavy skillet, or other frying kettle, heat 3 to 4 inches of oil to 370° F. Beat reserved egg whites to soft peaks; fold into batter.

4. Dip blossoms into batter, making sure they are completely coated. Drop into hot oil, frying several at once, but do not crowd in pan. Fry until golden, turning occasionally. Remove from pan with a slotted spoon and drain on paper towels. Sprinkle with salt and pepper, and serve immediately accompanied with Tomato Dipping Sauce.

Makes 30 appetizers or 10 first courses.

Tomato Dipping Sauce In a medium saucepan sauté shallots in olive oil over medium heat until softened and transparent. Add garlic and cook 30 seconds. Add oregano, thyme, basil, and sugar, then tomatoes, and bring to a boil, stirring. Reduce heat to simmer and cook, stirring occasionally to prevent scorching, until a rich sauce develops, thick enough to coat stirring spoon (about 30 minutes). Taste, add salt, pepper, hot-pepper sauce, and Worcestershire sauce; adjust seasonings if necessary. Serve hot, at room temperature, or cold. If a smoother, less chunky sauce is desired, purée in a blender or food processor, or strain through a sieve or food mill.

Makes 2 to 2½ cups.

Variation Combine ¾ pound softened goat cheese with 6 to 8 chopped sun-dried tomatoes. Use this mixture to fill zucchini blossoms. Twist ends of petals to enclose stuffing. Proceed with step 3 in main recipe.

■ CRYSTALLIZED FLOWERS

These flowers make lovely edible decorations for elegant desserts. Choose white or brightly colored flowers (not sprayed or treated in any way) with simple petal arrangements, such as small orchids, roses, sweet peas, and violets. This treatment also works well with grapes.

Wash blossoms quickly and gently pat dry with paper towels. Place 1 egg white in a small bowl; beat until foamy. Dip flowers, one at a time, in egg white or apply egg white with a small artist's brush; cover all parts of petals. Remove excess egg white so that petals won't stick together.

Sprinkle or sift superfine sugar over petals. Cover all egg white, shaking to avoid clumping. Blow softly on flowers to remove excess sugar. Place flowers on an aluminum foil–lined baking sheet. Let dry in cool area or in refrigerator for 2 to 3 days.

Recipes and Related Information
Candy, 93; Salad, 506.

FLUFF, TO

To lighten texture and remove lumps by tossing with a fork. Rice is commonly fluffed before serving to separate the cooked grains.

FLUTE, TO

To make an attractive edge on a pie crust by pinching the pastry with thumb and index finger into interconnecting V shapes or scallops. Decorative grooves or channels are also cut into mushrooms and other vegetables and fruits.

FOLD, TO; FOLD IN, TO

To incorporate a light, aerated mixture (usually beaten egg whites or whipped cream) into a heavier mixture without deflating the lighter mixture. This can be done with your hand, a rubber spatula, or a spoon, and with a down-up-and-over motion. It is a technique that even many experienced cooks perform improperly, but one that can be mastered with some practice and an understanding of its purpose.

Folding in beaten egg whites can have two goals: to lighten the texture of a batter or cream, and to act as a leavening agent for batters. Whipped cream also lightens a mixture and is often gently blended into sauces, soufflés, and other sweet and savory dishes.

When folding, first carefully stir about one fourth to one third of the beaten whites or whipped cream into the heavier mixture to lighten it. The resulting lightened mixture is easier to blend with the remaining whites or cream because mixtures of similar consistency can be more readily folded together.

Pour remaining whites or cream on top of the heavier mixture. Cut down through the center of the mixture, then scrape across the bottom of the bowl and up one side with a single, fluid lifting motion. This brings the mixture pushed by the spatula or spoon up and over the surface. As you fold, give the bowl a quarter turn with the other hand. Repeat the motion several times just until all the ingredients are blended (some streakiness is acceptable). Work quickly but lightly, taking care not to deflate the lighter mixture and therefore decrease volume of final product.

FOOD COLORING

The composition of food coloring and food dyes is highly regulated. Approved colorings vary from country to country. They may be artificial (derived from oil) or natural (derived from vegetables, plants, or insects). In general the natural colors are weaker and less stable. Most com-

mercial food processors prefer artificial colors because they are stronger, are more heat resistant, and are less expensive.

Use Food colorings tint an enormous array of processed foods, from baked goods to salad dressings. The home cook may find them useful in tinting icings, cakes, and confections. They should be used sparingly. Liquid colorings are volatile and should be added at the end of cooking.

Availability Most food colorings sold to home cooks are packaged in liquid form. Some cookware stores and bakery suppliers offer highly concentrated food coloring pastes, which are particularly useful for icings because they mix better with fat than do liquids. Pastes also impart a darker color than liquids, which create pastel hues.

Storage Keep in a cool, dark place. Pastes will last indefinitely; liquid colorings will last three to four years.

Beaten egg whites are carefully folded into a chocolate cake batter to lighten it before baking. A large bowl, here a copper one for beating egg whites, makes the process easier.

FOOD PROCESSOR

The European-designed and manufactured food processor made its debut in the United States in the early 1970s. Although it is still not standard equipment in the majority of American kitchens, many cooks have come to consider this extremely versatile, multi-functional machine their most valuable kitchen appliance. It makes quick work out of many tedious and time-consuming culinary chores. With one machine, a cook can chop, slice, shred, mix, and purée almost instantaneously. The more powerful processors have the muscle to knead heavy bread dough with little effort.

The food processor is composed of a motor-driven shaft, a work bowl that fits over the shaft, and various blades and disks that attach to the shaft inside the work bowl and rotate at high speed when the machine is on. Food is either placed directly in the bowl or fed in through a tube on the cover of a bowl.

Full-size food processors are most efficient when used for several consecutive tasks. It's often faster and easier to do a single small job by hand—chop one clove of garlic or one tablespoon of parsley—than it is to set up the machine and have to face cleanup afterward. On the other hand, a recipe that calls for a variety of chopped vegetables—say, to be sauteed and then puréed for a soup—is perfect for the food processor.

Recognizing that consumers appreciate the speed and power of these machines, but are reluctant to dirty them for processing spoonfuls of food, manufacturers have introduced compact versions ranging from small-capacity electric chopper-grinders (electric minichoppers) to small-sized food processors. The latter have small work bowls and interchangeable blades plus a chute attachment that sends food through the work bowl for processing and out into a freestanding container. Ideal for small quantities and small households, electric minichoppers are easy to use, affordably priced, and sized to take up a minimum of space. They cannot slice or shred, however.

Food processors vary in capacity and power, from the very compact for households of one or two persons to machines intended for cooks who prepare food on a large scale. Which processor to buy depends on how often you will use the machine and the amount of food you will need to prepare at one time. A large work bowl obviously holds more—some as much as 16 cups of shredded food, or up to 7 cups of liquid. These maximum-capacity machines need a powerful motor for peak performance and are thus highest in price. With the introduction of special whisk or beater attachments, food processors are now competitive with electric mixers for whipping egg whites and cream to airy clouds, but they still cannot match the ability of the mixer to make acceptable whipped potatoes. Full-size models also cannot grind coffee beans, grains, or hard spices—tasks the minichoppers perform very well.

Standard features with most models are a large feed tube; a multipurpose steel blade for blending, mixing, and puréeing; a plastic dough blade for breads; a slicing disk; and a shredding disk. Standard on some models is a whole-bowl feed tube that accommodates larger items such as an entire tomato or onion, or several all at once. Options vary according to the manufacturer. Among the options offered are a range of slicers and shredders, including the previously mentioned whisk; a French fry cutter; an attachment for making pasta; and a citrus juicer, with strainer insert. The juicer is an automated reamer, and the strainer functions like a motorized fine-mesh sieve to create refined purées by trapping seeds, skins, peels, and fiber from fruits and vegetables.

The machine is so fast that control of its speed is critical to obtaining a quality final product. Proper technique makes the difference between finely ground nuts and nut butter, or chopped onions and onion purée. Many models have a pulse function that turns the motor on and off in bursts, letting the cook monitor the processing more accurately. For best results when chopping watery vegetables such as onions, bell peppers, or celery, it's best to turn the motor on and off (pulsing) rapidly. The same pulsing technique is used to incorporate dry ingredients into a cake batter or liquid into a pastry. When slicing or shredding foods, the amount of pressure you apply is important. Generally firm foods require firm pressure and softer foods require light to medium pressure. However, all shredded cheeses require light pressure only.

Buy a food processor that has a direct drive, rather than one that is belt-driven. Also, as with any small electrical appliance, check the warranty, customer service records, and repair policy of the food processor you have selected before you pay for it.

FORCEMEAT

Derived from the French *farce* (stuffing), this rich, savory mixture is made of finely minced, ground, pounded, or puréed raw meat, fish, fowl, or game, plus a good deal of fat, usually pork fat. Forcemeat is classically used as the filling for pâtés and terrines. Sometimes chopped vegetables and nuts are blended in for textural contrast, herbs and spices for flavor, and some sort of liquor—brandy, Cognac, or Armagnac—for depth and perfume. Eggs and often a flour-based panada, a firm paste made of bread or cooked flour soaked in milk or water, are added to bind all the ingredients together.

Forcemeats can be coarse or fine; for a more varied consistency, they can be a combination of fine pieces and a purée. To make forcemeat before the advent of the food processor, pieces of meat were fed through a meat grinder or minced by hand. If a smooth paste was desired, the meat was pounded in a mortar and then rubbed through a fine sieve. The food processor has automated and shortened this labor-intensive process, although even a processed purée should be further refined by sieving.

Seasonings vary, but generally cold forcemeat-based dishes require more generous amounts to overcome the deadening effect chilling has on flavor.

Mousseline forcemeats, which resemble a soufflé, have been lightened with cream and bound with egg white and a panada. The feather-light quenelle, a French dumpling, is made from a mousseline forcemeat. Another classic mixture consists of rolled fillets of fish lined with this airy mixture and gently poached.

■ QUENELLES

This classic mousseline recipe is lighter and more delicate than the flour-based panada originally used for quenelles. Without the help of a food processor, making quenelles is a laborious task. The flesh of the fish must be first pounded with a mortar and pestle, then sieved to remove the connective tissue. With the processor, the fish is easy to purée. You still need to sieve it because small amounts of invisible connective tissue may remain in the puree. Keeping the ingredients cold helps them absorb the cream and makes the quenelles light. The ramekins called for in the variation are single-serving pottery baking dishes. They are available at most cookware stores.

- 1 pound sole or other white, firm-fleshed fish, cut in 1-inch pieces and chilled
- 1 egg
- 1 egg white
- 1 teaspoon salt
- ½ teaspoon white pepper
- 2 cups whipping cream, well chilled
  Boiling stock

1. In a food processor fitted with steel blade, purée sole. Then push puree through a sieve with a wooden spoon and return sieved purée to processor.

2. Add egg, egg white, salt, and pepper. Purée again. With machine running, slowly pour in cream and process until absorbed into fish mixture. Refrigerate the mousseline until ready for forming.

3. Use 2 tablespoons as a mold to form chilled mousseline into oval balls. As you work, dip spoons often in hot water. To form quenelles you can also use a large pastry bag with a plain tip.

4. Place formed quenelles in bottom of a large, well-buttered saucepan. Slowly pour boiling stock into pan to cover quenelles. Over low heat poach quenelles until they are firm (12 to 15 minutes).

Serves 6.

Variation   Using ramekins saves the cook from having to mold the mousseline and, if you wish, serves as the vehicle for an oyster surprise. The bain-marie (hot water bath) is essential for even poaching. Preheat oven to 350° F. Heavily butter six 4-ounce ramekins. Fill halfway with mousseline. Place a small, well-drained oyster in the middle of each ramekin. Cover top with remaining mousseline mixture. Place ramekins in baking dish and surround with boiling water. Water should come up almost to top of ramekins. Bake until a knife inserted into middle of mousseline comes out clean (15 to 20 minutes).

Serves 6.

■ CHICKEN QUENELLES

Quenelles can be served as a main course with a sauce, as a soup dumpling, or as an accompaniment to other dishes. Using ground chicken rather than the fish of the previous recipe, this version is flecked with specks of peppery watercress and can be served with the chicken stock in which it poaches. Ask the butcher to grind the chicken for you, or you can do it yourself in a food processor.

- ½ cup water
- ½ teaspoon salt
- 2 tablespoons butter
- ⅓ cup flour
- 1 egg
- 1 egg white
- 1 cup ground chicken
- 2 tablespoons whipping cream
- 2 tablespoons fresh watercress leaves
  Salt and white pepper, to taste
- 2 cups Chicken Stock (see page 560)

1. In a 2-quart, heavy-bottomed saucepan, combine the water, salt, and butter. Simmer over medium-low heat until butter melts.

2. With a wooden spoon, beat flour into butter-water mixture all at once. Cook over medium-high heat, beating continuously until mixture forms a ball and does not stick to sides of pan. Remove from heat.

3. Beat in egg, then egg white; set aside to cool completely.

4. In a medium bowl combine chicken, cream, watercress, and salt and pepper to taste. When flour mixture has completely cooled, blend with ground chicken mixture.

5. Simmer stock in a large, heavy-bottomed sauté pan or skillet over medium heat. Drop in quenelle batter, 1 tablespoon at a time, until pan is full. Simmer until quenelles puff and roll over easily (about 10 minutes). Remove with a slotted spoon. Repeat until all batter has been used.

Makes 20 quenelles.

TIMETABLE FOR FREEZING

Plan a constant turnover of the contents of a home freezer so that no food is kept too long. First in, first out is a good rule. Observe recommended storage periods listed below and in chart on opposite page.

Food	Storage Time at 0° F*
Fish and Shellfish	
Clams and scallops	3–4 months
Crab and lobster	1–2 months
Fatty fish (tuna, salmon, etc.)	1–3 months
Lean fish (haddock, sole, etc.)	4–6 months
Oysters	1–3 months
Shrimp	4–6 months
Meat	
Beef	
Roasts, steaks	6–12 months
Beef for stew	3–4 months
Ground beef	3–4 months
Beef variety meats (liver)	3–4 months
Corned beef, bologna, luncheon meats**	2 weeks
Lamb	
Roasts, chops, cubes	6–9 months
Ground lamb	3–4 months
Pork	
Roasts, chops, ribs	3–6 months
Ground pork	1–3 months
Ham***	2 months
Bacon, frankfurters***	1 month
Veal	
Roasts, chops, cutlets, cubes	6–9 months
Ground veal	3–4 months
Sausage***	1 month
Cooked meat	2–3 months
Poultry	
Chicken, capon, turkey, Cornish hens, small game	
Whole	12 months
Pieces	6–9 months
Giblets	2–3 months
Cooked poultry	
Pieces not in broth or gravy	1 month
Pieces in broth or gravy	6 months
Poultry dishes (casseroles, stews)	3–6 months
Goose, duck, game birds	
Whole	6 months

  *Foods stored longer than the recommended period will suffer a loss of quality, but will still be safe to eat. Storing foods at temperatures higher than 0° F shortens the storage period considerably.
 **Processed, cured, smoked, and ready-to-serve meat products do not retain their quality long.
 ***Do not freeze canned hams and canned picnics.

FREEZE, TO

Freezing has many advantages over other methods of food preservation. Frozen food tastes fresher, and it also retains its original color, texture, flavor, and nutritional value better than food preserved by other methods. And freezing is one of the simplest ways to put up food for later enjoyment.

If you expect to do a lot of freezing, you'll need a freezer rather than just the freezing compartment of a refrigerator. Home freezers reach and maintain the optimum temperature, 0° F, needed to preserve food quality better than refrigerator-freezer combinations. Fluctuations in temperature, common in the combination appliances, have an adverse effect on frozen food; with every 10° F above 0° F, storage life is cut by up to half.

BASIC FREEZER MANAGEMENT

To make the best use of your freezer, be sure foods are sealed airtight with wrapping material or containers designed for freezing. Use materials that are airtight, vapor-proof, and moistureproof.

Food loses quality if stored too long or at improper temperatures (although it can still be safe to eat). Keep an inventory of the foods you have in storage so that you'll know what's on hand and how long it has been there. Label each item with contents, entry date, weight, and number of servings. Periodically check the freezer temperature with a freezer thermometer (see THERMOMETER) to be sure that it is at 0° F or a little below.

FREEZING METHODS

Freeze foods only after they have cooled to room temperature. In each 24-hour period, freeze a maximum of 3 pounds of food per cubic foot of freezer space. Overloading slows down the freezing process, and foods frozen too slowly lose quality and may spoil.

QUICK-FREEZING

This is the recommended method of freezing packaged foods. To quick-freeze, place packages in a single layer close to the outside freezer walls, where freezing plates or coils are located. Allow space between packages so that air can circulate freely around them. Freeze packages 24 hours before sorting and stacking them.

TRAY-FREEZING

"Piece" foods, such as meatballs or drop cookies, keep best when tray-frozen. An advantage of this method is that pieces freeze individually and remain separate, allowing you to remove only as many as you need. Thawing is quicker, too. Another reason for tray-freezing is to firm up foods such as cakes and pies before packaging so that the packaging material will not adhere to them. To tray-freeze, spread unwrapped food on a baking sheet and freeze just until firm. Then immediately package as usual.

MEASURING QUALITY DURING STORAGE

Almost all food, whether plant or animal in origin, is subject to deterioration and eventual decay. To minimize loss of quality (and in severe cases, contamination) in frozen foods, you need to control the growth of microorganisms and enzymes to avoid oxidation.

Unlike canning, freezing does not sterilize foods by destroying the microorganisms present in them. Cold temperatures only inhibit the growth of microorganisms and slow down enzyme activity and oxidation. During thawing, spoilage organisms start to grow again; as the temperature of the food rises, so does the rate of growth of the organisms. The best protection against oxidation is to store food in airtight packages at the proper temperature for the recommended storage period.

The following clues indicate that foods may have suffered deterioration during freezing. If you discover any of these warning signs, chances are the food is still safe to eat, but the flavor will no longer be of top quality. You don't need to throw the food out unless it has developed off-odors, but plan to use it as soon as possible and take its condition into consideration when deciding on a cooking method.

Color Change   When foods are stored in the freezer too long, their colors fade. Vegetables, for example, turn a dull, drab color.

Freezer Burn   When foods are not carefully packaged, moisture is drawn out of them by the dry air of the freezer, resulting in freezer burn: a dry surface with grayish white spots. To protect against freezer burn, use proper packaging materials and be certain that packages are airtight.

Ice Buildup   Icy crystals inside the package indicate that the food has thawed, at least partially, and refrozen, or that the food didn't freeze quickly. To minimize the size of ice crystals, freeze foods as quickly as possible and maintain them at 0° F or lower.

Sauce Consistency   When food has passed its optimum storage period or has been allowed to thaw and refreeze, the consistency of the sauce may change. Starches may break down and the sauce may lose smoothness.

Texture Change   The texture of foods deteriorates when they have thawed and refrozen. Vegetables become soft and limp, meats toughen slightly, and the pasta in combination dishes may become soggy from absorbing moisture from the sauce.

THAWING FROZEN FOOD

Thawing in the refrigerator is the safest, although slowest, thawing method. Thawing foods at room temperature invites the risk of spoilage. If time is short, some foods, particularly poultry and meats, may be placed (in their

TIMETABLE FOR FREEZING

The length of time frozen food can be stored depends on the care with which the food was handled before freezing, the type of food, the quality of the packaging materials, and the maintenance of the proper storage temperature (0° F or less).

Food	Storage Time at 0° F*
Baked Goods	
Angel, chiffon, and sponge cakes	4–6 months
Biscuits	2–3 months
Butter and pound cakes	2–4 months
Cheesecake	4 months
Cookies	6–8 months
Cream puff and éclair shells	1–2 months
Fruitcakes	12 months
Muffins	6–12 months
Nut and fruit breads, coffee cakes, and steamed breads	2–4 months
Pancakes and waffles	1–2 months
Pie and tart shells	
Baked	3–4 months
Unbaked	6–8 weeks
Puff pastry	1–2 months
Yeast breads	
Baked	6–8 months
Unbaked	6 weeks
Eggs and Dairy Products	
Butter	
Salted	6 months
Unsalted	2–3 months
Buttermilk, for baking	1 month
Cheese	
Cream cheese	2 months
Hard and semihard natural cheese	2–3 months
Pasteurized process cheese	4 months
Soft cheese	2 months
Cream	
Whipped	1 month
Whipping (heavy)	2 months
Eggs: whole, yolks, or whites	9–12 months
Ice cream, ice milk, sherbets, and ices	1–2 months
Margarine	12 months
Milk	3 months
Yogurt, for baking	1 month

*Foods stored longer than the recommended period will suffer a loss of quality but will still be safe to eat. Storing foods at temperatures higher than 0° F shortens the storage period considerably.

freezer wrappings) in a plastic bag and thawed in a basin of cold water; this cuts thawing time about in half. A microwave oven is by far the fastest and easiest method of all. Your oven manual lists appropriate settings and approximate defrosting times.

Thaw most food in the freezer wrapping. However, cakes can be affected by the moisture that collects on the inside of the package as it warms to room temperature; therefore, loosen wrapping before thawing.

REFREEZING THAWED FOOD

If food feels cold, is still firm, and contains ice crystals, you may refreeze it without cooking it first. Be aware, however, that refreezing involves a loss of food quality and flavor and that refrozen food cannot be kept as long as freshly frozen food.

Once food has thawed, organisms that can cause spoilage begin to multiply. Therefore, unless you cook it first, do not refreeze food that has thawed completely. (You can, for example, cook thawed raw meat and then refreeze it.) Foods that have been held between 32° and 40° F for more than 24 hours should be used as soon as possible; they should not be refrozen. Seafood spoils quickly and should not be refrozen; cook it and use as soon as possible. Casseroles or dishes that have been precooked should not be refrozen. Discard any foods that have developed off-odors or off-colors.

To refreeze foods, label foods as refrozen, date, and use as soon as possible; spread the packages out in the freezer so that cold air circulates around them.

FRENCH FRY, TO

To fry directly in deep fat, traditionally without a protective coating of bread crumbs or batter, although batter-coated foods such as onion rings have come to be called French fried. The term most probably derives from a French preparation, *pommes frites*, fingers of deep-fried potatoes, and it has come to refer to any food so prepared.

> ***Recipes and Related Information***
> *Batter, 27; French-fried Potatoes, 468.*

FRICASSEE

This stew, usually of poultry, but also of veal (see Blanquette de Veau, page 593) or rabbit, is made with a white sauce. Sometimes the meat is first sauteed. The cooking liquid is most often white wine. After cooking, the sauce is bound with a white roux and enriched with egg yolk and cream.

FROSTING, ICING, AND FILLING

"The icing on the cake" has come to mean a detail that adds a special, delightful finale or flourish. The phrase of course comes from that magic moment when the baker turns artist. A coat of frosting transforms a basic cake or pastry into a stunning and distinctive creation. A line of filling, revealed in cross section with each slice, adds another level of visual and edible enjoyment. Decoration can be elaborate—applied in swirls and peaks or piped with a pastry bag. It can also be as simple as a coat of whipped cream, a sprinkle of confectioners' sugar, or a poured glaze made of just a few ingredients.

EQUIPMENT FOR CAKE DECORATION

Beautiful results are possible with tools you probably already have in your kitchen drawers and cabinets. However, if you bake a lot or are particularly interested in cake decoration, you may want to purchase some or all of the following equipment, which is available at better cookware shops or cake-decorating supply houses: pastry brushes (for applying glazes); flexible, narrow stainless steel icing spatulas in various sizes (both straight bladed and offset); toothpicks; skewers; a cake comb (a serrated metal triangle used to create grooves in frosting and icing); cardboard cake rounds (for supporting a cake as you apply decoration); cake-decorating turntable (raises cake closer to eye level and allows more even application of decoration); and a pastry bag and tubes. For a detailed description of specialty equipment for cake decoration, see CAKE AND PASTRY TOOLS.

FROSTING, FILLING, AND GLAZING BASICS

Any successful procedure, culinary or otherwise, is based on adequate preparation. Before you begin, have all equipment at hand and ingredients out and in the form or amount called for in the recipes. If the frosted cake or pastry must chill at any time during the decorating process, make sure that you have cleared a space for it in your refrigerator ahead of time.

Unless otherwise directed in the recipe, cakes must be completely cool before applying any decoration. If the top or sides of the cake or pastry are uneven, and if this will bother you, gently trim away the uneven area. Brush away crumbs, which, if left, will cause the frosting to roll away from the surface of the cake. An alternative is to seal the crumbs to the cake with a thin layer of melted jelly or preserves. If you don't want to see a fine line of brown crust, the characteristic golden surface of a baked cake, between cake and frosting, slice off the crust with a serrated knife. (However, if the cake or frosting is dark, the crust won't be noticeable.)

Set cake or pastry on a piece of cardboard (see Which Way Is Up?). For frosting a cake with a spatula, use a cardboard the same shape and size as cake; for frosting on a turntable or when applying a poured icing or glaze, the cardboard should be slightly smaller. Secure the cake to the cardboard with a tablespoon of frosting. Or, set on a flat plate that is several inches larger than cake or pastry and that has been covered around the rim with strips of waxed paper larger than the diameter of the plate.

APPLYING FILLING

If the filling was cooked, cool it before using. A metal spatula with a blade at least as long as the diameter of what is to be filled will give you the most control. If it is too small, its handle will continually drag against the surface of the cake or pastry. Scoop up the entire amount of filling at one time; set in center of layer. Spread from center to edges. If filling is soft, stop just short of the edge of the layer; this leaves room for the filling to spread when covered with another layer of cake or pastry.

APPLYING FROSTING OR ICING

If the cake or pastry is still rough even after you've trimmed it, coat with a very thin layer of frosting to even out the surface (it doesn't matter at this point if the cake shows through in spots); chill to set this precoat. Using a metal icing spatula, spread the sides with an even coating of frosting; be sure to carry frosting up the sides to the top of the cake, including any excess. Even the surface; it will be evened again, so this time it needn't be perfectly smooth. For the top, scoop up the entire amount of remaining frosting with the spatula and place in center of top of cake. Be sure to work with a clean spatula or crumbs may get into the frosting, creating an undesirable texture. With the spatula, smooth frosting evenly across top. For a decorative touch at the edge where top and sides meet, pipe a trim of frosting with a pastry bag. To create a smooth finish with buttercream frosting, dip knife or spatula in hot water; smooth around the sides, then across the top. This can only be done one time; repeated attempts will create lines. See photographs, page 247.

If frosting is to be textured or swirled, apply about a ¼-inch layer of frosting. Work on sides, then top. To create grooves, drag a cake comb or fork in straight or wavy lines around cake. (A cake-decorating turntable or lazy Susan is very helpful for this step; both raise the cake off the counter so your hand can maneuver around it better, and rotating produces a more uniform texture.) As a final textural touch, chopped nuts, crumbs, or flaked coconut can be pressed into the sides near the bottom. For swirls, use a knife, the back of a spoon, or metal spatula and pull frosting up in peaks; for ripples draw across frosting with knife or spatula in a wavy line. See photographs, page 247.

It is sometimes harder to get a really smooth finish when applying whipped cream. It will help if the whipped cream and the spatula or knife are chilled.

APPLYING A GLAZE

Glazes are used for European-type cakes, tube and loaf cakes of all kinds, fruit tarts, and pastries such as éclairs and cream puffs. For cakes, glazes add luster and visual appeal. Fruit tarts are glazed to impart a sheen and to make them look more appetizing, and, more practically, to keep the fruit juicy by protecting it from the drying effects of air. The temperature and consistency of a glaze are critical to its successful application; to make a glaze more fluid, it is sometimes better to loosen it by warming it slightly rather than by thinning it with more liquid (see Glacé Icing, page 250).

To glaze completely set cake on cardboard cut slightly smaller than its diameter (or glaze will pool on edges of cardboard). Set cake on wire rack resting on a baking sheet or on waxed paper to catch drips. Pour glaze over cake all at once. Tilt and rotate cake so that glaze flows and coats evenly. Never use a spatula to spread glaze or it will lose its sheen. Let cake rest on wire rack to allow excess to drip off and to allow glaze to set. Before transferring from rack to serving plate, run a thin-bladed knife around edge of cake to release it where glaze has stuck to the wires of the rack.

To glaze partially, apply glaze with a spoon in a network of random lines called drizzles, or pour on. For a drizzled effect, let the glaze run off the spoon in a thin stream as you move your hand back and forth over the surface of the cake. Some bakers prefer a thinner glaze for drizzling, but this is personal preference. Whatever the consistency, the glaze must be able to flow. To pour, put the glaze in a ladle or glass measuring cup with a lip. Let the glaze fall steadily from the ladle or cup as you move in a circular fashion around the cake. For tube cakes, apply more glaze on the outside of the cake than in the center.

To dip in glaze, a typical treatment for cream puff pastries, hold pastry in hand and dip; let excess run off and then set on tray to firm glaze. See photographs, page 247.

USING A PASTRY BAG
AND PAPER PIPING CONE

Learning to use a pastry bag and the simpler paper piping cone takes some effort and a bit of practice, but will greatly expand your decorating repertoire. See CAKE AND PASTRY TOOLS for a complete description of the pastry bag and tips.

The technique for either of these tools is not difficult; the skill is in learning how much pressure to apply and how to move the bag to create a particular effect (see photographs, page 246). To use, either a bag or piping cone is filled partway with frosting and gently squeezed. A ribbon of frosting is forced out of the bag or cone in a shape formed by the opening of the tip. Pastry bags have interchangeable metal tips that come in a variety of different sizes with openings of different shapes. With these tips, you can create stars, rosettes, ribbons, leaves, flowers, and many other designs. The paper cone is used for small

HOW TO USE A PASTRY BAG

Fold about one third of top over to form cuff. Set tip in place. To seal tip while filling bag, twist bag just above tip and push twisted portion of bag into tip.

Hold bag cuffed over one hand; fill no more than two thirds full. Hold bag by edges and shake to force filling into lower half of bag. Then twist top of bag below cuff so filling can't back up. Untwist small end of bag to open tip.

Grasp bag at neck with thumb and index finger of right hand; squeeze with fingers of right hand only. Guide bag with left hand while piping. Maintain even pressure; periodically twist bag to keep filling moving out of tip.

HOW TO MAKE A PAPER PIPING CONE

Cut a 10-inch square of parchment paper in half to form two triangles (enough for two cones). With 90-degree-angle point facing you, fold right-hand point in toward middle so that points meet, forming a cone. Repeat with opposite point.

Fold points into cone to secure. With a spoon or spatula, fill no more than half full with frosting, gently pushing frosting into cone to eliminate air pockets.

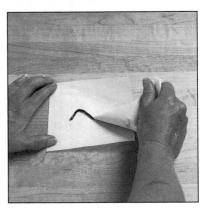

To contain frosting and to keep cone from unraveling, fold top of cone over several times. To form opening, cut closed tip of cone with scissors. Width of strand of frosting forced out of cone depends upon how much of tip is snipped off.

amounts of frosting, for line work, or for writing a message. The opening is created by snipping off part of the pointed end (see How to Make a Paper Piping Cone, above). Precut parchment triangles for making these cones are available in cookware stores.

It is important to not overfill the pastry bag or piping cone, so that you can control the bag. Allow the filling to flow from the bag. Keep the tip away from the surface of the cake—a half inch at least—so that the design can take shape without being squashed or destroyed, a common frustration for beginners. Practice with mashed potatoes rather than real frosting; their textures are similar. Pipe sample designs onto a piece of waxed paper, parchment paper, or other smooth surface. Repetition will lead to perfection. Before you decorate a cake, warm up with a few practice designs on a clean surface. If you make a mistake on the cake or pastry, scrape if off with a spatula and start over. Rechill the icing if it becomes too warm.

Any frosting or icing that is thick enough to hold its form when pressed through a tip and that is soft enough to flow smoothly out of the bag can be used to decorate a cake. Buttercream Frosting (see page 248) and Chantilly Cream (see page 252) are good choices for a pastry bag. Confectioners' Decorating Icing (see page 250) and plain, melted semisweet chocolate (cooled to 86° F) are commonly used with a paper cone.

HOW TO APPLY FROSTING

If cake is uneven, trim top. Coat with a thin layer of frosting to even surface. Don't worry if some of the cake's sides show through. The next layer will cover.

Spread sides with an even coating of frosting. Carry enough frosting up to top of cake so patches of cake are not visible. Excess frosting can be used to cover top.

Scoop up enough frosting to cover top completely . Spread to cover. Trim away any excess with spatula by holding against cake and rotating cake on turntable or with hand. Smooth with flat side of blade.

DECORATIVE TECHNIQUES

Piping   *Lay pastry bag at edge of cake. Squeeze gently as you slowly rotate cake. Use an open-star tip to create chains of rosettes, ribbons, or shells. Shown above is a ribbon.*

Swirls   *Form waves and swirls by drawing knife or spatula along frosting. Create peaks with knife, spatula, or spoon by dipping into frosting and pulling up.*

Textures   *Use a cake comb or fork. Make free-form grooves by resting comb against cake and dragging through frosting. For more uniform grooves, rotate cake slowly on turntable with comb touching.*

HOW TO APPLY GLAZES

Full glaze   *Pour on glaze all at once. Tilt and rotate cake so that glaze flows to cover completely. Do not use a spatula to even glaze.*

Drizzle and partial glaze   *Drizzle by letting glaze drip from spoon to form fine lines. Create a partial glaze by pouring glaze in a thin stream over cake as hand moves in circles over cake.*

Dipping   *Hold pastry upside down and dip into glaze. Set on tray, glaze side up, until set.*

■ BUTTERCREAM FROSTING

This creamy, rich, versatile frosting is used, in varying amounts, in many of the cake recipes included in this book. It works well with a pastry bag used for decorating. Buttercream frosting can be refrigerated for later use; before applying bring to room temperature (see Note).

For 1 cup

    2 egg yolks
    ⅓ cup sugar
    ¼ cup water
    ½ cup unsalted butter, softened

For 1½ cups

    3 egg yolks
    7 tablespoons sugar
    ⅓ cup water
    ¾ cup unsalted butter, softened

For 2 cups

    4 egg yolks
    ½ cup sugar
    ⅓ cup water
    1 cup unsalted butter, softened

For 3 cups

    6 egg yolks
    1 cup sugar (scant; 14 tablespoons)
    ½ cup water
    1½ cups unsalted butter, softened

1. In a medium stainless steel bowl, beat yolks until light.

2. In a heavy 2½-quart saucepan, combine sugar and water; stir over medium heat until sugar dissolves and syrup comes to a boil. As sugar is dissolving, wash down any sugar crystals that cling to sides of pan with a pastry brush dipped in cold water.

3. Boil syrup gently, without stirring, until it reaches 239° F (soft-ball stage). When syrup reaches the soft-ball stage, immediately remove from heat and pour into yolks, beating constantly as you pour. Continue to beat until the mixture is light, fluffy, and cool to the touch.

4. In medium bowl of electric mixer, cream butter. Gradually beat butter into yolk mixture, 2 tablespoons at a time, until smooth, shiny, and spreadable. At this point you may fold in some stiffly whipped cream or vanilla pastry cream to lighten the buttercream, if desired. Flavor the buttercream according to the chart at left. Use buttercream immediately or refrigerate until ready to use. Store up to 3 days in the refrigerator or freeze up to 2 months.

Note   If buttercream separates at any point after butter is added, the butter may be too cold. Add a little hot, melted butter, then beat until smooth. If buttercream has warmed up too much, refrigerate a few minutes, then beat until smooth. If using cold buttercream, remove from refrigerator, warm to room temperature (20 to 30 minutes), then beat frosting until smooth, shiny, and spreadable. Should the mixture separate as it loses its chill, add hot, melted butter as directed above.

■ CHOCOLATE FUDGE FROSTING

Use this dark, richly flavored frosting for layer cakes.

    6 ounces unsweetened chocolate
    1 cup butter
    2 cups confectioners' sugar
    2 eggs
    ¼ cup hot water
    2 teaspoons vanilla extract

1. In a double boiler melt chocolate and ½ cup butter; cool. In a medium bowl, cream remaining ½ cup butter, sugar, eggs, water, and vanilla until fluffy.

TO FLAVOR BUTTERCREAM FROSTING

Versatile Buttercream Frosting can be flavored in a multitude of ways to accompany many types of cakes. Add flavoring to the basic recipe as a last step.

Buttercream Flavor	Flavoring	Amount of Buttercream			
		1 cup	1½ cups	2 cups	3 cups
Chocolate	Semisweet chocolate (melted and cooled)	3 oz	4 oz	6 oz	8 oz
Citrus fruit	Finely grated orange or lemon rind	1 tsp	1½ tsp	2 tsp	3 tsp
Coffee	Coffee extract	To taste			
	Instant coffee dissolved in boiling water	2 tsp	1 tbsp	4 tsp	1½ tbsp
		1 tbsp	1 tbsp	1½ tbsp	2 tbsp
Fruit	Fruit purée	⅓ cup	½ cup	⅔ cup	1 cup
	Fruit liqueur	To taste; see Liqueur below			
Liqueur	Liqueur or brandy	2 tsp	1 tbsp	1½ tbsp	2 tbsp
Mocha	Semisweet chocolate (melted and cooled) and coffee extract	3 oz	4 oz	6 oz	8 oz
		To semisweet chocolate add coffee extract to taste or instant coffee in amounts under Coffee			
Nuts	Finely ground toasted nuts	3 tbsp	⅓ cup	½ cup	¾ cup
Praline	Finely ground caramelized nuts	2 tbsp	¼ cup	⅓ cup	½ cup
Vanilla	Vanilla extract	1 tsp	1½ tsp	2 tsp	1 tbsp
White chocolate	White chocolate (melted and cooled)	3 oz	4 oz	6 oz	8 oz

2. Add cooled chocolate mixture and beat on high speed until smooth and creamy. Use immediately.

Makes 2½ cups.

■ CARAMEL FROSTING

Although this frosting, also known as penuche, is most commonly paired with white or yellow cakes, try it with chocolate for something different. It has a rich brown sugar flavor, which complements chocolate quite well.

    2 cups firmly packed brown sugar
    ½ cup granulated sugar
    1 cup whipping cream
    ¼ cup butter
    1 tablespoon vanilla extract

1. In a large, heavy-bottomed saucepan, cook sugars, cream, and butter over low heat until sugars and butter are dissolved. Increase heat to medium and cook until mixture is 239° F on a candy thermometer (soft-ball stage); remove from heat and cool 15 minutes.

2. Stir in vanilla and beat mixture until it loses its shine and thickens to a spreading consistency; this may take 10 minutes or more and can be done in intervals, letting the mixture cool between beatings. Use immediately.

Makes 2 cups.

■ WHITE MOUNTAIN FROSTING

Probably this classic American boiled frosting got its name because of the way it peaks when beaten. Another name for it is Italian meringue (see MERINGUE). When made with brown sugar it is called sea-foam frosting. If you won't be using the frosting immediately, wait to add the vanilla extract or the optional orange or lemon rind; refrigerate, covered, up to 24 hours.

    1½ cups sugar
    ½ cup water
    4 egg whites
      Pinch cream of tartar (optional)
    2 teaspoons vanilla extract
    1 teaspoon grated orange or lemon rind (optional)

1. In a small, heavy-bottomed pan dissolve sugar in the water over low heat. Increase heat to medium and cook until 239° F on a candy thermometer (soft-ball stage).

2. As the sugar syrup approaches desired temperature, beat egg whites in a copper or stainless steel bowl until foamy; add cream of tartar if using a stainless steel bowl and beat until soft peaks form. Slowly pour hot syrup onto egg whites and beat at high speed until bowl feels cool to the touch.

3. Add vanilla and orange or lemon rind (if desired), and beat to incorporate. Use immediately.

Makes 3½ cups.

■ SEVEN-MINUTE FROSTING

Another cooked frosting, this recipe got its name because it takes approximately seven minutes to beat to the proper consistency.

    1½ cups sugar
    ¼ cup water
    2 egg whites
    1 tablespoon corn syrup
    ½ teaspoon cream of tartar
    1 tablespoon vanilla extract

1. In a large mixing bowl, combine sugar, the water, egg whites, corn syrup, and cream of tartar. Stand bowl over pan of simmering water and beat mixture at high speed with an electric mixer until light, fluffy, and of spreading consistency (about 7 minutes).

2. Remove from heat and continue to beat until mixture has cooled. Mix in vanilla. Use immediately.

Makes 2½ cups.

Citrus Seven-Minute Frosting   Omit vanilla extract; substitute ¼ cup fresh orange or lemon juice for the water and add 1 teaspoon grated orange or lemon rind to other ingredients.

Tropical Seven-Minute Frosting   Fold ½ to 1 cup chopped nuts, ½ to 1 cup chopped dried fruit, and 1 cup flaked coconut into cooled frosting.

Angel Food Cake and White Mountain Frosting are classics of American cooking. The cake is light, delicate, and pristine white. The pale frosting adds to the airy quality when applied in peaks and swirls. The recipe for Angel Food Cake is on page 82.

■ GLACE ICING

Icing in probably its simplest form, this recipe is made from confectioners' sugar and water. It is usually drizzled over yeast or quick breads, Danish, and other pastries, as well as all types of tube cakes. Although shiny and soft, the icing forms a thin crust when set, making it easy to handle. It can be flavored with melted chocolate, coffee, liqueur, or the suggestions given at the end of the recipe. It can be tinted to pastel shades with a few drops of food coloring, if desired. If used for coating rather than just drizzling, it should be a little thicker, enough to coat the back of a spoon. To maintain pouring consistency, set bowl of icing in warm water and stir continuously. Do not overheat the mixture or it will lose its sheen and the surface will crystallize. For a richer, shinier icing, use whipping cream instead of water. The recipe can easily be doubled or tripled.

  1½ **cups confectioners' sugar**
   3 **to 4 tablespoons water**

Into a medium bowl, sift sugar; add water and beat until smooth. The mixture should leave a thick trail when it falls back into the bowl from a spoon. If too thick, add a little more water. If too thin, add a little more sifted sugar. Use immediately.

Makes ½ cup.

Citrus Glacé Icing Substitute orange or lemon juice for the water; add ½ to 1 teaspoon very finely grated orange or lemon rind.

Cognac or Rum Glacé Icing Substitute Cognac or rum for the water.

Rich Glacé Icing Use 1 cup confectioners' sugar, reduce water to 1 tablespoon, and add 1 teaspoon softened butter along with water.

Vanilla or Almond Glacé Icing Add ⅛ to ¼ teaspoon vanilla or almond extract along with water.

■ CONFECTIONERS' DECORATING ICING

Another icing basic, this is quick, easy, holds its shape well, and isn't greatly affected by minor variations of temperature. It's perfect for piping and even for frosting because it is thicker than Glacé Icing.

   ½ **cup solid vegetable shortening**
 2½ **to 3 cups confectioners' sugar**
   2 **tablespoons whipping cream**
   1 **teaspoon vanilla extract**

1. In a medium bowl combine shortening, 2½ cups sugar, cream, and vanilla. Beat until completely smooth and spreadable (somewhere between the consistency of mayonnaise and peanut butter).

2. If icing is too thin, beat in remaining sugar a little at time until proper consistency is reached.

Makes 1 cup.

■ ROYAL ICING

Use this icing to add further decoration—birthday wishes or a special inscription—to cakes that have already been frosted with buttercream or another surface frosting. Use a pastry bag fitted with a writing tip or a fine-tipped paper piping cone (see page 246). Practice your decorations on waxed paper before adorning the cake: Make a pencil sketch on the waxed paper and then trace over it with icing. The icing can be tinted with food coloring. To use, Royal Icing should be stiff enough to hold its shape when piped out, but pliable enough to flow through the tip of the pastry bag or paper cone. When dry, it firms and hardens.

 1¼ **cups sifted confectioners' sugar**
  1 **egg white**
  1 **teaspoon strained lemon juice**

Beat ¾ cup of the sugar with egg white and lemon juice until thick and white (about 10 minutes). Add the remaining ½ cup sugar and beat until stiff. Icing may be tinted with food coloring at this point. To store icing for up to 1 week, lay a piece of plastic wrap directly on icing surface; refrigerate.

Makes ¾ cup.

■ BASIC GLAZE

Use a light-colored jam or preserve such as apricot for fair fruits or pastries, and a red or dark-colored glaze such as red currant or raspberry on red or dark fruits.

  ½ **cup fruit preserves or jelly**
  2 **tablespoons water or lemon juice**

1. In a small, heavy-bottomed saucepan, heat preserves and the water over medium heat until preserves are melted; remove from heat and force through a sieve to strain out any pieces of fruit or seeds.

2. Return to heat and cook until mixture reaches a thin coating consistency. Remove from heat and brush on pastry as directed in recipe.

Makes ½ cup.

■ CHOCOLATE GLAZE

This luscious glaze makes a smooth, chocolate layer when poured over a cake or pastry.

  6 **ounces semisweet chocolate,
     chopped into small pieces**
  4 **tablespoons unsalted butter**

1. Place chocolate in a double boiler or small stainless steel bowl set over a pan of hot, not boiling, water. Clarify butter by melting it in a small saucepan and skimming off white foam that rises to top.

2. When chocolate is just melted, stir in clarified butter. Set aside until chocolate is 86° F.

Makes about ¾ cup.

▪ ICING FONDANT

For the professional pastry maker and confectionery chef, fondant is a building block for many preparations, including many candies and frosting bases. It is labor-intensive (see page 96) and you may not want to prepare it yourself, but it does add a professional finish to cakes and pastries. Ready-made fondant is available from specialty-food stores. The following directions for thinning and flavoring will work with homemade or commercial fondant.

> **2 cups Fondant, homemade (see page 96)**
> **or commercially prepared**
> **¼ to ½ cup Sugar Syrup (see page 567)**

1. In a double boiler, place Fondant and ¼ cup Sugar Syrup. Warm over low heat; stir gently to avoid incorporating air bubbles. Do not overheat, or fondant will crystallize and dull. Add more syrup, if needed, to achieve desired consistency. If desired, add flavoring as Fondant melts (see variations).

2. Fondant is ready when it coats back of spoon evenly, without any spoon shining through. Use immediately; it will set on cooling.

Makes 2 cups.

Almond or Vanilla Fondant Add ¼ to ½ teaspoon almond or vanilla extract.

Chocolate Fondant Add 1 ounce melted unsweetened chocolate.

Coffee Fondant Substitute espresso or very strong coffee for the Sugar Syrup.

Orange or Lemon Fondant Substitute orange or lemon juice for the Sugar Syrup; add 1 teaspoon finely grated orange or lemon rind.

▪ PASTRY CREAM

Crème pâtissière

Pastry cream is a delicious, multipurpose custard (or pudding). It can be used by itself, as in vanilla pudding, or flavored and lightened with whipped cream or beaten egg whites. It is used as a filling for cream puff pastries, puff pastries, and cakes, and also in fresh fruit tarts. Pastry cream can be frozen successfully if either the flour or cornstarch is increased slightly to create a thicker cream. Thin pastry creams tend to separate when frozen. If pastry cream is lumpy or scorched, press through a sieve to remove lumps or bits of brown cream.

For 1¼ cups

> 1 cup milk
> 3 egg yolks
> ¼ cup sugar
> 2 tablespoons flour, sifted
> 1 tablespoon cornstarch, sifted
> 1 teaspoon vanilla extract

FLAVORINGS FOR PASTRY CREAM

Consider the main ingredients of the pastry which the pastry cream is to accompany, and choose a flavoring that will complement that taste.

Amount of Pastry Cream	Semisweet Chocolate	Dry Instant Coffee	Liqueur	Finely Ground Praline
1¼ cups	2 oz (melted and cooled)	2 tsp (dissolved in 1 tbsp boiling water)	1 tbsp	3 tbsp
1½ cups	2½ oz (melted and cooled)	2½ tsp (dissolved in 1 tbsp boiling water)	1½ tbsp	¼ cup
2½ cups	3 to 4 oz (melted and cooled)	4 tsp (dissolved in 1½ tbsp boiling water)	2 tbsp	⅓ cup

For 1½ cups

> 1¼ cups milk
> 4 egg yolks
> ⅓ cup sugar
> 3 tablespoons flour, sifted
> 1 tablespoon cornstarch, sifted
> 1 teaspoon vanilla extract

For 2½ cups

> 2 cups milk
> 6 egg yolks
> ½ cup sugar
> ¼ cup flour, sifted
> 2 tablespoons cornstarch, sifted
> 1½ teaspoons vanilla extract

1. In a medium saucepan bring milk to a boil; remove from heat.

2. In a medium bowl beat egg yolks with sugar until thick and pale. Beat in flour and cornstarch.

3. Pour hot milk into yolk mixture and whisk. Return to saucepan; cook over medium heat, whisking constantly, until mixture comes to a boil. Just before mixture begins to boil, it will become very lumpy. Whisk vigorously until smooth; continue to cook gently for 2 minutes, whisking constantly. (The mixture will thin slightly during this time.) Remove from heat and pour into a bowl; stir in vanilla and rub a piece of cold butter gently over the surface of the cream to prevent a skin from forming.

4. Pastry cream may be flavored when it has cooled slightly (see Flavorings for Pastry Cream, above). When pastry cream is cool, cover and refrigerate. It will keep up to 2 days in refrigerator.

■ CHANTILLY CREAM

A fancy name for sweetened, flavored whipped cream, Chantilly Cream is the preferred topping for many hot and cold desserts. Use it as a filling, to lighten other creams or fillings, or as a piped decoration. The following recipe can be doubled or tripled easily if you need more than one cup.

    ½ cup whipping cream
    1 tablespoon sifted confectioners' sugar
    ¼ teaspoon vanilla extract or 1 teaspoon liqueur

1. Chill cream, mixing bowl, and beaters (or whisk) before whipping the cream.

2. Whip cream until it begins to thicken; add sugar and vanilla. Continue beating until cream holds its shape on the beaters and forms peaks (cream should still look smooth and soft). Do not overbeat, or cream will become grainy or turn to butter. Slightly underbeat cream if you will be piping it from a pastry bag fitted with a star tip (the tip whips the cream a little more).

Makes 1 cup.

■ LEMON CURD

There are many different recipes for lemon curd, a delightful filling for any number of desserts—tarts, cake rolls, or layer cakes. Some use whole eggs, some egg yolks, and some a combination of the two. The primary differences among them are in their color and texture. A curd made with whole eggs is lighter in texture and holds its shape well, so is good for spreading. One made with only yolks is very thick and creamy and bright yellow. A mixture of whole eggs and egg yolks is paler than yolks only, but still very creamy.

    Juice and grated rind of 4 to 5 lemons
    1½ cups sugar
    1 cup butter, cut in pieces
    5 eggs, beaten

1. In a double boiler combine lemon juice, rind, sugar, and butter; stir over medium heat until sugar has dissolved and butter has melted.

2. Add eggs and beat with a whisk to combine, then continue stirring with a wooden spoon until mixture coats back of spoon. Do not let mixture boil or it will curdle.

3. Strain through a fine sieve to remove rind and refine to a creamy consistency. Cool, then refrigerate.

Makes 3 cups.

Variation To make curd using only yolks, substitute 10 yolks for the 5 whole eggs.

Recipes and Related Information
Cream Cheese Frosting, 86; Homemade Almond Paste and Marzipan, 7; Lemon Custard Glaze, 117; Maple Glaze, 183; Raspberry Glaze, 117; Whipped Cream Icing, 87.

FRUIT

Advances in transportation and refrigeration have vastly changed the kind of fruits seen in the marketplace in recent years. Exotic varieties from around the globe are now regularly available in urban supermarkets. The New Zealand kiwifruit, virtually unknown in America 30 years ago, is now commonplace. Increased curiosity about foreign cuisines and unusual foods has provided importers and wholesalers with a viable market—people willing to pay the additional cost of delicate handling and air freight on fragile, perishable fruits.

It is easy to understand the immense appeal of ripe fruits. Most are relatively low in calories and high in vitamins and fiber. Most can be enjoyed as is, without requiring further investment of time, expense, or calories. A ripe peach, for example, satisfies both hunger and sweet tooth. Most ripe fruits can serve as dessert by themselves.

Use Without a doubt fruit is most often enjoyed in its unaltered state. The apple eaten out of hand, the wedge of sweet melon, the bowl of fragrant berries—all are delicious without adornment. Fruits also lend themselves to countless other preparations, both raw and cooked.

Most American breakfasts include fruit in some form: a wedge of melon or half a grapefruit, a glass of orange or grapefruit juice, berries or bananas on top of cereal, or fruit preserves on toast.

Fruits that travel well are frequent choices in the typical American brown-bag lunch. Raisins, dried apricots, crisp apples, bananas, and juicy oranges are all good candidates for the lunch box.

As an appetizer, pair figs, melons, or pears with prosciutto. The moist sweetness of the fruit contrasts well with the salty pork. Grilled, bacon-wrapped dates or prunes offer the same pleasing contrast.

As a salad course, serve a refreshing fruit cup or macédoine, especially appealing at a warm-weather lunch. The presence of citrus, such as orange or grapefruit, will keep other fruits from browning (see ACIDULATED WATER). Half a grapefruit sprinkled with salt or a halved melon filled with port make light and appetizing beginnings to a meal.

In green salads, fruits add a refreshing tang. Grapefruit or pear sections provide contrasts of texture and flavor in a winter endive or spinach salad.

Fruits are occasionally served with main courses, especially if the centerpiece is pork, rabbit, or dark-meat poultry. Pork chops with applesauce, ham with spiced apples, squab with grapes, rabbit with prunes, and duck with pears or oranges are all examples of meat and fruit complements.

Pickles, relishes, and chutneys—tangy counterpoints to a sandwich or main course—often have a fruit base. Cranberries, which are both tart and sweet, make a piquant relish for the holiday turkey. In northern Europe, lingonberries are eaten as a relish with venison and other meats. Mango chutney, Italian *mostarda* (mustard fruits),

Use apples, oranges, and bananas as a basic mix for a fruit salad and vary it throughout the year by adding seasonal fruits, here kiwifruit and strawberries.

and watermelon pickles are yet more examples of fruits served as condiments for savory dishes.

Fruit and cheese, another successful marriage, are appreciated more in Europe than in America. Fresh berries are delicious with a soft fresh cheese such as ricotta. Other time-honored partnerships are apples and Cheddar or pears and blue cheese. Soft-ripened cheeses such as Camembert and Brie make well-suited accompaniments to firm fruits such as apples and pears.

In the context of a meal, fruits most often appear at dessert. Served raw sliced and sugared berries with cream or a chilled fruit salad with brandy or kirsch—they are among the easiest desserts for the cook. Satisfying hot or cold compotes are quickly assembled by poaching firm-fleshed fresh and dried fruits—apples, pears, apricots, quince, prunes—in sugar syrup. Baked with bread, biscuits, or bread-crumb topping, fruits are made into puddings, cobblers, and crisps.

When dipped in batter and fried, firm fruits such as peaches and apples make succulent fritters; encased in pastry and baked, they have homey appeal as dumplings. Juicy bush berries are especially good as fillings for double-crust pies; kiwifruits, strawberries, and raspberries are best shown off in open-faced tarts.

Fruits can be puréed for use in mousses, dessert sauces, and cream pies, and in frozen desserts such as sorbets and ice creams.

From breakfast to dinner, from hors d'oeuvre to dessert, fruit is suitable for almost any role.

Selection With many fruits, fragrance is the best indication of quality and ripeness. Melons, peaches, pineapples, and pears are very aromatic when ripe. Good solid color—for example, in cherries, berries, figs, pineapples, papayas, and mangoes—also indicates ripeness.

Individual fruit entries give additional tips on seasonality and selection. The most important point to remember in selecting fruit is to follow the seasons. Locally picked, vine- or tree-ripened seasonal fruit has far more flavor than out-of-season, hothouse, or cold-storage fruit or fruit that was picked immature for long shipping. Enjoy berries and melons at the height of summer, crisp apples in the early fall, citrus fruits when they're full and juicy in winter, and rhubarb, strawberries, and cherries in late spring. Farmers' markets are often the best source for truly ripe, full-flavored fruit.

Storage Some fruits—pears, peaches, persimmons and figs, for example—are extremely fragile when fully ripe and are almost always shipped underripe. They should be allowed to ripen at room temperature, then refrigerated as soon as they are ripe. Most fruits, however, taste better when they are not cold from the refrigerator; remove them from the refrigerator a half-hour or so before serving. See individual fruit listings for specific storage tips.

Preparation Most fruits should be washed gently just before using. Peel and slice with a stainless steel knife to avoid discoloration. Fruits that oxidize rapidly—bananas, apples, pears, feijoas—should be sprinkled with citrus juice or acidulated water to slow browning.

■ FRUIT FONDUE

Put the chocolate sauce in a heavy ceramic pot set over a candle to keep it warm. Around it arrange bowls of fruit and cubes of pound cake for dipping. Consider these additional accompaniments: apricots, bananas, figs, melon, peaches, orange sections, seedless grapes, glacéed fruits, marshmallows, and popcorn.

    ½ cup whipping cream
    8 ounces semisweet chocolate, finely chopped
    1 teaspoon vanilla extract
    2 tablespoons rum (optional)
    1 Pound Cake (see page 88)
    2 apples
    2 pears
       Juice of 1 lemon
    1 pint strawberries

1. Place cream in fondue pot or 1-quart saucepan; slowly heat. As soon as cream begins to form bubbles around edge, turn off heat and whisk in chocolate. When chocolate is completely melted, stir in vanilla and rum (if used).

2. Cut pound cake, apples, and pears into 1-inch-square cubes. Drizzle lemon juice over apples and pears. Wash and dry strawberries. Use fondue forks or bamboo skewers to dip fruit and cake into chocolate sauce.

Makes 1½ cups sauce, 6 to 8 servings.

■ FRUIT FOOL

Crushed raspberries, peaches, apricots, blackberries, or blueberries work equally well for this old-fashioned English dessert, although crushed gooseberries are the traditional choice. The juice released from the berries stains the whipped cream a lovely color.

    2 pints strawberries
    2 cups confectioners' sugar
    2 cups whipping cream
       Classic Scotch Shortbread (see page 144),
       for accompaniment

1. Wash strawberries and remove stems; pat dry. In a large bowl mash berries with a potato masher or fork. Sift confectioners' sugar over berries and stir to combine well. Macerate 1 hour.

2. Whip cream to soft peaks. Stir strawberries to mix berries and juices, and gently fold whipped cream into them. Some white streaks of cream may remain. Serve in stemmed goblets accompanied by shortbread cookies.

Serves 8.

FRY, TO

To cook in hot fat. Frying is part of almost every cuisine and a component of many cooking methods. Its appeal is in the wonderful flavor and crisp, browned surface of food cooked this way. Frying is particularly versatile, and when properly executed, it produces foods that are light and not at all greasy.

Within the broad category of frying, there are several subcategories, defined mainly by the amount of fat used and how much the food is moved around in the pan. Sautéing and stir-frying are the same technique, differentiated by national origin, typical ingredients, and type of pan used. Both methods require food cut to cook quickly—either in small pieces or in thin, even fillets. Sautéing, which comes from the classic French tradition, tends to use creamy sauces and few vegetables, and is done in a sauté pan, essentially a frying pan. Stir-frying, a technique most common in Asian cooking, usually involves a number of vegetables, but omits dairy products, and employs a wok. Deep-frying calls for total immersion of food in fat. Technically, there is also a fourth category of frying, panfrying, which is halfway between sautéing and deep-frying. Panfried foods are first dipped in a flour or crumb coating, then are cooked in an inch or more of hot fat.

Frying is an active, fast-moving cooking method that demands concentration and quick responses. The cook must be alert to alterations both in the food, as it changes from raw to cooked, and in the hot fat. Even a slight hesitation can make the difference between brown or burned, tender or tough meat.

WHICH METHOD TO USE?

Choice of method is often determined by what's on hand to cook with and the amount of preparation time available. Sautéed dishes are perhaps the simplest to put together. For a basic sauté, all that is needed are tender fillets of meat, poultry, or fish, a liquid to make the sauce, and seasonings. You'll want to pound poultry or veal to a uniform thickness, but further preparation is unnecessary. Deep-frying—chicken, for example—also calls for a minimum of ingredients—perhaps just a coating—and time. Stir-frying, although equally quick and simple, entails the most preparation. All ingredients must be cut to proper size; sauce ingredients should be portioned out and ready; marinades must be mixed and applied well ahead of cooking. Each of these methods is simplified with some planning and a well-stocked pantry and refrigerator.

FATS, OILS, AND TEMPERATURE

The high heat of frying rapidly cooks tender cuts of meat, sears their surface, retains moisture, and promotes browning. For all of the frying methods, fats and oils are the media by which heat is transferred to food. With a boiling point higher than water, fats and oils cook hotter, and therefore faster, than other liquids. Because heated fats caramelize sugars in the food, they encourage the characteristic browned surface on fried foods. Fat also keeps food from sticking to the pan.

HOW TO CHOOSE AN OIL

When frying, it is most important to use a fat that will stay intact at high heat. Eventually, any fat or oil will become hot enough to decompose. The point at which this breakdown occurs is called the smoke point. At this stage, smoke and an acrid gas are given off, the liquid begins to darken, and an unpleasant taste is imparted to food. Oils with high smoke points include safflower oil, grapeseed oil, corn oil, and peanut oil. Lard and solid vegetable shortening are also sometimes used for frying. Sesame and olive oils, which have lower smoke points, are less suitable for frying, and work better as seasonings.

The smoke point of an oil is lowered each time the fat is reused. After it has been cooked three or four times, it must be discarded. Bits of food afloat in the oil accelerate this breakdown; it is important to continually skim off crumbs from the hot oil and strain used oil through cheesecloth before storing. Exposure to air also lowers the smoke point. For this reason, a narrow, deep pot is preferred over a shallow, wide pan when a great deal of fat is used, as in deep-frying.

Select an oil that is appropriate to the recipe. An oil with a mild or neutral taste does not mask the flavor of the food. A stronger oil, such as peanut oil, imparts its own flavor and is used where additional taste would be desirable, such as in stir-frying.

FRYING TEMPERATURE

Not only is it critical that you choose a fat that stands up to high temperature, but you also need to maintain this high heat throughout the cooking process. Fluctuating temperature results in food that is either overdone on the outside and raw in the middle, or bland and greasy. An electric skillet or fryer with a built-in thermostat monitors temperature changes and corrects them automatically. With any other frying method, however, the cook needs to evaluate the cooking process and adjust the heat or the food as necessary. A deep-fat thermometer helps by indicating temperature variations. Experienced cooks often depend on their senses—sight, smell, and hearing—in addition to a thermometer, to judge when a fat is hot enough to use.

For deep-frying, drop a cube of bread into the hot oil and slowly count to 60. If the bread browns nicely, the oil is ready. If the bread burns, the oil is too hot. If the bread stays pale and becomes saturated with fat, the oil is not hot enough.

For sautéing with butter or a combination of butter and oil, watch for the butter to foam. Unclarified butter is quick to burn, so it must be watched carefully. With butter you can also be alert to the point of fragrance—the moment at which its characteristic aroma becomes apparent.

For all methods, the familiar sizzle when food meets hot fat is yet another indicator that proper frying temperature has been reached.

FRYING TECHNIQUE

Meat and other ingredients should generally be at room temperature at the time of cooking. Cold food immediately lowers the temperature of the fat below an optimum level. If food must be fried before it has warmed to approximately 70° F, cook only a few pieces at a time.

The surface of what is to be fried should be as dry as possible. Pat pieces of meat, poultry, and fish with a paper towel or, when appropriate, coat with flour, bread crumbs, or batter. Any surface moisture instantly converts to steam as it meets hot fat, causing fat to bubble up and possibly overflow sides of pan, and brings about an immediate drop in temperature as well. Overcrowding the pan also produces excess moisture and will steam, not brown, the food being cooked. Between batches, always allow oil to return to proper temperature.

Lightly cooked seasonal vegetables and green salads make good partners for fried fish, poultry, and meat. Deep-fried and sautéed foods are rarely served with elaborate garnishes. In this way, they keep their pure and simple character.

> ### Recipes and Related Information
> Deep-fry, 174; Fat, 216; Oil, 394; Panfry, 404; Sauté, 531;
> Stir-fry, 557.

FUNNEL

Narrow-necked funnels are a convenient way to channel liquids, particularly cooking oils, into bottles or other receptacles with a similar shape, to consolidate liquids from several sources, and to transfer finely milled grains and flours from their packages to your own storage containers. Some have screen inserts that trap bits of burned food or other undesirable matter as the liquid pours through; those for canning have very wide necks that permit easy filling of canning jars. Choose a funnel made of stainless steel, for its durability and because it won't interact with acidic foods or corrode. Canning funnels are usually plastic. Size is measured in inches across the top; depending upon how it will be used, a 4- or 6-inch funnel is most versatile.

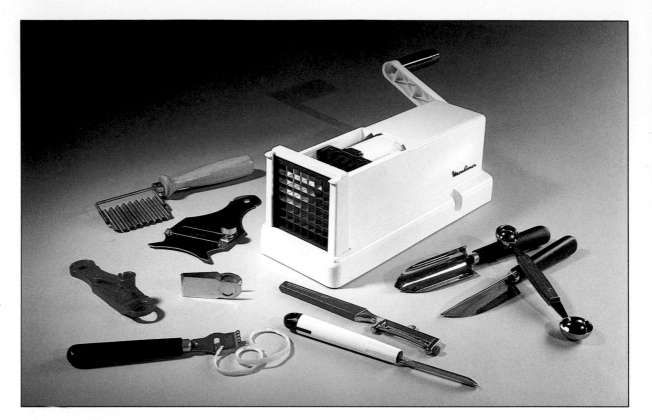

Those small kitchen tools known as gadgets can be useful if they are well made, if there is room to store them, and if the cook remembers to use them. Counterclockwise from top right are: French-fry maker, melon cutters, peelers, citrus zester and stripper, bean slicer, strawberry huller, truffle slicer, crinkle-chip cutter.

GADGETS: CUTTER, PEELER, AND ZESTER

Although dismissed by overly serious chefs as novelties or even space wasters, kitchen gadgets have a purpose and will earn their keep if they are well made and therefore perform their job well. What are gadgets? They encompass all those small devices that hang from racks or fill counter bins in housewares departments. They range from the familiar, such as citrus zesters and vegetable peelers, to the unidentifiable. Many are garnishing tools— the cutters that flute, hollow, and scallop all sorts of fruits and vegetables.

As is true of all cutting tools, unless the edges are sharp they won't work. Why mention the obvious? Unfortunately, some implements on the market are dull and therefore useless. So before you buy a tool, ask the salesperson for assurance that it will work.

ASPIC-TRUFFLE CUTTER

Usually sold in sets of 12 patterns, these tinned steel cutters are so tiny that a set will nestle in a box no bigger than 2 inches in length. These miniatures are used to punch out decorative garnishes from aspic, truffles, pastry, pimientos, olives, candied fruits, and cooked egg white. The many whimsical patterns include paisleys, circles, squares, triangles, clovers, hearts, spades, clubs, crescents, and alphabet letters. Dry the cutters immediately after washing or they will rust.

BEAN SLICER

Green beans look more delicate when cut lengthwise into thin pieces. This cutter is a combination guillotine and slicer. One blade chops off the stem and blossom ends; the other creates the narrow strips. The tool is made of molded plastic with stainless steel blades.

CITRUS STRIPPER

This tool cuts a ¼-inch-wide strip of rind from a lemon or orange. Use the resulting spirals to flavor a drink or preserve them in sugar syrup for decoration. To avoid pulling away the bitter white pith with the peel, set the cutting edge against the skin and pull it around the fruit without digging too deeply. Make short strips by cutting from stem to blossom end; cut longer ones by working around the midsection of the fruit. The tool also flutes mushrooms and cuts decorative channels in cucumbers, carrots, and other vegetables; when sliced they will have scalloped edges. Measuring about 6 inches long, the stripper has a molded plastic handle and a stamped, stainless steel blade.

CITRUS ZESTER

Five little holes at the blade end of this tool cut threads of colored rind when drawn across the skin of citrus fruit. Use the long threads as is or chop fine with a chef's knife or electric minichopper. Cooks who use this method for mincing rind love it. The alternative is rubbing the fruit against a metal grater, which always takes away some knuckle and bitter citrus pith with the rind, and is difficult to clean. Lemons and oranges with the rind removed should be saved for juicing; store them in a plastic bag in the refrigerator to prevent them from drying out. Measuring about 6 inches, the citrus zester has a molded plastic or wood handle and a stamped, stainless steel blade. If storage is tight, consider a combination zester-stripper (see photograph, opposite page).

CRINKLE-CHIP CUTTER

The wavy-edged blade of this cutter slices ruffled rounds and sticks of vegetables and cheeses. It is typically used on potatoes, carrots, squash, jicama, beets, and cucumbers. The blade is stainless steel, the handle molded plastic.

FRENCH-FRY MAKER

This device cuts a potato into the familiar, even sticks used to make French fries. A chef's knife can do this chore, but it will take longer and the results won't be as uniform. Of the two basic designs, the simplest has a sharp, stainless steel grid set in a cast aluminum frame. To use, the grid is placed on an upright end of a peeled potato and then pushed through to the bottom. The other type is larger and more mechanized. A slot in the plastic housing of the cutter holds the potato in place; a push of a lever sends the potato through the metal grid. The French-fry maker also cuts carrots and other root vegetables, and can be useful when preparing ingredients of equal size to be stir-fried.

MELON BALLER

This tool forms fruits and vegetables into little balls for fruit plates or salads. It also hollows cherry tomatoes and mushrooms for stuffing. The handle is plastic or wood and the bowl is stainless steel in graduated sizes. One- and two-scoop models are sold; round bowls are most typical, but oval and fluted ones are also available.

MELON V OR U CUTTER

This garnishing tool has a V- or U-shaped, stainless steel blade that cuts a zigzag (the V) or scalloped (the U) edge. Handles are wood or molded plastic. If garnishing is important to you, these cutters give an extra, decorative touch to foods used as containers, such as watermelon baskets and melon, lemon, and orange shells. The technique is simple and the effect attractive, although this tool is certainly not a high-priority item. To make shells, insert the tool so that successive cuts touch and are continuous around the circumference of the fruit. When the last cut reaches the first, the fruit will open. To make baskets with a handle, don't cut all the way around the fruit; instead, cut almost to the center, then up and down the other side and back around. Repeat on the opposite end to finish the handle and shape the basket.

PEELER

No matter what type of cooking you do, you always have to peel an apple, pear, potato, carrot, cucumber, eggplant, asparagus, or any of numerous other fruits and vegetables. Peelers have swivel or fixed blades; buy what feels comfortable in your hand and what works best. Choose a quality peeler. The better tools will stay sharper longer; some even have replaceable blades, or blades that reverse to accommodate both right- and left-handed cooks.

Specialty peelers, designed for particular vegetables and fruits, such as asparagus, avocado, and citrus, are also available.

STRAWBERRY HULLER

Why this small device that resembles squatty, wide tweezers works as well as it does is a mystery, but it neatly plucks the stem and leaves from a strawberry in a single motion without mashing the fruit. Also use it to pick tiny bones from fish.

TRUFFLE SLICER

This relatively simple and straightforward device is made of a sheet of stainless steel and has a shape that resembles a musical instrument you can't quite identify: long neck, pinched waist, and little legs. An adjustable blade projects from the upper surface. To use, the slicer is held at a 45-degree angle, supported by the legs, and the truffle is rubbed across the blade. It can also be employed to shave chocolate.

Recipes and Related Information
Basic Aspic, 265; French-fried Potatoes, 468; Garnish, 263; Truffle, 582.

GAME

Animals hunted for food or sport fall under the category of game. To the cook this includes both animals freshly killed by the hunter and those that are farm raised for the market. Small game animals include rabbit and hare, beaver, muskrat, raccoon, and opossum. Among the large game animals are venison (which usually refers to deer, but also includes other antlered animals such as caribou, moose, elk, and antelope), bison (American buffalo), wild boar, and bear. Duck, pheasant, and quail are some of the better-known game birds (see POULTRY). By strict definition, game also includes fish (see FISH).

Use Game furnishes some of the tastiest and most wholesome of all meat—it is rich in flavor, high in protein and minerals, and low in fat. Germans enjoy rabbit in *Hasenpfeffer*, a richly flavored stew that takes its name from the German words *Hasen*, which means hare, and *Pfeffer*, meaning pepper. Jugged hare is a Scottish rabbit

Although gumbos are most often associated with the Gulf Coast of Louisiana, these okra-thickened soups can be found throughout the Deep South. The version pictured here, featuring rabbit and oysters, is from the Georgia Sea Islands.

has been handled properly. Avoid those that are torn or that contain frozen liquid; a tear will expose the meat and allow it to dry out, while the latter could mean that the meat was thawed and refrozen, resulting in a considerable loss of quality. If you are fortunate enough to find fresh game, use the same criteria to judge the quality as you would for other meats and fowl—look for resilient flesh; avoid a slimy surface and an off odor.

Storage   Keep frozen game under proper conditions: in a freezer compartment able to maintain the recommended temperature of 0° F. Store fresh game in the coolest section of your refrigerator and use promptly.

Preparation   Thaw frozen game as you would other meat, then follow the recipe for specific preparation.

Cooking   Of all small game, rabbit is the easiest to find in the marketplace, and preparation methods for rabbit apply to most other small game as well; nearly any recipe for chicken, pheasant, or partridge can be adapted to rabbit, hare, or squirrel. The parts of large game, such as boar, buffalo, and venison, are similar to those of other meat animals (see BEEF, LAMB, PORK), so be guided accordingly in choosing a cooking method. Bison destined for market will have been raised similarly to beef cattle and will be as tender as fine grain-fed lean beef. Wild boar, a close relative of the domestic hog, generally tastes like the finest pork; recipes for pork are equally suitable for boar. Venison, the meat of deer and antelope, has a flavor that is faintly reminiscent of the finest, best-aged, most greaseless lamb.

■ GEORGIA RABBIT AND OYSTER GUMBO

The word *gumbo* comes from West Africa, where it means both okra and soups thickened with okra. African slaves brought the dish to America. This recipe is fairly peppery, so if hot food isn't your passion, you may want to reduce (or eliminate) the cayenne.

- 1 rabbit, cut into 6 or 8 pieces
     (see Cutting Up a Rabbit, opposite page)
- 2 quarts Chicken Stock (see page 560) or
     Fish Stock (see page 561)
- ¼ cup oil (preferably peanut, corn, or sunflower)
- ½ cup flour
- ½ pound okra, ends trimmed, sliced
     into ½-inch rounds
- 1 large green bell pepper, chopped
- 1 large onion, chopped
- 1 stalk celery, chopped
- ½ teaspoon cayenne pepper
- ¼ teaspoon dried thyme
- ¼ teaspoon salt, or to taste
- ¼ teaspoon freshly ground black pepper,
     or to taste
- 1 jar (1 pt) East Coast oysters, drained
- 2 to 3 cups cooked rice
     Tabasco sauce (optional)

stew, which sometimes uses rabbit blood as a thickener. Roast saddle of venison is a classic preparation. Ground venison, when mixed with a little beef fat for moistness, makes superbly flavored patties. Buffalo steaks are delicious when grilled, particularly over a smoky fire.

Availability   Both wildlife protection and food-safety laws restrict the commercial sale of meat from the wild animals of America. The only North American game animals that can be found readily in markets are those that have been farm raised. These include rabbit, bison, some deer, and the occasional raccoon or opossum, along with numerous types of game birds. However, farm-raised American game, along with game meats from other countries (especially the wide variety of ranch-raised game of New Zealand), are becoming increasingly available.

Some of the better-stocked, upscale supermarkets are beginning to carry buffalo, venison, and boar, along with rabbit and game birds, in frozen food cases. Rabbit can be found in many butcher shops, which can also provide game by special order. The alternative to buying game is hunting it, or sharing a hunter's bounty. However, this entry addresses game that is the most widely available commercially; consult a cookbook on game for information on the special requirements of handling and preparing freshly killed game.

Selection   The game you buy will most often be frozen; as with all frozen meats, check for signs that the package

1. Trim and discard all visible fat from rabbit (see Cutting Up a Rabbit, right). Put rabbit and stock in a large pot and bring to a boil. Lower heat to medium, partially cover, and simmer for 1 hour, skimming occasionally. Remove rabbit pieces with a slotted spoon and let cool. Leave stock over low heat, covered, to keep hot. When pieces are cool enough to handle, bone and reserve meat.

2. In a large, heavy skillet, heat oil over medium-high burner until oil is quite hot. Make a roux by stirring in flour a bit at a time, whisking vigorously to break up any lumps. Cook until roux turns peanut butter brown (about 10 minutes), stirring constantly and whisking whenever necessary to break up any lumps. Do not stop stirring or roux will burn.

3. When roux is the right color, add okra, green pepper, onion, and celery, stirring in vegetables carefully, in small batches, so their moisture does not make the roux burn. Lower heat to medium and cook until vegetables are tender (about 13 minutes), stirring frequently.

4. Add contents of skillet to stockpot and raise heat to high. Add cayenne, thyme, salt, pepper, and reserved rabbit meat. Bring to a boil, lower heat, and simmer 5 minutes, skimming occasionally. Add oysters, remove from heat, cover, and let stand 10 minutes.

5. Serve in large soup bowls over rice. Tabasco may be added at the table to raise the "heat" if desired.

Serves 4 to 5.

■ WILD BOAR MEDALLIONS OR CHOPS WITH TANGY BERRY SAUCE

Swift and simple but luxurious, the sauce for the boar will also go with venison medallions.

    1 **pound ½-inch-thick medallions cut from loin of boar** *or* **4 thick boar chops (approximately 6 oz each)**
       Salt and freshly ground pepper
    2 **tablespoons vegetable oil**

Tangy Berry Sauce

    ¼ **cup shallots**
    ¼ **cup balsamic vinegar**
    ¼ **cup dry red wine**
    ¼ **cup port**
    2 **tablespoons honey**
       Pinch cayenne
    ¼ **cup lingonberries or cranberries (fresh or frozen without juice)**
    2 **tablespoons unsalted butter, cut in small pieces**

1. Trim fat and silvery membrane from meat. Rub meat with salt and pepper and allow to stand at room temperature to develop flavor while sauce is prepared. If using boar chops, preheat oven to 300° F.

2. In a heavy skillet heat oil. Add meat and rapidly sauté on both sides until well browned. If using chops, transfer to a 300° F oven for 20 minutes to complete cooking. Place meat on a serving dish and nap with sauce.

Serves 4.

Tangy Berry Sauce In a small nonreactive saucepan, place shallots, vinegar, wine, port, honey, and cayenne. Stir well, adding berries. Bring to a simmer and cook over moderately low heat until liquid is very thick (about 20 minutes), stirring occasionally. Swirl in butter.

Makes about 1 cup sauce.

GARLIC

An odoriferous member of the lily family, garlic (*Allium sativum*) is a single bulb that consists of several small cloves, each wrapped in a papery skin and all held together by a papery outer skin. The long, gray-green leaves of the plant are usually cut off before the garlic is sent to market.

Use The pungent aroma and flavor of garlic make it valuable as a seasoning for savory dishes. It is generally peeled and minced to release its aromatic oils. Raw minced garlic is very strong, but cooking moderates its flavor. Long, slow cooking renders garlic very mild; even whole cloves soften and develop an almost sweet flavor.

Garlic is widely used in almost all the regions of the world, with the exception of Japan, England, and Scandinavia. Its indescribable flavor enhances numerous foods and dishes, including soup, salads, breads, sauces, meats, fish, vegetables, and eggs.

Availability California grows about 90 percent of the domestic crop. The predominant variety, harvested in midsummer, has ivory cloves sheathed in an off-white skin. A milder variety is harvested about a month earlier. Elephant garlic, which is not actually a garlic but a different species of allium, has especially large cloves and mild flavor. Mexican red garlic, harvested in January, has very small cloves and papery reddish skin. Mexican white garlic is generally harvested and shipped in March.

Thanks to this staggered harvest, fresh garlic is available the year around. Also in the market are granulated garlic, instant minced garlic, instant garlic powder, garlic salt, and minced garlic in oil. The first three products are pure garlic; the fourth is garlic powder combined with table salt; the fifth is pure garlic in oil.

Selection Choose fresh garlic that looks plump and feels firm. Avoid heads that are withered or have obviously bruised or darkened cloves.

Store Keep fresh garlic in a cool, dry, dark place with some air circulation. Try to leave heads whole because individual cloves dry out rapidly. Keep dried garlic products airtight in a cool, dry, dark place; they strengthen with age; replace every six months. Store minced garlic in oil airtight in the refrigerator for up to three months.

TIPS
CUTTING UP A RABBIT

Cut a cleaned, skinned rabbit along center of breast from neck to tail end to expose central cavity. With a small, sharp knife, detach and remove all organs from the cavity. (Liver and heart may be reserved for some other use, such as meat loaf or pâté.) Trim away and discard all tallowy fat in cavity, at leg joints, and along backbone. Thin white membrane over flesh may be left in place.

Rabbit can be cut into serving pieces much like chicken. Use both hands to dislocate front and hind leg joints by snapping them sharply away from body. Carefully sever from body with a knife or poultry shears. Repeat with other front leg, then with both hind legs. If desired, separate hind legs from thighs.

With torso of rabbit held between both hands, cavity facing you, break backbone between upper and lower back by snapping backward; finish by cutting along crack in bone. If desired, cut each torso piece in half by inserting knife along one side of backbone. If you wish, remove "armature" of annoying small bones by grabbing breast piece with both hands and snapping armature away from breastbone. Use sharp yanks with fingers or needle-nose pliers to remove small bones from flesh; most of meat remaining on breastbone will be boneless.

Preparation A few recipes call for whole unpeeled garlic cloves. To prepare them, simply separate individual cloves from the head and remove outer covering but leave the fine inner sheath.

Most recipes, however, call for peeled garlic. Mashing the clove lightly with the flat side of a knife helps loosen the skin. Peel, then cut away any bruised parts. If clove shows evidence of sprouting, cut it in half and remove the sprouting core.

Although many cooks prefer to use a garlic press for mincing garlic, others argue that the press breaks down the cell walls too severely, yielding a sharper, stronger flavor than garlic minced with a knife (see KNIFE, Cutting Techniques).

■ BAKED GARLIC

As it bakes in the oven, the garlic becomes sweet and has the texture of butter. It is delicious spread on crusty French bread along with cream cheese or turned into a garlic sauce for beef or lamb. Leftovers need never be discarded; whisk the garlic into soups or sauces for a wonderful flavor boost.

      6 whole heads garlic
      3 tablespoons olive oil
      1 tablespoon unsalted butter
      2 tablespoons water

1. Preheat oven to 325° F. Slice top from heads of garlic and trim roots even with base of bulbs. Remove some of the papery skin from outside of heads but do not separate cloves. Place heads in a 6-inch gratin dish, and drizzle each head with ½ tablespoon olive oil. Dot heads with butter and drizzle water over them.

2. Cover dish with aluminum foil and bake 1 hour and 15 minutes. Remove foil and bake 15 minutes more. Cool briefly before serving.

Serves 12 as a first course, 24 as an hors d'oeuvre.

■ GARLIC-HERB BREAD

This flavorful bread makes a superb accompaniment for a light salad or a hearty pasta dinner.

      1 small loaf (8 oz) French bread
      ¼ cup butter, softened
      1 medium clove garlic, minced
      1 to 1½ teaspoons finely chopped fresh oregano
         or ½ teaspoon dried oregano
      2 to 3 teaspoons freshly grated Parmesan cheese

1. Cut bread into 1½-inch-thick slices, or split in half lengthwise.

2. Blend together butter, garlic, and oregano. Spread on bread. Sprinkle with cheese.

3. Broil until top is light brown and bubbly (2 to 3 minutes).

Makes about 12 slices, or 1 split loaf (4 to 6 servings).

■ AIOLI

This classic French Provençal sauce—actually a garlic mayonnaise—can be the focus of a light meal if accompanied by cooked baby vegetables, particularly little potatoes and green beans, and a crusty baguette. Aioli is a wonderful sauce for grilled fish as well and is traditionally served with *bourride*, a French fish soup.

      3 to 6 cloves garlic
      1 cup Mayonnaise (see page 519)

Pound garlic using mortar and pestle. Add to Mayonnaise and blend well.

Makes 1 cup.

■ CHICKEN WITH FORTY CLOVES OF GARLIC

The garlic sweetens and softens as it roasts with the chicken. For a wonderful sauce, purée the cooked cloves and combine with the poultry juices. Note that the chicken must marinate for 30 minutes before roasting.

       1 lemon
       1 roasting chicken (2½ to 3 lb)
       1 teaspoon salt
       ½ teaspoon freshly ground pepper
      40 cloves garlic (about 3 heads)
       4 tablespoons unsalted butter
       2 tablespoons olive oil
       1 cup Chicken Stock (see page 560)
       1 small bunch parsley, minced, for garnish

1. Preheat oven to 375° F. Cut lemon in half and squeeze juice over chicken. Sprinkle salt and pepper over chicken and rub in. Marinate 30 minutes.

2. Remove papery husk from garlic heads. Separate cloves from heads but do not peel. In a 4- to 5-quart Dutch oven or heatproof casserole, brown chicken (breast side down) in butter and oil over medium heat (about 5 minutes). Add garlic cloves and stock to pan. Stir to coat with oil. Cover and roast 60 to 70 minutes.

3. Remove chicken to serving platter. Discard some of fat on surface of pan juices. Purée garlic cloves and remaining pan juices through a food mill or sieve (skin will be trapped by the food mill or sieve). Pour this sauce over chicken and sprinkle with parsley.

Serves 6.

Recipes and Related Information
Baked Garlic Grits, 272; Beef Soup au Pistou, 26; Braised Chinese Cabbage and Garlic, 73; Broccoli Sautéed With Garlic, 60; Garlic Butter, 68; Garlic Croutons, 506; Garlic Press, 282; Garlicky Pommes Anna, 466; Grater, 281; Hummus, 418; Leg of Lamb With Garlic, Potatoes, and Onions, 337; North Beach Garlicky Meat Loaf, 43; Pesto, 27.

GARNISH, TO

To decorate or embellish food with an edible condiment, which is called a garnish. The way food is presented—its arrangement, color, texture—affects how it tastes. If served with style, even the simplest food seems more flavorful. Good restaurants and good cooks know that a garnish should be harmonious with the food it accompanies and should never interfere with the taste of the food itself. A garnish accompanying a dish should always be edible and inviting. For a while, elaborate presentations of food and garnishes laid out in intricate patterns were in vogue. When done with skill, these are extremely beautiful, but they can be so artfully composed that many people

Citrus twist *Slice orange, lemon, or lime ¼ inch thick. Halve each slice. Slice flesh at center from rind to cut edge. Twist. Or, use a citrus stripper to cut a long ribbon of peel. Tie peel to form a knot with an equal amount of tail at either end.*

Fan *Green onions, radishes, and strawberries are all suitable for fans. For green onions: Trim off roots; trim away green tops, or leave some green for added color; make fine parallel slits, at least 1½ inches long, just at root end or at both ends. For radishes and strawberries: Keep leaves or stems; slice off root end of radish; with paring knife, make parallel slits to stem end. Fan out slices (fan strawberries gently since slices pull away easily). If desired, let radishes and green onions sit in cold water for several hours to open.*

Fluted mushroom *Use a citrus stripper or paring knife. Trim off mushroom stem. With a stripper: Start at top center; cut parallel, evenly spaced vertical grooves into mushroom cap. With a knife: Set blade at slight angle to cap and cut in from top center of cap to bottom. Finish V cut by cutting into cap at slight angle in other direction close to first cut. Remove strip. Continue around cap. The grooves can be cut on the diagonal for a spiral effect*

Radish rose *Trim away enough at root end so that radish sits flat. Slice off a small amount of stem end. With a paring knife make five overlapping shallow slices of equal width around radish (cut almost to bottom surface); these create "petals." Let radishes sit in cold water for several hours; they will swell and petals will open.*

Scored slice *Scoring makes an attractive fluted pattern on slices of firm vegetables—such as carrot, peeled or unpeeled cucumber, jicama—or fruits such as those in the citrus family. Use a citrus stripper to make wide grooves and a fork to make narrow ones. Score vegetable or fruit from top to bottom, then cut crosswise into slices of desired width.*

Tomato rose *Use firm tomatoes. With a sharp paring knife, first form a base for rose by cutting into skin across blossom end; then, without lifting knife, continue in a spiral around tomato, peeling skin away from flesh in one continuous strip of desired width. Roll up strip, peel side out, to form a flower; for stability, roll strip so that it rests on flat piece of skin from blossom end.*

hesitate to eat them. Today's trend seems to be toward a more approachable and less ornate style that emphasizes the natural appeal of the food.

Garnishes can be simple, such as the ubiquitous sprig of parsley, or extremely complicated. Japanese chefs who practice the art of *mukimono*—vegetable carving—are masters at creating fanciful, decorative shapes and spend years learning this traditional technique. Attractive garnishes need not take years of practice to master. A few basic ones serve to whet the appetite and provide color and texture.

Recipes and Related Information
Gadgets, 258; Knife, 328.

GELATIN

A natural protein, gelatin is found in the bones (especially young bones), skin, and connective tissues of animals. When heated in water, the protein is transformed into a gummy solution capable of thickening or setting a liquid. The presence of gelatin explains why a veal stock made with a high proportion of veal bones stiffens as it cools.

Culinary gelatin is derived from pig skin. It has little flavor in itself and is valued primarily for its ability to turn a liquid into a solid when chilled.

Use   Gelatin gives sturdy shape to sweet and savory mousses, molds, and puddings, to aspics and decorative coatings such as *sauce chaud-froid*, and to marshmallows and other jellied candies. One tablespoon powdered gelatin or four sheets leaf gelatin will set about 2 cups liquid.

Note   Because uncooked figs, papayas, and pineapples contain an enzyme that breaks down proteins, gelatin mixtures made with these uncooked fruits will not jell. The enzyme is destroyed by cooking, however; the cooked fruits will not inhibit jelling.

Availability   Most gelatin sold for home use in this country is powdered and packaged in paper packets, each containing 1 tablespoon (¼ ounce) gelatin. In addition to unflavored gelatin, most supermarkets offer a wide variety of fruit-flavored gelatins used primarily for molded gelatin dishes. Leaf gelatin, formed in thin clear sheets, is available from some specialty stores and bakery suppliers. Although it is less convenient than powdered gelatin (it must soak longer before use), it has a purer flavor than most powdered gelatin.

Storage   Keep unopened packets of powdered gelatin or leaf gelatin, wrapped airtight, in a cool, dry place. They will last indefinitely.

Preparation   Before adding to hot liquids, sprinkle 1 tablespoon powdered gelatin over ¼ cup cold water and allow to soften for about 3 minutes without stirring. To set cold liquids, soften powdered gelatin over cold water, then cook in a double boiler over (not in) hot water or in a heavy-bottomed saucepan over low heat until completely dissolved. Add to cold liquid.

Soften leaf gelatin by soaking in cold water to cover for 10 to 30 minutes (length of time depends upon brand). Then transfer softened sheets to a saucepan with a little water and cook over low heat, stirring, until gelatin dissolves. Leaf gelatin may be substituted for powdered gelatin, although its setting ability varies. In general, 1 package powdered gelatin has the setting ability of 4 sheets of leaf gelatin.

Jelled mixtures should be kept cold to hold their shape. Foods to be glazed with gelatin mixtures should be cold when the coating is applied.

Gelatin loses its setting ability when boiled. After adding gelatin to a liquid, do not allow to boil.

To unmold a gelatin-based dish, dip the mold quickly into a pan of very hot water—for no more than 5 seconds. If you see a slight movement of the food within the mold or a little melting at the edges as you try to slide the food from side to side, you know it is ready to be removed. Longer immersion in hot water will melt some of the gelatin, destroying detail and shape. Place a serving plate over mold, invert it rapidly, and give the mold a firm shake or tap. The dish should drop smoothly onto the plate. Sometimes it may be necessary to slip a thin-bladed knife between food and mold to release the vacuum that holds the gelatin in place. Then, if it fails to come right out, leave the mold inverted on the plate for a few minutes and let gravity take over. If possible, unmold at least 30 minutes in advance of serving so the dish can be returned to the refrigerator to firm up.

◼ BERRIES AND CHERRIES ROSE

Rosé wine is the piquant medium for this delicate summer salad with raspberries, strawberries, and sweet cherries.

    1 envelope unflavored gelatin
    2 tablespoons sugar
    ¾ cup boiling water
  1¼ cups rosé wine
    ½ cup *each* raspberries and halved strawberries
    1 cup pitted sweet cherries

Whipped Crème Fraîche

    ½ cup whipping cream
    1 tablespoon buttermilk or sour cream
    1 teaspoon sugar
       Dash freshly grated nutmeg

1. In a medium bowl mix gelatin and sugar. Add the boiling water and stir until gelatin dissolves completely; then stir in wine.

2. Refrigerate, stirring occasionally, until mixture begins to thicken and becomes syrupy. Fold in berries and cherries.

3. Pour into a 4-cup mold or six ¾-cup molds; refrigerate until firm (3 to 4 hours).

4. Unmold onto one or more serving plates. Serve with Whipped Crème Fraîche.

Serves 6.

Whipped Crème Fraîche Heat cream until barely warm to the touch (90° to 100° F). Stir in buttermilk. Let stand at room temperature (68° to 75° F) until cream begins to thicken (12 to 16 hours). Refrigerate at least 1 day before using. Add sugar and nutmeg to cream; beat until stiff.

Makes about ¾ cup.

■ GAZPACHO PATE

For a light and savory hors d'oeuvre to complement a summer meal, make this vegetable-filled, do-ahead pâté.

> 2 **envelopes unflavored gelatin**
> ¼ **cup white wine or water**
> 2½ **cups tomato juice**
> 1 **cucumber**
> 1 **green bell pepper**
> ½ **medium onion**
> 1 **ripe avocado**
> ¼ **cup parsley, minced**
> 1 **tablespoon fresh basil, minced,** *or*
>   **½ teaspoon dried basil**
> 1 **tablespoon fresh oregano, minced,** *or*
>   **½ teaspoon dried oregano**
> 1 **teaspoon cumin seed, toasted**
> 1½ **tablespoons olive oil**
> 1 **tablespoon red wine vinegar**
> 1 **tablespoon tomato paste**
> 1 **teaspoon kosher salt**
> ½ **teaspoon hot-pepper sauce, or to taste**
> 6 to 8 **romaine lettuce leaves**

1. In a 2-cup, stainless steel bowl, sprinkle gelatin over wine. Stir to combine and place bowl in a shallow pan of water. Add ½ cup of tomato juice to gelatin mixture. Place pan over low heat and stir mixture to dissolve gelatin. When mixture is clear, it is dissolved. Cool.

2. Dice cucumber, bell pepper, and onion into ¼-inch cubes. Peel, pit, and dice avocado.

3. In a blender or food processor, combine mixture of gelatin, wine, and tomato juice with one half of the cucumber, one half of the bell pepper, the onion, parsley, basil, oregano, cumin, oil, vinegar, tomato paste, salt, and hot-pepper sauce. Purée until smooth.

4. Stir the remaining tomato juice into the puréed mixture. Add the reserved cucumber and bell pepper, and the avocado. Pour into a 1½-quart mold and chill 4 to 12 hours.

5. Serve as a spread for breads or crackers.

Serves 10 to 12.

■ BASIC ASPIC

Whether made with the natural gelatin of cooked meat and poultry bones or with an unflavored, powdered gelatin, aspic can add a glistening touch to elegant meals.

> 2 **cups clarified Chicken or**
>   **Beef Stock (see page 560)**
> 1½ **envelopes unflavored gelatin**
> 2 **tablespoons red wine, white wine, fortified**
>   **wine, or liquor (such as vodka or gin)**
> ½ **teaspoon salt**

In a small bowl place ½ cup stock; sprinkle with gelatin and stir. Place remaining stock in a saucepan and bring to a boil. Stir in gelatin-stock mixture and wine. Cool to room temperature (about 20 minutes). Use as directed in your recipe.

Makes 2 cups.

Aspic Coat Prepare Basic Aspic; apply in a layer to serving tray or pâté. If adding a decoration, reserve about ¾ cup aspic for a glaze.

Aspic-Coated "Blossoms" Cut rounds of tomato skin, carrot coins, petals of hard-cooked egg white, black-olive diamonds, and chive stems; arrange on aspic-coated tray or food (see Aspic Coat) to form flowers. Pour over reserved aspic to secure and glaze decoration; chill to set.

Aspic "Jewels" Chill Basic Aspic in a shallow 9- by 13-inch pan 2 hours. Unmold and cut into cubes or other shapes. Use as a border for a tray or aspic-coated food.

Summer berries and cherries suspended in rosé wine make up Berries and Cherries Rosé. This subtle, delicate salad can also be served as a light dessert.

■ OEUFS EN GELEE

The beauty of this light luncheon dish is in the clarity of the stock used to make the aspic. Garnish with tomato slices and black olives, and serve with a crusty bread.

 2 **cups clarified Chicken or Beef Stock (see page 560)**
 1½ **teaspoons unflavored gelatin**
 1 **teaspoon dried tarragon**
 ½ **teaspoon salt**
 6 **sprigs fresh tarragon, parsley, or watercress**
 6 **hard-cooked eggs, peeled**
 6 **lettuce leaves, for garnish**
 12 **thin tomato slices, for garnish**
 12 **black olives, for garnish**

1. In a small bowl place ½ cup stock. Sprinkle gelatin over stock and stir. Place remaining stock in a medium saucepan and bring to a boil. Stir in gelatin-stock mixture, tarragon, and salt. Set aside to cool to room temperature (about 20 minutes).

2. Lightly oil a 4-cup ring mold. Line with tarragon sprigs. Place eggs horizontally in mold. Slowly pour half the cooled gelatin-stock mixture into mold. Chill 30 minutes; slowly pour remaining gelatin-stock mixture over eggs. Chill at least 5 hours.

3. To unmold, loosen edges with a knife. Fill a large pan with warm water about 1 inch deep. Lower egg mold into water and let sit 3 to 5 minutes. Remove mold and cover with a serving platter. Invert platter and mold; jelled mixture should fall onto platter. Lift platter off.

4. To serve, slice between each egg and garnish with lettuce leaves, tomato slices, and black olives.

Serves 6.

Recipes and Related Information
Bavarian Cream, 170; Charlotte Russe, 170; Lemon Roulade Charlotte, 171; Mousse, 372.

GIBLETS

The edible innards, or giblets, of birds, particularly chicken and turkey, consist of the gizzard, the heart, the liver, and often the neck. They are usually packaged by the processor in small paper bags and tucked inside the bird. Giblets are used to make gravy or are cut up and mixed into a bread stuffing.

Giblets for gravy are first simmered in water or stock to cover for about 30 minutes, then are cut up and blended with the pan drippings and stock.

Recipes and Related Information
Poultry, 468; Roast Turkey With Giblet Gravy, 474.

GINGER

A perennial herb, ginger grows from thick underground stems called rhizomes, which are the parts of the plant used in cooking. It is marketed both fresh and as a dried ground powder. Resembling a thick knobby root, fresh ginger has thin, pale brown skin and moist, pale gold flesh. It has a pungent, slightly hot flavor and a lively, fresh aroma. Young ginger, occasionally available in Asian markets, is cream-colored with pink-tipped shoots. It has a very thin, pale yellow skin, pale flesh with few fibers, and a particularly delicate flavor prized by Chinese cooks. Young ginger can be substituted for more mature ginger in all recipes, although you may want to increase the amount. Powdered ginger, which serves as a spice, has a delightful hot-sweet flavor. Sun-dried and finely ground, ginger is appreciated as a spice in many countries where fresh ginger is not used. Its flavor is only vaguely reminiscent of the fresh rhizome. The two are not interchangeable.

Use Fresh ginger plays a prominent role in the cooking of India and most other Asian countries. Fundamental to Chinese cooking, it figures in everything from soups to sweets. Minced ginger is added to oil in a wok before stir-frying vegetables or meats. Long, fine strips of ginger are scattered on fish before steaming to subdue fishy taste. Slices of smashed ginger are used to flavor marinades and steaming mixtures. Japanese cooks add ginger to marinades, soups, and dipping sauces. Pickled ginger is always served as a condiment with sushi. Korean cooks use ginger in seasoning mixtures for grilled meats, salads, and kimchee. Fresh ginger is used throughout Southeast Asia in noodle dishes, curries, salads, stir-fries, and steamed foods. In India, ginger contributes sharp flavor to curries and chutneys.

Ginger or ginger extract also flavors a wide variety of beverages, from ginger ale and ginger beer to the traditional English wassail bowl.

Ground ginger adds fragrance and spice to cakes, cookies, puddings, and quick breads. Moroccan cooks use it to flavor chick-pea and lentil soups, to season the stews served atop couscous and the meats used in *tajine*s (earthenware-pot stews). Swedish cooks rub pork with ginger before roasting it. Ground ginger complements carrots, beets, winter squashes, and most fruits. Add the spice to baked apples or peaches or to crumb toppings for fruit crisps.

Availability Fresh ginger is sold in all Asian markets and in most supermarkets throughout the year. Young ginger is available in some Asian markets from early summer through fall. Ground ginger is stocked on all supermarket spice racks.

Pickled Ginger Japanese markets carry two types of pickled ginger. One kind, *hajikamishoga,* is also known as blushing or bashful ginger because it is pale pink. Made from the whole shoots of young ginger pickled in rice vinegar, it is served with grilled fish. The pink color is natural.

The second variety, *benishoga* or *gari*, is served in sushi bars as a condiment. It is made from whole fresh ginger preserved in salt and vinegar, then grated in thin, wide slivers. It may or may not be dyed a pinkish red, and is usually packed in plastic tubs or bags.

Preserved Ginger Ginger preserved in sugar is available in a variety of forms: ginger stems, crystallized ginger, and preserved red ginger. The stems are the immature knobs of young ginger. Many Asian markets carry ginger stems in syrup. This product is usually packaged in a glazed, lidded crock but is also available in a plastic container without the extra syrup. Stems can be eaten after dinner as a sweet, or minced and added to baked goods, fruit compotes, and ice cream.

Crystallized ginger—bits of ginger preserved in sugar syrup, then coated with granulated sugar—is found in the spice section of supermarkets. It is used in the same ways as ginger in syrup.

Many Chinese markets carry preserved red ginger— ginger candied in red syrup. Packaged in jars, it adds color and piquant flavor to fruit dishes and salads. Chinese markets often carry another variety of preserved ginger, seasoned with sugar, salt, and licorice rhizome. Chinese cooks use it with fish and *congee* (rice porridge).

Selection When choosing fresh ginger, look for extremely hard rhizomes that snap easily into pieces. Avoid dry, shriveled stems that feel light for their size. For ground ginger, remember that packaged seasonings lose quality after a while; try to buy from a store that restocks its spice section fairly often.

Storage Keep fresh ginger in refrigerator crisper in a plastic bag with a paper towel to absorb moisture (to prevent mold, change towel occasionally). It will last for two to three weeks. Store ground ginger in a cool, dry, dark place; replace every six months.

After opening, store Japanese pickled ginger in its brine in the refrigerator for up to six months. Properly stored, ginger stems, crystallized ginger, preserved red ginger, and preserved ginger with licorice will keep indefinitely. Refrigerate jars of ginger stems after opening. Store crystallized ginger in an airtight container in a cool, dry place. Refrigerate preserved red ginger and preserved ginger in licorice in their jars.

Preparation Peel fresh ginger with a sharp knife, vegetable peeler, or ginger grater. Young ginger does not require peeling. Slice, mince, or grate as desired. To release ginger juice from slices, smash gently with the flat side of a large knife or cleaver. To grate ginger, use a Japanese or Chinese ginger grater with a series of fine teeth that rake the flesh off the fibers. The finest side of a box-shaped grater also works, although it is harder to clean. A knife is best for chopping ginger. If ginger is

firm, it can be chopped in the food processor using the metal blade; otherwise, don't use the food processor. With soft ginger, there is the possibility that the machine will smash or tear it instead of cutting it into discrete bits.

■ GINGERBREAD

Few recipes have so many variations. Gingerbread ranges from mildly spicy to dark and pungent, from soft as cake to hard as crackers. This recipe produces gingerbread that is firm, cakelike, and not too sweet.

2½ **cups flour**
2 **teaspoons baking soda**
½ **teaspoon salt**
1 **tablespoon ground ginger**
½ **cup solid vegetable shortening**
¼ **cup firmly packed dark brown sugar**
2 **eggs**
1 **cup *each* molasses and boiling water**

1. Preheat oven to 375° F. Generously grease and lightly flour an 8-inch-square pan. In a medium bowl stir and toss together flour, baking soda, salt, and ginger.

2. In large bowl of an electric mixer, beat shortening and sugar together until well blended. Beat in eggs, then add molasses and blend well. Stir in the water. Immediately add flour mixture and stir until batter is smooth.

3. Spread batter evenly in prepared pan. Bake until a toothpick or skewer inserted in center comes out clean (35 to 40 minutes). Remove from oven and set on a rack to cool. Serve warm or cold.

Serves 6 to 8.

In colonial New England, hard-textured gingerbread was often carried on journeys as an energy-rich snack, and slices of gingerbread were sold by food peddlers on the street. The spicy cake is still a favorite today, whether served as a snack, dessert, or even as an accompaniment to the main course.

GLACE

The French word for ice is *glace;* it can mean ice cream, the icing on a cake, or a glaze made from stock that has been reduced to the point where it is thick and syrupy. *Glacé* means iced or frozen, and usually refers to candied fruits (fruits preserved in sugar syrup), possibly because the surface has a sheen resembling ice.

Recipes and Related Information
Candied Fruit, 93; Candy, 93; Glace de Viande, 560.

GLAZE, TO

To coat a surface with a thin layer of syrup, chocolate, icing, melted jelly or preserves, egg wash, or other substance, in order to give it a shiny finish.

Recipes and Related Information
Egg Wash, 211; Frosting, Icing, and Filling, 244.

GOOSEBERRY

A small, round, thin-skinned fruit, the gooseberry looks somewhat like a grape. Its striated skin can be smooth or fuzzy. When ripe, the berry is green, pink, yellow, or white. Underripe gooseberries, best for cooking, are green. The English are probably the biggest consumers of gooseberries, although the commercial market even in England is small. In the United States, gooseberry cultivation is discouraged. In some states it is outlawed because the gooseberry, like the currant, is a carrier of white pine blight. A noninjurious hybrid strain is now grown commercially on a small scale in Oregon, Washington, and Michigan, adding to imports from New Zealand.

Use   Gooseberries are eaten raw, with milk and sugar, or cooked in pies, tarts, jams, jellies, and sauces. To make a popular English dessert, a gooseberry fool, fold lightly whipped cream into a gooseberry purée made from cooked, sweetened, and sieved fruit.

Availability   Fresh domestic gooseberries are sold in some specialty markets from May through August; imported New Zealand berries are on the market October through December. Canned gooseberries can be found in specialty stores and some supermarkets.

Selection   Choose underripe berries for cooking, ripe berries for eating raw.

Storage   Keep at room temperature or in the refrigerator crisper for up to two days.

Preparation   Remove tops and tails with scissors.

GRAIN

Among the many members of the grass family, fewer than a dozen are important to the human diet. But those few are very important, providing 70 to 80 percent of the caloric intake in less developed countries. Bamboo and sugar cane aside, these valuable grasses are called cereal grains after Ceres, the Roman goddess of agriculture.

The grains themselves are the seed kernels of cereal plants. According to the botanical definition, a grain is a complete fruit, containing all the genetic equipment for reproduction. Underneath the outer layer (or bran) is the endosperm—often the only part of the grain we eat—and the embryo (or germ).

After harvesting, some grains undergo processing to make them easier to cook and to prolong their shelf life. Some grains—such as barley, oats, and rice—have a tough inedible husk that must be removed before milling. Other processing steps may include polishing to remove the bran and germ, steaming or precooking to soften the kernel, and cracking, rolling, or grinding to shorten the cooking time.

Because most of the fiber, B vitamins, and oil and 25 percent of the protein in a grain are located in the bran and germ, processing significantly reduces nutritive value. Whole grains are slower to cook and quicker to go rancid, but they are definitely more nutritious than polished grains because bran and germ are left intact.

Use   Throughout the world, grains are a major part of the daily diet. In many countries, in fact, it is the rare meal that does not include grains. Where meat is scarce or where vegetarianism is widespread, some form of grain is the major dish in a meal. In contrast, in the wealthier nations of Western Europe and in the United States, grains are usually given a supporting, although appreciated, role.

Grains appear at every meal and in a multitude of guises. At breakfast, grains turn up as cooked and dry cereals, in breads, biscuits, and buns, and in pancakes and waffles. From the hominy grits of the American South to the creamy rice porridge (*congee*) of China, grains are a soothing and sustaining way to start the day.

At the midday or evening meal, grains can be the main event or a side dish. In southern China, a meal usually centers around steamed rice, with other dishes added as the market and budget permit. In Japan, rice is the foundation for every sushi variation; wheat- or rice-based noodles, simply garnished, are a popular Japanese lunch; and a large bowl of steamed rice is usually part of every main meal.

In India, rice is the staple for two thirds of the population, with wheat (in the form of bread) the predominant staple in the northern part of the country. Rice in the south and breads in the north are used to soak up the rich gravies and creamy lentil preparations typical of Indian cooking. An Indian meal may include little, if any, meat, but it always features rice or bread. Millet, also a popular grain in India, is eaten as a breakfast cereal or pilaf and is ground into flour for breads.

In Mexico, corn plays a fundamental role. It is dried and ground for use in tortillas, the principal breadstuff. Rice, usually partnered with beans, is a staple throughout Latin America. It accompanies stews or is layered with other ingredients and baked.

Grains add body and texture to soups and stews. They act as an absorbent foundation for saucy dishes and as an inexpensive and nutritious filler in casseroles. They can be ground for flour and used in breads; baked in puddings, both sweet and savory; cooked, cooled, dressed with a vinaigrette, and served as a salad, often garnished with meats, seafood, or vegetables; and cooked, seasoned, and combined with other ingredients to make a stuffing for meats, fish, poultry, and vegetables.

Grains are further processed to yield flour for breads, noodles, and breadstuff; cornstarch for thickening; and corn syrup for sweetening. In the breadth of their culinary uses and their nutritive value in the diet, grains are doubtless the most important cultivated crops.

Availability Many health-food stores offer a large variety of whole grains, either packaged or in bulk. Supermarkets stock some of the more popular grains, such as rice, barley, and cornmeal.

Selection Grains containing the bran and germ are subject to relatively rapid rancidity. When purchasing grains in bulk, try to buy from a store with a rapid turnover. Make sure the retailer takes the trouble to store the grains properly—in a covered container in a cool, dry place, and with a scoop provided for handling grains.

Storage Whole kernels of grain (groats) still contain the oil-rich germ and are thus more susceptible to rancidity than polished kernels. Cracked groats become rancid even more quickly because the oily germ is exposed. Buy whole groats or cracked groats in small quantities; they will keep in the refrigerator in an airtight container for up to six months. Polished kernels (with bran and germ removed) have a longer shelf life; they may be stored in a cool, dry place in an airtight container for up to one year.

The following section discusses the major culinary grains, their processing, availability, and traditional uses.

BARLEY

The tough outer hull on barley must be removed if it is to be used for anything but animal feed. To remove the hull, barley is pearled or polished between abrasive disks, then sifted. Three pearlings yield pot barley, which still has some of its bran intact. Most barley, however, is pearled five or six times to yield pearl barley, which is missing its hull, its bran, and most of its germ. Pearl barley may be further ground into barley grits, coarse, medium, or fine.

COOKING A VARIETY OF GRAINS

Grains add different tastes and textures, as well as important nutrients, to the diet. Grains with similar cooking times may be combined, as in Wheat Berry–Rice Pilaf (see page 276). Following steps for Measured Water Method for Brown Rice (see About Cooking Rice, page 274), prepare grains to use in various recipes.

Type of Grain	Cooking Method
Barley	*Groats:* Cook 1 cup raw in 4 cups liquid for 45 minutes to yield 3½ cups cooked. *Grits:* Cook 1 cup raw in 2½ cups liquid for 35 minutes to equal 3 cups cooked.
Buckwheat	Toasted buckwheat is known as kasha. *Groats:* Cook 1 cup raw in 2 cups liquid for 15 minutes to yield 2½ to 3 cups cooked. *Grits:* Cook 1 cup raw in 2½ cups liquid for 12 minutes to yield 2½ to 3 cups cooked.
Bulgur	*For pilaf:* Cook 1 cup raw in 2 cups liquid for 15 to 20 minutes to yield 2½ to 3 cups cooked. *For porridge:* Cook 1 cup raw in 4 cups liquid, uncovered, for 20 minutes to yield 3 cups cooked.
Cornmeal	Cook 1 cup raw in 3 to 4 cups liquid—depending on consistency—for about 25 minutes to yield 4 cups cooked.
Millet	Cook 1 cup raw in 1½ cups liquid 15 minutes; let rest, covered, 10 minutes, then fluff with a fork to yield 2½ cups cooked.
Oats	*Rolled oats:* Cook 1 cup raw in 2 cups liquid for 5 to 8 minutes to yield 1¾ cups cooked. *Groats:* Cook 1 cup raw in 2 cups liquid for 1 hour to yield 2 cups cooked. *Grits:* Cook 1 cup raw in 3 cups liquid for 25 minutes to yield 2½ cups cooked.
Quinoa	Cook 1 cup raw in 2 cups liquid for 10 to 15 minutes to yield 4 cups cooked.
Rice	See About Cooking Rice (page 274).
Rye	*Berries:* Cook 1 cup raw in 2 cups liquid for 30 to 40 minutes to yield 2¾ cups cooked. *Cracked:* Cook 1 cup raw in 2 cups liquid for 30 to 40 minutes to yield 2¾ cups cooked. *For porridge:* Cook 1 cup raw rye flakes in 4 cups liquid 25 minutes to yield 3 cups cooked. *For pilaf:* Cook as for cracked rye 15 minutes.
Semolina	Cook 1 cup raw in 3½ cups liquid for 25 minutes to yield 2¾ cups cooked.
Triticale	Cook 1 cup raw in 2 cups liquid for 30 to 40 minutes to yield 2¾ cups cooked.
Wheat	*Berries:* Cook 1 cup raw in 2 cups liquid for 40 to 60 minutes to yield 2¾ cups cooked. *Cracked:* Cook 1 cup raw in 2 cups liquid for 30 to 40 minutes to equal 2⅔ cups cooked.

About half the barley grown in this country is used for animal feed. An additional 30 percent is sprouted and ground for malt, an ingredient in beer. Barley has several culinary uses, too. It is added to soups and stews, eaten as a breakfast porridge (barley grits are especially suitable for breakfast cereal), steamed and eaten as a savory side dish, and baked with mushrooms and stock as a pilaf. Barley flour has poor gluten-forming ability, but can be blended with wheat flour in bread.

Baked in corn-shaped molds to give them their characteristic shape, corn sticks make a delicious accompaniment to hearty soups and stews.

Pearl barley is widely sold in plastic bags and in bulk. Pot barley and barley grits are sold in some health-food stores. Barley flour is also occasionally available in health-food stores.

BUCKWHEAT

Technically, buckwheat is not a cereal grain, for it is not a member of the grass family. Because it is treated as a grain in the kitchen, however, it deserves discussion here. Buckwheat has a full, nutty flavor that is even more pronounced when the grain is toasted.

Buckwheat groats add nutty flavor and texture to pilafs and stuffings; they may be mixed with rice or other grains, or with noodles. Steamed buckwheat grits make a hearty breakfast cereal. Buckwheat flour adds sturdy flavor to pancakes, Russian blini (yeast-risen pancakes), dumplings, Brittany crêpes, and breads.

Buckwheat is marketed either as whole unpolished kernels, called groats, or as ground kernels, called grits. The groats may be toasted or untoasted; the grits are usually toasted. Some supermarkets carry uncooked buckwheat groats or grits packaged as kasha (the Russian word for toasted buckwheat groats or grits). Buckwheat flour is available in health-food stores and some supermarkets.

Recipes: Blini, 602; Buckwheat Pancakes, 600.

CORN

The following section deals with dried corn and dried corn products. For information on fresh sweet corn, see CORN.

Cornmeal   Cornmeal is finely ground from dried white or yellow corn. Some health-food stores sell unbolted cornmeal, which includes both bran and germ. Most supermarket cornmeal, however, is ground from the kernel with the hull and germ removed.

Boiled cornmeal is eaten as a breakfast porridge with butter and syrup, or is molded, cooled, sliced, and fried for a breakfast dish or savory side dish. Cornmeal is used in a wide variety of puddings, muffins, corn breads, fried dumplings, and pancakes. It also serves as a coating for fried foods, such as catfish and trout. Italians cook coarsely ground cornmeal, called polenta, in water or stock to make a thick cornmeal mush, also called polenta. They serve it hot with butter, cheese, meat sauces, or roast fowl. They also chill it, slice it, and fry it, or reheat it in a baking dish, layered with cheese or meat sauce.

Cornmeal is sold in bulk or packed in boxes in the supermarket. Polenta is available in Italian markets and some supermarkets. Blue cornmeal (see opposite page) is available in specialty stores and by mail order. Store unbolted cornmeal in an airtight container in the refrigerator and use within three months. Regular cornmeal can be kept in a covered container in a cool, dry place for up to one year.

◼ OLD-FASHIONED
BUTTERMILK CORN STICKS

Corn sticks are quick breads made in the same way as muffins. They make a flavorful accompaniment to salads, chowders and soups, casseroles, and other savory dishes. To mold them into the traditional ear-of-corn shape, use a seasoned cast-iron corn-stick pan (see page 21). Corn sticks are best when served soon after baking; they don't keep well.

    1 cup *each* yellow cornmeal and all-purpose flour
    ¼ cup sugar
    2 teaspoons baking powder
    ¾ teaspoon salt
    ½ teaspoon baking soda
    1 egg
    1 cup buttermilk
    2 tablespoons vegetable oil

1. Preheat oven to 425° F. In a large bowl blend cornmeal, flour, sugar, baking powder, salt, and baking soda.

2. In a medium bowl beat egg with buttermilk and oil. Add egg mixture to cornmeal mixture and mix just until dry ingredients are moistened.

3. Divide batter evenly into 2 well-greased corn-stick pans (or greased standard muffin pans).

4. Bake until golden brown (15 to 20 minutes). Best when served warm.

Makes 14 to 16 corn sticks or 1 dozen muffins.

■ TEXAS JALAPEÑO-CHEESE CORN BREAD

This moist, multiflavored bread is a substantial side dish (and some Texans use sour cream in place of buttermilk to make it even heavier). New Mexico's famed (and somewhat odd-looking) blue corn bread follows, with coarsely ground blue cornmeal replacing the yellow. Corn bread does not keep well. However, the batter can be prepared as much as a day ahead and refrigerated, then baked when needed and served fragrant and warm.

> 1½ cups yellow cornmeal
> 1½ tablespoons flour
> ½ teaspoon salt
> 2 tablespoons sugar
> 1 tablespoon baking powder
> 1 small onion, minced (about ¾ cup)
> 1¼ cups buttermilk
> 1 can (8 oz) creamed corn *or* 1 cup fresh corn scraped with its "cream" from cob
> ½ cup melted butter
> 1 cup grated Cheddar cheese
> ½ pound chorizo, fried and finely chopped (optional)
> ¼ to ½ cup minced canned jalapeño chiles *or* 1 can (4 oz) diced mild chiles

1. Preheat oven to 400° F. In a large bowl stir together cornmeal, flour, salt, sugar, and baking powder. Add onion, buttermilk, corn, and butter; mix rapidly until flour is well moistened. (Batter may be refrigerated overnight.)

2. Grease an 8-inch-square baking pan or 10-inch cast-iron skillet. Pour in half the batter. Sprinkle on half the cheese, *chorizo* (if used), chiles, and remaining cheese. Cover with remaining batter and bake until firm (45 to 50 minutes). If top is not browned, broil about 5 minutes. To serve, cut into sixteen 2-inch squares or 8 wedges.

Makes 16 squares or 8 wedges, serves 8.

Texas Jalapeño-Cheese Corn Muffins Preheat oven to 425° F. Mix cheese and chiles into batter; do not use chorizo. Pour into 12 to 16 greased muffin cups and bake 20 to 25 minutes.

Texas Jalapeño-Cheese Blue Corn Bread Preheat oven to 350° F. Substitute coarsely milled blue cornmeal for yellow cornmeal; do not use chorizo. Bake 1 hour.

Food Processor Version Use metal blade to mince onion and shredding disk to shred well-chilled cheese.

■ BASIC POLENTA

Although polenta must be watched and stirred continuously as it cooks, diligence yields delicious results: a thick, creamy, golden pudding that has inspired cooks to create countless variations. Common throughout northern Italy, polenta can be eaten hot, with butter and cheese or shaved truffles. It can also be poured into a pan, cooled until firm, and sliced, then layered with meat sauces or with mushrooms and cheese, and baked until bubbly. Often it's reheated with a mantle of grated fontina or Gorgonzola cheese. Serve this recipe hot from the saucepan, to accompany grilled sausages, chicken, or chops.

> 4 cups water
> 1½ teaspoons coarse salt
> 1 cup polenta
> 4 tablespoons unsalted butter
> ¼ cup freshly grated Parmesan cheese

Bring the water and salt to a boil in a heavy saucepan. Gradually add polenta, whisking constantly. Stir in half of the butter. Cook over low heat, stirring constantly with a wooden spoon, 20 minutes. Mixture will become quite thick. Stir in remaining butter and Parmesan; serve hot.

Serves 4.

■ GRILLED POLENTA

When cooled until firm, then sliced and grilled, polenta makes a great companion to dishes rich in sauce. Serve it with braised rabbit or veal stew, Ragù Bolognese (see page 412), or with plump sausages sautéed with peppers.

> 1 recipe Basic Polenta
> Oil, for greasing rack

1. Oil an 8- or 9-inch loaf pan or a 1-inch-deep cake pan and fill with hot polenta. Cool, then chill until firm.

2. Prepare a medium-hot charcoal fire. Oil grilling rack. Slice polenta ½ inch thick. Grill on both sides until hot throughout. Polenta may also be successfully cooked on an indoor griddle. Serve immediately.

Serves 4.

Recipes: Pan-fried Catfish, 230.

Dried Blue Corn This variety of field corn with blue kernels is cultivated by Pueblo and Hopi Indians in New Mexico. The dried kernels are sold whole or ground into blue cornmeal. The cornmeal is used for blue corn tortillas, corn bread, pancakes, and mush. Baked goods made with blue cornmeal have a bluish gray tinge. Dried blue corn and blue cornmeal are available in some specialty markets or from mail-order sources.

Recipes: Texas Jalapeño-Cheese Blue Corn Bread, at left.

Dried Indian Corn Multicolored Indian corn is sometimes dried on the cob and sold in supermarkets for decorative use on autumn tables.

Dried Sweet Corn Dried either on or off the cob, sweet corn is still used in Pennsylvania Dutch cookery and is available in markets that cater to a Pennsylvania Dutch clientele. It is usually reconstituted in water, then added to soups or stews or made into a side dish.

Hominy This dried field corn has been heated and soaked in a basic solution to soften its hull, then hulled and the germ removed. It is then dried and sold in bulk or plastic bags as dried whole hominy. Look for it in Latin American markets.

When heated and soaked, the hull and germ removed, and finely ground, the dried corn is known as *masa harina* and is used to make tortillas, tamales, and other basic Mexican foods. Fresh prepared *masa* (corn dough) is available in many Latin American markets.

Mexican cooks also boil whole hominy until tender, then add it to soups, such as *menudo* (tripe soup), and to stews. When fully cooked, whole hominy has a sweet flavor and a firm but creamy texture.

Whole cooked hominy, both white and yellow, is also canned and sold in supermarkets. Southern cooks add whole hominy to scrambled eggs, simmer it in cream, or bake it in puddings.

Hominy Grits When cracked, dried whole hominy is called hominy grits. Quick-cooking hominy grits are ground finer than regular grits. Instant hominy grits have been precooked and dehydrated; they can be quickly re-hydrated in hot water. Hominy grits are eaten as a break-fast cereal, with butter and syrup; molded, cooled, sliced, and fried; and baked in puddings, cheese-topped casse-roles, and soufflés.

■ BAKED GARLIC GRITS

Hospitable southerners who want to help their northern friends develop a taste for grits are likely to introduce them to this elaborate and delicate version, which re-sembles a fallen cheese soufflé. Serve baked grits for brunch (the batter can be mixed the night before) or at dinner; they are especially suited to accompany roasts and barbecues. Use Cheddar cheese if grits will be eaten with a hearty dish, Swiss cheese if with a light main course.

   ½ **cup milk**
   3 **eggs**
   ½ **pound sharp Cheddar cheese or**
       Swiss cheese, grated
   2 **tablespoons freshly grated Parmesan cheese**
   8 **tablespoons unsalted butter, cut in small pieces**
   2 **medium cloves garlic, minced (about 2 tsp)**
   ¼ **teaspoon freshly ground pepper**
   1 **tablespoon snipped fresh chives or**
       minced green onion tops
   4 **cups water**
   1 **teaspoon salt**
   1 **cup quick-cooking hominy grits**
   1 **teaspoon butter**

1. Preheat oven to 325° F. In a medium bowl beat together milk and eggs. Add cheeses, unsalted butter, garlic, pepper, and chives. Set aside.

2. Bring the water and salt to a boil. Add grits, stir, and return to a boil. Lower heat to medium and continue cooking, stirring often, until grits are thickened (about 5 minutes). Pour out any unabsorbed water. Remove from heat, immediately pour cheese mixture into grits, and stir until cheeses and butter melt. (Grits may be prepared in advance to this point; cover and refrigerate up to one day until ready to serve.)

3. Grease a 2-quart casserole or soufflé dish with the 1 teaspoon butter. Spoon grits mixture into prepared casserole and bake until a knife inserted in center comes out clean (about 1 hour). Baked grits may be left in oven, with heat turned off, for 10 minutes before serving.

Serves 8.

Recipes: Menudo, 591.

MILLET

A small round yellow seed, millet does not require pro-cessing after harvesting. It is a common ingredient in bird-seed mixtures but is otherwise used infrequently in this country. It has a crunchy texture and a flavor resembling that of corn.

Millet may be steamed and eaten as a breakfast cereal with butter, maple syrup, and cream; cooked in stock like a pilaf or baked in a pudding; or when cooked added to stuffings or breads for texture and flavor.

Millet is sold in bulk in most health-food stores and in some supermarkets.

OATS

Whole oats must be hulled before they are fit for human consumption. Hulled whole oats are also known as oat groats. Steel-cut oats are groats that have been sliced with steel blades. Rolled oats (old-fashioned oats) are groats that have been steamed and flattened by rollers into flakes. Quick-cooking rolled oats are groats that have been cut into smaller pieces before rolling, yielding thinner flakes that cook more quickly. Instant oats are made from partially cooked groat pieces rolled even thinner than quick-cooking oats. Some brands of instant oatmeal are flavored with sugar and spices; most have salt added. Reg-ular and quick-cooking oats can be used interchangeably in recipes; using flavored instant oats alters the taste of a recipe that calls for regular or quick-cooking oats.

Apart from the morning bowl of oatmeal, oats do not figure largely in the American diet. Yet they are a flavorful and nutritious grain with several culinary uses. Although most Americans make their oatmeal from rolled oats, steel-cut oats also make a delicious cereal with chewier texture and slightly more nutritive value. Cooked whole oats can be added to soups or stews. Rolled oats are used in granola, cookies, muffins, and cakes. They can also be added, either raw or cooked, to yeast bread doughs. Cooked oatmeal contributes moisture and bulk to stuffings, breads, and meat loaves. It can also be molded, cooled, sliced, and fried like cornmeal mush. Oat groats can be ground into flour for baking.

Health-food stores generally stock oat groats, steel-cut oats, and rolled oats. Most supermarkets sell rolled, quick-cooking, and instant oats. Oat flour is available in some health-food stores.

■ OATMEAL GEMS

These chewy, slightly sweet muffins are good with soups and stews. The name *gem* refers to the old-fashioned cast-iron pans that produce a first-rate muffin with a crusty exterior and rounded top. If you don't have cast-iron gem pans, use plain muffin tins; for a similar result, try to find tins made of a heavyweight material. Leftover muffins are delicious split, toasted, and buttered. Note that the recipe calls for quick-cooking oats; however, regular oats can also be used as the two types are interchangeable in recipes.

    2 cups quick-cooking oats
 1½ cups buttermilk
    ¼ cup molasses
    2 tablespoons sugar
    2 eggs
    ½ teaspoon salt
    1 cup flour
    1 teaspoon baking soda

1. Preheat oven to 400° F. Grease standard muffin pans or line with cupcake papers. Combine oats and buttermilk in a medium bowl and let stand about 15 minutes.

2. Beat in molasses, sugar, eggs, and salt. Stir together flour and baking soda, then add to oat mixture and mix just until dry ingredients are moistened.

3. Fill prepared pans two thirds full. Bake until a toothpick inserted in a muffin comes out clean (about 20 minutes). Serve warm.

Makes about 16 muffins.

QUINOA

Relatively new to the American marketplace, quinoa (pronounced keen-wa) is actually an ancient food. Native to the Andean region of South America, it was a staple of the Incan diet. Quinoa has an excellent nutritional profile, with more protein than other grains. In contrast to other grains, its protein is complete (containing all the essential amino acids).

Although, like buckwheat, quinoa isn't technically a grain, it looks, cooks, and tastes like one. It can be substituted for rice in side dishes, casseroles, salads, and stuffings. It has a notably light texture and mild flavor. Look for quinoa in health-food stores.

RICE

An extremely important food crop, rice provides basic sustenance to half the population of the world. The cuisines of Japan, China, India, Indonesia, and Southeast Asia are all rice-based; few meals there are served without rice or a rice dish.

Thousands of varieties of rice are cultivated, but the most important distinction from the cook's standpoint is the length of the grain. Long-grain rice has a decidedly different texture when cooked than short-grain rice and is thus better suited to certain types of dishes.

Store rice in an airtight container in a cool, dry place. It will keep indefinitely.

Some cooks insist on washing or soaking rice before use. Although washing removes external starch particles that might cause stickiness, it also washes away any vitamin or protein enrichment (see Enriched Rice). On the other hand, some cooks claim that rinsing gives the rice a cleaner, lighter taste. Whether the nutritional loss is worth the improved flavor, or whether indeed the flavor improvement is noticeable, is a matter of personal taste.

Rice fits comfortably into most meals, whether as a background for highly seasoned dishes, as a vehicle for sauces, or as a filling accompaniment to simply prepared roasted or broiled meats and poultry.

ABOUT COOKING RICE

For a task that appears so simple, there is much disagreement about rice cookery. Some cooks prefer to boil rice in a large quantity of water until it is tender, pouring off the excess liquid and drying the grain in a slow oven. The advantages of this technique are that it does not require precise measurement and it yields a fluffy, dry grain; however, the discarded liquid contains valuable nutrients.

Other cooks steam rice. A precise quantity of liquid is brought to a boil, the rice is added, covered, and slowly steamed until done. This method produces moister, more nutritious kernels.

A third method, preferred by some Chinese cooks, calls for adding rice to precisely measured boiling liquid and simmering, uncovered, until much of the liquid is absorbed. Then the mixture is stirred, the pot covered, and the rice steamed until done. Stirring releases the starch from the kernels' surface and produces a stickier rice.

Yet another method, the pilaf method, calls for sautéing the grains in butter or oil first, then adding hot liquid, covering, and steaming until tender. The pilaf method produces distinct, flavorful grains. It is popular among Western cooks, but less so among Asian cooks, who prefer rice plain and dry.

The method chosen depends on the results desired. Here are more precise directions for different methods.

UNLIMITED WATER METHOD

Boil rice, uncovered, in an unlimited amount of salted water for 12 to 15 minutes until softened, but still firm at the core. Drain well in a sieve. Transfer to a shallow baking dish, cover, and steam in a 300° F oven 10 to 15 minutes, or until tender and dry. Toss with butter and serve. Timing given is for white rice; brown rice and wild rice can be cooked by this method, but will take longer.

MEASURED WATER METHOD

For White Rice Bring 1½ cups lightly salted water to a boil. Add 1 cup rice and stir once with a fork. Cover, reduce heat to low, and cook 18 minutes. Remove from heat and let stand 5 minutes. Fluff with a fork.

For Brown Rice Bring 2 cups lightly salted water to a boil. Add 1 cup rice and stir once with a fork. Cover, reduce heat to low, and cook 45 to 50 minutes. Remove from heat and let stand 5 minutes. Fluff with a fork.

For Wild Rice Bring 2½ cups lightly salted water to a boil. Add 1 cup wild rice and stir once with a fork. Cover, reduce heat to low, and cook 40 to 45 minutes. Remove from heat and let stand 5 minutes. Fluff with a fork.

CHINESE METHOD

Put 1 cup rice in saucepan with 2 cups cold, salted water. Bring to a boil over high heat, cover, and cook until water has been absorbed down to level of rice. Stir rice well with a spoon, cover, and reduce heat to low; cook about 15 minutes or until grains are tender. Fluff with a fork.

PILAF METHOD

Melt 2 tablespoons oil, Clarified Butter (see page 68), or a butter-oil mixture in a heavy-bottomed saucepan over moderate heat. Add 1 cup rice and stir to coat all grains with fat. Sauté rice 2 to 3 minutes, stirring constantly. Add 1½ cups boiling, salted water (2 cups for brown rice, 2½ cups for wild rice), cover, reduce heat to low, and steam until tender (15 minutes for white rice, 30 to 45 minutes for brown and wild rice). Remove from heat, let stand 5 minutes, and fluff with a fork.

COOKING RICE IN THE MICROWAVE OVEN

Using a microwave oven to cook rice saves cleanup and keeps the kitchen cool, but it won't save time. Rice will require the same number of minutes whether cooked by microwave or on top of the stove. If you choose the microwave method, use a larger container than seems necessary to prevent overflow. Reheat cooked rice 1 minute per cup at 100 percent power. Fluff all rice with a fork after cooking.

Type of Rice	Amount	Liquid	Cooking Time
Long-grain white	1 cup	2 cups	5 minutes at 100% power 15 minutes at 50% power
Brown	1 cup	2–2½ cups	5 minutes at 100% power 45–55 minutes at 30% power

Some Japanese rice is coated with cornstarch after milling to retard rancidity. It must be rinsed to prevent the cornstarch from making the rice gummy. Imported rice, such as Indian *basmati* rice, is not always as carefully cleaned as American rice. It should be picked over carefully to remove small pebbles and bits of chaff.

Arborio Rice Grown in the Po Valley of Italy, Arborio rice is a short-grain rice. Its high starch content is responsible for the distinctive creamy texture of Italian risotto. Arborio rice is also a good choice for rice puddings and soups.

Basmati Rice A particularly aromatic variety of long-grain rice, *basmati* is grown in India and Pakistan, and, more recently, in California. It is the preferred rice for Indian cooking, but its special fragrance and nutty flavor make it a delicious rice for use with Western dishes as well. Before cooking, it should be picked over for small stones, then washed well and soaked; follow cooking directions for white rice. Basmati is available in specialty stores, Indian markets, and some health-food stores.

Glutinous Rice A short-grain rice used in Asian cooking, glutinous, or sweet, rice has a high starch content and is very sticky when cooked. It is an ingredient in a variety of Asian sweets and snacks, such as molded rice puddings and dumplings. It is the variety used to make *mochi*, the Japanese chewy rice cake. It is not used as an everyday table rice.

Long-Grain Rice These varieties produce a kernel that is four to five times as long as it is wide, with tapered ends. The cooked grains tend to be separate, dry, light, and fluffy, making long-grain rice the best choice for salads and pilafs. Most of the rice served in America and in Western Europe is long-grain rice.

Short- and Medium-Grain Rice These varieties have short, rounded kernels; when cooked, the kernels are moist and slightly sticky, and tend to cling. The Japanese favor short-grain rice, perhaps because the grains are easier to pick up with chopsticks. Short-grain rice (also called pearl rice) has a higher proportion of waxy starch molecules (amylopectin) in its starch granules than long-grain rice, which explains the tendency of short grains to adhere. This quality is desirable in such dishes as croquettes, rice puddings, molded rice rings, and sushi.

■ BAKED RICE PUDDING

Long, slow baking results in a rich, sweet, golden cream, which is equally good warm or cold.

 Butter, for greasing pan
½ **cup raw short-grain rice (see Note)**
4 **cups half-and-half**
1 **cup whipping cream**
½ **cup sugar**
1 **teaspoon vanilla extract**

1. Preheat oven to 300° F. Generously butter a 2-quart ovenproof dish. Sprinkle rice over bottom of dish. In a large bowl combine half-and-half, cream, sugar, and vanilla; pour over rice, stirring to combine.

2. Bake 1 hour, stirring every 20 minutes. Raise heat to 350° F and bake until a creamy, golden crust forms (45 minutes to 1 hour). Serve hot or warm.

Serves 6.

Cold Rice Pudding   To serve cold, reduce amount of rice to ⅓ cup; just before serving fold in 1 cup whipping cream, whipped to soft peaks.

Raisin Rice Pudding   Fold into cream mixture 1 cup golden raisins that have been soaked in rum, if desired; pour over rice.

Note   If short-grain rice is unavailable, long-grain rice can be used, but will produce a thinner pudding.

■ FRIED RICE WITH HAM, EGG, AND CABBAGE

What started as a way to use leftover rice has become a popular dish in its own right—fried rice. Actually the rice is not really fried, but stir-fried in a little oil. The catchall found in some restaurants, dark brown with soy sauce, cannot compare with good homemade fried rice. Most fried rice dishes are seasoned with salt, not soy sauce, to preserve the color of the rice. Cloud ears, an ingredient in this recipe, are edible fungi used for their crunchy yet gelatinous texture. You'll find them in Asian markets and some well-stocked supermarkets.

   1½ ounces trimmed Smithfield ham
   2 to 3 tablespoons vegetable oil
   1 egg, beaten
   1 teaspoon minced fresh ginger
   1 clove garlic, minced
   ⅓ pound bok choy, cut crosswise into ¼-inch slices
   2 tablespoons cloud ears, soaked until soft and drained
   2 to 3 cups cooked rice, at room temperature (see About Cooking Rice, Chinese Method, opposite page)
   Salt, to taste
   ¼ cup Chicken Stock (see page 560)

1. Soak ham in water for 30 minutes. Drain and cut in thin slices. Heat wok or skillet over medium-high heat, and add 1 tablespoon oil. Pour beaten egg into pan and swirl to make a large, flat omelet. Cook egg just until set, transfer to cutting board, and cut into thin 1-inch strips.

2. Add remaining oil to pan. Add ginger and garlic; cook until fragrant. Add bok choy, ham, and cloud ears; stir-fry until heated through (about 2 minutes).

3. Add rice to pan and stir to break up clumps. Stir-fry vigorously, scraping up any bits of rice that cling to pan. When rice begins to brown, add salt to taste (allow for saltiness of ham), then add stock and egg strips. Turn heat to high and stir-fry until liquid is nearly all evaporated. Transfer to serving platter.

Serves 2 as a one-dish meal, 4 or more with other dishes.

■ LEMON RISOTTO

Serve this sprightly Italian rice dish before a fish main course. Add more stock to the rice mixture only after previous quantities have been absorbed.

   2 tablespoons plus 2 teaspoons unsalted butter
   2 tablespoons olive oil
   ¼ cup minced onion
   Grated rind of 1 lemon
   1½ cups Arborio rice
   4½ cups Chicken Stock (see page 560)
   ¼ cup plus 2 teaspoons fresh lemon juice
   ½ cup freshly grated Parmesan cheese
   Salt and freshly ground pepper, to taste

1. Melt 2 tablespoons butter in a heavy saucepan over moderately low heat. Add olive oil, then onion and lemon rind, and sauté slowly for 5 minutes. Add rice and stir to coat with oil. Turn up heat to high and toast, stirring, for 30 seconds. Immediately add ½ cup stock and reduce heat to medium-low. Stir constantly until stock is absorbed. Keep adding more stock, ½ cup at a time, stirring constantly and adding more only when the previous quantity has been absorbed. When all the stock is absorbed, stir in ¼ cup lemon juice. Rice should be tender. If not, add a little warm water bit by bit until rice is tender yet firm.

2. Stir in Parmesan and remaining butter. Cook briefly to blend and melt cheese. Season to taste with salt and pepper. Add remaining lemon juice and serve immediately in warm bowls.

Serves 4.

SPECIAL PROCESSING

All rice is processed before it reaches the commercial market. At the least, it is hulled. In addition, it may be polished, parboiled, precooked, or flavored.

Brown Rice   This type has been minimally processed. The tough hull has been removed, and the outer bran remains. Because of the presence of bran, brown rice is more nutritious than polished (white) rice but does take longer to cook.

Enriched Rice   In an attempt to replace some of the vitamins and protein lost through milling, the rice is sprayed after milling with vitamins in solution, then coated with protein powder and dried.

Flavored Rice   Some seasonings and/or other ingredients have been combined with the rice, which has been milled and possibly parboiled or precooked before being packaged.

Parboiled Rice This is also known as converted rice. The whole unhulled grain is soaked, drained, partially pressure-cooked, then dried and milled. The aim is to make converted rice more nutritious than regular white rice by diffusing the B vitamins from the bran and germ into the endosperm before the grain is milled.

Precooked Rice This is white rice that has been fully or partially precooked, then dehydrated.

White Rice An abrasive process mills or polishes the kernels and removes the bran and most of the germ. The result is white rice.

Recipes: Maki Zushi, 392; Nigiri Sushi, 233; Onion and Rice Soubise, 229; Red Beans and Rice, 32; Roast Chicken With Rice, Fruit, and Almond Stuffing, 470; Stuffed Green Peppers Mexicana, 426; Sushi Rice, 233.

RYE

Few Americans have ever cooked with whole rye berries, although many have made breads with rye flour. Rye grass thrives in poor soils and hard climates and is often planted where wheat would be unable to survive. The grain has a strong, distinctive flavor. It has no hull and does not require milling.

Whole cooked rye berries may be used in casseroles, soups, stuffings, or stir-fried dishes. Cracked rye is suitable for pilafs or breakfast cereals. Rye flakes may be used like rolled oats. Rye flour has poor gluten-forming ability and makes a heavy bread on its own; for that reason, rye breads usually contain some portion of wheat flour.

Whole rye berries, cracked rye, and rolled rye flakes are available in health-food stores. Rye flour is sold in most supermarkets, in bulk or packed in boxes or paper bags.

TRITICALE

A relatively new hybrid of wheat and rye, triticale is designed to be as productive as wheat, as hardy as rye, and more nutritious than either.

Cooked whole triticale may be used as any other whole grain: in pilafs, casseroles, soups, or stuffings. Triticale flour may be used, either by itself or mixed with wheat flour, in breads, cookies, pancakes, muffins, and other baked goods. The flour has a full, nutty flavor but has low gluten-forming abilities. For a lighter baked product, use 50 percent wheat flour.

Whole triticale berries and triticale flour are sold in health-food stores. Triticale flakes (rolled triticale) are available in some health-food stores.

WHEAT

In its worldwide importance, wheat is second only to rice. Although more people depend on rice than on wheat, more acreage is planted with wheat and more wheat is produced. Wheat was probably the first cereal cultivated, and it can thus be argued that wheat is responsible for changing the human race from nomads to settlers.

Although there are at least thirty thousand known varieties of wheat, the most important distinction for the cook is between hard and soft varieties. Hard wheats are relatively high in glutenin and gliadin, the two proteins that, when moistened, combine to form gluten. Gluten is the elastic substance that allows a bread dough to trap gases and hold a shape or a pasta dough to be rolled and stretched into noodles. Consequently, flours milled from hard wheats are the best choice for breads and pasta; flours milled from soft wheats are best for cakes, cookies, and quick breads.

The wheat berry, or whole kernel, may be processed to yield a variety of different products. Some of those products are described below; for further information on processed wheat products, see FLOUR.

Whole Wheat Berries The unprocessed kernels of wheat are called whole wheat berries. Because they still contain bran and germ, berries are slow to cook, but are correspondingly high in nutrition and flavor.

Whole wheat berries may be boiled or steamed for pilafs, stuffings, breads, and porridge. Berries may also be sprouted for use in salads, breads, or stir-fried dishes.

Look for whole wheat berries in health-food stores. Store them in an airtight container in a cool place or in the refrigerator for up to six months.

WHEAT BERRY–RICE PILAF

This pilaf offers an opportunity to try a mixture of different grains that lend balance, protein, and flavor to a meal. Triticale, a hybrid of wheat and rye, is an especially nutritious substitute for wheat berries. Barley can also be exchanged for the wheat berries.

- 2 tablespoons vegetable oil
- 1 onion, minced
- 2 carrots, finely diced
- 1 stalk celery, finely diced
- 1 cup wheat berries
- 1 cup brown rice
- ⅓ cup wild rice
- 4½ cups Chicken Stock (see page 560) or water
- ½ tablespoon kosher salt

1. Heat oil in a 2-quart saucepan over medium heat. Stir in onions, carrots, and celery, and cook until softened but not browned. Add wheat berries, brown rice, wild rice, stock, and salt. Stir to combine.

2. Cover pan and cook about 40 minutes over medium to low heat.

Serves 8.

Food Processor Version Cut onion, carrots, and celery into 1-inch pieces. Put in work bowl with metal blade and pulse 3 or 4 times. Scrape work bowl and pulse until desired texture is reached. Use as directed.

Wheat Bran The outer coating of the wheat berry is called the bran. Removed from the wheat berry during milling, it is often packaged and sold separately. Bran is valued principally as a source of dietary fiber, although it also contains B vitamins and protein.

Add bran to muffins, cereals, yeast breads, and quick breads for improved nutritive value. It is available in health-food stores and some supermarkets, both in bulk and in packages. Store bran in refrigerator in an airtight container; use within six months.

Recipes: Bran Muffins, 375; Refrigerator Bran Muffin Mix, 376.

Wheat Germ When wheat is milled for white flour, the bran and germ are removed. The oil- and protein-rich germ, often packaged and sold separately, is valued for the nutty flavor and nutrition it adds to dishes. Use wheat germ in breads, muffins, cookies, granola, and cooked cereals.

Wheat germ, toasted or raw, is available in bulk in health-food stores or in vacuum-sealed jars in supermarkets. It is sold flaked or as a coarse meal. Because of its high oil content, it is the most perishable part of the wheat kernel and goes rancid quickly. If purchasing wheat germ in bulk, buy it from health-food stores that keep it under refrigeration and have a rapid turnover. If the bulk wheat germ is not refrigerated, the vacuum-packed variety may be a better choice. Store bulk wheat germ in the refrigerator in an airtight container. After opening, keep vacuum-packed wheat germ in the refrigerator in the original container. If properly stored and sealed, bulk or packaged wheat germ will keep for two to three months.

Cracked Wheat Coarse, medium, or fine, cracked wheat is made from the whole unprocessed wheat berry cut with steel blades. When cooked, it has a nutty flavor and a slightly crunchy texture.

Eat cooked cracked wheat as a breakfast cereal, either alone or mixed with other grains. Use it for stuffings, pilafs, and cold salads. Cooked cracked wheat adds moist texture and nutty flavor to whole wheat breads.

Cracked wheat is available in health-food stores and some supermarkets, in bulk or packaged. Store it in an airtight container in a cool, dry place or in the refrigerator for up to six months.

Bulgur Whole wheat berries that have been steamed, then dried and cracked are known as bulgur. It has a nuttier flavor than cracked wheat and when cooked has a softer texture.

Use bulgur for salads, stuffings, breakfast cereals, and pilafs, or as an addition to bread doughs or meat loaves. Bulgur in coarse and fine grinds is available in health-food stores and some supermarkets, in bulk or packaged. Store in an airtight container in a cool, dry place for up to one year.

■ TABBOULEH

To use this Middle Eastern salad as an hors d'oeuvre, provide leaves of romaine to scoop up the mixture.

> 1 cup bulgur
> ⅓ cup fresh lemon juice
> 1 teaspoon salt
> ⅛ teaspoon freshly ground pepper
> ⅔ cup olive oil
> ½ cup *each* thinly sliced green onions and finely chopped parsley
> ⅓ cup fresh mint leaves
> 1 medium tomato, seeded and chopped
>   Inner romaine lettuce leaves, for accompaniment

1. Rinse bulgur and drain well. Cover with cold water and let stand for 1 hour. Drain well, pressing out moisture.

2. In a large bowl mix lemon juice, salt, and pepper. Using a whisk or fork, gradually beat in oil until well combined. To oil mixture add drained bulgur, onion, parsley, and mint; mix lightly. Cover and refrigerate until ready to serve (at least 2 hours).

3. Mound Tabbouleh in a shallow serving dish; sprinkle with tomato. Surround with romaine leaves, and use them as scoops for serving and eating.

Serves 4 to 6.

Semolina A pale ivory grain with a nutty flavor, semolina is ground from the endosperm of an especially hard wheat called durum wheat. Because durum wheat is high in glutenin and gliadin, the two proteins that form gluten when moistened, semolina dough is firm and elastic. The dough is so pliable that semolina is the flour used for most dried Italian pastas.

Generally, the coarse grind of semolina is preferred for cereals, the fine grind for pasta. (In Italy, semolina flour is used for factory-made dried pasta, not for homemade fresh pasta.) Use semolina for hot cooked cereal, puddings, and Italian *gnocchi*. Add finely ground semolina to bread dough for creamy color and nutty flavor.

Semolina is sold in Italian markets, some health-food stores, and some supermarkets, in bulk and packaged. It is available in coarse, medium, and fine grinds. Store in an airtight container in a cool, dry place for up to one year.

Couscous A semolina product, couscous is made from moistened semolina rolled into tiny pellets and dried. It is popular in Northern Africa, especially Morocco and Tunisia, where it gives its name to a dish built around it. A Moroccan or Tunisian couscous is an elaborate dish: a spicy stew of lamb, chicken, or fish and vegetables, or a sweet stew of dried fruits and nuts, rich in broth and served atop a mound of the steaming couscous grain.

Use couscous in casseroles, pilafs, or stuffings; enjoy it as a breakfast cereal with butter, sugar, and milk, or as a savory side dish for a roast or stew; or serve it in a traditional Tunisian or Moroccan couscous.

Couscous is sold in Middle Eastern markets, health-food stores, and some supermarkets, in bulk and packaged. A convenient instant version is available but yields a less desirable texture. Store in an airtight container in a cool, dry place; it will keep indefinitely.

■ COUSCOUS

Both the grain and the dish prepared from it are referred to as *couscous*. Traditionally the main ingredients—vegetables and chicken—cook in the bottom of a special *couscousière* while the couscous grains steam over it. You may also prepare the chicken and vegetables in one pan and cook the wheat grains separately. Quick-cooking or instant couscous is available to simplify this step.

       4 cups regular or instant couscous
       ½ cup unsalted butter
       3 tablespoons salt
       4 tablespoons vegetable oil
       4 onions, diced
       2 cloves garlic, minced
       2 teaspoons freshly ground black pepper
       1 teaspoon cayenne pepper
       ¼ gram saffron threads (1 vial)
       1 teaspoon ground turmeric
       2 tablespoons fresh ginger, minced
       2 tablespoons ground cinnamon
       6 cups water
       1 whole chicken (2½ to 3 lb)
       6 small red boiling potatoes, halved or
          quartered depending on size
       6 carrots, cut in 3-inch lengths
       3 zucchini, cut in 3-inch lengths
       3 golden zucchini, cut in 3-inch lengths
      12 ounces cooked chick-peas
       1 cup golden raisins

Spicy Harissa

       ½ teaspoon cumin seed
       ¼ teaspoon coriander seed
       1 clove garlic, minced
       1 red jalapeño chile, minced
       ¼ cup Chicken Stock (see page 560)
       1 tablespoon olive oil
       1 teaspoon cilantro, minced
       ½ teaspoon parsley, minced
       ⅛ teaspoon cayenne pepper
       ¼ teaspoon salt

1. If using regular couscous, rinse grains under running water, then soak in 8 cups water for 30 minutes (this allows them to swell later while they absorb flavors of stew). Drain couscous and pat dry with paper towels. Rub grains together to remove any lumps. Line colander or deep steamer with cheesecloth, add soaked couscous, place colander or deep steamer over a 4-quart pot of boiling water, and steam, uncovered, 30 minutes. (If colander and pan do not fit tightly you may have to wrap cheesecloth around bottom of colander to form a seal.) The goal is to have grains swell as large as possible and not become lumpy or soggy. For instant couscous follow instructions on package.

2. When couscous is cooked, place on a platter and spread out. Toss with 2 tablespoons butter and 1 teaspoon salt. Stir to remove any lumps. If preparing ahead, cover loosely with foil and reheat by steaming for 20 minutes.

3. Heat 4 tablespoons butter and oil in a large stockpot. Add onions and garlic; sauté 5 minutes. Add remaining salt, pepper, cayenne, saffron, turmeric, ginger, and cinnamon; cook 2 to 3 minutes. Add the water and bring to a boil. Reduce heat, place chicken in pan, cover, and simmer for 35 minutes. Add potatoes and carrots and simmer 15 minutes more. Add zucchini, chick-peas, and raisins; continue cooking 15 minutes.

4. To serve, put couscous into a large shallow bowl or platter and toss with remaining butter to remove any lumps. Place chicken in center of couscous. Surround with vegetables, and spoon pan juices on top. Serve Spicy Harissa as a condiment.

Serves 6 to 8.

Spicy Harissa Toast cumin and coriander seed in a small, dry skillet over medium heat for about 4 minutes. Purée with garlic, jalapeño, Chicken Stock, olive oil, cilantro, parsley, cayenne, and salt in blender or food processor.

Makes ½ cup.

WILD RICE

The seed of an aquatic grass, rather than a variety of rice, wild rice grows wild in Minnesota lakes and is cultivated in California. The grain is dark brown, slender, and even longer than long-grain rice.

Although Californians and Minnesotans defend the superiority of their products, there is little difference in flavor between the two. California rice is generally less expensive because it is harvested by machine. Most of the Minnesota crop is harvested by traditional hand methods.

Wild rice has a nutty, earthy flavor that is particularly appealing with game and dark-meat fowl. Ground into flour, it is used in combination with white flour for pancakes, waffles, crêpes, muffins, and other baked goods. Mix the grain with brown rice or white rice for pilafs and cold salads; stir it into soups; or use it as the foundation for a poultry stuffing.

Some supermarkets carry packaged wild rice or packaged rice blends containing wild rice. Check health-food stores and specialty shops for wild rice in bulk.

Recipes: Wheat Berry–Rice Pilaf, 276.

GRAPE

A prehistoric fruit, grapes have been known to man at least since Neolithic times and have been cultivated, possibly, since then. Today they are cultivated in many temperate regions of the world. The thousands of grape varieties are very sensitive to climate. Many varieties cultivated in California would not survive a New York winter, although dozens of hardier ones thrive on the East Coast. Grapes grow in clusters on vines. Ranging from ⅓ inch to more than 1 inch in diameter, they are oval or round, with smooth green, red, purple, or purplish black skins.

Use   Grapes are loosely classified as either table grapes or wine grapes, although there is considerable overlap. Because grapes grown primarily for wine—such as Cabernet Sauvignon and Riesling—rarely appear on the consumer market, they are not considered here. Most wine grapes, however, are very flavorful; if you live in a region where wine grapes are grown, seek them out.

Grapes are eaten out of hand or as part of fruit compotes, fruit salads, or chicken salad. They are the classic garnish for filet of sole or chicken breast prepared à la Veronique. Whole grapes can be pickled and used as a garnish, pressed for juice, or made into handsome preserves, conserves, and jellies.

Availability   Fresh grapes can be found the year around. Imports from the southern hemisphere fill in for the domestic crop in late spring. Check Common Table Grape Varieties for specific grape seasons.

Selection   Buy firm, plump grapes without signs of withering. Bunches should be well developed and fairly loose to allow for air circulation and to prevent mildew. Stem end should be green and healthy, not dry and blackened. White or green grapes are sweetest when color has a yellowish cast with a tinge of amber. Red grapes are best when red predominates.

Storage   Before refrigerating, remove any spoiled grapes. Store in a plastic bag in refrigerator; they will keep for up to two weeks.

▪ FLORENTINE GRAPE COFFEE CAKE

Serve this grape-dotted cake as part of an Italian-accented brunch along with frittata (see page 204) and caffè latte.

    1 teaspoon anise seed, coarsely crushed
    ½ cup sugar
    1 package active dry yeast
    ¼ cup each warm (105° to 115° F) water and
      warm milk
    ⅛ teaspoon salt
    ½ teaspoon vanilla extract
    ½ cup butter or margarine, softened
 2½ to 3 cups flour
    1 egg
    3 cups Concord or red seedless grapes

COMMON TABLE GRAPE VARIETIES		
The consumer market offers dozens of varieties of table grapes. These are some of the best-known varieties.		
Grape Variety	**Color**	**Availability**
Cardinal	Red	June
Catawba	Purple-red	September through October
Concord	Purple-black	September through October
Delaware	Pink	September through October
Emperor	Light red	September
Flame Tokay (seedless)	Red	September through November
Italia Muscat	Yellow	August through November
Perlette (seedless)	Green	Early June through July
Queen	Red	Late July through December
Red Malaga	Red	Late July through September
Ribier	Purple-black	July through February
Thompson Seedless	Green	June through November

1. In a small jar stir together crushed anise seed and sugar. Cover and let stand for 8 hours or overnight to blend flavors. Pour through a fine sieve to remove seed; discard seed.

2. Sprinkle yeast over the water in large bowl of electric mixer. Add 1 tablespoon of anise-flavored sugar. Let yeast-sugar mixture stand until yeast is soft (about 5 minutes).

3. Add 2 tablespoons anise sugar, warm milk, salt, vanilla, and butter.

4. Add 1 cup flour. Mix to blend, then beat at medium speed until smooth and elastic (about 3 minutes). Beat in egg until smooth. Stir in about 1½ cups more flour to make a soft dough.

5. Turn dough out onto a floured board or pastry cloth. Knead until smooth and satiny and small bubbles form just under surface (5 to 10 minutes), adding just enough flour to prevent dough from being sticky.

6. Turn dough in a greased bowl. Cover with plastic wrap and a towel; let rise in a warm place until doubled in bulk (1¼ to 1½ hours).

7. Punch dough down. Cover with inverted bowl. Let rest for 10 minutes.

8. Roll dough out on a floured surface to a large rectangle. Press into a greased, shallow 10- by 15-inch baking pan. Sprinkle evenly with grapes, then sprinkle grapes with remaining anise sugar.

9. Let rise until dough looks puffy (20 to 25 minutes). Preheat oven to 400° F.

10. Bake coffee cake until well browned (15 to 20 minutes). Let cool slightly in pan, then cut into generous strips. Best served warm.

Serves 8 to 10.

onion, and wine. Cover, reduce heat, and simmer 10 minutes; add grapes, cover again, and continue cooking until chicken is cooked through (about 10 minutes longer; test in thickest part with a small, sharp knife).

2. Using a slotted spoon, remove chicken and grapes to a heated serving dish; keep warm. Add cream to liquid in pan. Bring to a boil, stirring; cook until sauce is reduced and slightly thickened. Salt to taste. Pour sauce over chicken.

Serves 4 to 6.

GRAPEFRUIT

A relatively new citrus species, grapefruit was not acknowledged as such until 1830 and was not commercially cultivated until the late nineteenth century. Today, the United States produces about 90 percent of the world crop, with Florida growing about 70 percent. The most popular variety today is the (nearly) seedless Marsh, which has a yellow rind and yellow fruit. Thompson (also called Pink Marsh) and Ruby are pink-fleshed varieties developed in Texas. Ripe grapefruit is full of juice and has an invigorating flavor that is both sweet and tart.

Use   A large part of the Florida crop is processed for juice. Fresh grapefruit is generally eaten raw—by the half or peeled and sectioned. Grapefruit sections make a tangy addition to fruit salads and compotes and to green salads. Grapefruit and avocado are a particularly harmonious combination for a salad. For a hot brunch offering or as dessert, grapefruit halves can be dusted with white or brown sugar, dotted with butter and sprinkled with rum, then glazed under a broiler. Chilled grapefruit juice is enjoyed on its own in the morning, in combination with rum or vodka as a cocktail, or in fruit punches.

Availability   Fresh grapefruit can be found all year, but quality is best and prices lowest in winter. Grapefruit sections are available canned. Grapefruit juice is sold canned, bottled, and frozen.

Selection   Pick grapefruit that feels heavy for its size. Avoid soft, puffy fruit with pointed ends. Varieties with smooth, thin skin and good weight will be juicier than those with rough, thick skin. Surface blemishes do not affect quality.

Storage   Keep grapefruit at cool room temperature for five or six days or refrigerate for several weeks.

Preparation   The flesh of the grapefruit is firmly attached to the rind. A serrated grapefruit knife makes sectioning easier. Halve the grapefruit and run the knife around the perimeter of each half. Then cut around each section to separate it from interior membranes. Grapefruit spoons with serrated edges eliminate the need to section the fruit with a knife.

One of the most elegant ways to serve boneless chicken breasts is in a wine-cream sauce with seedless grapes.

■ CHICKEN BREASTS WITH GRAPES

Boneless chicken breasts can be cooked in an almost limitless variety of quick, elegant ways. Accompany these chicken breasts with fluffy rice and a fruity white wine such as Chenin Blanc.

> 3   **whole chicken breasts (3 lb), halved, boned, and skinned**
>   **Salt and freshly grated nutmeg, as needed**
> 2   **tablespoons butter or margarine**
> 1   **tablespoon orange marmalade**
> ¼   **teaspoon dried tarragon**
> 1   **green onion, thinly sliced (use part of top)**
> ⅓   **cup dry white wine**
> 1   **cup seedless grapes**
> ¼   **cup whipping cream**

1. Sprinkle chicken breasts with salt and nutmeg. In a large frying pan, heat butter over medium-high heat and brown chicken lightly. Add marmalade, tarragon, green

■ AVOCADO, JICAMA, AND GRAPEFRUIT SALAD

Avocado and grapefruit are often paired for their contrasting, yet complementary, textures and flavors. Crisp, juicy jicama adds even more textural interest.

   1 **large** *or* **2 small avocados**
   2 **medium Ruby grapefruit**
   ½ **pound jicama**
   2 **tablespoons olive oil**
     Salt and freshly ground pepper, to taste

1. Peel avocado and cut into wedges. Peel grapefruit and cut fruit into sections, reserving juice. Peel jicama and slice it into thin wedges about the length of the avocado wedges.

2. Alternate pieces of avocado, grapefruit, and jicama in a circle on a round serving plate or on individual plates. Combine reserved grapefruit juice, olive oil, and salt and pepper to taste. Drizzle dressing over salad.

Serves 4.

> ***Recipes and Related Information***
> *Citrus Reamer, 131; Knife, 328.*

GRAPE LEAF

In early to mid-summer, when the grape leaves on the vine are large, green, and tender, they may be harvested for culinary use.

Use Fresh grape leaves should always be blanched or brined before using. Middle Eastern cooks blanch grape leaves, then stuff them with rice or a mixture of rice and meat, and roll them into cigar-shaped dolmas. In France, grape leaves are used to protect and flavor some small cheeses. The flavor of mushrooms is enhanced when cooked in a pot lined with grape leaves. Wrapping quail, goat cheese, and anchovies with grape leaves before grilling over coals or baking imparts a special flavor. Some cooks put grape leaves in the brine for cucumber pickles to make the pickles crisp.

Availability Fresh grape leaves are not generally sold commercially, but cooks who live near vineyards will probably find vineyard owners willing to part with some for personal use. Grape leaves bottled or canned in brine can be purchased at Middle Eastern markets and some well-stocked supermarkets.

Storage Refrigerate grape leaves in their brine in an airtight, nonmetal container; they will keep indefinitely.

Preparation Blanch or steam fresh grape leaves briefly just to soften. Rinse canned or bottled grape leaves before use to remove brine flavor. Be careful when removing grape leaves from bottle or jar; they tear easily.

■ STUFFED GRAPE LEAVES

Fresh mint, plenty of garlic, and a little feta cheese enliven these classic Greek dolmas. These are a perfect hors d'oeuvre because, if you like, they can be prepared up to one week ahead. Refrigerate them in their cooking liquid and bring to room temperature before serving.

   1 **jar (1 lb) grape leaves preserved in brine**
   ¼ **cup olive oil**
   1 **tablespoon butter**
   ⅓ **cup minced shallot**
   2 **tablespoons minced garlic**
   3 **cups cooked rice**
   ¼ **cup dried currants**
   2 **tablespoons golden raisins**
   ¼ **cup chopped fresh mint**
   ¼ **cup finely minced parsley**
   1 **teaspoon chopped fresh dill**
   2 **ounces crumbled feta cheese**
     Salt, pepper, and fresh lemon juice, to taste
   3 **to 4 cups hot Chicken Stock (see page 560)**
     Cucumber-Mint Sauce (see page 294)
     Lemon wedges, for accompaniment

1. Preheat oven to 350° F. Blanch grape leaves in boiling water 45 seconds to remove briny flavor; drain and refresh under cold running water. Drain well and pat dry.

2. In a small skillet heat oil and butter. Add shallots and garlic and sauté over moderate heat until soft and slightly colored. Transfer to a large mixing bowl and add rice, currants, raisins, mint, parsley, dill, feta, and salt, pepper, and lemon juice to taste. Toss well with a fork to blend.

3. Lay a grape leaf out flat; put about 1½ tablespoons filling near base of each leaf. Roll leaf into a cigar-shaped package, tucking in sides as you roll. Repeat with remaining leaves. Transfer leaves to a roasting pan large enough to hold them snugly. Cover with stock and poach in the oven, covered, for 20 minutes. Cool in stock. To serve, mound grape leaves on a platter and accompany with Cucumber-Mint Sauce and a bowl of lemon wedges.

Serves 15 to 20.

GRATE, TO; GRATER, SHREDDER, AND MILL

To reduce food to shreds, flakes, or tiny particles by rubbing against a grater or by processing in a food processor, blender, electric minichopper, clean coffee grinder, or other similar-acting device. Also the category of specialized equipment that changes the texture of raw or cooked foods—cheeses, vegetables, fruits, meats, herbs and spices, nuts—to smaller pieces, even as fine as a powder, purée, or paste.

Traditionally these are hand tools, often having evolved as a faster, more efficient alternative to the knife, or as a better way of working with very hard or very soft foods. To a degree, some of this equipment (graters and shredders, in particular) have been replaced by electric machines such as the blender, food processor, or electric minichopper; yet they still have a place in the kitchen for processing small amounts of food. They also have the advantage of being able to grate or shred a substance directly onto prepared food or into a serving or work bowl.

Hand-operated mills are slower than electric machines, a seeming drawback that actually affords more control over what is produced—ground nuts as opposed to nut butter, for instance—and again are good for small amounts. Furthermore, food mills act as sieves to trap skins and seeds, while allowing the flesh of cooked fruits and vegetables to pass through as a purée.

Grater versus shredder: Made with a rough surface punctured with round holes whose ragged edges scrape fingers as well as food, a grater creates fine crumbs when food is rubbed against it. It is used to crumble hard cheeses such as Parmesan, to remove small amounts of citrus rind, and sometimes to crumb stale bread. Graters are difficult to clean without a toothpick. Shredders have flat holes with a cutting edge on one side that creates strings or ribbons when food is dragged across the surface. Some of these devices have slits, rather than holes; depending on the width of the slit, the resulting pieces range from fine to coarse. Grating crushes food to some degree and releases moisture and oils from such substances as onions and citrus. Shredding isn't as rough a process. Even if a machine can do the job better or faster, cooks still enjoy using this basic hand tool when they want a more direct involvement with food preparation.

BASIC GRATER-SHREDDERS

These tools are available as a single flat sheet of metal or in a box shape. Both types have a grip at the top. The flat grater has either rough holes or flat slits of uniform size. Each side of the box grater is perforated for different functions: fine holes for grating cheese and spices, and scraping citrus rind; medium holes for shredding cheese and citrus rind, onion, chocolate, and vegetables; large holes for processing vegetables, fruits, and cheeses; and slots for slicing fruit, vegetables, and cheeses. Buy grater-shredders made of stainless steel because they do not rust.

CHEESE GRATER

Some cheese graters are the standard rasp-type set over a receptacle. When a brick of cheese is rubbed across the grating surface, the pieces drop into the container. Others are rotary devices, an improvement in design over the basic grater because your hands need only to turn a handle rather than scrape over the grating surface. The rotary grater is made of stainless steel or stainless steel and plastic and has a double handle. The lower handle ends in a hopper that holds whatever is to be grated—a small piece of cheese, some nuts, or chocolate. The upper handle has a curved plate that is pressed against the cheese and keeps it in contact with the grater. To operate, one hand presses together the upper and lower handles to enclose a grating drum within the hopper, while the other hand rotates a crank attached to the drum. The grater comes with fine and medium grating drums and one for slicing. It is very efficient for grating small amounts.

FOOD MILL

One step better than a sieve for making purées, a food mill uses a rotary system to push cooked fruits and vegetables against a perforated disk. Like a sieve, it traps skin and seeds, creating a smooth purée—a filtering process that food processors can do only when equipped with a special attachment, and which blenders can't do at all. French models have three sizes of disks and sloping sides; American versions have a single, fixed disk and straight sides. The 3-quart size is the most popular; a 5-quart model is available as well.

GARLIC PRESS

This tool operates on brute force—yours—and produces extremely pungent garlic pieces by crushing the garlic flesh as it is forced through the holes, releasing the greatest amount of volatile oils. Many cooks prefer to mince garlic by crushing the unpeeled clove with the side of a knife, slipping off the peel, then chopping. The press is convenient. It has a small perforated receptacle and a plunger. Cloves of garlic are put into the receptacle and pushed through the holes by the plunger when the handles are squeezed. Some are described as self-cleaning because they are designed to push out any bits of garlic stuck in the holes. Made of cast aluminum, garlic presses come in various capacities and with various sizes of openings. So many of these devices don't work that it's best to ask a retailer to recommend one.

GINGER GRATER

Made of either porcelain or bamboo, this flat grater has a rough surface composed of rows of spiky notches that effectively grab at the fibrous flesh of fresh ginger as it is rubbed against it. It works much better for this purpose than a fine rasp-style grater, and if you cook with ginger fairly often, a ginger grater should be part of your *batterie de cuisine.* It is available at Asian markets and well-stocked cookware stores.

LEMON GRATER

Essentially a handheld version of a basic fine grater, this type is either curved or flat and is useful for grating small amounts of rind or cheese.

Graters, shredders, and mills are tools that change the texture of foods. Shown left to right, beginning with upper row: box grater, clamp-on rotary meat grinder, meat pounder, tomato press, nutmeg mill, salt and pepper mills, nut mill, food mill, garlic press, suction-bottom salad shredder, mortar and pestle, potato ricer, parsley mincer, ginger grater, nutmeg grater, cheese graters.

MEAT GRINDER

Although it has in part been replaced by the more practical and multifunctional food processor, the meat grinder is still preferred by some cooks for the consistency of the product it produces and its capacity for continuous operation. It grinds meat—fat and muscle—by forcing the food through steel blades and a perforated disk sized to produce coarse or fine pieces. Meat grinders are used to custom blend home-ground meats, poultry, and fish, and to prepare blends for pâtés, forcemeats, and sausages.

Three models are most commonly available and all work by rotary action, either hand-cranked or electrically powered: a clamp-on type that fixes to a kitchen counter or work table, one that is held in place by suction, and a third, freestanding, footed, commercial design. Larger capacity machines are more powerful and more efficient, producing more product per minute than smaller types. The best ones are made of cast iron, with steel blades, and come with a coarse and fine disk. The blades are very susceptible to rusting, and must be dried well and oiled after each use. A sausage-stuffing horn is optional for some models. Some heavy-duty mixers have meat-grinding attachments.

MEAT POUNDER

The primary purpose of this pestle with a flat base is to flatten fillets of meat and poultry so that they cook faster and more evenly. Pounders also tenderize by breaking down tough muscle fibers and do a good job crushing crackers and cookies for crumbs. Weight is important; the best ones are solid brass. Meat pounders are also made of stainless steel. Wooden versions (*champignons*, French for mushrooms) are used to purée cooked fruits and vegetables by rubbing them through a sieve. Some pounding mallets with square heads have one waffled surface for tenderizing.

MORTAR AND PESTLE

This simple pounder and bowl is a link to the earliest grinding tools used by mankind. For thousands of years, cooks have relied on these basic implements for crushing herbs, spices, and seeds, and grinding aromatic ingredients into seasoning pastes. The container is called a mortar, a name that evolved from the Greek word for wasting away—a reference to the breaking down of food as it is crushed. The pounding tool is the pestle. Although electric choppers and grinders make faster work of many of the tasks formerly performed by mortar and pestle, it is still an efficient—and satisfyingly hands-on—way to crush small amounts of herbs and spices and to mash garlic and cooked beans into a paste. Dried herbs should always be crushed or crumbled to release flavorful oils before using. Southeast Asian cooks insist that a curry paste pounded in a mortar is far superior in texture and flavor to one produced by machine.

Mortars and pestles come in many sizes and materials. Use small ones for herbs and spices, larger ones (1½ cups and more) for pastes. They are made of ceramic, stone, wood, or metal. To work, both inside of mortar and pounding end of pestle must be rough-textured and unglazed.

NUTMEG GRATERS AND MILLS

Because the perfume and flavor of most packaged spices fade quickly, and because you're never quite sure how long a spice has been sitting on the shelf before you buy it, it pays to buy whole spices and grind them yourself. If you've never encountered freshly ground nutmeg (or cinnamon), you'll be amazed at its intensity. Special tinned steel nutmeg graters, tapered in shaped, have one curved, grating side with the surface of a rasp and a second side that is flat. Some have a compartment at the top to hold a whole nutmeg. Nutmeg mills resemble wooden pepper mills. To operate, a whole nutmeg is inserted in the bottom. When the handle fastened to the top of the mill is rotated, the nutmeg is pressed against a cutting blade, producing a shower of ground spice.

NUT MILL

For a powdery sprinkling of nuts over a pastry or mousse, the rotary cheese mill is fine, but for the cup or more needed for tortes and nut crusts, consider using a nut mill. With an electric device, nuts can quickly pass from powder to butter because the action is so fast. A hand-operated mill affords more control. The rotary mill clamps to the countertop and feeds nut powder into a bowl you place under it. It functions almost identically to the cheese grater, except that a wooden pusher, rather than a curved plate, is used to keep nuts in contact with the grating surface. Very particular pastry cooks like this device because they think it does the best job and releases less oil than a food processor. Today, however, most cooks use a food processor for grinding nuts.

PARSLEY MINCER

For a few spoonfuls of fresh parsley, chives, basil, or other herbs, use a chef's knife or an electric minichopper. If you have room for storage, consider this specialty chopper. Made of stainless steel or plastic, it consists of a handle with a hopper at one end, which sits over rows of sharp teeth; the herb is minced as it passes through the hopper.

PEPPER MILL, SALT MILL

More and more recipes specify freshly ground pepper, black or white. As with all spices, when you grind your own peppercorns the flavor is fuller and richer. Look for a mill that is adjustable, permitting a range from fine to coarse grind. It should also be easy to load, work smoothly, and feel comfortable in your hand.

Salt mills are essentially the same as pepper mills and are used for grinding rock salt. Be sure to buy one with a hard plastic mechanism; metal will corrode.

POTATO RICER

Cooks dedicated to the potato ricer claim that this old-fashioned tool produces the best mashed potatoes. It resembles an oversized stainless steel garlic press, with a 3- to 4-inch basket. To use, set pieces of boiled potatoes in the basket, and squeeze to force out the potato in strands. All you have to do is mix the riced vegetable with butter, cream, and seasonings, and stir with a fork.

SALAD SHREDDER

A simple, basic device, the salad shredder appeals to afficionados of hand tools as an alternative to the food processor. It sits on the counter and has interchangeable disks that shred and grate. It is like a turtle when compared with electric kitchen machines, but affords more control and won't take away your skin as a rasp-type grater-shredder often does.

SALT MILL

See Pepper Mill.

SPICE GRINDER

Although some recipes refer to a spice grinder, implying that it is a particular tool, the term is a catchall for a number of crushing and grinding devices rather than a commonly available piece of equipment. Hand-operated or electric coffee grinders and electric minichoppers are considered spice grinders, as are traditional tools such as mortars and pestles and specialty tools such as nutmeg graters and mills, and pepper and salt mills.

TOMATO PRESS

When you've harvested your tomato crop and it's time to make tomato sauce in grand amounts, you'll appreciate the virtues of this hand-operated machine. It separates pulp and juice from hard-to-digest skin and bitter seeds in one operation and sends them through different openings into bowls that you provide. Also use it to core and seed apples. It has a cast aluminum body and plastic funnel and spout. For support, the device can either clamp to the edge of a counter or fasten to a work surface with suction. Consider one if you prepare tomatoes for cooking in quantity; otherwise the same results can be accomplished with a wire-mesh strainer or food mill. Be sure that the model you choose seals well, or your counter will be dripping with juice leaking from the machine.

GRATIN

This dish has a charactcristic crisp, golden brown crust developed by browning it in the oven or under the broiler just prior to serving. Typically the crust is composed of seasoned bread crumbs, grated cheese, or a white sauce. It is this crust that characterizes a gratin, not the food beneath it. Au gratin refers to food prepared as a gratin.

> **Recipes and Related Information**
> Broccoli Gratin, 61; Casseroles and Baking Dishes, 105.

GREASE, TO; GREASE AND FLOUR, TO

To coat with butter, solid vegetable shortening, or oil; for baking pans, to coat with grease and then to dust lightly with flour.

> **Recipes and Related Information**
> Cake, 79; Preparing Pan for Baking, 478.

GREEN ONION

Also known as scallion or bunching onion, the green onion is a young bulb onion harvested before it has formed a bulb. When harvested, green onions are generally about ¼ inch wide and are trimmed to about 10 inches in length for the commercial market. The stalks are white at the root end, shading to dark green leaves. Green onions have a mild onion flavor and a crisp texture.

Use Green onions are used wherever a mild onion flavor is desirable. They are often minced and added raw to salads, or sautéed and mixed into soups, stews, and vegetable dishes. Neatly trimmed whole green onions may be offered as part of a relish tray or antipasto platter. Green onions, along with ginger and garlic, are major aromatic ingredients in Chinese cooking. Lengths of green onion are used in Chinese stir-fries or to flavor steamed fish and shellfish; minced green onion garnishes Chinese soups. Brushes made by fringing the ends of a length of green onion are used to apply *hoisin* sauce to pancakes for Peking duck (see GARNISH, Fan).

Availability Fresh green onions are found the year around in supermarkets. They are almost always sold in small bunches, usually with clipped tops.

Selection Choose fresh-looking bunches.

Storage They will keep up to one week in a plastic bag in the refrigerator.

Preparation Trim hairy root end. Most Western recipes call for using only the white part; save the green leaves for stock. Many Chinese recipes call for both white and green parts.

■ GREEN ONIONS IN SILKY BEEF

These beef-wrapped green-onion rolls are featured at most Japanese *robata* restaurants—restaurants that specialize in simple charcoal grilling. In this recipe they are quickly sautéed in a skillet. A soy-based marinade tenderizes and flavors the beef; the green-onion center adds a pungent accent. Note that the rolls must marinate 1 hour or overnight.

> 1 pound very lean beef
> 2 dozen green onions
> ¼ cup soy sauce
> ¼ cup sugar
> ¼ cup peanut or corn oil
> 2 tablespoons rice wine
> 2 tablespoons water
> 1 tablespoon sesame seed, for garnish

1. Slice beef into thin strips about 5 inches long and 1½ inches wide. You should have about 18 strips.

2. Trim and clean green onions. Cut 18 green onions into 4-inch lengths, discarding green tops. Slice remaining green onions into thin rings; reserve for garnish.

3. Lay one 4-inch length of green onion in the center of each strip of meat, parallel to the 5-inch side. Roll meat around onion and secure with a toothpick. In a stainless steel, glass, or ceramic bowl, combine soy sauce, sugar, 2 tablespoons oil, wine, and the water. Pour marinade over green-onion rolls; cover and let marinate at least 1 hour at room temperature or refrigerate overnight.

4. Bring rolls to room temperature if necessary. Drain, reserving marinade. In a heavy skillet heat remaining oil over high heat. Add green-onion rolls and brown quickly all over, in stages if necessary to prevent crowding. Add the reserved marinade and continue cooking rapidly about 3 minutes.

5. Remove rolls to a cutting board and cut each one in half. Arrange on a serving platter and serve hot, garnished with chopped green onions and sesame seed.

Makes about 3 dozen small rolls.

> **Recipes and Related Information**
> Onion, 399; Watercress Dip With Green Onion and Basil, 521.

Greens sautéed with onions and bacon are standard southern fare, here paired with puffs of mashed potatoes and pork chops smothered with onions.

GREENS (POTHERBS)

Many of the sturdier leafy greens are also known as potherbs; although they may be eaten raw in salads when young and tender, these herbaceous plants most often end up in a pot with salt pork or a ham bone. They are delicate when young but are rarely marketed at that stage. The older, tougher leaves are too strong in flavor to eat raw, but boiling or stewing tenderizes and tames them.

Also see BEET, BROCCOLI RAAB, KALE, and SORREL. Other major potherbs are described below.

Use   In the American South, potherbs are traditionally boiled with smoked pork or fatback. In Italy, greens such as Swiss chard and broccoli raab are cooked in olive oil with garlic and served hot with pork, or seasoned with wine vinegar and eaten lukewarm as a salad. In Ethiopia, stewed collard greens are served with buttermilk curds as a traditional side dish for Ethiopian stews. Cooked kale or collard greens are traditional accompaniments to the Brazilian national dish, *feijoada completa.* Wilted greens also make a hearty addition to bean soups and minestrone. Stewed greens are particularly good with pork in any form, whether a single green cooked alone or a mixture of several. Most of these greens substitute well for each other, although they differ in the intensity of their flavor.

Availability   Many greens are sold inexpensively in supermarkets all year; peak availability is October through April.

Selection   Look for crisp greens with bright color; avoid those with woody stems or wilted, yellowed, or bruised leaves. Small leaves with thin stems are milder and more tender.

Store   Keep greens unwashed in a plastic bag in the refrigerator crisper. Greens are best and most nutritious when eaten immediately but will stay fresh for two to three days.

Preparation   Before use, wash greens well, in several changes of water if necessary. Discard any bruised or wilted leaves. If stems are woody or thick, they should be either peeled or cut away (and may be cooked separately). Cook small leaves whole; cut up large leaves.

Cooking   See BOIL, BRAISE, SAUTE, STEAM, STIR-FRY.

COLLARD GREENS

Like kale, collard greens are a member of the cabbage family. The dark green leaves strongly resemble kale, but they are flat and smooth, not crinkled.

DANDELION GREENS

Dark green, long and slender, dandelion leaves are less than 1 inch wide. When young, they are tender and delicate and are delicious in salads, especially with a hot bacon dressing. The leaves become bitter with age and must be cooked to mellow their flavor.

MUSTARD GREENS

These have a slightly fuzzy texture and may be flat or frilled at the edges. They are bright green and quite pungent, even when young. The spicy, bitter quality develops with age and only the youngest, handpicked leaves are likely to be suitable for eating raw.

SWISS CHARD

Both white- and red-ribbed varieties are available, with little discernible difference in taste. The ribs are wide, the leaves flat and deep green. Because ribs take longer to cook, they are trimmed away and cooked separately. The leaves are often cooked, then combined with the cooked stems just before serving. Chard is among the milder greens, stronger in flavor and sturdier in texture than spinach but milder than mustard, dandelion, and turnip greens. Italian cooks add it to soups; braise and serve it with oil and lemon; stuff the ribs with bread crumbs and deep-fry; and use as filling for ravioli.

TURNIP GREENS

Unless very young, strong-flavored turnip greens must be cooked to tame their taste. The dark green leaves are flat and smooth, with a narrow but often tough central rib. To mute their strong flavor, turnip greens can be cooked with other, milder greens or blanched before stewing.

■ COUNTRY-STYLE GREENS

Contrary to rumor, greens do not need hours of boiling in a sea of liquid, as this Mississippi recipe proves. What they do need, however, is the flavor of smoked slab bacon or ham. If you must substitute ordinary bacon or ham, you'll need twice as much. Greens are the traditional southern accompaniment to pork or ham; they also pair well with corn bread or candied yams.

> 2 **bunches fresh collard, turnip, or mustard greens**
> 1 **tablespoon lard or rendered bacon fat**
> 1 **medium onion, minced**
> ¼ **pound good-quality smoked slab bacon or smoked ham, cut in ½-inch dice** *or*
> ½ **pound ordinary sliced bacon or ham**
> 2 **cups water**
> **Salt and freshly ground pepper, to taste**
> **Dash of Louisiana-style hot sauce**

1. Trim away and discard tough stems of greens. To loosen grit, place leaves and remaining tender stems (you should have about 2 quarts) in a large bowl, cover with lukewarm water, and soak for 5 minutes. Rinse several times in lukewarm water to wash away any remaining sand.

2. Melt lard in a large, heavy, nonreactive pot with a lid. (Do not use an aluminum pot; if possible, use one with an enamel coating.) Add onions and bacon. Fry together over medium-high heat, stirring often, until onions wilt and bacon starts to brown (about 5 minutes).

3. Add greens and the water and bring to a boil over high heat. Cover, lower heat to medium, and cook until greens are tender, with just a little crunch (about 20 minutes).

4. Uncover, raise heat to high, and boil off some of the excess water (about 5 minutes). Season with salt, pepper, and hot sauce to taste, and serve hot (dish should be slightly soupy).

Serves 6.

GRILL, TO

To cook food on a *grill,* a grid of metal bars set over a heat source—charcoal, wood, gas, or electricity.

Grilled food is cooked by radiant heat (see RADIANT ENERGY) and direct contact. Rays of heat warm the outer surface and then, by conduction, move through the food's interior mass. Open-fire cookery may appear simple, but to be successful it requires constant attention. Starting the fire, maintaining an even temperature, achieving the correct distance from the heat, knowing when food is done, avoiding sudden flare-ups—all must be considered and understood.

GRILL VERSUS BARBECUE

The terms *grill* and *barbecue* are often used interchangeably for this cooking technique. Barbecue has, perhaps, a more informal connotation, redolent of casual entertaining and down-home cooking. Purists and the U.S. Department of Agriculture, however, consider only foods cooked by direct heat over wood or charcoal real barbecue.

Barbecue also refers to a type of food, which is an American institution, with strong roots in many different regions of the country. As varied as the different styles of barbecue are, they all share several common traits: Barbecue is the art of slowly cooking large pieces of meat over a smoky, cool (about 225° F) fire. Most barbecue is served with a tangy sauce at the table to moisten and flavor the meat. Each area has its own version, varying from a simple and pure North Carolina sauce made of cider vinegar and crushed red chiles to the spicy, vegetable-laden tomato sauces of the Southwest.

How does barbecue differ from grilled food? Barbecue has a distinctive smoky flavor and is served with a vinegar-based tangy sauce. Grilled food also has a smoky flavor, but is served plain or with one or more of a number of sauces. In general, grilled food is cooked quicker and is much more varied in style and taste.

TOOLS AND EQUIPMENT

Equipment for outdoor cooking is a matter of personal preference, available space, and frequency of use. Following are those tools that are most common.

GAS GRILL

On the market is a new generation of gas grills with sophisticated heat circulation and control. Versions with either lava rock or porcelain-coated metal bars both serve the same function, evenly emanating heat from the gas burners below and vaporizing drippings from the food above. Their primary assets are that the cook can control cooking temperature through (usually) three gas burners, which permit heat regulation to whatever temperature is required, and they are very easy to use. A major drawback of gas grills is their inability to give food a smoky flavor.

KETTLE-SHAPED GRILL

These grills are designed for cooking with the lid closed. Carefully located vents in the top and bottom provide air flow to keep the fire going while completely eliminating flare-ups. Thus, searing over a very hot fire can easily be accomplished without burning the food. If the coals are moved to each side of the kettle and a drip pan positioned in the center, food can also be cooked more slowly with the indirect-heat method of cooking. The two major drawbacks are the lack of hinged lids, which creates awkward juggling of equipment each time you open and close the grill, and the fixed grill position.

OPEN GRILL

These are not as easy to use as kettle-shaped grills, but are often less expensive. Since this type does not have a lid, the cook is likely to experience flare-ups during cooking. The best way to handle this is to use an open grill only for foods that don't have an oil-based marinade or are low in fat, such as fish or poultry. You can't use the indirect-heat method of cooking very well on an open grill because most of the heat diffuses in the air.

RECTANGULAR HINGED GRILL

Rectangular grills have the advantage of heat control because the grill can be raised or lowered. Briquettes, hardwood chips, or moistened fresh herbs can be added to the fire more easily than when using a kettle-shaped grill. A hinged lid makes opening and closing much easier. But, when it comes to heat control and evenness of cooking, kettle-shaped grills are better. The rectangular grill simply doesn't have the good heat circulation that a kettle-shaped grill does, and flare-ups are harder to control.

OTHER EQUIPMENT

Whether cooking in the kitchen or on the patio, your equipment should be close at hand and well organized. The following is considered basic for grilling.

Basting Brush   An inexpensive, twisted-wire brush works just as well as the more costly wooden-handled versions. The brush should have a long handle to keep the cook back from the fire while basting.

Charcoal Rails   Use charcoal rails to hold charcoal in even piles on each side of the drip pan for the indirect-heat method of cooking. Because the sides of the drip pan adequately perform the same function, charcoal rails are optional.

Drip Pans   These are essential for the indirect-heat method of cooking. Purchase disposable rectangular aluminum ones, 2 to 3 inches deep; because they are almost impossible to clean, they are usually used only once.

Grill Brush   There is less chance that food will stick to a clean grill. Scrub grill after each use with a special wire brush, available in hardware stores and supermarkets.

Instant-Read Thermometer   Internal temperature is an extremely accurate measure of doneness for many foods. An instant-read thermometer, well-suited for the fast pace of grill cooking, will give a very accurate reading within seconds of insertion.

Long-Handled Fork   Although long-handled forks are not recommended for turning foods (punctures will cause valuable juices to ooze out), they are very handy for removing large roasts from the fire, or for piercing food to check for doneness by looking at the color of the juices.

Mitts   Heavy-duty fireproof mitts are invaluable to protect the cook against unexpected fires. Find a pair that covers forearms as well as hands.

Roast Racks   Made of aluminum or stainless steel, V-shaped roast racks do an excellent job of holding large pieces of meat or poultry during cooking. If used with the indirect-heat method of cooking, the meat needn't be turned to cook evenly on all sides.

Skewers   Both metal and bamboo skewers are available. Metal ones can be used repeatedly; those made of bamboo are meant to be discarded after one use. Bamboo skewers need to be soaked 15 to 30 minutes so they won't flame (although even presoaked ones sometimes burn at the ends over very hot fires). If you have rosemary in your garden, strip away the needles, soak the branches for 30 minutes, and use as skewers; they imbue food with a wonderful rosemary flavor.

Spatula   Use an offset (angled-neck) stainless steel spatula with a blade that is 5 to 6 inches long. This blade will slide completely under most chops and fish fillets, preventing them from tearing and sticking to grill. Stainless steel won't rust and is easy to care for.

Spray Bottle   Always keep a spray bottle filled with water next to the grill to douse flare-ups.

Tongs   Perhaps the most useful grill tool, tongs should be at least 12 inches long and spring loaded. It's best to have two pairs—one for handling food and the other for moving hot briquettes. Tongs are preferred over long-handled forks because they don't puncture food (and allow natural juices to escape).

Wire-Hinged Baskets   These wire baskets will hold fish fillets, meat, hamburger patties, or even bread for toast between two hinged grills secured by a latch. The grills should be lightly oiled before food is set on them.

FUELS AND FRAGRANCES

Traditional hardwood briquettes now share shelf space with many other fuels. They all work well in the right situation; which fuel to use is a matter of personal preference. Many are available at well-stocked supermarkets, hardware stores, cookware stores, or can be ordered by mail through selected catalogs.

CHARCOAL BRIQUETTES

Briquettes are made from wood chips smoldered into carbon, then bound together with fillers and starch, and pressed into a uniform shape. Some brands add petroleum products to make "self-lighting" briquettes. A charcoal briquette fire is ready when the coals are completely coated with a thin layer of gray ash; at this point all of the additives have burned off. Briquettes burn evenly and consistently.

FRESH HERBS AND FRUIT RINDS

Thyme, bay, rosemary, oregano, and marjoram impart a pleasant flavor when added to the fire. Moisten fresh herbs with water (or wine or liquor) and toss them onto the coals just before the food goes on the grill. Lemon, orange, or lime rinds are other choices. Do not directly inhale the fumes of burning herbs or fruit rinds; they can be very powerful.

HARDWOOD CHARCOAL

Though not nearly as prevalent as mesquite charcoal, other hardwoods are carbonized in the same manner as mesquite into an excellent fuel. They impart a smokier flavor to food than does mesquite, but they are more costly and don't burn as hot. Using mesquite as the fuel and adding presoaked hardwood chunks as the smoke source work well.

HARDWOOD CHUNKS AND SAWDUST

Hardwood adds a unique smoky flavor to food cooked over it. Hickory, alder, mesquite, and apple wood are the most popular and available woods. For gas grills, hardwood chips work better than chunks. Use wood pieces ½ to 1 inch thick. Soak pieces in water at least 30 minutes before using. Place an old aluminum pie plate over the gas heating elements toward the back corner of the grill before turning the grill on. As the grill gets hotter, the chips will begin to smolder. With very high heat, the chips may flare up; have a spray bottle filled with water nearby.

MESQUITE CHARCOAL

Made from a Mexican hardwood, mesquite charcoal contains no additives or fillers of any kind. It burns very hot, perhaps twice as hot as charcoal briquettes and most other hardwood charcoals. This means you can use less of it and can cook at a higher temperature, which produces a tastier product. It imparts a subtle, natural flavor, which is not nearly as pronounced as fruitwoods, oak, or hickory. Mesquite coals can be used two or even three times before they need to be replaced. However, mesquite can be difficult to start, and can also emit burning embers into the air. Be careful, especially when windy outside, to avoid sending embers toward nearby trees or structures.

WOOD

You can use oak, hickory, cherry, apple wood, mesquite, or alder wood for outdoor cooking. But wood takes a very long time to burn down to usable coals and the coals are short-lived. A better use of these woods is as kindling; cut the remaining larger pieces into 1-inch chunks to add a smoky complement to your fire (see Hardwood Chunks and Sawdust, left). Never use softwood for either smoking or as a fuel. Their thick resins produce a distinctly unpleasant aftertaste. Be careful of burning any scrap wood. For instance, pressure-treated lumber (used in outdoor construction) contains chemicals that can be toxic.

The outdoor chef has many options when selecting equipment for grilling. Shown clockwise from upper left: open grill; wire-hinged basket (with hamburgers); charcoal and briquettes; charcoal chimney; kettle grill with cover; long-handled spatula, knife, and fork; aluminum drip pan; grill brush; rectangular hinged grill; basting brush; spray bottle; wire-bristle grill brush; portable gas grill; long-handled tongs.

TIPS

HOW MUCH FIRE? WHEN IS IT READY?

When determining the size of your fire, first envision the cooking surface your food will require. Spread briquettes in a single layer to an area about 1 inch past the edges of your imaginary boundaries. Adding about half again as much charcoal should provide enough for one hour's worth of fire. Usually 30 to 40 briquettes is sufficient for food for four people. If making a fire for slow cooking by the indirect-heat method, use about 25 briquettes on each side of the charcoal area, placing no charcoal directly beneath the food. Plan on adding 8 to 10 briquettes to each side per hour of additional cooking time.

A fire usually burns between 30 and 45 minutes before it is ready to be cooked over. Wait until the briquettes are covered with a light ash and are no longer flaming. Cooking over a direct flame will burn the outside of the food and leave the inside raw. Hold your hand flat over the fire at grill height. With a very hot fire, you will be able to hold your hand there for about 2 seconds; for a hot fire, about 3 to 4 seconds. If you can keep it there any longer than that, the fire has died down too much. Once the fire is ready, oil the grill and set in place to heat up for a few minutes before adding food.

STARTING THE FIRE

Whatever method you use, allow about 30 to 45 minutes for your fire to start. Have equipment and food ready.

CHARCOAL CHIMNEY

A very simple device, the charcoal chimney is an open-ended sheet-metal cylinder vented in the bottom, with a grate to hold the charcoal about 4 inches from the bottom. To use, fill chimney with charcoal, which is ignited from burning newspaper set under the grate. The coals will begin to smolder within 10 minutes; when they are ready, pour out of chimney into bottom of grill.

ELECTRIC STARTER

Check manufacturer's directions for starting a fire with an electric starter in your grill. In most cases, arrange briquettes in a pile on top of starter. Plug in starter and let it heat up. The briquettes should catch in about 10 minutes.

KINDLING

Although there are many personal styles of starting a fire with kindling, the basic method is to begin with newspaper sheets loosely crumpled or twisted into logs. Place paper logs in bottom of grill and top with a handful of dry kindling. Top with 5 or 6 briquettes and light the newspaper. If the briquettes don't light, keep adding paper and kindling until they do. Once the briquettes light, cover with more briquettes until all have caught.

LIGHTER FLUID

Follow all the manufacturer's safety precautions when using lighter fluid. Never squirt fluid directly onto a burning fire. The flame can easily travel back up the stream and ignite hand and arm. Also, never use gasoline, naphtha, paint thinner, or kerosene; they are difficult to control. Use only a product specifically labeled as lighter fluid.

PREPARING THE GRILL

Arrange the fire so that some areas of the grill do not have fire under them. If some of the foods are done more quickly than others, they can be moved to these cooler spots to keep warm while the remainder finish cooking. Also remember the following.

- Keep the grill clean. Use a wire grill brush to scrub off burned bits immediately after removing food from the grill; this avoids using soap and water, which will ruin the built-up seasoning on the grill.

- Have all tools ready and available before lighting the fire. Tongs, mitts, and a spray bottle are particularly important to have on hand. If barbecue tools are stored together in a portable bin or basket, they can be easily transported to the grill site.

- Have extra charcoal available in case the fire starts to die before the food is completely cooked.

GRILL COOKING METHODS

With the advent of covered grills, foods can be slowly cooked over indirect heat so that they become tender and stay moist during cooking. Depending on the type of food to be grilled and the desired result, grilling can be done over direct or indirect heat.

DIRECT-HEAT METHOD

Use the direct-heat method to sear foods to seal in their natural juices and to give a characteristic grilled look. For this method choose foods that are low in fat, such as poultry and fish, or that are quick-cooking—hamburgers, chops, skewered foods, vegetables, and fish fillets.

If using charcoal briquettes, start fire as described at left. When coals are covered with a light gray ash (after about 30 minutes), spread in a single layer. Place oiled grill over coals and let it heat 4 to 5 minutes. If you are using hardwood chips or chunks, spread them over coals just before cooking. They will immediately begin to smolder and smoke.

If using a kettle-shaped grill, keep lid closed for duration of cooking time; regulate heat by adjusting upper and lower vents. Lift lid only to turn the food.

If using a gas grill, turn on all three burners to high and close lid; grill should be ready in about 10 minutes. Leave burners on high, or turn one or more down, depending on the food being cooked and the desired effect.

INDIRECT-HEAT METHOD

With this method, you can now cook foods on the grill that were impossible to do even 10 years ago. Whole prime ribs, turkeys, and chickens will cook beautifully, without turning. Smaller cuts may need to be turned for even coloration and grill marks.

If using charcoal briquettes with a kettle-shaped grill, start fire as described at left. When coals are covered with a light gray ash, separate them into two piles on either side of the kettle. Place a disposable aluminum drip pan between the piles. If using hardwood chips or chunks or moistened fresh herbs, add them to the piles now. Put oiled grill in place and let it heat 4 to 5 minutes. Set food on grill directly over drip pan, close lid, and regulate temperature by adjusting the upper and lower vents. To first sear food, set directly over one pile of coals until browned, then move over drip pan.

If using a gas grill, preheat grill with all three burners on high. The grill will be ready in about 10 minutes. Turn off center burner and position disposable aluminum drip pan over it. Place oiled grill in position and let it heat 4 to 5 minutes. Set food on grill directly over drip pan; close lid and cook. Regulate temperature by adjusting the two outer burners. For a smoky complement using hardwood chips, see page 289. If using moistened fresh herbs, toss them directly onto the outside porcelain bars. These grills operate most efficiently when lid is closed. Open lid only to check on or to baste food, or to add more chips or herbs.

WHAT TO GRILL

We probably discovered by accident that fire made our food taste better. One can imagine a piece of raw meat or dry grain falling into a fire and the discovery upon its retrieval that its appearance had changed—and so had its flavor. With time, humans learned that if the meat was held a short distance from the fire, it cooked more evenly and was more digestible.

Through trial and error we not only learned techniques of open-fire cookery—how far the food should be from the flame to cook evenly and how long different foods need to cook completely—but also which foods taste best when prepared this way.

GRILLING FISH

Most fish have little internal fat to keep them moist during cooking. Care must be taken to ensure that they do not dry out on the grill. Marinades are usually unnecessary for fish. Be sure to lightly oil the grill to keep the delicate flesh of the fish from sticking to it. Avoid moving the fish too much and turn only once; excess movement will break the flesh apart. The best test for doneness is to press the flesh with your finger: Raw flesh is relatively soft and springy; properly cooked, the flesh is just firm; when overdone, it is hard and firm.

GRILLING MEATS

Most tender cuts of beef can be grilled directly over high heat. They can be cooked without a marinade, although one can be used for extra flavor. Less tender cuts should marinate to tenderize or should be grilled using the direct-heat method. Use the hand test (see When Is It Done? at right) as the best guide for doneness. A leg of lamb should marinate before grilling; lamb chops don't need further tenderizing. For skewered lamb dishes, use chunks cut from the shoulder or leg; be sure to marinate them for a tender and flavorful kabob. Pork has a tender, sweet flesh that accepts marinades beautifully, and its high internal fat content keeps the meat moist as it grills. Most cuts of pork can cook over direct heat; however, large roasts and heavily marinated cuts may cause flare-ups.

GRILLING POULTRY

Chicken is one of the most versatile foods for grilling. It accepts almost any marinade or sauce with beautiful results. Avoid boneless cuts, which tend to dry out quickly, unless skewering meat. For most recipes, use fresh fryers or broilers weighing between 3 and 4 pounds, well-sized to grill over direct heat if split. For larger birds, or to grill a whole bird, use the indirect-heat method. Poultry is done when a meat thermometer inserted in the thickest part reads 170° F, or when juices appear just slightly pink when skin is pierced. Game hens grill well also; flavor them as you would a chicken, and grill them using the direct-heat method of cooking.

GRILLING VEGETABLES

Like fish and poultry, vegetables have no way of staying moist when exposed to the high heat of a grill. They should be brushed with oil, and can be seasoned with fresh herbs or garlic. If cooked with other foods on a skewer, cut vegetables so that they will be done in the same amount of time as the other ingredients. Squash and eggplant are particularly good if sliced and grilled. Tomato, bell pepper, onion, and mushrooms are traditionally cooked on skewers. Consider blanching longer-cooking vegetables, such as carrots, before grilling so that they need less time to cook.

■ SANTA MARIA BARBECUED BEEF

The Santa Maria Valley on California's central coast has a tradition of outdoor barbecues going back to the early Spanish *rancheros*. Valley cooks have evolved a particular style—simply seasoned slabs of beef cooked over oak fires and served with a fresh tomato salsa and ham- and chile-flavored barbecue beans. (The locals insist on the pinquito bean, a small pink bean grown only in the Santa Maria Valley.) A 3-inch-thick top sirloin steak is the preferred cut of beef for a Santa Maria barbecue, but also suitable are the whole triangle tip and other small roasts from the sirloin tip. You might serve the barbecued beef with either Frijoles or Texas Jalapeño Pinto Beans (see page 35).

> 1 large sirloin steak or small roast (about 3 lb)
> 1 teaspoon *each* salt and garlic salt
> ½ teaspoon freshly ground pepper
> 1 cup Salsa Cruda (see page 521)

1. Trim meat of excess fat and tough membranes. If using a sirloin-tip roast, remove strings and butterfly (cut across grain almost through, then open like a book). Overall thickness should be 2½ to 3 inches. Combine salt, garlic salt, and pepper; rub generously all over meat. Set aside to season at room temperature for up to 2 hours, or longer in the refrigerator.

2. Two to three hours ahead of serving: Build a fire of oak or other hardwood, then allow fire to burn down to red-hot coals. Or, build a charcoal fire 1½ hours ahead and, when most of the charcoal is burning, add small chunks of oak. Sear meat over hottest part of fire, then move to a slightly cooler part and cook to taste. Total cooking time depends on size of meat, heat of fire, and type of grill (open or covered); thinner cuts over a hot fire may be medium-rare in 8 to 10 minutes per side, but with a cooler fire or a larger piece of meat allow 15 to 20 minutes per side.

3. Carve thin slices of meat on a cutting board with grooves to catch juices. Transfer slices to a warm platter and moisten with juices. Garnish with salsa; serve immediately.

Serves 6.

■ SINGAPORE SATAY

The flavor of Asian *satay*s is gained from their exotic marinades, and from rapid cooking that chars the glaze. The meat, cut small, is threaded on thin bamboo skewers (these are available from Asian groceries and souvenir shops, from cookware stores and well-stocked supermarkets). Thin metal skewers (or even lengths of metal wire) can also be used.

> 1 pound tender beef or lamb
> 4 small red onions, chopped (about 3 cups)
> 2 large cloves garlic, chopped (about 2 tablespoons)
> 3 stalks fresh lemon grass, chopped, *or*
>   1 tablespoon fresh lemon juice
> 1 teaspoon ground cumin
> 1 teaspoon ground ginger
> 1 tablespoon turmeric
> ½ teaspoon freshly ground pepper
> ½ teaspoon salt
> 1½ teaspoons brown sugar
> 3 tablespoons soy sauce
>   (preferably Chinese thin soy)
>   Peanut or corn oil, as needed

1. Cut meat into 1-inch cubes, carefully trimming away all fat and gristle. Place in a nonreactive container.

2. Purée remaining ingredients, except oil, in a blender or food processor and pour over meat. Marinate meat at least 3 hours at room temperature or overnight in refrigerator.

3. Soak bamboo skewers in water for at least 30 minutes. Thread meat cubes on skewers; reserve any unabsorbed marinade. Place oiled grill close to heat source over a wood fire or over a charcoal fire with wood chips scattered on top, and cook rapidly, turning and basting frequently with reserved marinade (or oil).

Serves 4 as an appetizer, 2 as an entrée.

■ FAJITAS

Fajitas are the strips of marinated and grilled skirt steak that give this popular southwestern dish its name. Note that the steak must marinate in the oil–lime juice mixture at least one day.

> 1½ pounds skirt steak, trimmed
> ¼ cup olive or peanut oil
>   Juice of 2 limes
> 1 tablespoon chopped cilantro
> 2 cloves garlic, crushed and peeled
> 1 teaspoon crushed red pepper *or*
>   1 jalapeño chile, seeded and finely diced
> ¼ teaspoon *each* salt and black pepper
> 8 to 12 large (8½ in.) flour tortillas
>   Guacamole (see page 15) *or* 3 avocados,
>   sliced and sprinkled with lime juice
>   Frijoles or Refried Beans (see page 35)
>   Salsa Cruda (see page 521)

1. To flatten and tenderize meat, pound steak with flat side of a meat mallet for about 1 minute per side.

2. In a medium bowl mix oil, lime juice, cilantro, garlic, red pepper, salt, and black pepper. Pour marinade over steak; cover and marinate in refrigerator, turning occasionally, for 1 to 4 days.

3. Prepare fire (using mesquite charcoal or chips) in barbecue. When fire is ready, remove steak from marinade and place on oiled grill. Baste occasionally with marinade until meat is cooked to taste (fajitas are usually served well-done). During the last few minutes of cooking, add tortillas to grill to warm (tortillas can also be wrapped, in twos and threes, in aluminum foil and heated in oven for 12 minutes).

4. Cut cooked steak across the grain in slices 1 inch long and 3 inches wide. Place slices on a warm platter. Place Guacamole, Frijoles, Salsa Cruda, and warm tortillas in separate serving dishes. Diners may wrap the steak and garnishes in a tortilla to eat burrito style, or they may place them separately on their plates and eat with a fork.

Serves 4 to 6.

■ BARBECUED PORK RIBS AND SAUSAGES

Texas barbecue calls for a grill with a cover and a supply of mesquite chips or mesquite charcoal since the meats are slowly smoked, rather than just grilled. Texas barbecue is also distinguished by the use of two separate sauces. The meats are continually basted with a "moppin' sauce," which should not contain sugar or tomatoes or it will burn. (Leftover basting sauce may be refrigerated for several weeks or frozen indefinitely.) At serving the cooked meats are dabbed with a "soppin' sauce"—the familiar, sweet-sour tomatoey sauce we associate with Texas cooking. This recipe is suited to a medium-sized barbecue grill and a medium-sized crowd.

> 6 pounds thick-cut pork country ribs
>   or back ribs, in slabs
> 6 to 12 mixed sausages of choice (hot links,
>   garlic sausage, kielbasa, chorizo, bratwurst,
>   and/or knackwurst)

Basting ("Moppin' ") Sauce

> ½ teaspoon salt
> 1 teaspoon freshly ground pepper
> 4 tablespoons fresh lemon juice
>   (2 lemons)
> 1 teaspoon garlic powder
> 2 teaspoons Texas chili powder
> 1½ teaspoons paprika
> 1 teaspoon Louisiana-style hot sauce
> 1 tablespoon Worcestershire sauce
> 2 cups Beef Stock (see page 560)
> ¼ cup bacon fat or butter
> ¼ cup vegetable oil

Texas-Style Barbecue ("Soppin' ") Sauce

- ¼ cup butter
- ¼ cup peanut oil
- ½ cup minced onion
- 4 cloves garlic, peeled and minced
- 1 cup Chicken Stock (see page 560)
- 1½ cups catsup
- ½ teaspoon Tabasco sauce
- ¼ cup molasses
- ¼ cup vinegar
- ¾ cup water
- 1 tablespoon fresh lemon juice
- 1 tablespoon liquid smoke flavoring
- 2 tablespoons Worcestershire sauce
- 3 tablespoons brown sugar
- 1 bay leaf, broken in half
- 1 teaspoon paprika
- 2 teaspoons dry mustard
- ⅛ teaspoon thyme
- ½ teaspoon cayenne pepper
- 1 teaspoon salt
- ½ teaspoon freshly ground pepper

1. In a barbecue with a cover, prepare fire with mesquite charcoal briquettes, or use another type of briquettes with mesquite chips. Let burn down to glowing white coals (45 minutes to 1 hour).

2. Meanwhile, prepare Basting Sauce and Texas-Style Barbecue Sauce.

3. When charcoal is ready, push the briquettes to the edges of the barbecue. (If there is room in your barbecue, place a flameproof pot filled with hot water in the center of the coals.) Mop pork slabs on the bony side with Basting Sauce and place mopped side down about 8 inches above the coals in the center of the oiled grill. Moisten the upper side with the sauce. Cover and smoke pork for about 2½ hours, basting every 15 minutes. Leave the bony side down until the last few minutes. If rack is closer than 8 inches to the coals, decrease cooking time to about 1 hour. Add a few fresh briquettes to the fire every 30 minutes. If using a circular grill with perforations in one side of the cover, rotate the perforations every 15 minutes to keep charcoal from going out.

4. When pork is nearly cooked, turn meaty side down and brown meat well. At the same time, add sausages to the grill, placing them directly over the coals, and grill, turning every few minutes until done through (10 to 15 minutes). Cut pork slabs into serving portions and cover with Texas-Style Barbecue Sauce. Serve sausages with the pork.

Serves 6 to 8.

Basting Sauce   Mix ingredients together in a 1½-quart saucepan and heat until fat melts.

Makes 2¾ cups.

Texas-Style Barbecue Sauce

1. In a heavy saucepan over medium heat, melt butter and oil. Add onion and sauté until it is slightly caramelized, about 5 minutes. Add garlic and sauté another 2 minutes.

2. Add remaining ingredients, raise heat, and cook at a full boil for 10 minutes, stirring frequently.

3. Reduce heat, cover partially, and simmer for 1 hour, stirring occasionally. Sauce may be refrigerated for up to one week and reheated when needed.

Makes about 4 cups.

A full-blown Texas ranch barbecue is an all-day affair. Grilled pork ribs are part of the selection of meats on a typical menu, which also might feature beans and roasted fresh corn on the cob slathered with chili powder–spiked butter.

■ BARBECUED CHICKEN WITH TWO SAUCES

To satisfy all tastes, you have a choice of two sauces—one sweet and tangy, the other with a little more punch. To get more sauce on the chicken, you might want to try this alternative: After the chicken pieces have been on the grill for about 40 minutes, remove them to a platter and set aside. Cut a piece of heavy-duty aluminum foil about 2 inches larger than the perimeter of the grill surface and roll up the edges to form a rim. Lay the foil on the grill. With a carving fork or skewer, poke 8 to 10 holes in the foil, spaced at regular intervals. Set the chicken on the foil-covered grill and generously coat with barbecue sauce. Grill another 20 minutes. The chicken will not be as brown as if cooked directly on the rack, but it will be more thoroughly coated with sauce.

   1 chicken (3 to 4 lb), cut up

Sweet and Mild Barbecue Sauce

   ½ large red onion, minced
   2 tablespoons butter
   ½ cup catsup
   ½ cup water
   2 tablespoons apple cider vinegar
   1 tablespoon brown sugar
    A few drops hot-pepper sauce

Hot and Spicy Barbecue Sauce

   ½ cup catsup
   ½ cup white wine
   2 teaspoons Worcestershire sauce
   2 cloves garlic, crushed
   ½ teaspoon chili powder
    A few drops hot-pepper sauce

1. Remove any excess fat from chicken pieces, wash chicken, and pat dry.

2. Prepare fire. When coals are ready, place chicken on oiled grill, skin side down. When seared, turn skin side up.

3. After 30 to 40 minutes, baste chicken with sauce, turning pieces frequently to prevent charring. Grill until the chicken springs back slightly when touched (50 to 60 minutes).

Serves 4.

Sweet and Mild Barbecue Sauce In a medium saucepan over moderate heat, sauté onion in butter. Add catsup, water, vinegar, brown sugar, and hot-pepper sauce. Stir until blended. Increase heat and bring sauce to a boil; reduce heat, and simmer 15 to 20 minutes. Cool.

Makes 1 cup.

Hot and Spicy Barbecue Sauce In a medium saucepan combine catsup, wine, Worcestershire sauce, garlic, chili powder, and hot-pepper sauce. Bring to a boil. Reduce heat and simmer 20 minutes. Cool.

Makes 1 cup.

■ BUTTERFLIED LEG OF LAMB WITH CUCUMBER-MINT SAUCE

In Middle Eastern cuisines there are two basic marinades for lamb. One is made with yogurt and onions, the other with lemon juice and onions. Either can be spread on any lamb cut. This dish uses the yogurt marinade with a spectacularly delicious result—a leg of lamb meltingly tender with a fragrant garlic flavor.

   1 onion
   1 cup plain yogurt
   1 tablespoon minced garlic
   1 bunch cilantro, stemmed and chopped
   ¼ cup olive oil
    Salt and pepper, to taste
   1 boneless leg of lamb (7 to 8 lb), butterflied

Cucumber-Mint Sauce

   1 cucumber
   1 onion
   1 teaspoon minced garlic
   ¼ cup chopped mint leaves
   1 cup plain yogurt
    Salt and pepper, to taste

1. Prepare marinade by puréeing onion in food processor or blender. Combine onion with yogurt, garlic, cilantro, olive oil, and salt and pepper.

2. Have a butcher bone and butterfly the leg of lamb to a uniform thickness. This is very important; otherwise, it will not cook evenly. The butcher should also trim the outside fat as closely as possible and remove all interior fat and connective tissue.

3. Rub the marinade into the meat and cover. Let rest at room temperature for at least 4 hours or refrigerate for up to 12 hours.

4. Prepare fire. When fire is ready, wipe excess marinade from meat and reserve remaining marinade in bowl. Sear both sides of meat over direct heat on oiled grill, then place lamb, skin side down, over drip pan, and close lid. You won't need to turn the lamb over during cooking. Baste occasionally with reserved marinade. Cook until meat is rare (130° to 140° F), about 45 minutes. Remove from grill and cover with foil. Allow to rest 10 minutes, for juices to collect in meat. To serve, divide leg into separate muscles—top round, bottom round, sirloin tip, and shank—and cut across the grain. Serve with Cucumber-Mint Sauce.

Serves 8.

Cucumber-Mint Sauce Peel cucumber, then quarter lengthwise and slice thin. Peel and finely dice onion and combine with cucumber, garlic, mint, and yogurt. Adjust seasoning with salt and pepper. Serve chilled.

Makes 2 cups.

NEW ENGLAND SHELLFISH ROAST

An interesting variation on a Cape Cod clambake, this recipe pulls out all the stops for a grand shellfish feast. Most of the work can be done prior to mealtime, making this dish ideal for entertaining.

    2 **live Maine lobsters (1½ lb each)**
    2 **dozen cherrystone clams**
    1 **dozen oysters**
    3 **pounds mussels**
  ⅓ **pound unsalted butter**
      Juice of 1 lemon
      Salt and freshly ground pepper, to taste
    1 **handful fresh thyme or fresh herb of choice**

1. To prepare lobster, insert knife between head and body to sever spinal cord. Cut lengthwise down the underside almost to the shell. Flatten lobster and remove the stomach, black vein, roe, and green matter (called tomalley). Wash lobsters thoroughly and pat dry. Crack claws.

2. Wash and scrub clams, oysters, and mussels. Remove beards from mussels.

3. In a small saucepan melt butter. Stir in lemon juice. Add salt and pepper to taste and set aside.

4. Prepare fire. When fire is ready, moisten thyme with water and toss on fire. Place all shellfish on oiled grill at once. Shellfish are done when the shells open (after 3 to 5 minutes). Remove carefully from fire to save juices that are in the shells. Drain these juices into saucepan. Place pan of lemon butter, pan of shellfish juice, and cooked shellfish on warming rack of grill until lobsters are done. Turn lobsters when flesh is slightly soft to the touch (6 to 8 minutes). Cook on other side an additional 2 minutes.

5. Serve with hot juices and lemon butter.

Serves 4 to 6.

GRILLED TUNA

A summertime specialty, this dish is a whole meal in itself. The variety of vegetables creates a colorful medley. To vary the effect, substitute broccoli, carrots, cauliflower, celery, sugar snap peas, baby squash, or another vegetable that seems enticing. Adjust the quantities of individual ingredients according to your taste.

    1 **bunch asparagus**
    2 **bulbs fennel, quartered**
  ½ **pound snow peas**
    8 **quarts boiling salted water**
    3 **red, yellow, or green bell peppers, cored**
    1 **pint cherry tomatoes**
    4 **tuna steaks (6 to 8 oz each)**
      Olive oil, for brushing

Grilled Tuna can be served on its own, as shown here, or on top of a bountiful assortment of fresh garden vegetables to make a spectacular salad.

Vinaigrette Sauce

  ½ **cup vegetable oil**
  ½ **cup fruity olive oil**
  ¼ **cup red wine vinegar**
    1 **tablespoon balsamic vinegar**
    2 **teaspoons Dijon mustard**
    1 **clove garlic, minced**
    1 **teaspoon salt**
  ¼ **teaspoon freshly ground pepper**

1. Prepare charcoal. Trim asparagus, fennel, and snow peas. Blanch these vegetables in the boiling water, then plunge them into ice water to stop cooking. Drain and set aside.

2. Cut peppers into strips. Remove stems from tomatoes and leave whole. Set aside.

3. Brush steaks with oil and grill 3 to 7 minutes per side (grilling time depends on size of steaks).

4. Place tuna steaks on platter. Surround with vegetables. Drizzle Vinaigrette Sauce over top.

Serves 6 to 8.

Vinaigrette Sauce Combine oils, vinegars, mustard, garlic, salt, and pepper. Mix well.

Makes about 1¼ cups.

Pheasant Brochettes With Baby Vegetables are an elegant grilled dinner. Tiny carrots and artichokes are available at specialty markets and better produce sections of supermarkets. Selected butchers will stock pheasant or accommodate special orders in the fall and early winter.

◼ PHEASANT BROCHETTES WITH BABY VEGETABLES

Baby vegetables are especially charming *en brochette.* They must be slightly precooked to match the cooking time of the pheasant. If desired, chicken or turkey can be substituted for the pheasant.

    2 **whole pheasants (about 2½ lb each)**
  12 **baby carrots, peeled and blanched**
    4 **baby artichokes, trimmed and parboiled**

Tarragon-Mustard Sauce

    ¼ **cup Dijon mustard**
    ¼ **cup tarragon vinegar**
    ¼ **cup vegetable oil**

1. Have butcher remove pheasants' necks (or do it yourself at home). Wash pheasants and pat dry. Remove breast meat from carcass; reserve carcass for stock.

2. Prepare fire. Slice each breast in half lengthwise and then into 6 equal pieces.

3. *To assemble:* Alternate pheasant strips with carrots on 8-inch metal or bamboo skewers, ending each skewer with a whole baby artichoke. (If using bamboo skewers, soak 30 minutes to keep them from burning.)

4. Prepare Tarragon-Mustard Sauce. Grill brochettes 5 inches from heat 6 to 8 minutes per side, basting frequently with sauce. Serve with remaining sauce.

Makes 4 brochettes, 4 servings.

Tarragon-Mustard Sauce In a small bowl combine mustard, vinegar, and oil; whisk vigorously to blend.

Makes ¾ cup.

◼ ALDER-GRILLED SALMON

Red alder provides the favorite wood for grilling seafoods in the Northwest. If you have a ready supply, you can build a fire entirely of this hardwood and let it burn down to glowing coals. An easier way is to add chunks of alder or other aromatic hardwoods (available in cookware and specialty-food stores) to a charcoal fire. Sauce is unnecessary, but you can melt butter with a squeeze of lemon juice in a pan on the edge of the grill.

    6 **salmon steaks (each 1 in. thick)** *or*
        2- to 3-pound fillet
        Vegetable oil
        Salt and freshly ground pepper, to taste
        Lemon wedges, for garnish

1. Prepare a hot charcoal fire in an open or covered grill. When charcoal is mostly lit, add alder or other hardwood chunks. Let fire burn until charcoal is covered with a light gray ash. Preheat grill thoroughly.

2. Meanwhile, prepare salmon. If using a large piece of fillet, slice diagonally into pieces of even size and thickness. Skin may be left on or removed according to taste. Rub salmon lightly with oil and sprinkle with salt and pepper. Refrigerate fish if necessary, but remove from refrigerator 30 minutes before grilling.

3. Place salmon on oiled grill, starting fillets bone side down on hottest part of fire. Cook until edges are turning opaque (4 to 6 minutes). Turn with a long-bladed spatula and cook until a skewer easily penetrates the thickest part (3 to 4 minutes). Serve immediately with lemon wedges.

Serves 6.

◼ VEGETABLE MIXED GRILL

Common vegetables are truly wonderful when grilled. They work equally well as a main course or as a complement to a grilled meat, fish, or chicken dinner. If fresh herbs are available, try adding them to the garlic rub. Serve with plenty of fresh aioli at the table.

    1 **medium eggplant (about 1 lb)**
    1 **pound zucchini**
    1 **pound yellow pattypan squash**
    2 **red bell peppers**
    1 **bunch green onions**
    ½ **cup olive oil**
    2 **tablespoons minced garlic**
        Salt and pepper, to taste
    1 **lemon (optional)**
    1 **cup Aioli (see page 262)**

1. Wash all vegetables and pat dry, leaving stems on eggplant, zucchini, and pattypan squash. Cut eggplant lengthwise into 1-inch-thick slices. Cut zucchini lengthwise into 1-inch-thick slices. Quarter pattypan squash. Stem and seed peppers and cut into quarters lengthwise. Remove roots from green onions.

2. On a baking sheet mix oil, garlic, and salt and pepper. Rub all surfaces of vegetables with oil mixture. Be sure surfaces of eggplant and squashes are well covered. Add more oil if necessary.

3. Prepare fire. *If using a gas grill:* Use presoaked hardwood chips for a smoky flavor complement. *If using charcoal:* Use presoaked hardwood chunks. When fire is ready, place all vegetables on grill. Quick hands and a pair of tongs are important because the oil covering will cause flare-ups; close the lid as soon as possible. Be sure to lay vegetables crosswise to grill so they don't fall through.

4. After 5 to 6 minutes, flip vegetables over with a spatula. Moisten with extra oil if surfaces appear to be drying out rather than cooking (eggplant is particularly susceptible to this problem). Close lid. Vegetables should be done in another 5 to 6 minutes. A squeeze of lemon juice on vegetables as they are cooking adds zip. Serve immediately with Aioli.

Serves 3 or 4.

> **Recipes and Related Information**
> Broil, 62; Temperature, 575.

GRIND, TO

To reduce foods such as coffee beans, nuts, seeds, seasonings, and meats into small particles. Grinding tools include hand or electric coffee grinders, salt and pepper mills, nut mills, food processors, electric minichoppers, electric blenders, and meat grinders (see GRATE).

Powders lose potency quickly; for optimum flavor and fragrance, it's best to store beans, nuts, berries, and seeds whole and grind them when needed.

GUAVA

A round to pear-shaped tropical fruit native to South America, the guava is generally 2 to 3 inches long and has several small, hard, but edible seeds embedded in its flesh. The many varieties are marked by a range of skin and flesh colors. The skin can be green, yellow, red, purple, or black, the flesh white, yellow, coral, or red. When ripe, the guava is highly scented and its moist flesh is sweet.

Use   Ripe guavas are halved and eaten from the shell or sliced and combined with other fruits. The halves can be peeled and poached in sugar syrup, at which point the seeds are easy to remove. Guava purées are delicious in sauces, sorbets, and mousses, or are cooked down into a firm paste that can be sliced. Guava paste is much appreciated in Mexico, where it is often served for dessert with crackers and a mild cheese or cream cheese. Because guavas are high in natural pectin, they make excellent jellies, jams, and preserves. Guava juice is enjoyed on its own or as part of other drinks.

Availability   California and Florida guavas are marketed from September through January, New Zealand varieties from March through June. Guava paste, guava juice, canned poached guava, and guava jelly are sold in Latin American markets.

Selection   Choose firm guavas for cooking. For eating raw, choose fragrant guavas that give slightly to gentle pressure. If purchased underripe, fruit will ripen if kept at room temperature.

Storage   Keep ripe fruit in the refrigerator for up to two weeks. To store guava paste, wrap airtight in plastic wrap, and keep in a cool, dry place for up to one month or refrigerate indefinitely. Leftover guava juice and canned guavas should be refrigerated in nonmetal containers.

Preparation   Trim stem and blossom ends. Peel fruit before slicing or puréeing.

HAZELNUT

Also known as the filbert, the hazelnut is the nut of trees of the genus *Corylus*. Round, oval, or elongated, it has a hard brown shell and pale gold flesh overlayed with a thin brown skin. Its rich, buttery flavor makes it a favorite of cooks and bakers.

Use   Before commercially grown hazelnuts are shipped, they are sorted to remove those that are substandard and air-dried to improve their longevity. Dried, unshelled nuts can be cracked and eaten raw. When toasted and shelled, hazelnuts are suitable as an hors d'oeuvre or as part of a nut mix. Hazelnuts are used in a variety of sweet and savory dishes and confections. Add toasted, chopped nuts to sautéed green beans, poultry stuffings, pâtés, sautéed pork, veal scallops, and salads. Minced hazelnuts contribute distinctive flavor to quick breads and cookies, ice cream, chocolate bars, and nougats. Finely ground hazelnuts are commonly part of European-style tortes, cakes, cheesecake, and tart doughs.

Availability   Hazelnuts in the shell are sold in some markets in the fall. Shelled hazelnuts are marketed in bulk in some health-food stores and in packages in some supermarkets and specialty stores.

Selection   Choose fresh hazelnuts that feel heavy for their size.

Sandwich together plain and cutout Linzer Hearts with raspberry jam to make a romantic offering for Valentine's Day.

Storage   Keep unshelled hazelnuts in a cool, dry place; they will maintain quality for up to six months. Freeze shelled hazelnuts for up to six months or store in the refrigerator for up to one month. Minced or ground hazelnuts should be used immediately.

Preparation   To remove the papery brown skin from shelled hazelnuts, toast them on a rimmed baking sheet in a preheated 350° F oven until the skin begins to flake (about 7 minutes). Then rub them against a wire sieve or wrap them in a dish towel and rub them against the towel to remove as much of the skins as possible.

Toasting brings out the full flavor of shelled hazelnuts. After skinning, continue toasting hazelnuts on a rimmed baking sheet in a preheated 350° F oven, shaking pan occasionally, until fragrant (about 5 minutes).

◼ LINZER HEARTS

Cut these valentine cookies from a traditional *linzer* dough—a butter-rich Austrian pastry with ground hazelnuts. The dough is made in 5 minutes, and the cookies bake in 10. When cool, give the hearts a snowy coat of confectioners' sugar.

　1½　**cups sifted flour**
　　¾　**cup granulated sugar**
　　½　**teaspoon ground cinnamon**
　　　　Pinch salt
　　　　Grated rind of 1 lemon
　10　**tablespoons chilled unsalted butter,**
　　　　cut into pieces
　2¼　**cups (approximately) finely ground hazelnuts**
　　1　**egg yolk**
　　　　Confectioners' sugar, for dusting

1. *To prepare in food processor:* In work bowl of food processor, combine flour, sugar, cinnamon, salt, and lemon rind. Process, using short on-off bursts. Add butter and process until mixture resembles fine crumbs. Transfer mixture to a large bowl; add hazelnuts and egg yolk and stir until well blended. Turn out onto a lightly floured board and knead briefly, just until mixture sticks together. *To prepare by hand:* In a large bowl stir together flour, sugar, cinnamon, salt, lemon rind, and hazelnuts. Turn mixture onto a cool work surface. With a pastry blender or 2 knives, cut in butter until mixture resembles fine crumbs. Add egg yolk and toss to blend. Knead briefly until mixture just sticks together.

2. Preheat oven to 375° F. Divide dough in half; enclose one half in waxed paper or plastic wrap and refrigerate. On a lightly floured surface, roll or pat unrefrigerated dough to a thickness of ¼ inch. Cut out cookies with a lightly floured, 2¼-inch, heart-shaped cutter. Transfer to ungreased baking sheets. Repeat with other half of dough.

3. Bake until lightly colored (about 10 minutes). Transfer to wire racks. When cookies are cool, sift confectioners' sugar over them. Store in an airtight container.

Makes about 4 dozen cookies.

Variation   To make the valentine hearts pictured at left, use a small, heart-shaped cutter to remove centers from half of the hearts cut in step 2. Bake large and small hearts and heart frames as directed. (Treat small hearts as miniature versions of above recipe.) When cool, lightly spread large hearts with raspberry jam. (You will need about ½ cup in all.) Sift confectioners' sugar on heart frames and set atop jam-spread hearts.

Makes 2 dozen cookies.

> ***Recipes and Related Information***
> *Biscotti, 8; Nut Tart, 443; Panforte, 186.*

HEAD

Certain vegetable plants have compact masses of leaves or buds. Individual lettuces, cauliflowers, and garlic bulbs, for example, are referred to as *heads*. Although some varieties of lettuce and cabbage actually don't form a true head, common usage groups them with those that do.

HEART OF PALM

The prized edible hearts of young palm trees resemble white asparagus spears. They have a silky texture and a delicate flavor resembling that of artichokes. The hearts are very costly because the whole palm must be cut down to reach them.

Use Raw hearts of palm may be sliced thin and added to salads. Cooked hearts of palm are usually treated like asparagus: served cold, with a vinaigrette or mayonnaise, or hot, with lemon butter.

Availability Rarely found fresh outside of Florida and tropical countries, hearts of palm are widely marketed water-packed in cans. They are sold at specialty food stores and well-stocked supermarkets.

Storage Transfer canned hearts of palm to a nonmetal container and refrigerate in their packing water for up to 10 days.

■ HEARTS OF PALM SALAD

As they are so difficult to extract from the palm tree, hearts of palm are costly to buy and definitely belong in the category of fancy foods. This salad is equally appropriate as a luncheon entrée (see Note below). The mixture of shrimp and hearts of palm must marinate in the mustard vinaigrette for several hours before serving to allow the flavors to blend sufficiently.

   1 tablespoon *each* tarragon vinegar and
       fresh lime or lemon juice
   2 teaspoons Dijon mustard
   1 clove garlic, minced
   ¾ teaspoon salt
   ½ teaspoon sugar
   ¼ teaspoon dried tarragon
       Dash cayenne pepper
   2 tablespoons olive oil
   ¼ cup vegetable oil
   1 can (14 oz) hearts of palm, drained and
       sliced in ¼-inch-thick rounds
   6 ounces small peeled, cooked shrimp
   1 head romaine lettuce
   1 medium tomato, cut in wedges, for garnish
   2 hard-cooked eggs, sliced, for garnish

1. In a medium bowl mix vinegar, lime juice, mustard, garlic, salt, sugar, tarragon, and cayenne. Using a whisk or fork, gradually beat in oils until mixture is slightly thickened and well blended. Lightly mix in hearts of palm and shrimp. Cover and refrigerate for 1 to 2 hours to blend flavors.

2. Line salad bowl or individual salad plates with outer leaves of romaine. Shred inner leaves and use to top whole leaves.

3. To serve, spoon hearts of palm mixture on bed of whole and shredded romaine. Garnish with tomato wedges and egg slices.

Serves 4.

Note This salad also makes a fine main dish for lunch. If you serve it as a main course, increase the shrimp to ½ pound to make 3 servings.

HEAT DIFFUSER

Several devices that diffuse heat from a gas or electric burner fall under this category. The simple wire trivet used to keep a carafe of coffee warm on the stove and raise glass and other sensitive materials a safe distance above direct heat is a heat diffuser. Another solution is a coated steel disk with 1-inch-high sides that introduce a cushioning layer of air between heat source and pan. Permitting gentle cooking and reducing scorching and burning, it operates on the principle that air is a less efficient heat conductor than metal and thereby slows heat transfer. Because metal is a very good heat conductor, the disk picks up the moderated heat and spreads it evenly across the diffuser and then by conduction to the pan. This diffuser maintains a low gas flame at a level that it would otherwise be unable to hold. A simmer plate, a third type, functions similarly; it is made of enameled cast iron and fits over a gas burner.

All of these heat diffusers are sized for home ranges; some have handles for easier lifting. They are inexpensive and worth having because they permit another dimension of control over cooking temperature, appealing for cooks who have electric ranges, which are difficult to adjust to slow cooking at low heat. For those who use the more flexible gas range, diffusers permit the flame to drop even lower than otherwise possible.

HERB

It is difficult to define and draw a firm line between herbs and spices. Some say that herbs are the leaves of herbaceous plants (plants with stems that are soft rather than woody, and which die entirely or down to the roots after flowering) and that spices are derived from the seeds, roots, bark, fruit, or flowers. By that definition, some plants, such as coriander, yield both herbs and spices. Others say that when the aromatic element comes from a tropical plant, it is a spice, and when it comes from a plant in a temperate zone, it is an herb.

For simplicity, this section deals with the aromatic leaves of herbaceous plants and refers to them as herbs. The aromatic roots, bark, stems, seeds, fruit, and flowers are considered spices and are treated under SPICE.

Use Herbs have a role as flavorings, fragrances, medicines, cosmetics, teas, dyes, and ornaments. Only their culinary uses are considered here. Herbs are valued in the kitchen for their aromatic essential oils. Rubbing, steeping, or heating the leaves releases their oils so they can be used to flavor and scent a dish or ingredient.

Herbs can be kept in the freezer for up to one year. Wash them in cold water after removing any deteriorating leaves. Pat them completely dry with paper towels, then package in small, airtight bags.

Some herbs are used extensively in one cuisine and hardly at all in another. Cilantro, for example, plays a major role in Latin American and Chinese cooking and a somewhat lesser role in Indian and Southeast Asian cooking. It is not used at all, however, in the cooking of Western or northern Europe.

Herbs are primarily used to accent and enhance the flavor of foods. An Italian tomato sauce without oregano is hard to imagine, although the dominant flavor of tomato sauce is always tomato. In a few dishes, however, the herb is the main or a major ingredient: basil in Italian pesto, parsley in Iranian *gormeh sabzi* (parsley and lamb stew), and watercress in a watercress soup.

As a flavor accent, herbs may be added to just about every dish in the cook's repertoire: soups, salads, stuffings, roasts, stews, sauces, marinades, breads, dressings and mayonnaise, pickles and jellies. As a garnish, herb-flavored butter (see BUTTER, Compound Butters) makes a simple, flavorful finish to grilled meats, fish, and poultry (use 1 tablespoon minced fresh herb to each ¼ cup softened butter). Herbs complement all types of meats, fish, fowl, vegetables, beans, grains, eggs, and cheese. The

mints and lemon verbena are occasionally paired with fruits, but otherwise, herbs rarely appear in sweet dishes.

As more and more Americans attempt to reduce their sodium intake, many are finding that herbs can enliven the blandness of a low-salt diet. In addition to their use in specific dishes, herbs are frequently incorporated into other ingredients such as mustards, vinegars, and salts. Herbs have also long been employed to brew tea (see below and TEA). Minced tarragon, chives, parsley, or cilantro adds a dimension of freshness and spark to storebought mustard or homemade blends. Almost any fresh herb is suitable for use in flavoring vinegars (see JAM, JELLY, PRESERVE, AND CONDIMENT). Herb-flavored salts (see HERB AND SPICE BLENDS) sprinkled on salad greens, fresh vegetables, and many cooked dishes add flavor without calories, often eliminating or greatly reducing the need for a sauce or dressing.

Teas brewed from the leaves of herbs are called tisanes. Most are made by infusion, that is, by steeping in hot water. Start with 2 to 3 teaspoons fresh or frozen leaves or 1 to 2 teaspoons dried herb per cup in a warm nonmetal teapot. Cover with the proper amount of boiling water and steep 5 to 10 minutes. Strain into cups. All herbal teas may be served iced. Just make them a little stronger to allow for the melting ice.

Availability   Dried herbs are widely marketed through supermarket spice racks, health-food stores, and specialty stores. For years parsley was one of the only fresh herbs regularly available in supermarkets; today hothouse cultivation brings a wide variety of fresh herbs to supermarkets throughout the year.

Selection   Purchase or gather fresh herbs only as they are needed. It is wise to buy dried herbs in small quantities. Some supermarkets and many health-food stores offer herbs in bulk. Try to buy them from a market with rapid turnover.

Storage   Fresh herbs are highly perishable. To preserve them in their fresh state, see individual herb entries. For longer storage, herbs may be dried, frozen, salt-cured, or packed in vinegar. Store dried herb leaves as whole as possible in airtight jars in a cool, dark place. Pulverize between the fingers or with a mortar and pestle just before use to release oils. When kept in a cool, ventilated place, home-dried herbs should retain freshness for one year. Commercially available herbs should last six months or slightly longer before beginning to lose flavor. Discard any that smell musty or dusty or that have lost their original punch. Frozen herbs are best used within one year. Once thawed, they cannot be refrozen. Salt-cured herbs and herbs packed in vinegar will keep indefinitely if properly stored in a cool, dark place.

Drying   For most herb leaves, drying is the time-honored method of preserving. Herbs to be used in cooking should be dried as whole as possible to retain flavor. See Drying Herbs, opposite page, for more information.

Freezing   This method is recommended for a few of the tender herbs, including basil, burnet, fennel, tarragon, chives, dill, and parsley. Tie a small bundle of the herb together and dip headfirst into boiling water for a few seconds. Immediately plunge into ice water and let cool in the water for a couple of minutes. (Blanching isn't necessary for basil, chives, and dill.) Remove leaves from stems and pack in small batches in plastic bags, label, and freeze. When ready to use, remove only the amount needed from the freezer. Add frozen herbs to foods to be cooked; let herbs thaw before adding to cold foods.

Packing in Vinegar   The French tightly pack tarragon leaves in little jars, then completely fill the jar with vinegar. They keep indefinitely in a cool, dark place.

Salt-curing   Some of the tender herbs such as basil, burnet, dill, fennel, and parsley can be packed in salt. Wash and drain, remove leaves from their stems, and place them in alternate layers with plain table salt in a container, beginning and ending with a salt layer. Fill completely and cover container with an airtight lid. Label and store in a cool, dark place. Remove salt from leaves just before using. They will keep indefinitely.

Preparation   Mince or chop herbs only just before using. Flavors are quickly lost as volatile oils are released by heat or oxidation. Add herbs to hot dishes at the last minute, unless it's a simmering stock. Steeping dried herbs brings out their flavor; steep for 15 minutes in a small amount of warm liquid—such as stock, butter, or water. If desired, add liquid as well as herbs to recipe.

SUBSTITUTING FRESH HERBS FOR DRIED

Because oils become concentrated in the drying process, dried herbs are generally more pungent than an equal quantity of fresh. The strength of the dried herb, however, depends on how it was harvested and preserved, how it has been stored, and how old it is. Follow this rule of thumb: ¼ teaspoon dried, finely powdered herb equals ¾ to 1 teaspoon dried, loosely crumbled herb equals 1½ to 2 teaspoons chopped fresh herb.

HERB AND SPICE BLENDS

The spice racks in supermarkets are filled with dozens of herb and spice blends. Many seem designed for specific uses, such as pizza spice and pumpkin-pie spice, although the packagers would contend that these blends have multiple functions. Others, the creations of well-known chefs or restaurants, are meant to provide home cooks with the unique blends needed to reproduce particular dishes.

Herb and spice blends are convenience products. Most are composed of spices and herbs found beside them on

---

Fresh herbs are one of the easiest foods to dry. Very low temperature and good air circulation are important to ensure that herbs dry properly to preserve flavor.

To dry in an oven   To dry herbs in a hurry, set oven at the lowest temperature. Wash leaves only if necessary to rinse away insects or dust; shake off water and drain well. Spread leaves on a cheesecloth-lined rack in the oven. Leave oven door open and stir leaves until they are crisp. They'll be ready in a few minutes.

To dry in a microwave oven   Place four or five stems of herbs on a double thickness of paper towels; cover with a single layer of towels. Turn on microwave at full power (high) until leaves are brittle (about 2 minutes for small leaves, 3 minutes for large). If leaves are not yet brittle, leave in microwave an additional 30 seconds.

To dry at room temperature   Hang herbs by their stems in bunches from the ceiling (called bunch-drying), or lay herbs flat on trays. Dry away from direct sunlight. An attic, covered porch, or kitchen that stays at 65° to 90° F is a good location. If you dry herbs in a covered area outdoors where dew collects, bring them indoors overnight.

Bunch-drying is ideally suited for herbs with long stems, such as marjoram, rosemary, and sage. Tie bunches at the stem ends, and hang upside down to dry. Bunches can be dried in small brown paper bags to keep dust from collecting on them and to catch seeds. Gather bag opening around steams and tie so that herbs hang freely inside bag. Cut several ½-inch holes in bags and suspend from the ceiling at varying heights to increase air circulation. Leaves and seeds will be thoroughly dry in one or two weeks.

Tray-drying works well for herbs with large leaves, such as basil, and herbs with short stems. Use stackable drying trays with mesh screens. Make one layer in each tray. If stacking trays, leave plenty of air circulation between them. Spread leaves or stems in a single layer. To protect against insects and dust, cover with cheesecloth. Turn leaves or stems each day or two. Most herbs dry crisp within one week to 10 days, depending on the weather. The crisper they are, the better they will keep. Remove from trays and package in airtight jars when crisp (see DRY).

STORING DRIED HERBS
When herbs are crumbly and feel dry, remove leaves from stems. Whole leaves keep their flavor longer than those that are crumbled before storage. Package in small glass jars. Inspect during the first week for moisture. If condensation appears, redry. Label and date containers. Store in a cool, dry, dark place. Properly stored, dried herbs retain their flavor and color for up to one year.

---

the supermarket shelf. Pumpkin-pie spice, for example, usually contains cinnamon, allspice, ginger, and nutmeg, all readily available in supermarkets. Garlic salt is often simply garlic and salt. Comparison shoppers quickly see that they can make many herb and spice blends at home for less than the cost of most commercial products.

If you maintain a large range of herbs and spices, properly stored and replaced every few months, you may find that your own blends are more satisfying than the commercial ones. Spice blends made from whole spices ground to order are far more pungent than storebought, preground blends. You can control the salt level and the balance of ingredients, eliminating a particular herb or spice or adding one to suit your palate.

Nevertheless, many recipes call for specific herb or spice blends and there is no denying their convenience. The major blends are described on the next two pages.

Use   Herb blends should be rubbed between the fingers to release their aromatic oils before adding to a dish. Spices can impart a raw taste if not given sufficient time to cook. Sautéing spices in oil or butter, if a recipe permits, will remove the raw flavor.

Availability   Most of the following blends are found in the spice section of any well-stocked supermarket. Other sources are suggested in the individual entries below.

Selection   Packaged seasonings lose quality after a while; try to buy from a store that restocks its spice shelves fairly often.

Storage   Store spice and herb blends in a cool, dark, dry place. Herb blends will keep for up to one year. Spice blends made of ground spices should stay pungent for up to six months. Those made of whole spices, for example, pickling spice, may be kept for one to two years.

HERB BLENDS

Some herb blends are proprietary and unique to the company that produces them; others are blended by almost all manufacturers. Theoretically, any herbs may be combined to make a blend, but only a few commercial blends enjoy widespread use. The following are among the most popular.

Bouquet Garni   The traditional bouquet garni consists of fresh parsley, fresh thyme, and a bay leaf tied together in a bundle and used to flavor stocks and soups. It is removed before serving. Some manufacturers pack a blend of dried herbs labeled bouquet garni that may include oregano, summer savory, marjoram, rosemary, basil, sage, thyme, dill, and sometimes tarragon. Herbs should be rubbed between the fingers when added to a dish. They can be used to flavor stuffings, soups, sauces, stews, and vegetable dishes. See BOUQUET GARNI.

Fines Herbes   This combination of fresh herbs is used often in French cooking. The traditional blend includes chervil, parsley, tarragon, and chives. Some manufacturers pack this combination of herbs, or a similar one, in dried form. Others pack fines herbes blends that do not bear a resemblance to the classic combination. One major brand consists of such pungent dried herbs as thyme, oregano, sage, rosemary, marjoram, and basil. Obviously, this blend is not a substitute for the fines herbes called for in French cookbooks, usually in combination with eggs, fish, and salads. More pungent fines herbes blends should be reserved for meats, tomato sauces, and eggplant preparations.

Herbes de Provence   Dried herbs typical of southern France—such as thyme, lavender, summer savory, basil, and rosemary—make up this aromatic blend. Use it to season lamb, chicken, tomato sauces, and other tomato-based dishes.

Italian Seasoning   This blend of dried herbs is intended to give a characteristic Italian flavor to dishes. Common components include oregano, marjoram, red pepper, basil, rosemary, thyme, and sage. Italian seasoning can be used with chicken and meats, with tomato-based dishes, squash and eggplant, pizza, and bean soups.

Poultry Seasoning   Usually a blend of sage, thyme, marjoram, savory, onion, black pepper, celery seed, or other herbs, poultry seasoning is always in powdered form. It can be used to season chicken, veal or pork dishes, stuffings, and biscuits.

SPICE BLENDS

Packers use different spices and proportions of spices in their blends. One major packer, for example, puts cinnamon, allspice, ginger, and nutmeg in pumpkin-pie spice. Another packer adds mace and cloves to the blend. The following descriptions are based on commonly available brands. Check the package label for a specific list of ingredients.

Apple-Pie Spice   This mixture usually contains such sweet baking spices as cinnamon, nutmeg, allspice, and cardamom. Use it in other fruit desserts or in spice cakes and cookies as well as in apple pie.

Beau Monde Seasoning   The components of this blend are salt, dextrose, onion, celery seed, and an anticaking agent. It is used to season meats, poultry, fish, sauces, stuffings, soups, and vegetable dishes.

Celery Salt   A mixture of salt and celery seed, celery salt is used to flavor soups, stuffings, meat loaves, Bloody Marys, baked fish, and dishes in which the flavor of celery is desired.

Chili Powder   Don't confuse this blend with ground red chile, which is made exclusively from ground dried chile pepper. Chili powder varies greatly from packer to packer. One major brand includes chili pepper, cumin, salt, allspice, garlic, oregano, cloves, and coriander. Chili powder adds characteristic hotness to such southwestern specialties as chili con carne, enchiladas with *salsa ranchera,* and barbecue sauce. It adds a lift to hamburgers, meat loaves, and tomato-based cocktail sauces. Sprinkle it over corn on the cob and baked fish for a touch of heat.

Crab Boil   Also known as shrimp spice, crab boil is popular among southern and New England cooks. It is a mixture of herbs and spices added to the water in which crab, lobster, shrimp, and crayfish are cooked. A typical version contains mustard seed, coriander seed, cayenne, bay leaf, dill seed, allspice, and cloves. Generally the mixture is added to boiling water and allowed to boil for 5 minutes before shellfish is added. Detailed directions for use appear on the package.

Curry Powder   A blend of cumin, coriander, turmeric, fenugreek, ginger, chiles, fennel, garlic, cinnamon, salt, mustard, cloves, black pepper, and more, curry powder imparts what Westerners perceive as a typical curry flavor to dishes. In fact, few Indian cooks would ever use a commercial curry powder, preferring instead to toast wholc spices and grind their own blend to order. Curry powder can also be used to flavor stuffed eggs, mayonnaise, cabbage salad, chicken and seafood salads, and chowders.

Five-Spice Powder Star anise, anise seed, clove, cinnamon or cassia, and Szechuan peppercorns ground to a powder are the typical spices in five-spice powder. Brands vary in pungency and balance; some even include cardamom or orange peel. Five-spice powder is used in Chinese cooking to flavor red-cooked meats—pork, chicken, duck, or beef simmered in soy sauce with ginger and spices—to marinate pork before barbecuing, and to season dipping sauces. It is available in plastic pouches in Chinese and other Asian markets.

Garam Masala Translating as *warm spice blend, garam masala* is an Indian blend that usually contains such elements as cardamom, black peppercorns, cloves, coriander, and cinnamon. The blend varies from region to region and from cook to cook. It is usually added to dishes near the end of their cooking time; occasionally, it is sprinkled atop a finished dish as a garnish. Garam masala may be purchased in Indian markets, but most Indian cooks blend and grind their own spices. This spice blend is added to countless Indian dishes in much the same way Americans use salt and pepper.

Garlic Salt This is a simple blend of salt and garlic. Some blends also contain parsley, modified food starch, sugar, and monosodium glutamate. Garlic salt can be used to make garlic bread or to add garlic flavor to soups, stuffings, tomato juice cocktails, roasts, and grilled meats and poultry.

Onion Salt A mixture of salt and onion, this blend can be used wherever the flavor of onion is desired, as in hamburgers and mcat loaves, roast meats, stuffings, soups, Bloody Marys, and other tomato juice cocktails.

Pickling Spice This pungent mixture is used to flavor vegetable and fruit pickles. It generally contains such ingredients as mustard seed, cinnamon, allspice, bay leaf, black pepper, ginger, red pepper, cardamom, turmeric, and mace.

Pizza Spice In addition to garlic, sugar, onion, and salt, pizza spice can contain unidentified ground spices. It is sprinkled atop pizza before or after baking.

Pumpkin-Pie Spice This powdered blend can contain cinnamon, ginger, nutmeg, allspice, mace, and sometimes cloves. It may be also used in custards, spice cakes, and cookies.

Quatre Epices *Four spices,* the translation of the French term, is a powdered mixture of white pepper, cloves, nutmeg, and ground ginger. French cooks use it primarily to flavor pâtés. *Quatre épices* is available in some supermarkets and in specialty stores.

Ras el Hanout Containing 50 or more exotic ingredients, this Moroccan spice is probably the most complex described here. Common flavorings include turmeric, ginger, allspice, cinnamon, cardamom, clove, nutmeg, peppercorns, and orrisroot as well as flowers such as rosebuds and lavender. *Ras el hanout* is used to flavor game, stewed lamb, stuffings, and other Moroccan dishes. It is available in Middle Eastern markets.

Seasoned Salt Formulas for this mixture vary from manufacturer to manufacturer. One popular brand includes salt, dextrin, sugar, garlic, monosodium glutamate, cornstarch, black pepper, celery seed, oleoresin paprika, cardamom, cumin, fenugreek, red pepper, sage, thyme, and turmeric. Seasoned salt can be sprinkled on salads, added to stuffings, and sprinkled on meats and fish before broiling.

Premixed seasonings are a convenience. Buy commercial blends or prepare your own from herbs and spices you use often. Freshly ground seasonings are always more pungent than packaged ones.

RECIPE MODIFICATION FOR HIGH-ALTITUDE BAKING

Baking at altitude (above 3,000 feet) can affect ingredients, proportions, and cooking times.

Feet Above Sea Level	Reduce Each Teaspoon Baking Powder by	Reduce Each Cup Sugar by	Increase Each Cup Liquid by
3,000–5,000	⅛ teaspoon	1 tablespoon	2 tablespoons
5,000–7,000	⅛–¼ teaspoon	2 tablespoons	2–3 tablespoons
7,000–10,000	¼ teaspoon	2–3 tablespoons	3–4 tablespoons
Above 10,000	¼–½ teaspoon	2–3 tablespoons	3–4 tablespoons
Over 3,000 feet:	Increase oven temperature by 25° F. Underbeat eggs (beat whites to soft peak stage).		
Over 10,000 feet:	Add one extra egg and increase each cup flour by 1–2 tablespoons.		

HIGH-ALTITUDE COOKING

At altitudes over 3,000 feet, foods cook differently than at sea level because of lower air pressure. Water boils at a lower temperature and food takes longer to heat; liquids evaporate more quickly; leavenings expand more; sugar becomes more concentrated; and batters have a greater tendency to stick to pans.

To compensate for these differences, increase cooking time for foods that are boiled, and raise oven temperature for baked goods by 25° F. Increase liquids, decrease leavenings, underbeat eggs and egg-based batters, decrease sugar, and butter and flour pans well or line with nonstick parchment paper. For baked goods, consult the chart above for exact recipe changes. Specific information about the effect of altitude on cooking in your area is available from cooperative extension agents of the U.S. Department of Agriculture or newspaper food editors.

EFFECT OF ALTITUDE ON BOILING WATER

Above 2,000 feet, the boiling temperature of water drops, as demonstrated in this chart.

Altitude	Water Boils at
Sea level	212° F
2,000 feet	208° F
5,000 feet	203° F
7,500 feet	198° F
10,000 feet	194° F
15,000 feet	185° F
30,000 feet	158° F

HONEY

Flower nectar gathered by bees and deposited in the waxy network of cells known as a honeycomb is the source of honey. Depending on the flower from which it is derived, honey can be quite strong and dark like buckwheat honey, or pale and delicate like clover honey. Among the best-loved honeys in the world are those made from thyme, orange, heather, rosemary, acacia, sage, and tupelo.

Use   The sweetness and spreadable texture of honey make it popular as a topping for breads, toast, biscuits, and corn muffins. As an ingredient in baked goods, it adds sweetness and moisture. Cakes, cookies, and breads with honey stay moist longer than those sweetened with sugar. Honey is traditional in Greek baklava (walnut-filled pastry), Israeli honey cake, Italian *panforte,* and in many Moroccan pastries. Moroccans also use honey to glaze poultry in several savory preparations. Honey is the principal sweetener in many confections, such as Turkish halvah and nougat.

Availability   Dozens of varieties of honey are marketed in the United States, but all are of three basic kinds: comb or straight from the hive; chunk, which contains bits of honeycomb; and extracted, the most common form. Extracted honey is removed from the comb with a centrifuge, heated to destroy yeasts, strained to remove wax and debris, then filtered for clarity. Honey is generally packed in jars or plastic squeeze bottles.

Selection   As honeys vary in flavor (see introduction), select one whose character will best complement its intended use.

Storage   Honey will keep indefinitely in a cool, dark place. Store it in an airtight container to prevent the absorption of moisture from the air.

Preparation   If honey becomes crystallized on standing, reliquefy by setting jar in a pan of hot water and warming gently over low heat.

■ SPICED FRENCH HONEY BREAD
Classic French *pain d'épice* does not contain eggs or shortening, but gets its moist richness from the inclusion of honey and cream.

- ½ teaspoon anise seed
- 1 teaspoon *each* baking soda and ground cinnamon
- ½ teaspoon *each* ground ginger and cloves
- ¼ teaspoon salt
- 3 cups flour
- 2 tablespoons dried currants
- ¼ cup firmly packed brown sugar
- ¾ cup honey
- ⅔ cup whipping cream
- ⅓ cup milk
- 1 teaspoon grated orange rind

1. Preheat oven to 325° F. Lightly grease and flour a 4½- by 8½-inch loaf pan. Whirl anise seed in a clean coffee grinder or electric minichopper until powdery.

2. In a large bowl combine ground anise seed, baking soda, cinnamon, ginger, cloves, salt, flour, currants, and brown sugar.

3. In a small bowl blend honey, cream, milk, and orange rind. Add honey mixture to flour mixture, stirring just until dry ingredients are moistened. Spread in prepared loaf pan.

4. Bake until a skewer inserted in center comes out clean (1 hour and 20 minutes to 1 hour and 30 minutes). Let cool in pan 5 minutes, then turn out onto a rack to cool completely. Wrap and let stand for at least 1 day before slicing thinly to serve.

Serves 8.

Recipes and Related Information
Baklava, 222; Honeyed Chicken With Apricots, 557; Panforte, 186; Sopaipillas, 182.

HORSERADISH

Native to Eastern Europe but cultivated today in the United States, horseradish is a pungent cylindrical root in the cabbage family. It has a rough, thin, light brown skin and a white flesh that, when sliced or grated, releases an acrid oil. Its origins are unknown, but today it grows in cool regions of the United States and Europe. The plant known as Japanese horseradish (see WASABI) is botanically unrelated, although it too is valued for its pungent root.

Use Because the pungent character of horseradish is highly volatile, the root is rarely cooked. Instead it is used raw as a condiment or as an ingredient in other condiments. Grated horseradish is part of most tomato-based cocktail sauces for shellfish. Mixed with whipped cream and/or sour cream, it becomes a favorite sauce for prime rib, boiled meats, and smoked fish. It adds a lively hotness to cream dressings for beets and coleslaw. Grated horseradish is the standard accompaniment to gefilte fish, fish cakes traditional on Jewish holiday tables.

Availability Grated horseradish bottled in vinegar is sold in most supermarkets. Some varieties are colored red with beet juice. Most supermarkets also carry bottled imitation horseradish flavored with oil of horseradish. Fresh horseradish root can be found in some markets fall through spring. It is most widely available in the spring, around the time of the Jewish Passover celebration, because it has a traditional function at the holiday table. Some European specialty markets also carry dried powdered horseradish.

Selection Choose a root of fresh horseradish that is smooth and unblemished.

Storage Keep horseradish in a paper bag inside a plastic bag in the refrigerator crisper for up to one week. Freeze whole fresh horseradish up to six months (see Preparation). Bottled horseradish should be refrigerated, tightly capped, in its original container. Because it quickly loses pungency, it should be used within one month. Store dried horseradish in an airtight container in a cool, dry place; it will gradually lose pungency but should stay vigorous for up to one year.

Preparation Scrub fresh horseradish and scrape away outer skin; halve and cut out center core.

◾ HORSERADISH CREAM SAUCE
The sharpness of horseradish livens up cool sour cream and makes a wonderful sauce for roasted meats.

> 1 cup sour cream
> 3 tablespoons freshly grated horseradish
> ½ teaspoon salt
> ⅛ teaspoon white pepper

Combine sour cream, horseradish, salt, and pepper. Serve chilled with hot or cold roast beef or other roasted, broiled, or grilled meats.

Makes about 1 cup.

HUCKLEBERRY

Although huckleberries resemble blueberries, they are unrelated. The huckleberry is the fruit of a native American plant of the genus *Gaylussacia*. Huckleberries are not cultivated; they grow wild, generally on low, spreading bushes, and they are generally smaller and darker than blueberries. Whereas blueberries have many tiny unnoticeable seeds, huckleberries have ten hard, rather large ones. They are also tarter than blueberries.

Use Many cooks prefer the huckleberry over the blueberry for pies because it is a tarter berry. Huckleberries can also be added to muffin and quick bread batters, or eaten fresh for breakfast with sugar and milk.

Availability Because huckleberries are not cultivated, they are generally available only to foragers.

Storage See BLUEBERRY.

Preparation Wash gently and dry quickly.

HUSK; HUSK, TO

The dry outer covering, as in the corn husk; also the act of removing the husk. Dried corn husks are the traditional wrapper for Mexican tamales.

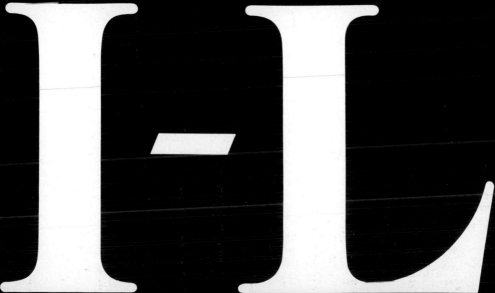

ICE CREAM AND FROZEN DESSERT

What we now know as ice cream—at first called cream ice—was introduced by a French chef to King Charles I of England in the early seventeenth century. Initially, frozen desserts were reserved exclusively for royalty and court nobility. However, by the end of the seventeenth century commoners, too, were indulging in these confections.

Despite the rapid spread of frozen ices and ice creams throughout Europe, the enormous and widespread popularity that ice cream enjoys today is a relatively modern, and largely American, phenomenon, thanks in no small way to the development of reliable refrigeration in the twentieth century. The familiar hand-cranked ice cream churn was invented by an American in 1846, the first ice cream cone sold in St. Louis in 1904, and during the 1920s and 1930s a variety of frozen desserts were invented in rapid succession—including Eskimo Pie, the Good Humor bar, and the Popsicle.

Today, a new generation of ice cream freezers for the home—smaller, easier to use, and more efficient than earlier versions—is inspiring ice cream enthusiasts to make homemade frozen desserts on a regular basis, not just for the occasional special party as was common when freezers were far bulkier and messier. Across America thousands of electric ice cream machines and prechilled canisters stand ready to swing into action at a moment's notice.

ICE CREAM FREEZERS

Preparing ice cream to be frozen doesn't require a lot of equipment other than an ice cream churn or freezer; the bowls, spoons, and saucepans used for everyday cooking fill most needs. The following describes the four basic categories of ice cream freezers—including the strengths and weaknesses of each.

SALT AND ICE-BUCKET FREEZER

This is the traditional ice cream churn that most of us remember from childhood. It has a large bucket with a smaller canister fit into it. Originally the bucket was made of wood and needed to be soaked in water before using to prevent leaks. Today most machines use a plastic or fiberglass bucket. The canister, made of stainless steel, has a removable lid; inside is a stationary paddle called a dasher. The blades are usually wood, plastic, or another soft substance, and are positioned so that they gently scrape the inside of the canister as it turns. The canister is continuously rotated by either a hand crank or an electric motor, while a mixture of about three-fourths ice and one-fourth rock salt in the bucket freezes the ice cream inside the canister. As an added convenience, some models require only ice cubes and ordinary table salt.

The hand-cranked model is less expensive than one that is motor-driven but requires 20 to 30 minutes of cranking for each batch of ice cream. Units equipped with electric motors produce slightly better results because of their consistent speed. Both models make excellent ice cream, but they do require messing with ice and salt. Be aware that some freezers of this type won't hold whole ice cubes, so the ice must be crushed before being put into the machine. In addition, the freezer of older models must be partially disassembled to check on the ice cream, occasionally resulting in some of the brine mixture splashing into the canister. Some newer freezers have the motor under the canister, so the ice cream can be checked without taking the machine apart.

REFRIGERATOR-FREEZER UNIT

Some ice cream freezers are designed to fit inside the freezing compartment of a refrigerator, with the power cord snaking out through the closed door. An electric motor churns the ice cream mixture and drives a small fan that circulates the cold air around the canister. The canister is stationary; the dasher turns. Their major advantage

---

FROZEN DESSERTS—THE REAL SCOOP

Much confusion exists over the names and definitions of particular types of frozen desserts as they cross the boundaries of many cultures and languages. To further complicate matters, common usage varies, especially regarding sherbets and sorbets. The following are broad definitions.

Frozen Yogurt A frozen dessert with yogurt as its base, it has a smooth texture very similar to ice cream, although less creamy, and a rich, slightly acidic taste. Frozen yogurt is usually flavored with fruit.

Gelato Italian *gelato* contains less air than most French or American ice creams, making it denser and firmer. The frozen-canister–type ice cream maker, which does not incorporate much air into the base during freezing, produces an ice cream that is similar to gelato. Use any recipe adapted from French Vanilla Ice Cream Base (see page 311) to make gelato. For richer ice cream, add more egg yolks (see Custard-Based Ice Cream).

Granita The Spanish name *granita* refers to the slightly grainy, granular texture of this type of sherbet, which is frozen without constant churning. In general, granitas have less sugar than sherbets. They should be served slightly thawed and slushy. Granitas may be whipped in a food processor with a metal blade just before serving. The resulting texture is nearly as smooth as that of a churned sherbet (see Sherbet, at right).

Ice This is the generic term for a sherbet (see Sherbet, at right).

Ice Cream Egg yolks, milk, cream, sugar, and flavorings form the base of this smooth, rich, frozen dessert. U.S. Food and Drug Administration standards require that to be labeled and sold as "ice cream," it must have at least 10 percent butterfat, at least 20 percent milk solids, and not more than 50 percent air. In France it is called *glace* (see GLACE), in Italy *gelato* (see Gelato, at left). There are two general American-style types: cooked custard-based ice cream and uncooked Philadelphia-style ice cream.

Ice Milk This is the generic name for frozen desserts that cannot be labeled ice cream because they contain too much air and/or too little butterfat.

Milk Ice This is a sherbet to which a small amount of milk or cream has been added, but not enough to make it an ice cream (see Sherbet, following).

Sherbet A water ice, sherbet is usually made from pulverized fruit pulp, fruit juice, and sugar syrup. It is often called by the French name *sorbet* and sometimes by the Italian name *sorbetto*. You may also see it called ice, water ice, Italian ice, or fruit ice. To make matters a bit more confusing, in parts of the United States "sherbet" contains milk or cream and is technically a milk ice. In these places water ices are usually called sorbets. The density of the sugar syrup used greatly affects the texture and flavor of a sherbet. French sorbets, made with a fairly light syrup, are slightly grainy and have an intense fruit flavor. Italian sorbettos, made with a heavier syrup, are smoother and sweeter.

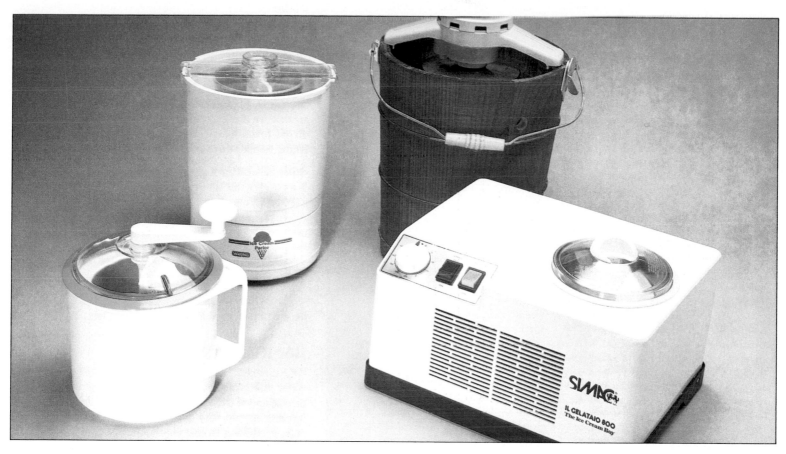

is that they don't require salt and ice. A major disadvantage is their limited availability.

PRECHILLED CANISTER FREEZER

The newest type of ice cream machine is sometimes called a Donvier-type after the Japanese company that invented it. This machine features a sealed, hollow metal canister that is filled with a special coolant. The canister must be held at 0° F in the freezer compartment of a refrigerator for 8 hours before use. Then the canister is removed and filled with the chilled ice cream mixture; a lid with a crank and dasher assembly is placed over it. The crank is rotated by hand every 2 or 3 minutes until the mixture is frozen, which is usually 12 to 18 minutes. The major disadvantage of this type of machine is that the canister takes up a fair amount of space in the freezing compartment. The primary advantages are that it's easy to use and, because of its special coolant, it freezes quickly enough to yield a product with surprisingly good texture—if the ice cream is eaten immediately. Because little air is incorporated during the churning process, the ice cream from this type of machine becomes very hard when stored.

FREEZER WITH SELF-CONTAINED REFRIGERATION

This is the Rolls Royce of ice cream machines, complete with its own refrigeration unit. Freezing coils are wrapped around the canister and a motorized dasher mixes the ice cream as it freezes. It is the easiest machine to use: Just pour in the ice cream mixture and turn the machine on. Because it lowers the temperature of the mixture quickly, this type of machine tends to yield the smoothest texture. Its chief drawbacks are high price and amount of counter space it occupies. Try not to store a self-contained machine away from where it is used; most must stand for 24 hours to allow the refrigerant to settle before use.

OTHER ICE CREAM–MAKING EQUIPMENT

The items listed below, most of which fall into the category of ordinary kitchen equipment rather than specialty tools, are helpful but not mandatory for making ice cream and other frozen desserts.

Blender and/or Food Processor Either machine makes it easier to purée fruit for ice creams and sherbets.

Candy Thermometer The best way to monitor the changes sugar goes through as it is heated is with a candy thermometer. A small, instant-read thermometer can also be used (see THERMOMETER).

Ice Cream Spades and Scoops Nonstick scoops contain a fluid antifreeze to ensure easy release of ice cream. Mechanical scoops have an arc-shaped blade that sweeps

Today's ice cream freezers make it simpler than ever to prepare frozen desserts at home on a regular basis. Among the most commonly available machines are (from left to right): prechilled canister freezer, salt and bucket freezer (ice cube and table salt type), salt and bucket freezer (crushed ice and rock salt type), freezer with self contained refrigeration.

ABOUT COOLING, FREEZING, AND STORING

Cooling an ice cream mixture thoroughly before churning is essential. It may be cooled slowly in the refrigerator or rapidly over an ice-water bath. If the mixture is warmer than 40° F when the freezing process begins, the increased churning time is likely to produce flecks of butter, especially in recipes that call for a high proportion of cream to milk. Although harmless, butter flecks are unpleasant and ruin the fine texture of homemade ice cream. (If butter forms in a batch of ice cream, allow ice cream to melt in the refrigerator. When liquid, strain the mixture through a fine sieve to remove the butter, then refreeze. The resulting ice cream will not be as smooth as if the recipe had been prepared properly, but it will be tasty and free of butter.)

EXPANSION DURING FREEZING

When filling an ice cream machine with ice cream mixture, stop at least 2 inches below the top of the canister. As ice cream freezes, it expands slightly. More important, the churning action incorporates air. This aeration, called loft or overrun, improves the texture of the finished ice cream and helps prevent it from becoming a solid block of ice.

If the freezing canister is filled two thirds and the finished ice cream reaches the top, the overrun is approximately 50 percent; if the canister is filled three quarters full and the ice cream reaches the top, the overrun is approximately 30 percent. High-quality ice cream has 20 to 50 percent overrun.

STORING AND SERVING TEMPERATURES

Ice cream and other frozen desserts should be stored at low temperatures to prolong their shelf life and protect their texture and flavor. Between 0° and 10° F is ideal. Ice cream should be allowed to warm slightly before serving, to about 30° F for serving. If ice cream is firmly frozen, transfer it from freezer to refrigerator 20 to 30 minutes before serving, or leave at room temperature for 10 to 15 minutes. Don't let ice cream thaw too much. Repeated thawing and refreezing will destroy its texture.

Although it is best to "ripen" most homemade ice creams in the freezer for several hours, they should be eaten within one or two days. Ice cream stored for long periods develops ice crystals on its surface and acquires a heavy, undesirable texture.

across the interior of the bowl to release ice cream. Spades have a wide flat surface instead of a bowl-shaped one. The numbers imprinted on the handles of many scoops indicate how many scoops of that size can be removed from one quart of ice cream. Scoops come in many sizes (see SPOON, LADLE, AND SCOOP).

Mixer   A hand-held or bowl mixer is useful for combining egg yolks and sugar, beating egg whites, and blending other commonly used ingredients (see MIXERS).

Molds   Plastic or stainless steel molds will allow you to layer ice cream into special shapes and several flavors of ice cream or sherbet in one frozen dessert. Although some molds are made specifically for frozen desserts, any type of mold of an appropriate size will work. To unmold a frozen dessert, gently immerse the mold nearly to the top in warm water to soften the ice cream around the edges. Then place a plate or serving tray upside down over the mold, and invert them both together (see MOLD).

Stainless Steel Mixing Bowls   A large stainless steel bowl with a flat bottom, set over a large kettle of boiling water, makes an excellent substitute for a double boiler, which is usually too small for the quantities involved in making ice cream. Stainless steel is better than glass or ceramic because it can be transferred from the heat to an ice-water bath without danger of breaking. Unlike other metals, stainless steel does not react with common ice cream ingredients, such as acidic fruits; aluminum and copper tend to discolor when they come in contact with acids and can impart a metallic taste.

Stainless Steel or Wooden Spoons   These types of spoons are preferred for ice cream making because they do not react with acidic ingredients and can tolerate extreme temperature changes.

Storage Containers   Ice cream should always be stored in a covered, airtight container to prevent it from absorbing odors from other foods and from forming crystals (the result of free moisture) on its surface. Any plastic container with a tight-fitting lid is fine. If the container is less than half full, it is a good idea to press a sheet of plastic wrap on the surface of the ice cream to seal it from the air.

Wire Whisk   In addition to performing mixing tasks when an electric mixer isn't available, a whisk is handy for stirring custard mixtures on the stove.

BASIC INGREDIENTS

For ice cream to have a smooth, creamy texture, both the water molecules and the fat globules in the mixture must be suspended evenly, so the ice crystals that form during freezing remain very small. The basic ice cream ingredients, in addition to contributing flavor, help maintain this balance.

Many commercial ice cream manufacturers use emulsifiers and stabilizers to improve the texture of their products, to mask or compensate for inferior ingredients, or to achieve an extended shelf life. Such artificial ingredients are never needed in homemade ice cream prepared in small quantities with fresh, wholesome ingredients. However, some noncommercial ice cream recipes call for such ingredients as cornstarch, instant vanilla pudding, gelatin, and flour in an attempt to simulate the texture produced by more expensive ingredients. Anyone who has tasted good homemade ice cream, made with pure, high-quality ingredients, will find it hard to offer such pseudoflavors to family and guests.

Cream   The butterfat in cream is primarily responsible for providing the rich, smooth texture of ice cream. In general, the higher the proportion of butterfat, the richer and smoother the ice cream. Resist the temptation to substitute all heavy cream for light cream, half-and-half, or milk in an ice cream recipe. Too much cream greatly increases the chance of producing ice cream flecked with butter. As a general rule, do not exceed a ratio of 75 percent cream to 25 percent milk.

Eggs   In many ice cream recipes egg yolks are cooked to form the custard base. They act as emulsifiers, keeping the fat globules in milk and cream from clumping together.

Fruit Most fruits used to flavor ice creams and sher bets contain naturally occurring pectin and a certain amount of fiber. Both of these substances help to keep both milk fat and water molecules in an even suspension as they freeze.

Milk The fat in milk forms small globules in the ice cream mixture and helps to keep the water molecules dispersed. The emulsifying action of the cooked egg yolks helps to keep these small fat globules from clumping together as they are churned. If they do form clumps, they will produce butter.

Sugar Water in which sugar has dissolved has a freezing point below 32° F. Because of the sugar present, not all the water in the mixture freezes. Sugar thus helps to keep the ice cream from becoming a solid block of ice.

CONTROLLING ICE CREAM TEXTURE

The texture of the finished ice cream depends on how fast it is processed. The faster the freezing process, the smoother the texture. You can control the rate of freezing by varying the amount of salt you use with the ice. Use about three fourths of a standard 26-ounce box of salt for relatively fast freezing and excellent across-the-board results. Using a whole box will shorten the freezing time, producing a finer, smoother texture; using half a box will lengthen the freezing time and give an icier texture.

CUSTARD-BASED ICE CREAM

Traditional, rich, custard-based ice cream is sometimes referred to as French custard. Egg yolks are cooked with sugar, milk, and cream to form a custard, to which flavoring is added. This method produces the richest and smoothest ice creams. The same ingredients combined in different proportions give somewhat varied results. For example, increasing the milk to 2 cups will produce a slightly lighter ice cream; adding 2 more egg yolks, for a total of 6, will make the ice cream richer. Experiment to find which combination of ingredients you prefer.

■ FRENCH VANILLA ICE CREAM BASE

This recipe is a foundation for most flavored ice creams. It produces consistently excellent flavor and texture regardless of the ice cream machine used. The texture can be varied by combining the ingredients in different proportions (see Custard-Based Ice Cream, above). If desired, for a more intense flavor, use 2 beans or double the amount of vanilla extract. Keep in mind that vanilla beans give a richer flavor than vanilla extract (see VANILLA BEAN). A vanilla bean can be used several times; remove bean from custard by straining custard through a fine mesh sieve. Rinse bean, dry thoroughly, and store airtight. As is true of all custards, be sure to use gentle heat when cooking the egg-yolk and cream mixture or the custard will curdle.

A DICTIONARY OF ICE CREAM DESSERTS

Many ice cream concoctions go by different names in different regions. The following definitions seem to be the ones most widely held.

Banana Split Adding a banana transforms a sundae into a banana split or royale. The traditional banana split has three flavors of ice cream, three different toppings, a banana sliced lengthwise, whipped cream, chopped nuts, and maraschino cherries.

Bombe Made in a spherically shaped mold, a bombe is layered with two or more flavors of ice cream, or ice cream and sherbet; each layer forms a shell for the next layer.

Ice Cream Soda An ice cream soda is composed of three basic parts: flavoring; carbonated water, such as seltzer water or club soda; and ice cream. Whipped cream is often added as a finish. To make the "perfect" ice cream soda, choose a large glass and put in about 2 tablespoons flavored syrup (use more or less to taste). Fill glass with carbonated water to within 2 inches of the rim. Mix well. Position a scoop of ice cream on the edge of the glass, balanced so that its bottom touches the surface of the soda. If desired, add a swirl of whipped cream. Serve with a long-handled spoon and a straw. Some famous combinations include the following:
Black and White Chocolate syrup and vanilla ice cream.
Black Cow Cola and vanilla ice cream.
Brown Cow Root beer and vanilla ice cream.
Strawberry Blondie Ginger ale and strawberry ice cream.

Milk Shakes, Malteds, Floats, and Frappes A milk shake is flavored milk shaken to a thick and foamy consistency, often with ice cream added. A malted is a milk shake to which malted milk powder has been added before blending—any amount from a single teaspoon to several tablespoons is fine. A float is a combination of fruit juice or a carbonated soft drink and a scoop of ice cream. A frappe is a frozen slush mixture made without dairy products; a simple sugar syrup is mixed with fruits or flavorings and partially frozen, then processed in a blender or food processor to the desired consistency. In some parts of the country a milk shake made with ice cream is called a frappe, and in still others a frappe is carbonated water mixed with ice cream.

Parfait and Coupe As served at the soda fountain, a parfait is a layered sundae in a long, slender glass. Simple to make, it is just alternating layers of ice cream and topping. A *coupe* is ice cream served with fruit topping.

Sundae This is the most free-form soda fountain creation, limited only by the imagination of the maker and the size of the dish. A sundae can be made with a single scoop of ice cream or a mountain of different flavors. There are no hard and fast rules of sundae making. One scoop, drizzled with one sauce and crowned with whipped cream, might suffice for some ice cream lovers, while others insist on a dish overflowing with a hodgepodge of nuts, syrups, toppings, fresh fruits, crushed candies, cookies, and whipped cream.

---

3 cups whipping cream
1 cup milk
¾ cup sugar
1 vanilla bean, split lengthwise, *or*
   1 tablespoon vanilla extract
4 large egg yolks

1. In a heavy-bottomed, 2-quart saucepan, heat cream, milk, sugar, and vanilla bean. (If you are using vanilla extract, do not add it until step 3.) Stir occasionally until sugar is dissolved and mixture is hot but not boiling.

2. Whisk egg yolks together in a bowl. Continue whisking and very slowly pour in approximately 1 cup of cream mixture. When smooth, pour back into pan.

3. Whisk constantly over low heat until mixture thickens enough to coat back of a spoon (about 5 minutes). Do not let mixture boil or it will curdle. Custard is done if line remains when finger is drawn across back of coated spoon. Remove vanilla bean. Add vanilla extract, if used.

Makes about 1 quart.

French Vanilla Ice Cream begins with a custard base. A custard has thickened sufficiently if it coats the back of a spoon and if a line drawn through the custard with your finger remains.

■ FRENCH VANILLA ICE CREAM

True ice cream aficionados will always return to the rich flavor of vanilla ice cream. It is delicious in its basic form or in any of the variations offered at the end of the recipe.

    French Vanilla Ice Cream Base (see page 311)
1 **vanilla bean, split lengthwise,** *or*
   1 **tablespoon vanilla extract**

1. Prepare French Vanilla Ice Cream Base, adding the vanilla with the vanilla in the base. Strain into a clean bowl and cool thoroughly.

2. Transfer to an ice cream machine and freeze according to manufacturer's instruction

Makes about 1 quart.

Butter Pecan Ice Cream   Prepare French Vanilla Ice Cream, but dissolve ¾ cup light brown sugar and 3 tablespoons unsalted butter in the French Vanilla Ice Cream Base instead of granulated sugar. Transfer mixture to an ice cream machine and freeze according to manufacturer's instructions; halfway through freezing process, add 1 cup chopped, toasted pecans.

Chocolate Ice Cream   Prepare French Vanilla Ice Cream Base. In a double boiler melt together 3 ounces semisweet chocolate and 1 ounce unsweetened chocolate. Slowly add ½ cup of the warm ice cream base to melted chocolate; whisk constantly to keep chocolate smooth. Return mixture to ice cream base; mix well and let cool. Continue with step 2, French Vanilla Ice Cream.

Chocolate Chip Ice Cream   Prepare French Vanilla Ice Cream through step 1. Transfer mixture to an ice cream machine and freeze according to manufacturer's instructions; halfway through freezing process, add 1 cup miniature chocolate chips.

Coffee Ice Cream   Prepare French Vanilla Ice Cream through step 1; add 2 tablespoons instant espresso powder and whisk until it is dissolved. Continue with step 2.

Fresh Fruit Ice Cream   Prepare French Vanilla Ice Cream through step 1. Peel, pit, chop, and mash 4 cups fresh fruit: peaches, nectarines, or apricots. Combine mashed fruit with ¼ to ½ cup sugar (less if fruit is very sweet, more if it is not sweet enough) and let sit 1 hour. Add fruit to strained ice cream base and continue with step 2.

Rum Raisin Ice Cream   Prepare French Vanilla Ice Cream through step 1. Soak ½ cup raisins in 3 ounces dark rum for 1 hour. Transfer ice cream mixture to an ice cream machine and freeze according to manufacturer's instructions; halfway through freezing process, add raisins and rum.

Strawberry Ice Cream   Prepare French Vanilla Ice Cream through step 1. Wash, hull, and mash 2 pints fresh strawberries. Combine mashed berries with ½ cup sugar and let sit 1 hour (more if berries are not sweet). Add strawberries to strained ice cream base and continue with step 2.

PHILADEPHIA-STYLE ICE CREAM

Philadelphia-style ice creams are uncooked. Some do not use eggs; others use whole eggs. Their texture is usually slightly grainier than custard-based ice creams because they lack the emulsifying action of cooked egg yolks to keep the water molecules separated as they freeze. However, bulky flavoring agents, such as significant quantities of fruit pulp or chocolate, can provide their own emulsifying action and make up for the lack of cooked egg yolks, greatly improving the texture of uncooked ice creams.

■ PHILADELPHIA-STYLE VANILLA ICE CREAM

Adding a whole egg to this recipe will give the ice cream a smoother texture.

  2 **cups whipping cream**
  2 **cups half-and-half**
 ¾ **cup sugar**
  2 **teaspoons vanilla extract**

1. Combine ingredients. Stir until sugar is dissolved.

2. Transfer to an ice cream machine and freeze according to manufacturer's instructions.

Makes about 1 quart.

PHILADELPHIA STYLE CHOCOLATE ICE CREAM

Chocolate acts as a smoothing agent to give this ice cream a velvety texture.

8 ounces semisweet chocolate
½ cup sugar
1 quart half-and-half
Pinch of salt

1. In a double boiler over low heat melt chocolate; set aside. Combine sugar, half-and-half, and salt. Stir until sugar is completely dissolved. Add melted chocolate, stirring until well mixed.

2. Transfer to an ice cream machine and freeze according to manufacturer's instructions.

Makes about 1 quart.

GELATO, FROZEN YOGURT, SHERBET, AND GRANITA

Gelato contains less air than American or French ice cream. The Donvier-type ice cream machine will produce the most gelatolike product because it does not incorporate much air into the base during freezing. To make gelato, use any recipe based on French Vanilla Ice Cream Base (see page 311). For frozen yogurt, any type of yogurt can be used, but one with a higher fat content yields a creamier result. Sherbets are based on a sugar syrup, which should be well cooled, like an ice cream base, before using. They make refreshing between-course palate cleansers, as do *granitas*.

LEMON FROZEN YOGURT

The combined acidic flavors of yogurt and lemon make this an especially refreshing dessert.

4 tablespoons sugar
4 containers (8 oz each) lemon-flavored yogurt
Rind of 2 lemons, finely chopped

1. Whisk sugar into yogurt until completely dissolved (about 2 minutes); stir in lemon rind.

2. Transfer to an ice cream machine and freeze according to manufacturer's instructions.

Makes about 1 quart.

SIMPLE SUGAR SYRUP FOR SHERBETS

This is the most traditional of syrups, somewhere between a French and an Italian type. It may be stored in the refrigerator for several weeks.

2 cups sugar
1 cup water

1. In a medium saucepan over high heat, cook sugar and water, stirring constantly until sugar dissolves and mixture reaches a full, rolling boil.

Fresh fruits such as peaches and raspberries make super sherbets. Serve two or three flavors together for a memorable dessert.

2. Immediately remove from heat and cool to room temperature. Strain, cover, and refrigerate until needed. Have the syrup well cooled (about 40° F) before using.

Makes about 3 cups.

STRAWBERRY SHERBET

This is an excellent, fresh-tasting sherbet that stores well for up to two weeks.

2 pints fresh strawberries *or* 12 ounces frozen strawberries, without syrup
1 cup Simple Sugar Syrup for Sherbets (see left)
Juice of ½ lemon

1. Wash and hull strawberries. Purée with sugar syrup and lemon juice in a blender or food processor.

2. Transfer to an ice cream machine and freeze according to manufacturer's instructions.

Makes about 1 quart.

Fruit or Berry Sherbet Any fruit that yields a good deal of pulp when puréed may be substituted for strawberries: other berries, peaches, pears, plums, or melons. If using blackberries or boysenberries, strain the purée before freezing, as in Raspberry Sherbet (below).

Raspberry Sherbet Substitute 2 pints fresh raspberries or 12 ounces frozen raspberries for strawberries. Before freezing, seed by straining through cheesecloth or a fine sieve. If using a sieve, do not grind seeds against mesh; this will adversely affect both color and flavor.

Ice cream bombes are layered desserts formed in a special melon-shaped mold. Frozen Watermelon Bombe features a vanilla ice cream "rind" with raspberry sherbet "flesh" and chocolate chip "seeds." A wash of food coloring tints the outside surface an appropriate green hue.

■ LEMON SHERBET

When fruits that provide a lot of juice but very little pulp—such as lemon, orange, grapefruit, and other citrus—are used in sherbet, the texture may become grainy because of the greater proportion of liquids to solids. The same is true of sherbets made from Champagne, wines, and liqueurs. Adding stiffly beaten egg whites to the sugar syrup base smooths the texture. The syrup base in such sherbets is called an Italian meringue (see Note).

> 2 large egg whites
> 2¼ cups sugar
> 1 cup water
> 1½ cups fresh lemon juice

1. In a large bowl beat egg whites until very stiff; set aside. In a medium saucepan over high heat, cook sugar and the water, stirring constantly until sugar dissolves and the mixture reaches a full, rolling boil. Remove from heat and slowly drizzle hot syrup into egg whites, whisking constantly until all the syrup is incorporated. Continue whisking and slowly add lemon juice. Stir over an ice-water bath or cover and refrigerate until cold.

2. Transfer to an ice cream machine and freeze according to manufacturer's instructions.

Makes about 1 quart.

Note Another technique for improving the texture of such sherbets is to increase the proportion of sugar syrup to 50 percent of the total volume of the mixture. The extra sugar helps to keep the ice crystals, which form during freezing, small.

■ WHITE ZINFANDEL GRANITA

Any dry white wine will work in this refreshing *granita,* which does not need an ice cream machine; it freezes in the freezer compartment of the refrigerator.

> 1½ cups water
> ¾ cup sugar
> 1½ cups white Zinfandel

1. In a medium saucepan bring the water, sugar, and half the wine to a boil, stirring constantly until sugar dissolves. Reduce heat and simmer 3 minutes without stirring.

2. Allow syrup to cool to room temperature, or cool in refrigerator. Add remaining wine to cooled syrup. Place in a shallow metal pan and freeze in freezer compartment of refrigerator.

3. Stir well every 30 minutes until firm, 3 to 4 times. Let warm slightly, and stir one final time before serving.

Makes about 1 quart.

SOME WELL-KNOWN FROZEN DESSERTS

Frozen desserts are favorite treats all over the world. Italians love *tortoni,* the French love profiteroles, and Americans love mud pie, among many others. The following recipes capture some of the distinctive flavors of a number of countries. Additional frozen desserts can be found in other entries in this book (consult Recipes and Related Information).

■ TORTONI

Your guests will never guess how simple this Italian treat is to prepare. Note that the mixture with almond-flavored liqueur must freeze at least six hours.

> 1 cup whipping cream
> ¼ cup confectioners' sugar
> ½ cup crushed amaretti cookies or chopped, toasted almonds
> 3 tablespoons almond-flavored liqueur
> 1 large egg white, at room temperature
> Crushed amaretti cookies, toasted almonds, or maraschino cherries, for garnish (optional)

1. In a medium bowl whip the cream and sugar to soft peaks. Fold in crushed cookies and liqueur.

2. In a separate bowl beat egg white until stiff but still shiny and moist. Fold into whipped cream mixture.

3. Spoon into a 1-quart bowl, parfait glasses, or paper-lined muffin cups. Garnish (if desired). Cover tightly and freeze at least 6 hours.

Serves 8.

■ MUD PIE

This is a favorite among coffee and chocolate lovers.

    1 recipe Hot Fudge Sauce (see page 522)
    1 Chocolate Crumb Crust (see page 436)
    1 quart Coffee Ice Cream (see page 312),
        softened
    ¾ cup whipping cream
    1 teaspoon vanilla extract
    1 tablespoon confectioners' sugar
    ⅓ cup toasted almonds, for decoration

1. Pour a thin layer of fudge sauce into the cooled Chocolate Crumb Crust and freeze until firm.

2. Spoon ice cream into the frozen crust and level the top. Press plastic wrap over ice cream and freeze at least 1½ hours.

3. Spread a generous layer of fudge sauce over ice cream. Freeze at least 30 minutes. Meanwhile, whip the cream with vanilla and sugar. Spread over the frozen pie. Decorate with almonds and freeze another 2 hours or longer.

Serves 8 to 10.

■ FROZEN WATERMELON BOMBE

This ice cream bombe looks like a watermelon. It's a treat for the eyes as well as the palate. The bombe must freeze in stages, so preparation must begin early the day it will be served, or the day before.

    1 quart French Vanilla Ice Cream (see page 312),
        slightly softened
    ¼ cup miniature semisweet chocolate chips
    1 quart Raspberry Sherbet (see page 313),
        slightly softened
    Green food coloring

1. Place an 8-cup melon-shaped mold in the freezer for at least 1 hour.

2. Line inside of mold with an even layer of Vanilla Ice Cream. Cover with plastic wrap, pressing against the ice cream to seal it tightly and fill any air pockets. Return mold to freezer for at least 4 hours.

3. Stir chocolate chips into Raspberry Sherbet to simulate watermelon seeds; remove plastic wrap from mold and fill cavity with sherbet. Top with plastic wrap and freeze until firm.

4. To unmold, dip quickly in lukewarm water and invert onto a chilled platter. Return to freezer to set exterior.

5. Paint outside of molded ice cream with green food coloring, varying shades to resemble stripes on a real watermelon. Cover well and keep frozen. Slice to serve.

Serves 8 to 10.

■ PEACH MELBA

The great French chef Escoffier created this dessert in honor of a popular opera singer, Nellie Melba.

    3 cups water
    2 cups sugar
    4 large peaches, peeled, halved, and pitted
    1 tablespoon vanilla extract
    1 cup fresh raspberries
    1 quart French Vanilla Ice Cream (see page 312)

1. In a medium saucepan combine the water and sugar; bring to a boil. Add peach halves. Lower the heat and simmer, covered, for 10 to 15 minutes. Remove from heat; let cool. Stir in vanilla, then chill.

2. In a small saucepan heat raspberries to boiling, stirring and mashing berries with a spoon; cool, then chill.

3. To serve, place prepared peach halves on chilled dessert plates. Top each half with a scoop of ice cream. Drizzle raspberry topping all over each serving.

Serves 8.

■ CHERRIES JUBILEE

This well-known flambéed dessert provides a colorful, dramatic ending to any dinner party.

    2 tablespoons sugar
    1 can (16 oz) pitted sweet or sour
        red cherries, with juice
    2 tablespoons kirsch
    1 tablespoon cornstarch
    1 pint French Vanilla Ice Cream (see page 312)
    ½ cup brandy

1. In a small saucepan over moderate heat, warm sugar and cherries with their juice until hot but not boiling. Make a paste of kirsch and cornstarch. Whisk into cherry mixture; heat, stirring, until thickened (do not boil).

2. Scoop ice cream into dessert dishes. Pour brandy into a ladle and hold it over a medium burner or candle for a minute to warm it slightly. To serve, light a match, ignite the warmed brandy, and pour it over cherry sauce. Stir until the flame dies down. Spoon cherry sauce over ice cream and serve at once.

Serves 4 to 6.

Recipes and Related Information
Ice Cream–Filled Profiteroles, 164; Papaya Ice Cream, 405; Prickly Pear Snow, 479; Rosé Pears and Ice Cream, 612; Sauce, 522; Watermelon Sherbet, 359.

INDUCTION

This method of heating uses magnetic energy to heat cookware made of magnetic materials. For this system a special electrically powered induction cook top is needed. Energy coils located under a ceramic surface convert electric current to high-frequency alternating current. When a pan made of a magnetic metal—steel or cast iron, for example—is set on the cooking surface, energy generated by magnetic force flows through the pan and causes the molecules in the metal to move at high speed and heat up.

Induction cooking is said to be as responsive as gas to change in temperature. It is also more energy efficient than either gas or traditional electric systems because only the cookware is heated, and energy does not escape into the air. As induction stove tops lack potentially hazardous open flames or exposed coils, burns and fires are less likely to occur. Maintenance is another benefit; the smooth surface is easy to clean.

The main drawback is the need for special cookware to make the system work. Conventional aluminum, aluminum-clad, copper, ceramic, and nonmagnetic stainless steel can't be used. The material must be one a magnet will cling to: cast iron, enameled cast iron, porcelain enamel on steel, magnetic stainless steel, or pans specially designed for induction cooking.

Induction cook tops plug into regular household current and are available in single and multiple burner units.

INFUSE, TO

To permeate a liquid with the soluble essences of herbs, spices, teas, or coffee by simmering. Usually the liquid is water, although other liquids can become infusions. Some recipes for custard, for example, require milk that has been infused with vanilla flavor, accomplished by warming the milk with a vanilla bean and letting it sit for 5 to 10 minutes.

> ***Recipes and Related Information***
> *Coffee, 134; Custard, 168; Tea, 573.*

JAM, JELLY, PRESERVE, AND CONDIMENT

Making jams, preserves, and pickled foods at home is not the labor-intensive, exhaustive endeavor that it used to be, thanks to modern equipment and the knowledge available today. Grandmother's summer kitchen yielded endless jars made from quantities of homegrown produce. The modern cook puts up small batches when time permits; these smaller yields cook faster and, as a result, retain more color and flavor. Quality is not being sacrificed to fit the needs of busy schedules, for home-canned foods far outshine expensive commercial products. Once you have begun to fill your pantry with these creations, you will no longer be satisfied with storebought preserves and pickles. You can also be confident that your jars of food contain only pure, clean, and healthful ingredients. When you have mastered the following basic recipes, you can create your own combinations.

ABOUT THE RECIPES

As a word of reassurance to those who are concerned about food contamination, this entry discusses techniques that deal with high-acid or brined foods. These fruits, pickles, and relishes can be safely canned at the boiling temperature (212° F). With this treatment, the organisms that cause spoilage and the enzymes that might deteriorate quality will be destroyed. We will not discuss the canning of meat, fish, or unbrined vegetables, which are susceptible to botulism contamination with improper handling.

BASIC EQUIPMENT

Organize supplies ahead and store them together. That way you'll be able to make up a small batch with very little effort. Most canning equipment is available at hardware stores or cookware stores. Jars and lids are also sold at well-stocked supermarkets.

Candy Thermometer   To monitor the temperature of the fruit as it cooks; a combination candy and deep-fat thermometer is the practical choice for most kitchens.

Jar Tongs   For lifting hot, filled jars from the water bath after processing.

Jelly Jars   Storage jars for jelly only; they are sealed with household paraffin rather than by water-bath processing. Fancy jars with brightly colored lids and a quilted pattern on the glass will enhance the appearance of your jellies, making them especially attractive to give as gifts. When you seal jelly with paraffin, you can use many sizes and shapes of jars and glasses, as long as they can withstand the boiling temperature needed to sterilize them.

Kettle   For cooking; choose a 6- to 8-quart, nonreactive, heavy enamel or stainless steel pot. Do not use aluminum or cast-iron pots since they may react chemically with the acids and salts in foods, thereby producing unpleasant colors and metallic flavors.

Labels   For identifying and dating jars.

Ladle   For transferring cooked food to jars.

Mason Jars   Storage jars; they are widemouthed, available in half pint, pint, or quart sizes, with two-piece dome caps. They have self-sealing lids that are held in place by a metal ring band. The lids are replaced after each use,

but the ring bands may be reused if they're not rusted or bent. Named for their inventor, John Mason, the jars are manufactured by several companies.

Paraffin (Household Wax)   For quick-sealing jellies that don't need to be sealed by water-bath processing.

Slotted Spoon   For skimming off foam that develops on surface of cooked food; done before filling jars so product won't be cloudy.

Water-Bath Canner   For processing; this pot is in addition to the cooking kettle. It has a rack that lifts the filled jars off the bottom of the pot and away from direct heat (see Useful Definitions, Water-Bath Process). Be sure to read instructions provided by manufacturer.

Widemouthed Funnel   For filling jars; don't use standard, narrow-necked funnels as they will clog.

Wooden Spoon   For stirring fruits or vegetables as they cook; choose ones with long handles.

USEFUL DEFINITIONS

Headspace   This is the air space between the food in the jar and the lid or paraffin, commonly ⅛ to ½ inch (follow recipe directions). Headspace allows for the expansion of food while it's being processed. Insufficient headspace will cause the seal to break and the contents to seep out.

Jell Point   This is the temperature at which a recipe will thicken properly. Test the jell point of a recipe with a candy thermometer or by using a frozen saucer. Jelly mixtures are ready at about 220° F, jams at 221° F to 224° F. Alternatively, drop a large spoonful of jelly or jam onto a saucer that has been kept in the freezer. The mixture will set up in 2 minutes, and you can tell how "tight" the jelly or jam will be when cooled. For convenience, you may want to keep a stack of saucers in the freezer.

Pectin   All of the recipes for jams, jellies, and preserves in this entry use a combination of fruit, sugar, acid, and pectin—a jelling agent. Natural pectin is found in the seeds, skin, and flesh of fruit. Some fruits, such as apples, cranberries, and most citrus fruits, are high in pectin. Fruits low in pectin are combined with a high-pectin fruit or commercial pectin. With the right amount of pectin, recipes will jell properly. Without it, the consistency might be either too runny or too thick and unspreadable. Commercial pectin is available in powdered or liquid form. Use only the form called for in the recipe.

Sealing   An airtight seal protects the processed food from airborne organisms that could cause spoilage, and ensures a long shelf life. The recipes in this section are sealed either with a layer of paraffin or, more often, with metal lids and ring bands. Lids and bands seal in the following way: During water-bath processing, the contents of the jars expand and some air is forced out of the jars. When the jars cool, the remaining air contracts, creating a partial vacuum that pulls the lids tightly against the jar rims and holds them in place. The vacuum and the sealing compound of the lid maintain the seal. As the jars cool, you may hear a loud popping noise. This is an indication that a jar has just sealed. Sealing is not always accompanied by a loud noise, however. To test for a seal, press the center of the lid of a completely cooled jar with your finger. If the lid stays down, the jar is sealed. Once jars

Making preserves doesn't require much specialty equipment. Shown from left to right are: thermometer; tongs; jar labels; widemouthed funnel; water-bath canner with rack; jars, lids, and rings; kettle; ladle; slotted spoon; wooden spoon.

PRESERVES AND CONDIMENTS: A PANTRY GUIDE

Is there a difference between jams and jellies, chutneys and relishes? Yes, sometimes only a fine one, but it might be helpful to know what each product actually is before you choose which recipes to make. Listed are definitions plus suggestions for use of each type.

Chutneys are fruits or vegetables cooked very slowly with sugar, vinegar, and spices. Uses: condiment served with Indian and Asian meals, barbecue glaze.

Conserves are two or more fruits cooked with sugar and raisins or nuts. Uses: spread, ice cream and dessert sauce, cake filling, condiment.

Fruit Butters are puréed, spiced, cooked fruit, slowly simmered in an open kettle or oven until thick and creamy. Uses: spread, meat glaze, barbecue baste.

Fruit or Herb Vinegars are flavored vinegars that sometimes steep for a number of weeks to deepen their flavor. Uses: salad dressing and pan glaze.

Jams are mashed fruits, cooked with sugar and sometimes with added pectin. Uses: spread, barbecue baste, meat glaze.

Jellies are fruit juices boiled with sugar. Fine jellies are clear and shimmering; when cut, they hold their shape. Uses: spread, cake filling (jelly rolls), meat and poultry glaze.

Marmalades are soft, clear jellies cooked with the peel and flesh of citrus. Uses: spread, ice cream topping, glaze for cheesecake.

Mustards are condiments made of mustard seed or powder. Uses: spread, dipping sauce, salad dressing.

Pickles and Relishes are fruits or vegetables pickled with vinegar or preserved with sugar. Uses: meat and sandwich condiment.

Preserves are whole or coarse fruit pieces cooked with sugar and sometimes with added pectin. *Preserves* is also a general term for several types of fruit spreads, including jams and jellies. Uses: spread, cake filling, barbecue baste, meat glaze, waffle and pancake topping.

---

have sealed, the flat lids will adhere to the jar rims, so you may remove and reuse the ring bands. If a jar fails to seal, refrigerate and eat contents within a short period. See Sealing Methods for more information.

Water-Bath Process   This is a method of heat processing to inactivate the enzymes in food and kill microorganisms that cause spoilage and to ensure an airtight seal. It can be safely used for such foods as jams, fruit preserves, and brined products because their high acidity inhibits the formation of toxins. To process, hot, cooked fruit is ladled into sterilized jars and covered with sterilized lids. The jars are set on a rack in the canner and enough water is added so that the jars are covered by several inches. The water is brought to a boil, the canner covered, and the jars boiled for the time specified in the recipe (timing begins when water comes to a boil). When done, jars are removed with tongs, cooled at room temperature for at least 12 hours, then stored.

SEALING METHODS

To be fully safe when sealing jellies, jams, preserves, marmalades, conserves, and chutneys, use the water-bath method. Jellies can be safely sealed with paraffin, but many people find it convenient to process jellies. This is a matter of personal preference. Try both sealing methods and decide which works best for you. Not all products must be sealed, however. Jars can be capped and stored in the refrigerator or freezer, but will not keep as long.

WATER-BATH CANNER METHOD

1. Harvest or purchase ripe, not bruised, produce. Wash and trim.

2. Check mason jars and discard those that are cracked or chipped, which will prevent airtight seals. Wash and rinse. If ring bands have been previously used, replace them.

3. Sterilize jars: Set jars in a kettle and cover with water. Boil 15 minutes. Turn off heat and let jars sit in the hot water until they are filled. The flat caps should be covered with water in a saucepan and boiled for 5 minutes. The outside ring bands do not need to be sterilized because they never touch food.

4. Cook recipe as directed. Keep heat low and watch for scorching. Test jelly for its jell point or doneness (see Useful Definitions, Jell Point).

5. Using ladle and widemouthed funnel, fill sterilized jars with prepared recipe, leaving a ¼-inch headspace or as recipe directs. Clean any spillage from mouth of jar with dampened cloth to ensure a perfect seal. Attach sterilized metal lid with tongs. Screw on outer ring.

6. Process filled jars: Set jars in rack of water-bath canner and set filled rack in canner. Keep jars from touching one another or the sides of the canner so water can freely circulate. Add enough hot water to cover jars by 2 inches. Put on canner lid. Bring water to a full rolling boil and process according to recipe directions (processing time varies from recipe to recipe; begin counting processing time when the water boils). Remove jars from canner with jar tongs. Cool on a folded towel. The cap will pop loudly as jars cool, and lid will indent in center. This can occur anytime within a 12-hour period. Test each jar after 12 hours to make sure it has sealed (see Useful Definitions, Sealing). Label and date each jar.

7. Store in a cool, dry, dark area. Jars will keep for several years.

JELLY METHOD (PARAFFIN SEAL)

1. Sterilize jelly jars as directed in Water-Bath Canner Method, step 3.

2. Prepare jelly according to recipe. Skim off any foam from mixture with a slotted spoon.

3. Using ladle and widemouthed funnel, fill jelly jars with prepared recipe, leaving ¼-inch headspace or as recipe directs. Wipe rims with a dampened cloth. Let cool.

4. Seal with paraffin: Melt household paraffin in a mason jar or heat-resistant glass measuring cup over boiling water. (Do not use a tin can or tea kettle to melt paraffin, as many books recommend; metal gets extremely hot and becomes difficult to handle. Heat-resistant glass doesn't absorb heat as dramatically and is easy to store.)

Paraffin is highly flammable; never melt over direct heat or let the water under the melting wax boil away. Pour a thin layer (⅛ inch) of paraffin over cooled jelly. A glass measuring cup with pouring lip simplifies this step. Tilt jar to be sure that paraffin touches sides. Let paraffin harden and set. Pour on another ⅛ inch in the same manner and let this set.

For convenience, set aside a jar or measuring cup to use only for storing and melting paraffin. Don't clean the container between uses; when needed, remelt what has hardened in the jar or cup, adding more if necessary.

5. Store in a cool, dry, dark area. Jars will keep for several years.

NONSEALING METHODS: REFRIGERATOR AND FREEZER

For small batches and for products that will be eaten soon after processing, it is unnecessary to seal sterilized jars. Refrigerate when cool, and use within two to three weeks. Pickles or relishes will keep up to one year in the refrigerator and actually become more delicious, with a deeper, fuller flavor, as they age and mature.

Some jam recipes have been specially developed for freezer storage. These use commercial pectin, are not processed, and need very little cooking. The final product is a jam with a bright color but a thinner consistency. The jars can be frozen for up to eight months. Once they are opened they must be refrigerated and eaten within three weeks (see Spicy Blueberry Freezer Jam, page 321).

Water-bath processed jars may also be frozen if pantry shelf space is at a premium. Be sure to leave ½-inch headspace in the jar to allow for expansion in the freezer.

■ STRAWBERRY JAM

This old-fashioned favorite has a fresh berry flavor and a clear, bright red color. It is the perfect spread for all types of breads and rolls. Spoon it on scones, English muffins, French toast, biscuits, muffins, or toast.

    2 quarts crushed strawberries
    3 tablespoons fresh lemon juice
    6 cups sugar

1. Measure berries and place in an 8-quart or larger pot.

2. Add lemon juice and sugar to berries; bring slowly to boiling, stirring occasionally until sugar dissolves.

3. Cook rapidly to the jell point until desired thickness is reached (about 30 minutes). As mixture thickens, stir frequently to prevent sticking.

4. When ready, remove pot from heat and skim off foam with a slotted spoon.

5. Quickly ladle into clean, hot, sterilized jars, leaving ¼-inch headspace; fasten lids.

6. Process in boiling water bath 10 minutes.

Makes about 8 half-pints.

■ SUMMER PEACH JAM

Full-flavored fresh fruit is the essence of distinctive jams, jellies, and preserves. Fresh peaches are available from about May through September, and reach the peak of their season in late summer. Be sure to select firm, fully ripe fruit that is free of blemishes and bruises. Never use overripe peaches. Note that the peaches need to be peeled before cooking: To peel, cut a small *x* in blossom end and drop whole fruit into boiling water for about 30 seconds; plunge into cold water, and slip off skin.

    5 pounds (about 12 large) firm, ripe peaches
    3 tablespoons fresh lemon juice
    5 cups sugar

1. Wash, peel, and pit peaches. Slice peaches into small pieces. Measure 10 cups of sliced peaches.

2. Place peaches, lemon juice, and sugar in a large bowl and allow to sit for 1 hour.

3. Transfer peach mixture to an 8-quart or larger pot and simmer until sugar is dissolved. Bring to a full boil.

4. Cook rapidly to the jell point until desired thickness is reached (about 25 minutes). Stir occasionally at first and then constantly as mixture nears jell point.

5. When ready, remove pot from heat and skim off foam with a slotted spoon.

6. Quickly ladle into clean, hot, sterilized jars, leaving ¼-inch headspace; fasten lids.

7. Process in boiling water bath 10 minutes.

Makes 8 half-pints.

■ APRICOT PRESERVES

Don't miss apricots at the height of their short late spring, early summer season—May through July. Fill crêpes or smother waffles with this marvelous preserve. Note that the fruit mixture must stand 4 to 5 hours before cooking. To peel apricots, follow the directions for peeling peaches given in the introduction to Summer Peach Jam.

    2 pounds firm, ripe apricots
    ¼ cup fresh lemon juice
    4 cups sugar

1. Peel, halve, and pit apricots. You should have 5 cups.

2. Thoroughly mix fruit with lemon juice and sugar. Cover tightly; let stand 4 to 5 hours in a cool place.

3. Heat fruit mixture slowly to boiling in a 6-quart or larger pot, stirring occasionally until sugar dissolves.

4. Cook rapidly until fruit is translucent (about 30 minutes). As mixture thickens, stir frequently to prevent sticking.

5. Quickly ladle into clean, hot, sterilized jars, leaving ¼-inch headspace; fasten lids.

6. Process in boiling water bath 15 minutes.

Makes 4 half-pints.

TIPS

FOR SUCCESSFUL FRUIT PRESERVES

- *Do not substitute ingredients or your recipe won't jell properly. The chemistry will change, and a failed product result.*
- *Never double recipes that call for commercial pectin as the thickener.*
- *Read the instruction booklets that accompany mason jars and commercial pectins.*

Always a favorite, Classic Orange Marmalade is chunky with fruit and peel and permeated with a rich citrus flavor. To best show off its warm, golden color, present it at the table in a clear serving bowl.

3. Place pot containing orange and lemon slices over medium heat and simmer until peel is tender (about 35 minutes). Remove from heat and let stand another 24 hours.

4. Measure fruits and their liquid and return them to pot, adding an equal amount of sugar. Bring to a boil, reduce heat to medium, and cook, stirring frequently, until jell point is reached (45 to 60 minutes).

5. Combine lemon juice and water strained from seeds, add to pot, and cook marmalade 10 minutes more, stirring constantly.

6. Quickly ladle into clean, hot, sterilized jars, leaving ¼-inch headspace; fasten lids.

7. Process in boiling water bath 15 minutes.

Makes 6 half-pints.

■ CRANBERRY CONSERVE

Modify tradition a bit this year with this cranberry conserve. It's one less thing you'll have to prepare for busy holidays, and it tastes terrific with turkey, chicken, and wild game.

> 1 unpeeled orange, very finely chopped
> 2 cups water
> 3 cups sugar
> 1 quart fresh or frozen cranberries
> 1 cup raisins
> ½ cup chopped walnuts or other nuts

1. Combine orange and the water in a 6-quart or larger pot; cook rapidly until peel is tender (about 20 minutes).

2. Add sugar, cranberries, and raisins. Bring slowly to boiling, stirring occasionally until sugar dissolves.

3. Cook rapidly until mixture starts to thicken (about 8 minutes). As mixture thickens, stir frequently to prevent sticking. Stir in nuts the last 5 minutes of cooking.

4. Quickly ladle into clean, hot, sterilized jars, leaving ¼-inch headspace; fasten lids.

5. Process in boiling water bath 15 minutes.

Makes 4 half-pints.

■ CLASSIC ORANGE MARMALADE

Traditionally, the finest orange marmalade is made from slightly bitter Seville oranges. They are hard to come by in this country, but if you can find them, by all means use them in this recipe. If you can't find bitter oranges, substitute sweet Valencia or navel oranges. Note that the fruit must sit for two 24-hour periods to soften the peel and release the natural pectin before cooking and processing.

> 6 bitter oranges (if available) or sweet oranges
> 2 sweet oranges
> 1 lemon
> 9½ cups water
>   Sugar, as needed
> 1½ tablespoons fresh lemon juice

1. Slice oranges and lemon very thinly. Remove seeds and place slices in a small bowl with ½ cup of the water; set aside.

2. Place lemon and orange slices in a large pot and cover with the remaining water. Soak 24 hours.

■ APPLE BUTTER

Old-fashioned apple butter is difficult to find in stores and very easy to make. It is delicious on toast and waffles, or eaten as a fruit dessert with cream.

> 6 pounds apples
>   Sugar, as needed
> ½ teaspoon ground cinnamon
> ½ teaspoon ground allspice

1. Slice, peel, and core apples. Put in a large kettle and add water to halfway up amount of apples. Cook over medium heat until softened (15 to 20 minutes); cool.

2. Preheat oven to 300° F. Purée apples in a blender or food processor. Measure purée. Add ½ cup sugar for each 1 cup purée. Put sweetened purée into a shallow glass baking dish. Stir in cinnamon and allspice.

3. Bake until butter is thick but not dry (2 to 2½ hours), stirring every 15 minutes.

4. Quickly ladle into clean, hot, sterilized jars, leaving ¼-inch headspace. Process in boiling water bath 10 minutes.

Makes 6 pints.

■ MINT JELLY

Traditionalists insist that the best accompaniment to roast lamb is a dollop of mint jelly. There is no comparison between artificially flavored commercial jellies and your own version, made with fresh mint leaves and stems.

>   1 cup chopped, solidly packed mint leaves
>   and tender stems
>   1 cup water
>   ½ cup apple cider vinegar
>   3½ cups sugar
>   5 drops green food coloring (optional)
>   1 pouch (3 oz) liquid fruit pectin

1. Put chopped mint into a 6-quart pot. Add the water, vinegar, and sugar; stir well.

2. Over high heat, stirring constantly, bring quickly to a full, rolling boil that cannot be stirred down.

3. Add food coloring (if desired) and pectin.

4. Return to a full, rolling boil. Boil rapidly 30 seconds.

5. Remove from heat. Skim off foam with slotted spoon. Strain immediately through two thicknesses of damp cheesecloth.

6. Ladle jelly quickly into hot, sterilized jars, leaving ½-inch headspace; seal with paraffin.

Makes 3 to 4 half-pints.

■ SPICY BLUEBERRY FREEZER JAM

Freezer jams glisten with the natural color and flavor of fresh fruit. Thinner than traditional cooked jams, they are simple, fast, and fresh tasting.

>   2½ pints blueberries
>   1 tablespoon fresh lemon juice
>   ½ teaspoon ground cinnamon
>   ⅛ teaspoon freshly grated nutmeg
>   5 cups sugar
>   ¾ cup water
>   1 package (1¾ oz) powdered fruit pectin

1. In a large bowl crush blueberries one layer at a time (crushing too many at a time inhibits free flow of juice).

2. Measure 3 cups crushed blueberries and place in a large bowl. Stir in lemon juice, cinnamon, and nutmeg. Thoroughly mix sugar into fruit. Let stand 10 minutes.

3. Combine the water and pectin in a saucepan. Bring to a full boil and boil 1 minute, stirring constantly.

4. Stir hot pectin liquid into fruit and continue to stir vigorously for 3 minutes to distribute pectin.

5. Ladle into freezer containers, leaving ½-inch headspace. Cover with lids and let stand at room temperature until set. (It may take up to 24 hours.) Store jam in freezer up to 8 months.

Makes about 6 half-pints.

PICKLES AND RELISHES

Making pickles and relishes is as easy as preserving, and many of the same principles apply. You will use water-bath canner, mason jars, and fresh, crisp produce. Pungent spices that have not lost their zest are important. You may want to grow your own herbs for the best quality possible. Kosher salt is used for brining because it does not have additives that would cloud the brine.

Follow the directions at the beginning of the chapter for using a water-bath canner. Store pickles and relishes in a cool, dark spot. Before using, let them age at least one month to mellow their sharp flavor.

■ BREAD AND BUTTER PICKLES

Most collections of early American pickled foods will include a recipe for Bread and Butter Pickles. These are sliced cucumbers, packed with onions, green peppers, and spices in a sweet-and-sour brine.

>   8 cups sliced pickling cucumbers
>   Salt
>   2 cups sliced onions
>   4 green bell peppers (with red on them if possible)
>   2 cups distilled white vinegar
>   2 cups sugar
>   1 tablespoon salt
>   2 teaspoons dry mustard
>   2 teaspoons turmeric
>   2 teaspoons celery seed
>   1 cinnamon stick, broken

1. Sprinkle cucumber slices with salt and let soak 1 hour. Rinse with cold water and drain.

2. Cut onion slices crosswise and cut peppers (remove seeds) in about 1½-inch lengths.

3. Combine vinegar, sugar, the 1 tablespoon salt, mustard, turmeric, celery seed, and cinnamon stick in large kettle; add cucumbers, onions, and peppers. Bring to a boil; cook until cucumbers start to look glassy (3 to 5 minutes).

4. Pack pickles into clean, hot, sterilized jars, leaving ½-inch headspace; fasten lids.

5. Process in boiling water bath 5 minutes.

Makes 5 to 6 pints.

With the addition of vinegar, these cucumbers and flavorings will become delicious Dill Spears.

■ GINGERED PEACH PICKLES

These pickles are delicious over ice cream or served with crème fraîche.

>   8 pounds (about 3½ qt) small peaches
>   3 pounds light brown sugar
>   1 quart cider vinegar
>   Fresh ginger (1-in. piece), peeled and crushed
>   2 tablespoons whole cloves, crushed
>   3 cinnamon sticks, broken up
>   1 whole clove per peach
>   Additional whole cinnamon sticks, for each jar
>   3 to 4 tablespoons brandy (optional)

1. Peel peaches and treat to prevent darkening. Halve and pit or leave whole.

2. Combine sugar and vinegar in a large pot; bring to a boil over medium heat and boil 5 minutes. Tie ginger, crushed cloves, and broken cinnamon sticks loosely in cheesecloth. Add to syrup and simmer 5 minutes.

3. Stick a whole clove in each peach. Add only enough peaches to boiling syrup to fill one 1-quart jar; cook until peaches are hot but not soft (about 2 minutes). Do not overcook. Remove peaches with slotted spoon and pack tightly in a clean, hot, sterilized jar along with a small stick of cinnamon. Repeat process until all peaches are packed in jars.

4. Bring syrup to a boil; remove spice bag. Pour hot syrup over peaches in jars, leaving ½-inch headspace. Add 1 tablespoon brandy (if desired). Fasten lids.

5. Process in boiling water bath 15 minutes.

Makes 3 to 4 quarts.

■ CORN RELISH

Corn relish tastes good with country-style cooking such as fried chicken, baked ham, and sausages of all kinds.

>   22 medium ears of corn (enough to make
>   10 cups kernels)
>   1 cup chopped red bell pepper (1 large pepper)
>   1¼ cups chopped celery
>   ¾ cup chopped onion
>   1½ cups sugar
>   2½ cups distilled white vinegar
>   2 cups water
>   1 tablespoon salt
>   1 teaspoon celery seed
>   2½ tablespoons mustard seed
>   ½ teaspoon turmeric

1. Cook ears of corn in boiling salted water 3 to 5 minutes. Plunge into cold water.

2. Drain corn. Cut kernels from cob with knife or corn kernel remover. Kernels should measure 10 cups.

3. In a large pot, combine kernels with remaining ingredients in large pot and simmer 15 minutes.

■ DILL SPEARS

Most pickling spices use dill as a major flavoring element. Dill weed (the feathery leaves) has a refreshing, cool quality; the small, hard, dried seeds are pungently warm and slightly bitter.

>   4 pounds pickling cucumbers, washed, blossom
>   ends removed, and cut into spears
>   3 cups distilled white or apple cider vinegar
>   3 cups water
>   ⅓ cup salt
>   3 peppercorns per quart
>   2 dill heads *or* 2 tablespoons dill seed per quart
>   1 clove garlic per quart

1. Combine vinegar, the water, and salt in a small saucepan and bring to a boil.

2. Add peppercorns, dill (or dill seed), and garlic to each clean, hot 1-quart jar.

3. Pack cucumber spears in jars. Fill jars with boiling pickling mixture, leaving ½-inch headspace; fasten lids.

4. Process in boiling water bath 20 minutes.

Makes about 3 quarts.

4. Immediately pack into clean, hot, sterilized jars, leaving ½-inch headspace; fasten lids.

5. Process in boiling water bath 15 minutes.

Makes 5 to 6 pints.

APRICOT AND CURRY CHUTNEY

Mention chutney, and mouths water for spicy East Indian dishes. Chutney is equally delicious with barbecued meats, roasts, poultry, chops, or cold cuts. In India, chutney is served fresh, but here it's more often preserved.

> 1½ pounds dried apricots, chopped (4 cups chopped)
> 1 quart water
> 1½ cups chopped onion
> ½ cup sugar
> 3 cups golden raisins
> 3 cups distilled white vinegar
> 1½ tablespoons grated fresh ginger
> 1½ to 2 teaspoons curry powder
> 2 cinnamon sticks (2 in. each)
> ¾ teaspoon salt

1. Combine apricots, the water, onion, and sugar in a 6-quart pot and simmer 5 minutes, stirring occasionally. Add remaining ingredients and cook 10 minutes more.

2. Remove cinnamon sticks and ladle chutney into clean, hot, sterilized jars, leaving ½-inch headspace; fasten lids.

3. Process in boiling water bath 10 minutes.

Makes about 4 pints.

HERB AND FRUIT VINEGARS AND MUSTARDS

Flavored vinegars are effective in salads and stir-fries or as pan glazes. They add zest to food and are satisfying to make. Collect different vinegars to flavor and see which ones you enjoy. Try Chinese and Japanese rice vinegars, wine vinegars, and apple cider vinegar. Wash and store empty wine bottles for vinegars. New corks are sold at hardware stores. The simple mustard recipe always works and is a great way to start to learn about this condiment.

HERB VINEGAR

The following is a basic method that can be used with any herb. Use about 4 ounces of fresh herbs or 2 ounces of dried herbs per quart of vinegar. Let the flavored vinegar sit for five or six weeks to deepen its flavor before using.

> Tarragon sprigs (or other fresh herb)
> White wine vinegar or rice vinegar

1. Wash fresh tarragon and pat dry with paper towels. Place a few sprigs in each sterilized bottle.

2. Pour vinegar into bottles and cap tightly.

3. Allow herbs to steep in vinegar for 5 to 6 weeks before using.

FRAN'S RASPBERRY VINEGAR

Use this raspberry vinegar in salad dressings, when poaching pears or apples, or to deglaze the sauté pan in which chicken or veal has been browned. This vinegar mellows as it ages. It keeps indefinitely, improving with time. Store in a cool, dark, dry place and refrigerate after opening.

> 12 pints raspberries (6 oz each)
> 1 cup sugar
> 2 quarts or more good-quality red or white wine vinegar

1. Rinse berries and place in large, clean, sterilized glass jars.

2. In a saucepan, combine sugar and vinegar, and bring to a boil, stirring until sugar dissolves.

3. Pour hot vinegar over berries. Berries must be completely covered with vinegar. Cover loosely and let stand in a cool place 3 to 4 weeks.

4. Strain mixture through a fine sieve into a saucepan, pressing gently to extract juice from berries. Bring to a boil, reduce heat, and simmer 10 minutes; skim off foam.

5. In the meantime, boil canning jars or glass bottles, completely immersed in water, for 15 minutes to sterilize. (Any type of bottle that can withstand the boiling temperature may be used.)

6. Ladle hot vinegar into hot, sterilized jars or bottles, leaving ¼-inch headspace; cap tightly.

Makes 2 quarts.

HOMEMADE MUSTARD

This recipe is basically foolproof. It makes the French-style wine mustard.

> ¼ cup dry mustard
> ¼ cup white wine vinegar
> ⅓ cup dry white wine
> 1 tablespoon sugar
> ½ teaspoon salt
> 3 egg yolks

1. Mix together all ingredients except egg yolks and allow to stand 2 hours.

2. Whisk yolks into mixture; transfer to top of a double boiler. Cook, stirring constantly, over hot, not boiling, water until mustard thickens (about 5 minutes).

3. Cool mustard. Cover and refrigerate up to 1 month.

Makes 1 cup.

Tarragon Mustard   Mix in ½ teaspoon crushed dried tarragon when adding egg yolks.

Lemon or Lime Mustard   Mix in ¾ teaspoon grated lemon or lime rind and 1½ teaspoons fresh lemon or lime juice when adding egg yolks.

JELLY-ROLL STYLE

This term takes its name from the dessert made from a sheet of sponge cake that is spread with jelly, rolled, and baked. When sliced, the cross section shows a spiral design of cake and filling. The term has come to mean a thin, flat piece of meat, fish, cake, bread, pastry, or other food rolled around a filling.

JERUSALEM ARTICHOKE

Also known as the sunchoke, the Jerusalem artichoke is a native American vegetable. Samuel de Champlain discovered it growing in Indian gardens in Cape Cod in 1604. Despite its name, it is not an artichoke but a tuber of a species of sunflower. The word *Jerusalem* may be derived from *girasole*, Italian for sunflower.

The fresh tubers have ivory flesh and a thin, light brown skin that may have a reddish hue. Ranging from 2 to 6 inches in length, they may be either rounded with fairly smooth skins or elongated with knobby protuberances. The tubers closely resemble fresh ginger.

When raw, the Jerusalem artichoke has a crisp texture like that of a potato and a delicate, somewhat nutty flavor. When cooked, the tuber has a texture resembling boiled turnips and a flavor reminiscent of artichoke. Most consumers are surprised to discover that the Jerusalem artichoke contains no starch.

Use   Slice or grate raw Jerusalem artichokes and add to salads, or marinate in vinaigrette and serve as a salad. Bake tubers in their skins as you would potatoes; slice and sauté or deep-fry; boil or steam, then sauté in butter, or peel and purée. Substitute for water chestnut in stir-fries. Purée for soup or preserve as relish or pickles.

Availability   Fresh Jerusalem artichokes are sold fall through winter.

Selection   Pick firm tubers without soft spots. For easy cleaning and preparation, choose those with smooth, regular shapes. Jerusalem artichokes are sold in bulk in some supermarkets; in other markets, they are scrubbed and packed in plastic bags.

Storage   If packaged in a plastic bag and kept in the refrigerator crisper, Jerusalem artichokes should remain crisp and firm for at least one week.

Preparation   Scrub well, using a stiff brush if necessary to remove dirt from knobs and crevices. Leave on skin or peel, as desired. Peeled raw Jerusalem artichokes oxidize rapidly; drop in acidulated water immediately to prevent browning. Drain just before using. The tubers are easier to peel if cooked first.

Cooking   See BOIL, DEEP-FRY, PUREE, SAUTE, STEAM.

JICAMA

The tuber of a tropical vine, jicama (pronounced *hee-ka-ma*) has long been important to Mexican cooks but only recently has been widely found in American supermarkets. It looks like a large, squat, knobby turnip with a rough earth-colored brown skin. The stark white flesh inside is as cool and crunchy as an apple and almost as sweet. Jicama is a member of the legume family and is also known as yam bean.

Use   Jicama can be eaten raw or cooked. In Mexico it is cut into slivers and served with ground chiles and lime as an appetizer. Cut into spears, it is perfect for dipping, and when dressed with citrus juice, chiles, and oil becomes a refreshing savory salad. Raw jicama adds crunchy texture and sweetness to fruit salads. Its natural sweetness and low calorie count make it an appealing dieter's snack. Substitute jicama for water chestnut in stir-fries, or prepare like a potato—boiled and mashed, or baked.

Availability   Fresh jicama appears all year in Mexican markets and some supermarkets, but peak availability is October through May. Some markets cut up large jicama and sell portions wrapped in plastic.

Selection   Jicama should be firm, without blemishes. It should feel heavy for its size.

Storage   Keep in a plastic bag in the refrigerator crisper for up to two weeks. Store small cut pieces in cold water to prevent drying out.

Preparation   Wash and peel, removing the fibrous white layer just underneath the skin.

▪ JICAMA WITH CHILE AND LIME

Jicama con chile y limon is commonly sold from little carts on the streets of Mexico. The mild flavor of jicama is an excellent foil for the bite of the ground chile and salt, and the tang of the lime juice. It is a delicious, simple to prepare snack or hors d'oeuvre.

> 1   **small jicama, peeled and cut into bite-sized wedges**
>   **Salt, to taste**
>   **Ground red chile, mild or hot, to taste**
> 2   **limes, cut into wedges**

1. Place jicama wedges on toothpicks and arrange on a platter. Sprinkle with salt and ground chile.

2. Serve with lime wedges. Each person squeezes a little lime juice over jicama before eating.

Serves 6 to 8 as an appetizer.

Recipes and Related Information
Avocado, Jicama, and Grapefruit Salad, 281; Nopalito Salad, 391.

JUICE EXTRACTOR

If you want to squeeze a pitcherful of fresh orange or grapefruit juice, you would use a reamer (see CITRUS REAMER). To press out the healthful juices from hard, raw fruits and vegetables such as carrots, apples, and cabbage, juice-bar style, you need this machine. All models function essentially the same: Pulp is finely grated so that its liquid is released, and as a result of centrifugal action, the juice is passed through a strainer that traps the pulp. More expensive models have a larger capacity and arc probably able to extract more juice. Some heavy-duty electric mixers and food processors have extractor attachments.

JULIENNE, TO

To cut into fine, even-sized sticks, which are also called matchsticks. These strips are used to garnish soups, stews, and salads; or, they can be steamed and served as a side dish. See KNIFE, Cutting Techniques, for information on how to julienne.

JUNIPER BERRY

A small, round, blue-black berry of an evergreen shrub native to Europe, the juniper berry is the principal flavoring in gin. It is about the size of a large pea and is extremely aromatic.

Use Apart from its importance in making gin, juniper is employed to flavor marinades for game of all kinds, for lamb, and for the German braised meat dish, sauerbraten. It is also traditionally added to Alsatian sauerkraut.

Availability Whole juniper berries are sold on most supermarket spice racks.

Selection Packaged seasonings lose quality after a while; try to buy from a store that restocks its spice section fairly often.

Storage Keep in an airtight container in a cool, dark, dry place for up to two years.

Preparation Toasting berries briefly in a warm skillet will bring out their fragrance. Crush berries gently with a mortar and pestle for use in marinades; crush finely for stuffings or sauces. They are pungent and should be used in moderation.

KALE

The leafy green vegetable known as kale, borecole, or cow cabbage is a non-head-forming member of the cabbage family and one of the first cabbages to be cultivated. Its dark green, ruffled leaves are high in vitamin C and calcium and very low in calories. It thrives in cold climates; indeed it is said that frost increases its sweetness. Collards belong to the same family but have smooth, flat leaves. Some markets now carry an ornamental kale, also known as salad savoy, which has handsome crinkly leaves bearing shades of rose, cream, purple, and green.

Use Because it thrives throughout cold Scottish winters, kale has long been an almost daily staple in the Scottish diet. Scotch cooks use it in colcannon (mashed potatoes with kale) and in lamb and barley soup. Portuguese cooks make a simple potato and kale soup called *caldo verde*. In the southern United States, kale is boiled with ham bone or salt pork, sometimes in conjunction with collards. Ornamental kale is edible but not choice; its best use is decorative.

Availability Fresh kale is sold fall through spring. Frozen kale is carried by many supermarkets.

Selection The best kale has crisp, dark leaves. Avoid bunches with limp, wilted, or yellowed leaves.

Storage It will stay fresh for several days in a plastic bag in the refrigerator crisper.

Preparation Wash well. Discard any limp or discolored leaves. Cut away tough stems. Shred, chop, or cook whole (cut large leaves in half).

Cooking See BOIL, STEAM.

■ STEAMED KALE AND PEARL ONIONS

If you've never tried kale, this simple steamed side dish would be a good introduction.

> ¼ pound pearl onions, peeled
> 1 bunch kale, coarsely chopped
> Lemon wedges, for garnish

Place onions and then kale in steamer over boiling water and cook until kale is wilted (8 to 10 minutes). Serve immediately with lemon wedges.

Serves 4.

KAMPYO

Also spelled *kanpyo*, these long, buff-colored, ribbonlike strips are made from dried gourd shavings.

Use *Kampyo* is employed in Japanese cuisine both as an edible string—to tie neat food packages—and as an ingredient in fillings for rolled sushi.

Availability   Look for kampyo in Japanese markets in 1-ounce plastic packets.

Storage   Leftover kampyo should be kept in a plastic bag in a cool, dry place. It will keep indefinitely.

Preparation   Kampyo must be softened before use. Wash first, then massage with a generous amount of salt to break down the fibers and increase absorbency. Wash again, then boil until soft. Drain.

KATSUOBUSHI

Along with kelp, *katsuobushi* (dried bonito) is the main flavoring agent in the basic Japanese stock called *dashi* (see Miso Soup, page 562). It is almost as hard as wood and must be shaved into flakes before using. The best dashi is made from katsuobushi that is shaved with a special utensil just before use. For convenience, many Japanese cooks purchase dried bonito flakes (*hanagatsuo* or *kezuribushi*).

Use   Dried bonito flakes are primarily used in dashi. They are also employed to flavor a soy-based dipping sauce for sashimi and as a garnish for some vegetable dishes such as chilled, boiled spinach.

Availability   Whole dried bonito is not generally sold in this country. Pale pink, dried bonito flakes are available in Japanese markets and some supermarkets, packed in boxes or plastic bags.

Storage   Leftover bonito flakes should be stored in an airtight container in a cool, dry place. Replace every six months because they lose flavor.

KIMCHEE

Almost every meal in Korea is accompanied by at least one kind of kimchee (also spelled *kimchi*), a fermented, pickled vegetable. The best-known kimchee, at least in this country, is made from cabbage, but in Korea it is also made from carrots, radishes, and other vegetables. Generally, the vegetables are grated or shredded, seasoned with salt, garlic, and red pepper, and left to stand for several days. Kimchee has a pungent fermented flavor and may be quite spicy and have a strong smell.

Use   For some families in Korea, kimchee is a winter replacement for fresh vegetables that are hard to find. It is served the year around, however, in much the same way pickles are served in this country. Its crunchy texture and pungent character are refreshing and revivifying.

Availability   Bottled cabbage kimchee is sold in many supermarkets; most Asian markets carry a larger variety of kimchee.

Storage   Refrigerate kimchee in a covered container; it will keep indefinitely.

KIWIFRUIT

Underneath the fuzzy brown skin of the kiwifruit is a lime green flesh studded with tiny black seeds. Its texture is moist and melonlike, its flavor refreshingly tart and sweet. Kiwifruit was practically unknown in this country until the late 1950s, when it began to be exported from New Zealand. Today it is also cultivated in California. Originally known as Chinese gooseberry, the fruit was renamed by exporters to avoid confusion with the green gooseberry (to which it is not related) and to identify it more strongly with their country.

Use   The delicate flavor of kiwifruit is best appreciated raw. Halve lengthwise and eat with a spoon, or peel, slice in rounds, and add to fruit salads. Sliced kiwifruit makes a striking garnish for fruit tarts and frozen desserts. It may also be puréed for sorbets or sauces. Like the papaya, the kiwifruit acts as a meat tenderizer. A halved kiwifruit can be rubbed over steaks or chops before grilling or broiling to tenderize them.

Availability   Fresh kiwifruits are sold all year in most supermarkets. The California crop is marketed from November through April; New Zealand imports take their place May through October.

Selection   Look for kiwifruits that are firm but not hard, with no soft spots. They should give slightly to pressure. Hard kiwifruits will ripen at room temperature if stored in a plastic bag.

Storage   Refrigerate ripe kiwifruit in a plastic bag for up to two weeks.

KNEAD, TO

When making bread, to work dough with hands into a smooth and malleable mass by pressing and folding. Kneading also forms and arranges gluten (a protein substance found in wheat-flour doughs) into an elastic network that gives structure to the finished product. A heavy-duty mixer with dough hook or a food processor using the steel blade will perform this task for you, but many bakers find kneading the most enjoyable part of the whole bread-making process and are reluctant to turn this step over to a machine.

Pastry and biscuit doughs are also kneaded. Unlike bread doughs, these mixtures are worked with a light touch just until all ingredients are combined. For flaky pastry, the kneading is even briefer—just until ingredients hold together.

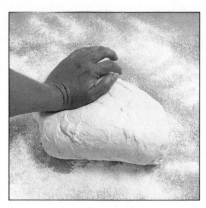

HAND-KNEADING BREAD DOUGH

With heel of hand, push dough away from you.

Bring end of dough back over with your fingers and give it a slight turn.

Repeat process until dough feels smooth, satiny, and elastic, and small bubbles appear just under surface of dough.

HAND-KNEADING PASTRY DOUGH

With fingertips, push the dough away from you and gently fold the top over; continue this motion just until the mass looks smooth and homogeneous.

Fraiser: Gather dough into a mound. Work small portions at a time, pushing away from you with heel of hand to smear dough across work surface.

To hand-knead rich, sticky bread doughs: For brioche, pick up, flip over, and throw back down; or pick up and slam down on surface without flipping. For very liquid doughs (baba, savarin, Kugelhopf), with the flat of your hand or a flat wooden spatula, slap the dough against the side of the bowl.

KNEADING BREAD DOUGH

Set dough on a lightly floured board; flour prevents dough from sticking. Using heel of your hand, push dough away from you; bring far end of dough back over with your fingers and give it a slight turn. Repeat the pushing, folding, and turning in a continuous, rhythmic, fluid motion until dough feels smooth, satiny, and springy, and small bubbles form just under surface. Depending on amount of flour you are working and how firmly you knead, this process can take anywhere from 8 to 15 minutes. Many bread recipes give a range for the amount of flour; use the lesser amount when mixing ingredients and add more flour as you knead if it seems appropriate. In the early stages of kneading, when dough is still sticky, you may want to sprinkle work surface occasionally with flour (taken from what is as yet unused from recipe). You also may want to scrape away any wet dough with a dough scraper before reflouring.

To knead with a heavy-duty mixer with dough hook, follow manufacturer's instructions.

KNEADING BREAD DOUGH IN A FOOD PROCESSOR

The food processor makes quick work of kneading any yeast dough. The plastic dough-kneading blade works best with more than 3 cups of dry ingredients; use the metal blade for less than 3 cups. Put all dry ingredients, including solid shortening, into work bowl. Mix all liquid ingredients together in a measuring cup. Start the motor and slowly add liquid in a stream only as fast as flour absorbs it (about 20 seconds). It is better to add more slowly than too quickly. Dough should gather into a ball and clean sides and bottom of work bowl. If dough is too dry, add more liquid by tablespoons through feed tube; if dough is too wet, add flour by tablespoons. Knead 60 to 90 seconds.

A food processor makes quick work of the usually time-consuming task of mixing and kneading yeast doughs. Use the metal blade for smaller batches, the plastic blade for larger ones.

Processor kneading not only saves time but also allows you to make moist, elastic doughs with the minimum amounts of flour. You can adapt any bread recipe to the processor without altering amounts of ingredients. Just remember to add liquid to dry ingredients as described above, and follow manufacturer's recommendations for maximum amounts.

KNEADING PASTRY, BISCUIT, AND RICH YEAST DOUGHS

For pastry such as pie and tart crusts, both the work surface and dough should be cool. With just the tips of your fingers, push dough away from you and fold top over gently. Continue this motion just until mass looks smooth and homogeneous. Biscuits require a minimum of handling—maybe only 12 to 15 turns.

Fraisage is a French term for working tart dough until pliable and blended but not tough by smearing it with the heel of the hand. To perform this technique, gather dough into a rough mound on a floured work surface. Work small portions at a time, pushing away from you. When pieces of dough are smooth, elastic, and peel away from surface in one piece, press all into a ball and shape crust as directed in recipe.

Rich yeast doughs such as brioche, *Kugelhopf,* baba, and savarin can be kneaded in a heavy-duty mixer which has both dough hook and flat paddle. For brioche, knead 5 minutes using a dough hook; for very wet and sticky baba and savarin, use the flat beater and knead 5 minutes. To hand-knead sticky doughs such as brioche, lay dough on a floured surface and pick up, flip over, and throw back down; or pick up and slam down on surface without flipping. Continue until pliable and smooth (about 10 minutes). Baba, savarin, and Kugelhopf, which have such a high proportion of liquid that they are almost like a batter, must be worked in a bowl. With the flat part of your hand or a flat wooden spatula, slap dough against side of bowl until smooth and elastic (about 5 minutes).

KNEADING PASTRY DOUGH IN A FOOD PROCESSOR

The metal blade makes pie doughs in seconds. Just follow these steps: Put flour and salt (and sugar, if called for) in work bowl. Add chilled fat cut into tablespoon-sized pieces. (Butter can be straight from the refrigerator. Vegetable shortening should be frozen.) Pulse 3 or 4 times. Add liquid through feed tube while pulsing very rapidly 20 to 30 times until just short of when dough looks like it will gather into a ball. Remove dough from work bowl and press together. Use as recipe directs.

Recipes and Related Information
Biscuit, 49; Flour, 234; Pie and Tart, 431; Yeast Bread, 613.

KNIFE

Good cooking begins with good cutting. A basic set of fine knives is probably the first purchase student chefs make. Although quality cutlery is costly, properly handled and well-maintained knives are a lifetime investment invaluable to their work. Fine knives can be sharpened to a keen, durable edge, feel better in the hand because they are well balanced, and are sturdily constructed to last for years. Professional chefs depend upon their personal collection of knives to such a degree that they rarely travel without them when they cook or teach away from their own kitchens.

Home cooks should select knives with the same discerning eye as the professional, and for the same reasons—ease of use, comfort, and value. Safety is another reason; a properly sharpened knife actually prevents accidents. Forcing a cut with a dull knife is one of the easiest ways to injure yourself.

SELECTING KNIVES

Top-quality knives are made of either carbon steel or an alloy—high-carbon stainless steel—that combines the softness of carbon steel and the rust-resistant attributes of stainless steel to produce a blade that can be honed to razor sharpness and won't discolor. Prior to the introduction of high-carbon stainless steel, carbon steel knives were long the favorite of chefs and serious home cooks because they take an edge so well, but were prone to stains and rust unless thoroughly dried immediately after washing.

The best blades are forged, or beaten into shape, by hand with anvil and hammer. Forging develops desirable characteristics in the metal impossible to obtain when shaped by machine. A handcrafted tool is also more aesthetically appealing than a machine-made product. Blades can be stamped or cut, processes that are automated and therefore less costly. Knives made by either of these methods are predictably less expensive than those that are hand-forged.

To be effective, the sharp edge of a blade must be thin enough to cut yet strong enough not to bend or ripple. It must, of course, be able to be resharpened when necessary. Grinding, the final step in the process of making a knife, imparts this strength to a very thin piece of metal. As with forging, grinding by hand produces a knife of superior quality. Hollow grinding, a machine process, produces an edge that can't be reground and is therefore best suited for serrated knives, which keep their factory-shaped edge indefinitely.

The part of the blade that extends into the handle is called the tang. A full tang extends completely into the handle and assumes the shape of the handle, adding balance and weight to a knife. This is an important feature for most tasks except some butchering and slicing procedures; knives for these tasks have partial tangs. Very heavy knives may have a rattail tang. Narrow and thin, and extending the length of the handle, this shape imparts strength but reduces heft. Better knives use metal rivets embedded in the handle on both sides rather than glue to hold the tang in place. On a riveted handle, the tang is a visible line of metal around the center of the edge of the handle. Choose a knife with a full or rattail tang, and with full rivets, not merely inlays.

A good handle is made of resin-impregnated wood so that it is smooth and waterproof. Polypropylene is another material commonly used for handles. Some companies use dense-grained natural hardwood handles that should not be cleaned in a dishwasher, but a good knife in any case should never be washed by machine because the heat will ruin its edge, as will harsh detergents and being knocked around in the utensil basket. Whatever the handle material, it should display a refined surface without crevices or recesses where food can hide and bacteria can grow. It should not have rough edges that can irritate your hand.

Before buying a knife, don't forget to pick it up to see how it feels in your hand. Due to slight differences in handle design, width, and material, knives of comparable quality may not be of comparable comfort. If you don't like to hold it, no matter how well made it may be, you won't use it and you'll have wasted your money.

As with cookware, don't feel compelled to purchase your knives in sets. While the price of a set may seem appealing, in reality there is better value in buying knives individually. That way you know you are getting only those you will use. Consider which you need based on your cooking style and storage space, then investigate what's available. Ask retailers for specific information regarding construction and quality for the brands they carry.

CARING FOR KNIVES

If you have invested in quality cutlery, take the time to care for it properly. Hard surfaces dull even the best of edges. Always cut on a surface that has some resilience. Wood is an excellent choice, as is polycarbonate, which gives much like wood. Avoid glass, metal, hard plastic, and ceramic tile (see CHOPPING AND CUTTING BOARD).

Fine knives should be washed immediately after use—don't soak—and dried thoroughly. Even if the handle is waterproof, good cutlery lasts longer and retains its appearance better when washed by hand.

Store knives in a slotted rack or drawer, or on a magnetic bar; never throw them bare-bladed into a drawer. Not only is this a safety hazard, but such cavalier treatment also damages the edges. If you want to store knives in a drawer, protect them with plastic sheaths, available at better cookware and cutlery stores.

SHARPENING KNIVES

A sharp edge is a necessity for good cutting and, again, for safety. For proper care, knives should be honed fre-quently, sharpened occasionally, and reground every one or two years, depending upon use.

SHARPENING STEEL

The easiest and best way to maintain a sharp edge on any knife is with a sharpening steel, if it is used correctly. If you don't already own a steel, buy one and learn to handle it; it will save you time, money, and frustration. The ideal steel is at least 12 inches long, not counting the handle, with a smooth or very finely ridged surface. The steel does not remove metal from the edge of a knife, as a whetstone does; rather, it realigns the cutting edge to keep it razor-sharp. If you use the steel every time you bring out your knife, it will hardly ever need to be sharpened on a stone or reground. Frequent, regular employment of a steel will maintain a good edge for up to two years.

To use a steel, hold steel in left hand, either out in front of you at chest level or vertically with tip resting on cutting board. Place heel of blade against steel near top, with blade making a 15- to 20-degree angle with steel. (Too wide an angle dulls the edge; too narrow an angle produces a brittle, fragile edge that dulls easily with use.) Maintaining gentle sideways pressure against steel, swing blade downward, drawing length of cutting edge across steel. Repeat on other side of knife. Alternate sides, making 10 or 12 strokes in all.

WHETSTONE

Eventually, even knives sharpened daily will need regrinding. The wedge-shaped edge will have worn down to such a degree that it must be re-created. A whetstone, made of an abrasive known as Carborundum, realigns the edge so that it will respond to the sharpening steel. If you haven't made a habit of using a steel regularly, a stone will bring a dull knife back to life. To use, draw the knife across the stone at the same 20-degree angle as with the steel, alternating sides, making 5 or 6 strokes on each side.

RODS

Other alternatives to the sharpening steel are ceramic or steel rods, which are available in three forms: a free rod that you use like a steel; a fixed rod on a stand that is already angled properly—to use, hold the knife perpendicular to the floor and draw across the rod; and a pair of crossed rods preset to a 20-degree angle.

AUTOMATIC HONER-SHARPENER

Until recently, electric knife sharpeners have done little more than grind away at the blade. A new machine, which uses a grinding wheel and two grinding pads studded with diamond particles, allows you to attain a sharper edge than previously possible with a home device. Magnets keep the knife at the proper angle in each slot; all you do is pull the knife through. The grinding wheel resets the edge, the coarse diamond pad sharpens, and the fine diamond pad hones. The machine uses household current.

A well-chosen selection of quality knives should last a lifetime. Shown clockwise from upper right: whetstone, automatic honer-sharpener, Asian knife, cleaver, utility and paring knives, poultry shears, kitchen scissors, chef's fork, shrimp deveiner, oyster knife, clam knife, tomato knife, avocado pitter, bread knife, ham slicer, boning knife, sandwich knife, fillet knife, chef's knife, sharpening steel.

A GUIDE TO BUYING KNIVES

Every kitchen should have at least four basic knives: a large chopping knife, a medium-sized slicing knife, a small paring knife, and a thin boning knife for delicate operations. A pair of good quality kitchen scissors will also prove invaluable. After that choose among the specialty knives as you see fit. Because good knives will last for years if well cared for, the most economical strategy in the long run is to invest in fewer knives of top quality rather than to accumulate a slew of cheaper slicers and choppers. Size is the blade measurement, excluding the handle.

Asian Knives Because of their large, rectangular blades, which look vaguely like those of Western meat cleavers, all Chinese knives, from lightweight vegetable knives to extraheavy, bone-chopping cleavers tend to be lumped together under the name Chinese cleaver. The name is misleading, however; only the heaviest of these knives are cleavers in the Western sense, that is, knives meant to chop through bones. At first you may find these large knives unwieldy, but with practice you will soon find them indispensable because they perform with such efficiency and are so versatile. These knives are numbered on the blade—the higher the number, the smaller and lighter the knife. Number 1, the heaviest, most closely corresponds to a true cleaver. The lighter versions are strictly for vegetables and boneless meats.

A medium-weight number 3 or 4 Chinese knife and the similar Japanese type with a narrower blade are called vegetable knives. Used like French chef's knives, they are good for slicing, dicing, and mincing; crushing garlic and ginger; and carrying chopped foods from cutting surface to cooking pan. They have wooden handles that some cooks use as pestles for grinding peppercorns and other spices.

Avocado Pitter Certainly not a necessary item, but if you typically have difficulty removing the pit from an avocado, this tool will make the process go more smoothly.

Boning Knife The extra-narrow, flexible, tapered blade of a boning knife affords maximum maneuverability when separating chicken breast from bone, the most common boning procedure for home cooks. These knives are typically 5 or 6 inches long.

Chef's Fork This two-pronged heavyweight fork performs many functions: transfers whole birds and roasts from pan to carving board or platter, holds meat and fowl in place during carving, and protects fingers from hot food by doing the lifting and moving.

Chef's Knife   Serious cooks consider this knife with its wide, slightly curving blade to be the most versatile and important of all cutting tools. Although its large size and deep blade may feel unwieldy at first, you will soon find it indispensable. Its primary function is chopping, done with a rocking motion that follows the arc of the blade or with rapid up and down movements. Not only is it good for slicing, dicing, and mincing, but its broad side can be used to smash garlic cloves or to flatten chicken breasts. The blade is also handy for scooping whatever you have just cut, from a bit of minced parsley to a pile of sliced celery, and transferring it to sauté pan or mixing bowl. The best of these knives has a thickening of the blade, called the bolster, between the blade and the handle, and sometimes a metal collar that extends past the bolster to the handle. The bolster improves balance by adding weight and also serves as a barrier to keep your hand from slipping into the cutting edge. These knives range in length from 6 to 13 inches; a 6- or 8-inch blade is probably the most popular size for home cooks. Some manufacturers call this knife a cook's knife.

Clam Knife   This knife tends to have a blunt, rather than a sharp edge, because clams have a different muscle structure than other bivalves. You can use an oyster knife for clams if you want to buy only one specialty tool. The technique for opening both bivalves is basically the same (see Oyster Knife).

Filleting Knife   Don't consider this knife part of your basic set, but if you like to fillet fish yourself, then it will earn its price tag. It has a paper-thin, extremely flexible blade that maneuvers superbly between flesh and super-delicate bones and skin. Two popular sizes are 6 and 10 inches; you will also find them well suited to slicing fragile cakes and pastries.

Grapefruit Knife   Some grapefruit lovers can't imagine life without this serrated cutter. The curved blade neatly separates flesh from membrane and from outer peel. A sharp paring knife does this job almost as well.

Kitchen Scissors   A pair of durable kitchen scissors is a necessity. Use them to snip fresh herbs, cut parchment paper to fit cake pans, trim poached eggs into neat ovals, groom houseplants and trim blossoms, prepare wrapping paper, double as poultry shears for halving game hens, and perform hundreds of other jobs. Some have many functions; they open cans and bottles, as well as cut. Scissors that come apart are easier to clean.

Meat Cleaver   These are meant to chop through bone. While the blades of chopping knives have a constant taper from the top to the cutting edge, the cleaver blade tapers slowly from the top to within an inch or so of the edge, then tapers quickly to the cutting edge. The result, technically known as a roll grind, is an edge that is not as fine as that of the chef's knife, but is capable of hacking through bones without denting or cracking. A cleaver can be used for coarsely chopping meats and vegetables, but its bulkier blade makes precise work, and especially thin slicing, more difficult. Choose a large knife; with practice you will find its extra size and weight working for you.

Oyster Knife   Opening oysters takes strength. Using this specially designed knife with its short, strong blade and hand guard makes the job easier. There are as many versions of bivalve knives as there are varieties of bivalves to open. To use, top of knife is inserted into hinge of oyster shell and twisted to pry shell apart.

Paring/Utility Knife   Use this knife as an extension of your index finger to make small cuts; used with a twisting motion of your hand and wrist, it is perfect for peeling and slicing fruits and vegetables, carving out the eyes of a potato, chopping or cutting up small amounts of herbs, and sculpting garnishes. Its shape resembles that of a chef's knife, but has less of an arc; a variation has an upwardly curved blade. Midsize paring knives are also called utility knives or sandwich knives. A 3- to 4-inch blade is typical for paring knives; utility knives have blades that are 6 to 8 inches long.

Poultry Shears   Made of heavy stainless steel or chrome-plated steel, poultry shears should have a spring-lever action for extra cutting power to work through bone and cartilage. Use them to disjoint all kinds of fowl or to divide little Rock Cornish game hens. A locking hinge at the handle secures blades for safe storage. Look for shears that come apart; they are easier to clean.

Serrated Knife   A serrated edge makes a clean cut through a firm crust or skin without crushing the delicate interior crumb or flesh. Serrated slicers do an excellent job cutting bread, and halving génoise, sponge, or butter cake layers for multitiered pastries (for an even cut, use a knife longer than the diameter of the cake; see photograph, page 85). Bread knives are 8 inches. Shorter serrated blades, around 5½ inches long, breeze through tomatoes—whose skin is notoriously resistant to all but the sharpest blades—with ease. They are also better suited than the longer bread knife for slicing a thin baguette loaf and for slicing fruits without forcing out the juice in the process. Use a back-and-forth sawing motion when cutting with a serrated knife.

Shrimp Deveiner   The arc of the blade, which duplicates the curved back of the shrimp, permits you to slice the shell and remove the black vein in one operation.

Slicing/Carving Knives   Designed to cut through cooked meats of all kinds, these knives have a pointed or round tip and long blades that are either flexible or rigid, depending on the piece to be cut. Rigid, more sturdy knives work better for slicing ham and roasts; poultry requires a thinner blade that can conform somewhat to its bone structure.

CUTTING TECHNIQUES

In the following descriptions of techniques, the right hand refers to the hand holding the knife, and the left hand to the one holding the food to be cut (with an apology to left-handed cooks). A French chef's knife and an Asian vegetable knife (Chinese or Japanese) are interchangeable in this discussion.

Work slowly at first until you get the hang of each technique; speed will come naturally. It is important to learn safe and efficient cutting habits. Give yourself plenty of room to work, stand in a comfortable position, relax, and focus entirely on the task at hand; you will find yourself cutting quickly and with minimum effort. Don't try to cut too much at one time. Work with a manageable amount so that you are aware of and can control what you are doing. The following techniques are illustrated in the photographs on the opposite page.

HAND POSITION

Holding food for safe and precise cutting is mostly a matter of keeping your fingers out of the way of the blade. For most cutting tasks, this means holding food against board with the fingertips of the left hand curled back away from blade. The blade then rides against the curved knuckles to guide the cut. As long as you do not lift the blade above the level of the knuckles and do not straighten out the fingers, you can avoid cutting yourself in this position.

The position of your hand depends upon the task. For precise cutting, grip handle close to blade, with thumb and forefinger grasping blade itself. Let the knife work with you by gripping it near its balance point. To find that point, lay the knife flat across the index finger. There are two basic blade positions: resting tip of knife on board and slicing with a rocking motion, or lifting entire blade, holding edge parallel to board, and slicing with a downward and forward motion. The former method allows more control, the latter more speed. For other grips, see Chopping, Paring, and Cleaver Chopping (following).

SLICING

Hold ingredient with fingers curled back and knuckles away from blade at a distance that equals one slice. Slice with a French chef's knife or Asian vegetable knife, using knuckles to guide blade, then move fingers back along food (or push food forward with thumb) to get into position for next slice.

SHREDDING AND JULIENNE CUTTING

To cut food into fine shreds, larger pieces, or julienne (matchsticks), first cut ingredient into slices of the desired length and thickness. Carrots and other slender vegetables may have to be sliced on a slant to achieve the right length. Stack slices, overlapping them slightly like shingles, and slice down through stack lengthwise, forming squared-off sticks. Shreds are very fine julienne pieces, less than ⅛ inch thick; matchsticks are twice as thick.

To shred green onions for garnish or stir-fries, first slice them into desired length. Slit white and pale green sections lengthwise, but do not cut all the way through. Open halves like a book and cut lengthwise into thin shreds. To shred hollow green tops, bundle them together under fingertips of left hand and carefully slice bundle into fine shreds.

DICING AND MINCING

These terms describe the same process, but differ in the size of the cut: Diced means cubes of ¼ to ½ inch, minced less than ⅛ inch, and finely diced somewhere in between. First cut (using a French chef's knife or an Asian vegetable knife) ingredient into shreds or matchsticks of the desired thickness, as described at left. Then gather sticks into a bundle and cut across into uniform cubes. Always try to keep food you are cutting in a shape that works with you. Cut round objects into sections, so that they lie flat.

Garlic, onion, and shallot are diced or minced by a slightly different method. First peel, leaving root end intact, then split in half lengthwise. Place cut side down on board and, positioning knife blade horizontally, make one or more cuts parallel to cutting board, almost to root end. Make a series of vertical, lengthwise cuts almost to root end, of the desired thickness. Slice across cuts toward root end to produce cubes. Discard root end.

SMASHING AND BRUISING

When an aromatic ingredient such as garlic, ginger, or green onion is used in large pieces to flavor a food, smashing or bruising it first helps release its flavor into the food. Cut to desired size, place pieces on board, and smack them smartly with broad side of blade. Another method is to place knife flat on top of food, then pound it with your fist. Watch out for cutting edge if using this technique.

To peel garlic, lay clove on a board. Hold flat side of a chef's knife just above it. Lightly pound knife, hitting garlic and loosening its skin. Pull skin off, cutting if necessary.

CHOPPING

Although uniform cubes (dice or mince) are sometimes unnecessary, cooking or processing will be faster if hard ingredients are cut into smaller pieces. You may also need to finely chop fresh parsley or other herbs. If the foods are very large, such as carrots or onions, first roughly cut up. For herbs, remove leaves from stems. Then place these pieces or leaves on cutting board. Grip knife a little farther out on handle than for slicing. Use left hand to press tip of knife down against board and chop with a rocking motion, pivoting knife back and forth across food. Chop to desired size with a rolling, downward and forward motion (not an up-and-down chop), scraping pile together.

If you hear your knife hitting cutting board along with vegetable, half your effort isn't reaching its target. Keep pile of food high and in a neat rectangle, if possible; remember not to chop too much at one time.

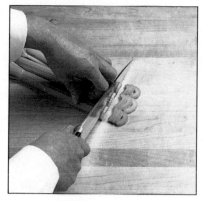

CUTTING TECHNIQUES

Hand position *For safety and to keep the food anchored while cutting, hold food against cutting board with fingertips curled back away from blade.*

Slicing *Hold food with knuckles away from blade at a distance that equals one slice. Slice, then move fingers back the width of another slice or push food forward that distance.*

Shredding and julienne cutting *Cut ingredient into slices of desired length and thickness. Stack slices, overlapping slightly, and slice lengthwise. The result will be squared-off sticks.*

Dicing and mincing *Cut food into shreds or matchsticks (see Shredding and Julienne Cutting). Gather pieces into a bundle and slice across into uniform cubes.*

Dicing/mincing garlic, onion, shallot *Place peeled, halved ingredient cut side down on cutting board. Position knife horizontally and make cuts parallel to board, almost to root end. Cut vertical, lengthwise cuts of desired thickness. Slice across cuts to root end.*

Smashing and bruising *Lay ingredient on cutting board and smack with broad side of knife blade or lay blade on food and pound it with fist. Use the latter technique to loosen garlic peel.*

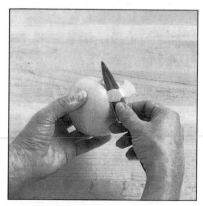

Chopping *Arrange pieces of food on board in a high, neat pile. Grip knife handle with one hand and use other to press tip of knife down against board; chop with a rocking motion across food.*

Paring *Lay blade on food, angled diagonally away from you. Cut in just the thickness of peel and draw knife toward you as you rotate food in opposite direction.*

Cleaver chopping *Hold cleaver with right hand well back on handle, thumb on top or on side. Swing down from wrist. Let gravity move the cleaver; lift knife and let fall.*

PARING

A paring knife is used like an extension of your index finger to make small precise cuts. The action centers more on the tip and end of the knife than with other knives. Hold a paring knife so that it moves with ease—index finger resting on top of blade and thumb gripping handle and serving as a balance. To peel away skin of a fruit or vegetable, grip paring knife as follows: grasp handle so that thumb rests against one side of blade and index finger lies along other side; handle should nestle in palm between fleshy pad and base of first finger. To peel, lay blade on fruit or vegetable, angled diagonally away from you. Make a cut just the thickness of the peel and draw the knife toward you as you rotate ingredient in the opposite direction. Skin should pull away in long strips.

CLEAVER CHOPPING

With a cleaver or heavier Asian vegetable knife, it is easy to chop meats to any texture, from rough cubes to a fine paste. Start by dicing meat, then change to a chopping grip (right hand well back on handle, thumb on top or on side). Swing from wrist for maximum chopping efficiency. With a good, heavy cleaver, little downward force is required; knife is simply lifted and allowed to fall. The left hand is not involved in this type of chopping. Stop every once in a while to scrape pile of pieces back together.

To chop through bones, as in cutting a chicken into braising pieces, hold knife as above. It may be unnecessary to hold food with other hand. For safety's sake, hold food as far away from where you will cut as possible. When you get to the last couple of inches, place food on board, get your left hand out of the way, take aim, and chop.

KOHLRABI

A member of the cabbage family, kohlrabi has a flavor reminiscent of both cabbage and turnip. It is moist and crunchy when raw; when cooked, its texture is like that of broccoli. Unlike the turnip, which it resembles, it is not a root, but a swollen, bulbous stem that grows above ground. The bulb may be pale green or purple outside; both varieties are white inside. Leaf stalks with leaves like those of turnips protrude from all sides (these stalks are generally trimmed away in the supermarket).

Use   Serve kohlrabi raw, or blanched and chilled, with a dip or marinated in vinaigrette. Steam or boil and dress with butter; add to soups or stews; purée with butter and cream; or use in any recipe in place of turnip. In Italy, raw or steamed kohlrabi is sometimes served with *bagna cauda* (a hot dip of butter, oil, garlic, and anchovies).

Availability   Fresh kohlrabi is sold in many supermarkets from May through November, with peak supply in June and July.

Selection   Choose small bulbs, about the size of a large egg; larger ones may be woody. If leaves are still attached, they should look fresh and perky. Avoid bulbs with cracks or blemishes.

Storage   Keep kohlrabi in a plastic bag in the refrigerator crisper for up to one week.

Preparation   Very young bulbs do not need to be peeled, but larger bulbs should be. If leaves are still attached, cut them off and boil or steam separately like spinach.

Cooking   See BLANCH, BOIL, PUREE, STEAM.

KONBU

Sun-dried kelp, called *konbu* (also spelled *kombu*) by both Japanese and Americans, appears in the market as a stiff, gray green sheet with a powdery finish. It must be rehydrated by soaking for use in the kitchen.

Use   Konbu imparts a delicate, fresh ocean taste to foods. Its primary function is as a flavoring for dashi, the basic Japanese stock (see page 563). Softened konbu is also wrapped around raw fish for several hours as a form of marinade; it is removed before serving. Pickled konbu is sometimes offered as a relish. Shredded konbu may be deep-fried or sautéed and used as a vegetable. Save steeped konbu sheets after making dashi, store in a plastic bag in the refrigerator, and use sheets as edible wrappers for other foods.

Availability   Dried konbu sheets are sold in Japanese markets and some health-food stores, packaged in plastic. One ounce is sufficient for four servings of dashi.

Storage   Unopened konbu will keep indefinitely in a cool, dry place. After opening, store in an airtight container in a cool place; it will keep for several months.

Preparation   Do not wash konbu. Wipe clean with a damp towel. Some Japanese cooks score surface lightly to release glutamic acid; others look down on this procedure. Steep sheets according to dashi recipe.

Recipes and Related Information
Miso Soup, 562; Sushi Rice, 233.

KUMQUAT

Resembling a miniature egg-shaped orange, the kumquat is rarely more than an inch long. Part of the citrus family, it is native to China but is now cultivated in Florida and California. Unlike other citrus, the skin of the kumquat is sweeter than its flesh.

Use Massage kumquat between fingers to mingle sweet skin and tart flesh, then eat the whole fruit raw. It can also be sliced and added to fruit salads. Kumquats make excellent preserves, marmalades, and relishes. Cooked or preserved kumquats can be used in a sauce for roast duck, pork, and turkey. Mince preserved kumquats and add to desserts or roll in sugar and serve as a sweetmeat.

Availability Fresh kumquats are sold in many supermarkets. They are stocked November through June, with peak availability from November through February. Whole kumquats preserved in syrup and bottled are carried by supermarkets and specialty stores. Preserved and sugared kumquats are found in Chinese markets during the Chinese New Year.

Selection Choose plump, firm kumquats; avoid those that look shriveled or dull.

Storage Fresh kumquats will keep in the refrigerator for up to one month. Kumquats preserved in syrup may be stored indefinitely at room temperature in the original jar; preserved and sugared kumquats will keep up to six months in a covered jar in a cool place.

LAMB

Humans learned to domesticate sheep tens of thousands of years ago. Indeed, for ancient civilizations, sheep were animals of incomparable value. Their wool provided clothing, their meat and milk sustenance. Furthermore, they were rugged animals capable of surviving extreme conditions.

The early importance of sheep and their offspring is evident in the role they played, and still play, in many religions. Lamb was the traditional sacrificial offering in early religious rites and is still part of many religious observances. Celebratory tables at the Christian Easter, the Jewish Passover, and the Muslim New Year are all traditionally graced with symbolic roast lamb.

The sheep that sustained earlier cultures was much different from modern lamb. Sheep were raised as much for their wool as for their meat and were often herded long distances in search of pasturage. By the time they were slaughtered, the meat was generally tough and had a strong flavor. Cooks developed ways to combat these two qualities. They might marinate it in acidic ingredients to tenderize it and mask its flavor; or they might stew it for several hours, often with fruits; or they might grind it and season it lightly.

Today's lamb, the result of sophisticated crossbreeding, is butchered at an early age and is mild and tender. Most lamb is slaughtered at 6 to 9 months; lamb older than 12 months cannot legally be sold as genuine lamb. If the animal were 12 to 24 months old at slaughter, the meat may be identified as yearling lamb and will be stronger in flavor. Some diners appreciate the rich, full flavor

of older lamb (known as mutton if older than 24 months), but most Americans prefer the more delicate flavor of young lamb. Some specialty markets offer baby lamb, also identified as milk-fed lamb, butchered at 3 to 5 months, or hothouse lamb, butchered at 6 to 10 weeks. It is extremely tender, pale in color, and delicate in flavor.

The term *spring lamb* has no legal definition and no longer has any practical meaning. In the past, sheep gave birth in September or October and the six-month-old spring lamb was a treat looked forward to by many diners for their Easter and springtime tables. Today's modern breeding and flock management enable sheep to give birth throughout the year.

Use Lamb is most appreciated today in the regions where it was first consumed: the Middle East, North Africa, and Greece. In these areas, it is safe to say that lamb is the preferred meat. Lamb is also widely eaten in India, France, Italy, Spain, England, China, and New Zealand, the world's chief sheep-raising country. It is much less popular in the United States, Latin America, Central and Eastern Europe, and is practically unknown in Japan and Southeast Asia.

Rack of Lamb With Herbs, an international favorite, makes a perfect combination with Zinfandel, strictly an American wine. The recipe is on page 338.

CUTS OF LAMB

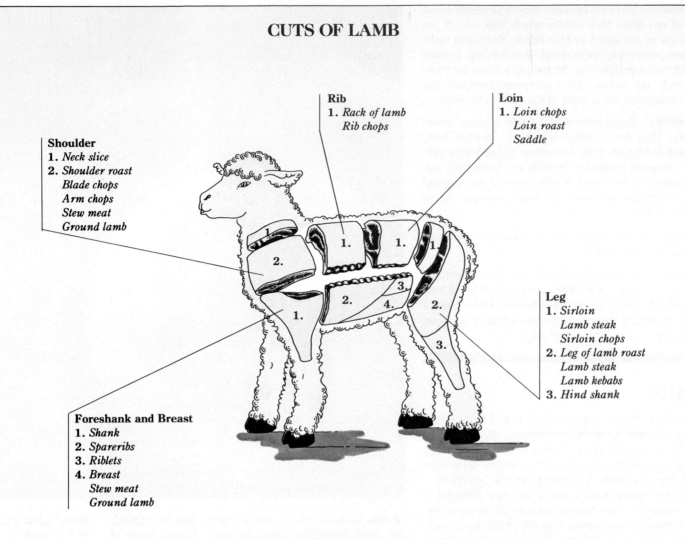

Shoulder
1. *Neck slice*
2. *Shoulder roast*
   Blade chops
   Arm chops
   Stew meat
   Ground lamb

Rib
1. *Rack of lamb*
   Rib chops

Loin
1. *Loin chops*
   Loin roast
   Saddle

Leg
1. *Sirloin*
   Lamb steak
   Sirloin chops
2. *Leg of lamb roast*
   Lamb steak
   Lamb kebabs
3. *Hind shank*

Foreshank and Breast
1. *Shank*
2. *Spareribs*
3. *Riblets*
4. *Breast*
   Stew meat
   Ground lamb

Lamb has fewer retail cuts than beef, but many of the same rules apply: The parts that do the least work are the tenderest. However, a lamb is a smaller, younger animal than a steer, and even the "tough parts" are usually more tender than the corresponding section of beef.

Shoulder This is the hardest-working muscle of the lamb, with the most fat, and plentiful bone. It is best suited for braising or stewing. The neck section of lamb is a stewing cut taken from the front of the shoulder. Boneless shoulder is sometimes sold as a roasting cut (although it is probably better braised). Chops cut from the shoulder (including both the blade chop with a long bone down the center, and the arm chop, with a round bone near the end) are fattier than the higher-priced rib and loin chops, but can be treated much the same way (baked, broiled, or panfried).

Foreshank and Breast Boneless rolled breast and bone-in breast are sometimes roasted (often with a stuffing inserted in a "pocket" cut in the center) but are more often braised, since they're rather fatty and not especially tender. Shank is always cooked in liquid, at length, until the meat starts falling off the bone. Economical lamb spareribs and riblets can be barbecued or braised, and are sometimes even roasted, but they are not entirely a bargain since the buyer is paying for a great deal of bone and a very little meat. Supermarket lamb stew meat, kebabs, and ground lamb are usually cut from the shoulder; the kebabs are from leaner shoulder meat than the stew or the ground lamb. Kebabs cut from the leg are far superior in leanness and tenderness.

Loin The whole loin roast (and the even less common whole saddle of lamb) are found at the butcher's only occasionally. Chops cut from the loin are found more frequently. These extremely tender chops can be broiled or panfried, and luxuriously sauced.

Rib The fine rib roast is sold as rack of lamb or, when bent into a circle, as crown roast. Chops from the rib are tender and juicy, whether left whole or, as in the case of the French chop, trimmed of the fatty meat from the end of the rib. Rib chops can be broiled or panfried, and double rib chops can be rapidly baked with a pocket cut for stuffing if desired. Like the loin, the rib portions of lamb are compatible with luxurious sauces.

Leg The back leg of the lamb is significantly more tender than the back leg of a steer. It may be cut into a whole leg (with the sirloin attached), a short cut leg (with sirloin trimmed off), a shank portion of the leg, and a center leg roast. These cuts are used primarily for roasting and grilling, but can be butterflied for barbecuing or cut off the bone for top-quality kebabs. Lamb steaks (to broil, panfry, or barbecue) are usually cut from either the center of the leg, or from the more tender sirloin just above the leg. Occasionally, lamb sirloin roast and sirloin chops can be found; these are both lean and tender. The hind shank, like the foreshank, is braised.

Spit-roasted suckling lamb is an Easter specialty in Greece. At other times, Greek cooks roast whole legs with oregano and white wine, or cook skewered lamb with herbs and serve it with yogurt. In the Middle East, ground lamb is massaged with cracked wheat to make kibbe, served raw or cooked. Ground lamb is used to stuff eggplants or grape leaves. In Iran lamb is marinated, grilled on skewers, and served with aromatic rice.

North African cooks braise lamb shoulder with vegetables for Couscous (see page 278) or stew it in a special covered clay pot called a *tajine*, often with fruits such as quince or prunes. In India lamb is curried, braised with spinach, or rubbed with spices and roasted in a *tandoor* (clay oven).

Milk-fed Spanish lamb is cooked in hot wood-burning ovens and served with potatoes. The French rub leg of lamb with thyme and lavender, stud it with garlic, and roast it, serving it with white beans or the green beans called *flageolets*. Italian cooks roast lamb with rosemary, or coat thin young chops with egg, bread crumbs, and Parmesan, and deep-fry them.

Irish lamb stew with potatoes and carrots; shepherd's pie from England, ground lamb topped with mashed potatoes; Finnish sauna-cured leg of lamb; and Mongolian hot pot are other ways that lamb is cooked around the world.

Availability   See Cuts of Lamb (opposite page).

Selection   All lamb sold retail is inspected by state or federal authorities for wholesomeness. About two thirds of lamb sold to consumers is also graded for quality. Lamb may be graded prime, choice, or good, depending primarily on the degree of marbling (intramuscular fat). Generous marbling contributes flavor and succulence. Most lamb sold at retail is graded choice.

In general, the paler the meat, the younger the lamb. Look for lamb with dry white fat, firm meat, and moist bones. Avoid buying lamb with yellowing fat or dark, mushy meat.

Storage   The larger the cut, the longer it may be refrigerated or frozen. Whole roasts, for example, may be stored longer than ground lamb. Large cuts may be refrigerated, well wrapped, for up to four days or frozen for up to nine months. Use ground meat within two days or freeze for up to four months. Defrost frozen meat slowly in refrigerator to promote reabsorption of melting ice crystals.

Preparation   Some cuts of lamb, such as the rack and the leg, are sold with part of the fat covering intact. Lamb fat has a strong flavor and should be trimmed away. However, be careful not to remove the fell, the papery outer membrane that holds the meat in shape. Cubed lamb for stew should be carefully trimmed of excess fat.

Cooking   See BRAISE, BROIL, GRILL, PANFRY, ROAST, STEW.

◼ LEG OF LAMB WITH GARLIC, POTATOES, AND ONIONS

Garlic slivers inserted into the lamb flavor the meat, and additional chopped garlic and roasting juices from the lamb give zest to the potatoes. Use a heavy roasting pan to prevent the vegetables from burning. Accompany this dish with green beans cooked until tender-crisp.

> 1   **leg of lamb (6 lb)**
> 4   **medium cloves garlic, peeled**
> 6   **tablespoons butter, softened**
> ½   **teaspoon dried thyme**
>   **Salt and freshly ground pepper, to taste**
> 2½ **pounds large, all-purpose white potatoes**
> 2   **tablespoons vegetable oil**
> 2   **large onions, thinly sliced**

1. Preheat oven to 450° F. Trim skin from lamb and remove as much excess fat as possible.

2. Cut 2 garlic cloves lengthwise into thin slices, then in thin slivers. Make slits in lamb about 1 inch deep with a small, sharp knife, spacing them fairly evenly. Insert garlic slivers in slits.

3. Chop remaining cloves with any remaining garlic slivers. Mix with butter, thyme, and salt and pepper to taste. Let stand at room temperature.

4. Peel potatoes, halve them lengthwise, and cut each half crosswise into slices about ¼ inch thick.

5. Set lamb on a rack in a large, heavy roasting pan. Spoon oil over lamb and sprinkle with salt and pepper. Roast 15 minutes. Reduce oven to 350° F and roast, basting lamb occasionally with juices, for 20 minutes.

6. Remove lamb and rack from pan. Put potato and onion slices in lamb juices in pan and mix well. Sprinkle with salt and pepper. Scatter garlic and butter mixture over potatoes. Replace lamb on rack in pan over vegetables.

7. Continue roasting, stirring vegetables occasionally, until lamb is done to taste (about 1 hour). To check, insert a meat thermometer into thickest part of lamb; lamb is rare at 130° to 140° F, medium at 145° F, and well-done at 160° F.

8. Transfer lamb to a carving board, cover loosely with aluminum foil, and let stand 10 minutes. Taste a relatively thick potato slice; if it is not tender, continue baking vegetables for a few minutes. Taste vegetables and add more salt and pepper, if needed.

9. Carve lamb; drain carving juices into a small saucepan and heat gently.

10. To serve, arrange lamb slices on a platter. Using a slotted spoon, transfer potato slices to platter or to separate serving dish. Pour juices remaining in roasting pan (mainly melted butter) into a small serving dish and heated carving juices into another.

Serves 10.

Meats that lack natural moisture benefit from larding, inserting strips of fat into the muscle with a special larding needle.

■ RACK OF LAMB WITH HERBS

Rosemary, oregano, thyme, and bay leaf, either alone or in combination, are delicious with lamb. Fresh herbs have more flavor, but dried herbs can also be used. The garlic- and herb-flavored salt rub in this recipe could easily be adapted to other cuts of lamb, such as a roast leg of lamb or a boned and rolled shoulder.

    1 **rack of lamb, 2 to 2½ pounds (see Note)**
    2 or 3 **cloves garlic, peeled, and thinly sliced**
    2 **tablespoons fresh herbs (see list above)** *or*
    1 **teaspoon dried**
    1 **teaspoon kosher salt**
    ¼ **teaspoon freshly ground pepper**

1. Preheat oven to 450° F. Remove excess fat from lamb. With tip of a knife, make several shallow incisions in meat and remaining fat, and push a slice of garlic into each cut (the garlic will infuse the meat with its flavor as the lamb roasts). If you are using fresh herbs, chop them finely together with any remaining garlic. If you are using dried herbs, crumble them finely.

2. Combine herbs, salt, and pepper; rub on lamb. Place lamb, fat side up, on a rack in a roasting pan.

3. Place lamb in oven, reduce heat to 400° F, and roast (without basting) to desired degree of doneness (about 25 minutes for medium rare; internal temperature should be about 140° F). Allow lamb to rest, loosely covered with aluminum foil, at least 10 minutes before serving. To serve, carve into chops.

Serves 2 to 4 (2 or 3 chops each).

Note For easier carving, ask the butcher to cut through backbone between ribs. After roasting, rack can then be neatly carved into chops with single ribs.

> ### *Recipes and Related Information*
> *Butterflied Leg of Lamb With Cucumber-Mint Sauce, 294; Cassoulet, 556; Couscous, 278; Dry Spice Rub for Lamb, 350; Moussaka, 209; Russian Marinated Lamb on Skewers, 453; Spring Lamb Stew With Fresh Peas, 420.*

LARD, TO

To add fat to lean meats by running strips of pork fat, known as lardoons, through the muscles with a larding needle (see NEEDLE AND FASTENER, Larding Needles), or by piercing the flesh with a thin knife and forcing the strips of fat through. This process adds flavor and moistness by increasing fat content. As the meat cooks, the fat melts, keeping the interior from drying out. Barding is another method of basting with fat; when you bard, the fat is wrapped around the outside of a piece of meat, rather than through its mass (see BARD). Seasonings, such as fresh herbs and garlic, are also used for internal flavoring, but not as a baste as they have no fat content. To add flavor, make shallow slits evenly around the roast and fill each slit with a sliver of garlic or piece of herb.

LEAVEN, TO

To lighten the texture and increase the volume of a batter or dough by the action of a natural agent such as air beaten into egg whites or the fermentation of yeast, or by using a chemical substance such as baking powder or baking soda, or by a combination. Each leavening agent contributes gases that expand and cause the dough or batter to rise.

> ### *Recipes and Related Information*
> *Baking Powder, 23; Baking Soda, 23; Yeast, 613.*

LEEK

A mild member of the onion family much appreciated in Europe, the leek resembles a giant scallion, with overlapping green leaves and a blanched white base.

Use Very young, pencil-thin leeks are tender enough to be sliced and eaten raw in salads. Older leeks should be poached or steamed and served hot or cold in the same way as asparagus: with vinaigrette, mayonnaise, or garnish of hard-cooked egg. Leeks add a mild onion flavor to soups, stuffings, and stews. Green leek tops add onion flavor to stocks. Whole leeks can be grilled, braised in stock, or baked and served as a side dish.

Availability Fresh leeks are sold all year, but supplies peak in fall and spring. Although some specialty markets now carry baby leeks as thin as young asparagus, most markets offer leeks an inch or more in diameter.

Selection Large leeks can be woody inside. Select small to medium leeks, without ragged or wilted leaves.

Storage Refrigerate in a plastic bag and use within three to five days.

Preparation To keep the base of the leeks white, dirt is piled up around the stalk. Although leeks are cleaned for market, dirt is often still trapped between the leaves. Wash well and remove any tough, ragged outer leaves. Trim roots from base. If cooking leeks whole, slit them lengthwise at least halfway down the stalk and run cold water between the leaves to wash away any dirt. If slicing leeks, slit them lengthwise through the base and wash well before slicing.

Cooking See BOIL, BRAISE, GRATIN, STEAM, STIR-FRY.

> ### *Recipes and Related Information*
> *Leeks Braised With Tasso, 59; Vichyssoise, 566.*

LEGUME

Technically, legumes are plants that carry their seeds in a pod. Beans of every shape and color, peas, and peanuts are all legumes. An exceptionally nutritious component in the human diet, they have, on average twice the protein of grains and a good dose of iron and B vitamins. With some legumes, such as peanuts and mature English peas, we eat only the seeds and discard the pods. Other legumes, such as sugar snap peas or Kentucky Wonder beans, are edible in their entirety. For more information on individual legumes, see BEAN, PEA, PEANUT.

LEMON

Although lemons are too tart to eat on their own, they are probably used more than any other fruit. Their lively tartness sharpens other flavors and gives a lift to all manner of foods.

Use Lemon is the principal flavor in a variety of desserts, from lemon ice cream and sherbet to lemon curd, lemon mousse, lemon meringue pie, and lemon cake. In addition, lemon juice and grated rind are used in many other desserts—especially fruit desserts—as a subsidiary flavor.

In the savory realm, lemon adds zest to sautéed or roasted chicken and is almost always served with fish and shellfish to heighten their flavor. A squirt of lemon juice in melted butter makes a lively dressing for cooked asparagus, broccoli, spinach, potherbs, green beans, and carrots. Italians serve the best young vegetables, such as celery hearts and baby artichokes, with nothing but lemon, salt, and olive oil. Moroccan cooks preserve lemons in salt, then use them to flavor stews and salads. Avocado is unthinkable without lemon alongside. Many melons and tropical fruits are also often served with a wedge of lemon. Lemon juice takes the place of vinegar in salad dressings and marinades. The acid juice of a lemon or lime is sometimes used to "cook" fish and shellfish. Seviche is an example.

Lemon juice enlivens such beverages as lemonade, iced tea, tomato juice, fruit punches, and cocktails. It is also valuable as an antioxidant: Rubbing lemon juice on cut bananas, apples, or pears inhibits browning; soaking some of these foods in acidulated water, an acidic mixture of lemon juice or vinegar and water, has the same effect.

Availability Fresh lemons are sold all year. Bottled lemon juice is also widely available in supermarkets.

Selection Choose firm lemons that feel heavy for their size. Generally, rough-textured ones have thicker skin and less juice than fine-skinned varieties.

Storage Refrigerated, lemons should keep for up to one month.

Preparation The desirable lemon oils are stored in the yellow peel. Be sure to grate only the yellow peel; the white pith is unpleasantly bitter. For directions on removing the rind, see GADGETS. To extract more juice from a lemon, press down on it as you roll it on a countertop or table. Lemons also yield more juice when slightly warm or at room temperature. If chilled, warm in a microwave on 50 percent power 1 minute. A citrus reamer is an effective way to juice and seed a lemon (see CITRUS REAMER).

■ LEMON CHICKEN BREASTS

This is a speedy interpretation of a popular Chinese chicken dish.

> 3 whole chicken breasts (2½ to 3 lb), halved, boned, and skinned
> 2 lemons
> 1 tablespoon *each* butter or margarine and vegetable oil
> 1 clove garlic, minced
> ⅓ cup Rich Chicken Stock (see page 560)
> 2 teaspoons *each* cornstarch and sugar
> 1 tablespoon *each* soy sauce and water
> Salt, to taste

1. Cut chicken crosswise into ½-inch-wide strips. Grate rind from 1 lemon and squeeze juice; reserve both. Halve other lemon; squeeze juice from one half and add to reserved juice. Slice remaining half lemon thinly and reserve for garnish.

2. In a large, heavy-bottomed frying pan or wok, brown chicken breast strips (about half at a time) on both sides in butter and oil over medium-high heat, removing them as they brown. When all chicken is browned, return to pan and mix in garlic.

3. Add stock and reserved lemon juice. Bring to a boil, cover, reduce heat, and simmer until chicken is just firm and opaque (5 to 6 minutes; do not overcook). In a small bowl blend cornstarch, sugar, soy sauce, and the water.

4. Add lemon rind and soy sauce mixture, bring to a boil over medium-high heat, and stir until thickened and smooth. Add salt if needed. Garnish with lemon slices.

Serves 4 to 6.

LEMON BALM

This perennial herb is appreciated for its lemon-scented, toothed leaves. The leaves add a minty lemon flavor to fruit salads, compotes, and stuffings. The leaves can be infused in hot water to make lemon tisane, a refreshing beverage that some say has medicinal properties. They are also used in cosmetics and fragrances. Fresh lemon balm is sporadically available in specialty markets; look for fragrant, sprightly leaves.

LEMONGRASS

Also known as citronella, lemongrass is a stiff, tropical grass that resembles a large fibrous green onion. It has yellowish white stems, gray-green blades and a delightful lemony aroma. An essential herb in Southeast Asian cooking, it adds a lemony flavor to many Vietnamese, Burmese, Thai, and Malaysian dishes.

Use   Lemongrass imparts a characteristic sourness to many Southeast Asian dishes, especially to soups and fish preparations. The gray-green blades are cut away and the stalks sliced crosswise very thinly. Generally, the large slices of lemongrass used in soup or sautés are considered flavoring agents and are not eaten. In Thailand, lemongrass is used in curry pastes and in hot and spicy shrimp soup; in Vietnam, it is part of meat stir-fries.

Availability   Now widely grown by Asian farmers in warmer areas of the United States, fresh lemongrass is sold in most Asian markets throughout the year. It is also available as dried blades, which must be soaked, and as a ground powder. Some health-food stores and herb shops carry ground lemongrass for use in teas.

Selection   Choose firm, unblemished stalks.

Storage   Keep in the refrigerator crisper for up to two months. Store dried and powdered lemongrass in a cool, dark, dry place; use within two months.

Preparation   Trim away the gray-green blades; wash stalks and slice thinly crosswise. Dried blades must be soaked for two hours in warm water before using. Most recipes call for the slices to be minced or pounded to a paste with other ingredients. Ground lemongrass can be added directly to a dish; substitute 1 teaspoon powder for each fresh stalk.

LEMON VERBENA

A woody deciduous shrub, lemon verbena has sharply lemon-scented leaves.

Use   The leaves of the lemon verbena shrub are employed to flavor beverages, cakes, puddings, and fruit compotes. Both fresh and dried leaves are infused in hot water to make tisane, a relaxing drink that some claim has medicinal value.

Availability   Fresh lemon verbena may occasionally be found in specialty markets. Dried lemon verbena is sold in herb stores and some health-food stores.

Selection   Look for fresh and fragrant leaves.

Storage   Keep fresh lemon verbena in a plastic bag in the refrigerator crisper and use within one or two days. Store dried lemon verbena in a cool, dark, dry place and use within a few months.

LETTUCE

Cultivated at least since 800 B.C., lettuce is today one of the most widely eaten vegetables in the Western world. In America and Western Europe, it is undoubtedly the major salad vegetable.

There are dozens of lettuce varieties but only four general types. Cos or romaine lettuce forms an elongated head with dark green, thickly ribbed outer leaves and a pale green inner heart. It is a sturdy lettuce that can take heavy or full-flavored dressings. Cabbagehead lettuce may be either crisphead, such as iceberg, or butterhead, such as Bibb, Boston, and limestone. Crisphead lettuces have tightly packed, solid heads with crisp, light green leaves; butterhead lettuces have soft leaves and loose, spreading heads. Looseleaf lettuce (also known as cutting lettuce or salad bowl lettuce) grows loosely from a central stem and does not form a heart. Oakleaf lettuce is a good example. The fourth type is stem lettuce, also known as celtuce or asparagus lettuce. Like romaine, it has a long edible stem and leaves; it is not commonly available commercially.

Use   Lettuces appear primarily in the salad bowl. Their refreshing flavor and crisp texture are best appreciated raw; because they are mostly water, cooking greatly alters their texture. French cooks, however, make lettuce soup and often cook shredded lettuce with steamed peas.

Frilly or colorful lettuces are often used to garnish serving platters. The outer leaves of cabbagehead lettuce are used as wrappers for some Chinese dishes, such as minced squab. Lettuce adds a crisp, crunchy texture to sandwiches and tacos.

Lettuce is the main or supporting ingredient in a virtually endless collection of salads, from a simple tossed green salad to the elaborate Cobb salad with diced bacon and chicken. It is almost always served with an oil- or cream-based dressing.

Availability   Stem lettuce is occasionally sold in Asian markets, but in general is not readily available commercially. The other lettuce varieties are carried in most supermarkets throughout the year.

Selection Crisphead lettuces should be firm and round, with green outer leaves that look fresh. Avoid heads with brown-tinged leaves. Heads that are especially hard, heavy, and white are probably overgrown and will have a large bitter core. Butterhead lettuces should have firm green leaves without brown edges; avoid heads with wilting or slimy leaves. Romaine lettuces should be full and compact. Avoid overly large heads, because outer leaves and ribs will be tough; reject heads with wilting leaves or rusty-looking ribs.

Storage Wash lettuce before storing. Dry thoroughly in a salad spinner or with paper towels, then wrap in paper towels, overwrap with a plastic bag, and store in refrigerator crisper. Leaf and butterhead lettuces will keep one or two days. Sturdier romaine and crisphead lettuces will keep three or four days.

Preparation Before washing lettuces, discard any wilted or bruised outer leaves. Twist out the central core, if any, or trim away base. Lettuce should be hand torn, not cut with a knife. Unless the recipe specifies otherwise, never dress a salad until just before serving; dressing makes leaves go limp and soggy.

■ CURRIED LETTUCE AND PEA SOUP

When fresh peas are in season, it's worth the effort of shelling them to make this piquantly seasoned soup. Otherwise, use about 2½ cups of frozen peas. When the soup is served hot, the curry flavor is assertive; chilled, the soup tastes more lemony.

   2 **pounds fresh peas in shells**
   2 **medium onions, finely chopped**
   1 **large clove garlic, minced**
   ¼ **cup butter or margarine**
   2 **tablespoons vegetable oil**
   2 **tablespoons curry powder**
   1 **teaspoon ground turmeric**
   2 **tablespoons flour**
   1 **small head butterhead-type lettuce, shredded (about 4 cups, lightly packed)**
      Grated rind and juice of 1 lemon
   2 **teaspoons sugar**
   4 **cups Rich Chicken Stock (see page 560) or canned chicken broth**
   1 **cup half-and-half**
      Salt, to taste

1. Shell peas (you should have about 2½ cups). Reserve about 2 tablespoons small peas to use as garnish.

2. In a 3½- to 4-quart saucepan, cook onions and garlic in butter and oil over medium heat, stirring often, until soft but not browned. Blend in curry powder and turmeric, then flour. Add shredded lettuce, lemon rind (reserve a few threads for garnish, if desired) and juice, sugar, and peas. Remove from heat and gradually blend in stock.

3. Bring to a boil, stirring, over medium heat; then cover, reduce heat, and simmer until peas are just tender (8 to 10 minutes). Blend in half-and-half. Taste, and add salt if needed.

4. Transfer mixture, about a third at a time, to food processor or blender, and process or whirl until smooth.

5. To serve cold, cover and refrigerate until thoroughly chilled. To serve hot, return to cooking pan and heat, stirring often, until steaming hot. Serve garnished with reserved uncooked peas and reserved lemon rind (if used).

Makes about 9 cups, 6 to 8 servings.

Recipes and Related Information
Caesar Salad, 506; Cream of Lettuce Soup, 563.

LIAISON

A mixture—such as a butter and flour roux, beurre manié, or beaten eggs and cream—used to thicken and enrich (add a luxurious finish to) soups, sauces, and stews is called a liaison. Other thickeners include flour, cornstarch, and even vegetable purées. Delicate egg-based thickeners must be warmed slightly before adding to hot liquid. To do this, pour a little of the hot sauce or soup into the mixture and whisk to blend. Pour back into the hot liquid and gently heat. Do not allow to boil or mixture will curdle.

Peas are cooked with tender lettuce and piquant seasonings to make creamy Curried Lettuce and Pea Soup, which can be enjoyed either hot or cold. Lemon zest or small peas make an appropriate garnish.

LILY BUD

Also known as golden lilies or golden needles, lily buds are the dried, unopened buds of tiger lilies. They generally measure 2 to 4 inches long and are golden brown, very slender, and wrinkled. They have a chewy texture and a mild, slightly musky flavor.

Use Chinese cooks use lily buds for texture in such dishes as Mu Shu Pork and hot and sour soup.

Availability Dried lily buds are sold in Asian markets packed in plastic.

Storage Dried lily buds may be kept indefinitely in an airtight container in a cool, dark, dry place.

Preparation Soak lily buds in cool water for 20 minutes, then drain and snip off any hard stems. Use whole or halve lengthwise.

LIME

Like lemons, limes are too tart to eat on their own, but they add a refreshing tang to many sweet and savory dishes. Florida, California, and Mexico are the major regions where limes are grown for the American market, with the Persian lime the most common variety. Florida also grows a small, round variety called the Key lime, which produces the juice used in the popular Key lime pie.

Use Limes are valued for the refreshing tartness of their juice and the aromatic oils in their skin. Lime wedges are often served with melons, and with tropical fruits such as papaya and mango. Lime juice gives a lift to a variety of cocktails, including the vodka gimlet and the daiquiri. Lime juice is added to marinades for chicken, pork, and fish. It is used extensively in Mexican cooking, in soups, salads, and fish dishes, the acidic juice "cooks" fish and shellfish, as in the popular Latin seviche. Juice and rind figure in a variety of desserts, including Key lime pie, lime curd, lime sherbet, and chiffon pie. Limes also make an excellent marmalade.

Availability Fresh limes come to market all year. When domestic supplies are low in the spring, they are supplemented with imports from Mexico and the West Indies. Bottled lime juice is also usually available in most supermarkets.

Selection Choose limes that are heavy for their size and that have a solid green color. Brown spots will not affect flavor, but avoid limes that are yellowish (they lack acidity) or hard and blackened (they are grainy).

Storage Refrigerated, limes should keep for approximately one month.

Preparation See LEMON.

■ KEY LIME PIE

This traditional recipe from Key West, Florida, takes less than 30 minutes to prepare.

  ½ **cup (scant) fresh lime juice (from about**
　　6 Key limes *or* 3 large, ripe regular limes)
  2 **to 3 teaspoons grated lime rind**
  1 **can (14 oz) sweetened condensed milk**
  4 **eggs, separated**
  1 **prepared Graham Cracker Crumb Crust (see**
　　page 118) or homemade baked pastry crust
  5 **tablespoons sugar, or to taste**

1. Preheat oven to 400° F. Stir together lime juice, lime rind, and condensed milk until mixture thickens to the consistency of heavy pastry cream (the acid of the lime juice thickens the milk). Beat egg yolks until thick and lemon colored; add to milk mixture to make a light custard. Turn custard into pie crust.

2. Beat egg whites until soft, droopy peaks form. Add sugar, 1 tablespoon at a time. (If a very sweet meringue is desired, use additional sugar.) Continue beating until meringue is shiny and forms stiff peaks.

3. Mound meringue over top of pie. Bake just until meringue is browned but still tender (about 10 minutes). Cool, then chill before serving.

Serves 8.

Recipes and Related Information
Cold Fillet of Sole With Cilantro, Lime, and Pomegranate, 232; Elotes, 158; Jicama With Chile and Lime, 324; Lime Chiffon Pie, 440; Lime Mustard, 323; Seviche, 234.

LITCHI

Also spelled litchee, lychee, and leechee, this tropical fruit is grown in China, Mexico, and the United States. The litchi tree produces a small oval fruit with a rough-textured, strawberry red hull. Underneath the hull, milky white pulp with a grapelike texture surrounds a hard brown seed. The flesh is sweet and moist. Dried litchis, also known as litchi nuts, are brown and shriveled with a prunelike flesh and a sweet, smoky flavor.

Use Peeled and chilled fresh litchis are eaten in fruit compotes and fruit salads. They can garnish chicken, duck, ham, or turkey salad. They are also sometimes added to stir-fried sweet-and-sour chicken or pork. Dried litchis are eaten out of hand as a snack.

Availability Fresh litchis are sold in Asian markets in June and July. Dried litchis and peeled, pitted litchis canned in syrup are also available in Asian markets.

Selection Select fresh litchis that look plump and firm; they should not be withered.

Storage   Refrigerate fresh litchis for up to 1 month or freeze indefinitely. Keep leftover canned litchis in their syrup in an airtight, nonmetal container in the refrigerator for one week. Refrigerated or frozen, dried litchis will keep indefinitely.

Preparation   Fresh litchis must be peeled and seeded; the leathery hull easily pulls away.

LOGANBERRY

A cross between the raspberry and the blackberry, the loganberry is red with a slightly elongated shape.

Use   It may be used in any way that blackberries or raspberries are. See BLACKBERRY and RASPBERRY.

Availability   Loganberries are found fresh in some markets in midsummer; canned loganberries are sold in some supermarkets.

Selection   See BLACKBERRY.

Storage   See BLACKBERRY.

LOQUAT

The fruit of a large evergreen shrub or tree often grown as an ornamental, the loquat is similar in texture and shape to the apricot and is usually 1 to 2 inches in diameter. The skin is yellowish gold; the flesh may be orange, yellow, or white, depending on variety. The loquat has large black seeds and a sweet-tart flesh that becomes sweeter as the fruit ripens. It is also known as the Japanese medlar.

Use   In China and Japan, peeled loquats are eaten as dessert or cooked with chicken. They can be made into jams, jellies, and preserves or can be dried for later use. Peeled and sliced or diced, loquats are added to fruit salads or compotes or cooked with roast pork.

Availability   Loquats must ripen on the tree and are too delicate to ship well. They are rarely available fresh, although some Asian markets carry them in the spring. Dried and canned loquats are sold in Asian markets.

Selection   Choose firm, unblemished loquats that give slightly to pressure.

Storage   In the refrigerator, loquats will last for up to two weeks. Dried loquats will keep indefinitely in the refrigerator or freezer. Leftover canned loquats may be stored in their syrup in a covered nonmetal container in the refrigerator for up to four days.

Preparation   Peel before using.

LOTUS ROOT

This thick, smooth-stalked vegetable has a thin, light brown skin and grows in six-inch increments resembling a string of fat sausages that may reach up to 4 feet long. The crisp ivory flesh is perforated with large holes. When the root is peeled and sliced crosswise, the slices exhibit a lacy snowflake pattern. The flavor is somewhat sweet and starchy.

Use   Lotus root may be thinly sliced, blanched, dressed, and served raw as a cold salad. Slices may also be deep-fried in tempura batter. Indian cooks incorporate lotus root in chutneys; Chinese cooks use the lacy slices to garnish platters. Because lotus root has the texture of potato, it may be substituted for potatoes in soups and stews. Lotus root starch, made from the ground root, is used as a thickener for Chinese soups and sauces and as a coating for fried foods.

Availability   Fresh lotus root is sold in Asian markets from July to February. It is also marketed as dried slices, sugared slices, or canned slices.

Selection   Choose firm, unblemished roots.

Storage   Refrigerated lotus roots will keep two to three weeks. Dried or sugared slices will keep indefinitely in a cool, dark, dry place. Leftover canned lotus root may be stored in water in a covered nonmetal container in the refrigerator for up to one week; change the water every other day.

Preparation   Lotus root discolors quickly; put peeled slices immediately in acidulated water to prevent browning. To soften dried lotus root, soak in acidulated water for one hour or until soft.

LOVAGE

The bright green leaves of this perennial herb look and taste a lot like celery. The flavor of the seeds is also celerylike.

Use   Lovage adds its pungent flavor to soups, stuffings, salads, and vegetable dishes. The ground seeds may be used to season breads, soups, roasts, and cheese dishes.

Availability   Fresh lovage is occasionally sold in some specialty markets. Lovage seed is carried in some specialty markets and herb stores.

Selection   Look for bright green leaves with no signs of wilting.

Storage   Place fresh lovage in a plastic bag and keep in the crisper; use immediately.

M

An assortment of fresh seasonal fruits macerated in sweet Muscat wine is a refreshing finish to a summer meal.

MACADAMIA CRISPS

Nuts of all sorts are a favorite ingredient for many kinds of cookies. These thin, crisp, buttery rounds are the perfect showcase for the rich flavor of elegant macadamia nuts. Fresh sweet cherries would be a juicy counterpoint to the crunchy texture of the cookies.

      1 **cup flour**
      ¼ **teaspoon baking soda**
      ½ **cup butter or margarine, softened**
   1 ¼ **cups firmly packed brown sugar**
      1 **egg**
      1 **teaspoon vanilla extract**
      1 **cup chopped macadamia nuts**

1. In a small bowl stir together flour and baking soda to combine thoroughly; set aside.

2. Preheat oven to 375° F. In mixer bowl combine butter and brown sugar, and beat until well blended. Beat in egg until fluffy. Add vanilla and mix to blend.

3. Gradually add flour mixture until just blended. Stir in macadamia nuts.

4. Drop by rounded teaspoonfuls, placed about 1½ inches apart, onto lightly greased baking sheets. Bake until cookies are golden brown (8 to 10 minutes). Let stand briefly on baking sheets, then remove to wire racks to cool completely.

Makes about 5 dozen 2½-inch cookies.

MACADAMIA NUT

Although the macadamia nut is native to Australia, most of the commercial crop now comes from Hawaii. Small and round, with a hard brown shell, the nut is almost always shelled and roasted in coconut oil before being marketed. The meat is cream colored, smooth and round, and very rich in flavor.

Use   Roasted and salted macadamia nuts are enjoyed as a cocktail snack. They can be minced and sprinkled on fish or sautéed vegetables. They are also used in desserts, including cream pies, cakes, and cookies.

Availability   Outside of their place of origin, macadamia nuts are almost always sold shelled and roasted. They are found in vacuum-packed tins or jars in most supermarkets.

Storage   Unopened tins and jars will keep indefinitely in a cool place. Once opened, the nuts should be used within one month or frozen for longer storage.

Preparation   For use in sweet dishes, salted nuts are often blanched first.

MACE

Surrounding the shell of the nutmeg is a fragile, lacy, red skin called mace. The mace is separated from the nutmeg at harvest and then ground separately or broken into flakes called blades. The flavor of mace is related to that of nutmeg but is more pungent and less sweet.

Use   Mace contributes pungent flavor to sweet breads, pound cake, cherry pie, and puddings. It is an ingredient in Indian and Moroccan spice blends and is added to many Indonesian curries. Blade mace is often used whole in pickles and clear soups.

Availability   Ground mace is found on most supermarket spice racks. Whole dried blade mace is sold in some Asian and Caribbean markets.

Selection   Packaged seasonings lose quality after a while; try to buy from a store that restocks its spice section fairly often.

Storage   Keep ground mace in a cool, dry, dark place; it is highly perishable and should be replaced every three to four months. For longer storage keep mace in the refrigerator. Blade mace will keep for one year in a cool, dry, dark place.

Preparation Ground mace can be added directly to dishes; blade mace can be used whole, or ground just before use in a pepper mill, clean coffee grinder, or electric minichopper, or with a mortar and pestle.

> **Recipes and Related Information**
> *Nutmeg, 393; Traditional Sugar-Cookie Cutouts, 149.*

MACERATE, TO

To place food in a flavored liquid to improve flavor and soften texture. This is the same process as marinating, a term usually applied to meats, fish, and vegetables. Macerating has come to be associated with fruits, most often fruits soaked in spirits.

▨ FRESH FRUIT IN WINE

Marinades for fruit serve to moisten and enhance the flavor of the fruit. An assortment of seasonal fruits steeped in sweet Muscat wine makes a light, refreshing dessert. A glass of the same wine makes a good accompaniment.

Blackberries or boysenberries shouldn't be used for this dish because they tend to disintegrate and their juice stains the whole dish. Casaba melon can be too soft to hold together in the marinade and watermelon adds a lot of liquid, diluting the flavor. Try to combine tart fruits such as oranges or pineapple with low-acid types such as pears or bananas, but don't use too much tart fruit or the acidity will overpower the wine. Choose three or four of the following, depending upon what is in season. Strawberries, hulled, split if large; cantaloupe, honeydew, or other firm melon, in cubes or balls; orange or tangerine sections, all white pith removed; peaches or nectarines, unpeeled, sliced; blueberries or huckleberries; red, green, or purple grapes, especially Muscat types; mango, peeled, seeded, and cut into wedges; papaya, peeled, seeded, and diced; pears, peeled, cored, and diced; fully ripe pineapple, in chunks; bananas, peeled and sliced.

> 4 cups assorted fresh fruit (see above)
> 1 cup sweet Muscat Blanc, Muscat Canelli, or Malvasia Bianca
> Fresh lemon juice, to taste (omit if using citrus fruits)
> Mint leaves or borage blossoms, for garnish

1. Combine cut fruit in a large bowl, pour in wine, and toss to moisten fruit thoroughly with wine. Marinate in refrigerator 1 to 4 hours.

2. Taste a piece of the sweetest fruit and a piece of the most tart. Add lemon juice if necessary. Serve in individual bowls or from a large bowl as part of a buffet. Garnish with a sprig of fresh mint or borage blossoms.

Serves 4.

MACHE

The French name for a hardy leafy green, *mâche* is perhaps better known in the United States as corn salad or lamb's lettuce. The leaves have a mild, slightly nutty flavor. Some varieties produce leaves that are slightly cup-shaped; others produce round, flat leaves.

Use Mâche serves primarily as a salad green, either alone or in combination with other greens. The mild flavor is a good counterpoint to stronger-flavored greens, such as arugula and chicory.

Availability Mâche is not widely grown commercially but may appear in some specialty markets in spring, fall, and winter. It also grows wild in much of North America.

Selection Choose only unblemished leaves with no signs of wilting.

Storage Place greens in a plastic bag in the refrigerator crisper and use within one or two days.

Preparation Wash and dry thoroughly. Trim roots and discard blemished or yellowed leaves.

MALT

When barley, or occasionally barley and corn, has been allowed to germinate partially and then is roasted and ground, the product is malt. When powdered malt is soaked in water, then heated and reduced to a syrup, the result is malt extract. Malted milk is powdered milk containing maltose (malt sugar) and dextrin (an unfermentable sugar).

Use The primary function of malt is in the making of beer and Scotch whisky. The malt provides the sugars needed by the yeast to ferment. In addition, the degree to which the malt is roasted is a major determinant of the final flavor of both beer and Scotch.

Malt extract, also known as malt syrup, is widely employed in commercial bakeries and can be easily used in the home kitchen. Malt, being hygroscopic (it readily absorbs and holds moisture), gives breads a moist texture; it improves the rising of dough and helps give a golden color to the crust. Only a very small quantity is needed to derive these benefits. For a standard two-loaf recipe, add 1 teaspoon malt syrup to the required liquid.

Malted milk powder was originally devised as food for invalids and infants, but it is now best known as a soda fountain ingredient, used to impart a toasty flavor to milk shakes. It is also a substance in the commercial manufacture of baked goods, cake mixes, and ice cream.

Availability Malt extract in jars or cans is sold in some supermarkets, health food stores, and stores that carry beer-making equipment.

Storage   If packaged in a tightly closed jar or other airtight container in a cool, dark, dry place, malt will keep indefinitely.

Preparation   Malt extract is very sticky. To make measuring easier, coat measuring spoon lightly with oil before adding malt extract. It will slip off the oiled spoon with little problem.

MANDARIN ORANGE

The mandarin orange is not one citrus fruit but many. The varieties of mandarin orange vary in size, color, flavor, and quantity of seeds. They can be as small as a golf ball or as large as a baseball. The skin can be a greenish gold or deep orange-red. The flesh can be seedless or full of seeds, and the juice sweet as honey or quite tart. What they have in common is their ease of peeling; mandarins are sometimes known as loose-skinned oranges or kid-glove oranges because they peel so readily. *Tangerine* is the name commonly used for deeply colored mandarins.

Use   Mandarin oranges are commonly eaten out of hand. Because they peel easily, they are an excellent lunch-box or picnic fruit. Their refreshing flavor is especially appealing at breakfast or at the end of a winter dinner. Mandarin oranges may be sectioned and added to fruit salad, green salad, or chicken salad. Sweet varieties may be squeezed for a breakfast juice. The juice may also be used in sorbets, marinades, and dessert sauces. The grated peel can flavor cakes, muffins, quick breads, stuffings, rice, and other grain dishes. Dried tangerine peel is used in Chinese cooking to add flavor to stews, stir-fries, and smoked poultry.

Availability   Mandarin oranges are in peak supply from November through March. Canned mandarin orange segments are also widely available in supermarkets. Dried tangerine peel is available in Chinese markets. Among the major mandarin orange varieties are the following:

Clementine   Sweet and juicy Algerian variety that can have few or many seeds.

Dancy   Small, with a rich red-orange color, a rich but acidic flavor, and many seeds.

Fairchild   An early variety that is sweet and juicy but with many seeds.

Honey   Exceptionally sweet, with many seeds.

Kinnow   Richly flavored, with a rind that is thin and relatively difficult to peel.

Satsuma   Sweet and almost seedless Japanese variety.

Tangelo   Cross between a mandarin orange and a pomelo or grapefruit, a Malaysian fruit that is the ancestor of the grapefruit. Tangelos range in color from pale yellow to deep orange, in size from medium-small to medium-large, with flavors and aromas that combine the best of both parents. The best-known variety is the Minneola, a large juicy fruit with a nipple-shaped stem end and few seeds.

Selection   Look for mandarins that feel heavy for their size. They should not have soft spots. Although some varieties are naturally puffy due to their loose skin, fruits that are extremely puffy may be overripe.

Storage   In the refrigerator, mandarin oranges will keep for up to one month. Refrigerate leftover canned mandarin orange segments in an airtight nonmetal container for up to one week. Store dried tangerine peel airtight in a cool, dark, dry place; it will keep indefinitely.

Preparation   Peel and section. Soften dried tangerine peel in cool water for about 30 minutes before using.

MANDOLINE

Before the food processor there was the mandoline. This tool for slicing, with adjustable blades, has long been used in professional kitchens to cut hard vegetables and fruits, such as carrots, cabbage, potatoes, beets, and apples, into uniform shapes. It functions  like a grater or shredder—food moves over the cutting surface and the cut pieces fall through the cutting slots. With it you can shred, slice, julienne, waffle cut, and shape French fries.

Resembling an old-fashioned washboard, the mandoline is long, narrow, and rectangular, with a body made of wood, plastic, or heavyweight stainless steel for professional models. The simplest models are single bladed, designed for shredding; in fact, they are sometimes dubbed slaw slicers. Other models have two blades of different thicknesses, or adjustable blades that permit a range of thicknesses. Food is held in place by a metal carriage that has a hinged lid and knob, and glides on tracks so your hand is protected from the cutting edges. Better models have foldaway legs that diagonally prop up the device.

All of these functions can also be done with a food processor, except for the waffle or ripple cut; however, if you don't have a processor, or if you enjoy using a hand tool for certain tasks, then the mandoline, long appreciated by professionals, might suit your needs.

Recipes and Related Information
Food Processor, 240; Grater, Shredder, and Mill, 281.

MANGO

The most commonly grown fruit in India, exceeding all other fruits combined, the mango is also extremely popular in the Caribbean and Mexico. When ripe, the fruit of the mango tree has a tantalizing perfume. Under its smooth thin skin is moist, golden orange flesh with a flavor reminiscent of peach, apricot, and papaya. The flesh clings to a large flat seed in the middle and must be cut away from it. The fruit must also be peeled before eating.

Of the hundreds of mango varieties of different sizes, shapes, and colors, those most common in the United States are round to oval, weigh from 6 ounces to 1 pound each, and have a skin that may be green with red patches or yellowish green with rosy parts. As a mango ripens, the warm red, orange, and yellow shades increase and the green fades.

Use   Mangoes can be eaten raw, either alone or in combination with other fruits, often garnished with tart lemon or lime wedges. Sliced ripe mangoes may be used in many desserts, such as compotes, cakes, and tarts; puréed mangoes can form the base of sherbets, whips, ice cream, beverages, and dessert sauces. Underripe mangoes are a chief ingredient in mango chutney and mango pickle; in India, they are prepared as a savory vegetable—cubed, braised with onions and warm spices, and served over rice.

Availability   Fresh mangoes are sold in Latin American and Indian markets and in well-stocked supermarkets and specialty produce markets from May to September, with peak supplies in June. Some Latin American markets also carry canned mangoes in syrup.

Selection   The sweetest mangoes have skins with a great deal of red or orange; all-green, hard mangoes will probably never ripen properly. Avoid shriveled, overripe mangoes with black spots on the skin.

Storage   Leave underripe mangoes at room temperature until color develops; ripe mangoes are very fragrant and give gently to pressure. To speed ripening, place mangoes in a paper bag pierced with a few holes. Refrigerate ripe fruit in a plastic bag and use within two or three days. Leftover canned mango may be refrigerated in its syrup in a covered container for up to four days.

Preparation   Mango halves cannot be readily pried away from the pit. To section a mango, cut vertically all the way around the fruit with a small sharp knife. Peel skin back, then cut flesh off the pit in long vertical slices. Ripe mangoes are messy and juicy, and mango juice stains; eat with caution.

Recipes and Related Information
Fresh Fruit in Wine, 347; Mango With Prosciutto, 358; Pavlova, 362.

MARGARINE

A substitute for butter, margarine is made from hydrogenated vegetable oils, predominantly soy and corn oil. Because it is cholesterol-free, less expensive, and lower in saturated fats than is butter, margarine is the preferred solid cooking fat in many American households today. Margarine is colored (see ACHIOTE) and fortified with vitamins to increase its similarity to butter (see BUTTER). Milk solids and diacetyl, a molecule that contributes a buttery flavor, are also added. Margarine is less frequently referred to as oleomargarine.

Use   Margarine may be substituted for butter in almost all recipes, although it will not impart the same rich, nutty flavor. It may be used for sautéing, for coating vegetables or bread, and for baking. It is unsuitable for butter-based sauces, such as Hollandaise and beurre blanc.

Availability   Margarine is readily found in all supermarkets, packaged in plastic tubs or in foil-wrapped sticks overwrapped with a paper carton.

Storage   Margarine should be refrigerated. It will keep for several weeks in the refrigerator or indefinitely in the freezer.

MARINADE; MARINATE, TO

A seasoned liquid or a paste of herbs and spices is a marinade. To marinate, let food sit in a wet or dry mixture to tenderize and/or increase the flavor of a food. Meats, fish, and even vegetables and fruit benefit from this treatment. Also see MACERATE.

Typically a wet marinade contains oil, seasoning, and an acid such as lemon juice, vinegar, or wine. The acid breaks down muscle fiber for a more-tender final product, while the oil adds moisture and, along with the seasoning, increases your appreciation of the food: Studies have shown that foods containing fat have a better mouthfeel. A dry marinade—a spice rub—is massaged into the food, infusing it with a particular blend of spices and dried herbs that grows stronger as the coating remains on the food.

Foods usually sit in marinades for at least one hour, or overnight, or in some cases longer, depending upon the desired intensity of flavor and the amount of preparation time available to the cook. For a short period of time—one hour or less—marinating foods can be left out at room temperature; otherwise keep in the refrigerator. If chilled, let food warm to room temperature (about 30 minutes) before cooking.

To prepare acid-based wet marinades, always use a nonreactive container, such as one made of glass or stainless steel, or a plastic bag to prevent adverse reactions or

Use marinades and bastes to tenderize and flavor meats, fish, and vegetables.

VERSATILE MARINADES AND DRY SPICE RUBS

To marinate, use a container that holds the food snugly in a single layer. Cover with plastic wrap. Leftover marinade can be refrigerated in a covered jar for several weeks.

Wet marinades can be mixed in a blender or by hand with a whisk. Make the dry spice rubs by combining all ingredients and mixing well.

Mustard and Herb Marinade

Use for lamb or chicken. Makes about 1 cup.

⅓ cup vegetable oil
¼ cup dry white wine
1 tablespoon *each* red wine vinegar and lemon juice
1 large clove garlic, minced
1½ tablespoons Dijon mustard
¼ teaspoon *each* salt and sugar
⅛ teaspoon *each* dried thyme, oregano, summer savory, and tarragon
Dash white pepper

Teriyaki Marinade

Use for beef, chicken, or fish. Makes about ¾ cup.

½ cup soy sauce
3 tablespoons sugar
2 teaspoons grated fresh ginger *or* ½ teaspoon ground ginger
1 clove garlic, minced
2 tablespoons dry sherry

Dry Spice Rub for Fish

Makes about 4 tablespoons.

2 teaspoons grated lemon rind
1 teaspoon garlic powder
1 teaspoon tarragon
1 teaspoon basil
2 teaspoons freshly ground black pepper
½ teaspoon cayenne pepper
1 tablespoon paprika
½ teaspoon salt

Dry Spice Rub for Lamb

Makes about 4 tablespoons.

1 teaspoon garlic powder
1 teaspoon fennel seed, bruised or crushed in a mortar with a pestle
½ teaspoon thyme
2 teaspoons freshly ground black pepper
½ teaspoon cayenne pepper
1 tablespoon paprika
1 teaspoon oregano
2 teaspoons rosemary
1 teaspoon basil
½ teaspoon salt

off-colors. Marinated foods are usually cooked by broiling, grilling, or roasting. Fat may cause flare-ups on the grill or in the broiler, so before cooking, drain off the marinade and pat away excess from the food. Also, the sugars present in some marinades lower the browning temperature. Cooks must be vigilant to see that the caramelizing sugars brown and do not burn.

To prepare dry spice rubs, wash and dry all food before marinating. For cuts of beef, lamb, and poultry, lightly oil all external surfaces. For fish, lightly coat with clarified butter. Then massage spice rub over external surfaces of food. Depending on type of spice mixture, use from 1 to 2 tablespoons of marinade per pound of beef, poultry, or fish. Let stand for one hour at room temperature before cooking to allow the spices to permeate the flesh.

Dry Spice Rub for Meat
Makes 3 tablespoons.

    1 teaspoon garlic powder
    1 teaspoon fennel seed, bruised or crushed
       in mortar and pestle
    ½ teaspoon thyme
    2 teaspoons freshly ground black pepper
    ½ teaspoon cayenne pepper
    1 tablespoon paprika
    ½ teaspoon oregano
    ½ teaspoon salt

Dry Spice Rub for Poultry
Makes 3 tablespoons.

    1 teaspoon garlic powder
    2 teaspoons tarragon
    ½ teaspoon sage
    1 teaspoon marjoram
    ½ teaspoon thyme
    2 teaspoons freshly ground black pepper
    ½ teaspoon cayenne pepper
    1 tablespoon paprika
    ½ teaspoon salt

■ TANDOORI CHICKEN

A tandoor is an Indian clay oven, but a conventional oven will work at home for this dish. The marinade and high heat turn the chicken very dark brown as it cooks. Marinating takes at least two hours, or overnight.

    2 whole chickens (about 3 lb each), quartered
    1½ teaspoons cumin seed
    1 teaspoon whole coriander, crushed
    ⅛ gram saffron threads (½ vial)
    2 tablespoons boiling water
    2 cloves garlic, minced
    1 teaspoon fresh ginger, minced
    1 jalapeño chile, minced
    1 tablespoon paprika
    1 cup plain yogurt
    3 tablespoons fresh lemon juice
    6 tablespoons unsalted butter, melted

1. Score chicken pieces in diagonal cuts through meat almost to bone in 3 or 4 places.

2. In a small, dry skillet, slowly toast cumin seed and coriander until barely browned (4 to 5 minutes). In a small bowl dissolve saffron in the boiling water.

3. Stir cumin seed, coriander, garlic, ginger, chile, paprika, yogurt, lemon juice, and 3 tablespoons of the butter into saffron. Mix thoroughly. Rub marinade into chicken and let marinate in the refrigerator for 2 hours or overnight.

4. Preheat oven to 500° F. Place chicken pieces on a broiler rack set in a shallow pan and roast 30 minutes.

Baste with remaining butter and turn to brown second side, just to color (5 to 8 minutes). Serve hot from oven.

Serves 8.

Recipes and Related Information
Spicy Red-Wine Marinade, 610; Wine in Cooking, 608.

MARJORAM

A perennial herb in the mint family, marjoram (also known as sweet marjoram) is often confused with oregano. It has a similar flavor and leaf shape, but is slightly milder and sweeter. The small green oval leaves are important to Mediterranean cooking.

Use Marjoram flatters many Mediterranean vegetables, such as tomatoes, beans, squash, and onions. Rub it on chicken, pork, and lamb before roasting; include it in meat loaves, sausage mixtures, and stuffings; or let it simmer in soups and tomato sauces. Because marjoram is delicate, it should be added to cooked dishes (such as soups and sauces) shortly before serving.

Availability Some specialty markets carry fresh marjoram the year around. Both whole dried leaves and ground marjoram are packed in jars and tins and are widely available on supermarket spice racks.

Selection Choose fresh leaves. Packaged seasonings lose quality after a while; try to buy from a store that restocks its spice section fairly often.

Storage Refrigerate fresh marjoram in a plastic bag and use as soon as possible. Store dried leaves or ground marjoram in a cool, dark, dry place. Replace leaves once a year, ground marjoram every six months.

Preparation Mince fresh leaves before adding to a dish. Rub dried leaves between fingers to release aromatic oils before using.

MATERIALS FOR COOKWARE

The materials used for cookware can play a role in the success or failure of the final product. Metals, glass, and ceramics each have properties that make them suitable for certain culinary jobs and undesirable for others. When choosing cooking equipment, it's as important to match the material to the task as it is to consider appropriate sizes and shapes. Use the chart on page 352 as a guide. For discussions of specific equipment, such as cookware or baking dishes, see particular entries.

COMMON MATERIALS FOR KITCHEN EQUIPMENT

For consistently successful results, choose cookware made of a material best suited for the job at hand. This chart describes the properties and suggested uses for the most common materials.

Type of Material	Advantages and Disadvantages	Care and Cleaning
Aluminum	A superior heat conductor, aluminum heats evenly and quickly. Can react with acidic foods, adversely affecting taste and color of food. Alkalies can cause pan to darken. Anodized aluminum has a fused-on coating that seals the metal, making it nonreactive and almost nonstick.	If necessary, scrub with coarse salt or mildly abrasive cleanser; rinse immediately. If darkened from oxidation, fill with water and vinegar or lemon juice, and boil 15 minutes.
Cast iron	Because cast iron absorbs heat slowly and evenly, it is good for baking and frying. Moisture can cause rusting. Seasoning before first use seals porous surface and keeps food from sticking. To season, rub inside of pan with vegetable oil; set over medium heat until oil begins to smoke (about 15 minutes); cool completely and wipe off excess oil with paper towels.	Retain seasoning by wiping clean with a paper towel; to remove food, scrub gently with a nylon pad. If used infrequently, coat cast iron with oil or wrap in plastic and store in dry place to keep rust-free and dry. Reseason when necessary.
Clad metals	These are a combination or sandwich of several metals for their best qualities: stainless steel for durability and resistance to corrosion, aluminum or copper for heat conductivity, and anodized aluminum for nonreactive and nonstick properties. Combination depends upon manufacturer.	Follow manufacturer's directions for care.
Copper	An excellent heat conductor, copper is well-suited for sauces and liquids. Copper cookware is usually lined with tin or stainless steel to prevent toxic interactions with certain foods.	Clean in hot, soapy water; dry at once. Brighten with commercial copper polish. Re-tin when necessary.
Earthenware, stoneware	Although poor heat conductors, they retain heat well and are good for baking and slow cooking. Both come glazed and unglazed. Porous unglazed clay bakers must soak in water prior to use; follow manufacturer's instructions. Stoneware is less porous and more durable than earthenware.	To clean earthenware soak in hot water, scrub with coarse salt, rinse, and air dry. Glazed stoneware is usually dishwasherproof.
Enameled metals	Cast iron or steel may be coated with a porcelain enamel that can chip and crack. Some have a dark, nonstick coating. Enameled steel is lighter than cast iron and has a thin, fragile glaze. Light-colored interiors can become stained.	Avoid knocking or hitting with metal utensils (wood utensils are preferable). Soak in hot, soapy water; avoid harsh abrasives. Follow manufacturer's directions for care.
Glass, glass-ceramic, porcelain	Poor heat conductors but good heat retainers, all are nonreactive, suitable for baking and, in a very few cases, for stove-top use; confirm at time of purchase. Glass and porcelain can crack or break if exposed to sudden changes of temperature. Glass-ceramic is impervious to sudden changes of temperature, so can go safely from freezer to oven, and sometimes to stove top.	Soak in hot, soapy water to remove any food stuck to surface. All are dishwasherproof.
Nonstick surfaces	Fused to interior of pan, nonstick surfaces permit almost fat-free cooking.	Wipe clean with a sponge and warm, soapy water; use only abrasives designed for these finishes.
Rolled steel	Appropriate for quick cooking, rolled steel absorbs heat rapidly. Often used for omelet pans, crêpe pans, and woks, it is susceptible to rust if exposed to moisture. Season and store as for cast iron.	See Cast iron.
Stainless steel	A poor heat conductor, stainless steel is best if clad with a good conductor such as copper or aluminum, or if entire pan or pan bottom contains a core of one of these metals. Stainless steel is sturdy, nonreactive, and easy to clean.	Wash in hot, soapy water; scrub with a nylon pad. Clean stubborn stains with stainless steel cleanser.

MEALY

This word is used to describe food that resembles crumbly and coarse meal. Cooked potatoes can have a mealy texture, which tastes dry and granular. The appearance of biscuit and pastry dough after the fat has been sufficiently cut into the dry ingredients is also described as mealy.

MEASURE, TO

To allot a specific quantity of food, whether dry or liquid; also, to determine the dimensions and volumes of pans, dishes, and molds.

To watch experienced cooks at work, it seems that they are casual to the point of recklessness about measuring—a pinch of this, a few splashes of that. Actually, they are more like tourists on a return visit: The recipe, like an itinerary, becomes the starting point for their explorations rather than a map to be slavishly followed. They have learned when exact measures are indispensable and when they are a matter of personal taste. Even without measuring tools, their dashes and splashes are remarkably accurate—the result of long practice.

Why measure? For one thing, measurements are a system of notation that helps ensure reproducible results. If the recipe is faithfully followed, the dish you make today should look and taste about the same as when you made it last month. If you share the recipe with grateful guests, they should rightly expect that their efforts will be as successful as yours.

Cooking is a science as well as an art. Precise measurements are sometimes critical to the success of a recipe; baking requires this type of attention. Many such recipes are balanced formulas. Amounts of ingredients are carefully chosen to interact in a specific way. Upset the balance more than just a bit or make improper substitutions and the final product will fail.

BASIC MEASURES

1 tablespoon	=	3 teaspoons
¾ tablespoon	=	2¼ teaspoons
½ tablespoon	=	1½ teaspoons
⅓ tablespoon	=	1 teaspoon
Pinch	=	Less than ⅛ teaspoon
1 cup	=	16 tablespoons
½ cup	=	8 tablespoons
⅓ cup	=	5⅓ tablespoons
¼ cup	=	4 tablespoons
1 gallon	=	4 quarts/8 pints/16 cups
1 quart	=	2 pints/4 cups
1 pint	=	2 cups
1 pound	=	16 ounces
¾ pound	=	12 ounces
⅔ pound	=	10⅔ ounces
½ pound	=	8 ounces
⅓ pound	=	5⅓ ounces
¼ pound	=	4 ounces

WEIGHT EQUIVALENTS OF SOME COMMON FOODS

Dry ingredients have different weights per cup. Even the weight of two identical measures of the same ingredient may vary depending on how it was added to the measuring cup—with a light touch or a heavy hand, sifted or unsifted, packed down or leveled off with knife or spatula. Professional cooks, in particular bakers, prefer to measure by weight. Home cooks who bake frequently might find it useful to purchase a scale (see Measuring Cups, Spoons, Scales).

Granulated Sugar

¼ cup	=	1¾ ounces
⅓ cup	=	2¼ ounces
½ cup	=	3½ ounces
⅔ cup	=	4½ ounces
¾ cup	=	5 ounces
1 cup	=	7 ounces
1½ cups	=	10½ ounces
2 cups	=	14 ounces

Solid Fats:
Butter, Margarine, Vegetable Shortening

2 cups/4 sticks/ 32 tablespoons	= 16 ounces
1 cup/2 sticks/ 16 tablespoons	= 8 ounces
½ cup/1 stick/8 tablespoons	= 4 ounces
¼ cup/½ stick/4 tablespoons	= 2 ounces
¼ stick/2 tablespoons	= 1 ounce
⅛ stick/1 tablespoon	= ½ ounce

All-purpose Flour

Flour	Unsifted	Sifted
2 cups	10 ounces	8½ ounces
1½ cups	7½ ounces	6¼ ounces
1 cup	5 ounces	4¼ ounces
¾ cup	3½ ounces	3 ounces
⅔ cup	3¼ ounces	2½ ounces
½ cup	2½ ounces	2 ounces
⅓ cup	1½ ounces	1¼ ounces
¼ cup	1¼ ounces	1 ounce

HOW TO MEASURE INGREDIENTS

Good cooks know not only when to measure accurately, but also how to measure correctly. When accuracy is critical, use the container that fills to the amount you need to measure—a half cup for that amount of flour, for example, instead of filling a full cup halfway. A liquid measuring cup won't be as accurate for dry ingredients because it can't be leveled off.

TO MEASURE DRY INGREDIENTS: POWDERS, CRUMBS, CHOPPED OR GRATED FOODS

Baking Powder and Baking Soda Use a measuring spoon of the correct size; dip into container and level off with edge of package lid, or with knife or metal spatula.

Crumbs and Chopped Foods Lightly fill measuring cup; level off with knife or spatula.

Flour Because particles of flour tend to pack, it is impossible to give an absolute value for the weight of a cup of flour. This will vary depending upon the method used to fill the cup, and whether the flour was sifted first (see Weight Equivalents of Some Common Foods). Many cookbooks and some recipes specify how to measure flour; follow cookbook or recipe instructions for good results. If a method is not specified, for consistent results choose one of the following and use it each time. Aerate or loosen flour by fluffing with a fork, then spoon lightly into measuring cup; don't tap or bang cup, since this will pack flour. Level off with knife or spatula. Or, aerate flour with a fork, scoop it up with measuring cup, then level off. If recipe calls for *1 cup sifted flour,* sift flour, then gently fill measuring cup. If it says *1 cup flour, sifted,* measure first, then sift.

Salt and Ground Spices Use a measuring spoon of the correct size; pour powder into spoon and level off with a knife or spatula.

Sugar Measure granulated white sugar as for Crumbs and Chopped Foods or by weight (see Weight Equivalents of Some Common Foods). Sift confectioners' sugar first (unless directed otherwise), then measure as for flour. For brown sugar, pack firmly into measuring cup so that when turned out it retains shape of cup. If lumpy, roll before measuring.

TO MEASURE LIQUIDS, OILS

Use a liquid measuring cup with calibrations marked on the inside. Fill to desired level; set on a flat surface and check at eye level. (Don't lift cup; it will not be as steady and reading won't be as precise.)

For easier removal of sticky liquids—such as honey, molasses, and syrups—from measuring cups, lightly grease the cup first, spray with vegetable cooking spray, or use a rubber spatula to scrape out food.

U.S. MEASURE AND METRIC MEASURE CONVERSION CHART

Metric equivalents are becoming increasingly common. Use this chart to translate between U.S. and metric measurements. For convenience, rounded measures for often-used quantities are also provided.

Formulas for Exact Measures					Rounded Measures for Quick Reference		
Measure	**Symbol**	**When You Know**	**Multiply by**	**To Find**			
Mass (weight)	oz	Ounces	28.35	Grams	1 oz		=30 g
	lb	Pounds	0.45	Kilograms	4 oz		=115 g
	g	Grams	0.035	Ounces	8 oz		=225 g
	kg	Kilograms	2.2	Pounds	16 oz	=1 lb	=450 g
					32 oz	=2 lb	=900 g
					36 oz	=2¼ lb	=1,000 g (1 kg)
Volume	tsp	Teaspoons	4.9	Milliliters	¼ tsp	=1/24 oz	=1 ml
	tbsp	Tablespoons	15.0	Milliliters	½ tsp	=1/12 oz	=2 ml
	fl oz	Fluid ounces	29.57	Milliliters	1 tsp	=1/6 oz	=5 ml
	c	Cups	0.237	Liters	1 tbsp	=½ oz	=15 ml
	pt	Pints	0.47	Liters	1 c	=8 oz	=250 ml
	qt	Quarts	0.95	Liters	2 c (1 pt)	=16 oz	=500 ml
	gal	Gallons	3.785	Liters	4 c (1 qt)	=32 oz	=1 liter
	ml	Milliliters	0.034	Fluid ounces	4 qt (1 gal)	=128 oz	=3¾ liter
Temperature	°F	Fahrenheit	5/9 (after subtracting 32)	Celsius	32° F	= 0° C	
					68° F	= 20° C	
	°C	Celsius	9/5 (then add 32)	Fahrenheit	212° F	=100° C	

TO MEASURE FATS

Spoon solid vegetable shortening and softened butter into dry measuring cups; level off. Sticks of butter or margarine usually have wrappers printed with tablespoon markings. There are 8 tablespoons in a stick of butter (see Weight Equivalents of Some Common Foods). For melted fats, measure in solid form and then melt, or melt and then measure as a liquid.

MEASURING BY WEIGHT

Quantity recipes and recipes from countries outside of the United States typically state ingredients by weight. This easy method has long been used by restaurant kitchens and professional bakers because it is consistent, exact, and reliable. Some recipes give weight equivalents; to convert those that don't, weigh the foods as you use them, and record weights for future reference (see Weight Equivalents of Some Common Foods).

THE METRIC SYSTEM

This decimal system of weights and measures (in units of ten) is based on the meter (for length), the kilogram (for dry weight), and the liter (for liquids). Unlike most countries of the world, the United States does not follow this system, but it is being routinely taught in American schools. More and more frequently, measuring tools sold in the U.S. have both pound and kilogram markings. See U.S. Measure and Metric Measure Conversion Chart.

TO MEASURE BAKING PANS AND DISHES

For best results, use the correct pan size. Recipes will describe a pan or dish in terms of shape (round, square, or rectangular), dimensions (9- by 13-inch, 8-inch), or volume (a 6-cup mold, a 2-quart dish). Many manufacturers stamp the size on the pan. If this hasn't been done, measure as follows.

Dimension With a ruler, measure length and/or width across the top of the pan from one inside edge to the other. Measure depth from the outside, bottom to top of one side. Scratch size on the pan for future reference. See BAKING PANS.

Volume The volume of a pan is measured by the amount of liquid it holds when filled to the rim. With a measuring cup, fill dish or pan with water; note capacity on the underside of the pan for future reference.

EQUIPMENT FOR MEASURING

Measuring tools are necessities for the cook. Buy measuring cups for liquid and dry ingredients, measuring spoons, and, if you have storage space, a scale with both American and metric weights. It makes sense to have several sets of cups and spoons—one set for liquids, the other for dry ingredients.

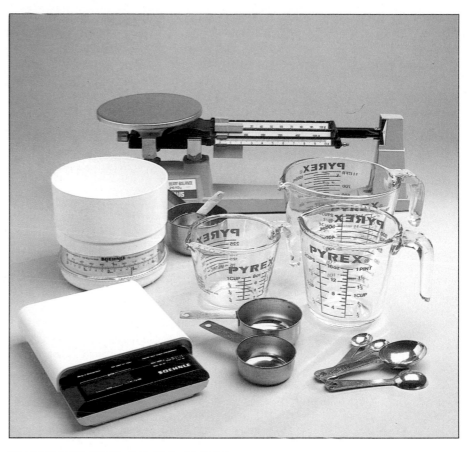

MEASURING CUPS, SPOONS, SCALES

Cups and spoons are standardized to measure liquid or dry ingredients. The standard liquid cup equals 8 fluid ounces or 236.6 milliliters. The standard dry cup equals 16 level tablespoons. The standard teaspoon equals 4.9 milliliters.

Cups for Liquids Cups for measuring liquids have a capacity of 1 quart or less, with a pouring lip and a handle. They are marked in divisions of quarts, pints, fluid ounces, and cups. Many have metric markings in millimeters as well. Buy sturdy cups with comfortable handles in several sizes. They are available in glass and plastic; some are microwave-safe. If buying plastic cups, be sure they are dishwasher-safe.

Cups for Dry Ingredients Made of stainless steel or plastic, these typically come in sets of 1 cup, ½ cup, ⅓ cup, ¼ cup, and sometimes ⅛ cup. Also available is a 2-cup measure that is handy for bakers. Buy several sets; if plastic, choose sturdy ones that can go in the dishwasher.

Measuring Spoons Like cups, these are sold in sets of individual spoons, typically including 1 tablespoon, 1 teaspoon, ½ teaspoon, ¼ teaspoon, and sometimes also ⅛ teaspoon. They are made of aluminum, plastic, or stainless steel. For use with liquids, fill to rim of spoon; for dry measure, fill and level off. If a recipe calls for a rounded or heaping spoonful, do not level off after filling the measuring spoon.

Precise measurements can sometimes mean the difference between the success or failure of a recipe. Shown clockwise from top: balance beam scale, measuring cups for liquids, measuring spoons, measuring cups for dry ingredients, electronic scale, spring scale.

Scales Whether you weigh ingredients routinely, only occasionally, or hardly ever, you will find a scale useful in the kitchen. Features to consider are capacity (how much do you need to weigh at one time?); accuracy (important for baking, but less so for estimating cooking times by weight); ability to zero out (scale can be reset to zero, which means that ingredients can be weighed one after the other in the same container, or that the reading will reflect only what's in the container and not the weight of the container as well); size (if it can sit on the counter, you will probably use it more); and readability (numbers can be seen easily).

There are three types of scales: spring, balance beam, and electronic. The spring model, the most inexpensive, is the least accurate because the spring mechanism loses elasticity over time. It usually has a plastic housing, American and metric markings, and ranges in capacity from diet portions to 6 to 10 pounds. Like the scale in a doctor's office, the balance beam scale is adjusted by weights that slide across a horizontal arm. It is very accurate, but can't zero out. Measurements are American and/or metric, and models can handle small amounts up to about 22 pounds. Materials are plastic or enameled cast iron. One manufacturer offers a balance scale with a small capacity, an adjusting wheel, and a hidden mechanism that can be reset to zero. Electronic scales need batteries and are priced to reflect their state-of-the-art status. They are the most precise, can zero out, have both American and metric measurements, and weigh diet-sized portions to about 10 pounds. Most electronic scales are plastic.

MELON

Like cucumbers and squash, melons are members of the Cucurbitaceae family, commonly known as gourds. There are dozens of melon varieties and, because they cross-pollinate readily, they are difficult to categorize. The somewhat random distinctions that taxonomists draw between melons are unimportant to the cook, who usually only wants to know how to find a ripe one. Suffice it to say that melons may be either smooth skinned or netted, hollow centered or solid fleshed, sweet or bitter.

Use Because melons are more than 90 percent water, cooking destroys their texture; they are almost always eaten raw. Two exceptions are the Chinese bitter melon and winter melon, which are always cooked. The high water content and natural sweetness make chilled melon an especially refreshing summer fruit. Melons are among the most appealing fruits—whether served in chilled wedges for breakfast or dessert; scooped into balls with a melon baller and added to fruit salad; seeded and filled with port, yogurt, cottage cheese, or ice cream; or puréed for a beverage or sorbet.

Availability The list below outlines some of the best-known melon varieties, their seasons, storage requirements, and recommended preparations.

Selection With few exceptions, you can tell a ripe melon by the fragrance. Most ripe melons also give slightly to pressure at the blossom end. Avoid melons that are soft or feel wet at the stem end. A melon that sloshes when shaken is probably overripe. See individual melons for further guidance.

Storage See individual melons.

BITTER MELON

Also known as balsam pear, the bitter melon looks like a warty cucumber. It is usually 6 to 10 inches long, light green, with bumpy ridges. The silvery green flesh is firm, with a spongy center containing pale brown seeds. Because of its high quinine content, it is indeed bitter; when presalted or parboiled and cooked, however, the bitter flesh develops more of a cool, mintlike character. It is popular in the summer for its refreshing qualities.

Chinese cooks use bitter melon in stir-fries with meats or seafood. They also steam it, stuff it with pork or shrimp, and add it to soups. Indian cooks use bitter melon as part of a spicy, mixed-vegetable preparation or stuffed with a spicy onion mixture and fried.

Fresh bitter melon is found in Asian markets from April through September. It is also available canned and dried. Choose small, firm melons with light green, shiny skin without brown spots. Refrigerate for up to one week. Leftover canned melon may be refrigerated in a nonmetal covered container for up to three days.

Most recipes call for soaking bitter melon in salt water for 30 minutes to remove bitterness. Alternatively, it may be cut up, sprinkled with salt, and allowed to drain for 30 minutes. A third method is to parboil the cut melon for 3 minutes before cooking.

CANTALOUPE

The cantaloupe is a muskmelon, a very fragrant melon with a raised netting on its skin. The netting is cream colored over a yellowish green background. The sweet, moist, orange flesh of the cantaloupe surrounds a hollow center partly filled with juice, pulp, and seeds.

Chilled cantaloupe may be halved, seeded, and eaten as is or cut into peeled wedges and draped with prosciutto (see Use, at left, for further suggestions).

Supplemented by Mexican imports in the winter, markets stock cantaloupe almost continually. Supplies peak in summer months and are lowest October through December. A ripe cantaloupe should have an enticing aroma and both ends should give slightly to pressure. Cantaloupe should have a smooth, symmetrical shallow basin at the stem end called a full slip. This indicates that the melon broke away naturally from its stem when it reached peak ripeness. Melons cut away from the stem before peak ripeness may show telltale stem fibers, scarring, or damaged tissue at the stem end; avoid these melons. Also avoid melons with pronounced yellow rind color (indicates overripeness); mold growth or moldy aroma; soft, wet tissue; or smooth spots without netting on the surface.

If melon is hard but properly colored, keep in a warm room for several days, away from sunlight, preferably in high humidity. Melons do not become sweeter after harvest, but they will soften and become juicier. When melon is aromatic and soft at stem and blossom ends, refrigerate. It will keep for up to one week.

CASABA

The round casaba melon has a golden yellow, slightly furrowed skin and creamy white to yellow flesh. Use like cantaloupe. Casabas are available from July through November, with peak supplies and peak quality in September and October.

Look for deep golden skin color and slight give at the blossom end. Casabas lack aroma. Avoid any with dark, sunken, water-soaked spots. Store like cantaloupe.

CHRISTMAS MELON

Also known as Santa Claus melon, this elongated variety resembles a small watermelon. The green skin sports yellow stripes; the flesh is creamy white to yellow and tastes like the casaba. Use like cantaloupe. Christmas melon is on the market in December, which accounts for its name.

A Christmas melon should have good aroma and give slightly at both ends. Avoid any with soft spots. Store like cantaloupe; this melon will keep up to one month under refrigeration.

CRENSHAW

Also known as Cranshaw, this melon has mottled green and yellow skin and salmon-colored flesh. It is quite large, weighing up to 9 pounds, and is highly aromatic. Its flesh has a rich, spicy taste. Use like cantaloupe. Crenshaws are available from July through October, with peak supplies in August and September.

The green skin turns yellow in parts at maturity. A ripe Crenshaw should be very aromatic and should give slightly at the blossom end. Store like cantaloupe; a Crenshaw will keep under refrigeration longer than a cantaloupe.

HONEYDEW

This large (average 6 pounds) oval melon has a smooth, creamy white to yellow-green skin and a pale green flesh. Pink-fleshed honeydew is occasionally available. The flesh is thick, juicy, and very sweet when ripe. Use like cantaloupe. Latin American imports supplement the domestic crop, making honeydew available almost all year. Peak supplies are June through October.

Look for yellowish white to creamy rind; a soft, velvety, slightly sticky feel; slight softening at blossom end; and faint, pleasant aroma. Avoid melons with flat white or greenish color, hardness, and cuts or punctures through the rind. Store like cantaloupe.

PERSIAN MELON

This melon resembles the cantaloupe but is slightly larger and rounder, with finer netting. The flesh is a delicate pink-orange and is thick, firm, and sweet. Use like cantaloupe. Persian melon is available from July through October, with peak supplies in August and September.

Choose melons with good aroma, slight give at both ends, no slick spots on the skin, and no dark or greenish black netting. Store like cantaloupe.

WATERMELON

The watermelon has solid flesh with small hard black seeds distributed evenly throughout. The hard skin is deep green and may be solid, striped, or mottled; the flesh is usually deep pink to red, although varieties with yellow flesh exist. Watermelons have an oblong shape, rather like a fat cucumber, and are generally quite large, often exceeding 30 pounds. The flesh is crisp and juicy and quite sweet when ripe. Seedless hybrids are grown commercially in some regions.

When cut into manageable wedges or rounds, watermelons can be eaten as is, for dessert or snack. Watermelon balls or cubes make a refreshing addition to fruit salads. Thick pieces of watermelon rind make excellent sweet pickles. A hollowed, scalloped shell filled with cut-up fruit is a dramatic addition to a buffet table.

In winter and spring, Mexican watermelons supplement the domestic crop, making the melons available almost continually. Domestic supplies are available June through September, with peak supplies in the hottest months. Because watermelons can be so large, they are frequently cut up by the retailer and sold in halves or quarters.

With cut melons, look for firm, juicy red flesh and dark brown or black seeds. Soft white seeds indicate immaturity. Avoid sections that are cracked or streaked with white. With uncut melons, look for a smooth and slightly dull rind (neither shiny nor very dull), filled-out and rounded ends, and a creamy underside. Store watermelons like cantaloupe.

WINTER MELON

Chinese winter melon is a very large gourd that somewhat resembles a greenish white pumpkin. Slightly more tall than wide, it has a hard ridged skin displaying a heavy white bloom. The large seed cavity contains pumpkinlike seeds. The flesh is snowy white with a delicate flavor, somewhat akin to a steamed cucumber.

Honeydew, cantaloupe, and watermelon balls make an attractive and naturally delicious salad.

Prosciutto and melon—the prosciutto ultra-thin and the melon ripe and cool— make a refreshingly simple appetizer.

■ MELON . . . OR PAPAYA . . . OR PEAR . . . OR MANGO WITH PROSCIUTTO

The combination of prosciutto and melon may be commonplace in Italian restaurants, but that doesn't mean it's dull. All that's required is paper-thin prosciutto and the sweetest, most fragrant melon you can find. The combination of salty ham with sweet, cold fruit is unforgettable. For a change of pace, or if melon is not available, substitute papaya, pear, or mango—or serve them all, complemented by a crisp, cold white wine.

> 1 **large ripe, sweet melon of any variety,** *or*
> 2 **ripe papayas, pears, or mangoes,** *or*
> **any combination of these fruits**
> **Half a lemon**
> 6 **ounces prosciutto, sliced paper-thin**
> **Freshly ground pepper**
> **Olive oil (optional)**
> 1 **tablespoon minced parsley, for garnish**

1. If using melon, cut away rind, then halve melon lengthwise. Scoop out seeds, then cut each half in half horizontally. Slice each quarter into pieces about ½ inch wide. If using papayas, pears, or mangoes, peel fruit, remove core or seeds, and slice into spears about ½ inch wide. Rub pears lightly with lemon to prevent browning.

2. Wrap fruit with prosciutto slices, allowing ends of fruit to show. Arrange on a serving platter. Dust with pepper, drizzle lightly with olive oil (if used), and garnish with parsley.

Serves 12.

■ WINTER MELON SOUP

This Chinese soup has gentle flavors and textures. The mild, slightly crunchy chunks of winter melon flesh absorb the flavors of a rich chicken stock, and bits of ham, ginger, and green onion provide little nuggets of stronger flavor. In a Chinese banquet, this soup is typically served inside a whole steamed winter melon, the rind of which has been decorated with carvings of dragons or other symbols of good luck. Winter melons are available at Asian markets.

> 4 **cups Rich Chicken Stock (see page 561)**
> 1 **ounce Smithfield ham, cut in thin slivers**
> 1 **teaspoon grated fresh ginger**
> **Salt and freshly ground pepper, to taste**
> ½ **pound winter melon, seeded, green rind removed**
> 2 **green onions, sliced**

Bring stock to a boil with ham and ginger. Season with salt and pepper. Cut winter melon flesh into wedges, and slice each wedge ¼ inch thick. Add melon and green onions to soup; simmer until melon becomes slightly translucent (about 3 minutes). Serve from pot or transfer to tureen; in either case, ham will settle to bottom, so stir soup with ladle while serving.

Serves 4 to 6.

Winter melon is always cooked. The peeled and diced flesh is added to stir-fries, especially with pork, chicken, or shellfish. A half melon may be carved out, steamed, and used as a decorative container for other foods, most often for a soup made with the pulp. Sugar-glazed winter melon is eaten as candy.

Fresh winter melon is sold in Asian markets in late summer and fall. Because it is so large, many markets sell it in pieces; it should preferably be cut to order. Select uncut melon that appears plump and well shaped. Cut melon should look juicy. Cover cut surfaces with plastic wrap and refrigerate; covered and properly stored, melon will keep three to five days.

To prepare, cut away all green rind. Halve melon; scoop out and discard seeds and fibrous center. Cut up flesh as recipe directs.

■ **WATERMELON SHERBET**

Any of your favorite melons can be substituted for the watermelon, if desired. For a charming presentation, use this recipe instead of the Raspberry Sherbet in Frozen Watermelon Bombe, page 315. Be sure the miniature chocolate chips, which serve as "seeds," are blended into the Watermelon Sherbet as directed. For more information on making frozen desserts, see ICE CREAM AND FROZEN DESSERT.

  ¼ **cup sugar, or more to taste**
  ¼ **teaspoon salt**
  1 **heaping quart chilled melon chunks,**
     seeds removed and juice reserved
     (the flesh from a 4-lb watermelon)
  2 **large egg whites**

1. Sprinkle sugar and salt over watermelon chunks and mix well. Once sugar has dissolved, taste watermelon for sweetness, and add more sugar (if desired).

2. In a food processor or blender, purée melon, its juice, and egg whites. Chill well, then transfer mixture to ice cream machine and freeze according to manufacturer's instructions.

Makes about 1 quart.

> ### Recipes and Related Information
> *Fresh Fruit in Wine, 347; Gadgets, 258.*

MERINGUE

A meringue is a foam of beaten egg whites mixed with sugar. The term refers both to the sugar-sweetened foam and to the shells, cake layers, and other baked desserts made from it.

There are two types of meringue, soft and hard, depending on the proportion of sugar to egg whites in the mixture. The soft type has less sugar and is used as a topping for pies and baked Alaska. Hard meringue has more sugar and is shaped into containers for fruits or cream, or piped into cookie kisses and other fanciful baked confections. Versatile Italian meringue possesses the characteristics of both hard and soft meringues and is used in similar ways.

MAKING MERINGUE

When making any meringue, the two most important steps in the process are whipping the egg whites to maximum volume without overbeating and adding the sugar slowly but thoroughly at the proper time so that it is completely incorporated and dissolved. Sugar sweetens the foam and helps it set in the oven, but if added to the whites too soon, it slows their ability to froth. If you are using an electric mixer, which works so fast that the whites can be overbeaten almost before you know it, adding some sugar earlier in the whipping process will work to your advan-

tage. Its delaying action will counteract the speed of the machine. To add sugar, beat egg whites to soft peaks, beat in approximately 1 teaspoon sugar per egg white (or as directed in recipe), beat to stiff peaks, then by hand fold in remaining sugar (in two or three batches, depending upon amount). For a complete discussion of beating egg whites, see EGG. Keep these points in mind as well.

- Eggs beat to greatest volume at room temperature, but separate easiest when cold.

- Keep all equipment—beaters and bowls—completely free of fat. Even a speck of fat can reduce the volume of beaten egg whites by as much as two thirds.

- A copper bowl and wire balloon whisk produce a superior egg white foam. If you don't use copper, add a pinch of cream of tartar to the whites just as they start to foam. A stainless steel bowl is the next best choice. Avoid these materials: aluminum, which will gray the egg whites; glass, which is slippery; and plastic, which is too difficult to clean so that it is absolutely fat-free.

- Although granulated sugar is used most often when making a soft meringue, you can, if desired, substitute superfine sugar, which is very easily incorporated and absorbs excess moisture from the whites that would otherwise bead on the surface of the meringue. Granulated sugar can be ground fine in a clean coffee grinder, electric minichopper, or food processor.

PROBLEMS AND HOW TO CORRECT THEM

Common problems with meringue are weeping (liquid oozing out of a meringue topping), beading (drops of amber sugar syrup forming on a meringue as it bakes), and an undesirable sticky, spongy texture. Weather is often the culprit. Making meringue on a humid or rainy day may cause the sugar to absorb moisture from the air. This moisture will end up as beads on the surface of the meringue or will produce a meringue that is soft and gooey. Beading is also the result of overworking the sugar in the foam or failing to dissolve it fully, not baking the meringue right away, undercooking, or baking at too high a temperature. Removing a hard meringue from the oven before it has dried out completely can give it a gummy, limp texture; it will be difficult to remove from the baking sheet. A fully cooked, properly dried out meringue will release without difficulty.

STORING MERINGUE

Once baked, meringues will stay crisp up to two weeks packaged airtight in a plastic bag and then in a sealed container. If you live in a humid climate, store them frozen. Pies don't store well; it's best to bake and serve them the same day. Let them sit out in a cool place until they are ready to eat.

**HOW TO MAKE
MERINGUE SHAPES**

Meringue Disk   *Draw a
circle the size of the disk;
beginning in center, pipe
meringue in a spiral to
fill circle.*

Meringue Kiss   *For each
kiss, point pastry bag
straight down and let a
small amount of meringue
fall onto baking sheet.
Pull back to cut off flow of
meringue.*

Meringue Shell   *Hold
pastry bag at an angle and
squeeze out meringue to
form oval of desired size.*

■ HARD MERINGUE
Swiss meringue

This is what most of us recognize as meringue. Light, delicate, and crumbly, it melts to a creamy texture when softened with a filling. This softening eases cutting and mingles the flavors, so fill about an hour or so before serving. Hard meringue is baked at very low heat, more to dry it out than actually cook it. A very white color is desirable, so don't let meringue brown.

    4 **egg whites, at room temperature**
       Pinch cream of tartar (optional)
    1 **cup plus 2 tablespoons sugar**

1. In a stainless steel or copper bowl, beat egg whites to soft peaks (if bowl is stainless steel, add pinch cream of tartar to whites when just foamy). Add 2 tablespoons sugar and continue to beat until stiff, glossy peaks form.

2. Gently fold in remaining sugar, taking care not to overwork meringue or it will deflate. Use immediately as directed in recipe.

Makes two 9-inch disks, five dozen kisses, or twelve to sixteen 3-inch shells.

Meringue Disks   Preheat oven to 200° F. Line two baking sheets with parchment paper. Draw a 9-inch circle on the back of each piece of parchment paper.
    To make with a pastry bag: Fill pastry bag fitted with a ½-inch plain tube tip half full with meringue. Working from center of circle out, let meringue fall from bag and move in concentric rings to form two 9-inch solid disks of meringue. Refill bag as necessary.
    To make by hand: With a spoon spread meringue evenly on the parchment inside of the two circles.
    Bake until crisp (1 to 1½ hours; if meringues begin to brown, reduce temperature to 150° F). When done, meringues will pull away easily from parchment paper. Remove from oven and cool on paper on wire racks. To serve, sandwich layers of buttercream, whipped cream, or mousse between disks, or use as desired. If not using immediately, package in a plastic storage bag or wrap in plastic wrap and store airtight until needed.

Meringue Kisses   Preheat oven to 200° F. Line a baking sheet with parchment paper.
    To make with a pastry bag: Fill pastry bag fitted with a ½-inch plain tip or number 4 rose tip half full with meringue. Hold pastry bag ½ inch above baking sheet, and with tip pointing straight down, press bag until a kiss of the desired size is formed, then pull back.
    To make by hand: Drop by rounded teaspoons onto parchment-lined baking sheet. For larger kisses, use a tablespoon.
    Bake until crisp (45 to 60 minutes; if meringues begin to brown, reduce temperature to 150° F). When done, meringues will pull away easily from parchment paper. Remove from oven and cool on paper on wire racks. Use

immediately, or package in a plastic storage bag or in plastic wrap and store in an airtight container until ready to use.

Meringue Shells   Resembling little eggs, these shells have an oval shape. Preheat oven to 200° F. Line a baking sheet with parchment paper.
    To make with a pastry bag: Fill a pastry bag fitted with a ½- to ¾-inch plain or star tip half full with meringue. Hold pastry bag at 45-degree angle and squeeze out meringue until desired width. Continue to squeeze, drawing bag toward you to create characteristic oval shape and smooth surface; stop pressure and pull back.
    To make by hand: Scoop up meringue with a soup spoon. Transfer meringue to a second spoon by sliding bowl of spoon under meringue to scoop it off first spoon. Repeat movement between spoons until desired shape. Carefully drop onto parchment-lined baking sheet. Or, for more irregularly shaped meringues, scoop up meringue with a soup spoon and drop onto parchment-lined baking sheet.
    Bake until crisp (1 to 1½ hours; if meringues begin to brown, reduce temperature to 150° F). When done, meringues will pull away easily from parchment paper. Cool on paper on wire rack. To serve, sandwich two meringue shells together with whipped cream. Accompany with fresh raspberry or other fruit sauce. If not using right away, package in a plastic storage bag or wrap in plastic wrap and store in an airtight container until needed.

■ SOFT MERINGUE
This meringue is used as a topping for pies and other desserts. It is a recipe you will probably use often. Amounts are given for 8-, 9-, and 10-inch pies.

For an 8- or 9-inch pie

    3 **egg whites, at room temperature**
    ¼ **teaspoon cream of tartar (optional)**
    ¼ **teaspoon cornstarch**
    4 **tablespoons superfine sugar**
    ½ **teaspoon vanilla extract**

For a 10-inch pie

    5 **egg whites, at room temperature**
    ½ **teaspoon cream of tartar (optional)**
    ½ **teaspoon cornstarch**
    6 **tablespoons superfine sugar**
    ¾ **teaspoon vanilla extract**

1. In a stainless steel or copper bowl, beat egg whites until foamy. Add cornstarch (if bowl is stainless steel, also add cream of tartar) and add 1 tablespoon sugar. Continue to beat until stiff peaks form.

2. Gently fold in vanilla, then remaining sugar, taking care not to overwork meringue. Use as directed in recipe.

Makes topping for 8-, 9-, or 10-inch pie.

◼ DACQUOISE

This is a hard Swiss meringue with ground almonds added for flavor and extra texture. You will see *dacquoise* under various names: Broyage, Progrès, Japonais, and Succès. The difference is primarily in the proportion of sugar to nuts. Almond meal made of nuts ground with their skins will be darker than meal made with ground blanched almonds.

   1½ **cups ground almonds**
   1½ **cups sugar**
    6 **egg whites**
   ½ **teaspoon cream of tartar (optional)**

1. In a small bowl combine ground almonds with all but 2 tablespoons of the sugar. Follow directions for Hard Meringue (opposite page), substituting sugar-almond mixture for plain sugar.

2. Follow directions for preparing Meringue Disks (opposite page). Use as needed.

Makes three 8-inch disks or two 9- to 10-inch disks.

◼ ITALIAN MERINGUE

There are many ways to use this hybrid between hard and soft meringues—as a topping for baked Alaska, as a base for many frozen desserts, and as the foundation for numerous frostings. Italian meringue has the highest proportion of sugar to egg whites; it pipes very well, and holds its shape well. Anything made with Swiss meringue can be made with Italian meringue, but it will be drier, crunchier, and more powdery. This meringue is also more stable than Swiss meringue, so it needn't be used immediately, and can even be refrigerated.

   1½ **cups sugar**
   ½ **cup water**
    4 **egg whites**
     Pinch cream of tartar (optional)

1. In a medium, heavy-bottomed saucepan (preferably a copper sugar pot), combine sugar and the water. Cook, stirring, over low heat until all the sugar has dissolved. Cook without stirring until the soft-ball stage (238° F on a candy thermometer) is reached.

2. As sugar syrup cooks, whip egg whites to soft peaks in a stainless steel or copper bowl (if bowl is stainless steel, add cream of tartar to whites when just foamy). Time this process so that egg whites are ready when sugar reaches soft-ball stage.

3. Remove sugar from heat. With electric mixer on high or beating furiously by hand with a whisk, slowly pour onto egg whites in a thin stream. Continue to whip mixture until it cools (8 to 10 minutes). Use meringue as recipe directs.

Makes two 9-inch disks, five dozen kisses, or twelve to sixteen 3-inch shells.

◼ ALMOND MERINGUE CAKE

Three layers of crisp almond meringue (*dacquoise*) are filled with Chocolate and Praline Buttercream or Coffee and Chocolate Buttercream (see page 248) and decorated with a border of buttercream rosettes.

   1 **recipe (three 8-inch disks) Dacquoise (at left)**
   3 **cups Buttercream Frosting (see page 248)**
    Toasted hazelnuts or almonds (optional), for garnish

To assemble cake: For an even-sided cake, carefully trim each of the three layers of Dacquoise to form an 8-inch circle. Use a sharp knife to avoid cracking meringue. There are two ways to fill layers with buttercream. You may either spread it on with a knife or decoratively pipe it onto each layer with a pastry bag fitted with an open-star tip. Decorate the top with stars and rosettes of buttercream. Small, whole, toasted hazelnuts or almonds can be used to decorate the center of each rosette.

Serves 8.

Variation Spread buttercream on the first two layers of meringue. Place third layer on top. Ice sides. Press toasted, chopped nuts onto sides of cake. Dust top with confectioners' sugar or decorate with rosettes.

Mousse Meringue Cake Prepare Chocolate Mousse (see page 127). Ice first two layers of meringue with mousse. Place third layer on top. Ice sides with mousse. Press chopped, toasted slivered almonds on sides of cake. Lightly dust top with confectioners' sugar. Cover and chill until ready to serve.

Layers of almond meringue separated by buttercream filling will enhance any table. For extra texture, press chopped nuts into the sides of the frosted cake.

■ PAVLOVA

A famous New Zealand dessert, Pavlova is said to have been created to commemorate a visit to that country by the well-known Russian ballerina, Anna Pavlova. It traditionally uses fruits from that part of the world—kiwifruit, passion fruit, bananas, and pineapple. Improved shipping has made exotic fruit more widely available in this country, but if you are unable to find the more unusual ones, any ripe fruit in season may be served. Select fruit with some acidity to balance the sweetness of the meringue. Note that the assembled Pavlova must refrigerate for at least one hour before serving, and then needs to sit out to warm to room temperature.

        1½ cups sugar
         2 tablespoons cornstarch
         6 egg whites
        ½ teaspoon cream of tartar (optional)
         1 teaspoon fresh lemon juice or vinegar
         1 teaspoon vanilla extract
         1 cup whipping cream
            Kiwifruit, passion fruit, pineapple, banana,
            mango, or other tropical fruit in season,
            prepared and attractively cut in pieces

1. Preheat oven to 250° F. Line a baking sheet with parchment paper. Draw a 6- or 7-inch circle on the paper to use as a guide. Set aside 3 tablespoons sugar. In a small bowl sift together remaining sugar and cornstarch to aerate and blend.

2. In a stainless steel or copper bowl, whip egg whites to soft peaks (if bowl is stainless steel, add cream of tartar to whites when just foamy). Add the 3 tablespoons sugar and continue to whip until stiff, glossy peaks form. Gently fold in half the sugar-cornstarch mixture. Add lemon juice, vanilla, and remaining sugar-cornstarch mixture; gently fold in.

3. Pour egg white mixture onto center of circle drawn on parchment paper. Shape meringue into a round approximately 6 to 7 inches in diameter, with sides higher than center so there is a small well in center. Bake until crisp on outside and firm to the touch (1 to 1½ hours). Let meringue shell cool on baking sheet in oven with door propped open.

4. One hour before serving, whip cream to soft peaks. Spread over center of baked shell and approximately halfway up sides. Decoratively arrange prepared fruit over whipped cream and refrigerate for at least 1 hour to let meringue soften and flavors blend. Serve at room temperature.

Serves 6.

Recipes and Related Information
Copper Egg-White Bowl, 155; Cream of Tartar, 162; Egg, 194; Whisk, 608.

MICROWAVE OVEN

The microwave oven is fast becoming America's most popular major appliance, according to manufacturers' sales figures. More than half of all homes in the U.S. have one, and the number is growing. Microwave cookery is quick, cool, and clean. Many foods cook in one fourth the time and with less energy than they would in a conventional oven or on a surface cooking unit. The microwave oven emits no heat—only the food gets hot—so the kitchen and the cook stay comfortably cool. Cleanup and maintenance are easy. Because food doesn't bake onto the dish or the oven walls, equipment and utensils wash clean with a sponge and soapy water, and the oven requires only an occasional wipe with a damp cloth to remove spills and spatters. Microwave ovens plug into regular household current and are sold in a range of sizes to fit into almost any space, so most kitchens can easily accommodate one.

HOW DOES IT WORK?

Microwaves are short, high-frequency radio waves. They are reflected by metal but pass through glass, paper, ceramic, and some plastics; they are attracted to the moisture, fat, and sugar content of food.

A magnetron tube inside each microwave oven converts electricity into high-frequency energy—the microwaves—and transmits the microwaves into the oven cavity. Because of their special properties, microwaves bounce off the metallic oven walls and are absorbed by food (they only penetrate a few inches, however). Inside the food, microwaves cause water molecules to vibrate very rapidly and rub against one another and adjoining molecules. This friction produces heat, which cooks the food as the heat travels toward the center of the food by conduction.

WHEN TO USE A MICROWAVE OVEN

The foods that do best in a microwave oven are those that are cooked in a conventional oven with moist heat. Because cooking time is brief and little water is used, vegetables retain vivid color, crisp texture, and valuable nutrients; fish is juicy, firm, and delicately flavored in minutes; and stews, casseroles, and sauced foods are done in less time and have minimal cleanup.

Microwave ovens are the ideal complement to the home freezer. With defrost capability, a microwave oven can thaw a frozen dish and then heat the food to serving temperature. Reheated foods stay fresh, with no warmed-over taste.

OTHER FACTORS TO CONSIDER

The microwave oven is a kitchen miracle worker for many tasks, but it isn't perfect. It will not brown most foods or produce a crisp crust, which limits its appropriateness for cooking meats and baking. Those baked goods that do not need a browned top—for instance, a sheet cake that will be frosted—may still not be as good when baked in a microwave oven as they would be when baked conventionally; the microwave performs best with rich batters baked in a round pan. Some dishes cook unevenly (this may be less of a problem with newer models). Bringing a liquid to a boil can take every bit as long in a microwave oven as on top of the stove, and cooking in large quantities can also negate the time savings. It's also quite easy—because of the unfamiliarity with either the oven or the recipe—to overcook foods. And it can be difficult to feel comfortable with a new cooking technology.

Enrolling in a microwave cooking class is a way to learn what the oven does best and how this appliance can be integrated into your individual cooking style. Introductory classes are sometimes offered by the retailer. Certainly read through the instruction booklet that accompanies your oven to become familiar with the features of that particular model and with microwave cooking in general.

WHICH OVEN FOR YOU?

Microwave ovens offer many options. They come full-size, midsize, and compact; portable or built-in; paired with a full-sized conventional oven in one unit, or combined with a convection oven in one unit.

For optimum benefits from the microwave, it's probably best to buy a single-purpose oven. If counter space is at a premium in your kitchen, lightweight models can be hung under a cabinet, or an oven can be set into existing cabinet space. Keep in mind, however, that smaller models usually hold less, which won't matter for one or two people, but it makes a difference when cooking for four or more. A smaller model is also less powerful—which means slower cooking.

Look for an oven with at least four power levels—High, Medium, Low, and Defrost. Some ovens have just one setting that is basically useful only for reheating; other models have as many as ten settings. Each setting corresponds to a percentage of power. Generally, High is 100 percent power, Medium is 50 percent power, and so on. Be sure to check manufacturer's instructions to learn with what percentage your oven is operating at each setting.

Most full-sized ovens feature 600 to 720 watts, and most recipes are written for ovens of this wattage. Some smaller ovens have less wattage, and therefore less power, at each setting. Recipes must be adjusted accordingly. Manufacturer's directions will guide you in making adjustments. It is increasingly common for recipes developed for the microwave oven to note the wattage required to prepare the dish in the specified amount of time.

MICROWAVE COOKING

As with most cooking, experience is the best teacher for using the microwave. The sooner you incorporate the microwave oven into your daily routine, the more quickly you will gain confidence and realize its full potential as a timesaving appliance.

Microwave cooking is based on time, not heat. To avoid overcooking, keep in mind the following variables:
- Shape of food: Thin pieces cook faster.
- Temperature at start of cooking: Chilled foods take longer to heat.
- Amount of food: When you double the quantity, the cooking time is nearly doubled.
- Composition of food: Low-moisture, high-fat, and high-sugar content foods cook faster.
- Density of food: Porous foods cook faster.
- Oven power: Ovens with higher wattage ratings cook faster at each power setting.
- Carryover cooking: Food continues to heat internally even after it is removed from the microwave, so always undercook to avoid drying out the food.

Because of all these variables, no recipe can give the exact instructions you will need for optimum results. Recipes should be considered guides to successful microwave cooking; some experimentation with your particular oven, as well as careful checking as dishes cook, will be required.

Uneven cooking—a major problem—is the result of uneven microwave penetration. Microwaves are attracted to corners and edges. In new models, stirrer fans in the oven wall help distribute the energy in a better pattern. Turntables serve the same purpose. To assure even heating, put the quickest-cooking area of the food in the center; arrange food in a circular pattern or use round dishes, if possible; rotate food during cooking time; stir food to bring cooked edges in and still-raw center portions out.

In microwave cooking, food is often covered to control moisture loss or to prevent spattering. If a recipe calls for a cover, use a tight-fitting lid or plastic wrap. For protection against spattering, use waxed paper, a paper towel, or a paper napkin. With high temperatures, pierce plastic wrap or lift a corner to allow steam to escape.

REHEATING AND DEFROSTING BAKED GOODS AT 50 PERCENT POWER

Baked goods can quickly dry out—even to the point of becoming rock hard—if overcooked. Try the shorter time first, and briefly return food to the microwave oven, if needed. Take into account that internal heat will continue to warm the food after it is removed from the microwave (carryover cooking).

Servings	Starting at Room Temperature	Starting Frozen
1	10–30 seconds	30 seconds–1 minute
2	15–40 seconds	45 seconds–1¼ minutes
3	20–50 seconds	1–1½ minutes
4	30–60 seconds	1½–2 minutes

Aside from wattage, other options include a temperature probe, dial or touch panel control, racks, turntables (developed to correct uneven cooking, they limit the size of the cooking dish to one that fits the turntable), clocks, and electronic programming, which permits multistage cooking—defrost/reheat or cook/hold, for example. The features you need will depend upon how you intend to use your oven. Some stores will allow you to exchange your oven for another model within a certain period of time if you decide that your first choice wasn't the right one.

UTENSILS AND EQUIPMENT

Before buying special cookware for use in your microwave, inventory what you have on hand. Most kitchens are already well stocked with microwave-safe cookware, which will not get hot in the oven, except where it comes in contact with hot food. (To test a dish for microwave use, place it in the oven along with a 1-cup measure filled with water. Microwave on 100 percent power for 1 minute. If the water is warm and the dish cool, the dish is microwave safe.) Use only plastic dishes or containers designed for microwave use. Most other plastics will be distorted by the heat of the food even though they are unaffected by the microwaves.

Among the items used for conventional cooking that you can also use in the microwave are heat-resistant glass baking dishes, pie plates, mixing bowls, measuring and custard cups, and ceramic serving dishes. Avoid metal and metal-trimmed cookware. Metal reflects microwaves; using it will give you uneven cooking and could cause arcing—sparks that may damage the oven. The one exception to the no-metal-in-the-microwave rule is aluminum foil, which is often used to shield fast-cooking areas of a dish—such as poultry wings and breast, or the corners of baked goods—to prevent overcooking.

Other cooking materials that you can use in the microwave include paper plates, paper napkins, paper towels, waxed paper, heavy plastic wrap, ovenproof cooking bags, and plastic-coated paper containers. The fact that you can cook with these disposable materials is another advantage of the microwave; cleanup can be as simple as throwing away the cooking container.

MICROWAVING FRESH VEGETABLES

Microwave ovens are excellent for cooking vegetables, which come out crisp-tender, with their natural colors still vibrant. And nutrition research indicates that many vegetables lose fewer water-soluble nutrients, such as vitamin C, when microwaved, due to the shorter cooking time and less amount of water needed. The shorter cooking time also better retains fresh flavor.

1. Refer to the chart on the opposite page to determine the approximate cooking and standing times for a given amount of a vegetable. Weights listed are for fresh vegetables as purchased, before trimming, peeling, and other preparation.

2. Cut vegetables into uniform pieces for even cooking. To speed cooking, shred or thinly slice vegetables, and peel the coarse outer layer from asparagus (unless the stalks are pencil-thin) and broccoli stems. Place in a round microwave-safe baking or serving dish. Put the woody stems of asparagus and broccoli, or thicker portions if vegetables are not of uniform size, toward the outside of the dish. Vegetables to be cooked whole and unpeeled,

such as potatoes and winter squash, need to be pierced with a fork to allow steam to escape. Left unpierced, the vegetable might explode. Arrange potatoes 1 inch apart in a star pattern on a paper towel, thicker ends toward the outside. See the opposite page for special instructions on cooking artichokes and corn on the cob.

3. Cook most vegetables with a few tablespoons of water to provide steam. Steam contributes both speed and even cooking. Cover the dish with a lid or plastic wrap.

4. Microwave on 100 percent power according to the time recommended on the chart. Halfway through cooking, stir vegetables, rearrange, or turn them over.

5. Let vegetables stand, covered, according to the time recommended in the chart. Standing time is very short or unnecessary for some vegetables, but for large, dense vegetables, such as winter squash or a whole head of cauliflower, it allows for thorough cooking without overdoing the outer edge.

6. Remember that cooking and standing times are approximate and will vary with the maturity, shape, size, and starting temperature of each vegetable.

7. Season vegetables with salt and pepper after cooking.

MICROWAVE TIPS

Making good use of the microwave oven can speed up food preparation in a number of ways.

Baking Cakes Dense, rich cakes made with whole eggs, pudding cakes, and cakes made with oil, such as a carrot cake, are best for microwaving. However, without careful timing, a cake can easily be overcooked since there is no browning to remind you that it is done. Never microwave light-textured cakes such as angel food cakes, sponge cakes, and chiffon cakes.

Baking Cookies Dark bar cookies, such as brownies, or bar cookies that will later be glazed with an icing should be cooked on 50 percent power, with the dish rotated two or three times during cooking. Check bar cookies carefully; they can easily overcook. Drop cookies are best baked in a conventional oven. In a microwave oven they won't brown, and so few can be cooked at a time that it may actually take longer to do the whole batch.

Blanching Prepare 1 pound of vegetables as you would for conventional cooking. Place in a glass casserole, add ⅓ cup water, and cover. Cook on 100 percent power until evenly cooked and brightly colored throughout (4 to 6 minutes). When done, cool and drain as directed for water blanching (see BLANCH).

Defrosting When defrosting, check food frequently. Do not allow hot spots to develop; these areas indicate cooking, not defrosting. Wait until hot spots cool, then continue, or shield them with a small amount of aluminum foil to deflect the microwaves.

MICROWAVING FRESH VEGETABLES

Cooking time assumes vegetable is covered and microwave is operating on 100 percent power (600 to 720 watt oven).

Type of Vegetable	Quantity	Cooking Time	Standing Time
Artichokes (See instructions, page 12)	1 (6–8 ounces each)	5–8 minutes	5 minutes
	2 (6–8 ounces each)	8–10 minutes	5 minutes
	4 (6–8 ounces each)	12–14 minutes	5 minutes
Asparagus (Pare stalks except if very thin)	1 pound, plus 2 tablespoons water	4–7 minutes	1 minute
Beans, green or wax Cut into 1½-inch pieces	1 pound, plus 2 tablespoons water	5–7 minutes	2 minutes
Broccoli Cut into spears (pare stalks)	1 pound, plus 2 tablespoons water	6–8 minutes	2 minutes
Brussels sprouts	1 tub (10 ounces), plus 1 tablespoon water	5–7 minutes	2 minutes
	1 pound, plus 2 tablespoons water	8–10 minutes	3 minutes
Cabbage Chopped or shredded	4 cups (about 1 pound), plus 2 tablespoons water	6–8 minutes	0 minutes
Wedges	4 (about 1 pound), plus 2 tablespoons water	5–7 minutes	2 minutes
Carrots Sliced into rounds	1 pound, plus 2 tablespoons water	6–8 minutes	1 minute
Cauliflower Cut into florets	1 pound, plus 2 tablespoons water	6–8 minutes	2 minutes
Whole	1–1½ pounds, plus 2 tablespoons water	11–13 minutes	3 minutes
Corn on the cob (*See instructions below)	1 ear	2–3 minutes	3 minutes
	2 ears	3–4 minutes	3 minutes
	4 ears	8½–10 minutes	3 minutes
Eggplant Cubed	1 pound, plus 2 tablespoons water	6–8 minutes	1 minute
Whole (pierce skin)	1–1¼ pounds	4–7 minutes	3 minutes
Onions Small, whole	1 pound, plus 2 tablespoons water	4–8 minutes	2 minutes
Parsnips Sliced	1 pound, plus 2 tablespoons water	6–8 minutes	2 minutes
Peas, green	1½ pounds, plus 3 tablespoons water	5–7 minutes	1 minute
Peas, snow (pea pods)	1 pound, plus 2 tablespoons water	4–6 minutes	1 minute
Potatoes, new Small, whole (pierce skin)	1 pound (6–8), plus 3 tablespoons water	8–12 minutes	3 minutes
Potatoes, white or sweet Whole (pierce skin)	1 (6–8 ounces each)	4–6 minutes**	5 minutes
	2 (6–8 ounces each)	6–8 minutes**	5 minutes
	4 (6–8 ounces each)	8–12 minutes**	5 minutes
Spinach Whole (wash leaves)	1 pound (water that clings to leaves is enough moisture)	4–6 minutes	0 minutes
Squash, spaghetti Whole (pierce skin)	1 squash (4–5 pounds)	15–20 minutes	5 minutes
Squash, summer	1 squash (1 pound), plus 2 tablespoons water	4–6 minutes	0 minutes
Squash, winter Whole (pierce skin)	1 squash (1 pound)	6–8 minutes	5 minutes
	2 squash (¾ pounds each)	7–9 minutes	5 minutes
Zucchini Sliced ½ inch thick	1 pound, plus 2 tablespoons water	4–6 minutes	0 minutes

*To cook in husk, remove silk, brush kernels with butter, and replace husk; sprinkle with water and arrange ears in spoke pattern, rotating once during cooking. To cook with husk and silk removed, rinse, brush with melted butter, and wrap with waxed paper, twisting ends to seal.

**Touch potatoes at end of cooking time. If they are very hard, cook another one or two minutes, then let them stand. They will finish cooking during standing time.

Heating Liqueur   Heat brandy or other liqueur for flamed entrées and desserts 30 to 45 seconds at 100 percent power.

Opening Bivalves: Clams, Mussels, Oysters   Soak and scrub shellfish in cold water, then arrange in a circle on a paper-towel–lined glass plate. Cover tightly with plastic wrap; cook at 100 percent power until shells open slightly (half a dozen oysters or a dozen mussels or clams takes 1 to 1½ minutes). Remove from oven and finish opening by hand.

Poaching Chicken   To cook chicken breasts for use in salads, soups, and fillings for entrées, microwave half of a breast in a covered casserole with ¼ cup vermouth or chicken stock and ¼ cup green onion for 8 to 10 minutes; cool and cut up.

Popcorn   Regular popcorn is only moderately successful when cooked by this method, leaving many unpopped kernels. If you wish to make popcorn in the microwave oven, use popcorn specially packaged for microwave use.

Precooking   The microwave oven can speed up outdoor grilling and produce more tender and juicy meats. For example, cook ribs, roasts, or fowl on 50 percent power until about half done, then transfer to the grill to finish cooking.

Reheating Foods   The microwave oven is almost unsurpassed in maintaining taste and texture when reheating foods. Points to remember include the following: 1. To reheat frozen foods, first thaw in refrigerator for easier reheating; 2. to attain even results, choose a dish close to the size of the food you are reheating; 3. to avoid overheating, begin reheating on 100 percent power, then lower to 50 percent power; 4. to reheat foods that absorb water during the initial cooking process (rice, noodles, vegetables, casseroles), add more cooking liquid (2 tablespoons per cup of food) to help food reheat evenly; 5. to reheat more than one item, reheat the food that can maintain the longest standing time first, then others in descending order (for example, a casserole, then a vegetable, then breads).

Steaming Fish   Steam 1 pound of fish in its own juices until moist and tender in 5 to 6 minutes. It will taste as if it were poached.

WHAT NOT TO MICROWAVE

Microwave cooking saves time and effort over conventional cooking in many cases. Some food's appearance, texture, and flavor are enhanced. However, certain dishes cannot be cooked in a microwave as successfully or as fast as with conventional methods.

Deep-fried Foods   Do not attempt to deep-fry in the microwave oven; temperature cannot be controlled and fats may spatter.

Eggs in Shells   Cook eggs in their shells by conventional methods; they may burst during microwave cooking.

Foods With Crisp, Browned Surfaces   Crispness and browning are best accomplished with conventional cooking methods.

Home-Canned Goods   Since safe internal temperatures cannot be accurately maintained, home canning should not be done in the microwave oven.

Pancakes and Crêpes   Although they can be warmed in the microwave oven, these foods need surface cooking to brown and crisp properly.

Rice, Dried Beans, and Pasta   Although rice cooks well in a microwave oven, no time is saved; dried beans and pasta also cook in the same amount of time as with conventional methods.

Turkey   For a bird over 15 pounds, conventional cooking is easier.

MILK

In the United States, the word *milk* commonly refers to cow's milk, although goats and sheep are valuable sources of milk outside the U.S. Milk as it comes from the cow is highly nutritious. It is a good source of protein (primarily from casein, a complete protein), carbohydrates (from lactose, a milk sugar that aids mineral absorption), fats (low-fat and nonfat milk have less fat), vitamins A, D, and B-2 (riboflavin), and minerals (especially calcium and phosphorus). Because milk is so nutritious, however, it is host to many microbes and is easily contaminated. For this reason, most milk is processed further (pasteurized) before it is sold.

Use   Undoubtedly a large share of the milk consumed in the U.S. is consumed as a beverage. Milk is also an ingredient of major importance to the home cook. Milk provides the base for other beverages: hot and cold cocoa, eggnog, and milk shakes, for example. It adds richness and softens bitter beverages such as coffee and tea. Milk moistens dry breakfast cereal and enriches hot cereal. It may be used in place of water or stock to give body and flavor to soups; fish chowders, for example, are usually milk based.

Milk plays a major role in the making of sauces, both sweet and savory. The classic custard sauce (*crème anglaise*) is milk based. One of the most basic savory sauces, béchamel, and its many derivatives are milk based. Milk is the primary liquid in most puddings, soufflés, and custards, including bread pudding, corn pudding, and *crème caramel*. Many ice creams, despite their name, are made with milk instead of cream; some fruit sherbets get their body from milk.

Due to its milk fat, milk adds moisture and richness to cakes, cookies, and bread doughs. It makes breads brown better, improves their keeping qualities, and gives a creamier, softer crumb. It is also the liquid of choice for most batters, including those for muffins, coffee cakes, waffles, popovers, and crêpes. Buttermilk is sometimes used for the tangy flavor it imparts to baked goods.

Milk is sometimes used as a soaking medium. Fish is dipped in milk before coating and frying in order to provide a moist surface to which the coating will adhere. Some cooks soak fish or chicken livers in milk for about an hour to rid them of strong flavors.

Poaching liquids for fish, sweetbreads, and cauliflower sometimes include milk to keep these foods white. Milk does not figure heavily in meat cookery. One exception, however, is the Italian favorite pork loin braised in milk; the milk cooks down into rich, nutty clumps that the Italians call *bruti ma buoni* (ugly but good).

Milk as it comes from the cow yields butter and cream; it is also the starting point for all yogurt and cheese.

Availability   The following remarks should clarify the differences among the many milk products available on supermarket shelves.

Acidophilus Milk   A cultured milk, acidophilus is pasteurized skim or low-fat milk with a bacterial culture added. The milk is immediately packaged and cooled, however, to prevent fermentation; thus it retains the flavor and texture of uncultured milk. When consumed, the bacterial culture is activated at body temperature. It is believed that these bacteria help maintain the balance of beneficial microorganisms in the intestinal tract. Acidophilus milk is often recommended for people taking antibiotics.

Buttermilk   Originally, buttermilk was the milky residue from churning cream into butter. Today commercial buttermilk is made by adding bacterial cultures to pasteurized milk (usually skim milk). The cultures convert the milk sugar (lactose) into lactic acid, producing a tartness in the buttermilk. Some processors add butter flakes to approximate the buttermilk of yesteryear. Buttermilk is drunk as a beverage by those who appreciate its smooth, creamy texture and buttery flavor. It adds a rich, creamy tang to cold soups and salad dressings; it imparts flavor and tenderness to pancakes, biscuits, quick breads, and cakes.

Chocolate Milk   This is pasteurized whole milk flavored with chocolate or cocoa and sweeteners. Chocolate low-fat and nonfat milks are also marketed.

Condensed Milk (also known as concentrated milk)   Although similar to evaporated milk, condensed milk has usually not been heat-treated for sterilization. Sweetened condensed milk is condensed milk with sweetener (usually sugar) added. It contains 40 to 45 percent sugar and cannot be substituted for evaporated milk in recipes.

Evaporated Milk and Evaporated Skimmed Milk   Both of these products have been heated to remove about 60 percent of their water, then sealed in cans and heat-treated for sterilization. One half cup of evaporated milk can be reconstituted with an equal amount of water to make 1 cup whole milk.

Extra-rich Milk   This form of milk contains either slightly more milk fat or slightly more nonfat milk solids.

Homogenized Milk   Most milk is homogenized after pasteurization, although homogenization is optional under federal standards. Homogenization is a method of dispersing milk fat throughout the milk to keep it from rising to the top as cream. After pasteurization, the milk is pumped at high pressure through extremely small openings and onto a hard surface. This breaks up the fat globules into such small particles that they remain dispersed in the liquid.

Low-Fat Milk   Some of the milk fat has been skimmed away to produce this product; it usually retains about 2 percent milk fat.

Nonfat Dry Milk (also known as powdered milk)   To make nonfat dry milk, the water is removed from pasteurized skim milk. It reconstitutes readily in warm water. Instant nonfat dry milk reconstitutes readily in cold water. These products are valued for their convenience and their long shelf life. They are also widely used in packaged mixes (such as cake and pudding mixes). Many commercial bakers find dry milk easier to work with than liquid milk.

Pasteurized Milk   To destroy potentially harmful microbes and improve its keeping quality, most milk is pasteurized: It is heated to 161° F and maintained at that temperature for 15 seconds. Ultrapasteurized milk is heated to 280° F and held there for at least two seconds; this process extends the refrigerated shelf life even further. Ultra-high-temperature (UHT) processed milk is treated like ultrapasteurized milk but is then packaged in sterilized containers and aseptically sealed. It may be safely stored unrefrigerated for at least three months.

Raw Milk   Milk shipped in interstate commerce must be pasteurized. Some states allow intrastate shipment of raw (unpasteurized) milk from certified herds. Because raw milk has not been pasteurized, it contains potentially disease-producing microbes and has a shorter refrigerated shelf life.

Skim or Nonfat Milk   To be labeled skim or nonfat, milk must be skimmed of as much fat as possible. Milk fat content must be less than 0.5 percent.

Whole Milk   To be labeled whole milk, a product must contain at least 3.5 percent milk fat and 8.6 percent solids that are not fat (proteins, carbohydrates, minerals, and vitamins).

TIPS

CALORIES IN MILK

Calorie counters may want to know that whole milk supplies about 160 calories per cup; low-fat milk, 140 calories; and skim milk, 90 calories. Because of its significantly lower fat content, skim milk cannot readily be substituted for whole milk in recipes. If calories are unimportant, 1 cup skim milk plus 1 tablespoon cream can be substituted for 1 cup whole milk in most cases.

Storage Fluid milk is highly perishable. It should be one of the last purchases in the supermarket and should be refrigerated immediately at home. Keep opened milk containers closed to prevent milk from absorbing other odors. Milk kept at room temperature for at least 30 minutes (in a milk pitcher, for example) should not be poured back into the original container. Refrigerate it in a separate container. Dry milk will keep indefinitely in a cool, dry place; store in an airtight container after opening. Reconstituted dry milk should be refrigerated. Unopened canned milk will keep indefinitely in a cool place; pour any unused canned milk into a clean container and refrigerate.

Pull Date All milk sold in interstate commerce is marked with a pull date to indicate when the product should be withdrawn from retail sale. The pull date is intentionally conservative to allow for additional storage time in the consumer's refrigerator.

Preparation Although many modern bread recipes instruct cooks to scald milk to destroy bacteria that might hamper the development of yeast, the pasteurized milk available today renders this step unnecessary. Some recipes call for heating milk for other reasons, however—dissolving sugar or melting shortening, for instance.

Recipes and Related Information
Basic White Sauce, 513; Cheese Sauce, 513; Crème Caramel, 169; Down-Home Mashed Potatoes, 466; New England Clam Chowder, 539; Scalloped Potatoes, 465.

MINCE, TO

Strictly defined, *mince* means to cut food into the finest dice possible, into pieces of even size. However, in common usage it has come to mean to chop very finely. Parsley is an ingredient that is typically minced.

MINT

The mint family of perennial herbs is quite large and includes such varied members as spearmint, peppermint, pineapple mint, pennyroyal, orange bergamot, and apple mint. Spearmint is most often used in cooking, although the others may be substituted. Mints have a strong aroma, a sweet, slightly hot flavor, and a cool aftertaste.

Use Whole mint leaves are often used to garnish salads or beverages; crushed mint leaves are important to some cocktails, particularly mint julep. Minced mint leaves add a cool, refreshing quality to coleslaw and fruit salads; mint also flatters peas, beets, carrots, onions, and cucumbers. Fresh mint contributes a delightful cool flavor to spicy Thai and Vietnamese salads and is used in the filling for Vietnamese spring rolls. Indian cooks incorporate mint in chutneys and curries. Moroccans make an aromatic sweet tea with mint leaves. Crushed mint leaves are also used to make the sweet jelly served with roast lamb in many English and American homes. Italian cooks employ mint in stuffings, vegetable soups, and dried bean dishes.

Mint extract and oil of mint are ingredients in a variety of desserts and confections, including ice cream, peppermint candies, and chocolate-covered mints. Mint and chocolate are often paired in desserts and candies; mint and fruit are another compatible team.

Availability Fresh mint is sold in some markets all year, with peak supplies in summer. Dried mint leaves, packed in jars and tins, are available on most supermarket spice racks. Mint extract is also widely sold in supermarkets.

Selection Choose fresh mint that show no signs of wilting or decay. For dried mint, keep in mind that packaged seasonings lose quality after a while; try to buy from a store that restocks its spice section fairly often.

Storage Prop fresh mint in a tall glass of water, cover with a plastic bag, and refrigerate; change water daily and use within three or four days. Store dried mint in a cool, dry, dark place; replace every year.

Preparation Wash and dry fresh mint; remove leaves from stalk; use whole or minced. Rub dried mint between fingers to release aromatic oils before adding to a dish.

Recipes and Related Information
Cucumber-Mint Sauce, 294; Mint Jelly, 321; Tabbouleh, 277.

MIREPOIX

A combination of aromatic vegetables added to soups, stocks, braises, and roasts, *mirepoix* increases the flavor of the food but is not necessarily included as part of the final dish. Mirepoix can be strained away or later puréed, mixed with pan juices, and used as sauce. Onions, celery, carrots, leeks, and sometimes parsnips are the classic mirepoix vegetables. *Brunoise* is a similar preparation, but the vegetables are cut in finer pieces (see BRUNOISE).

MIX, TO

To combine ingredients so that the result is blended and homogenous, or so that each substance is still somewhat distinguishable from one another but evenly dispersed.

MIXERS

There is no better way to whip cream, beat egg whites, and mix up light, airy cake batters than with an electric mixer. There are two types of mixers: portable and stand. The portable or handheld version is the simplest; the cook holds the machine with the beaters  inserted into a freestanding bowl and controls the movements of the mixer.

Portable mixers differ from one another primarily in power and speed settings. The high-quality ones may also come with dough hooks for kneading, and a few can be attached to a separate base that allows the mixer to function also as a stand mixer. Handheld mixers are lightweight, easy to store, and can be moved around the kitchen. On the other hand, the cook can't do other tasks while holding the mixer, and holding it can be tiring. Some portable mixers fade when working on stiff doughs.

Stand mixers range from light to heavy-duty. Electronic controls help maintain speed as the mixture gets heavier; some also have a timer. Bowl capacity is usually around 4 quarts, but other sizes are available. Some are very versatile, with a flat, open, paddle-type beater, plus a balloon whisk for whipping and a dough hook for kneading. Among the attachments are food grinders, juicers, slicer/shredders, sausage stuffers, pasta makers, grain grinders, and ice jackets.

Serious bakers are advised to buy a quality, heavy-duty stand mixer. Otherwise, most mixing can be done with a good portable.

Even on lowest speeds, electric mixers are fast; dry ingredients can erupt in a cloud that settles on your counter or even in your face before you realize what's happening. If you are adding many ingredients at one time— liquid and dry—cover the dry with the wet. This will have a blanketing effect that contains the flour in the bowl and out of your face.

Rotary eggbeaters are essentially portable electric mixers without the electric capability; your muscle is their power. They will quickly whip cream, aerate pancake and crêpe batters, and beat eggs, but will bog down in heavy mixtures such as dense cake batters. They function like a whisk and should have thin, rather than flat, wires so that as much air as possible is incorporated. Gear-driven beaters have the smoothest action. In these days of electric-powered, multipurpose mixing and processing machines, does the mechanical eggbeater warrant a spot in your kitchen? By all means, if you like using this tool and if it works for you. Be sure to select a rotary beater with a handle that you can grip comfortably.

MIXING BOWL

Every kitchen needs a generous assortment of these very versatile, multipurpose bowls, matched in capacity, shape, and material to the tasks done most often. Tall, narrow shapes are best for creaming and beating; the high sides prevent liquids or solids from  flying out of the bowl onto counter or face when quickly mixed with spoon, beater, or whisk. Wide and shallow bowls keep all ingredients in view and within reach; nothing gets lost on the bottom. They work for stuffings, salads, and ground-meat mixtures. Bowls with smoothly rounded bottoms make the best molds. These kitchen indispensables should more aptly be called mixing-stirring-folding-tossing-storing-holding-serving-molding-beating-marinating-organizing-heating-cooling bowls. Most cooks could think of dozens more uses for them. In general, use bowls larger than seems necessary for the job; the extra capacity will help control messes and reduce cleanup. Look for containers that sit flat on the work surface, are easy to pick up, and are not too heavy to move and store.

Any bowl-shaped container can serve as a mixing bowl. Those specially manufactured as such, however, are usually more durable. Typical materials include stainless steel, glass, ceramic, melamine plastic, and copper (for beating egg whites; see COPPER EGG-WHITE BOWL), in 1-quart through 8-quart capacities, and often in sets of three or four bowls. Smaller sizes (less than 1 quart) are handy for beating or separating a few eggs, setting out ingredients for stir-fries or other preparations in which ingredients are added in stages, and storing. It is unnecessary to purchase matching bowls, but sets usually come in the most practical sizes and nest for more compact storage. Overall, stainless steel is the preferred material. It is highly durable, nonreactive (it won't discolor batters, doughs, or high-acid foods), and resistant to thermal shock (it can withstand sudden changes of temperature—setting hot custard in a bowl of ice water, for example).

MOLD, TO; MOLD

To form into a shape with the hands, or by putting in a container (a mold) and then chilling or cooking until the food takes on the contour of the container. The receptacle that holds the molded food is called a mold. Meat loaves and pâtés, gelatin-based dishes, and candies are molded.

A mold does just that—gives food shape. Whether the food can maintain that shape on its own depends not on the mold but on the recipe—if it has gelatin, eggs, or another binding ingredient. Sometimes a mold will have the same

Molds are used to shape many types of foods: ice cream, gelatin, and pâtés, for example. They can be made of a variety of materials and in many configurations. Molds shown from top left to right: round gelatin/aspic, soufflé, pudding, terrines, ice cream (bombe and bird), coeur à la crème, custard, ramekin, pâté, timbale, oval gelatin/aspic.

name as the food it is most often associated with: timbale, angel food cake, *Kugelhopf*, charlotte, soufflé, gratin, and muffin have given their names to the specific pans used to prepare them.

ASPIC AND GELATIN MOLDS

For chilled gelatin-based dishes, metal molds cool the fastest and set the dish in the least amount of time. Porcelain or glass dishes will work also. The simpler the mold, the easier it is to remove its contents. On the other hand, some modeling enhances the appeal of an otherwise simple preparation. Select a mold that is sculptured but without deeply modeled, fine detail that would trap food. Clear, well-defined, simple patterns transfer best.

Molds are sold in hundreds of designs—fish, animals, birds, hearts, rings, crowns, stars, and turbans—in individual to buffet sizes, and formed of tin, copper, stainless steel, plastic, glass, and ceramic. Special oval ramekins for Oeufs en Gelée (see page 266), a light luncheon dish of poached eggs set in aspic, can be found in better cookware stores. Buy for pattern and use; very decorative copper or porcelain dishes make attractive kitchen accessories.

COEUR A LA CREME MOLD

To make this classic chilled French cheese dessert (see page 111), cheese with soft curds is blended with confectioners' sugar and cream, spooned into a heart-shaped porcelain mold or wicker basket (*coeur* means heart in

French), and drained. Fresh berries are often served with it. The mold is pierced to allow the liquid to drain off. Both individual molds and larger dishes are available.

ICE CREAM MOLDS

For fancy molded ice creams, the classic shape is a bombe, which resembles half a football. This mold holds 1 to 1½ quarts and comes with a lid. Another classic is one shaped like an elongated cantaloupe with deep, widely spaced ribs. It also has a cover and is sized the same. Both designs are made of tinned steel and can double as pudding molds.

PATE MOLDS AND TERRINES

By definition, the classic pâté is a rich, baked mixture of ground meats, seasonings, and fats—a Gallic meat loaf—encased in a pastry crust (*pâté en croûte*). The classic terrine, on the other hand, is a sort of pâté without a crust, named for the earthenware dish it is baked in. Few people except the French make these distinctions any longer; most American restaurants and cookbooks use the words interchangeably. The molds for pâtés and terrines are made of tinned steel, enameled cast iron, porcelain, and earthenware. Molds for pâté en croûte range from simple loaf pans to elaborate affairs of tinned steel with hinges, clips, or pins, often fluted or otherwise patterned. The sides and bottom separate for easy removal of the baked pâté. Terrine molds are simple loaf pans with covers. They are country-style and are rectangular or oval in shape. Some are finished to resemble a pâté en croûte—with a golden surface that resembles a baked crust, fluted, crimped, and topped with the image of an animal or bird to suggest the type of pâté encased within; the interior is glazed. Sizes are 2 to 4 quarts.

PUDDING BASIN

The English have long been consummate makers and eaters of steamed pudding; most households have special slope-sided glazed ceramic bowls just for this purpose. A gauzy pudding cloth, used to cover these dishes as they steam, is lovingly cleaned and folded after each use and set aside until the next time pudding is made. The basin is traditionally deep, wide at the top, and narrow at the bottom, with a flat base. It is rimmed so that the pudding cloth has something to rest against. Capacities range from 1 to about 3 quarts. Also available are fancier tinned steel pudding molds with covers.

SOUFFLE MOLD, CUSTARD CUP, AND RAMEKIN

To rise, a soufflé requires a straight-sided, flat-bottomed dish made of a heat-conductive material that encourages rapid expansion of the air trapped in the beaten whites. Because a soufflé is served in its baking dish, the dish should be attractive enough to bring to the table. Soufflé dishes are typically made of porcelain with ridged sides that replicate the pleated paper collars used by French chefs for hundreds of years to extend the sides of the dish and allow the soufflé to rise above it. The molds are usually rimmed for easier handling. Other materials include heat-resistant glass and stoneware. Dishes are typically 1, 1½, or 2 quarts, and ovenproof, since soufflés are classically baked, but soufflé dishes are also suitable for cold soufflés and mousses, for any baked casserole, and for serving dishes.

CUSTARD CUP

These heatproof ramekins with sloping sides are sized for individual servings of creamy baked custard or pudding, but perform other functions as well. Use them to hold ingredients for stir-fries, for melting chocolate and butter in a microwave oven, for serving condiments, for beating an egg or two, and for storing small amounts of leftovers. Choose from cups made of porcelain, heatproof glass, or glazed earthenware; the most useful size is about 5 ounces. Have at least one half dozen.

RAMEKIN

Any baking dish designed for a single serving can be accurately called a ramekin. Typically ramekins resemble scaled-down soufflé dishes, are porcelain or earthenware, and hold about 4 ounces of food. Use them for custards and sweet and savory mousses.

TIMBALE MOLD

Also known as a dariole mold, *timbale* comes from the French word for kettledrum, an apt description of its shape. The term refers to both the baking dish and the creamy meat, fish, or vegetable mixture cooked in it. As a preparation, timbales have several forms; the filling can be cooked alone, in a pastry crust like a pâté en croûte, or in a shell of macaroni or potato. Today timbales are often vegetable custards served with a meat, fish, or poultry main course. The molds hold about ½ cup, are made of stainless steel, and are tall, narrow, and straight or slope sided. They double as baking pans for the rich yeast bread called baba.

Recipes and Related Information
Blue Cheese Soufflé, 205; Chilled Lemon Soufflé, 207; Custard, 168; Frozen Watermelon Bombe, 315; Gelatin, 264; Hot Lemon Soufflé, 206; Pâté and Terrine, 416; Spinach Timbales, 579.

MONOSODIUM GLUTAMATE

Also known as MSG, or by its most common brand name, Accent, monosodium glutamate is technically a sodium salt made from glutamic acid. Although the process is little understood, monosodium glutamate appears to heighten the flavors of other foods, perhaps by increasing receptivity in the taste buds. In its commercial form, MSG is a coarse white crystal that resembles coarse salt.

Many diners experience reactions to monosodium glutamate, especially if eaten on an empty stomach—for example, in a soup served as a first course in a Chinese restaurant. Common reactions are facial tightness or numbness, burning sensations, and a feeling of pressure in the chest. Symptoms rarely last more than one hour.

Use Monosodium glutamate serves as a flavor enhancer in much the same way that salt does. It is sprinkled on meats before cooking or added to soups and stir-fries. Initially used only in Japan, it is now widely found in Japanese and Chinese kitchens. At home it should always be used in small quantities, if at all; it may be omitted from any recipe calling for it, although the salt level may need to be adjusted.

Availability Monosodium glutamate is found in the spice section of most supermarkets. A popular Japanese variety, Aji-No-Moto, is sold in Japanese markets and is offered as a table condiment in many Japanese restaurants.

Storage Monosodium glutamate will keep indefinitely in a cool, dark, dry place.

MOUSSE

A French word, *mousse* means frothy, which aptly describes the light and spongy character of this dish. It has an appealing soft and creamy texture and can be savory or sweet, cold or hot.

The main ingredients of a savory mousse are ground or puréed fish, poultry, cheese, or vegetables, plus cream, and beaten egg whites or whipped cream. If served hot, it is baked in a bain-marie until firm. If cold, gelatin is sometimes added to set the mixture. A dessert mousse is chilled or even frozen. It is easily made from a base of puréed fruit or melted chocolate, which is lightened with whipped cream or beaten egg whites and often thickened with gelatin.

■ CHILLED SAVORY MOUSSE

This cold mousse must be prepared at least four hours in advance of serving. Consider this a basic recipe and create your own versions by varying the main ingredients and seasonings. If desired, once the mousse has set, it can be covered with a thin layer of aspic and then chilled further until the aspic is firm. See Curried Chicken or Duck Liver Pâté in Aspic, page 416, for directions.

    1 **pound cooked, puréed meat or fish (chicken, veal, ham, rabbit, or salmon)**
    4 **tablespoons butter, softened**
    2 **cups Basic White Sauce (see page 513), cooled to room temperature**
    1 **envelope unflavored gelatin**
    ½ **cup Chicken or Fish Stock (depending on main ingredient; see page 560 or 561)**
    ½ **cup whipping cream**
        Salt and freshly ground black pepper, to taste
        Optional seasonings (choose any or all):
        ¼ teaspoon freshly grated nutmeg,
        ¼ teaspoon cayenne pepper, ½ teaspoon Worcestershire sauce
        Minced parsley or parsley sprigs, for garnish

1. In a large bowl blend together puréed meat and butter. Add cooled white sauce and mix with a wooden spoon until well combined or smooth (or mix in a food processor with a few short pulses so meat mixture doesn't become a paste).

2. In a small saucepan sprinkle gelatin over stock and let stand to soften (3 to 4 minutes). Dissolve gelatin over low heat; pour into meat mixture, and stir well. Whip cream to soft peaks and fold in. Taste and season with salt, pepper, and seasonings (if used).

3. Pour into a 5- to 6-cup soufflé or serving dish and smooth top. Cover tightly with plastic wrap and refrigerate at least 4 hours before serving to set mousse.

4. To serve, let sit out at room temperature at least 30 minutes. Decorate with minced parsley or parsley sprigs.

Serves 6 to 8 as a first course.

■ CHICKEN OR DUCK LIVER MOUSSE

A beautifully glazed mousse adds beauty to a pâté and cheese buffet. Since the aspic and mousse must set for several hours or more, this dish should be prepared a day ahead. If desired, make flower petals from pieces of tomato skin and black olives, and from skins from chives (see Aspic Glaze).

    1 **pound chicken or duck livers**
    1 **small onion, minced**
    1 **clove garlic, minced**
    1 **teaspoon salt**
    ½ **teaspoon dried thyme**
    ¼ **teaspoon allspice**
    ¼ **teaspoon white pepper**
    6 **tablespoons unsalted butter**
    2 **tablespoons brandy**
    1 **envelope unflavored gelatin**
    1 **cup whipping cream**

Aspic Glaze

    1 **recipe Basic Aspic (see page 265)**
    1 **tablespoon vegetable oil**
        Tomato-skin cutouts, for garnish
        Chives, for garnish
        Black olive pieces, for garnish

1. Prepare Aspic Glaze. Pour 1 cup Basic Aspic into an 8-inch square baking pan and chill for at least 2 hours (this chilled aspic will be cubed and used to garnish mousse).

2. In a medium skillet sauté chicken livers, onion, garlic, salt, thyme, allspice, and pepper in 2 tablespoons butter over medium heat until livers are brown on the outside but remain pink on the inside (about 12 minutes). Remove to a blender or food processor. Add brandy to skillet, scraping cooked-on bits to loosen; add to liver.

3. In a small saucepan soften gelatin in ½ cup of the reserved Basic Aspic. Dissolve gelatin over low heat, stirring until liquid is clear (2 to 4 minutes). Add to liver and purée to a smooth paste. Remove to a medium bowl. Stir in remaining butter. Cool at room temperature until mixture thickens slightly (about 20 minutes).

4. Whip cream to soft peaks; fold into liver mixture. Carefully spoon into aspic-coated mold. Cover with plastic wrap to prevent the mousse from drying out. Chill until firm (about 4 hours).

5. To unmold, loosen sides of mold with a knife. Pour 1 inch hot water into a pan larger than mold. Place mold in the hot water for about 2 minutes to loosen. Place a serving plate (at least 3 inches larger in diameter than mold) over mousse, invert, and lift mold from mousse. Dice 8-inch square sheet of Basic Aspic into cubes and surround the mousse.

Serves 12 to 20 as an appetizer.

Aspic Glaze Prepare Basic Aspic; set aside until cool but still liquid and reserve 1 cup aspic for mousse and for glaze. Coat 5-cup mold with 1 tablespoon vegetable oil. Pour ½ cup of reserved aspic into mold. Arrange tomato-skin cutouts, chives, and black olives in a decorative pattern to form flowers on aspic (if desired). Chill until firm (about 2 hours).

■ CHILLED FRUIT MOUSSE

A fruit mousse is easily made by thickening fruit purée with gelatin and enriching it with whipped cream. Reserve some of the berries for garnish. Like all cold, creamy mousses, this one is a boon to the busy cook because it can be prepared ahead of time.

    2 pints strawberries *or* 1 pint raspberries
    2 eggs
    2 egg yolks
    ½ cup superfine sugar
    1 envelope unflavored gelatin
    ¼ cup fresh lemon juice
    1 cup whipping cream

1. Rinse berries and pat dry; set aside some of the best-looking ones for garnish. If using strawberries, hull. Purée berries in a food processor or blender (to make 1 cup purée); strain through a fine sieve to remove seeds and set aside.

2. In a large bowl whip eggs, yolks, and sugar until thick, or until mixture drops off the beater in a ribbon. In a small saucepan sprinkle gelatin over lemon juice and let stand to soften (3 to 4 minutes). Dissolve over low heat. Pour in a thin stream into egg-sugar mixture; whip to combine. Add fruit purée and mix well. In a separate bowl whip cream to soft peaks and set aside.

3. Set bowl with mousse over ice and stir mixture until it is on the point of setting (it will have the consistency of cream whipped to soft peaks); remove from ice and fold in whipped cream. Pour immediately into a 6-cup mold or 6 individual ramekins. Refrigerate until set (2 to 3 hours). Serve with reserved berries.

Serves 6.

■ CHOCOLATE MOUSSE TORTE

Everyone loves chocolate mousse, especially when it's encased in a chocolate cookie-crumb crust that sparkles with the addition of large crystals of raw sugar. The torte must chill at least four hours, or overnight, so it's an excellent dish to make ahead for a party.

    2 cups chocolate cookie crumbs (one 8½ oz
       package chocolate wafers, crushed)
    ¼ cup coarse sugar
    ⅓ cup unsalted butter, melted
    1 recipe Chocolate Mousse (see page 127)
       Chantilly Cream (see page 252), for decoration
       Chocolate Curls (see page 126), for garnish

1. Preheat oven to 350° F. In a medium bowl combine crumbs and sugar. Pour in melted butter and stir to coat crumb mixture evenly with butter. Press into an 8-inch springform pan; bake 10 minutes. Cool and refrigerate.

2. Prepare Chocolate Mousse; do not chill, but pour into chilled shell. Refrigerate pie at least 4 hours, or overnight.

3. To serve, remove from pan, pipe spirals of Chantilly Cream around edge, and sprinkle cream with some Chocolate Curls (if desired).

Serves 8 to 10.

A double shot of chocolate— in the filling and in the sugar-speckled crumb crust—makes Chocolate Mousse Torte a favorite dessert of chocoholics everywhere.

Recipes and Related Information
Gelatin, 264; Mousse Meringue Cake, 361; Ribbon, 498; Sole Mousse, 377.

This tempting arrangement of muffins illustrates how easily this simple quick bread can be varied by changing a few ingredients.

MUFFIN

A muffin is a quick bread made from a mixture of 2 parts flour to 1 part liquid, plus one or more eggs, sugar, and other flavoring ingredients. Baking powder or baking soda is the leavening agent.

The classic muffin has a uniform shape, large in proportion to its weight, with a gently rounded top with a surface that is pebbled, somewhat like that of a cauliflower. The crust is an even golden brown and slightly shiny. The texture should be light, moist, and evenly grained, and the flavor pleasing, without tasting of baking powder or baking soda. The standard muffin is made in a pan with cups each measuring approximately 2¾ inches wide at the top and 1½ inches deep.

MAKING AND BAKING MUFFINS

Mix dry ingredients thoroughly to disperse the baking powder and/or baking soda evenly. The batter should be baked as soon as liquid and dry ingredients have been combined or leavening will lose some of its punch. As a timesaver, the dry ingredients can be combined ahead of time, as can the liquids. Unless the recipe indicates that it can be prepared in advance, though, don't blend the two mixtures until you are ready to fill the muffin pan and put it in the oven.

Always grease the pan, even if it has a nonstick lining. Coat with butter, shortening, or vegetable cooking spray, or use paper cupcake liners. Buy a heavyweight muffin pan that will conduct heat well. It will last for years, and your muffins will look better because they will rise higher. Fill standard muffin cups two thirds to three fourths full (unless directed otherwise in the recipe) with a spoon or measuring cup. If there isn't enough batter to fill all the muffin cups, fill the empty ones with water so the pan won't warp. Always preheat the oven for 10 to 15 minutes, and bake on the center rack. Muffins are done when the centers spring back when pressed lightly and when a toothpick inserted in the middle comes out clean.

Turn baked muffins onto a wire rack to cool. If some stick, tap bottom of cup lightly with your knuckles. If they still won't budge, let them sit in the pan briefly; steam that develops between muffin and pan will help dislodge them. If necessary, loosen around edges with a knife.

STORING MUFFINS

Plain muffins have the shortest life span. They should be eaten soon after baking. Muffins with fruits and vegetables, and those made with oil, stay moist longer. Don't store muffins or any bread in the refrigerator; they will quickly dry out. Muffins freeze extremely well. If not eaten the day they are made, place cooled muffins in a plastic bag, seal airtight, and freeze for six to twelve months. To reheat, bake frozen muffins, wrapped in aluminum foil, at 350° F for 15 to 20 minutes, or until thawed and heated through.

MONSTER MUFFINS

Muffins have become extremely popular as a take-out breakfast bread. On the assumption that you can't have too much of a good thing, the size of muffins has risen to huge proportions. Some are as large as 4 inches across and 2 inches tall, more a minibread than a single-serving bun. Although novel, these giants are often dry, especially if they must sit on a bakery counter for any length of time. Protect oversized homemade muffins from getting stale by freezing those not eaten right away.

Any of the muffin recipes in this section may be made in giant form by filling standard muffin cups to the top and increasing the baking time to 30 to 40 minutes. This time is approximate; some recipes will take longer than others. Test for doneness after about 20 minutes, then every 10 minutes or so. As the muffin batter will overflow onto the top of the muffin tin, remember to grease that surface as well as the molds.

■ BASIC MUFFINS

These basic muffins have a breadlike texture. To prepare them, the dry ingredients are typically sifted into a bowl, the liquid ingredients (including melted butter or shortening or oil) are then added together, and all are stirred just until moistened. Overbeating may cause tunnels in the muffins, which are elongated cells formed by bubbles of carbon dioxide trapped in the batter. Muffins may have peaked tops as well if overbeaten.

2½ cups flour
¾ cup sugar
1 tablespoon baking powder
  Pinch salt
¾ cup milk
½ cup unsalted butter, melted, or vegetable oil
2 eggs

1. Preheat oven to 350° F. Sift flour, sugar, baking powder, and salt together into a large bowl; make well in center. Mix milk, melted butter, and eggs together and pour into well; stir just to combine.

2. Pour into greased 2¾-inch muffin pans, filling two thirds to three fourths full. Bake until golden brown and a toothpick inserted in center comes out clean (25 to 30 minutes). Serve warm.

Makes 12 muffins.

Blueberry Muffins   Gently fold into batter 1 cup fresh or frozen blueberries.

■ BEST CAKE MUFFINS

If a more fine-grained, cakelike, and less crumbly texture is desired, try this recipe. Sugar and butter are creamed together before the liquid and dry ingredients are added, much as you would for a shortened cake batter.

1½ cups flour
2 teaspoons baking powder
½ teaspoon baking soda
  Pinch salt
½ cup butter
¾ cup sugar
2 eggs
1 teaspoon vanilla extract
⅔ cup milk

1. Preheat oven to 350° F. Grease muffin pan and lightly dust with flour. Sift flour, baking powder, baking soda, and salt together into a medium bowl and set aside. In a medium bowl cream butter and sugar together until light, fluffy, and a pale, ivory color. Add eggs, one at a

time, beating well after each addition (if mixture begins to curdle as you mix in eggs, add 1 tablespoon flour and beat on low speed until blended). Stir in vanilla and milk. Fold in dry ingredients.

2. Spoon batter into prepared 2¾-inch muffin pan, filling each mold three fourths full. Bake until golden brown and a toothpick inserted in center comes out clean (20 to 25 minutes). Serve warm.

Makes 12 muffins.

Blueberry Muffins   Gently mix into batter 1 cup fresh or frozen blueberries.

Cinnamon-Raisin Muffins   Sift ½ teaspoon cinnamon with dry ingredients; gently mix into batter ¾ to 1 cup dark or golden raisins.

Citrus–Poppy-Seed Muffins   Mix into dry ingredients 1 tablespoon grated lemon or orange rind and ¼ cup poppy seed.

Nut-Currant Muffins   Gently mix into batter ½ cup chopped walnuts or pecans and ½ cup dried currants.

■ BRAN MUFFINS

These muffins contain banana for moistness and richness, buttermilk for tang, and raisins for natural sweetness.

2½ cups whole wheat flour
1⅓ cups bran
3 tablespoons sugar
2 teaspoons baking soda
½ teaspoon salt
2½ cups buttermilk
1 egg
⅓ cup molasses
3 tablespoons butter, melted
1 ripe banana, mashed
2 cups raisins

Bran Topping

2 tablespoons bran
2 tablespoons raw sugar

1. Preheat oven to 400° F. Into a large bowl sift together flour, bran, sugar, baking soda, and salt. (Some of the flour and bran may not pass through sieve; remove what remains and add to sifted ingredients.)

2. In a medium bowl combine buttermilk, egg, molasses, melted butter, and banana. Add liquid to dry ingredients and stir just to combine. Fold in raisins.

3. Spoon into greased 2¾-inch muffin cups, filling each three fourths full. Sprinkle with Bran Topping. Bake until muffins are well browned and spring back when touched lightly (25 to 30 minutes). Serve warm.

Makes 12 muffins.

Bran Topping   Combine bran and sugar in a small bowl.

■ REFRIGERATOR BRAN MUFFIN MIX

Like all quick bread batters, muffins must be baked right after mixing. It isn't always convenient to pop into the kitchen at the break of day to stir up a fresh batch for a wonderful morning treat. One way to resolve this dilemma is to mix up a batter formulated to keep in the refrigerator, like this one for bran muffins. Also, see Freezing Batter, at left.

> 3 cups whole bran cereal
> 1 cup boiling water
> 1½ cups all-purpose flour
> 1 cup whole wheat flour
> 2½ teaspoons baking soda
> ½ teaspoon salt
> 1 cup raisins
> 2 eggs
> 1⅓ cups buttermilk
> ½ cup vegetable oil
> 2 teaspoons grated orange rind
> ½ cup each honey and light molasses

1. If baking muffins, preheat oven to 425° F. Place cereal in a large bowl; pour boiling water over cereal, stirring to moisten evenly. Set aside until cool (about 10 minutes).

2. Meanwhile, in a very large bowl stir together flours, baking soda, salt, and raisins.

3. Beat eggs into cereal mixture. Blend in buttermilk, oil, orange rind, honey, and molasses. Add cereal mixture to flour mixture, stirring just until dry ingredients are moistened. Bake muffins at once, or store in refrigerator for up to 2 weeks.

4. Spoon batter into greased 2¾-inch muffin pans, filling about two thirds full.

5. Bake until muffins are well browned and spring back when touched lightly (18 to 20 minutes). Serve warm.

Makes 2 to 2½ dozen muffins.

Recipes and Related Information
Baking Pans, 18; Quick Bread, 490.

MUSHROOM

Mushrooms are one of the most primitive foods eaten by mankind. Like molds, they are a member of the fungus family and a very simple plant. They reproduce by spores spread in the wind and subsist on decaying organic matter. The many different species vary considerably in color, shape, size, and flavor.

Use   Mushrooms are enjoyed both as a dish in themselves and as an ingredient in other dishes. Sliced mushrooms may be dressed with vinaigrette and eaten raw as a salad, or they may be added to mixed green salads. Sliced mushrooms are also used to garnish pizza. Small whole mushrooms may be pickled or cooked à la grecque. Sautéed in butter with parsley and garlic, mushrooms are enjoyed as a side dish or a topping for pasta. Creamed mushrooms are a delicious filling for patty shells and crêpes. Mushrooms add their woodsy flavor to stir-fries, sautés, and stews. They are an essential ingredient in Boeuf Bourguignonne and coq au vin. Mushroom caps may be stuffed and baked or coated with batter and fried. Minced mushrooms are used to flavor stocks and poaching liquids. Mushrooms are compatible with almost all meats and fish. They mix particularly well with grains, such as barley and wild rice. They make a delicious soup and an excellent addition to vegetable soups.

Availability   Although a few of the thousands of mushroom species can be cultivated, most cannot. Until recently in the United States, only one variety (*Agaricus bisporus*) was commercially cultivated, and the wild mushrooms in American forests were available only to those who knew how to forage for them. Today, however, several varieties are cultivated, and more and more specialty markets offer wild mushrooms provided by foragers. Some of the most commonly available varieties are discussed on the following pages.

Storage   Fresh mushrooms are very perishable and should generally be used within one or two days of purchase. Very damp wild mushrooms may be spread out on trays and kept in a cool place for one or two days. Otherwise, fresh mushrooms should be wrapped lightly in paper towels and refrigerated; never store them in a closed plastic bag, or trapped moisture will cause rapid deterioration. Dried mushrooms may be kept indefinitely in a cool, dry place in an airtight container. Canned mushrooms will also keep indefinitely in a cool place; after opening, any leftovers should be transferred to a nonmetal container and may be refrigerated in their canning liquid for up to four days.

Mushrooms can be successfully frozen but should be cooked first. Sauté in butter or oil, then freeze in airtight containers for up to one month.

Preparation   Because mushrooms readily absorb water, they should not be washed before using. They require special cleaning techniques to remove the dirt and tiny stones that may cling to them. A good mushroom brush or an old toothbrush is an effective tool for brushing away dirt and cleaning grit out of crevices. Lacking a brush, use a damp towel or paper towel to sponge off dirt.

Reconstituting Dried Mushrooms   Soak dried mushrooms in warm water until softened (usually about 30 minutes) or overnight in cold water. Lift mushrooms out of soaking liquid; the liquid may be strained through cheesecloth and used in soups, sauces, or stews. The softened mushrooms should then be swished in a large bowl of warm water; change the water several times to dislodge any remaining grit.

BUTTON (DOMESTIC)

Agaricus bisporus is the common supermarket button mushroom. Mild in flavor, it is cultivated in hothouses and is always available. Select button mushrooms with white caps that close tightly around the stem; gills should not be showing. Large sizes are good for stuffing or grilling. Smaller ones may be sliced raw for salads or eaten in stews, sautés, sauces, soups, and stuffings. Store in the refrigerator crisper, loosely wrapped in paper towels, and use as soon as possible.

■ COULIBIAC

Of Russian origin, *coulibiac* is traditionally prepared with salmon and wrapped in pastry. This creative variation incorporates sole mousse as well. Duxelles, finely minced mushrooms and shallots that have been cooked until all the liquid has evaporated, are part of classic French cuisine. The richly concentrated mushroom essence is used to impart flavor to sauces and other preparations, and as it is used here—as a stuffing.

> 2 eggs, beaten with 1 tablespoon water
> 1 salmon fillet, 1 inch thick (8 oz)
> 12 to 15 large spinach leaves, washed

Brioche

> 1 tablespoon active dry yeast
> 1 teaspoon sugar
> ¼ cup warm water
> 3 eggs
> 2¼ cups flour
> 1 teaspoon salt
> ½ cup plus 2 tablespoons unsalted butter

Duxelles

> 2 tablespoons unsalted butter
> 3 shallots, minced
> ½ pound mushrooms, finely chopped
> 3 tablespoons dry white wine
> Salt and freshly ground pepper
> 2 tablespoons whipping cream

Sole Mousse

> 2 pounds sole fillets, cut in pieces
> 2 egg whites
> Salt
> Freshly ground white pepper
> Freshly grated nutmeg
> 1½ to 2 cups whipping cream

To assemble the dish: Preheat oven to 350° F. Roll out Brioche dough in a rectangle about ½ inch thick and 10 inches wide by 20 inches long. Brush dough with the 2 eggs beaten with the water. Spread Duxelles over dough to within 2 inches of sides and 5 inches of ends. Spread half of Sole Mousse over Duxelles. Wrap salmon in spinach leaves and place in center of Sole Mousse. Cover with remaining mousse. Wrap dough around filling, sealing edges with water. Bake for 50 minutes.

Serves 8 as a first course, or 6 as an entrée.

Brioche In large bowl of electric mixer, dissolve yeast and sugar in the warm water. Beat in eggs, flour, and salt. Beat 1 minute. Cover and let rise 1 hour. Beat in butter and let rise 1 more hour.

Duxelles In a medium sauté pan, melt butter. Add shallots and sauté 1 minute. Add mushrooms, wine, salt, and pepper. Cook over low heat until all the moisture has evaporated from mushrooms (about 20 minutes). When mixture begins to look dry, add cream; continue to cook until it is quite thick. Remove from heat and reserve.

Sole Mousse Make certain fish, egg whites, and cream are cold; this allows mousse to absorb more cream. In food processor fitted with steel blade, place sole, egg whites, salt, pepper, and nutmeg. Purée, then, with machine running, slowly add 1½ to 2 cups cream, depending on desired texture. When cream has been absorbed, stop machine and chill mousse until needed.

■ MUSHROOMS STUFFED WITH HERB CHEESE

The mushrooms and stuffing can be prepared and assembled a day in advance of serving and chilled until needed. Broil right from the refrigerator; it is unnecessary to warm them to room temperature.

> 1 pound mascarpone cheese
> 4 small bunches basil, washed and minced to make 2 cups
> ½ cup pine nuts
> 16 large mushrooms, stems removed

1. Preheat broiler. In a medium bowl combine cheese and basil. Stir to blend well. Gently fold in pine nuts.

2. Spoon 1 tablespoon cheese mixture into each mushroom cap. Place mushrooms on broiler pan and broil 5 inches from heat until golden brown and heated through (3 to 5 minutes). Serve hot.

Makes 16 stuffed mushrooms.

CHANTERELLE

Also known as girolle, chanterelle is a wild mushroom available in yellow, white, and black varieties, although the yellow are the most common. They have a thick stem and a large wavy cap with gills underneath. Chanterelles may be sliced and sautéed with butter and garlic, with or without cream, and served on toast, pasta, or sautéed veal. Their full flavor is better suited to meats and poultry than to fish. Chanterelles are available fresh in specialty markets in the fall and winter. They are also available dried, brined, and canned.

Chinese Mu Shu Pork features cloud ear mushrooms plus shredded pork and vegetables. All is wrapped in a flour pancake and flavored with spicy-sweet hoisin sauce.

Fresh chanterelles should be moist but not soggy or wet; avoid those that look dried out or ragged. The stem should be white and dry inside. If not using immediately, see Storage. Flavor and texture are improved by long, slow cooking.

CHINESE CLOUD EAR

These irregular black mushrooms (also known as tree ears, wood ears, and black fungus) are available dried and packed in plastic bags in Asian markets. Before use, cover generously with warm water and soak until soft (about 30 minutes). Drain, then swish in a large bowl of warm water, changing water several times, to dislodge any dirt. Keep covered with cold water until use, then drain and dry.

Cloud ears have little flavor but are valued for their gelatinous texture and rich color. They are frequently used in Chinese stir-fries and soups, particularly hot and sour soup and Mu Shu Pork. They will keep indefinitely in an airtight container in a cool, dark place.

■ MU SHU PORK

In this version of a Beijing classic, pancakes wrap the filling in much the same way as tortillas hold a Mexican burrito together. In fact, packaged flour tortillas may be substituted for pancakes. Beef, chicken, pork, or dark-meat turkey can also be prepared mu shu–style.

> 3 green onions
> 1 tablespoon grated fresh ginger
> 1 tablespoon soy sauce
> 2 tablespoons water *or* half water and
>   half Shaoxing wine
>   Pinch sugar
> 3 tablespoons oil
> 2 eggs, lightly beaten
> ½ pound lean pork, cut in matchstick shreds
> ¼ cup shredded bamboo shoots
> ¼ cup *each* lily buds and cloud ears,
>   soaked in warm water and drained
> ¼ cup hoisin sauce

Mandarin Pancakes

> 2 cups flour, plus flour for dusting work surface
> ½ teaspoon kosher salt
> 1 cup boiling water
>   Sesame oil

1. Separate green onions into green tops and white bases. Cut white parts into shreds and combine with ginger. Cut green tops into shreds and set aside. Combine soy sauce, the water, and sugar; set aside.

2. Heat wok over medium heat. Add 1 tablespoon of the oil and swirl to coat sides of pan. Add eggs and cook just until set. Remove eggs to cutting board, and cut into thin strips.

3. Wipe wok clean and return to heat. Add remaining oil, and, when hot, add ginger–green onion mixture. Stir-fry until fragrant, and add pork. Cook just until pork loses its raw color. Add bamboo shoots, lily buds, and cloud ears; stir-fry 2 minutes longer. Add reserved soy sauce mixture and egg strips, increase heat to high, andcook until nearly all liquid is evaporated. Taste for seasoning, and transfer to serving platter.

4. Serve warm Mandarin Pancakes on a separate plate, with green onion shreds and hoisin sauce in small dishes. For each serving, spread a pancake with ½ teaspoon or so of the sauce, add a few green onion shreds, and top with some of the pork mixture. Roll pancake around filling and eat with fingers.

Serves 4 to 6 with other dishes.

Mandarin Pancakes

1. Place flour and salt in a bowl. Stir in the boiling water. Mix to form a firm dough. Place dough on dusted work surface. Knead briefly. Cover with an inverted bowl for minutes to cool.

2. Roll dough into a rope approximately 1½ inches in diameter. Cut rope into 16 pieces. Working with 2 pieces of dough at a time, flatten each piece into a small disk about 3 inches in diameter. While rolling each pancake, cover remaining dough with a towel to prevent drying. Drizzle a small amount of sesame oil on top of one disk. Place second disk over oil and press disks together. To form Mandarin Pancakes, roll out each layered disk into a 6-inch circle.

3. Heat an ungreased 8-inch skillet. Add layered pancakes. Cook for 3 minutes and turn over. Cook for 1 minute on second side. When properly cooked, pancakes appear dry but not brown. Remove from pan and gently pull apart the 2 pancakes. Wrap in aluminum foil and place in 200° F oven to warm while preparing remaining pancakes.

Makes 16 pancakes.

Variation   For a delicious vegetarian version of Mu Shu Pork, substitute 1 package fried tofu (see BEAN CURD), shredded, for the pork. Add ¼ cup shredded carrots and 2 black mushroom caps, minced, along with the bamboo shoots in step 3.

ENOKITAKE

A cultivated mushroom popular in Japanese cooking, *enokitake* (also spelled *enoki-daki*) are now available most of the year in supermarkets and Asian markets, usually packaged in plastic pouches. Enokitake have needle-thin, cream-colored stems about 3 inches long, topped by a tiny, cream-colored cap. Avoid those with signs of browning. They do not require cleaning. They have a spongy base that should be trimmed away. The delicate flavor is enjoyable both raw and cooked. Raw enokitake are used to garnish salads and other cold dishes. In Japan they are added to soups or wrapped in aluminum foil, sometimes with a morsel of chicken or fish, and grilled over charcoal.

MATSUTAKE

The cap of these wild mushrooms, highly prized in Japan, is dark brown, and the stem thick and meaty. They are very fragrant but tend to be tough. Most American mushroom cooks suggest that they benefit from long, slow cooking. Japanese cooks, however, wrap them in aluminum foil with sake and lemon and grill them over charcoal; they also add them to soups and stews. *Matsutake* can be grilled whole directly over charcoal with a basting of soy sauce; they can also be sliced and steamed in the same pot with rice. Fresh matsutake are available sporadically in late fall and winter, from either domestic sources or imported from Japan. Japanese markets also carry canned matsutake.

Fresh matsutake should be sponged clean and the stem ends trimmed. If not using immediately, see Storage. They will keep for one or two days.

MOREL

Highly esteemed in Europe and North America, morels have pitted, crinkly, cone-shaped brown caps that are hollow inside. In French they are called *morilles* and are featured in restaurants in the spring. They may be stewed in butter and cream and served over toast or pasta. They may be folded into an omelet or spooned into puff pastry shells. Their earthy flavor is especially good with chicken and veal.

Fresh morels are available in some specialty markets in the spring. They should look firm and moist and feel slightly spongy. Use immediately or see Storage. Because of the pitted cap, which easily traps small stones and dirt, morels require careful cleaning with a toothbrush or mushroom brush. Halve lengthwise for easier cleaning. Dried and canned morels are found in specialty markets.

▦ MOREL SOUP

This recipe calls for dried morels so you can make the soup in any season.

> 1 cup (1 oz) dried morels
> 1 medium onion, finely chopped
> 4 tablespoons butter or margarine
> 1 tablespoon flour
> ½ teaspoon *each* salt and dry mustard
>   Pinch freshly grated nutmeg
> 1 teaspoon catsup
> 1½ cups Chicken Stock (see page 560)
> 1 tablespoon fresh lemon juice
> 2 cups half-and-half
> 2 tablespoons dry sherry
>   Chopped parsley, for garnish

1. Place morels in a medium bowl; cover with hot tap water. Let stand until soft (about 30 minutes). Drain, reserving ½ cup of the liquid. Chop morels coarsely.

2. In a 3-quart pan over medium heat, sauté morels and onion in butter stirring often, until onion is soft and beginning to brown.

3. Sprinkle with flour, salt, dry mustard, and nutmeg; add catsup. Remove from heat and gradually blend in reserved soaking liquid and stock. Return to medium heat and bring to a boil; cover. Reduce heat; simmer until morels are tender (about 20 minutes).

4. Use a slotted spoon to remove about ¼ cup of the morels; set aside. Stir lemon juice into mixture in pan. Purée morel mixture in a blender or food processor.

5. Return morel purée to pan over medium heat. Gradually stir in half-and-half and reserved morels. Stir often until soup is steaming hot (do not boil). Taste and add salt if needed. Blend in sherry and serve at once, sprinkling each serving with parsley.

Makes about 5 cups, 4 servings.

Recipes: Three-Mushroom Chicken (see Oyster).

OYSTER

Both wild and cultivated oyster mushrooms can be purchased throughout the year. They have a smooth, broad, fan-shaped or shell-shaped cap that can be white, pale gray, tan, or brown. The underside of the cap is lined with fine gills. They may be quite large but are best when young and 1 to 1½ inches in diameter. They can be sliced and sautéed in butter or oil, with the addition of herbs, onions, garlic, and/or cream. Oyster mushrooms may be dipped in milk, then rolled in crumbs and fried; used in stuffings or soups; and grilled. They have a mild flavor; some claim they taste like oysters.

■ THREE-MUSHROOM CHICKEN

Although costly, wild mushrooms add a woodsy quality to this fricassee that the domestic variety can't match.

> 1   roasting chicken (4 to 5 lb), cut into serving pieces
> ⅓ cup flour
> ⅓ ounce *each* dried porcini, morel, and oyster mushrooms
> 2   tablespoons *each* oil and butter
> 2   shallots, thinly sliced
> 1½ cups dry white wine
> ¾ cup Chicken Stock (see page 560)
> ½ cup whipping cream
>   Salt and freshly ground pepper, to taste

1. Wash chicken pieces and pat dry. Dredge in flour and shake off excess. In a small bowl combine mushrooms. Cover with water; soak until soft (30 to 60 minutes).

2. Heat oil and butter in a large, heavy-bottomed skillet over medium-high heat. Add shallots and sauté until golden brown (about 3 minutes).

3. Add chicken to same skillet and sauté until golden brown (about 7 minutes per side).

4. Drain mushrooms, reserving water. In a small bowl combine ¾ cup of the mushroom water, the wine, and Chicken Stock. Add to skillet, stirring and scraping to loosen any browned bits that may have stuck to bottom of pan. Cook, covered, over medium-low heat until chicken is tender when pierced (20 to 25 minutes).

5. Squeeze all moisture from mushrooms; dice. Add to chicken and stir to blend. Add whipping cream; stir to blend. Season with salt and pepper. Cover; cook gently over low heat to blend flavors (3 to 5 minutes). Serve.

Serves 4 to 6.

PORCINI

This is the Italian name for *Boletus edulis*, occasionally marketed under its French name, *cèpe*. The *porcini* is one of the most highly prized edible mushrooms and grows only in the wild. Specialty markets may carry fresh porcini in the fall and winter; dried and canned porcini are available the year around. They have a light brown, smooth, rounded cap with a spongy underside and a thick, meaty stem. Porcini are generally sliced and cooked slowly in butter, olive oil, or bacon fat, often with garlic or shallots, parsley or other herbs, and sometimes cream. Braised porcini are delicious in pasta sauces, soups, and stews; they may also be minced and used in stuffings. They are delicious raw, sliced thin, and dressed with olive oil, lemon juice, and herbs. Porcini are very fragrant and have an earthy flavor. They are expensive but may be "stretched" by combining with button (domestic) mushrooms.

Recipe: Three-Mushroom Chicken (see Oyster).

SHIITAKE

Also known as black forest mushrooms, *shiitake* are a popular wild mushroom in Japan and have recently been successfully cultivated in the U.S. They are valued for their large, meaty, dark brown caps; the thin, tough stems are usually trimmed away. Shiitake have a smoky flavor that is appealing in Asian dishes. They may be grilled or broiled whole, or sliced and added to soups, noodle dishes, and stir-fries. They are sold fresh the year around in specialty markets; dried shiitake are widely available in Asian markets. Most Chinese cookbooks refer to shiitake simply as "Chinese black mushrooms." The fresh shiitake mushrooms that are now being raised commercially in North America lack the depth of flavor of the imported dried variety and should not be used as a substitute. They are good, however, in place of fresh mushrooms.

STRAW

The Chinese gave these mushrooms their unusual name not because they are long and slender, but because they are grown on beds of rice. These small mushrooms, usually less than 1 inch tall, have light brown, umbrellalike caps. Their mild flavor and slippery texture is best appreciated when in Asian soups and stir-fries. Highly perishable, straw mushrooms are usually canned, even for the local market. Look for them in Asian markets. Rinse well before using.

MUSTARD

Unlike other spices, ground mustard seed (mustard powder) has almost no aroma or character; however, when moistened with water, wine, or other liquid and allowed to stand 10 to 15 minutes, it becomes quite hot.

There are three main types of mustard seed: yellow, brown, and black. Yellow seed is used to make the familiar "ballpark" mustard. Brown seed, stronger in flavor, is used in Dijon-style mustard. A combination of yellow and brown seeds is used in powdered mustard. Black mustard seed, which is slightly milder, is used by Indian cooks.

Use Whole mustard seed is ground to make prepared mustards. Prepared mustard is used as a condiment for sandwiches, sausages, cold cuts, and cold meats. It adds pungency to mayonnaise, salad dressings, and sauces. Whole mustard seed is added to pickles and marinades. Indian cooks flavor many dishes with whole black mustard, including potatoes, cauliflower, cabbage, and green beans. In Chinese restaurants, mustard is served as a dip for fried foods, such as egg rolls.

Mustard seed is 30 to 35 percent oil. The oil pressed from mustard seed is used as a cooking oil in India. Mustard oil is pale yellow; aromatic and pungent when raw, it is milder when cooked. It is used in sautéing vegetables and fish and in making vegetable pickles. Mustard oil is available from Indian grocers. It should be stored in a cool place or in the refrigerator to retard rancidity.

The green leaves of the mustard plant are also edible; when young, they can be eaten raw in a salad and are excellent cooked as a potherb before they have developed the bitter flavor for which the more mature plant is known. See GREENS.

Availability Whole yellow mustard seed is sold on supermarket spice racks, as is powdered mustard. Whole black mustard seed is available from Indian grocers. In addition, supermarkets and specialty food stores carry a wide variety of prepared mustards. Some of the best-known types are described below.

American Mustard This familiar product is made from yellow mustard seed, salt, vinegar, and spices. Smooth and bright yellow (from the addition of turmeric), it is the condiment casually known as "ballpark" mustard, and the traditional spread for hot dogs and hamburgers.

Coarse-grain Mustard The rough texture of this fairly pungent mustard comes from the coarsely ground seed blended into it. Many manufacturers make a coarse-grain mustard. One of the best known is *moutarde de Meaux,* from the French town of Meaux. An English variety of coarse-grain mustard, known as whole-grain mustard, includes white wine, allspice, and black pepper. Enjoy coarse-grain mustards on sandwiches and with sausages.

Dijon Mustard Hot and smooth, this French mustard is made with brown mustard seed and white wine. It is excellent on sandwiches and in salad dressings. Dijon-style mustard is made in the same fashion but is not from Dijon. Both types of mustard often contain added herbs or spices, such as tarragon or green peppercorns.

English Mustard Made from a combination of dark and light mustard seeds, along with flour and turmeric, English mustard is bright yellow, smooth, and quite hot. It is often added to the cheese sauce for Welsh rarebit.

German Mustard A mild, sweet-and-sour variety, German mustard contains herbs, spices, and often caramel. It is good on cold-cut sandwiches and with German sausages. German-style mustard is made in the same fashion but is not from Germany.

Selection Testing prepared mustards is an adventure; new formulas appear regularly on the shelves of specialty stores and well-stocked supermarkets. If ordinary yellow mustard is your standard condiment, make a point of trying a few new ones. Mustards add flavor variety to many foods; use as a dip for grilled or broiled steak or hamburger in place of the more familiar catsup. When buying dry mustard, note that packaged seasonings lose quality after a while; try to buy from a store that restocks its spice section fairly often.

Storage Keep mustard seed and ground mustard in a cool, dry, dark place. They will keep for up to one year. After opening, prepared mustard should be refrigerated; it will keep indefinitely.

Preparation Whole mustard seed may be added directly to pickles and marinades. Indian cooks usually toast black mustard seed in hot oil to bring out its flavor before adding the remaining ingredients. To make prepared mustard from ground mustard, follow package directions; mixture must stand 10 to 15 minutes to develop full flavor. Also see Homemade Mustard, page 323.

■ MUSTARD MADNESS

This recipe is designed for a vertical roaster—an upright, tempered-steel frame used to roast chicken and smaller birds (see VERTICAL ROASTER). The vertical roaster cooks poultry faster than conventional methods because the metal frame, an excellent heat conductor, causes the bird to cook from the inside as well as the outside, sealing in the natural juices. After cooking, large game hens can be halved to make four servings. With a sharp knife or poultry shears, begin to cut at the breastbone and continue along this line all the way around the bird.

> 2 Rock Cornish game hens (1 to 1½ lb each)
> Salt, as needed
> Dijon mustard, as needed

1. Preheat oven to 450° F. Wash and dry game hens. Salt inside and out.

2. Set vertical roasters in a roasting pan containing ¼ inch of water. Lower game hens onto roasters. Truss wings to body of each bird. Paint each game hen with plenty of mustard.

3. Set pan on middle rack of oven and roast for 30 minutes.

4. When birds are done, remove from oven and allow to rest for 30 minutes on frames. Remove from frames to serve.

5. Serve accompanied with additional Dijon mustard.

Serves 2 to 4.

N&O

NAP, TO

To barely coat with one thin sheet, usually when covering a food with its companion sauce. *To nap* implies to add sauce with a light hand, applying in such a way that it covers the food completely.

NECTARINE

As is obvious from its appearance, the nectarine is a smooth-skinned relative of the peach. When ripe, the skin is a deep yellow-gold with a red blush. The flesh is similarly colored, and is very fragrant and juicy when ripe. Some nectarine varieties are clingstone, others freestone.

Use   The nectarine is commonly eaten out of hand, as a snack or dessert. It can also be sliced and enjoyed in pies, tarts, and cobblers, in compotes or fruit salads, and on breakfast cereal. Nectarine purée can be used in sherbets and ice creams, mousses, puddings, and whips.

Availability   The season for domestic nectarines runs from late March through September, with peak supplies in July and August. Imports from the southern hemisphere are available in some markets during the domestic off-season.

Selection   Look for nectarines with good fragrance and color; they should have a deep gold skin with a red blush. Avoid hard green fruit, although a hint of green is natural in some varieties. A ripe nectarine will give slightly to pressure but should not be overly soft. To ripen mature fruit, leave at room temperature for a few days.

Storage   Refrigerate ripe nectarines and use promptly.

Preparation   Nectarines do not require peeling but may be peeled for use in more elegant desserts. Sprinkle cut fruit with lemon juice to prevent browning.

▦ FROZEN NECTARINE TORTE

Peaches or plums also work well in this quick summer dessert, which would be a wonderful finish to a brunch.

>   2   **pounds ripe nectarines, peeled, seeded, and chopped**
>   1   **cup sugar**
>   1   **tablespoon fresh lemon juice**
>   1   **cup whipping cream**
>   1   **cup macaroon crumbs**

In a large bowl mash nectarines with sugar and lemon juice, mixing well. Whip cream to soft peaks and fold into nectarine mixture. Sprinkle ½ cup crumbs on the bottom of a 1-quart mold. Pour in nectarine mixture and top with remaining crumbs. Freeze until firm.

Serves 8.

NEEDLE AND FASTENER

These implements perform related functions: closing a cavity or pocket to hold in a stuffing or to improve appearance (lacing pins); drawing extremities (legs, wings) of a bird close to its body to form an attractive, compact shape (trussing needle, kitchen twine); holding meats, fish, fowl, and vegetables in place as they cook on a grill or under a broiler (skewers); or inserting strips of fat into lean meats to increase flavor and moistness (larding needle).

KITCHEN TWINE

For trussing or tying up poultry and meats, with or without a needle, or tying up cheesecloth bags of herbs for bouquet garni, use a heavy-gauge, natural-fiber string that can withstand high oven heat (linen is best because it won't burn under normal usage). Coated household sewing thread will impart a waxy taste to food, and nylon thread can melt. Uncoated cotton thread is satisfactory but is thin and may cut fingers when pulled tight.

LARDING NEEDLES

Of the two types of larding needles, one has a long, slender trough (about 10 inches) attached to a wooden handle. To use, strips of pork fat are set in the trough, then the needle is inserted into the roast with the grain of the meat and is rotated as it proceeds through from one end to the other. The needle is withdrawn slowly so that the fat is not pulled out. This process is repeated at regular intervals. A shorter version (about 6 inches long) has an eye, rather than a trough, and is designed for larding a shallow surface. Both needles are stainless steel. For an illustration of larding, see photograph on page 338.

POULTRY LACERS

These short, narrow shafts, with points at one end and loops or angled heads at the other, are used for closing poultry cavities, for securing pockets of stuffed meats, and for maintaining the shape of rolled meats. Widely available, they are made of stainless steel and come in sets of six pins with twine. The pins are set in place, then the twine is crisscrossed between skewers and pulled tight like the laces on a pair of boots. The loops or bent ends make it easier to remove the pins after roasting.

SKEWERS

Flat skewers are preferable because food won't slip when skewers are turned on the grill or under the broiler. Those made of stainless steel all have a loop or decorative head at one end so chunks of food won't slide off. Always soak bamboo skewers in water for at least 15 minutes before using on a grill or under a broiler so they won't burn. These picks make good cake testers as well. Sizes range from 8 to 14 inches.

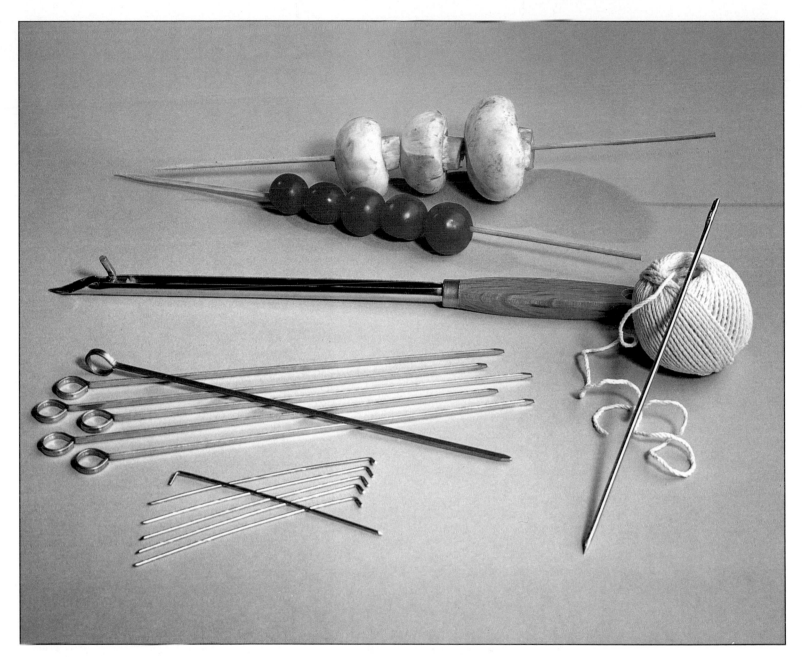

TRUSSING NEEDLE

Trussing holds the appendages of a bird together during roasting, makes a boned roast more compact so that it has a neater appearance and a more uniform shape that allows even cooking, and closes off the cavity of a bird or a pocket of stuffed meat. Trussing needles are made of stainless steel and are most commonly 8 inches long. They are used with uncoated heavyweight string made of a natural fiber (see Kitchen Twine, opposite page).

Recipes and Related Information
Bouquet Garni, 56; Lard, 338; Truss, 584.

NONREACTIVE

In the presence of an acidic food, certain metals—aluminum, cast iron, and unlined copper—produce a chemical reaction. The result is an off color or taste. When one of these foods—such as tomatoes, vinegar, lemon juice, or wine—is an ingredient in a recipe, most often you will be directed to mix or cook in a "nonreactive" or "nonaluminum" pan to avoid this undesirable reaction. Cookware made of stainless steel, enameled steel or cast iron, anodized aluminum, or a cladded metal doesn't interact with acids and is safe to use with acidic ingredients (see MATERIALS FOR COOKWARE).

Implements used by the cook to secure cavities or hold food in place include (top to bottom): bamboo skewers, larding needle, trussing needle, kitchen twine, metal skewers, poultry lacers.

An assortment of Chinese noodles of various shapes; clockwise from upper right: bean threads, two sizes of dried wheat-flour noodles, precooked rice noodles, and fresh wrappers—square for wontons and round for siu mai or potstickers.

NOODLE, ASIAN

Although many Westerners think of rice as the primary starch in Asian cuisine, noodles also play a major role. Unlike Western noodles, which are always made with wheat flour, those from Asia may have as their base wheat flour, rice flour, or vegetable starches such as yam, soybean, and potato. The best-known Asian noodle types are discussed on the following pages by country.

Due to the intertwined histories of Asian countries, noodle varieties overlap considerably throughout that part of the world. Wheat noodles (both with egg and without), rice noodles, and bean-starch or potato-starch noodles are employed in almost all these cuisines, as are small wrappers often made of rice flour. Although size and texture may vary slightly from country to country, substitutions are certainly possible and not problematic. Chinese egg noodles, for example, are widely available in supermarkets and are a fine substitute for Japanese *ramen*, Thai *bà mee*, Korean *gougsou*, or Philippine *pancit canton*.

Use The Asian cook uses noodles in a great variety of ways. Noodles give body to soup, as in the Vietnamese *phở bo* (beef noodle soup) or the chilled Korean beef and noodle soup called *naeng myun*. Noodles are boiled and then eaten both hot and cold, with toppings or with dipping sauces. Examples include spicy *dan dan mein* (egg noodles tossed with peanut sauce, a specialty of the Szechuan province of China) and Japanese *zaru soba* (cold buckwheat noodles accompanied with a soy-based dipping sauce). Noodles can be steamed, then stir-fried, as in the popular Thai dish called *pad Thai* (rice noodles tossed with bean sprouts, cooked egg, peanuts, and dried shrimp). Chinese cooks coil steamed vermicelli into thick pancakes, fry them on both sides until crisp, and top them with a stew or stir-fry.

Almost every Asian cuisine can boast a variety of noodle dumplings or stuffed noodle dishes. Examples include Chinese wonton and *fun* (sheets of steamed rice noodles, stuffed with shrimp and green onion), Japanese *gyoza* (pan-fried dumplings), and the Korean beef dumplings called *mandu*. In addition, noodles are used in stuffings, as in the Vietnamese *cha gio*, fried spring rolls filled with softened cellophane noodles, pork, and crab.

Availability If you live near an Asian neighborhood, you should be able to find all sorts of fresh Asian-style noodles and wrappers. Most well-stocked supermarkets carry some varieties.

Selection Buy fresh noodles from a market with a rapid turnover or from a store that receives fresh supplies daily.

Storage Fresh wheat noodles should be refrigerated and used within two or three days. If truly fresh when purchased, these noodles may be wrapped with plastic wrap overwrapped with aluminum foil, and frozen for up to three months. Rice-flour noodles are often stored at room temperature in markets because they stiffen when chilled; they may be stored at room temperature for two days or kept in the refrigerator for up to one week. To soften noodles stiffened by refrigeration, steam briefly in a covered steamer just until softened, then gently run hot water over noodles and drain. If very fresh, they may also be frozen for up to two months. Dried noodles of all kinds will keep indefinitely in a cool, dry place.

Preparation Many recipes using Asian noodles call for the noodles to be boiled prior to further treatment, whether combining with a sauce, stir-frying, or braising. If you are using homemade or packaged fresh egg noodles, fluff them a little first to loosen the clumps, then drop them into a large pot of rapidly boiling, lightly salted water. Stir immediately with long chopsticks or a spoon to separate the noodles, and begin testing them as soon as the water returns to a boil. Most will be done within a few seconds. Dried noodles take longer; follow package directions. Rice noodles generally do not need preliminary boiling if they are to be cooked in a sauce. Toss the noodles under running water by hand so you can feel when they are thoroughly cooled. Drain well and toss with a little oil to keep them from sticking. If sufficiently oiled and tightly wrapped, noodles can be kept for several hours or even overnight, covered, in the refrigerator.

CHINA

Noodles have been an important part of the Chinese diet since the Han Dynasty period (206 B.C. to A.D. 220), when the Chinese learned the technology of milling flour from an unknown neighbor to the west. Before this time, most grains were simply boiled whole, as rice is today; but finely milled flour could be combined with water, kneaded, and worked into various shapes, and cooked by various methods to produce noodles, dumplings, and breads.

Bean-Starch Noodles Also known as bean threads, glass noodles, cellophane noodles, silver noodles, Chinese vermicelli, transparent noodles, and long rice, these threadlike noodles are made from mung bean starch. Folded into skeins about 6 inches long, they are packaged in plastic or net bags. They may be soaked in hot water until soft (about 30 seconds), then used in stir-fries, soups, and salads. The soaked noodles have a slippery texture and a glassy look. Like dried rice noodles (see below), they may also be deep-fried without presoaking.

Dried Rice Noodles Also known as rice stick or rice vermicelli, these noodles made from rice flour are as thin as string. They are usually coiled into nests and packaged in plastic bags. Dried noodles may be deep-fried quickly in 400° F oil. They will puff dramatically into crisp, brittle white noodles, which provide the crunchy base for Chinese Chicken Salad. Dried noodles may also be soaked in warm water until soft and slippery, then stir-fried or added to soups.

Egg Noodles Chinese markets offer both fresh and dried egg noodles in several widths. Some supermarkets also carry fresh Chinese egg noodles. These wheat-based noodles cut in shoelace lengths are very popular in northern China, where wheat is the predominant starch. The noodles are added to soups for a quick lunch. They may also be boiled and served with meat or peanut sauce, or boiled, then fried into a crisp pancake and topped with a stew or sauce. Boiled noodles are also eaten cold dressed with oil, soy sauce, vinegar, and green onions.

Fresh Rice Noodles Many Asian markets carry cooked fresh noodles made from rice flour, which are sold in wide sheets or cut into ¾-inch widths. Soft, smooth, flimsy, and very bland, they absorb other flavors well. These slippery noodles are used in many dim sum dishes; served both cold and hot, they may be stuffed with ground pork or simply garnished with soy sauce, shrimp, and minced green onions. Narrow rice noodles are frequently used in soups or topped with stew for a quick, nourishing lunch.

Nonegg Noodles Chinese markets also offer both fresh and dried wheat noodles containing little or no egg. They are used in the same way as egg noodles.

Shrimp- and Crab-Flavored Noodles These dried noodles have been flavored with the roe of shrimp or crab. They are particularly good in soup but may be used as any other dried Chinese noodle.

Wonton or Egg Roll Wrappers The same dough in egg noodles is used for wonton skins and egg roll wrappers. These thin, square wrappers are available fresh in many supermarkets, packaged in plastic.

JAPAN

Noodles are among the most popular foods eaten in Japan, with buckwheat noodles (*soba*) more common in the north and wheat noodles (*udon*) in the south. At lunchtime, shoppers and workers throughout Japan stop for a quick bowl of noodles in one of that country's countless noodle shops. Also supplying the never-ending Japanese passion for noodles, street vendors can be found dishing up their wares at all hours of the day and late into the night. In the summer, many diners opt for chilled noodles served with a soy-based dipping sauce; in cold weather, the preference is for the warmth of noodles in steaming broth.

Harusame Also called *saifun*, *harusame* are long thin noodles made of potato and cornstarch. They are used in soups and salads or deep-fried for a garnish.

Hiyamugi These dried wheat noodles, about as long as spaghetti but slightly thicker, are packaged in bunches and tied with a cloth ribbon. They are usually eaten cold, served with garnishes and a dipping sauce.

Rice is an indispensable food in Asia. It may be cooked as a grain or ground and made into noodles or paperlike sheets.

Mai Fun This is the Japanese name for Chinese-style rice vermicelli. It is deep-fried and used as a salad base or garnish.

Ramen This is the Japanese name for Chinese-style egg noodles. Popular among the Japanese, they are often packaged with concentrated or dehydrated soup.

Soba Long, thin, and brownish gray, *soba* contains buckwheat flour. It may be eaten both cold with a dipping sauce or hot in broth. Variations include *cha soba* (a green-tinged buckwheat noodle containing powdered green tea) and *nama soba* (fresh soba made with egg and dusted with potato flour).

Somen These fine white wheat-flour noodles are similar to *hiyamugi*, but thinner. They are usually eaten cold. Variations include *cha somen* (containing powdered green tea) and *tomago somen* (containing egg yolk).

Udon Usually eaten in soup, with various garnishes, *udon* is a long, thick, wheat noodle with square edges. It is available both fresh and dried; fresh udon freezes well.

KOREA

Koreans are great noodle lovers and enjoy Chinese and Japanese noodles in addition to their own varieties. *Dang myun*, one specifically Korean variety, is a skinny, grayish tan noodle that resembles a cellophane noodle. It is made from potato and sweet potato starch and is cut in very long lengths. Like cellophane noodles, it is soaked in boiling water before use in soups and stir-fries. *Gougsou* is the long, thin, wheat flour noodle of Korea. It is widely used in hot and cold soups, garnished with vegetables and fish cake, and in stir-fries with fiery chili sauces. *Naeng myun* is a long, very thin noodle made from buckwheat flour and potato starch or cornstarch. It is boiled briefly and usually served cold in an icy broth with a variety of garnishes.

MALAYSIA, SINGAPORE, AND INDONESIA

The noodles available in these three countries are very similar to those found in China and elsewhere in Asia. *Laksa* is a thick rice vermicelli used in soups and curried dishes with coconut-milk sauces. *Beehoon* (or *bihun*), a thinner rice vermicelli, is used in curried dishes, stir-fries, and soups.

Bà mee (or *bakmie*) and *hokkien mee* are Chinese-style egg noodles used in curries and stir-fries. These countries also cook with a bean-starch noodle known as *sohoon* or *tunghoon* in Malaysia and Singapore and *sotanghoon* in Indonesia.

PHILIPPINES

Pancit is the Filipino word for noodle. As in China, the many varieties of pancit may be made with wheat, rice, or bean starch. *Pancit canton* is a long, round (as opposed to flat), Chinese-style wheat noodle; it is precooked and dried for use in soups and stir-fries. *Pancit mami* is a flat Chinese-style egg noodle used in soups; *pancit miki* is similar but contains less egg. *Miswa* is an extremely fine wheat noodle that cooks in seconds; it is an ingredient in soups. *Pancit luglug* is a thick, dried, rice vermicelli incorporated in soups. *Pancit sotanghon* is a bean-starch noodle used in stir-fries and stuffings. In addition to the many pancit dishes, Philippine cooks make a type of egg roll called *lumpia*. Lumpia wrappers are very delicate, thin, crêpelike rounds made with cornstarch. Stuffed with a variety of fillings, they may be eaten as is or deep-fried.

THAILAND AND BURMA

Most of the noodles used in Thailand and Burma have equivalents or close cousins among the Chinese noodles. Thai egg noodles, called *bà mee*, are made from wheat flour and are about the size of Chinese egg noodles or Japanese ramen. Available fresh and frozen in Asian markets, they are used in soups and stir-fries and in Burmese curries. In Burma they are known as *kyet-oo kaukswe*. A dried version called *kaukswe* is also used in Burmese curries.

Fresh wide rice noodles are known as *gwaytio* in Thailand and *kyasangi* in Burma. They may be purchased in either wide sheets or precut ribbons. A dried version called *hsan kwkse* is used by Burmese cooks. Thai cooks also use thin dried rice noodles, *jantaboon*, which are not as thin as Chinese rice vermicelli and must be soaked and boiled. The Thai version of dried rice vermicelli is known as *sen mee;* in Burma, it is *hsan kyasan*. Sen mee are used in the famous Thai noodle dish *mee krob* and in soups.

The Thai version of bean-starch noodles is called *wun sen*. In Burma, these noodles are known as *pekyasan*. They are used in soups and curries and in Thai salads, in combination with cool crisp greens and warm grilled meat.

VIETNAM

Some of the most widely used Vietnamese noodles are very similar to Chinese noodles. *Bánh phở* are flat rice noodles, available both fresh and dried. They resemble spaghetti but are slightly thinner and are primarily used in soups. *Bánh ưởt* are uncut rice-noodle sheets similar to fresh Chinese rice noodles. They are cut into widths for soups and stir-fries. *Bún* is a dried rice vermicelli similar to the Chinese product. When soaked, it is used in soups, grilled-meat salads, and stuffings for rice-paper rolls. *Bánh canh* are clear short noodles, slightly thicker than spaghetti, made from rice, wheat, corn, or other starches. The dried noodles are reconstituted quickly in boiling water, then used in stir-fries and soups. *Bún tau,* resembling Chinese bean-starch noodles, are an ingredient in stuffings and steamed meat loaves. *Bánh tráng* are translucent, round rice-paper wrappers used to make Vietnamese spring rolls and as a fresh wrapper for cooked meats.

■ STIR-FRIED NOODLES WITH SHREDDED PORK
Lo mein

This style of stir-frying noodles along with their toppings is sometimes called chow mein, but *lo mein* (mixed noodles) is more descriptive.

- ½ **pound thin Chinese-style egg noodles, boiled and drained**
- 4 **to 5 tablespoons oil**
- ¼ **cup Rich Chicken Stock (see page 561)**
- 1 **tablespoon soy sauce**
- 1 **teaspoon salt**
- 1 **tablespoon shredded fresh ginger**
- 2 **green onions, cut into 1-inch lengths**
- ½ **cup shredded pork**
- 2 **or 3 large leaves bok choy, cut into 2-inch slices**

1. Toss noodles with 2 tablespoons oil to coat evenly; set aside. (This may be done several hours ahead.) Combine stock, soy sauce, and salt; set aside.

2. Heat wok over medium-high heat, and add 1 tablespoon oil. Add ginger and green onions; cook until fragrant. Add pork and stir-fry until meat starts to lose its raw color. Add bok choy and stir-fry 1 minute longer, then transfer mixture to a warm plate.

3. Wipe wok clean with a paper towel and add 1 or 2 tablespoons oil. Reduce heat to medium. Swirl wok to cover sides with oil, then add noodles. Cook without stirring for 1 minute, then begin stirring and tossing noodles to brown them in places. Add a little more oil, if necessary, to keep noodles from sticking.

4. When noodles are heated through and lightly browned, add stock mixture and stir to loosen noodles from pan. Return pork mixture to pan and toss with noodles. Turn heat to high and continue cooking and stirring until liquid is nearly gone, then transfer to serving plate.

Serves 4 with other dishes.

■ SHANGHAI SPRING ROLLS

Manufacturers of Chinese noodles make very thin wrappers, 7 to 8 inches square, for spring rolls. If packaged spring-roll skins are too thick, roll them through the thinnest setting of a pasta machine to yield a rectangle twice the original size, then cut them in half.

- 16 **square spring-roll wrappers**
  Pork and Shrimp Stuffing (see page 191)
- ¼ **cup bean sprouts, cut into 2-inch lengths, or finely shredded bamboo shoots**
- 1 **egg white (optional)**
  Oil, for deep-frying

1. Place a wrapper with one edge toward you. Spread 1 tablespoon stuffing along edge to within ½ inch of end. Lay a few bean sprouts alongside stuffing. Roll up slightly to cover stuffing, fold in sides to seal ends, and roll up in remaining wrapper. Moisten edge with a little egg white or water to seal. Repeat with remaining wrappers.

2. Heat oil in a frying pan to 375° F. Fry rolls, a few at a time, until golden brown. Check a roll to make sure stuffing has thoroughly cooked, and adjust temperature or cooking time as necessary. Serve whole, or cut into bite-sized pieces.

Makes 16 rolls.

Crisp, fried Shanghai Spring Rolls are delicious dipped in either a sweet-and-sour sauce or hot Chinese mustard. When made with an egg-noodle wrapper, these rolls are known as egg rolls.

■ BEEF SOUP WITH NOODLES
Phở bo

Restaurants specializing in *phở*, a sort of soup-plus-salad served in a single bowl, are found in many Vietnamese cities, and they are an increasingly common sight in Vietnamese neighborhoods in this country as well. Phở (pronounced more or less *far*) is traditionally served for breakfast, but it is equally good to eat for lunch or a light supper. You will need to shop at an Asian market for many of the ingredients. Rice sticks are dried rice flour noodles.

    5 pounds meaty beef bones (ribs, neck, or shank)
    1 pound boneless stewing beef
      (chuck or short ribs; see Note)
    1 cinnamon stick
    3 pods star anise
    1 medium onion, sliced (include skin if clean)
   10 to 12 slices fresh ginger
      Salt or fish sauce, to taste
    ½ pound tender beef (sirloin or flatiron; see Note),
      thinly sliced
    2 cups bean sprouts
    2 or 3 fresh chiles, sliced
    2 medium tomatoes, cut into wedges (optional)
      Lemon or lime wedges
      Sprigs of fresh coriander, mint, or basil
    ½ pound rice sticks, cooked, boiled,
      drained, and cooled
    1 medium onion, sliced as thinly as possible
      Chile sauce

1. Rinse bones and place in a large stockpot. Cover amply with cold water. Bring to a boil and cook 15 minutes, skimming off foam that rises to surface. When foaming stops, add stewing beef, cinnamon, star anise, onion, and ginger. Reduce heat so stock barely simmers and cook from 6 to 12 hours. Begin checking stewing beef after an hour or so and remove when quite tender but not yet falling apart.

2. Strain stock, and skim off and discard fat from surface. Season to taste with salt or fish sauce. Stock may be prepared up to 3 days ahead and stored uncovered in the refrigerator.

3. Bring stock to a boil. Slice stewed and raw beef thinly across grain. Arrange bean sprouts, chiles, tomatoes (if used), lemon wedges, and herbs on a platter or individual plates. Warm deep soup bowls with hot water. Place some rice sticks in each bowl and top with cooked and raw beef and sliced onion. Ladle hot stock over all (heat of stock will cook raw beef). Serve immediately, each person adding sprouts, herbs, chiles, tomatoes, lemon wedges, fish sauce, and chile sauce to taste. Serve with both chopsticks and a soup spoon.

Serves 6 to 8.

Note Blade chuck roast or steak is often a good buy, and if you bone it yourself, it can provide both the stewing and the tender cuts for this dish. Look for a 3-pound roast or several steaks with a long, slender blade bone. The flatiron muscle on top of the blade bone (the opposite side from ribs and backbone) is tender enough for quick cooking, but the remaining muscles require longer cooking. The rib eye, the large round muscle alongside the ribs, falls somewhere between in tenderness, and is best reserved for another use, such as a Thai curry. Add the bones to the stockpot.

Variation Other cuts of beef, including organ meats, can be used in place of the stewing beef. Tripe is especially good to use this way. If shanks are used for the stock, the shank meat can be sliced and included in the soup. One of the most popular items in phở restaurants is beef tendons, which become tender and gelatinous when simmered in the stock for many hours. A similar soup may be made from chicken, in which case it is called *phở ga*. Use a 4- to 5-pound stewing fowl with giblets (but omit liver) and half the amount of spices and ginger. Simmer for only 2 to 3 hours. Remove cooked meat and shred it by hand, then assemble soup as directed above, with some sliced giblets in each bowl.

Recipes and Related Information
Chinese Chicken Salad, 508; Potstickers, 191; Wontons, 192.

NOPALES

The "leaves" or pads of the prickly pear cactus are nopales. The tear-shaped pads are pale green to dark green, with small sharp spines that are usually removed before the cactus reaches the market. Cooked nopales have a taste and texture comparable to green beans, with a subtle tartness that is quite special.

Use Nopales are frequently eaten in Mexico and the southwestern United States. They are steamed, diced, and added to scrambled eggs or tossed with tomato, onion, and vinaigrette to make a salad.

Availability Canned or bottled nopales and *nopalitos* (sliced or diced cactus) packed in vinegar or water are available in Latin markets and in well-stocked supermarkets in some parts of the country. Fresh nopales are occasionally found in Latin and southwestern markets.

Selection Select pale, thin nopales. The thicker, darker ones are less tender.

Storage Store fresh nopales in the refrigerator and use within a few days. Once opened, canned nopales should be transferred to a nonmetal container and refrigerated. Water-packed nopales will keep for one week in the original liquid; pickled nopales will keep indefinitely in their brine.

Preparation Some species are spineless. If you get the thorny kind, you'll have to scrape the spines from the sides and edges (use tongs to handle; the spines are nasty). Leave as much of the green skin as possible. Cut nopales into small pieces and cook until tender in well-salted water.

Cooked nopales may have a slippery quality somewhat like okra, but there are several ways to minimize this. One method is to rinse the cooked nopales, drain them in a colander, cover with a damp towel to keep them from drying out, and let them stand for about 30 minutes. Another way is to cook diced nopales in an ungreased pan with several chunks of onion and one or two cloves of garlic until nopales are no longer slippery (about 5 minutes). Rinse in a colander, then proceed with recipe.

■ NOPALITO SALAD

This lively salad from the southwestern United States is based on poached strips of nopales, dark-green cactus pads, and jicama, a large, root vegetable with white flesh and a slightly sweet, crunchy flavor.

½ small red onion
1 jar (12 to 14 oz) nopalitos tiernos en rajas (young nopal in strips)
1 or 2 canned or pickled jalapeño chiles, seeded and sliced (optional)
1 small *or* ½ large jicama
2 medium cucumbers, peeled
2 small green bell peppers, trimmed and seeded
2 small red bell peppers, trimmed and seeded
3 thick green onions
1 can (4 oz) sliced black olives
¼ cup minced parsley
2 heaping teaspoons minced cilantro
½ cup grated Monterey jack cheese or crumbled farmer cheese
2 ripe, firm avocados
1 jar (2 oz) sliced pimientos, drained and rinsed, for garnish

Lime Dressing

½ cup peanut or olive oil
⅓ cup fresh lime juice (about 4 small limes)
3 medium cloves garlic, crushed
½ teaspoon sugar
¼ teaspoon ground cumin seed
Salt and freshly ground pepper, to taste

1. Prepare dressing and chill for about 1 hour.

2. Slice onion into thin rings and place in a bowl of ice water. (This will take bite out of onion.)

3. Drain *nopalitos* and place in a large bowl. Nopalitos are usually packed with at least one jalapeño chile, along with other items such as onion slices and garlic. If a spicy salad is desired, halve jalapeño, remove seeds, cut

in strips, and mix with nopalitos. Remove other elements. If you prefer an extremely spicy salad, add one or both jalapeños.

4. Peel jicama with a small sharp knife by inserting knife tip just under beige skin and pulling off peel in strips. Discard tough flesh from root end and top. Julienne jicama into matchstick strips (about ¼ inch by ¼ inch by 1½ inches) and add to nopalitos. Julienne cucumbers, green peppers, and red peppers in matchsticks, and add to nopal mixture. Finely mince green onions, including crisp parts of green tops, and add to salad. Add olives, parsley, cilantro, and grated cheese.

5. Remove garlic from dressing and discard. At the last moment, slice avocados and add to salad. Immediately dress and toss salad to keep avocado from darkening. Let salad chill in refrigerator, marinating in dressing.

6. To serve, decorate top of salad with pimiento slices. Drain onions and scatter on top.

Serves 8.

Lime Dressing Whisk together oil and lime juice; stir in garlic, sugar, cumin, and salt and pepper, to taste.

Makes ¾ cup.

Nopales, the pads of the prickly pear cactus, make a stunning salad with a special southwestern flavor.

When rolled and sliced, the multiple ingredients in Makizushi form a beautiful mosaic. The sushi can be prepared a few hours ahead and stored in the refrigerator.

NORI

The Japanese word *nori* means paper-thin sheets of dried seaweed. It is consumed in great quantity by the Japanese, primarily in sushi and rice dishes. The sheets are dark green or dark brown and resemble carbon paper.

Use   Japanese chefs use nori to wrap sushi and rice balls. Besides holding fish or rice in place, the dark nori adds a visual contrast to the white rice and a pleasantly crunchy, faintly marine flavor.

Availability   Sheets of nori are usually found 10 to a package. They may be sold flat or folded in half, usually packaged in plastic. Some varieties are sold in tin canisters but they are more expensive. Some nori, identified as *yakinori,* is pretoasted by the manufacturer. *Ajitsuke-nori* has been brushed with soy sauce. Some manufacturers market nori in prepackaged bundles of short toasted strips; each package is an individual serving, to be crumbled on breakfast rice or wrapped around hot rice. Look for nori in Japanese markets.

Storage   Store leftover nori in an airtight container with the moisture-absorbing granules from the package or canister. Freeze nori if not using within a few weeks.

Preparation   Toasting brings out the full flavor and best texture in nori. Using tongs, wave one side only of a sheet of nori over a gas flame until the nori is crisp (a few seconds).

■ MAKIZUSHI

This rolled sushi is a favorite take-out food in Japan. You can make it a few hours ahead of time, but the seaweed, or *nori,* will not be as crisp. You need a mat to roll the sushi ingredients. Buy a special bamboo mat at an Asian market, or use an undyed, flexible straw place mat.

> 4   sheets nori, toasted
>   Sushi Rice (see page 233)
> 1   cucumber
> 1   pickled daikon (Japanese radish)
>   Wasabi, to taste
> ½   pound fish or shellfish, thinly sliced

1. Lay a sheet of nori on a bamboo or undyed, flexible straw mat. Spread one fourth of the Sushi Rice on nori, leaving a 1-inch margin along far edge of nori and a ½-inch margin along either side. Flatten rice with back of a wooden spoon.

2. Cut a strip of cucumber to equal width of nori. Repeat with pickled daikon. Place cucumber and daikon down center of nori (parallel to long end). Spread with thin layer of *wasabi*. Place slices of fish down center and gently press down to firm ingredients.

3. Lift bamboo mat with thumbs, holding ingredients with fingers, and roll so that nori wraps around filling. Roll tightly, and remove mat. Slice each roll into 6 to 8 pieces.

Makes 24 to 32 pieces.

NUT

Although the botanical definition is slightly different, the word *nut* commonly refers to a seed or fruit with an edible kernel surrounded by a hard or brittle shell. By this definition, nuts commonly used in the kitchen include almond, brazil nut, cashew, chestnut, hazelnut, macadamia nut, peanut, pecan, pine nut, pistachio nut, and walnut (see individual entries).

Use   Nuts play a great variety of roles in the kitchen. In their shells, nuts are often served as is, either as an appetizer with cocktails or as a dessert with a glass of port. Shelled nuts, either alone or in combination, can be roasted, salted or unsalted, and served with cocktails. Nut and dried fruit combinations are marketed as trail mix for hikers because of their long storage life.

Nuts add texture to almost every category of dish, from breakfast foods to desserts. At breakfast, nuts appear in dry cereals such as granola. They may be added to breakfast muffins or sprinkled on top of a fruit compote.

When toasted, nuts make a pleasing addition to salads and sautéed vegetables. Toasted walnuts with raw Belgian endive or sautéed almonds with green beans are just two among countless examples.

Because of their texture and oily richness, nuts are widely used in main courses. Buttery sautéed almonds or toasted pine nuts may be spooned on top of pan-fried sole. Chestnuts may be braised with chicken or game. Peanuts are the unusual ingredient in chicken and groundnut (peanut) stew (from western Africa). Iranian cooks braise duck in a walnut and pomegranate sauce.

Many types of breads and grains are especially complemented by nuts. Chopped walnuts add nutty richness to yeast breads and quick breads; chestnuts or toasted pecans are an ingredient in bread stuffings. Almonds or pine nuts are often added to rice pilaf for contrast.

As an enrichment or thickener, nuts may be used in soups and sauces, as in the Spanish *romesco* or the Mexican *chiles en nogada*. Nuts are even used in beverages: Ground almonds, for example, yield "almond milk" used to make orgeat, a syrup used as the base of a refreshing almond drink.

Nuts appear in many desserts: ice cream, cakes, pies, tarts, cookies, candies, soufflés, puddings, and dessert sauces. Pecan pie is a traditional Thanksgiving dessert in the southern United States; pecan pralines are another popular southern sweet. Almonds are used in nougat, nut brittle, and candy bars. Toasted ground walnuts or almonds can take the place of flour in a cake. Toasted nuts are sprinkled on top of sundaes and banana splits and are folded into cookie doughs and cake batters. Whole nuts can be candied in syrup and enjoyed as a sweetmeat.

Nuts are also valued for their edible oils. Hazelnut, walnut, almond, and peanut oils are widely used in the kitchen. See OIL for information on the various properties and uses of these nut oils.

Because of their high oil content, most nuts may also be ground into a thick spreadable paste. Peanut butter is probably the most popular example; its many uses and virtues are well known. Other nuts, such as almonds and hazelnuts, may be toasted or fried to develop more flavor, then ground into butter, seasoned with salt and/or sugar, and used as a spread.

Availability   See individual nut entries.

Selection   Unshelled nuts should feel heavy for their size. Shelled nuts turn rancid quickly; buy them from a market with a rapid turnover.

Storage   Their high fat content subjects nuts to rapid rancidity. Heat, light, and moisture promote fat oxidation; to retard rancidity, nuts should be kept in a cool, dark, dry place. Shelled nuts deteriorate faster than nuts in their shells. Freezing shelled nuts will effectively slow their decline. For specific storage instructions, see individual entries.

Preparation   *About skinning nuts:* Many nuts have thin papery skins that are often bitter or tannic. To remove these skins, nuts may be either blanched or toasted. After blanching briefly in boiling water, nuts are wrapped in a towel to steam, then rubbed with the towel to remove the skins. Skinned nuts should then be heated briefly in a 325°F oven to dry them out. This is an excellent method for almonds and pistachios. Hazelnuts and Brazil nuts may be toasted in a 325°F oven for about 10 minutes, then wrapped in a towel to steam. Skins may then be rubbed off easily.

About toasting nuts: Toasting nuts brings out their full flavor and crisps their texture. Nuts used in pastries, cakes, cookies, salads, sautés, and stuffings are almost always improved by a brief toasting in a 325°F oven. Use a rimmed baking sheet, shake sheet occasionally, and remove nuts when fragrant; they will crisp as they cool. When a recipe requires only 1 to 2 tablespoons toasted nuts, the preferred method is to place whole or ground nuts in a dry skillet over low heat. Stir constantly until aromatic oils are released and nuts color slightly (about 2 to 4 minutes depending upon size). Remove from pan to cool.

About grinding nuts: Because they are so rich in oil, nuts quickly turn to paste if grinding is not monitored. A nut mill (often preferred by serious bakers) will keep ground nuts dry and light. *To grind nuts in a food processor:* It's best to mix the nuts with some of the flour or sugar called for in the recipe. Even so, be careful not to overprocess (check every 10 seconds), or else you might get nut paste.

Recipes and Related Information
Food Processor, 240; Grate, Grater, 281.

NUTMEG

The seed of the apricotlike fruit of the nutmeg tree, nutmeg is encased in a hard shell that in turn is covered with a fragile webbed membrane called mace (see MACE). The mace is removed and the seed dried until the kernel rattles in the shell. The shell is then broken open and the nutmeg kernel removed. The kernel, the part used in the kitchen, is ovoid, dark brown, and about 1 inch in length. When grated it releases a slightly sweet and spicy aroma. Today, most nutmeg comes from Indonesia, Grenada, and Ceylon.

Use   Nutmeg is an excellent baking spice, used in pumpkin pie and custard pie, sweet breads, spice cakes, and cookies. It flatters all custard dishes and is traditionally sprinkled over eggnog. Nutmeg is often added to cheese sauce and other cheese dishes. Nutmeg complements spinach, potatoes, and winter squashes.

Freshly grated nutmeg is much more pungent and appealing than the storebought ground spice. With an inexpensive hand grater, home cooks can easily grate their own whole nutmeg.

Availability   Both whole and ground nutmeg are found on supermarket spice racks.

Selection Packaged seasonings lose quality after a while; try to buy from a store that restocks its spice section fairly often.

Storage Keep both whole and ground nutmeg in a cool, dark, dry place. Whole nutmeg will stay pungent for two years; replace ground nutmeg every six months.

Preparation Grate whole nutmeg just before using; add ground nutmeg directly to dish.

■ BAKED NUTMEG DOUGHNUTS

Although these doughnut-shaped rolls are baked, not fried, they resemble a doughnut in flavor. The dough does not require kneading and is light and puffy in texture.

    2 packages active dry yeast
    ¼ cup warm (105° to 115° F) water
    1⅓ cups warm (105° to 115° F) milk
    ¼ cup sugar
    2 teaspoons freshly grated nutmeg
    1 teaspoon salt
    ¼ teaspoon ground cinnamon
    ⅔ cup butter
    4½ to 5 cups flour
    2 eggs
    ½ cup Vanilla Granulated Sugar (see page 585)

1. Sprinkle yeast over the water in large bowl of electric mixer. Let stand until soft (about 5 minutes). Stir in milk, sugar, nutmeg, salt, cinnamon, and ⅓ cup butter.

2. Add 3 cups flour. Mix to blend, then beat at medium speed until smooth and elastic (about 5 minutes). Beat in eggs, then gradually stir in about 1½ cups flour to make a soft dough.

3. Transfer to a greased bowl, cover with plastic wrap, and let rise in a warm place until doubled (about 1 hour). Stir down dough.

4. Turn dough out on a well-floured surface (use some of remaining flour), and shape with floured hands into a flattened ball. Coat well with flour. Lightly roll out about ½ inch thick. Cut with a floured 2½-inch doughnut cutter. Place doughnuts about 2 inches apart on greased baking sheets.

5. Brush lightly with some of remaining butter, melted, and let rise until nearly doubled (about 30 minutes).

6. Preheat oven to 425° F. Bake until doughnuts are golden brown (about 10 minutes). Brush warm doughnuts with remaining melted butter and roll lightly in Vanilla Granulated Sugar.

Makes 3 dozen doughnuts.

> **Recipes and Related Information**
> *Apple Dumplings With Nutmeg Sauce, 193; Grate, Grater, 281; Herb and Spice Blends, 301.*

OIL

The edible oils used in the kitchen are expressed from a variety of sources: seeds (such as sesame); legumes (such as peanuts and soybeans); plants (such as safflower and corn); fruits (such as olives); and nuts (such as coconuts, walnuts, and almonds).

Oils differ in both flavor and cooking qualities. Some are well suited to high-heat frying; others should be used only for salads. Selecting the right oil for the job and understanding the special requirements of an oil are an important part of even the most basic cooking.

The most common edible oils are outlined under Availability, along with specific recommendations for use and handling. The Use section below applies generally to all edible oils.

Use Oils function in the kitchen as a lubricant, an ingredient, and a cooking medium. As a lubricant, oil keeps food from sticking to a pan or baking dish. Bread pans and cake pans are often brushed with oil (or butter) to make the finished loaf or cake easy to remove. Oil is an essential ingredient in many preparations. It provides the body for salad dressings and mayonnaise, which in turn provide lubrication for lettuces, cold vegetables, and sandwiches. It is the foundation of Italian pesto, yielding a cold sauce that spreads easily over hot pasta. Other oil-based sauces such as the French aioli (garlic mayonnaise) and rouille (garlicky red pepper sauce), the Spanish *romesco* (mayonnaise with red pepper and ground almonds), and the Italian *salsa verde* (parsley, onion, and garlic sauce) are spooned on top of soups for enrichment, spread on sandwiches, and served with boiled meats or seafood.

Oil also provides the required fat in some cakes, especially moist loaf cakes such as carrot cake. It is used to enrich bread doughs and batters. Some stronger tasting oils, such as Asian sesame oil, are used as flavorings; they are rubbed over steamed chicken and drizzled over stir-fried vegetables in the same way that a Western cook would add butter to a bowl of peas.

As a cooking medium, oils are essential to frying, whether sautéing, stir-frying, or deep-frying. In sautéing and stir-frying, a thin film of oil both keeps food from sticking to the pan and transfers heat to the food being cooked. Oil also imparts flavor. Foods sautéed in olive oil have a flavor quite different from those fried in peanut oil or vegetable oil. In sautéed dishes where the flavor of butter is important, oil is often added to the butter to raise the smoke point of the butter.

Availability The following are the most often used edible oils.

Almond Oil When imported from France, almond oil has a toasty almond flavor that is pleasing in salads and cold dishes. Its flavor is destroyed by heat. Use almond oil in mayonnaise, salad dressings, and cold poultry dishes.

The domestic product is considerably paler in flavor. Refrigerated, almond oil will keep for up to one year. Look for it in specialty stores and well-stocked supermarkets.

Avocado Oil   Derived from California avocados, this mild, buttery oil has a delicate flavor suitable for mayonnaise, salad dressings, and baked goods. Because it has a high smoke point, it can be used for sautéing, stir-frying, and deep-frying.

Coconut Oil   Used as a cooking oil in India and Malaysia, coconut oil imparts a coconut flavor to foods and can be heated to high frying temperatures. It is highly saturated and is solid when cool. Coconut oil is available in markets that carry Indian or Indonesian products. Refrigerated, it will keep for up to one year.

Corn Oil   This is a bland, unsaturated oil that is excellent for frying. It is also a major component in most margarine. Because it does not contain cholesterol, it is an oil of choice for many on low-cholesterol diets. Store in a cool, dark place for up to six months or refrigerate for up to one year. It is widely available in supermarkets.

Hazelnut Oil   This very expensive French import imparts a delicious toasted hazelnut flavor to cold dishes. Heating destroys its special flavor. It is strong and should be used with restraint. Use hazelnut oil in conjunction with a milder oil in salad dressings and mayonnaise, or drizzle it over green beans, artichokes, and asparagus. Refrigerated, it will keep for up to one year. It is available in specialty stores and well-stocked supermarkets.

Olive Oil   Pressed from the fruit of the olive tree, olive oil is a prized salad and cooking oil in the Western world. Indeed, 90 percent of the world's olive crop goes to oil. It is fundamental to the cooking of the Mediterranean: Spain, Italy, southern France, Greece, and Turkey. It is not well suited to deep-frying, for it smokes at moderate temperatures. However, it is excellent for sautéing and is an ingredient used for that purpose by almost all Mediterranean cooks. Olive oil is an ingredient in salad dressings, mayonnaise, sauces, soups, marinades, and even pastries in Mediterranean countries. Italians celebrate the new crop of olive oil by drizzling it on toasted bread; they also serve olive oil as a dip for raw vegetables, along with coarse salt and lemon.

Commercial olive oil is available in several different grades according to the degree of acidity. Although oils can be deacidified chemically, the best olive oil is naturally low in acidity because it is cold-pressed. These cold-pressed, low-acid oils are termed extravirgin olive oil (although chemically deacidified oils will also qualify for this term). In increasing level of acidity, olive oil is classified as extravirgin, superfine, fine, and virgin or pure.

The first, cold pressing of the olive gives the finest, fruitiest oil. Subsequent pressings in the presence of heat yield oil of lesser quality. Because the terms on olive oil labels do not necessarily indicate quality, it is important to experiment widely and find a brand that you like. The best oils have a clear, deep green appearance, a fruity aroma, and a flavor that is clean, light, often slightly peppery, and distinctly of the olive. Avoid heavy or bitter oils. Price is also not a good indication of quality.

The best extravirgin olive oils lose their character when cooked. They should be used in cold dishes or added to hot dishes at the end of cooking. For sautéing, select a mild olive oil.

Store olive oil in a cool, dark place for up to six months or in the refrigerator for up to one year. It will cloud in the refrigerator but will clear at room temperature. Olive oils in a wide range of quality are available in supermarkets and specialty markets. France, Italy, and Spain are the major exporters.

Peanut Oil   Among Chinese cooks, peanut oil is the most popular cooking oil. It imparts a faint peanut flavor to stir-fried foods, and it may be heated to high frying temperatures. Western cooks also find it suitable for salad dressings and sautéing. It is available in all supermarkets and in Asian markets. Some health-food stores also carry a cold-pressed peanut oil that is more perishable. Peanut oil will keep for up to one year in a cool, dark place. It will cloud at refrigerator temperature but will clear again when brought to room temperature.

Safflower Oil   This flavorless cooking oil can be heated to high frying temperatures. It is excellent for deep-frying but its bland, heavy character makes it less suitable for a salad oil. It is available in many supermarkets. Store in a cool, dark place, where it will keep for up to one year.

Sesame Oil   Pressed from sesame seeds, this oil is an important adjunct to Chinese cooking. Its toasty, nutty flavor adds an intriguing note to noodle dishes, soups, stir-fries, and dipping sauces. It is often rubbed over poultry or drizzled on fish after steaming. The Chinese rarely use it for cooking as heat would alter its flavor. Chinese sesame oil is available in some supermarkets and in Asian markets, packaged in a plastic squeeze bottle. It has a deep gold color and an arresting fragrance. A Japanese version of sesame oil is slightly lighter in color and flavor. Japanese cooks add it to the cooking oil used to make tempura. A cold-pressed sesame oil, available in health-food stores, has a much more pallid flavor and is not a substitute. Store Asian sesame oil in a cool, dry place for up to six months or in the refrigerator for up to one year. Cold-pressed sesame oil is more perishable; refrigerated, it will keep for up to six months.

Soybean Oil   A major cooking oil in America, it heats to high frying temperatures and has a bland flavor. Because of its lack of flavor, it is not a superior salad oil, but it does not contain cholesterol and is thus an oil of choice for many on special diets. Soybean oil is also used in margarine. It is available in supermarkets; store in a cool, dark place for up to one year.

Oils are used in the kitchen for lubrication and cooking, and as an ingredient. Depending on their source, they can range from pale colors to deeper hues.

The season's freshest produce is paired with a fine, seasoned olive oil for a light and brightly colored first course. For a more elaborate antipasto, add a selection of cured meats and a loaf of country-style bread.

at room temperature. However, most oils are considerably cheaper when bought in large containers. For convenience, pour off small amounts into airtight bottles to keep on the kitchen counter, storing the remainder airtight in a cool, dark place.

■ VEGETABLES WITH TUSCAN OLIVE OIL DIP

Italians living in Tuscany, the region that surrounds Florence, show off their finest oil and their freshest vegetables by serving them dipped in olive oil. You're offered a basket or a platter of crisp, colorful raw vegetables, along with a bowl of the best-quality oil seasoned with nothing but salt and pepper. You pinch (*pinzare*) the vegetables and join them in marriage (*matrimonio*) with the oil. If the oil is top-notch, there is no finer dip.

> 2 **cups fruity olive oil**
>   **Coarse salt and freshly ground pepper, to taste**
>   **Vegetables for dipping: Sliced bulb fennel, cherry tomatoes, carrot sticks, innermost celery stalks, endive leaves, cucumber spears (seeded), innermost hearts of baby artichokes, hearts of small lettuces, spears of young, tender zucchini**
>   **Lemon wedges, for garnish**

Season olive oil to taste with salt and pepper. Divide oil among small dipping bowls, one to a person. Arrange vegetables for dipping on a large, rustic platter. Offer each guest a dipping bowl, lemon wedges, and a small salad plate. You can also pour a little seasoned oil on each salad plate, arrange a bouquet of raw vegetables on top, and garnish the plate with a lemon wedge.

Serves 8.

Walnut Oil Imported from France, walnut oil has an appealing, fragrant, nutty quality. It is generally expensive, but a little goes a long way. It adds a rich, characteristic flavor to salad dressings and sauces. It may also be drizzled over cooked vegetables, such as asparagus and green beans, or used in the mayonnaise for a chicken salad. Heating destroys its special flavor. It is available in many supermarkets and in specialty stores. Refrigerate for up to one year.

Selection The cook should choose the oil that best corresponds to the character of the finished dish. Mediterranean dishes, for example, call preferentially for olive oil to convey an authentic Mediterranean flavor; most Chinese stir-frying is done with peanut oil. When deep-frying, it is important to choose an oil that can be heated to a desired high temperature without breaking down and smoking. Safflower, soybean, and corn oils have higher smoke points than peanut, olive, or sesame oils, and are therefore preferable for deep-frying (see FRY).

Storage Oils oxidize when exposed to light and heat. To extend their shelf life, store oils in a cool, dark place. The fragile nut oils are usually refrigerated. Other oils may be stored in the refrigerator to extend their useful life, but they may thicken and become cloudy at refrigerator temperature and be problematic for making salad. Some cooks prefer to buy small quantities and keep them

OKRA

An ancient native of Africa, okra was carried to America on the earliest slave ships. It was a staple of plantation cooking and important to Creole cooks. Gumbo, the Creole soup thickened with okra, is a contraction of the African name for the vegetable.

Okra grows in long slender pods; it may grow up to 9 inches in length but is usually 1½ to 3 inches when marketed. The fuzzy green pods may be ribbed or nonribbed. Inside are many small white seeds. When cooked, okra develops a mucilaginous quality, a characteristic that makes it a good thickener for soups and stews. The flavor of okra is mild, somewhat similar to that of green beans.

Use Okra can be blanched, cooled, dressed, and served as a salad, but it is generally served hot—braised, fried, or sautéed. It is a popular ingredient in the American South, particularly Louisiana. Southern cooks fry okra in cornmeal, stew it with bacon and rice, or pickle it. Louisiana cooks add it to gumbo or braise it with tomatoes.

Indian cooks fry sliced okra with onions and spices. Caribbean cooks stir it into cornmeal mush. Small whole pods may be cooked whole; large pods are usually sliced.

Availability   Okra is sold the year around in southern states. Elsewhere, it is most plentiful in the summer months. Most supermarkets carry frozen okra; some stock canned okra as well.

Selection   Small pods are generally more tender and sweeter than large pods. Choose small, bright green, crisp pods. Avoid any that are overlarge, stiff, shriveled, or blackened.

Storage   Wrap fresh okra in a plastic bag. Transfer left-over canned okra to a covered container. Keep both types in the refrigerator crisper up to four days.

Preparation   Wash just before cooking; trim stem ends. If slicing, slice just before cooking.

Cooking   See BOIL, BRAISE, DEEP-FRY, SAUTE, STEAM.

■ OKRA AND TOMATO STEW

Okra is related to both hibiscus and cotton. The sticky fuzz (removed long before the okra reaches the grocery store) makes it as nasty to pick as cotton. It is one vegetable that must be excluded from the current tendency to cook vegetables as briefly as possible (unless it is deep-fried). During cooking okra goes from crisp to slimy and finally to tender-crisp; it must be cooked long enough to recover from the slimy phase. The variations, native to the Georgia Sea Islands and the coastal lowlands, reflect the origin of okra, as they closely resemble West African dishes.

> 3 **strips bacon**
> 1 **medium onion, finely chopped**
> 1 **small green bell pepper, finely chopped**
> 1 **pound fresh okra, trimmed and sliced into rounds,**
>   *or* **1 package (12 oz) sliced frozen okra**
> 1 **teaspoon flour**
> 1 **pound fresh tomatoes, peeled and coarsely**
>   **chopped,** *or* **1 can (14 oz) tomatoes,**
>   **coarsely chopped**
> 1 **tablespoon light brown sugar**
>   **Salt and freshly ground pepper, to taste**

1. Cook bacon in a large skillet until crisp. Drain on paper towels, crumble, and reserve.

2. In bacon fat remaining in the skillet (about 3 tablespoons), sauté onion and green pepper over high heat, stirring until wilted (about 5 minutes). Add okra and cook over low heat for 10 minutes, stirring frequently.

3. Sprinkle flour over skillet and cook, stirring, until flour loses its raw aroma (about 1 minute). Add tomatoes, sugar, and salt and pepper, to taste. Stir in bacon. Continue to cook over low heat until okra is tender and mixture is slightly thickened (about 10 minutes longer).

Serves 4 to 6 as a side dish.

Lowlands Okra Pilau   Complete steps 1 and 2. Meanwhile, place 1 cup long-grain rice in 1½-quart saucepan with cover and add 2 cups cold water. Bring to a boil, stir once, cover, and cook over the lowest heat for exactly 12 minutes. Drain rice and add to okra along with tomatoes, salt, pepper, and bacon (flour and sugar are omitted). Cover skillet and continue to cook over low heat until rice is tender (about 15 minutes longer).

Serves 6 to 8 as a side dish.

Shrimp Okra Pilau   For a main dish, prepare Lowlands Okra Pilau and add 1 pound shelled medium shrimp and a dash of cayenne pepper during the last 7 minutes of cooking.

Serves 4 as a main course.

The sensuous texture and exotic flavor of well-cooked okra are set off perfectly by tart, fresh tomatoes in Shrimp Okra Pilau (recipe at left)—the mid-South's delicate version of Spanish paella or Louisiana jambalaya.

Whole olives are a traditional component of an Italian antipasto, along with cured meats, flavorful cheeses, and pickled vegetables.

OLALLIEBERRY

The olallieberry is a cross between the youngberry (a large, wine-colored berry named after its breeder) and the black loganberry (a relative of the blackberry, also named after its breeder). It is a very successful hybrid, widely grown in California. Resembling the blackberry, the fruit is shiny black, firm, and sweet. See BLACKBERRY for Use, Availability, Selection, and Storage.

OLIVE

The hardy olive tree, native to the Mediterranean, produces the small pitted fruit known as olives. There are dozens of olive varieties, the fruit varying slightly in size, shape, and flavor. Whether an olive is green or black, however, depends on if it has been left on the tree to ripen (black olives are ripe, green unripe).

Olives are too bitter to eat raw. They are either pressed for cooking oil or cured for table consumption. Table olives are cured with water, oil, brine, salt, or lye to dissipate their bitterness and preserve them.

Use   For information on olive oil, see OIL. Cured olives, both green and black, are a popular cocktail snack; their tangy, salty flavor is highly appetizing. Olives are almost always part of the Middle Eastern *mezze* (appetizer platter). Green olives are sometimes pitted and stuffed with pimiento, anchovies, or almonds. Whole pimiento-stuffed green olives are the classic garnish for martinis; sliced pimiento-stuffed green olives garnish a variety of savory dishes. Whole olives are used to garnish salads, such as the

Greek *horiatiki* salad (raw vegetables, feta cheese, and olives). Olives also lend their tangy flavor to pasta sauces, stews, and braised dishes. Greek beef stew often contains black olives. In one of the most popular Moroccan preparations of chicken, the bird is braised with preserved lemon and whole green olives. Minced olives can be added to bread doughs, stuffings, sandwich fillings, potato or pasta salad, and pizza toppings.

Availability   Most supermarkets carry pitted ripe California olives in cans and pimiento-stuffed green olives in jars. Some supermarkets and many specialty markets offer a larger variety of olives, both imported and domestic. The main varieties currently available are:

Alfonso   Brine-cured, ripe olive from South America, packed in vinegar for shipping; importer often bottles olives with olive oil.

Black (ripe) pitted   Lye-cured, shiny black California olive with pit removed; harvested green, then oxygenated to turn flesh black.

Dry-cured California   Salt-cured, wrinkled black olive rubbed with olive oil.

Dry-cured Moroccan   Salt-cured, wrinkled black olive; slightly bitter.

Gaeta   Salt-cured, wrinkled black Italian olive; often packed with herbs.

Greek-style   Brine-cured, purple-black California olive packed in vinegar.

Kalamata (Calamata)   Brine-cured, slit, black Greek olive packed in vinegar.

Liguria   Brine-cured, dark brown to black Italian olive.

Lugano   Brine-cured, purple-black Italian olive.

Morocco   Brine-cured, round, reddish black to black Moroccan olive, packed with leaves and twigs.

Nafplion (Naphlion)   Brine-cured, dark green, cracked Greek olive, packed in olive oil.

Niçoise   Brine-cured, then packed in olive oil; small dark brown to black French olive from Provence. This is the olive traditionally used for *tapénade.*

Nyons   Salt-cured, black French olive rubbed with olive oil; occasionally brine-cured.

Picholine   Brine-cured, smooth green French olive.

Ponentine   Brine-cured, purple-black Italian olive packed in vinegar.

Salona   Brine-cured, brown or purplish brown Greek olive with soft texture.

Sicilian-style   Brine-cured, green California olive, available cracked and uncracked.

Spanish-style Green olive from Spain or California. Lye-cured, then packed in salt and lactic acid brine; may be pitted or unpitted, stuffed or unstuffed.

Selection When purchasing brined olives in bulk, make sure they are well covered with brine.

Storage Leftover brined olives, whether purchased in bulk, cans, or jars, should be refrigerated in their brine in an airtight, nonmetal container; they will keep for several weeks, depending on the strength of the brine. If a white film forms on the surface of the brine, skim it off. When olives become soft, discard them. Oil-cured olives should be well coated with olive oil, stored in an airtight jar, and refrigerated.

■ TAPENADE

An earthy olive spread from southern France, *tapénade* is traditionally spread on grilled bread, bread sticks, or a chunk of a crusty country loaf. It's also delicious with cold roast beef or slathered on lamb chops just off the grill.

½ **pound large, black Greek olives or**
   Nicoise olives, pitted
1 **ounce anchovy fillets**
1 **clove garlic, minced**
2 **tablespoons capers**
2 **tablespoons olive oil**
   Freshly ground pepper, to taste

1. Place pitted olives in a food processor or blender. Add anchovies, garlic, capers, and olive oil; process or blend briefly. Mixture should be blended but still coarse. Transfer to a bowl and add black pepper to taste.

2. Spoon into crock or jar and cover with a thin layer of olive oil. Store in refrigerator up to 6 months.

Makes 1 cup.

> ***Recipes and Related Information***
> *Eggplant Relish, 208; Greek Salad, 507;*
> *Pissaladière, 446; Salade Niçoise, 510.*

ONION

The onion serves as a seasoning in almost all cuisines and is appreciated as a vegetable in many. Its flavor varies from sweet to strong, depending on variety and growing conditions. Its texture is crunchy when raw but softens with cooking. Cooking also tames the flavor. Chives, garlic, leeks, shallots, and green onions are also members of the onion family (see individual entries).

Use Onions are widely used as a seasoning in savory foods. Minced onions, either cooked or raw, are added to meat loaves and meatballs, stuffings, stews, soups, relishes and chutneys, tomato sauces, sautéed vegetables, meat and vegetable casseroles, savory tarts, bean and grain dishes, and salad dressings. In the realm of savory dishes, there are few places where the onion is unwelcome. Sliced onions are added raw to salads and sandwiches for their crunchy texture and pungent flavor. Sautéed onions are used as a pizza topping and as a partner to sautéed liver.

Onions are also eaten on their own as a vegetable or side dish. Small boiling onions can be pickled or creamed. Large onions can be cut into rings, coated with batter, and fried. Onion slices can be scalloped with butter and cream; they can be blanched, dressed, and served cold as a salad. Large onions may be hollowed out, stuffed or halved, and baked until soft. Very sweet varieties, such as the Granex, the Walla Walla, and the Maui onion, are best appreciated raw; some say the Maui onion is sweet enough to eat out of hand like an apple.

Availability Fresh onions are available the year around in a variety of shapes and sizes. Small pearl onions, not much bigger than a pearl, are sold in baskets wrapped in plastic; boiling onions are slightly larger (about 1 inch in diameter) and are sold either loose or in bags. These small onions are good for pickling, creaming, and adding to stews. Larger onions may be white, yellow, or purple, globe-shaped, flat, or torpedo-shaped.

Globe and Italian red onions are available all year. Bermuda onions (mild, flat, and either white or yellow) are found March through June. Spanish onions (large, round, mild, and yellow to red) are sold August through April. Red Torpedo onions are available in the early summer. Freeze-dried onions are found in most supermarkets.

Selection Choose firm onions without soft spots. Avoid sprouting onions or those with damp stem ends.

Storage Sweet, early summer onions do not store as well as late summer or fall varieties. Stored in a cool, dark, dry place, onions will keep for several weeks.

Preparation Peel, then slice, chop, or dice as directed (see KNIFE, Cutting Techniques). Many people find that cutting up onions makes their eyes water; this is due to an enzyme in the onion called alliinase, which bonds with sulfur in the onion when exposed to air and irritates the tear ducts. There is no known remedy, although some cooks suggest chilling onions before chopping.

Cooking See BOIL, BRAISE, GRILL, SAUTE, STEAM, STIR-FRY.

> ***Recipes and Related Information***
> *Asparagus With Lemon, Tomato, and Onions, 14;*
> *Basic Fritter Batter, 28; Carrot and Baby Onion Stew*
> *With Raisins, 101; Chive, 123; Garlic, 261; Green*
> *Onion, 285; Leek, 338; Leg of Lamb With Garlic,*
> *Potatoes, and Onions, 337; Onion and Rice*
> *Soubise, 229; Onion Soup With Beer, 565; Shallot, 535;*
> *Steamed Kale and Pearl Onions, 325; Thyme-Scented*
> *Chicken With Potatoes, Bacon, and Baby Onions, 578.*

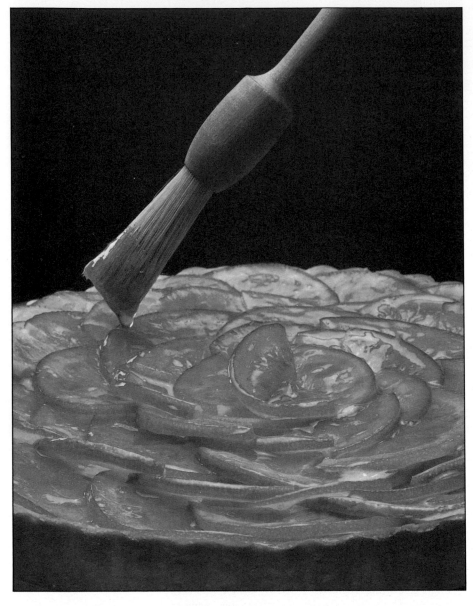

A glaze is being applied to this luscious Orange Custard Tart. The thin slices of candied orange resemble the petals of an opening flower.

Excellent eating oranges, they peel easily, separate easily into segments, and are seedless. For information on the loose-skinned citrus fruits known as mandarin oranges, see MANDARIN ORANGE.

The best-known bitter oranges are grown in Spain and are known as Seville oranges. They are too bitter to eat but provide excellent peel and juice for marmalade and orange liqueur.

Use   Sweet oranges are often eaten out of hand as a breakfast fruit, snack, or dessert. Orange sections or slices may be added to fruit salads or compotes and used to garnish chicken or turkey salad. Oranges and orange juice are used in such savory dishes as duck á l'orange, orange and red onion salad, and Mexican pork roast with orange juice. In America whole oranges are ground fine with cranberries and sugar to make a relish for holiday turkey. In Brazil sliced oranges are part of the national dish, *feijoada,* a bountiful spread of smoked and fresh meats, black beans, steamed rice, and cooked greens. The oranges are said to perk up the appetite for even more feijoada. In China, where oranges symbolize good fortune and prosperity, they are frequently offered at the end of a meal and are exchanged at the start of the new year. Oranges figure in an innumerable variety of desserts, including sherbet, cakes, curds, tarts, gelatin molds, and puddings. In France and Italy orange sherbet is often served in a hollow orange shell. Orange juice is enjoyed as a breakfast beverage, as an ingredient in cocktails and punches, and as a marinade for meats. Juice from blood oranges is particularly striking in a clear juice glass. *Maltaise* sauce, a variation on Hollandaise, is made with the juice and rind of blood oranges. Grated orange rind flavors custards, creams, doughs, stews, pastries, and cookies. Both sweet and bitter oranges can be used for marmalades, candies, and preserves.

Availability   Fresh oranges are found the year around, with peak supplies December through April. Domestic navel oranges are marketed from mid-November through mid-May. Valencias are available in every month but December and January. Orange juice is sold in all supermarkets, either frozen or bottled.

Selection   Look for firmness, heaviness, and bright-looking skin. Rich orange skin color is not a reliable indication of quality because the skin is frequently treated with vegetable dye. Fully mature oranges, particularly Valencias, will often regreen, turning greenish late in the season. Russeting, a brownish roughened area over the skin, often found on Florida and Texas oranges, does not affect eating quality and often occurs on oranges with thin skin and superior eating quality. Avoid lightweight oranges; those with very rough skin texture (indicates abnormally thick skin and less flesh); dull, dry skin with spongy texture (indicates aging and deteriorated quality); cuts or punctures; soft spots on the surface; and discolored, weakened areas of skin around stem end.

ORANGE

Because the orange tree cannot withstand frost, it is cultivated in a circumscribed area that includes Southeast Asia (where it originated), the Near East, North Africa, southern Spain and Portugal, Florida, southern California, Texas, and Arizona. The fruit is valued both for its juice and for its aromatic peel.

Both bitter and sweet varieties of oranges exist. Sweet oranges may be further divided into blood oranges, common oranges, and navel oranges. The blood orange develops pink or red flesh, juice, and rind. Many people think the distinctive flavor, usually described as resembling that of berries, is the most delicious of all the oranges. One of the best-known common oranges is the Valencia, valued for the quality and quantity of its juice. Navel oranges are known by the navellike appearance of the blossom end.

Storage Keep oranges in a cool place or refrigerate. They will store well for several weeks.

Preparation The desirable oils of the fruit are stored in the orange peel. When grating orange rind for all uses, be sure to grate only the orange rind; the white pith is unpleasantly bitter. Because vitamin C oxidizes rapidly, freshly squeezed orange juice contains considerably more than bottled or frozen juice; when serving as a breakfast beverage, squeeze juice just before serving for maximum nutrition.

■ ORANGE CUSTARD TART

This is a tart for orange marmalade fans. The thinly sliced, candied orange decorating the top has a taste that recalls the bitter orange flavor of orange marmalade. Note that the candied orange slices must stand in the sugar syrup overnight before using.

    2 to 3 small seedless oranges
    1 cup water
    ¾ cup sugar
    1 Sweet Tart Pastry (9½-inch; see page 441)
    3 eggs
    ⅔ cup sugar
    ¼ cup fresh orange juice
    1 teaspoon finely grated orange rind
    6 tablespoons unsalted butter, melted and cooled
    ½ cup apricot preserves
    1 tablespoon orange-flavored liqueur

1. Thinly slice orange (⅛ inch or less) with very sharp knife. In a wide saucepan combine the water and the ¾ cup sugar; bring to a boil to dissolve sugar. Add orange slices and simmer over very low heat until translucent (about 45 minutes). Remove from heat and let stand in syrup overnight.

2. Roll out tart pastry and use it to line a 9½-inch tart tin with removable bottom. Blind bake until partially baked.

3. Preheat oven to 350° F. Combine eggs, the ⅔ cup sugar, orange juice, and orange rind in a mixing bowl; whisk until well mixed. Whisk in melted butter. Pour into partially baked tart shell and bake until custard is set and knife inserted in center comes out clean (20 to 25 minutes). Cool to room temperature.

4. Decorate tart just before serving, if possible. Remove orange slices from syrup; drain well. Cut half of the slices in half. Cut remaining slices in quarters. Arrange a row of overlapping quartered slices along outer edge of tart on top of custard, with rounded edges of slices touching outer edge of tart. Then place a row of overlapping halved slices so they just overlap tips of first row. Continue with this pattern, alternating rows of overlapping quarters and halves, to center of tart. Form a very thin half slice into a cone shape for the center decoration. The tart top should now resemble the opening petals of a flower.

5. Heat preserves until melted; strain to remove solid pieces of fruit. Mix in liqueur. Brush glaze lightly over orange slices. Reserve leftover glaze for another tart.

6. Remove sides of tart tin and serve at room temperature. Tart should be stored in the refrigerator if not consumed within a few hours.

Serves 6 to 8.

Recipes and Related Information
Citrus Reamer, 131; Classic Orange Marmalade, 320; Cranberry-Orange-Nut Loaf, 492; Gadgets, 258; Mandarin Orange, 348; Orange Butter, 69; Orange Buttermilk Biscuits, 50; Orange Chantilly Cream, 605; Orange Chiffon Cake, 85; Orange Fondant, 251; Orange Loaf, 492; Orange Scones, 50.

OREGANO

A member of the mint family, oregano is also known as wild marjoram. This assertive herb has small green leaves and a fragrance identified with both Mediterranean and Mexican cooking.

Use Oregano is strongly associated by many Americans with Italian cooking; certainly it is important to many tomato sauces, pizzas, bean soups, and southern Italian stews. It is also frequently used by Greek cooks to flavor lamb, shrimp, baked fish, and stewed chicken. It flatters zucchini, tomatoes, eggplant, onions, green beans, and dried beans. Mexican cooks use a different variety of oregano to flavor tomato sauces, fish, seviche, soups, and roast pork. Dried oregano is offered as a garnish for some Mexican soups, including the tripe soup known as *menudo*.

Availability Two main varieties of oregano are sold in the United States today: European and Mexican. The European variety is milder and is occasionally found fresh in some specialty markets. It is readily available dried, either whole or ground, on supermarket spice racks. The more pungent Mexican oregano is dried and sold in Latin American markets.

Selection Choose bunches of lively looking, aromatic fresh herbs without signs of wilting or decay. Packaged seasonings lose quality after a while; try to buy from a store that restocks its spice section fairly often.

Storage Store fresh herb in a plastic bag in the refrigerator and use within three days. Store dried herb in a cool, dark, dry place. Whole dried leaves will keep for one year, ground leaves for six months.

Recipes and Related Information
Menudo, 591; Stuffed Vegetarian Pizza, 448.

Luscious golden papaya and the zest of fresh lime combine to create an exotic ice cream with a touch of the tropic.

PAN-BROIL, TO

A quick-cooking, dry-heat method performed on the stove top by cooking in a frying pan, using little or no fat, over moderately hot heat. The food sears on the surface and pulls away from the pan; any fat given off by the food is poured away during cooking. A special pan, called a grill pan or stove-top broiler, is specifically designed for pan-broiling. On the inside it has a ridged bottom so that food is raised up and fat drips below (see COOKWARE, Grill Pan). A heavy grill pan made of a material that conducts heat well, such as cast iron, does the best job.

PANFRY, TO

A dry-heat cooking method that cooks food in a small amount of hot fat. The terms *panfry* and *sauté* are often used interchangeably, but strictly speaking, less fat is used to sauté food than to panfry food.

Recipes and Related Information
Fry, 254; Sauté, 531.

PAPAYA

The papaya is a tropical fruit native to the New World, possibly to Mexico or the West Indies. Today it is cultivated in tropical or semitropical areas around the world, including Florida, Hawaii, India, Malaysia, China, Japan, and the Philippines.

The commercial variety common in the United States is the Solo papaya, a pear-shaped, smooth-skinned fruit that is usually about 6 inches long, about 3 to 4 inches wide at the widest part, and 1 inch wide at the neck. The Solo papaya weighs between 1 and 2 pounds. The skin is generally green when picked but it turns a vivid yellow-orange when ripe; the moist, melonlike flesh ranges from pastel orange to a deep salmon color. The papaya has a large seed cavity with numerous shiny black seeds that resemble caviar; although they are edible, they are usually discarded.

Use Chilled ripe papaya makes a refreshing breakfast fruit; it is seeded and usually served on the half shell with a wedge of lime. The seed cavity can be filled with ice cream or yogurt, if desired. Skinned and sliced or cubed, it can be added to a fruit salad or compote. Sliced papaya makes a handsome topping for a fruit tart. Puréed ripe papaya can be used in sherbets and ice creams, in quick breads, and in beverages. Green (unripe) papaya is made into pickles and chutneys, sliced and stewed with meats, and sautéed or baked with butter and brown sugar. For centuries, cooks have also taken advantage of an enzyme that is found in both the fruit and its leaves. Papain, the enzyme, is a natural tenderizer. Baking meat in papaya leaves or stewing meat with papaya, especially green papaya, will tenderize the meat. (Papain is the active ingredient in many commercial meat tenderizers.) Because papain inhibits jelling, raw papaya cannot be used in gelatin desserts; however, cooked papaya presents no jelling problems. Papaya seeds have a peppery flavor and may be used as a garnish or ground for use in salad dressings and marinades.

Availability Papayas are found sporadically all year but supplies peak in summer months. Bottled papaya juice is sold in some health-food stores.

Selection Choose papayas with good yellow color and an enticing fragrance. Slightly green papayas that are yellow over at least one third of the fruit will ripen in three to five days at room temperature. Ripe papayas are highly aromatic and give slightly to gentle pressure. Avoid fruit with dark spots or ones with softness at the stem end; this softness is the first sign of decay.

Storage Keep at room temperature until ripe, then refrigerate in a plastic bag and use within one week.

Preparation To eat on the half shell, cut in half and scoop out black seeds. Alternatively, peel with a vegetable peeler, halve, and seed.

■ PAPAYA ICE CREAM

Before mixing with the other ingredients that make up the base for this fruity ice cream, the papayas must be heated to deactivate papain, an enzyme that would otherwise break down the protein in milk and cream and impart a slightly bitter taste.

    2 large papayas
    2 cups milk
    2 cups whipping cream
    ½ cup sugar
    4 large egg yolks
    2 tablespoons fresh lime juice

1. Scoop papaya out of its skin and scrape out seeds. Finely chop fruit; place fruit in a small, heavy-bottomed saucepan and cook over very low heat until softened into a purée, stirring occasionally (about 15 minutes). Remove from heat and let cool.

2. In a medium, heavy-bottomed saucepan over medium heat, cook milk, cream, and sugar, stirring occasionally, until sugar is dissolved and mixture is hot, but not boiling. In a medium bowl whisk egg yolks to blend. Continue to whisk while very slowly pouring in approximately 1 cup of cream mixture.

3. When mixture is smooth, pour back into pan of hot liquid, whisking continuously, and cook until mixture thickens slightly and coats the back of a spoon (about 5 minutes; do not let mixture boil or it will curdle). Strain into a clean bowl and let cool.

4. Add papaya purée and lime juice to custard. Transfer to an ice cream machine and freeze according to manufacturer's instructions.

Makes about 1 quart.

> **Recipes and Related Information**
> *Ice Cream and Frozen Dessert, 308; Papaya With Prosciutto, 358.*

PAPRIKA

A ground spice derived from capsicum peppers, paprika varies in color and pungency according to the peppers used to make it. Most paprikas are relatively mild, range from orange-red to red, and contain the flesh only (not the seeds or veins) of dried capsicum peppers.

Use In America mild paprika is often used more for color than flavor. Bright red paprika adds visual appeal to stuffed eggs, baked fish, and a variety of cheese or vegetable casseroles. It is widely used in sausages, salad dressings, and condiments. In Hungary paprika is appreciated for its pungency, whether sweet, half-sweet, or hot. Paprika is virtually the country's national spice; it is the predominant flavor in many hearty soups and stews.

Gulyás (goulash) and *paprikás* are two categories of Hungarian dishes that are always liberally seasoned with paprika. Spanish paprika is used in Spain to flavor shellfish dishes, rice dishes, and sausages. In Morocco Spanish paprika seasons tomato and green pepper salads, carrot salad, and most dishes containing tomato.

Availability Ground paprika is widely available on supermarket spice racks. The best paprika is Hungarian, which may be sweet (mild), half-sweet, or hot. Spanish paprika is generally of lesser quality but is suitable for most dishes; it is always mild. Some specialty shops carry concentrated paprika paste in tubes.

Selection Paprika rapidly loses pungency. Try to buy from a store that restocks its spice section fairly often.

Storage To maintain its flavor and intensity, keep paprika in a cool, dark, dry place or refrigerate; replace every six months.

■ POUSSIN PAPRIKASH

Hungarian cooking is a lively blend of spicy and sweet. This recipe, a paprika-spiced fricassee, substitutes quick-cooking young poussins (under 6 weeks old) for the usual older and less tender chicken. Serve with buttered noodles with poppy seeds, creamed peas, and a tossed beet salad.

    2 poussins (1 lb each), halved
       Salt and freshly ground pepper
    3 tablespoons butter
    1 tablespoon vegetable oil
    1 large onion, thinly sliced
    ⅓ to ½ cup Chicken Stock (see page 500)
    1 tablespoon sweet or hot Hungarian paprika
    1 cup sour cream
    1 tablespoon flour

1. Wash poussins and pat dry. Season with salt and pepper; set aside.

2. In a medium, heavy-bottomed skillet over medium-high heat, heat butter and oil. Add poussins and sauté, starting skin side down, until golden brown (about 10 minutes per side).

3. Add onion and sauté until translucent. Add stock and paprika, stirring and scraping with a wooden spoon to loosen any browned bits that may have stuck to bottom of pan. Cook, covered, for 15 to 20 minutes. Remove poussins to serving platter.

4. In a small bowl combine sour cream and flour. Mix into sauce, stirring until well blended (about 1 minute). Pour over poussins and serve.

Serves 4.

> **Recipes and Related Information**
> *Bohemian Pork Goulash, 459; Budapest Borscht, 76.*

PARBOIL, TO

To cook foods partway in boiling water. This treatment is particularly helpful for stir-fries and sautés. By partially tenderizing longer-cooking ingredients such as carrots or broccoli, for example, their final cooking time will be faster and they can be combined with ingredients that finish quickly. Parboiling can be done in advance, which adds to its appeal as a time-saving preparation technique. Blanching is identical to parboiling except that foods are cooked only for a brief time (see BLANCH).

PARE, TO

In general, to remove the outer skin of a food, usually vegetables or fruits. A short-bladed paring knife or vegetable peeler is used. A narrower definition would be to trim away the irregular outer surface in order to produce pieces of uniform size that will cook at the same rate and have a more symmetrical final appearance. An example would be the classic garnish of pared nugget-shaped carrots or potatoes for roasted meats and poultry.

> **Recipes and Related Information**
> Gadgets, 258; Knife, 328.

PARSLEY

One of the most widely used culinary herbs, parsley is important to almost all the world's cuisines. With its fragile stems and sturdy, bright green leaves, parsley imparts a clean, fresh, slightly peppery flavor to dishes. The two main varieties are the curly-leaf type, widely available in supermarkets, and the flat-leaf Italian parsley, less common in American markets but quite common in Europe. Flat-leaf parsley is more pungent.

Use   The mild, fresh flavor of parsley harmonizes with almost all savory dishes. It is frequently mixed with other, more pungent herbs. Fines herbes (see HERB AND SPICE BLENDS) always include parsley, as does the classic bouquet garni (see BOUQUET GARNI). Minced parsley is a visually appealing garnish for soups, stews, sautés, meat loaves, and casseroles. Mixed with lemon rind and minced garlic, it becomes Gremolata, an Italian garnish for braised veal shanks (Osso Buco). Mixed with bread crumbs and minced shallots or garlic, it becomes *persillade*, which is spread on rack of lamb before roasting. It is a major component of the Italian *salsa verde* (green sauce) for boiled meats and of Middle Eastern Tabbouleh (cracked wheat, tomato, and parsley salad). Parsley sprigs can be deep-fried as a garnish for fried foods. They can be added to green salads or even lightly dressed and served as a salad on their own.

Availability   Fresh curly-leaf parsley is widely found all year in supermarkets. Flat-leaf Italian parsley is available in specialty markets and some well-stocked supermarkets. Dried parsley is sold on most supermarket spice racks. Given the ready availability and affordability of fresh parsley, there is little if any reason to use dried.

Selection   Whether curly-leaf or flat-leaf, look for bright green, vigorous bunches with a fresh, clean aroma. Avoid limp bunches with dull-looking leaves.

Storage   Wash well, shake off excess water, and wrap parsley in paper towels, then in a plastic bag. Store in refrigerator and use within three or four days.

Preparation   To mince parsley, separate leaves from stems. Finely mince leaves. Save stems to flavor stocks.

■ WARM PARSLEY SAUCE FOR SHELLFISH

Keep this sauce warm in a chafing dish and serve with chilled scallops, crab legs, or shrimp.

    4 cups parsley, leaves only
    2 cups whipping cream
    2 shallots, minced
    ½ cup dry white wine
    ¼ cup cold butter, cut into 4 pieces
       Salt and freshly ground pepper, to taste

1. Blanch parsley in boiling water 20 seconds; drain and transfer to a bowl of ice water to stop cooking and set color. Drain and dry thoroughly on paper towels. Chop by hand or in a food processor until almost puréed; set aside.

2. In a medium saucepan over high heat, reduce cream by half. In a medium skillet over high heat, cook shallots and wine until wine has almost evaporated. Whisk in hot reduced cream. Remove from heat and whisk in butter, one piece at a time, until incorporated. Add parsley and salt and pepper to taste.

Makes 1¾ cups.

> **Recipes and Related Information**
> Gremolata, 58; Osso Buco, 58; Piquant Parsley Dipping Sauce, 46; Tabbouleh, 277.

PARSNIP

It is easy to tell by sight that the parsnip is a member of the carrot family. This sweet-flavored root vegetable looks like an ivory-colored or pale yellow carrot. It is usually less uniform in thickness, however, being wider at the top and tapering to a very narrow root. Unlike carrots, parsnips are always eaten cooked; they are starchy and tough when raw. Cooked parsnips have a texture and flavor somewhere between carrots and sweet potatoes, although they remain pale yellow when cooked.

Use Parsnips are a delicious winter root vegetable. They may be peeled, sliced, and steamed like carrots, or boiled, then mashed with butter and cream. They may be cut into chunks and added to soups or stews, or baked in the oven with meat stock and butter.

Availability Parsnips are found in many supermarkets during winter months. They are sold with their tops clipped, either in bulk or in plastic bags.

Selection Look for small parsnips; larger ones may have woody cores. Avoid parsnips that are limp or shriveled or have splits or brown spots. Choose those that are reasonably uniform; misshapen ones that have to be severely trimmed are uneconomical.

Storage Keep in a plastic bag in the refrigerator crisper and use within three or four days.

Preparation Peel and trim ends.

Cooking See BOIL, BRAISE, PUREE, STEAM.

■ PARSLEYED PARSNIPS

If you've only used parsnips to flavor soups and stocks, you may be surprised to learn that they are also delicious on their own as a side dish to a winter meal. If you prefer small parsnips, they may be used whole. Larger ones are more appealing and will cook faster if cut in pieces.

    8 to 10 medium (1½ lb) parsnips, peeled,
        trimmed, and quartered
    2 tablespoons butter
    ¼ cup minced parsley
    ½ teaspoon dried basil

In a large, covered skillet cook parsnips in boiling water to cover until tender-crisp (about 15 minutes); drain. Add butter, parsley, and basil. Toss to coat parsnips.

Serves 4.

PASSION FRUIT

Also known by its Spanish name, *granadilla,* the passion fruit supposedly owes its English name to its flowers: Their markings, some say, resemble the instruments used in the Crucifixion. The fruit itself is small and egg-shaped, with a brittle, wrinkled skin. Both skin and flesh color vary by variety, but the most commonly available variety has a dark purple skin and a deep gold flesh with small black seeds. Some Latin markets carry a Mexican variety with yellow skin and grayish flesh. All have a soft, juicy pulp that is highly aromatic.

Use Passion fruit can be halved and eaten from the shell, seeds and all. The fruit can also be squeezed for its juice and the juice strained through a sieve to remove the seeds. Seeded passion fruit pulp, puréed in a blender, is a

Parsnips are a flavorful winter root vegetable that makes a tasty side dish when simply cooked and tossed with herbs and butter.

delicious flavor base for sorbets and ice creams, mousses, pies, and dessert sauces. Passion fruit juice adds an exotic accent to punches, cocktails, or fruit juice blends.

Availability Passion fruit is native to Brazil, but is now grown in California, Hawaii, New Zealand, and Australia. Fresh passion fruit is sold in Latin markets and some supermarkets between late February and early October. Bottled or canned passion fruit juice is sold in specialty markets, Latin markets, and some health-food stores.

Selection The skin of ripe passion fruit will be shriveled. The fruit will ripen if left at room temperature for several days.

Storage Refrigerate ripe fruit in a plastic bag and use within two or three days.

Preparation Halve and eat from the shell (the shell is not eaten); or scoop out the pulp and press it through a sieve to remove the seeds; or purée with seeds for use in ice creams, sorbets, and mousses.

Recipes and Related Information
Ice Cream and Frozen Dessert, 308; Mousse, 372.

Pasta comes in all shapes and sizes, from shells to strands to corkscrews.

PASTA

The word *pasta* is so closely associated with Italian cooking it is easy to forget that other cuisines use noodles, too. The huge realm of Oriental noodles is discussed in NOODLE, ASIAN. This section applies to Western noodles, which will hereafter be referred to as pasta, whether Italian or not.

Pasta is based on grain—usually wheat—which is combined with a liquid and kneaded to make a smooth dough or paste (hence the word *pasta*). The dough is then rolled out and cut or formed into the appropriate shape.

Today's markets offer dozens of pasta shapes and flavors. To make sense of the multitude, it helps to divide pasta into two categories: fresh and dried.

FRESH AND DRIED PASTA

Wheat flour and whole eggs are the basic ingredients of fresh pasta. Some cooks add a little olive oil to make the dough easier to work, and some add salt for flavor. However, neither oil nor salt is necessary for good results.

After the dough is blended and kneaded, fresh pasta is rolled out—by hand or by machine—and cut into the desired widths. Flat sheets can be cut into wide lasagne noodles or into superfine *capelli d'angelo* (angel's hair). Fresh pasta is also sometimes cut into little soup squares (*quadrucci*) or into large squares for ravioli or rectangles for cannelloni. See Guide to Fresh Pasta, opposite page.

Commercial dried pasta is made with water and durum wheat, a particularly hard (high-protein) wheat. Ground durum wheat, known as semolina, is preferred for dried pasta because it contributes to firm, elastic dough that is sturdy enough to be shaped by machine and to maintain a form. To shape the dough, it is pushed through dies or molds and then oven-dried. Semolina is sometimes used to strengthen homemade pasta, but it makes a dough that is difficult to work by hand.

Use   Italian cooks use fresh pasta with certain types of sauces and dried pasta with others. The two are not always interchangeable. In general, soft fresh pasta is used with butter-based and cream-based sauces, which coat the noodles nicely. Dried pasta is usually the choice for oil-based and shellfish sauces. Because it holds its shape so well, dried pasta is a better choice for heavy, chunky vegetable sauces. Ridged and shell-shaped pastas are more appropriate for meat sauces because they trap the bits of meat in their ridges and hollows. Dried pasta, such as elbow macaroni and small shells (*conchigliette*), is good in soup because it holds its shape. *Pasta e fagioli*, the Tuscan soup made of pasta and white beans, shows how a sturdy dried pasta can stand up to a thick bean soup.

Pasta may be used in every course of a meal, from first course to dessert. You can add body to a simple broth with angel-hair pasta or tortellini; thicker vegetable- or bean-based soups such as minestrone often incorporate short, stubby dried pasta. In the United States cold pasta salads are eaten as a first course or luncheon main course.

In Italy pasta is generally served as a first course, rarely as a main course. The variety of possible sauces is literally endless, incorporating butter or oil, cream, meats, vegetables, fish and shellfish, poultry, and eggs.

Besides being tossed in sauce, some pasta shapes— such as lasagne and ziti—may be layered with sauce(s) and cheese and then baked. Non-Italian baked pasta dishes include American macaroni and cheese, and *pastitsio*, a Greek dish consisting of layers of macaroni, cinnamon-spiced meat sauce, béchamel sauce, and cheese.

In Spain thin vermicelli noodles are fried in oil, then steamed to doneness in gradually added stock. Egg noodles can also be fried in butter until crisp. Chinese cooks coil cooked vermicelli into pillows and fry on both sides, then top the noodle pillows with a saucy stir-fry, which softens the noodles and partially coats them.

Pasta is almost always served as a separate course in Italy. In other countries, however, noodles are often an accompaniment to a main course. In France buttered noodles are frequently paired with roast chicken or a creamy veal stew. In America, too, buttered noodles are a common side dish with pot roasts, stews, and creamed chicken.

Pasta also turns up in sweet dishes. Sweet noodle *kugel*—noodles baked with cottage cheese, eggs, sugar, raisins, and cinnamon—is a popular dish among Jews of Middle-European descent. In France vermicelli is simmered in cream with sugar, spices, and lemon peel, then baked like a soufflé with egg yolks and beaten egg whites.

Availability Fresh pasta is sold in many specialty stores and Italian markets around the country and is found increasingly in supermarkets. Some brands include preservatives; check the package label. Many supermarkets also stock fresh (not dried) frozen pasta, such as ravioli, fettuccine, and tortellini. All supermarkets carry a few basic dried shapes, such as spaghetti, lasagne, and macaroni. For the more unusual shapes, look for imported dried pasta in specialty stores, Italian markets, and well-stocked supermarkets.

In addition to flour-and-water dried pasta and flour-and-egg fresh pasta, flavored pastas are increasingly available in the United States. Cooked, minced spinach or cooked and puréed beets can add color and subtle flavor to a pasta dough. Herbs, beets, tomatoes, carrots, squid ink, and saffron are some of the more common additions. There is even an Italian recipe for chocolate pasta. Flavored pastas are available both fresh and dried; look for them in specialty stores. They do not require special handling, although care should be taken to choose a compatible sauce.

GUIDE TO FRESH PASTA

Because different regions of Italy apply different names to the same cut, pasta nomenclature is confusing. Some of the more commonly used names for fresh pasta are:

Agnolotti Crescent-shaped dumplings, usually stuffed with meat or pesto.

Cannelloni Rectangles of pasta, usually about 3 inches by 4 inches, stuffed, rolled into tubes, sauced, and baked.

Fettuccine The favorite flat noodle of Rome, cut about ⅛ inch wide. Particularly good with cream sauces, as in fettuccine Alfredo (with butter, cream, and Parmesan).

Lasagne The broadest fresh noodle (also available dried), lasagne are cut about 2 inches wide. The cooked noodle is layered with vegetables, cheeses, béchamel and/or meat sauce, and baked in a casserole.

Pappardelle One of the widest fresh noodles, cut about ⅝ inch wide with a fluted pastry cutter to give it a frilly edge. Traditionally served with rich meat sauces, such as hare sauce (*pappardelle con la lepre*) or chicken-liver sauce.

Ravioli Two face-to-face squares of flat pasta stuffed with a filling of meat, cheese, or vegetables.

Tagliatelle The favorite flat noodle of Bologna. Very similar to fettuccine, although slightly thinner and wider. *Tagliatelle* are cut slightly less than ¼ inch wide. They are often tossed with *Ragù Bolognese*, a rich meat sauce.

Tagliolini and Tagliarini Similar names for the same shape: a long flat ribbon, rolled paper-thin, and cut less than ⅛ inch wide. Often used in broth.

Tortellini A small square topped with meat, vegetables, or cheese, then folded and twisted into a ring-shaped dumpling.

GUIDE TO DRIED PASTA

Manufacturers have created hundreds of dried pasta shapes. The most commonly available are the following.

Acini di Pepe Tiny "peppercorns" most often used in soups.

Bucatini Like spaghetti, but thicker and hollow. Often served *all'Amatriciana:* with tomatoes, *pancetta,* and hot-pepper flakes.

Capelli d'Angelo Angel-hair pasta, similar to fine spaghetti. Often served in broth.

Conchiglie Shell-shaped pasta; good with meat sauce since it captures bits of sauce in its hollows.

Ditali Thimbles; short ridged tubes, about ½ inch long; good with meat sauce. Shorter versions known as *ditalini* are used in soups.

Farfalle Butterflies; a flat noodle about 2 inches long and ¾ inch wide, pinched together in the middle to form a bow-tie shape. Good with tomato sauce or meat sauce.

Fusilli Long, spaghetti-length corkscrew noodles; good with thick, clinging, creamy sauces with bits of meat or vegetables.

Linguine A flat ribbon noodle similar to fettuccine; also available fresh. Often served with clam sauce or with pesto.

Lumache Shells larger than conchiglie (see above) and intended for stuffing. They are frequently filled with seasoned ricotta and topped with tomato sauce.

Macaroni Short, elbow-shaped, hollow noodles; good with meat sauce or cheese sauce, or baked American-style with cheese sauce and eggs. *Macaroni* is also a generic Italian word for dried pasta, usually spelled *maccheroni.*

Manicotti Large hollow tubes, usually stuffed with cheese or meat mixtures, then sauced and baked.

Penne Also known as *mostaccioli* (little mustaches), *penne* (quills) are tubes about 2 inches long, cut diagonally on the ends. They are generally paired with a tomato sauce.

Rigatoni Ridged, hollow tubes about 2 inches long and ½ inch wide. Rigatoni are delicious tossed with meat sauces, bits of which get trapped inside. They hold their shape well and may be baked in sauce.

Rotelle Short, 2-inch-long, corkscrew-shaped pasta; good with chunky sauces.

Ruote Cartwheels; *ruote* resemble little wagon wheels and are often served in soups.

Semi di Melone Melon seeds; tiny pasta shapes used in soups.

Spaghetti The familiar long rodlike pasta. Used with oil-based sauces, shellfish sauces, and tomato sauces. Thin spaghetti is known as spaghettini or vermicelli.

Ziti Long hollow rods, about the length of spaghetti. When cut into shorter lengths (about 2 inches long), they are known as ziti *tagliati,* although some manufacturers call these ziti, too. Use with hearty meat or mushroom sauces, or bake as for rigatoni.

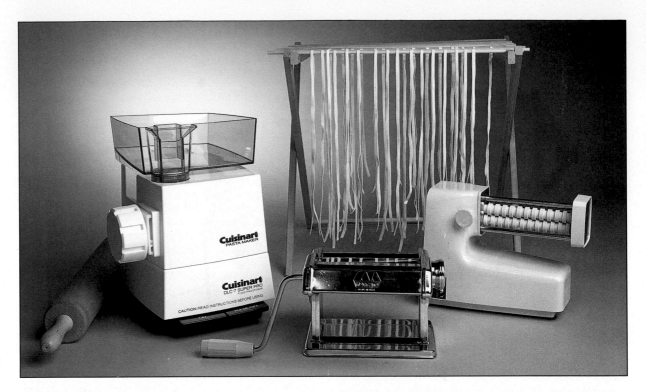

Specialty equipment for making pasta is becoming more commonplace in home kitchens. Shown from left: food processor with pasta-making attachment, wooden drying rack, hand-cranked pasta machine, electric pasta machine.

Storage   Fresh pasta is perishable. It will keep in the refrigerator, wrapped airtight, for about five days, or in the freezer for up to one month (it becomes dry and brittle if frozen longer). Do not thaw frozen pasta; cook directly from the frozen state.

Dried pasta will keep almost indefinitely if stored in a cool, dry place in an airtight container or tightly closed package. If unsauced, leftover cooked dried pasta such as macaroni or a similar shape may be lightly oiled and refrigerated for one or two days. Reheat briefly in boiling water or add to soups.

Cooking   Whether fresh or dried, properly cooked pasta should offer slight resistance to the tooth (al dente); it should not be soft or mushy. Because pasta is so bland, its firm texture is all the more important.

For best results, cook pasta in a large quantity of rapidly boiling, salted water—about 4 quarts of water to 1 pound of pasta. Bring water to a boil, drop pasta in all at once, stir, and cover the pot until the water returns to a boil. Then uncover and boil until pasta is al dente. In general, fresh flat noodles such as fettuccine cook in 60 to 90 seconds. Dried pasta may take 5 minutes or more, depending on its shape and age.

Drain cooked pasta immediately in a colander, shake colander to drain off excess water, then pour pasta into a warm bowl. Add sauce, toss, and serve immediately.

Pasta that is to be baked—such as lasagne, macaroni, or cannelloni—should be undercooked slightly when boiled; otherwise it will be too soft after baking. Drain well, then toss lightly with olive oil to keep noodles from sticking together as they cool.

PASTA-MAKING EQUIPMENT

A food processor makes the job of mixing fresh dough much faster, although the dough can easily be mixed and kneaded by hand. Rolling out the dough by hand, however, is a tedious task. If you plan to make pasta regularly, a hand-cranked pasta machine is a practical investment. An electric machine is even more convenient, but much more expensive. Some food processors have pasta-making attachments. Both hand-cranked and electric pasta machines are designed to make noodle preparation easier. The hand-cranked version thins the dough to the desired thickness, then cuts it into selected widths.

To use the machine, set its smooth rollers at their widest opening and feed a small piece of dough through the rollers until it is very smooth and elastic (about 8 or 10 times). Each time the dough strip comes out, fold in half before feeding it into the machine again. If dough gets sticky, dust it lightly with flour. Adjust the roller to next setting and pass dough through, this time leaving the strip unfolded. Pass through setting about two or three times. Continue feeding the strip of dough through the rollers (several times per setting), narrowing the opening down one step each time to thin the dough to the desired degree (don't roll too thin, however, or the pasta will fall apart when cooked). Repeat the rolling, folding, and rolling steps until all dough has been processed. Let pasta dry for about 15 minutes before cutting.

To cut dough, adjust the blades to the desired width. Put each dried strip of pasta through until cut, then hang or lay out to dry again, if necessary (pasta that is not dry enough will stick together when stored or cooked).

An electric machine completes the kneading operation as you feed it dough, fold dough over, and refeed. When the dough is smooth and elastic, the machine thins it to the desired thickness. After dough is set aside to dry for a few minutes, the dough strips are fed though the selected cutting disk, which quickly produces the desired width of noodle. Some versions have cutting disks that produce tubular noodles as well as flat forms.

A wooden drying rack, resembling a miniature version of the type used for drying laundry, is another piece of specialty equipment to consider. A pastry wheel, although not a necessity, is helpful for cutting strips or separating ravioli. A basic, quality hardwood rolling pin is necessary if you are rolling the dough by hand.

DOUGHS FOR HOMEMADE PASTA

Basic Egg Dough (see below) is probably the one you will use most often. However, the dough can also be varied with the addition of spinach, fresh herbs, or grated lemon rind. Serve the flavored doughs with a complementary sauce. Suggestions for use accompany each recipe.

■ BASIC EGG DOUGH

Fresh homemade pasta doughs are made with eggs, which provide moisture and make the dough softer and easier to knead than a flour-and-water dough.

  1½ cups unbleached flour
   1 teaspoon coarse salt
  1½ large eggs (see Note) or
      2 medium eggs, lightly beaten

1. *To mix by hand:* Put flour and salt in a bowl. Make a well in the center and add eggs. With a fork or with your fingertips, gradually incorporate all the flour to form a mass. Knead lightly to form a smooth ball. Cover with plastic wrap and let rest 20 minutes or overnight before rolling and cutting. *To mix in a food processor:* Put flour and salt in work bowl of processor fitted with metal blade. Begin processing. With the machine running, add eggs through the feed tube in a slow, steady stream. Process until mixture begins to come together but has not formed a ball. Stop machine and press a bit of dough between thumb and first finger. If it holds together, remove dough from bowl and knead by hand to form a smooth ball. If it doesn't hold together, process another 5 seconds, then knead by hand to form a smooth ball. Cover with plastic wrap and let rest 20 minutes or overnight before rolling and cutting.

2. *To roll by hand:* Lightly flour work surface. Start with one third of the dough at a time. Starting from the center and moving to the edge, roll the pasta using as few strokes as possible. If dough becomes too elastic, cover it for a few minutes with a damp cloth to prevent it from drying out. Roll out to ⅛ inch thick or slightly thinner.

To roll by machine: See Pasta-Making Equipment (opposite page), and follow manufacturer's directions for your machine.

3. *To cut pasta by hand:* Dust dough well with flour and let it rest to dry for about 10 minutes. Then roll up like a jelly roll, flatten the top slightly, and cut with a sharp knife across the roll into desired widths: ⅛ inch for fettuccine, ¼ inch for *tagliatelle.* After cutting the entire roll, open up the ribbons and spread noodles on a clean towel or waxed paper to dry, or hang noodles on a special wooden pasta drying rack, about 5 minutes or so before cooking; or wrap in plastic wrap and refrigerate.

Makes 1¼ pounds pasta.

Note Break 2 large eggs into a bowl. Whisk with a fork to blend. Measure volume and pour off one fourth.

■ SPINACH PASTA

Be sure to squeeze as much moisture as possible out of the blanched spinach or it will add too much water to the dough. Serve spinach fettuccine with Ragù Bolognese (see page 412) or use the pasta to make wider sheets for Lasagne Verdi (see page 414).

   1 recipe Basic Egg Dough (at left)
  ¾ pound fresh spinach, leaves and stems blanched,
      drained, squeezed dry, and finely minced

To mix by hand: Combine flour and salt in a bowl. In a separate bowl combine eggs and spinach. Make a well in flour and add spinach-egg mixture. Continue as directed for Basic Egg Dough. *To mix in a food processor:* Place spinach in work bowl of food processor along with flour and salt. Process until blended, then add eggs and continue as directed for Basic Egg Dough.

Makes 1¼ pounds pasta.

■ FRESH HERB PASTA

Fresh herbs can turn egg dough into a fragrant pasta that's delicious with just butter and cheese. Or use buttered herb pasta as a bed for a saucy stew, such as Osso Buco (see page 58). Use strong herbs such as rosemary and oregano in small quantities, rounding out the cup of herbs called for with mild parsley.

   1 recipe Basic Egg Dough (at left)
   1 cup mixed fresh herbs (basil, chives,
      parsley, chervil), loosely packed

To mix by hand: Combine flour and salt as directed for Basic Egg Dough. Mince herbs and combine in a separate bowl with beaten egg. Make a well in center of flour and add herb-egg mixture. Continue as directed for Basic Egg Dough. *To mix in a food processor:* Mince herbs and place in work bowl of food processor with flour and salt. Process until blended, then add eggs and continue as directed for Basic Egg Dough.

Makes 1¼ pounds pasta.

■ LEMON PASTA

This zesty pasta pairs well with steamed mussels or seafood sauces.

> 1 recipe Basic Egg Dough (see page 411)
> 1½ tablespoons grated lemon rind
> ½ teaspoon fresh lemon juice

To mix by hand: Combine flour and salt as directed for Basic Egg Dough. In separate bowl combine lemon rind and juice with eggs. Make a well in the center of the flour and add egg-lemon mixture. Continue as directed for Basic Egg Dough. *To mix in a food processor:* Place lemon rind in work bowl of food processor along with flour and salt. Process until blended. Combine lemon juice with eggs, then add to flour and continue as directed for Basic Egg Dough.

Makes 1¼ pounds pasta.

PASTA SAUCES AND PREPARATIONS

The sauces suitable for pasta are as numerous and varied as the cooks who make them. However, a few basics should be mastered by anyone who wants to perfect a repertoire of pasta dishes. A northern-style cooked tomato sauce, a cream sauce, a tomato-meat sauce, and basil-based pesto (see page 27) are not only useful on their own but also as building blocks for other dishes.

■ NORTHERN-STYLE TOMATO SAUCE

Cooks in northern Italy often enrich sauces with butter, add depth with vegetables and herbs, then simmer the sauce slowly to marry the flavors. This basic tomato sauce supports dozens of other dishes: lasagne, cannelloni, ravioli, baked vegetable casseroles, and braised entrées. If you can't get sweet, vine-ripened tomatoes, use the best available canned variety.

> 2 teaspoons olive oil
> 4 teaspoons butter
> 1 large carrot, peeled and diced
> 2 ribs celery, diced
> 1 onion, diced
> 2 tablespoons minced garlic
> 1 teaspoon flour
> 3 pounds ripe tomatoes, peeled, seeded, and chopped, *or* 1 can (28 oz) plum tomatoes, with juice, whirled briefly in a blender
> 1 tablespoon tomato paste
> Pinch sugar
> ¼ cup fresh chopped basil *or* 1 teaspoon dried basil
> 4 sprigs parsley
> 2 sprigs fresh oregano
> 1 bay leaf
> Salt and freshly ground pepper, to taste

Heat oil and butter in a large, heavy saucepan over moderate heat. When butter foams, add carrot, celery, onion, and garlic, and stew gently for 10 minutes. Stir in flour and continue cooking 5 minutes. Add tomatoes, tomato paste, sugar, basil, parsley, oregano, and bay leaf. Simmer, partly covered, for 1 hour. Remove bay leaf and herb stems. Pass sauce through a food mill or purée in a food processor if you prefer a smoother texture. Season to taste with salt and pepper.

Makes 4 cups.

Make-Ahead Tip Sauce may be made up to one week ahead and held in the refrigerator until needed. It may be frozen for up to one month.

■ PARMESAN CREAM SAUCE

Use this delicate sauce from northern Italy to dress up almost any pasta, fresh or dried. Toss fettuccine in it and you'll have a classic fettuccine Alfredo.

> 2 tablespoons olive oil
> 1 tablespoon butter
> 3 tablespoons minced shallots
> ½ cup whipping cream
> ½ cup freshly grated Parmesan cheese

Heat olive oil and butter in a skillet over moderate heat. Add shallots; cook gently until soft. Add cream; cook over low heat 3 to 4 minutes more, whisking to incorporate cream. Add Parmesan and remove from heat.

Makes about 1 cup.

Make-Ahead Tip Sauce may be made up to 4 hours ahead of serving and refrigerated. Reheat gently just before tossing with pasta.

■ RAGU BOLOGNESE

The cooking of Bologna is widely considered the richest in Italy. No dainty herbs and textures for the Bolognese: They add body to their tomato sauce with meat, lots of vegetables, and milk or cream. This sauce is especially good with sturdy pasta—such as shells or rigatoni—that has holes or ridges to trap it.

> ½ cup olive oil
> ½ cup unsalted butter
> 1½ cups diced onion
> 1 cup diced celery
> 1 cup peeled and diced carrot
> 2 pounds extralean ground beef
> 1¾ cups dry white wine
> 1 cup milk
> 5 pounds ripe tomatoes, peeled, seeded, and chopped, *or* 2 cans (28 oz each) plum tomatoes, with juice, whirled briefly in a blender
> 1 teaspoon kosher salt
> ⅛ teaspoon freshly grated nutmeg
> 1 teaspoon freshly ground pepper

1. Heat oil and butter in a medium stockpot over moderate heat. When butter foams, add onion, celery, and carrot and cook for 10 minutes. Add beef, breaking it up with a wooden spoon; cook until meat is lightly browned.

2. Add wine to sautéed beef-vegetable mixture; reduce heat to medium-low and simmer, uncovered, until wine is completely absorbed. Repeat with milk. Add tomatoes, salt, nutmeg, and pepper and simmer gently, uncovered, until mixture is reduced to a rich sauce (about 2½ hours). Taste and adjust seasoning. Serve immediately over egg noodles or cool and refrigerate.

Makes about 4 cups.

Make-Ahead Tip   Sauce may be made up to one week ahead of serving and refrigerated. It may be frozen for up to two months.

▪ WHITE CLAM OR MUSSEL SAUCE

Select the smallest clams available. The texture and flavor of canned imports from the Orient prove more authentic than our fresh cherrystone clams. Fresh mussels are even more flavorful than clams and are a showy presentation when arranged atop linguine, the classic pasta for this sauce. But any thin, dried pasta will work.

> 2 **pounds fresh clams or mussels** *or*
> 2 **cans (6½ oz each) chopped clams and their juice**
> ¼ **cup olive oil**
> 2 **cloves garlic**
> ⅓ **cup dry white wine**
> **Freshly ground pepper, to taste**
> 2 **tablespoons chopped parsley, for garnish**

1. If using canned clams, begin with step 2. If using fresh clams, scrub thoroughly with a stiff brush to remove any specks of sand or barnacles. Place clams in a metal colander and set in a large pot containing approximately 2 inches boiling water. Cover tightly and steam just until shells begin to open. Remove from heat and reserve a few shells with meat inside for garnish. Then remove meat from remaining shells. Dice meat and set aside. Strain juice from pan through a paper coffee filter, cheesecloth, or fine sieve; reserve ½ cup liquid to use for sauce.

2. In a large skillet heat 3 tablespoons of the olive oil over medium heat. Add garlic cloves; brown them lightly to flavor the oil; then discard garlic.

3. Add steamed fresh clams or canned clams along with their juice and white wine. Cook over medium-high heat until about half of the liquid has evaporated (about 2 minutes). Add pepper to taste and simmer 4 to 5 minutes.

4. Toss with cooked linguine and garnish with reserved clams or mussels in the shell and sprinkle with parsley.

Makes about 1½ cups.

▪ FETTUCCINE CARBONARA

The heat of the pasta cooks the eggs to yield a sauce made right in the serving bowl. Carbonara is a rich first course; follow it with a simple veal or chicken dish.

> 2 **tablespoons olive oil**
> 1 **tablespoon unsalted butter**
> 2 **tablespoons finely minced garlic**
> 8 **ounces pancetta (Italian bacon), in small dice**
> ⅓ **cup dry white wine**
> 2 **eggs**
> ⅓ **cup freshly grated Pecorino Romano cheese**
> ⅓ **cup freshly grated Parmesan cheese**
> 1 **recipe Basic Egg Dough (see page 411)**
> **Salt and freshly ground pepper, to taste**

1. Heat oil and butter in a skillet over moderate heat. When butter foams, add garlic and sauté until garlic is fragrant. Add *pancetta* and fry until lightly browned. Add wine and simmer until almost completely evaporated. Remove skillet from heat.

2. In a large serving bowl beat eggs lightly. Stir in Pecorino and Parmesan.

3. Cook pasta in plenty of boiling salted water until just done. Drain thoroughly and add to egg-cheese mixture. Toss well, then add hot pancetta mixture and toss again. Season with salt and plenty of pepper.

Serves 4.

A robust tomato sauce is important to countless Italian dishes, from lasagne and ravioli to braised meats and vegetables.

LASAGNE VERDI

Make your own spinach pasta for this recipe or substitute ¾ pound storebought noodles. This updated, extremely attractive version of a classic recipe is full of striking, contrasting colors and new combinations. The Lasagne With Meat Sauce variation is more traditional.

  1   recipe Spinach Pasta (see page 411)
      Olive oil, for moistening
  1   medium eggplant
  1   teaspoon kosher salt
  2   medium zucchini
 12   shiitake mushrooms *or*
      ½ pound domestic mushrooms
  3   leeks, cleaned
  1   tablespoon butter
  1   tablespoon olive oil
  3   cups Northern-Style Tomato Sauce (see page 412)
  ¾   cup freshly grated Parmesan cheese
  3   cups ricotta cheese
  ¾   cup grated Monterey jack or mozzarella cheese

1. Prepare Spinach Pasta. Cut pasta into lasagne-shaped noodles approximately 12 inches long to fit a 9- by 12-inch baking dish. Bring a large pot of salted water to a boil. Add lasagne noodles and cook until almost tender. Drain and refresh under cold water, drain again, and dry. Moisten noodles with olive oil and spread out on clean kitchen towels.

2. Preheat oven to 350° F. Slice eggplant in half. Slash ½-inch deep cuts into each half. Place halves on a towel and sprinkle with the salt. Let rest for 30 minutes. Place in colander, rinse, and pat dry. Place eggplant on a baking sheet and bake until tender (40 to 50 minutes). Cool slightly, then slice ¼ inch thick and reserve. Slice zucchini lengthwise into ⅛-inch-thick pieces and reserve.

3. Slice shiitake mushrooms about ¼ inch thick. Slice leeks into ½-inch-thick slices. In a large skillet heat butter and oil over medium heat, add leeks and mushrooms, and cook together for 10 to 12 minutes. Add tomato sauce to skillet; simmer for 15 minutes.

4. Spread one fourth of tomato-mushroom-leek sauce on bottom of baking dish. Place lasagne noodles on sauce, and cover with one third of the Parmesan cheese, half of the ricotta, and half of the Monterey jack. Cover cheeses with eggplant slices. Repeat layers using one third of the remaining sauce, one half of the lasagne noodles, half of the remaining Parmesan cheese, all of the remaining ricotta and Monterey jack cheeses, and the zucchini slices. Cover with one half of the remaining sauce and the remaining lasagne noodles. Top with remaining sauce and Parmesan cheese. Bake until warmed through and cheese is lightly browned (35 to 40 minutes). Cool 5 minutes before serving.

Serves 6.

Lasagne With Meat Sauce   Substitute 3 cups Ragù Bolognese (see page 412) for Northern-Style Tomato Sauce. Omit eggplant, zucchini, and leeks. Follow directions for Lasagne Verdi; bake about 30 minutes.

Serves 6.

PASTA PRIMAVERA

The typical *pasta primavera* is a veritable garden on a plate, with the most tender young vegetables tossed with herbs and thin pasta. You can readily substitute whatever is freshest in the market, but remember to aim for lively colors and contrasting textures. So that all the vegetables cook evenly, some are blanched before they are added to the other ingredients.

  1   pound sugar snap peas, strings removed, *or*
      1 cup shelled fresh peas
  1   pound fresh asparagus
  1   cup sliced slender green beans, in 2-inch lengths
  ½   cup thin carrot strips
  3   tablespoons olive oil, plus 1 tablespoon if using dried pasta
  2   tablespoons unsalted butter
  ½   cup diced red bell pepper
  ½   cup diced yellow bell pepper (optional)
  2   tablespoons pine nuts, toasted
  1   recipe Fresh Herb Pasta (see page 411) *or*
      ¾ pound dried spaghettini pasta
  1   cup thinly shredded romaine lettuce
  2   tablespoons snipped fresh chives
      Salt, to taste
  4   tablespoons minced parsley, for garnish
      Freshly grated Parmesan cheese

1. Bring a large pot of salted water to a rolling boil. Blanch peas, asparagus, beans, and carrots separately; when each batch is tender but crisp, remove to ice water to stop cooking. Drain well and pat dry. Save the cooking water.

2. Heat the 3 tablespoons olive oil and butter in a large, heavy-bottomed skillet over moderate heat. When butter foams, add red peppers and yellow peppers (if used) and sauté 1 minute. Add pine nuts and sauté 1 more minute. Add blanched and dried peas, asparagus, beans, and carrots, and toss until coated with butter-oil mixture and warmed through.

3. To cook pasta, bring reserved vegetable water to a rolling boil. If using dried pasta, add 1 tablespoon oil (if you are using fresh pasta, there is no need to add oil). Add pasta and cook until just done. Drain well and transfer to a warm serving bowl. Add hot vegetables to pasta with romaine and chives. Toss well, add salt to taste, then toss again. Divide pasta among warm serving plates. Garnish each portion with minced parsley; pass grated Parmesan separately.

Serves 4.

SPINACH RAVIOLI

Ravioli can be made with a variety of fillings and doughs. Be careful to match the dough and filling to make a compatible combination. These plump little pillows are made with a spinach dough stuffed with an unusual cheese and escarole mixture that is complemented by either tomato sauce or light Parmesan Cream Sauce. They're quite rich and should be followed with a simple main course. They can be prepared a few hours before serving and held on lightly floured baking sheets. Make sure they do not touch. Cover and refrigerate. They will freeze for up to three months; tray-freeze (see FREEZE) and wrap airtight.

    2 recipes Spinach Pasta (see page 411)
    1 recipe Northern-Style Tomato Sauce or
      1 recipe Parmesan Cream Sauce (see page 412)
    3 tablespoons minced parsley, for garnish
    ¼ cup freshly grated Parmesan cheese, for garnish

Cheese and Escarole Filling

    3 tablespoons minced leek or onion
    ½ tablespoon minced garlic
    3 tablespoons olive oil
    1 tablespoon butter
    1 large bunch escarole, washed and finely shredded
    1 teaspoon dried oregano
    2 tablespoons Marsala
    2 tablespoons whipping cream
    ¼ cup whole-milk ricotta cheese
    ¼ cup grated Bel Paese or
      grated mozzarella cheese
      Salt and freshly ground pepper, to taste
      Pinch freshly grated nutmeg

1. Roll dough out in sheets. Form ravioli as described in How to Make Ravioli (photographs at right).

2. Bring a large pot of salted water to a boil. Add ravioli to boiling water a few at a time; do not crowd the pot. Ravioli will sink, then float. After they begin to float, cook 2½ minutes. Remove one and taste for doneness. With a slotted spoon, remove cooked ravioli to a warm platter and keep warm in a low oven. Add remaining ravioli to boiling water in batches until all are cooked. Meanwhile, reheat tomato or cream sauce.

3. When all ravioli are on the platter, top with hot sauce. Garnish with parsley and Parmesan.

Serves 4 to 6.

Cheese and Escarole Filling Sauté leek and garlic in oil and butter over moderate heat until leek is very soft (about 15 minutes). Add escarole and oregano and sauté 2 minutes. Add Marsala, turn heat up to high, and cook until Marsala is almost completely evaporated. Reduce heat to medium and add cream. Stir to combine; simmer until cream thickens into a sauce (2 to 3 minutes). Remove from heat and cool slightly. Stir in cheeses; season to taste with salt, pepper, and nutmeg.

PASTA ROLL

The pasta roll can be made early in the day. Reheat by immersing in the boiling water 8 to 10 minutes. If you don't have a pot large enough to hold the full roll, cut pasta roll in half, wrap each half separately, and then poach.

    1 bunch spinach, julienned
    1 medium onion, diced
    2 cloves garlic, minced
    2 tablespoons unsalted butter
    1 tablespoon olive oil
    ½ pound ground veal or pork
    ½ pound boneless chicken breast, finely minced
    1 pound (2 cups) whole-milk ricotta cheese
    6 to 8 sprigs parsley, minced
    ½ teaspoon freshly grated nutmeg
    ½ teaspoon salt
    ½ teaspoon dried thyme
    ¼ teaspoon white pepper
    2 egg yolks
    1 cup freshly grated Parmesan cheese
    1 egg beaten with 1 tablespoon water
    ½ pound Basic Egg Dough (see page 411),
      rolled into 2 sheets (8 by 16 in. each)
      Northern-Style Tomato Sauce, for
      accompaniment (optional, see page 412)
      Melted butter and grated Parmesan cheese,
      for accompaniment (optional)

1. In a large skillet sauté spinach, onion, and garlic in butter and oil; set aside. In a large bowl or in food processor, mix veal and chicken breast (the processor will give you a smoother mixture).

2. In a large bowl mix cooked onion mixture with veal and chicken. Stir in ricotta cheese, parsley, nutmeg, salt, thyme, pepper, egg yolks, and Parmesan cheese.

3. Place egg-water wash in a small bowl. Lay out a piece of cheesecloth (larger than 16 inches square) on work surface. Place one sheet of dough on cheesecloth. Brush one long edge of dough with egg wash. Place second sheet of dough slightly overlapping first along long edge and press length to seal.

4. Spread prepared filling on pasta. Roll up jelly-roll style. Lay pasta roll along one edge of cheesecloth and roll up. Tie ends with string. In a fish poacher or a Dutch oven large enough to hold pasta roll, bring 6 quarts water to a boil. Gently lower roll into boiling water, reduce heat, and simmer 30 minutes. Remove from water and slice into 1-inch-thick pieces. Serve with tomato sauce or melted butter and Parmesan cheese, if desired.

Serves 8 as a main course.

Recipes and Related Information
Fettuccine With White Truffles, 583; Fusilli Salad, 508; Pesto, 27; Squid Marinara, 546.

HOW TO MAKE RAVIOLI

Roll pasta dough into sheets. Place mounds of filling, about ¾ teaspoon each, at regular intervals the length of the pasta. Brush lightly with cold water between mounds.

Place another sheet of pasta over the first and use fingers to press sheets together between mounds of filling.

Cut ravioli with a pizza cutter or pastry wheel. Use a fork to crimp and seal edges.

PATCH, TO

To repair cracks or tears in pie dough after it has been rolled out by sealing with a thin piece of leftover dough. Sometimes the patch is made stronger by gluing with water. It is better to patch pastry dough than to reroll it because rerolling will toughen it.

PATE AND TERRINE

A pâté is a spreadable paste of ground meats, livers, and seasonings. Its consistency can be airy and smooth like a mousse or more coarsely textured and country style. Ingredients for pâtés can be precooked and then combined, or the mixture can be processed and then baked in a crust, or in a mold that is often lined with pork fat. Special containers called terrine molds are traditionally used for pâtés, but any loaf pan of equal volume will work just as well (see MOLD). A terrine is made in a mold of the same name and was traditionally served in its mold. The pâté was freestanding. These definitions are, however, no longer rigidly followed. You will find the terms *pâté* and *terrine* used interchangeably.

Mixtures for pâtés are called forcemeats. These are made of fish, pork, lean veal, duck, game, or fowl, plus fat and flavorings, and are bound together with a bread or flour paste (see FORCEMEAT). Multicolored vegetable pâtés are increasingly popular.

Pâtés and terrines are served as appetizers or first courses. They are much like the American meat loaf, but have a richer, more luxurious texture and flavor. They are easy to prepare, especially with a food processor, although they may require costly or hard-to-find ingredients. Pâtés and terrines are wonderful for entertaining because they can be prepared well ahead; in fact, they improve when aged for several days.

■ CURRIED CHICKEN OR DUCK LIVER PATE IN ASPIC

The glistening aspic decoration belies the easy assembly of this curried liver pâté. Be sure to use a mold that is attractive enough to bring to the table.

    1 pound chicken or duck livers
    1 tart apple, diced
    1 small onion, diced
    4 tablespoons unsalted butter
    1 tablespoon curry powder
    ¼ cup Chicken Stock (see page 560) or apple brandy
    1½ tablespoons flour
    ½ teaspoon salt
    ¼ teaspoon freshly ground pepper
    1 egg
    1 baguette, sliced, for accompaniment

Aspic Glaze (see Note)

1. Preheat oven to 350° F. In a large skillet sauté livers, apple, and onion in butter over medium-high heat until livers are brown on outside but remain pink on inside (about 12 minutes). Stir in curry powder and cook 3 to 4 minutes.

2. Remove to a blender or food processor. Pour stock into pan, scraping cooked bits to loosen. Add pan juices to liver, and purée until smooth. Add flour, salt, pepper, and egg, and purée again until smooth.

3. Pour into a 3½- to 4-cup mold. Cover with aluminum foil, and place in a baking dish filled with about 1 inch warm water. Bake until knife inserted in center comes out clean (about 45 minutes). Remove from oven and cool. Chill for 1 hour and decorate with Aspic Glaze. Serve with baguette slices.

Serves 12 to 20 as an appetizer.

Note   See Aspic Glaze, page 372; use one half recipe Basic Aspic.

■ PATE MAISON

Set out this flavorful pâté with tiny French *cornichons* (pickles), a crock of Dijon mustard, and sliced baguettes. Cold and thinly sliced on French bread, it makes a splendid sandwich the next day.

    ½ medium onion, minced
    2 tablespoons butter
    ½ cup plus 2 tablespoons Cognac or Armagnac
    1 pound ground pork
    1 pound ground veal
    1 clove garlic, minced
    2 eggs, slightly beaten
    1 teaspoon salt
    ⅛ teaspoon freshly ground pepper
    1 teaspoon dried thyme
    1 chicken breast, boned and skinned
    1 pound pork fat, cut into ⅛-inch slices
    2 ounces pistachio nuts, shelled

1. Preheat oven to 350° F. In a small skillet sauté onion in butter over medium-high heat until translucent. Pour in ½ cup of the Cognac. Cook until Cognac is absorbed into onion (mixture will measure about ⅓ cup). Remove from heat and place in a large mixing bowl.

2. Add pork, veal, garlic, eggs, salt, pepper, and thyme. Mix with hands until thoroughly blended, or blend in food processor until light in texture and well blended.

3. Cut chicken breast into ½- by 3-inch slices. Put slices in a small bowl and add the remaining 2 tablespoons Cognac.

4. Line a 2-quart terrine or loaf pan with slices of pork fat. Press one half of ground meat mixture into pan. Cover with Cognac-soaked chicken, then pistachios. Press remaining ground meat mixture on top. Cover with another layer of pork fat.

5. Cover terrine with aluminum foil. Set in a pan of boiling water. Place on rack in center of oven. Bake until juices run clear yellow and pâté has shrunk from sides of pan.

6. When pâté is done, remove terrine and set on cooling rack. Place another loaf pan on top of pâté; fill with 3 to 4 pounds of weight (canned goods or bricks work well). Let pâté cool at room temperature for several hours, then refrigerate 2 to 3 days before slicing. To serve, unmold and slice.

Serves 10 as a first course.

■ HOT PORK AND HAM PATE IN BRIOCHE

French through and through, this hot pâté is baked inside a buttery brioche dough. The flavor of the pâté will intensify if the mixture is allowed to cure overnight in the refrigerator.

    2 tablespoons butter
    1 large onion, finely chopped
    1 clove garlic, minced
    ¼ cup brandy
    1 egg
    ½ cup soft bread crumbs
    1 pound ground pork
    2 cups ground baked ham
    ¼ cup finely chopped parsley
    ½ teaspoon *each* salt and dried thyme
    ¼ teaspoon ground allspice
    ⅛ teaspoon white pepper
    1 egg beaten with 1 teaspoon water

Brioche Dough

    1 package active dry yeast
    ¼ cup warm (105° to 115° F) water
    1 tablespoon sugar
    ½ teaspoon salt
    2 cups flour
    2 eggs
    ½ cup butter, softened

1. Prepare Brioche Dough and, while it is rising, make filling.

2. In a medium frying pan, melt butter and cook onion until soft but not browned. Mix in garlic and brandy; cook, stirring, until most of the liquid cooks away.

3. Beat the 1 egg in a large bowl. Mix in bread crumbs, then ground meats, onion mixture, parsley, salt, thyme, allspice, and white pepper. Cover and refrigerate until ready to enclose in dough.

4. Roll dough out on a generously floured board or pastry cloth to make a rectangle about 10 by 20 inches. Shape filling with your hands into a loaf about 4 by 8 inches. Place filling at one end of dough. Pinch dough to seal ends. With long sealed edge at bottom, place in a well-greased 5- by 9-inch loaf pan.

5. Cover lightly with waxed paper and let rise in a warm place until dough looks puffy (about 30 minutes); or cover and refrigerate for several hours or overnight, and let stand at room temperature until puffy looking (about 1 hour).

6. Preheat oven to 350° F. Brush dough lightly with beaten egg mixture. Bake until dough is well browned and juice runs clear when a long skewer is inserted in center (about 1½ hours).

7. Place pâté (still in pan) on a rack and let stand for about 15 minutes; then carefully remove loaf from pan and cut into 1-inch-thick slices. Serve warm.

Serves 6 to 8.

Brioche Dough   Sprinkle yeast over the water in large bowl of electric mixer; let stand for 5 minutes to soften. Mix in sugar and salt, then ½ cup flour. Beat at medium speed until elastic (about 3 minutes). Beat in eggs, one at a time, until smooth, then gradually beat in remaining flour. Add butter, 1 tablespoon at a time, beating well after each addition. Transfer to a greased bowl, cover, and let rise in a warm place until doubled (about 1½ hours). Stir dough down.

Pâtés, such as Pâté Maison, probably developed as a Gallic solution to the universal problem of what to do with leftovers.

quick-soak, cover with cold water, bring to a boil, and boil for 1 minute; cover, remove from heat, and let stand for 1 hour. Discard soaking liquid.

Cooking   *Fresh Peas:* See BOIL, SAUTE, STEAM, STIR-FRY. *Dried Peas:* See BOIL. Also see specific peas.

BLACK-EYED PEA

See Cowpea.

CECI BEAN

See Chick-pea.

CHICK-PEA

Also known as garbanzo beans or ceci beans, chick-peas are a staple in India and figure prominently in the cuisines of North Africa and the Middle East. Use chick-peas in salads, soups, and stews or as a side dish. They may be roasted and served as a snack; ground for flour for use in breads and fritters; puréed and seasoned for a dip; or added to the North African stew known as Couscous. Chick-peas are occasionally available fresh in the summer; the pod is a small, fuzzy, green oval with one or two seeds inside. Dried chick-peas are packaged in plastic bags or sold in bulk. For fresh peas, select full, light green pods without signs of drying.

To prepare fresh chick-peas, open the pod and remove the beans. Simmer beans, covered, in boiling water until tender. To prepare dried chick-peas, soak overnight or quick-soak (see Preparation); then simmer, covered, in 3 parts water to 1 part peas until tender (1½ to 2 hours).

■ HUMMUS

Serve this Middle Eastern dip with fresh raw vegetables, cracker bread, or toasted pita bread. Sesame tahini has the consistency of peanut butter. It's available in many supermarkets and specialty food stores. If it has separated, stir well before using.

> 2 **cans (15 oz each) chick-peas**
> 3 **cloves garlic**
> 2 **tablespoons fresh lemon juice, or more, to taste**
> 6 **tablespoons sesame tahini** *or*
>   **2 to 3 tablespoons peanut butter**
> ¼ **teaspoon ground cumin, or to taste (optional)**
>   **Salt, to taste**
>   **Finely chopped parsley, for garnish**

1. Drain liquid from 1 can chick-peas and put beans in a food processor or blender. Add peas from remaining can with their liquid, and garlic, lemon juice, and tahini; purée until smooth.

2. Add cumin (if used) and salt to taste, and purée a few seconds more. Serve garnished with parsley.

Makes 3 cups.

Hoppin' John, a richly flavorful dish of black-eyed peas, is traditionally served in the Deep South on New Year's Day.

PEA

All peas are members of the legume family, plants whose seeds are borne in pods. Some varieties, such as English peas and the French *petits pois,* are valued for their seeds only and are known as shelling peas. Some of the shelling peas—English peas, for example—are usually eaten fresh; others, such as pigeon peas, field peas (which, when split, are the common green or yellow split pea), and chick-peas, are usually dried.

The other major type of pea is the edible-podded pea, eaten in its entirety before the seeds develop. The Chinese snow pea is the best-known example.

Use   Depending upon their variety, peas may be used as a side dish or added to soups, salads, stews, rice and pasta dishes, and casseroles.

Availability   Fresh and dried peas are found in supermarkets and specialty produce stores; some health-food stores carry a selection of dried peas. This entry discusses the most common types of fresh and dried peas.

Selection   See specific peas.

Storage   Keep both shelling peas (in their pods) and edible-podded peas in a plastic bag in the refrigerator crisper and use within one or two days. Dried peas will keep for up to one year in an airtight container in a cool, dry place.

Preparation   Shelling peas should be shelled just before using. Open pod by removing string. Remove peas. Snow peas and sugar snap peas should be strung as well, although the pods should be left unopened. *About soaking and quick-soaking dried peas:* Most dried peas require presoaking to soften them before cooking. Cover with cold water and soak at least 8 hours or overnight. To

CHINESE SNOW PEA

Edible-podded Chinese snow peas are delicious when stir-fried quickly in oil by themselves or with other ingredients. They should be cooked only until hot throughout (one or two minutes). They may be stir-fried with Chinese black mushrooms, water chestnuts, and bean curd, or lightly glazed with oyster sauce. Snow peas can be added to soups or stews or served as a stir-fry side dish for all manner of Western dishes—from baked fish to roast pork, chicken, or beef.

Chinese snow peas are available the year around in Asian markets and in some supermarkets, with peak supplies in spring and fall. They should be bright green, and firm. Choose ones that are small and flat, with immature seeds. Avoid those with drying along the seam.

▮ STILTON SNOW PEAS

A quick blanching highlights the color and flavor of snow peas while retaining their crispness. The filled snow peas will hold in the refrigerator for several hours if loosely covered with plastic wrap to prevent drying out.

40 snow peas
3 ounces Stilton cheese, at room temperature
3 ounces cream cheese, softened
1 teaspoon chopped parsley

1. Remove stems from snow peas. Bring 3 quarts of water to a boil. Drop in snow peas and blanch for 30 seconds. Remove with slotted spoon and immediately place in ice-cold water to stop cooking. Remove from water and pat dry with paper towels. Carefully cut a 1- to 1½-inch slit in center of curved side of each snow pea with a sharp paring knife.

2. In a small mixing bowl, mix Stilton cheese, cream cheese, and parsley. Fill each snow pea through slit, using two spoons or a pastry bag fitted with a small star tip. Chill until serving time on paper-towel–lined baking sheets covered loosely with plastic wrap. To serve, arrange in a fan shape on an attractive plate.

Makes 40 appetizers.

Recipe: Shrimp With Snow Peas and Water Chestnuts, 606.

COWPEA

Also known as crowder peas, cowpeas are widely eaten in the American South and in Africa. They have a mealy texture and an earthy flavor that is complemented by pork, especially ham. The black-eyed pea is a type of cowpea. Use cowpeas in soups, stews, and salads or as a side dish. In the summer, cowpeas are occasionally available fresh, either shelled or unshelled. If you are buying unshelled fresh peas, select those with full, moist pods. Dried black-eyed peas and cowpeas are available packaged in plastic bags or sold in bulk; they should be used within one year of purchase. Black-eyed peas may also be purchased canned and frozen.

To prepare fresh cowpeas, open pod and remove beans. Cook fresh cowpeas in boiling water, covered, until tender. To prepare dried cowpeas, soak overnight or quick-soak (see Preparation); simmer, covered, in 3 parts water to 1 part peas until tender (about one hour).

▮ HOPPIN' JOHN

In the Deep South black-eyed peas eaten on New Year's Day are supposed to bring good luck in the coming year. In some areas residents insist that the peas bestow good luck only if they're prepared in Hoppin' John and served with cooked greens, which symbolize money. This recipe uses dried black-eyed peas. Note that the peas must stand for at least one hour or as long as overnight. Accompany Hoppin' John with Country-Style Greens. That recipe appears on page 287.

1½ cups (about ½ lb) dried black-eyed peas
1½ teaspoons salt, plus salt to taste
6 strips bacon, diced
1 medium onion, chopped
¾ cup long-grain white rice
2 tablespoons butter (optional)
   Salt and freshly ground pepper, to taste
   Dash of Louisiana-style hot sauce, to taste
½ cup minced green onions, including
   green tops, for garnish
3 tablespoons minced parsley, for garnish

1. Rinse peas and pick them over. Cover with 3 cups cold water, add 1 teaspoon of the salt, and let stand overnight. (For a quicker soak, to serve peas the same day, see Preparation.)

2. Drain peas, discarding water, and place in a large pot. In a separate pan, sauté bacon until crisp; add it to peas, reserving rendered drippings. Add onion, remaining ½ teaspoon salt, and 2 cups water. Bring just to a boil, lower heat, and simmer until peas are tender (about 30 minutes). A small amount of cooking liquid should remain; if liquid is absorbed too quickly during cooking, add fresh water by ¼ cups.

3. In separate pot, cover rice with cold water. Bring to a boil, stir once, cover, and lower heat to the barest simmer. Simmer rice for 20 minutes.

4. When peas are tender, add cooked rice to pot. Stir in 2 tablespoons reserved bacon fat or 2 tablespoons butter (if preferred), salt, pepper, and hot sauce to taste. Cover and simmer about 15 minutes longer so flavors mingle and rice absorbs some of the remaining cooking liquid. To serve, garnish with green onions and parsley.

Serves 6 to 7.

CROWDER PEA

See Cowpea.

ENGLISH PEA

Fresh shelled peas are best when steamed briefly in a covered saucepan in a small amount of boiling water. Steamed peas are usually buttered and occasionally creamed as well. French cooks add shredded lettuce to the steaming peas; other cooks add onion or green onion. Indian cooks braise peas with spices and cubes of firm homemade cheese. Italian cooks braise peas with prosciutto. Steamed peas can be cooled, then tossed with diced ham and mayonnaise for a summer salad. They can be mixed with other vegetables, such as carrots or corn, and served hot. They can be added to soups or stews and are particularly delicious with delicate meats such as veal or veal sweetbreads.

Fresh English peas are available in supermarkets the year around, with the domestic summer crop being supplemented by imports from Mexico. The domestic crop peaks in quantity and quality in the summer months. Both English peas and the tiny French *petits pois* are available frozen and canned. Fresh shelling peas are full of sugar at harvest but begin to convert their natural sugar into starch the moment they're picked. For that reason, the sooner the pea is cooked after harvest, the better. Buy English peas from a market with rapid turnover or, better yet, buy peas at local farm stands or farmers' markets, if possible. When selecting English peas, break a pod open and taste a pea; it should be sweet, not starchy. The pods should be well filled but the seeds should not be overlarge. Look for bright green pods; avoid those that have dry seams.

■ SPRING LAMB STEW WITH FRESH PEAS

Fresh mint seasons the lamb in this glistening stew. Serve with butter-fried potatoes and a leafy green salad tossed with your favorite dressing, crusty bread and butter, and fresh strawberries for dessert.

>   3 pounds boneless lamb leg or shoulder,
>   fat trimmed and cut in 1-inch cubes
>   Salt and white pepper, to taste
>   3 tablespoons butter
>   3 tablespoons vegetable oil
>   3 shallots, finely chopped
>   1 clove garlic, minced
>   1 large carrot, cut in ¼-inch-thick slices
>   3 or 4 sprigs fresh mint
>   1 cup Rich Chicken Stock (see page 560) or
>   canned chicken broth
>   1½ cups dry white wine
>   1½ to 2 cups shelled fresh peas

1. Sprinkle lamb lightly with salt and pepper. In a large, deep frying pan or Dutch oven, melt 2 tablespoons butter with oil. Add lamb, about a third at a time. Brown well, removing lamb as it browns. When all lamb is removed from pan, add shallots, cooking and stirring until they are soft and lightly browned. Mix in garlic and carrot.

2. Return lamb to pan. Add mint, broth, and wine. Bring to a boil, cover, reduce heat, and simmer until tender (45 minutes to 1 hour).

3. Remove lamb and keep it warm. Strain cooking liquid, discarding carrot and mint. Skim and discard surface fat. Return liquid to pan and bring to a boil over high heat. Cook, stirring, until slightly reduced and syrupy. Taste, and add salt if needed. Mix in peas and cook, stirring, for 1 to 2 minutes.

4. Cut remaining butter in pieces. Off heat, stir in butter, one piece at a time, until melted.

5. Return lamb to sauce, stirring to coat well. Spoon lamb into center of each warm plate. Surround with sauce and peas and serve at once.

Serves 6 to 8.

FIELD PEA

Small round peas grown especially for drying are known as field peas; they may be green or yellow. When split, they are called split peas. Whole field peas and split peas are boiled in about 4 parts water to 1 part peas until soft (about one hour). They can be boiled further to reduce them to a purée, then seasoned with butter or spices or made into soup. Bacon, sausage, or smoked pork make a pleasing addition to dried peas and dried pea soups. Whole field peas are available in plastic packages in some supermarkets and in bulk in some health-food stores. Split peas are available in plastic packages in most supermarkets and in bulk in most health-food stores.

Recipes: Curried Lettuce and Pea Soup, 341; Split Pea Soup, Black Forest Style, 565.

GARBANZO BEAN

See Chick-pea.

PETITS POIS

See English Pea.

PIGEON PEA

Also known as *gunga, goongoo,* or congo peas, pigeon peas are native to Africa and are widely eaten today in the Caribbean, Africa, and India. The dried peas are beige or pale yellow with red mottling; they are not widely available fresh. In the Caribbean cooks make pigeon peas into soup or dumplings or serve them with rice. Look for dried pigeon peas in health-food stores and markets catering to an Indian, African, or Caribbean clientele.

SPLIT PEA

See Field Pea.

SUGAR SNAP PEA

The sugar snap pea, a relatively new variety, is a cross between a shelling pea and an edible-podded pea. Its pod is still sweet and tender when the seeds are developed. Sugar snap peas are available in spring and fall in some supermarkets and specialty markets. Sugar snap peas should be bright green and firm, not limp. They should be plump, but not filled to bursting; avoid pods that are dried around the seam. Sugar snap peas need only brief blanching—a couple of minutes in a large quantity of boiling salted water, then draining, drying, and reheating in oil or butter. They should still be crunchy when served. Sautéed sugar snap peas make an excellent side dish for fish, poultry, pork, beef, or veal.

PEACH

The sweet, juicy peaches grown today probably bear little resemblance to the earliest peaches, native to China. Until modern horticulturists developed the strains we enjoy today, most peaches were small, fairly sour, and certainly more fuzzy than modern varieties. Today, there are thousands of named peaches. Some have stones that cling to the flesh (clingstone varieties); others are freestone. Some have white or pale pink flesh; others have yellow flesh. Some have white skins with a pink blush; others have a deep yellow skin with a reddish blush. Some are firm-fleshed varieties designed for canning; others are for eating out of hand. In any case, the peach is one of America's favorite fruits and one of the country's most important fruit crops.

Use A ripe peach eaten out of hand is a delicious breakfast food or snack. Sliced peaches can be added to fruit salads and gelatin salads; they also may be poached for compotes. Sliced and sugared peaches are often spooned on top of shortcake or soaked in wine or Champagne for an easy summer dessert. They can be baked with butter and sugar and macaroon crumbs, or with a cobbler dough or a fruit-crisp topping. Peaches can be puréed for sherbet and ice cream or made into jam or preserves. They can be pickled, home-canned in sugar syrup, or made into chutney. Peach juice makes a pleasing ingredient in fruit punches or cocktails.

Availability Domestic peaches are sold from early May to mid-September. Imports from the southern hemisphere may supplement the domestic crop in some supermarkets in the winter. Frozen peaches, canned peaches, and canned peach nectar are sold in most supermarkets.

Selection An appealing fragrance is the best clue to a ripe peach. Look also for fruit that gives slightly to pressure and has a yellow or creamy background color between its blushed areas. Avoid fruit with greenish undertones and fruit that is bruised or very soft.

Storage Peaches will keep in the refrigerator crisper for up to two weeks.

Preparation Peaches eaten out of hand do not require peeling. Most peaches are peeled for use in cooked dishes, however. Very ripe peaches are usually easy to peel; others may need to be blanched first. To blanch, cut a small *x* in the rounded end opposite the stem; dip fruit in boiling water for about 30 seconds, then plunge into ice water. Skin will peel away readily. Peaches oxidize and brown when exposed to air; rub or sprinkle with lemon juice to prevent browning.

▇ NUTTY PEACH PIE

For a variation, omit the nut topping and bake as a double-crust or lattice-top pie. Serve warm or at room temperature, topped with Chantilly Cream (see page 252) or with ice cream.

  1 **9-inch single-crust Nut Egg Pastry (see page 435)**
  5 **cups peeled, sliced freestone peaches (5 to 6 large peaches)**
  ½ **to ¾ cup granulated sugar**
2½ **to 3 tablespoons cornstarch**
    Dash freshly grated nutmeg
  1 **tablespoon fresh lemon juice**
  ⅛ **teaspoon almond extract**
  1 **egg white, lightly beaten (optional)**
  ⅓ **cup firmly packed light brown sugar**
  ½ **cup flour**
  6 **tablespoons unsalted butter**
  1 **cup chopped nuts (mixture of almonds and pecans)**

1. Preheat oven to 425° F. Line a 9-inch pie plate with Nut Egg Pastry. In a large bowl combine sliced peaches, ½ to ¾ cup granulated sugar (depending upon ripeness of peaches), cornstarch, and nutmeg. Allow to stand 15 minutes.

2. Stir in lemon juice and almond extract.

3. Lightly brush uncooked pie shell with a thin layer of egg white (if used) to make pie crust moistureproof. Pour filling into pie shell.

4. Mix brown sugar with flour; cut in butter until crumbly. Stir in nuts. Sprinkle mixture over peaches.

5. Bake for 15 minutes. Reduce oven to 400° F and continue baking for 35 to 40 minutes. Cover edges of crust with strips of aluminum foil, if necessary, to prevent excessive browning.

Makes one 9-inch pie.

Recipes and Related Information
Ginger-Peach Upside-Down Cake, 87; Gingered Peach Pickles, 322; Peach Filling, 627; Peach Melba, 315; Summer Peach Jam, 319.

This Nutty Peach Pie is baked in an almond pie crust and topped with an almond-pecan crumble. It's a perfect dessert for summer, when peaches are in season.

PEANUT

Actually a legume rather than a nut, the peanut has seeds that are encased in a fragile, dry pod. Like other legumes, the oval seeds may be split into two parts. The seeds are ivory-colored and covered with a papery brown skin. Peanuts have a buttery, nutty flavor that is intensified by roasting or frying.

Use   In this country half the peanut crop is made into peanut butter. Some portion of the remainder is sold in the shell; probably most of the unshelled peanuts marketed in this country are sold at sporting events. Shelled peanuts may be roasted or unroasted, salted or unsalted. They are used in candy bars and snack foods such as caramel corn, in nut mixes marketed as cocktail snacks, and in cookies. Chopped peanuts are added to salads and slaws, and to muffins and quick breads, and serve as a garnish for ice cream sundaes and sautéed vegetables. Peanuts are pressed for their oil, which is excellent for sautéing and frying and for salad dressings. Peanuts are popular in Africa, where they are known as groundnuts. African groundnut stew is a spicy chicken and tomato dish made with ground peanuts. Nigerian cooks grind peanuts into flour for bread. The Chinese eat seasoned and roasted peanuts as an hors d'oeuvre or grind them to make a sauce for noodles. Indonesian cooks make a spicy dipping sauce for skewered meats with ground peanuts, chiles, and coconut milk.

Availability   Most supermarkets carry peanuts both shelled and in the shell. Shelled peanuts are usually packed in vacuum-sealed jars or cans. Peanut butter, both smooth and chunky, is sold in all supermarkets. It may contain added sugar or preservatives. Natural peanut butter is available in most health-food stores. Chinese markets are a good source for raw peanuts.

Storage   Peanuts turn rancid quickly, shelled peanuts faster than unshelled. Store unshelled peanuts in the refrigerator or in a cool, dry, dark place for up to six months. Refrigerate shelled peanuts in an airtight container for up to three months, or freeze for up to six months. Natural peanut butter should be refrigerated after opening; it will keep for up to six months. Peanut butter containing preservatives will keep indefinitely in a cool, dry place.

Preparation   To toast peanuts, shell them, then arrange them on a baking tray and bake at 325° F until fragrant and lightly browned (8 to 10 minutes). Rub between towels to remove skins.

Recipes and Related Information
Choco–Peanut Butter Cookies, 145; Peanut Brittle, 96; Peanut Butter–Chocolate Chip Cookies, 141.

PEAR

Of unknown origin, pears today are cultivated in temperate zones all over the world. Among tree fruits grown in these zones, only the apple is more heavily planted. Of the 5,000 varieties of pears, only a few are of commercial importance in this country. Commercial varieties vary considerably in skin color, texture, and flavor. See Availability for a description of major types.

Use   Pears are probably most often eaten out of hand, as a breakfast food, dessert, or snack. Ripe pears are particularly delicious with a blue cheese such as Gorgonzola, Roquefort, or Stilton. Sliced pears are used in fruit salads and compotes. Pears may be poached, either whole or in halves, in a light wine syrup, raspberry syrup, or sugar syrup. They can be baked with butter and sugar or poached, sliced, and arranged on top of a fruit tart.

Availability   In addition to fresh pears, supermarkets also carry canned pears and canned pear nectar. The major commercial pear varieties include the following.

Anjou   This winter pear with greenish yellow skin and yellowish white flesh is globular in shape with a short neck. The Anjou is a hardy pear that ships and stores well; it holds its shape when cooked. It is available from October through May.

Bartlett   Also known as the Williams' pear, it is a popular summer pear with yellow skin and ivory flesh. There is also a variety with red flesh. It is very aromatic, very tender when ripe, with flesh that is sweet, juicy, and buttery. It is available from mid-July through November.

Bosc   This winter pear with an elongated shape and a russet brown skin has white flesh that is firm when ripe and quite sweet. Bosc pears hold their shape well when cooked and are excellent for poaching or baking.

Comice   Having perhaps the finest flavor and smoothest texture of generally available pears, this winter pear has a squat, almost neckless shape, a brownish green skin, and a white flesh. Ripe Comice are highly aromatic and fairly firm; they should not be allowed to get soft. A choice pear for eating out of hand, it has a buttery texture and a winy flavor. It also bakes well and makes fragrant sherbet. Look for Comice from October through January.

French Butter Pear   Also known as Beurre Hardy, this delicate pear does not cook well. However, it is exceptional for eating out of hand or with cheese. It has a brownish skin with a creamy flesh and a buttery texture that explains its name. It is available late summer through fall.

Seckel   This very small, brownish pear is often poached for a ham or turkey garnish or canned in a spiced syrup. It has a grainy texture and is available in some markets in late fall and winter.

Winter Nellis This firm, spicy pear (also spelled Nelis) has a squat shape and a dull green skin with russet dots. Because it is firm, it holds its shape well when baked. It is available from late fall through spring.

Selection Pears are one of the few fruits that won't ripen properly on the tree; for that reason, they are picked mature but hard and must be allowed to soften slightly before eating. Choose pears that are fragrant, free of blemishes, and beginning to color and soften.

Storage Hold pears at room temperature in a warm place until they give slightly to pressure. Refrigerate and use within a few days. Pears intended for cooking should be cooked when still fairly firm.

Preparation Pears do not require peeling for eating out of hand, although some have coarse or tannic skins that may be unpleasant. Peel as desired. Peeled pears oxidize rapidly; rub or sprinkle with lemon juice or store in acidulated water until ready to use.

■ BAKED PEAR TART

This tart looks especially pretty when baked in a scalloped tart band. Thinly sliced pear halves radiate from the center to form the petals of a flower.

This custard-filled pear tart is baked in a scallop-edged tart band. The top is dusted with confectioners' sugar to create a delicate flower pattern.

1	10-inch Sweet Tart Pastry for scalloped tart tin (see page 441)
6	tablespoons unsalted butter
1½	large eggs (beat second egg and use half)
½	cup plus 1 tablespoon granulated sugar
3	tablespoons sifted flour
4	ripe pears (Anjou or Bartlett)
2	tablespoons fresh lemon juice
½	cup apricot preserves
1	tablespoon pear liqueur or water
¼	cup confectioners' sugar

1. Position a 10-inch scalloped tart band on a flat baking sheet. (You may substitute a 10-inch tart tin with removable bottom or 10-inch circular tart band.) Roll out tart pastry and line tart band or tin. Trim dough even with top of tart band. Wrap and refrigerate 1 hour, or freeze for later use.

2. To make custard filling, cook butter over medium heat until butter browns. Immediately remove from heat and cool in pan 5 minutes. Place eggs in a mixing bowl and gradually whisk in granulated sugar. Whisk in flour. Whisk in melted butter and all of the browned bits that cling to bottom of pan (these give tart a delicious nutty flavor and aroma). Set aside until tart is assembled.

3. Preheat oven to 375° F. Peel pears. Cut each in half lengthwise, remove core and seeds, and place into a large bowl of cold water with lemon juice (this keeps pears white). Remove pear halves from water; dry well on paper towels. Using a sharp, thin knife held at a 45-degree angle to cutting board, slice each pear half crosswise in ⅛-inch slices, beginning at the narrow tip. Slide a narrow spatula under each sliced pear half, and transfer it to pastry-lined tart band. Center each pear half in a "petal" of the tart band, with narrow end of pear pointing toward center. Then push pear slices from narrow to wide end to fan them slightly. Trim tip off last pear half, slice, and place in center of tart. Pour custard filling in empty spaces around, but not on top of, pears. Custard should come only halfway up sides of tart.

4. Bake for 20 minutes at 375° F. Reduce oven to 350° F and bake until custard looks fully cooked (40 to 50 minutes longer). If edges of crust begin to brown too much, cover them with strips of aluminum foil. Cool completely.

5. To make glaze: Melt preserves over low heat. Strain to remove pieces of fruit; stir in pear liqueur. When tart is cool, brush pear halves with a thin coat of preserves. Then cover each pear half with an upside-down boat-shaped tartlet tin (or a cardboard pattern of the same shape). Cover center pear with an upside-down, small, round brioche tin, tartlet tin, or cardboard pattern. Sift a light layer of confectioners' sugar over tart. Carefully lift off tins.

6. Lift off tart band, slide tart onto a serving plate, and serve at room temperature.

Serves 10.

Recipes and Related Information
Pear With Prosciutto, 358; Rosé Pears in Chocolate Bath, 612.

Pralines (say praw-leens), usually associated with New Orleans, are traditionally served with strong, hot, black coffee with chicory.

PECAN

The pecan is a native American nut that is still not widely cultivated elsewhere. Most pecans today are grown in the South and Southwest, with Georgia the leading producer. Like the walnut, the pecan is a species of hickory. Its smooth, pale brown, oval shell often has black markings and is usually about an inch long. Some pecans are also dyed red to hide blemishes. The kernel is a rich, golden brown with an ivory interior; its flavor is rich and buttery, especially when toasted.

Use Pecans are widely used in the South and Southwest in pies, cakes, ice cream, pralines, and cookies. Pecans may be shelled, buttered, and roasted for a cocktail snack, or toasted, chopped, and added to salads and sautéed vegetables.

Availability Pecans are harvested in the fall and are available in their shells in some markets at that time. Most supermarkets and health-food stores carry shelled pecans, either in bulk or packaged, whole or chopped.

Selection Unshelled nuts should feel heavy for their size. Shelled nuts turn rancid quickly; buy them from a market with a rapid turnover.

Storage Because of their high oil content, pecans turn rancid quickly. Store unshelled pecans in a cool, dark, dry place and use within six months. Shelled pecans may be frozen for up to six months or refrigerated for up to three months.

Preparation To bring out their flavor, toast pecans on a baking sheet in a preheated 350° F oven until fragrant (six to eight minutes).

■ PRALINES

A mixture of caramelized sugar and nuts, pralines are usually crisp, but this recipe produces a softer candy. The use of buttermilk gives this version of the Louisiana classic a delicious tang. Traditionally these candies are eaten after a meal with strong black coffee.

    2 cups buttermilk
    2 cups sugar
    1 teaspoon baking soda
    ½ cup unsalted butter
    1½ cups coarsely chopped pecans

1. In a heavy-bottomed, 4- to 6-quart saucepan, combine buttermilk, sugar, baking soda, and butter. Cook over medium heat, stirring frequently with a wooden spoon and monitoring temperature with a candy thermometer. First the mixture will foam, then darken as it thickens. It is done when it reaches 238° F (soft-ball stage).

2. Remove mixture from heat and stir in pecans with a wire whisk. Beat mixture until it cools to about 220° F (on a candy thermometer). While it is still soft, spoon nut mixture onto waxed paper in 1- to 2-tablespoon mounds.

As pralines cool, they will become firm and can be removed from waxed paper.

Makes 2 to 3 dozen pralines.

Recipes and Related Information

Butter Pecan Ice Cream, 312; Chocolate-Pecan Waffles, 599; Pecan Applesauce Cake, 87; Pecan Buttermilk Waffles, 599; Pecan Lace Cookies, 142; Southern Pecan Pie, 439; The Stickiest Pecan Rolls, 629.

PEEL; PEEL, TO

The skin of a fruit or vegetable, also called the rind. To remove this skin.

Peeling tools include the fingers, a sharp paring knife, and a vegetable peeler. Sometimes heating facilitates peeling. Blanching some thin-skinned fruits and vegetables, such as peaches, plums, and tomatoes, splits the skin, which then pulls away in strips. Peppers can be peeled by scorching them over a flame or under a broiler or by roasting them in a hot oven until blistered, then sweating them in a paper or plastic bag 10 to 20 minutes. The moisture causes the skin to loosen. The easiest way to peel a clove of garlic is to cut off its root end and crush the clove with the side of a chef's knife; the skin will slip off. To skin nuts, toast in the oven until fragrant, then rub in a towel.

PEPINO

Like the potato, tomato, and eggplant, the pepino is a member of the nightshade family. The heart-shaped fruit is yellow with purple markings; the yellow flesh is aromatic, with a flavor reminiscent of cantaloupe, honeydew melon, and pear. It has a small seed cavity that contains inedible seeds.

Use Eat on the half shell with lemon or lime wedges. Add sliced, peeled pepino to fruit salads, compotes, and chutneys. Puree for sorbets. Sauté in butter to garnish duck or chicken.

Availability Fresh California-grown pepino is available in some supermarkets from August to December. Imports from New Zealand appear in the markets from February to June.

Selection Choose aromatic pepinos with good yellow skin color; a ripe fruit will give slightly to pressure.

Storage If fruit is slightly underripe, store at room temperature until it colors and softens. Refrigerate up to three days in a plastic bag in the refrigerator crisper.

Preparation Halve and remove seeds.

PEPPER

All peppers, whether sweet or hot, are members of the capsicum family and are native to the New World. The plant that produces peppercorns, *Piper nigrum,* is native to Asia and is not related.

Peppers are a rich source of vitamin C, superior even to citrus, and they contain as much vitamin A as carrots. For centuries, chiles (hot peppers) have been put to medicinal use, particularly as a topical healing agent. Even today, many commercial liniments contain oleoresin of capsicum. Ground hot peppers are said to be effective in homemade insecticides, and at least one commercial manufacturer exploits the irritative quality of hot peppers in a product designed to discourage thumb sucking. The color extracted from red pepper is used as a natural coloring agent in a variety of foodstuffs, including sausage and cheese. Similarly, some processors add pimiento to chicken feed to impart a deep yellow color to the birds' skin and fat.

Capsicum peppers range in flavor from mild and sweet to blisteringly hot. The heat comes from capsaicin, a compound found in the veins and seeds of hot peppers, but not in their walls.

Pepper nomenclature is confusing, as it varies from country to country. In the United States the mild peppers are known as sweet peppers; hot peppers are known either as hot peppers or chiles. In England all peppers are known as chiles, but hot ones are referred to as hot chiles. In Latin America hot peppers are chiles and mild peppers are pimientos. In the United States pimientos are just one variety of sweet red pepper. To add to the confusion, some varieties have several different common names.

The following discussion divides peppers into two types: sweet and hot. Although it is sometimes difficult to distinguish a sweet pepper from a hot one by sight, it is generally true that the smaller the pepper, the hotter. However, weather, soil, and degree of maturity can affect capsaicin content, making one pepper hotter than another of the same variety; even peppers on the same plant can vary in pungency. The following glossary should at least help you to distinguish mild, hot, and hotter.

SWEET PEPPERS

The most widely available sweet pepper is the bell pepper, named for its bell-like shape. Green bell peppers are the most common, but red, yellow, and even purple bells are increasingly available in specialty markets. Most green bells become red with age; red bell peppers are simply green bells that have been allowed to ripen on the vine. Consequently, red bells are sweeter than greens and are available later in the season. All bell peppers have a mild flavor and a crisp, crunchy texture.

Use Raw bell peppers add color and crunchy texture to salads and to raw vegetable assortments served with dips. Mediterranean cooks sauté strips of sweet peppers and serve them as a side dish or a garnish for braised salt cod or lamb. In Spain, Italy, and southern France, cooks roast and peel sweet peppers and serve them cool, as a salad, with lemon and oil. Middle European cooks stuff bell peppers with meat and/or seasoned rice or stew them with veal or chicken. In Japan strips of bell peppers are dipped in tempura batter and fried. Chinese cooks add bell pepper strips to stir-fries of all kinds.

Availability Green bell peppers are found in most markets the year around; peak season is August and September. The domestic red, yellow, and purple bells are harvested in late summer and fall, with some markets stocking imports from Mexico and Holland at other times of the year. Dehydrated bell pepper flakes are available on some supermarket spice racks.

Other sweet peppers include the following.

Bull's Horn A long, narrow, sickle-shaped green pepper with a pointed tip. Roast and peel it, then serve it whole with olive oil, garlic, and lemon. It is available in late summer and fall in some specialty markets. Select and store as for bell peppers.

Cubanelle A long (about 4 inches), tapered pepper that may be yellow or red. It has thick, meaty walls and is generally more flavorful than the bell pepper. Also known as the Cuban pepper, it is available sporadically in specialty markets. Select and store as for bell peppers.

Lamuyo Also known as European sweet pepper or rouge royal; a very sweet bell-shaped pepper, longer, larger, and more slender than the standard bell. Thick-fleshed and flavorful, it comes in a range of colors. Look for it in specialty markets in late summer and fall; select, store, and use as for bell peppers.

Pimiento A large, heart-shaped red pepper sold in some markets in late summer and fall. It has thicker, meatier flesh than the bell. Because of their thick walls, they are excellent for roasting and peeling. Bottled or canned peeled pimientos are available in most supermarkets. Select, store, and use as for bell peppers.

Sweet Banana A long banana-shaped yellow pepper that also comes in a hot variety (see Yellow Wax Pepper). It may be stuffed or pickled.

Selection Choose bell peppers that feel heavy for their size; they will have thick, meaty walls. Avoid any with soft spots or shriveled areas. Bell peppers should be firm and shiny.

Storage Keep peppers in a plastic bag in the refrigerator for up to one week.

Preparation If stuffing or slicing, ribs and seeds should be removed. To keep peppers whole for stuffing, cut about ¼ to ½ inch off top and scoop out or trim away seeds and white ribs. If peppers will be sliced, cut them in half, then trim away stem, seeds, and ribs.

Mixed sweet peppers make tricolored Peperonata, a lively late-summer antipasto. For a more substantial first course, pair the peppers with sliced mozzarella.

1. In a large skillet over medium heat, heat the ½ cup olive oil until it is hot but not smoking. Add garlic and onion and sauté, stirring until lightly colored (about 3 minutes).

2. Halve peppers; remove seeds and trim away white ribs. Cut lengthwise into strips ½ inch wide. Add all peppers to skillet at one time and stir to blend with garlic-onion mixture. Add tomatoes and salt and mix gently. Scatter oregano leaves across top. Cover and simmer slowly until peppers are soft (12 to 15 minutes). Remove from heat and transfer to serving bowl to cool.

3. Serve peppers at room temperature, garnishing the top with the sliced red onion and minced parsley. If desired, drizzle with the 2 tablespoons fruity olive oil just before serving.

Makes about 3½ cups.

■ STUFFED GREEN PEPPERS MEXICANA

These stuffed peppers have a sweetly spicy, south-of-the-border flavor. The peppers and filling can be cooked and the peppers stuffed ahead of time; store in refrigerator overnight, if desired, and let dish warm to room temperature before baking.

   6 medium-sized green bell peppers (about 2 lb)
   2 tablespoons butter or margarine
  ½ cup slivered almonds
   1 pound ground beef, crumbled
   1 large onion, finely chopped
   1 clove garlic, mashed
  ⅓ cup raisins
   1 tablespoon cider vinegar
   1 teaspoon *each* sugar and ground cinnamon
  ¾ teaspoon salt
  ¼ teaspoon *each* ground cumin and cloves
   1 can (15 oz) tomato sauce
 1½ cups cooked short-grain rice

1. Preheat oven to 350° F. Cut a thin slice from stem end of each pepper; carefully cut out seeds. Cook peppers, uncovered, in boiling salted water to cover, for 5 minutes; turn upside down to drain.

2. In a large, heavy-bottomed frying pan, heat butter over medium heat; add almonds and cook until lightly browned. Remove from pan with a slotted spoon; reserve. In the same pan cook ground beef and onion until lightly browned. Mix in garlic, raisins, vinegar, sugar, cinnamon, salt, cumin, cloves, and half of the tomato sauce. Simmer, uncovered, about 10 minutes. Mix in cooked rice and almonds.

3. Fill peppers with ground beef mixture. Arrange in an ungreased, deep, covered baking dish just large enough to hold the 6 peppers. Pour on remaining tomato sauce. (At this point peppers can be covered and refrigerated for several hours or overnight; if chilled, let dish sit out at room temperature for 30 minutes before baking.)

■ PEPERONATA

Mixed marinated peppers

Sweet peppers stewed slowly with tomatoes, herbs, and garlic are a popular summer first course in southern Italy. Serve them with crusty bread to mop up the aromatic juices, or offer Peperonata as part of a larger antipasto platter. Select meaty peppers that feel heavy for their size.

  ½ cup olive oil
   2 tablespoons minced garlic
  ½ yellow onion, minced
   2 red bell peppers
   2 green bell peppers
   1 yellow bell pepper (if unavailable, substitute another red or green pepper)
   2 tomatoes, peeled, seeded, and coarsely chopped
   2 teaspoons salt
  ¼ cup fresh oregano leaves
  ½ red onion, in paper-thin slices, for garnish
   2 tablespoons minced parsley, for garnish
   2 tablespoons fruity olive oil (optional)

4. Bake, covered, for 45 minutes; uncover, spoon sauce over, and continue baking for 15 minutes.

Serves 6.

HOT PEPPERS (CHILES)

Capsaicin, a compound found in the seeds and veins but not the walls of hot peppers, gives these peppers their heat. They range from the mildly spicy *pepperoncini* to the incendiary tabasco pepper. The jalapeño pepper, a pepper most diners consider very hot, usually measures 2,500 to 4,000 in Scoville Heat Units, the accepted measurement for heat in peppers. By comparison, the tiny tabasco may weigh in at 60,000 to 80,000 units!

Use Hot peppers are one of the world's most common seasonings. They add zest to all manner of dishes and are especially appreciated in hot climates, where their consumption has a cooling effect. Minced raw hot peppers are used in Mexican *salsa cruda* (fresh salsa), the ubiquitous table relish, or in guacamole. In fact few savory dishes in Mexico are prepared without chiles in some form, either fresh or dried; egg dishes, soups, stews, and appetizers are almost always enlivened with chiles. In the Hunan and Szechuan regions of China, hot red chiles give a lift to stir-fries and dipping sauces. Southeast Asian cooks use sliced green chiles in dipping sauces and soups; Thai curries are always liberally seasoned with green or red chiles. In this country, dried tabasco peppers are used to make one of America's most famous condiments, Tabasco Sauce. The well-known Texas specialty chili takes its name from its principal incendiary seasoning.

Availability Many supermarkets today stock at least a few fresh chiles, such as jalapeño and *serrano* varieties. Dried whole red chiles are often available in jars on the spice rack. In addition, many supermarkets carry canned or bottled chiles. For a wider selection of fresh, dried, and canned or bottled chiles, seek out a Latin or Asian market or a well-stocked specialty produce market. Most fresh hot chiles are available the year around, although supply of some varieties may be sporadic.

Recognizing the various chiles takes some practice and experimentation because there are dozens of varieties of similar shape and size. Many are sold in both fresh and dried states. The following are among the most common hot peppers.

Anaheim Also known as the New Mexico pepper, Rio Grande pepper, long green chile, or California pepper. This long (6 to 8 inches), slender green pepper is one of the mildest of the hot peppers. It is the pepper used for making *chiles rellenos* (fried cheese-stuffed chiles) in the southwestern United States. The mature Anaheim, a red pepper, is dried and ground for chili powder and paprika.

Ancho The correct name for the ripened and dried *poblano* (see Poblano; some markets incorrectly identify the fresh poblano as the Ancho, too). The dried ancho is perhaps the mostly commonly used chile in Mexico. It is about 5 inches long and dark brick red. Like the poblano, it may be slightly hot to hot. It is often ground for use in cooked sauces, such as mole.

Cayenne, Chile de Arbol, Thai Pepper Although not the same, they are similar: All are small, thin peppers marketed green, red, and dried. In Asian markets, they may be identified as bird peppers. The fresh red peppers are generally hotter than the green, but all are quite hot. The dried cayenne pepper can be soaked in vinegar and salt for a few days to make a pungent, liquid hot red-pepper sauce. Thai cooks use both fresh and dried bird peppers in dipping sauces, soups, and stir-fries.

Cherry Pepper A small round pepper that is pickled and bottled. Pickled red and green cherry peppers are available in many supermarkets. Slightly piquant, they make a colorful addition to a salad, an antipasto platter, or a sandwich plate.

Jalapeño A small (about 2 inches long), smooth-skinned green chile that is popular in Mexico and the southwestern United States. It is often pickled with carrots and onions and served as a table relish. Jalapeños are minced raw and used in salsas or split, deveined, stuffed with cheese or fish, and served as an appetizer. They are frequently canned, either whole, sliced, or in seeded strips. Jalapeño slices add zest to tacos, hamburgers, cheese dishes, and pizza. When ripened and smoked, jalapeños are known as *chiles chipotles.*

Pasilla A long (about 6 inches), narrow pepper with wide shoulders. When fresh, it is dark green to near black and may be identified in Latin markets as *chile chilaca;* when dried, it is chocolate brown. It has a deep, rich flavor and is moderately hot. Fresh ones are toasted and skinned before using in recipes; often they are cut into strips for use in soups, stews, and casseroles. Dried pasilla chiles are often ground for use in table sauces or seafood dishes.

Pepperoncini The small green pepper that is packed in vinegar, bottled, and sold in Italian markets and supermarkets. It is often used to garnish green salads or antipasto platters. A yellow variety, also pickled in vinegar and bottled, is imported from Greece and is available in some markets. Both are only slightly piquant.

Poblano Also known as the *chile ancho* (see Ancho). Ranging from 2½ to 6 inches in length and from dark green to near black, Ancho chiles are wide at the shoulder but taper to a point at the bottom. Flavor ranges from slightly hot to hot. They are usually roasted and peeled before using in recipes. Widely used in Mexico, they are stuffed with cheese, coated with batter and fried to make *chiles rellenos,* or are cut into strips for use in casseroles, soups, and sauces.

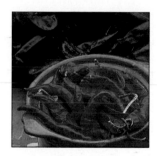

Whole chiles, mild or hot, will dry in several weeks at room temperature. When they are dry, crumble or grind them for use in chili recipes and other spicy-hot dishes.

Serrano A slender, very hot green chile, usually about 2 inches long. In Mexico it is used raw in guacamole and some salsas crudas and is cooked in other salsas. Serrano chiles are also commercially pickled.

Yellow Wax Pepper Also known as the Hungarian wax pepper or *chile guero*, it is pale yellow and usually about 5 inches long. It may be used raw in salsas; toasted, seeded, and used in salads; pickled and canned; and cooked in stews. It is extremely pungent.

Selection Fresh hot chiles should have a smooth skin without dry cracks. They should feel firm and look shiny.

Storage Wrap fresh chiles in paper towels and refrigerate for up to three weeks (they will sweat and deteriorate rapidly in plastic bags). Dried red chiles are perishable. Store them in an airtight container in a cool, dark, dry place for up to three or four months; for longer storage, refrigerate.

Preparation Hot peppers require caution in handling. Some people are extremely sensitive to the capsaicin in the pepper seeds and veins. The capsaicin irritates their skin and, if hands touch tongue or eyes, the discomfort can be severe. Wear rubber gloves when handling hot peppers until you can gauge your sensitivity. Always wash hands well after handling peppers.

Fresh hot chiles are often charred and peeled before use (see Roasting and Peeling Peppers, page 425).

Because the capsaicin in peppers is in the seeds and ribs, removing these parts significantly reduces a pepper's kick. If a recipe calls for whole hot peppers, you can reduce the heat by halving the peppers and cutting away seeds and ribs.

Dried red chiles can be ground in a pepper mill, clean coffee grinder, or electric minichopper, or with a mortar and pestle. When removing lid from appliance, keep head well out of the way bacause escaping fumes can burn.

Dried chiles are sometimes soaked in warm water to soften before using. Follow recipe instructions.

▪ NACHOS

This popular translation of a traditional Mexican snack offers a balance of flavors and textures.. Beer is the perfect beverage to cool the heat of the peppers. Another way to tame their spiciness is to remove the ribs and seeds.

   1 package (12 oz) corn tortilla chips
   ½ cup green jalapeños, minced
   ½ cup green onions, chopped
  2¼ cups shredded Monterey jack or
      sharp Cheddar cheese

Preheat oven to 400° F. Place tortilla chips in a single layer on 2 baking sheets. Sprinkle with jalapeños and green onions. Cover with shredded cheese. Bake until cheese melts (about 5 minutes). Serve warm from oven.

Serves 8 as an appetizer or 4 as a light lunch.

▪ CHILES RELLENOS

A classic Mexican dish, *chile relleno* is certainly a favorite in the United States. The chile relleno is a large, mild, green cooking chile that has been roasted, cleaned, and peeled; filled and dipped in batter; and fried until puffed and golden. In Mexico the chile relleno is always served in a sauce. There are three distinct schools of thought on the egg batter in which the chile is dipped: The batter may be flat, fluffy, or extra fluffy. The recipe that follows is right in the middle and the easiest to manage. If you want flatter chiles rellenos, just beat the eggs without separating them. For fluffier chiles rellenos, fold in one tablespoon flour for each egg in the recipe.

Although in Mexico the chile relleno is most often filled with a spiced shredded meat mixture, in the United States it is usually filled with cheese, as in this version. In Mexico the cheese-filled chile relleno is identified on menus as *Chile relleno con queso.* The chile relleno is usually served as a main dish but it can also be served as a vegetable side dish or as a brunch dish. For directions on how to roast chiles, see page 425.

A variation of chile relleno is *chile en nogada,* a classic in its own right that features a meat-and-fruit filling and a walnut cream sauce. The dish originated in Puebla, the walnut capital of Mexico, and is served traditionally on Mexico's two independence days.

   6 large, mild, green chiles, roasted and peeled,
      leaving on stems (or canned whole green chiles)
   ½ pound jack or Colby cheese, cut into strips
      approximately ½ inch wide, 2 inches long,
      and ¼ inch thick
      Flour
   4 eggs, separated
      Oil 1 inch deep, for frying
      Sour cream and cilantro, for garnish

Tomato Sauce

   1 tablespoon vegetable oil
   ½ cup chopped onion
   2 cloves garlic, crushed
   1 can (28 oz) solid-pack tomatoes, puréed
      briefly in blender
  3½ cups Chicken Stock (see page 560)

1. Carefully slit each chile lengthwise along one side; remove seeds and veins. Fill each chile with several strips of cheese, roll in flour, and set aside.

2. Beat egg whites until stiff; slightly beat yolks and fold into whites. Heat oil in a large skillet to 400° F. Drop a large spoonful of egg mixture into oil; lay a chile in the middle, top with another spoonful of egg, and smooth the egg to enclose all sides. Carefully baste the top with hot oil, to set. Cook until golden on the underside (about 1 minute); turn and cook again until golden on the underside. Drain on paper towels while preparing Tomato Sauce.

3. Carefully place the rellenos into the tomato sauce and simmer gently to heat thoroughly (about 15 minutes). Do not cook too long or batter will begin to break away.

4. Serve with some of the sauce, and garnish with a dab of sour cream and a few cilantro leaves.

Serves 3 to 6.

Tomato Sauce Heat oil in a large saucepan. Add onion and garlic and cook only until onion is soft. Add puréed tomatoes and stock, bring to a boil, reduce heat, and simmer 5 minutes.

Makes about 6 cups.

■ PINTO BEAN CHILI

This beef and pinto bean chili may strike you as the most traditional version.

> 1 **cup dried pinto beans, rinsed and drained**
> 3 **cups water**
> 2 **pounds boneless beef chuck, fat trimmed, cut in 1-inch cubes**
> 2 **tablespoons butter or margarine**
> 1 **large onion, finely chopped**
> 1 **clove garlic, minced**
> 2 **teaspoons salt**
> 1 **teaspoon ground cumin**
> 1 **tablespoon chili powder**
> 1 **can (1 lb) tomatoes**
> 1 **can (4 oz) diced green chiles**
> 1 **can (8 oz) tomato sauce**
>   **Shredded Cheddar cheese (optional)**

1. In a large, heavy saucepan, bring beans and the water to a boil. Boil briskly for 2 minutes; then remove from heat, cover, and let stand for 1 hour.

2. In a large, deep frying pan or Dutch oven, brown beef cubes well on all sides, about half at a time, in butter over medium-high heat, removing and reserving meat as it browns. When all the beef is removed from pan, add onion to pan and cook, stirring often, until soft and lightly browned. Return beef to pan. Mix in garlic, beans and their liquid, salt, cumin, chili powder, tomatoes (coarsely chopped) and their liquid, and green chiles.

3. Bring to a boil, cover, reduce heat, and simmer until beef and beans are tender (2 to 2½ hours).

4. Mix in tomato sauce and cook, uncovered, stirring occasionally, until chili is thickened to your taste (about 15 minutes).

5. Serve bowls of hot chili with cheese for sprinkling, if desired.

Serves 6 to 8.

Recipes and Related Information
Guacamole, 15; Salsa Cruda, 521; Salsa Verde, 580.

PEPPERCORN

The *Piper nigrum* vine, native to Asia, produces the world's most-used spice. Pepper berries grow in clusters around a stem, like grapes. As they ripen, the tiny berries change from green to yellow to red. The familiar black peppercorn is picked when slightly underripe, then sun-dried until it blackens and shrivels. The white peppercorn is the same peppercorn harvested ripe and hulled; it is less pungent than the black. Green peppercorns are soft, undried, underripe *Piper nigrum* berries. Pink peppercorns are pungent pink berries unrelated to *Piper nigrum.*

Use The importance of pepper to the world's cuisines and to world history cannot be underestimated. When Columbus and other explorers set off to search for trade routes to the Far East, they were hoping to find a shortcut to pepper. The pungent spice breathes life into dishes all over the world. Peppercorns are added to brines and marinades. Meats and fish are often seasoned with pepper before cooking; vegetables, soups, and salads with freshly ground black pepper. Cracked peppercorns are rubbed into the surface of a steak to make Steak au Poivre. Pepper is even used to heighten the flavor of strawberries and sweets. The milder and less visible white peppercorns are generally used with fish dishes. Green and pink peppercorns are a pungent seasoning for meats and fish.

Availability Black and white peppercorns, whole and ground, are found in most supermarkets. Some specialty markets carry a variety of peppercorns in bulk. The best black varieties are Tellicherry, Lampong, and Allepeppy; the best white varieties are Muntok, Brazilian, and Sarawak. Green and pink peppercorns may be packed in water or vinegar or freeze-dried; they are available in some supermarkets and most specialty markets.

Selection Packaged seasonings lose quality after a while; try to buy from a store that restocks its spice section fairly often.

Storage Keep ground pepper in a cool, dark, dry place and replace every three months. Whole peppercorns will keep indefinitely in a cool, dark, dry place. Once opened, green peppercorns in water will last for one week refrigerated airtight; green peppercorns in brine will last for a month in their brine in an airtight container in the refrigerator. Discard green or pink peppercorns when they turn dark. Store freeze-dried green or pink peppercorns in a cool, dry, dark place for up to six months.

Preparation Black and white peppers are most pungent when ground just before use. Keep a pepper mill on hand for easy last-minute grinding.

Recipes and Related Information
Steak au Poivre, 41; Tartar Sauce With Green Peppercorns, 520.

PERSIMMON

Of the two varieties of persimmon common in American markets, the Hachiya is the largest, weighing up to 1 pound. Its shape is like a large, elongated peach. It has a smooth, orange-red skin even before it is fully ripe. When underripe, the Hachiya is extremely tannic and unpleasant to eat. A fully ripe Hachiya persimmon has a silky flesh with the texture of pudding and a delightfully sweet flavor. Another variety, the Fuyu, is smaller, with a shape resembling a tomato. It has orange-red skin like the Hachiya and may be eaten when firm.

Use A ripe persimmon makes a delicious breakfast food or snack, halved and eaten like a melon, with a wedge of lemon or lime. The firm Fuyu persimmon may be sliced and used in winter salads or compotes. The Hachiya can be puréed for sorbets, ice cream, steamed puddings, cookies, and quick breads. Frozen Hachiya persimmons can be whipped in a blender to make a creamy dessert resembling a mousse.

Availability Both Hachiya and Fuyu persimmons are available from October through January. Dried persimmons are also sold in some health-food stores and Japanese markets.

Selection Choose persimmons with good color and without bruises or splits in the skin.

Storage Ripen Hachiyas at room temperature until as soft as a water-filled balloon; the process may take several weeks. Refrigerate and use immediately. The Fuyu persimmon should give slightly to pressure; ripen at room temperature if necessary. When ripe, refrigerate and use within a few days.

Preparation Slice Fuyus into horizontal slices or vertical wedges; discard stem. Remove stem from Hachiyas and halve or purée. Some Hachiyas contain a few black seeds, which should be discarded.

■ PERSIMMON PUDDING

During the cool months, when persimmons are plentiful, extend their season by freezing the pulp in 1-cup batches.

    1½ cups flour
     1 teaspoon baking powder
     1 teaspoon baking soda
     1 teaspoon ground cinnamon
     ½ teaspoon freshly grated nutmeg
     ¼ teaspoon salt
     3 ripe persimmons, pureed (see Note)
     1 cup sugar
     3 eggs
     1 cup buttermilk
     ½ cup whipping cream
     ½ cup butter, melted and cooled
        Whipped cream, vanilla ice cream, or Crème
        Anglaise (see page 168), for accompaniment

1. Preheat oven to 350° F. Butter a 10-inch baking pan or ovenproof dish. Sift together flour, baking powder, baking soda, cinnamon, nutmeg, and salt; set aside.

2. In a large bowl combine puree, sugar, eggs, and buttermilk; beat until smooth and creamy. Add cream and melted butter and beat again until smooth.

3. Fold in sifted flour mixture and pour batter into prepared pan. Bake until set (about 1 hour). The pudding will settle upon standing. Serve warm with whipped cream, vanilla ice cream, or Crème Anglaise.

Serves 8 to 10.

Note Persimmons must be very ripe. To remove pulp, halve fruit, discard seeds, and scoop out flesh; mash with a spoon if very soft or purée in a food processor.

PICKLE, COMMERCIAL

Although most Americans use the word *pickle* to describe a cucumber pickle, pickles may be made from a variety of fruits and vegetables. Pickles are preserved in a seasoned brine and used as a piquant condiment or counterpoint (see HERB AND SPICE BLENDS, Pickling Spice). The highly acidic brine prevents the growth of organisms that cause spoilage and gives pickles their long shelf life (see JAM, JELLY, PRESERVE, AND CONDIMENT, Pickles and Relishes). Besides cucumbers, other commonly pickled vegetables include peppers, onions, green tomatoes, green beans, red cabbage, beets, cauliflower, and okra. Commonly pickled fruits include watermelon rind, cherries, grapes, peaches, plums (popular in Japan), and melons. Other foods that are commonly pickled include ginger, pig's feet, herring, radishes, and walnuts.

Use The tangy flavor of pickles makes them useful as a piquant condiment. In America dill pickles are often served with sandwiches. In Japan pickles are served at almost every meal—radish pickles, cabbage pickles, eggplant pickles. Indeed, rice, pickles, and tea are the trio that ends traditional Japanese meals, both formal and informal. The French serve *cornichons* (tiny pickles) with pâté. The Italians serve *giardiniera* (pickled mixed vegetables) as part of an antipasto assortment. Northern Europeans eat pickled fish and meats as a first course. The English eat pickled walnuts with cold meats and cheese. Minced pickle or pickle relish adds a sweet-tart character to egg salad and tuna salad and to such cold sauces as tartar sauce and rémoulade sauce.

Availability Cucumber pickles are widely sold in supermarkets as dill pickles, sweet gherkins, kosher dills, sweet bread-and-butter pickles, sweet pickle relish, and dill pickle chips or slices. Some specialty markets and supermarkets carry other pickle varieties. Check specialty stores and ethnic markets for French cornichons, Italian giardiniera, Japanese pickled ginger, and pickled plums.

Bread-and-Butter-Pickles These are made from medium to large cucumbers packed in a sweet-tart brine.

Cornichons Made from tiny cucumbers, cornichons are tart French pickles usually about 1½ inches long. They are packed in a tangy brine, often with tarragon.

Dill Pickles These are tart cucumber pickles flavored with fresh dill.

Half-Sour and Sour Pickles These are garlic-flavored and prepared in a salt brine without vinegar; sour pickles develop their stronger flavor because they are left longer in the brine.

Kosher Dill Pickles Despite what their name implies, kosher dill pickles are not necessarily prepared according to Jewish dietary law unless otherwise indicated on the jar. They are dill pickles flavored with garlic.

Sweet Gherkins Quite sweet, these pickles are made with the tiny pickling cucumbers known as cornichons. They are often chopped for use in chicken or tuna salad.

Sweet Pickle Relish This is a sweet-tart mince of pickles, onions, and sweet red pepper.

Storage Unopened pickles should be kept in a cool, dark place, where they will keep for one or two years. Once opened, they should be refrigerated. Most pickles will keep for one year under refrigeration.

PIE AND TART

What makes a pie a pie and a tart a tart? You might call the tart a French cousin to the pie, for their similarities seem to put them in the same family. They both have a pastry crust and a filling and are usually served in wedges. However, while they are made from the same basic ingredients, the similarities between pies and tarts fade when you take a closer look at the nature of their crusts and the shape of the pans in which they are baked.

INGREDIENTS FOR PIES AND TARTS: WHAT EACH DOES

Pie and tart crusts have few ingredients—basically flour, fat, liquid, and some flavoring such as salt or sugar. Occasionally egg is added to impart strength and color to the crust. The proportion of these basic ingredients in the dough and how they are incorporated give a pastry a distinctive characteristic: tender or tough, crumbly or flaky.

Flour The main ingredient in a pastry dough, flour provides structure. Liquid added to flour develops a protein called gluten, which forms an elastic framework that holds the dough together and allows it to be stretched and rolled out without breaking. For pie and tart doughs, use all-purpose flour or white pastry flour (unbleached

is best). All-purpose flour is a blend of hard (high-gluten) and soft (low-gluten) white wheat flours. Pastry flour (not to be confused with cake flour) is a soft (low-gluten) flour that can be used in place of all-purpose flour; it is often difficult to find, however. Whole wheat flour adds a nutty flavor to pie and tart crusts. However, if it is used alone it produces heavy doughs that are difficult to mix and roll. A better product is a combination of all-purpose and whole wheat flours.

Fat Adding tenderness, or shortness, as well as richness to pastries, fat works by coating particles of flour to inhibit them from joining with water to produce gluten (see Flour). Pure fats, such as shortening and lard, have more shortening power than butter because, unlike butter (or margarine), they don't contain any moisture and therefore can't encourage gluten development. They produce flakier, more tender crusts. On the other hand, although a butter crust is less tender and flaky, it has a rich, buttery flavor and aroma. Sometimes the fat used is

Flour and shortening have been cut together in a bowl with a pastry blender. Ice water is waiting to be measured and added to complete the dough. In the background a glass pie plate holds an unbaked pastry crust finished with a rope edge.

an oil; the resulting pastry is crumbly, rather than flaky, because an oil has more coating power than a solid fat and so covers many more of the flour particles (rather than making layers). You can produce a good pie crust by using all shortening, all lard, all butter, or a combination of these in any of the basic pie crust recipes in this entry. Keep in mind the effect that the type of fat will have on the crust.

Liquid   Some liquid, usually water, is needed in a pie or tart dough so that the flour particles can form a dough; the liquid also acts as a leavening when it converts to steam during baking. However, the minimum amount of water should be used; too much liquid will make a tough crust. It is always better to begin by adding the smaller amount of liquid suggested in the recipe. If more liquid is needed, add a few teaspoons or 1 tablespoon at a time until the desired consistency is reached. For flakiness, use ice water or ice-cold liquids so as not to melt the fat.

Acid   Sometimes acidic lemon juice, vinegar, sour cream, or even crème fraîche is added to the dough to relax the gluten and tenderize the crust.

Salt   When added, salt improves the flavor and color of the baked crust.

Sugar   Although not all doughs contain sugar, those that do include it for the flavor and color it imparts when it caramelizes.

EQUIPMENT FOR MAKING PIES AND TARTS

It is entirely possible to make a pie crust with the fingertips and to roll it out on the countertop with a wine bottle. However, if you have some basic pastry-making equipment in your kitchen, the process will be faster and simpler. Unless you make many pies at a time, you really only need one pie plate, preferably heat-resistant glass or heavyweight aluminum; 9 inches is the standard size. For tarts, choose a fluted pan of tinned steel with a removable bottom. Miniature tinned steel tart pans are available for tartlets.

Also helpful are a pastry blender, a rolling pin (15 inches is a versatile length), a sharp knife and other cutters, a fluted pastry-cutting wheel, a ruler, aluminum foil or parchment paper, and metal or ceramic pie weights (or dried beans). Some recipes recommend that juicy pies or delicate tarts bake on a baking sheet; a heavyweight aluminum one is best. Some cooks like to use a cloth rolling pin sleeve and a pastry cloth on which to roll dough. The same results can be achieved by keeping the work surface and rolling pin lightly dusted with flour at all times when rolling out pastry.

Other equipment useful for pastry making includes kitchen staples such as wooden spoons, spatulas, measuring spoons and cups, mixing bowls, cooking racks, a quality portable or electric stand mixer with a strong motor, and a food processor with metal blade.

MAKING THE DOUGH

Pie crusts can be mixed with the fingertips, a wire pastry blender, two knives, the paddle attachment of a heavy-duty mixer, or a food processor. The process—called cutting in or rubbing in—literally whittles the fat into smaller and smaller flour-coated pieces (see CUT IN); the fineness of texture depends on the type of pastry you are making. For flaky pie crusts, the fat should be in discrete pieces that will then layer with the dough. For tarts, the fat is mixed in more uniformly.

Chill fat; when using more than one type, soften the fats, mix them together, and then chill this mixture. When using a food processor to make pastry that contains solid vegetable shortening, first measure and freeze the fat before cutting it into the flour. By doing this, the pastry will resist the heat produced by the action of the machine. If butter, margarine, or lard is used, the fat need only be chilled rather than frozen. Cut fats in quickly; overmixing results in oily pastry.

ROLLING OUT PIE AND TART PASTRY

Let chilled dough soften slightly before rolling. Place dough on lightly floured surface; sprinkle a little flour on top of dough or rub some on rolling pin. Roll out dough from center toward edge (easing pressure near edge of dough) ⅛ inch thick and 2 inches larger than the pie plate or 1½ inches larger than the tart tin. Carefully lift dough and give a quarter turn after each rolling, reflouring surfaces as needed to prevent sticking and tearing. Cupping hands slightly, occasionally reshape dough into a circle. If dough cracks or tears, brush a small flat piece of dough with water and apply as a patch (patching is preferred to rerolling, which toughens dough; see PATCH).

To Transfer Dough to Pie Plate or Tart Tin   Place rolling pin just to one side of center of dough. Lightly and gently drape half of dough over rolling pin, rest dough across pie plate, and unfold dough onto pie plate. Fit dough into plate with fingertips or a small ball of dough. For tart, trim dough even with top of tart tin or band. Do not stretch dough or crust will shrink as it bakes. Pie or tart shell may be frozen at this point.

For a Single-Crust Pie   Trim edge so it extends ½ inch to 1 inch beyond edge of pie plate. Fold edges of dough under. Finish edges (see opposite page). Blind bake or fill and bake.

For a Double-Crust Pie   Trim lower crust even with rim of pie plate. Roll out second piece of dough (for top) slightly thinner than bottom crust. Fill pie; brush rim of bottom crust with cold water. Place top crust on pie; press edges to seal; trim edge to ½ inch from rim and finish edges (see opposite page). Cut steam vents (slits or designs) in top crust before or after crust is on pie. Bake according to recipe directions.

DECORATIVE FINISHES

The top crust of a double-crust pie can be left plain or enhanced with applied cutouts made from dough scraps. Roll out scraps as thin as possible; use cookie cutters or a knife to cut out shapes that relate to the filling—little apples and leaves or berries and vines—or design your own: stars, flowers, even initials (see Apple Pie, page 437). Brush cutouts with water and press into place on the top crust. You may brush the top crust with one of the following glazes: milk and a sprinkling of sugar, cream, or, for a shiny brown glaze, egg or egg yolks lightly beaten with a pinch of salt and 1 teaspoon of water.

A woven lattice top allows the filling to show through and is extremely attractive (see Strawberry-Rhubarb Pie, page 498). To form a lattice, line pie plate with pastry and trim bottom crust to ½ inch beyond rim. Roll out a circle of dough 2 inches larger than rim of pie plate for lattice top; with a knife or fluted pastry wheel and a ruler, cut strips of dough ½ inch wide. Fill pie. Lay half of the strips of pastry, ¾ inches apart, across pie. Fold back every other strip at center. Lay a strip across the unfolded strips; unfold other strips over this. Fold back the alternating strips (ones that were flat the last time) and lay the next strip ¾ inch from the last. Continue until half of pie is covered with lattice pattern. Repeat this procedure on other side of pie. Trim lattice strips to match edge of bottom crust; lift lattice strips at edge and moisten rim of crust underneath; press lattice strips onto bottom crust at edge of pie. Flute edges.

To make attractive edges (see below for instructions for a variety of pastry crust edges) for single- or double-crust pies, allow pastry to extend ½ inch to 1 inch beyond rim of pie plate. Fold edge of dough under so it is even with the edge of the pie plate to create a raised, even rim.

Fork-fluted edge *Trim pastry even with rim of pie plate. Firmly press tines of fork into pastry around entire rim of pie plate.*

Fluted edge *Place left index finger on inside of rim, pointing toward outside of shell. Pinch pastry into V shape between right index finger and thumb; repeat along entire edge. Pinch again to sharpen points.*

Rope edge *Press thumb at an angle into pastry and pinch pastry toward thumb with bent index finger; repeat along entire edge.*

Ruffle edge *Place left thumb and index finger 1 inch apart on edge of pastry, pointing toward outside of shell. Gently pull pastry between them toward outside of shell with right index finger; repeat along entire edge.*

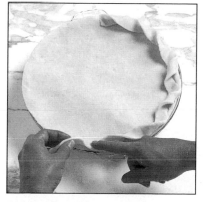

Spiral edge *Trim pastry even with edge of pie plate. Brush rim with water. Cut long, straight, ¾-inch strips of pastry. Press one end of strip to rim, twist strip, and press into rim with index finger after each twist.*

Lattice top *Fold back every other strip. Lay a strip across unfolded strips; unfold strips to cover pie and fold back the strips that were at first left lying flat. Lay next strip and repeat folding and unfolding procedure.*

BAKING PIES AND TARTS

Cooking time is only a general guideline as to when a pastry is ready to come out of the oven. For double-crust pies, the crust should appear golden brown, crisp, and dry; the filling should be bubbling through the steam vents. For single-crust pies and tarts, the crust edge should appear golden brown (but not burnt), crisp, and dry; the filling should be set (a knife inserted into the center comes out clean). If edges of crust begin to brown too much before pie is fully baked, cover with strips of aluminum foil.

More than one pastry can be baked in an oven at one time if there is sufficient room for air to circulate around the pans. Although experts do not recommend the microwave oven for baking pies since the crusts don't brown or become crisp, some bakers feel that the crusts are flakier than those cooked conventionally.

Crusts that may get soggy due to fillings such as custard and cream and crusts that will serve as a shell for an uncooked filling are often blind baked, which is a method used to prebake a pastry crust before it is filled. The pastry shell can be either partially baked or fully baked, depending on the way it is to be later filled. To keep the unfilled crust from puffing and distorting, it is usually lined with aluminum foil or parchment paper and then filled with dried beans or metal or ceramic pie weights and then baked. For shells to be fully baked, the weights are removed after the crust has baked for 15 to 20 minutes and has set; the crust is then pricked to allow steam to escape and baked further until golden brown. Fully baked blind-baked crusts are always cooled completely before filling (see BAKE BLIND).

Fruit tarts can get soggy from the juice exuded by the fruits. However, there are several ways to prevent soggy crusts and diluted pastry creams. After baking the crust, use a pastry brush to paint the inside of the crust with a thin layer of melted currant jelly. This will in essence waterproof the crust. Or, sprinkle crumbled vanilla wafers, ladyfingers, or stale white cake over the pastry cream before topping it with fruit. This will provide a dry barrier between the juicy fruit and the pastry cream and will help absorb the juices. Be sure to dry fruit well with paper towels before placing on tart. Assemble tart just before serving, whenever possible.

BASIC PIE CRUSTS

Pie crusts are most often a pastry of some sort, but biscuit and yeast doughs, crumbs, nuts, and meringues are used as well. Pies are known for their tender, flaky short crusts and are usually made with lard or shortening. Pie dough is easier to handle than tart pastry, and can be used to form double-crust and lattice-top pies with decoratively fluted edges. Because flaky pie crusts are fragile when baked, they must remain in the pie plate for support. A pie is served directly from the pie plate in which it is baked: a 1-inch deep plate or tin with a slanted, rimmed side.

Both Flaky Pastry (see below) and Egg Pastry (see opposite page) produce tender, flaky pie crusts and are appropriate for most single-crust, double-crust, or lattice-top pies. Flaky Pastry yields the flakiest crust, but Egg Pastry tastes buttery and is easier to handle.

Crumb crusts are just right for the chilled or frozen fillings—such as Bavarian cream, chiffon, or ice cream—of make-ahead pies and, best of all, they're easy to prepare: Just add a little sugar to the crumbs and stir in butter; press crumb crust mixture into pie plate, chill, and fill. There's no dough to roll or bake—an attractive feature during warm weather. For a crisper crumb crust, however, bake at 350° F for 10 minutes.

Cookie or cracker crumbs that are commonly used for crumb crusts include vanilla wafers, chocolate wafers, gingersnaps, dry macaroons, *amaretti* cookies, graham crackers, and zwieback or melba toast. Cracker and toast crumbs will need to be sweetened. For variety finely ground nuts, poppy seed, or sesame seed can be substituted for some of the crumbs.

Press-in crusts shortcut the process of rolling and shaping. Like nut crusts, they are quickly assembled and are essentially foolproof; the dough is set in the pie pan and worked with the fingers to cover the pan bottom and sides. They are a boon to those cooks who lack the time or the self-confidence to shape a crust by traditional methods.

■ FLAKY PASTRY

You will use this crust over and over again. It is tender and when cut reveals thin, flaky layers, the hallmark of a classic pie crust.

Single Crust (for one 9- to 10-inch pie)

- 1¼ cups flour
- ¼ teaspoon salt
- ½ cup cold solid vegetable shortening
- 3 tablespoons ice water

Double Crust (for one 9- to 10-inch double-crust pie or two 9-inch single-crust pies)

- 2¼ cups flour
- ½ teaspoon salt
- ¾ cup cold solid vegetable shortening
- 5 to 7 tablespoons ice water

1. Sift flour and salt together; place in a medium bowl.

2. Divide shortening in half. Cut half of shortening into flour mixture with fingertips, a pastry blender, two knives, or the paddle attachment of an electric mixer until mixture resembles coarse meal. (For food processor method, see end of recipe.) Then cut in remaining shortening until mixture resembles small peas.

3. Sprinkle ice water over mixture; toss with a fork to moisten dough evenly. Use as few strokes as possible and the minimum amount of water needed. Gently press dough into a ball. (For a double crust, divide dough into two portions and form 2 balls.) Flatten ball slightly with a few strokes with the side of your hand. Wrap dough with plastic wrap and refrigerate at least 1 hour. It will keep for 2 to 3 days in refrigerator or 1 month in freezer. To roll out dough see Rolling Out Pie and Tart Pastry, page 432.

Whole Wheat Flaky Pastry *For Single-Crust Pie:* Use Flaky Pastry recipe. Substitute 1 cup all-purpose flour and ⅓ cup whole wheat flour for the 1¼ cups flour, ¼ cup cold unsalted butter and ¼ cup cold vegetable shortening for the ½ cup shortening, and increase ice water to 3 to 4 tablespoons. Proceed as for Flaky Pastry. *For Double-Crust Pie:* Use Flaky Pastry recipe. Substitute 1¾ cups all-purpose flour and ⅔ cup whole wheat flour for the 2¼ cups flour, 5 tablespoons cold unsalted butter and 5 tablespoons cold vegetable shortening for the ¾ cup shortening, and increase ice water to 7 to 8 tablespoons. Proceed as for Flaky Pastry.

Food Processor Version Measure shortening; freeze until firm. Place flour and salt in work bowl of processor fitted with metal blade. Add half of the frozen shortening (cut into small pieces). Process with half-second pulses until mixture resembles coarse meal. Add remaining shortening; process with half-second pulses until mixture resembles small peas. Add ice water quickly through feed tube while pulsing; stop pulsing as soon as dough looks as if it will gather into a ball. Mixture should look crumbly but not dry. (Add more ice water, 1 tablespoon at a time, if necessary to moisten dough.) Gather dough into a ball, flatten slightly with side of hand, wrap, and refrigerate at least 1 hour.

■ EGG PASTRY

This pastry crust, made with butter and egg yolk, is easier to work with and tolerates handling better than does Flaky Pastry (see page 434). The butter and egg yolks lend a rich golden hue to the crust and improve the flavor. A little vinegar or lemon juice helps to soften the gluten and produce a tender crust. Egg Pastry is flaky, but somewhat sturdier than Flaky Pastry, so it's especially well suited for pies and tarts with moist custard fillings, rich pies, and certain freestanding deep-dish tarts. If you prefer, use all butter in this recipe. Nut Egg Pastry is less flaky and tender than Egg Pastry, but the nutty flavor is delicious.

Single Crust (for one 9- to 10-inch pie)

    1¼ cups flour
     ½ teaspoon sugar
     ¼ teaspoon salt
     ¼ cup *each* unsalted butter and solid
         vegetable shortening, combined and chilled
     ½ teaspoon vinegar
     1 egg yolk
     2 to 3 tablespoons ice water

Deep-Dish Tart (for one 9- to 10-inch tart)

    1½ cups flour
     ½ teaspoon sugar
     ¼ teaspoon salt
     ⅓ cup unsalted butter *and* 3 tablespoons solid
         vegetable shortening, combined and chilled
     ½ teaspoon vinegar
     1 extralarge egg yolk
     3 to 5 tablespoons ice water

Double Crust (for one 9- to 10-inch double-crust pie or two 9-inch single-crust pies)

    2¼ cups flour
     1 teaspoon sugar
     ½ teaspoon salt
     ½ cup unsalted butter *and* ¼ cup solid
         vegetable shortening, combined and chilled
     1 teaspoon vinegar
     2 large egg yolks
     4 to 6 tablespoons ice water

1. Sift together flour, sugar, and salt. Cut cold butter-shortening mixture into pieces and add to flour mixture. Cut into flour until mixture resembles coarse meal. (For food processor method, see below.)

2. Mix vinegar and egg yolk with smaller amount of ice water in a small bowl. Sprinkle liquid mixture over flour and toss with a fork to moisten dough evenly. Use as few strokes as possible and the least amount of water needed to moisten ingredients, only enough to gather dough into a ball. Add more water, 1 tablespoon at a time, if dough is too dry. Gently press dough into a ball; flatten ball with side of hand. (For a double crust, divide dough into 2 portions and form 2 balls.) Wrap dough with plastic wrap; refrigerate at least 1 hour. Dough will keep for 2 to 3 days in refrigerator or 6 to 8 weeks in freezer. To roll out dough, see Rolling Out Pie and Tart Pastry, page 432.

Nut Egg Pastry Use Egg Pastry recipe. Substitute ¼ cup finely ground nuts (almonds, pecans, hazelnuts, or walnuts) for ¼ cup of the flour. For a sweeter crust, add 3 tablespoons sifted confectioners' sugar to the flour. Finely grated orange or lemon rind can be added if desired. Proceed as for Egg Pastry.

Food Processor Version Mix butter and shortening together; freeze. Place flour, sugar, and salt in work bowl. Cut frozen butter-shortening mixture into pieces and add to bowl; using metal blade process with half-second pulses until mixture resembles coarse meal. Combine vinegar, egg yolk, and smaller amount of ice water and add quickly through feed tube while pulsing; stop as soon as dough looks as if it will gather into a ball. Mixture should look crumbly but not dry. (Add more water, 1 tablespoon at a time, if necessary to moisten dough.) Gather dough into a ball, flatten slightly with side of hand, wrap, and refrigerate at least 1 hour.

CREAM CHEESE PASTRY

Use this strong, relatively tough dough for very liquid fillings such as custards and chiffons. The addition of cream cheese strengthens the crust and adds an appealing tang to its flavor.

    1 **cup flour**
      Pinch salt
    4 **ounces cream cheese, softened**
    ¼ **cup solid vegetable shortening, chilled**
    3 **tablespoons ice water**

1. In a medium bowl sift flour and salt together. Cut in cream cheese and shortening until mixture resembles coarse crumbs.

2. Add the water and stir to moisten. Press dough into a ball and knead lightly until smooth.

3. Wrap with plastic wrap and refrigerate 30 minutes. Use as needed.

Makes one 9-inch crust.

CRUMB CRUST

These crusts can be made in as many flavors as there are types of crumbs; crushed vanilla or chocolate wafers, graham crackers, and gingersnaps are a few choices. Usually crumb crusts are chilled before use, to set the butter, but baking them briefly will achieve the same result.

    1½ **cups fine crumbs (see step 1)**
    ½ **cup unsalted butter, melted**
    ¼ **cup sifted confectioners' sugar (optional)**
      Ground cinnamon or nutmeg (optional)
    1 **egg white, lightly beaten (optional, see Note)**

1. Break crackers, cookies, cake, or bread into small pieces. Grind a small amount at a time in a food processor or electric blender. Place fine crumbs in a bowl.

2. Stir into crumbs, butter and, if used, sugar and cinnamon (taste crumbs for sweetness and spiciness before adding sugar or cinnamon; see Note).

3. Spread crumb mixture evenly over bottom and sides of a well-buttered 9-inch pie plate. Press an 8-inch pie plate onto crumb mixture to pack down and evenly distribute crumbs in the plate. Shape crumbs on rim of pie plate and press to mold.

4. To set crust, refrigerate for 30 minutes or bake in a preheated 325° F oven 10 minutes (cool before filling). Fill as directed in recipe.

Makes one 9-inch crust.

Chocolate Crumb Crust Either use chocolate wafer crumbs for fine crumbs or melt 2 ounces semisweet chocolate with the butter. Proceed as for Crumb Crust.

Note For a baked crumb crust that doesn't crumble, add one lightly beaten egg white to crumb mixture; bake as directed above.

PRESS-IN NUT CRUST

This is a nut version of a basic crumb crust. Use a Bavarian cream, mousse, or chiffon filling.

    1½ **cups finely ground nuts (almonds, hazelnuts, pecans, or walnuts)**
    ¼ **cup sifted confectioners' sugar**
    ¼ **cup unsalted butter, melted**
    1 **egg white, lightly beaten**

1. Preheat oven to 350° F. In a bowl combine nuts and sugar; stir in melted butter. Add egg white and mix well.

2. Spread nut mixture evenly over bottom, sides, and rim of a well-buttered 9-inch pie plate. Press an 8-inch pie plate into the nut mixture to pack down and evenly distribute nuts in the plate. Shape and flute the edges.

3. Bake until crust is set (10 to 15 minutes). Cool and fill as directed in recipe.

Makes one 9-inch crust.

Chocolate Press-In Nut Crust Melt 2 ounces semisweet chocolate with the butter. Proceed as for Press-In Nut Crust.

COCONUT FLAKE CRUST

Another simple crust, this one is delicious with cream or chiffon pies.

    3 **tablespoons unsalted butter, softened**
    1½ **to 2 cups flaked coconut**

1. Preheat oven to 325° F. Spread butter on bottom and sides of a 9-inch pie plate.

2. Distribute flaked coconut in an even layer over butter. Press coconut into butter. Bake until golden brown (about 15 minutes). Cool and use as needed.

Makes one 9-inch crust.

PRESS-IN PIE CRUST

Quick and simple, this crisp, tasty crust can be used for most pies and tarts and is always prebaked before filling.

    1 **cup flour**
    ¼ **cup confectioners' sugar**
    ½ **cup chilled unsalted butter**

1. Preheat oven to 400° F. In a medium bowl sift flour and sugar together. Cut in butter by hand until the size of coarse crumbs; or, use a food processor. Press dough evenly over bottom and sides of a 9-inch pie plate or tart pan with removable bottom. Chill 30 minutes.

2. Bake until light golden brown (10 to 12 minutes). Remove from oven, cool, and use as needed.

Makes one 9-inch crust.

Variation Mix in 1 teaspoon grated orange or lemon rind with flour and sugar. Substitute Vanilla Confectioners' Sugar (see page 585) for the confectioners' sugar.

A PIE SAMPLER

There are two main categories of pie fillings: fruit and berry laden and egg-thickened and sugar-based, such as pecan, custard, cream, and chiffon. However, don't neglect fillings of ice cream, Bavarian cream, and mousse.

◼ BASIC BERRY PIE

Unsweetened frozen berries can be used in this recipe, but if you are fortunate enough to have a source for wild berries, use them. Otherwise try cultivated varieties such as raspberries, blueberries, or blackberries. You'll want to vary the amount of sugar and add some lemon juice according to the tartness of the fruit.

    1   nine-inch double-crust Flaky Pastry (see
        page 434) or Egg Pastry (see page 435)
    1   pound (2 pt) fresh berries (see Note)
    ½   cup sugar
        Lemon juice, to taste (optional)
    3   tablespoons cornstarch
    1   tablespoon butter

1. Roll out half the pie crust and use it to line a 9- or 10-inch pie plate, letting excess hang over edge of pan. Combine berries, sugar, lemon juice (if used), and cornstarch in a large bowl and toss to coat berries evenly. Fill pie shell with berries, heaping them slightly in center. Dot with bits of butter.

2. Roll out remaining dough for top crust. Seal and flute edges of dough. Cut a round vent or 3 or 4 small radiating slashes in center of crust. Pie may be prepared to this point and refrigerated several hours before baking.

3. Preheat oven to 450° F. Place pie on baking sheet on lowest shelf of oven. Bake 15 minutes, reduce heat to 375° F, and bake until golden brown and bubbly (another 25 to 30 minutes). Cool on wire rack before serving.

Serves 8.

Note Use either blackberries, blueberries, boysenberries, olallieberries, or raspberries.

◼ APPLE PIE

Tart apples, such as Granny Smiths or pippins, make the best apple pie.

    1   nine-inch double-crust Flaky Pastry (see
        page 434) or Egg Pastry (see page 435)
    6 to 8 cups peeled, cored, and thinly sliced
        tart apples (6 to 8 apples)
    ¾   cup sugar, plus sugar for sprinkling (optional)
    ¾   teaspoon ground cinnamon
    ⅛   teaspoon freshly grated nutmeg
    2   tablespoons cornstarch
    2   teaspoons fresh lemon juice
    1   teaspoon finely grated lemon rind
    1   egg white, lightly beaten
    2   tablespoons cold unsalted butter
    1   egg yolk beaten with 1 teaspoon water

1. Preheat oven to 425° F. Roll out pastry for bottom crust and use to line a 9-inch pie plate. Roll out remaining pastry for top crust.

2. In a large bowl combine apple slices, the ¾ cup sugar, the cinnamon, nutmeg, and cornstarch; stir. Allow to stand 15 minutes. Mix in lemon juice and lemon rind.

3. Brush inside of bottom crust with egg white to moisture-proof crust. Arrange apple slices in pie shell in flat, snug layers. Create a higher mound of apple slices in center because apples cook down as they bake. Pour juices from bowl over apples; dot with butter.

4. Moisten rim of bottom crust and cover with top crust. Seal and finish edges; cut vents in top. Brush with egg yolk mixture.

5. Bake 15 minutes. Lower oven temperature to 400° F; continue baking until crust is golden brown (35 to 40 minutes). For a sugared crust, brush pie again with egg yolk glaze 5 minutes before pie is done; sprinkle with sugar.

Serves 6 to 8.

The top crust of this Apple Pie is decorated with pastry cutouts, a simple, yet impressive, treatment. See Decorative Finishes, page 433, for more about cutouts.

■ MINCEMEAT PIE

Mincemeat was originally made with minced or ground meats, usually beef or tongue, mixed with dried fruits and preserved with alcohol. Meat is absent from contemporary mincemeat recipes, although suet is used for richness. If you prefer a finer texture, grind all ingredients through the coarse disk of a meat grinder or in a food processor with metal blade, using a pulse action. The mincemeat recipe makes more than you will need for one pie, so use the leftover portion to make individual turnovers or to mix with apples for an especially flavorful apple-pie filling. To develop a rich, deep flavor, the mincemeat must be made six weeks before use. Prepared, storebought mincemeat can be substituted.

    1 nine-inch double-crust Flaky Pastry (see
       page 434) or Egg Pastry (see page 435)
    1 egg white, lightly beaten
    2 tablespoons sugar

Mincemeat

    1½ cups dark raisins
    1½ cups golden raisins
    1½ cups dried currants
     3 apples, peeled, cored, and chopped
     1 cup suet, finely chopped or ground by butcher
     1 cup firmly packed brown sugar
     1 cup candied citrus peel
     ½ cup almonds, sliced or slivered
        Grated rind and juice of 2 lemons
        Grated rind and juice of 1 orange
     ¼ teaspoon ground cinnamon
     ¼ teaspoon freshly grated nutmeg
     ⅛ teaspoon ground cloves
     1 cup brandy
     ½ cup sherry

1. Preheat oven to 400° F. Roll out pastry for bottom crust and use to line a 9-inch pie plate. Roll out remaining pastry for top crust.

2. Fill bottom crust with 3 cups mincemeat. Brush edges of crust with water; cover with top crust; press edges to seal, trim away excess dough, and finish edges as desired. Chill 10 to 15 minutes. Cut steam vents. Brush surface with egg white and sprinkle with sugar.

3. Bake 10 minutes; lower heat to 375° F and bake until golden brown (25 to 35 minutes). Serve hot, warm, or at room temperature.

Serves 6 to 8.

Mincemeat In a large bowl combine dark raisins, golden raisins, currants, apples, suet, brown sugar, citrus peel, almonds, lemon and orange rinds and juice, cinnamon, nutmeg, and cloves; mix well. Add brandy and sherry; stir to combine (more brandy may be added, if necessary, to moisten all the ingredients). Pack into sterilized jars; cover with parchment paper or waxed paper and screw on lid to acquire a tight seal. Let mincemeat ripen in a cool, dark, dry place for at least 6 weeks before using. Mincemeat will keep several months.

Makes about 1 quart.

■ PUMPKIN PIE

For lovers of this traditional Thanksgiving dessert, all the familiar spices and the smooth, creamy texture are here. This recipe yields two pies; if you don't serve them both, you can freeze half the filling or freeze the baked pie. If pie is frozen, thaw in the refrigerator overnight; then warm in a 350° F oven 15 to 20 minutes or serve cold.

    2 recipes 9-inch single-crust
       Flaky Pastry (see page 434)

Pumpkin Purée Filling

    1 pumpkin (about 2 lb)
    3 eggs
    2 cups whipping cream
    ¾ cup sugar
    1 teaspoon ground cinnamon
    ¾ teaspoon ground ginger
    ½ teaspoon freshly grated nutmeg
    ¼ teaspoon *each* ground cloves and ground allspice

1. Preheat oven to 400° F. Roll out Flaky Pastry for bottom crusts and use to line two 9-inch pie plates. Blind bake until partially baked.

2. Place pie shells on a baking sheet. Divide filling between two crusts. Bake 10 minutes; reduce heat to 350° F and bake until filling is set and a knife inserted near the center comes out clean (40 to 50 minutes). Serve warm or at room temperature.

Makes two 9-inch pies, serves 6 to 8 each.

Pumpkin Purée Filling

1. *To prepare pulp by baking:* Preheat oven to 350° F. Cut pumpkin in half. Scrape out seeds and strings. Place cut side down on a glass baking pan; add ⅛ inch water to pan. Bake until pulp is tender (1½ hours). Remove from oven and scrape pulp away from skin. *To prepare pulp by steaming:* Peel pumpkin with a sharp knife. Cut into 2-inch chunks. Place chunks in a vegetable steamer and steam until tender (20 to 30 minutes).

2. Purée pulp in food mill or food processor. Place purée in a fine-meshed sieve and drain well. Freeze purée after draining or use immediately. (If frozen, thaw purée in a fine-meshed sieve. A lot more water will drain off during the thawing process.)

3. In a medium bowl beat 2 cups cooked pumpkin purée just until smooth; add eggs, one at a time, beating well after each addition. Add cream, sugar, cinnamon, ginger, nutmeg, cloves, and allspice; beat to combine.

Makes about 2 cups.

■ SOUTHERN PECAN PIE

Pecan pie is a long-standing southern favorite that is generally among the most popular desserts at church suppers and elsewhere. Even the most iron-willed calorie watchers find it hard to resist this sweet seduction. Buy the freshest pecans you can find; they will be the crispest. Vanilla ice cream or whipped cream would be a good choice for an accompaniment.

>   1 **nine-inch single-crust Egg Pastry (see page 435)**
>   4 **eggs, lightly beaten**
>   ⅔ **cup firmly packed dark brown sugar**
> 1⅓ **cup light corn syrup**
>   ¼ **cup unsalted butter, melted**
>   ½ **teaspoon salt**
>   4 **teaspoons flour**
>   2 **teaspoons vanilla extract**
> 1¼ **cups coarsely chopped pecans**

1. Roll out Egg Pastry for bottom crust and use to line a 9-inch pie plate. Blind bake until partially baked.

2. Preheat oven to 375° F. In a large bowl combine eggs, sugar, corn syrup, butter, salt, flour, and vanilla; stir to blend. Mix in pecans. Pour into partially baked pie shell.

3. Bake until filling is set (30 to 40 minutes). Cover edges of crust with strips of foil, if necessary, to prevent excessive browning. Cool on wire rack.

Serves 8.

■ LEMON MERINGUE PIE

This version of lemon pie filling derives its rich yellow hue from egg yolks, butter, and lemon zest—no yellow food coloring here! The quick and easy lemon curd filling can be poured piping hot directly into a fully baked shell. Almonds are a good choice if you make a nut crust.

>   1 **nine-inch single-crust Flaky Pastry (see**
>   **page 434), Egg Pastry (see page 435), or**
>   **Nut Egg Pastry (see page 435)**
>   4 **eggs**
>   3 **egg yolks (reserve whites for Meringue Topping)**
>   1 **cup plus 2 tablespoons sugar**
>   ¾ **cup fresh lemon juice**
>   2 **teaspoons finely grated lemon rind**
>   9 **tablespoons unsalted butter, softened**

Meringue Topping

>   3 **egg whites (reserve yolks for filling),**
>   **at room temperature**
>   ¼ **teaspoon cream of tartar**
>   ¼ **teaspoon cornstarch**
>   4 **tablespoons superfine sugar**
>   ½ **teaspoon vanilla extract**

1. Roll out pastry for bottom crust and use to line a 9-inch pie plate. Blind bake until fully baked; let cool on a wire rack.

2. In a nonaluminum bowl combine eggs, egg yolks, sugar, lemon juice, and lemon rind. Place bowl over a pot of boiling water and whisk or stir over medium heat until mixture thickens to the consistency of mayonnaise (about 5 minutes). Do not boil or eggs will curdle.

3. Remove from heat; whisk in butter, 2 tablespoons at a time, until incorporated. Pour immediately into baked pie shell. Cool to room temperature before topping with meringue.

4. Preheat oven to 350° F. Spread meringue over pie, sealing to edges of crust all around. Bake until golden brown (10 to 15 minutes). Serve at room temperature. To cut meringue easily, dip the knife into water.

Serves 6 to 8.

Meringue Topping Beat egg whites until foamy. Add cream of tartar and cornstarch. Beat until whites form soft peaks. Add sugar, 1 tablespoon at a time, beating after each addition. Beat in vanilla and continue beating until stiff, glossy peaks form.

Two-layered Lemon Meringue Pie is a perennial favorite. To add some crunch, make an almond-based nut crust instead of the more expected flaky one.

■ CUSTARD PIE

It's best to eat a custard pie soon after it's baked. These pies typically develop a soggy shell if left to set and are prone to bacterial spoilage if not stored properly. If not eaten fairly quickly, keep in the refrigerator. However, the crust won't be as crisp.

> 1 nine-inch single-crust Flaky Pastry (see page 434) or Cream Cheese Pastry (see page 436)
> 2 eggs
> 4 egg yolks
> ½ cup sugar
> 1 cup milk
> 1 cup whipping cream
> 1 tablespoon vanilla extract
> Freshly grated nutmeg (optional)

1. Preheat oven to 325° F. Roll out Flaky Pastry for bottom crust and use to line a 9-inch pie plate. Blind bake until fully baked; cool.

2. In a medium bowl beat eggs, egg yolks, sugar, milk, cream, and vanilla until smooth and the sugar has dissolved.

3. Set baked shell on a baking sheet; strain custard into shell. Sprinkle with nutmeg, if desired. Bake until custard is set (30 to 40 minutes). Filling may be slightly wobbly in center when shaken, but will set as the pie cools.

4. Serve at room temperature or slightly chilled.

Serves 6 to 8.

Coconut Custard Pie   Follow recipe for Custard Pie. Reduce sugar to ⅓ cup and stir in ½ cup sweetened flaked coconut to custard. Ten minutes before end of cooking, sprinkle ¼ cup toasted flaked coconut over top of pie; finish baking.

■ BANANA CREAM PIE

For this classic American pie, choose bananas that are slightly firm but ripe. If you really love bananas, the filling can accommodate several more. Tossing the fruit in rum gives it a tropical accent. Cream pies are especially susceptible to spoilage if improperly stored. Refrigerate if not eaten within three hours.

> 1 nine-inch single-crust Flaky Pastry (see page 434) or Press-In Pie Crust (see page 436)
> 3 tablespoons flour
> 3 tablespoons cornstarch
> ⅔ cup sugar
> 3 cups half-and-half or milk
> 4 egg yolks
> 2 teaspoons vanilla extract
> 4 tablespoons butter
> 3 to 4 ripe bananas
> 2 tablespoons rum (optional)
> 1 to 2 cups whipping cream, whipped, or Meringue Topping (see page 439), for topping

1. Roll out pastry for bottom crust and use to line a 9-inch pie plate. Blind bake until fully baked; cool.

2. In a medium bowl sift together flour, cornstarch, and sugar. Add ½ cup of the half-and-half, the egg yolks, and vanilla; mix until smooth and creamy. In a medium, heavy-bottomed saucepan, heat remaining half-and-half and add to flour mixture, stirring until completely smooth; return to saucepan and cook over medium heat, stirring continuously. Bring to a boil and cook until starchy taste disappears (2 to 3 minutes). Pour custard into a bowl and dot with butter; set aside to cool.

3. Slice bananas and sprinkle with rum (if used). Fold into cooled custard and pour into pie shell.

4. Top with whipped cream or Meringue Topping and serve.

Serves 6 to 8.

Coconut Cream Pie   Use Coconut-Flake Crust (see page 436). For filling, reduce sugar to ½ cup. Fold 2 cups flaked coconut into custard before dotting with butter and setting aside to cool. If using Meringue Topping, sprinkle with ½ cup toasted coconut before browning.

■ LEMON OR LIME CHIFFON PIE

Chiffon pies are wonderful in a shimmery, ethereal way and make a refreshing summer dessert.

> 1 nine-inch crumb crust of Press-In Pie Crust (see page 436) or Press-In Nut Crust (see page 436)
> 1 envelope unflavored gelatin
> ¾ cup fresh lemon or lime juice
> 4 egg yolks
> ¾ cup sugar
> 1 teaspoon finely grated lemon or lime rind
> 3 egg whites
> 2 cups Chantilly Cream (see page 252), for garnish
> Strips of lemon or lime rind, for garnish

1. Roll out pastry for bottom crust and use to line a 9-inch pie plate. Bake as directed in recipe.

2. In a small saucepan sprinkle gelatin over ¼ cup of the lemon or lime juice and set aside to soften. In a double boiler combine egg yolks, ½ cup of the sugar, remaining ½ cup lemon juice, and grated lemon rind. Cook over medium heat, stirring constantly, until mixture thickens to consistency of whipping cream and coats the back of a spoon. Do not boil or mixture will curdle. Set aside.

3. Dissolve gelatin over low heat. Stir into lemon mixture. Set bowl over ice and stir until it is about to set (it will have the consistency of cream whipped to soft peaks). Beat whites to stiff peaks. Stir one third of whites into gelatin-lemon mixture to lighten, then fold in remaining whites. Pour into prepared pie shell, smooth top, and refrigerate until set (3 to 4 hours). Serve garnished with Chantilly Cream and rind.

Serves 6 to 8.

BASIC TART CRUSTS

A tart has a short crust made with butter and eggs and often sweetened with sugar. These ingredients make the pastry rich and crumbly rather than flaky. A tart is baked in a shallow, rimless, straight-sided tart tin with a removable bottom, or in a tart band positioned on a baking sheet. When baked, the once-fragile pastry develops enough strength to form a pastry shell that can support its filling without the help of the tart tin.

■ SAVORY TART PASTRY
Pâte brisée

This basic French tart dough is used for quiches and other savory pies. It is tough, strong and suitable for custard fillings that would make other types of dough soggy. This dough is made without sugar. For a touch of sweetness, if desired, add 2 tablespoons sugar with the flour and salt.

For one 9½- by 1-inch tart band or tin

    1½ cups flour
    ¼ teaspoon salt
    6 tablespoons cold unsalted butter
    2 egg yolks
    3 to 4 tablespoons ice water

For one 10- by 2-inch tart band or tin

    2 cups flour
    ½ teaspoon salt
    ½ cup cold unsalted butter
    2 egg yolks
    4 to 6 tablespoons ice water

1. Sift flour and salt together onto work surface; make a well in the center.

2. Place butter, yolks, and 3 tablespoons of the water in well. Using fingertips, pinch butter to mix with the water and yolks. With a dough scraper or pastry blender, gradually work flour into yolk mixture with a cutting motion to make coarse crumbs (if mixture seems dry and crumbly, add more water).

3. Gather crumbs into a rough mound. Work small portions of the dough against the work surface with the heel of your hand (pushing away from you), so that the dough is smeared across the work area surface (this is known as *fraisage;* it distributes the ingredients evenly through the dough).

4. When pieces of dough are pliable and peel away from the surface in one piece, press into a ball. Wrap well and refrigerate until firm (about 2 hours). Use as directed.

Food Processor Version   Put flour and salt in work bowl of food processor; process a few times to aerate. Add butter; process briefly to cut in. Add yolks and water and pulse rapidly just until mixture comes together. Turn out and continue with step 3.

■ SWEET TART PASTRY
Pâte sucrée

The high percentage of butter, large amount of sugar, and viscosity of the egg yolks in Sweet Tart Pastry produce a dough that is soft, moist, and sticky. The tender, crumbly, and fragile, rather than flaky, dough is quite suitable for delicate tart shells. This pastry can be difficult to roll. If covering a large area, press into shape with fingertips rather than spreading and thinning with a rolling pin. To ease dough into corners, use a ball of scrap dough for pushing and molding. This pastry dough patches without showing repairs.

For one 9½- by 1-inch tart band or tin

    1¼ cups flour
    ⅛ teaspoon salt
    ¼ cup sugar
    2 extralarge egg yolks
    ½ teaspoon vanilla extract
    6 tablespoons cold unsalted butter

**For one 10-inch scalloped tart band
or one 10- by 2-inch tart tin**

    1½ cups flour
    ¼ teaspoon salt
    ⅓ cup sugar
    3 large egg yolks
    ½ teaspoon vanilla extract
    ½ cup cold unsalted butter

1. Sift flour, salt, and sugar onto work surface; make a well in the center.

2. Place egg yolks and vanilla in center; mix with fork or fingertips to thoroughly blend ingredients.

3. Pound butter with rolling pin to soften; add to yolks. Using fingertips, pinch butter to mix with yolks. With a dough scraper or pastry blender, gradually work flour into yolk mixture with a cutting motion to make coarse crumbs.

4. Gather crumbs into a rough mound. Work small portions of the dough against the work surface with the heel of your hand (pushing away from you), so that the dough is smeared across the work area surface (this is known as *fraisage;* it distributes the ingredients evenly through the dough).

5. When pieces of dough are pliable and peel away from the surface in one piece, press into a ball. Wrap well and refrigerate until firm (about 2 hours). Use as directed.

Food Processor Version   Place salt, sugar, egg yolks, vanilla, and cold butter in work bowl of food processor and process using four rapid (1-second) pulses. Add flour and process with six to eight rapid pulses, until dough begins to clump (but doesn't form a ball). Turn out and continue with step 4.

Hazelnuts add texture and crunch to Nut Tart. For more flavor, toast the nuts before chopping.

■ SAND PASTRY
Pâte sablée

Use this sweet, short pastry dough to make crusts for tarts and tartlets or cookies. Once baked, this pastry has a sandy, crumbly texture—from which it gets its name—and is very fragile. The dough is difficult to roll and lift and so should be pressed into the baking pan. When made with a high-quality unsalted butter, it is exceptionally flavorful. Fill tartlets with seasonal fresh fruits or lemon curd. For cookies, cut into rounds and triangles and bake in a 350° F oven until slightly colored (five to eight minutes).

> 1½ **cups flour**
> **Pinch salt**
> ¾ **cup cold unsalted butter**
> ½ **cup confectioners' sugar**

1. Sift flour and salt onto work surface; make a well in the center.

2. Place butter and sugar in well. Using fingertips, pinch butter with sugar to make a smooth paste. With a dough scraper or pastry blender, gradually work flour into butter mixture with a cutting motion to make coarse crumbs.

3. Gather crumbs into a rough mound. Work small portions of the dough against the work surface with the heel of your hand (pushing away from you), so that the dough is smeared across the work surface (this is known as *fraisage;* it distributes the ingredients evenly through the dough).

4. When pieces of dough are pliable and peel away from the surface in one piece, press into a ball. Wrap well and refrigerate until firm (about 2 hours).

Makes one 8-inch tart shell or 4 to 6 tartlets.

A TART SAMPLER

Tart fillings can simply be flavored fresh fruit, fresh fruit on top of a layer of smooth pastry cream, a citrus curd, a custard with or without a fruit topping, or one similar to a pecan pie. See Baking Pies and Tarts (page 434) for suggestions on how to avoid a soggy tart crust.

■ FRESH FRUIT TART

A buttery, sweet crust, vanilla pastry cream, and fresh fruit combine to create a classic tart. Few pastries delight the eye and palate more than a tempting array of colorful fresh fruit tarts. The recipe below uses strawberries, kirsch-flavored pastry cream, and a red currant jelly glaze for a strawberry tart. When you vary the fruit, select a flavoring and glaze that will complement or heighten the characteristic taste of the fruit. When glazing the tarts, choose a jam or jelly that matches the fruit in color and flavor. Note that the pastry cream can be made up to three days ahead.

> 1 **Sweet Tart Pastry (9½ in.; see page 441)**
> 1 **cup milk**
> 1 **vanilla bean, split in half lengthwise,** *or*
> 1 **teaspoon vanilla extract**
> 3 **egg yolks**
> ¼ **cup sugar**
> 3 **tablespoons flour**
> 2 **tablespoons kirsch**
> ½ **cup stiffly whipped cream (optional)**
> 3½ **cups hulled, halved strawberries**
> **(approximately two 12-oz baskets)**
> 1 **cup red currant jelly**

1. Roll out tart pastry and use to line a 9½- by 1-inch tart tin that has a removable bottom. Blind bake until fully baked; cool; reserve.

2. To make pastry cream: In a heavy-bottomed saucepan, bring milk to a boil with vanilla bean; remove from heat and allow bean to steep in milk for 10 minutes. Remove vanilla bean, rinse off, and let it dry (it can be reused one more time). If using vanilla extract, add in step 4.

3. Beat egg yolks and sugar together until thick and light. Stir in flour.

4. Reheat milk to boiling. Whisk milk into yolk mixture and return to saucepan. Whisk over low heat until mixture boils; cook gently for 2 minutes, whisking constantly. Remove from heat and stir in vanilla extract (if using instead of vanilla bean). Transfer pastry cream mixture to a small container and cover surface with a piece of buttered plastic wrap or parchment paper. Cool to room temperature and store in the refrigerator, where it will keep 2 to 3 days.

5. Stir 1 tablespoon of the kirsch into pastry cream. If pastry cream is too thick, lighten by folding in ½ cup stiffly whipped cream.

6. To assemble tart; Spread a ½-inch layer of pastry cream in bottom of fully baked tart shell. Arrange a design of strawberries over the cream in concentric circles. You may use whole, halved, or sliced berries to form your design.

7. To make glaze: Heat jelly in a saucepan over low heat until just melted and bubbly. Stir in remaining kirsch. Brush surface of strawberries with a thin layer of glaze. Reserve leftover glaze for another tart.

Serves 6 to 8.

■ LEMON TART

This filling bears a slight resemblance to that of Lemon Meringue Pie (see page 439). Actually, it is more like a set custard than it is gelatinous and bouncy. This is an elegant, refined dessert that would look lovely garnished with piped rosettes of Chantilly Cream (see page 252) and candied violets. Check better cookware stores, and cake-decorating suppliers for candied violets.

- 1 Savory Tart Pastry (9½ in., with extra 2 tablespoons sugar; see page 441)
- 3 eggs
- 3 egg yolks
- ⅓ cup sugar
  Finely grated rind and juice of 3 lemons
- 1 tablespoon cornstarch
- 4 tablespoons butter, melted and cooled

1. Roll out tart pastry and use to line a 9½- by 1-inch tart tin that has a removable bottom. Blind bake until fully baked; cool.

2. Preheat oven to 350° F. In a medium bowl beat eggs, egg yolks, and sugar until combined; add rind and beat until mixture is smooth and light. In a separate small bowl, combine lemon juice and cornstarch and mix until smooth and well blended.

3. Combine the two mixtures; stir in butter. Pour lemon custard mixture into pie shell and bake until set and a knife inserted near center comes out clean (25 to 35 minutes). Let cool; serve at room temperature.

Serves 6 to 8.

■ NUT TART

Chez Panisse in Berkeley, California, is known for its nut tart. This version was inspired by the one served there. While hazelnuts are called for, any nuts will work as well. The dough is frozen, rather than just chilled, to better withstand the high heat of the cooked filling.

- ¾ cup whipping cream
- ¾ cup sugar
- 1 tablespoon frangelico or other hazelnut liqueur
- 1 tablespoon vanilla extract
- 1 cup hazelnuts, roughly chopped
- 1 nine-inch frozen Flaky Pastry (see page 434) or Savory Tart Pastry (9½ in., see page 441)

1. Preheat oven to 400° F. In a medium, heavy-bottomed saucepan, combine cream and sugar and stir over low heat until sugar has dissolved. Increase heat to medium and cook until mixture reaches 238° F (soft-ball stage) on a candy thermometer.

2. Remove from heat and stir in liqueur and vanilla; then add the nuts. Cool at least 10 minutes, then pour into frozen pie shell.

3. Bake until filling is a golden caramel color (25 to 30 minutes). Cool. Serve at room temperature.

Serves 6 to 8.

■ QUICHE LORRAINE

Quiche evolved in the area in eastern France that borders Germany; the word has its roots in *kuchen*, German for cake. Unlike the versions one commonly comes across in restaurants and specialty food stores today, some classic recipes for quiche Lorraine (like the version offered here) do not have cheese. The main ingredients are bacon, eggs, and cream. Pans for quiche are fluted, either metal (preferably with removable bottom) or porcelain, and are large—usually measuring 10 inches in diameter by 1½ inches deep (see BAKING PANS, FOR BATTER AND DOUGH, Quiche Pan). If a pie plate is used, only half the filling will be required; use extra filling for a second pie.

- 8 ounces bacon, diced
- 1 Savory Tart Pastry tart shell, partially baked (10 in., see page 441)
- 8 eggs
- 2½ cups half-and-half
- ½ cup whipping cream
- 1½ teaspoons salt
- ½ teaspoon ground white pepper
- ½ teaspoon freshly grated nutmeg

1. Preheat oven to 375° F. In a medium skillet sauté bacon over medium-high heat to remove some fat (about 8 minutes). Remove with a slotted spoon to a paper-towel–lined plate; cool briefly. Sprinkle over bottom of partially baked quiche shell.

2. In a large mixing bowl beat eggs and stir in half-and-half, cream, salt, pepper, and nutmeg. Pour into shell and bake until knife inserted in center comes out clean (about 1 hour). Remove from oven and cool 30 minutes before serving. Serve at room temperature.

Serves 8 to 10.

Recipes and Related Information
Baking Pans, 18; Beef and Mushroom Piroshki, 46; Cake and Pastry Tools, 89; Deep-Dish Chicken Pie, 472; Key Lime Pie, 342; Mud Pie, 315; Nutty Peach Pie, 421; Orange Custard Tart, 401; Raspberry-Almond Tart, 496; Sour-Cherry Pie, 120; Strawberry-Rhubarb Pie, 498.

PINEAPPLE

When the early European explorers found pineapple growing in the Caribbean and in Central and South America, they were immediately seduced by its sweet flavor. Taking it with them on their ships, they spread it to Africa, Madagascar, India, China, Japan, and the Philippines. Surprisingly, it wasn't widely cultivated in Hawaii until the late 1800s, and it wasn't readily available on the mainland until well into the twentieth century, when advances in shipping made transportation of ripe pineapples possible.

Pineapples do not ripen further after harvest; they must be left on the tree until their starch is converted to sugar. However, at that point, they are extremely delicate and perishable. Until the development of rapid, refrigerated shipping and air freight, most pineapples were shipped green. Today the American consumer can enjoy fruit that is almost fully tree-ripened.

The pineapple grown in Hawaii, the Cayenne, has a cylindrical pinecone shape and long, spearlike fronds. A second variety, the Red Spanish, is grown in Florida, Puerto Rico, and Cuba; it is squarish in shape. Yet a third variety, the Sugar Loaf, is exported to the United States from Mexico; it is an extralarge pineapple, weighing from 5 to 10 pounds.

Use   Pineapple is perhaps at its best eaten raw, in slices, wedges, or cubes. It may be added to fruit salads and chicken or turkey salad. Cubed pineapple adds a sweet-tart flavor to Vietnamese fish soup and Indonesian curries. Thai cooks add pineapple to noodles in coconut milk and serve the fruit with spicy ground pork. Pineapple slices may be grilled and served with roast pork or duck, or may be baked and served with ham. Caribbean cooks bake it with brown sugar and rum for dessert. Diced pineapple may be added to gelatin salads if cooked first. (Uncooked pineapple contains an enzyme that inhibits jelling.) Diced pineapple is also used in cream pies and cakes and is puréed for sherbet and ice cream. Pineapple juice is a refreshing breakfast beverage and an ingredient in some punches and tropical cocktails.

Availability   Pineapples are sold the year around; supplies peak March through June. Canned pineapple, in rings, cubes, or dice, is widely sold in supermarkets. Canned pineapple juice is also widely available in supermarkets. Dried unsweetened pineapple slices and candied pineapple are found in some health-food stores and specialty stores.

Selection   The best indications of ripeness are a strong sweet aroma and a rich yellow color. Avoid pineapples that are too green and those that have soft spots or dried-out leaves.

Storage   Keep pineapple in a plastic bag in the refrigerator and use within three to five days, preferably as soon as possible. Store leftover canned pineapple in an airtight, nonmetal container in the refrigerator and use within a few days. Refrigerate leftover canned pineapple juice in an airtight, nonmetal container; use within one week.

Preparation   To peel and section a pineapple, slice off frond and stand pineapple on stem end. Slice in quarters lengthwise. Cut away central core. Using a large sharp knife, cut flesh of each pineapple quarter away from rind by gradually sliding knife underneath flesh from one end to other end. Cube or dice. Alternatively, to make pineapple rounds, slice off frond and stand pineapple on stem end. Using a large sharp knife, slice away rind from top to bottom. Cut into rounds; core if desired.

Recipes and Related Information
Corer, 156; Sweet-and-Sour Pineapple Pork, 460.

PINE NUT

Two types of pine nut, also known as Indian nut or piñon, are available in this country. The more delicately flavored pine nut used in Mediterranean and Middle Eastern cooking is the seed of the stone pine; it is long, slender, and pale ivory, with a faint pine flavor. The other pine nut, broader at one end than the other, is found in Chinese markets; it is less expensive, but has a strong pine flavor that is not desirable in Mediterranean dishes.

Use   Chinese cooks garnish poultry and fish dishes with pine nuts. They also dip them in honey and fry them to make a sweet or use them to garnish tea cakes and pastries. Italians use pine nuts in pasta sauces and in the classic pesto sauce. They also add them to stuffings, sautéed vegetables (especially spinach), and cookies and ricotta cheesecake. Greek cooks sometimes put pine nuts in stuffed grape leaves.

Availability   Pine nuts are sold in small packages in specialty markets and in bulk in some health-food stores. Chinese markets and some specialty markets carry the stronger-flavored triangular variety.

Selection   Buy as fresh as possible.

Storage   Pine nuts, being high in oil, quickly turn rancid. Wrap tightly and freeze for up to six months or refrigerate for up to two months.

Preparation   The flavor of pine nuts is improved with toasting. Put nuts in a cold skillet over moderately low heat and cook, shaking skillet constantly so that nuts color evenly, until pine nuts are golden.

Recipes and Related Information
Mushrooms Stuffed With Herb Cheese, 377; Pesto, 27; Pine Nut Crescents, 146; Ricotta Cheesecake, 119; Sole With Almonds, Pine Nuts, and White Raisins, 533; Your Own Bridge Mix, 59.

PISTACHIO NUT

The fruit of a tree native to the Middle East and Central Asia, the pistachio nut is usually about ½ inch long and is covered with a tan shell that splits easily in half. The shell is sometimes dyed pink to hide blemishes. Inside, the edible kernel has a paper-thin brown skin, green flesh, and a yellow interior. It has a sweet, mild flavor. Most pistachios come from Iran and Turkey, although California pistachios are increasingly common.

Use Pistachio nuts are an ingredient in both sweet and savory dishes, especially in the Middle East. The green color makes them particularly valuable as a garnish for all manner of foods. French cooks use them to stud pâtés and galantines. Turkish cooks use pistachios to garnish savory rice dishes and sweet custards. In India pistachios are used in sweet, milk-based candies; one of the most popular Indian sweets is made of grated carrot, milk, sugar, and chopped pistachios cooked until thick. The nuts may be salted and roasted and eaten as a cocktail snack. They may also be blanched, skinned, and chopped or ground for use in ice cream, soufflés, and pastries. Most commercial pistachio ice cream is artificially colored and flavored with almond extract.

Availability Unshelled pistachios are sold in many supermarkets, either raw or roasted and salted. Raw pistachios are widely available in bulk in health-food stores. Middle Eastern markets are another good source for pistachios.

Storage Keep pistachios in the refrigerator for up to three months or in the freezer for up to six months.

Preparation Shell pistachios. To blanch and peel, boil 30 seconds, then drain and wrap in a clean dish towel. Rub nuts back and forth with towel, then unwrap and remove any unloosened skins by hand. Toast nuts in a 300° F oven to dry them out (about 10 minutes).

> ### Recipes and Related Information
> *Figs With Flavored Ricotta, 220; Pâté Maison, 416; Your Own Bridge Mix, 59.*

PIT; PIT, TO

Both the stone, or hard, central portion of a one-seeded (drupaceous) fruit such as a cherry or a peach, and the act of removing this stone. Sometimes a pit pulls away easily; to pit a peach, simply halve and pry stone away with a knife or your finger. Cherry and olive pits are much more tenacious. For pitting in quantity, consider a cherry pitter, which punches pits out much as a hole puncher removes circles of paper (see CHERRY PITTER).

PIZZA

Food historians and pizza-loving Neapolitans, residents of the Italian city most associated with this dish, concur that the famous open pie, made of thinly rolled bread dough topped with a seasoned mixture, probably originated with the flat breads of ancient Egypt. When the Greeks colonized southern Italy, they brought these breads with them. Although this is not the only explanation for the appearance of pizza in Italy, it is a popular one. There is little agreement, however, about the origins of the word *pizza*. The dictionary states that it grew out of the Latin *pinsere*, to beat or knead. Other sources suggest that it is the Neopolitan pronunciation of the Greek word *picea*, which specifically refers to these types of breads or pies.

For those who relish the dish, it matters little where it comes from or what we call it. However, Americans who visit Italy for the first time might not recognize pizza in all the guises it assumes in its native land. The familiar doughy pie topped with tomatoes and cheese is most common in the southern part of the country. Elsewhere the dough may be thicker and less chewy and the toppings as simple as some fresh herbs, mushrooms, or a slice of ham. Or, it may be paper-thin and crisp, with any number of toppings, sometimes with cheese, sometimes without. Neapolitan-style pizza is but one of a family of Italian bread-based foods that serve as plate and topping in one.

The current culinary interest in fresh, regional ingredients has broadened our definition of what makes a pizza, just as it has changed our view of so many other foods. The variations that have evolved from experimentations by many young chefs are closer in spirit to the pizzas of Italy. Banished are bland or oversalted prepared tomato sauces and rubbery cheeses, replaced by inventive combinations of fresh vegetables and meats, unusual cheeses, and creative flavorings. The emphasis is on using what grows naturally and nearby, which is what makes Italian pizza, or any food, so delicious. Pizza has become regional. Cities have given their names to particular styles; Chicago, New York, Boston, and New Haven each have a version.

Making pizza at home is no more difficult than baking bread. All you need is a hot oven and, for best results, a baking stone and a wooden baker's peel. You can also buy square terra-cotta tile at just about any tile supply store (see BAKER'S PEEL and BAKING STONE AND TILE). The stone or tile converts an oven into a home version of the commercial stone restaurant ovens. The wooden peel is the easiest way to move pizza in and out of the oven. With some advance preparation, the cook can make pizza from scratch as easily as pulling a storebought pizza from the freezer. Yeast doughs are tolerant of cold. If the dough is prepared in the morning, or even the night before, it can wait in the refrigerator, or even in the freezer; when needed, let it warm to room temperature. Then shape it, add toppings, and bake. If you have a favorite sauce, make it in quantity and freeze in recipe-sized portions.

FOOD PROCESSOR PIZZA DOUGH

Process dough to lumpy state, not a smooth ball; do not overprocess. Finish mixing by hand, if desired. If kneading by machine, process dough until ingredients are well mixed and dough forms a ball.

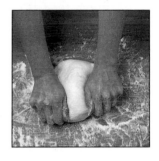

Place dough on a lightly floured surface and knead until it is smooth and silky, adding more flour if necessary.

On lightly floured surface, roll dough out to an even circle, ¼ inch thick, and place on tile.

PIZZA MARGHERITA

This familiar red (tomatoes), white (cheese), and green (basil) pizza is said to have been named after Queen Margherita of Italy, who loved the dish because it bore her country's national colors.

    1 cup grated whole-milk mozzarella cheese
    ½ cup whole fresh basil leaves
       Salt and freshly ground pepper, to taste
    ¼ cup plus 2 tablespoons olive oil
       Freshly grated Parmesan cheese
       Pinch chopped fresh oregano
       Cornmeal or rice flour, for dusting

Basic Pizza Dough

    1½ teaspoons active dry yeast (½ package)
    ¾ cup warm (105° to 115° F) water
    2 tablespoons olive oil
    2½ cups unbleached flour or bread flour
    1 teaspoon salt

Fresh Tomato Sauce

    3 medium tomatoes (about 1 lb)
    2 tablespoons olive oil
    1 clove garlic, minced
    1 tablespoon chopped fresh basil *or*
       ½ teaspoon dried basil
    ¼ teaspoon salt
    ¼ cup dry white wine

1. Preheat baking stone at least 30 minutes in a 450° F oven (475° F for a crisper crust). Roll pizza dough into a square or round and place on a baker's peel or baking sheet well dusted with cornmeal or rice flour.

2. Cover surface of pizza with Fresh Tomato Sauce, then cheese, then basil. Season with salt and pepper. Drizzle with ¼ cup olive oil, then dust with Parmesan cheese and oregano.

3. Slide pizza onto heated baking stone (as described in BAKER'S PEEL) and bake until well browned and puffy (20 to 25 minutes). Brush crust with remaining 2 tablespoons olive oil. Cut into small squares or wedges and serve hot or at room temperature.

Makes 2 medium pizzas or 1 large pizza.

Basic Pizza Dough   Dissolve yeast in the warm water in a small bowl; let proof 5 minutes. Stir in olive oil. In a large bowl combine flour and salt. Add yeast mixture and stir until dough just barely holds together (see also Food Processor Pizza Dough, on page 445). Turn dough out onto a lightly floured surface and knead until soft and silky, adding a little more flour if necessary. Put dough in an oiled bowl and turn to coat surface with oil. Cover bowl with plastic wrap and let rise in a warm place until doubled (about 1 hour).

Makes 2 medium pizza crusts or 1 large pizza crust.

Fresh Tomato Sauce   Pour boiling water over tomatoes; peel, then chop finely. Heat oil in a medium saucepan over medium-high heat. Add tomatoes and garlic. Mix in basil, salt, and wine. Bring to a boil, cover, reduce heat, and simmer for 15 minutes. Uncover and cook over medium-high heat, stirring often as sauce begins to thicken, until sauce is thick and reduced to about 1 cup (15 to 20 minutes).

Makes about 1 cup.

PISSALADIERE

All over the French Riviera, you find "the pizza of Nice": *pissaladière*. Baked in large sheets and cut into squares while still warm, it's handed to you on a fragile tissue to munch as you go. It features a mixture of seasoned onions, anchovies, and Mediterranean black olives.

Dough

    1½ teaspoons active dry yeast (½ package)
    ¼ cup warm (105° to 115° F) water
    ½ teaspoon sugar
    1¼ cups flour
    ½ teaspoon salt
    ½ teaspoon olive oil
       Cornmeal or rice flour, for dusting

Topping

    2 tablespoons olive oil (more, if needed)
    ¼ cup unsalted butter
    4 yellow onions, thinly sliced
    3 cloves garlic, minced
    1 teaspoon minced fresh thyme *or*
       ½ teaspoon dried thyme
       Salt and freshly ground pepper, to taste
    1 tin (2 oz) anchovy fillets in oil
    12 to 15 large black Greek olives, pitted
    ¼ cup minced parsley
    ¼ cup fresh basil leaves (optional)

1. *To prepare dough with electric mixer:* In a small bowl combine yeast, the water, and sugar and let proof 5 minutes. In large bowl of electric mixer, combine flour and salt. Using dough hook, begin mixing and add olive oil. Add yeast mixture and continue mixing. Dough hook will knead dough for you. Mix 5 to 7 minutes, or until dough is silky and no longer clings to sides of bowl. *To make by hand:* Put flour and salt in a large bowl, and stir in olive oil and yeast mixture by hand; knead by hand on a lightly floured surface until mixture is silky and smooth. For either method, place dough in a well-oiled bowl, turning to coat all surfaces with oil, and let rise, covered with a warm damp towel, for 1 hour.

2. To prepare topping: In a large heavy skillet over medium heat, heat olive oil and butter. Add onion and cook gently 5 minutes. Add garlic, thyme, salt, and pepper. Cook 20 minutes, or until onions are very soft but not brown. Taste; adjust seasoning if necessary. Put 2 anchovy fillets and half the olives in a blender. Add a few drops olive oil and blend. Add more oil as necessary to make a smooth paste.

3. To assemble Pissaladière: Preheat oven to 400° F. Roll dough out into a rectangle or circle. Transfer to a baking sheet well dusted with cornmeal or rice flour. Spread with anchovy and olive paste and cover with onion slices. Arrange remaining anchovies over onions in a crisscross pattern. Slice remaining olives; arrange between anchovies. Drizzle with a little olive oil and dust with 2 tablespoons each parsley and basil (if used). Bake until well browned (30 to 35 minutes). Cool slightly, then sprinkle with remaining herbs just before serving. Cut while still warm.

Makes 16 to 20 small cocktail squares or wedges.

■ DEEP-DISH PEPPERONI PIZZA

You'll need a special high-sided pan for this pizza (see BAKING PANS, FOR BATTER AND DOUGH, Pizza Pan). It resembles an oversized cake pan and measures about 15 inches in diameter and 2 inches deep. Once used, the pan should be wiped clean, not washed, so it will season. The dough is especially quick and easy to make because it uses quick-rise yeast (see YEAST). The dough can be mixed in a food processor as well as by hand. If you prefer, substitute browned, crumbled Italian sausage for the pepperoni.

>   3 **cups (1 lb) grated whole-milk mozzarella cheese**
>   1 **can (2¼ oz) sliced ripe olives, well drained**
> 2½ **cups (about ½ lb) thinly sliced pepperoni**
>   2 **recipes Fresh Tomato Sauce (opposite page)**
>   ⅔ **cup freshly grated Parmesan cheese**

Deep-Dish Pizza Dough

>   3 **to 3½ cups unbleached flour**
>   1 **package quick-rise active dry yeast**
>   ¾ **teaspoon salt**
> 1¼ **cups hot (115° to 125° F) water**
>   2 **teaspoons honey**
>   1 **tablespoon olive oil**

1. Preheat oven to 450° F. Grease a deep-dish pizza pan. Roll dough out on a floured surface to about a 14-inch circle. Use your hands to pat and stretch dough to fit into pan, pressing it against bottom and then up sides of pan to reach top edge.

2. Sprinkle half the mozzarella cheese over bottom of dough. Add olives in an even layer, then pepperoni. Spread evenly with sauce. Cover with remaining mozzarella cheese, then sprinkle with Parmesan cheese.

3. Bake on lowest rack of oven until crust browns well and cheese is richly browned (25 to 30 minutes). Cut in wedges and serve at once.

Makes 1 large pizza.

Deep-Dish Pizza Dough

1. In large bowl of electric mixer, combine 2½ cups of the flour, yeast, and salt. Stir to blend dry ingredients thoroughly. In a small bowl combine the hot water, honey, and oil; stir to blend well.

2. Add water mixture to flour mixture. Mix to blend, then beat at medium speed until smooth and elastic (about 5 minutes). Stir in about ½ cup more flour to make a soft dough.

3. Turn dough out onto a floured surface. Knead until dough is smooth and satiny (8 to 10 minutes), adding just enough flour (up to ½ cup) to prevent dough from being sticky.

4. Turn dough into a greased bowl. Cover with plastic wrap and a towel, and let rise in a warm place until doubled in bulk (30 to 40 minutes). Punch dough down, cover with inverted bowl, and let rest 10 minutes; use as directed in recipe.

The sunny flavors of southern France come together in Pissaladière, the earthy "street" pizza from Nice. Anchovies, garlic, onions, and olives are the soul of Pissaladière, at its best in casual settings and washed down with a sharp white wine.

A calzone is a savory Italian turnover made with a yeast dough. Fillings usually have cheese and often some type of sausage, ham, or salami.

■ CALZONE WITH SUN-DRIED TOMATOES

According to food historian Waverley Root, this form of pizza turnover originated in Naples. Calzone is named for the trouser leg some people think it resembles.

> 1 tablespoon oil from sun-dried tomatoes
> 1 medium onion, finely chopped
> 1 clove garlic, minced
> 1 cup (8 oz) ricotta cheese
> ¼ cup chopped sun-dried tomatoes
> 2 tablespoons chopped parsley
> Deep-Dish Pizza Dough (see page 447)
> ¼ pound sliced prosciutto or dry salami, cut into strips
> 2 cups (½ lb) grated whole-milk mozzarella cheese
> Cornmeal, for dusting
> Olive oil, for coating

1. In a medium skillet heat tomato oil over moderate heat; add onion and cook, stirring often, until soft but not browned. Mix in garlic, then remove from heat.

2. In a medium bowl mix ricotta cheese with dried tomatoes and parsley; stir in cooked onion mixture.

3. Divide dough into 2 equal portions. Roll each half out on a floured surface to a 12-inch circle. Spread half of the ricotta filling over half of each circle of dough, leaving about a ½-inch margin.

4. Sprinkle half of each circle with half of the prosciutto strips and 1 cup of the mozzarella cheese. Fold circles in half over filling, moistening and pinching edges together (or pressing with tines of a fork) to seal.

5. Preheat oven to 450° F. Sprinkle a large greased baking sheet lightly with cornmeal. Place calzone well apart on prepared baking sheet. Let rise until puffy (12 to 15 minutes).

6. Bake on center rack until crust browns well (about 15 minutes). Brush tops lightly with olive oil, then serve hot.

Makes 2 calzone.

■ STUFFED VEGETARIAN PIZZA

Students of pizza trace the concept of the stuffed pizza to Giordano's on Chicago's South Side. The idea has been carried far and wide by alumni of that restaurant's kitchen.

> 1 large onion, thinly sliced
> ½ pound mushrooms, thinly sliced
> 1 red or green bell pepper, cut in thin strips
> ¼ cup olive oil
> 2 cloves garlic, minced
> ½ teaspoon *each* salt and dried oregano
> ⅛ teaspoon *each* freshly ground pepper and dried marjoram
> Deep-Dish Pizza Dough (see page 447)
> 4 cups (1 lb) grated Monterey jack cheese
> Fresh Tomato Sauce (see page 446)
> ⅔ cup freshly grated Parmesan or Romano cheese

1. Preheat oven to 450° F. In a large skillet over medium heat, sauté onion, mushrooms, and red pepper in oil, stirring often, until onion is soft, mushrooms brown lightly, and mushroom liquid evaporates. Add garlic, salt, oregano, pepper, and marjoram; remove from heat.

2. Grease a deep-dish pizza pan. Divide dough into 2 portions, one about a third larger than the other. Roll larger portion of dough out on a floured surface to about a 14-inch circle. Use your hands to pat and stretch dough to fit into pan, pressing it against sides of pan to reach top edge.

3. Sprinkle evenly with 3 cups of the jack cheese. Spread vegetable mixture over cheese.

4. Roll out remaining dough to a 14- to 15-inch circle; place over vegetables, pressing edge against dough already in pan. Fold dough lining pan over top layer.

5. Spread tomato sauce over top layer of dough. Sprinkle evenly with the remaining 1 cup jack cheese. Top with Parmesan cheese.

6. Bake on lowest rack of oven until crust browns well and cheese is richly browned (25 to 30 minutes). Let stand for 2 to 3 minutes before cutting into wedges.

Makes 1 large pizza.

PLANTAIN

Also known as cooking banana or Adam's fig, the plantain is a member of the banana family commonly eaten in Latin America and the Caribbean. Unlike the more familiar yellow banana, the plantain must be cooked to be edible. It resembles a yellow banana but is larger and thicker skinned, with three or four well-defined sides. Plantains are green when unripe, turning yellow, then brown, then black when ripe. When cooked, they have a mildly sweet flavor comparable to winter squash.

Use Plantains may be peeled and fried in butter or oil and served as a side dish. They may also be roasted in their skins. In Cuba and Peru, plantains are sliced like potato chips and deep-fried. Like potatoes, plantain chunks are added to soups and stews. Venezuelan cooks use plantains to make cinnamon-scented, lightly sweet cakes that are served with pot roast. Mexican cooks fry boiled, mashed plantains in oil with onions and tomatoes and serve the dish with shrimp.

Availability Plantains are sold the year around in Latin and Caribbean markets. Some supermarkets also carry plantains.

Selection Plantains are usually shipped green but will ripen at room temperature. When ripe, they are dark brown or black and give slightly to pressure. Black skin does not indicate blemished flesh. Some recipes call for green plantains, which have a bland, starchy flavor.

Others call for half-ripe yellow plantains, which have a flavor similar to sweet potatoes. Still other recipes call for fully ripe black plantains, which have a flavor like bananas. Choose the degree of ripeness required by the recipe, or ripen plantains at home at room temperature. A green plantain will turn yellow-brown within one week and black within another week.

Storage Wrapped in plastic, ripe plantains will keep in the refrigerator for up to three days.

Preparation Ripe plantains are easy to peel, but unripe plantains are more difficult. To peel an unripe plantain, cut a lengthwise incision, then cut around the fruit in three places. Peel back skin with fingers.

■ FRIED PLANTAIN

Plantains are available in great variety in Mexico. This Mexican dish can be served as a vegetable or snack, similar to French-fried potatoes. If plantains are unavailable, select regular bananas that are not yet ripe.

   3 plantains or unripe bananas
   ½ cup butter
     Salt, to taste

1. Peel plantains and slice fruit crosswise into ½-inch-thick slices.

2. Melt half the butter in a skillet. Sauté plaintain slices, a few at a time, until tender and golden brown. Add more butter as needed. Salt lightly and serve.

Serves 6.

PLUM

The plum is one of the world's preeminent fruits, second only to the peach in commercial importance and first in the breadth of its geographic dispersion. The hundreds of plum varieties vary in size, color, and flavor. California alone grows at least 11 varieties in quantity. Generally speaking, plums have a thin, smooth skin and a very soft, moist flesh. All plums have a large center seed.

Use Plums are delicious eaten out of hand as a breakfast food or snack. They may be sliced and added raw to fruit salads or warmed in fruit compotes. Plums make excellent fruit tarts, crisps, and cobblers. They may be stewed for chutney, preserves, fruit butter, and jelly. In China plums are stewed with apricots, sugar, and vinegar to make a sweet-tart sauce served with roast duck. Plums are often distilled to make plum brandies such as slivovitz, *mirabelle,* and *quetsch;* in the United States, the sloe plum is used for gin. Plum blossoms are a fragrant addition to ice cream. The "plum" used in Japan to make pickled plums and plum wine is actually a variety of apricot. Similarly, the famous English plum pudding

usually contains a generous quantity of raisins and currants but no plums.

The prune is a variety of plum that can be dried without removing the pit. (Other plums would ferment if dried with the pit intact.) Although the word *prune* is most often applied to the dried fruit (see DRIED FRUIT, Prunes), some fresh plums are also known as prunes or prune plums. There are several varieties of prune plums, but the one that accounts for about 90 percent of domestic dried prunes is the French Agen. Other prune plums, such as the Italian prune and the sugar prune, occasionally appear fresh in markets in late summer.

Availability Fresh plums are in season from mid-May to September, with different varieties ripening at different times. Early varieties include the Santa Rosa, the Beauty, and the Burmosa; midseason varieties include the El Dorado, the Tragedy, and the Simka; late-season varieties include the Late Santa Rosa, the Casselman, the Laroda, the Nubiana, and the Queen Ann. The French prune plum is generally grown to dry for prunes but is available fresh in some markets in midsummer. The greengage plum, a green-skinned European plum, is not widely available in this country. Small beach plums grow wild along the Atlantic coast but are rarely grown commercially; they make excellent preserves and jelly.

Selection Choose plums that are firm but not hard; they should give slightly to pressure. Look for plumpness and full color. Avoid plums with breaks in the skin and brownish discoloration.

Storage Let firm plums sit at room temperature for one or two days to soften them slightly. Ripe plums should be stored in the refrigerator and consumed within three to five days.

■ HOT BUTTERED PLUMS

These fresh summer plums in a tart orange sauce are good to serve from a chafing dish, either alone or as a topping for crêpes or crisp waffles.

   ¼ cup butter or margarine
   ½ cup sugar
   2 teaspoons cornstarch
   ⅛ teaspoon freshly grated nutmeg
   4 cups quartered, pitted red plums
   ½ teaspoon vanilla extract
     Juice and grated rind of 1 small orange

1. In a large frying pan, melt butter over medium heat. Stir in sugar, cornstarch, and nutmeg. Mix in plums, turning to coat with sugar mixture. Cook, stirring occasionally, until juices form a thick sauce (3 to 5 minutes).

2. Remove from heat; gently stir in vanilla and orange juice and rind. Return to heat and stir until sauce boils and thickens slightly (2 to 3 minutes). Serve hot.

Serves 6.

As a timesaver, eggs can be poached in advance and rewarmed in hot water.

■ FRESH PLUM KUCHEN

The fresh, small blue prune plums of early autumn bake to crimson juiciness in this sugar-sprinkled dessert. The pastry is easy to prepare as it is pressed into the baking pan rather than rolled and then fit into the pan.

   ⅔ cup sugar
   ¼ teaspoon freshly grated nutmeg
   3 tablespoons flour
   1 tablespoon fresh lemon juice
   4 cups small blue prune plums, halved and pitted
   1 tablespoon butter or margarine
     Sugar, for topping
     Crème Fraîche (see page 161) or sour cream, for garnish

Kuchen Pastry

  1½ cups flour
   ¼ cup sugar
   ½ cup cold butter or margarine
   1 egg yolk
   ½ teaspoon vanilla extract

1. Preheat oven to 375° F. Press Kuchen Pastry into bottom and about halfway up sides of a 9-inch springform pan.

2. Mix sugar, nutmeg, and flour. Stir lemon juice into plums in a bowl, then mix lightly with sugar mixture. Arrange fruit, cut sides up, making two layers in pastry-lined pan. Sprinkle with any sugar mixture remaining in bowl. Dot with butter.

3. Bake on lowest rack of oven until pastry is well browned and plums are tender and bubbling (50 minutes to 1 hour). Sprinkle with sugar.

4. Remove pan sides and serve tart warm or cool with Crème Fraîche or sour cream spooned over each piece.

Serves 8.

Kuchen Pastry Mix flour with sugar. Cut in butter until crumbly. Beat egg yolk with vanilla. With a fork, stir egg mixture lightly into flour mixture. Using hands, press dough into smooth, flat ball.

PLUMP, TO

To soak dried fruits, particularly raisins and dried currants, in liquid to soften them, to have them absorb the liquid, and to fill out. This process is necessary only if the fruit is dry and hard. To plump raisins and dried currants, let the fruit sit in boiling water to cover for 5 minutes until softened. For a classic pairing, use rum. Alternatively, soak fruit in the liquid it will later be cooked in for at least 10 to 15 minutes, or even overnight. If plumping in alcohol, have it at room temperature, not hot.

POACH, TO

To cook food gently in liquid that is hot, but not quite boiling (about 210° F; the surface of the liquid will show some movement, with small bubbles just starting to appear). Almost any food can be poached, but the technique is particularly suited to fish, whether whole, in fillets, or in steaks; shellfish; and chicken, especially breasts. Cuts of beef and pork that require long cooking can also be poached. Eggs are poached in water and vinegar. Even fruit can be poached in syrup.

During poaching, a flavor exchange takes place between the liquid and the food. The liquid adds flavor to the food and in turn gains flavor from it. Chicken stock is the best liquid for poaching chicken, and fish stock or court bouillon—a mixture of water, wine, aromatic vegetables, and herbs—for poaching seafood. Although beef stock can be used to poach beef, it is not really necessary because the poaching meat turns water into a stock during the relatively long cooking time required for poaching.

Because the poaching liquid gains flavor from the food, it can be used to prepare an accompanying sauce. Many poaching liquids also make a good soup or broth.

Often food is poached in relatively large pieces because they remain more moist than small ones would. Many meats are poached with their bones in because the bones add flavor to both the food and the cooking liquid and help prevent the food from becoming dry.

Any good saucepan large enough to hold both food and enough liquid to cover is suitable for poaching. If you poach whole fish and have room to store a large piece of equipment, you may want to use a long, narrow fish poacher (see COOKWARE, Fish Poacher). It is best not to choose too large a pan because too much liquid would be needed to cover the food, and the liquid would lose flavor.

■ WINE COURT BOUILLON

Both wine and vinegar court bouillon are reusable. Just strain, reboil, and add about 1 cup of water to compensate for liquid lost in cooking. Bouillons freeze well, too.

   8 cups cold water
   4 cups dry white wine
   2 large onions, peeled and chopped
   2 carrots, peeled and chopped
   2 ribs celery, chopped
     Bouquet garni (see page 56)
   2 tablespoons salt
   ½ teaspoon black peppercorns

1. In a saucepan combine the water, wine, onions, carrots, celery, bouquet garni, and salt. Simmer for about 25 minutes. Add peppercorns and simmer for another 10 minutes. (Peppercorns tend to turn court bouillon bitter if they cook too long.)

2. Let liquid cool, then strain.

Makes about 10 cups.

◼ FISH FUMET

A fish fumet, or concentrated fish stock, is richer than court bouillon and will give more flavor to bland fish. A fumet may be a water-based stock made with a few vegetables and fish carcasses, or it may be a wine or vinegar court bouillon enriched with fish trimmings. If court bouillon is destined for a fumet, reduce it to concentrate flavor.

    2 **pounds fish heads and carcasses,**
       rinsed and broken into pieces
    1 **large onion, cut in chunks**
    1 **carrot, cut in ½-inch slices**
    1 **rib celery, cut in ½-inch slices**
       Bouquet garni (see page 56)
   10 **cups water**
    ½ **teaspoon salt**
   10 **black peppercorns**

1. In a large pan place fish trimmings, onion, carrot, celery, bouquet garni, the water, and salt. Bring to a boil over low heat, skimming occasionally as scum rises to surface. Simmer for about 20 minutes.

2. Add peppercorns, then continue to simmer for 10 more minutes. After 30 minutes of cooking, fish stock is done. Further cooking causes a bitter flavor.

3. Strain stock through a colander without pressing down on the mass. Pressing solids clouds stock, making it unsuitable for an aspic or a clear sauce.

Makes 8 cups.

◼ BASIC POACHED SHELLFISH

Poaching is an easy way to cook shellfish—the shells seal in flavors and juices. Use salted water as the poaching liquid or, for more flavor, court bouillon or fumet. To best control the temperature of the poaching liquid, have the liquid cold to begin and then bring both liquid and shellfish to a gentle simmer. Accompanied with a flavorful sauce, poached shellfish make a simple, delicious main course for any luncheon or dinner.

       Lobster, crab, shrimp, or crayfish
       Wine Court Bouillon (see page 450), or
       salted water to cover

1. Add shellfish to cold poaching liquid, then bring to a simmer. (Many people still plunge lobsters directly into boiling water, but this exposure to high heat toughens them. It is also less humane. The method of slowly heating the water also slowly numbs the lobster. The anesthetized animal expires when the water reaches about 80° F.)

2. Begin calculating cooking time when fish and liquid reach a simmer. Cook shellfish about 20 minutes per pound.

3. Lobster is done when a small leg can be pulled off easily. (Or insert an instant-read thermometer into vent hole at end of tail. A 165° F reading means lobster is

---

ABOUT POACHING

Do not overcook foods that are being poached. Also keep in mind the following.

POACHING FISH

- Use a cold poaching liquid for fish and shellfish, and heat just until surface of liquid barely moves. This prevents outside of fish from cooking before inside and helps prevent fish from falling apart. Also, if a whole fish is placed directly into hot liquid, the skin will split.
- When poaching a whole fish, first wrap it in cheesecloth. The cheesecloth preserves shape of fish and facilitates removal from liquid. Remove fish pieces with a slotted spatula. Handle all poached fish as delicately as possible.
- Almost all types of fish are suitable for poaching. The exception is fish with very soft, fatty flesh, such as sablefish, which tend to fall apart in the liquid.

POACHING MEATS

- Cook meats slowly and evenly. Prolonged boiling toughens meat and clouds broth.
- Leftover liquid can be used as stock. Leftover poached meat makes a delicious salad tossed with a vinaigrette dressing.

POACHING POULTRY

- Poaching produces an especially delicate poultry flavor. Poach whole birds or breasts. Boneless breasts are done in 6 to 7 minutes; whole chickens cook anywhere from 25 minutes to 2 to 3 hours, depending upon size and age.
- Poaching time for poultry starts just after liquid starts to move and scum has been skimmed from surface of water.
- Poached poultry is excellent for salads and sandwiches, or when a light, plain flavor is desired, without the color or fatty taste developed in sautéing.

---

fully cooked.) Lobster is not necessarily cooked through when shell turns red. In contrast, crabs and crayfish are finished when their shells change color. Shrimp are cooked when they change color and become opaque.

◼ PERFECTLY POACHED CHICKEN FOR SALADS AND SANDWICHES

When the cook wants an especially delicate poultry flavor, poaching is ideal. No matter how delicious the dressing or the sandwich fixings, if the chicken is dry the dish has little appeal. Poaching produces very moist meat.

    1 **chicken (fryer, roaster, capon, or stewing hen)**
    2 **medium carrots, coarsely chopped**
    2 **ribs celery, coarsely chopped**
    1 **large onion, quartered**
       Bouquet garni (see page 56)

1. Wash chicken, remove innards, and trim away excess fat. Place in a stockpot or Dutch oven with carrots, celery, onion, and bouquet garni. Add enough cold water to cover.

2. Bring slowly to a boil, partially covered. Skim. Reduce heat to medium-low and simmer gently, covered, until bird is just tender when pierced (see About Poaching, above). Poaching time starts just after the surface of the liquid barely bubbles and the scum has been skimmed away.

3. Remove bird from pot and set aside to cool. Strain broth and save for another use. When chicken is cool, remove meat from bones.

Makes 3 to 5 cups, depending on bird used.

One of the simplest and finest ways to cook salmon (or almost any fish) is to poach it in a court bouillon made with dry white wine.

■ POACHED FISH STEAKS WITH FRESH HERBS AND CREAM

Poached fish may be served plain, but it is usually better with a sauce. Often the poaching liquid itself can be the basis for the sauce. This recipe can serve as a model for countless dishes; it can be made with different varieties of fish, for example, or with mushrooms, tomatoes, or shellfish added to the sauce. The variations are limited only by your imagination.

    4 halibut, salmon, or turbot steaks (1 in. thick)
    ½ cup whipping cream
    4 cups Wine Court Bouillon (see page 450) or
       Fish Fumet (see page 451)
    2 tablespoons chopped fresh herbs, such as
       chives, parsley, basil, or chervil
       Salt and freshly ground pepper, to taste
       Rind of ½ lemon

1. Take fish and cream out of refrigerator at least 15 minutes ahead of cooking to let them come to room temperature.

2. Choose a deep skillet just large enough to hold fish steaks in one layer. Heat Wine Court Bouillon over moderate heat until it just reaches simmering point. Slide fish steaks into simmering stock. Adjust heat so stock simmers slowly, being careful not to let it boil.

3. Cook fish to the slightly underdone stage—about 7 minutes for salmon and 8 to 9 minutes for halibut or turbot. (To test for doneness, insert a thin skewer or toothpick into thickest part of fish. There should be some resistance in center.) Transfer almost-cooked steaks to a warm platter; cover loosely with aluminum foil to keep them warm.

4. Pour out half the liquid, reserving it for another use. Turn heat to high and boil stock until it is reduced by two thirds. Add cream and reduce sauce until it is slightly thickened. Turn down heat, stir in herbs, and season to taste with salt and pepper.

5. Return fish steaks to skillet to reheat slightly in sauce. Serve steaks topped with sauce and sprinkle a little lemon rind over top of each.

Serves 4.

Recipes and Related Information
Basic Poached Eggs, 199; Cold Fillet of Sole With Cilantro, Lime, and Pomegranate, 232; Rosé Pears in Chocolate Bath, 612.

POMEGRANATE

The pomegranate is an autumn fruit, about the size of a large orange. Most of the varieties produced in the United States have a red skin, but at least one variety, the Paper-Shell, has a yellow skin with a pink blush. Inside the thin hard skin are hundreds of small seeds, each one surrounded by juicy red pulp. The seeds are clustered in cells separated from each other by a bitter white membrane. Along with their surrounding pulp, the seeds can be eaten whole, or the juice may be expressed from them. Pomegranate juice is refreshingly both tart and sweet; however, it is a vivid reddish pink and it stains viciously.

Use Pomegranates are a refreshing snack or dessert eaten out of hand, although it requires some know-how to eat them (see Preparation). Pomegranate seeds make a bright red garnish for salads, fruit cups, desserts, and main courses. Turkish cooks sprinkle them on sweet custards; Arab cooks stuff baked fish with walnuts and pomegranate seeds. Pomegranate juice is used in punches and cocktails; although historically this juice was the basis for grenadine, a sweet pomegranate-flavored syrup used in many cocktails, many grenadine syrups today contain none. Pomegranate juice adds a sweet-tart flavor to marinades and basting sauces.

Availability Fresh pomegranates are sold from September through December, with peak supplies in October. Bottled pomegranate juice and syrup are available in Middle Eastern markets and some specialty stores.

Selection Choose fresh pomegranates that aren't rock hard, with plenty of color and without cracks or splits.

Storage They will keep in a plastic bag in the refrigerator for several weeks. Refrigerate pomegranate juice and syrup after opening. The syrup will keep indefinitely, but the juice should be used within a few days.

Preparation Perhaps the easiest way to eat a pomegranate out of hand is to roll it repeatedly over a hard surface to reduce pulp to juice; keep rolling until fruit feels soft and full of juice. Then carefully pierce fruit in one place with a skewer and suck out juice. Alternatively, slit fruit with a knife and pull it apart into sections. Use a small spoon or your fingers to dig seed clusters away from bitter membranes. To juice a fresh pomegranate, use a fruit juicer or a reamer, but wear an apron to protect yourself from spattering juice.

■ RUSSIAN MARINATED LAMB ON SKEWERS

Many Russian recipes call for the piquant, magenta juice of autumn pomegranates for marinating lamb. Serve the skewered lamb with a rice pilaf and lightly sautéed zucchini.

    ½ cup fresh pomegranate juice
    2 tablespoons fresh lemon juice
    1 small onion, finely chopped
    2 tablespoons vegetable oil
    1 clove garlic, minced
    ½ teaspoon salt
       Dash freshly ground pepper
    2 pounds cubed boneless lean lamb shoulder or leg
    2 green onions, thinly sliced (with part of tops),
       for garnish
       Lemon wedges and parsley sprigs, for garnish

1. In a shallow glass, ceramic, or stainless steel bowl, mix pomegranate and lemon juice, chopped onion, oil, garlic, salt, and pepper. Stir in cubed lamb. Cover and refrigerate for 4 to 5 hours or overnight.

2. Preheat broiler. Drain meat and divide it among six skewers. Broil, about 4 inches from heat, turning once, until well browned on both sides (8 to 10 minutes). Serve immediately, sprinkled with green onions and garnished with lemon and parsley.

Serves 6.

> **Recipes and Related Information**
> *Cold Fillet of Sole With Cilantro, Lime, and Pomegranate, 232.*

POPCORN

Some food historians and archaeologists believe that popcorn is the world's oldest form of corn (see GRAIN, Corn). It is at least 7,000 years old. Native Americans brought popcorn to the first Thanksgiving in 1621. The early settlers must have been surprised at the kernels' transformation: The hard dried corn, when heated in oil, bursts into a snowy white, fluffy ball. As millions of moviegoers know, its bland, faintly cornlike flavor makes it an excellent vehicle for melted butter and salt.

Use Popcorn is a snack food that has become a fixture at sporting events and in movie theaters. It is also coated with molasses and butter and mixed with peanuts to make caramel corn.

Availability Unpopped popcorn is sold in all supermarkets. Although a variety of home popcorn machines are available, it is easy to pop popcorn with only a heavy lidded saucepan (see Preparation). Special popcorn for making in a microwave oven is also widely available. Popped and flavored popcorn can be purchased from some mail-order sources and specialty stores.

Storage Unpopped popcorn should be stored in a tightly covered jar in a cool, dry place or in the refrigerator. It will keep for up to one year.

Preparation Add 1 tablespoon of oil to a 4-quart saucepan; set over high heat. When oil is hot, add ½ cup corn kernels. Cover pan and shake continuously over heat until popping ceases. Add melted butter and salt to taste. One-half cup unpopped popcorn makes about 1 quart popped corn. To make popcorn with a hot-air popcorn maker, follow manufacturer's directions.

The piquant, reddish pink juice of pomegranates is an ingredient in many Russian recipes for marinating lamb. Squeeze this fresh fall fruit to make a tasty marinade for broiling boneless cubes of lamb on skewers. Take the precaution of wearing rubber gloves while handling the pomegranate to protect your hands from vibrantly colored stains.

This moist, two-layer Poppy Seed Cake is decorated with Cream Cheese Frosting and poppy seeds. The striped effect is achieved by placing strips of paper over the top of the cake, then sprinkling the poppy seeds onto the icing. A variety of designs can be made by using different templates.

POPPY SEED

Poppy plants yield very small, edible seeds that may be white or black, depending on the poppy variety. They have a slightly sweet, nutty flavor that is appealing in pastries.

Use   Black poppy seeds are often sprinkled on top of breads to add color and texture. The seeds are cooked, sweetened, and used as a filling for strudel and the triangular Jewish pastry known as *hamantaschen*. Black poppy seeds are also used in cakes and salad dressings and are sprinkled over buttered noodles. White poppy seeds are used in Indian cooking; they are usually ground, then toasted in oil with ginger or garlic and used to thicken and flavor vegetarian dishes.

Availability   Most supermarkets stock black poppy seeds. Look for white poppy seeds in Indian markets. Jars or cans of black poppy seed paste or poppy seed filling are sold in Jewish delicatessens and specialty shops.

Selection   Packaged spices and seasonings lose quality after a while; try to buy from a store that restocks its spice section fairly often.

Storage   Poppy seeds have a high oil content and turn rancid quickly. Store airtight in a cool, dry, dark place. Use within six months; refrigerate for longer keeping. Leftover poppy seed paste should be put in a nonmetal container; it may be refrigerated for up to one month.

Preparation   To bring out the flavor of poppy seed, toast in a dry skillet over low heat, shaking skillet continuously, until seeds are crisp and fragrant (5 to 8 minutes). To grind, toast, then soak overnight in milk, drain, and grind in a blender, clean coffee grinder, or electric minichopper, or with mortar and pestle.

■ POPPY SEED CAKE WITH CREAM CHEESE FROSTING

A moist poppy seed layer cake is delicious with a cream cheese frosting.

   ⅔ **cup milk**
   ⅓ **cup poppy seed**
 2¼ **cups sifted cake flour**
   1 **tablespoon baking powder**
   ¼ **teaspoon salt**
 1¼ **cups sugar**
   ½ **cup butter, softened**
   2 **teaspoons vanilla extract**
   ½ **cup milk**
   3 **large egg whites**
   ¼ **cup sugar**
   2 **tablespoons poppy seed, for decoration**

Cream Cheese Frosting

   6 **ounces cream cheese, softened**
   ¼ **cup unsalted butter, softened**
   2 **cups sifted confectioners' sugar**
   1 **teaspoon fresh lemon juice**

1. Preheat oven to 350° F. Butter and flour two 8-inch-round cake pans; line bottom of each with a circle of parchment paper.

2. Bring the ⅔ cup milk to a boil. Remove from heat and stir in poppy seed; cool to room temperature.

3. Sift together flour, baking powder, and salt; set aside. Cream the 1¼ cups sugar and butter together; beat until light. Add vanilla.

4. Combine poppy seed mixture and the ½ cup milk. Add this mixture alternately with flour to creamed mixture, adding one third of each mixture at a time.

5. Beat egg whites until they hold soft peaks. Add the ¼ cup sugar, a little at a time, and beat until whites hold stiff, glossy peaks (do not overbeat). Gently fold into batter. Divide batter evenly between the two cake pans. Bake until cake draws away from sides of pans or cake tester comes out clean (about 30 minutes). Cool in pans 10 minutes, then turn out onto wire racks to finish cooling.

6. Frost with Cream Cheese Frosting. Decorate with poppy seed.

Serves 6 to 8.

Cream Cheese Frosting   Cream together cream cheese and butter. Add confectioners' sugar and lemon juice; beat until creamy. If frosting is too runny, add more sugar. If it is too stiff, add a little milk.

Recipes and Related Information
Citrus–Poppy Seed Muffins, 375; Poppy Seed Filling, 627.

PORK

By most accounts, today's domesticated pig is a descendant of the wild boar. Humans began raising pigs for the table possibly as early as the Mesolithic period; today, pork is the most widely eaten meat in the world.

Historically pork has always been a mainstay of peasant diets. The animals, being scavengers, are easy to feed, they are extraordinarily prolific (producing on average 11 offspring per litter, two times a year), and they are usable down to the last hair. Not only do people make edible use of every part of the inner body, they also know how to treat the skin for leather, the hair for upholstery and insulation, and the inedible parts of the fat for lubrication.

In the days before refrigeration, much of the meat was salted or otherwise processed for long keeping. Even today, only about one third of pork meat is sold fresh. Although we no longer need to store pork for long periods, we have developed a taste for the various hams and sausages created over the years.

Because fresh and cured pork products differ greatly from a cook's standpoint, they are discussed separately in the following sections.

Use Depending on the cut, fresh pork may be roasted, broiled or grilled, panfried, poached, or braised. A fresh leg (ham), for example, may be marinated in wine and herbs, then roasted. A crown roast makes an elegant party dish, either simply roasted or roasted and stuffed. Panfried or grilled pork chops are a popular American dish, often paired with applesauce or sautéed apples. Swedish cooks stuff boneless pork loin with plumped prunes before roasting; plumped dried apricots could be substituted for the prunes. American cooks baste spareribs and baby back ribs with barbecue sauce and either roast or grill them. The Chinese consume large quantities of fresh pork: They braise slabs of fresh belly bacon in soy sauce; braise sparerib nuggets with black beans; steam pork meatballs with cabbage; roast whole pigs; and stir-fry strips of marinated pork with mushrooms, eggs, and lily buds, then wrap the mixture in thin pancakes for Mu Shu Pork. Pork is widely used in Mexico, too—as a filling for tamales, enchiladas, and tacos, and as an ingredient in hearty soups. Seasoned ground pork makes an excellent filling for stuffed cabbage leaves or savory pies. It is also the basis for countless types of sausage (see SAUSAGE).

Flavorful cured pork products are eaten alone or used as an ingredient in many types of preparations. See specific cured pork entries.

Availability Fresh pork is sold widely in all supermarkets, although most do not carry a large variety of cuts. For a larger selection, seek out Latin, German, or Asian markets or specialty butchers.

Cured pork products are widely available in supermarkets and specialty markets. The more popular of these products are described in a separate section, beginning on page 460.

Selection Fresh pork should have a pale pink to pink color (loin cuts are generally lighter than shoulder and leg cuts) and white fat. Both flesh and fat should be firm to the touch. Like all fresh meat, it should smell fresh, with no off-odor. See specific types of cured pork for selection information.

Storage Fresh pork should be kept in the coldest part of the refrigerator. Prepackaged meat may be stored in its original wrapper. Pork wrapped in butcher paper should be unwrapped, set on a plate, and covered loosely with aluminum foil or waxed paper. Refrigerate and use within two or three days. Large cuts will keep slightly longer, ground meat slightly less.

For longer storage, pork may be frozen immediately after purchase. Remove original wrapping; place in plastic wrap and overwrap with freezer paper or aluminum foil. Large cuts may be frozen for up to six months, chops or ground meat for up to three months. Thaw slowly in freezer wrapping in refrigerator.

Store leftover cooked pork, covered, in coldest part of refrigerator within two hours of cooking. Use within four to five days. For storing cured pork see specific types.

Preparation Fresh pork does not require special preparation. Extra fat may be trimmed away from roasts or chops if desired. Before cooking, some cooks prefer to brine fresh pork for several days to firm and flavor the meat. To make a brine for 6 pounds of pork, dissolve ½ cup sugar (granulated or brown) and ¼ cup salt in 2 gallons warm water. Lightly bruise herbs and spices in a mortar (bay leaf, peppercorns, juniper berries, cloves, and thyme are traditional) and add to the warm liquid. Let liquid cool completely, then pour over pork in a clean container. Keep pork submerged with a weighted plate for two to four days. Remove from brine, rinse, and pat dry.

Cooking See BRAISE, BROIL, GRILL, PANFRY, POACH, ROAST, STIR-FRY. For cooking cured pork see specific types.

FRESH PORK

Fresh pork has not been salted, brined, smoked, or otherwise cured. It has a mild, faintly sweet flavor. Recipes for fresh pork begin on page 457.

DRY-HEAT COOKING

Virtually all the major parts of the pig take to roasting and barbecuing. Pork may be roasted at a higher temperature than beef or lamb without becoming too dry because its veins of fat will baste the lean parts throughout the roasting. When grilling, however, it's best to cook slowly, so that the inside will cook through before the outside burns. Chops, cutlets, and slices are generally cooked like beef steaks—by panfrying, broiling, or grilling.

CUTS OF PORK, FRESH AND CURED

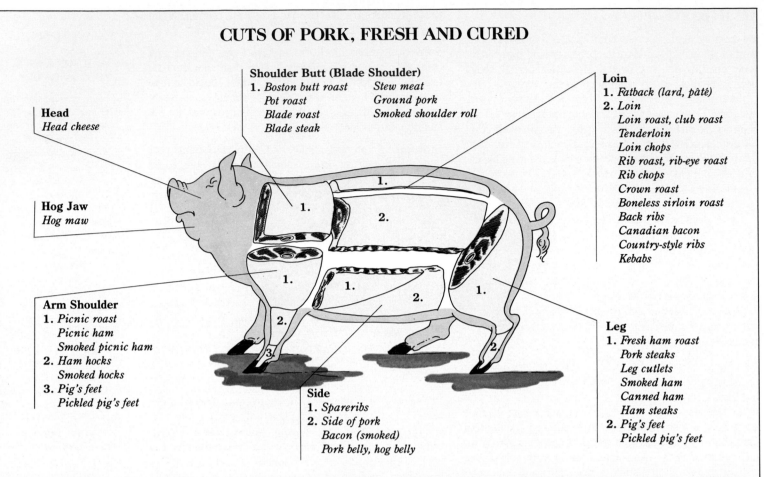

Head
Head cheese

Hog Jaw
Hog maw

Arm Shoulder
1. Picnic roast
   Picnic ham
   Smoked picnic ham
2. Ham hocks
   Smoked hocks
3. Pig's feet
   Pickled pig's feet

Shoulder Butt (Blade Shoulder)
1. Boston butt roast   Stew meat
   Pot roast   Ground pork
   Blade roast   Smoked shoulder roll
   Blade steak

Side
1. Spareribs
2. Side of pork
   Bacon (smoked)
   Pork belly, hog belly

Loin
1. Fatback (lard, pâté)
2. Loin
   Loin roast, club roast
   Tenderloin
   Loin chops
   Rib roast, rib-eye roast
   Rib chops
   Crown roast
   Boneless sirloin roast
   Back ribs
   Canadian bacon
   Country-style ribs
   Kebabs

Leg
1. Fresh ham roast
   Pork steaks
   Leg cutlets
   Smoked ham
   Canned ham
   Ham steaks
2. Pig's feet
   Pickled pig's feet

Like any animal raised for the table, the pig offers a variety of cuts of varying degrees of tenderness. This chart should help you decipher the available retail cuts of pork and determine the best cooking methods for each.

Pork has fewer primal or wholesale cuts than beef, and a smaller variety of retail cuts are found at the market. The choice of cut for a particular dish is less critical than with beef; even the "tough" parts of the pig are relatively tender.

Shoulder Butt The economical pork shoulder butt (also called Boston butt) has relatively dark, flavorful meat that is divided into many small muscles, each sheathed with a thin coat of fat and divided by thicker streaks of fat and sinew. Pork shoulder makes the most luscious and juicy of all roasts and steaks—at first taste it seems like the pig's answer to beef prime rib—until one encounters the inevitable streaks of sinewy fat. Thus the shoulder is often braised to dissolve those portions, and its sauce carefully degreased (see DEGREASE). Shoulder meat can also be used in a Szechuan-style stir-fry or be cut into kebabs or stew meat, and it's a perfect cut for making homemade country sausage.

Arm Shoulder The picnic portion of the arm shoulder is the foreleg of the pig. It is mainly sold as a small ham. When found fresh it can be treated much like the shoulder butt. The ham hock is the bottom end of this cut. Typically the fresh picnic shoulder is roasted, but it can also be braised or cut into kebabs, and the hocks (which are nearly always smoked) are flavor boosters for beans, greens, and meat stews. The feet of the pig are both fatty and bony and are definitely a developed taste. They are usually pickled.

Leg The cut sold as leg of pork is the hind leg, which is usually smoked for ham. When sold unsmoked it's commonly labeled fresh ham and may be marketed with or without the bone. As a roasting cut, it's just the opposite of the Boston butt: The meat is pale, very lean and fine-grained, but somewhat dry; it tends to be tough when roasted. A roasted fresh ham makes a spectacular company dinner; even with the best of care, however, it will not be quite as tender as a roasted loin. Fresh ham is often braised to compensate for its lack of intrinsic moisture. It can also be cut up for lean kebabs, stir-fries, and other dishes calling for pieces of pork. The ham butt section is the meatiest portion of a fresh ham; the ham shank is much bonier.

Side The lower rib cage of a hog contains the spareribs and the side of pork. The side, which is the source of smoked bacon and salt pork, is rarely found unsmoked except in Asian markets, where it is called pork belly and is highly prized. Italian *pancetta* is also a form of unsmoked side of pork. Country-style ribs do not come from the side at all, but from the loin.

Loin The most prized cut, whether for roasting, barbecuing, stir-frying, or panfrying, is the loin. This is the source of most pork chops, pork steaks, and the most elegant pork roasts, including the crown roast (a bone-in loin, with the bones cracked and bent in a circle). Pork loin roasts and chops may be sold with or without bones; they may be divided in the market into a blade or rib, an end (the source of country-style ribs and of rib chops), a center cut (the source of the most expensive pork chops, rarely sold as a roast), and a sirloin end (the source of the tenderloin). The tenderloin may also be found in some markets sold on its own; it's a small strip of muscle, rounded at one end and pointed at the other, with a thin coating of fat. The tenderloin measures about 12 inches long and 3 inches at its widest. It is a superb cut for rapid roasting or for scallops, medallions, mignons, cutlets, and stir-fries. The opposite end of the loin, the rib end, also contains a tender, lean, and somewhat larger fillet piece. If you find this pork tenderloin in the market, you can grill it or use it for a roast, a stir-fry, scallops or medallions, kebabs, or a stew.

■ MARINATED FRESH HAM, ROASTED OR BRAISED

Fresh ham (the uncured leg of the pork) is a festive dish when roasted, but it actually responds better to braising. This recipe, which calls for an overnight marinade to lend the meat juiciness, can be cooked either way. This treatment is also superb with a boneless shoulder butt.

- 1 **cup dried figs, halved**
- 3 **cups unsweetened apple cider**
- 1 **large sweet onion, thinly sliced**
- ½ **fresh ham (4 to 5 lb boneless, or 5 to 6 lb bone-in)**
- 4 **cloves garlic, peeled and slivered**
- 1 **cup Calvados or applejack**
- 2 **teaspoons dried thyme, crumbled**
   Salt and freshly ground pepper

Mustard Maple Glaze

- 2 **tablespoons lard or vegetable oil**
- 2 **tablespoons grated onion**
- ½ **cup real maple syrup**
- ¼ **cup cider vinegar**
- 1 **tablespoon coarse mustard**
- ¼ **teaspoon freshly ground pepper**
- ⅛ **teaspoon hot-pepper sauce**

1. Barely cover figs with apple cider and let stand at room temperature overnight. Pour remaining cider into a small saucepan, bring to boil over moderate heat, and reduce by about a third (boil about 20 minutes). Remove from heat and add onion while still hot. Let cool.

2. Cut slits in ham and push in slivers of garlic. Combine cider mixture with Calvados and thyme, place ham in a large bowl, and pour liquid over ham. Marinate overnight or longer, covered with plastic wrap, turning several times.

3. Remove ham from refrigerator and from marinade, rub all over with salt and pepper, and allow to come to room temperature. Preheat oven to 400° F. Drain figs and add liquid to marinade. Strain marinade and reserve. For a boneless ham, stuff figs along the cleft in the center, where the bone used to be. For a bone-in ham cut (with a boning knife) a long cleft right next to the bone and stuff figs in cleft.

4. Place ham, fat side up, on a rack in a large shallow roasting pan; bake 40 minutes. If braising ham, wipe meat dry and brown in a very hot skillet filmed with oil.

5. *To roast:* Reduce oven temperature to 325° F, and baste generously with marinade every 20 minutes. One hour before ham is done, brush with Maple Mustard Glaze, and pour off drippings. Freeze drippings to degrease (see DEGREASE). Continue to roast ham (brushing with glaze every 15 minutes) until it reaches an internal temperature of 160° F. When ham is done, place on a platter. Remove drippings from freezer, skim off fat, and heat remaining drippings to boiling. Slice ham and nap with drippings. Serve warm. *To braise:* Place browned ham in a heavy casserole large enough to hold it. Pour on marinade. Bring liquid to a boil, cover, lower heat, and simmer about 2 hours, until cooked through (or cook, covered, in a 325° F oven for the same length of time). Remove ham to a warm platter, spoon fat off liquid (or pour off liquid and freeze briefly to degrease), and pour liquid into a saucepan. Heat to boiling and boil for about 10 minutes to slightly reduce sauce. Slice ham and place on serving dish. Nap with sauce and serve warm.

Serves 6 to 8.

Mustard Maple Glaze In a small, heavy-bottomed saucepan, heat lard over medium heat until fragrant and rippling. Add onion, reduce heat to low, and cook, stirring, 1 minute. Add maple syrup, vinegar, mustard, pepper, and hot-pepper sauce. Increase heat to medium-high and boil, stirring occasionally, until mixture reduces to ½ cup (about 15 minutes).

Makes ½ cup.

■ TUSCAN HERBED PORK ROAST

This austere, elegant bone-in pork loin from the area around Florence, Italy, derives its flavor from a generous infusion of garlic and herbs. To turn it into a festive crown roast, ask the butcher to bend it into a circle and fasten the ends (or do it yourself, using kitchen string to fasten). When roasting is complete, turn roast bones up, place paper frills over the ends of the bones, and fill the center with vegetables. Braised carrots and roasted new potatoes are a popular choice.

- 12 **cloves (1 bulb) garlic, peeled**
- 2 **tablespoons dried rosemary** *or*
   3 **tablespoons fresh rosemary**
- 1 **teaspoon salt**
- 1½ **tablespoons coarsely ground pepper**
- 2 **tablespoons olive oil**
- 1 **bone-in pork loin roast (about 5 lb)**
   Fresh rosemary sprigs, optional

1. In a blender, food processor, electric minichopper, or clean coffee grinder (or by hand, using a garlic press and a mortar and pestle), purée together garlic, rosemary, salt, pepper, and olive oil. With a small, sharp knife, make slits through pork (at least three slits per rib). Insert herb purée in each slit. Tie fresh rosemary sprigs (if used) across pork. If possible let pork stand for 2 to 3 hours to reach room temperature and allow herb mixture to penetrate meat.

2. Preheat oven to 350° F. Place pork, bone side down, on a roasting pan. Roast until an instant-read thermometer inserted in thickest part of meat reads 160° to 150° F for pink or 160° F for well-done. Remove pork from oven and let rest about 10 minutes before slicing. Serve hot, tepid, or cool.

Serves 6 to 8.

In Braised Pork With Prunes, a favorite in much of Europe, the sweetness of the prunes is a perfect accompaniment to the richness of the meat. It is best served with a simple side dish such as white rice or steamed potatoes.

■ STUFFED PORK CUTLETS

This quick and easy recipe, common to Italy, Spain, and the Italian-speaking area of southern Switzerland, can easily be varied. For an Italian version similar to veal saltimbocca, stuff the cutlets with prosciutto and a good mozzarella (such as buffalo milk) or Bel Paese cheese. For a French-Swiss version pair packaged sliced ham with Gruyère or Emmentaler. For an all-American version use Cheddar or Monterey jack with thinly sliced Smithfield or a similar delicatessen ham.

> 8 boneless lean pork cutlets (from loin or butt), each about ¼ inch thick
> 4 thick (¼ in.) slices mild cheese (4 to 6 oz)
> 4 thin slices prosciutto, Smithfield, or packaged ham (about 2 oz)
> 1 egg, lightly beaten
> 1 to 1½ cups Italian-style seasoned dry bread crumbs
> ¼ cup light olive oil or vegetable oil
> 1 lemon, cut in 4 wedges, for garnish

1. Trim away any fat or connective tissues from pork. Between two sheets of waxed paper, pound each cutlet with flat end of a meat mallet (or a heavy can) until flattened to about ⅛ inch thick. Trim cheese and

prosciutto to a size slightly smaller than that of the cutlets. Top half of the cutlets with a slice of cheese and a slice of ham. Cover with remaining cutlets and pound edges lightly to seal.

2. Holding each cutlet "sandwich" together, dip both sides in egg, then into bread crumbs to coat completely. Place on waxed paper.

3. In a heavy 10-inch skillet, heat oil over high heat until rippling. Lower heat to medium-high and add cutlets (covering with a spatter shield, if desired). Cook until cooked through (about 5 minutes per side). Remove from pan with slotted spatula, draining off oil, and serve hot, garnished with lemon wedges.

Serves 4.

MOIST-HEAT COOKING

When stewed or braised, pork shows off its adaptability. The loin, fresh hams, and the juicy shoulder butt are excellent cuts for braising. If there's time, the meat benefits from a night in a marinade. It is then braised in the marinade with enough extra liquid (stock, juice, or wine) to come about two thirds of the way up the meat (see the braising variation of Marinated Fresh Ham on page 457).

■ BRAISED PORK WITH PRUNES

Rice and boiled carrots make a good accompaniment for this dish because they complement the honey-lemon sauce and the prune garnish.

> 1 boneless pork loin roast or shoulder roast (2½ lb), rolled and tied
> Salt and freshly ground pepper
> 2 tablespoons vegetable oil
> 1 tablespoon butter
> 2 medium onions, finely chopped
> 1 cinnamon stick (2 in. long)
> 1 cup Chicken Stock (see page 560)
> ½ cup water
> 1 cup pitted prunes
> 2 tablespoons mild honey
> 2 teaspoons fresh lemon juice

1. Pat meat dry. Season on all sides with salt and pepper.

2. In a heavy casserole brown pork on all sides in oil and butter over medium-high heat. Remove pork to a plate.

3. Reduce heat to low, stir in onions, and cook, stirring occasionally, until softened (about 5 minutes).

4. Return pork to pan and add any juices from plate. Add cinnamon, stock, and the water, pushing cinnamon stick into liquid. Bring to a boil. Reduce heat to low, cover, and simmer, turning pork over from time to time, 1½ hours.

5. Add prunes to liquid, cover, and cook until meat is very tender when pierced with a knife (meat should register an internal temperature of 150° F on a meat thermometer) and prunes are tender (about 30 minutes).

6. Stir honey into pork cooking liquid and cook, un-covered, over low heat, basting pork often, for 5 minutes. Transfer meat to a plate with 2 wooden spoons, leaving as much of the chopped onions as possible in casserole. Remove prunes to a bowl with a slotted spoon.

7. Skim as much fat as possible from cooking liquid. Boil liquid over high heat, stirring often, until it thickens (about 5 minutes). Transfer pork to a carving board and discard strings. Cut pork in slices about ½ inch thick.

8. When sauce has thickened, add lemon juice. Add more salt and pepper, if needed. Discard cinnamon stick.

9. Return prunes to casserole and reheat over low heat. Set pork slices gently on top, cover, and reheat over low heat 5 minutes. Pork can be kept, covered, up to 2 days in refrigerator; reheat pork and prunes in sauce over low heat, covered.

10. Arrange pork slices on a platter or on plates, and spoon sauce and prunes over and around slices.

Serves 4 to 5.

■ BOHEMIAN PORK GOULASH
Dill seed and caraway seed accent this traditional pork goulash. Noodles are a good foil for the creamy sauce.

> 2 pounds lean boneless pork, cut in ½- by 2-inch strips
> Salt and white pepper
> 1 tablespoon *each* butter (or margarine) and vegetable oil
> 2 medium onions, thinly sliced and separated into rings
> 1 clove garlic, minced
> 1 tablespoon sweet Hungarian paprika
> 2 teaspoons caraway seed
> ½ teaspoon dill seed
> 1 bay leaf
> 1 cup Beef Stock (see page 560) or Rich Chicken Stock (see page 561)
> ⅓ cup dry white wine
> 1½ teaspoons cornstarch blended with 1 tablespoon water
> ⅔ cup sour cream
> Chopped parsley, for garnish

1. Sprinkle pork strips on all sides with salt and pepper. In a large, heavy frying pan over medium-high heat, melt butter with oil; add pork strips, about half at a time, and brown well on all sides, removing them as they brown. When all pork is browned, spoon off all but about 2 tablespoons of the pan drippings (if necessary).

2. Add onions and cook, stirring often, until rings are soft and begin to brown. Mix in garlic, paprika, caraway seed, and dill seed. Return pork strips (along with any accumulated juices) to pan. Add bay leaf. Pour in stock and wine. Bring to a boil, cover, reduce heat, and simmer until pork is tender (45 to 50 minutes).

3. Remove and discard bay leaf. Blend in cornstarch mixture and cook, stirring, until sauce boils and thickens. Remove pan from heat and blend in sour cream.

4. Return to low heat and stir gently until heated through. Do not boil. Taste and add salt if needed. Sprinkle with parsley.

Serves 4 to 6.

OTHER WAYS WITH PORK
The following recipes show pork's versatility. Supermarket ground pork is as high in fat as sausage (about 30 percent); consumers concerned about fat and economy may want to grind their own.

■ CAILLETTES
What the French call *caillettes* (little quail) are actually well-seasoned rounds of ground pork, rice, and spinach. Serve as individual hors d'oeuvres or pack this mixture into a bacon-lined loaf pan or terrine mold. Bake until the juices run clear, and serve with a fresh tomato sauce.

> 2 pounds chicken livers
> Salt and freshly ground pepper, to taste
> 2 tablespoons flour
> 2 tablespoons olive oil
> 2 shallots, finely minced
> 2 pounds lean ground pork
> 1 cup cooked white rice
> 1 pound fresh spinach, washed, stemmed, and chopped
> ½ cup minced parsley
> 2 cloves garlic, minced (optional)
> 1½ teaspoons minced fresh thyme *or* 1 teaspoon dried thyme
> 3 eggs, lightly beaten
> 1 pound caul fat (available at some butcher shops) or thinly sliced bacon

1. Preheat oven to 425° F. Trim livers of any fat or tough spots, chop them coarsely, and put in a bowl. Sprinkle with salt and pepper, to taste, and flour.

2. In a large skillet over medium heat, heat olive oil. Add shallots and sauté until they are softened but not browned (about 10 minutes). Add livers and sauté over medium-high heat 3 to 4 minutes, or until they are barely browned outside but still pink within.

3. Transfer livers to a bowl, leaving shallots in skillet. Add pork to skillet and sauté 5 minutes, or until pork loses its raw red color but is not fully cooked.

4. Mix together livers, shallots, pork, rice, spinach, parsley, garlic (if used), thyme, and eggs. Shape into 1½-inch balls. Wrap each ball in a small square of caul fat. Place on a cookie sheet and bake until crisp and golden brown (20 to 25 minutes).

Makes about 100 small Caillettes.

ABOUT PORK LARD

The firm white fat of the pig can be rendered to make lard, a valuable cooking medium and cooking ingredient in many cuisines. Much of the fat rendered for lard comes from the back and is also known as back fat. Leaf lard, which many consider to be the finest, is rendered from a sheet of fat that surrounds the kidneys.

Chinese cooks use lard to give a light texture to shrimp paste and pastry doughs. They also appreciate its rich flavor in stir-fried dishes. Lard gives a crisp texture to fried foods but they must be eaten immediately; as the foods cool the lard congeals and the coating softens.

Mexican cooks rely on lard to give flavor and lightness to flour tortillas and tamale doughs. Boiled beans are enriched with lard or refried in lard for even more enrichment. Lard, the basic cooking fat, is used for sautéing chicken, pork, and other meats. Even Mexican *buñuelos* and *sopaipillas* (dough fritters) are made with lard.

Like all solid fats, lard is never used in cold dishes because it congeals at room temperature.

To render pork fat for lard, cut 1 pound of back fat or leaf lard into small pieces. Place in a saucepan with ¾ cup cold water. Bring to a boil and simmer until water boils off and all the fat has been rendered (about 20 minutes). There will be some solid bits (cracklings) that refuse to give off any more fat. Strain fat through cheesecloth into a clean jar. Refrigerate, covered, for up to three months.

Look for fresh leaf lard or back fat in Asian and Latin markets. It can be refrigerated for up to one week or frozen for two to three months. It must be rendered and resolidified for use in doughs. Most supermarkets also offer rendered lard in solid blocks packaged in paper cartons. Often made from inferior fat, it contains preservatives that allow it to be stored at room temperature.

■ SWEET-AND-SOUR PINEAPPLE PORK

Excessively sweet and syrupy restaurant versions of this dish, loaded with MSG and food coloring, have given sweet-and-sour dishes a bad name. The original idea was and still is a good one: tender cubes of deep-fried pork with stir-fried vegetables and unsweetened pineapple in a sauce more sour than sweet. Make an extra effort to find red bell peppers because they supply the color that gives the dish much of its appeal. Prepare the Beer Batter 3 to 24 hours ahead. Rice vinegar and the light and dark soy sauces are available at Asian markets, specialty markets, and well-stocked supermarkets.

> ¾ pound boneless pork shoulder or loin (equivalent to 1½ lb thick loin chops or country-style spareribs), cut into ½-inch cubes
> 1 tablespoon light soy sauce
> ¼ cup Chicken Stock (see page 560) or water
> ¼ cup plus 2 tablespoons rice vinegar
> 2 tablespoons dark soy sauce
> 1½ to 2 teaspoons brown sugar
> ½ teaspoon white pepper
> 2 teaspoons cornstarch dissolved in ¼ cup water
> Oil, for deep-frying
> 2 tablespoons grated fresh ginger
> 2 cloves garlic, minced
> 3 thick green onions, white parts sliced and tops cut into 1-inch pieces
> 1 large *or* 2 small red bell peppers, seeded and cut into 1-inch squares
> ½ cup pineapple wedges (fresh or canned in their own juice), drained

Beer Batter

> 2 eggs
> 1⅓ cups flour
> 1 teaspoon kosher salt
> 1 tablespoon vegetable oil
> ¾ cup beer

1. Toss pork cubes with light soy sauce and marinate for 30 minutes. Combine stock, vinegar, dark soy sauce, sugar, white pepper, and cornstarch mixture; set aside.

2. In a wok or other deep pan, heat oil to 350° F. Drain pork cubes thoroughly and dredge in Beer Batter. Deep-fry until crisp and golden brown (about 3 minutes). Drain on paper towels; transfer to warm serving platter.

3. Remove all but 2 tablespoons oil. Increase heat to medium-high. Add ginger, garlic, green onion bottoms, and red pepper; stir-fry until fragrant. Add pineapple and stock mixture, bring to a boil, and cook until thickened. Pour sauce over pork; garnish with green onion tops.

Serves 4 to 6 with other dishes.

Beer Batter   Separate eggs. Combine flour, salt, egg yolks, and oil; blend thoroughly with a spoon. Stir in beer; beat to a smooth consistency. Cover and refrigerate for 3 to 24 hours. Just before frying, beat egg whites to soft peaks and fold into batter.

Recipes: Bohemian Cabbage Rolls, 74; Hot Pork and Ham Pâté in Brioche, 417; Potstickers, 191; Stuffed Whole Cabbage, 74.

CURED PORK

Fresh pork is cured in a variety of ways. Salting—either with a dry salt rub or with a brine—draws out the natural moisture, making the meat inhospitable to harmful organisms. In addition to salting, pork is often smoked and/or air-dried to draw off additional moisture.

Although these curing processes were originally developed to yield pork that could be kept for long periods at room temperature, today's methods usually do not cure pork to that degree. Hams and bacon are injected with brine and then smoked to give them flavor. They are not sufficiently cured, however, to be stored at room temperature; they must be refrigerated. Exceptions are the country hams that are salted and aged in a procedure that may take up to one year. Italian-style prosciutto and Smithfield and Virginia hams are of this type.

BACON

Cured and smoked pork belly is the source of bacon. Most bacon today is made by pumping a brine solution into a pork belly with mechanical needles. By this method, the bacon can be cured in a matter of hours. Some processors put smoke flavoring in the brine; others smoke the bacon after brining. The added water is part of the reason that most modern bacon shrinks considerably in the frying pan.

Originally, bacon was made with a dry cure. Salt, sugar, and sodium nitrate were rubbed into the bacon. The bacon was left to cure for a couple of weeks and then smoked. Dry-cured bacon is still available from some small local processors but it has virtually disappeared from the national marketplace.

Pan-fried bacon is a breakfast food in America, a daily partner to eggs and toast in some households. It's the *B* in the BLT and is welcome on other sandwiches, from egg salad to fried oysters. Crumbled bacon adds crunchy texture and flavor to spinach salad and Cobb salad. The hot fat from rendered bacon is sometimes the basis for a warm salad dressing or is used for frying. Strips of bacon can be draped over meat loaf for basting or wrapped around hamburgers. Italian cooks use a variety of unsmoked peppered bacon called *pancetta*. They render bits of pancetta and toss it with eggs and hot pasta to make Fettuccine Carbonara. They wrap salmon cubes in pancetta, then skewer and grill them. Pancetta adds a peppery, baconlike flavor to sauces, stews, soups, and pizza.

All supermarkets carry packaged sliced bacon. Thick-sliced bacon and slab (unsliced) bacon are available from some butchers and specialty markets. Dry-cured bacon can be purchased by mail order. Most supermarkets also carry bacon bits in jars in the spice section; artificial bacon bits are also sold in supermarkets. Pancetta appears in the market as a flat slab of seasoned pork belly, that is rolled into a thick sausage shape. It is available in Italian and specialty markets sliced to order in thin rounds, which can then be unwound into baconlike rashers.

Being high in saturated fat, bacon is perishable. Store sliced bacon in its original wrapping in the refrigerator for no more than one or two weeks. It may be wrapped airtight and frozen for up to two months. Slab bacon will keep longer, up to several weeks in the refrigerator. Dry-cured bacon can be stored in a cool, dry place for several months. Pancetta will keep in the refrigerator for up to three weeks or in the freezer for up to three months. Store real bacon bits in the refrigerator for up to two months; imitation bacon bits will keep indefinitely in a cool dry place.

Unsmoked bacon should have white fat and pale pink meat; smoked bacon will have yellowish fat and rosy meat. To prepare remove rind from slab bacon before slicing, or slash rind in several places to keep bacon from curling. Sliced bacon should be put into a cold heavy skillet and cooked over low heat.

A lid that fits inside the skillet over the bacon will keep the rashers from curling. Turn bacon over when browned on one side and continue cooking to desired crispness (5 to 10 minutes total cooking time). Drain on paper towels. Pancetta can be rendered in the same fashion. Both pancetta and bacon can be cut into small dice before rendering. Rendered bacon fat can be strained off and stored in a covered container in the refrigerator.

Recipes: Country-Style Greens, 287; Fettuccine Carbonara, 413.

CANADIAN BACON

Called back bacon in Canada and England, Canadian bacon is a cured and smoked meat product made from the lean pork loin. It resembles ham much more than bacon, both in appearance and in flavor. Canadian bacon comes ready to eat. In addition to using the loin sliced, you can also bake it whole and glazed, like a ham.

Canadian bacon is usually sliced into rounds, panfried, and served with breakfast eggs. It figures in Eggs Benedict, a popular brunch dish of poached eggs, Canadian bacon, English muffins, and Hollandaise sauce. The loin can also be baked whole and glazed, like a ham, or sliced and eaten as a snack or sandwich meat.

Packaged Canadian bacon, both whole and presliced, is available in many supermarkets and from specialty meat markets. Presliced Canadian bacon should be refrigerated and used within three to four days or wrapped airtight and frozen for up to one month. Whole Canadian bacon can be stored slightly longer.

Recipes: Eggs Benedict, 200.

HAM

A cured meat product, ham is made from fresh pork hind legs. The curing method varies depending on the style of ham desired. The ham may be cured with a dry salt mixture or with a brine flavored with various spices. After salting or brining, the ham may be smoked and/or air-dried. The following describes some of the most popular styles of ham.

Canned Ham   Whether domestic or imported, canned ham is usually made by immersing the meat in a brine and simultaneously injecting it with brine to speed the cure. After curing, the ham is usually smoked. Most hams are then partially or fully cooked and are labeled accordingly: heat-and-serve, ready-to-eat, or fully cooked. Ready-to-eat and fully-cooked hams do not require further cooking, although they may be heated, if desired. Heat-and-serve hams should be baked in a moderate (325° F) oven until the internal temperature is 150° F. Canned and packaged hams, both boneless and bone-in, whole or in parts, are widely available in supermarkets; they should be refrigerated even before opening, unless labeled sterilized. After opening, use within a week.

Prosciutto   With few exceptions, this salted and air-dried Italian-style ham should not be cooked. It may be thinly sliced and eaten raw, often with figs or melon, or it may be stirred into cooked dishes—such as pasta or steamed peas—at the last minute.

Look for prosciutto in Italian markets and specialty markets. A whole prosciutto is much too large for most families, and markets that carry it are prepared to slice it to order or sell it in chunks. Thin-sliced prosciutto dries out quickly; slice prosciutto or buy it sliced only as needed. Should you care to buy one, a whole uncut prosciutto will keep for at least one year if stored in a cool, dry place. Once prosciutto is cut, keep exposed surface covered and use within a few weeks.

Smithfield, Virginia, and Other Country Hams These hams are usually made from corn- or peanut-fed hogs. In a typical procedure (which varies from producer to producer), the legs are salted for about four weeks, then washed, coated with peppercorns, refrigerated for about two weeks, then smoked for about 10 days. After smoking the meat is aged for 6 to 12 months. The resulting ham may be served raw like prosciutto (see page 461), in very thin slices because it is quite salty. In the South, however, it is often cooked. To cook a Smithfield ham (or similar country ham), soak the ham for 12 to 24 hours in several changes of cold water. Using a stiff brush, scrub off any surface mold. Then cover with cold water, bring to a boil, and simmer until the small bone near the shank moves easily (15 to 20 minutes per pound). Save the cooking water for cooking greens. Slice away ham rind with a sharp knife. If desired, coat fat with brown sugar and bread crumbs and bake in a hot (400° F) oven until glazed (about 20 minutes). Let cool to room temperature before slicing thinly. Country ham can be sliced, covered with gravy, and served with grits; added to bean or vegetable dishes; or served cold with hot biscuits. Smithfield hams are available from some specialty markets and mail-order sources. See Prosciutto (page 461) for storage directions.

■ CIDER-BAKED COUNTRY HAM

In this treatment the ham is baked with cider so that simmering on the stovetop is unnecessary.

    1 Smithfield ham or country-style ham (12 to 14 lb)
    4 cups apple cider
    ½ cup bourbon
    Brown sugar, for glaze

1. Soak ham in several changes of cold water for at least 24 hours. Scrub under cold running water with a stiff brush and wipe dry.

2. Preheat oven to 350° F. Place a long sheet of heavy aluminum foil across the bottom of a shallow roasting pan with ends of sheet extending from each side of pan (foil should be long enough to make a tent for ham). Place ham on foil, pour on cider, and seal foil around ham. Bake until ham is cooked through and tender (about 4 hours).

3. Remove ham from oven and allow to cool until it can be handled. Discard aluminum foil. Remove drippings (save fat if desired). Gently and carefully remove skin, leaving a thick layer of fat. Score fat in a diamond pattern with a sharp knife, and return ham to oven for 15 minutes to heat surface. Slide out oven shelf so that ham is fully exposed. Heat bourbon in a small saucepan and pour it over ham. Be sure that nothing flammable is near oven opening. Using a long match and exercising great caution, light bourbon. When flames die

down, spread brown sugar over fat, and slide oven shelf back in. Continue baking until sugar forms a dark melted glaze (about 15 minutes).

Serves 8 to 10.

■ COUNTRY HAM SLICES WITH RED-EYE GRAVY

All ham slices will be enlivened by this surprising sauce. The secret is black coffee.

    4 slices (½ in. thick) country or old-fashioned ham, cooked or uncooked (see Note)
    4 tablespoons rendered drippings from baked ham or vegetable oil
    ¼ cup firmly packed light brown sugar
    ½ cup strong black brewed coffee

1. Score through fat at edges of ham slices to keep them from curling. Heat drippings in a large, heavy skillet. Add ham and sauté over medium heat, turning several times, until lightly browned on both sides (20 to 25 minutes if using uncooked slices, about 10 minutes if cooked).

2. Remove ham and keep warm. Stir sugar into pan juices and cook at low heat, stirring constantly, until sugar dissolves. Add coffee and simmer until gravy turns rich brown (about 5 minutes); do not boil. Pour gravy over ham and serve.

Serves 4.

Note If you are using uncooked slices of a salty, dry-cured ham, add 1 cup of water to skillet along with ham. Ham will absorb all the water by the time it is cooked through; add more water if original amount is absorbed too quickly.

SALT PORK

Cut from the pork belly, salt pork is white fat streaked with lean meat. It is salted like bacon but not smoked. Most salt pork is extremely salty and should be blanched before use. Cover with cold water, bring to a boil, simmer 3 minutes, and drain. Fry a small amount and taste; if too salty, blanch again. After blanching, it can be diced, rendered (see RENDER), and used to add flavor to green beans, cabbage, or bean soups. Rendered salt pork can be added to cornbread or dumplings. It is a traditional flavoring in clam chowder and baked beans. In the American South, it is often cooked with potherbs such as collards or mustard greens.

    Many supermarkets carry packaged salt pork in 6- to 8-ounce chunks. It is also available from most meat markets. Salt pork can be refrigerated, tightly wrapped, for up to a month or frozen for several months.

Recipes: Boston Baked Beans, 34; New England Clam Chowder, 539.

POTATO

Although they were introduced late, potatoes are a significant part of the American diet today and are now common on all continents. Native to Central and South America, the potato was unknown in Europe until the late sixteenth century and didn't arrive in North America until the early eighteenth century. Because it is hardy and easy to grow, it is always one of the least expensive vegetables in the market. Widespread cultivation of the potato has made it one of the world's most important food crops.

Use Because potatoes are so important to the diets of people all around the world, it is difficult to give a meaningful overview of the ways they are used. In the United States potatoes are typically boiled, mashed, baked, sautéed, or fried. Mashed potatoes may be combined with another puréed vegetable, such as celeriac, chestnuts, or parsnips. Baked potatoes are served whole, with butter and/or sour cream. Raw potatoes may be sliced thin and sautéed, or grated and sautéed to make hash browns. Cooked, cubed, and sautéed potatoes are often flavored with onion and green pepper and served with breakfast eggs. When potatoes are cut into finger-length strips and deep-fried, they are known as French fries and are a staple of the American fast-food industry, especially as the accepted companion to hamburgers.

The French slice potatoes thinly and bake them with butter and cream to make a gratin Dauphinois; when meat stock is used instead of cream and when a topping of grated Gruyère cheese is added, the dish becomes gratin Savoyard. Vichyssoise, a cold potato and leek soup, is now a classic. Italian cooks make dumplings called *gnocchi* from potatoes. Germans and Hungarians add mashed potatoes to bread for improved flavor and texture. Swedish cooks bake potato strips with cream and anchovies to make Jansson's temptation and, like the Germans, fry thin pancakes of grated potatoes. *Lefser* is a Norwegian flatbread based on potatoes and cooked on a griddle. Russian cooks add boiled potatoes to herring salad and bake grated potatoes into pudding with onions and egg. Potatoes are also distilled into vodka in the Soviet Union. In Peru, where potatoes have long been a staple, they are boiled and garnished with a spicy chile and cheese sauce. Indian cooks deep-fry potato slices in chick-pea batter, sauté them with aromatic spices, or curry them. Potatoes are not widely used in Asia, but are known there. Almost everywhere in the world, potatoes are a major food source.

Apart from their use as a food, potatoes are a good salt absorber. An oversalted soup can occasionally be salvaged by adding potato slices and simmering until the salt is sufficiently absorbed. The potatoes are discarded before serving.

Availability Potatoes are sold in supermarkets the year around. There is no peak season because crops in different areas mature at different times and potatoes

store well. Potatoes are also available in the freezer case, in the form of frozen French fries, hash browns, and other precooked shapes. Canned boiled potatoes are also found in supermarkets, as are dried potato flakes and instant mashed potatoes.

The main potato varieties, and their suitability to various cooking tasks, are as follows.

Red Skinned (New) This type has a thin red skin and a crisp white flesh. It is a waxy potato, excellent for boiling in the skin and serving whole. Because it cubes neatly after boiling and absorbs dressing readily, it is good for potato salad. Red-skinned potatoes may also be rubbed with olive oil and baked whole; they will maintain their firm, waxy texture. There are several varieties of red-skinned potatoes, but they are rarely identified by variety in the supermarket.

Russet or Idaho This standard baking potato is generally 4 to 6 inches long, about 2 inches in diameter, with a rough brown skin. The ivory flesh is dry and fluffy when baked. It is a good potato for mashing and for deep-frying, as it does not readily absorb the frying oil.

French fries are the most popular of all potato dishes. Serve them with a thick grilled steak or with fried fish in the English tradition of fish and chips. The recipe is on page 468.

White Rose A waxy potato, the White Rose is a long, white potato with a thin ivory-colored skin. It is best for boiling but may be baked or deep-fried. Like the russet, it is recommended for French fries because it does not readily absorb the frying oil.

Other potatoes that are becoming increasingly available include:

Blue Included in this category are such varieties as Blue Carib and All Blue. They have grayish blue skin and inky blue flesh. Delicate in flavor, they should simply be boiled and buttered.

Finnish Yellow Wax As its name suggest, this light-skinned variety has yellow meat and a waxy texture. Boil in the skin and dress with butter or use in potato salads.

German Fingerling This is a small, light-skinned potato with a lumpy shape and yellow flesh. It has a waxy flesh and should be boiled whole and buttered, or coated with olive oil and baked in a covered casserole until tender when pierced with a knife.

Rose Fir Small and waxy-fleshed, the Rose Fir has thin pink to red skin. It has a creamy texture and delicate flavor and is best when simply boiled and buttered.

Selection The most important distinction to draw between potato varieties is between the starchy or mealy types (best for baking) and the waxy types (best for boiling). A starchy type falls apart when boiled; a waxy type does not develop the desired dry, fluffy texture when baked. See Availability.

When selecting potatoes, look for firm specimens. New potatoes should be of a fairly uniform size to make cooking easier. Mature baking potatoes should be dry and well shaped, without sprouting. Avoid potatoes with a greenish cast. They have been exposed to too much light, either sunlight or artificial light, and may be bitter.

Storage Potatoes keep best in a cool, dark, dry place. Do not refrigerate. They should keep for two to three weeks without sprouting.

Preparation Peel if desired; otherwise, scrub skin well. Potatoes oxidize quickly; drop peeled potatoes into water immediately to slow browning.

Cooking See BAKE, BOIL, DEEP-FRY, PANFRY, PUREE, STEAM.

■ BASIC BAKED POTATO

Use russet potatoes for baking. Remember to pierce the potatoes just after removing them from the oven. Potatoes cook much faster in a microwave oven, even when you are cooking a number of them (see chart, at right). They need to be pierced before they cook.

> **3 large baking potatoes (1½ to 2 lb total)**
> **Oil or melted butter, for coating**
> **Butter, sour cream, snipped fresh chives, crumbled cooked bacon, for garnish (optional)**

1. Preheat oven to 400° F. Rub potatoes all over with oil. Set on baking sheet or directly on oven rack.

2. Bake until tender (about 45 minutes). Immediately pierce with a fork. Slit lengthwise or slice in half, and top with a pat of butter, sour cream, snipped fresh chives, or crumbled cooked bacon (if desired).

Serves 3 to 6.

POTATOES IN THE MICROWAVE OVEN

Choose whole potatoes of even size; pierce in several places with fork. Cook at 100 percent power the following times (for 6- to 8-ounce potatoes). Touch potatoes at end of cooking time. If they are very hard, cook another one or two minutes, then let them stand. They will finish cooking in the standing time.

Amount	Approximate Cooking Time	Standing Time
1	4–6 minutes	5 minutes
2	6–8 minutes	5 minutes
4	8–12 minutes	5 minutes

■ DUCHESSE POTATOES

An old-fashioned potato ricer makes quick work of mashing potatoes and eliminates offending lumps. Duchesse Potatoes are an embellished version of simple American fare.

> **4 large russet or other baking potatoes (about 2½ lb)**
> **½ teaspoon salt**
> **¼ teaspoon white pepper**
> **6 tablespoons unsalted butter**
> **2 egg yolks**
> **1 egg beaten with 1 tablespoon water, for coating**

1. Peel and coarsely dice potatoes; place in a 4-quart saucepan and cover with water. Bring to a boil, reduce heat, and simmer until tender (25 to 30 minutes); drain. Force potatoes through a ricer or mash with a potato masher. Stir in salt, pepper, 5 tablespoons butter, and egg yolks. Cool briefly.

2. Preheat oven to 400° F. Butter a baking sheet with remaining butter or line with parchment paper. Place potato mixture into a pastry bag fitted with a 1-inch open-star tip (to give a fluted design) and pipe mounds 2 inches by 2 inches in diameter onto prepared baking sheet. Alternatively, form into egg-shaped mounds with two tablespoons and place on prepared baking sheet. Brush potatoes with egg wash. Bake until golden brown and crusty (about 20 minutes).

Serves 8.

POTATO PANCAKES

Homemade applesauce and sour cream can turn this simple side dish into a satisfying meal. Shred potatoes with a grater or in a food processor fitted with a shredding disk.

    3 large baking potatoes, peeled and shredded
    1 small onion, minced
    1 teaspoon salt
    ½ teaspoon freshly ground pepper
    1 egg
    4 tablespoons dry bread crumbs
    ½ cup vegetable oil, for frying
       Sour cream and applesauce, for garnish

In a large bowl, stir together shredded potatoes, onion, salt, pepper, egg, and bread crumbs. In a medium, heavy-bottomed skillet, heat oil over medium heat. For each pancake, use 2 to 3 tablespoons potato mixture; flatten in skillet to about ½ inch thick. Sauté pancakes until crisp and golden brown (12 to 15 minutes); turn and cook second side 6 minutes. Remove from pan and serve with a dollop of sour cream and a scoop of applesauce (if desired).

Serves 6.

POMMES SOUFFLES

Twice-fried Pommes Soufflés are thinly sliced potatoes that puff into little pillows during the second dip in hot oil. For a perfect result use mature, starch-filled potatoes. Be sure to keep the oil at a constant temperature. There are always some failures, which are edible, so be prepared to make extra if presentation is important. The recipe can be made partially ahead and finished just before serving.

    2 large russet potatoes (about 1½ lb)
       Oil, for frying

1. Peel potatoes and cut each into a perfectly symmetrical rectangular block. Slicing along length (which is with the grain), cut perfectly uniform, ⅛-inch slices. Cut each slice in half. Trim corners, if desired, to form hexagonal shapes. Reserve in ice water for at least 15 minutes.

2. In a heavy-bottomed saucepan or wok, heat 4 inches of oil to 250° F. Remove potatoes from ice water and dry thoroughly. Immerse potato slices, one at a time, in hot oil. When slices rise, spoon hot oil over them and continue cooking until edges start to look translucent (about 6 minutes). Remove with a wire skimmer and drain on paper towels. Potatoes may be prepared ahead to this point and reserved; reserve oil in pan as well.

3. Just before serving, heat same oil to 375° F. Carefully lower partially fried potato slices into hot oil; they should puff immediately. Cook until golden brown and crisp (3 to 4 minutes). If some have not puffed, return to hot oil one more time. Remove with a wire skimmer and drain on paper towels. Serve immediately.

Serves 8.

POTATO NESTS

The nests are dramatic edible containers that can be filled with sautéed cherry tomatoes, sautéed leeks and peas, caramelized pearl onions, or even Pommes Soufflés. The nests can be prepared ahead and reheated in the oven. To shape the nests, you must use a special two-piece wire basket designed just for this preparation (see photograph, at right). Before using the potato-nest basket for the first time, it is important to season the baskets so the potatoes won't stick to them. To season, heat oil to 375° F in a heavy-bottomed kettle. Place basket in hot oil and let sit for about 5 minutes. Turn off heat and leave basket in oil about 1 hour. Remove basket from oil and wipe dry.

    2 large russet potatoes (about 1½ lb)
       Oil, for frying

1. Peel potatoes, julienne, and set in bowl of cold water to keep from turning brown. In a heavy-bottomed kettle or wok, heat 4 inches of oil to 380° F. Remove one eighth of potatoes from water and thoroughly pat dry (or they won't brown properly). Place in larger basket of seasoned potato-nest fryer in a ¼-inch thick layer. Fit smaller basket over potato layer and secure tightly.

2. Hold fryer basket handle with a hot pad (wire will get too hot to hold safely in bare hand). Immerse in hot oil and deep-fry for about 4 minutes. Still protecting hand, lift fryer from oil and carefully remove small inner basket. Return potato-lined outer basket to hot oil and fry until golden brown (about 1 minute more).

3. Remove and loosen potato nest from wire basket and drain on paper towels. These may be prepared several hours ahead and reheated in a 300° F oven 5 to 8 minutes. Fill with your choice of filling and serve.

Serves 8.

SCALLOPED POTATOES

This traditional American dish is a perennial favorite accompaniment to roasts—meat or fowl. It is rich with a garlic-flavored cream sauce.

    2   tablespoons unsalted butter
    2½   pounds russet potatoes, peeled
    2   cups whipping cream
    1   cup milk
    1   clove garlic, minced (optional)
    1½   teaspoons salt
    ½   teaspoon freshly ground pepper

1. Preheat oven to 350° F. Grease a 3-quart baking dish with butter. Slice potatoes ⅛ inch thick; layer in baking dish.

2. In a medium bowl stir together cream, milk, garlic (if used), salt, and pepper. Pour over potatoes and bake until potatoes are tender when pierced with a knife (1 hour and 10 minutes). Serve hot.

Serves 8.

A basket fryer gives shape to foods such as shredded potatoes as they cook in deep fat. The resulting edible nest makes an attractive container for a variety of vegetables. See Potato Nests, at left.

■ POMMES ANNA

This rich potato "cake" is one of the classic dishes of French cuisine. A well-buttered, 8-inch cast-iron skillet is the perfect size and shape for this dish.

    8 large baking potatoes
    8 tablespoons butter, melted
    1 tablespoon vegetable oil
    1 tablespoon salt
    ½ teaspoon freshly ground pepper

1. Preheat oven to 475° F. Slice potatoes ⅛ inch thick; soak slices in ice water to prevent browning. At baking time, drain and pat dry.

2. In a heavy, 8-inch skillet, arrange one fourth of the potato slices in overlapping circles to fill pan. Shake pan gently while filling to keep potatoes from sticking. Season with ¼ teaspoon salt and ⅛ teaspoon pepper and drizzle with 2 tablespoons of the butter. Repeat layers with remaining ingredients.

3. Sauté on top of stove over medium heat 10 minutes, then bake for 1 hour. To serve, loosen potatoes by running a knife around edge of pan. Place a flat serving dish over pan, invert serving dish and skillet together, and lift skillet from potatoes. Serve immediately.

Serves 8.

Garlicky Pommes Anna   Add 4 cloves minced garlic to melted butter before pouring over potato layers.

Parmesan Pommes Anna   Mince 5 shallots and stir into melted butter with ¼ cup freshly grated good-quality Parmesan cheese.

■ DOWN-HOME MASHED POTATOES

Mashed potatoes need not be uniformly smooth; in fact, a few small lumps improve the texture. Nor should the milk be premeasured and heated; the quantity needed will depend on the type and age of the potatoes. (Mealy baking potatoes that have been stored for a long time take more milk than new potatoes.) Simply pour milk in gradually, beating after every addition, until potatoes are just right. A few minutes in the oven before serving will reheat and puff up the potatoes. If you have a potato ricer, use it to mash the potatoes.

    1 medium-large (about 11 oz) potato per person
    1 tablespoon butter for each potato
      Milk, as needed (¼ to ½ cup per potato)
      Salt and white pepper, to taste
      Paprika, for garnish

1. Bring a large pot of salted water to a boil. Meanwhile, peel potatoes and quarter or halve them (depending on size). Drop potatoes into pot as they are peeled, even if water is not quite boiling. Cook potatoes over high heat until fork-tender (about 25 minutes after water comes to a boil). Some pieces can be left a little underdone. Drain well.

2. Place potatoes and butter in a large bowl. Using a potato masher or fork, coarsely mash them together. Make a well in center and pour in a small amount of milk.

3. With an electric mixer (*not* a blender or food processor, which will turn potatoes into a starchy goo), beat potatoes, adding more milk a little at a time as needed, until desired texture is obtained. Tasting carefully, add salt and pepper. At this point, potatoes can be set aside, uncovered, until the rest of dinner is nearly ready. A half hour before serving time, preheat oven to 350° F.

4. Mound potatoes in an ovenproof casserole, sprinkle with paprika, and bake uncovered 20 minutes.

■ TWICE-BAKED POTATOES WITH WISCONSIN CHEDDAR CHEESE

For special occasions, potatoes put on company manners—here halved, their flesh scooped from their shells, mixed with seasonings, and returned to the shell to bake. This dish is convenient because it can be prepared ahead, then baked to serve with a sumptuous beef roast.

    3 large baking potatoes (1½ to 2 lb total)
    3 tablespoons butter or margarine
    ¼ teaspoon salt
    ⅛ teaspoon ground white pepper
    1 egg yolk, beaten with 3 tablespoons milk
    2 tablespoons snipped fresh chives
    1½ cups (6 oz) grated sharp Cheddar cheese (Wisconsin, if possible)

1. Preheat oven to 400° F. Scrub potatoes and pierce each in several places with a fork. Rub all over with butter, using about 1 tablespoon. Bake potatoes until tender in the center when tested with a fork (about 45 minutes).

2. Remove potatoes from oven and cut each in half lengthwise. Reduce oven temperature to 350° F. When potatoes are cool enough to handle, scoop out centers, leaving a shell about ¼ inch thick. Place shells in a shallow baking pan.

3. In a medium bowl combine hot scooped-out potato, remaining butter, salt, and pepper; add egg yolk mixture. Using an electric mixer, beat until fluffy and well combined. Stir in chives and 1 cup cheese.

4. Mound potato mixture into hollowed-out shells, dividing it evenly. Sprinkle with remaining cheese. (Potatoes can be prepared ahead to this point. Cover and refrigerate for up to one day; let stand at room temperature for about 30 minutes before baking.)

5. Bake until potatoes are heated through (15 to 20 minutes).

Serves 6.

BAKED POTATO SKINS

These crisp shells are delicious served as is. To serve as part of a brunch menu, fill with scrambled or poached eggs or Cheddar cheese.

> 6 small baking potatoes (4 to 5 in. long)
> ¼ cup butter or margarine
> ¼ teaspoon paprika
> Pinch white pepper

1. Preheat oven to 400° F. Scrub potatoes, pat dry, and rub skins lightly with a little of the butter. Pierce potatoes in several places with a fork.

2. Bake potatoes until tender when pierced (45 minutes to 1 hour). When cool enough to handle, cut in halves lengthwise and scoop out potato, leaving a thin shell about ⅛ inch thick. Reserve potato for other dishes.

3. Place skins on a baking sheet. Melt butter in a small pan with paprika and white pepper. Stir. Brush insides of potato skins with butter mixture.

4. Bake potato skins until crisp and golden (18 to 20 minutes). (For variety, try adding grated Cheddar cheese, crumbled bacon, green onion, or chives.)

Serves 6.

COTTAGE FRIED POTATOES

Give Cottage Fried Potatoes a down-home appeal by cooking, slicing, and frying them with the skins on.

> 5 medium potatoes
> 2 tablespoons *each* butter or margarine
> and vegetable oil
> ⅛ teaspoon paprika
> Salt and coarsely ground pepper

1. Scrub potatoes well. Cook, in their skins, in boiling salted water until about half cooked (15 to 20 minutes). Without peeling, slice potatoes about ⅛ inch thick.

2. In a large, heavy frying pan over medium-low heat, melt butter with oil and paprika. Add potatoes. Sprinkle lightly with salt and pepper.

3. Cook, using a wide spatula to lift and turn potatoes occasionally, until they are brown and crusty on all sides (20 to 25 minutes). Turn carefully to keep slices from breaking.

Serves 4 to 6.

HASH BROWN POTATOES

This is actually a seasoned potato cake made of shredded cooked potatoes crisply fried with a touch of onion.

> 5 medium potatoes
> ¼ cup finely chopped onion
> ½ teaspoon salt
> Pinch white pepper
> 2 tablespoons *each* butter or margarine
> and vegetable oil

1. Cook potatoes, in their skins, in boiling salted water until about half cooked (15 to 20 minutes). When cool enough to handle, slip off skins. Shred potatoes coarsely into a bowl. Mix lightly with onion, salt, and white pepper.

2. In a heavy, well-seasoned or nonstick 9- to 10-inch frying pan over medium heat, melt butter with 1 tablespoon oil. Add potatoes, pressing down with a spatula. Cook over low heat (without stirring) until potatoes are brown and crusty on bottom (12 to 15 minutes).

3. Loosen edges with a spatula. Cover pan with a plate, invert potatoes onto it, and add remaining tablespoon oil to pan. Swirl to coat pan well. Slide potatoes back into pan and cook until bottom is well browned and crusty (12 to 15 minutes).

4. Serve from pan or invert onto a warm serving plate.

Serves 6.

A trio of delicious potato dishes—cottage fries, potato skins, and hash browns—makes delicious breakfast fare. Serve with eggs and sausage, ham, or bacon.

◼ FRENCH-FRIED POTATOES

Most types of potatoes can be fried, but russets or other baking potatoes are especially suitable because they absorb less oil. Putting the raw potatoes in cold water removes excess starch so they do not stick to one another during frying. Because French fries are best when fried twice, this recipe calls for a first frying at a relatively low temperature, followed by a second frying at a high temperature. This method makes meal preparation easy because after the first frying the potatoes can stand at room temperature until just before serving.

    2 pounds large baking potatoes, peeled
    8 cups (at least) vegetable oil, for deep-frying
      Salt

1. For the best results, read DEEP-FRY and SAUTE before beginning if these are techniques you don't use often.

2. If potatoes are over 4 inches long, halve them crosswise. Cut in lengthwise slices about ⅜ inch wide, then cut each slice in lengthwise strips about ⅜ inch wide. Trim irregular edges. As they are cut, drop potato sticks into a large bowl of cold water.

3. Rinse potatoes and drain well in a colander. Using paper towels, thoroughly pat them dry in small batches. This step is very important because fat will bubble up violently if potatoes are even slightly wet.

4. Line trays with two layers of paper towels. Heat oil in deep fryer or deep, heavy saucepan to about 340° F on a deep-fat thermometer, or test oil with a piece of potato (oil should foam up around it).

5. Dip a frying basket or a large skimmer into hot oil, then put about one third to one half of the potatoes in basket or skimmer and carefully lower into hot oil. Do not overfill because fat that bubbles up vigorously when potatoes are added can be dangerous. If using a basket, leave it in oil during frying; remove skimmer.

6. Fry potatoes until tender but pale (about 5 minutes). Check by pressing one; it should crush easily. Use slotted skimmer to remove potatoes to towel-lined trays. Reheat oil before adding next batch. Potatoes can be left for a few hours at room temperature.

7. About 10 minutes before serving, heat oil in deep fryer or deep, heavy saucepan to about 375° F on a deep-fat thermometer. Line more trays with two layers of paper towels.

8. Carefully put about half of the potatoes in frying basket or large skimmer. Carefully lower into hot oil. Fry until golden brown (about 2 minutes). Lift out basket or remove potatoes with skimmer and let drain briefly over pan. Transfer to towel-lined trays. Repeat with remaining potato slices.

9. Sprinkle potatoes with salt and toss gently. Serve immediately.

Serves 4.

◼ HOMEMADE POTATO CHIPS

Better than any store-bought chip, this homemade version is fried twice for extra crispness. As a welcome bonus, the potato skins can be buttered and baked until golden and crisp. For best results leave a little potato flesh on the skins when you peel them.

    3 large russet potatoes
      Peanut or corn oil, for deep-frying
      Coarse salt

1. Peel potatoes. Slice potatoes ¼ inch thick and place in a bowl of ice water until ready to fry.

2. In a heavy skillet or deep fryer, heat at least 3 inches of oil to 375° F. Dry potatoes well between kitchen towels. Add potatoes to hot oil and fry until lightly golden. Drain on paper towels.

3. Raise temperature of oil to 400° F and refry potatoes until very crisp and golden. (If doubling or tripling recipe, do second frying with fresh oil.) Drain on paper towels, salt lightly, and serve immediately.

Makes about 5 dozen chips.

Recipes and Related Information
Chive Potato Salad, 123; Church-Social Potato Salad, 506; Leg of Lamb With Garlic, Potatoes, and Onions, 337; New Potatoes With Caviar, 107; Thyme-Scented Chicken With Potatoes, Bacon, and Baby Onions, 578; Vichyssoise, 566.

POULTRY

Domesticated birds fattened for the table are referred to as *poultry*. Chicken, duck, turkey, squab, Rock Cornish game hen, and goose are the best-known examples of poultry in this country, although pheasant, partridge, and other game birds are now being raised on a small scale in some regions.

Twentieth-century scientific breeding has changed the shape of the birds we eat, giving us poultry with broad, meaty breasts and little fat. Improved efficiency in poultry raising has changed the shape of the poultry business: Most chickens today are raised in confinement to keep their muscles from toughening, and they are fed a specially formulated diet to bring them quickly to market weight. Increased efficiency in poultry processing has kept the price of chicken low, making it probably the most popular meat on the American table. However, many claim that today's supermarket chicken tastes bland compared with chicken that has been allowed to range freely for its feed. For those interested in tasting the difference, free-range chickens are being raised for specialty markets in some parts of the country; they are more expensive and usually tougher than supermarket chicken, but some consumers may find that their flavor outweighs the other drawbacks.

Use Poultry appears on the table as an appetizer, in soups, salads, and sandwiches, and as a main course. Jewish chicken soup with matzo balls, southern fried chicken, Peking duck, German roast goose with apples, and roast turkey with stuffing and giblet gravy are among the many ways that cooks around the world use poultry.

POULTRY PRIMER

At the market, poultry is grouped by species (such as chicken, turkey, and duck), and by class (for example, broilers, fryers, and roasters). Within each class, birds may be grouped by physical characteristics, primarily age, which in turn determine the cooking method (see Which Bird To Buy?, at right).

Type	Age	Size	Cooking Method
Chicken			
Poussin	Under 6 weeks	1 lb	Broil, Grill, Roast, Sauté
Rock Cornish game hen	4–5 weeks	1–1½ lbs	Broil, Grill, Roast, Sauté
Broiler	7–9 weeks	1½–2 lbs	Broil, Grill, Roast, Sauté
Fryer	9–12 weeks	3–4 lbs	Broil, Grill, Fry, Roast
Roaster	10–20 weeks	Over 5 lbs	Braise, Fry, Roast, Stew
Capon	16–20 weeks	6–9 lbs	Roast
Stewing chicken	Over 10 months	4–6 lbs	Braise, Stew, Make stock
Turkey			
Fryer-roaster	Under 16 weeks	4–8 lbs	Roast
Young turkey			
Hen	14–22 weeks	7–15 lbs	Roast
Tom	14–22 weeks	15–25+ lbs	Roast
Mature turkey	Over 15 months	12–25 lbs	Stew, Make stock
Other			
Duckling	8–16 weeks	3–5½ lbs	Broil, Roast
Young goose	Over 6 months	4–14 lbs	Roast
Pheasant	6 weeks	2–3 lbs	Bake, Roast
Quail	Under 6 weeks	¼–½ lb	Broil, Grill, Roast, Sauté
Squab	Under 6 weeks	¾ lb	Broil, Grill, Roast, Sauté

Availability Poultry is sold in many forms: fresh and frozen, whole, ready-to-cook parts, and processed meat products such as rolls, delicatessen meats, and hot dogs. Most supermarkets carry fresh chicken and fresh turkey parts all year. Chinese markets are a good source for fresh duck and quail. Most specialty butchers can order fresh goose, duck, quail, squab, or poussin with sufficient notice. See specific poultry entries.

Selection Fresh poultry is very perishable. When purchased, it should not have an off-odor or off-color and should be quite dry. If poultry is packaged, there should not be any accumulated liquid on the tray or in the bag. Prepackaged fresh poultry often has a "sell by" date stamped on the label. This date, seven days after the bird was processed, is the recommended final day for store sale. Refrigerated at a cold temperature, the bird will keep several more days. For unwrapped poultry, ask the butcher how fresh it is and how soon it should be cooked.

When buying frozen poultry, avoid torn packages or birds with signs of freezer burn. Pink-tinged ice indicates the bird thawed and was refrozen; it will likely be dry.

Storage Fresh poultry should be used within one or two days of purchase, or frozen immediately. Refrigerating fresh poultry does not kill organisms that cause food spoilage; it only slows their growth. Spoiled meat will have a definite off odor and a slimy surface. Discard any meat that is of questionable freshness.

Prepackaged poultry can be left in its package, with transparent wrapping intact, for refrigerator storage. If the wrapping is torn, or if chicken is wrapped in butcher paper, unwrap, set the poultry on a plate, and cover loosely with aluminum foil or waxed paper.

Cooked poultry can be refrigerated for three or four days, well wrapped to keep it from drying out. Freeze for longer storage. Cooked poultry in broth or gravy should be refrigerated for only one or two days. Raw or cooked poultry should not be left at room temperature for more than one or two hours.

To freeze fresh poultry, wrap tightly in plastic wrap and overwrap with freezer paper; freeze for up to one year. Frozen poultry, if not to be used right away, should be placed immediately in home freezer. Remove store wrap; rewrap in fresh plastic and overwrap with freezer paper. Freeze for up to one year. See FREEZE, Timetable for Freezing.

For best quality, thaw frozen poultry slowly in refrigerator in its wrapping, allowing three to four hours defrosting time per pound. A large turkey may take up to three days; small birds should take one to two days. Frozen parts will thaw in one day.

For quicker thawing, thaw in waterproof, completely sealed wrapping under cold running water, or in cold water that is changed frequently to maintain a consistent temperature. A 5- to 9-pound bird will thaw this way in 4 to 6 hours. A bird over 9 pounds needs 8 to 12 hours.

TIPS

WHICH BIRD TO BUY?

Younger birds are more tender and are best suited for roasting, baking, grilling, sautéing, and frying. The terms to look for are the following.

- *For chicken: Rock Cornish game hen, broiler, fryer, roaster, and capon*
- *For turkey: young turkey, fryer roaster, young hen, and young tom*
- *For duck: duckling, young duckling, broiler duckling, fryer duckling, and roaster duckling*
- *For goose: young goose*
- *For pigeon: squab*

  Older birds need long, slow cooking with moist heat to break down tough connective tissue; they should be used in stews, braises, and fricassees, or for stock.

- *For chicken: mature chicken, hen, fowl, and baking and stewing chicken*
- *For turkey: mature turkey, yearling turkey, and old turkey (hen or tom)*
- *For duck and goose: mature and old.*

Thaw poultry at room temperature only if you are able to monitor the process carefully, because bacteria that can cause food poisoning grow rapidly at this temperature. To thaw a turkey, place the unwrapped frozen bird in a double-walled brown bag or several thicknesses of newspaper. The paper keeps the surface of the bird cold while the interior thaws. Frozen small birds and frozen parts can be thawed in their wrappings. Refrigerate or cook thawed poultry as soon as possible.

Preparation All raw poultry should be cleaned and washed before cooking. Remove any clumps of visible fat around neck and tail. Remove innards (neck and giblets) from cavity. Use tweezers or fingernails to pull out any stray feathers or hairs. Wash quickly inside and out, pulling out any bloody bits from inside the bird. Pat dry with paper towels. Some whole birds are trussed, or tied together, before roasting for a more attractive appearance (see TRUSS). For a discussion about specific poultry techniques, see also BONE, CARVE, DISJOINT.

Cooking See BROIL, BRAISE, DEEP-FRY, GRILL, POACH, SAUTE, STEW, STIR-FRY, STOCK AND SOUP.

CHICKEN

As a mild-flavored meat, chicken lends itself readily to variation; in fact chicken is compatible with almost every herb, spice, and vegetable in the marketplace. When you consider the hundreds of ways that Americans prepare chicken and add to that the thousands of chicken dishes common to the rest of the world, it is clear that the options for the curious cook are virtually unlimited. As a lean, low-cholesterol meat, it is welcome in the diets of the many Americans trying to reduce their intake of fat and cholesterol.

Chicken figures in the cuisine of almost every country in the world. In this country fried chicken, roast chicken, and some form of baked chicken are in almost every cook's repertoire. Chicken is made into pot pies, stewed with dumplings, poached to make a flavorful broth that is the basis of countless soups, and chopped or sliced for a cold salad or sandwich filling.

In Mexico chicken is shredded to make fillings for tacos, enchiladas, and tamales. French cooks are famous for coq au vin (chicken in red wine). Italians roast chicken with rosemary or sauté it alla cacciatore. Spanish cooks pair chicken with rice, tomatoes, sausage, and shellfish to make paella. Chicken Kiev, deep-fried boneless breasts rolled around seasoned butter, is a Russian specialty. In Japan chicken is marinated in soy sauce, rice wine, and ginger and grilled, or steamed with cooked rice and egg to make the popular lunch dish called *donburi*. Chinese cooks stir-fry chicken with all manner of vegetables and seasonings; they also braise a whole chicken in soy sauce or smoke it over tea leaves.

In India chicken is highly spiced and braised in curries, or marinated in yogurt and spices and roasted in the tandoor (clay oven). In West Africa chicken is simmered with tomatoes and peanuts to make groundnut stew.

Both fresh and frozen chickens are widely available in supermarkets, either whole or cut into parts. Whole chickens are almost always less expensive, but some cooks prefer the convenience of precut, packaged parts. It is easy to cut up a chicken, and the method is well worth learning (see BONE, DISJOINT). The cook who buys whole chickens not only saves money but also gets the useful fat, the tasty giblets, and the bony parts for stock. Chickens may be cooked whole or cut into parts. The legs, thighs, breasts, and wings are the choice parts, with the bony wing tips, neck, and back often reserved for making stock.

Chickens are marketed in several different sizes, each with particular cooking requirements. See Which Bird to Buy? on page 469 for more information.

◼ ROAST CHICKEN WITH RICE, FRUIT, AND ALMOND STUFFING

Although roasting chickens are slightly more flavorful than frying chickens, both can be roasted. The stuffing for this chicken is a variation of rice pilaf. If you like, serve the rice as a side dish with any roast, instead of as a stuffing. In this case, cook the rice for a total of 18 minutes.

½ cup slivered almonds
¼ cup vegetable oil
1 small onion, finely chopped
1 cup long-grain rice
1½ cups hot water
½ cup strained, fresh orange juice
   Salt and freshly ground pepper, to taste
1 small apple, peeled, halved, and cored
½ cup raisins
¼ teaspoon ground cinnamon
1 roasting chicken (3½ to 4 lb)

1. Preheat oven to 400° F. Toast almonds in a baking dish in oven, stirring occasionally, until lightly browned (about 5 minutes). Transfer to a bowl and let cool.

2. In a deep frying pan, heat 3 tablespoons of the oil over low heat. Add onion and cook, stirring often, until tender (about 5 minutes). Increase heat to medium, add rice, and sauté for 2 minutes. Add the hot water, orange juice, salt, and pepper; bring to a boil. Reduce heat to low, cover, and cook for 10 minutes.

3. Dice apple. After rice has cooked 10 minutes, add apple and raisins to rice and stir very lightly with a fork. Cover and cook for 5 minutes; rice will be nearly tender. Stir in cinnamon and reserved almonds. Taste and add more salt and pepper, if needed.

4. Sprinkle chicken with salt and pepper on all sides. Spoon enough rice stuffing into chicken to fill it, but do not pack it too tightly; reserve extra stuffing at room temperature.

5. Set chicken on a rack in a roasting pan and roast until juices run clear when a skewer is inserted into thickest part of leg (about 1 hour). If juices are pink, continue roasting chicken a few more minutes. Transfer chicken to a carving board. Let stand 5 to 10 minutes before carving and serving.

6. Heat the remaining 1 tablespoon oil in a frying pan over low heat. Add remaining stuffing and cook, stirring often with a fork, until rice is tender and hot (about 3 minutes). Spoon into a serving dish.

7. Serve chicken and its stuffing on a platter. Serve remaining rice separately.

Serves 4.

■ CHICKEN KIEV

Unlike other coated foods, Chicken Kiev must be fried cold so that the butter trapped inside the chicken roll stays frozen. If allowed to thaw, the butter would leak out during frying. The herbed butter must be frozen one hour before you prepare the chicken rolls, and then the chicken rolls must chill one to two hours before they are cooked. If the rolls seem to be browning too quickly, remove them when they are golden and finish cooking in a 325° F oven 10 to 12 minutes.

> ½ **cup butter, softened**
> 2 **tablespoons chopped parsley**
> 1 **clove garlic, crushed**
> 1 **tablespoon snipped fresh chives**
> ½ **teaspoon salt**
> **Freshly ground pepper, to taste**
> 4 **small whole chicken breasts, halved, boned, and skinned**
> 1 **egg, lightly beaten**
> 2 **cups dry bread crumbs**
> 4 **cups vegetable oil, for frying**
> **Watercress sprigs, for garnish**

Sauce Gruyère

> 3 **tablespoons butter**
> 3 **tablespoons flour**
> 1 **cup half-and-half**
> ½ **cup grated Gruyère cheese**
> **Salt and freshly ground pepper, to taste**

1. In a medium bowl, using a wooden spoon, blend butter with parsley, garlic, chives, salt, and pepper (or blend mixture in food processor). Shape into a rectangular block, wrap in waxed paper, and freeze until solid (about 1 hour).

2. Wash chicken breast halves and pat dry. Pound breast halves between two pieces of waxed paper to ¼ inch thick. Cut frozen butter into eight sticks. Place one stick in the center of each half breast. Fold edges of breasts over butter and roll up tightly, completely enveloping butter with meat.

3. Brush each chicken roll with beaten egg. Put bread crumbs on a large square of waxed paper or on a plate, and coat rolls thoroughly with crumbs.

4. Transfer chicken rolls to a baking sheet, cover lightly with waxed paper, and refrigerate 1 to 2 hours to set coating.

5. In a heavy-bottomed, 3-quart saucepan, heat oil to 365° F as registered on a frying thermometer. Deep-fry rolls until golden brown all around (about 8 minutes per roll).

6. Gently remove with a slotted spoon to a baking sheet lined with paper towels. To hold, keep warm in a 200° F oven.

7. Serve Chicken Kiev with Sauce Gruyère and garnish with watercress.

Serves 8.

Sauce Gruyère In a small saucepan over medium heat, melt butter. Whisk in flour and cook briefly. Pour in half-and-half and cook until thickened. Stir in grated cheese and season with salt and pepper.

Makes about 1½ cups.

Diners delight in the burst of herbed butter released as they cut into Chicken Kiev. In the recipe at left, parsley, chives, and garlic flavor the butter; in classic versions, tarragon is the frequently used herb.

ABOUT CHICKEN LIVERS, GIBLETS, AND FAT

Chicken livers are enjoyed by many diners as a dish in themselves. Some supermarkets and all specialty poultry markets carry chicken livers, either fresh or frozen. Fresh livers and thawed frozen livers are perishable and should be used within one or two days; they may be tightly wrapped and frozen for up to three months (do not refreeze thawed livers). Pat them dry, flour them lightly, and sauté them in bacon fat with onions, bacon, and mushrooms; or sauté them in butter with Marsala; or sauté them with onions and chop them with hard-cooked eggs to make chopped chicken livers. Cooked livers may be added to stuffings or served with pasta, rice, or toast. After trim-ming away tough outer skin and connective tissue, chicken giblets (heart and gizzard) may be chopped, sautéed, and added to stuffings or gravy.

Save any fat you pull from the neck or tail cavity. Render it slowly in a skillet over low heat with a little water, and store it in a tightly covered jar in the refrigerator (see RENDER). It will keep for one month; freeze for longer storage. Use chicken fat in place of butter for sautéing or spreading on bread. In Germany it is known as *schmaltz* and is important to the Jewish kitchen. Schmaltz is used in chopped chicken liver, in Matzo Balls, and wherever a flavorful cooking fat is desired.

■ DEEP-DISH CHICKEN PIE

Let this homey American dinner pie warm a cold winter evening. To speed up preparation, cook the filling a day or two ahead and refrigerate it, covered. To serve, bring it to room temperature and proceed with step 3.

    1¼ cups flour
    ¼   teaspoon salt
    ¼   cup butter, cut in pieces
    2   tablespoons lard, cut in pieces
    1   egg
    2   tablespoons cold water

Chicken Filling

    1¼ cup butter
    1   small onion, chopped
    ¼   cup finely chopped celery
    3   tablespoons flour
        Pinch *each* freshly ground pepper and
        freshly grated nutmeg
    2   cups Chicken Stock (see page 560)
    6   cups cubed cooked chicken
    ½   cup fresh or frozen peas
    ¼   pound mushrooms, quartered
    2   small carrots, peeled and sliced
        Salt and freshly ground pepper, to taste

1. Sift flour and salt into a bowl. Cut butter and lard into flour with a pastry blender until mixture is crumbly.

2. Separate egg and reserve white. Beat yolk with 1 tablespoon of the water and pour liquid into flour mixture. Stir with a wooden spoon until mixture begins to form a ball. With floured hands, lightly shape into a ball. Cover dough with waxed paper and refrigerate 1 hour.

3. Preheat oven to 425° F. Make filling and while it cools, roll out cold pastry on a floured surface into a 12-inch circle. Mix reserved egg white with remaining tablespoon of the water; brush onto one side of pastry.

4. Pour cooled chicken mixture into a straight-sided, 9-inch-diameter baking dish about 2 inches deep. Place pastry, glazed side down, over filling. Trim pastry, flute edge, and cut slits in crust to allow steam to escape. Brush top with egg wash.

5. Bake until pastry is golden brown (30 to 40 minutes). Serve immediately.

Serves 8

Chicken Filling In a saucepan over medium heat, melt butter; add onion and celery and cook until soft. Stir in flour; cook until thickened. Add pepper and nutmeg. Gradually stir in stock, stirring constantly, until mixture bubbles and thickens. Mix in chicken, peas, mushrooms, and carrots. Season with salt and pepper to taste. Set filling aside to cool.

■ CHICKEN CURRY WITH CONDIMENTS

Curry is not one spice but several, commonly consisting of cumin, coriander, black mustard seed, fenugreek, and turmeric (for the yellow color). The spiciness can be enhanced with the addition of chile pepper, although commercial curry powders are fiery enough for many palates. The condiments associated with traditional curry are both spicy and soothing: cilantro *raita*, cucumbers in yogurt, tomato chutney, mango chutney, minced green onion, coarsely chopped peanuts, shredded coconut, deep-fried garlic chips, diced green bell pepper, dried currants, and always lots of steamed *basmati* rice.

    6   boneless, skinless chicken breasts
    2   tablespoons vegetable oil
    3   tablespoons unsalted butter
    1   medium onion, diced
    2   cloves garlic, minced
    1   apple, diced
    1   green bell pepper, diced
    1   jalapeño chile, minced
    2   tablespoons curry powder
    ¼   cup flour
    1½ to 2 cups Chicken Stock (see page 560)
    ½   teaspoon salt

1. Cut chicken breasts into 2-inch cubes. Heat oil in a 14-inch skillet and sauté the chicken pieces over medium heat until lightly browned (about 12 minutes). Remove and reserve.

2. Melt butter in the same 14-inch skillet over medium heat. Stir in onion and garlic, and sauté until lightly browned (6 to 8 minutes). Stir in chicken pieces, apple, bell pepper, chile, curry powder, and flour. Cook for 5 minutes. Stir in Chicken Stock and simmer for 20 minutes to meld the flavors. Season with salt.

Serves 8.

■ CHICKEN MARENGO

Napoleon's chef created this dish for his commander-in-chief in 1800 after the Battle of Marengo. It was said to have been made from locally available ingredients—chicken, tomatoes, and garlic. This version also includes mushrooms, green pepper, and olives. It is a very flavorful poultry stew, and like all stews it improves if made ahead and gently reheated just before serving. Serve with rice pilaf.

```
12   pearl onions
 1   roasting chicken (3 to 3½ lb), cut in pieces
 2   teaspoons salt
 ½   teaspoon freshly ground pepper
 ¼   cup olive oil
 4   tablespoons unsalted butter
 1   clove garlic, minced
 1   small onion, sliced
 1   green bell pepper, sliced
 5   small plum tomatoes, cut in large dice
 1   teaspoon dried oregano
 1   teaspoon dried basil
 1   cup dry white wine
 1   cup Chicken Stock (see page 560)
 ½   pound mushrooms, halved
 ½   cup pitted black olives, halved
 2   tablespoons parsley, minced
```

1. In a large saucepan bring 1 quart of water to a boil. Blanch pearl onions for 1 minute. Trim root end, slip off skins, and cut an *x* in root end of each onion, reserve.

2. Season chicken pieces with salt and pepper. In a 4- to 5-quart Dutch oven, sauté chicken legs in oil and butter over medium-high heat 5 minutes; add breasts and brown another 5 minutes. Add garlic, onion, bell pepper, tomatoes, oregano, basil, wine, stock, and reserved onions to chicken. Reduce heat and simmer 20 minutes.

3. Add mushrooms and black olives to chicken and cook 10 more minutes. To serve, sprinkle with parsley.

Serves 6.

Recipes: Barbecued Chicken With Two Sauces, 294; Chicken Breasts With Grapes, 280; Chicken Breasts With Sherry, Cream, and Mushrooms, 611; Chicken in Half-Mourning, 583; Chicken or Duck Liver Mousse, 372; Chicken Quenelles, 241; Chicken Soup With Dumplings, 189; Chicken Stock, 560; Chicken With Forty Cloves of Garlic, 262; Chinese Chicken Salad, 508; Country Fried Chicken, 176; Curried Chicken or Duck Liver Pâté in Aspic, 416; Golden Chicken Stew With Cheese Dumplings, 192; Honeyed Chicken With Apricots, 557; Lemon Chicken Breasts, 339; Paper-Wrapped Chicken, 175; Perfectly Poached Chicken for Salads and Sandwiches, 451; Rich Chicken Stock, 561; Tandoori Chicken, 351; Three-Mushroom Chicken, 380; Thyme-Scented Chicken With Potatoes, Bacon, and Baby Onions, 578.

ROCK CORNISH GAME HEN AND POUSSIN

The Rock Cornish game hen is a hybrid bird with a dressed weight of about 1¼ pounds. The hens have a delicate flavor and all-white meat; they make attractive, if large, single servings.

The poussin is a young chicken slaughtered at less than six weeks. Its dressed weight is about 1 pound. It makes a large single serving or a small serving for two. Its flavor is delicate.

Rock Cornish hens and poussins can be used in similar fashion. Whole birds may be roasted, braised, or sautéed; roasted birds may be stuffed. Because of their small size, they are usually served either whole or halved. They may also be split down the backbone, flattened, and grilled or broiled. Their delicate flavor is complemented by butter and herbs. Almost any preparation for whole chicken may be adapted to Cornish hens and poussins.

Most supermarkets carry frozen Cornish hens the year around. A specialty butcher may be able to obtain fresh Cornish hens by special order. Fresh poussins are increasingly available in specialty markets; they may require special order.

See Selection, Storage, and Preparation for more information.

Recipes: Game Hens Coq au Vin, 58; Poussin Paprikash, 405.

TURKEY

This big-breasted, mild-flavored bird, native to the New World, was probably served at the first Thanksgiving. Today's domesticated turkey is not only a fixture on most Thanksgiving tables but is now increasingly appreciated the year around. As an inexpensive, low-calorie meat, it is suitable for dozens of preparations.

Despite the increased availability of turkey, it is still closely associated in most American minds with Thanksgiving and Christmas. The brown-breasted turkey, surrounded by cranberry sauce and sweet potatoes, is a modern reminder of the turkeys eaten by the Pilgrims at the first Thanksgiving. The turkey giblets (heart and gizzard) are minced and added to the gravy.

In this country turkey is also used in soups, casseroles, sandwiches, and salads. Sliced turkey breast, smoked or unsmoked, is popular fare for buffets and parties. Turkey may be creamed and served over spaghetti or rice. Thinly sliced raw turkey breast may be used in any preparation calling for veal scaloppine.

In Italy turkey breasts are breaded and fried, then baked with mozzarella and prosciutto. In Hungary turkey parts are wrapped in bacon, panfried, then braised in stock and sour cream. Greek cooks stuff turkey with a mixture of ground lamb, chestnuts, pine nuts, apples, rice, and bread crumbs. In Mexico turkey is braised with *mole poblano,* a dark chile sauce enriched with chocolate.

TIPS

COOKING CHICKEN AND TURKEY IN THE MICROWAVE OVEN

Chicken pieces cook quickly and are tender and juicy when cooked in a microwave oven. Because they cook so quickly, pieces get neither brown nor crisp. Before cooking brush chicken with a mixture of gravy browner and oil to add color, or coat with seasoned crumbs. Cover dish with waxed paper during cooking and rotate dish a half turn halfway through cooking. Microwave at 100 percent power: 2 chicken pieces, 4 to 6 minutes; 4 pieces, 6 to 10 minutes; 6 pieces, 8 to 12 minutes. Let chicken stand 5 minutes to finish cooking.

Small turkeys (6 to 12 pounds) can be microwaved successfully. Before cooking brush turkey with a mixture of gravy browner and oil to add color. Cook turkey (breast side down for half the cooking time; turn breast side up to finish) at 100 percent power, 6 to 7 minutes per pound, or at 50 percent power, 11 to 13 minutes per pound. Let turkey stand 20 minutes before carving to finish cooking.

Moist and tender, a beautifully roasted turkey is the festive focus of any celebration, whether for the holidays or for another special occasion.

Most turkeys are marketed as young turkeys, which means they are 14 to 22 weeks old, either female or male (see Poultry Primer, page 469). Despite a long-held belief to the contrary, there is no difference in quality between a hen and a tom; hens are merely smaller.

See Selection, Storage, and Preparation for more information.

■ ROAST TURKEY WITH GIBLET GRAVY

There are many ways to roast a turkey: plain (without a cover), in a foil tent, in a paper bag, and, according to one probably tall story, in a sleeping bag. This basic recipe recommends roasting the turkey unstuffed for an optimally moist bird. Garlic butter is rubbed under the skin to flavor the breast, and chopped onion, parsnip, and carrot are added to the pan to flavor the drippings. The recipe prepares a small turkey that will serve 10 to 15 persons. For a larger bird, cook according to the timetable on page 500; use a meat thermometer as the most accurate means of determining when the turkey is done. It is unnecessary to increase the amounts of the other ingredients when cooking a larger bird.

>   1   turkey (10 to 12 lb)
>   1   clove garlic, crushed
>   1   cup butter, softened
>   Salt
>   2   onions, cut in large chunks
>   2   parsnips, cut in large chunks
>   2   carrots, cut in large chunks

Giblet Gravy

>   Giblets and neck from turkey
>   ¼   cup butter
>   ¼   cup flour
>   Salt and freshly ground pepper

1. Preheat oven to 450° F. Remove innards from turkey and save for Giblet Gravy. Wash turkey and pat dry.

2. Gently free skin from breast meat, starting at neck end and continuing to tail.

3. Mix garlic with butter. Stuff garlic butter under breast skin. For a crisper skin, also butter outside surface. Salt turkey inside and out.

4. Truss turkey (see page 584) and set on a rack in a roasting pan. Surround with chunks of onion, parsnip, and carrot.

5. Set pan on middle rack of oven. Roast at 450° F for 30 minutes. Reduce oven to 325° F and continue to roast for another 1½ hours, or until done to suit, basting every 15 minutes.

6. When turkey is done, remove from pan and allow to rest for 20 to 30 minutes before carving. Set aside pan with drippings to make gravy.

Serves 10 to 15.

The efforts of turkey farmers and marketers to make turkey more than a one-season food are visible in the supermarket. Fresh whole turkeys, as well as turkey parts and processed turkey products, are now widely available the year around. The forms in which turkey, fresh or frozen, are available include: whole birds; halves and quarters; boneless roasts; bone-in and boneless whole, halved, and sliced breasts; fillets; drumsticks; wings; drummettes; thighs; and ground turkey.

Convenience options include prebasted birds, injected with natural ingredients intended to keep the bird moist (properly roasted, a bird will be moist and juicy without prebasting, however); frozen stuffed birds; and pop-up or retractable thermometers that activate when the bird has reached an internal preset temperature determined by the manufacturer.

Giblet Gravy

1. Place giblets and neck from turkey in a saucepan and cover with water. Bring to a boil, then reduce heat and simmer 20 to 30 minutes. Drain giblet stock and reserve.

2. Cut giblets in small cubes and reserve.

3. When turkey is done, remove it from pan and set aside to rest while the gravy is being made. Add at least 1 cup water to roasting pan. Blend water with drippings, stirring and scraping with a wooden spoon to loosen any browned bits that may have stuck to bottom of pan. The water and pan drippings together should equal 2 cups. Reserve this liquid.

4. In a saucepan, melt butter. Whisk in flour and cook over medium heat until golden brown. Stir in reserved giblet stock and liquid from pan drippings. Stir constantly until thickened.

5. Season with salt and pepper. Stir in giblet cubes and serve with roast turkey.

Makes 2 cups.

DUCK

In its domesticated form, the dark-meated duck usually weighs about 4½ pounds. Because it is fattier and bonier than chicken or turkey, a 4½-pound duck will only feed two. Most of the meat is in the breasts, although the legs also offer enjoyable eating.

The rich meat of duck is complemented by fruit. The roasted bird is often partnered with cherries, oranges (as in duck à l'orange), figs, apples, or other fruit. Duck is almost always roasted or grilled because of its considerable fat content. Because the legs take longer to cook than the breast, some cooks remove the breast first and serve it separately; when the legs have finished cooking, they are served as a separate course, often with a green salad. Raw boneless duck breasts may be sautéed or grilled. They have a richness comparable to beef and may be served in similar fashion—with green peppercorns or red wine sauce, for example. Cold roast duck may be used in salads or sliced and served with chutney. In France duckling is considered a spring treat and is often served with spring vegetables such as peas or turnips. In China duck is a favored bird, prepared in dozens of ways. Among the many possibilities: It may be steamed, rubbed with soy sauce, and deep-fried; smoked over tea leaves; or air-dried, roasted, and served in the elaborate series of dishes that constitute Peking duck.

Inventive cooks have created uses for almost all parts of the duck. Chinese cooks braise the gelatinous duck feet. Duck fat is particularly flavorful, good for frying potatoes or omelets. Duck skin may be cut into small pieces and rendered for cracklings to sprinkle over salads. French cooks stuff the duck neck with a sausage mixture, sew it closed, and roast it. Duck liver makes a delicious pâté or may be sautéed in butter and served on toast. Duck foie gras, an expensive delicacy, is the buttery liver from specially fattened ducks. Cooked foie gras is served hot or cold, usually with toast.

Frozen duck is sold in many supermarkets. Fresh duck is available increasingly in specialty markets and is almost always available in Asian poultry markets. Imported duck foie gras is marketed in tins in specialty stores. Recently, domestic fresh duck foie gras has appeared on the market. As of this writing, it is available from specialty wholesalers catering primarily to the restaurant trade.

See Selection, Storage, and Preparation for more information.

■ BROILED DUCK BREASTS WITH APRICOT-MUSTARD GLAZE

Usher in the first cool night of autumn with elegant broiled duck glazed with mustard and apricot jam. To complete the menu, serve Pommes Anna (see page 466), Sautéed Cherry Tomatoes (see page 582), and Baked Pear Tart (see page 423).

> 2 **whole ducks (about 4½ lb each)**
>   **Salt and freshly ground pepper**
> 1 **clove garlic, slivered**

Apricot-Mustard Glaze

> ½ **cup apricot jam**
> 3 **tablespoons Dijon mustard**
> 3 **tablespoons soy sauce**
> 3 **tablespoons honey**
> 1 **clove garlic, minced**

1. Wash ducks and pat dry. Remove innards. Bone ducks so that breasts are removed with skin attached. Reserve duck carcasses for stock and duck legs for another recipe (they can be used for Chinese Duck Salad, page 476).

2. Split duck breasts to make 4 half breasts. Remove visible fat from underside of skin. Season lightly with salt and pepper. Prick holes in skin covering breasts and insert garlic slivers.

3. Prepare Apricot-Mustard Glaze. Brush glaze on both sides of breast halves.

4. Preheat broiler. Broil breast halves, skin side down, about 6 inches from heat for 6 minutes. Turn and broil 2 to 3 minutes more. Be careful not to burn duck (if necessary, lower rack to slow cooking).

5. To serve, slice breasts on the bias and serve with remaining Apricot-Mustard Glaze.

Serves 4.

Apricot-Mustard Glaze   In a small bowl or jar with a lid, thoroughly combine jam, mustard, soy sauce, honey, and minced garlic.

Makes about 1 cup.

Leftovers can be glamorous, as demonstrated by Chinese Duck Salad, served cold on a bed of shredded lettuce and puffy rice vermicelli.

1. In a large, heavy-bottomed skillet, bring stock to a boil. Add duck legs, cover, and return to a boil. Reduce heat to medium-low and simmer, covered, until cooked (about 25 minutes). Remove duck legs and cool completely. When cool, remove skin and discard. Tear meat off bones and cut into small cubes.

2. In a medium bowl combine soy sauce, ginger, and garlic. Add duck meat and toss to coat. Cover and refrigerate 8 to 24 hours.

3. When ready to assemble salad, heat oil in wok to 365° F (measure with a deep-fat thermometer). Fry rice vermicelli, a handful at a time, until it puffs (30 to 60 seconds). Be careful not to let it brown. Remove with slotted spoon and drain on paper towel. Set aside.

4. Place lettuce in a large bowl. Remove duck from marinade with slotted spoon, drain, and pat dry. Toss with lettuce, green onions, and almonds, then with Soy Dressing. Serve surrounded with rice vermicelli.

Serves 4.

Soy Dressing In a small bowl or jar with a lid, combine oil, vinegar, sugar, and soy sauce.

Makes about 2¼ cups.

Recipes: Chicken or Duck Liver Mousse, 372; Curried Chicken or Duck Liver Pâté in Aspic, 416.

GOOSE

Like the duck, the goose is a dark-meat bird with a high proportion of bone and fat. Most of the meat is in the breast. In England, France, Scandinavia, and Germany, goose is the traditional choice for the Christmas feast. Its rich meat is flattered by the flavors of fruit such as apples, prunes, and pears. Because of its high fat content, it is almost always roasted. Some cooks prefer to put onions, apples, and bread in the cavity to flavor the bird and absorb fat; they then cook the stuffing separately to keep it from absorbing all the fat.

A whole goose offers other attractions for the cook. The long neck may be used like a sausage casing, stuffed, tied, and roasted. The fat is very flavorful, excellent for frying potatoes or eggs or for chilling and spreading on toast. In France some geese are force-fed to encourage the development of large livers; this foie gras, an expensive delicacy, resembles an extremely rich, smooth, and buttery pâté. After cooking it may be served hot or cold, usually accompanied by warm toast.

Frozen geese are available in some well-stocked supermarkets the year around. More supermarkets stock frozen geese at Christmas time. Look for fresh geese in specialty markets at Christmas time; most markets require advance ordering.

See Selection, Storage, and Preparation for more information.

■ CHINESE DUCK SALAD

Make this salad to use up the duck legs left over from Broiled Duck Breasts (see page 475). To toast almonds, cook in a small dry skillet over medium-high heat, stirring with a spoon, until golden brown (about 5 minutes).

    4 **cups duck or Chicken Stock (see page 560)**
    4 **duck legs, washed and patted dry**
  ½ **cup soy sauce**
    1 **tablespoon minced fresh ginger**
    1 **clove garlic, minced**
    2 **cups vegetable oil**
    3 **ounces rice vermicelli**
    1 **head iceberg lettuce, washed and shredded**
    2 **green onions, thinly sliced**
  ½ **cup toasted slivered almonds**

Soy Dressing

    1 **cup oil**
  ¾ **cup rice wine vinegar**
  ½ **cup sugar**
    2 **tablespoons soy sauce**

■ BRAISED GOOSE IN HARD CIDER

The hard cider in the pan juices infuses the goose with a wonderful apple flavor.

    2 stalks celery, coarsely chopped
    1 carrot, peeled and coarsely chopped
    1 parsnip, peeled and coarsely chopped
    1 medium onion, quartered
    1 goose (about 14 lb)
       Salt and freshly ground pepper
    4 cups hard cider

Pan Gravy

    ¼ cup flour
    2 cups goose or Chicken Stock (see page 560)
       Salt and freshly ground pepper

1. Preheat oven to 450° F. In a large roasting pan, place celery, carrot, parsnip, and onion.

2. Remove giblets from goose. Wash goose and pat dry; remove excess fat. Pierce skin of goose several times with the tip of a knife. Sprinkle inside and out with salt and pepper. Tie legs together and set goose on vegetables in roasting pan.

3. Roast in center of middle rack of oven for 30 minutes. Reduce heat to 325° F. After roasting for an additional 1½ hours, pour hard cider into bottom of pan. Roast 1½ more hours (a total of 3½ hours), or until done to suit. Periodically skim fat from pan with a bulb baster.

4. When goose is done, remove it from oven; allow it to rest 30 minutes before carving. Serve with Pan Gravy.

Serves 10 to 12.

Pan Gravy Skim off all but ¼ cup fat from pan juices. Place roasting pan with juices over medium-high heat. Add flour and cook until golden brown, stirring constantly. Add stock, stirring and scraping with a wooden spoon to loosen any browned bits that may have stuck to bottom of pan. Cook and stir until texture of gravy is smooth and velvety. Season with salt and pepper.

Makes 3 cups.

SQUAB

The squab is a pigeon bred for the table. The dressed bird usually weighs under 1 pound and has dark meaty breasts with a rich flavor. Squabs are generally roasted or braised, with or without a stuffing. In China squab meat is minced, stir-fried, and served with lettuce wrappers; or is fried whole, carved, and served with a fragrant pepper salt. French cooks serve braised squab with spring peas.

Frozen squabs are available from some specialty markets. Fresh squab may be ordered from some butchers; some Asian poultry markets also carry fresh squab.

See Selection, Storage, and Preparation for more information.

■ SMOKED, STUFFED SQUABS WITH CALVADOS

Smoking the squabs is easy. You will need a kettle grill with cover for this recipe, as the birds smoke while they grill. Soak apple cuttings in water mixed with apple juice for two to four hours. When the fire is hot, put the cuttings on top of the coals, place the squabs on the grill, and set the cover in place.

    ⅓ cup apple juice
    ⅓ cup Calvados or applejack
    ⅓ cup vegetable oil
    2 squabs (about ¾ lb each)

Stuffing

    ¼ cup Calvados or applejack
    ½ pippin apple, cubed
    1 shallot, minced

Calvados Sauce

    ½ cup apple juice
    ¼ cup Calvados or applejack
    1 tablespoon cornstarch mixed with
       2 tablespoons water

1. Make Stuffing. Set aside.

2. In a medium bowl combine apple juice, Calvados, and vegetable oil to make marinade.

3. Wash squabs and pat dry. Set in a pan just big enough to hold both birds. Pour marinade over squabs and marinate in refrigerator for 4 hours.

4. Remove squabs from marinade, reserving marinade for basting, and pat squab dry.

5. Insert Stuffing into squabs and tie legs together with kitchen string; tuck wings under.

6. Prepare fire. When coals are ready, grill squabs 5 inches from heat, breast side down, with cover on grill so that smoke can penetrate meat.

7. After 15 minutes turn squabs breast side up. Continue grilling, basting frequently with marinade, until breast meat springs back slightly when touched (about 10 minutes).

8. To serve, snip kitchen string and remove. Spoon out Stuffing and serve on the side. Smother squabs with Calvados Sauce.

Serves 2.

Stuffing In a small bowl mix together Calvados, apple, and shallot.

Makes about ½ cup.

Calvados Sauce In a small saucepan stir together apple juice, Calvados, and cornstarch paste. Simmer until thickened.

Makes ¾ cup.

QUAIL

Small, dark-meat birds, quail weigh about ½ pound each. Most recipes call for at least two per person. The legs and wings are inconsequential; most of the meat is in the breast. Quail are almost always cooked whole, roasted, braised, panfried, or deep-fried. They may be wrapped with bacon before roasting for added flavor and moisture. They may be stuffed with fresh herbs and then roasted; deep-fried and served with Chinese roasted pepper salt; or panfried in bacon fat and served for breakfast.

Frozen quail are available from some specialty butchers, who can also provide fresh quail by special order. Some Chinese markets also carry fresh quail.

See Selection, Storage, and Preparation for more information.

■ SAUTEED QUAIL WITH RED CURRANT SAUCE

The delicate quail, in their deep red sauce, would make a romantic Valentine's Day menu. Carry out the holiday motif by serving red caviar on toast hearts as a first course.

- 4 quail
  Salt
- 2 tablespoons butter
- 1 tablespoon vegetable oil

Red Currant Sauce

- ¼ cup red currant jelly
- ¼ cup canned gooseberries with juice
- 1 tablespoon red wine vinegar
- ⅛ teaspoon *each* ground cinnamon, ground nutmeg, and ground ginger

1. Wash quail and pat dry; truss. Sprinkle with salt. Heat butter and oil in a medium, heavy-bottomed sauté pan or skillet over medium-high heat.

2. Add quail and sauté until golden brown on all sides (about 4 minutes). Reduce heat to medium-low, cover, and cook until tender (12 to 15 minutes). Remove quail and set aside. Leave drippings in pan for sauce.

3. To serve, discard trussing strings. Return quail to sauté pan; pour sauce over quail and warm gently over medium heat for 2 minutes. Arrange birds on serving platter and spoon sauce over.

Serves 2.

Red Currant Sauce In a small bowl combine jelly, gooseberries with juice, vinegar, and spices. Transfer to a small saucepan and cook over medium heat until jelly melts (about 3 minutes). Pour mixture into sauté pan, stirring and scraping with a wooden spoon to loosen any browned bits that may have stuck to the bottom of the pan. Cook over medium heat until heated through.

Makes about ½ cup.

POUND, TO

To flatten meat to a uniform thickness, usually about ¼ inch, for even cooking and an attractive appearance. Veal scallops are often compressed to ⅛ inch, which enables them to cook in mere seconds. Pounding also tenderizes tougher cuts by breaking down connective tissue that is difficult to chew. To prevent meat from tearing, place it between two sheets of plastic wrap. With the flat bottom of a meat pounder (not the edge, which will shred meat), pound with a downward stroke until meat is evenly flattened.

PREHEAT, TO

To warm an oven or broiler to a specified temperature before food is set in it. Heating oil or another fat in a skillet before adding food serves the same preparatory purpose as does preheating an oven, although it isn't called preheating. Foods that cook in dry heat—baked goods and roasts particularly—need that burst of hot air provided by a preheated oven before cooking or to create a crisp outer coat. Deep-fried foods will be soggy and greasy if cooked at too low a temperature. Preheating is less important for foods that use moist heat, such as stews and casseroles, or for oven-cooked foods that take several hours or more to finish. Most recipes will specify preheating, but some don't, so use your own judgment as to when the step will make a difference in the final product.

PREPARING PAN FOR BAKING

To release cooked food more easily and cleanly, baking pans, casseroles, and baking sheets are often coated with a thin layer of butter, oil, or shortening, or a light film of vegetable cooking spray as a first step. Some pans are also dusted with flour, sugar, crumbs, or grated cheeses. These coatings give batters, including sweet and savory soufflés, something to cling to as they rise. The layer of sugar, crumbs, or cheese adds a crisp coating or sandy texture as well as more flavor to the finished product.

Personal preference most often dictates which fat to use, and whether you want it to be neutral or flavored. Butter imparts a rich, distinctive taste; vegetable shortening, oils, and vegetable cooking spray do not have a flavor of their own. Applying the fat in a thin, even layer is really more important than which fat you choose. If the coating is unevenly applied, there is a chance the food will stick in the bare areas. If the layer is too thick, the food will be greasy. Liquid fats can be wiped on with a pastry brush, with your fingers, or with paper towels. Use your fingers or paper towels for solid fats.

Lining pans with parchment paper, aluminum foil, or waxed paper is another way to prevent sticking. It also facilitates cleanup. Cookies baked on parchment-lined baking sheets can be transferred to cooling racks simply by sliding the paper onto the rack. Sugar-rich meringues are easier to remove after baking if piped onto paper-covered baking sheets.

Nonstick pans should always be coated. Most recipes give instructions for preparing pans for baking. If not, experiment with different methods and use the one that works the best for you.

Recipes and Related Information
Baking Pans, for Batter and Dough, 18; Cake, 77.

PRICKLY PEAR

Also known as tuna, cactus pear, Indian fig, and barbary fig, the prickly pear is the fruit of the prickly pear cactus. It is an egg-shaped fruit, slightly larger than an egg, with skin that ranges from yellow to red. The skin has sharp spikes that are usually removed before it is sent to market. The sweet, moist flesh ranges from salmon or pink to magenta and contains small, hard seeds.

Use Peel and eat raw with lemon or lime (discard seeds). Purée for sorbet, ice cream, and dessert sauce.

Availability Fresh prickly pear can be purchased from September through December in Latin markets and some supermarkets.

Selection Choose firm but not rock-hard fruit with a shiny appearance. Hard ones will soften at room temperature in a few days.

Storage Refrigerate ripe prickly pears in a plastic bag and used within two or three days.

Preparation Remove any remaining sharp spines with pliers. Cut off ends, then peel fruit back from top to bottom with a sharp knife. To remove seeds, press fruit through a sieve or pass through a food mill.

◼ PRICKLY PEAR SNOW

Prickly pear tastes like a seedy watermelon. Prickly pear syrup is delicious as a topping on ice cream, in milk shakes, and in this light, refreshing, "southwestern nouvelle cuisine" sorbet. The sorbet will keep packaged airtight in the freezer two to three weeks.

½ cup sugar
1 cup water
6 prickly pears
1 tablespoon fresh lime or lemon juice
2 egg whites
Pinch cream of tartar
½ teaspoon orange-peel liqueur

1. Heat sugar and the water together in a heavy, 2-quart saucepan over low heat, stirring occasionally until sugar dissolves. Simmer mixture for 10 minutes until it has reduced slightly and thickened but has not yet started to color.

2. Meanwhile, wearing thick rubber or leather gloves, halve prickly pears and spoon out pulp. (Handle prickly pears with care. Even storebought ones may have a few tiny spines that will stick to fingers. Discard shells before removing gloves.) Add prickly pear pulp and lime juice to reduced sugar mixture, and simmer until fruit is mushy (about 20 minutes).

3. Briefly purée prickly pear mixture in a food processor or blender. With a wooden spoon, push purée through a strainer into a bowl. Discard seeds left in strainer. Pour syrupy purée into two pie pans and freeze until partly solid (2½ hours), stirring purée after 1 hour and again 30 minutes later.

4. Beat egg whites with cream of tartar until they are stiff but not dry. Remove frozen purée from freezer and stir again (or purée again in food processor if it has become too firm to stir). Blend in orange liqueur, then fold purée into egg whites. Place sorbet in a serving bowl, cover with plastic wrap, and return to freezer until it chills to the consistency of ice cream (3 to 4 hours). Before serving, place in refrigerator for 30 minutes to soften slightly.

Serves 6 to 8.

Variation Use the syrup yielded at the end of step 3 as a sauce for vanilla ice cream or fresh fruit salad, or to lend a brilliant beet-red color to any fruit dessert.

PROOF, TO

A bread-baking term, *proof* is used two ways. The first meaning refers to the test for the potency of yeast: In a small bowl put ½ cup warm (about 110° F) water. Sprinkle in a pinch of sugar and 1 tablespoon active dry yeast (1 package) or 1 crumbled, compressed, small yeast cake. Stir and let sit 5 to 10 minutes to soften. If the yeast is alive, the surface of the liquid will form a thick foam. There's the proof. A lack of foam indicates that the yeast is most likely dead; discard that batch and begin again with a fresher package.

Proofing also describes the second rising of a yeast dough after it has risen, been punched down, and shaped. The dough sits in a warm spot (75° to 80° F) until it has doubled in bulk and retains the mark of your finger if pressed into it.

Recipes and Related Information
Yeast, 613; Yeast Bread, 613.

PREPARING BAKING PANS

To grease pan, use fingers, paper towel, or brush if using liquid fat. Apply a thin, even layer of butter, margarine, vegetable shortening, or oil, or spray with a fine mist of vegetable cooking spray. Use a light touch or surface of baked good will be gummy.

If lining pan with parchment paper, use pan as a template. Set pan on paper and trace around it with a pencil. Cut out just inside of pencil line. Set in pan and smooth to fit; remove and trim if too large.

If called for, dust pan lightly with flour, crumbs, or sugar. Hold pan at an angle over paper or sink, and tap gently to loosen excess coating. Let excess fall from pan.

PUFF PASTRY

Also called *pâte feuilletée*, puff pastry holds the distinction of being the most versatile, intriguing, and delicious of all the pastry doughs. Like conventional pie and tart pastry, puff pastry is made from very basic ingredients—flour, salt, water, and butter. The dough is much richer in butter than the others, however, and the butter is worked into the dough in a unique manner—not in one step, but repeatedly, through a series of rollings and foldings. What results are paper-thin sheets of dough separated by equally fine layers of fat. During baking the fat melts and releases steam that causes the dough to rise up to ten times its original height.

The dough is leavened solely by steam and hot air, rather than by yeast or chemical leaveners. Folding traps air within the dough. During baking the air fills the many spaces left by the butter when it melts. The air expands from the heat and puffs the pastry. Moisture from water in the dough and from the many layers of butter convert to steam when heated during baking, which also causes the dough to rise.

Close inspection of the airy, golden brown pastry reveals hundreds of separate, crispy layers, one upon the other. The estimate is that more than 700 layers are created by the time the dough and butter have been rolled and folded the traditionally recommended six turns. The flavor and aroma of puff pastry are rich and buttery.

Volumes could be written on the attributes of puff pastry and its many sweet and savory applications. It can be made into pastry cases for all sorts of fillings in many shapes and sizes, freestanding pastry decorations, applied pastry decorations, hors d'oeuvres, cookies, and wrappers for meat, fish, cheese, and fruit *en croûte*.

PUFF PASTRY BASICS

The reputation of puff pastry for being temperamental and time-consuming causes many novice bakers to shy away from attempting to make it. Admittedly, making puff pastry is not a one-step procedure. But the process is neither difficult nor time-consuming. Each step actually takes only 5 to 10 minutes to accomplish. Between steps, the dough rests in the refrigerator for about one hour. If you subtract the resting time from the total amount of time needed to make the dough, you will see that actual working time is only 30 to 40 minutes.

Puff pastry dough is made from two basic elements: (1) a smooth, elastic dough called the *détrempe* and (2) a block of butter beaten until pliable. When dough and block of butter are the same temperature and consistency, the butter is wrapped up in the dough, and this lump of dough-wrapped butter is given six turns. To give the dough a turn, it is rolled out into a rectangle, folded into thirds like a business letter, and rotated a quarter turn (90 degrees) on the work surface. Each turn is an exact repetition of this rolling, folding, and turning process.

The end product of this turning is virgin puff pastry: puff pastry that has been given six turns and has not been rolled out, cut out, or shaped in any way. Some pastries require virgin puff pastry and some pastries can be made with puff pastry trimmings and scraps.

Don't throw away the trimmings left over after virgin puff pastry is cut. Layer scraps, wrap, and refrigerate for at least one hour. (They can be stored up to two days in the refrigerator or can be frozen for up to one month.) The scraps can then be rolled out into a sheet and used. All pastries can be made with virgin puff pastry, but in some cases—where a high, puffy rising is unnecessary—the scraps will suffice. They can be used quite successfully for the following: as the base for a dessert or as one of the layers of a dessert; for *mille-feuilles* or napoleons; as pastry cases for pies (blind baked without filling) to be used as a first course, an entrée, or a dessert.

INGREDIENTS FOR PUFF PASTRY

Use the ingredients recommended in the recipe. A combination of pastry flour and all-purpose flour yields a dough that will roll out easily and has enough strength to be rolled out without tearing and baked without breaking. The resulting dough can hold its shape when baked, but remains tender. You can use 50 percent pastry flour (soft flour) and 50 percent all-purpose flour (a combination of hard and soft flours) or 75 percent pastry flour and 25 percent hard flour (bread flour high in gluten). Fresh, cold, unsalted butter and ice water are essential.

PREPARING PUFF PASTRY

To produce the characteristic layers of dough and butter, the butter should be neither too soft nor too hard. Ideally, the dough and butter should be of equal temperature and consistency, which is why the détrempe is chilled before the first rolling. Very soft butter will blend too thoroughly with the dough. The result will be crumbly rather than multilayered and flaky, much like a short pie crust. Butter that is too hard will shear through the dough, leaving holes that will allow steam and air, which leaven the dough, to escape.

The butter also should be plastic, which means that it can be manipulated. Usually, a recipe recommends that you beat the cold butter with a rolling pin to make it pliable, although not work it so much that it loses its chill.

Temperature is critical, not only for butter but for all the ingredients, the equipment, and the room you are working in. The goal is to keep everything cool enough so the layers of butter stay separate from the layers of dough. Try to make puff pastry during the coolest part of the day, and on a day when you plan to be home for several hours. On warm days, chill the work surface and rolling pin for 30 minutes. If you have room, you can chill a portable marble slab or cutting board in the refrigerator. Otherwise, place on the work surface a rimmed baking sheet filled with ice cubes.

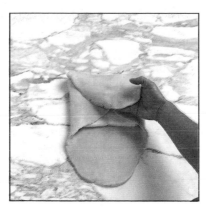

WORKING WITH PUFF PASTRY

Roll chilled détrempe (dough) into a rounded cross shape. Work surface and rolling pin should be chilled and lightly floured. When rolling, do not press down hard on dough; use even pressure. Roll dough thinner at edges.

Place square of cold butter in center of dough cross. Wrap butter in dough as shown. If dough seems warm, return to refrigerator 10 minutes before rolling.

Complete wrap as if forming an envelope. Then for each turn, roll dough into a rectangle. Fold in thirds as if you were folding a business letter. Rotate a quarter turn clockwise (90 degrees), square edges, and either roll again or refrigerate, as directed in recipe. Remove any excess flour by brushing dough with a pastry brush before and after folding.

The dough also should chill between every two turns. This firms up the butter and relaxes the dough, making it easier to roll out without compressing the layers. The dough should also be allowed to rest in the refrigerator again just before it's baked so the baked puff pastry will maintain its original shape and size.

A marble work surface is best for puff pastry, as it is for other pastry doughs. It naturally maintains a temperature 20° F cooler than the air, and because it is nonporous, pastry won't stick to it. However, marble is expensive and quite heavy. An alternative is a cutting board made of white polycarbonate if you can find one of sufficiently large size. If you have one of these portable boards, make a lot of pastry, and have room in your refrigerator, store board on a refrigerator shelf to keep it at the proper cold temperature. Countertops made of plastic laminate are also suitable for making puff pastry. Chill when necessary with ice cubes and tray as described in Preparing Puff Pastry (see opposite page).

**CUTTING PUFF PASTRY:
UNBAKED AND BAKED**

Always cut puff pastry dough when cold and use a sharp knife. Cut straight down into dough with a clean, sharp movement. Do not drag knife through warm dough or you will seal layers of dough together, making it difficult for them to separate and rise to their fullest volume. Always trim away folded edge of puff pastry; if left, folded edge won't rise. Large pastries like vol-au-vents (see page 483) sometimes shrink out of shape in the oven. To help them rise straight, cut them at a slight angle: Slant the knife so that the edge of the pastry is slightly wider at the bottom. Flip pastry so top is wider. As it bakes, the pastry will rise evenly.

To make rectangular puff pastry cases out of baked pastry dough, slice puff pastry horizontally with a serrated knife. This will create a case, with a top and bottom, like a box, which can be filled with your choice of filling.

To serve pastry, cut with a serrated knife held at a 45-degree angle to the pastry. Use a gentle sawing motion. Cut carefully because puff pastry is very fragile and flaky. Using a nonserrated knife may crush pastry and cause it to splinter.

**REFRIGERATING OR FREEZING
PUFF PASTRY**

After four turns, unbaked dough may be wrapped in plastic wrap and refrigerated for two to three days, or it may be wrapped well and frozen for one month. Thaw, wrapped, in refrigerator (several hours or overnight). Before using, give pastry one more turn. It is best not to freeze pastry in a self-defrosting freezer for more than one week.

After dough is cut and shaped, let it rest for up to one hour in the refrigerator. Then it should be either baked immediately or frozen as follows: Place pastry on a tray, freeze, remove from tray, wrap well, and freeze for up to one month. Frozen puff pastry shells and other puff pastries may be blind baked without thawing; brush with egg wash and bake.

Baked pastries don't refrigerate well. To freeze, cool completely, freeze on a tray until firm, wrap well or place in freezer containers, and freeze for six to eight weeks. Loosen wrapping and thaw at room temperature. Crisp pastry in 350° F oven 5 to 10 minutes.

■ **CLASSIC PUFF PASTRY**
Pâte feuilletée

To keep the pastry light and puffy, don't apply too much pressure to the dough when rolling or give the dough an excessive number of turns.

> 1 **cup plus 1 tablespoon unbleached all-purpose flour**
> 1 **cup plus 1 tablespoon unbleached white pastry flour**
> 1 **teaspoon salt**
> 3½ **tablespoons cold unsalted butter, cut into small pieces**
> ½ **cup plus 1 tablespoon ice water**
> 1 **cup cold unsalted butter**

1. *In a food processor:* Place flours, salt, and the 3½ tablespoons butter in bowl of food processor fitted with metal blade. Process with 1-second pulses until butter is cut into flour and resembles coarse meal. *To make by hand:* Combine flours and salt. Cut in butter with pastry blender or two knives.

2. Put flour mixture in a medium bowl and sprinkle with a scant ½ cup ice water; toss with fingertips to moisten. Add more water, a few drops at a time, until mixture is just moist enough to be gathered into a ball. Knead two or three times to form a soft, smooth ball of dough.

3. Cut an *x* into top of dough, ½ inch deep, with a knife; wrap well. Refrigerate until firm (2 to 3 hours). Can be refrigerated overnight.

To Wrap Butter in Détrempe and Give Dough Six Turns

1. Remove *détrempe* from refrigerator. Let sit out to warm slightly (10 minutes).

2. Place butter between two pieces of waxed paper on work surface and beat with rolling pin to soften. Beat until butter is pliable and smooth but still cold. Pat butter into a 6-inch square.

3. When détrempe and butter are the same temperature and consistency (test by inserting a finger into each), roll out détrempe into a rounded cross shape (see photographs, page 481) 12 inches in diameter on an ice-cold, lightly floured surface (marble is best). Roll edges of dough thinner than center.

4. Place square of butter in center of dough and wrap dough around it as shown (see photographs, page 481).

5. Return dough to refrigerator for 10 minutes if it has warmed up too much in wrapping process.

6. Place cool dough on a cold, lightly floured surface with vertical seam pointing toward you. Press dough down with rolling pin to flatten slightly. Begin rolling dough at end farthest from you, always rolling away from you, never sideways or toward you. Ease up on rolling pin when you come to ends of dough to avoid pushing butter

out of the dough. As you roll out dough and fold it, keep sides and ends parallel and thickness even. If butter breaks through dough at any time during rolling process, dust problem areas generously with flour and then continue rolling dough.

Turn 1   Roll dough into an 8- by 18-inch rectangle, with the short side facing you. Brush dough with soft pastry brush to remove flour. Fold bottom third of rectangle up (brush away any flour with pastry brush), then fold top third down, as if it were a business letter. Dust off excess flour and rotate dough a quarter turn clockwise (90 degrees) so seam is on your left. Square up edges by tapping them with rolling pin.

Turn 2   Roll out dough as before. Fold in thirds as before (like a business letter). Square up edges of dough. Mark dough with two finger indentations to indicate number of turns. Wrap and refrigerate for 1 hour. After 1 hour proceed to turns 3 and 4. Do not store dough longer than 1 hour.

Turn 3   Remove dough from refrigerator and allow to warm slightly if very stiff and cold. Place seam on your left, and roll and fold as if for turns 1 and 2.

Turn 4   Turn dough a quarter turn clockwise (90 degrees) and roll and fold again. Mark dough with four finger indentations, wrap, and refrigerate at least 1 hour, or until ready to use. Dough can be frozen at this point or refrigerated 2 to 3 days.

Turns 5 and 6   Give dough two more turns and roll out to thickness specified in recipe. Cut or shape as directed. Rest 1 hour. Bake at 450° F unless otherwise indicated. After dough has been given six turns, it is best to roll out, shape it, and either bake it or freeze shaped dough. The best time to store unshaped puff pastry dough is after four turns.

Makes 21 ounces puff pastry.

■ **QUICK AND EASY PUFF PASTRY**

This quick method is like the one for Classic Puff Pastry in that it calls for repeated rolling, folding, and turning. The difference is in how the butter is incorporated into the dough. (Note that the butter must be frozen 30 minutes before using.) With this method, you can achieve very similar results with half the effort. The finished product is exceptionally light and flaky, suitable for tarts, twists, and turnovers. The dough may be frozen, well wrapped, for several months, or refrigerated for up to three days. If it is frozen, thaw in refrigerator overnight before using.

> 1⅓ **cups all-purpose flour**
> ⅔ **cup cake or pastry flour**
> 1 **teaspoon salt**
> 14 **tablespoons unsalted butter, cut in pieces and frozen 30 minutes**
> ½ to ¾ **cup very cold whipping cream**

1. Combine flours and salt in a bowl or on a marble work surface. Cut in butter coarsely until it is reduced to ¼-inch bits. Add ½ cup cream and mix gently, adding additional cream if necessary, until mixture just forms a ball. Amount of cream will vary depending on humidity and type of flour.

2. Roll dough out on a lightly floured surface into a rectangle measuring approximately 8 by 20 inches. Fold the two 8-inch ends toward center until they meet in middle. Then fold one half over the other. Wrap in plastic and refrigerate dough 1 hour. Repeat rolling and folding process twice, refrigerating dough 1 hour after each time. Repeat rolling and folding one more time. Puff pastry is now ready to use.

Makes about 1 pound puff pastry.

■ VOL-AU-VENT

One of the classic French pastry cases for either savory or sweet fillings, a vol-au-vent looks lovely as a centerpiece for a first course or as the featured dish on a buffet table. The pastry is shaped and trimmed so that a lid is formed from the upper pastry layer. A *bouchée* is a miniature vol-au-vent. *Bouchée* is the French word for *little mouthful,* which is just what they are: little mouthfuls of flaky, filled pastry. Bouchées are a useful part of an hors d'oeuvres repertoire, for they can be partnered with just about any type of filling, including mushrooms and chopped chicken livers sautéed in wine, creamed chicken or sweetbreads, spicy curried crab or shrimp, or creamed asparagus.

> Classic Puff Pastry (opposite page)
> 2 egg yolks, beaten with a pinch of salt

1. Roll out pastry ¼ inch thick. Using a plate as a guide, or your own pattern made of cardboard, cut out two 8-inch circles. Cover and refrigerate dough circles 30 minutes. Gather pastry scraps and reroll ⅛ inch thick; cover and refrigerate.

2. Place one circle of pastry on a parchment-lined baking sheet. With a 5-inch-diameter plate or cardboard pattern as a guide, cut a circle in center of other round of chilled dough, but do not cut through. Brush egg wash around outer 3 inches of full circle, making sure that egg does not drip down sides of dough. Cover with second circle, pressing dough just gently enough to seal two pieces together. Freeze 10 minutes. Remove rolled scraps from refrigerator and cut into fancy shapes for decorating lid of pastry.

3. When dough is chilled but not frozen, mark a chevron pattern with a very sharp knife on surface of outer rim of upper circle. Use egg wash to glue on decorative cutouts made from scraps. Freeze 20 minutes (if freezing longer, wrap well with plastic wrap).

4. Preheat oven to 425° F. Remove pastry from freezer and brush surface with beaten egg, making sure that egg does not drip down sides. Bake until golden brown and

puffy (25 to 35 minutes). If dough starts to brown too much before pastry is ready, lower temperature after about 20 minutes to 400° F.

5. Remove from oven and carefully cut around inner circle of dough with a very sharp knife and a gentle, sawing motion. Remove this lid and, with a fork or spoon, scoop out any soft, uncooked dough from inside. Cool completely and fill with desired filling.

Makes 1 Vol-au-Vent.

Bouchées Follow Vol-au-Vent recipe, but cut out rounds with a 2-inch biscuit cutter. Use a small sharp knife or a 1-inch biscuit cutter to make small lids on half of the 2-inch rounds. Brush unmarked 2-inch rounds lightly with egg. Position marked rounds directly on top. Transfer to parchment-lined baking sheets and chill or freeze 10 minutes, if desired; brush again with egg wash and bake in a preheated 475° F oven 5 minutes; reduce heat to 400° F and bake an additional 5 to 8 minutes or until done. Cool Bouchées on a rack. When cool, remove lid and scoop out the soft centers.

Makes about 12 Bouchées.

This fresh fruit tart band is filled with pastry cream, topped with peach halves and blueberries, and then glazed with apricot jam. This dessert can be made with almost any fruits in season. The recipe is on page 485.

A red-hot metal skewer burns caramelized lines into the sugar on top of Mille-Feuilles. The Mille-Feuilles features three layers of puff pastry filled with vanilla pastry cream.

■ MILLE-FEUILLES

In French *mille feuilles* means *a thousand leaves,* and that is what you get—many thin, delicate leaves of puff pastry. Here they are layered with rum pastry cream to form the base for Mille-Feuilles and for napoleons. Both preparations begin with a long, narrow pastry that is either dusted with confectioners' sugar (for Mille-Feuilles) or iced with marbled glaze (napoleons). Assembled as a large pastry, it is then cut into small servings. Puff pastry is very flaky and should be cut with a serrated knife and a sawing motion. It is best when assembled just before serving. Puff pastry trimmings can be used instead of virgin puff pastry.

> 2½ cups Pastry Cream (see page 251)
>   Classic Puff Pastry with 6 turns (see page 482)
>   1 cup apricot jam, melted and sieved
>   2 teaspoons rum
>   ¼ cup whipping cream
>   1 cup toasted sliced almonds, coarsely chopped
>   ⅓ cup confectioners' sugar

1. Prepare Pastry Cream and chill.

2. Roll out Classic Puff Pastry into a 12- by 18-inch rectangle, ⅛ inch thick; chill until firm (about 20 minutes). Cut into three equal rectangles that measure 6 inches by 12 inches each. Prick each rectangle all over. Place on parchment-lined baking sheets, cover, and refrigerate 30 minutes. If you have an oven and baking sheets that will accommodate the 12- by 18-inch sheet of puff pastry, this large sheet can be pricked all over and baked whole. Then, after baking, it can be cut into three equal strips with a serrated knife.

3. Preheat oven to 425° F. Cover pastry strips or whole sheet with parchment paper. Set another baking sheet on top of each pastry layer to weight dough. Bake 10 minutes. Lift up baking sheet and parchment paper, prick dough again, replace top baking sheet and parchment, and bake 5 minutes more. Reprick dough. When pastry is browning and appears to be set, remove baking pan and parchment paper from top of pastry. When pastry is crisp, golden brown, and thoroughly baked, remove from oven. Transfer to wire racks and set aside to cool.

4. Trim pastry rectangles with a serrated knife so they are all the same size. Reserve flattest layer for top. Cut out a cardboard rectangle slightly smaller than puff pastry rectangles to use as a base for the cake. Wrap cardboard with aluminum foil.

5. Place one of the three pieces of puff pastry on the foil-wrapped cardboard. Brush this pastry with a thin layer of warm apricot jam. Stir rum into Pastry Cream. Whip cream until stiff and fold into Pastry Cream (see Note).

6. Spread half of Pastry Cream on first layer of pastry. Place second layer on top. Brush with a thin layer of jam. Spread all but ¼ cup of remaining cream on second layer. Place third layer of pastry on top with smoothest side up. Ice long sides of cake with remaining cream and press toasted almonds on sides.

7. Sift a fine layer of confectioners' sugar evenly over top of cake. Heat a long metal skewer over stove burner (gas burners work best) until red-hot. Hold skewer at a 45-degree angle to long sides of cake with point angled toward top left corner of cake. Burn lines in the confectioners' sugar 1½ inches apart on top of cake. Reheat skewer as necessary to create dark caramelized lines in the sugar. To create a crosshatch pattern, burn another set of lines beginning with skewer angled toward upper right corner of cake.

Serves 6.

Note If you must assemble cake several hours before serving, you can add a small amount of gelatin to Pastry Cream. Sprinkle 2 teaspoons gelatin over 2 tablespoons water or rum. When gelatin is spongy, place bowl over hot water (double boiler) and stir to dissolve gelatin. Cool over ice until syrupy. Stir into Pastry Cream just before folding in whipped cream.

PUFF PASTRY TART BAND

Showcase fresh seasonal fruits in a puff pastry tart band. Create colorful combinations of flavors and textures by using more than one kind of fruit on a tart. Raspberries can be combined with sliced figs or fresh poached peaches. Or arrange peach halves down the center of the band and edge with fresh blueberries. Let each peach half equal one serving. Kiwi slices look pretty with strawberries. Puff pastry scraps may be used in place of virgin puff pastry to make tart band.

> 1¼ **cups Pastry Cream (see page 251)**
> ½ **recipe Classic Puff Pastry with 6 turns (see page 482)**
> 1 **egg yolk lightly beaten with 1 teaspoon water**
> 1 **tablespoon fruit liqueur or brandy**
> ¼ **cup whipping cream or Crème Fraîche (see page 161)**
> 3 **cups fresh raspberries, hulled, halved strawberries, or sliced fruit**
> ¼ **cup apricot preserves, sieved (for light-colored fruits) or currant jelly (for dark fruits)**
> 1 **tablespoon liqueur or brandy**

1. Prepare Pastry Cream and chill.

2. To prepare tart band: Roll out Classic Puff Pastry into an 8- by 16-inch rectangle that is ⅛ thick. Cover and refrigerate until firm.

3. Cut out three cardboard templates with the following dimensions: 5 inches by 15½ inches, ⅞ inch by 15½ inches, and ⅞ inch by 3¼ inches .

4. When dough is well chilled, use cardboard templates and a long, sharp knife to cut out one 15½- by 5-inch rectangle of dough for tart base, two 15½- by ⅞-inch strips of dough for side walls of tart, and two 3¼- by ⅞-inch strips of dough for ends of tart.

5. Place large rectangle of puff pastry (base) on a parchment-lined baking sheet. Prick all over with a fork. Brush 1-inch border at edge of dough with cold water. Place thin strips of dough on moistened border to form tart walls and lightly press into place. Score edges of tart with back of a small knife, making ⅛-inch-deep marks every ¼ inch along border. Cover and refrigerate 30 minutes.

6. Preheat oven to 425° F. Brush top only of narrow strips (walls) with egg wash. Bake 20 minutes, or until tart is puffed and light brown. Lower oven to 400° F and bake until golden brown and done. Cool completely on wire rack before filling.

7. To assemble tart: Stir fruit liqueur into Pastry Cream with a wooden spoon. Stiffly whip cream into Pastry Cream. Spread a ¼-inch layer of cream on bottom of tart. Arrange fresh fruit on top of cream. Melt preserves or jelly in small saucepan until bubbly; stir in liqueur to make glaze. Brush glaze over fruit.

Serves 6 to 8.

CHEESE PALMIERS

Rolled in sugar, dainty *palmiers* (palm leaves) can be eaten with dessert; rolled in salt or grated cheese, they become a savory to enjoy with cocktails or wine.

> **Quick and Easy Puff Pastry (see page 482)**
> 1½ **cups freshly grated Parmesan cheese**

1. On a surface covered with grated Parmesan, roll out puff pastry dough into a rectangle 8 inches wide by 12 inches long by ⅛ inch thick.

2. Fold two 8-inch sides toward center, meeting in middle. Dust surface lightly with cheese. Then fold top half of dough down over bottom half. Dust dough with any remaining Parmesan. Chill dough, wrapped in plastic, for 1 hour.

3. Preheat oven to 350° F. Cut roll into ¼-inch widths. Place on ungreased baking sheets, widely separated. Bake until golden brown (20 to 25 minutes). Serve warm, or cool on a rack and store in an airtight container for up to 2 weeks.

Makes about 50 palmiers.

Quick puff pastry dusted with Parmesan can be turned into buttery Cheese Palmiers, to serve warm or cool with cocktails or red wine. Provide plates or large napkins: The palmiers are deliciously flaky.

To make Raspberry Feuillantines, a puff pastry rectangle is baked, then split horizontally and filled with vanilla pastry cream, raspberries, and Chantilly Cream. Use a large open-star tip to pipe the cream.

■ RASPBERRY FEUILLANTINES

Feuillantines are rectangles of puff pastry that are decorated and baked to form pastry cases. These elegant containers are a perfect pastry to follow any dinner party. Here they hold kirsch-flavored pastry cream, fresh raspberries or strawberries, and Chantilly Cream.

> 1¼ cups Pastry Cream (see page 251)
>   Classic Puff Pastry with 6 turns (see page 482)
> 1 egg yolk lightly beaten with 1 teaspoon water
> 1 tablespoon kirsch or other liqueur
> 4½ cups fresh raspberries, or halved or quartered fresh strawberries
> 2½ cups Chantilly Cream (see page 252)

1. Prepare Pastry Cream and chill.

2. To prepare feuillantines: Roll out Classic Puff Pastry into a 12- by 14-inch rectangle that is ¼ inch thick. Place on a parchment-lined baking sheet and refrigerate until very firm (about 20 minutes).

3. Meanwhile cut out a cardboard rectangle that is 2¾ inches by 5 inches to use as a pattern. Using this pattern, cut out eight rectangles of puff pastry from chilled dough with a sharp knife. Turn each rectangle of dough over and place on parchment-lined baking sheet. Cover and refrigerate 1 hour.

4. Gather scraps into a ball; chill. When scraps are firm, roll out very thin. Place on a baking sheet and freeze briefly to chill dough. Cut out small leaves, flowers, stems, and other designs from dough to decorate tops of

rectangles. Brush tops of rectangles with egg wash. Arrangle cutouts decoratively on top of each rectangle. Chill 20 minutes. Rectangles may be frozen at this point. The frozen puff pastry dough may be baked unfilled and without thawing.

5. Preheat oven to 425° F. Brush top of each rectangle with egg wash. Bake 20 minutes. Lower oven to 400° F and continue baking until golden brown and puffy. Cool on wire racks. Store in dry place at room temperature until ready to fill.

6. To assemble: Split each rectangle in half horizontally with a serrated knife, creating a bottom and a top. Remove any uncooked dough from center. Place bottoms on dessert plates.

7. Stir kirsch into Pastry Cream. Spoon 2 tablespoons Pastry Cream into each bottom. Sprinkle fresh berries on top of cream.

8. Prepare Chantilly Cream. Place Chantilly Cream in a pastry bag fitted with a large, open-star tip. Pipe a layer of rosettes on top of berries. Place puff pastry tops on filled bottoms. Decorate plate with a few berries. Serve immediately while pastry is still warm.

Makes 8 pastries.

> ***Recipes and Related Information***
> *Brie or Camembert in Puff Pastry, 112; Cake and Pastry Tools, 89.*

PUNCH DOWN, TO

A bread-making term that means to put your fist gently into risen yeast dough to deflate it. At this point the dough has lightened from a heavy mass into an inflated foam due to the action of the gases given off by yeast during fermentation. These gases are trapped by strands of gluten formed when the dough was mixed and cause this gluten network to expand.

Yeast doughs are punched down to avoid overstretching and breaking the gluten strands. This step also creates more gas bubbles, which means a wider distribution of carbon dioxide in the dough and a more even grain when the bread is baked.

Actually, you don't really have to punch the dough; if you lift it gently, it will collapse in the same way.

Recipes and Related Information
Yeast, 613; Yeast Bread, 613.

PUREE, TO; PUREE

To blend, sieve, or process food into a soft, smooth consistency; the food that results from this process. A purée is a thick liquid made from finely ground, cooked vegetables, fruits, grains, or legumes. Familiar purées include applesauce, mashed potatoes, and pumpkin pie filling. Purées are the primary flavor base for many ice creams, mousses, pâtés, soups, and sauces. Purées add more nutrition when thickening a soup or sauce than do flour, fat, or dairy products.

Prepare food for puréeing by washing, trimming blemishes, and removing seeds. Skins should be scrubbed but do not always have to be removed. Hard-skinned vegetables, however, such as pumpkins and winter squash, should be peeled; peeling most other foods is a matter of personal taste. Cook food until tender in stock or water, then purée with some of the cooking liquid (for soups) or a few tablespoons of butter (for vegetables). Most fruits and vegetables puree best while still warm. Mash food with a potato masher, if desired, then purée by pressing through a fine strainer; or cut into uniform pieces and purée in a food processor or blender, or with a food mill. Although unnecessary, using a blender or food processor is the easiest method. A food mill is useful for puréeing fibrous vegetables such as celery and watercress.

Different foods can be cooked separately or combined for purées. Nonstarch foods such as beans and tomatoes produce very liquid purées, which are good for sauces. Starchy vegetables such as carrots, potatoes, and parsnips produce thicker purées.

Serve purees immediately, or store in the refrigerator for up to four days or in the freezer for up to one month. Reheat in a double boiler or in a heavy-bottomed saucepan over low heat.

In general, 1 pound of trimmed and cleaned raw fruits and vegetables makes about 2 cups of purée. Thick-skinned vegetables and pitted fruits are an exception. For these foods, about 1 pound of raw food yields 1 cup of purée. One-half pound of beans makes 2½ cups of purée. When using purée as a thickener, 1 cup of puréed potato or a similar starchy vegetable is enough to thicken 2 quarts of vegetable soup.

■ VEGETABLE PUREES

A delicious variation for serving vegetables, purées are good with broiled, baked, or sautéed meats. Almost any vegetable is suitable; the list below gives some suggestions. If you wish to serve more than one, prepare them separately and serve them side by side or swirled together on the plate. Purées can also be made into soup (see instructions at end of recipe).

> 1 **pound fresh vegetables, trimmed**
> 1 **tablespoon butter or margarine**
> ¼ **to ½ cup half-and-half**
> **Salt and freshly ground pepper, to taste**

1. Cut vegetables into pieces of even size. Steam until tender in a small amount of water. Drain, reserving any liquid for soups, if desired.

2. Place vegetables and butter in food processor or blender. Process until smooth.

3. With machine running, slowly add half-and-half to make a smooth, creamy purée. Season to taste with salt and pepper.

Serves 4 to 6.

Variation Herbs and spices add another dimension to vegetable purées. Here are a few suggestions.

Broccoli Add a pinch of cayenne pepper.

Carrots Add fresh or dried dill to taste.

Cauliflower Add curry powder or ½ cup shredded Swiss or Cheddar cheese. Dust with paprika or serve with a purée of contrasting color.

Parsnips Add ground allspice or ground nutmeg to taste.

Spinach Add ground nutmeg to taste.

Zucchini, pattypan, or crookneck squash Add a few sprigs of dill.

Puréed Vegetable Soup Blend vegetable purée with enough chicken or beef stock to make a soupy mixture. Gently heat in saucepan until warmed throughout.

Recipes and Related Information
Ice Cream and Frozen Dessert, 308; Mousse, 372; Pâté and Terrine, 416; Persimmon Pudding, 430; Pumpkin Purée Filling, 438; Sauce, 512; Stock and Soup, 558.

Q&R

QUICK BREAD

Aptly named, quick breads are relatively fast to assemble and bake because they are made with leavenings other than yeast and therefore don't require a preliminary rising before they are put in the oven. Cream puffs, popovers, biscuits, muffins, corn bread, pancakes and waffles, sweet loaves, and quick coffee cakes are all members of this family of baked goods.

Quick breads may be grouped by the type of leavening used and/or by whether they are made from a batter or a dough. Cream puffs and popovers (and their English sibling, Yorkshire pudding) are leavened by steam. Others depend on baking powder and/or baking soda for their volume. Batter-based quick breads include popovers, pancakes, and waffles, each made from a thin, runny mixture known as a pour batter, which has an equal amount of flour and liquid. By increasing the proportion of dry to liquid ingredients, a pour batter thickens into a drop batter, used for some biscuits, corn bread, loaves, and dumplings. Even thicker are soft doughs, which have a three to one ratio of flour to liquid. They are stiff enough to be manipulated by hand. Cut biscuits, scones, and doughnuts are made from soft dough.

All quick breads have a tender, moist, and light texture. The crumb can be slightly coarse and breadlike like the classic muffin, flaky like a biscuit, or velvety like a cake, depending on how the ingredients are mixed together. For batters (muffins, sweet loaves, and corn bread), the dry ingredients are well combined and then quickly, but with a light hand, blended with the liquids. Overworking the batter may cause tunnels or other undesirable characteristics. For doughs (biscuits and scones, for example), solid shortening (butter, margarine, or vegetable shortening) is added to the dry ingredients and the mixture worked until the particles of shortening are uniformly the texture of coarse crumbs. For many fruit and/or nut loaves, fat is creamed with sugar and eggs, dry ingredients are folded in alternately with liquid, and nuts and/or fruit are added last.

Diversity, as well as fast assembly, adds to the appeal of quick breads. By experimenting with ingredients and their proportions, as well as with the way you mix and shape the batter or dough, you can produce endless variations of a basic recipe.

The following recipes are for sweet loaves. Other types of quick breads are covered elsewhere; see Recipes and Related Information on page 493.

BAKING, COOLING, AND STORING QUICK BREAD LOAVES

Sweet quick bread loaves, served with a spread such as butter, jam, or whipped cream cheese, are a delightful accompaniment to coffee or tea. They are moist, keep well if wrapped airtight, and actually improve in flavor if left to sit for a day. Like all quick breads, they can be made in minutes and generally bake in one hour or a little less.

For best results, use the pan called for in the recipe. Even if the pan has a nonstick finish, it should be greased and floured before filling. Typically, the pans used for quick bread loaves are the standard 5- by 9- by 3-inch size or the slightly smaller 4½- by 8½- by 2½-inch version. Many recipes make enough batter for two loaves; if you make these breads often, buy two pans of the same size. Some recipes, such as Boston Brown Bread, bake in coffee cans or vegetable cans. Fill pans one half to two thirds full and spread batter with a spatula to distribute it evenly. Bake in the center of a preheated oven until a wooden skewer inserted in the center comes out free of crumbs. It is usual, even characteristic, for a crack to form across the top of a quick bread loaf, so don't consider the bread a failure if this occurs.

If possible, let the cooled loaves ripen at least several hours, preferably overnight, wrapped well in plastic wrap and aluminum foil. They should stay fresh three or four days. To freeze, wrap tightly in plastic wrap and aluminum foil and label; they will maintain quality two to four months. Thaw in wrapping at room temperature. To warm, set loaf in a baking pan, cover loosely with foil, and heat in a 350° F oven about 10 minutes (longer if not at room temperature).

■ ZUCCHINI BREAD

Try this flavorful version of a favorite loaf bread to use up a bountiful zucchini crop. If possible, prepare the bread a day ahead to better develop its taste and ease of slicing.

       3 cups flour
       1 tablespoon baking powder
       1 teaspoon salt
      ½ teaspoon ground cinnamon
      ½ teaspoon freshly grated nutmeg
      ½ teaspoon ground cloves
      ¼ teaspoon ground allspice
      ½ cup milk
       2 eggs, lightly beaten
      ½ cup vegetable oil
    1½ cups firmly packed brown sugar
    2½ cups grated zucchini
       2 cups chopped walnuts

1. Preheat oven to 350° F. Grease and lightly flour two 4½- by 8½-inch loaf pans.

2. In a large bowl sift together flour, baking powder, salt, cinnamon, nutmeg, cloves, and allspice. In a small bowl combine milk, eggs, oil, and sugar; pour into dry ingredients, stirring to combine. Add zucchini and walnuts, and stir just to combine.

3. Divide batter evenly between prepared pans and bake until a wooden skewer inserted into the center comes out clean (about 1 hour). Cool in pans on wire rack 15 minutes; turn out onto wire rack to cool completely.

Makes 2 loaves.

■ TOASTED COCONUT-BANANA BREAD

A generous measure of coconut lends a tropical taste to this favorite fruit-nut bread. It's the perfect use for almost overripe bananas. For best flavor, wrap the cooled bread and let sit at least one day.

   1 **cup grated coconut**
   2 **cups flour**
   1 **tablespoon baking powder**
   1 **teaspoon ground cinnamon**
  ½ **teaspoon** *each* **salt and baking soda**
  ¾ **cup sugar**
   1 **cup finely chopped walnuts**
   1 **egg**
  ¼ **cup milk**
  ⅓ **cup vegetable oil**
   1 **teaspoon vanilla extract**
   2 **soft, ripe bananas**

1. Preheat oven to 350° F. Grease and lightly flour a 4½- by 8½-inch loaf pan. Spread coconut in a shallow pan and bake, stirring occasionally, until lightly toasted (12 to 15 minutes). Set aside to cool.

2. In a large bowl mix flour, baking powder, cinnamon, salt, baking soda, and sugar. Stir in walnuts and coconut.

3. Beat egg with milk, oil, and vanilla until well combined. Mash bananas (you should have about 1 cup); blend with egg mixture. Add banana mixture to dry ingredients, stirring just until blended.

4. Spread in prepared pan and bake until loaf is well browned and a wooden skewer inserted in the center comes out clean (50 to 60 minutes).

5. Cool in pan 15 minutes on wire rack; turn out onto wire rack to cool completely.

Makes 1 loaf.

■ PUMPKIN HARVEST BREAD

Spicy and moist, pumpkin bread makes a fine and somewhat unconventional accompaniment to hearty autumn fare such as bean soup or baked beans.

   2 **cups flour**
   2 **teaspoons baking powder**
   1 **teaspoon ground cinnamon**
  ½ **teaspoon freshly grated nutmeg**
  ¼ **teaspoon** *each* **salt, baking soda,**
      ground ginger, and ground cloves
  ¼ **cup granulated sugar**
  ½ **cup chopped walnuts**
  ¼ **cup raisins**
   2 **eggs, lightly beaten**
  ½ **cup firmly packed brown sugar**
   1 **cup canned pumpkin**
  ½ **teaspoon vanilla extract**
  ⅓ **cup butter or margarine, melted and cooled,**
      or vegetable oil

1. Preheat oven to 350° F. Grease and lightly flour a 4½- by 8½-inch loaf pan. In a large bowl sift together flour, baking powder, cinnamon, nutmeg, salt, baking soda, ginger, cloves, and granulated sugar. Mix in walnuts and raisins.

2. In a medium bowl beat together eggs, brown sugar, pumpkin, vanilla, and butter. Add pumpkin mixture to flour mixture, stirring just until dry ingredients are moistened.

3. Spread in prepared pan and bake until loaf is well browned and a wooden skewer inserted in the center comes out clean (50 to 55 minutes).

4. Cool in pan 15 minutes on wire rack; turn out onto wire rack to cool completely.

Makes 1 loaf.

For an inviting family meal, accompany an autumn supper of baked beans with chunks of garlic sausage and slices of Pumpkin Harvest Bread.

Boston Brown Bread, which dates from colonial times, gets its characteristic reddish brown color from molasses, often used by colonists as a substitute for more costly sugar.

■ TANGY LEMON LOAF

Lemon breads have always been a popular accompaniment to tea. They are, in fact, called tea breads for that reason. An orange variation is given at the end of the recipe, as is a variation for the perennial holiday favorite, Cranberry-Orange-Nut Loaf. This cakey bread slices and tastes even better if allowed to rest for 12 hours before serving.

    3 **cups flour**
    1 **tablespoon baking powder**
    1 **teaspoon salt**
   ½ **cup butter, softened**
    1 **cup sugar**
    1 **tablespoon finely grated lemon rind**
    2 **eggs**
    1 **cup milk**
   ½ **cup fresh lemon juice**
    1 **tablespoon vanilla extract**

1. Preheat oven to 350° F. Grease and lightly flour two 4½- by 8½-inch loaf pans. In a medium bowl sift together flour, baking powder, and salt; set aside.

2. In a large bowl cream butter and sugar until light and fluffy; add rind and beat until a pale, ivory color. Add eggs, one at a time, beating well after each addition (should the mixture begin to curdle, smooth texture by stirring in 1 or 2 tablespoons flour).

3. In a small bowl combine milk, lemon juice, and vanilla. To creamed butter mixture, gently fold in flour mixture alternately with the liquid, adding one third of each at a time; don't overwork batter. Divide batter evenly between prepared pans, smooth tops, and bake until a wooden skewer inserted in the center comes out clean (about 1 hour).

4. Cool in pans on wire rack 15 minutes; turn out onto wire rack to cool completely.

Makes 2 loaves.

Orange Loaf Substitute orange rind and juice for the lemon. If desired, fold 1 cup dried currants or raisins into batter before pouring into pans.

Cranberry-Orange-Nut Loaf Substitute orange rind and juice for the lemon. Fold 1 package (12 ounces) cranberries, chopped, and 1 cup walnuts, chopped, into batter before pouring into pans.

■ BOSTON BROWN BREAD

Boston has produced a number of memorable dishes, including this steamed brown bread. Studded with raisins and dark with molasses, this bread is customarily served with a big pot of baked beans on Saturday or Sunday night. Since it predates the common use of ovens, it is steamed and therefore remains quite moist and dense. Boston Brown Bread is also tasty spread with softened cream cheese and served as an accompaniment to afternoon coffee or tea. To make it you will need a cylindrical mold such as an empty 1-pound coffee can or two empty 1-pound fruit or vegetable cans.

   ½ **cup** *each* **rye flour, whole wheat flour, and cornmeal**
 1¼ **teaspoons baking soda**
   ½ **teaspoon salt**
    1 **cup buttermilk**
   ⅓ **cup molasses**
   ½ **cup raisins**

1. Have ready several quarts of water boiling on the stove and a deep kettle with a tight-fitting lid. In a medium bowl stir and toss together flours, cornmeal, baking soda, and salt.

2. Stir together buttermilk and molasses, add to dry ingredients along with raisins, and stir until thoroughly incorporated.

3. Pour batter into a buttered 1-pound coffee can or divide it equally between two 1-pound fruit or vegetable cans about 3 inches in diameter and 4 to 5 inches high. Cover tightly with aluminum foil.

4. Place can(s) in kettle on a rack and pour in boiling water to come halfway up the sides. Cover kettle and set over low heat. Regulate temperature so that water barely bubbles. Cook for about 2 hours if using large mold, about 1½ hours if using small ones. A wooden skewer plunged into the middle of a loaf should come out clean.

5. Remove mold(s) from water, let stand about 5 minutes, then unmold onto a rack to cool completely.

Makes 1 large loaf or 2 small cylindrical loaves.

■ FRUITED COFFEE RING
Mixed dried fruits make a colorful mosaic in a sugar-dusted bundt cake. Brown sugar and nuts swirled through the batter add further appeal.

    1 package (8 oz) mixed dried fruits (about 1½ cups)
    2 cups flour
    2 teaspoons baking powder
    ¼ teaspoon salt
    ¾ cup butter or margarine, softened
    ¾ cup granulated sugar
    1 teaspoon vanilla extract
    2 eggs
    ¾ cup milk
    ¼ cup butter or margarine, melted
      Confectioners' sugar, for dusting

Brown Sugar Mixture

    ⅔ cup firmly packed light brown sugar
    1 tablespoon flour
    1 tablespoon ground cinnamon
    ⅓ cup finely chopped walnuts

1. Preheat oven to 350° F. Grease well and lightly flour a 9-inch bundt pan or other tube pan with a capacity of 9 to 10 cups. Place dried fruits in a medium bowl and cover with boiling water. Let stand 10 minutes, then drain fruits and pat dry with paper towels. Chop finely.

2. In a medium bowl stir together flour, baking powder, and salt.

3. In large bowl of electric mixer, cream the ¾ cup butter with the granulated sugar until light and fluffy. Blend in vanilla. Then add eggs, one at a time, beating well after each addition.

4. Add flour mixture to creamed mixture alternately with milk, mixing to blend after each addition. Stir in dried fruits.

5. Spoon a third of the batter into prepared pan. Sprinkle with half of the Brown Sugar Mixture, then with 2 tablespoons of the melted butter. Add another third of the batter, remaining Brown Sugar Mixture, and melted butter. Top with rest of the batter; spread to cover sugar mixture completely.

6. Bake until coffee cake tests done when a long skewer is inserted (55 to 65 minutes).

7. Let stand in pan on a wire rack for about 15 minutes, then invert and remove pan. Cool, then dust with confectioners' sugar before serving.

Serves 8.

Brown Sugar Mixture In a small bowl combine sugar, flour, cinnamon, and walnuts; mix well.

Recipes and Related Information
Baking Pans, for Batter and Dough, 18; Baking Powder, 23; Baking Soda, 23; Batter, 27; Biscuit, 49; Dough, 179; Doughnut and Fried Bread, 179; Dumpling, 189; Preparing Pan for Baking, 478; Waffle and Pancake, 598; Yorkshire Pudding, 40.

QUINCE

In appearance, the quince lies somewhere between an apple and a pear. It can be pear-shaped, but it is usually more squat, like an apple. When ripe its skin is yellow, with green hints. Its flesh is hard and yellowish white, with small seeds, like those of an apple, at the core. Although quince was eaten raw in antiquity, it is formidably tart, and today is almost always cooked, usually with large amounts of sugar. When well cooked, quince turns a salmon pink and develops an alluring fragrance.

Use In North Africa and the Near East, sliced quince is added to stews, especially stews of fatty meats such as pork and mutton. Iranian cooks stuff baked quince halves with spiced ground meat mixtures. Quince can be cooked to a purée and sweetened like applesauce or cooked with an abundance of sugar to make marmalade. Quince has a high pectin content; if the softened pulp is cooked with considerable sugar and cooled, it forms a firm gel capable of being sliced and known as quince cheese or quince paste. In Spain and Latin America, quince paste is often served with a mild cheese or cream cheese for dessert. Because of its high pectin content, sliced quince is sometimes added to other fruit preserves to encourage jelling. Cooked quince can be added to fruit compotes or made into cobblers, crisps, and tarts.

Availability Quince is an autumn fruit, at its peak from late October through December. Quince paste is available in Latin markets, where it is known as *membrillate*.

Selection Select firm quince with good yellow color and a regular shape, and without serious blemishes. For preserves or jelly making, small blemishes or small worm holes can be cut away.

Storage Quince will keep up to one month in the refrigerator.

Preparation If a recipe requires, quince can be quartered, cored, and peeled like apples.

▪ PARISIAN COMPOTE

Quinces are the golden apples of Greek mythology given by Paris to the goddess Aphrodite as a symbol of love. At first taste, their flavor resembles that of apples. Cooked quince can be mistaken in appearance for apple as well. However, unlike an apple, a quince leaves a tart aftertaste. For an interesting variation, substitute quinces in recipes otherwise made with apples or pears.

3	pears
3	quinces or Golden Delicious apples
1	cup water
½	cup white wine
½	cup sugar
2	tablespoons honey
½	vanilla bean
1	cinnamon stick
16	walnut halves, toasted, for garnish

1. Peel and quarter pears and quinces; set aside. In a 2-quart saucepan, combine the water, wine, sugar, and honey, and stir to blend.

2. Bring mixture to a boil over medium-high heat and stir until sugar is dissolved. Add vanilla bean, cinnamon stick, and quinces. Reduce heat to medium-low and simmer for 18 minutes.

3. Add pears and continue cooking for 15 minutes more. Using a slotted spoon, remove fruit to a serving dish, and discard vanilla bean and cinnamon stick. Boil juices until reduced by half. Pour liquid over fruit. Garnish with walnut halves.

Serves 8.

RADIANT ENERGY

In addition to conduction and convection, radiation is one of the principal means of heat transfer. Radiant heat uses electromagnetic waves of energy to raise the temperature of an object. Both the broiling element of an oven and the glowing hot coals of an outdoor grill emit radiant energy. The process is fast and direct because heat is transferred directly from source to object, unlike convection, for example, which needs an intermediary such as air or liquid to do the transmitting. Usually, however, cooking involves a combination of processes. Broiled and grilled foods are cooked by both radiant energy and direct contact. Waves of radiant heat warm the outer surface of the food and then by conduction—direct molecule by molecule contact—move through its interior mass.

Recipes and Related Information
Broil, 62; Conduction, 138; Convection, 138; Grill, 287.

RADICCHIO

A variety of Italian chicory, radicchio has only recently been cultivated in this country. The Veneto variety grows in small, loose heads with red leaves and white ribs; the Treviso variety is more slender and tapered, like Belgian endive, with reddish purple leaves and white ribs. Other varieties beginning to appear on the market display a variety of coloring, from rose-pink to mottled green and red. The sturdy leaves have a crunchy texture and slightly bitter flavor. Radicchio in all its varieties is a strikingly beautiful salad "green," known in Italy as *un fiore che si mangia* (an edible flower).

Use   In Italy radicchio is a favorite winter salad green, and is most often simply dressed with vinaigrette. Americans usually prefer to temper the bitter flavor by mixing radicchio with other salad greens. The leaves may also be grilled and dressed with olive oil and salt, or floured and fried as an accompaniment to meats.

Availability   Radicchio is primarily found in winter and early spring, although some markets may carry it sporadically throughout the year.

Selection   Look for crisp, fresh leaves; avoid those with discolored ribs or signs of wilting or decay.

Storage   Radicchio will keep in a plastic bag in the refrigerator crisper for several days.

Preparation   Discard any bruised, limp, or discolored leaves. Trim root end. Wash, dry, and tear leaves into bite-sized pieces.

RADISH

Although most Americans are familiar only with the small, round, red radish, radishes are a remarkably varied group. They include the long, carrot-shaped white daikon used in Japanese cooking; the large, round black radish; and the slender, carrot-shaped red radish. Round radishes range in size from a small Brussels sprout to a large rutabaga; tapered radishes may be 2 to 12 inches in length. Radishes may be white, red, red with white markings, dark brown, or black. All have crunchy texture and peppery flavor. Generally, those grown in hot weather with little water will be hotter than radishes grown in early spring.

Use   In America radishes are generally eaten raw. They are sliced or grated for salads and eaten whole with sandwiches. They are also used to garnish platters of cold meats or vegetables. The French eat mild spring radishes with bread and sweet butter. Scandinavians garnish open-faced sandwiches with sliced radishes and use them in spring soups. In China radishes are carved into flowers and fans to garnish platters and may be marinated in sugar, vinegar, and soy sauce. In Japan the giant, mild daikon radish is grated and served as a relish with sashimi. Rounds of daikon simmered in dashi and soy sauce are served as a hot vegetable with chicken and shellfish. Grated daikon is usually mixed into the dipping sauce for Japanese tempura (batter-fried foods) and is mixed with grated carrots in a cool salad. In addition daikon is one of the most commonly pickled vegetables in Japan; as a pickle, it is eaten at the end of the meal with rice. In Africa young, tender radish tops are steamed, highly seasoned, and served like potherbs. Peppery radish sprouts add a lift to salads and sandwiches.

Availability Radishes are sold all year, with the Asian types more readily available in Asian markets. Radish sprouts are found in some health-food stores.

Selection Radishes should feel firm and crisp, not spongy. The interior should be firm and solid; older radishes may be pithy or hollow and will likely be hot. If leaves are attached, they should be fresh, not wilted.

Storage Remove any leaves before refrigerating. Small radishes should be refrigerated and used within three or four days. Daikon and larger radishes will keep under refrigeration for up to two weeks.

Preparation Scrub well and trim away leaves, tops, and tips. Slice, grate, or serve whole, as recipe directs.

■ AMANA COLONIES RADISH SALAD

One group of German immigrants, the Amana Society, founded seven villages near Cedar Rapids, Iowa, in the nineteenth century. For many years the residents dined in communal kitchens. Their fare, of which this radish salad is typical, reflected both their German heritage and the abundant harvest of the rich Iowa farmland.

    3 bunches radishes
    1 teaspoon salt
    ½ cup sour cream
    1 tablespoon apple cider vinegar
    ⅛ teaspoon white pepper
    2 tablespoons snipped fresh chives
      Butter lettuce leaves

1. Remove and discard radish leaves and roots. Cut radishes into thin slices (about 3 cups); this is easily done with the slicing disk of the food processor. Mix radish slices lightly with salt. Place in a colander and let stand to drain for 30 to 45 minutes. Blot dry with paper towels.

2. In a medium bowl blend together sour cream, vinegar, white pepper, and chives. Add drained radishes and mix lightly to coat with dressing. Cover and refrigerate until ready to serve (up to 2 hours).

3. Serve salad in a bowl lined with butter lettuce leaves.

Serves 6.

RANCIDITY

The deterioration of fats and foods that contain fats, such as nuts, oils, butters, and other dairy products, is caused primarily by prolonged exposure to air. Rancidity is characterized by an offensively rank smell and taste. Fats should be stored away from light and heat, both of which can initiate molecular changes that promote rancidity. Iron and copper also encourage oxidation of fats; for this reason aluminum or stainless steel pots are preferred for deep-frying.

Glazed fresh raspberries top rich almond cream in this striking and elegant summer fruit tart. The recipe is on page 496.

Recipes and Related Information
Butter, 67; Fat, 216; Oil, 394.

RASPBERRY

Like blackberries, raspberries are thorny members of the rose family. They are among the most aromatic and intensely flavored berries. Commercial raspberries may be either red or black, although red are far more common. Recently, a few specialty growers have offered golden raspberries, a mutant of the red berry that tastes very much like it. Like the blackberry, the raspberry is a collection of small drupes clustered around a central white core. Unlike the blackberry, however, a ripe raspberry pulls away from its core when harvested, creating a hollow center in the berry.

Use Raspberries, being delicate, are at their best when raw. They may be sprinkled with sugar and drizzled with milk or cream for a simple summer dessert. They may be

One of the most pleasing desserts is fresh raspberries topped with a rosette of whipped cream.

crushed for use in dessert sauce, mousse, ice cream, and sherbet. Raw raspberries make a handsome tart and a colorful addition to fruit salads. Raspberries may be combined with other fruits, such as peaches or nectarines, in cobblers and crisps. In France they are distilled to make a fragrant liqueur.

Availability Raspberries, a summer fruit, mature as early as May in some parts of the country and as late as November in others. Peak availability is in June and July. Frozen raspberries are found in most supermarket freezer cases.

Selection Raspberries are generally packed in plastic or cardboard containers and mold quickly. Check carefully to be sure a basket does not contain moldy berries. A cardboard basket that is stained on the bottom probably includes crushed berries. Raspberries should have a full red, black, or gold color and be highly perfumed; the green caps should not be attached.

Storage At home, invert berries onto a paper-towel–lined tray. Discard any moldy berries. Refrigerate and use within one or two days.

Preparation Raspberries rarely require washing. If they appear dusty, rinse quickly just before using.

■ RASPBERRY-ALMOND TART

This tart can be prepared hours before serving because the crust won't get soggy if the tart must sit awhile before serving: The almond cream filling insulates the crust from the juicy berries. In addition this tart lends itself to a myriad of colorful fruit toppings including whole strawberries, blueberries, sliced persimmons, sliced poached pears or peaches, kiwifruit, fresh currants, mandarin orange segments, or poached rhubarb.

    1 Sweet Tart Pastry (9½-inch; see page 441)
    7 tablespoons unsalted butter, softened
 1¼ cups sifted confectioners' sugar
 1¼ cups finely ground blanched almonds
    1 small egg, lightly beaten
    1 cup red currant or red raspberry jelly
    1 tablespoon raspberry-flavored liqueur or kirsch
    2 to 3 cups fresh raspberries

1. Roll out tart pastry and use it to line a 9½-inch tart tin with removable bottom. Blind bake until partially baked; cool.

2. Preheat oven to 350° F. In a large bowl cream together butter and sugar. Stir in ground almonds. Add egg and stir until well mixed. Spread almond mixture evenly over bottom of partially baked tart shell. Bake for 25 to 30 minutes. Cool on wire rack.

3. In a heavy-bottomed saucepan heat jelly over low heat until just melted and bubbly. Stir in liqueur. Brush surface of tart filling with a thin layer of warm jelly just before placing fruit on tart.

4. Arrange whole raspberries very close to one another in concentric circles on top of filling. Reheat jelly-liqueur mixture and brush it lightly on tops of berries to glaze them. Carefully lift tart so that it releases from pan sides and serve.

Serves 6 to 8.

Recipes and Related Information
Fran's Raspberry Vinegar, 323; Raspberry Feuillantines, 486; Raspberry Glaze, 117; Raspberry Sauce, 522; Raspberry Sherbet, 313; Raspberry Vinegar and Shallot Dressing, 521.

RECONSTITUTE, TO

To restore a dehydrated food to liquid form or a condensed food to full strength by adding water. Also, to rebuild a sauce that has separated. For starch-bound sauces, a good whisking after heating is usually all that is needed. To reconstitute Hollandaise sauce, beat 1 egg yolk with 1 tablespoon of water in a double boiler until thick and fluffy. Then slowly add curdled sauce, beating constantly, until fully incorporated.

RED PEPPER SPICE

Spice packers market several different products made from ground dried capsicum peppers (both sweet and hot), including cayenne pepper, paprika, and ground red pepper. The varieties and combinations of peppers used in each blend vary from packer to packer. Some manufacturers do not make a distinction between cayenne pepper and ground red pepper. Others pack both, making the ground red pepper a milder blend than the cayenne pepper. Red pepper flakes—also called crushed red pepper, pizza pepper, or pepperoni *rosso*—are a product of blended dried red chiles, but are ground coarse rather than fine.

Most commercial blends of ground red pepper are indeed hot; how hot is a matter of the style of the packer. Most cayenne pepper is blended from pungent Chinese, Indian, African, and Mexican chiles. Most ground red pepper is blended from milder California, Louisiana, Carolina, and Turkish capsicums. Although brands of red pepper flakes vary in pungency, they can be extremely hot and should be used with caution.

Use Ground red pepper adds piquancy to sauces, chili, stews, egg dishes, pizza, soups, and sausages, and to any other dish that needs a lift. Use with restraint as brands vary in pungency. Red pepper flakes are used as a table condiment to add heat to pizzas, salads, pasta, and other dishes at the discretion of the diner. In the kitchen red pepper flakes can add zest to soups, tomato sauces, steamed shellfish, and fresh sausage.

Availability Ground red pepper is sold in bulk in some health-food stores and ethnic markets; it is widely available on supermarket spice racks packed in bottles, tins, and bags. Red pepper flakes in jars and tins are found on supermarket spice racks. Some health-food stores sell red pepper flakes in bulk.

Selection Packaged seasonings lose quality after a while; try to buy from a store that restocks its spice section fairly often.

Storage Keep ground red pepper and red pepper flakes in an airtight container in a cool, dark, dry place. Replace every six months.

Recipes and Related Information
Cayenne Pepper, 107; Paprika, 405; Pepper, 425.

REDUCE, TO

To boil rapidly to decrease volume and intensify flavors. As the liquid evaporates, it also thickens and concentrates the essences. The end product is called a reduction. Typically, a recipe requires that a mixture cook until one third to one half of its original volume has boiled away (*one third* usually applies to sauces, and *one half* most often refers to wine reductions). Seasoning should be added after reducing; if added at the start of cooking, these flavors also intensify and the final product might become overseasoned. The reduction process is also used to produce a sauce from a vegetable purée; the purée alone is cooked down to produce an intense, yet light, flavor.

A wide, heavy-bottomed saucepan is best for reducing. The larger the surface area of the pan, the faster the liquid can evaporate. The thick bottom permits better control of heat.

Recipes and Related Information
Sauce, 512; Stock and Soup, 558.

REFRESH, TO

To plunge boiled foods—most often vegetables—immediately after cooking into cold water or an ice bath to halt the cooking process, set color, and crisp texture. It is considered by professional cooks as the sister process to blanching, the critical finish that ensures a superior final product. Food should be refreshed only briefly—just long enough to chill it completely and stop it from cooking further. It should then be drained to prevent sogginess.

Recipes and Related Information
Blanch, 52; Boil, 54.

RENDER, TO

To extract an animal fat from its connective tissue by melting. Lard, from pork, and chicken fat are two rendered fats used in cooking. Rendering is a slow process, done in a heavy-bottomed pan over low heat. It continues until all the fat drains out, the tissue has turned brown and crispy, and any impurities have sunk to the bottom of the pan. The remaining clear fat is strained carefully through filter paper. The crisp bits left in the pan after the fat is strained off are considered a delicious, though rich, delicacy known as cracklings. In traditional Jewish cooking, they are called *greben*, if derived from chicken or goose fat, and are mixed into stuffings or chopped liver, as well as served as a snack.

Many bakers prefer lard for pastries because it is a pure fat, without the water or milk solids found in butter and margarine, and so has more shortening or tenderizing power than fats with moisture. Lard and rendered chicken fat have long been favorites for frying, for basting roasts, and for making sauces because they contribute rich flavor. As evidence more clearly links high intake of animal fats and certain diseases, this practice is losing favor among health-conscious cooks.

Recipes and Related Information
Pie and Tart, 431; Pork, 455; Poultry, 468.

RHUBARB

Although botanically a vegetable, rhubarb is considered a fruit by most cooks and diners. Its long, celerylike stalks are edible; the leaves and roots contain oxalic acid, which is toxic. Rhubarb may be either hothouse- or field-grown. Hothouse rhubarb has pink stalks, yellow leaves, and few strings; field-grown rhubarb has red stalks and green leaves. Generally, hothouse rhubarb has a milder flavor. Rhubarb is extremely tart when cooked and is usually generously dosed with sugar.

Use Rhubarb is also commonly known as pie plant, a good clue to its most frequent use. It is excellent in pies, especially when tossed with spices and flour to thicken its abundant juices. Rhubarb is also frequently combined with strawberries or pineapple in double-crust or lattice-topped pies. It may be stewed with sugar and served warm or cold, with or without cream. To make rhubarb fool, an equal quantity of whipped cream is folded into stewed, cooled rhubarb. The vegetable makes a delicious crisp and cobbler; it is also fermented to make wine.

Availability Hothouse rhubarb is sold in some supermarkets almost all year. Field-grown rhubarb is a spring crop, harvested in April and May.

Selection Look for crisp, unblemished stalks. Avoid any that are limp or wilted.

The tart, refreshing flavor of rhubarb paired with the sweetness of strawberries makes a delicious pie. The addition of raisins and ginger gives it an unusual twist. The lattice-top crust lets the strikingly colorful filling show through.

2. In a large bowl combine strawberries, rhubarb, raisins, sugar, flour, and ginger; let stand 15 minutes.

3. Brush inside of bottom crust with egg white. Pour filling into shell. Dot with butter.

4. Moisten rim of bottom crust with water and cover with top crust or lattice top; seal and finish edges.

5. Place pie on a rimmed baking sheet and bake 20 minutes. Lower oven to 400° F and continue baking until crust is golden brown (40 minutes). Cover edges of crust with strips of aluminum foil, if necessary, to prevent excessive browning.

Serves 8.

RIB

A single branch from a head of celery is a rib or a stalk, although some books and chefs use the term *stalk* to mean the entire head. Ribs can be as much as a foot long. They were so named perhaps because they slightly resemble human ribs and because they have a stringy ribbing on their outer surface. To continue the parallel to human anatomy, the innermost celery ribs are called the heart.

RIBBON

This term is used to describe the consistency of a batter or mixture of egg and sugar beaten to the point of optimum incorporation of air. At this stage, the mixture will fall slowly from the whisk or beater and leave a ribbonlike trail on top of the mixture in the bowl. The trail remains on top for a few seconds before sinking into the rest of the mixture. This consistency applies to any air-lightened mixture, such as génoise and meringue.

> ***Recipes and Related Information***
> *Cake, 77; Egg, 194; Meringue, 359.*

RICE, TO

To force cooked root vegetables—such as potatoes—through a special tool that resembles a giant garlic press. The food is extruded in little pellets resembling grains of rice. Cooks fond of mashed potatoes say the best versions—which are not pasty or lumpy—are processed with a potato ricer.

> ***Recipes and Related Information***
> *Down-Home Mashed Potatoes, 466; Grate, Grater, 281; Potato, 463.*

Storage   Refrigerate and use within two or three days.

Preparation   Wash stalks and remove leaves. Cut stalks crosswise into ½-inch widths. Place in a saucepan with sugar (about ½ cup per pound) and a little water; cover and simmer over moderately low heat until tender.

▪ STRAWBERRY-RHUBARB PIE

For a delicious treat, raisins and ginger are added to this Strawberry-Rhubarb Pie.

> 1   nine-inch double-crust Flaky Pastry (see page 434) or Egg Pastry (see page 435)
> 2   cups washed, hulled, and halved strawberries
> 4   cups sliced, young, unpeeled rhubarb stalks
> ⅓   cup raisins
> 1⅓ cups sugar
> 6   tablespoons flour
> ¼   teaspoon ground ginger
> 1   egg white, lightly beaten
> 1½ tablespoons unsalted butter

1. Preheat oven to 425° F. Roll out pastry for bottom crust and line a 9-inch pie plate. Roll out remaining pastry to form top crust or lattice top.

RIND

This is the skin or peel of a fruit; in particular citrus fruit such as lemon, orange, and grapefruit. Citrus rinds are often candied or preserved in sugar syrup, and used as decoration. The outer colored portion, also called the zest, is removed in strips, fine threads, or finely grated pieces to infuse baked goods, beverages, sauces, soups, and other dishes with its essence and perfume. Special gadgets are available to remove the zest. The citrus zester has five tiny holes that cut threads of zest when dragged across the rind; the citrus peeler cuts a single ¼-inch piece.

Recipes and Related Information
Candy, 93; Gadgets, 258; Peel, 424; Zest, 631.

ROAST, TO

To cook raw food with currents of hot, dry air in order to make food edible and more flavorful. Roasting and its twin, baking, are the same process. Generally, roasting refers to the cooking of whole meats, including poultry, often with added fat. Most other oven-cooked foods—fish, bread, or cut-up poultry, for instance—are referred to as baked. On the other hand, ham is baked and chestnuts are roasted. These distinctions are more a matter of usage than an indicator of any real difference.

A roast is a cut of meat or poultry cooked, uncovered, by dry heat (without the addition of moisture). Most roasts are cooked in a shallow pan to permit good air circulation; the result is even heat penetration. A roast is usually placed fat side up, which lets the fat that melts during cooking baste the meat as it drains. A rack or trivet in the bottom of the pan holds the meat out of the drippings.

ROASTING BASICS

Roasting is ideal for the most tender cuts of meat. Not all cuts that are labeled roast, however, are truly suitable for roasting. For beef, lamb, and pork, the rib roast (sometimes called a rack) is the most popular cut for roasting. In the case of pork and lamb, this type of roast is sometimes tied by the butcher into a crown roast. Another popular cut for this cooking method is the loin, especially of pork and veal. Leg of lamb, veal, and pork also provide excellent roasts. Roasts should be relatively large so that they remain succulent. All types of poultry can be roasted, from small Rock Cornish game hens (suitable for one or two servings) to chickens, ducks, and turkeys.

ROASTING BEEF

Ask a dozen people how to roast a cut of beef and you'll get a dozen different answers. Some advocate roasting beef at a high temperature for a short time; others advocate low temperatures and long cooking times; still others prefer moderation or a combination of the two methods, starting out at a high temperature, then reducing it. Some cooks roast beef at a very high temperature for a short time, then turn off the oven and let the roast finish cooking in the retained heat. All these methods have advantages and drawbacks, defenders and detractors. How you roast beef is largely a matter of personal preference.

Slow, even cooking will produce a roast with a uniform interior color. A medium-rare roast will be medium-rare from the interior to the exterior and from one end to the other. Another advantage of slow-cooked meat is that it shrinks less during cooking, so you get more meat for your money. However, slow-cooked roasts do not have a crisp browned crust. Also, some cooks like to have a range of doneness on one roast, which is impossible to achieve with the slow-cook method.

High-temperature roasting produces the crisp, well-browned crust preferred by many diners. Some cooks also claim that a quickly formed crust helps to lock in meat juices, yielding a juicier, more flavorful roast. However, high-temperature roasting is not recommended for large cuts such as a standing rib roast, which would burn on the outside before it cooked through in the middle. Also, high-heat roasting causes fat to spatter on oven walls, leaving a dirtier oven to clean.

ROASTING OTHER MEATS

When lamb, a lean meat, is cooked by a dry-heat method, it dries out and, when overcooked, develops strong flavors. With the exception of baby lamb, lamb should always have at least a tinge of pink in the center. The delicate flavor of baby lamb is best when the meat is well-done. Lamb roasts to a higher internal temperature than beef for comparable stages of doneness (see Guide to Internal Temperatures, page 575).

Milk-fed veal has a delicate flavor that is fully developed only when the meat is fully cooked. Cooking it to rare or medium-rare does not show veal at its best. However, its lack of internal marbling means that veal can easily dry out. The best solution is to roast it in a slow (325° F) oven and bard the roast well (cover with a thin layer of fat to add moisture; see BARD).

Pork roasts are delicious, and since they are fattier cuts than beef roasts, they are moist and juicy without additional basting. A medium oven (350° F) is appropriate for a pork roast. Many roasting timetables recommend cooking pork to an internal temperature of 170° F to ensure that potentially harmful parasites that can be present in fresh pork are killed. However, pork is safe to eat if cooked to an internal temperature of 150° F, and will still be appetizing.

Whether to roast poultry at a steady high heat or at an initial high temperature that is then reduced for the remainder of cooking is basically a matter of personal preference. Again, what is most important is to produce a roasted bird that is moist, yet cooked to the desired internal temperature. The current recommendation is to roast

ROASTING TIMETABLE

Many factors affect the cooking time of any roasted meat, including its size and shape, whether it was chilled or at room temperature when put in the oven, and the reliability of the oven. For best results use an instant-read thermometer to monitor internal temperature, a very accurate indicator of doneness. See When Is It Done, at right.

Type of Meat	Weight (Pounds)	Oven Temperature	Internal Meat Temperature
Beef			
Prime rib	6–8	325° F	125°–130° F (rare)
			140°–145° F (medium)
Rib eye (Delmonico)	4–6	350° F	125°–130° F (rare)
			140°–145° F (medium)
Tenderloin, half	2–3	425° F	125°–130° F (rare)
Tenderloin, whole	4–6	425° F	125°–130° F (rare)
Top loin (New York)	5–7	325° F	125°–130° F (rare)
			140°–145° F (medium)
Top round	8–10	325° F	125°–130° F (rare)
			140°–145° F (medium)
Top sirloin	6–8	350° F	125°–130° F (rare)
			140°–145° F (medium)
Lamb			
Leg			
Boneless	5–8	375° F	130°–145° F (rare, medium-rare)
Bone-in	10–12	375° F	130°–145° F (rare, medium-rare)
Rack	1½–3	400° F	130°–145° F (rare, medium-rare)
Shoulder			
Boneless	3–5	325° F	130°–145° F (rare, medium-rare)
Bone-in	7–10	325° F	130°–145° F (rare, medium-rare)
Pork			
Boston butt	4–6	350° F	145°–155° F (medium, medium-well)
Leg (fresh ham)			
Whole (boneless)	10–14	350° F	145°–155° F (medium, medium-well)
Whole (bone-in)	12–16	350° F	145°–155° F (medium, medium-well)
Loin			
Boneless	3–5	350° F	145°–155° F (medium, medium-well)
Center	3–5	350° F	145°–155° F (medium, medium-well)
Blade loin or sirloin	3–4	350° F	145°–155° F (medium, medium-well)
Shoulder			
Boneless	3–5	350° F	145°–155° F (medium, medium-well)
Bone-in	5–8	350° F	145°–155° F (medium, medium-well)
Spareribs	3–5	325° F	145°–155° F (medium, medium-well)
Poultry			
Under 6 pounds			
(Broiling and frying	1	425° F	170°–175° F (medium)
chicken, duck, game	1½–2	425° F	170°–175° F (medium)
hen, pheasant, poussin)	2½–3½	425° F	170°–175° F (medium)
Over 6 pounds			
(Capon, roasting	6–8	450°/325° F*	170°–175° F (medium)
chicken, turkey)	8–10	450°/325° F*	170°–175° F (medium)
	10–12	450°/325° F*	170°–175° F (medium)
	12–14	450°/325° F*	170°–175° F (medium)
	14–16	450°/325° F*	170°–175° F (medium)
	16–20	450°/325° F*	170°–175° F (medium)
	20–24	450°/325° F*	170°–175° F (medium)
Veal			
Leg, boneless	5–8	325° F	140°–145° F (medium, medium-well)
Loin, boneless	4–6	325° F	140°–145° F (medium, medium-well)

*Begin roasting in a 450° F oven for the first 30 minutes; reduce oven to 325° F for remainder of cooking.

until the breast is cooked, 170° to 175° F on a meat thermometer. The thigh joint may be pink at this stage. If this is objectionable, the bird can be carved in the kitchen and the dark meat returned to the oven to cook further. If the bird is stuffed, remember to add 20 to 30 minutes to the cooking time to be sure that the stuffing reaches a safe temperature, which is about 165° F. Or, the stuffing may be baked separately in a covered casserole.

PREPARATION

To prevent lean meats from drying out and to add extra flavor, a roast can be marinated; basted as it cooks with roasting juices, oil, melted butter, or a marinade; or covered with a layer of fat (barding) or softened butter. The liquids can be sprinkled, spooned, or brushed over the food. Barding is recommended for lean cuts of beef, veal, chicken, and small birds, such as game hen and squab, but not for duck and goose, which are already fatty. Poultry will look better if trussed before roasting (see TRUSS).

Roasts are usually set on a rack in a roasting pan; the pan should be large enough so that no part of the meat extends beyond its edge; otherwise, some meat juices will drip into the oven. If the pan is much too large, however, the juices will burn. To roast a small bird or a relatively small cut of meat, you can use a heavy, shallow baking dish instead of a roasting pan. A rack provides open space beneath the roast so that heat can reach the underside, and allows any drippings to fall to the pan below. Without a rack, the bottom of the roast will stew in the pan juices instead of staying dry and crisp. The meat is roasted uncovered so that it will be cooked by dry heat rather than by the steam that would form under a cover.

WHEN IS IT DONE?

There are two aspects to doneness. First, the roast must achieve a safe internal temperature; second, it should be done to the cook's individual taste. The Roasting Timetable at left can help you estimate how long to cook a roast in the oven. However, it should be considered only a guideline. The most reliable indicator is internal temperature (see Guide to Internal Temperatures, page 575) measured with a meat thermometer (see THERMOMETER). Bring meat to room temperature before roasting. Let roast sit out for 10 to 30 minutes (depending upon size) before carving. The meat will reabsorb juices as it rests, making it firmer and easier to slice (see CARVE).

To use a standard meat thermometer, insert in thickest part of muscle before roasting. Make sure thermometer does not touch bone. An instant-read thermometer is not set in place before roasting; it is inserted during roasting and will give an accurate reading within seconds.

Recipes and Related Information
Beef, 37; Lamb, 335; Pork, 455; Poultry, 468; Veal, 591.

ROSEMARY

A pungent herb native to the Mediterranean, rosemary has dark green, needlelike leaves with a faint camphor flavor. When used in excess, the leaves can impart an acrid taste. The rosemary plant, with its tiny blue flowers, is a hardy perennial often grown by home gardeners as an ornamental.

Use Sparingly used, rosemary flatters most meats, especially pork, lamb, veal, and chicken. Whole sprigs may be added to the fire when grilling meats or may be dipped in oil and used to baste grilling meats. Rosemary also complements potatoes, beans, and bean soups.

Availability Fresh rosemary is sold in some supermarkets and specialty markets all year. Dried rosemary is widely available on supermarket spice racks.

Selection All packaged seasonings lose quality after a while; try to buy from a store that restocks its spice section fairly often.

Storage Keep fresh rosemary in a plastic bag in the refrigerator for up to one week; frozen in plastic bags, the leaves will keep indefinitely. Store the dried herb in a cool, dark, dry place. Whole dried rosemary will keep for up to one year; ground rosemary should be discarded after about four months. Fresh rosemary sprigs can be tied in bunches and air-dried; remove dried leaves and store them as for dried whole rosemary.

Preparation Rosemary leaves should be chopped or pulverized to release their oils.

Recipes and Related Information
Dry Spice Rub for Lamb, 350; Rack of Lamb With Herbs, 338.

RUTABAGA

The yellow rutabaga is a member of the cabbage family and is, in fact, a cross between a turnip and a wild cabbage. It resembles the turnip in its round, slightly squat shape. Unlike the turnip, however, its flesh is golden yellow and its skin yellow deepening to purple at the top. When cooked, the flesh is sweet and firm.

Use Rutabaga, also known as a Swede or a Swedish turnip, is a highly underutilized vegetable in light of its appealing sweet flavor. Peeled, boiled, and buttered, it makes a delicious companion to meats, especially ham, duck, and pork. It can be added to winter soups and stews or sliced thinly and baked with stock and buttered bread crumbs. Rutabagas can be sliced and parboiled, then panfried with apples as a side dish for pork chops. Mashed with butter and cream or stock, rutabagas are a delightful and overlooked winter dish.

Availability Fresh rutabagas are found in some supermarkets all year but are most plentiful in fall and winter.

Selection Look for firm, unblemished roots; avoid spongy ones. They should feel heavy for their size. Small rutabagas are particularly sweet; large rutabagas may have a woody interior.

Storage Rutabagas should be stored in a cool, humid place, where they will keep for several weeks. They can also be refrigerated for at least one month.

Preparation Peel thick skin; cube, slice, or dice as recipe directs.

Cooking See BAKE, BOIL, STEAM, SAUTE, STIR-FRY.

■ SHERRIED OXTAIL SOUP

Thick, rich oxtail soup suggests a German menu. Start the meal with a creamy beet and herring salad, and accompany the soup with a wonderful homemade rye bread, sliced thickly and served slightly warm.

> 3 **pounds oxtails, cut into segments**
> **Salt, white pepper, ground allspice,**
> **and flour, for coating**
> 2 **tablespoons butter**
> 3 **onions, chopped**
> 3 **carrots, shredded**
> 1 **small rutabaga (about ½ lb), peeled and sliced**
> 1 **small celeriac (about 12 oz), peeled and cubed**
> 5 **cups water**
> 1 **teaspoon** *each* **salt and paprika**
> ⅛ **teaspoon** *each* **white pepper, cayenne pepper,**
> **and dried thyme**
> 1 **bay leaf**
> ½ **cup dry sherry**

1. Sprinkle oxtails lightly with salt, white pepper, and allspice, then coat lightly with flour. Heat butter in a 5- to 6-quart saucepan or Dutch oven; brown oxtails well on all sides in heated butter, removing them as they brown. When all are browned, pour off most of the drippings. Add onions and carrots; cook, stirring occasionally, until onion is limp and lightly browned. Return oxtails to pan with rutabaga, celeriac, the water, the 1 teaspoon salt, paprika, the ⅛ teaspoon white pepper, cayenne, thyme, and bay leaf. Bring to a boil; reduce heat, cover, and simmer until meat is very tender (about 4 hours).

2. Skim off fat, then strain soup. Return liquid to kettle. Discard bay leaf. Remove meat from bones and add to broth. Purée strained vegetables in blender or food processor with a little broth. Mix puréed vegetables into broth.

3. Boil soup gently, uncovered, to reduce liquid slightly (about 20 minutes). Stir in sherry. Add salt to taste.

Serves 4 to 6.

S

Paella, a Spanish casserole of poultry, sausage, shellfish, and vegetables, uses a saffron-infused chicken stock to tint the rice a warm golden yellow.

SAFFRON

It isn't hard to understand why saffron is the most expensive spice in the world. Made from the dried yellow-orange stigmas of a species of crocus, saffron must be picked by hand. Each crocus blossom yields three stigmas; about 225,000 stigmas make 1 pound.

Fortunately, a little saffron goes a long way. Just a few threads dissolved in hot liquid can add a rich golden color to a pot of soup or rice. Its distinctive flavor and aroma are indescribable but immediately recognizable; if overused, saffron can have an unpleasant medicinal taste.

Use   Saffron imparts color and flavor to many Mediterranean, North African, and Middle Eastern dishes. Paella and many other Spanish rice recipes are seasoned with saffron. It can be found in Italian *risotto alla Milanese* and Mediterranean fish soups such as bouillabaisse, and is present in most Moroccan versions of couscous, in Iranian rice dishes, and in Indian curries, tandoori dishes, and pilafs. In Sweden, Spain, and Italy, saffron is added to buns, breads, and cakes. The Pennsylvania Dutch are also great consumers of saffron, adding it to chicken and noodle dishes and soups.

Availability   Saffron is packed both in thread form and as a powder. It is widely carried in supermarkets; some store it on the spice rack and others require customers to request it.

Selection   Because powdered saffron quickly loses its pungency, threads are preferred. Powdered saffron is sometimes adulterated with turmeric or other powders that are less expensive.

Storage   Keep saffron, whether powder or threads, in a cool, dark place and use within six months.

Preparation   Saffron must be heated to release its color and flavor. To dissolve powdered saffron or saffron threads, steep for 2 minutes in a small amount of hot water or other liquid used in the recipe; add infusion directly to dish, straining out threads if desired (it is not necessary). For fullest flavor, add saffron near the end of the cooking process.

■ PAELLA

Traditionally, this rice-based Spanish dish is cooked in a shallow, wide-bottomed pan known as a paella pan.

- 1 chicken (3½ lb), cut into 8 pieces
- 1 teaspoon salt
- ½ teaspoon freshly ground black pepper
- 1 teaspoon dried oregano
- 4 cups Chicken Stock (see page 560)
- ¼ gram (1 vial) saffron threads
- 4 tablespoons olive oil
- ½ pound spicy Italian or Spanish sausage
- 2 onions, diced
- 3 cloves garlic, diced
- 4 tomatoes, diced
- 1 bell pepper, diced
- 2 cups uncooked long-grain rice
- 1 pound fresh peas *or*
  1 package (10 oz) frozen tiny peas
- 1 pound prawns, shelled
- ½ pound clams in the shell, scrubbed
- ½ pound mussels in the shell, scrubbed

1. Wash chicken pieces and pat dry. Season with salt, black pepper, and oregano. Let rest for 30 minutes. Meanwhile, in a medium saucepan, heat stock; add saffron, turn off heat, and let steep.

2. In a 6- to 8-quart Dutch oven, sauté chicken in oil over medium heat until golden brown (about 7 minutes). Turn and brown 5 minutes. Remove to paper-towel–lined plate and reserve. Add sausage and brown, turning to cook all sides, for about 5 minutes. Remove sausage to a paper-towel–lined plate and reserve. Cut sausage in half. Add onion and garlic to Dutch oven and sauté 5 minutes. Add tomatoes, bell pepper, rice, reserved chicken, and saffron stock to cover and simmer 20 minutes. Add halved sausages, peas, and prawns. Stir to mix well. Cover and cook 10 minutes. Add clams and mussels. Cover and cook 15 minutes. Fluff the rice and serve in casserole dish.

Serves 8.

SAGE

A member of the mint family native to the southern Mediterranean, sage is one of the more pungent herbs in the cook's pantry. Sage leaves are long, narrow, grayish green ovals with a coarse texture. They are aggressive in aroma and flavor, slightly musty or camphorlike, especially when subjected to heat.

Use   Sage is especially appreciated in Italian and English cuisines. Italians use it to flavor dried-bean dishes and pork. To make the famous saltimbocca, a whole sage leaf is sandwiched between a veal scallop and a slice of prosciutto; the "package" is skewered with toothpicks and sautéed in butter with wine. English cooks use sage in stuffings and blend it with cream cheese or cottage cheese to make a sandwich spread. They also layer Derby cheese with the juice of fresh sage leaves to make the green-streaked Sage Derby. In America minced sage is popular as a sausage seasoning; it is also a virtual fixture in turkey stuffings. Because of its pungent character, it should be used with restraint.

Availability   Some well-stocked supermarkets and specialty markets now carry fresh sage the year around. Dried, rubbed (crumbled) sage and ground sage are sold on supermarket spice racks.

Selection   Choose fresh sage with a strong aroma and no signs of wilting. Packaged seasonings lose quality after a while; try to buy from a store that restocks its spice shelf fairly often.

Storage   Fresh sage can be stored for a few days in the refrigerator if wrapped in a paper towel and placed inside a plastic bag. It can also be preserved in salt: Wash and dry the leaves, then layer them with salt in a jar or freezer container. Cover and refrigerate or freeze indefinitely; wash salt off leaves before using. Dried, rubbed, and ground sage quickly go musty; keep in a cool, dark, dry place and replace every three months.

■ SALTIMBOCCA

This Roman dish is a good example of the Italian penchant for whimsical food names; it is so succulent it almost leaps into your mouth (*salta in bocca*). The success of the dish depends on tender, milk-fed veal and fresh sage. Serve with a light red wine or a rich Italian Chardonnay.

- 1¼ pounds leg of veal, cut into 12 scallops
  Salt and freshly ground pepper
- 12 fresh sage leaves
- 12 paper-thin slices prosciutto
- 2 tablespoons unsalted butter
- 3 tablespoons dry white wine
- 1½ tablespoons minced parsley, for garnish

1. Place each scallop between pieces of plastic wrap and, using a mallet or the bottom of a skillet, pound to a uniform ⅛-inch thickness. Salt and pepper scallops lightly. Put a sage leaf on each and cover with a slice of prosciutto. Secure prosciutto to scallop with toothpicks.

2. Melt 1 tablespoon of the butter in each of two large skillets. Add scallops and brown quickly on both sides. When scallops are just barely cooked, transfer them to a warmed serving platter; remove toothpicks.

3. Scrape juices and browned bits from one skillet to the other. Add wine to skillet with juices and reduce slightly over high heat. Pour sauce over scallops; garnish with parsley.

Serves 4.

SALAD

Interestingly, the word *salad* comes not from anything to do with the green and leafy foods we most often associate with it, but from *sal*, the Latin word for *salt*, the first salad dressing. Salt was used as an early preservative to keep herbs and other plants fresh. These salted foods could be considered the original salads.

Eventually, all manner of ingredients were added to the simple mixtures. Today a salad can consist of so many different types of ingredients and be served in so many ways that it almost resists definition, except to call it, as does the dictionary, a hodgepodge. However, whether cold or hot, appetizer, first course, main course, post-entrée refresher, all vegetable, all fruit, with meat, or meatless, most salads share a common characteristic: a sauce or dressing of some sort. After that it's up to personal taste and the creativity of the salad-maker. For salad dressing recipes, see SAUCE, Dressings.

■ CAESAR SALAD

Here is that classic, said to have been created by a hotel chef in Baja, California, in the 1920s. Some versions require merely rubbing the serving bowl with garlic; but including it in the dressing results in a more pronounced flavor. Adorning the salad with your own homemade croutons adds a special touch. The lettuce can be washed, dried, and torn in advance, then refrigerated until needed (see Leafy Green Salads, opposite page).

    1 egg
    8 cups torn romaine lettuce
    3 tablespoons fresh lemon juice
    1 clove garlic, minced
    1 teaspoon Dijon mustard
    ⅓ cup olive oil
    6 flat anchovy fillets, drained and finely chopped
       Freshly ground pepper
    ⅓ cup freshly grated Parmesan cheese
    1 cup Garlic Croutons (at left)

1. Place egg on a spoon and carefully lower it into a small pan of boiling water. Immediately remove pan from heat; let egg stand in water 1 minute. Remove egg and place in cold water.

2. Place romaine in a large salad bowl; if done ahead, cover and refrigerate.

3. In a medium bowl mix lemon juice, garlic, and mustard. Using a whisk or fork, gradually beat in oil. Mix in anchovies.

4. Bring to the table egg, salad bowl, dressing, pepper mill, cheese, and croutons. Grind pepper generously over greens. Add dressing to greens and mix gently. Break in prepared egg and mix well. Sprinkle with cheese and croutons and mix again. Serve at once.

Serves 4.

■ CRISPY COLESLAW

This slaw (the word *cole* comes from *Kohl,* the German word for *cabbage*) is a favorite accompaniment to hamburgers or delicatessen-style sandwiches.

    ½ cup *each* mayonnaise and sour cream
    ½ teaspoon salt
    1 teaspoon sugar
    2 teaspoons mustard
    1 tablespoon *each* horseradish and apple cider vinegar
    1 medium-sized green cabbage (1½ to 2 lb), thinly shredded
    1 medium carrot, shredded
    6 green onions (tops included), thinly sliced
    ¼ cup chopped parsley

1. In a medium bowl combine mayonnaise, sour cream, salt, sugar, mustard, horseradish, and vinegar; stir until well blended.

2. In a large bowl combine cabbage, carrot, green onions, and parsley. Pour dressing over vegetables; mix lightly to coat well. Cover and refrigerate to blend flavors for at least 2 hours (up to 8 hours).

Serves 6 to 8.

■ CHURCH-SOCIAL POTATO SALAD

This soulful potato salad combines elements from traditional French, German, and Creole recipes. It has green and red onions and celery for crunch and a tangy cayenne-spiked dressing for punch.

    4 large potatoes, peeled and halved
    ½ cup chopped red onion
    ¼ cup sliced green onion
    1 stalk celery, chopped
    4 hard-cooked eggs, peeled and chopped

Dressing

    3 tablespoons vinegar
    1¼ cups vegetable oil
    2 tablespoons Dijon mustard
    1 teaspoon horseradish
    1 teaspoon salt
    1 teaspoon dried tarragon
    ½ teaspoon cayenne pepper
    ½ teaspoon freshly ground black pepper

1. Boil potatoes until tender (20 minutes), cool, and chop into chunks.

2. Combine red onion, green onion, and celery. Add to potatoes and blend gently. Add Dressing, fold in hard-cooked eggs, mix gently, and chill.

Serves 4 to 6.

Dressing Combine all ingredients and beat until smooth. Set aside.

TOMATOES WITH MOZZARELLA AND BASIL

This classic is a salad for summer, when the tomatoes and basil are at their best. Use only sweet, vine-ripened tomatoes, and visit a cheese merchant for the finest whole-milk mozzarella. A hot loaf of crusty bread should be on the table, too.

8 ounces fresh whole-milk mozzarella or imported buffalo-milk mozzarella, at room temperature
4 tomatoes, at room temperature, cored and thinly sliced
½ cup extravirgin olive oil
Juice of 1½ large *or* 2 small lemons
¼ cup shredded fresh basil leaves
Kosher salt and freshly ground pepper
Additional basil sprigs, for garnish

1. Slice cheese into rounds about ⅛ inch thick. On a large serving platter or on individual salad plates, arrange alternate slices of cheese and tomato in a concentric pattern.

2. In a small bowl combine olive oil, lemon juice, and basil. Whisk well. Spoon dressing over salad. Season with salt and pepper. Garnish with basil sprigs and serve immediately.

Serves 4 as a first course.

GREEK SALAD

This leafy salad is refreshing before, with, or after a Greek-style main course. During warm weather you can make it a main dish for two or three people simply by doubling the amount of cheese. Feta cheese, made from goat's milk, is available in the refrigerator section of most supermarkets and from cheese markets.

½ cup Greek olives
4 cups each torn red and green leaf lettuce
½ cup slivered mild red onion
1 medium tomato, chopped
1 small green pepper, seeded and slivered
½ cup crumbled feta cheese

Oregano Dressing

1 tablespoon red wine vinegar
2 teaspoons fresh lemon juice
1 clove garlic, minced or pressed
½ teaspoon *each* salt and dried oregano
⅛ teaspoon coarsely ground pepper
¼ cup olive oil

1. In a small bowl combine dressing with olives; cover and let stand for 30 minutes at room temperature.

2. In a salad bowl combine lettuce, onion, tomato, and green pepper. Mix lightly with olives and Oregano Dressing. Sprinkle with cheese.

Serves 4 to 6.

LEAFY GREEN SALADS

The basic salad ingredient, lettuce, tastes and looks best if treated carefully between market and table. A green salad will be the most satisfying if the greens are crisp, well dried, and cold before you add dressing. If greens are too wet, the dressing will not cling to them and the flavor will be diluted.

How much can you do ahead? Greens can be torn, placed in a plastic bag or covered in the bowl in which the salad will be mixed, and refrigerated for several hours before serving. The dressing can also be made in advance. An oil and vinegar dressing can stand out at room temperature for several hours; a creamy one should be covered and refrigerated.

With the exception of shredded lettuce and cabbage for certain salads, greens will be most pleasing if torn rather than cut. In the United States lettuce is usually served in bite-sized pieces; in France the most familiar salad is made with whole leaves of butter lettuce (which are folded with the fork, never cut, to eat).

When it comes to selecting and combining greens, choose from among many available flavors and appearances. Romaine and iceberg lettuces provide crispness; butter and oakleaf lettuces contribute softness and varied shapes; the color of red-leaf lettuce and radicchio brightens the mixture. A few shredded leaves of sorrel lend a pleasant tartness; curly endive adds texture and interesting bitterness; spinach gives a coarse quality. For a sharp bite, include watercress, arugula, or Belgian endive.

The addition of herbs and flowers expands the range of ingredients even more. Nasturtiums, chrysanthemums, violas, violets, alyssum, daylilies, roses, and dianthus are just a few of the edible flowers with which you can enhance your salad (as long as they are free of chemical sprays). Herb flowers add lovely flavor and color, although the flavors of the herbs themselves are intense, so use them judiciously.

Mix the salad at the last possible moment before serving in order to prevent the lettuce from wilting. Since greens should be handled gently, the phrase *tossed salad* is a bit misleading. When mixing a salad, use two large spoons or a pair of salad servers with a light, up-and-over motion—rather like folding egg whites into a soufflé. Many professional chefs prefer to toss greens with their hands, considering that technique the least bruising.

Figure on about 8 cups of lightly packed greens for four servings of a mixed salad. For this quantity of lettuce, you will need about ⅓ cup of an oil-and-vinegar dressing or ⅓ to ½ cup of a creamy one. Too much dressing will overwhelm the greens, but too little will leave them tasteless and bland.

Oregano Dressing In a small bowl mix vinegar, lemon juice, garlic, salt, oregano, and pepper. Using a whisk or fork, gradually beat in oil until well blended.

Makes about ⅓ cup.

CARROT-RAISIN SALAD

Walnuts add texture to this longtime favorite salad. Make it at least one hour before serving so the flavors can blend.

½ cup mayonnaise
2 tablespoons sour cream
1 tablespoon cider vinegar
½ teaspoon sugar
¼ teaspoon salt
3 large carrots, grated
1 cup raisins
1 cup walnuts, coarsely chopped

In a 2-quart bowl stir together mayonnaise, sour cream, cider vinegar, sugar, and salt. Toss carrots with dressing to coat well. Add raisins and walnuts. Let salad marinate for 1 hour before serving.

Serves 6 to 8.

FUSILLI SALAD

Corkscrew-shaped spaghetti is called *fusilli*. A creamy dressing such as this one will best cling to the long spirals.

    8 cups water
    1 tablespoon salt
    8 ounces dry fusilli
    2 tablespoons olive oil
    1 teaspoon white wine vinegar
    2 teaspoons chopped fresh basil
    1 clove garlic, minced
    ½ cup whipping cream
    1 egg yolk
       Salt and freshly ground pepper
    ½ cup raw peas
    ½ cup cubed yellow squash
    ½ cup cubed tomato

1. In a large pot over medium-high heat, bring the water and salt to a boil. Add pasta, stir well, and cover. Return to a boil and cook pasta until just tender.

2. Drain pasta in a colander and transfer to a large bowl. Toss with 1 tablespoon of the olive oil, vinegar, and basil. Set aside to cool.

3. In a medium saucepan sauté garlic in remaining tablespoon olive oil. Pour in whipping cream and heat to just below boiling. Turn off heat.

4. In a small bowl mix a little of the hot cream with egg yolk. Pour mixture back into cream sauce; blend well to thicken sauce. Season with salt and pepper and set aside to cool.

5. In a medium skillet with a small amount of water, lightly steam peas and yellow squash. When they are tender-crisp, toss with tomato and pasta. Pour sauce over all, toss again, and serve at room temperature.

Serves 4.

MIXED VEGETABLES VINAIGRETTE

Use whatever vegetables are in season for this salad; the ones listed below make a summertime version. Earlier in the year a similar salad might feature artichoke hearts or asparagus. In fall and winter use cool-season vegetables such as broccoli, cauliflower, and celery root.

    1 pound slender green beans
    2 large red or yellow bell peppers
    1 medium cucumber, peeled, seeded,
       and thickly sliced
    ½ teaspoon salt
    1 head escarole or red-leaf lettuce
    1 pint cherry or yellow pear tomatoes
    2 teaspoons *each* Dijon mustard and white
       wine vinegar
    6 tablespoons olive oil
       Salt and freshly ground pepper, to taste
       Basil leaves and flowers, for garnish

1. *The day before:* Trim green beans and cut into 2-inch lengths. Immerse in rapidly boiling salted water until tender but still bright green and a little crunchy. Drain, rinse immediately in cold water to stop cooking, and refrigerate. Roast and peel peppers (see page 425). Working over a bowl to catch juices, cut peppers into strips, discarding seeds and ribs. Refrigerate peppers with their juices.

2. *On day of serving:* Toss cucumber slices with salt and drain in a colander 15 minutes. Wash escarole, tear into bite-sized pieces, and dry thoroughly. In a large salad bowl combine greens with beans, peppers, cucumbers, and tomatoes; reserve pepper juices for dressing.

3. In a small jar combine mustard, vinegar, olive oil, and reserved pepper juices. Stir or shake to combine. Taste for seasoning and, if necessary, add salt and pepper. Just before serving, pour dressing over salad and toss to coat vegetables evenly. Garnish with basil leaves and flowers.

Serves 6.

CHINESE CHICKEN SALAD

Although the Chinese do eat cold chicken dishes, "Chinese chicken salad" is strictly a Chinese-American invention. It is very popular in Chinese restaurants in the United States. For a hotter version, use chile oil (available at Asian markets) in place of all or part of the sesame oil.

    1½ tablespoons soy sauce
     1 tablespoon *each* peanut oil and sesame oil
     2 teaspoons black vinegar
        Pinch of sugar (optional)
        Oil, for deep-frying
     2 ounces bean threads
     1 large chicken breast *or* 2 chicken legs,
        poached or steamed
     2 green onions, shredded
     1 tablespoon shredded fresh ginger
     3 stalks celery, cut in thin diagonal slices
        Large leaves of lettuce or Chinese cabbage
        Coriander sprigs, for garnish

1. In a medium bowl combine soy sauce, peanut and sesame oils, vinegar, and sugar (if used); set aside for at least 15 minutes to allow flavors to develop.

2. In a wok or other deep pan, heat oil to 375° to 400° F; add bean threads. They will rise instantly and form a loose disk. Fry about 15 seconds per side; remove and drain on paper towels.

3. Remove chicken meat from bones and shred by hand or with a knife. Toss chicken, green onion, ginger, and celery in soy sauce mixture. Line plate with lettuce leaves; top with fried bean threads. Arrange chicken mixture on top and garnish with coriander.

Serves 4 to 6 with other dishes.

CRAB SALAD LOUIS

To a generation or two of Californians, crab Louis (pronounced *loo*-ee) is a salad with a tomato-flavored mayonnaise dressing. According to some historians, however, the original Louis dressing contained not a speck of mayonnaise. Whatever it contains, Crab Salad Louis has remained a favorite. All versions have a few elements in common—crab or other shellfish and sliced hard-cooked egg on a bed of lettuce, with a dressing containing bottled chili sauce. Two versions of the dressing follow.

  ½ **head lettuce**
  ½ **cup cooked crabmeat**
  1 **hard-cooked egg, sliced**
      Freshly ground pepper
      Snipped fresh chives

Louis Dressing I

  2 **tablespoons white wine vinegar or
      fresh lemon juice**
      Pinch of salt and freshly ground pepper
  ½ **teaspoon dry mustard**
  ¼ **teaspoon paprika**
  ½ **teaspoon Worcestershire sauce**
  ½ **cup olive oil**
  ¼ **cup chili sauce**
  2 **tablespoons chopped fresh herbs
      (parsley, chives, tarragon, or a blend)**

Louis Dressing II

  ¼ **teaspoon dry mustard**
  1 **tablespoon fresh lemon juice**
      Dash of Worcestershire sauce
  ¼ **cup olive oil**
  ⅓ **cup mayonnaise**
  ⅓ **cup chili sauce**
  1 **tablespoon chopped fresh herbs
      (parsley, chives, tarragon, or a blend)**

Line a large individual salad bowl with outside leaves of lettuce. Tear remaining lettuce and arrange in bowl; place crabmeat in center. Place egg slices around outside; sprinkle with pepper and chives. Before serving, pour ¼ cup dressing over salad; serve remainder on the side.

Serves 1 as a main course, 2 as a first course.

Louis Dressing I Combine vinegar, salt and pepper, mustard, paprika, and Worcestershire; beat with a wire whisk until dissolved. Beat in oil, then chili sauce and herbs. Chill well and stir before serving.

Makes 1 cup.

Louis Dressing II Combine mustard, lemon juice, and Worcestershire; beat to dissolve, then beat in oil. Add mayonnaise, chili sauce, and herbs; blend thoroughly. Chill before serving.

Makes 1 cup.

BOMBAY TUNA

This sweet, tangy, and crunchy mixture—tuna combined with apple, currants, chutney, and almonds, and flavored with mustard and curry powder—is equally good as a salad or as a sandwich.

  1 **can (6½ oz) tuna packed in water, well drained**
  ½ **cup cubed unpeeled apple (pippin
      or other tart variety)**
  ⅓ **cup diced celery**
  1 **green onion, sliced**
  ¼ **cup slivered almonds or coarsely
      chopped toasted almonds**
  2 **tablespoons dried currants**
  ¼ **cup mayonnaise**
  2 **teaspoons chutney, finely chopped**
1½ **teaspoons Dijon mustard**
  ½ **teaspoon curry powder, or to taste**

1. In a medium bowl, combine tuna, apple, celery, green onion, almonds, and currants.

2. Stir mayonnaise, chutney, mustard, and curry powder into tuna mixture.

Makes 3 salads or 4 sandwiches.

Experts may argue over what makes an authentic Louis dressing, but the countless diners who order Crab Salad Louis regularly in California seafood restaurants probably don't care. Whether made with crab or shrimp, Louis salads are among the state's most popular dishes.

Red Fruit Plate is a spectrum of reds, oranges, and pinks. Each bite-sized piece can be dipped in the tasty Cream Cheese Dressing, which is flavored with plum jam.

2. Arrange lettuce leaves on a large salad plate. Place tuna in center of lettuce-lined plate. Arrange beans, quartered beets, green pepper strips, hard-cooked eggs, and tomatoes around tuna. Decorate vegetables with anchovy fillets and olives.

3. Drizzle dressing over ingredients after they have been set on plate, or marinate each ingredient in a little dressing and then arrange.

Serves 4.

■ RED FRUIT PLATE WITH CREAM CHEESE DRESSING

A jewel box of summer fruits, ranging in color from pink through crimson to burgundy, makes an eye-catching summer salad arrangement.

Red-leaf lettuce
1 cup sweet cherries with stems
1 basket (2 to 3 cups) strawberries
8 figs, sliced crosswise
4 wedges (about 1½ in. thick) watermelon
2 nectarines, pitted and cut in wedges
4 red plums, halved and pitted
1 bunch (about 1 lb) red seedless grapes

Cream Cheese Dressing

1 package (3 oz) cream cheese
1 tablespoon fresh lemon juice
2 tablespoons plum jam
¾ cup whipping cream

Line 4 plates with lettuce. Divide fruits among the 4 plates, arranging them with red surfaces up. Serve with Cream Cheese Dressing to spoon over each serving.

Serves 4.

Cream Cheese Dressing   Soften cream cheese; beat until creamy. Gradually add lemon juice, jam, and cream, beating until thick. Refrigerate for about 1 hour to blend flavors.

Makes about 1½ cups.

■ SALADE NIÇOISE

Traditionally, this showcase salad from the south of France near Nice consists of tuna, anchovies, capers, beans, and tomatoes, but any seasonal favorites may be successfully included.

½ pound thin green beans (haricots verts, if possible)
1 bunch small beets
1 small head lettuce, torn into bite-sized pieces
1 can (6½ oz) tuna, packed in olive oil, drained
1 green bell pepper, cut in thin strips
2 hard-cooked eggs, quartered
2 tomatoes, quartered
1 can (2 oz) anchovy fillets
16 black Niçoise olives or
oil-packed olives from Italy or Greece
Mustard Vinaigrette (see page 520)

1. Trim ends from green beans; in a large pot bring 3 quarts water to a boil. Boil beans until tender-crisp and bright green (about 7 minutes). Using a slotted spoon, remove to a bowl of ice water to stop cooking and to chill. Trim leaves from beets (do not peel beets). Boil beets in the same 3 quarts water until tender (15 to 20 minutes depending on size). Slip skins from beets while still warm, then quarter.

SALAMANDER

In mythology the salaman-  der is a beast able to endure fire without being burned. Over the centuries, some literary chef gave this name to a tool used to brown foods. This special oven, found in professional kitchens, has an overhead heat source designed to glaze gratins (see GRATIN) or caramelize the sugar topping of desserts such as Crème Brûlée. For glazing and browning, the home cook can use the broiler set to high heat or a portable salamander. This utensil, also sometimes called a crème brûlée iron, is a small, heavy, iron disk attached to a long rod ending in a wooden handle. To use, heat the disk to red-hot over the stove burner; for caramelizing sugar, press the head into the sugar until it reaches the desired state; for browning savory dishes, hold the head close to the surface and move across from one side to the other.

The salamander is easier to control than a broiler, which is important for cold custards; the sugar will melt with the concentrated infusion of heat, but the custard won't heat up as well.

SALT

This is the most common culinary seasoning in the world. Available in unlimited quantities from the sea and rocks, it also is naturally present in the human body and is in many foods. Although excessive salt consumption is believed to promote hypertension, some salt intake is essential to the human diet.

WHEN TO SALT

There is considerable disagreement among cooks about the proper moment in the cooking process to add salt. Because salt draws out moisture, many cooks claim that salting roasts after cooking results in a juicier roast. However, other cooks claim that moisture loss is immaterial for roasts cooked immediately after salting; they claim that salting before cooking results in better flavor than merely salting the surface of the food after cooking. Most cooks agree that salt sprinkled on meats or vegetables prior to cooking in a microwave oven will toughen the foods.

Some cooks insist that dried beans should be salted after cooking since salt toughens them otherwise. The same cooks, however, will add a salty ham bone or salt pork to the bean cooking liquid. There seems to be no agreement; experiment and decide for yourself.

Many cookbooks and recipes suggest adding a pinch of salt to egg whites while beating them. In fact the salt destabilizes the foam. If salt is desirable for flavor, add it at the end of the beating process.

Use   The most prominent function of salt is as a seasoning. When used in moderation, it heightens the flavor of food. Dishes prepared without salt often seem bland and flat. Starchy foods—potatoes, rice, beans, and bread—seem to beg loudest for the flavor-enhancing quality of salt, but even sweet baked goods benefit from a pinch.

Salt also functions as a preservative. For thousands of years salt has been employed to withdraw moisture from bacteria and mold cells in food, slowing cell growth considerably. In the presence of a lot of salt, the cells may even dry up. This inability of bacteria and mold cells to survive in a salty medium is what preserves such items as salt cod. (In the past, it preserved bacon and salt pork, although neither is salted enough today to be preserved by salt alone.) Processors add salt to butter and cheese to flavor them and to prolong their refrigerated life.

Salt contributes to the pickling process by establishing a high-acid, low-pH, anaerobic (oxygen-free) environment in which bacteria are unable to live. Salting cabbage, for example, generates a brine which, if allowed to ferment, produces an environment inhospitable to bacteria. The result is sauerkraut, which can be preserved for long periods without refrigeration if kept submerged in brine.

Withdrawing moisture from foods with salt can also improve flavor. Salting cucumber and eggplant, for example, removes the bitter juices.

Added to the water in which vegetables are boiled, salt improves flavor and raises the boiling point of the water slightly, enabling the vegetables to cook more quickly and therefore better retain color and nutritive value.

Salt can also lower the freezing point of water, which is why it is added to the ice packed around ice cream freezers. Without salt the surrounding brine pack would never get cold enough to freeze the ice cream.

Cooking foods in hot salt is a popular technique in some cuisines, and surprisingly, these foods do not taste particularly salty. Chinese cooks bake whole chickens in salt; Spanish cooks similarly bake whole fish. The salt is heated in the oven, then the food is completely buried in it and returned to the oven. Because salt is a more even conductor of heat than air, the food cooks evenly and quickly and the finished product is especially moist despite salt's proclivity to draw moisture out.

Availability   Most supermarkets carry the following salt varieties. Sea salt is also found in most health-food stores and in specialty markets.

Common or Table Salt   Most table salt, which is fine grained, contains additives to keep it from clumping. Iodized salt is supplemented with iodine to reduce the incidence of goiter.

Kosher Salt   This coarse-grained salt has no additives and is about half as salty as table salt. Some cooks prefer it for salads and uncooked dishes because they like its texture. Others object to the texture and use it only where it will dissolve, such as in soups or water used to boil pasta or vegetables.

Pickling or Canning Salt More finely ground than table salt, pickling or canning salt has no additives that might cloud pickles.

Rock Salt Coarse-grained rock salt is crystallized salt found in rocks. It is less refined than table salt. Because it is used, along with ice, to pack around the outside of ice cream freezers to speed the rate of freezing, it is sometimes referred to as ice cream salt.

Sea Salt As its name suggests, sea salt is obtained from sea water; its texture can be coarse or fine. The best varieties come from England, France, and the United States and have a fresh, light taste.

Storage Store salt in a closed container; it will keep indefinitely.

Recipes and Related Information
Gravlax, 233; Ice Cream and Frozen Dessert, 308.

SANDWICH GRILLING IRON

The French version of a grilled cheese sandwich, *croque-monsieur* has a filling of a slice of ham topped with Swiss, Emmentaler, or Gruyère cheese; *croque-madame* uses chicken as the meat. To cook, the sandwich is sautéed in butter in a skillet or browned in  a cast-aluminum grilling iron that impresses the bread with a decorative shell pattern. The iron, which sits directly on the burner unit of a stove, consists of two plates joined with a hinge at the back. Each plate has two shell-shaped impressions. Heatproof handles allow safe movement of the iron. A version without the shell design is also available and is slightly smaller in size.

Aside from the classic sandwiches, consider these combinations, all on buttered bread: fresh peaches or other fruit; whipped cream cheese and jam; asparagus tips with basil butter; or thin slices of red onion with romaine lettuce and mayonnaise.

To use, butter the grilling-iron plates or spray them with vegetable cooking spray. Clean by washing gently and wiping dry.

SAUCE

Broadly defined, a sauce is any fluid dressing, including relishes and condiments. An exquisite sauce has always been the hallmark of fine cuisine and the test of a cook's expertise. A well-made sauce is impressive even when it may actually be easily and quickly prepared. It implies luxury and competence and mastery of a revered culinary art. Most of all, however, sauces are a treat to the palate, in both flavor and texture.

A sauce is basically a thickened liquid—usually stock, milk, cream, melted butter, or wine, but other liquids are sometimes used. The most common thickeners are flour, or other starches, and egg yolks. Some sauces contain no thickeners but gain body by being reduced or boiled until they are concentrated. Once a liquid has been thickened, it needs only seasonings to give it flavor. The preparation of a sauce usually involves the following steps: gently simmering the ingredients, skimming away any impurities that may rise to the surface, and reducing to add body and ripen the flavor.

Sauces can be thought of as belonging to groups. They are categorized according to their major ingredients and their thickening agent. The major sauce families are white and brown sauces, which are thickened with flour and made with milk or stock; tomato sauces; butter sauces; flourless cream sauces, which are thickened by reduction; and dressings.

Each family of sauces has a different use. In general the white sauces, butter sauces, and flourless cream sauces are served with seafood, light meats, and vegetables, and the brown sauces are served with dark meats. Tomato sauces are served with pasta, fish, fowl, and some light meats. Dressings, of course, are for salads. However, because saucing is such a question of taste, there are many exceptions to these guidelines.

Once you master the techniques of preparation, you can vary any sauce to suit your own preference or particular need. Remember, however, that sauces are meant to enhance, not to disguise, the flavor of food. Add new seasonings gradually and taste the sauce before adding any additional flavor.

Use heavy saucepans of good quality so that flour-thickened sauces will not stick or burn and egg yolks will not curdle. A small whisk, which can quickly and easily reach all parts of the saucepan, is also essential. A food processor or blender is an invaluable aid in making some sauces, especially those in the mayonnaise family, which otherwise require prolonged whisking.

WHITE SAUCES

The simplest of the hot sauces, white sauces are quickly made with ingredients usually at hand. This group can be subdivided: the milk-based white sauces and the stock-based, cream-colored *velouté* sauces.

The techniques for making both types are similar. Both are thickened with a light roux—a mixture of butter and flour that is cooked until bubbling and until the starchy taste of the flour has dispersed. The liquid is added only after the roux cooks long enough to toast the flour lightly. If the roux is not properly cooked, or if too much flour is used for the amount of liquid, the sauce becomes unpleasantly pasty and sticky.

Flour tends to cause lumps if not combined properly with the liquid. To avoid lumps, the liquid should be whisked into the roux rather than mixed in with a spoon. Whisking, which blends the mixture more thoroughly, should be constant while the liquid is being added and until the sauce comes to a boil.

A roux gives a creamy texture to these sauces, which are often further enriched with cream and egg yolks. With or without added enrichment, white sauces can be quite rich, although they are lower in calories than butter sauces and flourless cream sauces.

Almost all vegetables, light-meat chicken and turkey, fish, and shellfish can be served with a white sauce. For poultry and seafood, velouté is generally preferred because then the stock is related to the dish. Fish stock reinforces the fish flavor and poultry stock enhances the flavor of a chicken or turkey dish.

Almost any flavoring can be added to these basic sauces. Cheeses—from the mild Swiss cheeses to the sharper Parmesan or tangy blue cheeses—are popular additions to milk-based sauces. Fresh herbs, Dijon mustard, and spices such as curry powder and paprika also excite the palate.

White sauces can be made up to two days ahead and then refrigerated or frozen. If sauces are to be enriched with egg yolks, however, it is best to add the yolks after the sauce has been reheated. Reheat white sauces in a medium saucepan over low heat, whisking often.

■ BASIC WHITE SAUCE

Also known as béchamel, this is a classic French sauce usually made with milk (but sometimes enriched with cream) and a white roux. Sauces derived from Basic White Sauce are often served with vegetables but also accompany eggs, fish, pasta, and sometimes poultry. White sauce can also be mixed with cooked vegetables to make creamed vegetables or poured over vegetables, sprinkled with grated cheese, and baked as a gratin. Béchamel is sometimes layered in baked lasagne and is the secret to making macaroni and cheese creamy. A thicker version of the sauce, made with more flour, is the base for soufflés; a thinner version, made with less flour, is the foundation for cream soups.

    1 cup milk
    1½ tablespoons butter
    1½ tablespoons flour
        Salt and white pepper, to taste
        Freshly grated nutmeg

1. In a small, heavy-bottomed saucepan, bring milk to a boil. Remove from heat. Melt butter in a small, heavy-bottomed saucepan over low heat. Whisk in flour. Cook, whisking constantly, until mixture is well blended and bubbly (about 2 minutes). Let cool slightly.

2. Gradually pour milk into flour mixture, whisking. Return pan to heat and bring to a boil over medium-high heat, whisking constantly. Add pinch of salt, pepper, and nutmeg. Reduce heat to medium-low and simmer, uncovered, whisking often, for 5 minutes.

3. Taste and add more salt, pepper, and nutmeg, if needed. If not using sauce at once, dab top with butter to prevent a skin from forming. Sauce can be refrigerated, covered, for up to 2 days or frozen. To reheat, whisk over medium heat. Serve hot.

Makes 1 cup.

Cheese Sauce Bring 1 cup Basic White Sauce to a simmer in a small, heavy-bottomed saucepan over medium heat, whisking often. Remove from heat and whisk in ¼ cup freshly grated Parmesan, Gruyère, or sharp Cheddar cheese until melted. Quickly whisk in 1 egg yolk (if sauce is to be part of a baked dish, but do not reheat sauce with yolk, which may curdle) or 2 tablespoons butter (if sauce is to be used as an accompaniment). Taste and add salt and pepper.

Cream Sauce Bring 1 cup Basic White Sauce to a simmer in a small, heavy-bottomed saucepan over medium heat, whisking often. Whisk in ¼ cup whipping cream. Simmer sauce, whisking often, until slightly thickened (about 2 minutes). Taste and add salt, pepper, and nutmeg, if needed. If desired, stir in 1 tablespoon chopped fresh chives, tarragon, parsley, or basil. Serve hot.

One of the classics of French cuisine, béchamel is the base of many sauces. Made with milk or cream, it is white, smooth, and rich enough to be pleasurable in itself—over fish, poultry, or vegetables—yet adaptable enough to accept other flavorings.

Madeira Sauce dresses up any roast, poultry, or meat. If you keep brown sauce in the freezer, it can be prepared in just a few minutes.

flour into butter. Cook, whisking constantly, until mixture turns a light beige color (about 3 minutes). Remove from heat and let cool slightly.

2. Gradually pour stock into flour mixture, whisking. Bring to a boil over medium-high heat, whisking constantly. Add pinch of salt and pepper. Reduce heat to medium-low and simmer, uncovered, whisking often, for 5 minutes.

3. Taste and add more salt and pepper, if needed. If not using sauce at once, dab top with butter to prevent a skin from forming. Sauce can be refrigerated, covered, up to 1 day or frozen.

Makes 1 cup.

Creamy Velouté Sauce Bring Velouté Sauce to a simmer in a medium, heavy-bottomed saucepan, whisking often. Whisk in ¼ cup whipping cream and bring to a boil. Simmer, whisking occasionally, until sauce thickens slightly (about 2 minutes). If desired, stir in 1 tablespoon chopped fresh chives, tarragon, parsley, basil, or dill. Taste and add salt and white pepper, if needed.

BROWN SAUCES

Like white sauces, brown sauces are thickened with a roux of butter and flour cooked together, although the roux for brown sauces is cooked until it has just taken on some color. This roux gives color to the sauce. The liquid used in the sauce, usually beef or veal stock, also adds a warm brown appearance. Even darker is the roux used as a thickener and flavoring agent in Louisiana cooking; it deepens to a rich red-brown.

Brown sauces are served mainly with dark meats, especially beef and lamb, and with duck; they are good with roast poultry and poached eggs as well. They reinforce the taste of meat and enhance it with additional flavorings. Brown sauces are not served with seafood or vegetables, although vegetables can accompany the meats served with these sauces.

These sauces are often served on the side as an accompaniment to a beautifully browned roast or steak, so as not to hide the color of the food. Not usually thick, they moisten food without coating it or clinging to it.

A favorite flavoring for brown sauce is wine, especially a fortified wine such as port or Madeira. The flavor and color of tomatoes also complement these sauces. Fresh herbs are another popular addition. A small amount of butter can be stirred into the sauces, but often this enrichment is not necessary because the meat they accompany is rich enough.

Brown sauces can be made up to three days ahead and refrigerated or frozen. Reheat them in a heavy saucepan over medium heat, whisking often. If they contain fresh herbs or fortified wines, add more of these flavorings after reheating to compensate for flavor lost during the process of chilling and reheating.

■ **VELOUTE SAUCE**

Like Basic White Sauce, Velouté Sauce is generally used as a base for other sauces served with fish, chicken, turkey, veal, and eggs. Often the fish, poultry, or meat is poached in stock, which gains more flavor and is then used to prepare the *velouté*. To vary the sauce, consider combining white wine with the stock.

 1 **cup Chicken Stock (see page 560) or Fish Stock (see page 561)**
 1½ **tablespoons butter**
 1½ **tablespoons flour**
     Salt and white pepper, to taste

1. Bring stock to a boil in a small, heavy-bottomed saucepan. Remove from heat. Melt butter in a small, heavy-bottomed saucepan over low heat. Whisk

■ BASIC BROWN SAUCE

This rich, meat-flavored sauce is the basis for all brown sauces. It is generally not used as is, but is flavored with Madeira, mushrooms, or other ingredients. These sauces are served mainly with beef and lamb, as well as some poultry and egg dishes. Brown sauce freezes well and can be used as needed to turn any broiled, roasted, or sautéed meat into a festive dish.

> 2 tablespoons vegetable oil
> 2½ tablespoons flour
> 2 cups Beef Stock or Brown Veal Stock
>   (see page 560)
> 1 onion, coarsely chopped
> 1 carrot, diced
> 1 tomato, diced
> 1 bay leaf
> 1 sprig fresh thyme *or* a pinch of dried thyme
> 5 parsley stems
> 2 teaspoons tomato paste
>   Salt and freshly ground pepper, to taste

1. In a medium, heavy-bottomed saucepan, heat oil over low heat; add flour and cook, whisking constantly, until mixture is golden brown. Be careful to keep it from burning. Remove from heat.

2. Gradually whisk stock into flour mixture. Add onion, carrot, tomato, bay leaf, thyme, and parsley. Bring to a boil, stirring constantly. Reduce heat to low and simmer, uncovered, stirring frequently, for 1 hour.

3. Stir tomato paste into sauce, season lightly with salt and pepper, and simmer 1 minute. Strain through a fine sieve. If not using sauce at once, dab top with butter to prevent a skin from forming. Sauce can be refrigerated, covered, up to 3 days, or frozen.

Makes about 1½ cups.

■ MADEIRA SAUCE

Serve with grilled or sautéed steaks or with roast beef, veal, chicken, or turkey.

> 1½ cups Basic Brown Sauce (above) or
>   Quick Brown Sauce (at right)
> 4 tablespoons Madeira
>   Salt and freshly ground pepper, to taste
> 1 tablespoon butter (optional)

1. In a medium, heavy-bottomed saucepan, bring brown sauce to a boil over medium heat, whisking often.

2. Whisk in 2 tablespoons of the Madeira, add salt and pepper, and simmer, uncovered, over medium-low heat for 10 minutes.

3. Add remaining 2 tablespoons Madeira and bring just to a simmer. Remove from heat and stir in butter, if desired. Taste and add more salt and pepper, if needed. Serve hot.

Makes about 1½ cups.

■ QUICK BROWN SAUCE

This version of brown sauce provides a quick substitute for Basic Brown Sauce (at left), although this recipe produces a sauce that is lighter in color and texture and not quite as rich; it also includes tomatoes and tomato paste for additional flavor.

> 1 tablespoon vegetable oil
> 1 onion, diced
> 1 carrot, diced
> 2 cups Beef Stock, Brown
>   Veal Stock, or Chicken Stock
>   (see page 560)
> 2 ripe, medium fresh tomatoes *or*
>   4 drained canned plum tomatoes, diced
> 4 tablespoons cold water
> 1 tablespoon tomato paste
> 1 tablespoon potato starch or cornstarch
>   Salt and freshly ground pepper, to taste

1. In a medium, heavy-bottomed saucepan, heat oil over medium-high heat. Add onion and carrot and sauté, stirring often, until well browned. Be careful not to let vegetables burn.

2. Add stock and tomatoes to saucepan. Bring to a boil, stirring constantly. Reduce heat to very low, cover, and simmer 30 minutes.

3. In a small bowl whisk the cold water into tomato paste. Add potato starch and whisk to form a smooth paste. Gradually pour into simmering sauce, whisking constantly. Bring sauce back to a boil, whisking. Season very lightly with salt and pepper. Strain sauce, pressing on vegetables.

4. If not using sauce immediately, dab surface with a small piece of butter to prevent a skin from forming. Sauce can be refrigerated, covered, up to 3 days, or frozen.

Makes about 1½ cups.

Brown Sauce With Herbs Bring 1 cup Quick Brown Sauce or Basic Brown Sauce (at left) to a simmer in a small, heavy-bottomed saucepan over low heat. Remove from heat and stir in 1 to 2 tablespoons chopped fresh tarragon, chives, basil, or parsley. If desired, stir in 1 tablespoon butter.

TOMATO SAUCE

Favorites in many cuisines, tomato sauces are good with almost every food, from meats to fish and pasta. The best tomato sauces are those made with fresh tomatoes, although canned ones can be used as well. In fact, when tomatoes are not plentiful, canned tomatoes may be a better choice; they will often have more flavor than what is offered fresh in the market off-season. Because tomatoes are the star ingredient and determine the final flavor of the sauce, they must be ripe. Sometimes the appearance of

---

TIPS

HOW TO MAKE PERFECT GRAVY

For many people, a beef roast or a turkey just isn't a meal without rich brown gravy. Here are some ideas for making your gravy smooth and flavorful.

- *Think of gravy as a thickened sauce. First remove the meat from the roasting pan, then pour or spoon off the fat and measure it. For each cup of gravy, measure 1 to 2 tablespoons of fat into a saucepan. Discard the rest.*

- *Loosen the drippings in the pan with liquid— beef or chicken broth, water, or red or white wine (or a combination of these). Heat and stir to loosen brown bits, and pour the liquid into a measuring cup; if there are large undissolved bits, pour liquid through a sieve. Don't add too much liquid, or the flavor will be weak.*

- *For each cup of liquid, measure 1 to 2 tablespoons flour. Stir the flour into the fat in the saucepan and heat until bubbly. Remove from heat. Using a wire whisk, gradually stir in the liquid. Return to heat and cook, stirring constantly, until mixture is thickened. Boil 3 to 5 minutes more. Salt to taste.*

- *If you prefer a creamy gravy for pork or chicken, use a liquid of about half milk, and half broth or water.*

TIPS

SAVE THAT SAUCE!

White and Brown Sauces Always whisk all over the surface of the pan, including the edges, to avoid sticking.

When making a white or brown sauce ahead, dab the surface of the hot finished sauce with butter to prevent a skin from forming during storage.

Thaw frozen white and brown sauces before reheating.

Butter Sauces Add the butter gradually to Hollandaise and béarnaise sauces; otherwise they may separate.

If a Hollandaise or béarnaise sauce separates, whisk 1 tablespoon of the separated sauce with 1 tablespoon of cold water until the mixture is smooth. Gradually whisk in the remaining separated sauce. If this does not work, start again by whisking 1 egg yolk and 1 tablespoon of water in a small, heavy-bottomed saucepan over low heat until thick, as in the recipes; then very gradually whisk in the separated sauce and any remaining butter.

Dressings All vinaigrettes can be made ahead but will separate upon standing. To re-emulsify a dressing, simply shake or whisk it.

When making mayonnaise, add the oil to the yolks slowly; otherwise, the mayonnaise separates.

If mayonnaise separates, beat it gradually into 1 teaspoon of Dijon mustard or 1 egg yolk.

tomatoes is misleading because they are red on the outside but turn out to have disappointingly pale flesh. To avoid these, choose tomatoes that are not too firm and that have a strong aroma of tomatoes. No extra thickening is required for most tomato sauces because the tomato pulp thickens the sauce as it cooks.

Herbs and tomatoes are natural partners. Besides the familiar tomato-loving herbs—basil, thyme, and oregano—almost any fresh herb or good-quality dried herb can flavor a tomato sauce. Members of the onion family, especially yellow onions, leeks, shallots, and garlic, can be chopped, sautéed, and cooked with the tomatoes to increase depth of flavor.

Although tomato sauce is delicious alone, it is so versatile that it can also be mixed with most other sauces. Add a few tablespoons to Basic White Sauce (see page 513) or Velouté Sauce (see page 514) to make an orange-colored sauce that is good with fish. Combine tomato sauce with a brown sauce and serve with roast tenderloin of beef, or mix with one of the butter sauces, such as Béarnaise (see page 518) and use with steaks, veal, and eggs.

■ BASIC TOMATO SAUCE

The flavor of this chunky sauce is fresh because the tomatoes cook only briefly. This sauce is good with pasta, fish, chicken, meat, eggs, and vegetables. There are many ways to vary the flavor of the sauce: Butter or olive oil can replace the vegetable oil; thyme and bay leaves as well as a variety of fresh herbs can be added to the finished sauce (basil is especially good, but tarragon, oregano, and cilantro also add an interesting change of flavor). Adding a tablespoon of tomato paste brightens the sauce. When tomatoes are out of season, use 2½ pounds (undrained weight) of canned whole plum tomatoes; drain them well and chop them. For a very smooth sauce, purée Basic Tomato Sauce in a food processor or blender.

>   2 tablespoons vegetable oil
>   ½ onion, chopped
>   1 clove garlic, finely chopped
>   2½ pounds ripe tomatoes, peeled, seeded,
>   and chopped
>   Pinch dried thyme
>   1 bay leaf
>   Salt and freshly ground pepper, to taste

1. In a medium, heavy-bottomed skillet, heat oil over low heat. Add onion and cook, stirring occasionally, until soft but not browned (about 7 minutes). Stir in garlic and cook 30 seconds.

2. Add tomatoes, thyme, bay leaf, and salt and pepper. Cook over medium heat, stirring often, until tomatoes are soft and mixture is thick and smooth (about 20 minutes).

3. Discard bay leaf. Taste and add more salt and pepper, if needed. Sauce can be refrigerated, covered, up to 2 days, or frozen. Serve hot.

Makes about 1½ cups.

BUTTER SAUCES

Probably the most popular group of sauces, these are rich and silky in texture because their main ingredient, butter, not only enriches but also constitutes the body of the sauce. Butter sauces are reserved for special occasions and for the most festive foods, such as lobster, scallops, fresh salmon, and asparagus.

Although butter sauces can be made quickly, they also demand the most care and can separate if not prepared properly. They are emulsions, or fragile combinations of fat (in this case heated butter) and liquid. If the butter separates from the liquid, the sauce loses its lovely texture and becomes watery and unattractive. Hollandaise and béarnaise sauces, which contain egg yolks in addition to the butter, lose their smoothness if the egg yolks curdle, or cook into small bits resembling scrambled eggs. To avoid both problems, whisk the sauce constantly and do not cook it too long or over too high a flame. They should be served warm, not boiling hot.

Because these sauces are so sensitive to heat, it is best not to serve them on heated plates. Often they are served separately, in sauceboats. A small amount of the rich sauce is all that is needed: 3 tablespoons per person is usually enough with most foods.

Butter sauces should not be prepared ahead. If some sauce is left, however, do not discard it; store it in the refrigerator or freezer. Leftover sauce cannot be reheated to its former smoothness, but it can be whisked in small pieces into another sauce, especially a velouté or tomato sauce, or stirred into dishes such as hot cooked rice, pasta, or vegetables for a special flavor.

■ HOLLANDAISE SAUCE

One of the most delicate of sauces, Hollandaise is a favorite with poached fish, shellfish, and vegetables. Also try it with poultry: Enrich the basic sauce with whipping cream, or mix chopped fresh tomatoes into room-temperature Hollandaise and serve over cold poached chicken breasts. The predominant flavor in the sauce is butter. A small amount of lemon juice is added as a seasoning. Many cooks increase the amount of lemon juice, especially when serving the sauce with fish. Hollandaise can be held up to 45 minutes in a double boiler set on a warming tray.

>   3 egg yolks
>   3 tablespoons water
>   Salt
>   ¾ cup unsalted butter, clarified (see page 68)
>   Pinch cayenne pepper
>   ¼ teaspoon strained fresh lemon juice, or to taste

1. In a small, heavy-bottomed nonreactive saucepan, combine egg yolks, the water, and salt; whisk briefly. Cook over low heat, whisking vigorously and constantly, until mixture is creamy and thick enough that whisk leaves a visible trail on bottom of pan. (Be careful not to let mixture overheat or egg yolks will curdle. Remove pan from heat occasionally so that it does not become too hot; sides of pan should be cool enough to touch.) When yolk mixture becomes thick enough, remove it immediately from heat and whisk for another 30 seconds.

2. With saucepan off heat gradually whisk in clarified butter drop by drop. After sauce has absorbed about 2 or 3 tablespoons butter, add remaining butter in a very thin stream, whisking vigorously and constantly. Stir in cayenne and lemon juice. Taste and add more salt, cayenne, and lemon juice, if needed.

3. Serve sauce as soon as possible. It can be kept warm in saucepan for about 15 minutes if set on a rack above warm water, but it must be whisked frequently. It can also be kept warm in a thermos.

Makes about 1 cup.

■ QUICK HOLLANDAISE SAUCE

Using a blender or food processor to prepare Hollandaise sauce makes a more stable emulsion, but the sauce will lack some of the body and flavor of the traditional preparation. This quick version can be served with the same foods as the traditional Hollandaise sauce. There is no need to heat the egg yolks in a saucepan; the butter, heated until bubbling, cooks the egg yolks slightly. A quick version of Béarnaise sauce (see page 518 for the traditional recipe), is offered at the end of the recipe.

> **3 egg yolks, at room temperature**
> **1 tablespoon water**
> **   Salt**
> **¾ cup unsalted butter, clarified (see page 68)**
> **   Pinch cayenne pepper**
> **½ teaspoon strained fresh lemon juice, or to taste**

1. In a blender or food processor, process egg yolks with the water and salt until the color lightens and they are very well blended. Heat butter to just bubbling. With machine running, gradually incorporate hot butter drop by drop into yolk mixture. After 2 or 3 tablespoons butter have been added, pour remaining butter through in a fine stream, with machine still running.

2. Add cayenne and lemon juice and process briefly to mix. Taste and add more salt, cayenne, and lemon juice, if needed.

3. Serve sauce as soon as possible. To keep it warm for about 15 minutes, transfer to a saucepan placed in a pan of warm water, and whisk sauce frequently. It can also be kept warm in a thermos.

Makes about 1 cup.

Quick Béarnaise Sauce   Prepare the liquid flavoring for Béarnaise Sauce, page 518, step 2, and substitute it for the water in Quick Hollandaise Sauce. In step 2 of Quick Hollandaise Sauce, omit lemon juice. Stir 1 tablespoon chopped tarragon and 1 tablespoon chopped parsley into finished sauce.

THICKENERS FOR SAUCES AND SOUPS

The same thickeners are employed for both sauces and soups. Listed below are the most commonly used thickening agents and enrichments. Where appropriate, guidelines are offered.

Beurre manié   An uncooked paste of equal amounts of butter and flour, beurre manié is used to build up sauces that are too thin. To make beurre manié, knead flour and butter together with fingers, or mash with a fork or spoon. For a soup use 1 tablespoon flour and 1 tablespoon butter to thicken 1 cup of liquid. For a sauce use 2 tablespoons flour and 2 tablespoons butter to thicken 1 cup of liquid. Extra beurre manié can be stored, wrapped in waxed paper, in the refrigerator for about 10 days.

Butter swirls   Although used mostly as a finish, butter swirls will thicken sauce and soup slightly. Add bits of butter to the sauce or soup at the end of cooking and swirl in the pan to create a spiral; do not stir; 1 or 2 tablespoons will be enough to finish most sauces and soups.

Cornstarch   A sauce thickened with cornstarch is glossy and translucent. Cornstarch is a familiar ingredient in Asian cuisines. To avoid lumping, always add cornstarch mixed with liquid, in paste form. To thicken 1 cup of liquid, mix 1 tablespoon cornstarch with 2 tablespoons water.

Egg yolks and cream   When combined, egg yolks and cream act as both thickener and enrichment. For a prepared sauce that is already somewhat thick, mix 1 egg yolk with 2 to 3 tablespoons whipping cream for 1 cup of sauce. If the sauce is quite thin, 2 to 3 yolks may be needed to thicken sufficiently. Pour a little of the hot sauce into the combined yolk and cream and whisk to blend. Pour this mixture back into the sauce and gently heat. Do not allow it to boil or it will curdle. To thicken 6 cups of soup, use 2 egg yolks and ¼ cup of whipping cream. Proceed as for a sauce.

Flour   One of the most familiar thickeners, flour contains insoluble proteins that make the sauce opaque (cornstarch is close to a pure starch). Flour should be added as a paste, and then the sauce should be allowed to simmer a few minutes; uncooked flour imparts a strong, undesirable cereal taste. Or, add flour as a roux (see Roux at right).

Reduction   This process slowly simmers sauce over low heat until the volume of the sauce decreases and the flavor is greatly concentrated. Cooks in a hurry should avoid reduced sauces, although the patient sauce maker will be rewarded with a bonus of extra flavor. Straining is necessary at times to produce a smooth sauce. Because flavor will intensify as the sauce cooks down, seasoning should be added after reduction. The reduction process is also applied to vegetable purées; the purée alone is cooked down to produce an intense yet lightly flavored sauce.

Roux   The most common thickener, roux is equal parts of flour and butter cooked over medium heat to form a paste. One of the secrets of successful sauce making is a properly cooked roux. The combination of butter and flour adds body and flavor to sauces and soups. The paste can be used immediately, or stored in the refrigerator up to 2 weeks. There are three kinds of roux: white, blond, and brown. White roux is barely cooked, just enough to remove the taste of the flour; it is used in cream sauces. Blond roux is cooked to a pale golden color and is used in sauces where a white color is not as essential. Brown roux is cooked until it gives off a nutty aroma; it is used for brown and flavorful sauces. In making roux, heat the butter carefully, or use clarified butter (see page 68). Do not let the butter brown or burn. When adding the flour, whisk vigorously to blend. It will take 2 to 3 minutes over medium heat to cook out the flour taste. For a soup use 1 tablespoon butter and 1 tablespoon flour to thicken 1 cup of liquid. For a sauce use 2 tablespoons butter and 2 tablespoons flour to thicken 1 cup of liquid.

Vegetable purées   Used with soups in place of roux, these purées provide a unique taste. Vegetable purées add bulk so that another thickener is usually not required. However, cream is often added to a vegetable-purée–based soup for richness. Vegetables suitable for puréeing and adding to soups include beans (such as lentil, black bean, and split pea), tomato, carrot, cucumber, zucchini, potato, and leek. The quantity of purée needed to thicken a soup varies with the vegetable; add it in small amounts until the desired consistency is achieved.

Whipping cream   By itself, whipping cream is considered a thickener and an enrichment. Reduced, cream is one of the preferred thickening agents for sauces in nouvelle cuisine. For soups add cream at the end of cooking, in whatever amount produces the desired flavor and consistency.

■ BEARNAISE SAUCE

A zesty version of Hollandaise sauce, béarnaise is prepared like a Hollandaise, except the egg yolk mixture is flavored with tarragon, vinegar, wine, and shallots. Pepper is added in two forms—as cracked peppercorns that cook in the vinegar and as freshly ground pepper at the end. Serve the sauce with broiled fish, especially salmon, with steak, or with poached eggs. (For a quick version, see Quick Hollandaise Sauce, page 517. For hints on saving a separated sauce, see page 516.)

    ½ teaspoon black peppercorns
    2 tablespoons white wine vinegar
    3 tablespoons dry white wine
    2 shallots, chopped
    3 tablespoons dried tarragon
       Hollandaise Sauce (see page 516)
    1 tablespoon *each* chopped fresh tarragon
       leaves and chopped parsley
       Salt and freshly ground pepper, to taste

1. In a small heavy-bottomed saucepan, combine peppercorns, vinegar, wine, shallots, and dried tarragon. Bring to a boil and reduce until ingredients are barely moist. Set aside.

2. Prepare Hollandaise Sauce and then whisk in reduction. Add fresh tarragon leaves and parsley. Taste and add salt and pepper, if needed.

3. Serve sauce as soon as possible. It can be kept warm for about 15 minutes in pan if set on a rack above warm water, but it must be whisked frequently. It can also be kept warm in a thermos.

Makes about 1 cup.

■ BEURRE BLANC

This is the most popular butter sauce in modern French cooking and has become a great American favorite as well. It is a delicate sauce thickened only with butter. Although not traditional, cream is used in this recipe to allow the sauce to be held longer. Serve it with poached or steamed fish, shellfish, and vegetables. It is also good with poached chicken breasts. Leftover beurre blanc cannot be reheated because it would separate, but it can be used instead of plain butter to enrich flour-thickened sauces or stirred into hot cooked vegetables, pasta, or rice.

    2 large shallots, finely chopped
    2 tablespoons white wine vinegar
    3 tablespoons dry white wine
    2 tablespoons whipping cream
       Salt and white pepper, to taste
    1 cup softened butter, cut into 16 cubes

1. In a small, heavy-bottomed, nonreactive saucepan, combine shallots, vinegar, and wine. Bring to a boil, reduce heat to medium, and simmer mixture, uncovered, until liquid is reduced to about 2 tablespoons.

2. Whisk in cream and reduce heat to low. Simmer mixture, whisking occasionally, until liquid is reduced to about 3 tablespoons. Mixture can be prepared up to this point as much as 1 day ahead, covered, and refrigerated.

3. If chilled, simmer shallot mixture and season lightly with salt and pepper; reduce heat to low. Add one cube of butter, whisking constantly. When butter is nearly blended in, add another cube, still whisking. Continue adding one cube at a time, whisking constantly. The sauce should be pleasantly warm and should thicken. If it becomes too hot and drips of melted butter appear, remove saucepan immediately from heat and whisk sauce well; add next 3 or 4 cubes of butter off heat, whisking constantly. When temperature of sauce drops again to warm, return to low heat and continue adding butter cubes. Remove from heat as soon as last cube is added.

4. Strain sauce if desired. Taste and add salt and pepper, if needed. Serve sauce as soon as possible. It can be kept warm in saucepan if set on a rack above a pan of warm water, but it must be whisked frequently to prevent separation and the temperature must be kept constant. It can also be kept warm in a thermos.

Makes about 1 cup.

FLOURLESS CREAM SAUCE

The traditional cream sauce gets its body from flour. This type of sauce is richer than the traditional ones because reduced cream gives the sauce its body; the liquid is boiled with cream until a portion of the water evaporates and the sauce thickens naturally.

These sauces are not as thick as the white sauce; they are light in texture and are very quick to make. Nearly as rich as butter sauces, they usually contain white wine and can also be flavored with stock or with the same ingredients as any white or *velouté* sauce. Like white, velouté, and butter sauces, flourless cream sauces are good accompaniments to seafood, light meats, and vegetables.

These sauces can be made ahead and refrigerated for up to two days. Reheat them in a heavy, uncovered saucepan, whisking often.

■ MUSTARD CREAM SAUCE

Serve this sauce with broiled or sautéed fish fillets, sautéed veal scallops, chicken breasts, turkey breast slices, or pork chops. Prepare the sauce with chicken or veal stock to accompany poultry or meats and fish stock for fish.

    1   tablespoon butter
    2   shallots, finely chopped
    ¼   cup dry white wine
    ½   cup Chicken Stock (see page 560),
         Brown Veal Stock (see page 560), or
         Fish Stock (see page 561)
         Salt and freshly ground pepper, to taste
    1¼   cups whipping cream
    1½   to 2 tablespoons Dijon mustard

1. In a medium, heavy saucepan, melt butter; add shallots and cook, stirring, until softened (about 2 minutes).

2. Add wine, stock, and salt and pepper; simmer, stirring, until liquid is reduced to about 2 tablespoons. Stir in cream and bring to a boil, stirring. Reduce heat to medium and cook, stirring often, until sauce is thick enough to coat a spoon (about 7 minutes). At this point, sauce can be kept, covered, 1 day in the refrigerator.

3. Reheat sauce, if necessary, over medium heat, whisking. Reduce heat to low and whisk in 1½ table-spoons mustard. Taste and add more salt, pepper, and mustard, if needed. Serve hot.

Makes about 1 cup.

DRESSINGS

Served cold or at room temperature, dressings are sauces used on salads. The foods they accompany are also usually cold or at room temperature, although some dressings are good with hot food. Homemade dressings taste much fresher and better than commercial types and they are free of preservatives.

The two basic dressings are vinaigrette and mayonnaise. Most other dressings are variations of these. Vinaigrette is light and clear, making it ideal for greens and colorful salads, which are most appealing when the ingredients show through the dressing. It is also good with salads containing rich ingredients such as beef or duck. Mayonnaise-based dressings are richer and creamier and complement lean ingredients such as fish and chicken

Like butter sauces, dressings are emulsified sauces or blends of fat and liquid; unlike butter sauces, dressings are not blended over heat. The ingredients are simply whisked gradually together or are whirled in a blender or a food processor. Vinaigrette is not stable and therefore must be whisked just before using. An egg yolk binds mayonnaise together, making it relatively stable.

Differing versions of both types of dressings can be produced by varying the kind of vinegar and oil used, and both benefit from the addition of chopped fresh herbs and condiments such as mustard or capers.

■ MAYONNAISE

Mayonnaise can be prepared in a bowl, blender, or food processor. This mayonnaise made in a food processor with a whole egg will not be as rich or as thick as one made with egg yolks alone. Mayonnaise can be refrigerated, covered, for up to one week.

   2 egg yolks (or 1 large egg),
      at room temperature (see Note)
      Salt and white pepper, to taste
   1 teaspoon Dijon mustard
   2 tablespoons white wine vinegar or
      strained fresh lemon juice
 1½ cups vegetable oil, at room temperature
   1 tablespoon warm water (optional)

1. *To prepare with a whisk or mixer:* In a medium, heavy bowl, whisk egg yolks with a pinch of salt and pepper, mustard, and 1 tablespoon of the vinegar. Begin whisking or beating in oil drop by drop. When 2 or 3 tablespoons oil have been added, whisk or beat in remaining oil in a very fine stream. Stir in remaining vinegar. *To prepare with a food processor or blender:* Process 1 whole large egg with a pinch of salt and pepper, mustard, 1 tablespoon of the vinegar, and 1 tablespoon of the oil in a blender or food processor until well blended. With machine running, pour in remaining oil, about 1 teaspoon at a time. After ¼ cup oil has been added, pour in remaining oil in a fine stream, with machine still running. Add remaining tablespoon vinegar and process briefly to blend.

2. Taste and add more salt and pepper, if needed. If mayonnaise is too thick, gradually beat in 1 tablespoon warm water.

Makes about 1½ cups.

Note When preparing the mayonnaise in a blender or food processor, use 1 whole large egg instead of two yolks, if you wish. In this case, reduce the oil used to 1¼ cups.

Make perfect mayonnaise by blending fresh ingredients by hand or with a blender or food processor. The homemade flavor is worth the extra effort.

A Mexican table setting is incomplete without a bowl of salsa. The ingredients common to most red salsas are onions, garlic, tomatoes, fresh cilantro, and, of course, chiles.

■ TARTAR SAUCE WITH GREEN PEPPERCORNS

Green peppercorns give extra zip to tartar sauce, a traditional accompaniment to fried fish. The sauce is also delicious with fried vegetables, especially cauliflower, and with cold chicken or turkey. For added interest, use green peppercorn mustard or herb mustard instead of Dijon mustard.

    1 cup Mayonnaise (see page 519)
    1 tablespoon Dijon mustard
    2 tablespoons chopped parsley
    1 tablespoon chopped green onion,
        preferably green part
    1 hard-cooked egg, chopped
    1 tablespoon drained capers, rinsed and chopped
    2 teaspoons drained green peppercorns
    1 tablespoon chopped dill pickle
    1 teaspoon strained fresh lemon juice (optional)
        Salt and pepper, to taste

1. In a bowl mix mayonnaise and mustard until thoroughly blended. Stir in parsley, green onion, egg, capers, peppercorns, and pickle.

2. Taste and add lemon juice (if desired) and salt and pepper, if needed. Sauce can be refrigerated, covered, up to 2 days.

Makes about 1¼ cups.

■ VINAIGRETTE DRESSING

This popular salad dressing is perfect for green salad because it coats the greens lightly. It is also good with almost any salad ingredient, from raw or cooked vegetables to meats, fish, and pasta. Herb vinaigrette is especially good with seafood salads. Although vinaigrette is usually associated with cold dishes, it also makes a quick and pleasant sauce for hot food, especially fish, poultry, and meat.

There are many ways to vary the basic dressing. Replace the vegetable oil with olive, walnut, or other oil. Use white wine vinegar or red wine vinegar for dressings used every day; or try Champagne vinegar, sherry vinegar, or tarragon vinegar for special occasions.

    2 tablespoons wine vinegar or
        strained fresh lemon juice
        Salt and pepper, to taste
    6 tablespoons vegetable or olive oil

1. In a small bowl whisk vinegar and salt and pepper until salt dissolves.

2. Whisk in oil. Taste, and add more salt and pepper, if needed. Dressing can be refrigerated, covered, up to 1 week. Whisk before using.

Makes about ½ cup.

Caper Vinaigrette   With the oil, whisk in 1 tablespoon chopped capers and 2 tablespoons chopped parsley. As capers are salty, add salt to the dressing with a light touch. This dressing flatters grilled fish and fish salads.

Herb Vinaigrette   Just before using, add 1 tablespoon chopped parsley, chives, basil, or tarragon. For a more intense tarragon flavor, make the dressing with tarragon vinegar and add chopped fresh tarragon.

■ MUSTARD VINAIGRETTE

This dressing is thicker than most vinaigrettes because the oil is whisked in gradually. In addition the mustard helps to thicken it. Instead of plain Dijon mustard, you can use a grainy type or a flavored version such as herb mustard or green peppercorn mustard. If desired, add capers for more texture and flavor.

    1 teaspoon Dijon mustard
    3 tablespoons red wine vinegar
    1 clove garlic, minced
        Salt and pepper, to taste
    9 tablespoons olive oil
    1 tablespoon capers (optional)

1. Whisk mustard, vinegar, garlic, and salt and pepper together in a small bowl. Gradually pour in oil in a fine stream, whisking constantly.

2. Mix in capers, if used. Adjust seasoning, if needed. Dressing can be refrigerated, covered, up to 1 week. Whisk before using.

Makes about ¾ cup.

■ RASPBERRY VINEGAR AND SHALLOT DRESSING

This pink dressing has a wonderful aroma of raspberries. Use it to flavor poultry salads and to add unexpected zip to simple green salads. The dressing is made quickly in a food processor, but it can be prepared in a blender or bowl instead if the shallot is finely chopped by hand. If you are using a blender, combine the chopped shallot with the other ingredients in step 1 and continue with the rest of the recipe. If you prefer to prepare the dressing by hand, follow the procedure for Vinaigrette Dressing (opposite page), adding the chopped shallot at the beginning.

   ½ small shallot, peeled and halved
   3 tablespoons raspberry vinegar
      Salt and pepper, to taste
   ½ cup plus 1 tablespoon vegetable oil

1. Chop shallot until fine by dropping pieces one by one down feed tube of a food processor while blade is turning. Add vinegar and salt and pepper; process until combined.

2. As blade is turning, gradually pour in oil. Dressing will thicken slightly. Taste and add more salt and pepper, if needed. Dressing can be refrigerated, covered, up to 2 days. Whisk before using.

Makes about ¾ cup.

OTHER SAUCES

In addition to the classic sauces, we enjoy many other types throughout a meal, as dipping sauces for hors d'oeuvres, as accompaniments to the main course, and as toppings for all kinds of desserts.

■ CURRY SAUCE

A smooth and silky curry dip works magic on hard-cooked eggs, boiled shrimp and crab, or a basket of snow peas and hearts of bok choy. Or, serve it with thinly sliced cold chicken, smoked turkey, roast pork, or ham. The sauce keeps up to two weeks in the refrigerator.

   ¼ cup honey
   1 cup Chicken Stock (see page 560)
   2 tablespoons hot curry powder
   1 tablespoon ground coriander
   ½ teaspoon cayenne pepper
   ½ teaspoon white pepper
   ⅓ cup Dijon mustard
  3⅓ cups Mayonnaise (see page 519)

1. In a small saucepan combine honey and stock. Heat and stir until honey dissolves. Add curry powder, coriander, cayenne, and white pepper. Continue cooking over moderate heat until mixture is reduced to ¾ cup.

2. Remove from heat and cool completely. Add mustard and Mayonnaise. Mix well.

Makes about 4 cups.

■ WATERCRESS DIP WITH GREEN ONIONS AND BASIL

This dip is a showstopper—a nutty, coarse-textured creation fragrant with basil and brilliantly green. Beside it arrange a basket of crudités: cherry tomatoes, cauliflower and broccoli florets, snow peas, endive leaves, zucchini and carrot spears, artichoke hearts, and radishes or fennel. The dip keeps up to 10 days in the refrigerator. To stem the watercress easily, hold the base of the watercress in one hand. With the other hand, pull along the stem. All the leaves on one stem will come off with this one movement.

   3 cups watercress, stems trimmed
   ¾ cup fresh small basil leaves
   ¼ cup minced garlic
   ½ cup good-quality olive oil
   1 cup freshly grated Parmesan cheese
   ¾ cup whipping cream
   ½ cup finely ground walnuts
   ¼ cup minced green onions
      Salt and freshly ground pepper, to taste
   1 tablespoon milk or water (optional)

1. In a blender combine watercress, basil, garlic, olive oil, and grated Parmesan cheese. Blend until pasty. Add cream and blend only until ingredients are mixed (do not overblend).

2. Transfer mixture to a bowl and stir in walnuts and green onion. Add salt and pepper. Mixture will thicken as it stands; if desired, add milk or water to thin it out before serving.

Makes 2 cups.

■ SALSA CRUDA

This basic uncooked salsa is found on the tables of practically every restaurant in Mexico. It is an indispensable presence at a Mexican meal and should be a part of any repast with a Mexican theme. Set it out as a dip for fried tortilla chips or as a sauce for grilled or broiled seafood. It is delightful spooned onto raw oysters or steamed mussels on the half shell; or try it wrapped up in a warm soft tortilla with crispy *carnitas* or pork in green chile.

   1 yellow onion, peeled and minced
   3 fresh ripe tomatoes, peeled, seeded,
      and coarsely chopped
   2 tablespoons minced cilantro
   1 clove garlic, minced
   1 small green chile, minced, or more to taste
   1 tablespoon fresh lime juice
      Salt, to taste

In a small bowl combine all ingredients except salt no more than 1 hour before serving. Do not add salt until the last minute. Salsa is best when freshly made.

Makes about ¾ cup.

CILANTRO RAITA

While this *raita* can be made without the chiles, the zest they add is a delicious contrast to the creamy coolness of the yogurt.

    8 tablespoons cilantro
    1 clove garlic
    ½ jalapeño chile
    1 teaspoon kosher salt
    1 cup plain yogurt

Mince cilantro, garlic, and chile. Stir this mixture and salt into yogurt. Chill.

Makes 1¼ cups.

SOY-BASED DIPPING SAUCES

Soy sauce with a little something mixed in provides an endless variety of dipping sauces. Each of the following recipes makes an individual serving.

Shellfish Dipping Sauce Combine 1 tablespoon soy sauce, 1 teaspoon grated fresh ginger, and ½ teaspoon rice vinegar. This sauce is especially good with steamed crab or shrimp.

Soy and Chile Oil Dipping Sauce Combine 1 tablespoon soy and ½ teaspoon chile oil (or to taste). Use with steamed dumplings.

Soy-Ginger Dipping Sauce Combine 1 tablespoon soy sauce, ½ teaspoon grated or finely minced ginger, and a few drops sesame oil. Use with poached or steamed chicken.

Soy and Mustard Dipping Sauce Combine 1 tablespoon soy sauce and Dijon mustard, to taste. Use with dumplings or vegetables with pork stuffings.

SWEET-AND-SOUR DIPPING SAUCE

This sweet-and-sour sauce tastes good with fried appetizers, because it is not too sweet. Try it with fried shrimp or Shanghai Spring Rolls (see page 389).

    ½ cup water
    ¼ cup rice wine vinegar
    3 tablespoons brown sugar
    1 teaspoon tomato paste
    1 tablespoon minced fresh ginger
    1 clove garlic, minced
    1 teaspoon soy sauce
    1 teaspoon cornstarch

1. In a small, heavy-bottomed saucepan combine ¼ cup of the water, the vinegar, sugar, tomato paste, ginger, garlic, and soy sauce; bring to a boil. Reduce heat and simmer 5 minutes.

2. Dissolve cornstarch in remaining water and add to sauce. Simmer until glossy. Strain before serving.

Makes ⅔ cup.

RASPBERRY SAUCE

Perhaps no other fruit sauce better complements so many desserts than this very simple, extremely delicious raspberry purée. It is a sauce you will use over and over again.

    2 cups fresh or thawed frozen raspberries
    4 to 5 tablespoons confectioners' sugar,
      sifted (optional)
    1 to 2 tablespoons kirsch (optional)

Purée raspberries in a food processor or blender until very smooth. Strain into a bowl, pressing the purée through the mesh. If you are using fresh or unsweetened frozen berries, whisk in 4 tablespoons sugar. Taste and add more sugar, if needed. Add kirsch, if desired. Refrigerate until ready to use. Sauce can be kept, covered, up to 2 days in refrigerator.

Makes about 1 cup.

STRAWBERRY SAUCE

For the best natural flavor, buy strawberries in the peak of their season. Serve with pound cake, poached or raw fruit, or over ice cream.

    2 cups strawberries, chopped
    ½ cup sugar
    2 to 4 tablespoons water (optional)

In a small bowl combine strawberries and sugar; let stand about 1 hour. In a small saucepan over medium heat, cook berry mixture about 5 minutes, mashing berries as they cook. Add the water 1 tablespoon at a time if berries are not very juicy. Serve hot or cold.

Makes about 2 cups.

HOT FUDGE SAUCE

What would any ice cream sundae be without thick, rich, chocolatey Hot Fudge Sauce?

    6 tablespoons unsalted butter
    ½ cup water
    4 ounces unsweetened chocolate
    1 cup sugar
    3 tablespoons light corn syrup
    ⅛ teaspoon salt
    2 teaspoons vanilla extract

1. In a heavy-bottomed 1-quart saucepan, melt butter in the water over medium heat. Bring to a boil, stirring constantly.

2. Add chocolate, stirring occasionally, until it melts. (Do not worry if chocolate lumps at this point; it will smooth out later.)

3. Add sugar, corn syrup, and salt. Boil 5 minutes. Remove from heat and add vanilla. Serve hot.

Makes about 2 cups.

■ OLD-FASHIONED BUTTERSCOTCH SAUCE

Butter and brown sugar are the characteristic flavors paired to make butterscotch.

½ cup unsalted butter
1 cup firmly packed light brown sugar
3 tablespoons light corn syrup
½ cup whipping cream

In small, heavy-bottomed saucepan, melt butter. Stir in brown sugar, corn syrup, and cream. Bring to a boil over medium heat. Cool slightly before serving.

Makes about 1½ cups.

■ OLD-FASHIONED CHOCOLATE SAUCE

This sauce is the kind your mother might have made, with a slightly grainy texture.

8 ounces bittersweet chocolate
½ cup light corn syrup
½ cup whipping cream
2 teaspoons vanilla extract

In a 1-quart saucepan, melt chocolate over low heat. Add corn syrup and stir until smooth. Stir in cream and vanilla. Serve warm or at room temperature.

Makes about 1½ cups.

Recipes and Related Information

Aioli, 262; Bittersweet Chocolate Sauce, 164; Blueberry Sauce, 599; Calvados Sauce, 477; Compound Butters, 68; Cream Sauce, 209; Cucumber-Mint Sauce, 294; Dijon Mayonnaise Dipping Sauce, 46; Fresh Tomato Sauce, 446; Green Sauce, 530; Gremolata, 58; Horseradish Cream Sauce, 305; Horseradish–Sour Cream Dipping Sauce, 46; Mustard Sauce, 233; Northern-Style Tomato Sauce, 412; Nutmeg Sauce, 193; Parmesan Cream Sauce, 412; Pesto, 27; Piquant Parsley DippingSauce, 46; Ragù Bolognese, 412; Tempura Dipping Sauce, 28; Texas-Style Barbecue Sauce, 293; Tomato Dipping Sauce, 238; Tomato Sauce, 428; Tomato-Shallot Sauce, 206; Warm Parsley Sauce for Shellfish, 406; Wasabi Dipping Sauce, 233; White Clam or Mussel Sauce, 413.

SAUCE AND CONDIMENT, COMMERCIAL

Today's cook faces a nearly endless range of packaged sauces and condiments. These items give characteristic flavor to many dishes or provide a piquant counterpoint to a finished dish. This section describes some of the most widely available sauces and condiments.

Use Sauces and condiments provide the seasoning or garnishing without which many dishes would be bland or uninteresting.

Availability Check well-stocked supermarkets, ethnic markets, and specialty stores for the more exotic sauces and condiments.

Selection See specific sauce or condiment.

Storage See specific sauce or condiment.

BEAN PASTE, BROWN

Asian brown bean paste is a thick sauce made from fermented yellow soybeans, flour, water, and salt. Some varieties are quite smooth; others contain some whole beans. It adds saltiness, rich flavor, and body to bland vegetable and bean curd dishes and is used to season fish, beef, pork, and duck. Brown bean paste is available in cans and jars in Asian markets and well-stocked supermarkets. Store in a covered container in the refrigerator; it will keep for up to one year. Stir in peanut or sesame oil if sauce gets too thick or stiff.

CATSUP

The word *catsup* (also spelled *ketchup)* derives from *ketsiap,* a pickled fish sauce used centuries ago in China. The word has since been altered and applied to a variety of quite different condiments. In Indonesia *kecap manis* is a sweet, soy-based condiment. Early English ketchups were fermented relishes made of walnuts or mushrooms. The modern American version is a tomato-based product, seasoned with vinegar, sugar, onion, garlic, and spices. Catsup is widely used as a condiment for hamburgers, hot dogs, and French fries. Its sweet-tart tomato flavor is important to some versions of barbecue sauce, meat loaf, baked beans, and Chinese sweet-and-sour pork.

Pakoras are deep-fried Indian vegetable fritters. The refreshing coolness of the accompanying sauce, yogurt-based Cilantro Raita, makes a good foil for the highly seasoned fritter batter. The fritter recipe can be found on page 106.

Bottled catsup is available in all supermarkets. Unopened, it will keep indefinitely in a cool pantry. Store opened catsup tightly capped in refrigerator; it will keep indefinitely.

CHILE PASTE WITH GARLIC

Made of ground red chiles, soybeans, salt, oil, and garlic, this Chinese condiment adds a full-flavored spiciness to stir-fried dishes. To use, add a small amount to the oil in the wok when stir-frying. Chile paste is packed in jars and is available in Chinese markets. Store chile paste in an airtight jar in refrigerator; it will keep indefinitely.

CHILE SAUCES

The chile sauces outlined below are moderately thick to very thick. For information on thin chile-based sauces, see Hot-Pepper Sauce.

The array of commercial chile sauces is practically infinite, varying by manufacturer and by country of origin. The following categories should be helpful in identifying chile sauces for particular needs.

American Chili Sauce Most American-style chili sauces are thick, mild, tomato-based products heightened with horseradish or chili powder. They are bottled and widely available in supermarkets. Their primary use is in cocktail sauces for shellfish.

Chinese Chile Paste With Garlic See Chile Paste With Garlic (above).

Chinese Chile Sauce Simultaneously hot, sweet, and sour, this thick sauce is made from ground red chile, apricot, lemon, and garlic. It is added in small quantities to pickled vegetables, fish dishes, and stir-fries.

Indonesian Chile Paste *Sambal* is the generic word for Indonesia's chile-based condiments, which range from mild to fiery hot and may be raw or cooked. The contents of bottled sambals vary, but the main varieties found in this country are *sambal ulek* (*oelek*), made of ground fresh red chiles, salt, and vinegar; *sambal bajak* (*badjak*), similar to sambal ulek but flavored with dried shrimp or with nuts and onions; and *sambal manis,* sweeter and milder, containing onions and spices. Sambals add a lift to stir-fries, noodle dishes, and dipping sauces for spring rolls or grilled meats. Look for them in Asian markets.

Thai Chile Sauce *Nam prik* is the generic name for Thai chile sauces, of which there are many. Some type of nam prik is almost always on the table, to be used as a dipping sauce for spring rolls or grilled meats or to perk up soups or noodles. Some cooks make their own, although bottled versions are common. Most are based on red chile, garlic, sugar, salt, and vinegar and have a catsuplike consistency. However, some Thai chile sauces also contain dried shrimp, shrimp paste, fish sauce, coconut cream, tamarind liquid, shallot, or peanut. One of the most widely distributed brands in the United States is Sriracha sauce, a smooth, pourable blend of red chile, garlic, sugar, salt, and vinegar. Sriracha sauce and other bottled Thai chile sauces are sold in Asian markets.

Tunisian Chile Paste Known as *harissa,* Tunisian chile paste is made of dried red chile, garlic, olive oil, and occasionally caraway seed. It is packed in jars, cans, and tubes and sold in Middle Eastern markets. Harissa is used to season olives and is thinned with lemon juice and oil for use as a marinade for brochettes, a dressing for salads, or a condiment for couscous.

DRIED SHRIMP PASTE

Shrimp paste in various guises is essential in several Asian cuisines. From Chinese shrimp paste (*hom har jeung*) to Thai (*kapee*), Indonesian (*trasi*), Vietnamese (*mam ruoc*), and Philippine (*bagoong*) varieties, shrimp paste imparts a pungent, salty fish flavor to many Asian dishes. In that sense, it is the Asian equivalent of Western anchovies or anchovy paste. Chinese shrimp paste is made from dried ground shrimp in brine. Many of the Southeast Asian shrimp pastes are made from salted, fermented dried shrimp or anchovies.

Chinese shrimp paste adds a lively shrimp flavor to pork, fish, bean curd, vegetable, and fried rice dishes. Thai shrimp paste is an ingredient in most Thai curries and dipping sauces. Vietnamese cooks use shrimp paste to enliven soups and sauces. Filipinos employ bagoong as a table relish, adding it to stews, grilled fish, and steamed rice. Indonesian trasi is added to fried rice and to the spicy sambals (chile sauces) used as condiments. Characteristic to all of these cuisines, shrimp paste turns up in dozens of sauces, soups, stews, noodle and rice dishes, and sautés.

All these pastes have a strong odor and should be used sparingly; however, cooking moderates both odor and flavor. Look for dried shrimp paste in ethnic markets. They are available either fresh (liquid, usually bottled) or dried (in paper-wrapped bricks, cakes, plastic tubs, or jars). They range in color and texture from the grayish pink, pourable Chinese shrimp sauce to the chocolate-brown Indonesian trasi, which is sold in firm bricks or sausagelike rolls. Dried shrimp paste can be stored, tightly wrapped, in a cool, dry place for months. Liquid shrimp pastes should be covered and refrigerated after opening.

FISH SAUCE

Pourable sauces made from salted fermented fish are an important seasoning agent in most Southeast Asian cuisines. They go by different names in Thailand (*nam pla*), Vietnam (*nuoc mam*), the Philippines (*patis*), Burma (*ngan-pya-ye* or *ngapi*), Indonesia (*petis*), and China (*yu lu* or *yu chiap*), but all have a salty and strong flavor. Although brands differ in strength, in general the Philippine fish sauce is milder than the Vietnamese and Thai varieties. These fish sauces are also referred to as fish's gravy.

Fish sauce adds a pungent, fishlike flavor to dipping sauces, soups, stir-fries, salad dressings, noodle and rice dishes, and a variety of other preparations. Like salt in Western cooking, it is used to heighten flavors, but fish sauce should not be noticeable itself. Bottled fish sauce is available in Asian markets. Opened fish sauce will keep indefinitely if tightly capped and refrigerated.

GRAVY BROWNER

Commercial gravy browner is a liquid product based on caramel and water; most brands also contain seasonings such as dried vegetables, salt, dried herbs, and spices. Gravy browner adds a rich brown color and some flavor to stews, sauces, and soups. Although it duplicates the color that roasted veal and beef bones give to stock, it does not impart the intense, meaty flavor derived from real bones. It is also used to contribute appetizing color to microwaved roasts that do not develop color from surface caramelization. Brush on a mixture of gravy browner and water for meats and gravy browner and oil for fowl. Gravy browner is available in jars in most supermarkets. Follow package directions to use.

GRENADINE SYRUP

Historically, grenadine syrup was derived from pomegranate juice. Today most bottled grenadine syrup is made with artificial flavors and colors and contains no pomegranate juice at all. The syrup has the cherry red color of pomegranate juice and a vaguely similar flavor.

Grenadine syrup figures in a variety of drinks, such as the tequila sunrise and the Shirley Temple. It can also be spooned over ice cream or added to sparkling water or lemonade for sweetness and color. Some brands of grenadine syrup contain a small amount of alcohol; check the label. Bottled grenadine is available in liquor stores and some supermarkets. Store grenadine containing alcohol in a cool place after opening; syrup without alcohol should be refrigerated after opening. Both will keep indefinitely.

HOISIN SAUCE

A sweet, jamlike sauce based on fermented soybeans, commercial *hoisin* sauce may also contain flour, sugar, chile, garlic, vinegar, and red beans. Hoisin sauce is used in Chinese cooking both as an ingredient and as a table condiment. It adds a sweet, pungent flavor to stir-fried shellfish, chicken, pork, and vegetables. It is often spread on the pancakes served with Peking duck or barbecued pork. In stir-frying, hoisin sauce is usually added to the wok before the main ingredients to give the sugars a chance to caramelize. It comes packed in cans and jars and is sold in Chinese markets. To store, transfer canned hoisin sauce to an airtight nonreactive container; bottled sauce may be kept in its bottle. Hoisin sauce will keep indefinitely in the refrigerator. If it thickens, thin with sesame or peanut oil.

HOT-PEPPER SAUCE

Most of the hot-pepper sauces available in this country are made of hot fresh or dried peppers and vinegar. Tabasco Sauce, a brand named after the region in Mexico where the peppers originated, is certainly the best known. Tabasco Sauce is made from fresh peppers that are ground, salted, and aged in oak barrels for three years before being mixed with vinegar. Several other commercial hot-pepper sauces are based on whole fresh peppers packed in vinegar or sherry.

Hot-pepper sauce adds a lift to tomato juice cocktails, gumbo, cooked greens, seafood stews, oysters, eggs, barbecue sauce, and a variety of Cajun and Creole dishes. In the American South, it is a common table condiment to be added at will to any savory dish. Brands vary considerably in pungency; it takes only a few drops of the most incendiary varieties to add zest to a dish. Tabasco Sauce is available in supermarkets. Other brands of liquid hot-pepper sauce—Crystal, Red Rooster, and Louisiana Hot Sauce—are also sold in some supermarkets and in specialty stores.

Hot-pepper sauce will keep for six months in a cool, dark place but begins to lose flavor if stored longer. Refrigerated, it will keep indefinitely. For information on thick chile-based sauces, see Chile Sauces, page 524.

MISO

Also known as soybean paste or bean paste, miso is made from boiled soybeans that are crushed and fermented. It is an extremely important part of the Japanese diet, eaten in some form almost daily. There are several varieties of miso, made by adding another grain to the soybeans. Yellow miso is made from soybeans and rice and is slightly sweet; it is good for dressings. Red miso is made from barley and soybeans; it is heartier and good in soups. A very dark, thick miso is also available, made primarily from soybeans.

In this country miso is best known as the milky ingredient in Miso Soup, a light, slightly nutty soup that often introduces a meal in a Japanese restaurant. In Japan miso soup is often served for breakfast. Miso is thinned with dashi for use as a salad dressing; it is also brushed on grilled skewered vegetables and seafood to make a category of dishes known as *dengaku*.

Most supermarkets carry at least one variety of miso and Japanese markets carry several. Miso is packed in tubs, jars, tubes, and plastic bags and is usually stocked in the refrigerated section. Refrigerate miso and use within three months; it loses flavor upon standing. Thin miso with dashi before adding to soup to ensure that it blends smoothly.

MUSTARD

See MUSTARD.

ORANGE FLOWER WATER

A highly perfumed, clear liquid, orange flower water is distilled from fresh orange blossoms. In Morocco orange flower water is sometimes used to scent the water poured over hands before dining. Middle Eastern cooks use it to scent rice dishes, puddings, cookies, cakes, and pastries. It is an ingredient in some cocktails, such as the Ramos gin fizz. The fragrance of orange flower water dissipates with air and heat; for maximum effect, add it to cooked dishes when they are cool or cooling. Orange flower water is available in liquor stores and some supermarkets. Store in a cool, dark place; it will keep for several months but will gradually lose strength.

OYSTER SAUCE

This thick, pourable brown liquid is made by fermenting dried oysters with soy sauce and brine. The best oyster sauces are fermented for several years before bottling. They are widely used in Cantonese cooking as a flavor enhancer. Chinese cooks use oyster sauce to impart richness and body to many dishes. It is added to stir-fried meats and vegetables and is offered as a table condiment for roast pork and cold chicken. Oyster sauce in bottles, jars, and cans is readily available in Asian markets. It will keep indefinitely in the refrigerator. Some brands contain cornstarch and will thicken a sauce slightly; adjust ingredients accordingly. Because oyster sauce is salty, most recipes calling for it do not require salt.

PLUM SAUCE

Made from plums, apricots, chiles, vinegar, and sugar, this thick Chinese condiment is dark amber in color, with a sweet-tart, slightly hot flavor. Also known as duck sauce, it accompanies roast duck, pork, spareribs, and egg rolls. Plum sauce is sometimes used as a basting sauce for roast duck and as a sauce enrichment in stir-fried dishes. Plum sauce, bottled or canned, is widely available in Chinese markets. Once opened, canned plum sauce should be transferred to an airtight nonreactive container; it may be refrigerated for up to one year.

ROSE WATER

A highly perfumed, clear liquid, rose water is distilled from fragrant rose petals. A more concentrated form is known as rose essence. Rose water is a popular flavoring in Middle Eastern cooking, added to orange salads, rice pudding, and custard-filled pastries. In India, where rose flavoring is also appreciated, rose essence is preferred and used in a version of ice cream, in the yogurt drink called *lassi,* in sweet carrot pudding, and in the syrup served with fried dessert dumplings. Iranian cooks make a sherbet of rose water, sugar, and water. Rose water is also required in some exotic cocktails. The essence is much stronger than the water and should be added drop by drop.

Bottled rose water is available in some supermarkets, liquor stores, and specialty markets. Rose water and rose essence are sold in Middle Eastern and Indian markets. Store rose water and rose essence in tightly closed bottles in a cool, dark place. They will keep for at least one year but lose strength with age. Because these fragrances are alcohol based, they are volatile (dissipating with heat). Add them to cooled or cooling mixtures for maximum effect.

SOY SAUCE

Essential to Chinese and Japanese cooking, soy sauce is a fermented product based on soy beans. Most brands also contain wheat. Tamari is essentially the same as soy sauce but is made without wheat (see Tamari). Although brands and styles vary in color and flavor, most soy sauce is dark brown. Japanese soy sauce has a relatively sweet flavor and is less salty than either Chinese or American varieties. Chinese soy sauce is extremely salty. Black soy sauce, specified in some recipes, has molasses added; it is richer and saltier in flavor than regular soy sauce. Most American-made soy sauce falls between the two styles. The most widely distributed brand, Kikkoman, is light bodied, light flavored, and lacks the sweetness of the Japanese brands and the saltiness of the Chinese. Synthetic soy sauces made from hydrolized soy protein, which are also manufactured in this country and have wide distribution, are a poor substitute for the real thing.

Soy sauce is used by Chinese and Japanese cooks in much the same way that Westerners use salt—as a flavor enhancer. In China it is not considered a table condiment; rather, it is added to foods before or during cooking. Soy sauce adds a distinctive fermented flavor to almost all stir-fried dishes, whether of meat, chicken, fish, or vegetables; it adds a brown gloss to steamed chicken and roast duck; it flavors noodle dishes, both hot and cold. In Japan soy sauce is on the table to be used as a dipping sauce for sushi, sashimi, and tempura; it is used in soups such as *shabu-shabu* and provides the base for dozens of basting sauces brushed on pork, seafood, or chicken while grilling.

All supermarkets stock American-made soy sauce in bottles or cans. Many also stock synthetic soy sauce and low-sodium soy sauce. Asian markets stock imported soy sauces from China and Japan. Because of its high salt content, soy sauce does not require refrigeration. It will keep indefinitely in a cool, dark place. Low-sodium soy sauce must be refrigerated.

STEAK SAUCE

Although steak sauces vary from manufacturer to manufacturer, most are liquid to semiliquid condiments with a sweet-sour-salty balance of flavors. The most popular brand in this country, A-1 Sauce, contains tomato paste, vinegar, corn syrup, raisins, orange peel, and other herbs, spices, and seasonings. Other popular brands contain chile peppers, molasses, or soy sauce.

Sprinkle steak sauce on steaks, chops, or hamburgers before or after grilling or add to barbecue sauces and marinades. Most supermarkets carry a variety of bottled steak sauces, which should be stored in the refrigerator after opening; steak sauce will keep indefinitely.

SWEET-AND-SOUR SAUCE

The contrast of sweet-and-sour flavors is important to Chinese cooking but bottled sweet-and-sour sauce was created for the American palate. Most commercial versions of this sauce are thick with cornstarch and may contain food coloring. The texture and flavor they impart are far removed from the texture and flavor of authentic Chinese sweet-and-sour dishes. In the American kitchen, the sauce can be used to glaze ham or spareribs. Bottled sweet-and-sour sauce is available in most supermarkets and some Asian markets. After opening, store lidded jar in the refrigerator; it will keep indefinitely.

TABASCO SAUCE

See Hot-Pepper Sauce.

TAMARI

A cultured and fermented liquid soybean product, tamari resembles soy sauce, but is thicker and stronger in flavor than soy. It is used in Japan as a dipping sauce and a base for basting sauces. Tamari is available in many health-food stores and Japanese markets. A salt-free tamari is also available in some markets. Refrigerate tamari after opening; it will keep indefinitely.

THAI CURRY PASTE

In Thai cooking, many dishes seasoned with a paste of herbs and spices are known as curries. The major types of curry paste in Thailand are red (based on red chile peppers), green (based on green chiles and coriander), and yellow (based on yellow chiles and turmeric). Many cooks make their own curry pastes regularly, altering them with herbs and spices to suit individual tastes. However, bottled curry pastes are widely available and are acceptable to many Thai cooks.

Check Asian markets for bottled Thai curry paste. After opening, store lidded jars in refrigerator; they will keep for several weeks.

WORCESTERSHIRE SAUCE

A liquid condiment reputedly devised by two British chemists in the nineteenth century, Worcestershire sauce today is a fixture in most American refrigerators. The exact formula is a secret, but the label lists vinegar, molasses, tamarind, anchovies, and spices. It is dark brown, with a distinctive flavor that incorporates sweet, sour, salty, and spicy elements. It can be sprinkled on hamburgers or

steaks before or after cooking; some cooks add it to barbecue sauce, marinades, and basting sauces. It is used in most renditions of Caesar salad, in cocktail dips and cheese spreads, in English steak and kidney pie, in steak tartare, Welsh rarebit, and Bloody Marys.

Bottled Worcestershire sauce is available in supermarkets. Refrigerate after opening; it will keep indefinitely.

SAUSAGE

Highly seasoned ground pork is the basis for most of the world's sausages, although some delicious sausages are made using chicken, turkey, game birds, and even seafood. Perhaps the best definition is that sausage is made from ground meat, usually stuffed in a casing (but not necessarily), usually highly seasoned with herbs and/or spices, and frequently laced with such flavorful additions as cubes of fat, truffles, pistachios, peppercorns, wine, or chiles.

Grilled Italian sausages and sautéed bell peppers and onions are robust accompaniments to omelets. Cook the meat outdoors on a grill or indoors in a skillet.

A piquant green sauce unites all elements in Boiled Dinner Bolognese (recipe is on page 530). If you wish, serve the cooking broth as a first course. Or, strain and freeze it to use later as the base for your next bollito misto.

Use   Sausage is used in sandwiches, stuffings, pasta sauces, savory pies and pastries, soups, casseroles, and stews. From breakfast links to the midday hot dog to a dinner of grilled wurst and potatoes, sausage satisfies American appetites all day long.

Availability   Most of the sausage available in the United States is made there or in Canada. Imported pork products must conform to extremely strict federal regulations and are, at this writing, essentially unavailable in the United States.

The major types of sausages sold in America are described in the following pages. Although supermarkets carry a variety of fresh and cured sausage, the best sausages are generally found in ethnic markets and specialty stores. Italian, German, and French markets are good sources for sausages made by traditional European methods.

Selection   An off odor is the first clue to deterioration in sausage; avoid any that smell strong or sour. Fresh sausage is especially perishable and should be bought from a market with a rapid turnover.

Storage   Because it is so perishable, sausage should be refrigerated and used within two or three days or it can be frozen for up to two months. If the meat has been

lightly smoked, it can be refrigerated for up to one week. Cooked sausages can be kept for up to one week in the refrigerator or two months in the freezer; if vacuum-packed and unopened, they can be refrigerated longer. Semidry sausages may be kept at room temperature for two or three days; for longer keeping, refrigerate for up to three weeks. Dry sausages may be stored unsliced at cool room temperature for six weeks; after slicing, refrigerate and use within three weeks. Both semidry and dry sausages may be frozen for up to three months, but with some loss of flavor and texture.

FRESH SAUSAGE

Made from raw ground and seasoned meat, fresh sausage is often bound with eggs, bread crumbs, or cereals. It may or may not be stuffed in a casing and may or may not be smoked. It must be cooked before it is served. Some of the better-known types of fresh sausage are described below.

Bockwurst   A German-style veal sausage, occasionally with pork added, *bockwurst* is usually first boiled, then grilled or panfried. It is traditionally served with potatoes, mustard, and German beer.

Chaurice   See Chorizo.

Chorizo   Both Mexican- and Spanish-style *chorizos* are available. The Mexican type is made from fresh pork and is highly seasoned with vinegar, chiles, garlic, and cumin. It is stuffed into casings and made into links, but most recipes call for removing the casings and crumbling and frying the chorizo. Spanish-style chorizo is usually made from smoked pork and is firmer than the Mexican version; it can be grilled in its casing and sliced for use in soups and bean dishes. *Chaurice* is the Cajun version, made of ground pork highly seasoned with garlic and hot red pepper.

Cotechino   This large, Italian-style pork sausage is usually seasoned with garlic, pepper, fennel seed, and wine. The sausage is poached whole and served hot, with potato salad, lentils, or other boiled meats and vegetables as part of a *bollito misto* (mixed boil).

Crêpinette   A French-style sausage that is shaped into a patty and wrapped in caul fat, most *crêpinettes* are made of ground pork and seasoned with herbs, although ground chicken, cooked spinach, and nuts such as pistachios and chestnuts are other common additions. They may be panfried without any fat, or brushed with butter, coated with bread crumbs, and grilled.

Italian Link Sausage   Most Italian markets carry hot and sweet versions of this link sausage. Both are pork sausages seasoned with garlic, wine, and fennel, but the hot version has red pepper, too. To cook, the sausages are poached briefly, then panfried or grilled. The meat can be removed from the casings and used on pizzas or in sauces or stuffings.

Saucisson à l'Ail This French garlic sausage is comparable to Italian *cotechino* without fennel. It is usually served with lentils, potato salad, mashed potatoes, or white beans.

Weisswurst This white German sausage is made from veal. After steaming it can be eaten in a bun with mustard or cut up and added to stews and soups.

COOKED SAUSAGE

Although the following sausages are generally sold fully cooked and ready to eat, many taste better when hot; they are usually reheated before serving.

Andouille Usually salted and smoked, *andouille* is a large French-style tripe sausage that is most often eaten cold in thin slices. *Andouillette* is a similar but smaller sausage, made of tripe and spices stuffed in a sausage casing; it is not usually smoked. Andouillettes are usually grilled and served hot with mashed potatoes, potato salad, or French fries.

Blood Sausage The British call this sausage *black pudding;* the French, *boudin noir;* Cajuns, *boudin rouge;* and the Germans, *blutwurst.* It is made from pork blood, pork fat, and seasonings. French varieties usually contain bread crumbs and cream; English varieties may include barley or oatmeal; Cajun blood sausage commonly contains cayenne pepper and garlic. They are generally grilled or sautéed in butter or bacon fat and served hot with French fries, potato salad, mashed potatoes, or sauerkraut.

Bologna Spelled baloney in American markets, *bologna* is the term applied to a large variety of lightly smoked sausages that are sliced thin and eaten cold. Bologna may be made of pork, beef, turkey, veal, ham, or a combination. It may be fine or coarse textured and lightly or richly spiced. Bologna is usually served in thin slices as an appetizer or sandwich filling.

Boudin Blanc This smooth-textured French-style white sausage is made of pork, veal, and/or chicken, usually bound with cream, onions, and bread crumbs. *Boudin blanc* is usually panfried or grilled before serving and is often accompanied by mashed potatoes.

Bratwurst A German-style pork or pork and veal sausage, bratwurst may be fresh or cooked. If fresh, it must be boiled first. Fresh bratwurst is often simmered in beer, then panfried or grilled, and served with sauerkraut. Cooked bratwurst is reheated—either steamed, panfried, or grilled—before serving.

Braunschweiger See Liverwurst.

Frankfurter Today, *frankfurter* is a generic name for a huge variety of sausages, also known as wieners or hot dogs. Frankfurters may be made of pork, beef, turkey, chicken, or a combination; kosher franks are all beef. Frankfurters range from the tiny cocktail size (24 to a pound) to foot-long dogs (4 to a pound), but most are about 4 inches long and 8 or 10 to a pound. Frankfurters are usually steamed or grilled before being served in buns with such optional accompaniments as mustard, relish, chili, and sauerkraut. Frankfurters may also be cut into chunks and added to stews or soups, such as old-fashioned split pea soup.

Head Cheese Composed of small pieces of hog's head bound in gelatin, head cheese is usually seasoned with white wine and spices. It is sliceable and commonly served cold with vinaigrette and a salad.

Knockwurst Similar to frankfurters, but usually thicker and more highly seasoned, knockwurst (or knackwurst) are German-style sausages that may be cooked whole and served like hot dogs or may be sliced and added to potato salad.

Liverwurst and Braunschweiger Both variations on the same theme, these two sausages are smooth textured, spreadable, and usually made of pork liver (sometimes beef or goose liver). American-style liverwurst is usually not smoked, but German-style braunschweiger usually is. Both are served as an appetizer with crackers or as a sandwich filling.

Thuringer Several types of German-style sausage are called Thuringer. It may be fresh, in which case it must be poached before serving, then panfried or grilled. Or it may be semidry, smoked, and ready-to-eat. The semidry type is often served as an appetizer, thinly sliced, or cut up and added to split pea or bean soups.

SEMIDRY AND DRY SAUSAGE

Semidry sausages have been smoked to remove some of the moisture. They are often called summer sausages, a legacy from prerefrigeration days. Because they were partially dried, they could be kept for some time without spoiling, even in warm weather.

Fully dry sausages may be smoked or unsmoked but have been dried from one to six months for preservation. They usually have a slightly shriveled exterior and are firm enough to slice thinly.

Cervelas A semidry French-style pork sausage, *cervelas* is usually seasoned with garlic. To serve, it is poached, then sliced and accompanied with mustard and potato salad. It is also occasionally poached, then wrapped in brioche dough and baked.

Cervelat The name *cervelat* is applied to a variety of Middle European–style summer sausages. Most are made of pork or beef and are smoked. They may be thinly sliced as an appetizer or diced and added to salads, soups, or bean dishes.

Kielbasa This is the Polish word for sausage, usually applied in this country to a smoked, semidry sausage seasoned highly with garlic, pepper, paprika, and herbs. Most American-made *kielbasa* is shaped into long, thick links that may weigh a pound or more. They are usually made of pork but some contain beef or veal as well. Kielbasa can be sliced and eaten cold, but it is usually poached and served with potatoes, lentils, or sauerkraut. It may also be sliced and added to soups and stews or used in recipes that call for garlic sausage.

Linguiça A Portuguese-style pork sausage seasoned with red pepper and garlic, *linguiça* is similar to chorizo but generally thinner, firmer, and milder. It is diced and scrambled with eggs or added to omelets. It may be added to soups, or cut into chunks, skewered, and grilled.

Mortadella Smooth-textured mortadella is an Italian-style pork sausage larded with cubes of fat and black peppercorns. Most domestic mortadella is about 6 inches in diameter; in Italy it can be much wider. Mortadella is thinly sliced and eaten cold as an appetizer; it may also be diced and added to stuffings.

Pepperoni Another dried type of Italian-style sausage, pepperoni is made of beef or pork, usually 1 to 1½ inches in diameter, and highly seasoned with red and black pepper. It is thinly sliced and served as an appetizer or a pizza garnish.

Salami Including a variety of dried, sliceable sausages made throughout Europe, most salami is made of raw pork or beef that is highly seasoned, stuffed into casings, and air-dried. It is usually not smoked. Popular salami made in the United States include Genoa and French Lyonnaise types, the latter identified as *saucisson sec*. Salami is usually sliced thin and served as an appetizer or sandwich filling. Jewish delicatessens often scramble eggs with sliced kosher all-beef salami.

■ HOMEMADE PORK SAUSAGE

Pork butt often contains a generous proportion of fat. Trim off some of it if you prefer a leaner sausage—but not all of it. Fat makes the sausage juicy and carries the flavors of the seasonings. Grind the meat, using a meat grinder or a food processor, then mix in savory seasonings.

　2 pounds boneless pork butt, cut in 1-inch cubes
　1 clove garlic, minced or pressed
1½ teaspoons dried sage
　1 teaspoon salt
　½ teaspoon *each* coarsely ground black pepper
　　and dried summer savory or marjoram
　¼ teaspoon *each* ground allspice and dried thyme
　⅛ teaspoon cayenne pepper

1. *To make in a meat grinder:* Using coarse blade, grind pork cubes twice. *To make in a food processor:* Spread pork cubes in a single layer on a baking sheet and place in freezer until meat is firm but not frozen (about 20 minutes). Then process, using short on-off bursts, until meat is coarsely ground.

2. Using mortar and pestle or blender, combine garlic, sage, salt, black pepper, summer savory, allspice, thyme, and cayenne thoroughly. Add to ground meat and mix well until seasonings are evenly distributed. (Use your hands, if desired.)

3. Wrap well and refrigerate for 8 hours or overnight to blend flavors.

4. Form into patties and cook in a frying pan over medium-low heat until well browned and crusty, or use in recipes as directed.

Makes 2 pounds.

■ BOILED DINNER BOLOGNESE

A dazzling array of meats and vegetables, each added at just the right stage to achieve tenderness, makes up the Italian simmered dinner known as *bollito misto*. Look for the distinctive, plump *cotechino* sausage in Italian delicatessens; if it isn't stocked regularly, perhaps the dealer can order it for you. It contributes a lot of flavor to the dish.

　　1 beef rump roast (3½ to 4 lb)
　　12 cups water or Beef Stock (see page 560)
　　1 fresh beef tongue (2½ to 3 lb)
　　1 veal shank (1 to 1½ lb), cut through bone
　　　into 3 sections
　　1 large onion, finely chopped
　　4 large carrots
　　2 stalks celery, sliced
　　5 sprigs parsley
　　1 tablespoon salt
　　¼ teaspoon *each* whole allspice and
　　　black peppercorns
　　1 cotechino sausage (1 to 1½ lb)
　　4 to 6 leeks, well rinsed, with coarse
　　　outer leaves discarded and leafy tops
　　　trimmed to about 5 inches
　10 to 12 small red potatoes, scrubbed (unpeeled)
　　1 small savoy cabbage (about 1 lb),
　　　cut into 8 wedges

Green Sauce

　½ cup olive oil
　¼ cup white wine vinegar
　3 green onions, coarsely chopped
　1 cup lightly packed parsley sprigs
　2 tablespoons capers
　1 clove garlic, minced
　1 tablespoon anchovy paste
　　Pinch freshly ground pepper
　¼ cup lightly packed fresh basil leaves *or*
　　1 tablespoon dried basil
　　Salt (optional)

1. Preheat oven to 500° F. Place rump roast in a shallow, heavy roasting pan. Bake, uncovered, turning once, until meat is well browned (20 to 25 minutes). Transfer roast to a 10- to 12-quart, heavy-bottomed kettle with cover. Add a little of the water to juices left in bottom of roasting pan, stirring to loosen any brown drippings that may be stuck to pan bottom and to blend water, juices, and drippings; pour water-drippings mixture over roast in kettle.

2. To kettle add tongue, the 3 pieces of veal shank, and chopped onion. Slice one of the carrots and add it to meats with celery, parsley sprigs, salt, allspice, pepper-corns, and remaining water. Bring to a boil over medium heat, cover, reduce heat, and simmer for 2 hours. Add sausage, cover again, and cook for 1 hour more until meats are tender.

3. Meanwhile, cut remaining carrots lengthwise into quarters; cut quarters crosswise into halves. Add carrot pieces to kettle with trimmed whole leeks and whole unpeeled potatoes; cook until meats and potatoes are tender (about 45 minutes).

4. With a slotted spoon remove tongue and set it aside. Remove rump roast, veal shank, and sausage to a large, heated platter. Surround with leeks, potatoes, and carrots. Cover lightly with foil and keep warm while preparing cooked tongue.

5. Cut off and discard bones and gristle at thick end of tongue. Slit the skin on the underside, and starting at the thick end, peel it off. Add tongue to meats and vegetables on platter.

6. Add cabbage wedges to gently boiling broth and cook, uncovered, until cabbage is tender when pierced with a knife and bright green (8 to 10 minutes). While cabbage cooks, prepare Green Sauce. Add cooked cabbage to meats and vegetables on platter.

7. If you wish to serve broth as a first course, strain through a wire sieve, taste and salt if needed, and serve it hot. Then carve meats and serve with vegetables and Green Sauce.

Serves 10 to 12.

Green Sauce In a food processor fitted with a metal blade or a blender, combine olive oil, wine vinegar, green onions, parsley sprigs, capers, garlic, anchovy paste, pepper, and basil. Process or whirl until smooth. Taste and add salt if needed. Serve at room temperature.

Makes about 1¼ cups.

Recipes and Related Information

Barbecued Pork Ribs and Sausages, 292;
Cassoulet, 556; Choucroute Garni, 75; Red Beans
and Rice, 32; Split Pea Soup, Black Forest Style, 565;
Stuffed Mirliton, 110.

SAUTE, TO

Sautéing has been done for centuries, with the French and Chinese its most accomplished practitioners. In fact sauté-ing and stir-frying are the same technique (see STIR-FRY). In its strictest culinary application, sauté, from the French *sauter* (to jump), means to rapidly cook small, uniformly sized pieces of food over high heat in oil or fat in a specially designed straight-sided, shallow pan with an extralong handle. To keep the food from sticking, the pan is kept in constant motion, so the food "jumps" in the pan. More typically, sautéed food is turned, rather than tossed. Any skillet made of a material that conducts heat well can be substituted for a sauté pan.

When the food is browned on all sides, it is removed from the pan, set aside, and kept warm while the juices are made into an accompanying sauce. Deglazing removes caramelized bits of food from the bottom of the pan and incorporates them into the liquid that is the base for the sauce (see DEGLAZE).

Sautéed Beef Steaks Marchand de Vin is a beef- and red-wine-lover's dream dish—tender, aged beef and a deglazing sauce of good red wine, enriched at the last minute with a bit of butter. The recipe is on page 533.

The tastes of toasted nuts and sweet raisins offer an interesting contrast to the mild-flavored fish in Sole With Almonds, Pine Nuts, and White Raisins. Sauté the nuts in clarified butter to bring out their flavor.

WHAT FOODS CAN BE SAUTEED?

Meats of the highest quality are most suitable for sautéing. Among the dark meats, thin beef steaks and relatively small lamb chops are ideal because they cook through in the time it takes to brown them. Sautéing is also a favorite way to cook chicken livers or thin slices of beef or calf's liver. It is a perfect technique for cooking slim pieces of tender light meats, such as veal chops, and slices of veal scallop, chicken breast, or turkey breast. Food should be uniform in size so the pieces cook quickly and evenly; for this reason slices of meat or poultry are often pounded before being sautéed.

Any fish fillet can be sautéed. Try to choose fillets that are relatively firm fleshed and do not appear to be falling apart. Short fish fillets are easiest to sauté because there is less chance of breakage during turning or transferring to the serving platter. Cut fillets in half before cooking them if they are too long to be handled easily. Very thin fillets such as sole require only about 2 minutes of sautéing on each side. Fish steaks up to 1 inch thick and small whole fish are suitable for sautéing, too, as are shrimp and scallops.

Almost any vegetable can be sautéed. Those that are naturally tender, such as peppers, mushrooms, and zucchini, can be cut into small pieces and sautéed. Others, such as broccoli and cauliflower, should first be blanched to soften them slightly. The blanching process is actually a timesaver: Cut vegetables in appropriately sized pieces, blanch in boiling water and refresh in cold water to stop cooking; then just before serving, sauté vegetables briefly in butter to heat and flavor them.

GETTING STARTED

A successful sauté depends upon three factors. First, the fat must be hot. If it is not hot enough, the food will stick to the pan, the outside won't be seared, and the juices will escape. Second, the food must be absolutely dry. Moisture on the food forms a layer of steam between the food and the fat that prevents searing and browning. Third—and many cooks overlook this factor—the pan must not be too crowded. Space between pieces of food is a prerequisite for thorough browning. Crowding causes steaming, rather than searing, and results in the juices escaping from the food into the pan. It is equally important not to allow too much space between pieces of food in too large of a pan (the more the food covers the fat, the less likely the fat will burn).

Oil alone, or a combination of butter and oil, is used for sautéing. Oil can withstand higher temperatures without burning than butter and is often the choice for searing meats. Butter gives a lovely flavor, but burns easily at higher temperatures; restaurant chefs often add 1 or 2 tablespoons of cooking oil to the butter to raise the temperature at which it will begin to smoke. Or, they use clarified butter (see page 68), which can heat to a higher temperature without deteriorating than unclarified butter.

To protect the delicate flesh of white meats, poultry, and fish from sticking to the pan, cooks often flour these foods lightly before sautéing. Floured meat browns more easily than uncoated meat and has an appetizing appearance. If a nonstick pan is used, these foods can be sautéed without being floured but they will not brown as well. Red meat does not require flouring because the higher fat content helps to keep it from adhering to the pan.

Although the coating has a protective function, it too should be treated with care. Floured food should not be allowed to sit for more than a few minutes because moisture from the food will make the coating gummy. For the same reason, the coated pieces of food should never be piled one on top of the other.

THE SAUTE PANTRY

If the simplicity and speed of sautéing appeal to you, consider having the following on hand as staples in the refrigerator and pantry.

In the refrigerator   Butter (including clarified butter), cream or half-and-half, eggs, sauce bases, and stock. Freeze stock and sauce bases that will be held longer than a few days.

On the shelf   Bread crumbs, flour, herbs and spices, oils, canned tomatoes and tomato purée, red and white wine, sherry, and brandy.

Equipment   Sauté pan or skillet, wooden spoons, slotted spoons, spatula, meat pounder, and paper towels.

■ SOLE WITH ALMONDS, PINE NUTS, AND WHITE RAISINS

This is a variation of a Venetian dish called *sfogi in saòr,* which means savory soles.

¼ cup white raisins
2 cups dry white wine
5 tablespoons Clarified Butter (see page 68)
¼ cup slivered almonds
6 sole fillets
1 teaspoon salt
½ teaspoon freshly ground pepper
4 tablespoons flour
3 tablespoons unsalted butter
2 tablespoons minced shallot
  Salt and freshly ground pepper, to taste
2 tablespoons pine nuts

1. Soak raisins in white wine for 30 minutes. Remove raisins and reserve both wine and raisins.

2. In sauté pan heat the 5 tablespoons clarified butter. Add almonds to pan and sauté until they begin to color. Remove almonds with slotted spoon and drain on paper towels.

3. Sprinkle fish with the 1 teaspoon salt, ½ teaspoon pepper, and flour. Add fish to pan and sauté each side to a golden brown. Remove fish to a warm platter. Add the 3 tablespoons butter to pan. When butter has melted, add shallot and cook until soft. Add reserved wine and raisins. Cook for 2 to 3 minutes and season to taste with salt and pepper. Add pine nuts to sauce and pour over fish.

Serves 6.

■ SAUTEED VEGETABLE MEDLEY

This quick side dish pairs well with most roasted meats.

¾ pound small new potatoes, quartered
1 large carrot, cut in sticks
4 small white onions, peeled and halved
2 tablespoons butter
½ pound (20 medium) mushrooms, halved
1 teaspoon dried basil
  Grated Parmesan, Romano, or Sapsago cheese, for garnish (optional)

1. In a large saucepan cook potatoes in boiling salted water to cover for 10 minutes; drain and set aside. Blanch carrot and onions briefly and refresh in cold water to stop cooking.

2. Meanwhile, in a large skillet melt butter; then add mushrooms to skillet and sauté.

3. Add potatoes, carrot, and onions to skillet, and sauté briefly with mushrooms.

4. Add basil; toss vegetables to mix. Garnish with cheese, if desired.

Serves 4.

■ SAUTEED BEEF STEAKS MARCHAND DE VIN

This simple dish, "wine merchant style," relies on two basic ingredients: good beef and good red wine.

1½ to 2 pounds tender beef steaks (filet mignon, strip, sirloin), ¾ to 1 inch thick
  Salt and freshly ground pepper, to taste
2 tablespoons minced shallot
4 tablespoons butter
½ cup red wine

1. In a heavy skillet over medium-high heat, rub a piece of fat trimmed from steak. Cook steaks, turning once and season after turning with salt and pepper. Test for doneness by pushing on steak with finger: A rare steak offers slight resistance; when medium-rare, it springs back lightly; when medium or beyond, it gets increasingly stiff and resistant. Remove steaks to warm plates.

2. Cook shallot in meat juices until translucent. Add a little of the butter if the pan is nearly dry. Add wine, bring to a boil, and reduce by two thirds. Remove pan from heat, swirl in butter, check seasoning, and spoon the sauce over the steaks.

Serves 4.

Recipes and Related Information

Broccoli Sautéed With Garlic, 60; Chicken Breasts With Grapes, 280; Chicken Breasts With Sherry, Cream, and Mushrooms, 611; Sautéed Cherry Tomatoes, 582; Sautéed Quail With Red Currant Sauce, 478; Trout With Almonds, 231.

SAVORY

An herb native to the Mediterranean region, savory is of two types: summer savory, an annual, and winter savory, a hardy perennial. The two have a related peppery flavor, but summer savory is milder.

Use Summer savory flatters egg dishes, fish soups, and summer vegetables. Winter savory complements dried bean dishes, meats, sausages, and stuffings.

Availability Look for dried summer and winter savory, both whole and ground, in well-stocked supermarkets. Fresh savory is carried sporadically by specialty markets.

Selection Fresh savory should be crisp and green, with no signs of wilting or decay. Packaged seasonings lose quality after a while; try to buy them from a store that restocks its spice section fairly often.

Storage Dried savory will keep one year in a cool, dark, dry place. Refrigerate fresh savory wrapped in paper towels and plastic wrap.

Sautéing is a fast-moving process in which food is cooked quickly in a shallow pan and turned frequently with a spatula.

SCALD, TO

To heat milk so that tiny bubbles form around the inside edge of the pan, although milk should not boil. To dip foods in boiling water or to pour boiling water over them (the same as blanching).

Before milk was pasteurized, scalding was a sanitary measure. Although unnecessary for sanitation today, some recipes specify scalding in order to improve flavor and shorten cooking time. Yeast bread recipes suggest scalding for outmoded reasons. Most custards use heated milk, although it's wisest to let scalded milk cool slightly before mixing with eggs to avoid curdling.

SCORE, TO

To cut shallow lines partway through the top layer of a dough to create a decorative pattern, or into meats to tenderize and allow a marinade to penetrate more fully. The lines are usually in a crisscross, diamond pattern.

SCUM

Impurities that float to the top of a stock, sauce, or other liquid are called scum. They often form a gray, filmy covering on the surface of the liquid. This layer is removed by skimming with a special long-handled spoon with a wire or perforated bowl (see SKIM).

SEAR, TO

To brown meat with intense heat in order to seal in the juices and to impart color and more flavor; this is done in a skillet or in the oven. Searing is often the first step when preparing a stew or braise.

SEED, TO; SEED

To remove, from a fruit or vegetable, the seeds, which are the portion normally capable of germination. The method of seeding depends on the size of the seed and how easy it is to access. Some seeds, such as those in watermelons and cherimoyas, are large enough to be removed by hand when you encounter them while eating or preparing fruit. Seeds that run in the core of a vegetable, such as a cucumber or zucchini, can be removed by scraping with a spoon or with a special coring tool (see CORE). Apple and pear seeds are removed through coring. Tomatoes are seeded by squeezing cut pieces gently or by being puréed and then strained. Berries can be seeded only by being puréed and then strained through a fine-mesh sieve. Citrus seeds revealed in slices and wedges get picked out with the point of a knife; when citrus fruits are juiced through a reamer with a strainer basket, the seeds are trapped by the strainer.

SEPARATE, TO

To divide a whole egg into yolk and white. Also, to become divided into two distinct parts, as when a custard curdles into liquid and gel or when the ingredients in an emulsion cease to be in suspension.

> ***Recipes and Related Information***
> *Curdling, 167; Custard, 168; Egg, 194; Emulsion and Emulsifier, 212.*

SESAME SEED

The tiny sesame seed is the seed of an herbaceous plant native to Indonesia and East Africa. The creamy white variety is the most common, but a black variety is used in southern Indian cooking. Sesame seeds have a mildly sweet, nutty flavor that is enhanced by toasting.

Use Sesame seeds are pressed for oil, which may be made in several different styles (see OIL). The seeds themselves are a valued cooking ingredient in the Middle East, India, China, Japan, and Korea. Middle Eastern cooks blend sesame seeds into a paste called tahini, which they use to season dressings and dipping sauces (see TAHINI). In India sesame seeds are added to pilafs, stuffings, sauces, chutneys, and candies. Chinese cooks use both black and white sesame seeds as a garnish, in candies, and as part of a coating for fried foods. In addition the Chinese use toasted white sesame seeds to make a paste that is used in salad dressings and noodle dishes. In Japan white sesame seeds are ground and added to salad dressings; black sesame seeds garnish grilled squid and hand-shaped rice balls wrapped in seaweed. Cooks in Korea use great quantities of sesame seed, sprinkling it over braised beef ribs and grilled chicken and adding it to chicken salad, meatballs, noodle dishes, and mixed vegetables.

Sesame seed is also found in confections all over the world. In the United States, for example, it is sprinkled on breads for a nutty garnish; in the south, where it is known as benne seed, it is baked into crackers.

Availability White sesame seeds are found commonly in jars or tins on supermarket spice racks. Health-food stores often stock them in bulk. Asian, Middle Eastern, and Indian markets also carry sesame seeds, often including black as well as white varieties.

Storage Because of their high oil content, sesame seeds go rancid quickly at room temperature. However, they will keep in the refrigerator or freezer indefinitely.

Preparation Toasting brings out the full flavor of sesame seeds. To toast, cook them in a dry skillet over moderately low heat, shaking pan constantly, until they are lightly browned and fragrant (about 3 minutes).

■ SESAME FRIED FISH FILLETS

This Chinese version of the familiar three-step batter uses sesame seeds rather than bread crumbs. If black sesame seeds are available, mix them with the white variety for an attractive and textured coating reminiscent of multicolored beach pebbles.

    1 pound fillet of catfish or other lean white fish
    2 teaspoons minced fresh ginger
    2 green onions, minced
    2 tablespoons Shaoxing wine or dry sherry
       Pinch of salt
       Oil, for deep-frying
    ¼ cup cornstarch
    1 egg, lightly beaten
    ¾ cup white sesame seed
    ¼ cup black sesame seed
       Soy and Mustard Dipping Sauce
       (see page 522), for dipping

1. Slice fish crosswise into two-bite-sized slices, about ¼ inch thick. Place in a shallow bowl, sprinkle with ginger, green onion, wine, and salt, and marinate in refrigerator for 30 minutes to several hours.

2. In a wok or other deep pan, preheat oil to 375° F. Drain fish and pat dry with paper towels. Have cornstarch in one shallow bowl, beaten egg in another, and combined sesame seeds in a third. Dip a piece of fish in cornstarch and shake off excess; dip into egg (use a wire skimmer or tongs to avoid getting egg on hands; coating will stick to hands, rather than fish); then roll in sesame seeds until coated.

3. Fry until white sesame seeds are light tan (3 to 4 minutes). Drain on paper towels and serve with Soy and Mustard Dipping Sauce.

Serves 4 to 6 with other dishes.

SET, TO

To firm up or to solidify. Gelatin in the presence of cold, and egg protein when heated, cause foods to congeal. Also, as melted chocolate hardens, it sets.

> ### Recipes and Related Information
> *Chocolate, 124; Custard, 168; Egg, 194; Gelatin, 264; Mousse, 372.*

SHALLOT

A mild member of the onion family, shallots grow in clusters of several small bulbs, each of which is rarely larger than a walnut and may be much smaller. They are sheathed in a papery reddish brown or yellowish brown skin that is easily removed. The white flesh is tinged with red or purple.

Use Shallots are valued for their gentle onion flavor. Favored by French cooks for sauces, salad dressings, and some soups, shallots are also essential to the classic French butter sauces such as beurre blanc and its variations. They may be pickled and used as a garnish for cold meats or braised whole as part of a vegetable stew.

Availability Shallots are found in most supermarkets. In some stores they are packaged in netting or in cellophane-wrapped boxes. Many supermarkets also stock freeze-dried shallots.

Selection Select firm shallots that are not sprouting.

Storage Keep shallots in a cool, dry place with some air circulation, such as a basket. Under proper conditions, they will keep for up to one month. Store freeze-dried shallots in a cool, dark, dry place for up to six months; they lose flavor with time.

Preparation Remove papery outer skin; trim away root end. Reconstitute freeze-dried shallots according to package directions. See KNIFE, Cutting Techniques, for a description of how to mince shallots.

Two colors of sesame seeds—white and black—add visual interest to the coating of Sesame Fried Fish Fillets.

OPENING BIVALVES

Oysters   Wearing work gloves or using a heavy cloth, hold oyster with deep cup of oyster down. Insert tip of oyster knife into hinge and twist to open shell. Slide knife along inside of upper shell to sever muscle; slide knife under flesh to sever bottom muscle.

Clams   Refrigerate bivalves for a few hours or freeze 30 minutes; they will be easier to open. Slide blade of clam knife between the two shells. Work knife between shells toward hinge until you can pry shells apart. To sever muscles, slide blade along inside of one shell and under clam.

Mussels   Debeard by pulling out threads of tissue that protrude from the shell. Mussels die soon after debearding; prepare immediately. Open as you would a clam.

SHELL, TO

To remove the natural outer covering, or shell, of a food. Typically the term refers to nuts; eggs; seafood such as crab, mussels, and oysters; and to vegetables such as peas and beans.

SHELLFISH

All shellfish fall into one of three categories: crustaceans (crabs, shrimp, prawns, lobsters, crayfish); mollusks (including univalves such as abalone and conch, and bivalves such as mussels, clams, oysters, and scallops); and cephalopods (such as squid and octopus), which, despite being classed as shellfish, do not have shells. Even within these categories, flavors and textures vary greatly. To discuss the best ways to select, store, and prepare shellfish, it is helpful to consider the major varieties separately.

Use   Shellfish preparations are among the world's best-loved dishes. Favorites include Louisiana boiled crayfish, French steamed mussels with white wine and onion, baked clams on the half shell with buttered bread crumbs and bacon, Chinese stir-fried crab with black bean sauce, grilled lobster with drawn butter, and fried shrimp.

Availability   Shellfish are marketed fresh and frozen. The best quality and selection are usually found at a specialty fish market. Some merchants keep crabs and lobsters in holding tanks for live purchase.

Selection   Shellfish deteriorate rapidly after harvesting. Buy from a reputable dealer with a rapid turnover. Carefully frozen shellfish are preferable to "fresh" shellfish that have been out of the water too long.

Periodically during the summer months, local fish-and-game departments declare some sections of coastal waters temporarily unsafe due to the presence of toxic organisms that could be taken up by bivalves. Before harvesting bivalves from coastal waters, check with local fish-and-game authorities to make sure warnings are not in effect.

Storage   Refrigerate fresh shellfish immediately after purchase. If possible, store on a bed of ice in the refrigerator, loosely covered with a clean towel.

Preparation   See individual shellfish entries for specific preparation tips.

Cooking   See BAKE, BOIL, BRAISE, BROIL, DEEP-FRY, GRILL, SAUTE, STEAM, STIR-FRY.

ABALONE

The abalone is a univalve, its mushroom-shaped flesh hiding underneath a large, one-sided shell. The highest concentrations of abalone are found along the coasts of California, Mexico, Japan, and Australia. The flesh is very chewy and must be tenderized by pounding. The texture is silky, the flavor briny and mild.

Scaloppine-like abalone steaks are usually floured lightly and fried quickly in butter. To prepare, remove shell the same way you would shuck a clam (see Opening Bivalves, at left), then scrub off or carefully cut away the outer black skin. Cut thin steaks across the muscle or cut thin strips with the grain. Pound with a mallet or the side of a cleaver to about ¼-inch thickness. Slash meat with a sharp knife to prevent it from curling during cooking. The meat may also be finely minced or ground for use in shellfish cakes or croquettes; small tenderized (pounded) strips may be deep-fried.

The harvesting of fresh abalone in California is highly regulated. Abalone is sporadically available in the shell in the spring and autumn and is easiest to find in Asian fish markets. Some markets sell tenderized steaks. Abalone is also sold canned, dried, and frozen.

Fresh abalone should be alive when purchased; if live, the exposed muscle will react when touched. Abalone flesh should smell sweet, not fishy. Refrigerate and cook within one day. Frozen abalone may be stored in the freezer for up to three months; thaw in the refrigerator. Once opened, canned abalone should be kept covered with water in a covered container; change water every two days. Keep dried abalone tightly wrapped in a cool, dry place; it will keep indefinitely.

■ ABALONE STEW

The classic use for abalone is as a steak quickly sautéed in butter for less than one minute on each side. This stew gives another savory use for these univalves. Fresh abalone needs to be pounded to tenderize it, but if purchased frozen or canned, that has been done.

   1 **pound abalone steaks**
  ⅓ **cup unsalted butter**
   1 **cup finely chopped onion**
   1 **large clove garlic, peeled and minced**
  ⅓ **cup finely chopped red or green bell pepper**
   1 **bay leaf**
   1 **can (8 oz) tomato sauce**
   2 **cups water**
   3 **potatoes, peeled and cut in ½-inch cubes**
  ½ **teaspoon salt**
  ⅓ **teaspoon cayenne pepper**

1. Cut abalone in ½-inch cubes; reserve. In a large saucepan over medium heat, melt butter and sauté onion, garlic, and bell pepper until onion is soft and pale gold in color (about 5 minutes). Add bay leaf, tomato sauce, the water, potatoes, salt, and cayenne.

2. Cover and simmer until potatoes are almost tender (about 15 minutes). Add abalone cubes and simmer until abalone is tender (4 to 5 minutes).

Serves 8.

PREPARING SQUID

Rinse squid in cold water. Cut off tentacles just above eye. Squeeze the thick center part of tentacles, which pushes out the hard beak. Discard beak.

Squeeze the entrails from the body by running your fingers from the closed to the cut end. Pull out the transparent quill that protrudes from the body.

Slip a finger under the skin and peel it off. Pull off edible fins from either side and skin them.

PREPARING AMERICAN LOBSTER

Hold lobster right side up on a firm surface. With a sharp knife, pierce the shell and flesh at the center of the cross-shaped mark behind the head.

Cut in half lengthwise. Remove and discard gravel sac near the head and intestinal vein in tail. Remove the gray-green tomalley (liver) and any roe from body; reserve for flavoring sauces.

Twist off and save claws. With sharp knife, separate each of the two halves between tail and body. Slice tail between every other shell segment, leaving shell intact. Crack claws and joints, leaving shell in place.

PREPARING SHRIMP AND CRAYFISH

Shrimp Remove legs. Peel a bit of shell from head end of body. Holding the peeled section with hand, pull tail with other hand and shell will come off.

Slit shrimp down outside curve and remove the intestinal vein. On larger shrimp the intestinal vein contains grit that would interfere with the taste of the recipe. Often on medium shrimp grit is not present and the intestinal vein need not be removed before serving.

Crayfish To remove tail, hold crayfish securely on firm surface, right side up. Lift center tail flap and twist carefully to free it from body. Holding crayfish firmly with one hand, pull tail flap away from crayfish to remove intestinal vein.

PREPARING HARD-SHELL CRABS

Hold crab firmly against work surface. Kill it instantly by stabbing crab just behind the eyes with the point of a sharp knife. Turn crab over. Gently fold back and then twist or pull off apron or tail flap. The attached intestinal vein will pull out along with apron; discard both. Turn crab right side up.

With one hand, hold on to crab body where apron was removed and use other hand to pry up and tear off top shell. Discard shell. Remove gills from each side of crab and take out grayish, saclike sand bag. Pull out and discard mandibles from front of crab.

Holding body where legs are attached, apply pressure so that crab splits in half along center of body. Fold back halves and twist apart. Twist off claws and legs where they join the body. Crack them with a nutcracker and remove the meat.

PREPARING SOFT-SHELL CRABS

Cut across the eyes with kitchen shears or a sharp knife. Reach into the cut and pull out the gray saclike stomach, called the sand bag. Discard the stomach.

Turn crab over, lift up flap or apron, and fold it down away from body. Gently pull out the apron and attached intestinal vein. Discard apron and vein.

Turn crab right side up. Lift flaps at each side near the legs, then scrape off and discard the spongy gills.

CLAMS

A bivalve, the clam has edible flesh inside two hinged shells. Atlantic clams include the small soft-shell steamers and the hard-shell quahogs, which range in size from littlenecks to cherrystones to large chowder clams that must be ground or minced. Pacific clams include the hard-shell littleneck, the soft-shell razor clam, and the large geoduck, which has an elephantlike trunk protruding from its shell.

With the exception of the chowder clam, Atlantic clams are often shucked and eaten on the half shell or in raw clam cocktails. Most West Coast clams are too tough to eat raw. Clams may be steamed open with wine and garlic, then eaten as is or added to chowders or pasta sauces. Clams on the half shell are often topped with a seasoned bread mixture or herb butter and baked until hot.

Fresh clams are sold in the shell or shucked. Both East and West Coast varieties are available the year around but are better in the colder months. Clams are also canned and smoked. Fresh unshelled clams should be alive when purchased; if live, the shells will be tightly closed or will close when touched. Reject any that refuse to close tightly. Store live clams in the refrigerator, covered with a damp cloth. Cook and eat within one or two days. Scrub clam shells well. To shuck, see Opening Bivalves, page 536.

■ NEW ENGLAND CLAM CHOWDER

As with any traditional clam chowder, the amount of salt you add depends on the saltiness of the clam broth and salt pork; be sure to taste before seasoning.

    20 medium-sized clams, scrubbed, *or*
        1 quart shucked clams
     2 tablespoons butter
    ¼ pound salt pork, rinsed in cold water
        and diced finely
    1½ cups diced onion
     8 cups clam broth, reserved from steaming clams,
        or bottled clam juice
     3 cups peeled, cubed potatoes, cooked in
        salted water
     3 cups half-and-half
        Salt and freshly ground white pepper, to taste
        Butter, for garnish
        Oyster crackers or pilot crackers,
        for accompaniment

1. If necessary, steam clams and remove and discard shells. Strain clam broth and reserve.

2. In a large kettle place the 2 tablespoons butter with salt pork. Cook over low heat to render fat and brown pork. Remove pork pieces (cracklings) with slotted spoon and reserve.

3. Add diced onions to fat and cook until they begin to soften. Add clam broth or clam juice to kettle and bring to a boil. Reduce heat and simmer for 5 minutes. Chop clams into small pieces and add to kettle along with cooked potatoes.

4. Cover and simmer for 10 minutes. Add half-and-half to kettle and heat gently. Return pork cracklings to kettle and season with salt and pepper.

5. Serve in warm bowls with a pat of butter in each bowl and plenty of freshly ground pepper. Pass the crackers.

Serves 8.

■ MANHATTAN CLAM CHOWDER

This is the red version of the well-known New England Clam Chowder, which is white. The saltiness of the clams, salt pork, and clam broth affects the amount of additional salt and pepper required.

    ¼ cup salt pork, finely diced
     1 green bell pepper, diced
     1 onion, minced
     3 medium boiling potatoes, peeled and diced
     2 cups ripe tomatoes
        (about 3 large tomatoes), diced
    ½ teaspoon dried thyme
        Salt and freshly ground black pepper, to taste
    ⅛ teaspoon cayenne pepper
     3 cups Fish Stock (see page 561) or
        bottled clam juice
     2 cups shucked steamed clams
        Crusty bread, for accompaniment

1. In a 4-quart saucepan sauté salt pork over medium heat. Add bell pepper and onion, and cook until softened (3 to 5 minutes). Stir in potatoes, tomatoes, thyme, salt, pepper, cayenne, and Fish Stock.

2. Cover and simmer 25 minutes. Add clams, and cook 10 minutes more. Serve steaming hot with crusty bread.

Serves 6 to 8.

Recipes: Cioppino, 556; Steamed Clams, 611; White Clam or Mussel Sauce, 413.

CONCH

Also known as whelk, the conch is a univalve, its sweet flesh almost completely encased in a beautiful rose-tinged, whorled shell. The flesh is tough but may be tenderized by long, slow cooking or by pounding and parboiling. In the Caribbean, conch is eaten raw in a cold cocktail with lemon, onion, and minced tomato, or minced and made into conch chowder.

The meat may be ground, bound with a fritter batter, and deep-fried. It may be sliced thin, pounded, floured, and sautéed in butter like abalone or slowly stewed with wine and herbs. Italians call it *scungilli* and braise it with marinara sauce.

Conch is harvested the year around off the coast of Florida. It is sold in the shell or shucked. A Pacific coast variety is occasionally available in Asian markets on the West Coast. Conch is also marketed frozen (both cooked and raw) and canned, especially along the Atlantic coast and in the Gulf states.

Fresh conch should smell sweet, not fishy. Refrigerate and cook within one day. After opening, canned conch should be covered with water and stored in an airtight container; refrigerate and use within three days. Store frozen conch for up to three months; thaw in the refrigerator before using.

Conch meat is difficult to extract from the convoluted conch shell. Use a hammer to knock a hole in the shell about 1 inch below the crown. With a small, sharp knife, sever the muscle where it attaches to the crown. Grasp the portion of the conch meat that protrudes from the shell and pull to extract it. Trim away the soft parts from the crown end of the meat and cut out the intestinal vein. Peel off the skin, using a knife to cut away any parts that cling. Cut away the hard, flat operculum at the foot of the meat.

CRABS

The Atlantic and Pacific coasts harbor a variety of different crabs, all of which yield sweet white meat. Crabs are eaten both cold and hot, in the shell and shelled. The Dungeness crab and blue crab have edible body and claw meat. In the Alaskan king crab and spider crab, the edible meat is concentrated in the legs and claws; in the southern Atlantic stone crab, the edible meat is only in the claws.

Crabs are often boiled or steamed and served whole. Hot, steamed crabs in the shell are usually accompanied by lemon butter. Cold crab in the shell is usually accompanied by mayonnaise or a tomato-based cocktail sauce. Crab in the shell is added to a variety of hearty soups from gumbo to Cioppino. Chinese cooks stir-fry crabs with ginger and green onion or black bean sauce. Soft-shell blue crabs—crabs that have just molted their hard shells—are entirely edible; they are generally panfried in butter and eaten shell and all.

Crabmeat is often sold cold as a first-course cocktail, with lemon, mayonnaise, or cocktail sauce. Shelled crabmeat may be baked with seasoned cracker crumbs and butter; mixed with mayonnaise and bread crumbs, formed into cakes and fried; made into stuffings for trout; creamed and served in pastry shells; added to soups; or made into cold or hot mousses. Caribbean cooks season the meat highly, stuff it back into the shell, and bake it. Crabmeat may also be used as a filling for enchiladas, tacos, quiche, or crêpes.

Pacific Dungeness crab is available fresh from Washington state to Baja, California, from October through May; it is sold either live or precooked. Fresh Dungeness crabmeat is available locally and is shipped canned or frozen to other parts of the country.

Soft-shell blue crabs from the Atlantic and Gulf coasts are available from April through September; they are airfreighted fresh to some urban markets and are widely sold frozen. Hard-shell blue crabs are available all year, with local seasons depending on water temperature. The she-crab is a female blue crab with orange roe; she-crab soup, containing both meat and roe, is popular in the southern Atlantic states. Florida stone crab claws are enjoyed fresh locally and are frozen for shipment. The legs and claws of Alaskan spider and king crabs are frozen and sold the year around. Frozen Alaskan king crab legs are available in most fish markets.

Canned crabmeat is widely available in supermarkets; most of it is from spider crabs (sometimes identified as "snow crab"), although some markets carry Alaskan king crabmeat or Dungeness crabmeat.

Fresh uncooked crabs should be alive when purchased; if they are alive, they will be active and kicking. Avoid any sluggish or still ones. Refrigerate fresh crab immediately and cook that day. Cooked crabs and crabmeat should smell sweet when they are purchased. Refrigerate and use within three days. Once opened, canned crabmeat should be stored in an airtight nonreactive container in the refrigerator and used within two days. Fresh meat may be frozen for up to three months, although there will be some loss of flavor and texture. Thaw frozen crabmeat slowly in the refrigerator. Blot dry before using to keep it from watering down the dish in which it will be used. The liquid from canned crabmeat is usually used in recipes. All crabmeat should be picked over carefully to remove any bits of the shell or cartilage.

■ MARYLAND CRAB CAKES

Nothing can match the sweetness of Chesapeake Bay crab, but this dish is worth making with other types as well. The homemade Tartar Sauce that accompanies it is wholly different from the commercially bottled product.

> 1   **pound crabmeat (preferably from Maryland blue crabs)**
> 1   **cup soft bread crumbs**
> 1   **large egg, lightly beaten**
> ¼   **cup mayonnaise**
> 1   **tablespoon mustard**
> 1   **teaspoon Worcestershire sauce**
> 2   **tablespoons minced parsley**
> ¼   **teaspoon white pepper**
>   **Dash Tabasco Sauce**
>   **Oil, for frying**
>   **Lemon wedges, for accompaniment**
>   **Tartar Sauce With Green Peppercorns (see page 520), for accompaniment**

1. If you are using something other than Maryland blue crab, taste a pinch of it; if it is too salty, rinse briefly under cold running water.

2. Carefully pick over crabmeat, removing any shell and other inedible bits; leave crab in large lumps. Gently mix in bread crumbs.

3. Combine egg, mayonnaise, mustard, Worcestershire, parsley, pepper, and Tabasco. Gently blend this mixture with crabmeat.

4. Form crab mixture into six thick patties. Wrap individually in plastic wrap and refrigerate for 30 minutes to firm the mixture.

5. Pour ¼ inch of oil into a large skillet; heat until aromatic and rippling (about 350° F). Add crab cakes and fry, turning once, until golden on both sides (about 3 minutes per side). Serve immediately with lemon wedges and Tartar Sauce With Green Peppercorns.

Serves 6.

Recipes: Chilled Savory Mousse, 372; Cioppino, 556; Crab Salad Louis, 509.

CRAYFISH

The crayfish (also known as crawfish or crawdad) is a freshwater crustacean harvested from rivers and ponds. It resembles a tiny lobster and is usually about 4 inches long. The prized parts are the sweet white tail meat and the fat in the head, which adds richness to crayfish dishes.

Important to Louisiana Cajun and Creole cooking, crayfish are steamed and served in the shell, cold or hot. They are added to gumbos and jambalaya and made into stews, bisques, salads, and pies.

Crayfish are available, either live or cooked, in some markets from spring through fall. They are farmed in Louisiana in flooded fields and are airfreighted around the country and to Europe. Frozen whole crayfish or frozen tail meat is available in some markets or by mail. Uncooked crayfish should be alive when purchased; avoid any that are sluggish or still. Refrigerate immediately and cook within one day. Cooked crayfish should smell sweet when purchased. Refrigerate and use within two days. Frozen crayfish will keep for up to three months. Thaw frozen crayfish slowly in the refrigerator; do not refreeze. See Preparing Shrimp and Crayfish, page 537.

Fresh crayfish are sometimes muddy; soak in cold water for 10 minutes. Crayfish are cooked in their shells, then shelled to retrieve the tail meat.

▇ BOILED SEAFOOD DINNER

The liquid prepared in step 2 constitutes a homemade crab boil. It can be reused three or four times. Refrigerate and use within a week, or freeze. If you can't find blue crabs or live crayfish, use just shrimp (about 6 pounds should be enough for 12 people).

> 5 pounds live crayfish
> 2 gallons water
> 2 cups salt
> 1 cup fresh lemon juice
> ½ cup cayenne pepper
> ¼ cup black peppercorns
> 2 teaspoons whole allspice
> 1 tablespoon whole cloves
> 1 tablespoon thyme
> 12 bay leaves
> 2 teaspoons whole celery seed
> 2 tablespoons coriander
> 3 heads garlic
> 6 onions, halved
> 24 small red potatoes
> 12 blue crabs
> 3 pounds shrimp
> 12 ears corn, cut in half widthwise

1. Purge crayfish by soaking in cold salted water. Drain and rinse; repeat this process until the soaking water is no longer muddy. Set crayfish aside.

2. In a 4- to 5-gallon pot, bring the 2 gallons water and salt to a boil over high heat. Add lemon juice, cayenne, black peppercorns, allspice, cloves, thyme, bay leaves, celery seed, and coriander; continue boiling for 20 minutes.

3. Add garlic, onions, and potatoes; boil another 10 minutes. Add crabs and boil 5 minutes. Add crayfish and continue boiling for 5 minutes. Add shrimp and corn and boil until shrimp are pink and firm (5 to 7 minutes). Drain boiled food through a colander suspended over a large pot.

4. Serve seafood and vegetables in large, shallow bowls or on platters.

Serves 12.

LOBSTER

Two varieties of lobster are taken in American waters. The spiny lobster, a warm-water crustacean found along the coasts of Florida and California and in the Gulf of Mexico, contains meat in its tail only; the American lobster, found in the Atlantic from New England to southern Canada, has edible meat in both tail and claws. The spiny lobster has a rough, reddish brown shell and no claws; the bluish black American lobster has large claws with sharp pincers. Both types turn bright red when cooked.

Lobster is usually poached, steamed, baked, or grilled and may be eaten cold or hot. Cold lobster is generally served as a first-course cocktail or in a salad with mayonnaise or vinaigrette. Hot lobster is often served in the shell with melted butter and lemon. Lobster shells are used to flavor bisques and aromatic sauces and butters. The meat is used in soups, casseroles, soufflés, and sautés, or it may be creamed and served in a pastry shell. Split lobsters are topped with buttered bread crumbs and baked. Chinese cooks stir-fry lobster meat with black bean sauce or with ginger and green onion.

This spicy boiled dinner uses three crustaceans found fresh in Louisiana: blue crabs, crayfish, and shrimp. Or, if you prefer, any of these can be used alone.

Moules Mariniere is an adaptation of a classic French dish that never fails to please even the most discriminating palate. Easily prepared and economical, this recipe may well become a mainstay in your seafood repertoire.

Spiny lobsters are available live or cooked the year around in some markets. Frozen spiny lobster tails (often identified as rock lobster or *langouste*) are widely available. American lobster, also known as Maine lobster, is usually sold live from tanks and is available all year; some markets sell whole cooked American lobsters.

Live lobster should be active when taken from the tank; avoid sluggish ones. Cooked lobsters should smell sweet; their tails should be tightly curled underneath the body, a sign that they were alive when cooked. Refrigerate live lobsters and cook within one day. Cooked lobster should be eaten within two days. Frozen lobster may be stored up to three months; thaw slowly in the refrigerator.

Live lobsters are usually cooked whole. However, some recipes call for splitting and cleaning the lobster before cooking; see Preparing American Lobster, page 537. Prepare a live spiny lobster by setting it on its back on a firm surface; with a heavy, sharp knife, stab point into mouth to sever spinal cord. Turn lobster over and split in half lengthwise; use a rubber mallet, if necessary, to force knife through body. If starting with a cooked spiny lobster, begin preparation by splitting in half. With both cooked and uncooked lobsters, rinse viscera from body and intestinal vein from tail under cold running water.

■ LOBSTER SALAD

This salad is best with your own mayonnaise, made with lemon juice instead of vinegar. Prawns and crab can be added to the salad for variety. Note that the salad should chill for two hours before serving; chilled plates keep the salad cool longer.

>   3 cups cooked lobster meat
>   (2 live lobsters, approximately 1½ lb each;
>   see Basic Poached Shellfish, page 451)
>   2 stalks celery, diced
>   1 red bell pepper, diced
>   1 small bunch chives, snipped
>   1 shallot, minced
>   1 cup Mayonnaise (see page 519; use fresh lemon
>   juice instead of vinegar)
>   1 head Bibb lettuce, separated into leaves
>   1 lemon, cut into 8 wedges, for garnish (optional)
>   8 parsley sprigs, for garnish

1. Cube the cooked lobster into large pieces (about ¾ inch each). In a 2-quart mixing bowl, place lobster, celery, bell pepper, chives, and shallot. Add mayonnaise and stir well to combine. For best flavor chill at least 2 hours before serving.

2. To serve, wash the lettuce leaves, then pat dry. Place one leaf on each chilled salad plate. Serve about ½ cup salad on each lettuce leaf. Garnish each plate with lemon wedge and parsley sprig, if desired.

Serves 8.

Recipes: Basic Poached Shellfish, 451.

MUSSELS

Bivalves with a smooth, bluish black shell, mussels have flesh that ranges from deep yellow to orange. They are found clinging to rocks along both Atlantic and Pacific coasts and are successfully produced by aquaculture in New England. Most of the commercial harvest is from the East Coast; due to toxic substances in the water, Pacific coast mussels are usually quarantined during the summer.

Fresh mussels are steamed in the shells, usually with white wine, oil, and garlic, until they open; they are then eaten from the shell with melted butter or tossed with pasta. They may be shelled, chilled, and used in salads or shellfish cocktails. Mussels may also be grilled over coals until they open. Steamed mussels and their liquid may be made into soups or added to shellfish stews. They may also be steamed open, then dressed with butter and bread crumbs and baked on the half shell. In most recipes, mussels can be substituted for clams.

Fresh East Coast mussels are sold the year around. West Coast mussels are available from November through April. They are generally marketed live, in the shell, although some East Coast markets sell shucked mussels. Canned smoked mussels are also available in most markets. Mussels in the shell should be alive when purchased. Their shells will be tightly closed or will close when touched; discard any that refuse to close. Refrigerate, covered with a damp cloth; cook within one day. Store cooked, shucked mussels in a tightly closed container in the refrigerator; use within two days. Scrub mussel shells well with a stiff brush. See Opening Bivalves, page 536.

■ MOULES MARINIERE

This version of a classic French dish features a richly flavored cream sauce. Fennel adds a hint of licorice to the cooking stock. For directions on how to debeard a mussel, see photograph on page 536.

   6 dozen mussels
   4 shallots, chopped
   1 bay leaf
  ½ teaspoon fennel seed
   1 cup dry white wine
   1 cup whipping cream
   3 egg yolks
     Juice of 1 lemon
   2 tablespoons unsalted butter
     Salt and pepper, to taste
     Chopped parsley, for garnish

1. Scrub and debeard mussels. Soak them in a bowl of cold water or in sink for 30 minutes. Any sand will leach out and sink to bottom of bowl.

2. In a large stockpot simmer shallots, bay leaf, fennel seed, and wine for 5 minutes. Add mussels and steam for 5 minutes; all mussels should open in that time. If doubling recipe, it will take longer for mussels to open. Transfer mussels to a large bowl and keep them warm.

3. To make sauce, strain mussel stock and boil until reduced to about 1½ cups. In a medium bowl beat together cream, egg yolks, and lemon juice. Add 1 cup of mussel stock to cream mixture in a thin stream, then pour the mixture back into the remaining stock. Heat very gently, stirring constantly so that egg yolks do not scramble. Turn off the heat and stir in butter. Season with salt and pepper, if necessary.

4. Divide mussels among 6 large, shallow soup bowls. Ladle sauce over each bowl and sprinkle each with chopped parsley. Place a large bowl on the table for mussel shells.

Serves 6.

Recipes: Cioppino, 556; White Clam or Mussel Sauce, 413.

OYSTER

The oyster is a bivalve that lives in shallow, temperate, and tropical waters. Inside its rough, hard, gray shell is the soft, briny flesh that is appreciated both raw and cooked. Today, several varieties of oysters are commercially farmed on both Atlantic and Pacific coasts of the United States.

Most of the oysters of the world are probably eaten raw on the half shell, with lemon, vinegar, or cocktail sauce. However, there are also dozens of delicious ways to cook them. They may be grilled over coals until their shells open. They may be shelled, poached, and served in a cream sauce or simmered in milk or cream with butter for an oyster stew. Oysters on the half shell may be topped with herb butter or buttered bread crumbs and baked. Whole oysters may be wrapped in bacon and broiled or simmered in butter with hot-pepper sauce and served atop toast. Oysters are added to bread stuffings for turkey or fish and are baked in double-crust pies. Deep-fried cornmeal-coated oysters may be eaten hot with lemon or tucked into a loaf of French bread to make an Oyster Loaf (see page 544). Smoked oysters are usually eaten as an appetizer with crackers or mixed into cream cheese–based dipping sauces.

Most varieties of oysters are available fresh the year around but are better in the colder months. They spawn during the summer and their flesh gets fatty, making them less appealing on the half shell. Oysters are usually sold live in the shell; some varieties are also available shucked in jars or smoked and packed in tins.

Today's commercial oysters are carefully monitored for the toxin that shellfish can ingest in the summer months, and thus present no danger to diners. Unshelled oysters should be alive when purchased; if live, their shells will be tightly closed. Discard any with open shells. Store them in the refrigerator cup side down, covered with a damp towel; use within three days. Shucked oysters should be refrigerated in their liquor and used as soon as possible. See Opening Bivalves, page 536.

■ OYSTER LOAF

Food has always played a prominent role in San Francisco. During the rowdy days of the city in the late 1800s, carousing husbands often carried home an oyster loaf—not candy or flowers—after a late night out as a peace offering to their annoyed spouses. This makes an excellent first course for up to six people or dinner for two.

  1 loaf French bread (about 1 lb)
  8 tablespoons unsalted butter
  ¼ teaspoon freshly grated nutmeg
  ¼ teaspoon cayenne pepper
  ½ teaspoon freshly ground black pepper
  1 teaspoon salt
  ½ cup flour
  ½ cup milk
  1 egg
16 medium oysters, shucked, *or*
    2 jars (10 oz each) oysters
  ¾ cup dry bread crumbs (see step 1)
  3 tablespoons vegetable oil, for frying
    Juice of 1 lemon
    Tartar Sauce With Green Peppercorns,
    for accompaniment (see page 520), optional

1. Preheat oven to 400° F. Slice top off loaf of bread. Scoop out soft center, leaving a ½-inch-thick crusty shell. Break soft bread into crumbs and place on a baking sheet. Toast 10 minutes; reserve. Coat inside of bread shell with 3 tablespoons of the butter. Place shell on baking sheet and toast in oven until golden brown (about 10 minutes); reserve.

2. In a small bowl stir together nutmeg, cayenne, pepper, salt, and flour. In another small bowl beat together milk and egg. Dip oysters in seasoned flour, then in egg-milk mixture, and finally in bread crumbs. Place on a plate and chill 1 hour.

3. In a medium skillet sauté oysters in oil and remaining butter over medium heat until golden and crusty on first side (about 4 minutes). Turn; sauté second side 2 minutes. Place cooked oysters in bread shell and pour pan juices over. Serve drizzled with lemon juice and accompanied with Tartar Sauce With Green Peppercorns (if desired).

Serves 4 to 6 as a first course, 2 as a main course.

Recipes: Hangtown Fry, 202.

SCALLOPS

The scallop is a bivalve found on the Atlantic and Gulf coasts. The edible part is the sweet white muscle that holds together the two fan-shaped, hinged shells. The larger sea scallop is about 5 inches across, with a muscle that may be 1 inch wide and ½ inch thick; it is found in water from the mid-Atlantic to the New England coast. The smaller bay scallop is about 2 inches across, with a muscle considerably smaller than that of the sea scallop. Bay scallops are found in Atlantic estuaries. The Florida calico scallop is about the same size as the bay scallop, but the calico is a deep-sea scallop.

Scallops may be baked with buttered bread crumbs or herb butter; sautéed with butter, herbs, and wine or cream sauce; added to soups, shellfish stews, and pasta sauces; floured and deep-fried; poached and eaten cold in salads; or skewered and grilled. They may be marinated for seviche or eaten raw in sushi.

Fresh sea scallops are available all year but supplies are more plentiful in summer. They are almost always sold shucked; they die quickly out of the water. However, live sea scallops are occasionally available in some markets. Bay scallops are available fresh in fall and winter on the East Coast, where they are most prevalent; they, too, are almost always sold shucked. Frozen bay and sea scallops are widely available in fish markets.

Fresh shucked scallops should smell sweet, not fishy. Refrigerate immediately and use within one or two days. Scallops may be frozen for up to three months; thaw slowly in the refrigerator.

■ COQUILLES ST. JACQUES

Scallops come in two sizes, tiny bay scallops (about 100 to the pound) and the larger and more variably sized sea scallops (from 20 to 40 per pound). The larger scallops take slightly longer to cook; if they are cut in thirds or quarters, their cooking time will match that of the smaller bay scallops.

  3 shallots, minced
  ¼ cup parsley, minced
  1 clove garlic, minced
  4 tablespoons unsalted butter
  ¾ cup dry white wine
    Bouquet garni (see page 56)
  1 pound bay scallops
  ½ cup soft bread crumbs
  2 tablespoons freshly grated Parmesan cheese
  2 tablespoons butter, melted
  ½ teaspoon salt
  ⅛ teaspoon freshly ground pepper

1. Preheat broiler. In a large, heavy-bottomed sauté pan, sauté shallots, 2 tablespoons of the parsley, and garlic in the 4 tablespoons butter over medium-low heat until soft but not browned (about 10 minutes). Add wine and bouquet garni and simmer 10 minutes.

2. Cut scallops so that all are approximately the same size. Add to pan and cook 4 to 6 minutes (scallops will appear opaque but slightly resilient when done). Remove bouquet garni and divide scallops among 4 shallow gratin dishes or shells.

3. In a small bowl stir together bread crumbs, Parmesan, melted butter, remaining parsley, salt, and pepper. Sprinkle about ¼ cup over each dish of scallops. Place on op rack of oven and broil until golden brown and slightly crisp (2 to 3 minutes).

Serves 4.

SHRIMP AND PRAWNS

Shrimp are saltwater crustaceans and prawns are found in fresh water. However, most consumers and fish markets use the word *prawn* to designate a large shrimp. Shrimp are found on all coasts: From the southern Atlantic and the Gulf of Mexico come brown, white, and pink varieties; from the California coast come spot shrimp known as Monterey prawns. The flesh is firm and white and, when cooked, has coral striations. The flavor is sweet and slightly briny.

Fresh shrimp and prawns may be cooked and served in the shell, either hot or cold. Hot shrimp in the shell are often accompanied by melted lemon butter, cold shrimp by mayonnaise or tartar sauce. Cooked peeled shrimp are used cold in salads and shellfish cocktails and hot in casseroles, crêpe fillings, curries, and fish stuffings. Shrimp may be sautéed, stir-fried, poached, grilled, or braised, either peeled or in the shell. Peeled shrimp may be battered and fried. Shrimp are an important part of Louisiana Cajun and Creole cooking, turning up in bisques, jambalaya, gumbo, and *étouffée* (stew). Crushed shrimp shells may be used to flavor sauces and butters for shellfish dishes.

Monterey prawns (spot shrimp) are available from spring through fall, either whole or with heads removed. Gulf shrimp are available the year around and are almost always sold with heads removed. Almost all shrimp have been frozen at some point in the shipping process, although they may be thawed for retail sale. Most fish markets carry cooked and peeled shrimp as well as raw shrimp in the shell. Canned and frozen shrimp are also available in most markets.

Shrimp, both raw and cooked, should feel firm and smell sweet; avoid any with an ammoniated odor. If buying thawed frozen shrimp, be sure they have not been thawed more than one or two days. Uncooked shrimp should be refrigerated immediately and cooked as soon as possible. Cooked shrimp may be refrigerated for up to three days. Shrimp may be frozen for up to three months; thaw slowly in the refrigerator.

Deveining is optional with small shrimp; with large shrimp, the black intestinal vein may be gritty and therefore should be removed. See Preparing Shrimp and Crayfish, page 537.

■ SHRIMP CREOLE

In French and in the culinary vernacular of New Orleans, *creole* means to cook with tomatoes and sweet bell peppers, and usually to accompany with rice.

     4 tablespoons butter
     1 large onion, diced
     1 large stalk celery, diced
     1 large green bell pepper, diced
     2 cloves garlic, minced
     ½ teaspoon dried thyme
     ½ teaspoon salt
     ½ teaspoon white pepper
     ½ teaspoon cayenne pepper
     ½ teaspoon freshly ground black pepper
     1 tablespoon flour
     ¼ cup dry white wine
     1 cup peeled and diced tomatoes
     1 cup Chicken Stock (see page 560)
     2 bay leaves
       Hot-pepper sauce, to taste (optional)
     2 pounds shrimp (24 to 30 per lb in shells),
       shelled and deveined
     6 to 8 cups cooked rice, for accompaniment

1. In butter in a large skillet, sauté onion, celery, bell pepper, and garlic over medium heat until lightly browned (about 6 minutes).

2. In a small bowl mix thyme, salt, white pepper, cayenne, black pepper, and flour; stir into onion mixture and cook 2 minutes. Stir in wine, tomatoes, stock, bay leaves, and hot-pepper sauce (if used). Reduce heat and simmer 20 to 25 minutes.

3. Remove bay leaves. Stir in shrimp and simmer until bright pink (3 to 4 minutes). Serve with hot rice.

Serves 6.

Recipes: Boiled Seafood Dinner, 541; Cioppino, 556; Fritto Misto With Caper Mayonnaise, 176; Pork and Shrimp Stuffing, 191; Potstickers, 191; Shellfish Bisque, 564; Shrimp-Crowned Eggs, 199; Shrimp Okra Pilau, 397; Shrimp With Snow Peas and Water Chestnuts, 606; Spinach-Shrimp Soufflé, 205; Stuffed Mirliton, 110; Tempura Batter, 28.

SQUID AND OCTOPUS

Squid and octopus are cephalopods, mollusks with a distinct head, eyes, a beak, and muscular tentacles. Both have mottled skin overlaying smooth white flesh; when cooked, both are chewy and firm. In general the octopus is tougher and requires longer, slower cooking. Both squid and octopus have a somewhat off-putting appearance, but they are inexpensive and highly versatile.

Both squid and octopus are served in Japanese sushi bars; the octopus is always boiled first. Squid may be cut into rings and sautéed, deep-fried, or added to shellfish

If you've been hesitant about trying squid, tomato-based Squid Marinara just might change your mind. Serve with a crusty bread to mop up the wonderful sauce.

soups; the rings may also be poached and served cold in a seafood salad. Whole squid bodies may be skewered and grilled teriyaki-style or stuffed and baked. Italian cooks typically use squid in pasta sauce. The black squid "ink" is used in Italy to color and flavor rice and pasta dishes. Octopus takes well to slow-cooking methods, such as braising in red wine or in tomato-based sauces. If tenderized first, it may be grilled.

Squid is found on both coasts the year around and is sold fresh and frozen, either whole or cleaned bodies (tentacles removed) only. Octopus is also sold fresh or frozen, whole or in pieces, raw or cooked. It is readily available in fish markets that cater to a Japanese clientele. Fresh squid and octopus should smell sweet, not fishy. Refrigerate and cook within one or two days. Cooked squid and octopus should be refrigerated and eaten within three days. Frozen squid or octopus may be stored for up to three months; thaw slowly in the refrigerator.

See Preparing Squid, page 537. Octopus requires tenderizing before use; simmer for 20 to 25 minutes in salted water before adding to a soup, stew, or sauce.

■ SQUID MARINARA

This flavorful, peppery squid dish may be eaten hot or cold. It also makes a wonderful sauce for pasta. Spaghetti would be a good choice.

    4 pounds squid
    ⅓ cup fruity olive oil
    4 cloves garlic, minced
    4 cups crushed tomatoes in purée
    1 teaspoon dried oregano oregano leaves
       (not powdered), crumbled
    1 teaspoon dried basil *or* 6 fresh basil leaves
       Salt and freshly ground black pepper, to taste
    ¼ cup chopped Italian parsley
    1 teaspoon red pepper flakes

1. Clean squid (see Preparing Squid, page 537). Cut the bodies crosswise into ¾-inch-wide pieces. Also cut the tentacles if they are large.

2. In a heavy casserole or Dutch oven, heat oil. Add squid and sauté for 5 to 6 minutes. Add garlic and stir for 1 minute.

3. Add tomato, oregano, basil, salt, and pepper. Cover and cook until squid are tender (about 20 minutes). Stir in parsley and red pepper flakes. Adjust seasonings to taste.

Serves 8.

Recipes: Cioppino, 556; Fritto Misto With Caper Mayonnaise, 176.

SHORT

Dough with a high proportion of fat to flour. Short pastry and cookie doughs are tender and crumbly. By waterproofing the flour particles, fat limits the development of gluten, a structure-building offshoot of flour proteins created when flour mixes with liquid. Without this structure, the dough is more brittle, but it tastes so rich and wonderful you hardly mind the crumbs.

Recipes and Related Information
Classic Scotch Shortbread, 144; Sand Pastry, 442.

SHUCK, TO

To remove the outer covering of clams, oysters, and mussels; nuts; the husk of corn; the same as *to shell* and *to husk*. For information on opening bivalves, see SHELLFISH.

SKIM, TO

To remove surface fat or other impurities from a soup, stock, stew, or sauce with a skimmer, a spoon, or a ladle.

Recipes and Related Information
Degrease, 177; Spoon, Ladle, and Scoop, 551.

SKIN, TO

To remove the skin of poultry, fish, or game. Particular preparations, such as boned chicken breasts and fish fillets, are traditionally served skinless for reasons of taste, digestion, or aesthetics.

SLASH, TO

To notch the fat of a steak at even intervals all the way around or to make shallow cuts in the surface of a thin piece of veal. By doing this the meat will stay flat as it cooks; otherwise it will curl as it shrinks to its final size.

SLIVER, TO; SLIVER

To cut a thin and usually short stick of food, as fine as a splinter. The term is most often used to describe garlic cut this way; the garlic pieces are inserted into slits cut into roasts, particularly lamb, in order to flavor the meat internally as it cooks.

SMOKE POINT

The temperature at which a fat decomposes and gives off smoke and an acrid gas. Different fats break down at different temperatures; it is worthwhile knowing the smoke point of common fats since it is this characteristic that determines a fat's suitability for frying. For example, cooks appreciate the delicious flavor butter imparts to food, but know that it can't reach frying temperature without burning; vegetable oils (such as safflower, corn, peanut, and grapeseed oils) stay intact at higher temperatures and are often combined with butter in order to raise the smoke point of butter. See FRY for more information about the smoke points of different fats and about frying.

SORREL

Also known as sour grass and dock, sorrel is a leafy, deep-green member of the buckwheat family. Sorrel leaves, with their slender stems, somewhat resemble spinach, but the flavor is markedly different. Cooked sorrel has a pronounced lemonlike tang that is especially appealing in cream sauces, stuffings, and soups.

Use Very young sorrel leaves may be added to salads with other greens. Otherwise, sorrel is almost always cooked. When simmered in butter and cream, it makes a delicious partner to salmon and trout. French cooks stuff whole shad with sorrel purée and make a sorrel soup thickened with eggs and cream; Eastern European Jews make a cold sorrel and sour cream soup called *schav*.

Availability Sorrel grows wild throughout North America and is cultivated commercially. Fresh sorrel is marketed sporadically in supermarkets the year around, although it is most easily found in the spring. Specialty markets also carry cooked sorrel in jars.

Selection Look for green leaves with no sign of yellowing. Sorrel wilts readily after harvesting but flavor is not compromised.

Storage Wash and dry leaves; wrap in paper towels, then enclose in a plastic bag and refrigerate for up to four days. Bottled sorrel should be refrigerated after opening and used within one week.

Preparation Remove leaves from stems.

When food needs to be blended, spread, turned, or lifted, cooks will usually reach for one of these long-handled tools with flat blades. Shown from top to bottom: offset spatulas, rubber scrapers, turners.

SPATULA, SCRAPER, AND TURNER

The word *spatula* has the same Latin root as do spoon, spade, sword, and oar; the spatula functions similarly to all of these implements. Like a spoon or spade, it can scoop or lift; a spatula with a serrated edge can slice much like a knife; and with the same motion as an oar dipping into water, a spatula can cut through soft mixtures to blend them more thoroughly.

There are actually several tools that perform spreading, mixing, lifting, and turning tasks: the familiar rubber-headed scrapers; the long, thin, flexible metal spreaders; and the rectangular, shovel-type, angled-neck turners. Their uses overlap to some degree, but not completely. Each is called a spatula, but can be referred to by other names as well.

METAL SPATULAS

Serious pastry makers depend on these long, narrow-bladed culinary tools. Flexible-bladed spatulas are useful for spreading frostings, toppings, fillings, and batters. The more rigid ones are for lifting and transferring pastries and cakes from a baking sheet to work surface or serving dish. Any metal spatula can be used for moving delicate decorations around the work area. You may find them sold as icing spatulas. Shorter, stubbier-bladed ones are called sandwich spatulas. Versions of both types come with one serrated edge for slicing breads, cake layers, and even tomatoes and cucumbers. If you are a dedicated pastry maker, buy the best-quality spatula you can find; otherwise quality is less important. Most have wood handles, with 10- or 13-inch-long blades; the blade of a sandwich spatula is about 4 inches long. Buy one long enough to reach across the diameter of a cake or pastry.

RUBBER SCRAPERS

Basic to any kitchen, these have flat, hard rubber blades and handles of wood, plastic, or nylon. They are primarily scraping tools, for cleaning the last bit of batter out of a mixing bowl or reaching every crevice in a can of food. They are also used commonly for folding and mixing. The somewhat pliant material and design of the blade—one long edge is straight and turns at a sharp right angle while the other curves as it nears the top—conform to the shape of the container or bowl to remove cleanly the contents without damaging the surface.

Have at least two or three scrapers of differing handle lengths and blade sizes. They are typically 10 inches overall, with a 2½-inch-wide by 3¾-inch-long blade. Longer handles or bigger blades can be helpful for deep bowls or large quantities. Some come with half-width blades to fit into narrow spaces. Match the size and shape to the task: If the handle is too short, you will end up with puffs of batter on your hand and wrist; if it is too long, it will be

▓ SORREL SOUP

Sorrel has an acidic, lemony flavor that adds an appealing tang to many dishes, particularly soups.

> 1 large onion, chopped
> 2 cloves garlic, minced
> 3 tablespoons unsalted butter
> 3 medium potatoes, peeled and diced
> 5 cups tightly packed sorrel leaves *or* 3 cups spinach and 2 cups sorrel, julienned
> 1 teaspoon freshly grated nutmeg
> ½ teaspoon salt
> ½ teaspoon freshly ground black pepper
>   Dash cayenne pepper
> 2 quarts Chicken Stock (see page 560)
> ½ cup sour cream, for garnish
> ¼ cup snipped fresh chives, for garnish

1. In a 4-quart saucepan cook onion and garlic in butter over medium-low heat until lightly colored (about 15 minutes). Add potatoes, sorrel, nutmeg, salt, pepper, cayenne, and stock to saucepan. Bring to a boil, reduce heat, and simmer, partially covered, 50 minutes.

2. Purée in blender or food processor. Serve hot soup immediately or chill 4 hours and serve cold. Garnish with a swirl of sour cream and chives.

Makes about 9 cups.

awkward to use. When selecting a scraper, check to see if the rubber head has an odor; if so, your food may end up with a rubbery aroma. Also, match the rigidity of the head to the task: For some scraping jobs, you might want the head to bend; others may need a stiff head. Scrapers designed for professional kitchens will last the longest.

TURNERS

Chances are that you use a turner almost daily, whether for flipping pancakes, rotating hamburgers and steaks, or sliding an omelet from the pan. They function as extensions of your hand, and are metal with a square or rectangular blade and a wood or plastic handle (those with wood handles should be hand washed). Unlike icing and sandwich spatulas, these angle sharply where the blade meets the handle, allowing you to raise your arm a safe distance from the heat while dropping the blade down into a skillet or sauté pan. When the blade itself angles, the turners are called offset spatulas. They are commonly sold as pancake turners. Heavier blades are better for lifting; lighter, thinner blades can more easily work their way between food and pan. They are available either solid or perforated; the latter type of blade permits cooking fats to drain off.

SPATZLE MAKER

To make Spätzle (see page 190), tiny dumplings that are a favorite food in Germany and Austria, a soft egg batter is forced through a Spätzle maker into boiling water, where they cook like dumplings. Most typically the machine is a slotted stainless steel colander; the

dough sits in the bowl and is extruded through the holes with the turn of a crank. Another style resembles a potato ricer or an oversized garlic press, with openings about ¼ inch in diameter. Still another type of Spätzle maker is similar to a flat grater. A plastic housing that holds the dough slides on a track that is set on a perforated stainless steel plate; the housing is moved back and forth across the track, forcing the dough through the holes and into the pot of water.

SPICE

Few foods have changed the shape of world history more than spices. The struggle for control of the spice-producing lands has led to vicious piracy, sabotage, and wars; the search for spice trade routes led to the discovery of the New World.

Why were spices such a treasure? In the days before refrigeration, they were often used by European cooks to mask the flavor of strong foods. Recipes from Roman times through the Renaissance call for lavish use of spices, developing people's taste for very highly seasoned dishes. Taste aside, cooking with spices was a status symbol, an obvious sign of wealth.

Today, with spices readily available and food kept fresh by refrigeration, spices are used by most cooks as a subtle enhancer, not a mask. Although some cuisines depend heavily on spices and others hardly at all, it is a rare dish that is not touched by spices in some way.

Although difficult to define and draw a firm line between herbs and spices (see HERB), one workable definition holds that spices are derived from the seeds, roots, bark, fruit, or flowers of plants and that herbs are the leaves of plants with nonwoody stems. By that definition some plants—such as coriander—yield both herbs and spices.

Use Spices add richness and dimension to other foods and prepared dishes. They are grace notes, not essential to make the dish work technically (a spice cake would still rise without spices) but conspicuous by their absence.

Cooks located in warm climates use spices the most lavishly—no doubt because most spices originate in tropical or semitropical climates. Indian cooks employ an extensive array of spices: cloves, cardamom, ginger, nutmeg, pepper, cumin, cinnamon, and more. Latin American cooking is also laced with spices, especially cumin and cinnamon. Ethiopian and North African cooking is particularly spicy, with African cooks depending on pepper, ginger, cloves, nutmeg, fenugreek, and cinnamon. As might be expected, Indonesia—which encompasses the original Spice Islands, the Moluccas—also is noted for dishes that are rich in spices, particularly pepper, nutmeg, mace, and cloves.

In northern Europe spices including ginger, nutmeg, anise, cinnamon, and cloves are added to cookies and cakes especially at Christmas. Sweden's saffron-scented Lucia Buns and Germany's peppery *Pfeffernüsse* cookies are examples of traditional holiday baking. Scandinavian rye breads are often scented with caraway. Allspice flavors Swedish pickled herring and liver paste; juniper berries are used with game; and the famous liquor aquavit (Scandinavia's preferred distilled spirit) is flavored with caraway or other spices. Spanish cooks use cinnamon in desserts. French and Italian cooks are more inclined to use herbs than spices, but they do use a pinch of nutmeg in their basic cream sauces; older Italian recipes may call for cinnamon, ginger, or cardamom. Greek cooks employ cinnamon and clove in tomato-based stews of lamb or beef. Middle Eastern cooks are avid users of saffron.

Spices are far less important in cooking of the Far East. Rather, the Japanese and Chinese depend more on garlic, ginger, and soy sauce. However, star anise is prevalent in Chinese cooking and turns up in Vietnamese and Thai dishes, too.

Availability All supermarkets carry a wide assortment of spices in whole and ground forms. Health-food stores, ethnic markets, and specialty stores are another good source for spices. For information on a particular spice, see individual entries; for information on commercially prepared blends, see HERB AND SPICE BLENDS.

Selection When possible, buy spices in whole form and grind them yourself. Whole spices stay fresh much longer than ground, and freshly ground spices are far more pungent than those that are preground. Buy from a merchant who stores spices correctly: in a cool, dark, dry place.

Storage Whole spices will keep for up to two years under ideal conditions; ground spices for about six months.

Preparation Whole spices such as cloves, peppercorns, and cinnamon stick can be added directly to stews and soups and strained out before serving. For easy removal, wrap them in a cheesecloth bag tied with string or use a tea infuser. Whole spices can be ground with a mortar and pestle, or in a pepper mill, clean coffee grinder, or electric minichopper. Some recipes specify toasting spices lightly before grinding to bring out their flavor.

SPINACH

Leafy, green spinach probably originated in southwestern Asia, in the vicinity of modern-day Iran. Although introduced late to Europe, it caught on quickly. Today spinach is appreciated for its sprightly, fresh flavor and high content of vitamins A and C, iron, and folic acid.

Use Raw spinach has recently become popular as a salad green, often tossed with crumbled bacon and egg. Spinach also is wilted in butter or oil and served as a side dish; creamed and served with fish; puréed for soups, soufflés, and quiches; or minced and worked into pasta dough. Iranians enjoy *gormeh sabzi*, lamb braised with spinach and herbs; Indian cooks, using different spices, make a similar preparation called *saag gosht*. In Greece minced spinach is combined with eggs, feta cheese, and seasonings, then layered with filo dough and baked to make *spanakopita*.

Availability Fresh spinach is sold in most supermarkets the year around, with peak supplies from March through June. There are several varieties of spinach, some with flat smooth leaves, others with crinkly leaves. What appears in some markets as "New Zealand spinach" is neither spinach nor from New Zealand. Despite a fuzzy texture its leaves resemble spinach in color and flavor and can be used in its place. All supermarkets also carry canned and frozen spinach.

Selection Look for bright green leaves; avoid any that are wilted or slimy. Small, tender leaves, which impart a delicate flavor, are preferred for salads.

Storage Wrap fresh spinach in plastic and keep in the refrigerator for up to three days.

Preparation Spinach is grown in sand and can be very gritty. Wash well, in several changes of water if necessary, and remove tough stems. For salads, dry leaves thoroughly.

Cooking See SAUTE, STEAM, STIR-FRY.

■ CHAFING DISH SPINACH SALAD

Heated just until it begins to wilt, spinach makes a dramatic first course salad to prepare at the table—if you are a bit of a culinary exhibitionist.

> 2 **bunches (about ¾ lb each) spinach**
> 1 **tablespoon olive oil**
>   **Freshly ground pepper**
> 4 **slices bacon, crisply cooked, drained, and crumbled**
> 2 **hard-cooked eggs, grated**
>   **Lemon wedges, for garnish**

Mustard Dressing

> 2 **tablespoons tarragon wine vinegar**
> 1 **tablespoon Dijon mustard**
> 1 **small shallot, finely chopped**
> ½ **teaspoon sugar**
> ¼ **teaspoon salt**
> ⅓ **cup vegetable oil**

1. Remove and discard stems from spinach; you should have about 15 cups leaves. If done ahead, place in a bowl, cover, and refrigerate.

2. In a deep, broad chafing dish, heat olive oil over moderately high heat. Add several grindings of pepper, then crumbled bacon. Stir to heat through.

3. Add spinach and mix lightly just until spinach begins to wilt (about 1 minute). Remove from heat at once. Mix gently but thoroughly with Mustard Dressing. Serve salad on individual plates.

4. Garnish each serving with egg and a lemon wedge.

Serves 4 to 6.

Mustard Dressing In a small bowl blend together vinegar, mustard, shallot, sugar, and salt. Using a whisk or fork, gradually beat in oil.

Makes about ½ cup.

Recipes and Related Information
Cream of Spinach Soup, 563; Ground Beef and Spinach Stuffing, 592; Parmesan-Spinach Soufflé, 205; Spinach-Ham Soufflé, 205; Spinach Omelet, 203; Spinach Pasta, 411; Spinach Ravioli, 415; Spinach-Shrimp Soufflé, 205; Spinach-Stuffed Breast of Veal, 592; Spinach Timbales, 579; Vegetable Purées, 487.

SPOON, LADLE, AND SCOOP

Spoons don't resemble your arm and hand by chance; they serve as an extension of your body to mix, beat, and otherwise move food around. You could use your hand as a spoon (and many cooks prefer to mix and toss dry ingredients, batters, and salads that way), but most cooks use a long-handled spoon to maintain clean hands and to prevent exposure to overly hot or cold foods. The ubiquitous wooden spoons and spatulas, solid and slotted cook's spoons, wire and perforated skimmers, ladles of all sizes, and multifunctional scoops and paddles are kitchen work horses and basic culinary equipment.

COOK'S SPOONS

These long-handled metal spoons are preferred to wood ones for stove-top use because they can take high heat without burning, won't absorb cooking flavors, and don't harbor bacteria. They can scratch pans, however, so are best for mixing large quantities, such as soups or stews with many ingredients, where there is less chance that the bowl of the spoon will drag against the pan's interior. Use a spoon with a solid bowl for transferring and serving, and the slotted type for removing solid foods from liquid. However, when lifting fried foods from hot fat, a wire skimmer (at right) lets more fat fall back into the pan than a slotted spoon. Choose a cook's spoon made of heavy, sturdy stainless steel, that, as a poor heat conductor, keeps the spoon from heating up when set in hot liquids. Generally, these spoons measure from 11 inches to 13 inches overall (yours should be long enough to reach into your deepest pot, or several may be preferred if a very long one seems unwieldy for most tasks).

WOODEN SPOONS AND SPATULAS

Utensils made of wood have a comfortable feel—both in your hand and against the sides of mixing bowls and cookware. A poor heat conductor, wood won't get hot or cold, so it can be held without worry. Wooden spoons and spatulas are such basic equipment that it's hard to imagine any kitchen counter without a crock filled with them in several sizes. Use them to stir, mix, and fold both hot and cold foods, and to transfer mixtures from a bowl to a pan or plate.

Do you need both spoons and spatulas? These tools function the same, although their shapes differ: Spoons tend to have rounded handles and end in a bowl; spatulas have slightly flattened handles and a flat or gently curved paddle. Some cooks prefer spatulas when folding mixtures together because of the shape. If you are curious, buy both a spoon and paddle and see which you prefer. It won't be a wasted purchase because both can be used over and over, and a collection of these wooden tools enhances your

batterie de cuisine. Overall lengths range from 8 to 16 inches; bowl shapes vary also. Buy tools that fit comfortably into your mixing bowls, saucepans, and stockpots. Those made of a hard wood such as boxwood are preferred because they won't split and are less porous, and therefore less likely to absorb food flavors. However, they shouldn't be cleaned in the dishwasher or soaked in water. After using, rinse and dry well.

SKIMMERS

Tools for removing solids from liquids, skimmers are made in several styles to suit their various purposes: for removing foods from hot fat or liquid, and spooning off the frothy scum that rises to the surface of stocks and preserves. Skimmers for transferring food are either metal perforated with many small holes or are wire. The first type has a long metal handle ending in a shallow disk. It functions like a slotted spoon in that it permits liquid to pass through its perforations; but because it has so many more holes, it won't trap unwanted fat as does a slotted spoon. Its bowl is only slightly concave so that it can pass over the surface of a stock or bubbling pot of jam and lift off only the scum. Another type of spoon for removing scum has a fine wire mesh, instead of holes, in a stainless steel frame. Skimmers for deep-fried foods have

A tangy mustard dressing coats the warm, wilted greens of Chafing Dish Spinach Salad. For a special presentation, toss the salad at the table in an attractive serving dish.

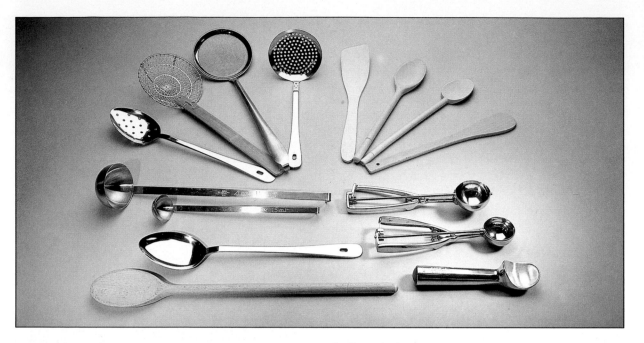

Spoons and stirrers of all types function as an extension of the cook's hand. Shown clockwise from bottom left: large wooden and metal cook's spoons; small and large ladle; perforated metal cook's spoon; Asian wire skimmer, wire-mesh skimmer, perforated-bowl skimmer; wooden cook's spoons; spring-operated ice cream scoops; insulated scoop.

wire bowls—either in a mesh crosshatch pattern or in concentric rings held in place by a wire frame. The long handles are either metal or, if Japanese or Chinese (used for tempura or wok cookery), bamboo. Wire skimmers are very versatile and have their place as part of basic equipment.

LADLES

For serving soups and sauces, ladles are invaluable. The deep bowl set at a right angle to a long handle is the design for reaching into saucepans and deep pots. Stainless steel is the most durable material for ladles. Bowl sizes range from 1 ounce to 8 ounces for metal and are about 4 ounces for plastic.

SCOOPS

Shaped like a ladle or shovel, scoops are tools used for dipping into soft foods such as ice creams, vegetable purées, salads, drop cookie batters, grains, and powders. Bowl-shaped scoops remove foods from containers in neat rounds or ovals, which, along with portion control, is their appeal. Other scoops have a more utilitarian function: They resemble high-sided shovels or garden trowels and are essentially large-capacity spoons used to transfer flour, rice, and grains from a storage bin or bag to a mixing bowl. Some scoops are spring operated, with a scraper that pushes out perfect rounds of food with the press of a lever. Some scoops, such as those used at ice cream shops, are filled with a chemical that keeps the metal warmer than the frozen dessert and able to dip into even the hardest ice cream with relative ease. Materials include chrome, stainless steel, aluminum, and plastic.

SQUASH

The many varieties of squash are all members of the gourd family and are native to the New World. Squash (and other gourds) can grow quite large; in the garden, they are recognized by their trailing vines, large leaves, and handsome blossoms. Summer squash varieties are eaten while soft and immature; most winter varieties are allowed to mature, developing hard skins and starchy meat.

Because summer and winter varieties vary so greatly in flavor and handling requirements, they are considered separately below.

Use   Summer squash varieties may be boiled, sautéed, steamed for use as a side dish, or battered and deep-fried. They may be brushed with oil and grilled, or baked with butter and bread crumbs. When hollowed out, they can be refilled with a seasoned stuffing of their own flesh. Summer squash can be puréed for soup or added to soups, or eaten raw in salads or with dipping sauces. The delicate squash blossoms can be stuffed, battered, and deep-fried.

Winter squash varieties may be cut into wedges or halves and baked in their skins until tender; peeled, cut into chunks, and boiled or steamed until tender; or cooked and mashed with butter, brown sugar, and cream. Small halves may be stuffed with a seasoned meat mixture and baked. Cooked peeled pieces can be puréed and added to soup, or used as a filling for pastas and pies, or as part of a batter. The hard seeds of winter squash may be cleaned, toasted, and salted for a delicious companion to cocktails.

Availability   Summer squash varieties have a thin edible skin and soft, barely developed seeds. They exist in a wide range of shapes, colors, and sizes. Although most abundant in summer, Mexican imports make many summer squash available virtually the year around. Squash blossoms are found in some specialty markets and some Italian markets in summer.

Winter squash are excellent keepers and may be stored for several months. Their flesh is generally moist when cooked and ranges from starchy to quite sweet. Some winter squash are available the year around, but peak supplies are in fall and winter.

The major varieties of summer squash include the following.

Crookneck Squash A yellow squash with a slightly pebbly skin, crookneck has a bulbous base tapering to a slender crooked neck.

Pattypan Also known as cymling squash, pattypan is bowl-shaped, about 3 inches in diameter, with a scalloped rim. It may be white, yellow, or pale green.

Scallopini Although similar in shape to pattypan, scallopini has a speckled green skin like that of a zucchini.

Zucchini Cylindrical and smooth-skinned, zucchini is a squash that can be as small as a finger but is usually about 6 inches long in commercial markets. Zucchini now come in yellow as well as shades of gray, green, and black.

The major varieties of winter squash include the following.

Acorn This dark green squash may have distinctive orange markings. A small squash, it is usually about 4 inches in diameter and 6 to 8 inches wide, with deep ridged furrows in the skin. The flesh is yellow to orange; the seed cavity is relatively large. Because of its size, acorn squash is excellent for baking on the half-shell with butter and brown sugar or for stuffing.

Banana Shaped like its namesake, banana squash may grow up to several feet in length. The skin is yellowish pink, the flesh orange.

Butternut Usually 9 to 12 inches long, with a bulbous base, butternut has buff skin and yellow to orange flesh.

Hubbard Recognized by its warty gray-green or dark green skin, Hubbard squash often weighs 12 pounds or more. The yellow flesh is sweet and is excellent in pies.

Pumpkin Large pumpkins may 100 pounds or more. They tend to have watery, bland flesh and are best used as jack-o'-lanterns. However, some pumpkin varieties, such as the sugar pumpkin, are grown for their eating qualities. Their flesh is quite sweet, suitable for baking and for pies. Pumpkin seeds are delicious when toasted.

Spaghetti Squash When baked, the flesh of spaghetti squash separates into spaghettilike strands. The squash itself may be up to 1 foot in length and 8 inches in diameter. Its smooth skin is bright yellow, its flesh pale yellow and rather bland.

Turban Available in a variety of shapes, sizes, and colors, the turban squash is recognized by its topknot.

Selection Choose firm summer squash with no brown spots. Smaller squash are generally sweeter. Pick winter squash that are firm and have hard skins; they should be heavy for their size. Precut wedges should look moist but not mushy.

Storage Keep summer squash in a plastic bag in the refrigerator for up to three days. Squash blossoms are extremely perishable. Arrange on a paper-towel–lined tray, refrigerate, and use within one day. Refrigerate precut squash and use within one week. Uncut winter squash will keep several months in a cool, dark, dry place.

Preparation *For summer squash:* Trim ends (peeling isn't necessary); cut into chunks or slices before cooking. *For winter squash:* Cut into wedges or halves with a large, heavy knife; remove seeds; peel squash using a sharp knife. To bake whole spaghetti squash, pierce with a fork in several places. Set squash in a baking dish with one inch of water. Bake in a preheated 375° F oven until tender when pierced with a fork (45 to 75 minutes, depending on size). Cool 5 minutes, then cut in half lengthwise. Scoop out seeds. Use a fork to separate flesh into spaghettilike strands.

To toast squash seeds, rinse them well and dry thoroughly. Toss seeds with oil to coat lightly. Salt to taste and arrange on a baking sheet. Toast in a 325° F oven until crisp (about 15 minutes). Cool on paper towels.

Cooking *Summer squash varieties:* See BOIL, DEEP-FRY, GRILL, SAUTE, STEAM, STIR-FRY. *Winter squash varieties:* See BAKE, BOIL, STEAM.

▓ BAKED SQUASH SLICES

For eye appeal, alternate squash slices in the baking dish.

> 1 **small acorn squash**
> 1 **large zucchini squash**
> **Olive oil, for drizzling**
> **Salt and freshly ground pepper, to taste**

1. Wash both squashes. Halve acorn squash; remove seeds; and peel. Cut zucchini in half lengthwise. Cut both squashes into ¼-inch-wide slices and arrange in shallow baking dish.

2. Drizzle oil over squash and season to taste. Cover and bake in 450° F oven until tender (15 to 20 minutes).

Serves 4.

Recipes and Related Information

Deep-fried Zucchini Blossoms, 238; Mediterranean Eggplant Spread, 208; Pumpkin Harvest Bread, 491; Pumpkin Pie, 438; Pumpkin Purée Filling, 438; Vegetable Purées, 487; Zucchini Bread, 490.

STAR ANISE

This pungent spice is a dark brown, eight-pointed star about ½ inch in diameter. Star anise is native to China.

Use   Star anise lends its licoricelike flavor to Asian soups, stews, and marinades. It is one of the five components of five-spice powder. Red-cooked Chinese beef, pork, and poultry always contain star anise. The spice is included in the smoking mixture for Chinese tea-smoked chicken and duck. Peanuts and soybeans are simmered in liquids seasoned with star anise, then cooled and eaten cold as a snack. Star anise also flavors the poaching liquid used for Chinese marbleized tea eggs. Both Thai and Vietnamese versions of beef noodle soup are flavored with star anise.

Availability   Star anise is available in packages in Asian markets.

Storage   Keep star anise in a cool, dark, dry place for up to one year.

Preparation   Many recipes call for a given number of star anise "points," which consist of both the seed and the hard seed covering. The points may be added directly to a stock or stew, but, for easy removal, wrap points in cheesecloth before adding.

Recipes and Related Information
Beef Soup With Noodles, 390; Herb and Spice Blends, 301.

STEAM, TO

To cook food by the heat of steam. Food is placed on a rack above, but not in direct contact with, boiling liquid. The rack is set in a pan that is covered, to keep the steam from escaping. Steam from boiling liquids swirls around food and cooks it with intense, moist heat.

Steaming is an excellent method in terms of nutrition. Whereas water-soluble vitamins might be washed away during boiling, steaming keeps vitamin loss to a minimum. Steamed vegetables also retain their color better than those that are boiled or cooked in oil. Steaming can also be especially efficient; with Chinese-style stacking steamers, many different foods can be cooked at once over a single heat source. But the greatest virtue of steaming is in the texture and flavor of the finished dish. There is no better way to preserve the delicate taste and texture of a perfectly fresh fish than to cook it gently with steam. This method is suitable for whole fish, fillets, and fish steaks. Scallops and shrimp also are very tender and succulent when steamed. Some holiday puddings and breads, such as plum pudding and Boston Brown Bread (see page 492), are traditionally steamed.

HOW TO STEAM

The factors that govern successful steaming are simple: The steam must circulate freely in the steamer; the liquid should never touch the steamed food; and the liquid should never boil dry. If you are using stacking steamers, the heat source must be strong enough to circulate the steam through the racks. If, upon lifting the lid, it is evident that the steam is not reaching the top rack, remove the top rack so the steaming is efficient. Keep a separate pot of water boiling in order to replenish the steaming water while maintaining the temperature of the steam.

Steaming is a cooking method done to perfection in a microwave oven. In minutes fish steams in its own juices to a moist and tender result. Vegetables cook to crisp-tender and are vibrantly colored. For more information see MICROWAVE OVEN or the manufacturer's instructions that accompany your microwave oven.

Several types of steamers are available. Chinese bamboo or metal steamers are convenient because the trays can be stacked and several foods can be steamed at once. You can make any deep saucepan into a steamer by setting a folding steamer rack inside and covering the pan tightly. To steam small amounts of food, you can improvise a steamer by setting a colander or strainer in a large saucepan and covering it tightly. See COOKWARE, Steamers, for more information.

■ STEAMED SALMON STEAKS WITH BLACK BEAN SAUCE

This recipe features some of the basic ingredients of Chinese cooking, including garlic and salted fermented black beans. Both ingredients lend themselves beautifully to braising, stir-frying, and steaming. The beans have an indefinite shelf life when stored in an airtight container. They are sold in Asian markets and are usually labeled "salted black beans." If you don't have a wok, any large pan with a domed lid will work just as well.

   4 **salmon steaks (each 1 inch thick)**
   1 **teaspoon salt**
   4 **green onions, flattened with the side of a cleaver and cut in 2-inch-long sections, plus 2 green onions, shredded**
   4 **slices of peeled fresh ginger the size of a quarter coin, shredded, plus 1 teaspoon minced, peeled fresh ginger**
   2 **tablespoons salted fermented black beans, covered with water for 5 minutes, rinsed, and drained**
   2 **tablespoons soy sauce**
   2 **cloves garlic, peeled and coarsely chopped**
   1 **tablespoon dry sherry or dry vermouth**
   ½ **teaspoon sugar**
   4 **tablespoons peanut oil**
     White pepper, to taste
     Fresh cilantro, for garnish

1. Blot salmon dry and sprinkle with salt. Place half of the 2-inch-long green onion sections and half of the shredded fresh ginger on the bottom of a shallow, heat-resistant plate. Arrange salmon steaks in a single layer on top of ginger and green onions. (Use 2 plates and 2 steamers, stacked, if necessary.) Scatter the remaining green onion sections and shredded fresh ginger over the salmon steaks.

2. Combine beans with soy sauce, garlic, sherry, sugar, and the 1 teaspoon minced ginger. Spread ingredients evenly over fish.

3. Fill a wok with boiling water to 1-inch from the bottom of a bamboo steamer. Bring the water to a boil. Put the plate of fish in the steamer, cover, and place the steamer in the wok. Steam over medium heat for 10 minutes. When done, remove from wok. Uncover steamer, tilting lid away from you.

4. In a small pan heat peanut oil until hot and almost smoking. Meanwhile, sprinkle white pepper and shredded green onions over salmon steaks set on plate in steamer. Carefully pour oil over the entire surface of each steak to coat completely. The oil should sizzle. Serve hot, garnished with fresh cilantro.

Serves 4 to 8.

STEW, TO

To cook slowly over low heat, causing a wonderful exchange of flavors among the ingredients. It is an ideal cooking method to use with inexpensive cuts of meat. The gentle cooking in moist heat tenderizes the meat and makes it succulent. Yet economy is not the only reason to prepare a stewed dish. These cuts are also most flavorful and produce the best-tasting sauces.

A stew is usually made of small pieces of meat covered completely with liquid—water, stock, wine, or a combination; usually other ingredients such as vegetables and seasonings are added for flavor. The meat may or may not be browned first, and the cooking liquid becomes the sauce, which can be thickened naturally by boiling until reduced in volume or by adding flour or another thickening agent (see SAUCE).

Stews and braises, including casseroles, ragouts, and daubes, are almost identical preparations, the main difference being the amount of liquid used and the way the meat is cut up. Braising calls for less liquid and the meat is usually whole or in large pieces. A stew has more liquid and the meat is generally in small pieces.

Stews offer considerable opportunity for the cook to be creative, as long as the ingredients have similar cooking times. Hardier root vegetables such as onions, carrots, and parsnips, prized for their sweet flavor, hold up well when cooked for a long time. More delicate additions that will lose their color when overcooked, such as mushrooms,

---

STEAMING BASICS

Steaming can be done over boiling water, in butter and water, and in a paper package, a technique called *en papillote*. A note of caution: Steam can cause severe burns. When removing the cover from a steaming pot, open it away from you and let the steam dissipate before you reach or look inside. Long sleeves or long oven mitts can protect your wrists from steam burns. Exercise the same care when steaming in a microwave oven: Pierce plastic wrap or lift a corner of a covered dish to allow the steam to escape.

- When steaming over water, be sure the food is at least 1 inch above the surface of the boiling water so that vigorously bubbling water cannot boil the food.
- To steam vegetables over boiling water, use a metal steamer or a colander. Place it over a few inches of water in a 2- or 3-quart saucepan with a tight-fitting lid. Bring the water to a boil, add the vegetables, and steam until crisp-tender (5 to 20 minutes).
- To butter steam vegetables, add vegetables and about ¼ inch of water to melted butter in a large skillet; cover tightly and steam over medium-high heat until tender. Butter steaming is particularly suited for long, thin vegetables such as asparagus or whole green beans; it is a very quick way to cook cut-up vegetables because the skillet offers a large surface area over which to spread them.
- Steaming food in parchment paper saves cleanup and calories: The paper encases the food, assuring flavor by sealing in natural juices and flavorings, and eliminates the need for a cooking pan. Very little, if any, fat is needed for this method. Fish is particularly well-suited for this technique, but other delicate foods, such as pieces of boned poultry, can also be prepared this way. Cook the packages in a conventional or microwave oven. Parchment paper is available in well-stocked supermarkets and better cookware stores.

---

potatoes, peas, and green beans, should be mixed in during the final 20 to 30 minutes. If the dish is made ahead, these more delicate vegetables go into the pot during the reheating period.

FINISHING, STORING, AND REHEATING STEWS

For even heating a heavy pan with a tight-fitting cover is necessary. It should be made from materials that are efficient heat conductors, such as enameled cast iron or clad metals (see MATERIALS FOR COOKWARE).

One of the most attractive features of stews is that, although they may take time to prepare, once done they keep well and need only to be reheated to serve.

Stews are wonderful do-ahead meals, tasting even better a day or so after cooking, when the flavors have had a chance to blend. They will keep up to one week in the refrigerator and up to two months in the freezer.

No matter when the dish is to be served, immediately or later on, any fat should be skimmed away after cooking. This is most easily accomplished when the dish has cooled and the fat has congealed on the surface. If it is to be refrigerated or frozen, cool it first at room temperature.

To reheat from the refrigerator, use a very low temperature to just warm the meat, avoiding further cooking. If raw vegetables are to be added at this point, increase the heat to medium-low and cook, covered, until the vegetables are tender and cooked through (10 to 20 minutes). To reheat from the freezer, first thaw the stew, then refrigerate until ready to reheat.

■ CASSOULET

In the southwest of France, cassoulets are as different and as personal as an individual's name. Some are made with goose or duck, many with lamb, and others with only pork products. White beans and sausages are common to them all. To develop flavor, this stew must slow-cook for hours; like all stews, it is best made ahead and reheated. Before cooking, the beans must soak 12 hours or overnight or 1 hour for the quick-soak method (SEE BEAN, Preparation).

    1 pound Great Northern or small white beans
    ¼ pound salt pork, diced
    1 onion, quartered
    1 carrot, coarsely diced
       Bouquet garni (see page 56)
    3 cloves garlic, minced
    1¼ teaspoons salt
    ½ teaspoon freshly ground pepper
    1 duck (about 4 lb), quartered
    ½ pound pork loin, cut in 2-inch cubes
    ½ pound *each* mild sausage links and spicy
       sausage links
    4 tablespoons bacon fat or vegetable oil
    1 onion, diced
    3 tomatoes, peeled, seeded, and chopped
    ½ cup Chicken Stock (see page 560) or
       Beef Stock (see page 560)
    ½ cup dry bread crumbs

1. Place beans in a 6-quart stockpot and cover with water. Soak beans 12 hours or overnight; drain and discard any broken beans.

2. Return beans to stockpot; cover with water. Add salt pork, quartered onion, diced carrot, bouquet garni, and garlic. Cover, reduce temperature to low, and simmer 2 hours. Remove bouquet garni and discard. Add 1 teaspoon of the salt, and ¼ teaspoon of the pepper; reserve beans in pot.

3. Preheat oven to 400° F. Place duck pieces in a roasting pan, and sprinkle with remaining salt and pepper. Reduce oven temperature to 350° F.

4. In an 8-quart Dutch oven, sauté pork loin cubes and sausages in 2 tablespoons of the bacon fat over medium heat until browned and cooked through (12 to 15 minutes); remove meats and reserve.

5. To same pan add diced onion, tomato, and stock, stirring to combine. Cover and simmer 15 minutes. Stir in cooked beans.

6. Add quartered duck pieces, pork loin, and sausages to bean mixture. Mix to cover meat with beans. Sprinkle dry bread crumbs over beans, drizzle with remaining bacon fat, cover pan, and bake 1 hour. Remove cover and continue cooking 20 minutes more. Serve hot in big, deep, country-style bowls.

Serves 8 to 10.

■ CIOPPINO

Northern California's own version of the typical Mediterranean fisherman's stew features the local Dungeness crab along with other shellfish and fish in a fragrant, tomato-flavored broth. For an authentic flavor, serve with San Francisco Sourdough French Bread (see page 619).

    1 to 2 pounds fish heads and bones (preferably
           rockfish, halibut, or other lean, white fish)
    1 cleaned and cracked Dungeness crab *or* 1 pound
       king crab legs (shell and fat reserved; see Note)
    2 medium onions, sliced
    8 sprigs parsley
    ½ teaspoon fennel or anise seed, cracked
    12 peppercorns, cracked
    1 cup dry white wine
    4 cups water
    3 tablespoons olive oil
    3 cloves garlic, chopped
       Pinch red pepper flakes
    1 red or green bell pepper, seeded and diced
    1 large can (28 oz) Italian-style tomatoes
    2 tablespoons minced fresh basil *or*
       ½ teaspoon dried oregano
       Salt and freshly ground pepper, to taste
    2 to 3 pounds assorted fish and shellfish
           (clams or mussels, scrubbed; lean, white fish,
           in 1-inch cubes; shrimp, peeled and deveined;
           squid, cleaned and cut into rings)

1. Wash fish heads and bones well, removing any bits of blood or organs. Split heads and chop large sections of bone into smaller pieces. Place in a large saucepan or stockpot with crab shell, 1 onion, parsley, fennel seed, peppercorns, wine, and the water. Bring to a boil, reduce heat, and simmer 30 to 45 minutes, skimming off any foam that rises to surface. Strain stock.

2. In a large soup kettle, heat olive oil over medium heat. Add garlic, remaining onion, pepper flakes, and bell pepper; sauté until wilted. Add tomatoes, basil, reserved crab fat (if available), and stock; bring to a boil and simmer until slightly thickened (about 30 minutes). Season with salt and pepper, allowing for salty clam juices (if clams are used).

3. Arrange fish and shellfish in order of cooking time. Add clams and uncooked crab 10 minutes before ready to serve; halibut, 8 minutes; shrimp, cooked crab, mussels, and rockfish or ocean perch, 5 minutes; and squid, 2 minutes. Serve hot in large soup bowls.

Serves 4 to 6 as a main dish.

Note Some fishmongers will clean and crack crabs— either live or cooked—for you. For information on cleaning and cracking crabs yourself, see page 538. Whoever cleans the crab should save the top shell for the stock and reserve the tasty fat from the corners of the shell for the tomato broth. Uncooked crab fat is olive green and turns pale yellow when cooked.

■ HONEYED CHICKEN WITH APRICOTS

If you enjoy chicken combined with fruit, try this dish during apricot season. It's good with brown rice.

    1   chicken (3 to 3½ lb), cut in quarters
        (reserve giblets for other uses)
        Salt and ground allspice
    1   tablespoon *each* butter or margarine and oil
    1   medium onion, thinly slivered
    1   small clove garlic, minced or pressed
    ½   teaspoon *each* ground turmeric and
        ground ginger
    ¼   teaspoon ground coriander
    1   cinnamon stick (2 to 3 in.)
    ½   cup water
    ¼   cup honey
    1   lemon, thinly sliced, with seeds removed
    4   apricots, pitted and quartered

1. Sprinkle chicken lightly on all sides with salt and allspice. In a large, deep skillet over medium heat, melt butter with oil. Add chicken and brown well on all sides.

2. When chicken pieces are nearly browned on last side, discard all but a scant 2 tablespoons of the drippings. Then add onion and garlic around chicken. Sprinkle with turmeric, ginger, and coriander. Add cinnamon stick.

3. Add the water and honey. Arrange lemon slices in a single layer over chicken. Bring to a boil, cover, reduce heat, and simmer until chicken is tender (45 to 50 minutes).

4. Remove chicken and lemons to a warm, deep serving platter and keep warm. Bring liquid to a boil over high heat, stirring to blend in brown drippings from skillet, and reduce until syrupy. Add apricots, turning them in the sauce just long enough to glaze and heat through.

5. Spoon sauce and apricots over chicken and serve.

Serves 4.

> ### *Recipes and Related Information*
>
> *Abalone Stew, 536; Basic Boeuf en Daube, 42;
> Blanquette de Veau, 593; Boeuf Bourguignonne, 43;
> Bohemian Pork Goulash, 459; Boiled Dinner
> Bolognese, 530; Carrot and Baby Onion Stew With
> Raisins, 101; Couscous, 278; Golden Chicken Stew With
> Cheese Dumplings, 192; Okra and Tomato Stew, 397;
> Portuguese Fish Stew, 232; Spring Lamb Stew With
> Fresh Peas, 420.*

STIR, TO

To mix with a slow, wide, circular motion, usually with a spoon, to combine ingredients. Stirring custards keeps the mixture from setting and stirring flour-based sauces prevents lumps.

STIR-FRY, TO

To cook bite-sized pieces of meats and vegetables quickly over high heat in a small amount of oil. Sautéing and stir-frying are basically the same technique; the difference between them is primarily cultural. Stir-fried preparations, reflecting the Chinese palate, include many vegetables. Dairy products, so important in the sauces used with French sautés, are not used.

In stir-frying the food is cooked by both the heat of the pan and the heat carried by the oil. As the name implies, the ingredients are stirred in the pan almost constantly during cooking so they cook evenly. It is an ideal way to preserve the colors, flavors, and textures of foods, and to maintain nutritional value as well.

The cooking pan, a wok, is slope-sided and deep, and requires less oil than does a sauté pan or skillet (see COOKWARE, Wok, for information about this pan and companion equipment for it). Less fat means that stir-fried foods have fewer calories than other fried foods. Each piece of meat or vegetable gets immersed in the small pool of oil that collects in the bowl of the wok and is quickly seared and cooked. However, if you don't have a wok, a large skillet or electric skillet can be substituted. Bear in mind, however, that the flat-bottomed skillet will require more oil to keep the food from sticking.

GETTING STARTED

Stir-frying is as simple to execute as other frying methods, but it is usually complex in preparation. Because everything happens quickly in stir-frying, organization is essential. The speed of the method requires that chopping and slicing be done in advance, sauces and spices premeasured, and thickening agents blended.

To smooth the preparation, shop for and ready all the ingredients a day ahead; store the ingredients in individual bowls in the refrigerator until needed. About 30 minutes before cooking, allow them to come to room temperature. To save time and counter space, try to combine ingredients that will go into the wok at the same time. Don't mix liquid and dry ingredients unless instructed specifically to do so. Before the wok is heated is the time to assemble all the tools you will need as well. If you want to keep the dish hot for any length of time before serving, turn the oven on a low setting to warm the plate and hold the finished dish until ready.

For best results heat the wok first, then add the oil in a thin stream around the outside of the pan. As the oil slides down the hot sides, it both heats to the perfect cooking temperature and oils the sides of the wok to keep the food from sticking. If you accidentally pour in too much oil, do not try to pour it out of the wok; instead, swab the excess out with a paper towel and discard. After cooking rinse the wok out immediately with hot water and return it to the heat to dry; otherwise, be sure to wash it as soon as possible and then dry it thoroughly.

Sauces, fresh snow peas, Asian mushrooms, and fresh ginger are common ingredients in stir-fried dishes. If you enjoy making these types of preparations, keep these foods in your pantry or refrigerator.

Stir-frying is an ideal way to preserve the flavor and crunchy texture of fresh asparagus. Here Beef With Asparagus makes for a springtime treat.

■ BEEF WITH ASPARAGUS

When asparagus is in season, virtually every Chinese restaurant features this simple but delicious stir-fry.

- 2 teaspoons minced fresh ginger
- 2 tablespoons Shaoxing wine or dry sherry
- 3 tablespoons dark soy sauce *or* 2 parts light and 1 part black soy sauce (see Note)
- ½ teaspoon sesame oil
- ½ pound lean beef, thinly sliced into strips
- 1½ teaspoons cornstarch
- 2 to 3 tablespoons vegetable oil
- 1 pound asparagus, cut diagonally into 2-inch pieces

1. In a medium bowl combine ginger, wine, soy sauce, and sesame oil. Toss beef strips in soy mixture; marinate for 30 minutes to several hours.

2. Drain beef well and reserve marinade. Combine marinade with enough water to make ⅓ cup. Dissolve cornstarch in this mixture.

3. Heat wok over high heat and add 1 tablespoon of the oil. Add beef to pan; stir-fry until meat loses the raw color (about 1 minute). Remove meat from pan.

4. Add remaining oil to wok. Add asparagus and stir-fry over medium heat until just heated through. Return beef to pan; add reserved marinade. Increase heat to high and cook until sauce thickens. Serve immediately.

Serves 4 to 6 with other dishes.

Variation When asparagus is not in season, sliced Chinese or Western-style broccoli can be used in its place. Blanch, if desired (see BLANCH).

Note For a richer sauce, reduce soy sauce in marinade to 1 tablespoon dark soy; add 2 tablespoons oyster sauce to pan in step 4.

> ### *Recipes and Related Information*
> *Green Onions in Silky Beef, 285; Lemon Chicken Breasts, 339; Mu Shu Pork, 378; Shrimp With Snow Peas and Water Chestnuts, 606; Stir-Fried Noodles With Shredded Pork, 389.*

THE STIR-FRY PANTRY

Ingredients for stir-fried dishes are not always easy to find. Try well-stocked supermarkets or specialty food stores; they frequently have an ethnic foods section where many ingredients used for Asian cooking can be found. If you are fortunate enough to have access to Asian markets, your shopping will be simplified and the range of dishes you can prepare much expanded.

In the refrigerator Snow peas, fresh ginger, fresh garlic, green onions, chicken stock. If you wish to hold stock longer than a few days, freeze it.

On the shelf Canned bamboo shoots, canned water chestnuts, dried mushrooms, soy sauce, oyster sauce, hoisin sauce, hot-pepper sauce, peanut oil, sesame oil, rice wine, rice wine vinegar, pale dry sherry, cornstarch. (Most of these ingredients can be stored for a long time without refrigeration.)

Equipment Wok with cover, wooden spoons, chopsticks, slotted spoon.

STOCK AND SOUP

To the French, stocks are the foundation of all cuisine. These rich brews develop from slow-cooking meats, bones, and vegetables in liquid in order to extract their nutrients and flavor and to draw out other natural materials that add desirable body and texture. The purpose of stocks is to provide a base of flavor upon which a recipe can be built. Stock is the starting point, or critical ingredient, of a multitude of dishes, particularly soups and sauces. Beef stock has the deepest flavor and color, and is followed by chicken stock; fish stock is the lightest.

Basically, soup is a liquid that has been cooked with additions intended to impart enough flavor and nutrients so that the final product becomes an appealing food. In cooking, soups are categorized as *clear* (broths, consommés) or *thickened* (cream soups, vegetable purées), *light* (broths, consommés, bouillon, light cream soups) or *hearty* (dense vegetable soups and thick cream soups).

INGREDIENTS FOR STOCKS AND SOUPS

A stock of good quality is the offspring of an arranged marriage between mildly flavored vegetables, incorporated for their sweetness and aroma, and meat and bone, used for their flavoring and thickening properties. Water is the medium that brings these elements together.

Because the ingredients of stock are often free or cost very little, stock is economical to prepare. Beef and veal bones are available from butcher shops and at many supermarkets. Chicken wings or necks for chicken stock are found in almost every supermarket; poultry bones and carcasses left over from other preparations can be frozen for later use in a stock. Fish bones for fish stock can be obtained at seafood markets.

Although all the components of soups do not need to be crisp, fresh ingredients heighten flavor and visual appeal. This does not mean that leftovers have no place in a soup. Yesterday's cooked vegetables, steamed rice, or roast chicken, when added to a flavorful homemade stock, makes a delicious dish.

EQUIPMENT FOR MAKING STOCKS AND SOUPS

Although not a difficult process, making stock is time-consuming, so it's most practical to prepare a large quantity in one session—some to use right away and the rest to freeze. Use a large, heavy-bottomed stockpot with at least an 8-quart capacity or a Dutch oven (see COOKWARE). Also helpful, but not necessary, is a chinois, which is a conical sieve with a very fine mesh (see COLANDER, STRAINER, AND SIEVE) used to strain cooked stock. You can substitute a colander lined with several thicknesses of finely woven, dampened cheesecloth for a chinois, but do not use cloth with a loose weave.

Soup making requires little equipment other than a large saucepan and a wooden spoon. The pan should be heavy and a good heat conductor so the ingredients will cook evenly. A food processor or blender is convenient for puréeing and chopping ingredients.

PREPARATION BASICS

For stocks ingredients should always be covered with cold water, which is more effective for drawing out flavorful essences than hot water. The liquid is slowly brought to a boil and then simmered for the remainder of the cooking time. The slow simmering, as opposed to a continuous boil, allows fat and albuminous material (scum) to rise to the surface, where it can be skimmed off at regular intervals. The skimming is important to obtain a refined stock.

An especially clear stock results if the ingredients simmer uncovered. This is practical for fish stock, which is ready after only 20 minutes of simmering, but less so for the others because the liquid evaporates rapidly and water needs to be added frequently. A compromise is to cover the stock partially as it simmers so that steam can escape but the liquid does not evaporate too quickly.

Soups are so diverse in type and in composition that the best preparation is to follow the recipe as directed.

COOLING AND DEGREASING STOCK

Stock should be cooled quickly so that it can be refrigerated or frozen as soon as possible. If left too long in a warm kitchen, stock can spoil. To cool stock quickly, put bowls of strained stock in the sink and fill the sink with enough cold water to come almost to the rim of the bowls. To speed the cooling, add ice cubes to the water in the sink. Change the water when it becomes warm. Refrigerate the stock when it has cooled to room temperature.

Before using, fat should be removed so the stock will be clear and will not taste greasy. Even stocks that were skimmed frequently while they cooked will still contain some fat (except for fish stock, which contains very little fat). The easiest way to remove fat is to refrigerate the stock. As it cools, the fat solidifies on the surface and it can be scraped off with a spoon. However, if you are not planning to use the stock right away, let the layer of congealed fat sit on the chilled liquid since it acts as a shield, protecting the stock from bacterial contamination. To remove fat from hot stock, skim the fat from the surface with a spoon or wire skimmer. Then draw strips of paper towels or a paper coffee filter across the surface.

STORING AND REHEATING STOCKS AND SOUPS

Most soups and stocks can be made ahead, refrigerated or frozen, and reheated. Cool soups and stocks to room temperature before you refrigerate or freeze them; store in covered containers. Use refrigerated stocks or soups within three to five days. Stocks can be kept up to about one week if brought to a boil for 10 minutes every other day. Freeze stocks in portion-sized containers—1- or 2-cup size for sauce making, larger for soups—or in ice cube trays. Once frozen, transfer the cubes to plastic storage bags for easy access. Remember to leave an inch or so of headroom in the larger storage containers to allow for the expansion of the liquid as it freezes. Most stocks can be frozen about six months; soups will freeze for about four months. Always boil refrigerated or frozen stock before using in a recipe.

Refrigerated soups should be reheated in a saucepan over medium-low heat. Stir vegetable purée soups, cream soups, and velouté soups frequently during reheating to prevent scorching and sticking. It is best not to reheat soups containing egg yolks, which may curdle. Soups containing thickeners such as flour, potatoes, or rice thicken on standing; when reheating the soup, stir in a few tablespoons of additional liquid if necessary. Many fresh herbs lose their flavor when reheated; if the herb is already in the soup, it is good to add a little more of it after reheating. Try to defrost frozen soups before reheating.

Stock frozen in a plastic container can be defrosted quickly by the following method: Set container, uncovered, in a pan of hot water for a few minutes until the stock at the edges and bottom defrosts. Then push on the bottom of the container and slip the frozen stock into a saucepan. Cover the saucepan and heat the stock over medium-low heat until it melts and can be measured. Measure the desired amount. Freeze remaining stock immediately.

BASIC STOCK

Stock making needn't be a weekly ritual, but it is a procedure with which all good cooks should be comfortably familiar. Homemade stocks add a special dimension to cooking. A supply of the following basic stocks, stored in serving-sized portions in your freezer, will actually simplify meal preparation, as well as improve its presentation. After sautéing a chicken breast, a pan sauce can be quickly assembled from pan juices, some stock, and seasonings. Adding fresh vegetables and cooked meat to already prepared broth makes a flavorful soup.

■ BEEF STOCK

The bones and vegetables in this recipe are first roasted to give the stock a brown color and a rich flavor. For the best flavor, use knuckle bones with some meat attached. If possible, use a mixture of beef soup bones and veal knuckle bones; the combination will make a more flavorful stock, with the veal bones also serving as a natural thickener. Or, if desired, use only veal bones (see variation). Meat scraps, completely trimmed of fat, can be added to the stock during the last quarter of cooking time.

  4 **pounds beef soup bones, chopped in a
few pieces by the butcher**
  2 **medium onions, unpeeled, root end
cut off, quartered**
  2 **medium carrots, scrubbed but not
peeled, quartered**
  2 **stalks celery, cut in approximately 2-inch pieces**
  2 **bay leaves**
10 **stems parsley (without leaves)**
  4 **cloves garlic (unpeeled)**
½ **teaspoon black peppercorns**
½ **teaspoon dried thyme**
16 **cups (approximately) cold water**

1. Preheat oven to 450° F. Roast bones in a roasting pan, turning occasionally with a slotted metal spatula,

until they begin to brown (about 30 minutes). Add onions, carrots, and celery; roast until browned (about 30 minutes).

2. Drain off fat. With a slotted spatula, transfer bones and vegetables to a stockpot, kettle, or other large pot. To ingredients in stockpot add bay leaves, parsley stems, garlic, peppercorns, thyme, and enough of the cold water to cover.

3. Bring just to a boil. Add a little more cold water to reduce to below boiling; stir once. Bring back just to a boil and reduce heat to very low so that liquid bubbles very gently. Skim off foam that collects on surface. Partially cover and cook, skimming foam and fat occasionally, for 4 to 6 hours. During first 2 hours of cooking, add hot water occasionally to keep ingredients covered.

4. Strain stock through a colander lined with several thicknesses of dampened cheesecloth, discarding solids. If stock is not to be used immediately, cool to lukewarm. Refrigerate until fat rises to the surface and congeals (about 8 hours). If stock will be used within 3 to 5 days, leave fat; skim fat when ready to use. If stock is to be frozen, skim fat.

Makes about 8 cups.

Brown Veal Stock Substitute veal bones, preferably knuckle bones, for the beef bones.

Glace de Viande (Meat Glaze) Use this concentrated essence to flavor sauces and soups or to glaze meats. Boil stock, uncovered, over high heat until syrupy and reduced by about seven eighths. Let cool; it will become gelatinous. Store, covered, for 1 week in the refrigerator, or cut into tablespoon-sized cubes and freeze.

■ CHICKEN STOCK

The process for stock making is the same regardless of which bird is the main ingredient. Chicken and turkey are most common in stock, but other fowl, such as duck or pheasant, are also used. The most flavorful result is produced from an older bird such as a stewing hen. However, use whatever parts are available—carcass, cooked scraps, wing tips, giblets (excluding livers), skin, or any leftovers. For more flavor you can brown the bones, carcass, necks, and back. Cook in a 450° F oven until brown (15 to 30 minutes); watch carefully, turn occasionally, and drain off all fat.

  3 **pounds chicken wings, chicken backs, or
a mixture of wings, backs, necks, and
giblets (except livers)**
16 **cups (approximately) cold water**
  2 **medium onions, peeled and quartered**
  2 **medium carrots, peeled and quartered**
  2 **bay leaves**
10 **stems parsley (without leaves)**
½ **teaspoon black peppercorns**
½ **teaspoon dried thyme**

1. Put chicken in a stockpot, kettle, or other large pot. Add enough of the cold water to cover. Bring just to a boil. Add a little more cold water to reduce to below boiling; stir once. Bring back just to a boil and reduce heat to very low so that liquid bubbles very gently. Skim off foam that collects on surface.

2. Add onions, carrots, bay leaves, parsley stems, peppercorns, and thyme. Adjust heat to keep surface just breaking with bubbles, but not boiling. Partially cover and cook, 2 to 3 hours, skimming foam and fat occasionally.

3. Strain stock through a colander lined with several thicknesses of dampened cheesecloth, discarding solids. If stock is not to be used immediately, cool to lukewarm. Refrigerate until fat rises to surface and congeals (about 8 hours). If stock will be used within 3 to 5 days, leave fat; skim fat when ready to use or if freezing stock.

Makes about 10 cups.

Rich Chicken Stock For a more strongly flavored stock, add beef, pork, or veal bones and trimmings. Increase the simmering time by 1 hour or more to extract additional flavor and body. Or, follow the recipe for Chicken Stock, but begin with a previous batch of stock in place of water. The resulting "double stock" will make an excellent soup. Cutting up chickens regularly is a good way to keep a batch of stock fresh, and it gets richer with each extraction. Rich stock can always be diluted with water when a basic or thin stock is needed.

◼ FISH STOCK
The best bones for fish stock come from mild fish, such as sea bass or halibut. Do not use bones from strong-flavored fish, such as tuna or mackerel. If bones are not available, substitute 1½ pounds of fish pieces for chowder. Concentrated fish stock is called fumet (see page 451).

    2 pounds fish bones, tails, and heads
    1 tablespoon unsalted butter
    1 medium onion, sliced
    ½ cup dry white wine
  7½ cups cold water
    1 stalk celery, cut in approximately 2-inch pieces
    1 bay leaf
    8 stems parsley (without leaves)
    ½ teaspoon dried thyme

1. Put fish bones in bowl in sink. Let cold water run over bones for 5 minutes.

2. Melt butter in stockpot, kettle, or large saucepan over low heat. Add onion and cook, stirring often, until soft but not brown (about 10 minutes).

3. Add fish bones, wine, the water, celery, bay leaf, parsley, and thyme. Mix well. Bring just to a boil and skim thoroughly to remove foam. Reduce heat to low and simmer, uncovered, skimming occasionally, for 20 minutes.

4. Pour contents of pot through a fine wire-mesh strainer into a bowl without pressing down on the mass; discard solids. (Pressing down on the solids will cloud the liquid, making it unsuitable for an aspic or a clear sauce.)

5. If not using immediately, cool to room temperature. Pour into 1- to 2-cup containers. Refrigerate, covered, up to 2 days or freeze up to 3 months.

Makes about 6 cups.

◼ VEGETABLE STOCK
This vegetable-based stock adds a fresh flavor to other preparations, although it lacks the intensity and stick-to-the-ribs quality of broth made from chicken or beef bones. It can be used as a substitute for chicken or beef stock in recipes for puréed or cream soups, or as the cooking liquid in any full-meal soup or stew. If you follow a vegetarian diet, this stock will work well as a foundation for many nonmeat dishes.

    2 leeks
    2 tablespoons vegetable oil
    2 yellow onions, peeled and chopped
       into ½-inch pieces
    9 small cloves garlic, coarsely chopped
    2 small carrots, peeled and cut into ½-inch rounds
    1 parsnip, peeled and cut into ½-inch rounds
    3 small potatoes, quartered
    2 stalks celery, cut into ½-inch slices
    ½ pound mushrooms, halved
    1 teaspoon dried thyme
    1 bay leaf
    1 teaspoon dried oregano
    4 sprigs parsley
   10 cups cold water
    2 teaspoons kosher salt
    ½ teaspoon pepper
    2 tablespoons miso (see page 525)

1. To clean leeks: Cut off hairy root ends of leeks; remove and discard coarse outer leaves. Discard green tops. Split remaining stalk lengthwise, cutting, from leafy end, to within 1 inch of root end. Soak in cold water for several minutes. Separate leaves under running water to rinse away any clinging grit. Chop leeks across width into ½-inch pieces.

2. Heat oil in a 6-quart stockpot over medium heat. Add leeks, onions, and garlic. Stir to coat with oil and cook about 5 minutes. Add remaining ingredients. Bring to a boil, skim impurities from surface, and reduce heat to low. Cook for 30 minutes. Strain into a 3-quart bowl. Discard vegetables.

3. Stock can be stored in the refrigerator in a covered container for up to 5 days or frozen in an airtight container for up to 1 month.

Makes about 10 cups.

A SOUP SAMPLER

Soup has a thousand faces. It can be part of a meal or the meal itself. It can be as plain as the unadorned soothing chicken broth we all sip as a tonic when we are ill or as sophisticated and stylish as a sparkling consommé or a delicate cream soup that might begin an elaborate, multi-course dinner. In between are a myriad of combinations, textures, and consistencies which make soup cookery a delightful adventure for the creative cook.

■ CLASSIC BEEF CONSOMME WITH VEGETABLE JULIENNE AND MADEIRA

This consommé provides a light first course with a concentrated beef flavor. Made from beef stock, it is clarified by simmering with egg whites. Ground beef and chopped vegetables cook in the stock together with the whites and give the soup its rich flavor. Preparing consommé does demand patience because quite a bit of whisking is required at the beginning of the clarification process.

> 1 small leek
> 4 cups Beef Stock (see page 560)
>   Salt and freshly ground pepper
> 3 egg whites
> ½ pound very lean ground beef
> 1 medium carrot, quartered lengthwise and cut in thin slices
> 1 medium stalk celery, halved lengthwise and cut in thin slices
> 2 medium tomatoes, cored and diced
> ¼ cup Madeira

Vegetable Julienne

> 1 small stalk celery
>   Reserved white and light green part of leek (see step 1)
> 1 small carrot
> 1¼ cups Beef Stock (see page 560)
>   Salt and freshly ground pepper

1. Prepare and clean leek. Use dark green part of leek for making consommé and cut it in thin slices; reserve white and light green part for vegetable julienne.

2. Skim fat thoroughly from surface of stock. In a large, heavy saucepan heat stock until warm. Remove from heat and skim off any remaining fat by quickly drawing strips of paper towel over surface. Season stock to taste with salt and pepper.

3. In a large bowl whisk egg whites lightly until foamy. Add leek, beef, carrot, celery, and tomatoes, and mix thoroughly with egg whites. Slowly ladle in about 2 cups stock, stirring well after each addition. Slowly pour in remaining stock and mix well. Return to saucepan.

4. Cook mixture over medium heat, using large whisk to stir constantly. Stop whisking as soon as mixture just begins to bubble and looks milky; mixture should reach about 180° F on a thermometer. Continue cooking 1 or 2 more minutes, until a foamy crust forms on surface of soup, indicating that filter of egg whites has risen to top.

5. Reduce heat to low. Using ladle make small hole in egg white filter near side of pan so that soup bubbles mainly in hole. Cook, uncovered, for 45 minutes without stirring mixture or moving saucepan. Remove from heat. Taste liquid for seasoning, adding more salt and pepper through hole if necessary, but do not stir.

6. Line a large strainer with several layers of dampened, wrung-out cheesecloth. Set strainer above a medium saucepan, leaving room for consommé to drip through into saucepan without coming in contact with strainer. Slowly and carefully begin to ladle consommé into strainer, beginning where hole was made. When most of consommé is ladled through, carefully slide egg white filter and remaining consommé into strainer. Let soup drip through but do not press on filter. If consommé is not very clear, strain it again through mixture in cheesecloth. Discard solids in cheesecloth.

7. Remove any remaining fat by quickly drawing strips of paper towel over surface of consommé. Soup can be prepared ahead up to this point and kept, covered, up to 2 days in refrigerator.

8. Bring consommé nearly to a boil and stir in Vegetable Julienne and Madeira. Serve hot in small soup bowls.

Makes 3½ to 4 cups, 3 to 4 servings.

Vegetable Julienne Peel celery, using a vegetable peeler to remove strings. Cut celery, reserved white and light green part of leek, and carrot into 1½-inch-long pieces. Cut carrot pieces lengthwise into ⅛-inch-thick slices, then cut each piece again lengthwise at ⅛-inch intervals to make thin strips. Cut celery and leeks into thin lengthwise strips about same size as carrot strips. Put vegetable strips in medium saucepan and add Beef Stock and a pinch of salt and pepper. Bring to a boil and skim off any foam. Reduce heat to low, cover, and simmer until tender (about 8 minutes). Drain vegetables; reserve cooking liquid. (This liquid can be reused as stock. Do not add it to consommé, or consommé will cloud.)

■ MISO SOUP

Protein-rich miso soup is traditionally served as a prelude to a Japanese meal of tempura or sushi. One-half cup of cooked, diced spinach, whole bean sprouts, or cubed tofu can be added to make a more substantial offering. Dried bonito flakes (*katsuobushi*, see page 326) and strips of seaweed (*konbu*, see page 334) are made into a flavorful broth known as dashi that gives the character to this national dish.

> 2 tablespoons red miso (see page 525)
> 1 green onion, sliced in thin rounds
> 2 mushrooms, sliced thinly
> 2 radishes, cut in thin circles

Dashi

- 1 **ounce konbu (dried kelp)**
- 1 **quart cold water, plus more as needed**
- 1 **ounce katsuobushi (dried bonito flakes)**

Bring dashi to a boil. Stir in miso to thoroughly dissolve the miso paste. Stir in green onion, mushrooms, and radishes. Boil for 5 to 8 minutes and serve in small bowls.

Makes about 4 cups, 3 to 4 first-course servings.

Dashi   In medium stockpot put konbu and the 1 quart cold water. Heat slowly, just below a boil, about 10 minutes (do not boil or flavor will be too strong). At this point konbu should be soft; if not, add ¼ cup cold water and cook until soft (about 1 minute). Remove konbu with slotted spoon and set aside. Bring stock to a boil; add ¼ cup cold water and katsuobushi. Boil, then immediately remove from heat. Let flakes settle (about 1 minute), then skim off any foam and strain soup.

Makes 3 to 4 cups.

■ CREAM OF ANY VEGETABLE SOUP

Use this creamy base to make soup from whatever vegetable is in season. Some possibilities are given here, but try your favorite vegetable or a combination. The soup can be served hot or chilled.

- ¼ **cup butter**
- 1 **medium onion, thinly sliced,** *or*
  1 **bunch green onions, sliced**
- 2 **tablespoons** *each* **flour and noninstant, nonfat dry milk**
- 1 **quart whole milk, at room temperature**

1. In a large pot melt butter. Add onion and sauté until softened.

2. Stir in flour and dry milk and cook until bubbly.

3. Gradually add whole milk, stirring until soup is smooth. Heat, stirring occasionally, until soup thickens. Add your choice of vegetable (see recipes below).

4. In a blender or food processor, whirl until smooth. Serve hot or chilled.

Cream of Asparagus   Remove tough stem ends from 1 pound asparagus. Cut spears into 1-inch pieces. Add asparagus and ½ cup chopped celery to soup in step 3 and simmer until tender (5 to 7 minutes). After processing add dry sherry to taste (optional).

Cream of Broccoli   Coarsely chop 1 pound broccoli. Add to soup in step 3 and simmer until tender (6 to 8 minutes). After processing add dry sherry to taste (optional).

Cream of Carrot   Scrub 8 to 10 carrots; slice. Add to soup in step 3 and simmer until tender (10 to 12 minutes). After processing stir in 1 to 2 teaspoons dried dill.

Cream of Cauliflower   Coarsely chop 1 medium head cauliflower. Add to soup in step 3 and simmer just until tender (10 minutes). After processing stir in ½ cup shredded Cheddar cheese.

Cream of Lettuce   In step 3 add 3 to 4 cups shredded iceberg lettuce. Cook, covered, for 3 minutes. After processing stir in dry sherry to taste (optional). Sprinkle with paprika or nutmeg.

Cream of Mushroom   In the basic recipe replace 2 cups of the whole milk with 2 cups Chicken or Beef Stock (see page 560) or 1 can (14½ oz) broth. In step 3 add 1 pound (40 medium) mushrooms, sliced or chopped, and ¼ cup chopped parsley. Cook, covered, until mushrooms are soft (about 5 minutes). After processing stir in 1 cup plain yogurt or sour cream. Sprinkle with nutmeg.

Cream of Spinach   Remove stems from 2 bunches fresh, cleaned spinach and coarsely chop leaves (or thaw two 10-ounce packages frozen chopped spinach). Add to soup in step 3 and simmer 3 minutes. After processing season with ¼ teaspoon dried thyme and stir in 1 cup plain yogurt. Garnish with sieved egg yolk.

Cream of Watercress   Remove stalks from 3 bunches watercress. Add to soup in step 3. Cook, covered, for 3 minutes. After processing garnish each serving with a dash of nutmeg and a slice of lemon.

Low-calorie Cream of Any Vegetable Soup contains no cream—nonfat dry milk helps thicken the roux. Once the base is made, add a puréed vegetable for both color and nutrition. For the finishing touch, stir one tablespoon of Champagne or sherry into each serving.

▪ SHELLFISH BISQUE

A bisque is a special type of shellfish-flavored cream soup. It would be a wonderful first course of an extra-special dinner. It has a rich stock, seasoned with brandy, root vegetables, bacon and salt pork, and herbs. Shellfish Bisque can be made with crab, lobster, abalone, shrimp, clams, or mussels, to name a few appropriate seafoods. Since much of the flavor is in the shell, it will enhance the broth to cook the shellfish in the liquid unshelled, then strain it before proceeding. Wash the seafood carefully before cooking to remove any sand or debris.

    2 quarts clam juice
    ¼ cup brandy
    1 onion, minced
    4 shallots, minced
    4 cloves garlic, minced
    1 stalk celery, minced
    1 carrot, peeled and minced
    6 sprigs parsley
    4 bay leaves
    2 live lobsters (approximately 1¼ lb each)
    2 pounds unshucked clams
    1 pound prawns
    ¼ cup salt pork, diced
    ½ cup bacon, diced
    2 onions, diced
    2 stalks celery, diced
    2 teaspoons dried thyme
    ½ cup flour
    3 medium boiling potatoes, unpeeled
    3 cups whipping cream
    1 teaspoon white pepper
    ⅛ teaspoon cayenne pepper

1. In a 6-quart kettle place the clam juice, brandy, onion, shallots, garlic, celery, carrot, parsley, and bay leaves. Bring to a boil, add live lobsters, cover, and simmer 15 minutes.

2. Remove lobsters from broth and set aside to cool; when cool, remove lobster meat from shells and discard shells. Add clams and prawns to broth and cook over medium heat for 2 to 3 minutes. Strain broth into a mixing bowl and reserve. Remove prawns and clams from vegetables. Peel prawns, remove clams from shells, and reserve meat of both. Discard shells and vegetables.

3. In kettle sauté diced salt pork and bacon until crisp; add diced onions and celery and cook for 8 minutes. Stir in thyme and flour and cook over low heat for 5 minutes. Add reserved poaching liquid and whisk until thickened. Cut potatoes into ½-inch dice and add to the soup. Simmer 20 minutes. Add cream, white pepper, and cayenne; stir to heat through (about 10 minutes). Dice lobster into bite-sized pieces. Add lobster, prawns, and clams just before serving.

Makes 12 cups, 6 servings.

▪ CRANBERRY BEAN MINESTRONE

If you shop in a neighborhood with an Italian heritage, you may have seen fresh cranberry beans in the markets in September and October. Sold in pods flecked with cranberry red, they need to be shelled before cooking. Though fresh, the beans still take half an hour or longer to cook.

This colorful soup takes advantage of the special character of these beans. If you can't find them, make the soup using 2 cups of different kinds of cooked dried red or white beans, or drained canned kidney or pinto beans.

Serve the soup with thick slices of crusty Italian bread, red wine and for dessert, fresh pineapple flavored with a little kirsch.

    1½ pounds fresh cranberry beans
     2 tablespoons olive oil
     1 pound mild Italian pork sausages
     1 large onion, finely chopped
     1 large carrot, cut lengthwise in quarters,
        then thinly sliced
     1 stalk celery, thinly sliced
     1 large clove garlic, minced or pressed
     1 red or green bell pepper, seeded and chopped
    ¼ cup chopped parsley
     1 teaspoon dried basil
    ½ teaspoon dried oregano
    ¼ teaspoon dried marjoram
     1 large can (about 30 oz) tomatoes packed
        in tomato sauce
    3½ cups Beef Stock (see page 560) *or*
        2 cans (14½ oz each) regular-strength beef broth
    ½ cup dry red wine
    ¼ cup tiny soup pasta (pastina)
     4 cups coarsely shredded fresh spinach leaves
        Salt (optional)
        Grated Parmesan cheese, for garnish

1. Split bean pods and slip out beans as if shelling peas. (You should have about 2 cups beans.)

2. In a 5- to 6-quart Dutch oven, heat oil over medium heat. Remove casings from sausages and crumble meat into Dutch oven; cook sausage until lightly browned, stirring often. Mix in onion, carrot, and celery; cook, stirring often, until onion is soft. If drippings are excessive, spoon off and discard most of the fat.

3. Coarsely chop tomatoes (reserving liquid). To Dutch oven add shelled beans, garlic, bell pepper, parsley, herbs, tomatoes and their liquid, and stock. Bring to a boil, cover, reduce heat, and boil gently until beans are nearly tender (30 to 40 minutes).

4. Stir in wine and pasta, and boil gently, uncovered, until pasta is tender (10 to 12 minutes). Add spinach, stirring just until it is wilted. Taste and add salt if needed.

5. Serve with Parmesan cheese to sprinkle over each serving to taste.

Makes 12 to 14 cups, 4 to 6 servings.

■ SPLIT PEA SOUP, BLACK FOREST STYLE

Garnish with fresh parsley and sliced green onions just before you serve this tangy pea soup dotted with veal frankfurter slices. Accompany it with light rye bread, red and green cabbage slaw with sour cream dressing, and tart apples for dessert. Beer or, better yet, an Alsatian Gewürztraminer is a good beverage to go with the soup.

- 2 tablespoons butter or margarine
- 2 medium onions, finely chopped
- 2 medium carrots, diced
- 1 stalk celery, thinly sliced
- 1 medium potato (about ½ lb), diced
- 1 large smoked ham hock (about 1 lb) *or* 1 meaty ham bone
- 1 package (12 oz) green split peas, rinsed and drained (approximately 1⅔ cups)
- 1 bottle or can (12 oz) beer
- 6 cups water
- 1 teaspoon dried thyme
- 2 teaspoons whole mustard seed, crushed
- ⅛ teaspoon ground cloves
- ½ pound veal frankfurters, sliced ½ inch thick
- 2 tablespoons cider vinegar
  Salt (optional)
- ¼ cup *each* chopped parsley and sliced green onions

1. In a 5½- to 6-quart kettle over medium heat, melt butter. Add onions, carrots, and celery, and cook, stirring occasionally, until vegetables are soft but not browned.

2. Add potato, ham hock, split peas, beer, the water, thyme, mustard seed, and cloves. Bring to a boil, cover, reduce heat, and simmer, stirring occasionally, until ham and peas are very tender (2 to 2½ hours).

3. Remove ham hock. When it is cool enough to handle, remove and discard bones and skin. Return meat to soup in large chunks.

4. Add frankfurter slices and reheat to serving temperature. Blend in vinegar. Add salt to taste. Stir in parsley and green onions, and serve at once.

Makes about 12 cups, 6 servings.

■ ONION SOUP WITH BEER

This hearty soup would make a perfect late-night supper.

- 6 medium onions (2 to 2½ lb)
- ⅓ cup butter or margarine
- 2 cloves garlic
- 3 tablespoons flour
- 1 teaspoon paprika
- 1 bottle or can (12 oz) dark beer
- 8 cups Beef Stock (see page 560) or canned regular-strength beef broth
- 6 to 8 slices French bread, cut about 1 inch thick
- 6 to 8 tablespoons freshly grated Parmesan cheese
  Salt and freshly ground pepper, to taste
- ½ to ¾ pound Swiss cheese, shredded (2 to 3 cups)

1. Cut onions in half lengthwise, then cut across the grain into lengthwise slivers. In a 5- to 6-quart kettle over medium heat, melt butter. Add onions, cover, and cook until limp (about 10 minutes). Uncover and cook, stirring often, until onions are lightly browned (about 15 minutes). Reduce heat to medium-low if onions begin to brown too quickly.

2. Mince or press one of the garlic cloves. Add minced garlic, flour, and paprika to onions, stirring to blend flour into mixture. Remove from heat and gradually stir in beer and 2 cups of the stock. Return to heat and bring to a boil, stirring. Cover, reduce heat, and simmer for 1 hour.

3. Meanwhile, place bread slices on a baking sheet. Peel remaining clove of garlic, cut it in half, and with it rub both sides of each bread slice. Bake in 325° F oven until crisp and lightly browned (40 to 45 minutes). Sprinkle each slice with 1 tablespoon of the Parmesan cheese.

4. After soup has simmered for 1 hour, add remaining 6 cups stock; bring to a gentle boil. Season to taste.

5. Divide soup among ovenproof bowls. Top each with a slice of toasted French bread. Sprinkle Swiss cheese over bread slices. Place bowls on a baking sheet about 6 inches below broiler. Broil until the cheese is bubbling and lightly browned (6 to 8 minutes). Serve at once.

Makes 10 to 12 cups, 6 to 8 servings.

The flavors of split peas, veal frankfurters, and vegetables meld together to produce a robust Split Pea Soup, Black Forest Style.

■ GAZPACHO, UXMAL STYLE

Replete with crisp vegetables, this soup can be kept in the refrigerator for up to three days.

> 1 large can (28 oz) whole tomatoes and their liquid
> 1 tablespoon red wine vinegar
> 3 tablespoons olive oil
> 1 cup tomato juice
> 1 clove garlic, minced
> 1 teaspoon salt
> ½ teaspoon *each* sugar and dried oregano
> 1 stalk celery, finely chopped
> 1 small green chile, seeded and finely chopped *or* ⅛ teaspoon cayenne pepper
> ½ cup peeled, seeded, and chopped cucumber
> ¼ cup *each* finely chopped mild red onion and seeded green bell pepper
> ¼ cup sliced pimiento-stuffed green olives
> 1 avocado, peeled, seeded, and diced
> Lime wedges, Garlic Croutons (see page 506), sour cream, crumbled crisp bacon, and cilantro sprigs, for accompaniment

1. Reserving 2 whole tomatoes, purée remainder and liquid, vinegar, olive oil, tomato juice, garlic, salt, sugar, and oregano.

2. Pour purée into a large bowl. Finely chop reserved tomatoes and add to purée; add celery, green chile, cucumber, onion, bell pepper, and olives. Cover and chill from 8 hours to 3 days.

3. Just before serving, mix in avocado. Serve cold; pass small bowls of condiments to add to taste.

Makes about 7 cups, 6 to 8 servings.

■ VICHYSSOISE

The French name leads some to think that this classic originated in France, but it is thought to have been created in the kitchen of a New York hotel.

> 5 medium leeks (2 to 2½ lb)
> 2 tablespoons butter
> 1 small onion, finely chopped
> 3 medium smooth-skinned potatoes (1 to 1¼ lb), peeled and diced
> 2 teaspoons salt
> ⅛ teaspoon white pepper
> 4 cups boiling water or Chicken Stock (see page 560)
> 1 cup milk
> 2 cups half-and-half
> 1 cup cold whipping cream
> Salt, to taste
> Snipped fresh chives, for garnish

1. Cut off root ends and tops of leeks. Clean, drain, and slice them about ¼ inch thick.

2. In a 3- to 4-quart saucepan over medium heat, melt butter. Add leeks and onion and cook, stirring often, until soft but not browned. Mix in potatoes, salt, pepper, and the boiling water. Bring to a boil, cover, reduce heat slightly, and cook until potatoes are very tender (25 to 30 minutes).

3. Purée mixture, about half at a time, in a blender or food processor until smooth. Return to cooking pan. Blend in milk and half-and-half. Stir over medium heat until steaming hot. Strain into a large bowl. Cover and refrigerate 3 to 5 hours or overnight.

4. Using a whisk, blend in whipping cream. Taste and add salt if needed. Serve sprinkled with chives.

Makes 9 or 10 cups, 8 to 10 servings.

Recipes and Related Information

Beef Soup au Pistou, 26; Beef Soup With Noodles, 390; Budapest Borscht, 76; Chicken Quenelles, 241; Chicken Soup With Dumplings, 189; Country Watercress Soup, 607; Curried Lettuce and Pea Soup, 341; Escarole Soup, 213; Gnocchi Verde, 190; Matzo Balls, 189; Menudo, 591; Morel Soup, 379; Sherried Oxtail Soup, 501; Sorrel Soup, 548; Vegetable Purées, 487; Winter Melon Soup, 358; Wontons, 192.

STRAWBERRY

Its intense fragrance, its natural sweetness, and its brilliant red color have made the strawberry one of the world's best-loved fruits. Strawberries grow wild on several continents, including North America, and have been cultivated since at least the fifteenth century. However, it has taken years of experimentation and crossbreeding to produce a strawberry that can tolerate shipment. Today's commercial California berry, much hardier (and some say less flavorful) than its ancestors, is often shipped as far away as Europe.

Use Strawberries and cream are a marriage made in heaven, but the berries are also flattered by a sprinkling of lemon, rum, or wine. Slightly underripe berries can be sugared to bring out their sweetness. Some say that a little freshly ground black pepper also brings up the flavor of the berries. Strawberries are a favorite in ice cream, sherbet, sorbets, dessert sauces, chiffon pies, tarts, mousses, soufflés, and fruit salads. Strawberry shortcake is an American classic.

Availability When the weather cooperates, California strawberries are found from Valentine's Day through November. Elsewhere strawberries arrive on the market later and depart earlier. In most parts of the United States, supply and quality peak in May and June. Some specialty markets are beginning to offer tiny *fraises des bois* ("wood strawberries"), which have an almost candy-like flavor. They are exceedingly delicate and always expensive. Frozen strawberries are available in most supermarkets.

Selection Ripe strawberries have a full color and fragrance. Avoid berries with white shoulders and with faint or no aroma. Berries in plastic baskets can easily bruise and mold; look the basket over carefully for decomposing berries.

Storage Refrigerate for up to three days; berries will last longer if arranged in one layer on a paper-towel–lined tray. Wash berries just before using.

Preparation Wash quickly and pat dry; remove hulls and inner white core with a knife or strawberry huller.

Recipes and Related Information

Berries and Cherries Rosé, 264; Berry Shortcake, 50; Chilled Fruit Mousse, 373; Dipped and Stuffed Strawberries, 128; Fresh Fruit in Wine, 347; Fresh Fruit Tart, 442; Fruit Cobbler, 51; Fruit Fondue, 254; Fruit Fool, 254; Gadgets, 259; Red Fruit Plate With Cream Cheese Dressing, 510; Strawberries in White Chocolate, 128; Strawberry Ice Cream, 312; Strawberry Jam, 319; Strawberry-Rhubarb Pie, 498; Strawberry Sauce, 522; Strawberry Sherbet, 313.

SUGAR AND SYRUP

The range of sugars and syrups employed in the kitchen is quite broad—from powdery confectioners' sugar to thick dark molasses. Each is used primarily as a sweetener, but the choice of sweetener affects texture, keeping qualities, flavor, appearance, and taste.

Use Sugars and syrups are valued as sweeteners, but they also play other roles. In baking, sugar imparts a tender crumb and a brown crust and improves keeping qualities. Up to a point, sugar promotes yeast growth. It gives stability to whipped egg whites, creating firm meringues that can stand up to baking or poaching. Sugar is also a preservative: In sufficient quantity it slows or prevents the growth of harmful bacteria in foods. Syrups are widely used as toppings; see also specific syrups.

Availability Granulated sugar, brown sugar, confectioners' sugar, superfine sugar, sugar substitutes, corn syrup, honey, maple syrup, and molasses are available in all supermarkets; check health-food stores for blackstrap molasses, fructose, and turbinado sugar. Coarse sugar can be found at bakers' supply stores. Demerara sugar is more common in English markets than in American ones, but can be found in some supermarkets. Rock sugar is available in well-stocked supermarkets, Asian markets, and specialty stores.

Storage If kept in an airtight container in a cool, dry place, all sugars will keep indefinitely. Once opened, maple syrup and molasses should be stored in the refrigerator. Store corn syrup, tightly capped, in a cool, dry, dark location.

SUGAR SYRUPS

A sugar syrup is a solution of sugar dissolved in water; it varies in concentration, depending on the ratio of water to sugar. Typically, a *simple sugar syrup* is used for poaching fruit, diluting fondant, and for adding to frostings and sherbets. To make a simple syrup, sugar and water are cooked over low heat until the granules dissolve; the heat is increased and the mixture boiled for 1 minute. For flavor, lemon or orange juice may be added to the water; extracts or liqueur may be stirred in after the syrup has boiled. A thin syrup is 3 parts water to 1 part sugar; a medium syrup is 2 parts water to 1 part sugar; a heavy syrup is equal amounts of water and sugar. A *soaking syrup* is a concentrated, flavored sugar syrup; it is used for soaking cakes and as a light glaze. If the syrup is boiled further, it begins to change character and pass through stages of concentration. See CANDY for a further discussion of these stages.

Eventually, sugar begins to change color, deepening from a pale yellow to dark brown, then rich mahogany; its flavor deepens as well. This change is called caramelization and gives its name to the chewy candy, caramel. It also adds color and flavor to such well-known dishes as *crème caramel*, crème brûlée, and *pralines*, and to sauces, soups, and gravies.

To caramelize sugar, cook sugar and water in a heavy-bottomed saucepan (or a special copper caramelizing pot) over low heat until sugar dissolves. The mixture can be stirred at this point (although not once the sugar dissolves or it will crystallize) and the sides of the pan should be brushed down with a damp brush to remove any sugar crystals. When sugar is dissolved, increase heat to high and cook *without stirring* until sugar deepens to the desired color. The color of the liquid changes very quickly, so monitor the process and remove from heat as soon as it is ready. To keep the color for later use, set pan in bowl of ice; this will prevent the syrup from cooking further. It will thicken as it cools; warm on stove to reliquefy.

BROWN SUGAR

A mixture of granulated sugar and molasses, brown sugar is moist and clingy when fresh. Exposure to air dries it out, but adding a slice of apple or bread to the box will restore moisture. Dark brown sugar contains more molasses than light brown sugar. Both can be substituted for granulated sugar; they will impart a slightly darker color and a subtle molasses flavor. Brown sugar tends to trap air between the crystals and should be firmly packed when measured.

CASTOR SUGAR

Also spelled *caster sugar*, castor sugar is the British equivalent of superfine sugar. The term is often encountered in old American or English recipes.

COARSE SUGAR

Also called decorator's sugar, coarse sugar is used for garnishing breads, cakes, cookies, and pastries.

CONFECTIONERS' SUGAR

Also known as powdered sugar, confectioners' sugar is made by grinding granulated sugar to a powder. Because it absorbs moisture easily, many packers add a small amount of cornstarch to prevent caking. Confectioners' sugar is most useful in uncooked dishes such as frostings and coatings because it doesn't leave a grainy texture. It should be sifted before measuring.

HOW TO CARAMELIZE SUGAR

Dissolve sugar in water over low heat in a heavy-bottomed pan. In the early stages of cooking, the liquid is nearly colorless.

Once the sugar has dissolved, increase heat to high. Do not stir or undesirable crystals will form. As the liquid cooks, it will begin to turn a golden, honey color.

Caramelized sugar is a rich, warm brown. Be sure to monitor the liquid as it cooks because the color changes occur very quickly.

CORN SYRUP

Derived from corn kernels, the thick, pourable corn syrup has certain advantages in cooking. It keeps other sugars from crystallizing, which makes it valuable in candy making. Because it is hygroscopic (it absorbs moisture), it helps keep baked goods moist. Dark corn syrup has caramel color and flavor added.

DEMERARA SUGAR

Not as highly refined as granulated white sugar, demerara sugar is a light brown or amber cane sugar that resembles light brown sugar, but is not as moist. It is common in Great Britain. Granulated or light brown sugar can be substituted for it.

FRUCTOSE

This is one of the two simple sugars (monosaccharides) that make up table sugar (sucrose). Because it is the sugar found naturally in fruits, some people believe it is less refined and more nutritious than sucrose. However, the granulated fructose in retail stores is refined from high-fructose corn syrup, not from fruit. It is sweeter than sucrose and is not directly substitutable in cooking.

GRANULATED SUGAR

Certainly granulated sugar is one of the most useful staples in the kitchen. White granulated sugar is about 99.8 percent sucrose, derived from sugarcane or sugar beets. In the United States pure cane sugar is preferred for home cooking, with beet sugar reserved for commercial food processing.

HONEY

See HONEY.

MAPLE SYRUP

Boiling the sap of maple trees produces maple syrup. The syrup is graded according to color, which is a good indication of quality. The palest, most delicate syrups are Fancy Grade. Grade A, Grade B, and Unclassified syrups have progressively darker color and stronger flavor. Maple syrup is the traditional American companion to pancakes, waffles, and corn cakes. Some people drizzle it on hot oatmeal, fried doughnuts, or cornmeal mush. It adds a delicious buttery flavor to ice cream, puddings, frostings, chiffon pies, spice cakes, and apple pies. It can be used to glaze a ham, spareribs, or cooked carrots. Pure maple syrup, imitation maple syrup, and maple-flavored syrup (with real maple flavoring) are available in most supermarkets. Some specialty stores and mail-order sources offer Fancy Grade maple syrup. Refrigerate after opening and use within a few months.

MOLASSES

The refining of cane sugar produces molasses, a by-product. Light molasses is the residue from the first boiling of sugarcane juice; the second boiling yields dark molasses. Blackstrap molasses is the very dark, strongly flavored residue of the third boiling; high in minerals, it is usually found in health-food stores. Molasses may be sulfured or unsulfured depending on whether sulfur was used in the sugar-making process.

Light molasses can be used as a topping for pancakes or hot cereal. Dark molasses is used to flavor many New England dishes. It improves the keeping qualities of breads and other baked goods and imparts a dark color and distinctive flavor to pies, breads, baked beans, and gingerbread. It adds richness and sweetness to barbecue sauce.

ROCK SUGAR

The crystallized sugar known as rock sugar may be clear or slightly amber. The Chinese use it to impart sweetness and sheen to stews and braises. It can be coarsely crushed with rolling pins and used to decorate cookies or cakes.

SUGAR SUBSTITUTES

Synthetic sugars approved for consumer use today include saccharin and aspartame. Both are sweeter than granulated sugar and are not directly substitutable in cooking.

SUPERFINE SUGAR

A fine grind of granulated sugar, superfine sugar is useful in sweetening cold beverages, raw fruits, and meringues because it dissolves so readily.

TURBINADO SUGAR

When raw sugar crystals are washed with steam in a centrifuge, they yield turbinado sugar. These coarse amber crystals have the subtle molasses flavor of brown sugar.

Recipes and Related Information
Caramels, 95; Crème Brûlée, 170; Crème Caramel, 169; Pralines, 424.

SUNFLOWER SEED

The fruit of the sunflower is a small ivory seed encased in a thin black and white shell that is soft enough to split with one's teeth.

Use Most sunflower seeds are pressed for the oil, which has industrial uses. However, the seeds themselves have a pleasant nutty flavor and crunchy texture. They can be sprinkled on salads or added to breads and granola. Unshelled seeds are roasted and salted, then eaten from the shells as a snack. Sunflower seeds are very high in protein; they can be ground to flour in a blender and then added to breads for protein enrichment.

Availability Sunflower seeds are sold roasted and unroasted (raw), salted and unsalted, in the shell and shelled. Many supermarkets carry roasted and salted sunflower seeds in packages. Check health-food stores for raw, unsalted, or shelled sunflower seeds in bulk.

Storage Keep unshelled sunflower seeds in a cool, dark, dry place; refrigerate shelled sunflower seeds. Both should be used within one month.

SWEAT, TO

To draw out the juices of a food by cooking over low heat in a fat, such as butter. At this stage, before the food has begun to brown, beads of moisture will appear on the surface. Vegetables are often given this preliminary step to remove rawness and to develop their flavor before other ingredients are added.

SWEET POTATO

A native of the New World, the sweet potato is not a potato at all but a member of the morning glory family. It has thin yellow-brown skin and golden yellow flesh. What Americans call yams (see YAM) are actually a variety of sweet potato distinguished by a copper-colored or purplish skin and deep orange flesh. American yams generally have a denser texture than sweet potatoes.

Use In the United States sweet potatoes are baked whole and eaten with butter; boiled and mashed with butter; or cubed, boiled, then glazed with butter and honey, brown sugar, or maple syrup. Sweet potatoes are present in some form on most American Thanksgiving tables. Sweetened and mashed sweet potatoes can be combined with eggs, milk, and spices and baked in a pie crust. Japanese cooks fry slices of batter-covered boiled sweet potato for tempura. In Peru chunks of boiled sweet potato are simmered in stews or served as a garnish for seviche.

Availability Sweet potatoes are sold in most supermarkets the year around, although supplies are lowest in the summer months. Canned sweet potatoes are carried by most supermarkets.

Selection Choose firm, smooth-skinned sweet potatoes without soft spots, cracks, or blemishes.

Storage Sweet potatoes are poor keepers; they may be stored in a dark, humid place for up to two weeks.

■ **MAPLE-GLAZED SWEET POTATOES**
The crusty brown slices, just slightly sweet, are good for breakfast with bacon and eggs or as a vegetable accompaniment to either poultry or ham.

   3 to 4 (about 2 lb) medium sweet potatoes
   6 tablespoons butter
   ¼ teaspoon *each* salt and freshly ground pepper
   ¼ cup maple syrup

1. Peel sweet potatoes, quarter them lengthwise, then cut crosswise with a sharp knife or food processor into ⅛-inch-thick slices.

2. In a large skillet over medium heat, melt butter. Add potatoes and season with salt and pepper. Toss for 1 minute or so to thoroughly coat potatoes.

3. Lower heat, cover pan, and continue to cook for about 10 minutes more. Toss occasionally to prevent sticking. Potatoes should be just tender when pierced; if not, cook a few minutes longer.

4. Add maple syrup and raise heat to medium. Cook uncovered for 5 to 10 minutes more, tossing or stirring occasionally, until potatoes are thoroughly glazed.

Serves 4 to 6.

SWISS CHARD

Also known simply as chard, Swiss chard is a variety of beet grown for its leaves rather than for its root. Two varieties are commonly cultivated: green chard, with deep green leaves and white ribs and stems, and red chard, with similar leaves and beet red ribs and stems. Both are full-flavored greens with a bitter edge.

Use Chard, both red and green, is boiled and eaten as a potherb (see GREENS). It may be seasoned with a piece of salt pork or bacon or, in the Italian fashion, with olive oil, garlic, and lemon. Italian cooks also fill raviolis with cooked and seasoned chard, add chard to soups, and bake it with Parmesan cheese.

Availability Swiss chard is most plentiful fall through spring but is available in many markets the year around.

Selection Look for crisp leaves with no browning or bruised spots.

Storage Keep in a plastic bag in the refrigerator and use within three or four days.

Preparation Because ribs take longer than leaves to cook, they should be handled individually. Cut leaves from ribs; cut ribs into smaller pieces. After cooking, combine ribs and leaves or serve separately.

Cooking See BOIL, BRAISE, STEAM, STIR-FRY.

T-Z

TAHINI

Common to Middle Eastern cooking, tahini (also spelled tahina) is an oily paste made of ground raw (untoasted) sesame seeds. A similar Chinese paste, much darker and nuttier in flavor, is made with toasted sesame seeds.

Use Tahini seasons many well-known Middle Eastern dishes. Combined with lemon juice, garlic, minced parsley, and salt, it makes a dip known as *taratoor*. This sauce is particularly delicious with wedges of pita bread, grilled fish, or cold steamed vegetables. It may also be used as a dressing for green salads. Lebanese cooks add it to eggplant purée to make *baba ganoosh* and to chick-pea purée to make hummus. Falafel, the fried balls of cracked wheat and chick-peas popular in the Middle East, are served in pita bread with sliced tomato and a spoonful of tahini dipping sauce.

Availability Bottled and canned tahini are sold in Middle Eastern markets, health-food stores, and some supermarkets.

Storage Because of its high oil content, tahini turns rancid quickly. It should be refrigerated after opening and used within one or two months.

Preparation Stir tahini well before using to reincorporate the oil floating on top.

TAMARIND

Also known as the Indian date, tamarind is the fruit of a large evergreen tree that grows in India, the East and West Indies, the Pacific islands, and the American tropics. The tree produces a brown pod in the shape of a flat snap bean, 3 to 7 inches long. As the fruit inside matures, the pod becomes very brittle. Inside the pod is a dark brown pulp surrounding firm white seeds. The pulp—the edible part of the fruit—is very sticky and both tart and sweet at the same time, resembling the taste of a sour prune.

Use Tamarind imparts an intriguing flavor, both sweet and tart, to beverages, candies, condiments (it is an ingredient in Worcestershire sauce), marinades, and chutneys. Indian cooks make a sweet and spicy chutney from tamarind pulp. Filipino cooks add tamarind to soup broth to give it a cool, sour taste. In Indonesia chicken is marinated in tamarind-flavored water and spices before frying. In Vietnam tamarind flavors a peanut dipping sauce for grilled shrimp paste wrapped around sugarcane.

Availability Whole tamarind pods are found in Latin American, Indonesian, Indian, and Southeast Asian markets. Most of these markets also carry tamarind pulp in firm bricks, concentrated pulp in jars, and instant powder. Dutch or Indonesian markets also offer tamarind syrup for use in beverages.

Storage Tamarind pods, dried pulp, and instant powder can be stored indefinitely in a cool, dark, dry place. Fresh pulp or reconstituted dried pulp will keep one to two weeks in the refrigerator; freeze for longer storage. Tamarind syrup should be refrigerated after opening.

Preparation With the exception of the instant powder, tamarind must be softened before use. To prepare whole pods, crack brittle shell and put fruit (pulp and seeds) in a bowl. Cover with water, break fruits up with fingers, and let stand overnight. Squeeze fruit with fingers to separate seeds from pulp. When pulp is very soft, press it through a sieve and discard seeds. If using tamarind pulp in blocks or tamarind concentrate, simply put a small piece in a bowl and cover with boiling water. When it is soft (30 minutes or more), press it through a sieve to separate it from seeds. Some recipes call only for the tamarind soaking liquid, not the pulp.

TAPIOCA

The starchy food known as tapioca derives from the root of the cassava, a South American and African plant.

Use Tapioca serves both as a thickener and as a dessert in itself. Tapioca starch (also known as tapioca flour) is an excellent thickener for sauces and fruit fillings that must be frozen because it does not break down when thawed. It is also used to thicken glazes for fruit tarts because it does not cloud the glaze. Pearl tapioca, dried barley-sized balls of tapioca starch, can be made into a creamy cooked custard or baked pudding, akin to rice pudding. Pearl tapioca is occasionally used to thicken soups.

Availability Tapioca starch is found in Latin American markets, Asian markets, and health-food stores. Pearl tapioca and instant pearl tapioca are available in most supermarkets.

Storage Both tapioca starch and pearl tapioca will keep indefinitely in a cool, dark, dry place.

Preparation Tapioca starch can be used as a thickener in the same manner as cornstarch. After adding it to a liquid, do not boil or tapioca may turn stringy.

■ TAPIOCA PUDDING

The tapioca pearls glisten in this soothing childhood favorite. Note that the pudding cooks slowly.

    2 cups half-and-half
    2 cups milk
    ⅓ cup sugar
    1 tablespoon vanilla extract
    ½ cup pearl tapioca

1. Preheat oven to 300° F. Generously butter a 1½-quart ovenproof dish.

2. In a medium bowl stir together half-and-half, milk, sugar, and vanilla. Add tapioca and stir well. Pour in prepared dish and bake until a creamy, golden skin has formed on the surface (2 to 2½ hours).

3. Serve hot or warm.

Serves 4 to 6.

Recipes and Related Information
Cornstarch, 159; Pie and Tart, 436.

TARRAGON

A perennial herb, tarragon has slender, spiky green leaves rarely more than an inch long. The leaves have a pungent aroma and flavor, reminiscent of anise.

Use   Tarragon is used often in French cooking, where it is considered one of the four fines herbes (sweet herbs—chervil, parsley, chives, and tarragon) added to eggs and many other dishes. It is the principal flavoring in béarnaise sauce, a relative of Hollandaise. It is particularly compatible with fish and shellfish, tomatoes, chicken, eggs, and salad greens. Tarragon is an ingredient in many recipes for green goddess dressing and tartar sauce. The whole herb is also used to flavor vinegar; tarragon vinegar is delicious in salad dressings.

Availability   Fresh tarragon can be found in well-stocked supermarkets and specialty markets; it is most plentiful in the summer. Dried tarragon is found on all supermarket spice racks.

Selection   Choose fresh tarragon with rich green leaves that show no signs of wilting or drying. Packaged seasonings lose quality after a while; try to buy from a store that restocks its spice section fairly often.

Storage   Refrigerate fresh tarragon wrapped in damp paper towels and overwrapped in plastic; it will keep for one week. The leaves can be removed from the stems, packed tightly in a clean jar, then covered with white wine vinegar and refrigerated for up to one year. Store dried tarragon in a cool, dark, dry place, and use within one year.

Preparation   Mince fresh tarragon. Tarragon packed in vinegar should be squeezed lightly to remove as much vinegar as possible before using. Dried tarragon should be crumbled between the fingers to release its essential oils when adding it to a dish.

Recipes and Related Information
Basic Single-Serving Omelet With Herbs, 203;
Béarnaise Sauce, 518; Herb, 299; Herb Vinegar, 323;
Tarragon Mustard, 323; Veal Chops With
Tarragon, 593.

TEA

Although the term *tea* traditionally refers to the leaves of the oriental shrub *Camellia sinensis*, it has come to apply to all drinks made from leaves, flowers, seeds, roots, or bark steeped in hot water. In a broad sense all teas are herbal teas since they are made from edible plant parts. Current usage, however, classifies Asian teas separately from caffeine-free herbal teas.

Use   Teas may be brewed for consuming either hot or cold. They are frequently served with such optional additions as lemon, sugar, honey, or milk.

Availability   Asian tea is widely sold in American supermarkets. Most supermarket tea is blended tea, packed in disposable tea bags for convenience, although some markets now stock loose tea in airtight canisters. Instant iced tea is also widely available. For a large selection of premium-quality loose teas, it may be necessary to visit a specialty store, a health-food store, or an Asian market. Many supermarkets and health-food stores now also sell a wide variety of caffeine-free herbal teas.

Selection   Some of the world's most popular teas—such as English breakfast, Irish breakfast, and Earl Grey—are blends of tea leaves from various sources. Individual teas

Although paraphernalia for making coffee abounds, the preparation of tea has remained a fairly simple and straightforward process that requires little equipment. Shown clockwise from top right: teapot, sugar bowl and cream pitcher, ceramic tea infuser, tea-bag rest, metal tea infuser, cup with strainer, teapot with strainer, tin of loose tea leaves, cup with infuser.

TEATIME: IN A POT, IN A CUP, OVER ICE

To brew a pot of tea   To keep the tea from cooling too quickly, warm teapot by filling it with boiling water; let stand for 1 or 2 minutes, then pour off water. Meanwhile, fill teakettle with fresh cold water from the tap. Bring water to a full, rolling boil. Put 1 teaspoon tea leaves per 6-ounce cup in the teapot. Add appropriate amount of boiling water. Cover and let steep 3 to 6 minutes for black tea, 6 to 8 minutes for green and oolong teas, and 8 to 12 minutes for herbal teas. Stir once, then pour into warm cups through a strainer (some teapots are equipped with a built-in strainer). The lengthy steeping brings out the full flavor of the tea.

To brew a cup of tea   Warm a teacup by filling it with boiling water; let stand for 1 or 2 minutes, then pour off water. Bring fresh cold water to a rolling boil in a teakettle. Put 1 teaspoon of leaves in a tea ball or perforated infusing spoon. Set ball or spoon in warmed cup; pour in boiling water. Infuse 3 to 6 minutes for black tea, 6 to 8 minutes for green and oolong teas, and 8 to 12 minutes for herbal teas. Stir once with infuser, then remove infuser and serve.

To brew iced tea   Make an extrastrong pot of hot tea and allow it to cool completely.

Then strain tea into an ice-filled glass. This method will produce a cloudy tea. To prevent cloudiness (which does not affect flavor), make a cold-water infusion: Measure 3 tablespoons tea leaves per quart of cold water; combine in a pitcher, cover, and refrigerate for several hours, then strain over ice.

EQUIPMENT FOR BREWING TEA

The preparation of tea requires very little equipment. Select a teapot that retains heat well: Porcelain or glazed earthenware is a good choice. For catching tea leaves as you pour from teapot to teacup, you will need a strainer. The simplest ones are miniature versions of the mesh baskets used to drain cooked vegetables and pasta. More elegant strainers are chrome or even silver-plated. If brewing tea by the cup, buy an infuser. This can take the form of a mesh or perforated metal ball or a perforated spoon. The infuser is filled with tea leaves, immersed in a cup of hot water, then removed when tea has brewed to suit. Also on the market are electric teakettles imported from England; they automatically bring water to the proper boil and maintain the temperature, ever ready for that next cup of tea.

are named for their place of origin—Darjeeling, Ceylon, Keemun, and Assam, for example. Both blends and individual teas may be flavored with citrus peel, flower blossoms, or spices.

The name of a black tea sometimes reflects the size of the tea leaves. Because large leaves brew slower than small leaves, teas are usually sorted by size for more efficient brewing. Souchong (as in Lapsang souchong) denotes large leaves. Pekoe denotes medium-sized leaves. Orange pekoe teas are made of the smallest leaves.

Green tea leaves are easy to identify by their appearance. Oolong teas are also relatively easy to distinguish from black teas by their color. When in doubt, ask the merchant for guidance.

Storage   Teas should be stored in an airtight container in a cool, dark, dry place. They may be kept for up to one year without loss of flavor.

Preparation   Brewing tea is a simple process, but many people sidestep the few procedures necessary to brewing a superior cup of tea. See Teatime: In a Pot, In a Cup, Over Ice, above. For herbal teas, see HERB.

ASIAN TEAS

Despite their differences, the many types of Asian tea available to the consumer all come from the same plant, *Camellia sinensis,* an evergreen bush in the camellia family. The differences among teas derive from where they are grown and how they are processed. Native to Southeast Asia, the plant from which tea leaves are obtained has been cultivated in China at least since the fourth century. It thrives in tropical and subtropical climates; today most of the commercial crop comes from China, Japan, India, Indonesia, Sri Lanka, and Taiwan. The choicest teas, such as Darjeeling from the foothills of the Himalayas, are grown in high altitudes. On any given bush, the best pluck consists of the smallest leaves and the unopened leaf buds.

TYPES OF ASIAN TEAS

After plucking, the leaves are subjected to one of three different processes, depending on the type of tea desired. The countless varieties of tea are classified by their processing: fermented (black), unfermented (green), and semifermented (oolong).

Black Tea   This is the type most familiar to Westerners. First the teas leaves are withered in the sun. Next, they are mechanically bruised to break their leaf cells, then left in a warm place for a few hours to ferment. This fermentation is unlike the yeast fermentation that turns grape juice into wine; the word is used in a broad sense to describe the action of enzymes on the tannin and the natural oils in the tea leaves. During this process, leaf color deepens and flavor and astringency develop. Finally, the leaves are fired to stop the fermentation process and preserve them. An expert fermentation supervisor knows just when to fire the leaves for desired color and flavor. Black teas have a rich reddish brown color and a full aroma and flavor.

Green Tea   Leaves for green tea are steamed immediately after harvesting to prevent fermentation and to make them pliable. They are then rolled to crush the leaf cells. The final step is to fire or dry them with a blast of hot air. Green teas have a pale color and less aroma and flavor than black tea.

Oolong Tea   To make oolong tea, the leaves are given an intermediate treatment—they are allowed to ferment partially and then are steamed to stop the process. They yield a tea somewhere between green and black tea in color, flavor, and body.

HERBAL TEAS

These teas are made from just one kind of herb or a mixture of several, with flowers and spices added. When brewed, they are sometimes known as tisanes or infusions. Popular herbal teas include chamomile, linden, jasmine, lemon verbena, hibiscus, and rose hip. The leaves and flowers of virtually any edible plant can be dried for a tisane. Most yield a pale beverage with a subtle aroma.

TEMPERATURE

The measure of the hotness or coldness of a material is its temperature. In cooking, temperature can be expressed in degrees (a 375° F oven) or with words (cook over simmering, not boiling, water). Recipes use degrees when the desired result is indicated by a particular temperature or is the product of it: "cook sugar syrup to 238° F (soft-ball stage)" or "roast for 45 minutes at 325° F." Words substitute when it's less critical to hit a temperature right on the mark: "Bring to room temperature" is a familiar cooking instruction that means to about 72° F.

Professional chefs consider internal temperature the best way to tell when food has reached a particular stage of doneness. A beef roast that is approximately 125° F in its interior will always be rare, whether cooked at 325° F or 425° F and regardless of how long it took to reach that temperature. Use the chart at right as a guide for judging when roasted, broiled, or grilled meats and poultry are done. An accurate meat thermometer or instant-read thermometer should be basic equipment in every kitchen.

TEMPERATURE EQUIVALENTS

This chart gives degrees Fahrenheit and descriptions of some common cooking temperatures.

Stage	Temperature
Freezer	0° F
Freezing	32° F (water)
Refrigerator	40° to 45° F
Cool room temperature	60° to 65° F
Room temperature	68° to 77° F
Warm room temperature	75° to 79° F
Lukewarm	98.6° F
Scalding	149° F
Simmering	210° F (water)
Boiling	212° F (water)

Oven Temperature	
Very slow	Below 300° F
Slow	300° F
Moderately slow	325° F
Moderate	350° to 375° F
Hot	400° to 425° F
Very hot	450° to 475° F
Extremely hot	500° F and above

GUIDE TO INTERNAL TEMPERATURES

Note that the internal temperature denoting a particular stage of doneness isn't the same for all types of meat. Suggested temperatures may be lower than may appear on a meat thermometer or in older recipes; the temperatures in this chart reflect the greater accuracy and reliability of home ovens and broilers today and the preference for meats that are less well-done.

Type of Meat	Rare	Medium	Well-done
Beef	125°–130° F	140°–145° F	160° F
Lamb	130°–140° F	145° F	160° F
Pork		145°–150° F	160° F
Poultry		170°–175° F	180° F
Veal		140°–145° F	160° F

THERMOMETER

Are your cookies underdone or burned? Does your frozen food lose quality sooner than expected? Is your turkey dry and tasteless, your roast medium when you really wanted rare? These can all be problems of temperature, whether of the cooking or storing environment—oven or freezer—or of the food itself. Experienced cooks know that ovens have hot and cool spots, and actual temperature can vary 25° F or more from its setting. They have learned that, for roasts, internal temperature is a better indicator of doneness than time. They also recognize that the freezing compartment in many combination refrigerator-freezers doesn't maintain the recommended setting of 0° F. Reliable thermometers are invaluable kitchen tools because their data helps the cook be more accurate and have more control over the cooking process.

TWO BASIC TYPES

Regardless of their application, thermometers are one of two types: bimetal or glass-tube.

Bimetal thermometers have a face, like a dial, and a pointer. The pointer moves by action of a spring made of two metals welded together, which react differently to heat. A change in temperature causes the spring to wind or unwind and move the pointer around the dial. Bimetal thermometers are less accurate than the glass-tube type, but the dials are easier to read and they hold a temperature reading longer. Use them when it is less critical to measure to a precise degree, such as for roasting and baking. For use in appliances, these thermometers come mounted on a stand to set on a shelf or rack and with a hook for hanging. To serve as a food probe, the dial is fastened to a stem. Select bimetal thermometers with shatter-resistant faces and clearly marked dials. Some have magnifying covers, a real advantage, or movable red arrows to mark a particular reading.

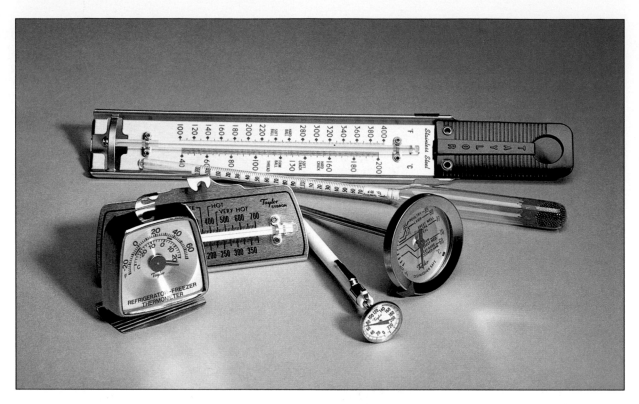

Specialized thermometers are designed for use with appliances and food. Shown top to bottom: candy and deep-fat, hydrometer, meat, instant-read, oven, refrigerator-freezer.

Instant-read thermometers are stem-type bimetal devices designed for quick response when inserted into meat, poultry, yeast doughs, and hot liquids. They have slender stainless steel shafts and a face with large numbers that register from 0° to 220° F. Unlike traditional meat thermometers that remain inserted in food throughout cooking, instant-read devices are inserted periodically, read, and removed. They will respond very quickly—in about 20 to 30 seconds. They are very versatile and highly recommended.

Glass-tube models register temperature by the expansion or contraction of a fluid—mercury or a colored liquid—trapped in a thin column of glass. The tube rests against a scale typically marked in 2°, 5°, or 10° F increments. The temperature graduations are occasionally marked on the tube itself. Glass-tube thermometers are very accurate and responsive, but are fragile and more difficult to read than a dial type. Magnifying lenses are an advantage, as are scales with dark numbers marked on a white or light background.

TO TEST FOR ACCURACY

It only makes sense that a thermometer be as accurate as possible, or why bother to use it. Use the boiling point of water, 212° F, as a reference point for probe and glass-tube stand models. Bring water to a boil, immerse either stem or entire unit (whichever is appropriate), and note the reading. If the reading is off and the model is adjustable, set it to 212° F; if you cannot reset it, note the difference, and adjust for it when you use the thermometer. For stand thermometers with dials, set in oven, refrigerator, or freezer alongside one that you know is accurate; compare readings.

Some thermometers have a narrow temperature range that stops below the boiling point. To verify accuracy, compare with one you know to be accurate or against a laboratory model, sold at scientific equipment stores.

SPECIALTY THERMOMETERS

Some thermometers are designed for multiple uses. They usually have a wide temperature range; certain probe models are suitable for roasting, testing yeast doughs, and determining the internal temperature of foods cooked in a microwave oven. Single-application models are marked to suit their purpose. Oven thermometers begin at around 100° F and climb to about 600° F. Freezer thermometers register from -40° F to 80° F. Candy and deep-fat thermometers, often one dual-purpose device, usually start at 100° F and stop at 400° F, a range that covers all the stages of working with sugar, plus the usual frying temperature range of 365° to 390° F. Meat thermometers mark from 100° F to 220° F.

What are the benefits of specialty thermometers? Their narrow temperature range means greater accuracy. Because fewer numbers need to be indicated on the dial or scale, the markings are larger and thus clearer. Some have special adaptations, such as hooks or stands, for ease of use. As with any equipment, select the thermometers that suit your needs. A well-known brand, backed by the retailer, is always a sensible choice.

CANDY AND DEEP-FAT THERMOMETERS

When working with sugar syrups, it's critical to know the concentrations. Concentration of a sugar syrup can be measured by its appearance—threads, soft-ball stage, rigid strands, or deep brown color—or by its temperature reading on a candy thermometer. These devices are preferably glass-tube types (although bimetal ones are available and do work), and the most practical are set on a stainless steel frame with a plastic extension at the top for easy handling. They usually have a clip so that, once the sugar syrup comes to a boil, the thermometer can be attached to the side of the pan, partially immersed in the liquid, to register the temperature without the cook having to hold the device in place.

For fried foods that are neither soggy and pale from cooking at too low a temperature nor burned on the outside and underdone within from an overly high temperature, hot oil must be kept at the recommended level—usually between 350° and 400° F. Deep-fat thermometers resemble those for candy making, although the upper register is usually slightly higher.

Combination candy and deep-fat thermometers are commonly available and are a practical choice for most households. Make sure that the markings accommodate both procedures.

FREEZER THERMOMETER

Foods keep best in the freezer at 0° F. Although they are still safe to eat if stored at higher temperatures, color, flavor, and texture begin to deteriorate above 5° F. For each 10 degrees above zero, the storage life of food is cut up to half. It's a good idea to monitor the temperature of the freezer section with a freezer thermometer. Place the thermometer toward the top and front of the freezer. Leave it overnight without opening freezer door. If the temperature is above 0° F the next day, adjust the temperature control and take another reading. Freezer thermometers have hooks to hang on the front of a loaded freezer shelf.

HYDROMETER

A candy thermometer measures the concentration of sugar syrup by noting its heat. When making ice cream and sorbets, you may also want to measure density, which affects both texture and flavor—smooth and sweet, grainy and intense. The lightness or heaviness (the density or specific gravity) of a syrup, the result of how much water evaporates from cooking, is expressed in degrees Baumé (named after the French chemist who developed the scale). Taking this measure requires a hydrometer, a glass tube roughly the shape of an ordinary fever thermometer and about one third larger in size, and which is marked from 0° to 40° Baumé. To use, a solution is poured into a tall container and the hydrometer dropped in and allowed to float. The measure of density is taken at the point where the stem rises above the surface of the liquid. Hydrometers are not a usual part of a well-equipped kitchen, although they are used extensively in restaurants and commercial food preparation. You may want one if you make a lot of frozen desserts or fruit syrups. However, most recipes are designed to work without such a precise measure.

MEAT THERMOMETER

A meat thermometer measures the inside temperature of a turkey, chicken, or roast while it is in the oven. Roasting charts should be regarded as very general guidelines because there are many variables to consider—how an oven heats, the shape of the food being cooked, how often the oven door is opened, the cook's definition of doneness. Internal temperature as measured by a thermometer gives a better indication than time alone whether or not food has reached a particular stage. Meat thermometers are of two types: one that stays in food throughout cooking or the instant-read type. Cooks today tend to prefer the latter as it has a thinner shaft that won't puncture as big a hole in the food as well as a larger dial that is easier to read. Instant-read thermometers are meant for quick use so you can take a range of readings.

OVEN THERMOMETER

A variation of plus or minus 25° F from the set temperature is considered normal for even the best-quality home ovens. If you regularly use an oven thermometer, you can adjust the oven setting to match the actual heat produced and avoid guesswork and failed recipes (directions for this adjustment are in the owner's manual of your oven). Both bimetal and glass-tube stand models with hook are available. Because internal temperature can vary, place the thermometer where you will be cooking, generally on the center rack. Heat the oven to the desired temperature and check thermometer (preferably through the oven window) when oven indicates it has reached the preset temperature. If necessary, adjust oven dial, wait until the new temperature has been reached, and read thermometer again. A folding model, which uses a glass tube protected in a stainless steel case, is extremely accurate and is the instrument of choice for those who service ovens. Used for spot checks at timed intervals, it isn't left in the oven throughout the cooking period. Because of its high quality, it is considerably more expensive than other models.

Recipes and Related Information
Candy and Confection, 94; Deep-fry, 174; Freeze, 242; Ice Cream and Frozen Dessert, 308; Roast, 499; Temperature, 575.

THYME

A Mediterranean native of the mint family, thyme is one of the most widely used herbs on the pantry shelf. Its subtle aroma and flavor make it a "background" herb, rarely the major seasoning in a dish but one that gives complexity to countless culinary preparations.

Use   Thyme is a common herb throughout the Mediterranean. In southern France and Greece, it is almost always paired with lamb and often with chicken. Thyme flavors shellfish stews and chowders, gumbo, poultry stuffings, and dried bean dishes. It is often used with tomatoes and dishes with tomato sauce, as well as with eggplant, onions, or green beans. A lemon-scented variety, called lemon thyme, enhances the flavor of fish, chicken, and veal.

Availability   Some supermarkets and specialty markets sporadically offer fresh thyme, with the best availability in the summer months. Dried thyme and ground thyme are found on all supermarket spice racks.

Selection   Choose fresh herbs that have good green color; avoid those that are wilted. Packaged seasonings lose quality after a while; try to buy from a store that restocks its spice section fairly often.

Storage   Refrigerate fresh thyme in damp paper towels overwrapped in plastic; it will keep for up to one week. Store dried thyme and ground thyme in a cool, dark, dry place. Dried thyme will keep up to one year, ground thyme up to six months.

■ THYME-SCENTED CHICKEN WITH POTATOES, BACON, AND BABY ONIONS

The combination of potatoes, bacon, and baby onions is a favorite addition to braised chicken dishes in French cooking. This dish is often regarded as a symbol of good home cooking. Homemade chicken stock will produce a more flavorful, full-bodied sauce. If possible, make stock in quantity and store in the freezer.

> 1   **frying chicken (3½ lb), at room temperature**
> ¼   **pound bacon, preferably thick sliced, cut crosswise in ¼-inch strips**
> 16 **baby onions, peeled**
>   **Salt and freshly ground pepper, to taste**
> 1   **tablespoon vegetable oil**
> 2   **tablespoons butter, at room temperature**
> 3   **tablespoons dry white wine**
> ¾   **cup Chicken Stock (see page 560)**
> 2   **sprigs fresh thyme *or* ½ teaspoon dried thyme**
> 6   **medium-sized oval potatoes (about 1½ lb total), peeled, halved lengthwise, and put in a bowl of cold water**
> 2   **teaspoons flour**

1. Remove neck and giblets from chicken. Pull out fat from inside of chicken on both sides near tail. Cut off tail and wing tips. Thoroughly pat chicken dry. Sprinkle on all sides evenly with salt and pepper.

2. Heat bacon in a large, heavy, oval casserole over medium-low heat until some fat is rendered. Raise heat to medium-high. Add onions and sauté with bacon, shaking pan often. When bacon browns, transfer it to paper towels using a slotted spoon. Continue to sauté onions, turning them over carefully until they are browned on all sides. Transfer to paper towels. Discard all but 1 tablespoon fat from pan.

3. Add oil and 1 tablespoon butter to casserole and heat over medium-high heat. When foam subsides, set chicken in hot fat on its side so that leg is in contact with fat; brown side of chicken. Using two wooden spoons, turn chicken gently onto its breast and brown it. Turn chicken on other leg and brown it. Lastly, turn chicken on its back and brown it. Remove chicken from casserole.

4. Add wine, stock, and thyme to casserole, and bring to a boil, stirring to dissolve any brown bits in pan. Return chicken to casserole, placing it on its back. Reduce heat to low, cover, and simmer for 20 minutes.

5. Meanwhile, trim each potato half to an oval shape, using paring knife to round any sharp angles. Keep potatoes in bowl of cold water until ready to cook.

6. Put potatoes in large saucepan and cover with fresh water. Bring to a boil. Add pinch of salt, cover, and simmer over medium heat until nearly tender (about 20 minutes). Drain thoroughly.

7. While chicken cooks, mash remaining 1 tablespoon butter in a small bowl with a fork until softened. Mix in flour until mixture becomes a uniform paste.

8. After chicken has simmered 20 minutes, add onions, cover, and continue cooking until chicken juices run clear when thickest part of leg is pierced with a thin skewer (about 25 minutes); if juices are still pink, cook a few more minutes and test again.

9. When chicken is tender, transfer to a platter with two wooden spoons, reserving juices in casserole. Cover chicken with aluminum foil and keep it warm. If onions are tender, remove with slotted spoon; if not, cook a few more minutes until tender. Spoon onions into a bowl and add bacon.

10. Bring chicken cooking liquid to a boil. Reduce heat to low. Add potatoes, salt, and pepper; cover. Cook potatoes until they are just tender (about 10 minutes), carefully turning them often. With a slotted spoon, remove potatoes to a dish; keep warm.

11. Skim off as much fat as possible from chicken cooking liquid. Boil liquid until it is reduced to about ¾ cup; discard thyme sprigs (if used).

12. Pour liquid into a small, heavy saucepan and bring to a simmer. Gradually whisk butter-flour paste into simmering sauce, a small piece at a time, whisking constantly. Bring to a boil, whisking.

13. Return vegetables and bacon to sauce, and heat 2 minutes over low heat to blend flavors. Taste and add more salt and pepper, if needed. Discard any liquid that chicken has released onto platter. Spoon sauce and vegetable-bacon mixture around whole chicken and serve immediately. Carve chicken at the table.

Serves 4.

TIMBALE

Both the mold and the dish made in it are called a timbale. The name is French, meaning kettledrum, an apt description of its shape (see MOLD). A traditional timbale was a dish cooked in a pastry crust. Today it more often is an individually sized, custard-based vegetable or fish dish served as a first course or a side dish. The molds are small, designed for a single serving.

■ SPINACH TIMBALES

Timbales can be baked ahead and served at room temperature, a time-saving feature a cook will appreciate. As they are prepared in individual molds, each sized for a single portion, they simplify serving. These extremely flavorful spinach molds are an excellent accompaniment to poultry.

- ½ **cup whipping cream, warmed**
- 1 **egg**
- ¼ **teaspoon salt**
- ⅛ **teaspoon mild Hungarian paprika**
  Pinch freshly grated nutmeg
- ½ **cup cooked, chopped spinach, drained and squeezed dry**
- 3 **tablespoons freshly grated Parmesan cheese**
- 2 **tablespoons minced shallot**
- 1 **tablespoon minced parsley**

1. Preheat oven to 325° F. In a medium bowl mix together cream, egg, salt, paprika, and nutmeg. Add spinach, Parmesan cheese, shallot, and parsley. Stir to blend.

2. Generously butter two 1-cup timbale or soufflé molds. Fill molds about two thirds full with mixture. Place molds in a small glass baking dish. Fill dish with hot water to reach about three fourths up sides of molds.

3. Place dish with molds in center of middle rack of oven. Bake until timbales are golden brown and a knife inserted in center comes out clean (20 to 30 minutes).

4. To unmold, run a knife around inside edge of each mold. Invert molds onto dinner plates, tap sharply with a knife, and lift off. Serve timbales hot or at room temperature.

Serves 2.

TIMER

Although most ovens these days have built-in timers, hearing them requires us to stay nearby—captive in the kitchen. Timers that we can carry with us allow us to pursue other tasks around the house while a turkey roasts, a cake bakes, or a soufflé rises. The old-fashioned hourglass still does the job, but it has become outmoded—not because it lacks trendy gears or circuits, but because it does not sound an alarm to remind us that a cooking process requires our attention. It is also unable to measure very brief units of time such as one minute or less. Timers with alarms are of two basic types: spring-action and digital.

Spring-action timers are activated by rotating a dial to the desired number of minutes; the mechanism ticks off the seconds until the dial returns to zero and then alerts you with a buzzer, beep, or bell that the time has elapsed. Battery-operated, digital timers are electronic and therefore more expensive than spring-action models. However, some can monitor four separate tasks at one time, and can measure seconds, minutes, and hours. Although most spring-action timers must be reset for more than 60 minutes, the digital timer can be programmed for almost 10 straight hours.

When deciding which timer is best for you, also consider: *Accuracy*—Some timers have play; do you need exact measurements for the type of cooking you do most frequently? *Loudness*—How loud is the alarm and how long will it ring? Will you be in the same room as the timer or will you need to hear it from some distance away? Also, some sound once for several seconds and shut off; others continue to ring until they are turned off or the battery dies. *Readability*—Are the numbers easy to read? Is the display large enough to be clear?

TOMATILLO

Despite its name and appearance, the tomatillo isn't a variety of tomato. A native of Mexico, the tomatillo is related to the ground cherry and the cape gooseberry. It resembles a small green tomato encased in a papery husk. Mexican cooks, confusingly, call it *tomate verde* (green tomato). Its texture is like that of a firm tomato; its flavor is lemony or applelike.

Use The tomatillo is rarely eaten raw in its native land, although some American diners enjoy its tart flavor in salads. In Mexican cooking, where it is an important ingredient, it is husked and simmered in water about 10 minutes to soften slightly, then puréed and used in salsas and stews. The ubiquitous *salsa verde,* a table condiment applied to tacos, enchiladas, and quesadillas, is made of ground tomatillos, onion, and chiles. Tomatillos are added to pork stews and to the several Mexican dishes cooked *en mole verde* (in green mole).

Availability Fresh tomatillos are sold in Latin markets and some specialty markets, with peak supplies August through November. Canned, husked tomatillos are available in Latin markets.

Selection When buying them fresh, tomatillos should be firm and unblemished. They turn yellow as they ripen, but the green ones are more desirable for their firm texture and tart flavor.

Storage Refrigerate fresh unhusked tomatillos in a paper bag for up to three weeks. Leftover canned tomatillos should be transferred to an airtight nonmetal container and refrigerated; they will keep for up to five days.

Preparation Husk and wash fresh tomatillos to remove the sticky residue on the surface. Simmer (do not boil) until just tender when pierced with a knife (about 10 minutes). Drain and purée or use as recipe directs.

■ SALSA VERDE

This green salsa has an unusually fresh flavor that results from the blending of tomatillos and cilantro. It is particularly good with pork, chicken, and fish dishes.

> 1 jalapeño *or* 2 serrano chiles, fresh or canned, chopped
> 1 can (12 oz) tomatillos, drained, *or* 8 fresh tomatillos, cooked and drained
> 2 cloves garlic, chopped
> 3 tablespoons finely minced white onions *or* 2 green onions, finely chopped
> ¼ cup cilantro leaves
> ¼ teaspoon salt
> ¼ cup water

1. Place chiles, tomatillos, garlic, white or green onion, cilantro, and salt in a blender or food processor and blend briefly to a purée.

2. Add the water in small amounts and blend to desired consistency.

Makes about 1½ cups.

TOMATO

Native to the lower Andes (parts of modern Ecuador, Peru, and Bolivia), the tomato is a New World plant. The early explorers took tomato seeds back to Europe, but for many years the tomato was considered only an ornamental plant. Botanists correctly recognized it as a member of the deadly nightshade family and assumed that it was poisonous; in fact, only the leaves and stems are toxic. Up until the middle of the nineteenth century, Americans also refused to eat tomatoes. Even then, most cookbooks of the time instructed that tomatoes be cooked for three hours. The taste for raw tomatoes is primarily a phenomenon of the twentieth century.

Use Today tomatoes are used throughout the world in countless ways, in appetizers, soups, salads, sauces, stews, and side dishes. They rarely appear at dessert, although New England cooks turn green tomatoes into a sweet green tomato pie. More typically, Americans quarter them and add them to salads, halve them and stuff them with egg salad or shrimp salad, slice them and layer them in sandwiches for moisture, and cook them with sugar and spices to make bottled catsup. Mexicans mince tomatoes with onions, cilantro, and chiles to make salsa, an everyday table condiment.

Italian cooks, famous for their tomato recipes, turn tomatoes into aromatic sauces for pasta, toppings for pizza, and luscious salads with anchovies, herbs, and olive oil. They are fundamental to the cooking of the Mediterranean region, where they figure in such famous dishes as French ratatouille, Moroccan tomato and green pepper salad, Spanish gazpacho, Greek shrimp with tomatoes and feta cheese, and Italian *pizza alla Napoletana.* Tomatoes are relatively little used throughout Asia. They are not part of the Japanese diet and were not introduced to China until the 1930s. In India tomatoes are used raw in a chopped salad and are added to a variety of stews and vegetable dishes. They appear on the Swedish smorgasbord and, in the form of tomato paste, flavor a Norwegian butter spread on grilled mackerel. South African tomatoes are, by some accounts, among the best in the world.

Even unripe tomatoes have culinary uses. In the American South, and in the upper midwestern and Plains states, green tomatoes are sliced, dipped in flour or cornmeal, and fried or simmered with onions and spices to make green tomato relish.

Availability Fresh tomatoes are sold in most supermarkets the year around, but vine-ripened tomatoes are available only during the summer and fall. Vine-ripened tomatoes have superior flavor but are extremely fragile. For that reason, most tomatoes that must be shipped any distance are picked and shipped green and allowed to ripen in warming rooms. Hydroponic tomatoes (grown in water without soil) and greenhouse tomatoes often have a lovely appearance but generally lack flavor.

The following are popular tomatoes.

Cherry Tomato This bite-sized, round tomato is often used as a garnish or a salad tomato.

Sauce Tomato Also known as the plum tomato, Roma tomato, Italian tomato, or paste tomato, this egg-shaped variety has thick meat and few seeds. The meaty texture makes it excellent for sauces.

Slicing Tomato This large, slightly squat tomato is probably the most familiar, with a shape well suited to slicing. It has a large seed cavity and lots of juice, which make it better for eating raw than for cooking.

Yellow Pear Tomato A relatively recent addition to specialty markets, this tiny pear-shaped tomato is less than an inch long and is generally used in the same way as cherry tomatoes.

Supermarkets and specialty stores stock a wide variety of prepared tomato products.

Canned Tomatoes These tomatoes are available in several forms in supermarkets, such as peeled whole tomatoes, peeled and crushed tomatoes, whole tomatoes with added basil, and peeled whole plum tomatoes. In general, Italian packers pick canning tomatoes riper than American processors do; compare imported Italian canned tomatoes with American brands. Canned tomatoes are convenient for soups, sauces, casseroles, and stews. In most cooked dishes, they are preferable to unripe fresh tomatoes.

Canned Tomato Sauce Available in all supermarkets, tomato sauce is a convenience product, useful in making sauces, casseroles, and stews.

Sun-Dried Tomatoes A recent addition to most markets, sun-dried tomatoes were initially imported from Italy, but are now produced domestically as well. Sun-drying gives tomatoes a chewy texture and an almost candylike flavor. To keep them moist, they are generally packed in olive oil. Use sun-dried tomatoes as a garnish for sandwiches, pizza, salads, and soups. They add a rich tomato flavor to pasta sauces and stews. Most brands are extremely salty and should be used with restraint.

Tomato Paste Available in cans and, increasingly, in tubes, tomato paste is highly concentrated and is usually used in small amounts. Tubes of tomato paste are especially convenient because they allow the cook to use only the amount required and refrigerate the rest indefinitely.

Selection Choose fresh tomatoes by their color and aroma. Vine-ripened tomatoes have good color and a noticeable fragrance. They should be neither overly soft nor overly firm. Avoid any with blemishes or splits.

Storage Firm, underripe tomatoes can be stored in a warm, sunny spot for a few days; they will soften and improve in flavor. Ripe tomatoes can be left at room temperature for a day but should be refrigerated for longer storage; once ripe, use tomatoes within a few days. Any leftover tomato sauce should be transferred to an airtight nonmetal container, refrigerated, and used within a few days. Leftover canned tomato paste should be transferred to an airtight nonmetal container and covered with a film of olive oil to prevent oxidation. In that condition, it may be refrigerated for two weeks or frozen indefinitely.

Cover unused sun-dried tomatoes with olive oil and keep refrigerated in an airtight container; they will keep several months.

Preparation Wash and core large tomatoes. Remove caps on cherry tomatoes, if present. *To peel tomatoes:* Cut a skin-deep *x* in the blossom end of each tomato. Drop into boiling water and blanch 15 seconds. Lift out with a slotted spoon and drop into a bowl of ice water. Skin will slip off easily. Alternatively, spear tomatoes with a fork and hold them over a gas or charcoal flame, turning them until skin splits. *To seed tomatoes:* Halve them horizontally. Hold each tomato half over a bowl, cut side down, and squeeze to remove seeds.

■ FRIED GREEN TOMATOES
Early cold snaps in the upper midwestern and Plains states often catch unripened tomatoes on the vine. Green tomato preserves are one way to use these tart fruits; an even faster way is to panfry them to serve as a vegetable.

> 4 **medium-sized green tomatoes**
> **Salt and freshly ground pepper, to taste**
> ⅓ **cup (approximately) flour**
> **Vegetable oil, for frying**
> 1 **egg, lightly beaten**

1. Slice tomatoes about ½ inch thick. Sprinkle lightly with salt and pepper. Dust slices with flour on all sides.

2. Pour oil into a large frying pan to a depth of about ¼ inch. Place over medium heat. While oil heats, dip tomato slices into egg to coat all sides.

3. Fry tomatoes, about half at a time, turning once, until golden brown on all sides. Serve hot.

Serves 6.

■ TOMATOES AU GRATIN
For a more attractive presentation, halve the tomatoes with a zigzag cut. The tomatoes can broil along with salmon steaks or lamb chops.

> 2 **large tomatoes, halved**
> 2 **tablespoons melted butter**
> ½ **cup freshly grated Parmesan or Romano cheese**
> ¼ **cup dry bread or cracker crumbs**
> ½ **teaspoon *each* paprika and dried basil**
> 2 **tablespoons dry white wine, tomato juice, or chicken broth**

1. Gently squeeze tomato halves to remove seeds.

2. Combine butter, cheese, crumbs, paprika, basil, and wine. Divide evenly among tomato halves, pressing lightly into tomatoes.

3. Broil on oiled aluminum foil until crumb mixture is slightly browned and tomato is warmed through (about 10 minutes).

Serves 4.

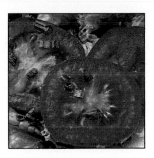

Fresh tomatoes in season have a naturally sweet flavor that needs only a simple dressing and some fresh herbs to show it off.

Sweet cherry tomatoes make a colorful and quick sauté. Buy them at the height of their season, when they are most flavorful; this simple treatment of olive oil and herbs is all they need.

■ SAUTEED CHERRY TOMATOES

This is a quick summer vegetable dish that gets its flavor from fresh herbs and tomatoes in the peak of their season.

    1 tablespoon olive oil, butter, or margarine
    1 pint cherry tomatoes, stemmed
    2 to 3 tablespoons finely chopped parsley *or*
      a mixture of parsley and fresh basil, oregano,
      or thyme
      Salt and freshly ground pepper, to taste

1. Heat oil in a large skillet over medium heat. Sauté tomatoes, stirring occasionally, for 2 to 3 minutes. Cook until tomatoes are soft, but do not let them burst.

2. Sprinkle with herbs. Toss to coat. Season to taste with salt and pepper.

Serves 6.

Recipes and Related Information

Asparagus With Lemon, Tomato, and Onions, 14; Basic Tomato Sauce, 516; Calzone With Sun-Dried Tomatoes, 448; Dried Tomatoes, 188; Fresh Tomato Sauce, 446; Northern-Style Tomato Sauce, 412; Okra and Tomato Stew, 397; Tomato Dipping Sauce, 238; Tomato Sauce, 428; Tomato-Shallot Sauce, 206; Tomatoes With Mozzarella and Basil, 507.

TONGS

Like spatulas and knives, tongs function as extensions of your hand. They permit you to turn steaks, hamburgers, bacon, and sausages at a safe distance from heat or spattering grease, and to pluck ears of corn or other vegetables from boiling water. Tongs can stand in as spaghetti and salad servers. Unlike a fork, tongs hold food without piercing the surface, so juices aren't lost. One type resembles heavy wire scissors and has handles and open loops for grasping. Another works like tweezers by spring action; the gripping end is wider than the shaft and sometimes has small teeth to enable a more secure hold. Made of stainless steel or chromed steel, tongs average 8 or 9 inches in length.

TOSS, TO

To mix by gently flipping or lifting food to combine or coat, as in tossing a salad. In restaurant kitchens this is often done with the hands to better feel the amount of dressing on the greens. In fact, many serious cooks do a great deal of mixing with their hands because they enjoy the tactile experience and because touch develops a more direct sensitivity to the food they are preparing.

TRUFFLE

The truffle, like the mushroom, is a fungus that grows in symbiosis with trees, specifically oak trees. Because the truffle grows underground and doesn't break the surface, it must be hunted with dogs or pigs trained to sniff it out. The impossibility of cultivation and the difficulty and unpredictability of the hunt make truffles one of the world's most expensive foods.

The two most prized varieties are the black truffle (found primarily in the Périgord and Quercy regions of France and the Umbria region of Italy) and the white truffle (found primarily in the Piedmont region of northern Italy). The black truffle has an earthy aroma and flavor that it imparts to any food it is cooked with. The white truffle is even more aromatic, with a garlicky, slightly cheesy aroma.

Use White truffles are rarely cooked; instead they are grated over hot foods as they are served. Pasta, polenta, or risotto with shaved white truffles is a great specialty of the Piedmont region. White truffles are also shaved over melted fontina cheese to make *fonduta,* the Italian version of fondue. Black truffles are used to garnish and flavor pâtés and terrines, especially those made of foie gras (fatted goose or duck liver). Black truffles flavor scrambled eggs, omelets, even mashed potatoes. Minced black truffles are added to sauces for beef, pheasant, and other rich meats and poultry.

Availability Fresh truffles are found in late autumn to winter. In season, they are imported to the United States and are sold at specialty markets. Many specialty markets also carry canned black truffles (whole or in pieces) and tubes of truffle paste throughout the year. While they cannot match the intense aroma of the fresh item, they are more available and more affordable.

Selection Choose aromatic, well-shaped truffles without blemishes.

Storage Truffles are perishable and are best used immediately. To store for a few days, bury truffles in a bed of rice in a covered glass jar and refrigerate, or bury them in a basket of whole fresh eggs and refrigerate.

Preparation Use a mushroom brush or an old toothbrush to gently clean truffles. Black truffles should be peeled (save the peel to flavor soups or sauces), then sliced paper-thin, with either a knife, vegetable peeler, or truffle slicer (see GADGETS). White truffles do not require peeling; shave them with a truffle slicer over hot food.

■ FETTUCCINE WITH WHITE TRUFFLES

This dish is delicious served as a starter for or alongside delicately flavored salmon.

> 2 tablespoons butter
> 1 tablespoon minced shallot
> 1 cup whipping cream
> 1 white truffle
> 2 ounces Italian fontina cheese
>   Salt and freshly ground pepper, to taste
> 1 pound fettuccine, preferably fresh, cooked in lightly salted water

1. Boil water for pasta. The sauce will take about 5 minutes to make, so time pasta accordingly.

2. Melt butter in a large skillet over medium heat. Add shallot and cook until soft and translucent. Pour in cream, turn heat to high, and reduce cream by half.

3. While sauce is reducing, use a vegetable peeler or truffle slicer to shave off enough tiny slices of truffle to make about 1 tablespoon.

4. When cream begins to thicken, add cheese and stir until it is melted. Season sauce to taste, turn down heat, and keep it at a simmer until pasta is ready.

5. Drain pasta thoroughly. Add truffle shavings to sauce, then immediately toss pasta in sauce. Serve immediately on warm plates with a little freshly ground pepper.

Serves 3 or 4 as a main dish, 6 as a first course.

■ CHICKEN IN HALF-MOURNING

This classic French dish gets its name from the circles of black truffles stuffed under the skin of the chicken. They show through as black shadows when the bird is cooked.

> 1 can (25 g) black truffles *or* 1 fresh black truffle, about 1¼ inches in diameter
> 2 tablespoons Madeira (if using fresh truffle)
> 2 whole chickens (3 to 3½ lb each)
> 1 medium onion, sliced and separated into rings
> 1 medium carrot, sliced
> 1 stalk celery, sliced
> ¼ teaspoon white peppercorns
> 3 sprigs parsley
> 4 cups Rich Chicken Stock (see page 561) *or* 2 cans (14½ oz each) chicken broth and ½ cup water
> 3 tablespoons butter or margarine
> ¼ cup flour
> ½ cup whipping cream
> 2 tablespoons fresh lemon juice
>   Salt

1. Drain and reserve liquid from canned truffles. Cut 12 thin slices from a truffle; finely chop rest of truffle(s). Place in bowl with liquid (or Madeira, if a fresh truffle).

2. Rinse chickens and pat dry; reserve giblets for another use. Remove and discard any excess fat. With two fingers, reach into each chicken from neck end and carefully loosen skin from flesh across breasts and tops of drumsticks. Using 6 truffle slices for each chicken, gently slide truffles under skin across breast and tops of drumsticks. Fasten neck and body cavities of each chicken with a skewer. Place chickens side by side in a deep, heavy Dutch oven just large enough to hold them both.

3. To chickens, add onion, carrot, celery, peppercorns, parsley, and stock. Bring stock to a boil over medium heat; then cover, reduce heat, and simmer until chickens are very tender when thighs are pierced with a fork (about 1½ hours). Remove chickens to a warm platter; cover with aluminum foil and keep warm.

4. Strain cooking liquid, discarding vegetables. Skim and discard fat. Return liquid to a boil over high heat, uncovered, until reduced to 2½ cups. Remove from heat.

5. In a 2- to 3-quart saucepan over medium heat, melt butter. Blend in flour; cook and stir until bubbly. Remove from heat; gradually blend in the 2½ cups reduced chicken broth. Cook, stirring until thickened and boiling. Blend in cream and return to a boil, stirring often. Stir in lemon juice and chopped truffles plus liquid (or Madeira). Add salt, if needed.

6. Spoon about a third of the sauce over and around chickens; serve remainder in a warm sauceboat. Use poultry shears to cut chickens into quarters to serve.

Serves 8.

TRUSSING POULTRY

Fold wing tips under ribs. Force legs down into wing joints to stabilize bird. Cut a piece of twine about four times length of bird (to measure, drape string around bird as shown above).

Lay string across and under neck opening; draw string up over wings and under drumsticks. Pull ends toward you between drumstick and breast on each side and cross over.

Bring string over ends of drumsticks, making sure it goes across end of breastbone. Take string under bird, flip bird over, and tie tightly with a half bow. Snip away extra string. Bird is now ready for cooking.

TRUSS, TO

To secure the appendages of a bird close to the body. Trussing holds the bird together during cooking so that, when finished, it has an attractive appearance and even shape. With stuffed poultry, trussing keeps the stuffing from falling out.

There are many ways to truss poultry. The simple tie method shown here is easy for the home cook to employ. If you wish, you can augment this method by closing up the cavity with small poultry skewers. It is very important to tie the bird tightly; the more tightly the string is drawn, the better and more rounded the cooked bird will be. Use a kitchen twine made of natural fiber and of as heavy a gauge as you can find. Very thin twine may cut into your hands when you are making the final pull. Some birds come with the legs held together by a metal clip, which serves the same purpose as trussing. Remove all trussing, whether by metal clip or string, before the bird is served.

Recipes and Related Information
Needle and Fastener, 384; Poultry, 468.

TURMERIC

Like its relative ginger, turmeric is a rhizome—an underground stem. It resembles ginger externally, but its color and flavor are very different. Turmeric has a bright yellow-orange color and a pungent, slightly acrid flavor.

Use Because of its vibrant color, turmeric is used as a fabric dye in Asia; in this country, it is sometimes employed to color margarine and other dairy products. It adds color and flavor to American-style mustard and is a major ingredient in commercial curry powders and in many homemade Indian spice blends. Turmeric is also used to color and flavor pickles, Indonesian rice dishes, and Balinese roast pig. Slices of fresh turmeric are used by Southeast Asian cooks to flavor and color soups.

Availability Fresh turmeric is sold in a few Southeast Asian markets; dried whole turmeric is sometimes available in Indian and Southeast Asian markets. Dried ground turmeric is found on supermarket spice racks.

Selection Packaged seasonings lose quality after a while. Try to buy from a store that restocks its spice section fairly often.

Storage Ground turmeric will keep in a cool, dark, dry place for up to six months.

TURNIP

A sweet, crisp-textured root vegetable, the turnip has the squat round shape of a spinning top. Its flesh is white, its thin skin white with purple shoulders. When grown in cool climates and picked young, the turnip is mild, crisp, and sweet; turnips grown in hot weather can develop hot flavors, and older turnips can be woody inside. Turnip greens are also edible when young (see GREENS).

Use Young turnips can be peeled, sliced, and eaten raw with dips or in salads. More often, however, turnips are boiled or steamed, then tossed with butter and parsley. Turnips can also be boiled and mashed with butter and cream, pureed for soup, or added to soups. In France turnips are a sign of spring and are often paired with roast duck on spring menus.

Availability   Turnips are sold in many supermarkets the year around but are best in the cool months.

Selection   Turnips should be firm to the touch, not spongy or rubbery, and should feel heavy for their size. Avoid large turnips, which may be woody inside.

Storage   Turnips will keep several weeks in a cool, humid place or in the refrigerator.

Preparation   Wash, trim ends, and peel.

Cooking   See BOIL, STEAM, STIR-FRY.

> **Recipes and Related Information**
> *New England Boiled Dinner, 42; Winter Salad of Beets and Turnips, 48.*

UGLI FRUIT

The ugli fruit is a cross between three citrus fruits: the grapefruit, the orange, and the tangerine. It is about the size and color of a yellow grapefruit, but its thick rind is bumpy. Its pink flesh is sweeter than both the grapefruit and the orange, and it has few seeds.

Use   Ugli fruit, which is grown in Jamaica, is most often eaten out of hand like an orange. However, it may be used in any of the ways oranges and grapefruits are: in sherbets, sorbets, or fruit salads, for example.

Availability   Ugli fruit is sold in some specialty produce markets in the winter.

Selection   The skin of ripe ugli fruit has a hint of orange.

Storage   Refrigerate and use within one week.

Preparation   Ugli fruit peels easily. Peel and section as you would an orange, or halve and section as you would grapefruit.

UNMOLD, TO

Both *unmold* and *turn out* have the same meaning when used in a recipe: to remove food from its container, with the implication that the food is firm enough to hold its shape when out of the mold. *Unmold* describes removing a gelatin-based mixture from a mold. *Turn out* usually refers to removing a baked pastry from the pan in which it was baked.

Oiling mold or spraying with vegetable cooking spray will aid unmolding. The best method is to dip mold quickly into a pan of very hot water; this should take at the most 5 seconds (less for cream-based mixtures). If you notice a slight movement of the food within the mold, or a little melting at the edges as you try to slide it from side to side, you will know it is ready to be removed. Too much

time in hot water will melt some of the gelatin, destroying detail and shape.

If molding onto a serving plate, first rinse plate with cold water. The water will make the plate slick, which will allow you to center the food by sliding it gently in place. Place serving plate over mold, invert it rapidly, and give mold a firm shake or tap. Molded food should drop smoothly onto plate. Sometimes it may be necessary to slip a thin-bladed knife between food and mold to release the vacuum that holds food in place. Then, if it doesn't come right out, leave mold inverted on plate for a few minutes and let gravity do its work. If a chilled mold, return to refrigerator to firm up before serving.

Cakes, cupcakes, muffins, and loaf breads are turned out by inverting the baking pan over a wire cooling rack and lifting off the pan. Some recipes suggest letting baked product sit in its pan for 10 or 15 minutes before turning out; the steam that builds up as the food cools will help release food from pan. To remove tarts from tins with loose bottoms, push up the removable bottom and allow sides of tin to fall away from tart. For tarts baked in a tart band, lift off the ring, then slide tart onto a cooling rack.

> **Recipes and Related Information**
> *Gelatin, 264; Mold, 369.*

VANILLA BEAN

The vanilla bean is the pod of an orchid native to Central America. When ripe and ready for handpicking, the pod is yellow and odorless. Its characteristic aroma and dark color develop during a period of slow sunning and drying. Whole commercial vanilla bean is generally about 4 to 5 inches long and chocolate brown. Slit open lengthwise, the pod reveals hundreds of minuscule black seeds, which appear as specks in many high-quality vanilla ice creams.

Use   Vanilla is prized for the flavor it imparts to other dishes, primarily sweets. It is the most popular ice cream flavor in America, and it enhances other custard desserts as well. Vanilla is almost always used to flavor flan (*crème caramel*), custard sauce (*crème anglaise*), pastry cream, and rice pudding.

Vanilla adds its intriguing taste to most cakes and cookies and is often used to flavor whipped cream. Vanilla is also appealing with many fruit desserts. Pears, peaches, apples, or apricots may be poached in a syrup flavored with vanilla beans; it is commonly added to applesauce and banana desserts. It is often paired with chocolate because it heightens the chocolate flavor. The Aztec emperor Montezuma was said to have flavored his hot chocolate with vanilla. Vanilla Sugar (see Fragrant Vanilla Sugar, at right) can be sprinkled on strawberries, pie crusts, and ricotta cheese; many cookie recipes call for rolling the finished cookies in vanilla sugar.

TIPS

FRAGRANT VANILLA SUGAR

When either granulated or confectioners' sugar is infused with the flavor and perfume of vanilla bean, the result is a delicious product that can be substituted for plain sugar.

Vanilla Granulated Sugar   Split a vanilla bean in half lengthwise. Place both halves in a tall jar. Fill jar with 1 to 2 cups granulated sugar. Cover and let stand for at least 24 hours for sugar to absorb vanilla flavor. Replenish sugar as you use it. Vanilla will continue to flavor sugar for up to one year.

Stirring may dislodge some of the tiny seeds inside the split vanilla bean. They're a potent flavor as they become distributed throughout the sugar. If these tiny specks become too numerous, strain sugar through a fine sieve as you use it, returning seeds to sugar in jar.

Vanilla Confectioners' Sugar   Substitute confectioners' sugar for granulated sugar in the directions given above.

Availability Whole vanilla bean is found in the spice section of most supermarkets and specialty food stores. All supermarkets carry bottled pure vanilla extract and imitation vanilla extract. Pure extract is more expensive but is far superior in flavor. Specialty stores may offer several brands of pure extract for you to choose from.

Selection Whole vanilla beans should be pliable and should have a fine white "bloom" of vanillin crystals on the outside. Avoid any that are excessively hard and dry. The best pure vanilla extract has a rich, well-balanced aroma and flavor.

Many American tourists are tempted to bring back vanilla extract from Mexico where it is inexpensive and exceptionally strong. However, some "pure" Mexican vanilla extract may be adulterated with coumarin, a plant derivative with vanilla flavor. Unfortunately, coumarin is mildly toxic. To be safe, purchase Mexican vanilla extract only from a source that can guarantee its purity.

Storage Vanilla bean can be stored for several months in a tightly covered jar in a cool place; if the bean is to be used again after cooking, rinse, wipe bean free of liquid, and store as directed. Store vanilla extract in a cool, dark place for up to one year.

Preparation Like all alcohol-based extracts, vanilla extract is highly volatile (its flavor dissipates when exposed to air and heat). For maximum effect, add it to cool or cooling liquids. Whole vanilla bean can be added to a sauce or simmering liquid, then strained out. Rinsed and dried, the bean can be reused. Alternatively, split the vanilla bean lengthwise and scrape the seeds into the simmering liquid.

Recipes and Related Information
Custard, 168; Extract and Essence, 213; Ice Cream and Frozen Dessert, 308.

VARIETY MEAT

The term *variety meats* (or *offal*) is applied to the innards and the extremities of the animals we eat. In the United States these are among the least appreciated items in the meat case, although they are also among the most affordable and most delicious. In other countries, variety meats are often highly prized; European, Latin, and Asian cooks have developed countless dishes that take advantage of the special flavors and textures of variety meats.

Use Around the world, variety meats are enjoyed in appetizers, soups, salads, and main courses. In Italy sweetbreads and kidneys are used as a garnish for pasta and risotto. Tongue is often eaten cold as a salad or sandwich filling. Brains are also occasionally eaten cold, with mayonnaise or vinaigrette. As a main course, variety meats can be sautéed, braised, grilled, or fried. Delicate

tripe is better suited to slow braising or to the hearty soups popular in Mexico and Spain. Kidneys can be grilled with bacon, and brains can be coated with batter and fried.

Availability Few American supermarkets stock fresh variety meat because the meats are highly perishable and there is not a strong demand for them. Ethnic markets and supermarkets with a large Latin, Asian, or black clientele have a larger selection of variety meats. Most butcher shops can order them for you. A discussion of the most-available variety meats follows.

Selection Because variety meats are highly perishable, freshness should be your first consideration when purchasing. It is advisable to buy from a butcher who can attest to the freshness of the meats and who will let you smell and inspect the items before buying. Freezing tends to damage the delicate texture of most variety meats. However, if they were frozen while still very fresh, were carefully wrapped, and were thawed slowly, they are a better choice than meats that are labeled fresh but are actually several days old.

Storage Again, remember that fresh variety meats are perishable and keep only a few days. If purchased fresh, variety meats should be refrigerated and used within two days. If purchased frozen, they can be kept in the freezer for up to three months; thaw slowly in the refrigerator before cooking.

Preparation See specific variety meats.

Cooking See BRAISE, FRY, GRILL, POACH, SAUTE.

BRAINS

In the United States, the brains offered on restaurant menus are almost invariably calf's brains, prized for their smooth texture and delicate flavor. However, pork, beef, and lamb brains are also available to cooks who seek them out. Check specialty butchers and ethnic markets for brains; they may have to be ordered in advance.

Brains consist of two symmetrical, ridged lobes held together by a thin membrane. They should be firm and plump, with a moist, shiny surface, and with no off-odor. Soak the brains in cold water for 30 minutes, changing the water several times, to draw out blood and make the membrane easier to remove. Peel away the membrane; soak brains an additional hour to whiten them.

Some recipes call for poaching brains in a seasoned court bouillon until firm (about 25 minutes for calf's brains). After poaching, they may be sliced and served with vinaigrette or with brown butter, coated with batter and fried, or scrambled with eggs. Other recipes call for a brief blanching (about 5 minutes) to be followed by further cooking. After blanching, they may be floured and pan-fried in butter; coated with butter and bread crumbs and baked; or sautéed with mushrooms and cream.

BRAINS IN BROWN BUTTER SAUCE

This is the classic recipe for brains, and for good reason—the sauce has just the right amount of tartness to give the tender unctuousness of the brains a little bite. If desired, with this recipe poaching can be omitted; the brains will be a little stronger tasting, but even more tender.

    1 pound lamb's or calf's brains, soaked,
       trimmed, and, if desired, poached (see page 586)
       Salt and white pepper, to taste
    ½ cup Clarified Butter (see page 68)
    1 tablespoon drained capers
    ¼ cup plus 1 tablespoon minced parsley
    ¼ cup fresh lemon juice
    ¾ cup sifted flour
    2 tablespoons unsalted butter
    1 tablespoon olive oil
    1 large lemon, cut in 8 wedges

1. Slice brains ½ inch thick. Dust lightly with salt and pepper and set aside. In a slow oven, gently warm a small, heavy bowl and a plate that will cover the bowl comfortably.

2. In a medium saucepan, heat Clarified Butter over medium heat; let darken to golden brown, then remove from heat. Stir in capers and the ¼ cup parsley; pour into warmed bowl (reserving saucepan), cover with plate, and return to oven to keep warm.

3. Pour lemon juice into saucepan used to cook butter. Over high heat, cook down lemon juice to about 1 tablespoon. Season with salt and pepper; add to warm butter mixture, cover with plate, and return to oven to keep warm.

4. Dredge brain slices in flour; shake off excess. In a large skillet, heat the 2 tablespoons unsalted butter and olive oil over medium heat. When butter stops foaming, add brains; increase heat to medium-high and brown on both sides until golden (about 3 minutes per side). Remove slices with a slotted spoon to a serving dish; pour reserved butter sauce over them, and serve garnished with 1 tablespoon parsley and lemon wedges.

Serves 4.

CHITTERLINGS

The large intestines of pigs are called chitterlings. Some markets sell whole chitterlings; others slit them and cut them into sections. Fresh chitterlings should be pinkish beige and moist; they may have a strong odor. To prepare, cut into lengths and slit open. Soak two hours in several changes of acidulated water; drain, dry, and pull off fatty inner lining.

Chitterlings may be simmered three to four hours with tomato sauce, herbs, and spices; they may be marinated or highly seasoned and stuffed into chitterling casings to make sausages. Sausages made of tripe or chitterlings are known as *andouilles* in France and are quite popular.

EARS

Fresh pig's ears should be pale pink and dry, with a smooth, not sticky, texture. To prepare, scrape ears with a small knife or stiff brush to remove any hairs; to singe off stubborn hairs, hold ear over an open flame. They should be parboiled 5 minutes, then rinsed and kept in acidulated water until ready to cook. French cooks stew pig's ears with pig's feet, vegetables, and herbs. German cooks dice the parboiled ears and braise them with peas, herbs, and potatoes. In Portugal the ears are braised whole until tender with herbs, garlic, tomatoes, and peppers.

FEET

Calf's feet are a rich source of gelatin and are often added to veal stock or a slow-cooked stew to give it body. Moroccan cooks make a highly spiced stew of calf's feet, bulgur, and chick-peas. In Germany pig's feet are stewed with sauerkraut; in France they are braised until tender, then rolled in butter and bread crumbs and broiled. In Greece,

Delicate sweetbreads are enriched with a wine-flavored sauce and fresh, sautéed mushrooms. The recipe appears on page 590.

Steak and Kidney Pie is traditional lunchtime fare in pubs throughout England. Broiled tomatoes and a hearty English beer or ale are appropriate accompaniments.

where lamb is popular, lamb's feet are simmered until tender and served with egg and lemon sauce. Chicken feet are used by cooks all over the world to give body to chicken stock. Chinese cooks braise duck feet with black beans and serve them as dim sum, a tea-house snack.

Select feet that are moist; avoid those that are sticky, dry, or blemished, or that have an off-odor. Scrape or singe off any stray hairs. Some recipes call for feet split lengthwise; a butcher can easily do this for you.

Recipes: Menudo, 591.

FRIES

The testicles of lamb, pigs, beef, and veal are known as fries. They are also sometimes referred to as mountain oysters; beef and veal fries are sometimes also known as Rocky Mountain oysters or prairie oysters. Fries should be plump and firm, with their outer skin intact. To prepare, slit the three layers of skin with a small sharp knife without slitting the flesh; pull off the skin. Soak fries in several changes of acidulated water to draw off any blood. Cover fries with cold salted water, bring to a boil, and simmer until firm (6 to 7 minutes). Drain and pat dry. They may then be sliced, coated with egg and bread crumbs, and fried; dipped in fritter batter and fried; browned slowly in butter and spices; or simmered in a highly seasoned tomato sauce. Fries are highly perishable.

GIZZARD

Chicken gizzard, the equivalent of the stomach in other animals, is tough but flavorful if properly prepared. It has a tough membrane that must be trimmed away. The gizzard may then be diced and browned slowly in butter with other giblets for giblet gravy, stuffing, or stew. Cajun cooks add finely ground cooked gizzards and black pepper to steamed rice to make dirty rice. Fresh gizzards should be plump and shiny, without an off-odor.

Recipes: Roast Turkey With Giblet Gravy, 474.

HEAD

Recipes for pig's, lamb's, goat's, or calf's head are common in many cuisines. Mexican families may roast a whole goat, including its head, as a celebration dish; Greek families do the same with goat or lamb. Whole heads may be boned, laid flat, and wrapped around a stuffing; they may be halved and baked with vegetables until tender; or they may be boned, poached, and served hot with vinaigrette, *salsa verde* (Italian parsley and caper sauce), or fresh tomato salsa and hot tortillas.

Ask the butcher to remove the eyes and to bone or split the head, as the recipe requires. Soak the head in several changes of acidulated water to draw out blood. Keep in acidulated water if cooking that day; otherwise, pat dry, wrap in plastic, and refrigerate for up to three days.

HEART

The deep-red heart muscle is richly flavored but tough if not properly handled. To prepare heart, trim away any visible fat, fibrous tissue, and tubes. Large beef hearts may be stuffed, tied, and braised whole. In Peru beef heart is served as an appetizer, after being cubed, marinated, skewered, and grilled over coals. Hearts can be braised with wine, herbs, and vegetables or cut in julienne strips and stir-fried with vegetables and soy sauce. Poultry hearts can be minced, sautéed in butter, and added to stuffings or gravy. To keep large hearts tender, they should either be sliced thinly and cooked quickly or kept whole or in large pieces for slow braising.

KIDNEY

Lamb and pork kidneys consist of a single lobe; beef and veal kidneys are multilobed. Beef, lamb, and pork kidneys are dark red; veal kidneys are slightly lighter. Kidneys have a rich flavor and firm texture and are appealing on their own or added to other dishes. English cooks have many kidney dishes in their repertoire, including the famous Steak and Kidney Pie and kidneys broiled with bacon or braised with mushrooms and cream. The English also find a place for kidneys on the breakfast table. Chinese cooks stir-fry pork kidneys with vegetables; French cooks braise kidneys with mustard or mushrooms and cream, or grill them with herb butter.

Beef, veal, and pork kidneys should be plump, firm, and encased in a shiny membrane. Lamb kidneys are often sold encased in their fat, which should be off-white. Avoid kidneys with a strong odor.

To prepare kidneys, trim away any fat and connective tissue and pull off the outer membrane. Beef and veal kidneys should be halved to allow for easier removal of fat and tissues.

▪ STEAK AND KIDNEY PIE

Some of the most typical and enjoyable English foods can be found in pubs (public houses), especially at noontime. There you are likely to find well-prepared cold plates, fine cheeses, and exceptional meat pies such as this well-known preparation. The pie may be assembled in advance (through step 3), covered, and refrigerated for several hours before baking. Accompany Steak and Kidney Pie with a green vegetable and a crisp salad. The pastry is easily made from frozen puff pastry shells, available in the freezer cases of specialty food stores and well-stocked supermarkets. The frozen shells will thaw to a consistency suitable for rolling in about 20 minutes.

- 6 tablespoons flour
- 1½ teaspoons salt
- ¼ teaspoon *each* ground pepper, dried thyme, chervil, marjoram, and summer savory
- 2 pounds boneless top round steak, cut in ½-inch cubes
- ½ pound beef or lamb kidneys, sliced
- ½ pound mushrooms, quartered
- 2 tablespoons butter or margarine
- ½ cup dry red wine or Beef Stock (see page 560) or regular-strength canned beef broth
- 6 frozen puff pastry patty shells (10-oz package), thawed
- 1 egg, beaten with 1 teaspoon water

1. Preheat oven to 325° F. In a large bowl mix flour, salt, pepper, thyme, chervil, marjoram, and savory. Mix in steak cubes and kidney slices, coating well with flour mixture.

2. Sauté mushrooms in butter until lightly browned.

3. Place half the beef and kidney mixture in a 2-quart, 2-inch-deep baking dish. Top with mushrooms, then with remaining meat. Pour on wine or stock.

4. Arrange the patty shells, overlapping slightly, on a floured board or pastry cloth. Roll out pastry into a slightly larger shape than the top of the casserole. Lay pastry over meat mixture; trim and flute edge, sealing it to baking dish. Pierce or slit top in several places to allow steam to escape. Trim with pastry scraps cut into decorative shapes, if desired.

5. Brush pastry with egg mixture. Bake until meat is tender (insert a long wooden skewer to test) and pastry is well browned (1½ to 2 hours). Serve immediately.

Serves 6 to 8.

LIVER

Appreciated by cooks throughout the world, liver has a rich flavor and smooth texture. Beef, veal, pork, lamb, duck, and chicken all have delectable livers that may be used in countless ways. Beef and veal livers can be roasted whole but they are usually sliced and pan-fried. Calf's liver with onions is a popular Venetian dish. Chicken livers can be fried with bacon and served with rice or pasta. Duck livers make an unctuous, savory mousse or a rich topping for pasta. Chopped liver, that staple of the Jewish delicatessen, is usually made with beef liver but may also contain chicken liver; it is served as an appetizer with crackers or as a sandwich filling. German cooks make delicate calf's liver dumplings to float in soup. Chinese cooks stir-fry pork liver with green onions and mushrooms. Goose liver is made into a rich, creamy spread by Middle European cooks. The famous fatted goose and duck livers of France (foie gras) are one of the world's greatest delicacies, served cold in the form of a terrine or pâté, or sliced, pan-fried, and served hot.

Liver should be firm and moist, with a shiny appearance, and without any off-odor. True calf's liver is easy to distinguish from beef liver by appearance: Calf's liver is a pale reddish brown; beef liver is a dark reddish brown that verges on purple. To prepare livers, trim away any visible fat and tough connective tissue. Calf and beef livers, if purchased whole, both have a thin exterior membrane that should be pulled off. Liver is sometimes soaked in milk for one hour before cooking to "sweeten" it. Cook liver briefly and quickly; overcooked liver is dry, tough, and disagreeable.

Recipes: Curried Chicken or Duck Liver Pâté in Aspic, 416; Chicken or Duck Liver Mousse, 372.

SWEETBREADS

The thymus glands of calves or young lambs, sweetbreads gradually shrink as the animal ages. They are delicate in taste, smooth and soft in texture, and are considered a delicacy by many diners. Calf's sweetbreads are readily available from most specialty butchers, either fresh or frozen. Lamb sweetbreads may require special ordering. Sweetbreads should be plump and firm, with the exterior membrane intact.

Soak sweetbreads in several changes of cold water for one hour to draw out any blood. Then blanch in simmering acidulated water for 3 to 5 minutes (depending on size) and plunge into cold water to firm them. When cold, drain them and trim away any membranes and connective tissues. If serving whole, chill several hours under a weight to firm and shape; otherwise, separate with hands into smaller lobes.

Sweetbreads may be braised with peas or with mushrooms and cream; wrapped in bacon, skewered, and grilled; or braised in butter and served atop spinach or sorrel purée. They are also sautéed, poached, and broiled.

■ **SWEETBREADS AND
MUSHROOM-MARSALA SAUCE**

The exuberance of Marsala and the luxury of sautéed mushrooms unite in a light, buttery sauce that bathes sweetbreads in a warm, rich Italianate glow. Serve with French-fried potatoes to dip in the sauce, and follow with a tartly dressed green salad.

          ½ cup unsalted butter
          1 small onion, minced
          1 medium carrot, finely diced
          2 tablespoons minced shallot
          ¼ cup finely diced mild cooked ham
          ½ pound mushrooms, sliced
        1½ to 2 pounds sweetbreads, soaked,
             blanched, trimmed, weighted, and sliced
             if pieces are large (see page 589)
             Salt and freshly ground pepper, to taste
          ½ cup Marsala
          1 cup Beef Stock (see page 560) or
             canned consommé
          ¼ teaspoon dried marjoram
          3 tablespoons minced parsley
        1½ tablespoons flour

1. Preheat oven to 350° F. In a flameproof, heavy-bottomed, 2-quart casserole, melt 3 tablespoons of the butter over low heat. Add onion, carrot, shallot, and ham; cover and cook over low heat until tender (about 10 minutes). Uncover and add mushrooms and 3 more tablespoons butter. Set remaining 2 tablespoons butter aside to soften. Increase heat under casserole to medium and sauté vegetables until mushrooms darken and begin to soften.

2. Season sweetbreads with salt and pepper. Combine with vegetable mixture in casserole. Pour on Marsala and stock; add marjoram, 2 tablespoons of the parsley, and additional salt and pepper to taste. Cover and bake 45 minutes.

3. Remove casserole from oven. With a slotted spoon, remove sweetbreads and most of the vegetables to a bowl. Set a colander over bowl and invert bowl over casserole so that liquid from sweetbread mixture drains back into casserole. Set sweetbread mixture aside in bowl, covered, and keep warm.

4. Over highest heat, boil down liquid in casserole until reduced by ½ to 1 cup, stirring frequently and scraping sides and bottom of casserole. Meanwhile, work remaining 2 tablespoons butter together with flour to make beurre manié. When liquid has reduced, add beurre manié to casserole. Lower heat to medium, and cook, stirring constantly, until butter melts and sauce thickens (about 1 minute). Correct seasoning. To serve, spoon sweetbreads onto a serving dish or individual plates. Pour on sauce and garnish with remaining parsley.

Serves 4 to 6.

TAIL

Beef tails (usually identified as oxtails) and pig's tails are appreciated by many diners for their rich meat and gelatinous texture. Slow braising tenderizes them and softens the gelatinous cartilage. Both oxtails and pig's tails may be stewed in wine with herbs and aromatic vegetables. The pieces can also be braised, then coated with butter and bread crumbs and broiled.

Fresh oxtails are almost always sold pretrimmed and sliced. They should have bright red meat and white fat. Pig's tails are available from ethnic markets; the meat should be firm and rosy red, the fat creamy white.

Recipes: Sherried Oxtail Soup, 501.

TONGUE

Fresh tongue—whether beef, veal, lamb, or pork—should be firm, and with no off-odor. Tongue has a rich flavor and firm meaty texture and is appealing on its own or in combination with other foods. Small whole lamb tongues can be pickled or preserved in aspic. Whole tongue can be poached and served hot or cold with mayonnaise, vinaigrette, or *salsa verde* (Italian parsley and caper sauce); it may be braised with wine and vegetables and served hot in a rich sauce. Poached tongue may also be cubed and tossed with cold vegetables and a vinaigrette for a salad. Whole tongue may be corned or smoked, thinly sliced, and served in sandwiches, traditionally on rye bread with mustard.

Fresh tongue should be soaked in several changes of cold water for two to three hours to draw out blood before cooking. A corned tongue should then be blanched 5 minutes and rinsed to remove excess salt. Poach fresh or corned tongue in court bouillon until tender (1½ to 2 hours for beef tongue, 30 minutes for lamb tongue). Drain; when cool enough to handle, trim away fat and gristle and peel off skin, which is easier to remove while tongue is hot.

Recipes: Boiled Dinner Bolognese, 530.

TRIPE

The muscular lining from two of the four parts of a ruminant's stomach is called tripe. Beef tripe is the most common; some butchers may be able to obtain veal and lamb tripe by special order. Smooth-textured tripe comes from the first stomach; honeycomb tripe, which owes its name to its appearance, comes from the second stomach. Fresh tripe should have an ivory color and no off-odor. By the time it appears in the market, it has already been cleaned, soaked, and precooked. It should be rinsed in cold water and patted dry.

Tripe is extremely bland, which is partly its virtue. During long, slow cooking with vegetables, herbs, and gelatinous meat such as calf's feet, it absorbs their flavor and becomes tender. Tripe can be cooked as little as one or two hours, but it is often encased in a tightly sealed container and braised slowly for up to 24 hours. French cooks braise tripe with onions, carrots, and cider for at least 12 hours to make *tripe à la mode de Caen.* Spanish cooks braise tripe with tomato and sweet peppers or simmer it with chick-peas and *chorizo* to make a one-dish meal. Italian cooks braise tripe in tomato sauce and then garnish it with basil and Parmesan cheese.

■ MENUDO
Tripe soup

To hear Mexicans talk of the beneficial effects of menudo, one would expect to find it included in the pharmacopoeia, along with other medicines and remedies, instead of in a cookbook. It has the reputation for fighting the ailments of the *cruda,* or hangover, and is therefore traditionally served on New Year's Day.

  1 **calf's foot, cut into pieces**
  3 **pounds tripe, washed, trimmed of fat, and cut into 1-inch squares**
  4 **quarts water**
  2 **teaspoons salt**
  3 **ancho chiles (see Note)**
  1 **fresh Anaheim chile (see Note)**
  1 **large onion, chopped**
  3 **cloves garlic, crushed**
  1 **teaspoon freshly ground pepper**
  2 **cans (29 oz each) hominy, drained, *or*
      5 cups cooked hominy**
  ½ **cup cilantro**
      Lime wedges, chopped onion, fresh mint, dried oregano, salsa, or sliced jalapeño, for garnish

1. Place calf's foot, tripe, the water, and salt in a large stockpot. Bring to a boil, reduce heat, and simmer, uncovered, for 2½ hours, skimming occasionally.

2. Remove and discard stems and seeds from chiles; crumble chiles into a blender or electric minichopper, and process until finely ground.

3. Remove calf's foot from pot. Remove any meat remaining on the bones and discard the bones. Coarsely chop meat and return it to soup. Add onion, garlic, pepper, and ground chiles, and continue to cook, uncovered, for another 2½ hours.

4. Add hominy and bring soup to a boil; reduce heat and simmer 1 to 2 hours. Soup will be finished in 1 hour, but an additional hour of cooking will improve the flavor. Stir in cilantro during the last 30 minutes of cooking.

5. Serve soup with garnishes passed separately.

Serves 8.

Note Two to three tablespoons mild ground red chile without spices may be substituted for the *ancho* and Anaheim chiles.

VEAL

The meat of young calves, usually no more than four months old, is the source of veal. (After six months, calf meat is considered beef.) The palest, most delicate veal is from milk-fed calves. Even young calves, if fed a grass diet, will develop red meat with stronger flavor. Veal is prized for its tender texture and mild flavor and subsequent versatility in the kitchen.

Use The delicate flavor of veal is appreciated by European cooks, with Italians having perhaps the widest repertoire of veal dishes: veal scaloppine (thin cutlets), veal stews and braises, stuffed whole breast of veal, and veal stuffings for pasta. French cooks also have a way with veal stews and sautés; Austrians are famous for their breaded veal cutlets. In Spain veal is stewed with sausage and peppers, and veal kidneys are cooked with sherry.

Veal bones are high in natural gelatin and are thus preferred by many cooks for making stock (see STOCK AND SOUP). A stock made with veal bones and some meaty veal pieces will have the rich body and mild flavor that is desirable in many French sauces.

Quickly cooked Veal Chops With Tarragon make a delicious foil for the subtle flavors of a Pinot Noir. An assortment of fresh vegetables will complete the meal nicely. The recipe is on page 593.

Selection   Because veal comes from young animals, it lacks the extensive intramuscular fat (marbling) typical of good beef. The best indication of quality in veal is its color. Look for veal with pale meat and white fat. Its texture should be fine, not coarse.

Successful veal cookery requires selecting the right method for each cut. Despite the fact that this meat comes from animals with underdeveloped muscles, all veal is not necessarily tender. It lacks the intramuscular marbling that acts as shortening by coating the muscle fibers and making them easier to cut. In addition, some cuts of veal are high in collagen, a protein which can be softened by long, slow cooking but which toughens if improperly handled. See Cuts of Veal at left.

Storage   Follow storage directions for BEEF.

Preparation   Trim off or slash the membrane that surrounds each veal scallop to prevent the meat from curling in the pan. In most recipes, scallops are pounded before cooking to flatten them as thin as possible (see POUND).

Cooking   Veal is generally cooked by moist-heat methods because it does not have enough natural fat to baste itself. Even when roasted, veal is either basted with a liquid or cooked in a covered pot in order to develop moisture in the form of steam. In many recipes, veal is paired with a sauce to compensate for its lack of flavorful fat. Veal chops, although lean, can be broiled or grilled; watch carefully to see that they don't overcook and get dry. Boneless roasts are braised or roasted in the oven. See BRAISE, BROIL, ROAST.

CUTS OF VEAL

The primal cuts of veal are similar to those of a full-grown beef steer (see page 38), but there are fewer of them. The rump, round, and hind shank, for instance, are all considered a part of the leg, and the breast is a single cut.

Ground veal   The breast and/or the shoulder are the cuts that are ground. Unless it has been mixed with beef suet, it contains only 20 percent fat or less. If the veal has not been ground with a meat grinder, it is relatively difficult to process at home; the meat is too slippery to shred well in a food processor.

Leg of veal   Most commonly, the leg is boned and sold as a roast. Butchers also divide the leg into its separate muscles and then slice the muscles thinly to make cutlets and scallops; the center cut of the leg (which is often labeled as a round) is probably the major source of these prized cuts. (More reasonably priced veal scallops can be cut at home from a boned leg.) Occasionally one finds other versions of leg of veal: Veal "round" roasts may actually be from the leg rather than the shoulder, as are bone-in rump roasts (cut from the area where the leg joins the hip). These and the center cut leg, are more tender than the shank half leg, which is occasionally sold as a roast but should really be braised.

Loin of veal   The loin includes numerous smaller cuts, not all of them available from a typical meat case. Loin chops are, of course, the most familiar, and can be sautéed, broiled, braised, or baked. The next most common cut from this section is the boneless rolled loin roast. This and several cuts from the leg are perhaps the most suitable cuts of veal for genuine roasting; all require basting. The rolled loin can be unrolled, filled with stuffing, and rerolled (tied in several places with kitchen twine) for an elegant roast. A bone-in loin includes the T-bone, and is a V-shaped cut that's also suitable for roasting.

Shoulder of veal   This cut is much more tender than the corresponding part of a steer, although tougher than the rib, loin, or leg. The shoulder is excellent for stewing and braising. Although this cut contains many membranes, long, slow cooking breaks down the chewiness. Boneless shoulder is often sold as a roast as well. Veal neck, a cut from the shoulder, is quite tough and must be cooked slowly by moist heat. Shoulder of veal is sometimes cut into steaks, which, despite the steak designation, should be braised, rather than grilled.

Veal breast   Although tough, bony, and (for veal) rather fatty, the breast is always economical. With the bone in, the breast can be cut into riblets and grilled. More popular are boned breasts, with a pocket cut in them for stuffing. Ground veal is usually made from this cut. It is much less fatty than other ground meats.

Veal foreshank   Usually this cut is sold under its Italian name, *osso buco*. Although tougher than the hind shank (which is often sold as part of the leg), and full of membranes, it is perhaps the richest-flavored cut when cooked slowly in liquid long enough to dissolve the sinews. The bones also yield delicious marrow. Veal foreshank is a common ingredient in meat stocks (and the sauces and soups based on meat stocks), yielding the gelatin that makes stocks rich and substantial. This cut is usually sold at a very reasonable price, but it has a very high ratio of bone to meat. As meat for stock, however, where the bones play a major role as a thickener, it's a superb value.

Veal rib   Occasionally veal rib is sold as an entire rack or a crown roast for use as a roast. More often, the rib section is cut into tender, flavorful chops.

Veal sirloin   Not common in butcher shops, veal sirloin is the portion of the loin next to the leg. It's a delicious cut, but since a calf is so much smaller than a steer, it's a bony one; as a result, this cut yields relatively little meat for its premium price. Veal sirloin chops are high-priced and delicious. Many butchers also cut the boned sirloin into veal scallops, although genuine veal scaloppine is supposed to be cut from the center portion of the leg.

■   **SPINACH-STUFFED BREAST OF VEAL**

Breast of veal, a large and dramatic-looking dish, is actually cooked covered for part of the time to keep the meat moist. With its meaty stuffing of ground beef, spinach, and cheese, this baked veal breast is frankly Italian. Accompanied by a salad or green vegetable, it will serve a large group economically and well.

1   breast of veal (3 to 3½ lb)
2   tablespoons olive oil or vegetable oil
1   cup *each* Chicken Stock (see page 560) or full-strength canned chicken broth and dry white wine

Ground Beef and Spinach Stuffing

½   pound ground beef
1   medium onion, chopped
1   clove garlic, minced or pressed
¼   pound small mushrooms, thinly sliced
1   package (9 or 10 oz) frozen chopped spinach, thawed and squeezed dry
½   cup soft bread crumbs
1   cup grated Monterey jack cheese
1   egg, slightly beaten
½   teaspoon *each* salt and dried basil
⅛   teaspoon freshly ground pepper

1. Have butcher cut pocket in veal breast for the stuffing. Preheat oven to 325° F.

2. Fill pocket with stuffing and fasten open end with small metal skewers. Place meat in large roasting pan. Brush with oil. Pour on ¾ cup each of the stock and the wine. Cover with foil and bake until meat is very tender (2 hours). Increase oven temperature to 350° F and continue baking, uncovered, for 25 to 30 minutes longer. Brush occasionally with pan drippings to brown meat. Remove meat to heated platter and keep warm.

3. To loosen pan drippings, add remaining ¼ cup each of broth and wine, stirring over high heat until liquid is reduced by about one third. Serve sauce separately. To carve veal, cut between rib bones.

Serves 6 to 8.

Ground Beef and Spinach Stuffing Crumble ground beef into a large frying pan and brown it in its own drippings. Mix in onion, garlic, and mushrooms. Cook, stirring occasionally, until onion is soft and begins to brown. Remove from heat; mix in spinach, then bread crumbs, grated cheese, egg, salt, basil, and pepper.

◼ BLANQUETTE DE VEAU

This is the classic French white stew. Although it appears to want color, do not leave the carrots in for the traditional presentation. The recipe can be made almost completely in advance and finished just before serving (see Note). Serve over rice pilaf or steamed potatoes.

    1 pound mushrooms
    2 tablespoons fresh lemon juice
    4 tablespoons butter
    ½ teaspoon salt
    ½ teaspoon white pepper
    3 tablespoons brandy or
        Brown Veal Stock (see page 560)
    5 cups Brown Veal Stock (see page 560) or
        additional water
    3 cups cold water
    4 pounds veal shoulder, trimmed of fat
        and cut into 2-inch cubes
    2 medium onions, cut in quarters
    6 carrots, cut in quarters
        Bouquet garni (see page 56)
    ½ pound small onions
    3 tablespoons flour
    ¼ cup whipping cream (optional)
    2 egg yolks (optional)

1. Toss mushrooms with lemon juice. In a medium skillet sauté mushrooms in 2 tablespoons of the butter over medium heat 1 to 2 minutes. Season with salt and pepper. Remove mushrooms with a slotted spoon and set aside. To avoid possible flare-ups, remove pan from heat, then add brandy, stirring to remove any cooked bits. Reserve liquid.

2. In a 6-quart kettle add the 5 cups Brown Veal Stock, 2½ cups of the cold water, and cubed veal shoulder. Bring mixture to a boil; add remaining water and remove from heat. Skim away any scum that has risen to the surface and return kettle to heat; add onions, carrots, and bouquet garni. Reduce heat to low and simmer, covered, for 1½ hours.

3. Bring 1 quart of water to a boil. Blanch small onions for 1 minute. Trim the root end, slip off the skins, and cut an *x* in the root end of each onion. Heat remaining butter in a small skillet and sauté onions over low heat until barely browned (about 15 minutes); remove onions with a slotted spoon and reserve buttered skillet.

4. Remove onion and carrot pieces from stock; set aside. In the small skillet, whisk flour into melted butter and cook briefly. Whisk 1 cup of stock into flour mixture. Return flour-stock mixture to veal, stirring thoroughly to combine. Add reserved mushrooms, their cooking liquid, and small onions to veal. Simmer for 15 minutes.

5. In a small bowl stir cream and egg yolks (if used) together; whisk into veal, and cook over low heat for 1 to 2 minutes (do not allow to boil or yolks will curdle).

Serves 8.

Note The recipe can be made through step 4 up to four days ahead. Refrigerate covered. When ready to continue, bring back to a simmer and continue with step 5.

◼ VEAL CHOPS WITH TARRAGON

If pale pink, milk-fed, eastern veal is available in your area, by all means try this simple, elegant treatment. The redder, beefier-tasting veal typical of the West can be prepared the same way.

    4 veal rib chops, ¾ to 1 inch thick
    2 or 3 sprigs fresh tarragon, plus leaves
        for garnish (see Note)
    1 teaspoon kosher salt
    ¼ teaspoon freshly ground pepper
    ½ cup unsalted Chicken, Brown Veal, or Beef Stock
        (see page 560) *or* ¼ cup canned broth mixed with
        ¼ cup water

1. Trim excess fat from chops. Finely chop half the tarragon and combine it with the salt and pepper. Rub salt mixture over both sides of chops.

2. Heat a large skillet (nonstick or well-seasoned cast iron) over medium heat. Add chops; cook until center springs back readily when pressed with a fingertip (3 to 4 minutes per side). Remove chops to a warm platter or to individual plates.

3. Deglaze skillet with stock, scraping up any browned drippings. Add remaining tarragon leaves. Reduce sauce by half, taste for seasoning, and correct if necessary.

4. Spoon sauce over chops, decorating each with tarragon leaves.

Serves 4.

Note If fresh tarragon is unavailable, substitute 1 teaspoon crumbled dried tarragon leaves to season the chops and omit the additional tarragon from the sauce and as the garnish. Or, use tarragon leaves packed in vinegar (available at specialty shops), well drained, in place of fresh leaves.

Meats such as veal or poultry that lack natural fat are sometimes wrapped in a layer of exterior fat to keep them moist during cooking. This technique is called barding.

■ VITELLO TONNATO

Because this dish of cold, sliced leg of veal with tuna sauce must be made in advance, it works beautifully for a buffet. To serve, fan veal slices on platter and spoon sauce over meat. The piquant, creamy sauce—sparked with anchovy, garlic, capers, and vinegar—needs to refrigerate for a day to marry the flavors and the veal also needs to chill overnight.

    1 can (6½ oz) tuna, drained
    2 anchovy fillets
    1 clove garlic, sliced
    ¼ cup olive oil
    2 tablespoons white wine vinegar
    1 tablespoon whipping cream
    1 tablespoon capers, drained
       Leg of veal (4 lb), boned and rolled

1. Preheat oven to 350° F. In a blender or food processor purée tuna, anchovies, garlic, olive oil, vinegar, and cream. Stir in capers; chill (this sauce is better when made a day in advance so flavors can blend).

2. Place veal on a rack in an 8- by 12-inch roasting pan. Roast about 45 minutes (to an internal temperature of about 140° F). Cool briefly and refrigerate overnight.

3. To serve, slice veal ¼ inch thick, arrange on a platter, and pour tuna sauce over pieces.

Serves 8 to 10.

■ WIENER SCHNITZEL

Any thin slice of meat is a *schnitzel* in German, but veal is the meat of choice. This preparation—Viennese (Wiener) style—consists of paper-thin veal scallops coated with seasoned crumbs and sautéed until golden brown. To keep the bound coating from slipping off in the skillet, the cutlets must sit 30 minutes before cooking. See variations at end of recipe for other classic veal scallop dishes. Use milk-fed veal from the leg for these quick sautés. When pounded to an even ⅛-inch thickness, the little scallops cook through quickly and remain tender.

    2 pounds veal scallops
    1 egg
    1 tablespoon water
    1 teaspoon salt
    ½ teaspoon freshly ground pepper
    1 cup dry bread crumbs
    4 tablespoons unsalted butter
    2 tablespoons vegetable oil
    1 lemon, for garnish
       Red Cabbage With Apples (see page 75),
       for accompaniment
       Boiled parsleyed potatoes, for accompaniment

1. Lightly pound veal cutlets with a wooden mallet to tenderize and flatten to about ⅛ inch thick, or have the butcher do it for you. In a shallow, small bowl, beat egg with the water. In another shallow, small bowl, mix salt, pepper, and bread crumbs.

2. Dip veal slices in beaten egg to coat thoroughly, then dip in seasoned bread crumbs. Place on a plate and chill 30 minutes.

3. In a large skillet sauté one half of the veal in 2 tablespoons butter and 1 tablespoon oil over medium heat 2 minutes; turn and cook second side 2 minutes. Reserve in 200° F oven while preparing remaining veal with remaining butter and oil. When all are cooked, remove to a serving platter and drizzle with lemon juice. Serve with Red Cabbage With Apples and boiled parsleyed potatoes.

Serves 6.

Schnitzel à la Holstein   Prepare veal as above. Prepare Basic Poached Eggs (see page 199) or Basic Fried Eggs (see page 200) and serve on top.

Veal Marsala   Prepare as for Veal Scaloppine (below), reducing cooking time to 20 to 30 seconds on each side (they will finish cooking in the sauce). Transfer cooked veal to a plate. Add 1 tablespoon butter and 1 tablespoon finely minced garlic to skillet; sauté until fragrant, then add ¾ cup Marsala wine. Bring to a boil and reduce until about half original volume. Remove pan from heat, swirl in 3 more tablespoons butter, cut into small pieces. Season to taste with salt and pepper. Return veal to pan briefly just to warm through. Divide scallops and sauce onto dinner plates and garnish with minced parsley.

Veal Parmigiana   Prepare veal as above, adding 1 teaspoon dried basil and 1 teaspoon dried oregano to bread crumb mixture. Prepare 4 cups Basic Tomato Sauce (see page 516). Place veal on an ovenproof serving platter, coat each piece with ½ cup tomato sauce, place a 1-ounce slice mozzarella cheese on each piece, and bake in a preheated 400° F oven until cheese melts (about 3 minutes). Serve immediately.

Veal Picatta   Prepare as for Veal Scaloppine (below); reserve in a 200° F oven while preparing lemon sauce. Over very low heat, add 6 tablespoons fresh lemon juice and ¼ cup minced parsley to skillet and scrape all browned bits from sides and bottom of pan. Add 4 tablespoons butter and stir until butter melts. Remove veal to a serving platter, pour sauce over, season with salt and freshly ground black pepper to taste, and garnish with lemon slices and minced parsley.

Veal Scaloppine   Pound veal and lightly sprinkle with salt and freshly ground black pepper. Dredge veal lightly in flour, shaking off excess. Sauté in butter and oil quickly on both sides (less than 1 minute per side). Serve immediately.

Recipes and Related Information
Brown Veal Stock, 560; Osso Buco, 58; Saltimbocca, 505.

VEGETABLE

The American vegetable marketplace has expanded dramatically in the recent past. Today's supermarket stocks a much greater variety of vegetables than consumers could have imagined just 10 years ago.

The new marketplace owes its breadth in part to a curiosity about other cuisines. Many supermarkets carry a wide assortment of Chinese vegetables and Latin chiles in addition to Japanese mushrooms, Thai eggplants, and Belgian endive. Americans have also begun to demand the variety of vegetables that they find in restaurants: baby squash and squash blossoms, radicchio, and wild mushrooms. Growers, aided by progressive seed companies, have taken an interest in supplying markets and restaurants with these unusual and exotic vegetables. Another factor affecting the growth of the marketplace is the increased interest in nutrition—in reducing intake of meat, and in raising the proportion of high-fiber foods in our diet. All these recent developments provide challenge and constant delight for the curious cook.

Baby vegetables include both special miniature varieties of common vegetables and regular varieties picked when immature. Fully mature miniatures add natural sweetness and a whimsical touch to a dish; regular varieties harvested when young may or may not have fully developed flavor.

For helpful information on purchasing, storing, and preparing most of the vegetables currently available, check the individual vegetable entries in this book.

Use Although most Americans think of vegetables as secondary to meat, in many cuisines vegetables take center stage. In China vegetable stir-fries are embellished with a small amount of meat rather than the reverse. In India, even among nonvegetarians, meals based on vegetables are common.

Around the world, vegetables are appreciated at all times of the day, from breakfast through dessert. Ethiopians often eat a breakfast of boiled beans flavored with onions and tomatoes; the English enjoy baked or stewed tomatoes in the morning, and the American coffee-shop breakfast wouldn't be complete without fried potatoes. At the other end of the day are the vegetable-based desserts, ranging from carrot cake and sweet potato pie to sugar-dusted Italian squash-blossom fritters.

Vegetables are served in salads, casseroles, sautés and stir-fries, stews and braised dishes, pickles, pasta, soups, and side dishes. Some vegetables are so highly prized that they are often served as a separate course: steamed asparagus, sautéed wild mushrooms, sliced beefsteak tomatoes, whole steamed artichokes, or hot corn on the cob can launch a meal in simple but memorable style. Other vegetables are usually given a supporting role: Onions and garlic, for example, are appreciated more for the aromatic qualities they lend to other dishes than as dishes in themselves.

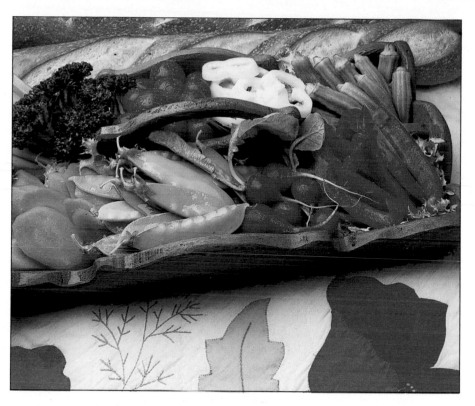

Baby vegetables can be used in all standard preparations; they are particularly appealing served whole.

Availability Buying vegetables in season is the best way to get superior quality. When prices are lowest, quality is usually at its best because the domestic harvest is at its peak. Vine-ripened autumn tomatoes from a local supplier have little in common with midwinter tomatoes shipped green from Mexico. Learn to enjoy vegetables to the fullest during their season and to forgo them at other times of the year. The good cook takes pleasure in following the seasons and the well-ordered parade of colors in nature. The first asparagus, June peas, and the first sweet corn of summer give way to the sunset colors of peppers and tomatoes, followed by the earthy winter comfort of mushrooms, rutabagas, and fennel.

The season for most farmed baby vegetables corresponds with the season for the regular varieties.

Selection Without exception, vegetables are best the moment they are harvested. The longer it takes to get a vegetable from the field to the market, the more flavor and texture suffer. For best quality, patronize local farmers' markets; most likely the vegetables were grown nearby and picked within the previous 24 hours. Alternatively, look for a market that knows how to care for its vegetables by keeping them cool and neatly trimmed, and by making an effort to stock locally grown produce. Fresh vegetables have good, bright color and firm texture. Carrots, celery, and root vegetables should feel firm, not spongy; leafy greens should be crisp, not wilted; asparagus and beans should be sturdy, not limp.

Crudités—raw fresh vegetables—are always welcome as part of an hors d'oeuvres buffet. Throughout the year, the produce market yields a varied palette of fresh vegetables. Choose the best the season has to offer, prepare them in bite-sized pieces, and arrange them in an eye-catching still life, with a dip or two alongside.

Storage The more quickly you use the vegetables you buy, the better. Some vegetables, such as peas and corn, quickly convert sugar to starch after harvest; they should be cooked the day they are purchased. Others, such as hard-shelled winter squash, can withstand long storage but do not improve in flavor after harvest.

Most vegetables, including baby vegetables, which are particularly perishable, should be refrigerated until use, preferably in a vegetable bin. Potatoes, garlic, onions, and shallots are exceptions, however; refrigerating them encourages rot. Store them in a cool, airy place. Hard squashes can be refrigerated but don't require it; they will keep in a cool, airy place for several months.

Preparation For most vegetables, wash and dry; peel and trim as necessary. Some baby vegetables, such as carrots and potatoes, have very delicate skins that do not require peeling.

Cooking See BLANCH, BOIL, BRAISE, BROIL, GRILL, MICROWAVE OVEN, PARBOIL, PUREE, STEAM, STIR-FRY.

VEGETABLE COOKING SPRAY

Most pan sprays are made of vegetable oil, alcohol, lecithin (a vegetable compound used as an emulsifier), and a propellant. They are a boon to those on low-calorie or low-cholesterol diets because they eliminate the need to grease baking pans or skillets. Most commercial brands instruct the user to apply the coating while the pan or skillet is cold.

Stored in a cool place, cooking sprays will keep indefinitely. Widely available in supermarkets, they are usually stocked next to the cooking oils.

VERTICAL ROASTER

To a great degree, food cooks by conduction—the slow, molecule-by-molecule transfer of heat from outside to center mass. If heat could somehow reach both the interior and the exterior at the same time, cooking time would be faster and food would cook more 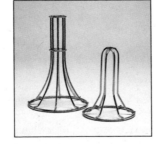 evenly. That's why dense or delicate cake batters are often baked in tube pans and why a baked potato will be done sooner with a nail tapped through the center. It's also the clever idea behind the vertical roaster for poultry.

These open, upright frames of stainless steel wire conduct heat to the internal cavity of fowl set on them. When roasted this way, poultry cooks faster and stays juicier than with conventional methods because the metal frame is an excellent heat conductor that promotes cooking from the inside as well as the outside. The frames are available for chickens and Rock Cornish game hens (see Mustard Madness, page 381).

VINEGAR

When a naturally fermented alcohol—such as sherry, wine, or apple cider—is attacked by a type of airborne bacteria called acetobacter, the alcohol is converted to acetic acid, creating vinegar. Winemakers take precautions to keep acetobacter from attacking their wine, but vinegar manufacturers take the opposite approach. Most encourage the growth of acetobacter by inoculating their base material with a starter culture. By this method, manufacturers can promote a consistent and desirable flavor.

The variety of vinegars available to consumers has increased dramatically in recent years. Formerly, distilled white vinegar, apple cider vinegar, and wine vinegar were the only readily available options. Today, well-stocked supermarkets and specialty shops offer a variety of herb-flavored vinegars, such as tarragon and dill; fruit vinegars, such as raspberry and blueberry; Champagne vinegar; sherry vinegar; Japanese rice vinegar; malt vinegar; and the famous Italian *aceto balsamico* (balsamic vinegar), made from wood-aged wine. See Availability for descriptions of specific vinegars.

The commercially available flavored vinegars are generally expensive, yet flavored vinegar is easy to make at home (see JAM, JELLY, PRESERVE, AND CONDIMENT).

Use High-quality vinegar has a fruitiness and refreshing acidity that give a lift to many dishes. Perhaps the most common use for vinegar is in salad dressing. Almost any type of salad—whether of mixed greens, cold vegetables, cold rice, or shellfish—benefits from the jolt of acidity that vinegar provides. Vinegar also acts as a tenderizer in meat marinades by denaturing the surface proteins. Vinegar in egg-poaching water (about 2 tablespoons per quart) will keep the whites from spreading and make the eggs more tender. In a Hollandaise sauce or related sauce, vinegar keeps the protein in the egg yolk from coagulating when the sauce is cooked. Vinegar acts as an antioxidant, slowing the browning of foods such as avocado and celery root, and as a preservative, preventing the growth of harmful bacteria in pickles.

The flavor of vinegar is essential to many dishes around the world. Most pickles wouldn't be pickles without the vinegar that preserves and flavors them. American diners, especially those from the Deep South, like to flavor cooked greens such as spinach with vinegar. English fish and chips are always served with strong malt vinegar as a condiment. Japanese salads get their distinctive taste in part from mild, slightly sweet rice vinegar. Italians enrich sauces with the mellow balsamic vinegar; the finest balsamic vinegar is used, drop by drop, as a table condiment. Modern French cooks add sherry vinegar to sautéed calf's liver and pair raspberry vinegar with duck livers. The basic dressing known as vinaigrette derives its name from the French word for vinegar (*vinaigre*); usually made from 3 parts oil to 1 part vinegar, this versatile sauce is used to dress green salads and salads of cold vegetables, leeks, fish, and grains. Champagne vinegar with minced shallots and black pepper is a popular condiment for raw oysters in France. In China black vinegar made from rice is used to dress cold noodle dishes and to enrich stir-fries.

Availability The following are among the most widely used vinegars today; they are sold in supermarkets and specialty stores.

Apple Cider Vinegar Made from the juice of apples, apple cider vinegar has an aroma and flavor that distinctly suggest the fruit. Its fruity quality is appealing in dressings for cabbage salads and fruit salads. It is also widely used in pickling.

Balsamic Vinegar Made from the juice of a white grape, balsamic vinegar is aged for several years in wood barrels. The vinegar is dark brown, with a mellow sweet-and-sour character that is greatly appreciated by Italian cooks. In Italy balsamic vinegar enriches stews, dresses salads, and even perks up the flavor of strawberries. The finest balsamic vinegar is carefully aged for decades and is extremely expensive.

Distilled White Vinegar The flavor of distilled white vinegar, which is made from grain alcohol, is too coarse for most salad dressings, but it is widely used in pickling.

Raspberry Vinegar Macerating raspberries in white wine vinegar and then straining the vinegar produces raspberry vinegar. The fruit imparts a pale raspberry color and an unmistakably raspberry flavor and aroma. The fruity character is appealing when with chicken, duck, and liver, and in salads with a fruit component.

Rice Vinegar Used in Chinese and Japanese cookery, rice vinegar is clear to pale gold in color, with a mild and subtly sweet flavor. Asian cooks use rice vinegar in noodle dishes, salad dressings, dipping sauces, and pickles.

Sherry Vinegar A fragrant, slightly nutty vinegar made from Spanish sherry, it is best in salad dressings; with green beans, asparagus, and chicken or duck; or to deglaze the skillet after sauteing chicken or calf's liver.

Wine Vinegar Either red or white, good-quality wine vinegar has a pleasing aroma and is pungent without being harsh. Generally, red wine vinegar is used with dark meats, in marinades, and in salads where its color is not objectionable. Use white wine vinegar with fish, in potato salads, or in pickles where a clear vinegar is preferred.

White wine vinegar is the base for many commercial herb vinegars.

Storage Keep bottles of vinegar tightly capped; store in a cool, dark place for up to six months.

PORK ADOBO

The famous adobo is a classic dish of the Philippines. Like the curries of other countries, adobo probably originated as a way of preserving meat. In this case the preserving agent is vinegar, not chiles or other spices. The following version calls for boiling cubes of pork in a vinegar and garlic mixture until the liquid evaporates and the cubes begin to fry in their own rendered fat. Use pork with some visible fat, either from the shoulder or the nearby section of the loin (usually sold as "country-style spareribs").

    1½ pounds boneless pork, in 1-inch cubes
    ½ cup rice vinegar
    6 cloves garlic, minced
    3 tablespoons soy sauce or fish sauce
    ¼ teaspoon freshly ground pepper
    1½ cups water
    1 bay leaf

1. In a bowl combine pork cubes, vinegar, garlic, soy sauce, and pepper; marinate 1 to 3 hours in the refrigerator.

2. Transfer all ingredients to a non-aluminum saucepan, add 1 cup of the water and bay leaf, and bring to a boil, uncovered. Adjust heat so meat cooks at a lively simmer but does not boil too rapidly.

3. Cook until liquid is nearly gone, then reduce heat further. Mixture will sizzle and pop as the last bits of water evaporate; then the pork cubes will begin to brown in the remaining fat. Turn cubes to brown evenly and remove from heat if mixture shows signs of scorching.

4. Remove pork cubes to serving dish. Add ½ cup of the water to pan and bring to a boil, stirring to scrape browned bits from pan. Pour over pork. Serve with rice.

Serves 4 with other dishes.

Variation Follow Pork Adobo recipe. Use a mixture of chicken, cut into braising pieces (1 to 2 inches long with bones), and boneless pork. Cook only until liquid is reduced to ½ cup, then brown meats in a separate pan: In a large skillet add 1 to 2 tablespoons vegetable oil (enough to coat bottom of pan). Heat oil over medium-high heat and brown chicken and pork pieces well. Transfer browned meats to a warm platter and cover with sauce.

Recipes and Related Information
Fran's Raspberry Vinegar, 323; Herb Vinegar, 323; Raspberry Vinegar and Shallot Dressing, 521; Vinegar Dressing, 233.

TIPS

COOKING WITH VINEGAR

Because vinegar is highly volatile, its flavor dissipates with heat and air. To retain its pungent character in a cooked dish, add vinegar to the dish only after removing it from heat. If a less pungent flavor is desired, add the vinegar while the dish is cooking and allow vinegar to boil off slightly.

WAFFLE AND PANCAKE

A thin mixture called a pour batter—the amount of liquid and dry ingredients are about equal and are wet enough to be pourable—forms the base for waffles and all types of pancakes. Most pour batters are classified as quick breads because they use a leavening other than yeast; blini, a buckwheat pancake, is the exception since it is yeast leavened. Like all quick breads, pour batters are fast to assemble and cook. Pancakes and waffles are popular breakfast foods; crêpes and blini appear on hors d'oeuvres trays as first courses, as desserts at elegant dinners, and on the menus of the trendiest restaurants.

INGREDIENTS AND METHOD

Dry ingredients include flour, baking powder or soda, salt, sometimes sugar, and often spices. These are blended and then combined with the liquid additions: milk, oil or melted butter, and eggs. For a light and delicate finished product, the eggs can be separated into yolks and whites: The yolks are added with the liquids and the whites beaten and folded into the batter as the final step.

Frequently, the same batter can be used for either pancakes or waffles; the difference is in how the batter is cooked. For pancakes, spoonfuls of batter are dropped onto a preheated griddle or skillet and cooked on both sides until golden brown. For waffles, the batter is poured onto the grids of a preheated waffle iron and baked until crisp and golden brown. See specific recipes for information on other food products.

Although pancakes, waffles, and other types of pour-batter products cook quickly, it is important not to rush them. When underdone, they are brown on the surface and unpleasantly liquid on the inside. To cook, the pan or appliance should be preheated to the proper temperature: For nonelectric pans, a drop of water will jump when it hits the hot pan; for thermostatically controlled devices, a light signals readiness. Flip pancakes when the surface appears dry and the bubbles around the edge have set. Cook waffles until steam is no longer given off or until the indicator light on an automatic waffle maker denotes that the waffles are ready.

EQUIPMENT

Although drop batters and doughs are stiff enough to hold their shape, a pour batter requires a special pan or iron if it is to have a distinctive form or imprint (see WAFFLE IRON AND PANCAKE PAN). Otherwise, when spooned onto a flat cooking surface—a griddle or skillet—the batter will spread in a gradually widening circle until set by heat.

A new griddle or skillet should be seasoned before use (see MATERIALS FOR COOKWARE). A well-seasoned pancake griddle or waffle iron should not be washed after using. Wipe away any clinging bits with a little oil and a paper towel, and store in a dry place. If the pan you are using isn't reserved only for pancakes, and isn't seasoned, you may need to add a thin coat of oil to it during preheating; if the batter contains fat, this may not be necessary.

Other equipment useful for making pancakes, waffles, and similar products includes pancake turners, whisks or wooden spoons for mixing the batter, an electric mixer for beating egg whites, and a mixing bowl. If you make these foods often, you may want to look for a batter bowl, which is an oversized liquid measuring cup with a 2-quart capacity; it is large enough to hold the batter and has a convenient pouring lip.

■ BASIC WAFFLES

If you are using a stove-top waffle iron, cook batter at least 1 minute for crisp waffles, preferably 2 minutes, after steam stops rising from iron. The top should lift without resistance. Serve waffles immediately after cooking for best texture and flavor, accompanied with butter and maple syrup, fresh fruit, or even ice cream. If they must be held, keep them warm in a 350°F oven 3 to 5 minutes. Serve on warm plates and warm any sauce served with them as well. Don't stack waffles or they will lose their crispness and get soggy. Extra waffles can be frozen, well wrapped, and toasted, but they won't have the same crispy flavor as when freshly made.

> 1¾ cups flour
> 1 tablespoon baking powder
> Pinch salt
> 2 tablespoons sugar
> 2 cups milk
> 3 eggs, separated
> 6 tablespoons butter, melted
> Pinch cream of tartar (optional)
> Butter and warm maple syrup, for topping

1. Sift together flour, baking powder, salt, and sugar into a medium bowl. Make a well in center of mixture. In another bowl combine milk, egg yolks, and melted butter. Pour into well in flour mixture; stir until smooth and creamy. This can also be done in a blender or food processor, but don't overwork or batter will be tough.

2. Preheat waffle iron according to manufacturer's directions or until a drop of water sizzles and bounces when placed onto hot iron.

3. In another bowl beat egg whites to soft peaks (if not using a copper bowl, add cream of tartar to whites when just foamy). Fold one third of beaten whites into batter to lighten, then fold in remaining whites.

4. Pour enough batter onto lightly oiled waffle iron to spread into corners (about 1 cup batter for a 4-square waffle iron). Cook 2 minutes after moment when steam stops escaping from sides of waffle maker. When waffles are cooked sufficiently, iron should release them easily. Serve immediately with butter and syrup.

Makes 4 cups batter, four 4-square waffles.

Cornmeal Waffles   Prepare Basic Waffles, but substitute ¾ cup cornmeal for 1 cup of the flour. Spread with cream cheese and chopped jalapeño chile, and serve with soup or eggs.

■ BUTTERMILK WAFFLES

This batter makes a light, tender waffle. Also try one of the variations: pecan, blueberry, or chocolate.

    1¾ cups flour
     1 teaspoon baking powder
     1 teaspoon baking soda
     2 tablespoons sugar
     2 cups buttermilk
     ½ cup butter, melted
     2 eggs, separated
        Pinch cream of tartar (optional)

Prepare as for Basic Waffles.

Makes 4 cups batter, four 4-square waffles.

Blueberry Buttermilk Waffles   Fold 1 cup washed and dried blueberries into batter before cooking.

Chocolate-Pecan Waffles   Substitute ¼ cup unsweetened cocoa powder for ¼ cup flour called for in recipe. Use a total of 6 tablespoons sugar. Mix in 1 teaspoon vanilla extract to buttermilk mixture. Fold in 1 cup chopped pecans to batter before cooking.

Pecan Buttermilk Waffles   Fold 1 cup pecan pieces into batter before cooking.

■ BELGIAN WAFFLES
WITH BLUEBERRY SAUCE

Yeast-leavened Belgian waffles are rectangular and have an extradeep grid made with a special waffle iron (see page 603). They can also be made in a regular waffle iron.

     1 package active dry yeast
     ¼ cup warm water
     2 cups flour
     ¼ cup sugar
     ¼ teaspoon salt
     ¼ cup butter or margarine, melted and cooled
     2 tablespoons vegetable oil
    1½ cups water
     ½ teaspoon vanilla extract
     2 eggs, separated
        Whipped cream (optional)

Blueberry Sauce

     ⅓ cup butter
     ⅔ cup sugar
     3 tablespoons light corn syrup
     ¼ cup water
     2 tablespoons grated lemon rind
     ¼ teaspoon freshly grated nutmeg
    1½ cups fresh or frozen unsweetened blueberries

1. Sprinkle yeast over the ¼ cup warm water in a small bowl; let stand about 5 minutes to soften. In a large bowl mix flour, sugar, and salt. Beat in butter, oil, the 1½ cups water, and vanilla until smooth. Then beat in egg yolks and yeast mixture.

2. Beat egg whites until they form soft peaks; fold gently into batter. Cover and refrigerate several hours or overnight; stir down batter.

3. Place a seasoned 6- by 7½-inch Belgian waffle iron directly over medium heat, turning it over occasionally, until a few drops of water dance on grids (or preheat an electric model). Spoon about ½ cup batter onto lightly oiled iron, spreading it just to cover grids.

4. Close iron and turn occasionally until waffle is well browned (4 to 5 minutes in all). Transfer waffles to wire rack unless served immediately.

5. If waffles are made ahead, cool, wrap in aluminum foil, and freeze. Reheat in a preheated 325° F oven, uncovered, in a single layer on baking sheets until hot and crisp (about 10 minutes).

6. Serve hot, with Blueberry Sauce. Top with whipped cream (if desired).

Makes 9 waffles.

Blueberry Sauce   Combine butter, sugar, and corn syrup in a medium saucepan. Cook over medium heat, stirring, until mixture boils. Stir in the water and boil 2 minutes. Add lemon rind, nutmeg, and blueberries. Cook, stirring, until mixture boils.

Makes about 1¾ cups.

Belgian waffles have deep grids, the better to trap delicious syrups and sauces. Blueberry Sauce, shown here, is served hot and is flavored with fresh nutmeg and grated lemon rind.

BASIC PANCAKES

Making pancake batter yourself is almost as easy as using a mix and always tastes better. For quick breakfasts, you can have the dry ingredients combined, all ready to stir into the egg mixture. Do this while the pan is heating. If the batter thickens too much upon standing, thin with a little extra liquid. Leftover batter can be stored in the refrigerator in an airtight container overnight, but the pancakes made from it won't be as light because the baking powder will have lost some of its punch. Always preheat the skillet or griddle before pouring on the batter. Test for readiness by shaking a few drops of water on the pan surface. The pan is ready to use if the water skips, sizzles, and quickly evaporates. Pour batter onto griddle or pan, and cook until the bubbles that form begin to burst and the edges look dry. Turn and cook on the other side.

    1¾ cups flour
    ¼ cup sugar
    2 teaspoons baking powder
    ½ teaspoon salt
    2 eggs
    4 tablespoons butter, melted
    1¼ cups milk
        Butter and warm maple syrup, for topping

1. Sift flour, sugar, baking powder, and salt into a medium bowl. Add eggs, butter, and milk and beat until smooth and creamy; set aside.

2. If using an electric skillet, preheat to 350° F; preheat lightly oiled griddle or skillet over medium heat until a few drops of water dance on the surface. For each pancake pour ¼ cup batter onto hot griddle and cook on first side until bubbles that form begin to pop and edges look dry. With a spatula, turn and cook until second side is a rich, golden brown.

3. Serve at once with butter and syrup.

Makes 8 to 12 four-inch pancakes.

Buckwheat Pancakes Prepare batter with 1¼ cups all-purpose flour and ½ cup buckwheat flour.

Whole-Grain Pancakes Prepare batter with 1 cup all-purpose flour and ¾ cup whole wheat flour.

BUTTERMILK PANCAKES

The addition of buttermilk provides a little tang and makes these pancakes extratender.

    1 cup cake flour
    2 teaspoons sugar
    1 teaspoon baking powder
    ½ teaspoon baking soda
        Pinch salt
    1 egg
    1 cup buttermilk
    2 tablespoons butter, melted, or vegetable oil
        Butter and warm maple syrup, for topping

1. Sift flour, sugar, baking powder, baking soda, and salt into a medium bowl. Add egg, buttermilk, and butter, and beat until smooth and creamy; set aside.

2. If using an electric skillet, preheat to 350° F; preheat lightly oiled griddle or skillet over medium heat until a few drops of water dance on the surface. For each pancake pour ¼ cup batter onto hot griddle and cook on first side until bubbles that form begin to pop and edges look dry. With a spatula, turn and cook until second side is a rich, golden brown.

3. Serve at once with butter and syrup.

Makes 8 to 12 four-inch pancakes.

Blueberry Buttermilk Pancakes Fold ½ to 1 cup rinsed and dried blueberries into batter before cooking.

BUTTERMILK BLINTZES

Unlike crêpes, which are cooked on both sides, the pancakes for blintzes are browned on one side only. They are then wrapped around a sweetened cheese filling and fried to brown the outside. Making blintzes is a lengthy operation. If you make them ahead, you can cover and refrigerate the filled blintzes for up to 24 hours. When ready, brown quickly and serve hot. The name for this Jewish dish is from the Yiddish *blintse*, which in turn evolved from the Russian *blinets* (diminutive of *blin*, or pancake). Note that the batter must chill for one hour before using.

    ¾ cup flour
    ¾ teaspoon baking soda
    ½ teaspoon salt
    2 tablespoons sugar
    1 cup buttermilk
    ½ cup water
    3 eggs
    2 tablespoons vegetable oil
    3 to 4 tablespoons *each* butter or margarine
        and vegetable oil, for frying
        Sour cream and cherry preserves, for topping

Cheese Filling

    1 package (8 oz) cream cheese, softened
    1 egg
    2 tablespoons confectioners' sugar
    ½ teaspoon vanilla extract
    ¼ teaspoon ground cinnamon
    2 cups (1 lb) pot cheese (also called farmer cheese)

1. In blender or food processor, combine flour, soda, salt, sugar, buttermilk, the water, eggs, and the 2 tablespoons oil. Whirl or process until batter is smooth, stopping motor once or twice to scrape flour from sides of container. Cover and refrigerate for at least 1 hour before using.

2. Make blintzes in a lightly oiled 6- to 7-inch crêpe pan, but brown them on first side only and cook until top surface is dry to touch. Stack blintzes to cool.

3. To fill each blintz, place about 2 tablespoons of Cheese Filling in center of browned side of each pancake. Fold in opposite edges about 1 inch, then fold in remaining edges to enclose filling, overlapping in center to make a slightly rectangular envelope. Set blintzes aside, folded side down.

4. In a large frying pan over moderately high heat, melt 2 tablespoons butter with 2 tablespoons oil. Fry filled blintzes without crowding until golden on each side (1 to 1½ minutes on each side). Add more butter and oil to pan as needed.

5. Drain blintzes well on paper towels and serve on warm plates, topped with a dollop each of sour cream and cherry preserves.

Makes 20 to 24 blintzes.

Cheese Filling In a large bowl beat cream cheese with egg, confectioners' sugar, vanilla, and cinnamon. Then beat in pot cheese.

Makes about 3 cups.

■ SWEDISH PANCAKES

These small, moist, delicate pancakes are traditionally made in a *plett*, a cast-iron griddle with shallow, 3-inch-diameter depressions to hold the batter (see page 604). If you don't have this pan, the pancakes will taste just as good. Serve them in the Swedish manner, with butter and lingonberry preserves, or with your favorite fruit-flavored syrup. Imported lingonberry preserves can be found at specialty food shops and well-stocked supermarkets.

⅔ cup flour
½ teaspoon baking powder
⅛ teaspoon salt
2 eggs, separated
1 cup milk, at room temperature
¼ cup half-and-half
¼ cup butter or margarine, melted and cooled
Butter and lingonberry preserves or syrup, for topping

1. Sift flour, baking powder, and salt onto a square of parchment paper or waxed paper; set aside. In a large bowl beat egg yolks with milk and half-and-half. Beat in melted butter, then add flour mixture. Stir to combine.

2. Beat egg whites until stiff peaks form. Carefully fold into batter.

3. Set a lightly oiled Swedish pancake pan, griddle, or skillet over medium-low heat until a few drops of water dance on the hot surface. Use about 2 tablespoons batter for each pancake. Cook pancakes until golden brown on each side, turning once very carefully with a spatula. Serve hot with butter and lingonberry preserves or syrup.

Makes about 2 dozen 3-inch pancakes.

■ DUTCH BABIE

This oven pancake is said to have originated at a small family restaurant in Seattle. Very similar to Yorkshire pudding, it uses eggs, flour, and milk, although the proportion of eggs is much higher. The recipe can be doubled or even tripled, as long as it is baked in a shallow pan in a 425° F oven.

4 eggs
1 cup milk
1 cup flour
Pinch *each* salt and sugar
¼ cup butter
Confectioners' sugar, fresh lemon juice, and fruit in season, for garnish

1. Preheat oven to 425° F.

2. In a blender combine eggs and milk on high speed. Add flour, salt, and sugar in two batches, blending well after each addition until smooth and creamy.

3. Place butter in a 12- to 14-inch shallow ovenproof pan or skillet and set in oven to melt. Swirl pan to coat evenly with butter and pour in batter. Bake until puffy and golden brown (20 to 30 minutes).

4. Serve immediately in baking pan, dusted with confectioners' sugar and sprinkled with lemon juice. Accompany each serving with an assortment of fresh, seasonal fruit.

Serves 6 to 8.

Buttermilk Blintzes should be made, filled, and folded ahead of serving time and refrigerated. They can be browned later, and served hot with cherry preserves and sour cream.

HOW TO MAKE CREPES

Pour batter into greased pan, tilting pan so batter forms a thin, even covering over entire bottom.

Cook crêpe 45 to 60 seconds. Small holes will be visible on top side; bottom will be browned. Turn and cook other side.

Remove crêpe to a platter, board, or sheet of waxed paper to cool.

■ BLINI

Yeast-risen buckwheat pancakes were a fixture on the tables of imperial Russia, served dripping with butter and caviar, or with sour cream and smoked fish. Made in a smaller cocktail size, they are novel topped in many different ways: with sour cream and chutney, with sour-cream herring, with crème fraîche and smoked trout, with a slice of grilled sausage, with melted herb butter and tiny shrimp, or with melted butter and smoked oysters. Serve piping hot, with chilled vodka, Champagne, or cocktails. They may be made ahead of serving time.

  2   **cups all-purpose flour**
  ½   **cup buckwheat flour**
  1   **package active dry yeast**
  2   **teaspoons sugar**
  2   **egg yolks**
  3   **cups lukewarm (100° F to 105° F) milk**
  3   **egg whites**
  2   **tablespoons unsalted butter**

1. In a medium bowl sift together all-purpose and buckwheat flours. In a small bowl, dissolve yeast and sugar in ½ cup warm milk and set aside to soften a few minutes. Make a well in flour and add egg yolks. Gradually stir in yeast mixture and remaining milk, incorporating yolks and flour.

2. Cover bowl with a towel and place in a warm area. Let rise until doubled in bulk. Beat egg whites to soft peaks and fold into batter.

3. Melt butter on griddle or in large skillet. Form Blini by dropping heaping tablespoons of batter onto hot griddle. Cook on both sides until golden brown.

Makes 2 dozen Blini.

■ BASIC CREPES

In France, their country of origin, crêpes are served as a snack, a lunch or supper dish, or—depending on flavoring and embellishment—a dessert. Wrap hot-off-the-griddle crêpes around a number of mixtures: tiny shrimp warmed in a saucepan with a little sour cream, chopped tomatoes, shallots, and thyme; sausage and cheese; crumbled blue cheese and chopped walnuts; or grated Gruyère and crumbled bacon. Use cooled (but not chilled) crêpes to wrap around pencil-thin asparagus, or spread with chutney, then top with paper-thin slices of smoked ham or turkey and roll up.

  1   **cup flour**
  ¾   **cup water**
  ⅔   **cup milk**
  3   **eggs**
  2   **tablespoons vegetable oil**
  ¼   **teaspoon salt**

1. In blender or food processor, combine flour, the water, milk, eggs, oil, and salt. Whirl or process until batter is

smooth, stopping motor once or twice to scrape flour from sides of container.

2. Cover and refrigerate batter for at least 1 hour. Blend batter well before making crêpes.

3. Add just enough batter to make a thin coat to a lightly oiled 6-inch pan. Cook each crêpe until set (about 60 seconds); turn and cook other side (about 45 seconds). Transfer to a sheet of parchment or waxed paper. Do not stack crêpes until they are completely cool.

Makes 16 to 20 crêpes.

Make-Ahead Tip Completely cooled crêpes may be stacked, wrapped in aluminum foil, and refrigerated for up to five days or frozen for up to two months. Thaw in cool oven.

■ CREPES SUZETTE

A quick-witted French chef transformed a failure into what has become a culinary classic—crêpes suzette. While the chef was preparing a dessert of crêpes with a liqueur sauce, the sauce caught fire. After tasting the sauce, he realized that the flames gave it extra depth. The dish was served in triumph. The batter makes enough crêpes for a double recipe. Extra pancakes can be frozen for later use. They are delicious with any fruit filling or ice cream.

  6   **eggs**
  6   **cups half-and-half**
  1   **cup water**
1¼   **cups milk**
  2   **cups flour**
  2   **tablespoons butter, melted**
  1   **tablespoon sugar**
  1   **teaspoon salt**
  ¼   **cup brandy or Cognac**
    Additional butter, for cooking crêpes
  ½   **cup brandy**

Orange Butter Sauce

  6   **tablespoons butter**
    Grated rind of 2 oranges
    Grated rind and juice of 2 lemons
    Juice of 4 oranges
  ¼   **cup sugar**
  ½   **cup orange-flavored liqueur**

1. In a large bowl combine eggs, half-and-half, the water, milk, flour, melted butter, sugar, salt, and brandy. Whisk together well. Batter will be slightly lumpy. Transfer batter to blender in batches and blend until smooth. Let batter rest at room temperature 45 minutes or refrigerate overnight before using.

2. Heat a nonstick 7-inch skillet or crêpe pan over moderately high heat. Add 1 teaspoon butter and swirl to coat pan. When butter foams, add 3 tablespoons batter and quickly tilt pan to coat bottom of skillet thinly.

Cook crêpe until set (60 seconds); turn and cook other side (about 45 seconds). Transfer to a sheet of parchment paper or waxed paper. Continue with remaining batter.

3. To make Orange Butter Sauce: Melt butter in chafing dish or large shallow pan. Add orange and lemon rinds and juice and cook over medium-low heat until reduced by one third. Add sugar and stir to dissolve. Add orange-flavored liqueur and heat through.

4. To assemble: Reduce heat under sauce to low. Using 18 crêpes altogether and freezing remainder for another use, lay crêpes one by one in pan and coat with sauce. Fold each crêpe in half, and then in half again, making small triangles. Arrange triangles, overlapping them around edge of pan. Continue until all have been coated, folded, and arranged in pan.

5. Pour brandy over warm crêpes and carefully ignite, shaking pan to distribute sauce throughout dish. As soon as flames subside, transfer crêpes with sauce to warmed plates.

Serves 6.

Make-Ahead Tip Completely cooled crêpes may be stacked, wrapped in aluminum foil, and refrigerated for up to five days or frozen for up to two months. Thaw in cool oven.

WAFFLE IRON AND PANCAKE PAN

Some fascinating utensils have been designed to produce uncommon pancakes and waffles. If you enjoy varying your breakfast and brunch repertoire, you will probably want to purchase one or more of these. For more information on seasoning pans, see MATERIALS FOR COOKWARE.

WAFFLE IRONS

The iron in which waffles are baked and which gives them their distinctive gridlike pattern may be round, square, or rectangular. Some are electric; others are designed for use on top of the range, either gas or electric. In any case, the grids of a waffle iron—like the surface of a crêpe pan or a pancake griddle—should be seasoned well and then never washed. Season the grids before first use, as you would a cast-iron pan (see MATERIALS FOR COOKWARE), or if finished with a nonstick surface, follow the manufacturer's directions for seasoning. If you don't use the waffle iron often, brush grids lightly with vegetable oil or spray with vegetable cooking spray before heating iron.

Belgian Waffle Iron Belgian waffles, the hit of the 1964 world's fair in New York, are thick, with deep pockets. At the fair they were piled with fresh strawberries and whipped cream, but they are equally delicious with ice cream or fruit sauces. Belgian waffle irons come in stove-top and electric models, and with plain and nonstick grids. They are of cast aluminum.

Electric Waffle Makers A built-in thermostat takes the guesswork out of making waffles: It heats the unit to a predetermined temperature and signals you that it's ready to use. Pour on the batter, close the lid, wait a few minutes, and the light on the appliance will go on again when the waffle is ready to eat. The grids are made of cast aluminum, either plain or with a nonstick finish, and in regular or Belgian-waffle style. Some models feature reversible grids that become a griddle or have embossed disks for making *pizzelle*, thin, crisp Italian wafers.

Heart-Shaped Waffle Iron Like the *plett* (used to make Swedish pancakes, see page 604) this utensil is from Scandinavia. Circular, with five interlocking hearts, it is made of aluminum, usually with a nonstick finish. To use, the iron is first preheated, then the batter is poured over the grids. The iron is set on the burner of the stove to cook for several minutes, then is turned to finish on the other side.

PANCAKE PANS

Another name for pancakes is griddle cakes because they are best made on a wide shallow griddle. If you make pancakes frequently, consider buying a rectangular griddle. Its shape is well suited for making several servings of pancakes at a time instead of the one or two possible in a round frying pan (see COOKWARE). The following are pans for specialty pancakes.

Blini Pan A blini pan is so small some people mistake it for a one-egg frying pan. It has a bottom diameter of 3½ to 4 inches in order to shape the diminutive Russian pancakes. Otherwise, it is like a standard crêpe pan and should be seasoned and cared for in the same way.

Crêpe Pan Although a crêpe pan resembles an omelet pan in that it is fashioned of rolled steel, it differs in one important respect—it has a flat, well-defined bottom to give the crêpe a sharp edge. The sides of an omelet pan, on the other hand, curve gently into the bottom. Season as you would a cast-iron pan. Reserve it strictly for crêpes and you will never need to wash it. After each use, wipe away any crumbs with a paper towel dipped in a little oil; store in a dry place to prevent rust. Before the next use, rub a little oil over inside surface of sides and bottom as pan heats.

Crêpe pans range in size from 5 to 8½ inches (diameter of pan bottom, not top edge). Most recipes specify 6- to 7-inch crêpes.

A Breton crêpe griddle is notable for its larger size—11 to 15 inches in diameter. Not as deep as smaller crêpe pans, it has a shallow, upturned rim that contains the crêpe batter. Made of cast aluminum or cast iron, it also can be used as a griddle for modest conventional pancakes and grilled sandwiches.

Waffles and pancakes are made from batters that take on the shape of the cooking pan. Shown clockwise from top left: electric waffle iron with nonstick grids, stove-top heart-shaped waffle iron, stove-top Belgian waffle iron, Swedish pancake pan (plett), crêpe pan.

Swedish Pancake Pan (Plett) Designed to shape the small, delicate, eggy pancakes from Scandinavia, this pan can also be used to make blini. In one respect a *plett* is even more convenient than the standard blini pan because it can accommodate several pancakes at a time. The pan is a large (about 10 inches in diameter) cast-iron griddle containing seven shallow, 3-inch-round depressions. Season and treat it as you would any other cast-iron pan.

Recipes and Related Information
Batter, 27; Waffle and Pancake, 598.

WALNUT

The walnut is an ancient food of undetermined origin, although most scholarly speculation centers on Persia. Today, it is second only to the almond in world popularity. The edible portion of the nut is encased in a semi-hard, light brown, two-part shell. The meat inside consists of a pair of irregularly shaped halves connected, "back to back," near their midpoints. Of the several walnut species, only two are of commercial importance: the mild-flavored English walnut and the native North American black walnut, which has a stronger, richer flavor but is quite difficult to shell.

Use Toasted shelled walnuts can be served as a cocktail snack or incorporated in a cocktail mix of buttered, roasted, and salted nuts. Walnuts in the shell are a traditional after-dinner companion to port. Toasted walnuts add nutty flavor and texture to green salads, vegetable dishes, breads, cakes, pies, and cookies. In sufficient quantity and finely ground, they take the place of flour in some cakes. Italian cooks make a sauce of ground walnuts and cream for stuffed pasta squares known as *pansotti*. Turkish cooks make a smooth ground walnut sauce for cold shredded chicken. In Iran cooks stew chicken or duck in a sweet-and-sour pomegranate sauce with ground walnuts. Bulgarian cooks make a refreshing cold soup, called *taratòr*, with cucumber, ground walnuts, yogurt, garlic, and dill. In America cooks use the native black walnut in ice cream and quick breads.

Availability Fresh English walnuts in the shell are sold in many supermarkets and specialty markets in the fall. Packaged English walnut halves and walnut pieces are available in supermarkets all year; bulk shelled English walnuts are carried the year around by some supermarkets and health-food stores. Shelled black walnuts are available from mail-order sources. The difficulty of shelling them makes them hard to find commercially.

Selection Fresh walnuts in the shell should feel heavy for their size.

Storage If stored in a cool, dry place, fresh walnuts in the shell will keep for several months. Shelled walnuts should be refrigerated or frozen because they go rancid quickly. They will keep for about two months in the refrigerator, about one year in the freezer.

Preparation Toasting brings out the flavor of walnuts; for toasting directions and times, see NUT.

■ GREEK WALNUT TORTE

A torte is a light cake, with nuts and/or crumbs substituting for part or all of the flour. Here, flour is omitted altogether, replaced by ground walnuts and dry bread crumbs. The torte is delicately scented with orange, both in the cake itself and in the whipped cream frosting. Since egg whites are the only leavening agent, it is important to beat them properly and to fold them into the batter without deflating them (see EGG, Beating Eggs, and FOLD).

      1 pound shelled walnuts
      6 tablespoons dry bread crumbs
      9 egg yolks
      ¾ cup sugar
      2 teaspoons finely grated orange rind
      2 tablespoons strained fresh orange juice
      9 egg whites
      ¼ cup sugar
      3 tablespoons orange-flavored liqueur
    1½ teaspoons finely grated orange rind
         Candied orange rind, for garnish

Chocolate Glaze

      1 to 2 ounces semisweet chocolate
      ¼ cup unsalted butter, clarified

Orange Chantilly Cream

      1 teaspoon unflavored gelatin
      2 tablespoons cold water
    1½ cups whipping cream
      ¼ cup sifted confectioners' sugar
      1 tablespoon orange-flavored liqueur

1. Preheat oven to 350° F. Butter and lightly flour two 10-inch-diameter by 2-inch-high cake pans or two 9½-inch-diameter by 3-inch-high springform pans. Line bottoms with circles of parchment or waxed paper.

2. Finely grind walnuts, 1 cup at a time, with 1 tablespoon of the bread crumbs, in food processor or small jar of blender. Bread crumbs and ground walnuts should equal 4 cups.

3. In large bowl of electric mixer, lightly beat egg yolks. Gradually add the ¾ cup sugar, and beat until mixture falls from beater in a ribbon and leaves a slowly dissolving trail on the surface (ribbon stage). Beat in orange rind and orange juice. Stir in walnut mixture.

4. In a large bowl, beat egg whites until they form peaks; gradually add the ¼ cup sugar and beat until they are stiff but still glossy. Stir one fourth of the whites into batter to lighten it. Gently fold in remaining whites. Whites should be completely incorporated but not deflated.

5. Divide batter equally between two cake pans. Bake until cake is springy to the touch and begins to pull away from sides of pan (30 to 40 minutes). Cool in pan 5 minutes, then remove sides of pans (if using springform pans) and allow to finish cooling on wire racks.

6. To assemble cake: Split each cake layer in half horizontally with a long, serrated knife. Place one layer on cake plate; brush with 2 teaspoons orange-flavored liqueur. Spread one third of Chocolate Glaze evenly over cake and sprinkle ½ teaspoon orange rind over glaze. Repeat these steps for the next two layers. Top with fourth layer of cake; brush with remaining orange-flavored liqueur. Ice sides and top of cake with Orange Chantilly Cream. Place remaining cream in a pastry bag fitted with an open-star tip. Decorate border with rosettes of cream or a chain of shells. Refrigerate until ready to serve. When ready to serve, place a 1-inch piece of candied orange rind in the center of each rosette to mark each slice.

Serves 10 to 12.

Chocolate Glaze In a double boiler melt chocolate over hot (not boiling) water. Remove from heat and stir in clarified (tepid) butter. Cool mixture to tepid (86° F).

Orange Chantilly Cream Soften gelatin in the cold water; in a double boiler stir over hot (not boiling) water until gelatin dissolves; cool until syrupy. Beat whipping cream until slightly thickened; add dissolved gelatin, confectioners' sugar, and orange-flavored liqueur. Continue beating until soft peaks form and hold their shape when beaters are lifted from bowl. Do not overbeat; cream should look soft and glossy.

> **Recipes and Related Information**
> *Braised Celery With Walnuts, 109; Walnut-Apple Strudel, 222; Your Own Bridge Mix, 59.*

WASABI

A variety of aquatic plant unique to Japan, *wasabi* comes from an edible root that has a tough brownish green skin and a pale green flesh. The flesh is finely grated to make a pungent condiment similar to horseradish.

Use Wasabi is most often encountered in sushi bars. Sushi chefs put a thin swipe of wasabi atop the rice and underneath the fish when making Nigiri Sushi (see page 233). They also serve a small mound of wasabi with sashimi (thinly sliced raw fish), which the diner mixes to taste with soy sauce to make a dipping sauce for the sashimi. Similarly, wasabi is often served with cold noodle dishes, to be added to the dipping sauce. Japanese cooks also pickle vegetables such as eggplant with wasabi and mustard.

Availability   Fresh wasabi is rarely if ever seen in this country. Powdered wasabi in tins is sold in many supermarkets and in all Japanese markets. Wasabi paste in tubes is available in some Japanese markets.

Storage   Powdered wasabi, stored in a cool, dry place, will keep indefinitely. Wasabi paste should be refrigerated after opening.

Preparation   For powdered wasabi, add just enough tepid water to powder to form a paste. Mix until smooth. Let stand 10 minutes to develop flavor. Paste wasabi is ready to use right from the tube.

WATER CHESTNUT

A tuber that grows in east Asian marshes, the water chestnut is now cultivated in the southeastern United States. It has a squat round shape with a pointed tip. Underneath its dark brown skin is cream-colored flesh as crisp and sweet as that of an apple. Young, fresh water chestnuts are best; flavor becomes starchy and less sweet with age.

Use   Water chestnuts, essential to Chinese cooking, add texture to countless soups, stir-fries, and stuffings. Chinese steamed dumplings are typically filled with a mixture of seasoned minced shrimp or ground pork and water chestnuts. The refreshing, clean taste and crisp texture of water chestnuts make them an appealing nibble at the start of a meal. American cooks sometimes wrap them in bacon and broil them to serve as an appetizer.

Availability   Fresh water chestnuts are occasionally available in Chinese markets. Canned water chestnuts, both whole and sliced, are sold in supermarkets and Chinese markets.

Selection   Fresh water chestnuts should feel rock hard and should have a smooth, not wrinkled, exterior.

Storage   If firm, fresh water chestnuts will keep up to two weeks refrigerated in a plastic bag. Canned water chestnuts, once opened, should be transferred to an airtight nonmetal container and covered with fresh water; they will keep for two to three weeks if the water is changed every few days.

Preparation   Fresh water chestnuts may be muddy. Rinse well just before using; peel. Unless using immediately, cover peeled water chestnuts with cold water to prevent discoloration. Canned water chestnuts can be blanched for 15 seconds in boiling water, then shocked in cold water, to rid them of their canned taste.

■ **SHRIMP WITH SNOW PEAS AND WATER CHESTNUTS**

This Chinese stir-fry is a study in crisp textures and complementary colors. Splitting the shrimp lengthwise causes them to curl into spirals when cooked.

> ½ **pound shrimp, peeled and split lengthwise**
>   **Pinch salt**
> 2 **tablespoons Shaoxing wine or dry sherry**
>   **Oil, for stir-frying**
> 1 **tablespoon minced fresh ginger**
> ½ **pound snow peas, stems and strings removed**
> ½ **cup sliced water chestnuts (preferably fresh)**
> 1 **tablespoon soy sauce**
> ½ **teaspoon cornstarch, dissolved in ¼ cup water or stock**

1. Toss shrimp with salt; add wine; marinate for 20 minutes to several hours.

2. Drain shrimp and reserve marinade. Heat wok over high heat; add oil. Add ginger, stir-fry until fragrant, and add shrimp. Stir-fry until shrimp are mostly opaque (2 to 4 minutes, depending on size).

3. Add snow peas and water chestnuts; stir-fry until just heated through. Add reserved marinade, soy sauce, and cornstarch mixture. Bring to a boil and cook until sauce thickens. Serve immediately.

Serves 4 to 6 with other dishes.

WATERCRESS

A member of the mustard family, watercress grows wild and profusely in shallow, slow-moving creeks. For the commercial market, it is cultivated in streams and harvested by waders. Watercress has small, round, dark green leaves on stems slightly thicker than parsley. The leaves and stems have a peppery taste.

Use   Watercress makes a peppery addition to green salads and sandwiches or a lively base for chicken or egg salad. In France cooks make watercress soup, thickened with potatoes and cream. The English put a sprig of watercress on dainty tea sandwiches.

Availability   Fresh watercress is sold by the bunch in most supermarkets the year around. Supplies peak in late spring and early summer.

Selection   Look for watercress with healthy green leaves; avoid any bunches with yellowing or slimy leaves.

Storage   Untie bunch at home and remove any bad sprigs; wash gently in cool water, dry thoroughly, then wrap in paper towels, overwrap in plastic, and refrigerate. Use within two to three days.

Preparation   Cut away any overly thick stems.

Stir-fried Shrimp With Snow Peas is even better when made with fresh water chestnuts, available in Chinese markets and some specialty markets.

THE TIGER
Third sign of the zodiac
Magnetic, aggressive, adventur...
...an unpre...

■ COUNTRY WATERCRESS SOUP

This creamy soup, which can be served hot or cold, is lightly thickened with potato. Serve the soup hot with Garlic Croutons (see page 506) or cold with French bread. This soup thickens as it chills. If it becomes too thick, gradually stir in another 2 to 3 tablespoons of cream or milk just before serving.

        2 medium leeks
        2 bunches watercress (10 oz total)
        1 medium potato
        2 tablespoons butter
        1 medium onion, sliced
     1½ cups Chicken Stock (see page 560)
           Salt and white pepper, to taste
     1½ cups milk
       ¼ to ½ cup whipping cream
           Freshly grated nutmeg

1. Wash and trim leeks. Cut white and light green parts of leeks in thin slices; reserve dark green part for other uses. Thoroughly rinse watercress, discard large stems, and reserve only upper, leafy third of each bunch. Reserve 8 to 12 attractive watercress leaves for garnish. Plunge bunches of watercress into large saucepan of boiling water. Bring back to a boil, drain immediately, and rinse under cold running water. Drain thoroughly and squeeze dry. Peel potato and cut in thin slices.

2. Melt butter in heavy saucepan over low heat. Add onion and leeks and cook, stirring often, until soft but not brown (about 10 minutes). Add watercress bunches and cook, stirring, for 2 minutes. Add potato, stock, and a pinch of salt and pepper, and bring to a boil. Reduce heat to low, cover, and simmer, stirring occasionally, until potatoes are tender (about 20 minutes).

3. Purée soup through a food mill, or in a blender or food processor. Strain to remove stringy parts of watercress.

4. Return soup to saucepan and add milk. Bring to a boil, stirring occasionally. Add ¼ cup cream and bring again to a boil. If soup is too thick, stir in remaining cream. Add nutmeg. Taste and add salt and pepper, if needed.

5. Prepare garnish by dipping a small strainer containing reserved watercress leaves into a small saucepan of boiling water for 30 seconds. Rinse under cold water to stop cooking and drain.

6. Serve soup hot or cold. To chill hot soup, cool slightly, then cover and refrigerate until thoroughly cold (several hours or overnight). Ladle soup into bowls and garnish with blanched watercress leaves.

Makes 4 to 5 cups, serves 4.

Recipes and Related Information

Cream of Watercress, 563; Watercress Dip With Green Onions and Basil, 521.

WHIP, TO

To beat rapidly in a circular motion in order to increase the volume of a mixture by incorporating air into it; done with a whisk, rotary beater, or electric mixer. The action is vigorous—the whisk doesn't move around the mixture, but enters and leaves it so as to pull in the maximum amount of air.

Essentially, whipping is stirring; instead of using a single spoon, however, you use a beater or whisk consisting of 12 to 25 wires bent into a bulbous shape. Therefore, each stir represents a dozen or more stirs. The whisk has become such a standard tool for this procedure that the term *to whisk* has come to mean *to whip*.

Recipes and Related Information
Cream, 160; Egg, 194; Whisk, 608.

WHISK, TO; WHISK

To beat rapidly to incorporate air into a mixture (see WHIP); also the utensil used to perform this task. Like spoons and spatulas, whisks are beating tools, used to smoothly incorporate ingredients. Unlike them, however, whisks perform an additional function—that of  incorporating air, which causes a mixture to lighten or expand. Whisks are made of stainless steel wires in a range of thicknesses, shapes, and sizes depending on how they will be used. They are traditionally an integral part of the French chef's *batterie de cuisine;* in American home kitchens the electric mixer and food processor have taken over many of their functions—particularly for beating egg whites and whipping cream. However, the open design of the whisk is still invaluable for mixing sauces, batters, and dressings. Although using a whisk is more labor-intensive, many cooks prefer to whip egg whites and cream by hand. Studies indicate that egg whites whipped in a copper bowl with a balloon whisk produce the greatest volume and the finest, most stable foam.

Whisks are available with wires that are flexible or rigid, thin or heavy-gauge, and gathered in an open, elongated, or flat shape; match the whisk to your purpose. As a guideline, use a balloon whisk, which resembles an oversized light bulb and has anywhere from 12 to 25 thin, flexible wires, when you want to incorporate as much air as possible—as when beating egg whites and whipping cream. For blending, use one with a less open shape. Thinner wires work well for light mixtures and for aerating flours and other powders; heavier wires will stand up in denser batters and sauces. A flat whisk, which looks like a standard whisk cut in cross section, is angled for mixing in shallow dishes or pans, and is particularly useful for beating eggs and reaching around the edges of a saucepan to draw any lumpy portions of a sauce into the mixture.

Don't use a fine-gauge whisk or one with wires joined close together for heavy batters; they lack the strength to move easily through a thick liquid, and the wires will trap the batter inside the whisk. Check construction to make sure that food can't collect where wires and handle meet. A whisk with a stainless steel handle can go in the dishwasher; one with a wooden handle must be washed by hand, but tends to be more comfortable to hold.

Recipes and Related Information
Copper Egg-White Bowl, 155; Egg, 194.

WINE IN COOKING

Apart from its pleasure as a beverage, wine has an important place in the pantry. Wherever wine is enjoyed at the table, cooks have learned to take advantage of its special properties in the kitchen. White or red, sweet or dry, wine can enhance a range of different dishes.

Use Wine has three main uses in the kitchen: as a marinade ingredient, as a cooking liquid, and as a flavoring in a finished dish.

Selection So-called cooking wines sold in stores are unsuitable for most culinary purposes. They have been salted to the point that they are unfit to drink so that they may be sold in stores without liquor licenses or in dry states or localities. It is far better to use an unadulterated table wine or a fortified wine (such as sherry or Madeira).

Storage All wines should be stored in a cool, dark, well-ventilated place with moderate humidity. They should preferably be stored on their sides to keep the cork moist; a dry cork will shrink and allow air to enter. Ideal storage conditions are less important if the wine will be used within a few weeks; the longer you plan to keep the wine before using, the more important it is to store it properly.

Leftover table wines can be refrigerated and used for cooking if held for only one or two weeks. If you have at least a half bottle of wine left over, pour it off into a clean half bottle, cork it, and store in the refrigerator. Without air space at the top, the rebottled wine will keep for up to one month.

WINE AS A MARINADE

Marinating food—especially meat and poultry—in wine contributes flavor and tenderness. As well as adding a flavor of its own, wine helps food absorb the flavors of herbs, vegetables, or spices. The moderate acidity of wine also helps penetrate and tenderize meats.

Both red and white wines are suitable for marinades. It's unnecessary to use a fine wine, although you should use a well-flavored wine you wouldn't hesitate to drink. Dry wines are traditional for savory marinades, but a sweet wine can add an appealing flavor to game birds, such as squab or quail.

Wine is also used as a marinade in fruit desserts. In this context, fruits are said to macerate in wine. Peaches macerated in red wine or strawberries macerated in sparkling wine make refreshing summer desserts. Generally super-fine sugar is added to taste in order to balance the acidity of the wine (see MACERATE).

WINE AS A COOKING LIQUID

Cooking directly in wine adds flavor and necessary moisture. Fish poached in white wine or chicken braised in red wine are just two examples among many of wine as a cooking medium. Poaching in wine is ideal for delicate foods, such as fish. The poaching liquid may be a simple court bouillon of wine and water flavored with aromatics or a fumet, a wine-based fish stock. Fruits, too, are often poached in a wine syrup, made by boiling wine and water with sugar and such flavorings as cinnamon or vanilla bean. Wine syrups can also be drizzled over whole just-baked cakes as a flavoring and glaze.

Steaming in wine is a technique most often used with shellfish. Clams or mussels are put into a pot with white wine, shallots or onions, and herbs; the pot is covered and the liquid brought to a boil. The shellfish open as they steam in the wine and are imbued with its flavor.

Braising meats and poultry in wine—first browning the meat or poultry in oil or fat, then adding wine and cooking slowly in a covered pan—is a technique common to some of the world's most satisfying dishes. Not only does the wine moisten and tenderize tougher cuts of meat, but its distinctive flavor also enhances the sauce. The long, slow cooking and the typical final reduction of the sauce concentrate the flavors of the wine.

This concentration, however, can be a mixed blessing. Red wines, especially, can dominate a sauce and should be used with caution. Sometimes a concentrated flavor is desirable, as in the classic Burgundian coq au vin or in dishes made with game or red meats. But with other braised dishes, even if you plan to serve a red wine, cooking with a white wine may produce the best flavors.

WINE AS A FLAVORING

Fortified wines such as sherry and Madeira are often stirred into soups at the last moment or even at the table. A spoonful of sherry or a dash of Madeira are the classic finishing touches for some consommés and cream soups. Usually the soup is not cooked further after the wine is added to avoid dissipating the flavor of the wine.

Wine is also used to deglaze a roasting pan or a skillet in which foods have been roasted or sautéed. Deglazing is

the first step in creating a delicious assortment of sauces. Whether you are working with a beef roast, pan-fried chicken, or sautéed fish fillets, the deglazing procedure is the same: Pour off excess fat, add aromatics if desired (herbs, onions, garlic), then add wine and bring it to a boil, scraping drippings loose from bottom of pan. After alcohol has boiled out of wine, other liquids such as cream or stock may be added and reduced to make a sauce.

Most recipes for wine sauces call for reducing, which simply means boiling down the sauces until the volume has been cut by about half. Reducing is an essential technique to many great sauces. Reducing a wine-based sauce eliminates the alcohol while it concentrates the flavor of the wine. Such sauces must be made with care. Reducing a wine sauce too far can make it too acidic and boil away most of the flavor.

Good cooking begins with the best ingredients. Good, inexpensive wine from a high-quality winery is an important pantry item.

Sautéed Chicken Breasts With Sherry, Cream, and Mushrooms (see page 611) is a fine complement to Chardonnay or other full-flavored white wines. The sauce lends itself to endless variations; in place of the mushrooms, try almonds or other nuts, artichoke hearts, or even a mixture of raisins and unsweetened coconut.

2. Combine ground spices, wine, vinegar, onion, garlic, and ginger in a glass, ceramic, or stainless steel bowl large enough to hold poultry.

3. Marinate whole or cut-up birds in refrigerator, covered, overnight, or for up to three days. Turn birds frequently to marinate them evenly.

4. Remove birds from refrigerator 30 minutes before cooking. Drain thoroughly and discard marinade. Roast, grill, or broil (stuffed or unstuffed) according to any standard recipe.

Makes about 1 cup (enough for a whole fryer or duck or for 2 or 3 Rock Cornish game hens).

■ PORK ROAST WITH WHITE-WINE MARINADE

Two days of marinating in a mixture of white wine, spices, and herbs gives roast pork a little of the flavor of wild boar. Be sure to marinate the pork in a nonaluminum container such as stainless steel, ceramic, or glass.

> 1 teaspoon fennel seed
> 2 teaspoons coriander seed
> 1 teaspoon black peppercorns
> 1 teaspoon salt
> ¼ teaspoon ground ginger
> 1 pork loin roast (about 3½ lb with bones)
> 1 cup Gewürztraminer or Sauvignon Blanc
> 1 large sprig fresh sage *or* ½ teaspoon dried sage
> 1 large sprig fresh thyme *or* ½ teaspoon dried thyme
> 1 bay leaf
> 8 small new potatoes

1. Two days ahead: Coarsely grind fennel, coriander, and pepper in a clean coffee grinder, electric mini-chopper, or with a mortar and pestle. Combine ground spices with salt and ginger. Rub this mixture all over pork roast. Put roast in a stainless steel, ceramic, or glass bowl, pour in wine, and crumble herbs into bowl. Marinate roast in refrigerator, turning it several times a day to marinate it evenly.

2. On cooking day: Remove roast from refrigerator at least 1 hour before cooking. Preheat oven to 450° F. Drain roast thoroughly and discard marinade.

3. Pat roast dry with paper towels and place it, fat side up, on a rack in a roasting pan. Put roast in hot oven, reduce heat to 325° F, and roast to an internal temperature of 170° F (25 to 30 minutes per pound). Add potatoes to roasting pan for the last 30 minutes to roast in drippings.

4. Let roast rest about 15 minutes before carving into ½-inch slices. Serve with roast potatoes and a full-flavored dry white wine or a lighter red wine.

Serves 4.

■ SPICY RED-WINE MARINADE

This recipe, similar to the white-wine marinade (at right), but based on a red wine, is especially good for roasted, broiled, or grilled poultry. For a sweeter taste, use ruby port instead of a dry wine.

> ½ teaspoon *each* whole coriander, fennel, black pepper, and juniper berries
> ¾ cup dry red wine
> 2 tablespoons red wine vinegar
> ½ onion, sliced
> 2 or 3 cloves garlic, minced
> 1 tablespoon minced fresh ginger *or* ½ teaspoon ground ginger

1. Grind coriander, fennel, pepper, and juniper berries together in a clean coffee grinder, electric minichopper, or with a mortar and pestle.

■ STEAMED CLAMS

When simply steamed in a seasoned broth, clams, mussels, or oysters make a tasty first course. Serve in shallow bowls with crusty bread to scoop up the juices. Steam the clams (or other shellfish) in a nonreactive saucepan so the acid in the wine will not impart a metallic flavor.

    4   pounds (about 32 medium) clams
    8   cloves garlic, minced
    2   large shallots, minced
    ½   teaspoon salt
    1   cup dry white wine
    6 to 8 sprigs parsley, minced, for garnish

1. Wash clams, scrubbing exterior, to remove any sand. Place clams in a deep, 4-quart, nonreactive saucepan. Add minced garlic and shallots to saucepan with clams. Sprinkle with salt and add wine.

2. Bring to a boil, reduce heat, and simmer for 2 minutes. Discard any clams that fail to open. Garnish with parsley.

Serves 4.

■ BEEF BRAISED IN RED WINE

This is not a dish for subtle wines; it works best with a full-flavored wine with ample acidity. A Petite Sirah or a Zinfandel with plenty of character will fill the bill nicely. Serve the same type of wine as a beverage. Although braised beef can be cooked on top of the stove, it is easier to maintain the slight simmer in a low oven. A slow cooker or other covered electric cooker also works well, but you will still need to do steps 1 through 3 on top of the stove.

    2½ pounds boneless chuck roast
    1   tablespoon oil or chicken or duck fat
    ⅓   pound shallots, peeled and left whole
    ½   bottle dry red wine
        Bouquet garni of parsley, bay leaf, thyme,
        and celery leaves
    ½   teaspoon salt
    ½   teaspoon freshly ground pepper
    4   dried tomato halves, chopped, or
        8 dry-cured olives, pitted and chopped

1. Preheat oven to 225° F. Cut meat into large cubes (2 to 2½ inches), trimmed of excess fat and gristle. Dry cubes of meat with a paper towel. (This allows them to brown more easily.)

2. Heat oil in an ovenproof casserole over medium heat. Brown cubes of meat a few at a time. (Don't try to brown too many at a time or they will stew rather than brown.) Transfer cubes to a plate as they brown and add more as space allows.

3. When all meat has been browned, brown shallots in the same fat. Pour out any fat remaining in pan. Add wine, bring to a boil, and reduce heat to a simmer. Return meat cubes to pan. Add bouquet garni, salt, pepper, and tomatoes.

4. Cover pan and place it in oven. Bake 3½ to 4 hours, adjusting heat, if necessary, so sauce barely simmers. Meat should be very tender and should absorb flavor of sauce.

5. Turn off oven. Remove cooked meat and shallots to a serving platter and return them to oven to keep warm. Discard bouquet garni and bring sauce to a boil on top of stove. Reduce sauce by a third. Taste and correct seasoning.

6. Pour sauce over meat and serve with buttered noodles, steamed potatoes, or polenta.

Serves 6.

■ CHICKEN BREASTS WITH SHERRY, CREAM, AND MUSHROOMS

If you are serving a first course before this dish, you can cook the chicken breasts first, then hold them in the oven for 15 minutes or so. The sauce will only take about five minutes to prepare, so you will be able to sit down and enjoy the first course before serving the entrée.

    4   chicken breast halves, boned and skinned
    ¼   cup flour
    ½   teaspoon salt
    ½   teaspoon pepper
    2 to 4 tablespoons butter
    2   tablespoons vegetable oil
    ¼   pound mushrooms, sliced
    1   tablespoon chopped garlic
    1   green onion, chopped
    ¼   cup dry sherry
    ½   cup whipping cream

1. Preheat oven to 200° F. Trim all bits of fat and membrane from chicken breasts. In a shallow bowl combine flour, salt, and pepper. Dredge breasts in seasoned flour and shake off excess. Have a warm, ovenproof plate ready.

2. In a large skillet over medium heat, heat butter and oil together. Add chicken breasts and cook just until the thickest part springs back when pressed (about 3 minutes per side). Remove to warm plate, cover loosely with aluminum foil, and keep warm in oven while you prepare sauce. (Recipe may be prepared to this point up to 15 minutes ahead of serving time.)

3. If butter has browned, pour it out and add another 2 tablespoons butter to pan. Add mushrooms, garlic, and green onion, turn heat to high, and sauté until mushrooms begin to soften. Add sherry, bring to a boil, and reduce by half. Add cream, bring to a boil, and reduce to a thick sauce. Taste for seasoning and correct if necessary.

4. Return chicken breasts to skillet to coat them with sauce. Serve topped with mushrooms and sauce.

Serves 4.

TIPS

COOKING WITH WINE

Wine can be used in place of part or all of the cooking or marinating liquid in countless recipes as long as you remember the following.

- *Boiling down wine concentrates its flavors, including acidity and sweetness. Be careful not to use too much or the finished dish may be excessively sweet or sour, or taste too strongly of wine.*

- *Whether quickly making a deglazing sauce or simmering a dish over a long period, allow enough cooking time after adding the wine for the alcohol to evaporate. Boiling a sauce rapidly in a shallow pan will cook off the alcohol in 1 or 2 minutes, but slow simmering in a deeper pan may take 15 minutes or more. Taste sauce before serving to be sure. Avoid adding wine to a sauce just before serving, or the dish may taste unpleasantly alcoholic. The last-minute addition of wine to some soups (see Wine as a Flavoring, page 609) is one delicious exception.*

- *Remember that wine does not belong in every dish. More than one wine-based sauce in a single meal can be monotonous. Use wine in cooking only when it has something to contribute to the finished dish.*

The elegant appearance of Rosé Pears in Chocolate Bath belies its ease of preparation.

■ ROSE PEARS IN CHOCOLATE BATH

Poach the pears and mix the sauce ahead of time; then assemble this elegant dessert just before serving.

2½ cups red table wine
⅓ cup sugar
½ cinnamon stick, broken
⅛ teaspoon ground coriander
3 whole cloves
    Grated rind of ½ orange
    Grated rind of 1 lemon
4 Bartlett pears, peeled
1 cup Old-fashioned Chocolate Sauce
    (double recipe; see page 523)
2 to 3 tablespoons Cognac, orange-flavored
    liqueur, or almond-flavored liqueur
    Mint sprigs, kiwifruit slices, or
    candied violets, for garnish

1. In a medium saucepan combine wine, sugar, cinnamon, coriander, cloves, and orange and lemon rinds. Bring to a boil. Add pears, reduce heat, and simmer just until tender (8 to 10 minutes).

2. With a slotted spoon remove pears. Halve and core if desired. Place one pear upright in each of 4 champagne or sherbet glasses.

3. Mix chocolate sauce and Cognac. Pour around pears and garnish as desired.

Serves 4.

Nut-Filled Pears in Chocolate Bath Poach pears as directed in steps 1 and 2. Halve pears horizontally, cutting in a sawtooth pattern to flute. Core, and stuff each half with a mixture of chopped nuts, raisins, dried dates, and dried apricots. Reassemble pears and surround each one with Old-fashioned Chocolate Sauce.

Rosé Pears and Ice Cream Poach pears as directed in steps 1 and 2. Halve vertically and core. Place a scoop of ice cream, sherbet, or frozen yogurt in each of 4 champagne or sherbet glasses. Lean 2 pear halves against each scoop.

Rosé Pears in Vanilla Cream Poach pears as directed in steps 1 and 2. Mix 1 to 2 tablespoons Cognac into 1 cup Stirred Custard (see page 168). Whip 1 cup whipping cream and fold into custard. Place cream in bottom of serving glasses. Add pears and garnish with mint.

Recipes and Related Information
Boeuf Bourguignonne, 43; Cheese, 110; Choucroute Garni, 75; Classic Beef Consommé With Vegetable Julienne and Madeira, 562; Fresh Fruit in Wine, 347; Game Hens Coq au Vin, 58; Marinade, 349; Stilton Crock With Port Wine, 114; Sweetbreads and Mushroom-Marsala Sauce, 590; Veal Marsala, 594; Wine Court Bouillon, 450; Winter Fruit Compote, 186.

WORK, TO

To stir or knead a mixture; implies manipulation and resistance. This is a common term used in recipes for bread doughs: "Work the flour into the dough" is a typical instruction. Although it most often refers to hands-on processes, it more generally can mean any vigorous blending of somewhat stiff, resistant mixtures whether by hand or by machine.

Recipes and Related Information
Knead, 326; Yeast Bread, 613.

YAM

The true yam, *Dioscorea,* is a tuber cultivated in Africa and Asia. (For information on the vegetable Americans call yam, see SWEET POTATO.) There are several varieties of *Dioscorea* in various shapes, sizes, and colors, but all have a high starch content. The Japanese mountain yam looks like a large old bone. It is usually peeled, grated, and eaten raw; when grated, it has a gluey consistency and mild flavor. The African giant yam or white yam may grow to weigh 100 pounds. It has a barklike skin, a white flesh, and a mild, starchy flavor.

Use The Japanese yam serves as a binder in some processed foods and as a garnish for noodle dishes and rice. The giant yam is a staple in Africa. In West Africa it is pounded into a paste called Fufu, which may be made into dumplings or used as a thickener for soups and stews. African cooks also slice yams and deep-fry them like potato chips, boil them in milk, or slice and bake them like potatoes with sliced onions, bread crumbs, and cheese. In the Caribbean, yams may be simply steamed and buttered, or grated, bound with egg, and fried in oil.

Availability True yams are occasionally found in Japanese, African, or Latin markets in this country. Some African and Latin markets also stock canned white yams from West Africa.

Selection Yams should be firm, unblemished, and unwrinkled. Smaller ones are preferable.

Storage Keep in a cool place or in the refrigerator for up to one week.

Preparation The Japanese yam should be peeled and finely grated. The yam may be irritating to sensitive skin; wear gloves while peeling or peel under cold running water. African or Caribbean varieties should be peeled and cooked. Cut peeled yam into chunks or slices and add to stews or boil in salted water until tender.

Cooking See BOIL, DEEP-FRY, STEAM.

YEAST

Although wild yeasts have existed since the origins of civilization, their actions were not fully understood until the work of Louis Pasteur in the 1850s. Pasteur's studies of fermentation made it possible for scientists to cultivate yeasts. Today cultivated yeast strains are made and marketed expressly for breads, wines, and beers.

Use Yeast makes bread rise and is responsible for the fermentation of grape juice into wine and barley mash into beer. The yeast feed on the sugars in the dough or the juice, converting the sugars to carbon dioxide and alcohol. In the case of bread, the carbon dioxide gas is trapped within the dough and makes it rise. In the case of wine, the carbon dioxide escapes but the alcohol remains. In beer making, trapped carbon dioxide provides natural carbonization. For the home cook, the principal value of yeast is as a leavening agent in breads.

Availability Yeast for baking is widely stocked in supermarkets, packaged either as active dry yeast or as fresh yeast in moist cakes. One yeast cake is equivalent to one ¼-ounce package active dry yeast (1 tablespoon dry yeast). Some health-food stores also carry active dry yeast in bulk. Recently available in the market is quick-rise yeast, a high-activity yeast strain that makes doughs rise up to 50 percent faster than regular yeast does.

Selection Check expiration date on package.

Storage Fresh yeast is more perishable than dry; refrigerate and use within three weeks of purchase. Bulk dry yeast should be stored airtight in a covered container. Both packaged and bulk dry yeast should be kept in a cool, dark, dry place and used within six months.

Preparation To activate dry yeast, sprinkle it over a bowl of warm (about 110° F) liquid; let soften 1 minute. Stir with a fork to dissolve yeast. Set aside to proof 5 to 10 minutes. Proofing verifies that yeast is still active. Within 10 minutes, yeast should produce a foamy layer on surface of water. If not, discard yeast and liquid, and begin again with a fresh package. To activate fresh cake yeast, place it in a bowl of warm (about 110° F) liquid; mash with a fork to blend and stir until smooth. Set aside to proof 10 minutes. Discard if yeast does not begin foaming within 10 minutes.

About Proofing: In the days when the effectiveness of commercial yeast was less predictable, proofing was essential. However, the baker's yeast produced today is extremely reliable and, if used before the expiration date on the package, should not require proofing. Indeed, many modern recipes call for adding dry yeast directly to bread dough.

Recipes and Related Information
Fermentation, 219; Leaven, 338; Proof, 479.

YEAST BREAD

Making fresh yeast-leavened bread at home is a pleasure that, if planned, can fit into most schedules. The rewards are many: the warm, relaxed kneading and shaping; the wonderful yeasty aroma that permeates the air during baking; and finally, the delight of biting into a fresh, full-tasting bread.

The world of bread is a temptingly varied one, and is much more inviting than the standard sliced white loaf frequently associated with the word *bread*. The slender, crusty French baguette and rich brioche, the dark, fragrant German rye, and the simple, chewy Italian loaf are just a few of the forms that bread takes in other cultures.

TYPES OF YEAST BREADS

All yeast breads are made from a soft dough; approximately 3 parts flour to 1 part liquid is the usual ratio. This proportion can vary somewhat as flours differ in their capacities to absorb liquid, which is why most bread recipes give a range for the amount of flour. At its most basic, bread is a combination of flour, yeast, salt, and a liquid. With the addition of eggs, sugar, milk, butter, spices, nuts, raisins, and other ingredients, the basic dough becomes richer, sweeter, and more cakelike. Flours ground from grains other than wheat also impart a special characteristic to a bread; rye, cornmeal, and oats add texture and distinctive flavor to the dough.

Examples of a straightforward yeast bread are the familiar white or whole-grain loaf. Brioche is a golden bread rich in eggs and butter and a favorite for breakfast when spread with more butter and homemade preserves. Babas and savarins also are abundantly buttery and are so sweet that they are served as a dessert, drenched in liqueur. Croissants, Danish pastries, sweet rolls, babas, and savarins are yeast leavened, but because of the high proportion of butter to flour in their doughs, they are as much a pastry as a bread.

Breads vary in shape as well—from the familiar loaf to free-form rounds and braids, to those molded in special fluted or flared tins. What these varied breads have in common is that they use yeast as a leavener. In a dough, yeast gives off carbon dioxide gas, which, along with the steam produced by liquid ingredients, causes the dough to expand and rise. Quick breads are leavened chemically; they use either baking powder or baking soda (or a combination of the two) rather than yeast (see QUICK BREAD).

INGREDIENTS FOR BREADS: WHAT EACH DOES

Most bread recipes call for the same few basic ingredients—flour, liquid, yeast, and salt—often plus shortening, eggs, and sugar or other sweetener. The nature of the ingredients, their proportion, and the way they are combined make all the difference in the final product.

The ingredients that go into a loaf of bread are simple—flour, other grains and cereals, yeast, eggs, milk, and sugar and honey. But their combined effect is wonderfully complex.

Flour   This is the fundamental component—the foundation—of most breads. Wheat flours have the ability to make gluten, an elastic protein that gives structure to breads and all baked goods. Gluten is formed when liquid combines with two of the proteins contained in wheat flour. Beating, stirring, or kneading develops the gluten further into a strong cellular network to hold the gases and steam that are given off during the bread making and baking processes and inflate the finished product and make it light. Nonwheat flours have little or no gluten and produce breads that are dense and low rising; they are often combined with wheat flour for best results. See FLOUR and GRAIN.

Liquid   In some form, liquid is present in most breads. It helps to distribute the yeast evenly in the flour and is a medium in which sugar and salt can dissolve. Doughs made with water generally yield crisper breads with more crust than doughs made with milk. Used in yeast breads, milk adds richness, makes a bread with a finer crumb and softer crust, and can help retard staling. Before pasteurization, milk used in a bread recipe was first scalded; this was thought to destroy some enzymes that adversely affected bread quality. However, scalding isn't necessary with pasteurized milk (see MILK).

Yeast   When fed the correct amounts of food, moisture, and warmth, yeast, which are tiny plants, multiply rapidly. A small amount of sugar supports the growth of yeast, but too much sugar slows the rate. For this reason, rich doughs with a high proportion of sugar take longer to rise than leaner ones. Yeast is sold in two forms: cake (compressed) and active dry yeast (standard and quick-rise). Yeast is very heat sensitive: Too little heat and it will not multiply; too much and it will die. The optimum temperature varies according to the type of yeast. Both cake yeast and active dry yeast are most effective at about 110° F. Quick-rise active dry yeast will tolerate a range of temperatures from 90° to 115° F. See YEAST.

Salt   In addition to flavoring bread, salt also helps to control the rate of fermentation of yeast breads and to make the dough easier to handle. In very hot weather, an environment that may cause a yeast dough to rise too rapidly, the addition of extra salt will slow down the reaction.

Sugar   From sugar, a yeast dough gets sweetness and an immediate source of food for the yeast; sugar also imparts tenderness to the crumb and color to the crust.

Fat   Butter, margarine, shortening, and oil are the usual forms fat takes in a yeast dough, although their addition is optional. Fat helps produce a tender loaf with a nice, brown crust.

Eggs   A dough made with one or more eggs has a rich flavor and color.

BREAD-BAKING EQUIPMENT

The *batterie de cuisine* for baking bread ranges from the simplest baking sheet or loaf pan to a sleek heavy-duty mixer. Here are some of the basic tools many bakers use regularly.

Food Processor   This appliance is good for mixing and kneading dough. More and more bread recipes are offering a variation for preparing doughs this way. Check the instructions for your machine to determine the capacity for heavy dough. Placing too much dough in the machine can damage the motor.

Measuring Utensils   Have both liquid and dry measuring cups, and two sets of measuring spoons (one for liquids and one for powders). A spatula will come in handy to level off dry ingredients or to loosen baked breads from pans. A dough thermometer (also called an instant-read thermometer; see THERMOMETER) is helpful to determine that the liquid used in a yeast bread is at the proper temperature.

Mixer   A heavy-duty mixer takes much of the work out of the labor-intensive task of making bread. Its strong motor can beat a fairly heavy dough to develop sufficient elasticity so that the dough requires less kneading later. These mixers often are equipped with a special dough hook, designed for yeast breads; many practiced bread makers use the dough hook of the mixer to knead the dough until it is almost ready to set aside to rise, then finish the job with a minute or two of hand-kneading to be sure the dough feels just right.

Molds Breads can be baked in a variety of pans, including the traditional loaf pans and fluted brioche molds, or they can be shaped by hand and set on a flat baking sheet. As with other cookware, a heavy metal pan made of a material that will absorb and hold heat well, will produce the best product. Clay is also well-suited for baking bread; some baking surfaces are soaked in water before baking so that the steam released in the oven will produce a crisp crust. For more information, see BAKING PANS.

Other Utensils A pastry brush is useful for applying glazes, wire racks are necessary for cooling the finished bread, and a serrated knife is the proper tool for making clean slices without tearing the crumb.

PREPARING YEAST DOUGHS

All ingredients should be at or near room temperature, about 72° F, since yeast thrives in a warm environment. The liquid is usually somewhat warmer, 105° to 115° F. On a cold day, rising time may be speeded if the mixing bowl is warmed in a low oven before use.

Often the first step in a recipe is to soften the yeast in warm water with some sugar; the yeast sits for about 5 minutes and then other ingredients are added. Some recipes specify proofing the yeast by leaving it longer, for 10 to 15 minutes; if within 10 minutes the surface bubbles and foams, the yeast is alive and can be used successfully. If a reaction fails to occur, the yeast and liquid should be discarded, and the process repeated with a fresh package. However, commercial yeast is reliable enough that, if a package is used before the marked expiration date, proofing shouldn't be necessary. Some recipes mix in the yeast directly with the dry ingredients.

KNEADING THE DOUGH

Flour is added last and then the dough is manipulated by hand, with a wooden spoon, in a heavy-duty electric mixer, or in the work bowl of a food processor. Working the dough disperses the ingredients and develops a strong network of gluten. Kneading continues until the dough takes on a silken elasticity and fine bubbles or blisters can be discerned just below the surface. More flour is added to bring the dough to a workable consistency. See KNEAD for a further discussion of this technique and information on using a food processor for making yeast doughs.

THE RISING PERIOD

When the dough has been sufficiently kneaded, it is set aside to rise. Confusingly, this stage is also called proofing (see PROOF). During rising the yeast continues to grow, giving off carbon dioxide gas that gently and slowly expands the dough. The first rising takes 1 to 1½ hours; during that time the dough generally doubles in bulk. The second and third risings, if called for, are for shorter periods. Some recipes have only one rise. However, flavor improves and a finer texture results if the dough has several long, slow risings.

For rising, the dough is shaped into a ball and placed in a lightly oiled bowl, then turned to coat the entire surface. This light covering of oil keeps the dough moist and prevents it from forming a skin that will inhibit expansion. The bowl is covered with plastic wrap or a clean kitchen towel and set in a warm, draft-free place, the environment needed for yeast doughs to rise to maximum volume (usually about 80° to 85° F). Commercial bakeries have special proofing ovens; at home doughs rise nicely in a gas oven warmed by a pilot light or in an electric oven that has been turned on at 200° F for 1 minute, then turned off. As a test to determine if the dough has risen sufficiently, dent it gently with your index finger. If the dent remains, the dough is ready. If the depression fills up and nearly disappears, the dough needs more time.

SHAPING THE DOUGH

When the dough has doubled, it is punched down or deflated by hitting it with your fist or by gently picking it up and setting back down into the bowl. This step keeps the dough from overstretching and subsequently breaking the gluten network and creates a bread with a more even grain by widely distributing the bubbles of carbon dioxide that developed during the rising period. The dough is then shaped (see Shaping Loaves and Rolls at right), set in a pan or on a baking sheet, and usually left to rise a second time. Baking pans and baking sheets should be well greased; they also may be lightly dusted with flour or sprinkled with cornmeal. After rising and before baking, loaves are sometimes slashed with a sharp knife or a razor blade, or snipped with scissors. This is done both for decorative effect and to allow excess gas, which would otherwise cause the dough to tear, to escape during baking.

BAKING, COOLING, AND STORING YEAST BREADS

Within minutes after being placed in a preheated oven, a yeast dough rises dramatically. This expansion, called oven spring, continues until the yeast is killed by the heat and the structure of the bread sets; some doughs may increase in volume by almost 80 percent during this time. A light, crispy bread can be produced by baking directly on a high-fire baking stone or on an unglazed quarry tile, the home version of a commercial brick oven (see BAKING STONE). Commercial bakery ovens produce breads with superior crusts by injecting a fine spray of water into the oven cavity. Home bakers can approximate this mechanism by setting a pan filled with hot water on the floor of a gas oven or on the lowest shelf of an electric oven. In addition, spray the oven interior several times during the first 10 minutes or so of baking with a fine mist of water. Remove the pan of water toward the end of baking time in order to allow the bread to dry and brown.

SHAPING LOAVES AND ROLLS

Forming a standard loaf Shape dough into a rectangle that is as long as the loaf pan and slightly less than twice as wide as it is long. At narrow end, roll dough tightly, jelly-roll style. Pinch ends and seam to seal; turn ends under, if necessary.

Making a braid Place ropes across baking sheet. Braid, tapering to a rounded point at both ends. Pinch ends to seal; turn ends under, if necessary.

Shaping rolls Bowknots: Tie strands of dough loosely into knots. *Cloverleaf Rolls:* Arrange 3 balls of dough in each cup of muffin pan. *Fantans:* Lay stacks of dough strips horizontally in each cup of muffin pan as shown here or vertically as shown in photograph, page 618. *Parker House Rolls:* Fold circles of dough in half.

TIPS

YEAST BREADS AND THE MICROWAVE OVEN

Rising time for yeast doughs can be shortened if done in a microwave oven that can operate at 10 percent power. See Micro-Rise Method, page 364.

Yeast breads baked in a microwave oven are pale, low in volume, and tough. However, already baked breads and rolls can be defrosted and reheated in seconds in a microwave. The secret is to reheat bread only until it's warm. Overheating will cook the bread, and it will come out of the microwave oven hard and tough. See Reheating and Defrosting Baked Goods at 50 Percent Power (page 363) for specific times.

The bread is done when it has developed a beautiful golden color and sounds hollow when tapped; however, color and touch are not always reliable indicators of doneness, so use baking time as well. Typically, a loaf of bread needs 40 minutes to 1 hour to bake.

Remove baked bread from pan or baking sheet immediately and cool on a wire rack to prevent bottom from getting soggy. If serving, slice with a serrated bread knife and a sawing motion. After the bread is completely cool, store at room temperature, tightly wrapped in plastic wrap, aluminum foil, or an airtight plastic bag. Unless you live in an environment of exceptionally high humidity, storing bread in the refrigerator will cause it to dry out more quickly than it will at room temperature. Breads enriched with eggs, butter, and fruit such as raisins keep longer than plain breads because of their higher fat and moisture contents. Home-baked yeast breads also freeze beautifully.

Freezing bread shortly after it has cooled is the best way to preserve it in peak condition. Choose a freezer wrapping that is both moistureproof and vaporproof in order to keep the bread from drying out or absorbing other flavors and odors. The wrapping should be sturdy enough not to tear when freezer packages are shifted. Use frozen breads within four to six months of baking.

Do not glaze, ice, or sugar-dust coffee cakes and rolls that you plan to freeze. Add these decorations after thawing and shortly before serving. Remove frozen breads several hours before (or the night before) you serve them. Let them thaw at room temperature, then serve as is or warm in the oven. A microwave oven is ideal for thawing or reheating breads; see Reheating and Defrosting Baked Goods at 50 Percent Power (page 363). However, breads heated in the microwave steam rather than bake, and will not be crisp.

◼ OVERNIGHT WHITE BREAD

These homey loaves rest—shaped and ready to bake—in the refrigerator until the next day.

    2 **packages active dry yeast**
    ½ **cup warm (105° to 115° F) water**
    2 **tablespoons honey**
    1⅔ **cups warm (105° to 115° F) milk**
    1½ **teaspoons salt**
    2 **tablespoons butter or margarine**
    5½ **to 6 cups flour**
       Oil, for greasing
    1 **teaspoon butter or margarine, softened (optional)**

1. In a large bowl of electric mixer, sprinkle yeast over the warm water. Add 1 teaspoon of the honey. Let stand until soft (about 5 minutes).

2. Stir in milk, remaining honey, salt, and the 2 tablespoons butter.

3. Add 3 cups flour. Blend, then beat at medium speed until smooth and elastic (about 5 minutes). Stir in about 2 cups more flour to make a soft dough.

4. Turn dough out onto a board or pastry cloth coated with some of the remaining ½ to 1 cup flour. Knead until dough is smooth and satiny and small bubbles form just under surface (10 to 15 minutes), adding just enough flour to prevent dough from being sticky.

5. Cover ball of kneaded dough with plastic wrap and a kitchen towel; let rest for 30 minutes.

6. Punch dough down and divide into two equal portions. Shape each into a loaf (see photograph, page 615). Place shaped loaves in greased 4½- by 8½-inch loaf pans. Brush lightly with oil.

7. Cover with plastic wrap and refrigerate for at least 3 hours (up to 24 hours). During this time, dough should nearly double in bulk.

8. Remove from refrigerator and let stand at room temperature for 1 hour.

9. Preheat oven to 375° F. Bake until loaves are well browned and sound hollow when tapped (35 to 40 minutes). Remove loaves from pans and cool on wire racks. Rub ½ teaspoon of the soft butter (if desired) over top crust of each loaf while warm.

Makes 2 loaves.

◼ QUICK-MIX HONEYED WHEAT BREAD

Using quick-rise active dry yeast, you can produce a light, fine-textured whole wheat bread that is faster to make than most yeast breads for several reasons. You mix the yeast with the other dry ingredients without first softening it in hot water; the dough needs only one rising and it rises faster than most whole-grain breads.

    5¼ **to 5¾ cups all-purpose flour**
    2 **cups whole wheat flour**
    2 **packages quick-rise active dry yeast**
    2 **teaspoons salt**
    2 **cups milk**
    ½ **cup water**
    ½ **cup honey**
    2 **tablespoons vegetable oil, plus oil for greasing**

1. In large bowl of electric mixer, combine 4 cups all-purpose flour, whole wheat flour, yeast, and salt; stir to blend dry ingredients thoroughly.

2. In a 1½- to 2-quart saucepan, combine milk, the water, honey, and oil; place over medium heat, stirring to blend well, until hot to touch (110° to 115° F).

3. Add milk mixture to flour mixture. Mix to blend, then beat at medium speed until smooth and elastic (about 5 minutes). Stir in about ¾ cup of the remaining all-purpose flour to make a soft dough.

4. Turn dough out onto a board or pastry cloth coated with some of the remaining ½ to 1 cup flour. Knead until dough is smooth and satiny and small bubbles form just under surface (about 10 minutes), adding just enough flour to prevent dough from being sticky.

5. Cover dough and let rest for 10 minutes.

6. Divide dough into two equal portions. Shape each into a loaf (see photograph, page 615). Place shaped loaves in greased 4½- by 8½-inch loaf pans. Cover lightly with waxed paper or plastic wrap. Let rise in a warm place until doubled in bulk (40 to 45 minutes).

7. Preheat oven to 375° F. Bake until loaves are well browned and sound hollow when tapped (30 to 45 minutes). Remove loaves from pans and let cool on wire racks.

Makes 2 loaves.

BRAIDED EGG BREAD

Poppy or sesame seed speckles the crust of this traditional Jewish bread, *challah*. It is a wonderful bread for sandwiches and makes delicious French toast. For an illustration of shaping a braided loaf, see photographs, Shaping Loaves and Rolls, page 615.

> 3 **packages active dry yeast**
> 3 **tablespoons sugar**
> 1 **cup warm (105° to 115° F) water**
> 5 **cups flour**
> 1 **tablespoon salt**
> ½ **cup warm (105° to 115° F) milk**
> ¼ **cup butter, softened**
> 3 **eggs**
>   **Oil, for greasing**
> 2 **egg yolks**
> 1 **tablespoon water**
>   **Pinch salt**
>   **Poppy or sesame seed, for sprinkling**

1. In a small bowl dissolve yeast and sugar in the warm water and set aside a few minutes to soften. Sift flour and the 1 tablespoon salt and set aside.

2. In a large bowl combine milk, butter, and the 3 eggs; stir in yeast mixture. Slowly add flour, one cup at a time, to make a soft dough. Turn out onto a lightly floured surface and knead until dough is smooth, satiny, and elastic. (The mixing and about 5 minutes of kneading can be done in a heavy-duty electric mixer; finish kneading by hand.)

3. Turn dough in a lightly oiled bowl. Cover and let rise in a warm place until doubled in bulk (about 1 hour). Punch down, knead lightly, and divide dough into 6 portions.

4. Roll each portion of dough into an 18-inch-long strand. Place 3 strands side by side diagonally across a large, greased baking sheet. Braid, being careful not to overstretch dough. Pinch ends of braid and tuck under to seal. Repeat for second loaf.

5. Let rise until almost doubled in bulk (about 45 minutes). Preheat oven to 400° F. Combine egg yolks, the 1 tablespoon water, and salt; brush lightly over braids. Sprinkle evenly with seeds.

6. Bake until loaves are golden brown and sound hollow when tapped lightly (35 to 40 minutes).

Makes 2 braided loaves.

FRENCH BAGUETTES

This recipe contains no fat of any kind and only a little sugar, so the bread it produces is very lean. It will taste best when it's freshly baked (within 1 hour or less of baking). To freshen it, sprinkle with a little water and reheat in the oven. Or, freeze bread as soon as it has fully cooled; to reheat, let it stand at room temperature for about 15 minutes, then warm it in a 350° F oven. Special black steel or stainless steel baguette pans, which typically hold two loaves, are available at better cookware stores.

> 1 **package active dry yeast**
> 2 **cups warm (105° to 115° F) water**
> 1 **teaspoon sugar**
> 2 **teaspoons salt**
> 5½ **to 6 cups unbleached flour**
>   **Oil, for greasing**

1. In large bowl of electric mixer, sprinkle yeast over ¼ cup of the warm water. Add sugar. Let stand until yeast is soft (about 5 minutes).

2. Stir in the remaining 1¾ cups water and salt. Add 4 cups of the flour. Mix to blend, then beat at medium speed until smooth and elastic (about 5 minutes).

3. Gradually beat in about 1 cup more flour to make a soft dough.

4. Turn dough out onto a board or pastry cloth floured with some of the remaining ½ to 1 cup flour. Knead until dough is springy and small bubbles form just under surface (10 to 15 minutes), adding just enough flour to prevent dough from being sticky.

5. Turn dough in a greased bowl. Cover with plastic wrap and a towel; let rise in a warm place until doubled in bulk (about 1 hour).

6. Punch down dough; knead dough lightly into a ball on a floured surface. Cover with inverted bowl and let rest for 10 minutes.

7. Divide dough into 3 equal portions. Shape each into a slender oval loaf 16 to 18 inches long by rolling the ball of dough under palms of hands to elongate it. Place in greased baguette pans or well apart on a large, greased baking sheet. Let rise until puffy but not quite doubled (20 to 25 minutes). Preheat oven to 450° F. With a razor blade make 3 diagonal slashes, about ½ inch deep, down center of each loaf.

8. Before baking use an atomizer filled with cold water to spray shaped loaves with a fine film of moisture. Place in oven, then spray twice more at 3-minute intervals. Bake until bread is well browned (25 to 30 minutes in all). Slide onto wire racks to cool.

Makes 3 loaves.

TIPS

SPECIAL FINISHES

Although the natural, brown mat surface of a freshly baked loaf is extremely appealing, the appearance may be further enhanced by brushing the crust with a glaze or sprinkling the bread with seeds, spices, or herbs to develop textural interest. For shine, brush with an egg wash (see page 211). For a soft crust, brush with milk, buttermilk, cream, melted butter, or margarine. For a sweet glaze, brush with honey or a sugar syrup. Sesame seeds, poppy seeds, caraway seeds, fennel seeds, or finely chopped garlic or onion are a few topping suggestions; try mixing several herbs and spices for a fuller, more complex taste.

The dough for Golden Dinner Rolls can be shaped in a variety of ways. Shown here are Bowknots, Parker House Rolls, Cloverleaf Rolls, and Fantans.

1. In large bowl of electric mixer, sprinkle yeast over the water. Add 1 tablespoon of the sugar. Let stand until yeast is soft (about 5 minutes).

2. Add remaining sugar, milk, salt, and softened butter.

3. Mix in 2½ cups of the flour; beat until smooth and elastic (about 5 minutes). Beat in eggs, one at a time. Then stir in about 2 cups more flour to make a soft dough.

4. Turn dough out onto a board or pastry cloth coated with some of the remaining ½ to 1 cup flour. Knead until dough is smooth and satiny and small bubbles form just under surface (8 to 10 minutes), adding just enough flour to prevent dough from being sticky.

5. Turn dough in a greased bowl. Cover with plastic wrap and a towel. Let rise in a warm place until doubled in bulk (about 1 hour), or refrigerate (6 hours to 2 days).

6. Punch down dough. On a lightly floured surface, knead into a smooth ball; cover with inverted bowl and let rest for 10 minutes. Shape into one or more of the types of rolls shown in photograph at left and in Shaping Loaves and Rolls on page 615 (directions for specific rolls given below). Place on baking sheets or in baking pans as directed.

7. Let rise until almost doubled in bulk (30 to 45 minutes; 1 to 1¼ hours if dough has been refrigerated). Preheat oven to 400° F.

8. Brush rolls lightly with melted butter. Bake until golden brown (12 to 15 minutes). Transfer to wire racks to cool. If you wish, brush warm rolls with a little more melted butter for a softer crust.

Makes about 2 dozen rolls.

Bowknots   Divide dough into 24 equal portions; roll each portion with your hands on a lightly floured surface to make a strand 6 inches long. Tie loosely into a knot. Place on greased baking sheets.

Cloverleaf Rolls   Pinch off small pieces of dough and shape into smooth 1-inch balls. Dip into melted butter, then place three balls in each cup of a greased standard muffin pan.

Fantans   Roll dough out to about ⅛-inch thickness on a lightly floured surface. Brush with melted butter. Cut dough into strips 1 inch wide. Stack 6 strips on top of one another; cut stacked strips into 1½-inch pieces. Place each stack horizontally (as shown on page 615 or vertically, as shown in photograph on this page) in cup of greased standard muffin pan.

Parker House Rolls   On a lightly floured surface, roll dough out to ¼-inch thickness. Brush with melted butter. Cut into 2½- to 3-inch circles. Use handle of a wooden spoon to make a depression just off center across each circle. Fold along depression and place on greased baking sheets with larger portion on top.

■ **GOLDEN DINNER ROLLS**

One basic dough can be formed into four varieties. Shape all the rolls alike, or try two or three different kinds. The finished rolls are pictured in the above photograph. Shaping Loaves and Rolls, page 615, illustrates how to form the dough into each type of roll.

   2 packages active dry yeast
   ½ cup warm (105° to 115° F) water
   ⅓ cup sugar
   ¾ cup warm (105° to 115° F) milk
   1 teaspoon salt
   ¼ cup butter or margarine, softened, plus
       melted butter or margarine for brushing
   5 to 5½ cups flour
   2 eggs
       Oil, for greasing

■ SOURDOUGH STARTER

If you are using a dry starter mix, prepare it according to package directions. Most starters require several days to establish, so plan ahead. Once you have an established starter—whether you began with dry mix or with a borrowed starter—each time you bake with it, the first step is to combine the starter with flour and water and let the mixture ferment overnight. This procedure, which replenishes the basic starter and provides the additional quantity for baking, is given in the following recipe.

Sourdough starters should be stored only in glass, ceramic, or food-grade plastic containers. Never use metal containers, which might react chemically with the starter. Caps should also be nonreactive. A glass jar or ceramic crock with a clamp top and a rubber gasket is ideal. From time to time, when the starter is being replenished, the container should be washed.

If the starter will not be used for more than one week, it should be replenished by the process given here, and the excess discarded.

    1 cup sourdough starter
       Equal parts warm (105° to 115° F) water
       and flour (at least 1 cup each)

1. Combine starter and the water in a large bowl. Stir in flour and beat to a smooth batter.

2. Cover bowl with plastic wrap and set aside in a warm (about 75° F) place. Let mixture stand until it is bubbly and sour, and a clear liquid begins to collect on surface (6 to 12 hours depending on liveliness of starter).

3. Stir starter, scoop out 1 cup of sponge, and place it in storage container; refrigerate until next use.

■ SAN FRANCISCO SOURDOUGH FRENCH BREAD

Even if you do not live near the Golden Gate, you can make a delicious sourdough bread. However, it takes time for the dough to get really sour. Try it on a weekend or some other time when you can let the dough ferment and rise at a leisurely pace. The traditional shapes for San Francisco sourdough bread are a long, oval French loaf and a 12-inch round, 3 to 4 inches thick.

    1   cup sourdough starter
         (see Sourdough Baking, above)
    3   cups warm (105° to 115° F) water
    6½   to 7 cups bread flour
    1   tablespoon salt
         Oil, for greasing
    1   package active dry yeast
         Cornmeal, for dusting
    1   egg, beaten with ¼ cup milk or water (optional)

1. Two nights ahead: Follow the procedure in step 1 of Sourdough Starter (above), adding 2½ cups of the warm water and 2½ cups of the flour to the 1 cup of starter. Mixture should sit 8 to 12 hours.

SOURDOUGH BAKING

A sourdough starter is a living culture of yeast cells and leavening bacteria. It must be replenished regularly by the addition of more flour. The easiest way to do this is the way pioneers of the Old West did daily: They mixed the starter with additional flour and water and then allowed the whole mixture to ferment overnight. Some of it was ladled back into the crock to form the starter for the next day, and the rest was used for pancakes, breads, and other baked goods.

Now that reliable dry yeasts are available, cooks do not need to keep a starter alive in order to bake bread. However, the characteristic flavor of sourdough has remained popular. Although it is possible to make sourdough breads by using only the starter for leavening, this technique results in a dense bread. Most commercial sourdough is made with a combination of starter and another leavener, either yeast or baking soda.

The easiest way to make a sourdough starter is from a commercial packaged mix, available in many specialty shops and supermarkets. Of course, if you know someone who has a good starter, perhaps you can borrow a cup or so. Once established, a starter can be kept alive indefinitely.

2. Next day: Return 1 cup sponge to storage container. To remaining sponge add salt and 2½ cups flour. Stir until dough is too stiff to work. Spread 1 cup flour on board, turn out dough onto board, and knead until dough is smooth and resilient (8 to 10 minutes). Add more flour as necessary to keep dough from sticking; knead until flour is thoroughly incorporated.

3. Place dough ball in lightly oiled bowl and turn to oil all surfaces. Cover bowl with plastic wrap and let rise 4 to 6 hours in a warm place. Punch down dough, cover again, and refrigerate overnight.

4. On day of baking: Remove dough from refrigerator and allow to return to room temperature. In a large bowl warmed with hot water, dissolve yeast in ½ cup warm water (105° to 115° F). Add dough and knead to incorporate yeast mixture. Add ½ cup flour and knead in bowl until surface is not too sticky, then turn dough out onto a floured surface and knead until smooth, adding additional flour as needed.

5. Return dough to oiled bowl and let rise, covered, until doubled in bulk (about 1 hour). Punch down and let rise again if time allows; otherwise, proceed to form loaves.

6. Preheat oven to 350° F. Punch down dough after rising. Form into loaves and place on baking sheets dusted with cornmeal; allow room between loaves for rising. Cover with a towel and let dough rise until nearly doubled in bulk. If desired, brush tops lightly with egg mixture. Slash tops making shallow cuts with a sharp knife or razor blade (lengthwise or diagonal on long loaves, crosshatched on round loaves). Bake on lowest shelf of oven until crust is golden brown and loaves sound hollow when tapped on bottom (about 1 hour). Cool on wire racks.

Makes two 16-inch loaves or 12-inch rounds or four baguettes.

Note For a more substantial crust, see Baking, Cooling, and Storing Yeast Breads, page 615.

The Italian flat bread called focaccia is a popular children's snack but it can also accompany a meal. Serve this onion-and-herb version with soup or salad for a casual lunch.

2. While dough is rising, heat butter in a skillet over low heat. Add onion and sauté until onion is soft but not browned (about 15 minutes). Remove from heat and stir in basil, ½ teaspoon of the salt, and pepper. Reserve.

3. Mix in remaining 2 cups flour to dough. Combine the 2 tablespoons olive oil and the remaining ¾ cup warm water; add to dough. Beat until dough forms a mass. Turn out onto a lightly floured surface and knead until dough is shiny and smooth (8 to 10 minutes). Transfer dough to a lightly oiled bowl and turn to coat all sides with oil. Cover and let rise until doubled in bulk (about 1½ hours).

4. Preheat oven to 450° F. Punch dough down into a 13- by 15-inch rectangle. Transfer to a baking sheet sprinkled with cornmeal. Spread top with onion mixture. Drizzle with additional olive oil. Sprinkle with remaining coarse salt and bake until golden (about 15 minutes). Cool slightly on a rack; serve warm.

Makes one 13- by 15-inch rectangle.

■ PUMPERNICKEL

Dark and hearty, this free-form loaf makes wonderful sandwiches and provides a filling and satisfying accompaniment to robust soups.

> 2 packages active dry yeast
> 2 tablespoons sugar
> ½ cup warm (105° to 115° F) water
> 4 to 5 cups dark rye flour
> 2 cups whole wheat flour
> 1 teaspoon salt
> 2 cups warm (105° to 115° F) milk
>   Oil, for greasing
> 2 tablespoons butter, melted

1. In a small bowl dissolve yeast and sugar in the warm water and set aside to soften a few minutes. Sift together 4 cups rye flour, whole wheat flour, and salt; set aside.

2. In a large bowl combine milk and yeast; add flour mixture, one cup at a time, until a smooth dough forms (add additional rye flour, if needed, to make smooth dough). Turn out onto a lightly floured surface and knead until smooth, satiny, and elastic (10 to 12 minutes), or dough can be kneaded in a heavy-duty electric mixer.

3. Place dough in a lightly oiled bowl, brush with melted butter, cover with plastic wrap, and let rise in a warm place until almost doubled in bulk (about 1 hour). Punch down and knead lightly 2 minutes. Divide dough in half and shape into two free-form loaves. Set loaves on a greased or parchment-lined baking sheet, brush again with melted butter, and let rise until almost doubled in bulk (about 45 minutes).

4. Preheat oven to 375° F. Bake loaves until they are well browned and sound hollow when tapped (about 30 minutes). Cool on wire racks.

Makes 2 loaves.

■ FOCACCIA

By most accounts, *focaccia* is reckoned to be Italy's oldest bread—a simple yeast dough flattened and baked on a stone slab in a wood-fired hearth. Quite likely, it's the grandfather of the famous Neapolitan pizza. Today's cooks can easily make this versatile country bread at home, even without the stone and the hearth. Garnished as you like— here, with sautéed onions and basil—it can partner salads and soups, sliced tomatoes and cheese, or cocktails.

> 1¼ cups warm (105° to 115° F) water
> ¾ teaspoon sugar
> 1 package active dry yeast
> 2¾ cups unbleached flour
> 3 tablespoons unsalted butter
> ½ cup minced onion
> ⅓ cup minced fresh basil
> 1½ teaspoons coarse salt
> ½ teaspoon freshly ground pepper
> 2 tablespoons olive oil, plus olive oil
>   for greasing and drizzling
>   Cornmeal, for dusting

1. In a large bowl combine ½ cup of the water, sugar, and yeast. Set aside 10 minutes to let yeast soften. Stir in ¾ cup flour, cover, and let rise 2½ hours.

■ SWEDISH RYE BREAD

This dark, fragrant rye bread from Sweden is perfumed with orange, fennel seed, and honey.

2 packages active dry yeast
½ cup warm (105° to 115° F) water
4 to 5 cups all-purpose flour
2½ cups rye flour
1 tablespoon salt
2 cups warm (105° to 115° F) milk
¼ cup honey or molasses
¼ cup firmly packed brown sugar
¼ cup unsalted butter, softened
   Finely grated rind and juice of 2 large
   oranges (approximately ¾ cup juice)
1 tablespoon fennel seed
   Oil, for greasing

1. In a large bowl of a heavy-duty electric mixer, combine yeast and the water and set aside to soften a few minutes. Sift together 4 cups all-purpose flour, rye flour, and salt; set aside.

2. Stir milk, honey, brown sugar, butter, orange rind and juice, and fennel seed into yeast mixture. Add flour mixture, one cup at a time, to yeast mixture, mixing well after each addition, to make a soft, pliable dough (add additional all-purpose flour, if needed, to make a soft dough). Knead 5 minutes in mixer or by hand on a lightly floured surface until smooth, satiny, and elastic (10 to 12 minutes). If prepared completely in mixer, turn out and knead 1 to 2 minutes. Place dough in a lightly oiled bowl, cover with plastic wrap, and let rise in a warm place until doubled in bulk (about 1 hour).

3. Punch down dough; turn out onto a lightly floured surface and knead gently 1 minute. Divide dough in half and shape into 2 round loaves. Set loaves on greased or parchment-lined baking sheets. With a sharp knife or razor blade, slash a cross about ¼ to ½ inch deep on surface of each loaf. Let rise until almost doubled in bulk (35 to 45 minutes).

4. Preheat oven to 350° F. Bake bread until it is golden and sounds hollow when tapped (50 to 60 minutes).

Makes 2 loaves.

■ BATTER BREAD

Batter breads are among the simplest to prepare because they aren't shaped. Instead, they bake in a pan.

1 package active dry yeast
½ cup sugar
½ cup warm (105° to 115° F) water
4 cups flour
1 teaspoon salt
½ cup warm (105° to 115° F) milk
¼ cup unsalted butter, softened
3 eggs
   Oil, for greasing

1. In a small bowl dissolve yeast and sugar in the warm water and set aside to soften a few minutes. Sift together flour and salt; set aside.

2. In a large bowl combine milk, butter, and eggs; stir in yeast mixture. Slowly add flour, one cup at a time, until a soft dough forms. Turn out onto a lightly floured surface and knead for at least 5 minutes by lifting and throwing the dough down as for brioche (see KNEAD), or use a heavy-duty electric mixer.

3. Place dough in a lightly oiled bowl, cover with plastic wrap, and let rise in a warm place until doubled in bulk (about 1 hour).

4. Generously butter an 8- or 9-inch round cake pan. Punch down dough, knead lightly, and place in pan. Let rise until almost doubled in bulk (35 to 45 minutes).

5. Preheat oven to 375° F. Bake until bread is golden and sounds hollow when tapped (50 to 60 minutes).

Makes 1 loaf.

■ BEER BREAD

Beer in the dough acts as an additional leavening agent; use dark beer for a bread with a greater depth of flavor.

2 packages active dry yeast
1 teaspoon sugar
½ cup warm (105° to 115° F) water
4 to 5 cups all-purpose flour
3 cups whole wheat flour
2 cups beer (Guinness or other dark beer)
⅓ cup molasses
4 tablespoons butter, melted
2 teaspoons salt
   Oil, for greasing bowl and baking sheet
3 tablespoons warm water, for brushing

1. In a small bowl dissolve yeast and sugar in the warm water and let soften briefly. Sift together 4 cups all-purpose flour and whole wheat flours.

2. In a large bowl combine beer, molasses, butter, and salt; stir in yeast mixture. Add flour, one cup at a time, to make a soft dough (add more all-purpose flour, if needed, to make a soft dough). Turn out onto a lightly floured surface and knead until smooth, satiny, and elastic (5 to 10 minutes). Or, mix and knead 5 minutes in a heavy-duty electric mixer, and then finish kneading by hand.

3. Place dough in a lightly oiled bowl, cover, and let rise in a warm place until doubled in bulk (about 1 hour). Punch down, knead lightly, divide, and shape into two loaves; set on greased baking sheet. Brush lightly with warm water and let rise until almost doubled in bulk (about 45 minutes).

4. Preheat oven to 400° F. Bake until loaves are well browned and sound hollow when tapped (30 to 35 minutes).

Makes 2 loaves.

■ CLASSIC BRIOCHE

Here is a good brioche: It is fine textured, light, and tastes of butter and eggs. It can be baked as a loaf or in small brioche molds. After the first rising, you can also use this dough to make delicious raised doughnuts (see page 183). Brioche dough is sticky and can be difficult to knead. Try the method suggested in the recipe, or the one described in KNEAD, Kneading Pastry, Biscuit, and Rich Yeast Doughs. Like all breads, brioche can be made to suit your schedule. After the dough has had its first rise, you can punch it down and refrigerate it for up to a few days before forming and baking, if desired.

     1 package active dry yeast
     2 tablespoons sugar
     ½ cup warm (105° to 115° F) milk
    1½ teaspoons salt
     2 eggs
     2 egg yolks
    3¼ to 3½ cups flour
    12 tablespoons butter (softened if mixing
        by hand, chilled otherwise)
     1 egg mixed with 2 teaspoons water, for glaze
        Oil, for greasing

To Mix by Hand

1. In a large bowl sprinkle yeast and sugar over warm milk, stir, and let stand a few minutes to dissolve.

2. Add salt, eggs, and egg yolks and mix well.

3. Add 2 cups of the flour and beat vigorously until batter is smooth and heavy. Drop in softened butter, 1 tablespoon at a time, and beat after each addition until incorporated. If some tiny lumps of butter remain, don't worry; they will blend in later.

4. Add 1 cup of the remaining flour and mix well until a rough mass forms, then scrape out onto a lightly floured surface. Knead for a couple of minutes, sprinkling on a little more flour as necessary to keep dough from being too sticky. Stop kneading and let rest for about 5 to 10 minutes. Continue kneading for a few minutes more, until dough is smooth and elastic.

5. Place in a greased bowl, cover, and let rise until dough is puffy and slightly more than doubled in bulk (about 1 hour).

6. Punch down dough. Cover and refrigerate for one or two days at this point, if desired. (The dough will continue to rise until it is thoroughly chilled; just punch it down every hour or so.)

7. *To make brioches:* Cut dough in half, and on a lightly floured surface shape each piece into an even rope about 10 inches long. Cut each rope into 7 pieces, each about 1½ inches long. Plump each piece of dough into a smooth ball by holding it in one hand as you tuck the edges underneath with the fingers of your other hand, thus forming a tight round with a seam on the bottom.

Cover with a towel and let rest for 10 minutes. To form brioches, generously butter 14 brioche molds or muffin tins. Pick up a piece of dough and pinch it with your fingertips, gently stretching the ball to elongate it slightly as you pull away a marble-sized piece of dough—but don't detach it completely. To form the topknot, place dough on floured surface, lay your index finger on top of the stretched portion, then roll your finger back and forth, to pull out the small end of dough about another inch. Twist the topknot 3 or 4 times and press it firmly back into the larger base. The final shape resembles a tiny snowman with a fat body and a tiny head. Place in one of the prepared molds, pressing down firmly around the edges. Form the remaining balls the same way. Place filled molds on a baking sheet, cover loosely with a towel, and let rise until a little more than doubled in bulk and puffed well over the tops of the molds.
To make a loaf: Butter a 9- by 5-inch loaf pan. Form dough into a smooth loaf and place it in pan. Cover and let rise until doubled in bulk (about 1 hour). After rising, use a sharp, pointed knife or razor blade to make a ½-inch-deep slash lengthwise down the center.

8. Preheat oven to 375° F. Before baking, paint top of each brioche (or the loaf) with egg glaze, taking care not to let it run down into molds.

9. Bake small brioches (on a baking sheet) for about 20 minutes, turning pan once or twice during baking if they brown unevenly. Bake loaf for about 50 minutes; if it browns too much, cover loosely with a tent of foil for the remainder of the baking time.

10. Remove from oven and turn out onto racks (if any stick, pry them out with a knife point) to cool completely before wrapping for storage or freezing. To reheat, place on a baking sheet in a 350° F oven for about 10 minutes.

To Mix With a Processor

1. In a small bowl sprinkle yeast and sugar over warm milk, stir, and let stand a few minutes to dissolve.

2. Pour yeast mixture into bowl of a food processor fitted with steel blade. Add salt, eggs, and egg yolks and whirl for a few seconds.

3. Add 2 cups of the flour and process again until smooth. While blade is turning, drop in chilled butter, 2 tablespoons at a time. Continue to process until smooth.

4. Add another 1½ cups of the flour. Process again until dough comes together and forms a rough ball that revolves around the bowl; process for 30 seconds more. Continue with step 5 of To Mix by Hand for the rising and forming. (Some food processors tend to strain while kneading a dough. If yours labors or stalls, remove dough and continue kneading by hand.)

Makes fourteen 3-inch brioches, or 1 loaf.

■ SAVARIN

This wonderfully rich yeast cake was said to be named for the French gastronome, Brillat-Savarin. It is prepared in a ring mold, soaked with sugar syrup, and served with the center filled with whipped cream and fresh fruit. Cubes of fresh pineapple are suggested here, but any seasonal fruit will be equally flavorful and attractive. Babas au Rhum (see variation) are almost identical to a savarin, but have currants mixed into the dough, are made in special cup-shaped molds, and receive a special drenching in rum. Be sure to butter the molds well.

  1 package active dry yeast
  ¼ cup warm (105° to 115° F) water
  ¼ cup sugar
1⅔ cup flour
  1 teaspoon salt
  3 eggs
  ½ cup unsalted butter, softened, plus
     butter for greasing
  ¼ cup rum, plus rum for sprinkling
  1 cup whipping cream, whipped,
     for accompaniment
  1 cup fresh pineapple cubes or
     other fresh fruit in season

Soaking Syrup

  2 cups sugar
  2 cups water

1. In a small bowl dissolve yeast and sugar in warm water and set aside to soften 5 minutes. Sift together flour and salt; set aside.

2. In a large bowl combine eggs, butter, and the ¼ cup rum. Add yeast mixture, then slowly add flour, 1 cup at a time; mix to a smooth batter. Knead by slapping dough against side of bowl with hand (see KNEAD, Kneading Pastry, Biscuit, and Rich Yeast Doughs), or with a heavy-duty electric mixer and flat beater attachment. Cover batter with plastic wrap and let rise in a warm place until doubled in bulk (about 1 hour).

3. Preheat oven to 375° F. Generously butter a 10-inch savarin mold. Punch down dough, knead lightly, then place in prepared mold. Let rise again until almost doubled in bulk (30 to 40 minutes). Bake until golden brown and high (30 to 40 minutes).

4. Let cool in pan on wire rack 10 minutes; turn out from pan onto a rimmed plate or large, square baking dish. Pour hot Soaking Syrup over bread; sprinkle with rum to taste. Pour off any excess syrup. To transfer to a serving plate, cover bread with savarin mold and invert. Lay serving plate on surface of bread and invert; bread will drop out onto plate.

5. Fill center of Savarin with whipped cream and fresh fruit. Serve at room temperature or chilled.

Serves 6 to 8.

Soaking Syrup   Place sugar and water in a medium, heavy-bottomed saucepan. Dissolve sugar in water over low heat, stirring; increase heat to medium-high and boil 3 minutes.

Babas au Rhum   Prepare Savarin up through kneading dough, step 2. Mix 1 cup currants into dough, cover with plastic wrap, and let rise until doubled. Punch down and divide dough among 10 to 12 well-buttered baba molds, filling each approximately two thirds full. Let rise until dough fills mold (25 to 30 minutes). Bake in a 375° F oven until golden brown and high (about 20 minutes). Cool in molds 10 minutes, invert, and soak with hot Soaking Syrup. Cool, then sprinkle with rum, to taste; drain off excess syrup and serve at room temperature or slightly chilled.

Makes 10 to 12 Babas.

Rich, cakelike brioche display their characteristic topknots. Shown are four stages of individual brioches: balls of dough; dough elongated to form topknots; unbaked brioches with topknots in place; and baked brioches.

Flaky croissants are shaped from triangles of butter-flecked dough that are rolled from the wide end toward the point, then curved into a crescent.

■ CROISSANTS

With so many steps, croissant making might seem like quite a difficult task at first glance—but it's really not hard, perhaps just a bit time-consuming. The technique of building thin layers of butter between layers of yeast dough will be familiar if you have ever made puff pastry, and even if you haven't, instructions are detailed enough for beginning bakers. Follow directions carefully and you should not have any trouble producing the lightest, flakiest croissants you've ever had.

  1 package active dry yeast
1¼ cups warm (105° to 115° F) milk
  2 teaspoons sugar
1½ teaspoons salt
2¾ cups flour
  1 egg mixed with 1 teaspoon water

Butter Mixture

1¼ cups cold butter
  3 tablespoons flour

1. In a large bowl sprinkle yeast over warm milk, add sugar, stir, and let stand for a few minutes to dissolve. Add salt and flour, then mix vigorously but briefly, just until you have a rough, sticky dough that holds together. Set aside for about 5 minutes while preparing Butter Mixture.

2. Wipe work surface clean, sprinkle it generously with flour, and turn dough out onto it. Flour the dough, which is quite soft, and push, pat, and roll it into a rectangle about 10 by 14 inches. Unwrap Butter Mixture and place it on bottom half of dough, leaving about a 1-inch border on 3 sides. Lift up the top of the dough, working it loose with a spatula or scraper if it sticks to work surface, and flip it over the butter. Pinch edges to seal. Give the dough a quarter turn, so sealed flap is to your right.

3. Using smooth, even strokes, roll to a 9- by 17-inch rectangle. Check to see if it is sticking and sprinkle with flour if necessary—don't be afraid to pick it up and look. Fold bottom third of dough up over the middle, then flip top third down to cover it. Turn again so flap is to your right and roll out again to 9 by 17 inches. Fold in thirds as before, flour lightly, wrap in plastic wrap, place in a plastic bag, and chill for about 30 minutes. At this point, the first two turns are finished.

4. Roll chilled dough again to 9 by 17 inches, fold in thirds, wrap in plastic wrap and a plastic bag, and refrigerate for 45 minutes. (If at any time dough becomes soft and resists rolling out, or if butter breaks through in large, smeary patches, stop working, dust dough with flour, then slide onto a baking sheet and chill for about 20 minutes.)

5. Roll out and fold dough again, thus completing four turns. Wrap and chill for at least 1 hour (or for a few hours or overnight if it's more convenient) before forming croissants.

6. Roll dough out to 10 by 20 inches, keeping sides as even as possible. With a sharp knife, cut in half lengthwise, then cut each half into four 5-inch squares. Cut each square in half diagonally to make 2 triangles.

7. Working with one triangle at a time, pick up the 2 closest points, at the base, and gently stretch them out to about 7 inches. Hold these 2 points down with one hand and use the other hand to wiggle and stretch the other, farthest point out to about 7 inches or more. Starting at the base, roll up stretched dough just like a crescent roll. Pull points down, toward one another, to form a crescent shape.

8. Place croissants about 2 inches apart on baking sheets. Cover with a towel and let rise until puffy and doubled in size (about 1½ hours). If you've used 2 baking sheets and your oven can hold only 1 sheet on the same rack, chill 1 sheet for the first hour or so, to slow rising, so baking times are staggered.

9. Preheat oven to 425° F and place a rack on middle level. Brush each risen croissant with egg mixture and bake until well browned and puffy (12 to 15 minutes). If they are not browning evenly, quickly turn pan around from front to back once or twice during baking. If some are done before others, just remove them with a spatula. Transfer croissants to a rack to cool for a few minutes before serving. Wrap and freeze what you won't use in a day. (To reheat, unwrap and set on a baking sheet, still frozen, and place in a 400° F oven for about 7 minutes.)

Makes sixteen 4-inch Croissants.

Butter Mixture   Cut butter into tablespoon-sized bits, dropping them onto work surface, then sprinkle with flour. Tear off two good-sized sheets of waxed paper and set aside. Begin mashing butter and flour together by smearing across work surface with the heel of your hand; gather butter mixture into a pile with a spatula or pastry scraper, then repeat smearing a couple of times, until butter is smooth and workable, but still cold. With floured hands form butter into a small, rough rectangle and place it between sheets of waxed paper. Roll and pat butter into a larger, 6- by 8-inch rectangle, keeping sides as even as possible. Set aside while you roll out yeast dough.

■ DANISH PASTRY DOUGH

Danish pastry dough is slightly richer than croissant dough because it contains eggs and a little more sugar.

> 2 **packages active dry yeast**
> 1 **cup warm (105° to 115° F) milk**
> 2 **eggs, at room temperature**
> 2 **teaspoons salt**
> ¼ **cup sugar**
> 3¼ **cups all-purpose flour**

Butter Mixture

> 1½ **cups cold butter**
> ¼ **cup all-purpose flour**

1. In a large bowl sprinkle yeast over warm milk, stir, and let stand a few minutes to soften. Add eggs, salt, and sugar and mix well. Pour in flour and mix briefly, just until you have a rough, sticky dough that holds together. Set aside for about 5 minutes while preparing Butter Mixture.

2. Scrape clean surface of work area used for Butter Mixture, sprinkle it generously with flour, and turn yeast dough out onto it (dough will be quite soft). Sprinkle top of dough with flour, then roll and pat into a 10- by 14-inch rectangle. Unwrap Butter Mixture and set it on bottom half of dough, leaving a 1-inch border on 3 sides. Gently lift up unbuttered top flap and flip it down over butter. Pinch the edges to seal, then use a wide spatula or scraper to help lift dough package and give it a quarter turn, so the sealed flap is to your right.

3. To roll out and fold dough, follow steps 3, 4, and 5 of Croissants (see page 624), except roll out Danish dough a little larger, to an 8- by 20-inch rectangle, since you are working with more dough. After you've completed all the turns, form and bake the pastries (see A Variety of Danish Shapes and Fillings, page 626)—or if it is more convenient, wrap dough in plastic wrap and a plastic bag, and refrigerate overnight before forming and baking.

Makes about 2 dozen pastries, depending on shapes.

Butter Mixture   Cut cold butter into tablespoon-sized chunks, dropping chunks onto work surface. Sprinkle butter pieces with flour. Blend butter and flour by smearing them out in front of you with the heel of your hand; gather up the mixture and smear again three or four times until butter is perfectly smooth and workable but still cold. Flour your hands and pat mixture into a rectangle about 4 by 5 inches. Place between two sheets of waxed paper or plastic wrap and pat and roll into a larger, 7- by 9-inch rectangle, keeping edges as even as possible. Set aside for a moment.

Danish pastries are the flakiest and most buttery of all sweet rolls. Shown here are icing-topped Cinnamon Rolled Danish. The recipe appears on page 626.

A VARIETY OF DANISH SHAPES AND FILLINGS

The recipe for Danish Pastry Dough makes about two dozen pastries, and each shape (directions follow) requires half the dough. For variety, make two different shapes and at least two fillings. After you cut the dough in half, wrap and chill the piece you are not working on.

Fillings can be made a day ahead since they all keep well if covered and refrigerated (or frozen). Use the leftovers as cake or cookie fillings, and serve fillings made with fruit over ice cream or puddings.

If you need to use two baking sheets when baking the Danish and can't fit both pans on the same oven rack, refrigerate one rack after forming and let the other batch rise at room temperature. The chilled batch will rise more slowly, so baking times will be staggered.

If you're going to freeze a Danish, omit any icing called for after baking. Ice the pastries after reheating in a 400° F oven for about 5 minutes and they'll look and taste freshly made.

The amount of filling used in each Danish may not look generous, but it's better to have too little than too much, which would bubble up and leak out during baking. Be sure to press very firmly when sealing the edges of unbaked pastries, using your fingertips or the tines of a fork so that the pastries don't pop open in the oven (although this happens occasionally despite all precautions).

■ CINNAMON ROLLED DANISH

  ½ cup dried currants
  ½ recipe Danish Pastry Dough (see page 625)
  4 tablespoons melted butter
  ½ cup Cinnamon Sugar (see page 145)
  ½ cup chopped walnuts or pecans
  1 egg beaten with 1 teaspoon water
    Glacé Icing (see page 250)

1. In a small bowl pour boiling water over currants and set aside while you roll out dough.

2. On a floured surface roll dough into an 11- by 17-inch rectangle. Brush with melted butter, then sprinkle evenly with Cinnamon Sugar. Sprinkle on nuts. Drain currants and pat them dry with paper towels, then distribute them over dough. Press ingredients into the dough with your fingertips. Starting with a long side, roll into a tight cylinder, like a jelly roll. Cut into 1-inch slices and place about 2 inches apart on baking sheets. Cover with a towel and let rise until puffy and almost doubled in bulk (45 minutes to 1 hour). Brush each slice with some of the egg mixture.

3. Preheat oven to 400° F. Bake until well browned (12 to 14 minutes). Transfer to wire racks to cool; brush with Glacé Icing while still warm.

Makes about 18 rolls.

■ TURNOVERS

  ½ recipe Danish Pastry Dough (see page 625)
  1 egg beaten with 1 teaspoon water
  1 cup Prune, Date, Apricot, or Apple Filling
    (see page 627)
    Glacé Icing (see page 250)

1. Roll dough on a lightly floured surface into a 12- by 16-inch rectangle. Cut lengthwise into three strips, 4 by 16 inches, then cut each strip into four 4-inch squares.

2. Brush the edges of each square with some of the egg mixture, then place a generous tablespoonful of the filling in the center of each. Fold the squares in half diagonally, to make triangular-shaped turnovers, and press the edges firmly with your fingers to seal. Place about 2 inches apart on baking sheets, cover with a towel, and let rise until puffy and nearly doubled in bulk (about 45 minutes). Brush with remaining egg mixture.

3. Preheat oven to 400° F. Bake until golden brown and puffy (12 to 15 minutes).

4. Cool on racks and brush with icing while still warm.

Makes 1 dozen Turnovers.

■ BEAR CLAWS

  ½ recipe Danish Pastry Dough (see page 625)
  1 egg beaten with 1 teaspoon water
  1 cup Date, Poppy Seed, or Nut Filling
    (see page 627)
    Glacé Icing (see page 250)

1. On a lightly floured surface, roll dough into a 12- by 16-inch rectangle. Cut lengthwise into three strips, 4 by 16 inches, then cut each strip into four 4-inch squares.

2. Brush edges of each square with some egg mixture. Place about 1 tablespoon of filling in the center of each, spreading it slightly down toward bottom and across center. Fold top half of dough down to cover filling and press edges firmly to seal. Make about seven ½-inch-long cuts across long, sealed edge of each rectangle, spacing cuts about ½ inch apart. Gently bend each rectangle into a curve, so cuts open slightly, forming claws. Place about 2 inches apart on baking sheets. Cover with a towel and let rise until almost doubled in bulk (about 45 minutes or a little longer). Brush each pastry with some of the remaining egg mixture.

3. Preheat oven to 400° F. Bake until puffy and well browned (12 to 14 minutes). Cool Bear Claws on wire racks and brush each with a little icing while still warm.

Makes 1 dozen Bear Claws.

Pain au Chocolat   Omit filling. Finely chop 6 ounces semisweet chocolate. Brush edges of squares with beaten egg; sprinkle the center of each with 1 tablespoon chopped chocolate. Fold over and pinch the edges to seal but do not make any cuts (shapes should be rectangular). Let rise; bake and ice as directed for Bear Claws.

PINWHEELS
½ recipe Danish Pastry Dough (see page 625)
1 cup Prune, Nut, or Apple Filling (below and right)
1 egg beaten with 1 teaspoon water
Glacé Icing (see page 250)

1. On a lightly floured surface, roll dough into a 12- by 16-inch rectangle. Cut lengthwise into three strips, 4 by 16 inches, then cut each strip into four 4-inch squares.

2. Separate squares. With a small, sharp knife, make diagonal cuts at corners of each, cutting in from corner to about ½ inch from center. Place a generous tablespoon of filling in middle of each. One by one, fold over alternating points from edge to center, overlapping them a bit. Wet overlapping points with drops of egg mixture, then pinch firmly together so they stick. Place about 2 inches apart on baking sheets, cover with a towel, and let rise until almost doubled in bulk (45 minutes to 1 hour). Brush with some of the egg mixture.

3. Preheat oven to 400° F. Bake until puffy and golden brown (12 to 14 minutes). Transfer to racks to cool and brush each with icing while still warm.

Makes 1 dozen Pinwheels.

APPLE FILLING
4 medium-sized apples, peeled and cored
⅓ cup sugar
2 tablespoons dried currants
2 tablespoons chopped walnuts
1 teaspoon fresh lemon juice

Shred apples on the coarse side of a grater into a bowl. Mix in sugar, currants, walnuts, and lemon juice.

Makes about 1½ cups.

APRICOT FILLING
1 cup (6 oz) finely chopped dried apricots
3 tablespoons sugar
¼ cup chopped almonds

Put apricots in a small saucepan, cover them with water, and simmer over moderate heat until tender. Drain thoroughly. Purée apricots in a food processor or pass through a food mill, then beat in sugar and almonds.

Makes about 1¼ cups.

Peach Filling Substitute 1 cup (6 oz) coarsely chopped dried peaches for the apricots.

CHEESE FILLING
1 cup cottage cheese
2 tablespoons sugar
3 tablespoons flour
1 egg yolk
2 teaspoons grated orange rind
¼ cup dried currants (optional)

Press cottage cheese through a strainer or food mill 2 or 3 times, until it is fairly smooth, or simply whirl for several seconds in a food processor. Add sugar, flour, egg yolk, orange rind, and currants (if used); mix thoroughly.

Makes about 1¼ cups.

DATE FILLING
1 cup (8 oz) finely cut pitted dates
½ cup water
¼ cup firmly packed brown sugar
2 teaspoons grated orange rind

In a small, heavy saucepan, combine dates, the water, brown sugar, and orange rind. Cook over low heat, stirring frequently, until mixture is thick enough to hold a shape and dates have absorbed the water.

Makes about 1½ cups.

Fig Filling Substitute 1 cup (8 oz) finely cut dried figs for the dates and reduce the sugar to 2 tablespoons.

NUT FILLING
1 cup walnuts, hazelnuts, or almonds
¼ cup sugar
1 egg white
1 tablespoon butter, softened

By hand or in a food processor, chop nuts into very fine pieces—about ⅛ inch, or the size of coarse bread crumbs. Combine with sugar, egg white, and butter, and beat until blended.

Makes about ¾ cup.

POPPY SEED FILLING
½ cup poppy seed
1 egg
1 egg white
5 tablespoons confectioners' sugar
¼ cup dry bread crumbs

Combine poppy seed, egg, egg white, confectioners' sugar, and bread crumbs and mix until thoroughly combined. Set aside for 20 minutes or so before using.

Makes about ¾ cup.

PRUNE FILLING
1 cup (8 oz) finely cut pitted prunes
⅓ cup water
¼ cup firmly packed brown sugar
1 tablespoon fresh lemon juice

In a small, heavy-bottomed saucepan, combine prunes, water, and sugar. Simmer gently for several minutes, stirring frequently, until mass is thick enough to hold a shape and prunes have absorbed the water. Stir in lemon juice.

Makes about 1½ cups.

CHRISTMAS PANETTONE

Legend has it that this Milanese bread has a lofty dome to honor the *duomo* or cathedral in many a Lombardian town. Food historian Waverley Root relates that it's a custom for the children of Milan to leave a bowl of panettone soaked in water on windowsills on New Year's Eve for the camels of the bearers of gifts to the Christ Child.

    2 packages active dry yeast
    ½ cup warm (105° to 115° F) water
    ⅓ cup sugar
    ¼ cup warm (105° to 115° F) milk
    ½ teaspoon salt
    ¼ teaspoon freshly grated nutmeg
    ⅔ cup butter or margarine, softened
    2 teaspoons grated orange rind
    1 teaspoon vanilla extract
    3¾ cups flour
    2 eggs
    2 egg yolks
       Oil, for greasing
    ¼ cup Marsala
    ½ cup golden raisins
    ⅓ cup *each* slivered candied cherries and
       diced mixed candied fruits
    ¼ cup pine nuts or slivered almonds
       Confectioners' sugar

1. In large bowl of an electric mixer, sprinkle yeast over the warm water; add 1 teaspoon of the sugar. Let stand until yeast is soft (about 5 minutes).

2. Add remaining sugar, warm milk, salt, nutmeg, butter, orange rind, and vanilla. Add 2 cups of the flour; mix to blend, then beat until smooth and elastic (about 5 minutes).

3. Beat in eggs and egg yolks, one at a time. Gradually beat in remaining 1¾ cups flour; when all has been added, beat at medium speed until batter is elastic (about 3 minutes).

4. Transfer batter to a greased bowl. Cover and let rise in a warm place until bubbly (about 1 hour). While batter is rising, pour Marsala over raisins in a small bowl; set aside.

5. Stir batter down; then stir in raisin mixture, cherries, candied fruits, and pine nuts until well distributed.

6. Spread batter in a well-greased, lightly floured, 9½- to 10-cup charlotte mold (about 7½ inches in diameter and 4 inches deep) or panettone pan. Let rise until doubled (30 to 45 minutes). Preheat oven to 325° F.

7. Bake until bread is well browned and a skewer inserted in center comes out clean (1 to 1¼ hours). Let stand in pan on wire rack for about 15 minutes, then remove pan and transfer to rack to cool (rounded side up). Dust with confectioners' sugar while warm.

Serves 10 to 12.

STOLLEN

During the Christmas holidays German bakeries are full of these light, fruit-filled loaves.

    1 package active dry yeast
    ½ cup sugar
    ¼ cup warm (105° to 115° F) water
    1 cup warm (105° to 115° F) milk
    ½ cup butter, melted
    1 egg
       Grated rind of 1 lemon
    ½ teaspoon salt
    4 to 5 cups flour
    ½ cup dark raisins
    ½ cup golden raisins
    ½ cup slivered almonds
    ½ cup candied peel
       Oil, for greasing
    2 tablespoons butter, melted
       Glacé Icing (see page 250)

1. In a small bowl dissolve yeast and 2 tablespoons of sugar in the warm water; set aside briefly to soften.

2. In a large bowl combine milk, butter, egg, lemon rind, salt, and the remaining sugar; add yeast mixture. Add 4 cups flour, one cup at a time, to make a soft dough (add more flour, if needed, to get texture). In a heavy-duty mixer with dough hook or by hand on a floured surface, knead dough until smooth, satiny, and elastic (at least 5 minutes). Knead in raisins, almonds, and candied peel.

3. Place dough in a lightly oiled bowl, cover, and let rise until doubled in bulk (about 1 hour). Punch down and knead briefly. Halve dough; shape each piece into an oval; fold each oval in half along the long side. Place on a greased baking sheet, brush with melted butter, and let rise until almost doubled in bulk (about 45 minutes); brush again with butter. Preheat oven to 350° F.

4. Bake loaves until golden and hollow when tapped (about 30 minutes); cool. Drizzle with Glacé Icing.

Makes 2 loaves.

KUGELHOPF

This Alsatian specialty originated in Austria, where it is known as *gugelhopf*.

    2 packages active dry yeast
    1 teaspoon sugar
    ½ cup warm (105° to 115° F) water
    2½ cups flour
    1 teaspoon salt
    3 eggs
    ½ cup butter, softened
       Oil, for greasing
    ½ cup whole blanched almonds
    ½ cup dried currants
    ½ cup golden raisins
       Confectioners' sugar, for dusting

1. In a small bowl dissolve yeast and sugar in the warm water and set aside a few minutes to soften. Sift together flour and salt and set aside.

2. In a large bowl beat together eggs and butter; add yeast mixture, then slowly add flour, one cup at a time, to make a soft dough. On a lightly floured surface, knead slowly (see page 327) at least 5 minutes (or use a heavy-duty electric mixer).

3. Place dough in a lightly oiled bowl, cover, and let rise until doubled in bulk (about 1 hour). Generously butter a 9-cup Kugelhopf mold or other tube pan; arrange almonds decoratively around sides of mold (butter will cause nuts to adhere to pan sides). Punch down dough, add currants and raisins, and knead lightly to mix in; set in mold. Let rise until almost doubled in bulk (about 45 minutes).

4. Preheat oven to 375° F. Bake until golden brown (40 to 50 minutes). Cool 10 minutes in pan on wire rack, then turn out of pan onto wire rack and cool completely. To serve, dust with confectioners' sugar.

Serves 10 to 12.

■ THE STICKIEST PECAN ROLLS

Wonderfully gooey through and through, these rolls are at their most appealing served warm.

> 2 **packages active dry yeast**
> ½ **cup warm (105° to 115° F) water**
> ¾ **cup granulated sugar**
> ½ **cup warm (105° to 115° F) milk**
> 1 **teaspoon salt**
> 2 **teaspoons grated orange rind**
> ½ **cup butter or margarine, softened, plus**
>   **½ cup butter or margarine, melted**
> 4½ **to 5 cups all-purpose flour**
> 2 **eggs**
> ½ **cup whole wheat flour**
>   **Oil, for greasing**
> 1 **cup firmly packed brown sugar**
> 1 **cup pecan halves**
> 1 **cup coarsely chopped pecans**

Cinnamon Filling

> 1 **cup sugar**
> 1½ **teaspoons ground cinnamon**

1. In large bowl of electric mixer, sprinkle yeast over the water. Add 1 tablespoon granulated sugar. Let stand until yeast is soft (about 5 minutes).

2. Add remaining granulated sugar, milk, salt, orange rind, and softened butter.

3. Add 3 cups all-purpose flour. Mix to blend, then beat at medium speed until smooth and elastic (about 5 minutes). Add eggs, one at a time, beating until smooth after each addition. Stir in whole wheat flour, then about 1½ cups more all-purpose flour to make a soft dough.

These are The Stickiest Pecan Rolls you'll ever taste, with nuts both inside and out and a hint of orange in the dough.

4. Turn dough out onto a board or pastry cloth coated with some of the remaining ½ cup all-purpose flour. Knead until dough is smooth and satiny and small bubbles form just under surface (12 to 15 minutes), adding just enough flour to prevent dough from being sticky.

5. Turn dough in a greased bowl. Cover with plastic wrap and a towel; let rise in a warm place until doubled in bulk (1¼ to 1½ hours).

6. While dough rises, prepare baking pan. Pour ¼ cup of the melted butter into a 9- by 13-inch baking pan; tip and tilt to coat pan evenly. Sprinkle evenly with brown sugar, then with pecan halves.

7. Punch dough down. Cover with inverted bowl and let rest for 10 minutes. Roll dough out on a floured surface into an 18-inch square. Brush with remaining melted butter. Sprinkle with Cinnamon Filling, then with chopped pecans. Starting from an 18-inch side, roll dough jelly-roll fashion; moisten long edge and pinch to seal. Cut into 12 equal slices.

8. Arrange slices, cut sides down, in prepared baking pan. Cover lightly with waxed paper. Let rise until doubled in bulk (about 1 hour). Preheat oven to 350° F.

9. Bake until well browned (30 to 35 minutes). Let stand in pan on rack for 1 minute; then invert carefully onto a serving tray. Let stand with pan in place for 30 seconds, then remove pan. Serve warm.

Makes 1 dozen rolls.

Cinnamon Filling   In a small bowl mix together sugar and cinnamon.

Enjoy Chocolate-Swirled Babkas, a sweet yeast bread, with afternoon coffee or tea.

■ CHOCOLATE-SWIRLED BABKAS

Topped with streusel and bursting with fudgy cocoa filling, these rich, sweet loaves are a New York bakery favorite.

  2 packages active dry yeast
  ½ cup warm water (105° to 115° F) water
  ⅓ cup sugar
  ⅔ cup warm (105° to 115° F) milk
  ½ teaspoon *each* salt and vanilla extract
  3 tablespoons butter or margarine, softened, plus 3 tablespoons butter or margarine, melted
4½ to 5 cups flour
  3 eggs
    Oil, for greasing
  1 cup coarsely chopped walnuts

Cocoa Filling

  ⅓ cup unsweetened cocoa
  ⅔ cup sugar

Streusel Topping

  2 tablespoons butter or margarine, softened
  ¼ teaspoon ground cinnamon
  ⅓ cup confectioners' sugar
  ¼ cup flour

1. In large bowl of electric mixer, sprinkle yeast over the water. Add 1 teaspoon sugar. Let stand until yeast is soft (about 5 minutes).

2. Mix in remaining sugar, milk, salt, vanilla, and softened butter.

3. Add 2½ cups flour. Mix to blend, then beat at medium speed until smooth and elastic (about 5 minutes). Separate one of the eggs; reserve white for glaze. Beat in egg yolk and remaining whole eggs, one at a time. Stir in about 1½ cups more flour to make a soft dough.

4. Turn dough out onto a board or pastry cloth coated with some of the remaining ½ to 1 cup flour. Knead until dough is smooth and satiny and small bubbles form just under surface (10 to 12 minutes), adding just enough flour to prevent dough from being sticky.

5. Turn dough in a greased bowl. Cover with plastic wrap and a towel; let rise in a warm place until doubled in bulk (45 minutes to 1 hour).

6. Place dough on a floured surface and punch down. Cover with inverted bowl and let rest for 10 minutes.

7. Divide dough in half. Roll out each half on floured surface to a 10- by 20-inch rectangle. Brush 1½ tablespoons of the melted butter over each rectangle, leaving about a ½-inch margin on all edges. Sprinkle half of the Cocoa Filling over buttered surface of each rectangle, then sprinkle each rectangle with ½ cup walnuts.

8. Starting with a 20-inch side, roll each rectangle of dough tightly, jelly-roll style. Pinch edge to seal.

9. Zigzag each roll back and forth to fit into a well-greased 4½- by 8½-inch loaf pan.

10. Let rise until almost doubled in bulk (35 to 45 minutes). Preheat oven to 350° F. Beat reserved egg white with 1 teaspoon water; brush egg white mixture over loaves. Sprinkle each loaf with half of the Streusel Topping.

11. Bake until coffee cakes are well browned (30 to 35 minutes). Carefully remove loaves from pans and let cool on wire racks.

Makes 2 coffee cakes.

Cocoa Filling   In a small bowl mix cocoa and sugar until well combined and no lumps remain.

Streusel Topping   In a medium bowl beat butter with cinnamon until fluffy; gradually beat in sugar, then mix in flour until crumbly and uniformly combined.

■ VANILLA FRENCH TOAST

French toast is a delicious way to finish yesterday's loaf. Use any type of slightly stale, dense-textured bread (bakery or homemade). Allow thicker slices to sit in the dipping liquid for a while, or they will be dry in the middle.

  4 eggs
  1 cup milk
  1 teaspoon vanilla extract
  8 slices day-old bread (preferably a dense-textured rather than an airy commercial type)
  ¼ cup butter (preferably clarified)
    Confectioners' sugar, Cinnamon Sugar (see page 145), or warmed syrup, for accompaniment

1. In a shallow dish beat eggs and milk together with vanilla.

2. Dip bread into this mixture. In a large frying pan or on a griddle fry dipped bread in 2 tablespoons butter until well browned and crisp on each side, turning once (add remaining butter as needed).

3. Serve hot, sprinkled with confectioners' sugar or Cinnamon Sugar, or drizzled with syrup.

Serves 4.

YOGURT

When milk is held for several hours at a temperature of about 110° F, lactic acid–producing bacteria will grow and cause the milk to coagulate. The result is yogurt, a fermented milk product with a thick, creamy texture and a tangy flavor. Although the earliest yogurt was probably made by accident—perhaps when a desert nomad put milk in a goatskin bag and hung it next to the warm body of a camel—today's commercial yogurt is made under strictly controlled conditions.

Use Widespread acceptance of yogurt is fairly recent in this country, although it has been popular throughout the world for hundreds of years. In Greece yogurt is eaten as a breakfast food with the aromatic local honey. Throughout the eastern Mediterranean and the Middle East, yogurt is used as a dipping sauce, a basting medium, a condiment, a soup base, and a dessert. Middle Eastern cooks often mix yogurt with garlic and dill or mint and serve it as a sauce for grilled lamb or fish. Indian cooks incorporate yogurt in marinades and stews; tandoori dishes (baked in a clay oven) are marinated first in yogurt and aromatic spices. Indians also make *lassi,* a cold yogurt drink, which may be either sweet or salty. *Tzatziki,* chopped cucumber and garlic in yogurt, is a popular Greek appetizer. In Iran grated cucumbers are combined with yogurt, raisins, onions, and salt to make a cold soup.

In America yogurt is also eaten at breakfast, as a quick lunch or snack, or as a dessert with fruit. It may be used as a substitute for sour cream—for example, a salad dressing, dip, soup garnish, or baked potato topping. Frozen yogurt is a popular snack food.

Availability Yogurt is available in plain and flavored styles, made with whole milk, low-fat milk, or nonfat milk. Many of the flavored versions are fruit-based, containing fruit purée or fruit preserves. Some fruit yogurts have the fruit on the bottom of the container; others are Swiss style, with the fruit dispersed throughout. Other flavors, such as coffee and vanilla, are also popular.

Some snack shops and restaurants also sell frozen yogurt, which usually contains added sugar, stabilizers, and extra nonfat milk solids. Some soft-serve yogurt is made by blending yogurt in equal parts with ice cream.

Storage Refrigerate both commercial and homemade yogurt and use within one to two weeks. Commercial yogurt containing preservatives can be stored longer.

COOKING WITH YOGURT

Yogurt will curdle if exposed to excessive heat. When used in sauces and other cooked dishes, it is generally added at the last minute, with the pan removed from the heat. Alternatively, yogurt can be stabilized by adding 2 teaspoons of cornstarch per cup. The stabilized yogurt can be brought to a boil, but should not be cooked more than one or two minutes.

■ HOMEMADE YOGURT

High-quality yogurt is easy to make at home and has the benefit of being extremely fresh and flavored to your liking. An electric yogurt maker is helpful for maintaining a warm temperature but is unnecessary. The heat of the pilot light in a gas oven is usually sufficient. You can also place the containers in a warm water bath and change the water as it cools.

> 1 **quart milk (whole, low-fat, or nonfat; see Note)**
> 1 **rounded tablespoon plain yogurt (commercial or homemade)**

1. In a medium saucepan heat milk just to boiling; remove from heat and let stand, covered, until temperature drops 100° F.

2. Stir in 1 rounded tablespoon of plain commercial unpasteurized yogurt or yogurt from a previous homemade batch. Pour into five 8-ounce containers with lids. Cover and set in a warm place (115° F to 120° F) until mixture coagulates (8 to 10 hours).

3. Refrigerate until cold. Serve as is or with fruit, or use as required in other recipes.

Makes 1 quart.

Note For creamier texture, add ⅓ cup nonfat dry milk per quart of milk.

ZEST

The colored, outermost layer of the skin of citrus fruits, as opposed to the bitter white pith and the flesh itself, is the zest. It contains the essential oils that carry the flavor of the fruit; when grated or pared away in fine strips and chopped, it is often used to flavor baked goods, sauces, and sautés. Any of the citrus zests can be used with great success as a seasoning or as a replacement for salt. See GADGETS for directions on how to remove and chop zest.

Ribbons of bright yellow lemon zest may be used to flavor many foods. An easy way to remove the zest in strips is with a citrus stripper, as shown here.

> ***Recipes and Related Information***
> *Lemon, 339; Rind, 499.*

INDEX